Chance, Cause, Reason

Chance, Cause, Reason

An Inquiry into the Nature of Scientific Evidence

Arthur W. Burks

The University
of Chicago Press

Chicago and
London

The University of Chicago Press, Chicago 60637
The University of Chicago Press, Ltd., London

Printed in the United States of America

Library of Congress Cataloging in Publication Data

Burks, Arthur Walter, 1915–
Chance, cause, reason; an inquiry into the nature of scientific evidence.

Bibliography: p.
1. Evidence. 2. Induction (Logic) 3. Chance.
4. Causation. I. Title.
BC171.B87 160 74-11617
ISBN 0-226-08087-0
ISBN 0-226-08088-9 (pbk.)

ARTHUR W. BURKS is professor of Philosophy and of Computer and Communication Sciences at the University of Michigan. He was a principal designer of the ENIAC, the first general-purpose electronic computer, and contributed to the original design of stored-program computers. He has edited *Essays on Cellular Automata*, John von Neumann's *Theory of Self-Reproducing Automata*, and the last two volumes of the *Collected Papers of Charles Sanders Peirce*. He has published articles in *Mind*, *Philosophical Review*, *Philosophy of Science*, *Review of Metaphysics*, and other journals. [1977]

For my wife Alice

Contents

Tables xii
Figures xiii
Preface xv

1 Concepts and Problems

1.1 Questions and Answers 1
1.2 Mathematics and Empirical Science 2
1.2.1 Logical and empirical statements 2
1.2.2 The logical and empirical status of geometry 7
1.2.3 The logical modalities 10
1.3 Specifying the Meaning of a Technical Term 12
1.4 Inquiry and Argument 15
1.4.1 Kinds of logic 15
1.4.2 The logic of empirical inquiry 17
1.5 Deductive and Inductive Arguments 21
1.5.1 Deductive arguments 21
1.5.2 Inductive arguments and probability 23
1.6 Problems and Methods 28
1.6.1 The four main problems of this book 28
1.6.2 Theories and models in empirical science 31
1.6.3 The methods of this book 33
1.7 Conclusion 36

2 The Calculus of Inductive Probability

2.1 Introduction 39
2.2 The Calculus of Inductive Probability 40
2.2.1 Axioms 40
2.2.2 Truth-functional and modal logic 42
2.3 Some Theorems of the Calculus of Inductive Probability 45
2.3.1 Probability and the logical modalities 45
2.3.2 Multiplication principles 48
2.3.3 Addition principles 51
2.4 Relative Frequency 57
2.5 Bayes' Theorem and Induction 65
2.5.1 Bayes' theorem 65
2.5.2 Confirmation by repeated experimentation 71
2.5.3 The confirmation theorem 76
2.5.4 Applications to induction 85
2.6 Unconditional Probability 92
2.7 Summary 95

3 Alternative Inductive Logics and the Justification of Induction

3.1 Three Inductive Logics 99
3.2 Inductive Logics for Simple Models of Reality 104
3.2.1 Simple models of reality 104
3.2.2 Carnap's inductive logics 107
3.2.3 Induction and statistical uniformity 114
3.2.4 Inductive logics and Bayes' method 118
3.3 Hume's Thesis on the Justification of Induction 128
3.3.1 Alternative inductive logics and Hume's thesis 128
3.3.2 Historical comment 134
3.3.3 Speculative character of Hume's thesis 137
3.4 Frequency Theories of Probability 142
3.4.1 The frequency theory of empirical probability 142
3.4.2 The frequency theory of inductive probability 150
3.5 Summary 161

4 Probability and Action

4.1 Introduction 165
4.2 Peirce's Pragmatism 166
4.2.1 The pragmatic principle of meaning 166
4.2.2 Sameness of meaning 168
4.2.3 Analysis 169
4.2.4 The descriptive component 171
4.2.5 The normative component 175
4.2.6 Probability and pragmatism 176
4.3 The Traditional Theory of Utility 179
4.3.1 Utility and Choice 179
4.3.2 Quantitative probabilities and valuations 185
4.3.3 Infinite utilities 188
4.3.4 Two paradoxes of utility 193
4.3.5 Insurance and gambling 199
4.3.6 Simple ordering of preferences and uncertainties 207
4.4 The "Book" Theorem 213
4.5 Summary 216

5 The Pragmatic Theory of Inductive Probability

5.1 Introduction 247
5.1.1 Preview 247
5.1.2 Historical remarks 249
5.2 The Calculus of Choice—Grammar 254
5.2.1 The marking "game" 254
5.2.2 Choice and act trees 256
5.2.3 Complete sets of trees 259
5.3 The Calculus of Choice—Simple Ordering 262
5.3.1 Marking and logical equivalence axioms 262
5.3.2 Simple ordering of preferences 266
5.3.3 Simple ordering of uncertainties 270
5.4 The Calculus of Choice—Normal Forms 272
5.4.1 Normal form axiom 272
5.4.2 Comparative values 277

5.4.3 Comparative probabilities 281
5.5 The Calculus of Choice—Quantitative 286
5.5.1 Utilities and quantitative probabilities 286
5.5.2 Proof of the main theorem 291
5.5.3 Savage's axiomatic system 299
5.6 The Pragmatic Theory of Inductive Probability 305
5.6.1 Introduction 305
5.6.2 The normative use of the calculus of choice 306
5.6.3 Probability statements and logical truth 312
5.6.4 Conclusion 318
5.7 Closely Related Theories of Inductive Probability 320
5.7.1 The a priori theory 320
5.7.2 The personalistic theory 325
5.8 Summary 327

6 The Logic of Causal Statements as a Formal Language

6.1 Introduction 337
6.2 The Structure of the Logic of Causal Statements 342
6.2.1 Grammar 342
6.2.2 Axioms 345
6.2.3 Proofs and theorems 350
6.3 An Abstract Interpretation 351
6.3.1 Examples 351
6.3.2 Modal models 358
6.3.3 Logical truth 362
6.4 The Mechanical Character of a Formal Language 367
6.4.1 Arithmetization of a formal language 367
6.4.2 Gödel's incompleteness theorem 372
6.4.3 Machines and algorithms 380
6.4.4 Machines and formal languages 388
6.5 Some Theorems of the Logic of Causal Statements 396
6.5.1 Derived rules of inference 396
6.5.2 Some metatheorems 407
6.5.3 Paradoxes of implication 412
6.6 Summary 416

7 The Logic of Causal Statements as a Model of Natural Language

7.1 Introduction 421
7.2 Laws of Nature 424
7.2.1 Laws and theories 424
7.2.2 Causal laws 427
7.3 Subjunctives and Dispositions 435
7.3.1 Causal modalities and subjunctives 435
7.3.2 Causal dispositions 440
7.3.3 Elliptical causal implication 444
7.4 Causality 451
7.4.1 Causes and effects 451
7.4.2 Contravening causes and completeness 457
7.5 Iterated Modalities 464

7.5.1 Change of dispositions 464
7.5.2 Comprehensive modal logics 467
7.6 Conclusion 474

8 The Dispositional Theory of Empirical Probability
8.1 Introduction 479
8.2 A Fair Coin 480
8.2.1 Dispositional model of the fair coin hypothesis 480
8.2.2 Causal and probabilistic dispositions 487
8.2.3 Dispositional models of atomic empirical probability statements 497
8.3 Dispositional Models of Empirical Probability Theories 503
8.3.1 Empirical probability theories 503
8.3.2 The dispositional theory of empirical probability 511
8.3.3 The positivistic theory of empirical probability 519
8.3.4 Prior probabilities and empirical probability 528
8.4 Alternative Theories of Empirical Probability 531
8.4.1 The frequency theory of empirical probability 531
8.4.2 Peirce's dispositional-frequency theory of probability 533
8.4.3 The personalistic account of empirical probability 538
8.5 Summary 542

9 Cause and Chance in Space-Time Systems
9.1 Introduction 549
9.2 Space-time Systems 551
9.2.1 Induction and repetition 551
9.2.2 Indexical symbols and properties 554
9.2.3 Cellular automata 562
9.2.4 Local and global laws 568
9.3 Causality in Nature 571
9.3.1 Uniformity of nature 571
9.3.2 Determinism 574
9.3.3 Near-determinism 577
9.3.4 Tychism 581
9.4 Determinism and Chance 585
9.4.1 Embedded subsystems and probability 585
9.4.2 Entropy and randomness 592
9.4.3 Determinism and randomness 597
9.5 Summary 603

10 The Presupposition Theory of Induction
10.1 Introduction 607
10.2 The Epistemological Status of Causal Necessity 608
10.2.1 Empirical and a priori concepts 608
10.2.2 Causal necessity is a priori 613
10.2.3 Causal necessity is irreducibly modal 619
10.3 Causal Models of Standard Inductive Logic 622
10.3.1 Possible causal systems 622
10.3.2 Verification of causal laws 627
10.4 The Presupposition Theory of Induction 632
10.4.1 The a priori aspect of inductive probability 632
10.4.2 Epistemological status of the presuppositions 636

10.5 Historical Antecedents 639
10.5.1 Keynes' principles of induction 639
10.5.2 Kant's theory of causality 643
10.6 Summary of the Presupposition Theory 647

11 Chance, Cause, and Reason

11.1 Fundamental Concepts 651
11.2 Questions and Answers 655
11.3 A Unified Theory of Probability, Causality, and Induction 657

Bibliography 659

Index 673

Tables

1 Branches of Logic 16
2 The Most Likely Number of Successes 59
3 Probability and Frequency 60
4 Calculation Format for Bayes' Theorem 68
5 Bayes' Method of Finding an Unknown Probability 78
6 Success of Bayes' Method in Finding the True Hypothesis 80
7 Success of Bayes' Method in Estimating an Unknown Probability 82
8 Convergence of Opinion of Two Investigators Who Start Inquiry With Different Prior Odds 90
9 Universe Descriptions of a Model With Two Individuals and Two Basic Properties 106
10 Alternative Inductive Logics for a Model 111
11 Parallelism Between Some Concepts of Classical Thermodynamics and Some Concepts of Inductive Logic 115
12 Variance of Acts 195
13 Normal Form Acts for Two Consequences and Four Possible Universes 261
14 Truth Table for "$(P \vee Q) \vee (\sim P \vee Q)$" 346
15 Some Basic Conjunctions of a Model of the Ancestral Relation 356
16 Gödel Numbers 367
17 Illustration of the Conditional Proof Algorithm 399
18 Illustration of the Generalization Rule Algorithm 401
19 Illustration of "Height" as Defined for the Exchange Rule Algorithm 404
20 Illustration of the Exchange Rule Algorithm 406
21 Comparison of Five Kinds of Implication 446
22 Iterated Modal Operators Compared with Iterated Modal Predicates 471
23 Modal Structure of a Causal Model of Standard Inductive Logic 624
24 Three Classifications of Statements Compared 645

Figures

1	Choice tree for gambling	219
2	Act tree for Fig. 1	219
3	Act tree for indifference	220
4	General form of choice and act trees	220
5	The sure-thing paradox	221
6	Utility function that justifies insuring	222
7	Utility function that justifies gambling	223
8	Utility function that justifies simultaneous insuring and gambling	224
9	Preference relations among acts	225
10	Pragmatic manifestation of "P is more likely than Q"	225
11	Pragmatic manifestation of equal probabilities	226
12	An extended act tree	226
13	Ungrammatical and grammatical trees	227
14	Normal-form choice tree	228
15	Non normal-form choice trees	229
16	Examples of the logical equivalence axiom	230
17	Illustration of the first part of the logical equivalence axiom	232
18	Illustration of the second part of the logical equivalence axiom	233
19	Example involving both parts of the logical equivalence axiom	234
20	Example of the subsct axiom	235
21	Transitivity of preference	235
22	Subset axiom applied to an extended tree	236
23	Violation of the invariance axiom	236
24	Joint example of logical equivalence and invariance axioms	237
25	Ordering of uncertainties axiom	238
26	Probabilistic impossibilities	238
27	Normal form of an extended tree	239
28	Probabilistic impossibilities and normal form	240
29	Illustration of the trimming and normal form algorithms	241
30	Proof of a reduction theorem	242
31	Proof of the partial act theorem	243
32	Proof of a lemma on comparative values	243
33	An act tree in which every choice maximizes a utility function	244
34	Proof of theorem [18]	245
35	Automata primitives	381
36	Finite automaton	382
37	Tape units	385

38 Turing machine $\mathfrak{M}$ 386
39 Universal Turing Machine $\mathfrak{U}$ 387
40 Construction of theorem and non-theorem enumeration machines 390
41 Construction of a decision machine for theoremhood 391
42 Construction of a truth enumeration machine 394
43 Two-dimensional cellular space 563
44 Partial history of a deterministic cellular automaton 565

Preface

This is a treatise in the philosophy of science for readers with some knowledge of mathematics and science. An intermediate understanding of symbolic logic would be helpful; but it is not essential, since the text develops its own logic and since whatever is expressed in symbols is also stated in English. The problems discussed are philosophical, concerning the nature of scientific evidence and related concepts: probability, causality, and inductive reasoning.

Because the book has been a long time in preparation, an explanation of its development may be of interest. In 1960, I began to edit for book publication my articles on the foundations of science. As I brought my views together into a single system, however, I soon felt the need for deeper analyses; and these analyses led in turn to further problems. The work went through several such stages, with interruptions for other duties. It has been written in such diverse places as Ann Arbor (Michigan), Urbana (Illinois), Munich (Germany), Kanpur and Ranikhet (India), and Stanford (California). The result, sixteen years later, is the present volume.

While the doctrines are those of my earlier articles, the ideas are now better organized, more detailed, and, I hope, more refined. The most important materials not previously published are: the calculus of choice, which I evolved as a formal tool for the pragmatic theory of inductive probability (chap. 5); the positivistic theory of empirical probability (chap. 8); the analysis of determinism and its relation to chance (chap. 9); and, last, the formulation of my presupposition theory of induction in terms of cellular automata and causal modal models (chap. 10).

The main philosophical influences on my work may be seen in terms of problem, method, and solution. Broadly speaking, I use the modern tools of symbolic logic and probability theory to redo the classic controversy between David Hume and Immanuel Kant concerning the nature of causality and induction. My solution is the presupposition theory of induction. I agree with Hume that there is no noncircular justification of induction, and with Kant that the concept of causal necessity is a priori rather than empirical. My formulation of the presuppositions owes much to John Maynard Keynes.

As a graduate student, I was convinced by C. H. Langford that neither material nor logical implication is adequate for causal relations, and I began to develop the logic of causal statements at that time. From Rudolf Carnap I learned how to combine symbolic logic and probability theory in formal models of induction, though my philosophy of induction is radically different from his. My debt to Charles Peirce is more general. As did others before me, I found pragmatism useful for explicating the concept of probability, though I do not think pragmatism should be applied to metaphysics. My dispositional theory of empirical probability arose from my analysis of causal dispositions, with a hint from Peirce's suggestion that a probability is a "would be."

I owe a great debt both to institutions and to individuals. I have received valuable support from the National Science Foundation (two grants), the American Council of Learned Societies, and the Center for Advanced Study in the Behavioral Sciences, as well as from my own institution. The University of Michigan has provided time for research and opportunities to discuss my ideas with colleagues and students. The university has also provided specific aid from the Horace H. Rackham Endowment Fund, including a publication subsidy.

I want to thank my colleagues and friends, especially Richard B. Brandt and Charles L. Stevenson, for many stimulating discussions of my work. And I wish to acknowledge the indispensable assistance of my graduate students, in particular Frederick Suppe, Gunnar Niemi, Steven Boer, Rainer von Konigslow, Soschichi Uchii, Andrew Lugg, Janine Idziak, and Harry Gensler; I am deeply grateful for the time and the personal commitment implicit in their astute observations. Alice Gantt has done most of the typing, a very exacting job. My wife Alice has studied the manuscript and has contributed invaluably to both its composition and its exposition.

The book is designed to be read in either direction. The first chapter states the problems, the last chapter indicates where the solutions are given, and each intermediate chapter has its own summary. The reader can start with the problems and see how they are solved, or he can begin with the conclusions and see how they were reached.

1 Concepts and Problems

1.1 Questions and Answers

In his *Dialogues* Plato states the Sophists' "paradox" of inquiry:

> And how will you enquire, Socrates, into that which you do not know? . . . if you find what you want, how will you ever know that this is the thing which you did not know?
> . . . a man cannot enquire either about that which he knows, or about that which he does not know; for if he knows, he has no need to enquire; and if not, he cannot; for he does not know the very subject about which he is to enquire.*

Plato invoked his theory of innate knowledge (theory of recollection) to resolve the paradox. Such a severe measure is not necessary, insofar as scientific inquiry is concerned. The job may be done by a simple distinction: knowing what question is being asked *vs.* knowing the answer to that question. Inquiry begins with a question and ends with an answer.

Learning from someone who knows is analogous to inquiring into the unknown, and the Sophists had a corresponding "paradox" of the learner:

> Do those . . . who learn, learn what they know, or what they do not know?†

The resolution is along the same lines: To learn a result we must understand the language in which it is expressed.

And yet there is a deeper point to the Sophists' paradoxes. Inquiry is guided by questions, and it is humanly impossible to comprehend (or to frame) some questions until one knows the answers to many others. One who understands no quantum mechanics can hardly make a mistaken pronouncement on the subject. Scientific knowledge is a highly complex, structured system. Its interconnected parts are arranged in a hierarchy, with the higher levels resting on the lower ones. Hence in science both learning and inquiry proceed by successive approximations. From this point of view the answer to the Sophists' paradoxes is: One learns what he partially knows.

Philosophy of science, the subject of this book, is not itself a science; nor is it well developed and highly organized, though it has sciences of this sort

* *Meno* 80.

† *Euthydemus* 276.

within its domain of subject matter. Yet philosophy of science is complex and interdependent, so that the above remarks apply to it in part. As a consequence, one cannot fully explain the subject's content and scope at the outset. In this introductory chapter we give some tentative formulations of the problems to be solved and the methods to be used, but improved versions will be given later on.

Our main question is: What is the nature of scientific knowledge? (Thus this is also a treatise in epistemology or theory of knowledge.) The question breaks down into several others: What are the essential characteristics of causes, effects, and laws of nature? What is probability, and how is it related to chance and scientific evidence? What are the roles of reason and experience, of discovery and argument, in science? Clearly these questions can lead in many different directions; we shall want to make some distinctions to show what kinds of answers we are seeking.

1.2 Mathematics and Empirical Science

1.2.1 Logical and empirical statements

Mathematics is the queen of the sciences; still, it is fundamentally different from the empirical sciences. This point may be illustrated by contrasting the infinitesimal calculus with Newton's mechanics. Historically the two arose together: Faced with the problem of gravity, Newton developed the calculus as a tool for solving it. He used both the calculus and the empirical facts contained in Galileo's law of falling bodies and in Kepler's three laws of planetary motion to confirm his law of universal gravitation. In this case the empirical science (here the theory of celestial and terrestrial motion) and the mathematics (here the calculus) evolved together, each stimulating and aiding the other.

We can, however, distinguish and order them. Whatever its origin, the calculus has since been formulated and organized as a systematic and rigorous subject, independent of the theory of motion and, indeed, independent of any empirical data. In this formulation the propositions of the calculus are established by deduction from axioms and definitions by means of rules of inference. What is significant for us here is that in this way of proceeding the propositions of the calculus are shown to be true by reasoning, reflection, and computation, with observation and experiment playing no role. Contrast the methods used to show that Newton's law of universal gravitation is true. Reasoning, thinking, and computation must be used, for the connection between the law itself and observable facts is remote, and mathematics is needed to make it. But Newton's law cannot be established by purely reflective inference alone; there are many possible formulas to choose from, and observation or experiment or both are required to decide among them. Thus Kepler believed that the gravitational influence of the sun falls off inversely with the distance, while according to Newton's law it falls off inversely as the square of the distance. Mathematical reasoning is required to decide between these alternative hypotheses, but it is not sufficient.

What we have found to be true in the particular case of the calculus and the law of gravity holds for mathematics and empirical science generally. There are two fundamentally different types of science (in the sense of systematized knowledge), distinguished by the methods used to establish the truth or falsity of statements in the science. Putting the matter oversimply: Mathematical questions can be settled in a study, while those of empirical science require a laboratory. This methodological distinction between mathematics and empirical science is paralleled by a corresponding distinction between "logically true-or-false statements" and "empirically true-or-false statements," in a way we shall now explain.

As we use the term, a *statement* is an element of language that is either true or false. We will use "proposition" as a synonym of "statement," and for variety we will sometimes say "sentence" when we really mean "statement." The distinction between a sentence and a statement is subtle and complicated, but for our purpose the following remarks should suffice. Strictly speaking, a sentence belongs to a particular language. Sentences of different languages may express the same statement, as do "four plus seven equals eleven" and the German "*vier und sieben ist elf*." A sentence may be called a statement when it is regarded as representing any sentence that expresses the same statement as it expresses.

Many different kinds of statements occur in mathematics and empirical science, but the most basic and important statements of the former subject are logically true-or-false, while the most basic and important statements of the latter subject are empirically true-or-false. One can usually classify a statement as logically true-or-false (or as empirically true-or-false) without knowing whether it is true or false; and at the moment we are interested in the epistemological status of a statement (e.g., Is it logically true-or-false?) rather than its truth-status (e.g., Is it true?).

In the balance of this subsection we shall develop the distinction between logically true-or-false and empirically true-or-false statements by means of examples and explanatory remarks.

Examples of logically true statements are

[1] $87 \times 113 = 9831$

[2] The acceleration of a body is its time rate of change of velocity

[3] If x is the father of y, then y is not the father of x.

Examples of logically false statements are

[4] The circle can be squared with ruler and compass

[5] $19 \times 21 = 409$

[6] Every proposition is both true and false.

Thus the joint class of "logically true-or-false" statements includes: all propositions of deductive logic, e.g., [6]; all statements of arithmetic and pure mathematics, e.g., [1], [4], and [5]; definitions, e.g., [2]; and statements of ordinary language that are necessarily true or necessarily false, e.g., [3]. Note well: The "logically" of "logically true-or-false" covers propositions of mathematics and ordinary language not usually said to belong to deductive logic.

Examples of empirically true statements are

[7] The ammeter reads 0.7 [when it actually does]

[8] The planetary orbits are approximately elliptical

[9] If two bodies were alone in space and the first were fixed, the second would be accelerated toward it at the rate GM/R^2, where M is the mass of the first, R the distance between them, and G the universal gravitational constant.

Examples of empirically false statements are

[10] The ammeter reads 0.5 [when in fact it reads 0.7]

[11] That bird is a white swan

[12] All swans are white.

Thus the category of "empirically true-or-false" statements includes various kinds of propositions of empirical science: observational reports, e.g., [7] and [10]; descriptive laws or generalizations from these reports, e.g., Kepler's law [8]; and abstract theories explaining laws, e.g., Newton's law of gravity [9]. It also includes observational reports, e.g., [11], and empirical generalizations, e.g., [12], of everyday life.

Some points about the distinction between logical and empirical statements need to be made before we can define these classes more precisely. Our answer to the Sophists' paradox of inquiry is that understanding the meaning of a statement (logical or empirical) must in the nature of the case precede inquiry directed at determining whether that statement is true or false (see sec. 1.1). Moreover, it is by means of this understanding that the inquiry is directed and that the goal of the inquiry is recognized if and when reached. Now understanding a proposition presupposes a knowledge of some language in which that proposition may be expressed; and learning a language is an empirical matter, involving experience, observation, and induction. Hence deductive logic and mathematics are in some sense dependent on experience and induction, though not in a sense that contradicts our characterization of logically true-or-false statements.

Consider next the relation between (a) understanding a logical or empirical statement, (b) the ability to recognize and judge proof or evidence that the statement is true or false, and (c) the capacity to plan and direct investigations that will terminate in proof, disproof, verification, or disconfirmation of the statement. State (a) is a necessary condition of (b) and of (c); (a) often results in (b), less often in (c); but (a) is not a sufficient condition of either (b) or (c). That is, one may understand a statement without being able to verify it, even without being able to recognize a proof or disproof of it.

Consider the following example. I have just taken a coin from my pocket, tossed it on the floor, and without looking at it replaced it in my pocket so that there is no trace left of whether it fell heads or tails. Hence

[13] The coin fell heads

is an empirical statement of which no one will ever be able to decide the truth or falsity.

Of course in this case we know how in principle to verify proposition [13], for we could have looked at the coin. But it is not always so. Indeed, at any given time mathematics and empirical science are filled with unresolved questions, and in many cases no one knows how, even in principle, to settle the question. A famous example is

[14] Four colors suffice to color a map so that no two adjacent countries will have the same color.

This statement is easily understood, but no one knows how to prove or disprove it. Moreover, it is conceivable that a topologist will one day construct a proof of it that cannot be understood by many who understand the statement itself.

An example from empirical science is

[15] There is an annual stellar parallax.

Both Aristarchus and Copernicus recognized that [15] is a consequence of their heliocentric theory, but neither knew how to show it true. A more theoretical example is

[16] Absolute space exists, and is filled with the ether.

Newton conjectured this, and he attempted to account for the force of gravity and the reflection and refraction of light by means of the ether. Later the ether was commonly believed by physicists to be the medium that sustained waves of light. But various observational results, particularly the famed experiment of A. A. Michelson and E. W. Morley, have shown [16] to be false.*

The net effect of this whole subsection is to give a meaning to the technical terms "logically true-or-false" and "empirically true-or-false." The essential points are as follows. The truth-value of a **logically true-or-false statement** *can be* established, in principle, by defining, intuiting, reflecting, calculating, and reasoning alone, without the use of observation or experiment. An **empirically true-or-false statement** can be confirmed or disconfirmed, in principle, by observation, experiment, defining, reflecting, calculating, and reasoning; an empirically true-or-false statement cannot be confirmed or disconfirmed without the use of observation and/or experiment, but defining, reflecting, calculating, and reasoning may not be required. We conclude this subsection by making five further points about how we employ these terms.

First, the use of the italicized "can be" in the definition of "logically true-or-false" is essential, since some mathematical questions can also be settled by empirical means. Electrical engineers use network analyzers to study and predict the behavior of electric utility distribution systems. If the laws of electricity were not known, a network analyzer could be used for the experimental investigation of these laws. Actually these laws are known; and, in fact, the engineers use the network analyzer to obtain the solutions of mathematical problems empirically. Similarly, aerodynamicists sometimes use wind tunnels to solve mathematical equations.

Second, we spoke of "confirming" or "disconfirming" an empirical statement rather than determining its truth-value, since in many cases one cannot prove an empirical statement to be true (or false) but can establish only a probability that it is true (or false).

Third, we did not say that an empirical statement can be confirmed or disconfirmed by observation and experiment alone. This would do for many cases, e.g., [7], [10], [11], [13], above; but it would exclude those that cannot be confirmed or disconfirmed without the use of mathematics, e.g., [8], [9], [15], and [16].

Fourth, more could be said here about what should be included under reasoning and what should be included under observation and experiment. We need not do so now, for we have drawn the distinction between "logical" and "empirical" sharply enough for our initial purposes; but later we will refine it with respect to the distinction between deductive and inductive reasoning (pp. 312–16; see also p. 636).

Fifth, we have given positive characterizations of both "logically true-or-false" and "empirically true-or-false," rather than defining one as the

* Newton, *Mathematical Principles of Natural Philosophy*, pp. 636–37, 671–76. Whittaker, *A History of the Theories of Aether and Electricity*.

The relation between verification and understanding is discussed further in sec. 4.2.4.

negation of the other with respect to a class of cognitive, non-normative propositions. We wish to leave open at this time the possibility that certain cognitive propositions are neither logically true-or-false nor empirically true-or-false, and we will argue later that such indeed is the case (secs. 5.6.3, 10.4.2).

For the sake of convenience we sometimes use "logical" instead of "logically true-or-false," and similarly for "empirical," though of course it is odd to say that "3 + 5 = 19" is logical. The terms "analytic," "synthetic" and the terms "a priori," "a posteriori" are often used for the same or a similar distinction (see sec. 10.5.2).

1.2.2 The logical and empirical status of geometry

We may illustrate the logical-empirical distinction with a historical example. Euclid created the first axiomatic system. His plane geometry contained definitions and axioms, followed by proofs of all known theorems. The axioms seemed to be intuitively true, the theorems to follow demonstratively from the axioms, and so both axioms and theorems seemed to have been shown true by reasoning alone. Thus all the statements of Euclid's geometry appeared to be logically true, and they were so regarded by mathematicians and philosophers for two millennia. Yet there was a paradox. The statements of geometry were taken to refer to physical space and thus to have factual content. But logically true statements do not tell us anything about how things actually are, as contrasted to how they might be. Kant saw this paradox and, to resolve it, said that geometry is both synthetic (telling us about the structure of space) and a priori.* Non-Euclidean geometry, providing a very different resolution, was discovered shortly after Kant wrote.

N. I. Lobachevski and F. Bolyai proposed one alternative to Euclid's plane geometry early in the nineteenth century, and G. R. Riemann and F. Klein proposed another alternative later in that century.† Lobachevskian, Euclidean, and Riemannian geometry all have the same fundamental concepts and definitions and for the most part the same axioms. They differ with respect to whether lines can be infinite in length (they can be in the first two geometries, not in the third), with respect to the parallel postulate, and in many respects that follow from these. One version of the parallel postulate is stated in terms of the number of straight lines that can be drawn through a point, parallel to a given line: infinitely many parallels

* *Critique of Pure Reason*, p. 70; *Prolegomena*, p. 17. See pp. 643–46 below.

† See Sommerville's *Non-Euclidean Geometry* and Coxeter's *Non-Euclidean Geometry*. Useful short accounts are found in Courant and Robbins, *What is Mathematics?*, pp. 214–27; Richardson, *Fundamentals of Mathematics*, pp. 414–38; and Stabler, *An Introduction to Mathematical Thought*, pp. 11–19.

can be drawn in Lobachevskian geometry, exactly one parallel in Euclidean,* and none in Riemannian. The following alternative theorems exhibit an important respect in which the three geometries differ.

[17] The sum of the angles of a triangle is *less than* 180 degrees

[17′] The sum of the angles of a triangle is *exactly* 180 degrees

[17″] The sum of the angles of a triangle is *more than* 180 degrees,

in Lobachevskian, Euclidean, and Riemannian geometry, respectively.

The axioms and theorems of plane geometry state connections among certain key terms, such as "point," "line," "straight line," "plane," and "congruent." These are often called "undefined terms," because they are not defined within the axiomatic or formal system itself. They can be defined outside the system, in which case we say they are "interpreted." Euclid and other Greeks had an ordinary interpretation of "point," "line," "plane," etc., in mind when doing geometry; but developments in modern mathematics and logic show that sometimes it is best when working with proofs not to give an interpretation to the undefined terms of the system. As David Hilbert once remarked of geometry, "One must be able to say at all times—instead of points, straight lines, and planes—tables, chairs, and beer mugs."†

The distinction between an "interpreted" and "uninterpreted" term is an important one; let us digress a moment to enlarge upon it. The statement

[18] All *A* are *B*

is only partially interpreted, the symbols "*A*" and "*B*" being free variables. Such a "statement form" is neither true nor false as it stands; but is true on some interpretations, i.e., for some values of the free variables, and false on others, i.e., for other values of the free variables. Thus [18] is true for A = men and B = mortal, false for A = cows and B = horses. On the other hand, the statement form "all *A* are *A*" is true on all interpretations and hence is true as it stands. It is sometimes convenient to treat a statement form as if it were a statement intended to cover all interpretations. For example, [18] may be treated essentially as if it were the statement

[18′] For all *A* and *B*, all *A* are *B* .

When statement forms are construed in this way the notions of logically true-or-false and empirically true-or-false apply automatically to them. For example, "All *A* are *A*" is logically true but "All *A* are *B*" is not. Consequently, it is convenient to use *statement* to include statement forms (sen-

* Euclid's parallel postulate was framed differently. *The Thirteen Books of Euclid's Elements* 1:202.

† Reid, *Hilbert*, p. 57.

tences with free variables) as well as statements in the strict sense. See further Section 6.3 (An Abstract Interpretation).

The pure mathematician leaves the undefined terms of geometry ("point," "line," "plane," etc.) uninterpreted so that the question of truth and falsity is not applicable to the axioms and theorems. For he is interested in whether or not the theorems follow from the axioms, that is, whether or not the proofs are valid. Logical (deductive) validity does not depend on the particular interpretation, since an argument form is valid if and only if every argument resulting from an interpretation of that form is valid. Euclid's proofs are full of holes, but when these are filled the axioms logically imply the theorems. Similarly, there are rigorous axiomatizations of Lobachevskian and Riemannian geometry, and in each of these the axioms logically imply the theorems. For example,

[19] The axioms of Lobachevskian geometry imply [17]

[19′] The axioms of Euclidean geometry imply [17′]

[19″] The axioms of Riemannian geometry imply [17″]

are all logically true.* There is thus an important element of truth in pure geometry, but it concerns the relation of the axioms to the theorems of the system, not the truth status of the axioms or theorems in themselves.

The matter is different when the undefined terms are given their normal interpretation in reference to physical space. The three pure geometries thereby become three physical geometries, each empirically true-or-false. The question then concerns a suitably defined physical triangle. Space is Lobachevskian, Euclidean, or Riemannian, according to whether the sum of the angles of this physical triangle is less than, equal to, or greater than 180 degrees.

One important interpretive definition of "straight line" is

[20] A straight line is the path of a beam of light in a vacuum.

This definition has been used implicitly in many applications of geometry to surveying, physics, and astronomy. When all the undefined terms of plane geometry are interpreted by definitions like [20], the sentences [17], [17′], and [17″] become empirically true-or-false statements about physical space.

There is a commonly told story that K. F. Gauss did attempt to test the empirical statements of physical geometry. Whether the story is true or is just a fairy tale of the community of scholars, it illustrates the point well. Supposedly, Gauss wished to determine which of the statements [17], [17′], and [17″] is true when these are interpreted by definition [20], i.e., when applied to the sum of the angles of a triangle whose sides are formed by beams of light. Gauss is said to have measured the sum of the angles of a

* These sentences are intended as abbreviations for sentences in which the axioms and the statements they imply are actually written out.

large triangle with mountaintops for vertices and to have found that [17′] was true within the accuracy of his experiment.

Now I have never seen any documentation of the story that Gauss made measurements for the purpose of determining whether space is Euclidean. We do know he was a surveyor and in this capacity he did triangulate (measure the angles of large triangles) in Germany. And he invented the heliotrope to facilitate the process.* The heliotrope operated with reflected light from the sun, so that lines established by its use were paths of light beams. Moreover, Gauss had already discovered non-Euclidean geometry at the time he did his triangulation, though he never published his revolutionary discovery for fear of ridicule and damage to his reputation.† Hence it is possible that part of his motive in triangulating was to test [17′], and it seems very likely that he thought of his surveying findings in connection with non-Euclidean geometry even though this was not his function as a surveyor.

In any case, Gauss measured large triangles on the surface of the earth, and these measurements showed that [17′] was true within the accuracy of the method. Whether [17′] is true for *very* large astronomical triangles is still an open and complicated question of cosmology, the prevailing opinion among scientists having changed from time to time. The situation is complicated by the fact that even if Lobachevskian or Riemannian geometry is true, the sum of the angles of a triangle may be very, very close to 180 degrees. If the measured sum of the angles deviates from 180 degrees by more than the experimental error, Euclidean geometry is refuted, while if the measured sum of the angles deviates from 180 degrees by less than the experimental error, the question as to which interpreted geometry is correct remains unanswered. In the latter case, the choice of which geometry to use is a matter of convenience.

Thus geometry provides a good example of a subject in which empirically true-or-false and logically true-or-false statements are intimately related.

1.2.3 The logical modalities

It is now opportune to introduce a few of the symbols of mathematical logic to be used in subsequent chapters.

Consider the class of all statements that are either logically true-or-false or empirically true-or-false. Small letters will be used as variables for which statements belonging to this class may be substituted.

* Dunnington, *Gauss*, chap. 10.

† See, besides the other references in this subsection, Wolfe's *Non-Euclidean Geometry*, p. 48, Bonola's *Non-Euclidean Geometry*, p. 67, and Engel and Stackel's *Die Theorie der Parallellinien*, p. 226.

We use a square "$\Box$" to mean "is logically true," i.e.,

[21] $\Box p =_{df} (p \text{ is logically true})$.

The sign "$=_{df}$" means "equals by (explicit) definition"; "$\Box p$" is the symbol defined (the *definiendum*) and the right-hand side is the defining expression (the *definiens*). The square is also translated "it is logically necessary that"; the qualifying "logically" is required because in Chapter 6 we will introduce a concept of causal necessity.

We can build more definitions on this one.

[22] $(p \rightarrow q) =_{df} \Box(\text{if } p \text{ then } q)$

[23] $(p \leftrightarrow q) =_{df} \Box(p \text{ if and only if } q)$.

The single-headed arrow is read "logically implies" (sometimes "logically entails") while the double-headed arrow is translated "is logically equivalent to." Since a (correct) definition is a special case of logical truth, equality by definition is a special case of logical equivalence. Other kinds of implication and equivalence will be defined in Section 2.2.2 and in Chapter 6.

We require just four more symbols in this section. The negation symbol "$\sim$", the conjunction symbol "&", and the disjunction symbol "v" will be formally defined in Section 2.2.2; it suffices for the present to translate them as "not," "and," and "and/or," respectively. The diamond "$\Diamond$" is read "is consistent" or "is logically possible"; it is defined by

[24] $\Diamond p =_{df} \sim\Box\sim p$.

We can readily show by substitution and the law of double negation ($p \leftrightarrow \sim\sim p$) that

[25] $\Box p \leftrightarrow \sim\Diamond\sim p$.

The following are self-evident

[26] $\Box p \rightarrow p$

[27] $p \rightarrow \Diamond p$,

i.e., a logical truth is true, and a true proposition is logically possible.

The symbols "$\Box$", "$\Diamond$", "$\rightarrow$", and "$\leftrightarrow$" are called modal symbols because by means of them one can distinguish modes of truth and falsity. Let us see how they can be used to distinguish logical truths and falsehoods from empirical truths and falsehoods.

The idea of logical falsehood (self-contradiction) is easily expressed with the square

[28] $\Box\sim p \leftrightarrow (p \text{ is logically false})$,

and combining this with definition [21] gives

[29] $(\Box p \vee \Box\sim p) \leftrightarrow (p \text{ is logically true-or-false})$.

Since our universe of discourse is, by definition, limited to statements that are either logically true-or-false or empirically true-or-false, we have

[30] $\sim(\Box p \vee \Box\sim p) \leftrightarrow$ (p is empirically true-or-false) .

By elementary logical manipulation, using definition [24], this becomes

[31] $(\Diamond p \,\&\, \Diamond\sim p) \leftrightarrow$ (p is empirically true-or-false) ,

i.e., a statement is empirical if both it and its negation are logically possible. Hence

[32] $(p \,\&\, \Diamond p \,\&\, \Diamond\sim p) \leftrightarrow$ (p is empirically true) ,

which by means of result [27] reduces to

[33] $(p \,\&\, \Diamond\sim p) \leftrightarrow$ (p is empirically true) ,

i.e., an empirically true statement is a true statement whose negation is logically possible. Similarly,

[34] $(\sim p \,\&\, \Diamond p \,\&\, \Diamond\sim p) \leftrightarrow$ (p is empirically false) ,

and by means of formula [27]

[35] $(\sim p \,\&\, \Diamond p) \leftrightarrow$ (p is empirically false) ,

i.e., an empirically false statement is a false statement that is logically possible.

The logically true statements [21], [28], [29], [31], [33], and [35] summarize our classification of statements (see pp. 340–41).

1.3 Specifying the Meaning of a Technical Term

We must digress for a moment to reflect upon exactly what it was we were doing in the last section, since it illustrates a typical and basic type of philosophical activity.

Subsection 1.2.1 was devoted to specifying the meaning of the technical terms "logically true-or-false" and "empirically true-or-false" as we use them. These meanings are partly new, partly old, being in line with the ordinary uses of the words "logical" and "empirical," but also being more precise, less ambiguous, and more specialized than the ordinary uses. It is important to realize that that whole subsection has been employed to give a sense to these two terms, and that the examples and qualifications played an essential role in this enterprise. Insofar as Subsection 1.2.1 was successful, the reader will now know what is meant by these terms as they are used in this book.

There are other, more familiar, ways of specifying the meanings of terms, such as explicit definitions and axiomatic systems. For example, the explicit definition [21] (sec. 1.2.3) completely identifies the meaning of the square for one who already knows the meaning of "logically true," the definiendum "□*p*" being introduced by the definition as a synonym for the definiens "*p* is logically true." Axiom systems may also be used to specify the meaning of a term or set of terms. In Section 1.2.2 we mentioned that Euclidean plane geometry may be studied as an uninterpreted system, in which case its axioms and theorems are neither true nor false; and that it may also be so interpreted that its axioms and theorems are empirically true-or-false. There is a third way of construing this same axiom system: as an implicit definition of the concepts of Euclidean straight line, Euclidean plane, etc. One *defines* Euclidean planes, straight lines, etc., as those entities satisfying or making true the axioms of Euclidean geometry. Note that in this way of viewing the axiomatic system, the axioms are true by definition rather than being empirically true-or-false. But there is no magic here, for it is now an empirical question as to whether any Euclidean plane (in this sense) exists; just as when we define a centaur to be an animal that is half-man and half-horse, it is an empirical question as to whether there are any centaurs.

It is sometimes possible to specify a set of statements constituting a subject and then to give an axiomatic system such that every statement or its negation is a theorem of that system. Such an axiomatization is called "complete." There are complete formulations of Euclidean plane geometry.* An incomplete axiomatic system will leave certain questions open, i.e., there will be some statement about the subject matter such that neither it nor its negation is a theorem. If this statement is logically true-or-false, the incomplete system may not by itself completely define a term or set of terms; nevertheless, an incomplete system can partially characterize the meaning of a term. Some cases begin with a subject matter that is informal, intuitive, and not well defined; that is, it is not clear at the outset exactly which statements belong to the subject matter and which do not. But it may still be clear that on the intended interpretation certain statements do belong to the subject matter and are true by virtue of the meanings of their terms, i.e., are true by definition. And such statements may form the basis of an axiomatic system that, while not defining the terms in question, helps delineate and specify their meaning. Examples of this use of an axiomatic system to help specify the meaning of a term are given in Chapter 2 (for "probability") and in Chapter 6 (for "causal necessity").

A careful study of definition is beyond the scope of this work, but one more component of definition deserves brief mention. This is the use of examples, either abstract ones like sentences [1] through [16] of Section 1.2.1, or concrete objects, events, or experiences. One type of definition, called "ostensive definition," relies heavily on concrete examples picked out

* Wilder, *Introduction to the Foundations of Mathematics*, p. 37. "Completeness" has many different senses, but these differences are irrelevant here.

by pointing and indicating. For instance, one might ostensively define "chair" by exhibiting chairs of various kinds as examples of the term and pieces of furniture that are not chairs as non-examples of the term. Some symbols may be needed to explain what is going on, but the burden of the definition would be carried by designated examples. Different kinds of chairs may be shown to insure that the extension of the term defined is as broad as that of "chair"; if all the chairs shown were iron, the ostensive definition would be of "iron chair" as well as of "chair." To insure against too broad an extension, examples of objects that are not chairs may be presented as cases where the term is not applicable; since every object correctly called a "chair" is also correctly called a piece of "furniture," sofas and tables may be presented as examples of objects that are not chairs to show that "chair" rather than "furniture" is being defined.*

It is clear from the foregoing that one *specifies the meaning of a term* by establishing relations between it and other, presumably understood, terms; and/or between the term and examples, objects, events, and experiences. Explicit definitions, ostensive definitions, axiomatic systems, and the material of Section 1.2.1 all function in this way to communicate some information, partial or complete, about the meaning of a term. An explicit definition equates the definiendum to the definiens; an ostensive definition relates the definiendum to objects and experiences; an axiomatic system interrelates a whole cluster of terms by means of formation rules, definitions, axioms, and rules of inference. In philosophy it is traditional to define one's terms before beginning to philosophize with them; our use of informal remarks, examples, explicit definitions, and axiomatic systems to specify the meanings of our key terms constitutes a continuation and extension of this tradition.

The reader may wonder why we did not give explicit or axiomatic definitions of "logically true-or-false" and "empirically true-or-false," rather than use the informal procedure of Section 1.2.1 to specify the meanings of these terms. The reason is that it would be useless to attempt explicit definitions at this stage of our inquiry, for any term in the definiens would need as much informal specification of meaning as that given "logically true-or-false" and "empirically true-or-false" in Section 1.2.1. More generally, formal definitions of very basic and fundamental concepts, including those of probability and causality, presuppose considerable informal specification of meaning. In the beginning, all one can usefully do is specify the meanings of such foundational terms by informal remarks, examples, and qualifications. Later, after the groundwork is laid, more formal procedures for specifying meanings are in order. The concept of inductive probability provides a good example of this overall procedure: its meaning will be

* Ostensive definitions are closely related to empiricist theories of meaning. See my paper "Empiricism and Vagueness."

specified first informally (sec. 1.5.2), then by means of the traditional calculus of probability (chap. 2), next in connection with a formal model (sec. 3.2), and finally by means of an axiomatic system governing choices (chap. 5). Other terms whose meaning will be specified in successive stages are "utility" (secs. 4.3.1, 5.5.1), "standard inductive logic" (secs. 3.1, 3.2, 10.3), and "logically true-or-false" (secs. 1.2.1, 5.6.3). We shall review the definitions of these terms in Chapter **11**.

When specifying the meaning of a technical term of considerable importance to this work, we print the word or phrase in question in **boldfaced type,** unless, of course, it is a novel symbol like the square of Section 1.2.2. *Italics* are used in the same way for terms of lesser importance, e.g., "definiens" in Section 1.2.3 and "model" in Section 1.6.2, and also for emphasis.

1.4 Inquiry and Argument

1.4.1 Kinds of logic

We said in the beginning that we wished to study the nature of scientific knowledge. We now see that there are two basic kinds of such knowledge: that of mathematics on the one hand, and that of empirical science on the other. The problem of the former, i.e., of the nature of logical truth and falsity, belongs to the philosophy of mathematics and is not central to our investigation, though we will make frequent reference to logical truth and falsity. In contrast, the problem of the nature and ground of empirical truth and falsity is one of the central topics of the philosophy of science and is the main problem of this treatise. This problem is intimately related to the subject of inductive logic. In order to clarify this relationship and the distinction between deductive and inductive logic, we will now present an overall discussion of the branches of logic.

We begin with some very broad concepts of reason and logic and gradually delineate our subject matter by successively narrowing these concepts. Rules, procedures, algorithms, methods, and recipes are all different, but they may be viewed in a common light, as a system of instructions (simple or complex) to be followed in a given type of situation. All of them may be covered by the word *rule*, if we widen it to include complex systems of rules providing for many cases and alternatives. Each instance of reasoning has a starting point and a terminus: it begins with a question, a problem, some data, a premise, or a hypothesis; and ends (it is hoped) with an answer, a solution, an explanation, a conclusion, or a consequence. This process is governed by a rule that is applicable to other (similar) instances. *Reasoning* proceeds by rules, implicit or explicit, and is always general: there must be other cases covered by the same rule. *Logic* studies and evaluates the most general, common, and basic rules of reasoning, together with related matters.

As we noted in connection with the calculus and Newton's theory of gravity (p. 2), there is a difference between how a subject develops and how its results are best arranged to show their grounds. This leads to the following bifurcation of logic. The **logic of inquiry** studies rules that are useful in solving problems, answering questions, and arriving at important results; it evaluates these rules in terms of applicability, simplicity, and utility. Charles S. Peirce called this "the logic of abduction."* It has also been called "heuristic logic" and "the logic of discovery." The **logic of argument** treats rules for deriving conclusions from premises and relating evidence to hypotheses and theories, judging these rules to be valid or fallacious, correct or incorrect, reliable or unreliable. To draw an analogy: The logic of inquiry is concerned with the dynamics of reasoning, the logic of argument with the statics of it.

TABLE 1

BRANCHES OF LOGIC

		TYPE OF STATEMENT	
		Logically true-or-false	Empirically true-or-false
TYPE OF ACTIVITY	Inquiry	Logic of mathematical inquiry	Logic of empirical inquiry
	Argument	Deductive logic	Inductive logic

Independently of the above division, logic may be dichotomized according to whether it treats logical or empirical statements. The two divisions give rise to four branches of logic, as shown in Table 1. We will say a few words about each of these branches before treating in more detail the ones particularly relevant to this book.

The **logic of mathematical inquiry** studies the investigation of logically true-or-false statements; for example, how to discover proofs, how to make mathematical generalizations. The **logic of empirical inquiry** studies inquiry aimed at empirical truths, emphasizing the methods of the empirical sciences. The principles of the two logics of inquiry are similar.

The arguments used to establish or refute logically true-or-false statements are called deductive arguments. The logic of deductive arguments (called **deductive logic**) studies deductive arguments, though not all of them. "Logically true-or-false," as defined in Section 1.2.1, covers all statements of

* *Collected Papers*, vols. 1, 2, 5. See also the present writer's "Peirce's Theory of Abduction."

mathematics; hence all proofs of mathematics (including proofs by mathematical induction!) are deductive arguments. But deductive logic does not study all of these, since then it would be identical with mathematics rather than being at most a part of it. It is difficult to draw the line between deductive logic and the rest of mathematics, especially since mathematical logic is the most important part of deductive logic. Very roughly, the distinction is this: Deductive logic treats the most foundational and general types of deductive arguments, while mathematics emphasizes those that depend on the specific subject matter of that branch of mathematics in which they occur. The logic of causal statements (chaps. 6 and 7) is a part of deductive logic.

Deductive arguments are also used to derive one empirically true-or-false statement from another. But empirically true-or-false statements often transcend the evidence for them, and so empirically true-or-false statements cannot be confirmed or disconfirmed by deductive arguments alone. For this one needs, in addition, inductive arguments. The logic of inductive arguments studies the most general, universal, and fundamental types of inductive arguments, leaving the more detailed and specific forms to the individual sciences and statistics. We call this subject **inductive logic,** but it should be noted that the name "inductive logic" is often used to refer to a mixture of the logic of empirical inquiry and the logic of inductive arguments.

Our chief concern is with the foundations of inductive arguments. But to put our view of inductive logic in proper perspective, let us discuss first the two other branches of logic closest to it: the logic of empirical inquiry (in sec. 1.4.2) and deductive logic (in sec. 1.5.1).

1.4.2 The logic of empirical inquiry

We begin by listing some of the rules of procedure belonging to this branch of logic: Given a vague problematic situation, formulate a precise and definite question concerning it. Systematically consider and organize the possible solutions to a problem suggested by what is known in the field at the time. Search related fields for useful analogies (Darwin, for example, adapted an idea from Malthus' work on population to the theory of evolution). Take a scientific or mathematical method or technique developed to solve a certain kind of problem and search for other areas in which it may be successfully and usefully applied. Given a difficult problem, formulate simpler problems whose solutions will probably contribute to the solution of the original problem. On the basis of given data and known laws, construct a hypothesis to explain the data, derive a consequence from the hypothesis, test this consequence, and then iterate the whole cycle. Given two competing hypotheses, devise and perform a crucial experiment to decide between them.

If the arguments for each of two alternative hypotheses are otherwise equal, choose the simpler hypothesis.*

At this point one may well object that these are not really rules, but merely suggestions, and that in the very nature of the case there can be no *logic* of empirical inquiry (as distinguished from the logic of inductive arguments). Success in solving scientific problems requires creativity, genius, insight, careful preparation, determination, and hard work—and these are either native endowments or acquired skills or a combination of the two. One cannot become a scientist merely by learning these "rules."

There is much truth in this. Rules vary widely in two important respects: the extent to which applying them is mechanical and automatic (though explicit and nonhabitual), and the extent to which success is guaranteed. The decision procedures of deductive logic lie at one extreme: Carrying out a decision procedure is a purely mechanical, automatic process and one is sure to get an answer to the question "Is this argument valid?" (see sec. 6.4). The rules of inquiry cited above stand at the opposite extreme: great ingenuity and knowledge are required for applying them, and success is highly problematic.

But other things must be said to keep the picture in proper balance. A great deal of scientific work that passes for creative is not really so and can surely be reduced to rules. Moreover, we should not confuse the fact that the logic of empirical inquiry *is now* in a primitive state with the conjecture that most of human problem solving *cannot* be mechanized. Note should be taken here of the existence of a new tool for the mechanization of inquiry: the electronic digital computer (sec. 6.4.3). Extensive attempts to reduce discovery in limited areas to rules programmable on a computer are currently being made under the headings "artificial intelligence" and "adaptive systems."† Finally, while deductive logic is highly developed at the present time and the logic of mathematical inquiry is by contrast extremely primitive, not so much discrepancy in state of development exists between the logic of empirical inquiry and inductive logic. Consequently, issues of the latter two subjects are often closely intertwined.

This last point may be illustrated in connection with the rule of simplicity. As formulated above, this rule applies to competing hypotheses concerning the same phenomena. Two cases occur: The competing hypotheses are logically equivalent, or they are not.

Consider the first case. If the two alternative hypotheses are logically

* Many of these rules and modifications of others also belong to the logic of mathematical inquiry. For further examples of rules in this subject see Polya's *How to Solve It*.

† See, for example, *Self-Organizing Systems* (edited by Yovits and Cameron) and *Computers and Thought* (edited by Feigenbaum and Feldman). See also sec. 10.2.1 (Empirical and a priori concepts).

In my opinion, we will acquire a deep and detailed understanding of the processes of discovery only when we can study computers programmed to solve difficult problems.

equivalent, they have the same observable consequences and are really alternative formulations of the same empirical hypothesis. In this case one does not need to decide which of two contradictory descriptions of nature is true, but only which of two alternative formulations of the same empirical materials he wishes to work with; clearly this choice should be made for the convenience of inquiry. By definition, the simpler of these two hypotheses is the more convenient to use, and hence the simpler should be adopted. Thus we have derived one version of the rule of simplicity from a general principle of economy of research: Investigation should be planned to obtain a maximum of information (results) from a given expenditure of effort and money. Obviously, many of the rules of empirical inquiry may be derived from this principle of economy.

Consider next the second case: The two competing hypotheses are *not* logically equivalent. This case is best discussed by means of an illustration from the history of science, namely, the famous controversy between Galileo and the Roman Catholic Church regarding the geocentric and heliocentric hypotheses. These two hypotheses were sometimes regarded as alternative ways of calculating the apparent motions of the planets. As such they were essentially logically equivalent. Now the Church had no objection to the heliocentric hypothesis treated in this way, but Galileo was not satisfied so to regard it. He insisted that the earth really did move while the sun and the stars stood still, whereas the Church maintained that the earth stood still while the sun and stars moved. Interpreted in this way, the heliocentric and geocentric hypotheses were not logically equivalent, but had different empirical consequences. An examination of these consequences will show something about the relation of empirical inquiry to inductive arguments.

The observable consequences on which the two hypotheses differed fall into two classes: those that follow from the particular hypothesis itself, and those that are not derivable from the hypothesis itself but only from it together with theories about related subjects. The phenomenon of stellar parallax belongs to the first class. The heliocentric hypothesis states that the earth revolves around the sun yearly while the stars stand still; if so, the stars should appear in different directions at different seasons, i.e., when the earth is at different positions in its orbit. No such shift was observed, though we know *now* that this was due to limitations of the instruments available, for stellar parallax was not observed until about three-hundred years later. A consequence belonging to the second class is the fact that a freely falling body moves straight down. Neither the geocentric hypothesis nor the heliocentric hypothesis by itself implies anything about terrestrial motions, but taken in conjunction with the established Aristotelian theory that an unsupported object will move straight to its natural place, the geocentric theory implies it should fall straight down (as it does) while the heliocentric theory implies that it should fall west (since on this theory the earth is rotating and its surface is moving east).

It is difficult even now to assess the evidential weight these arguments should have had, but a good case can be made for the following evaluation. The absence of parallax was evidence in favor of the geocentric hypothesis; for while it could be explained on the heliocentric hypothesis by saying that the stars were too distant for the parallax to be observed, the stars did not appear to be that distant; moreover, at that time there was no reason other than the heliocentric hypothesis to believe that they were that distant. Likewise, I think, the fact that unsupported bodies do not fall west was evidence for the geocentric hypothesis, for the following reasons.

A fundamental rule of the logic of argument is the **rule of total evidence,** which states that one *should* use all the information (evidence, knowledge) available to him in deciding whether a proposition is true or false, probable or improbable, and in deciding what degree of probability to use in acting on a proposition.

A special case of the rule of total evidence is the rule that one should employ established theories from related areas in judging the adequacy of a new theory. Now the Aristotelian theory of falling bodies was probably the most adequate theory concerning terrestrial motion at the time of the controversy between Galileo and the Roman Catholic Church—there were alternatives in the making, but there was no satisfactory substitute until Newton developed his theory of gravity. Hence, insofar as these two consequences (parallax and direction of fall) are concerned, the evidence seemed to be on the side of the geocentric theory. There was also evidence we have not discussed, and its bearing is likewise controversial; but in my opinion, when one includes all the information known to Galileo and the Catholic Church, except considerations of simplicity, the balance weighed on the side of the geocentric hypothesis.

The factor of simplicity worked in the opposite direction. Now it was not the case, as is so often asserted, that Copernicus' heliocentric theory involved fewer circles and epicycles than the current versions of Ptolemy's geocentric theory.* But though the Copernican machinery for generating the paths of the planets was more complicated than the Ptolemaic machinery, the opposite was true with respect to the paths themselves. The paths of the planets, taken all at once, are simpler when referred to the sun as origin than when plotted with the earth as origin, since in the former case they do not have retrograde motion, whereas in the latter they do. Consequently the heliocentric theory was easier to work with than the geocentric theory. This factor of simplicity was very important in the development of science, for Kepler would not have arrived at his three laws of planetary motion had he been using the geocentric rather than the heliocentric theory.

* Koestler, *The Sleepwalkers*, p. 192, and Price, "Contra-Copernicus . . . ," p. 217.

In my opinion inductive logic and the logic of empirical inquiry give opposing judgments at this point, considerations of evidence and argument favoring the geocentric theory and considerations of economy and fruitfulness favoring the heliocentric theory. The matter is quite different when one includes Kepler's work, and it is definitely settled in favor of the heliocentric theory by Newton's theory of gravity; but this does not affect the point under discussion. Of course, with only the information available to Galileo and the Catholic Church, the investigator need not and should not choose one hypothesis and completely reject the other, as they did. In such circumstances both hypotheses should be held for further consideration and investigation (see sec. 2.5.1).

On the account just given, the simplicity of a hypothesis is a matter of research economy and heuristics and so is the concern of the logic of inquiry rather than the logic of argument. But one might also hold that simplicity and evidence are not entirely separate matters, and that simplicity has an evidential value as well as an economic one (cf. pp. 570–71, 634–35). We need not pursue this issue here, however, for we have attained the goal of this subsection, which was to describe the logic of empirical inquiry and show how it is interconnected with inductive logic.

1.5 Deductive and Inductive Arguments

1.5.1 Deductive arguments

Consider the deductive argument

[36] All my pets are parakeets, all parakeets are parrots, therefore all my pets are parrots.

Arguing is a special kind of reasoning and reasoning is governed by rules. In arguing, one asserts the premises as true (at least tentatively) and then claims the conclusion is true because it follows by a correct (valid) rule from true premises. In this case the rule is

[36′] *From* All A are B *and* All B are C *to infer* All A are C.

There are many ways of judging a rule of deductive inference. We can ask that it be useful, easy to apply, etc. But since inquiry aims at truth, an essential character of a good rule is that it always takes us from true premises to a true conclusion. "Valid" is defined with respect to this requirement. Thus rule [36′] and argument [36] are both valid, but the deductive rule

[37′] *From* All A are B *and* All C are B *to infer* All A are C

is invalid, for it would allow one to draw a false conclusion from true premises, as in the invalid argument

[37] All dogs are mammals, all Japanese spaniels are mammals, therefore all dogs are Japanese spaniels.

Now what shall we say of the validity of the rule

[38′] *Given* x is copper, *to conclude* x conducts electricity ?

Since copper does in fact conduct electricity, every instance of this rule, e.g.,

[38] This wire is copper, therefore this wire conducts electricity,

that has a true premise will have a true conclusion. To know that this rule takes us from a true premise to a true conclusion, however, we must transcend deductive logic and mathematics and enter the realm of empirical science. Now it is convenient to define "valid" for deductive arguments in such a way that questions of validity can be settled within mathematics itself. This we proceed to do.

We define *deductive argument* to cover rules governing deductive arguments as well as the arguments themselves, e.g., both [36′] and [36]. We next set up a correspondence between deductive arguments and conditional (if . . . then . . .) statements. Given a deductive argument with *premises* $\Phi_1, \Phi_2, \ldots, \Phi_N$ and *conclusion* θ, its *corresponding conditional* is

$$\text{If } (\Phi_1 \& \Phi_2 \& \ldots \& \Phi_N), \text{ then } \theta \quad .$$

Note that the antecedent of the hypothetical is the conjunction of all the premises, and the consequent is the conclusion. Finally, we define a deductive argument (or rule of inference) to be *valid* if its corresponding conditional is *logically* true; otherwise it is *invalid*.

We give these definitions because they are simple and satisfactory for our purposes, but as analyses of the corresponding notions of ordinary language they are deficient in crucial respects. A deductive argument involves the claim that the conclusion follows logically from the premises, but it is much more than this: it is a putative proof of the conclusion from the premises that proceeds by intuitively acceptable steps and that serves some purpose. A few examples will illustrate this point. An "argument" consisting of Euclid's axioms and postulates as premises and his last theorem as conclusion has such a large intuitive gap that it is not even an argument in the ordinary sense of the term. Likewise, the following two pieces of discourse serve no useful purpose and hence would hardly be called arguments, even though in each case the conclusion follows from the premise in a single intuitive step.

[39] The Wizard of Oz is a fictional character, therefore the Wizard of Oz is a fictional character.

[40] Caligula was so named because of his boots, therefore either the number six is a prime or it is not.

In a formal language, the notion of an intuitively acceptable step is modeled by the notion of "immediate consequence," and the notion of "valid deductive argument" is modeled by the notion of "proof" (sec. 6.2.3). But it is very difficult to characterize these notions for natural languages, and the notion of serving some purpose is not a formal notion at all. We shall return to these issues later (sec. 6.5.3). For the present, note that our definition of "valid deductive argument" captures an important part of the ordinary notion (the claim that the conclusion follows logically from the premises) and will suffice for our purposes.

The conditionals corresponding to the deductive arguments given earlier are

[36″] If all my pets are parakeets and all parakeets are parrots, then all my pets are parrots.

[37″] If all dogs are mammals and all Japanese spaniels are mammals, then all dogs are Japanese spaniels.

[38″] If this wire is copper, then it conducts electricity .

The conditional [36″] is logically true and argument [36] is accordingly valid. Conditional [37″] is not logically true, and so argument [37] is invalid. Conditional [38″] is true, but not logically true; therefore argument [38] is invalid, though one can construct a valid argument from it by adding

[41] Copper conducts electricity

to the premise.

It is sometimes said that deductive logic is concerned with validity, not truth. This idea is expressed in the remarks: In mathematics "we never know what we are talking about, nor whether what we are saying is true,"* and "If all the logicians in the world were laid end to end they would never reach a conclusion!" Now of course deductive logic does not settle the truth-status of empirical statements. But we have so defined deductive validity that questions of validity are replaced by questions about logical truth. Thus deductive logic deals with logically true-or-false statements as well as with arguments and rules of inference.

1.5.2 Inductive arguments and probability

We begin, as before, with an argument. Let us take as premise a complete description of what Ignaz Semmelweis knew about puerperal fever at the end of 1847.† Around 1840, in the medical students' clinic of the maternity department of Vienna General Hospital, from 5 to 16 percent of the

* Russell, *Mysticism and Logic*, p. 75.
† *Encyclopaedia Britannica* 24:631.

patients died of this disease. The rate was much lower in the midwives' clinic of the same department. Such explanations as overcrowding, fear, and mysterious atmospheric influences were offered, but Semmelweis examined them all and found them wanting. Moreover, when the students and midwives interchanged clinics, death followed the students. The patients would die in rows, but women who entered after delivery were spared. At last a colleague who "had received a punctured wound in one finger from the knife of one of his students" died of the disease. "At once," Semmelweis wrote, "I recognized the identity of the diseases."* The medical students often came into the maternity clinic from the dissecting-room, washing their hands with soap and water only. Starting in May 1847, Semmelweis had the students wash with chlorinated lime water. Shortly before this the mortality rate had been more than 12 percent, but by the end of the year it had fallen to 3 percent.

Semmelweis' conclusion was that the students' hands had been spreading the infection and that his policy of disinfection caused the decrease in mortality. Clearly this conclusion does not follow deductively; it is logically possible that the premise should have been true and the conclusion false. Moreover, there was a *chance* that the cause of the mortality decrease was something else, e.g., the natural abatement of an epidemic. But the premise does constitute good *evidence* for the conclusion. It is not *likely* that the conclusion should be false; i.e., given the premise it is *probably* true. The inductive argument can thus be stated

[42] *D, therefore probably C,*

where the premise *D* contains the data presented in the first paragraph of the present subsection and the conclusion is

(*C*) The students had been spreading the infection and the practice of disinfection caused the decrease in mortality.

Thus as "therefore" is the characteristic mark of a deductive argument, so "therefore probably" is the characteristic mark of an inductive argument, though of course synonyms may be used and these terms may be present implicitly rather than explicitly.

At this point it would seem natural to proceed as we did with deductive arguments (sec. 1.5.1), formulating a rule of inference and then a corresponding hypothetical. The situation is quite different here, however. Inductive arguments are much more complicated and intractable than deductive arguments. (Witness that inductive logic is much less developed than deductive logic.) Thus it is very difficult to formulate a general rule of inference governing argument [42]. Attempts have been made to formulate general rules of induction, for example by Francis Bacon and John Stuart

* Céline, *The Life and Work of Semmelweis*, p. 114.

Mill (pp. 101–2); and while these rules are of interest and are an essential part of inductive logic, they are not so easy to apply as are rules of deductive argument. The chief problems come when one attempts to express formally and in general terms the following aspects of an inductive argument: First, it is evidentially significant whether the data were gathered by a fair and unbiased procedure, i.e., constitute a "fair sample"; second, general background information (as contrasted to the specific data at hand) bears on the initial plausibility of the conclusion; and third, bona fide causal connections must be distinguished from accidental correlations.

We shall return to these important problems (secs. 3.1, 3.3, and chap. 10). But at present we can bypass them and go directly to the task of formulating a statement corresponding to an inductive argument. Now probability is a matter of degree, the degree of probability being conditional on (relative to) the evidence. One can see this by keeping the conclusion (C) of [42] constant and varying what data are included in the premise (D): the probability decreases tremendously if reference to the effects of the chlorinated lime water are deleted; it increases if a description of Semmelweis' later work is added; and it becomes conclusive if the contributions of Pasteur and Lister are included. To make all this explicit we replace the inductive argument by the statement

[42′] The probability of C on condition D is high ,

or, more succinctly,

[42″] $\mathbf{P}(C, D)$ is high .*

We have thus replaced an inductive argument by a corresponding probability statement, and the question of the validity or correctness of the inductive argument becomes a question of the truth of the corresponding probability statement. The two processes of replacing a deductive argument by a corresponding conditional and an inductive argument by a corresponding probability statement are analogous though different.

There are also cases where the probability is a real number. A silver coin is to be tossed in the usual way and bets are to be made on the proposition

(T) This silver dollar will fall tails on the next toss .

The total evidence available is

(E) This silver dollar looks symmetrical, and most symmetrical coins fall tails approximately half the time.

Because of the symmetry the probability is precise.

[43] $\mathbf{P}(T, E) = 1/2$.

* In some texts this is written "$P(C|D)$ is high."

The word "probable" has many meanings; the same is true of "chance," "likely," "plausible," etc. The foregoing specifies the meaning of "probable" that we are most interested in. We call probability in this inductive, evidential sense **inductive probability** (or **P**). "$\mathbf{P}(c, d)$" may be read "the probability of c on d," "the probability of c on condition d," "the probability of c relative to d," or "the probability of c on evidence d," with or without the qualifying word "inductive." Of course this evidential sense of probability occurs not only in science, but in law, history, philosophy, statistics, and everyday life as well.

Our discussion has shown that the basic form of an inductive probability statement is

[44] $\mathbf{P}(c, d) = x$.

We call a statement of this form an **atomic inductive probability statement.** An atomic inductive probability statement has three components in addition to the probability operator **P**: the statements c and d and the term x. Term x expresses the extent or degree to which the premise or condition d gives evidential support to (substantiates, confirms, corroborates, renders probable) the conclusion c. Term x may be a single quantity (real number) as it is in the calculus of probability (chap. 2). But x may also be a vague term like "low" or "high" (cf. "proved beyond a reasonable doubt"). This issue is discussed further in Section 4.3.2 (Quantitative probabilities and valuations).

There is another important difference between the non-numerical case [42″] and the numerical case [43]. As we noted a moment ago, it is difficult to formulate the general rule of inference governing the Semmelweis argument and to find other examples of the same rule. In contrast, the event of tossing a coin by the usual procedure is easily repeated, either with this coin or with another one. Because of this repeatability feature, inductive probability statements like [43] are easily confused with a quite different kind of atomic probability statement, which we will introduce after making an observation about the application of inductive probabilities.

Suppose you toss the silver dollar repeatedly, with the result

(R) This silver dollar was tossed many times by the usual procedure and fell tails about 70 percent of the time.

Were you wrong in believing [43]? Clearly you are surprised and will change your behavior and expectations concerning the coin. But [43] is still true; it simply is not applicable now that R is known. By the rule of total evidence (p. 20) you should no longer base your actions and expectations on [43], but rather on

[45] $\mathbf{P}(T, E\&R) = 0.7$

The evidence statements in [43] and [45] differ, and hence there is no incompatibility in both [43] and [45] being true.

Still, a coin that tends to fall tails half the time is intrinsically and physically different from a coin that tends to fall tails 70 percent of the time. Whether the coin has one characteristic or the other is an empirical matter that can be settled by tossing the coin. Moreover, these characteristics can be described by means of the term "probability." Consider the following two statements about the sequence of tosses of the silver dollar:

[46] The probability that this silver dollar will fall tails is 0.5

[47] The probability that this silver dollar will fall tails is 0.7.

Suppose these statements are made with the intention of deciding between them on the basis of how the coin actually falls when it is tossed. Thus, if *R* turns out to be true, statement [47] will be accepted as likely and statement [46] will be rejected as unlikely. When statements [46] and [47] are understood in this manner, they are clearly empirically true-or-false.

We call statements of this kind **atomic empirical probability statements** and the sense of probability used in them **empirical probability,** symbolized "$\mathbf{P}_e$". Let "τx_n" mean that the silver dollar falls tails on the *n*th toss. The empirical probability statements concerning the silver dollar may be written

$$\mathbf{P}_e(\tau x_n) = 0.5$$

$$\mathbf{P}_e(\tau x_n) = 0.7 \quad ,$$

or more briefly

[46′] $\mathbf{P}_e(\tau) = 0.5$

[47′] $\mathbf{P}_e(\tau) = 0.7$.

Empirical probability statements occur also in conditional form, that is, with two "argument" places (pp. 92–93). Thus one might consider the sequence of deaths in a large city and determine of each whether it was caused by lung cancer (γ) and whether the dead person smoked (σ). He could then ask whether death by lung cancer was correlated with smoking, that is, whether $\mathbf{P}_e(\gamma, \sigma) = \mathbf{P}_e(\gamma, \text{not-}\sigma)$. Empirical probability statements are very common in the empirical sciences, and they will be studied extensively in Chapter 8.

The question immediately arises as to whether there really are two different kinds of probability, inductive and empirical. This is a difficult question; we later discuss it at length (sec. 3.4). It suffices at present to note that there are two important prima facie differences between inductive probability and empirical probability. In the first place, an atomic empirical probability statement is clearly empirical, whereas it is doubtful that an atomic inductive probability statement is empirical. Thus result *R* is empirical evidence for "$\mathbf{P}_e(\tau) = 0.7$" and against "$\mathbf{P}_e(\tau) = 0.5$." But R is not evidence for "$\mathbf{P}(T, E\&R) = 0.7$" or evidence against "$\mathbf{P}(T, E) = 0.5$." These two inductive probability statements express an assessment of the bearing of certain evidence statements on T, so that a change in evidence is no reason for changing one's belief in either of them, though by the rule of total evidence it is a reason for applying one rather than the other. Since inductive probability was defined in terms of inductive reasoning, prima facie an atomic inductive probability statement is logically true-or-false rather than empirically true-or-false.

In the second place, the subject matter of an inductive probability statement may differ from that of an empirical probability statement. An empirical probability statement is defined for a sequence of events, not for a single event, whereas an inductive probability statement may refer either to a sequence of events or to a single, isolated event. Thus "$\mathbf{P}_e(\tau) = 0.7$" refers to a sequence of tosses of the silver dollar, stating that tails tend to come up 70 percent of the time. In contrast, "$\mathbf{P}(T, E\&R) = 0.7$" refers to a single toss of the coin, saying that relative to evidence $E\&R$ the inductive probability of the *next* toss being a tail is 0.7.

Notice that in order to state how a piece of evidence bears on an empirical probability statement we need to use the concept of inductive probability. Thus, relative to evidence E, "$\mathbf{P}_e(\tau) = 0.5$" is (inductively) more probable than "$\mathbf{P}_e(\tau) = 0.7$," while relative to evidence $E\&R$, "$\mathbf{P}_e(\tau) = 0.5$" is (inductively) much less probable than "$\mathbf{P}_e(\tau) = 0.7$." This suggests that the concept of inductive probability is more fundamental than the concept of empirical probability. We argue in Chapter 8 that this is in fact the case.

1.6 Problems and Methods

1.6.1 The four main problems of this book

We are now able to state our main problems more specifically. We began with the question: What is the nature of scientific knowledge? We later limited ourselves to empirical science and still later to the nature of scientific evidence. The rationale of the relation of scientific evidence to what it is evidence for is to be found in the rules of inductive argument. Since inductive arguments involve probability and chance, scientific evidence involves reasoning about chances.

In the last section we reduced inductive arguments to atomic inductive probability statements, i.e., statements of the form $\mathbf{P}(c, d) = x$. In this way our concern for the foundations of inductive arguments (sec. 1.4.1) becomes an interest in the foundations of inductive probability. Our problem may be stated: What is the nature of an atomic inductive probability statement? But this question too calls for further specification. Here one can move in either of two directions. On the one hand, he can distinguish various kinds of inductive arguments and hence kinds of atomic inductive probability statements, abstract their form, and formulate general rules for evaluating them. This approach is descriptive and stays close to the details of actual scientific arguments. Alternatively, one can ask broad questions about atomic probability statements in general. Given the present state of knowledge of scientific method, this approach is necessarily somewhat remote from actual inductive arguments and is accordingly speculative and philosophical. Both the descriptive and the speculative approaches to inductive arguments and probability have been followed—the former usually under the title "inductive logic" (sec. 1.4.1), the latter generally as philosophy of science—and this is as it should be. Correctly viewed, these two approaches supplement one another in the way that observation and theory interact in empirical science. In the present study, however, we choose to concentrate on the speculative approach to the problem of the nature of atomic probability statements. Hence our first main question is: (I) *What is the general nature of an atomic inductive probability statement?*

Now the reduction of inductive arguments to atomic inductive probability statements converts the problem of assessing the correctness or validity of an inductive argument into the problem of determining the truth-status of an atomic inductive probability statement. It is therefore important to ask how we know that an atomic inductive probability statement is true. Is its truth established by reason and reflection, or by observation and experiment? Thus one broad but basic problem about inductive probabilities arises in connection with the classification of statements into the logical and the empirical (sec. 1.2.1). Do atomic inductive probability statements fit into this classification, and if so, where? Our second main question is, then: (II) *Is an atomic inductive probability statement logically true-or-false, empirically true-or-false, or neither?* The logical-empirical dichotomy is closely associated with the distinction between the mathematical and the empirical sciences; thus this is tantamount to asking whether the ground of inductive inference is fundamentally mathematical in nature, or essentially empirical, or neither.

Empirical probability statements play a fundamental role in empirical science, e.g., in genetics, statistical mechanics, and quantum theory. Therefore we need to understand them and their relation to inductive probability statements. Hence our third main question is: (III) *What is the general nature of an atomic empirical probability statement, and how are empirical and inductive probability related?*

The mathematics of probability is young—about three-hundred years old.* Theories of probability that provide answers to the sort of questions

* Todhunter, *A History of the Mathematical Theory of Probability.*

we have raised are even younger, about half as old. We shall discuss the main ones: the frequency theory (sec. 3.4), the a priori theory (sec. 5.7.1), and the more recent personalistic theory (sec. 5.7.2). We use some of the features of the latter two in developing our own two theories of inductive probability: the pragmatic theory of inductive probability (sec. 5.6) and the presupposition theory of induction (sec. 10.4).

Another important stream of thought, traditionally not associated with probability theory, has a definite bearing on our first two questions. The concept of an inductive argument is an old one, and philosophers have been discussing the foundations of inductive inference for a long time, their discussions centering on the concept of cause with little reference to probability. The central issue was stated and argued most clearly by David Hume and Immanuel Kant. Hume defined causality in terms of experience and argued that any attempt to justify (provide a basis in reason for) induction must be circular. Kant held an opposed view: he argued that the concept of cause is a priori and attempted to justify (provide a rational ground for) induction. The concept of probability played only a minor role in their discussions. But since this concept is intimately related to scientific evidence and hence to the causal laws established by means of such evidence, the central issue is better stated by using both the concept of probability and the concept of causality.

In short, an adequate theory of inductive probability must take account of both chance and cause. Admittedly, the term "cause" is used less in science now than formerly, largely as a result of two developments in science: the prominence of statistical and indeterministic theories and laws, and the tendency to study systems and states thereof rather than events and things. And because of these and other developments, the concept of causality needs reanalysis. Nevertheless, the fundamental question discussed by Kant and Hume, when restated in terms of probability, is an important philosophical question. Their question was: What is the nature of causality, and what is the role in experience of the necessary connection between cause and effect? Thus we are led to our fourth and last main question: (IV) *What is the nature of causal necessity and how are causal necessity and inductive probability related?*

Some of the deductive properties of causal necessity are formalized in my logic of causal statements (chap. 6). My presupposition theory of induction contains an account of the relation of causal necessity to inductive probability (sec. 10.4).

We thus have four basic questions about probability and causality. The formulation of some of them will be refined later (pp. 92, 144, 313, and 511). All four are interrelated and hence their answers will be also. A single theory answering all the questions is presented in Chapter 11.

1.6.2 Theories and models in empirical science

The methods we use to study these four problems can be most easily explained after a brief discussion of the role of theories and models in empirical science.

Reality is a host of complex systems: dynamical, biological, chemical, evolutionary, thermodynamical, ideological, etc., etc. Because of their complexity, to learn about any one of them man must begin with a simplified, idealized view or model of it and, on the basis of empirical data, improve this model by successive approximations. Hence a scientific theory represents certain aspects or features of reality, but not all. No theory can tell us everything about reality, because reality is more complex than any theory could be.

These idealizations and simplifications of a theory should be, and usually are, made explicit. For example, in his law of falling bodies Galileo deliberately excluded the effects of friction and of the buoyancy of air; he was really studying free fall in a vacuum, though he could not produce even an approximate vacuum. This idealizing aspect of science is manifested in the fact that scientific results are often framed in terms of perfect entities, e.g., a perfect vacuum, an ideal gas, a frictionless body.

Sometimes the factor of idealization appears in connection with a model. The words "model" and "theory" are used in various ways, often interchangeably, but for our purposes we distinguish them sharply. A hypothetical, constructed, imagined, or actual structure or system is a *model* of an actual system or aspect of reality when it is sufficiently similar to or isomorphic with that system or aspect of reality. A *theory* is a statement or system of statements asserting something about the universe, a part of it, or some aspect of it. Some theories are statements about models, saying, in effect, that the given model is similar to reality in certain respects. For example, the kinetic theory of gases takes as a model for a gas a system of small spheres that bounce back and forth against the walls of a container but exert no force on each other and cannot rotate. Here the theory itself can be interpreted as asserting that the given model fits reality in certain enumerated respects, e.g., that the billiard ball model applies only to gases whose molecules possess no appreciable rotational energy.

A model may be used to represent an aspect or part of reality. Mathematical formulas and systems of equations are also used for this purpose. A theory may say that a formula fits reality in certain respects. For example, Galileo's law of falling bodies may be formulated as the assertion that in the absence of friction, buoyancy, etc., the formula "$v = gt$" describes the motion of a freely falling body. Though formulas and models play similar roles in theories, a formula is not, in general, a model. The difference lies in the way the two represent their objects. Peirce distinguished iconic signs, which represent their objects by being similar to them or possessing the same structure, from symbols, which represent their objects by conventional rules.* To apply this distinction to models and formulas: A model is an icon, a formula is a symbol.

Compare Niels Bohr's model of the atom with the mathematical description of modern quantum mechanics. Bohr imagined an atom to consist of electrons moving in orbits around a nucleus, as the planets move around the sun. The modern physicist can give a much better account of the behavior of the atom by using the formulas of quantum mechanics than by using Bohr's model. It is important that these formulas do not represent the atom in a sufficiently direct or iconic way to make them models in our sense of the term. Indeed, it was essential to the success of quantum mechanics to give up the search for models and to be satisfied with more abstract and symbolic formulas.

The discrepancies between a model or formula on the one hand and reality or nature on the other fall into two classes, then, according to whether they are or are not due to deliberate simplification. This distinction is crucial in testing and applying a law or theory. Clearly a theory should not be tested or applied in circumstances where the excluded aspects make a significant difference. To say that according to Galileo's law the acceleration of a falling object is independent of the shape and density of the object and that hence a feather and a stone will fall at the same rate in air is simply to misapply the law. An explanation of why the stone and feather fall at different speeds requires an appeal to the behavior of the air, and the atmosphere is deliberately excluded from Galileo's law. On the other hand, Galileo's law does imply that a body is uniformly accelerated in a vacuum, while in fact (by Newton's law, [9], p. 4) its acceleration increases slightly as it approaches the ground. This disparity between law and nature is very small, but it is not the result of a deliberate simplification by Galileo, not being known to him.

What we desire is knowledge of the whole, and hence we want a comprehensive theory as well as a true one. Moreover, a particular way of simplifying reality may be inadequate and fruitless. Consequently, both intended and unintended differences between model or formula and reality count against the theory, though not at all in the same way. The first reveal the need for a model or formula of wider scope that will include the given model or formula as a special case, while the second show that the given theory must be revised or rejected. Science makes progress in both directions. To use our Galileo example once more: Contemporary physics can describe and predict the behavior of many objects acted on by both frictional and

* *Collected Papers*, vol. 2, book 2. The distinction is discussed in my "Icon, Index, and Symbol."

gravitational forces; and the theories of Newton and Einstein give a more accurate account of the effect of the earth's gravity than did Galileo's.

We stated earlier that a model is an icon, a formula is a symbol. Now two formulas may be similar, in which case one may be used to represent the other iconically, the first becoming a model of the second. Likewise, a system of formulas or an artificial language can be a model of a natural language; examples will be given later.

1.6.3 The methods of this book

In the present work we make much use of the method of simplifying and modeling just described. But philosophy of science is not a science, and we cannot expect this method to produce results of the same kind and certainty here as it does in science.

We present three main types of modeling in turn. The first is modeling of language. Chapter 2 contains a formal axiomatic system for probability, called "the calculus of inductive probability," and Chapters 6 and 7 describe a formal language for causality, called "the logic of causal statements." Each of these axiomatic, mathematical systems is an artificial language and as such is a highly idealized model of ordinary language with respect to the terms ("probability," "causality") that are axiomatized. These models are of interest in the study of actual language, since they provide a formal system with which ordinary usage may be compared and contrasted. This is not our main purpose in presenting them here, however. Rather, these artificial languages are to provide a basis for our two theories of inductive probability, the pragmatic theory and the presupposition theory.

They do this by helping to specify the meanings of the two key terms of this book, "inductive probability" and "causality"; see Section 1.3. Consider "probability" as an example. We specified the meaning of this term somewhat in Section 1.5.2, but it will become clear in Chapter 3 that this specification is not sufficient to enable us to discuss our questions about probability in the way we wish. Hence the informal remarks of Section 1.5.2 need to be augmented by the axiomatic treatment of probability presented in Chapter 2, as well as by some of the materials in Chapter 3. See also Section 10.3, "Causal Models of Standard Inductive Logic."

For our axiomatic languages to be useful as specifications of the meanings of "probability" and "causality" they must fit ordinary usage in certain respects. Our four main questions were originally phrased in ordinary language, and while the subsequent discussion of them will draw on the artificial languages of Chapters 2 and 6, it will be conducted for the most part in everyday language. If the new languages were not models of ordinary language in the relevant respects, we would not be answering our original questions but different ones.

On the other hand, these new languages, as in the case of any model, must be simplified with respect to actual discourse. There are two main reasons for this. The first is a matter of sheer complexity. Ordinary language is complex, and the notions of probability and causality are more intricate than most. In the case of formal, axiomatic modeling of language there is a further reason for deviating from actual language. It is that language is at once somewhat under man's control and capable of improvement. Recall that the central task of logic is to study rules of reasoning (sec. 1.4.1). The rules underlying actual reasoning are sometimes explicit, more often implicit, and they usually fall in between. One task of logic is descriptive: to formulate rules of inference that rational people actually use, and to evaluate them as correct, reliable, good, successful, etc. But, traditionally, logic has also had a normative function: to study and propose new rules (rules that one should or might use) and modifications of old ones.* Our formal language of probability has many normative elements (sec. 2.1; see also sec. 5.6.2).

The use of mathematical logic to model ordinary language is a kind of applied mathematics, for it involves the application of a purely logical, mathematical structure to reality. It is also closely related to *analysis* in the technical philosophical sense of this term. The notion of analysis will be discussed later (sec. 4.2.3); here we will characterize it only briefly. The term, statement, or argument analyzed is called the *analysandum;* that which is to be substituted for the analysandum is called the *analysans.* The analysans should have approximately the same meaning as the analysandum but should be superior to the analysandum in certain respects. When analysis is carried out by means of a formal system, the analysans is a formal entity, e.g., a formula or a sequence of formulas, serving as a model of the analysandum.

Our second type of modeling is of decision-making in conditions of uncertainty. Chapter 5 contains the calculus of choice, which is an axiomatic system of rules for making choices. Like logical rules, rules of choice are normative as well as descriptive, and the calculus of choice is used to model ideal choice behavior as well as actual choice behavior. Decision-making involves inductive reasoning as well as valuation, so that rules of choice are closely related to probability rules and the calculus of choice is closely related to the calculus of probability.

Our third type of modeling is of the universe as a whole. Chapter 3 is entitled "Alternative Inductive Logics and the Justification of Induction." In it we wish to show that there are inductive logics that, while "irrational" in the ordinary sense of this word, are logically conceivable and, in a certain sense, are bona fide alternatives to standard inductive logic. To show that these alternatives are indeed consistent we need to work them out in complete detail. We do this for highly simplified models of reality, and we then generalize from these models to reality. The inductive logics developed from

* See my "Peirce's Conception of Logic as a Normative Science."

these models are also discussed in connection with the pragmatic theory of inductive probability. In Chapter 10 these models are extended to embody causal laws (as defined in chaps. 6 and 7), the extended models providing a basis for the presupposition theory of induction. Both kinds of models are very simple qualitative systems consisting of discrete events and a limited number of basic qualities and general laws.

Both the pragmatic and the presupposition theories of inductive probability are epistemological theories of the relation of the human mind as knower to the world as known. Consequently they involve generalizations from the models just mentioned to the actual situation. We now discuss briefly the extent of the gap between model and actuality, and also consider how and to what degree it may be bridged.

Science employs many methods, which vary from one branch to another and alter from time to time. Though the methods change less through history than the results obtained by means of them, the variations in method are significant. Nevertheless, for our purposes we may ignore most of these differences. In addition, the separation of empirical science from mathematics (sec. 1.2.1) and of argument from inquiry (sec. 1.4.1) entails isolating inductive arguments from the context in which they occur. Our formal languages are highly simplified models of actual languages. Finally, our models of reality are simple, qualitative, discrete, finite systems, whereas reality is actually a tremendous complex of systems governed by quantitative laws and is probably continuous and infinite. These restrictions and simplifications add up, of course, to an extreme idealization of actual scientific method and the universe to which it is applied.

Science pays close attention to the gap between model and reality and attempts to formulate accurately the scope of a model. It spans this gap between model and fact by meticulous observation, rigidly controlled experiment, and the mathematical derivation of quantitative predictions from the theory. Today we can verify that Galileo's law of falling bodies holds (approximately) for a vacuum by conducting an experiment in vacuo. Galileo could not do this, but he did minimize the effects of friction in his famous inclined plane experiment; and while he had only rough laws for friction and bouyancy he bolstered his case by careful observations, reflections, and experiments on the effects of these factors.

No such techniques and controls exist for handling simplification and idealization in the philosophy of science. Aside from the normative element in logic, we wish our theories to fit the facts, and hence we appeal to empirical data. These data are very general qualitative and comparative observations about scientific method and the universe it is used to investigate. But the distance between our qualitative, discrete, finite model universes and the actual universe is much greater than the distance between a model in science and that aspect or part of reality it models. Consequently our theories of inductive probability and causality are highly schematic and programmatic. At the appropriate places we shall ask, of course, whether our results depend upon limitations in the model or are in fact true of the reality being modeled. But in the end each decision on this point is necessarily tentative and speculative.

1.7 Conclusion

This book is concerned with the ultimate nature of the knowledge acquired by the empirical sciences.

The empirical sciences are to be distinguished from mathematics. The latter investigates logically true-or-false statements by reasoning and reflection; whereas the former inquires into empirically true-or-false statements, using observation and experiment as well as reasoning and reflection. There are two main aspects of an empirical science: its methods and its results.

The empirical sciences are based on reliable and tested methods of observation and experiment that may or may not involve instruments and apparatus. These methods are public in the sense that any qualified observer, at least in principle, can repeat the observation or experiment to check the results. Experimental work is generally guided by theories and models, and it is often assisted by mathematics. In turn, empirical data usually suggest new theories and models. In this way scientific methods are employed to establish (confirm or disconfirm) empirically true-or-false propositions about natural phenomena (physical, biological, mental, etc.) that are of general interest and importance. While these methods change over time, they are more invariant and stable than the results of empirical science.

At any given time an empirical science has results in the form of a body of confirmed empirically true-or-false statements, including descriptions of apparatus, reports on observations and experiments, predictions, generalizations, laws, and theories. These statements are interconnected by deductive and inductive arguments. Inductive arguments establish their conclusions with probability rather than with certainty, and hence there is always a chance that a scientific statement is erroneous. Consequently, these statements should be held tentatively, and investigation should aim at replacing them with more comprehensive, more accurate, and better confirmed results.

We have not attempted to define "empirical science" or to give necessary and sufficient conditions for a subject to be an empirical science, but only to formulate the most important characteristics of empirical science generally. Some of these characteristics may be absent from a specific empirical science, particularly at the beginning. For example, early theories of motion were not based on experiments, and biology has only recently made significant use of mathematics.

It should be noted that many of the characteristics just enumerated apply also to inquiries into empirically true-or-false statements not belonging to empirical science; thus a detective may use scientific method to discover the criminal, and a repairman may run a "controlled experiment" to locate a fault in a television set. Consequently, what we say about evidence in science also applies to evidence in other disciplines such as law and engineering. These other disciplines have their own unique problems with evidence, however, that do not interest us. Thus legal evidence usually relates to particular events not observed under controlled conditions and not repeatable, whereas scientific evidence generally relates to laws and repeatable events. The contrast is not so great as it might seem, for some scientific theories deal with unique and unrepeatable events (e.g., the origin of our solar system) or histories (e.g., the geological history of the earth); but still there is a difference. At any rate, science best displays the most general and important characteristics of evidence, which are what concern us here.

The foregoing makes clear that scientific knowledge is a complicated phenomenon with many dimensions. In the present work we wish to concentrate on just one of these dimensions: the nature of scientific evidence and inductive arguments. Now, the conclusion of an inductive argument is qualified by "probably," for there is always some chance that the conclusion is false though the premise is true. Hence inductive arguments are closely related to atomic inductive probability statements and may be reduced to such statements, subject to a certain amount of simplification and idealization. Two basic questions then arise: What is the general nature of an atomic inductive probability statement, and is an atomic inductive probability statement logically true-or-false, empirically true-or-false, or neither?

A concept of empirical probability also plays an important role in empirical science. Our third main question is: What is the general nature of an atomic empirical probability statement, and how are empirical and inductive probability related?

The nature of scientific knowledge and evidence has often been discussed in connection with causal laws. An important traditional philosophical question is: Are causal laws "merely" summaries of facts, or do they involve some kind of necessity? Since probability is basic to scientific evidence and knowledge, this question needs to be reexamined in terms of probability. We are thus led to our fourth main question: What is the nature of causal necessity and how is it related to probability?

These four problems in probability and causality will be investigated by the use of model languages for probability and causality and of very simple, qualititive, discrete models of the universe. The solutions offered will be speculative. The last chapter, "Chance, Cause, and Reason," provides an overview of the entire work.

2 The Calculus of Inductive Probability

Part of our knowledge we obtain direct; and part by argument. The Theory of Probability is concerned with that part which we obtain by argument, and it treats of the different degrees in which the results so obtained are conclusive or inconclusive.*

2.1 Introduction

As a preliminary to investigating the internal nature of atomic inductive probability statements we shall study some interrelations among them, utilizing a well-established axiomatic system for probability that we refer to as the "traditional calculus of probability." This formal calculus is widely applied in mathematics, logic, and science and is capable of many interpretations. Indeed, the question of which interpretation or interpretations are basic is the main topic of the foundations of probability. The **traditional calculus of probability** is defined by axioms [1]–[4] in Section 2.2.1, provided the symbol "**P**" in these axioms be uninterpreted, i.e., provided the meaning of this symbol be left open. The logical and arithmetical symbols in the axioms are interpreted in their normal way, and elementary principles of arithmetic are used in deriving theorems; and since the axioms are statement forms, the question of their truth or falsity cannot arise.

Three different interpretations or applications of the traditional calculus of probability interest us. The calculi of frequency probability (p. 145), empirical probability (p. 516), and inductive probability result from interpreting "**P**" as frequency probability ($\mathbf{P}_f$), empirical probability ($\mathbf{P}_e$), and inductive probability (the "**P**" of sec. 1.5.2), respectively. The **calculus of inductive probability** is the most important of these interpreted systems for us, and it will be developed at length in the present chapter.

An atomic inductive probability statement form "$\mathbf{P}(c, d) = x$" contains the statement variables "c" and "d" and the numerical variable "x." Small letters, with or without subscripts, will be used as variables for which logically true-or-false and empirically true-or-false statements may be sub-

* Keynes, *A Treatise on Probability*, p. 3.

stituted. Capital letters will be used to abbreviate specific statements of either kind.

The use of statement variables in "$\mathbf{P}(c, d) = x$" is subject to the restriction that "d" ranges only over logically possible statements; that is, the probability of a statement is never defined relative to a contradiction or a logical impossibility. For example, "$\mathbf{P}(C, D\bar{D}) = x$" is ill-formed. On the other hand, "$\mathbf{P}(D\bar{D}, C) = 0$" is well-formed and, indeed, true, provided C is logically possible. The variable "x" in "$\mathbf{P}(c, d) = x$" ranges over non-negative real numbers. It will be proved that x cannot be greater than one, so in fact $0 \leqq x \leqq 1$ (theorem [8]). This restriction of degrees of probability to single real numbers is an important idealization to be discussed at length later (secs. 4.3.2, 5.5.1, and 5.6.2).

As the reader proceeds, it should be evident that the calculus of inductive probability formalizes some of the actual rules of usage governing probability in inductive reasoning, subject only to the qualification that there are discrepancies between any model and what it models. We give a number of examples during the course of the chapter to illustrate this correspondence.

The calculus of inductive probability is a normative as well as a descriptive model of ordinary reasoning about inductive probability. This reasoning is sometimes confused, inconsistent, or fallacious, and for such cases the calculus of inductive probability provides rules and principles that, on reflection, seem better than the rules and principles actually used. Examples will illustrate this point also.

2.2 The Calculus of Inductive Probability

2.2.1 Axioms

The calculus of inductive probability specifies a body of statements about inductive probability. All of these may be deduced as *theorems* from four statements, which are taken as *axioms*.*

The first axiom presupposes a definition: Two statements c and d are **mutually exclusive on condition** e when e logically implies that c and d are not both true, i.e., $e \rightarrow \sim(c\&d)$.

[1] If c, d are mutually exclusive on condition e, then $\mathbf{P}(c \vee d, e) = \mathbf{P}(c, e) + \mathbf{P}(d, e)$.

This axiom relates disjunction to addition. The second axiom relates conjunction to multiplication.

[2] $\mathbf{P}(c\&d, e) = \mathbf{P}(c, e) \times \mathbf{P}(d, c\&e)$.

The next axiom relates logical implication to probability.

* This axiom system is from Hosiasson-Lindenbaum's "On Confirmation." Another axiom system will be presented in sec. 2.6.

[3] If $d \rightarrow c$, then $\mathbf{P}(c, d) = 1$.

The last axiom allows logically equivalent conditions to be exchanged within the scope of a probability operator.

[4] If $e \leftrightarrow f$, then $\mathbf{P}(c, e) = \mathbf{P}(c, f)$.

There are several preliminaries to be covered before we begin to prove theorems from these axioms.

Note first that, except for [3], these axioms do not contain atomic probability statements as constituents. Nevertheless, they, and the theorems that follow from them, may be used to deduce some atomic probability statements from others. An example will make this clear. Let G signify that cards are to be drawn from a well-shuffled bridge deck, with the proviso that a card once drawn is not replaced. The probability of drawing a one-eyed jack on the first trial is 2/52 since there are two such jacks in the deck of 52 cards; i.e., $\mathbf{P}(J_1, G) = 2/52$. The probability of drawing a one-eyed jack on the second trial is 1/51 if the first card drawn is a one-eyed jack, since in this case there is only one such jack left; i.e., $\mathbf{P}(J_2, J_1\&G) = 1/51$. By axiom [2], then, the chance of drawing two one-eyed jacks in succession is 2/52 x 1/51. Thus we have deduced the atomic probability statement "$\mathbf{P}(J_1\&J_2, G) = 2/2652$" from the atomic probability statements "$\mathbf{P}(J_1, G) = 2/52$" and "$\mathbf{P}(J_2, J_1\&G) = 1/51$" by means of axiom [2].

It is often convenient when writing probability formulas to drop a condition common to all the probability terms under consideration; the condition G of the preceding example is such a condition. Dropping G gives $\mathbf{P}(J_1\&J_2) = \mathbf{P}(J_1)\mathbf{P}(J_2, J_1)$. We frequently drop this common condition, but it should be remembered that the result is an abbreviation for a longer formula that makes the condition explicit. Thus "$\mathbf{P}(J_1)$" abbreviates "$\mathbf{P}(J_1, G)$" while "$\mathbf{P}(J_2, J_1)$" abbreviates "$\mathbf{P}(J_2, J_1\&G)$" (cf. sec. 2.6, Unconditional Probability).

We next comment on the terminology used in the calculus of probability. Probability may be predicated of statements or propositions, as we have done. Axiom [1] may be read: If c and d are mutually exclusive statements, the probability of their disjunction is the sum of the probabilities of c and d. Probability may also be predicated of events. Axiom [1] would then read: The probability of either of two mutually exclusive events occurring is the sum of the probabilities of the events taken singly. Either mode of speech is permissible, and in fact we will find it convenient to use both. Of course, since we originally specified inductive probability as an evidential relation holding between statements (sec. 1.5.2), the former usage is the primary one for us.

The calculus of inductive probability constitutes a part of inductive logic (see sec. 3.1). Now just as reasoning may be used in verifying an empirical statement (p. 6), so we build inductive logic around a core of deductive logic. Consequently, we use elementary arithmetic, truth-functional logic, and modal logic in proving theorems of the calculus of inductive probability.

2.2.2 Truth-functional and modal logic

Each statement within the scope of the probability operator "**P**" has one of the two truth-values, *true* and *false*, although the investigator often does not know which. A number of useful sentential connectives may be defined in terms of the truth-values of the statements they connect. Some of these truth-functional connectives are as follows.

Negation: $\sim p$ is true if and only if p is false; "$\sim p$" may also be written as "$\bar{p}$." *Conjunction:* $p \& q$ is true if and only if both p and q are true; "$p \& q$" may also be written "pq." *Disjunction:* $p \vee q$ is true if either p or q is true, or if both are true; otherwise it is false. The symbols for conjunction and disjunction may be used to connect more than two statements: for example, $p \& q \& r$ is true if and only if all three conjuncts p, q, and r are true, while $p_1 \vee p_2 \vee \ldots \vee p_N$ is true if and only if at least one of its disjuncts is true. *Material implication:* $p \supset q$ is true if either p is false or q is true, while $p \supset q$ is false only when p is true and q false. *Material equivalence:* $p \equiv q$ is true when p and q have the same truth-value, and it is false when they have different truth-values. *Material inequivalence:* $p \not\equiv q$ is true when p and q have different truth-values, otherwise false.

We digress a moment to talk about the symbols, and also to talk about talking about the symbols. Synonymous symbols, e.g., "$\sim p$" and "$\bar{p}$," are introduced to allow flexibility in writing formulas. For example, we think "$p\bar{q} \vee \bar{p}q$" is more perspicuous than "$(p \& \sim q) \vee (\sim p \& q)$," but prefer "$\sim (p \vee q)$" to "$\overline{(p \vee q)}$" and "$\sim (p\bar{q} \vee \bar{p}q)$" to "$\overline{(p\bar{q} \vee \bar{p}q)}$."

Strictly speaking, in defining the truth-functional connectives one should distinguish the object language, in which one talks about the non-linguistic part of the world, from the metalanguage, in which one talks about the object language. Instead of saying "$\sim p$ is true if and only if p is false" we would say "The result of substituting a statement s for the variable 'p' in '$\sim p$' is true if and only if s is false." The letter "p" cannot itself be true or false: it is here used as a variable for which one can substitute statements that are either true or false. Compare "His hat is red" with " 'Red' has three letters."

But a symbolism that rigidly reflects this distinction between object language and metalanguage is more complex than is necessary for the present informal treatment of language. It is needed only when a language is treated formally, as in Chapter 6 (The Logic of Causal Statements as a Formal Language), and except for that chapter we use informal modes of expression. It should be noted that there are many ways of indicating a symbol is being talked about. Thus "The word red has three letters" and even "Red has three letters" (in appropriate context) convey the same meaning as " 'Red' has three letters." Similarly, quotation marks are not needed around an expression that is set off from the text, as in the quotation from Keynes at the head of this chapter.

Let us now return to the truth-functional connectives defined at the beginning of this subsection. These symbols are often translated into English: "$\sim$" as "not," "&" as "and," "v" as "either . . . or . . . or both," "$\supset$" as "if . . . then . . . ," "$\equiv$" as "if and only if," and "$\not\equiv$" as "either . . . or . . . but not both." The translations, both forward and in reverse, are at best approximate and in many cases downright bad. We have time to mention just a few of the differences between ordinary language and truth-functional logic in the present study. The words "or," "and," "if . . . , then . . . ," etc., are used to connect statements about related matters, while the truth-functional connectives are allowed to connect arbitrary statements. For example, the compound statement "(Malintzin was Cortes' mistress)& $(2 + 3 = 5)$" is a well-formed and true statement of truth-functional logic, but its two conjuncts are not even remotely connected and it would never serve any function in ordinary discourse.

The translation of "if . . . , then . . ." into material implication is particularly bad. Material implication was defined truth-functionally, that is, so that the truth-values of p and q determine the truth-value of the material conditional "$p \supset q$." In contrast, the "if . . . , then . . ." of ordinary language is rarely if ever truth-functional. Of course, if p is true and q is false, "if p, then q" is false. But if p is false or q is true, the truth of "if p, then q" depends on what relations there are between p and q. Some examples will make the difference between ordinary implication and material implication clear. Suppose a valuable wine glass is stored so that it cannot be broken. Since its antecedent is false,

(The glass is broken) $\supset$ (The earth will explode)

is true, while the ordinary English sentence

If the glass is broken, *then* the earth will explode

is obviously false. Similarly "(Mercury is made of smoked cheese) $\supset$ (Eisenhower was a very poor President)" is true, but since the constitution of the planets had nothing to do with Eisenhower's executive abilities the corresponding "if . . . , then . . ." statement is clearly false. Consider finally "If it rains tomorrow the sidewalk will nevertheless remain dry, for it will not rain tomorrow."

These failures stem from the fact that to use material implication is only to assert something about the truth-values of antecedent and consequent, whereas "if . . . , then . . ." is used to assert a stronger connection between these components. For example, the "if . . . , then . . ." of "*If* all horses are watches and all watches are quadrupeds, *then* all horses are quadrupeds" may be correctly translated by the logical implication of Section 1.2.3.

The relevant contrast here is between two kinds of logic that treat of statements. A logic whose only operators and connectives are truth-functional (such as "$\sim$", "&", "$\supset$") is a *truth-functional logic*. Modal operators, such as necessity ($\Box$) and possibility ($\Diamond$), and modal connectives, such as logical implication ($\rightarrow$) and logical equivalence ($\leftrightarrow$), are clearly not truth-functional. A logic of necessity, possibility, etc., is called a *modal logic* because by means of it one can distinguish modes of truth; for example, one can distinguish logical truth from empirical truth. These distinctions cannot be made by truth-functional connectives, and for this reason modal logics are much better models of natural languages than truth-functional logics. Chapter 6, "The Logic of Causal Statements as a Formal Language," contains a modal logic covering the causal modalities (causal necessity, causal possibility, etc.) as well as the logical modalities and including quantifiers as well as connectives. This modal logic is used as a model of natural language in Chapter 7, "The Logic of Causal Statements as a Model of Natural Language."

Though modal logic provides better models of natural language than does truth-functional logic, the latter does capture some basic aspects of the functioning of natural language and is, moreover, simpler to work with. As with any model, no harm can come from using the simpler, less adequate model, provided the differences between model and reality are kept well in mind (see sec. 1.6.2). Let us, then, discuss further the extent to which truth-functional logic is a useful model of natural language.

There are two extremes. Some uses of sentential connectives in ordinary language are essentially truth-functional. For example, "It rained today *and* it rained yesterday" is true just in case both conjuncts are true. At the other extreme, ordinary language connectives that are not truth-functional nevertheless have an important truth-functional core. The most important connective of this sort is "if . . . , then . . ."; let us look at it in more detail.

The form "if . . . , then . . ." often expresses more than a conditional. It sometimes expresses a biconditional, and in a contrary-to-fact subjunctive it implies that the antecedent is false (see sec. 7.3.1). But even in such cases, "$p \supset q$" is implied by "if p, then q." Thus material implication is the truth-function that best expresses the conditional aspect of "if . . . , then . . . ." Another way of stating it is to say that material implication expresses the truth-functional core of "if . . , then . . . ." This is borne out by a comparison of material and logical implication. As noted earlier, "if . . . , then . . ." sometimes expresses logical implication. Now the concept of logical implication can be analyzed into those of logical necessity and material implication: $(p \rightarrow q)$ if and only if $\Box(p \supset q)$, showing that the symbol "$\supset$" renders part of the meaning of "if . . . , then . . . ." Logical equivalence may be analyzed similarly: $(p \leftrightarrow q)$ if and only if $\Box(p \equiv q)$. More generally, truth-functional logic is the core or basis of modal logic (see sec. 6.2).

Let us look further at the relation of logical necessity to truth-functional logic. Consider an expression built up from given statements or statement variables by means of truth-functional connectives. Any such expression is defined to be a *tautology* if it is true for all possible assignments of truth-values to its constituent statements and variables. The law of excluded middle "$p \vee \sim p$" is a tautology, as is "(red is a color) v (red isn't a color)," which is an instance of it. But "(red is a color) v (blue is a color)" is not a tautology; for though it is true, the result of substituting falsity for both constituent statements is false. Clearly, every tautology is logically necessary. The converse, however, is not the case. Thus "$(7 + 5 = 12) \vee (8 + 9 = 17)$" is a logical truth, but it is not a tautology, for falsity results from substituting falsity for both disjuncts. Hence "tautologyhood" is a special case of logical necessity.

Though we use both truth-functional and modal logic in proving theorems of the traditional calculus of probability, we try to do this in an intuitively simple way. The reader who needs a better intuitive understanding of these logics or wishes a rigorous treatment of them is referred to Chapter 6. When employing truth-functional logic, one does well to capitalize on its truth-functional character by thinking of formulas in terms of truth-values. For example, it is easily seen that "$(p \not\equiv q) \equiv [(p \vee q)(\bar{p} \vee \bar{q})]$" is a tautology; for the left-hand side asserts that p and q have opposite truth-values, which is equivalent to saying that at least one of the pair p, q is true and at least one of the pair is false.

2.3 Some Theorems of the Calculus of Inductive Probability

2.3.1 Probability and the logical modalities

Axioms [3] and [4] involve the logical modalities. Axiom [3] states that logical necessity is a limiting case of probability. Now if q is necessary, then $p \supset q$ is necessary, i.e., if $\Box q$, then $p \rightarrow q$. Hence the theorem

[5] If $\Box q$, then $\mathbf{P}(q, p) = 1$;

that is, a logical truth has a probability of one. For example, $\mathbf{P}(2 + 7 = 9$, It is raining$) = 1$. Of course, the state of the weather has no evidential bearing on any arithmetical proposition. Moreover, the form $\mathbf{P}(c, d) = x$ originally arose from an inductive argument whose premise d and conclusion c were both empirical statements. Why, then, do we apply the operator $\mathbf{P}$ to necessary statements? The answer is that to do so makes it easier to derive theorems. This fact will be illustrated in the proof of the next theorem.

The subtraction principle is

[6] If $e \rightarrow (c \not\equiv d)$, then $\mathbf{P}(c, e) = 1 - \mathbf{P}(d, e)$.

Proof: "$(c \not\equiv d) \equiv [(c \vee d) \& \sim(cd)]$" is a tautology. Hence from $e \rightarrow (c \not\equiv d)$ it follows that (α) $e \rightarrow (c \vee d)$ and (β) $e \rightarrow \sim(cd)$. Statements (α) and [3] yield $\mathbf{P}(c \vee d, e) = 1$. Formula ($\beta$) states that c and d are mutually exclusive relative to e, and so by axiom [1] we have $\mathbf{P}(c \vee d, e) = \mathbf{P}(c, e) + \mathbf{P}(d, e)$. The theorem then follows by simple arithmetic.

It is a special case of the subtraction principle that the probability of any proposition is one minus the probability of its negation.

[7] $\mathbf{P}(c, e) = 1 - \mathbf{P}(\sim c, e)$.

Proof: $e \rightarrow (c \not\equiv \bar{c})$. Combining this with theorem [6] gives theorem [7]. Since the range of "$\mathbf{P}(c, e)$" is restricted to non-negative real numbers (p. 40), all probabilities are non-negative and

[8] $0 \leqq \mathbf{P}(c, e) \leqq 1$

is a simple corollary of theorem [7].

Let us illustrate the subtraction principle. The probability of a fair die falling with the four up is 1/6. Hence the probability of *not* getting a four is 5/6. By axiom [2] the probability of not getting a four on any of three successive tosses is $(5/6)^3$. Hence by the subtraction principle the probability of getting a four on *at least one* of three fair tosses of a die is $1 - (5/6)^3$ or 91/216.

It should be noted that the notion of "fair" is a knotty and complex one in many probability contexts. This problem will be discussed later (sec. 8.2). In the meantime we will use "fair" only to avoid lengthy descriptions of the evidence.

Theorem [5] states that a logical truth has a probability of one. It is easy to show now that a logical falsehood, i.e., a logical impossibility, has a probability of zero. Substituting "$\sim c$" for "q" and "d" for "p" in theorem [5] gives: If $\Box \sim c$, then $\mathbf{P}(\sim c, d) = 1$. By theorem [7], $\mathbf{P}(c, d) = 1 - \mathbf{P}(\sim c, d)$. Hence if $\Box \sim c$, then $\mathbf{P}(c, d) = 0$. That is, if c is logically false, $\mathbf{P}(c, d) = 0$ no matter what d is.

Axiom [4] allows the exchange of logically equivalent statements in the second argument position of the probability operator. The next theorem allows the exchange of the statements c and d in the first position of the probability operator provided that the general evidence e ***logically implies*** that c and d are equivalent.

[9] If $e \rightarrow (c \equiv d)$, then $\mathbf{P}(c, e) = \mathbf{P}(d, e)$.

Proof: Assume that $e \rightarrow (c \equiv d)$. "$(c \equiv d) \equiv (c \not\equiv \bar{d})$" is a tautology, and so $\Box[(c \equiv d) \equiv (c \not\equiv \bar{d})]$. Substituting its logical equivalent for "$(c \equiv d)$"

in "$e \rightarrow (c \equiv d)$" gives "$e \rightarrow (c \not\equiv \bar{d})$." By the subtraction principle we have $\mathbf{P}(c, e) = 1 - \mathbf{P}(\bar{d}, e)$. Theorem [7] tells us that $\mathbf{P}(d, e) = 1 - \mathbf{P}(\bar{d}, e)$. Hence $\mathbf{P}(c, e) = \mathbf{P}(d, e)$.

As a special case of [9] we have

[10] If $c \leftrightarrow d$, then $\mathbf{P}(c, e) = \mathbf{P}(d, e)$.

Proof: Assume $c \leftrightarrow d$. This is equivalent to $\Box(c \equiv d)$. The latter implies $\Box[e \supset (c \equiv d)]$ and hence $e \rightarrow (c \equiv d)$. Then apply theorem [9].

Axiom [4] and theorems [9] and [10] together constitute the *exchange principle*, a principle that allows logically equivalent statements to be exchanged in probability contexts. Consider this example. A fair coin is fairly tossed two times. Let T_1 and T_2 mean that it falls tails on the first and second tosses respectively. It is desired to calculate the probability that it falls tails at least once, i.e., $\mathbf{P}(T_1 \vee T_2)$. Now

$$(T_1 \vee T_2) \leftrightarrow (T_1\bar{T}_2 \vee \bar{T}_1T_2 \vee T_1T_2) \quad ,$$

since a disjunction is true if either disjunct or both disjuncts are true. Hence by the exchange principle

$$\mathbf{P}(T_1 \vee T_2) = \mathbf{P}(T_1\bar{T}_2 \vee \bar{T}_1T_2 \vee T_1T_2) \quad .$$

To continue the example, applying [1] twice we get

$$\mathbf{P}(T_1\bar{T}_2 \vee \bar{T}_1T_2 \vee T_1T_2) = \mathbf{P}(T_1\bar{T}_2) + \mathbf{P}(\bar{T}_1T_2) + \mathbf{P}(T_1T_2) \quad ,$$

and using axiom [2] we finally obtain

$$\begin{aligned} \mathbf{P}(T_1 \vee T_2) &= \mathbf{P}(T_1)\mathbf{P}(\bar{T}_2, T_1) + \mathbf{P}(\bar{T}_1)\mathbf{P}(T_2, \bar{T}_1) + \mathbf{P}(T_1)\mathbf{P}(T_2, T_1) \\ &= 3(1/2)(1/2) = 3/4 \quad . \end{aligned}$$

The following modal argument was used in the proof of theorem [9] and deserves comment:

$$e \rightarrow (c \equiv d)$$
$$\Box[(c \equiv d) \equiv (c \not\equiv \bar{d})]$$
$$\therefore\ e \rightarrow (c \not\equiv \bar{d}) \quad .$$

The conclusion is derived from the first premise by substituting "$c \not\equiv \bar{d}$" for its *logical equivalent* "$c \equiv d$." Note that material equivalents cannot in general be exchanged in modal contexts. For example, the argument

$\Box$[(Amundsen discovered the South Pole in 1911) $\supset$
(The South Pole was discovered in 1911)]

(The South Pole was discovered in 1911) $\equiv$
(Amundsen died in 1928)

$\therefore$ $\Box$[(Amundsen discovered the South Pole in 1911) $\supset$
(Amundsen died in 1928)]

is clearly invalid, for the premises are true while the conclusion is false. *Thus the principle that material equivalents can be exchanged for each other is not valid in modal logic.* It is valid in truth-functional logic, for in that subject all connectives are defined in terms of truth-values. For example, the argument

(Amundsen discovered the South Pole in 1911) $\supset$
(The South Pole was discovered in 1911)

(The South Pole was discovered in 1911) $\equiv$
(Amundsen died in 1928)

$\therefore$ (Amundsen discovered the South Pole in 1911) $\supset$
(Amundsen died in 1928)

is valid. But, generally speaking, in a modal logic only logical equivalents can be exchanged (see the exchange rule of sec. 6.5.1).

With respect to the principle of exchanging equivalents, the calculus of inductive probability resembles modal logic rather than truth-functional logic. The exchange principle justifies exchanging equivalents for one another in $\mathbf{P}(c, d)$, but there is a modal requirement: the condition for exchange involves logical equivalence or logical implication, and hence the notion of logical necessity. The exchange principle does not warrant exchanging statements that are merely materially equivalent. Consider the fair coin again. Let T_1, T_2 mean that it falls tails on the first and second tosses respectively, and let F mean that the tosses and the coin are fair. Suppose it falls tails both times, so that "$(T_1T_2) \equiv T_1$" is true. Then the argument

$$\mathbf{P}(T_1, F) = \mathbf{P}(T_1, F)$$

$$[(T_1T_2) \equiv T_1]$$

$$\therefore \mathbf{P}(T_1T_2, F) = \mathbf{P}(T_1, F)$$

has true premises and a false conclusion and is therefore invalid. Contrast theorem [10].

2.3.2 *Multiplication principles*

The calculus of inductive probability is called a "calculus" because it enables one to calculate the probability of a statement from the probabilities of its truth-functional constituents. Since all truth-functional connectives can be defined in terms of negation and disjunction or by means of negation and conjunction, principles concerning these connectives play a fundamental role in the probability calculus. Theorems [6] and [7] enable one to calculate the probability of a statement from the probability of its negation, axiom [2] to calculate the probability of a conjunction from the probabilities of its conjuncts, and axiom [1] to calculate the probability of a disjunction from the probabilities of its disjuncts for the special case of mutually exclusive events. In the current subsection we shall develop other principles for conjunction and in the next subsection further principles for disjunction.

Axiom [2] applies to a conjunction with two conjuncts. It may be generalized to cover an arbitrarily long conjunction. The result is called the *general multiplication principle.*

[11] $$\mathbf{P}(a_1a_2 \ldots a_N, b) = \mathbf{P}(a_1, b) \times \mathbf{P}(a_2, a_1b) \times \mathbf{P}(a_3, a_1a_2b) \times \ldots \times \mathbf{P}(a_N, a_1a_2 \ldots a_{N-1}b) \quad .$$

Proof: We prove this by means of the deductive rule known as "mathematical induction." For $N = 1$ equation [11] becomes $\mathbf{P}(a_1, b) = \mathbf{P}(a_1, b)$, which is obviously true. By means of axiom [2] and the exchange principle (for regrouping conjuncts) it can be shown that: If equation [11] holds for N equal to some integer i, then equation [11] holds for N equal to $i + 1$. We have thus established

(a) Equation [11] holds for $N = 1$

(b) If equation [11] holds for $N = i$,
then equation [11] holds for $N = i + 1$.

Applying the rule of *mathematical induction* to premises (a) and (b) yields the conclusion

(c) Equation [11] holds for every N, i.e., for $N = 1, 2, 3, \ldots$.

Conclusion (c) is the general multiplication principle.

To illustrate the general multiplication principle we calculate the probability of drawing four diamonds in succession from a standard deck, *without replacing* the cards as they are drawn. Let D_1, D_2, D_3, D_4 mean that the first, second, third, and fourth cards drawn are diamonds, and assume that the cards are properly shuffled before the drawings begin. Then

$$\begin{aligned}\mathbf{P}(D_1D_2D_3D_4) &= \mathbf{P}(D_1)\mathbf{P}(D_2, D_1)\mathbf{P}(D_3, D_1D_2)\mathbf{P}(D_4, D_1D_2D_3) \\ &= (13/52) \times (12/51) \times (11/50) \times (10/49)\end{aligned}$$

or approximately 0.0026.

The problem is different, of course, if after each card is drawn it is *replaced* and the deck reshuffled; here the general multiplication principle gives $(13/52)^4$, which is 1/256 or approximately 0.0039. This problem can also be solved by means of a corollary of the general multiplication principle.

Before we present this corollary, we must define the concept of an independent set of events. The intuitive idea is that the probability of a given event does not depend on the outcome of the other events of the set. Thus in a succession of fair throws of a fair coin the probability of a head on one throw does not depend on (is independent of) how the coin falls on the other throws. Again, if cards are drawn in succession from a *well-shuffled* deck, and after each drawing the card is *replaced* and the deck well-shuffled again, the chance of getting an ace on a given draw is *not* affected by what happens on the other draws. We proceed now to formalize the idea of a set of statements being independent.

Consider a set of statements $a_1, a_2, a_3, \ldots, a_n, \ldots$. To say that a_2 is independent of a_1 on condition b is to say that $\mathbf{P}(a_2, b) = \mathbf{P}(a_2, a_1b) = \mathbf{P}(a_2, \bar{a}_1b)$; that is, the probability of a_2 does not depend on the truth or falsity of a_1. For example, let G_1 state that cards are fairly drawn from a well-shuffled deck, with the proviso that after each drawing the card drawn is replaced and the deck is carefully shuffled again. Then $\mathbf{P}(D_2, G_1) = \mathbf{P}(D_2, D_1G_1) = \mathbf{P}(D_2, \bar{D}_1G_1) = 1/4$, and D_2 is independent of D_1 on condition G_1. In contrast, let G_2 describe the same conditions except that the card drawn is not replaced. Then $\mathbf{P}(D_2, G_2) = 13/52$, $\mathbf{P}(D_2, D_1G_2) = 12/51$, $\mathbf{P}(D_2, \bar{D}_1G_2) = 13/51$, and D_2 is not independent of D_1 on condition G_2.

Thus $a_1, a_2, a_3, \ldots, a_n, \ldots$ constitute an independent set if the probability of a_n does not depend on the truth or falsity of any of the other a's. This notion of independence is a probabilistic one, to be contrasted with the logical notion of independence. Since the latter will be used in defining the former, we explain it first.

Consider a finite set of statements $a_1, a_2, \ldots, a_N$. A *basic conjunction* is a conjunction of one term for each $n = 1, 2, \ldots, N$, each term being either a_n or $\bar{a}_n$. There are thus 2^N basic conjunctions of the a's: $a_1a_2 \ldots a_N$, $a_1a_2 \ldots \bar{a}_N$, $\ldots$, $\bar{a}_1\bar{a}_2 \ldots \bar{a}_N$. The notion of logical independence may now be defined as follows: $a_1, a_2, \ldots, a_N$ are **logically independent on condition** b if and only if, for each basic conjunction γ of the a's, it is logically possible that $b\gamma$ [i.e., $\Diamond(b\gamma)$]. When the a's are logically independent on condition b, the basic conjunctions of the a's describe a set of "universes" that are logically possible relative to b. The notion of a set of logically possible universes will be used frequently in this book (see especially secs. 3.2, 6.3, and 9.2.3).

Note that the general multiplication principle [11] assumes that $a_1a_2 \ldots a_{N-1}b$ is logically possible, else some of the probability terms on the right would not be defined. In our application of this principle a stronger condition will usually be satisfied, the condition that $a_1, a_2, \ldots, a_{N-1}, a_N$ are logically independent on b.

We now define the concept of probabilistic independence, first for finite sets of statements and then for infinite sets. To define the independence of a statement a_n from the remaining a's, we need a method for referring to the truth-functional combinations of these other a's; let $\tau_{\bar{n}}$ range over all truth-functional compounds of the a's other than a_n. Then $a_1, a_2, \ldots, a_N$ are **independent on condition** b if and only if

(1) $a_1, a_2, \ldots, a_N$ are logically independent on condition b, and

(2) for each n ($1 \leqq n \leqq N$) and for each $\tau_{\bar{n}}$ such that $\Diamond(\tau_{\bar{n}}b)$,

$$\mathbf{P}(a_n, \tau_{\bar{n}}b) = \mathbf{P}(a_n, b) \qquad .$$

This is the definition for finite sets of statements.

The definition of independence for infinite sets of statements is: a_1, $a_2, \ldots, a_n, \ldots$ are independent on condition b if every finite subset of the a's is independent on condition b.

This definition of probabilistic independence is formulated in terms of a set of statements, the definition requiring that each a_n be independent of all the other a's. Most applications are to ordered sets, or sequences; this is so for the usual case of drawings with replacement. An alternative definition of independence can be given in terms of a sequence of trials $a_1, a_2, \ldots,$ $a_n, \ldots$. It is the same as the definition given above, except that $\tau_{\bar{n}}$ is restricted to truth-functions of a's earlier than a_n, that is, to truth functions of $a_1, a_2, \ldots, a_{n-1}$. The two definitions may be proved equivalent by means of [2], [9], [12], [23], and the fact that any truth-functional formula can be expressed in "disjunctive normal form," i.e., as a disjunction of basic conjunctions of its component statements.

After this extended background, we can formulate the *special multiplication principle.*

[12] If $a_1, a_2, \ldots, a_N$ are independent on condition b, then

$$\mathbf{P}(a_1a_2 \ldots a_N, b) = \prod_{n=1}^{N} \mathbf{P}(a_n, b) \qquad ,$$

where the right-hand side of the equation abbreviates "$\mathbf{P}(a_1, b) \times \mathbf{P}(a_2, b) \times \ldots \times \mathbf{P}(a_N, b)$." For example, the probability of getting all heads in five fair tosses of a fair coin is $(1/2)^5$, or 1/32. The special multiplication principle may be proved from the general multiplication principle [2] and the definition of independence by the use of mathematical induction.

2.3.3 *Addition principles*

We first extend axiom [1] to cover an arbitrary number of statements. This requires extending the concept of "mutually exclusive" also to cover an arbitrary number of statements: $a_1, a_2, \ldots, a_N$ are mutually exclusive on condition b if and only if b logically implies that at most one of $a_1, a_2, \ldots, a_N$ is true. The *special addition principle* is

[13] If $a_1, a_2, \ldots, a_N$ are mutually exclusive on condition b, then

$$\mathbf{P}(a \vee a_2 \vee \ldots \vee a_N, b) = \sum_{n=1}^{N} \mathbf{P}(a_n, b) \qquad ,$$

where the right-hand side of the equation abbreviates the summation "$\mathbf{P}(a_1, b) + \mathbf{P}(a_2, b) + \ldots + \mathbf{P}(a_N, b)$." Theorem [13] follows from axiom [1] by means of mathematical induction and the definition of "mutually exclusive." As an example, suppose one card is drawn from a bridge deck, and S = the card drawn is a spade, A = the card drawn is a red ace, D = the card drawn is the nine of diamonds; then $\mathbf{P}(S \text{ v } A \text{ v } D) = \mathbf{P}(S) + \mathbf{P}(A) + \mathbf{P}(D) = 13/52 + 2/52 + 1/52 = 4/13$.

A frequently applicable method of solving probability problems is to divide or partition the situation into nonoverlapping (mutually exclusive) alternatives that cover all the cases (are jointly exhaustive). The statements $a_1, a_2, \ldots, a_N$ are **jointly exhaustive on condition** b if and only if b logically implies that at least one of $a_1, a_2, \ldots, a_N$ is true.

The case of mutually exclusive and jointly exhaustive events is of special interest. Here b logically implies that exactly one of the a's is true, so that (relative to b) the a's constitute a "partition" of the universe of logical possibilities (see p. 287). Note that the basic conjunctions of the a's are mutually exclusive and jointly exhaustive on b.

To say the a's are jointly exhaustive on condition b is to say $b \longrightarrow (a_1 \text{ v } a_2 \text{ v } \ldots \text{ v } a_N)$; applying axiom [3] to this gives $\mathbf{P}(a_1 \text{ v } a_2 \text{ v } \ldots \text{ v } a_N, b) = 1$. Combining this with the special addition principle gives

[14] If $a_1, a_2, \ldots, a_N$ are mutually exclusive and jointly exhaustive on condition b, then $\sum_{n=1}^{N} \mathbf{P}(a_n, b) = 1$.

Suppose now that the a's are equally probable with respect to b as well as being mutually exclusive and jointly exhaustive. Then $\mathbf{P}(a_n, b) = 1/N$ for $n = 1, 2, \ldots, N$. Using the special addition principle [13] we obtain the *principle of counting equiprobable cases*.

[15] If $a_1, a_2, \ldots, a_N$ are mutually exclusive, jointly exhaustive, and equally probable on condition b, then for $n = 1, 2, \ldots, N$, $\mathbf{P}(a_1 \text{ v } a_2 \text{ v } \ldots \text{ v } a_n, b) = n/N$.

In words: The probability of an event is the number of favorable (n) equiprobable cases divided by the total number (N) of equiprobable cases. For example, the probability of getting a heart in a fair draw from a bridge deck is 13/52, there being 13 favorable cases out of 52 equiprobable cases.

The principle of counting equiprobable cases is a very useful rule for calculating probabilities and hence deserves further illustration. Let α be the probability that if a bridge hand contains the ace of spades then it contains a second ace, and let β be the probability that if a bridge hand contains at least one ace then it contains a second ace. Is $\alpha = \beta$? Intuitively these two probabilities seem to be the same. To know that a hand contains the ace of spades is to know more than to know that it contains an ace, but this additional information does not seem relevant to whether there is a second ace in the hand. Let us see if intuition is correct here.

To compute α and β by means of the principle of counting equiprobable cases we need to count the number of bridge hands containing the ace of spades and one other ace, the number of bridge hands containing the ace of spades, etc. This can be done by means of the concept of a combination and the use of the factorial operator "!" on integers. Thus $n!$ equals $n \times (n - 1) \times (n - 2) \times \ldots \times 2 \times 1$. A "combination" of a set of objects is any selection of one or more of the objects without regard to order. The *number of combinations of n things taken r at a time* is called C_r^n. It is proved in textbooks on probability that $C_r^n = n!/[(n - r)!r!]$. For example, the number of combinations of the four letters w, x, y, z taken two at a time is $C_2^4 = 4!/[2!2!] = 6$; these combinations are wx, wy, wz, xy, xz, yz.

The number of bridge hands containing the ace of spades and at least one other ace is $C_{12}^{51} - C_{12}^{48}$, the number of hands with the ace of spades less the number of hands with the ace of spades and no other ace; the number of bridge hands containing the ace of spades is C_{12}^{51}; α equals the first of these numbers divided by the second, and turns out to be approximately 0.56. The number of bridge hands containing at least two aces is $C_{13}^{52} - C_{13}^{48} - 4C_{12}^{48}$, the total number of hands less the number of hands with no aces and less the number of hands with exactly one ace; the number of bridge hands containing at least one ace is $C_{13}^{52} - C_{13}^{48}$; to obtain β we divide the first of these numbers by the second, getting approximately 0.37. Thus $\alpha \neq \beta$, which is contrary to what was expected! Here is a situation where intuition and the calculus of probability give opposing results. Because of this conflict the present problem is called the "paradox of the second ace."*

A paradox has been characterized as an argument that proves an unbelievable conclusion from impeccable premises by unimpeachable rules! Clearly, to resolve a paradox we must abandon something. In this case we have a conflict between intuition (which says that $\alpha = \beta$) and a formalism (which yields $\alpha \neq \beta$ as a result). And in this instance everyone, on reflection, accepts the result of the calculus and abandons intuition. But to one who is not familiar with the formula for counting combinations the paradox may nevertheless be puzzling. We can dispel the mystery by analyzing a miniature version of the problem. A two-card hand is fairly dealt from a deck consisting of the two black aces and the four kings. Let T = the hand contains two aces, S = the hand contains the ace of spades, and L = the hand contains at least one ace. The problem is to calculate $\mathbf{P}(T, S)$ and $\mathbf{P}(T, L)$. We can solve this as before, by means of the principle of counting equiprobable cases, but the miniature problem is so simple that we can enumerate all the cases and thereby avoid the formula for counting combinations. There is one hand containing two aces, namely $A_s A_c$. There are five hands containing the ace

* Ball, *Mathematical Recreations and Essays*, p. 44.

of spades: A_sA_c, A_sK_s, A_sK_h, A_sK_d, A_sK_c; and there are nine hands containing at least one ace: A_sA_c, A_sK_s, A_sK_h, A_sK_d, A_sK_c, A_cK_s, A_cK_h, A_cK_d, A_cK_c. Using the principle of counting equiprobable cases we have:

$$\mathbf{P}(T, S) = \frac{\text{Number of hands with two aces}}{\text{Number of hands with the ace of spades}} = 1/5$$

$$\mathbf{P}(T, L) = \frac{\text{Number of hands with two aces}}{\text{Number of hands with at least one ace}} = 1/9$$

and so $\mathbf{P}(T, S) \neq \mathbf{P}(T, L)$ as before.

The foregoing analysis should dissolve the paradox of the second ace. S logically implies L, but not conversely, and so S contains more information than L, namely, that the ace in question is in fact the ace of spades. Prima facie, this additional information is not relevant to T, and hence the result $\mathbf{P}(T, S) \neq \mathbf{P}(T, L)$ appears paradoxical, but the above analysis shows that this additional information is in fact relevant. It is worth noting that the additional information is not relevant when the evidence concerns the first card dealt rather than the whole hand. Let S' = the first card dealt to the hand is the ace of spades, and L' = the first card dealt to the hand is an ace. In this case the order of cards within a hand must be distinguished, whereas in the original problem order is irrelevant. By the principle of counting equiprobable cases, $\mathbf{P}(T, S')$ equals the number of ordered hands with two aces whose first card is the ace of spades, divided by the number of ordered hands whose first card is the ace of spades, or 1/5. Similarly, $\mathbf{P}(T, L')$ equals the number of ordered hands with two aces, divided by the number of ordered hands whose first card is an ace, or 2/10. Hence $\mathbf{P}(T, S') = \mathbf{P}(T, L')$. In comparing this variant with the original problem, we observe that to verify S or L one must, in general, look at both cards in the hand, whereas to verify S' or L' one need examine only the first card of the hand.

We turn next to the problem of calculating the probability of a disjunction when the alternatives are not mutually exclusive. Consider the probability of obtaining at least one deuce when two dice are thrown. The probability of a single die falling deuce is 1/6, so that it might seem that the desired probability is $1/6 + 1/6$. The fallacy of this reasoning is apparent, however, when it is applied to the question "What is the probability of at least one deuce when seven dice are thrown?"; for here it yields 7/6, contradicting the fact that no probability can exceed one. The source of the error is clarified by a careful reading of the special addition principle, which holds only when the alternatives are mutually exclusive; that is not the case here, because all dice could fall deuce. How can we calculate probabilities for non-exclusive alternatives? We can reduce them to a set of mutually exclusive alternatives. In the terminology of truth-function theory, this means expressing a nonexclusive disjunction in disjunctive normal form.

"Or" in the sense of "and/or" means that either one or the other disjunct is true, *or both*; hence $(c \vee d) \leftrightarrow (c\bar{d} \vee \bar{c}d \vee cd)$. Exchanging logical equivalents by theorem [10] we obtain

$$\mathbf{P}(c \vee d, e) = \mathbf{P}(cd \vee c\bar{d} \vee \bar{c}d, e) \quad .$$

Since the disjuncts on the right are mutually exclusive, the special addition principle applies, giving

$$\mathbf{P}(c \vee d, e) = \mathbf{P}(c\bar{d}, e) + \mathbf{P}(\bar{c}d, e) + \mathbf{P}(cd, e)$$

and hence

$$\mathbf{P}(c \vee d, e) = [\mathbf{P}(cd, e) + \mathbf{P}(c\bar{d}, e)] + [\mathbf{P}(cd, e) + \mathbf{P}(\bar{c}d, e)] - \mathbf{P}(cd, e) \, .$$

By reasoning similar to that used above,

$$\mathbf{P}(c, e) = \mathbf{P}(cd \vee c\bar{d}, e) = \mathbf{P}(cd, e) + \mathbf{P}(c\bar{d}, e) \quad ,$$

$$\mathbf{P}(d, e) = \mathbf{P}(cd \vee \bar{c}d, e) = \mathbf{P}(cd, e) + \mathbf{P}(\bar{c}d, e) \quad .$$

Combining all these results, we get the *general addition principle.*

[16] $$\mathbf{P}(c \vee d, e) = \mathbf{P}(c, e) + \mathbf{P}(d, e) - \mathbf{P}(cd, e) \quad .$$

Thus the probability of a disjunction is the sum of the probabilities of the disjuncts *decreased* by the probability that both disjuncts are true. In our example, the probability that at least one of two dice will fall deuce is $1/6 + 1/6 - 1/36 = 11/36$.

The general addition principle does not generalize easily to arbitrarily long disjunctions. These will be handled in a different way. By the subtraction principle

$$\mathbf{P}(a_1 \vee a_2 \vee \ldots \vee a_N, b) = 1 - \mathbf{P}(\overline{a_1 \vee a_2 \vee \ldots \vee a_N}, b) \quad .$$

The formula "$(\overline{a_1 \vee a_2 \vee \ldots \vee a_N}) \equiv (\bar{a}_1\bar{a}_2 \ldots \bar{a}_N)$" is a tautology (called De Morgan's law) and hence $[(\overline{a_1 \vee a_2 \vee \ldots \vee a_N}) \leftrightarrow (\bar{a}_1\bar{a}_2 \ldots \bar{a}_N)]$. Applying the exchange principle we get the desired theorem

[17] $$\mathbf{P}(a_1 \vee a_2 \vee \ldots \vee a_N, b) = 1 - \mathbf{P}(\bar{a}_1\bar{a}_2 \ldots \bar{a}_N, b) \quad .$$

We illustrate this theorem by calculating the probability of getting at least one ace in three successive draws from a well-shuffled deck, *without* replacement. Let A_1, A_2, A_3 mean that an ace is obtained on the first, second, and third draw, respectively. By theorem [17]

$$\mathbf{P}(A_1 \vee A_2 \vee A_3) = 1 - \mathbf{P}(\bar{A}_1\bar{A}_2\bar{A}_3) \quad .$$

Using the general multiplication principle and the subtraction principle we get

$$\begin{aligned}\mathbf{P}(A_1 \vee A_2 \vee A_3) &= 1 - \mathbf{P}(\bar{A}_1)\mathbf{P}(\bar{A}_2, \bar{A}_1)\mathbf{P}(\bar{A}_3, \bar{A}_1\bar{A}_2) \\ &= 1 - \tfrac{48}{52}\tfrac{47}{51}\tfrac{46}{50} \quad ,\end{aligned}$$

or approximately 0.217.

Now consider the question: What is the probability of getting at least one ace in three successive draws *with* replacement? The answer is found in the same way, except that the special multiplication principle may be used. The probability turns out to be $1 - (48/52)^3$ or approximately 0.213. For this special case we can derive a corollary from theorem [17] by means of the subtraction principle and the special multiplication principle.

[18] If $a_1, a_2, \ldots, a_N$ are independent on condition b, and

$\mathbf{P}(a_n, b) = x$ for $n = 1, 2, \ldots, N$; then

$$\mathbf{P}(a_1 \vee a_2 \vee \ldots \vee a_N, b) = 1 - (1 - x)^N \quad .$$

This enables us to calculate the probability of at least one deuce when many dice are thrown. Let D_n mean the nth die falls deuce. Then $\mathbf{P}(D_n) = 1/6$. Hence

$$\mathbf{P}(D_1 \vee D_2 \vee \ldots \vee D_N) = 1 - (5/6)^N \quad .$$

For seven dice the probability of obtaining at least one deuce is approximately 0.721; for twenty-five dice it is about 0.990; and for thirty-eight dice it is about 0.999.

Before concluding this section, let us pause to review our general method of solving problems by means of the calculus of inductive probability. There are three general steps. First, one writes the problem in truth-functional notation. Thus, suppose we wish to calculate the probability that when two cards are drawn in succession from a bridge deck without replacement, either the first will be an ace (A_1) and the second will not ($\bar{A}_2$), or else the first will be a king (K_1) and the second a queen (Q_2). Symbolically, we wish to compute $\mathbf{P}(A_1\bar{A}_2 \vee K_1Q_2)$. The second general step is to reduce this to atomic probabilities by means of the theorems of the calculus of inductive probability. Which theorems to apply may be determined from an inspection of the truth-functional connectives involved and the conditions of the problem. Since the main connective of "$A_1\bar{A}_2 \vee K_1Q_2$" is a disjunction, and since the events involved are exclusive, the special addition principle [13] may be applied to give

$$\mathbf{P}(A_1\bar{A}_2 \vee K_1Q_2) = \mathbf{P}(A_1\bar{A}_2) + \mathbf{P}(K_1Q_2) \quad .$$

Each term on the right involves a conjunction, and the general multiplication principle [11] applies, giving

$$\mathbf{P}(A_1\bar{A}_2 \vee K_1Q_2) = \mathbf{P}(A_1)\mathbf{P}(\bar{A}_2, A_1) + \mathbf{P}(K_1)\mathbf{P}(Q_2, K_1) \quad .$$

Finally, the negation on A_2 may be eliminated by the subtraction principle, giving

$$\mathbf{P}(A_1\bar{A}_2 \vee K_1Q_2) = \mathbf{P}(A_1)[1 - \mathbf{P}(A_2, A_1)] + \mathbf{P}(K_1)\mathbf{P}(Q_2, K_1) \quad .$$

Each of these transformations is made by means of the calculus of inductive probability. The third general step is to reach outside the calculus of probability to determine the values of the atomic probabilities involved: $\mathbf{P}(A_1) = 1/13$, $\mathbf{P}(A_2, A_1) = 3/51$, $P(K_1) = 1/13$, $\mathbf{P}(Q_2, K_1) = 4/51$. Finally, these values are substituted in the formula to give the answer

$$\mathbf{P}(A_1\bar{A}_2 \text{ v } K_1Q_2) = (1/13)(1-3/51) + (1/13)(4/51) = 52/663 \quad .$$

2.4 Relative Frequency

Inductive probability is closely related to frequency. This relation is important, because inductive probabilities as such cannot be directly observed, whereas frequencies can be. Moreover, confusion about this relation is common (see pp. 149, 532). In the present section we offer informally and without proof some of the theorems about frequencies found in the calculus of inductive probability.* The theorems proceed from inductive probabilities to frequencies; they enable one to reason inductively from information about the probabilities governing a process to conclusions concerning the frequencies to be expected. In Section 2.5 some theorems are given that enable one to proceed in the opposite direction, inferring results about inductive probabilities from observed frequencies. Since both types of inference are inductive, the concept of inductive probability in these theorems is more fundamental than the concept of frequency. In the next chapter (sec. 3.4.2) we shall discuss attempts to define inductive probability in terms of frequencies.

We will confine ourselves to finite and infinite sequences of independent and equiprobable trials or events, and we begin with some definitions. Consider the sequence $x_1, x_2, x_3, \ldots, x_l, \ldots$, with the outcome of x_l being either ϕ or $\bar{\phi}$. The statement "ϕx_l" asserts that x_l is ϕ, while the statement "$\overline{\phi x_l}$" asserts that x_l is not ϕ. Each "ϕx_l" expresses the occurrence of a certain event, while each "$\overline{\phi x_l}$" expresses the occurrence of the complement event; for example, "ϕx_l" might signify that a coin falls tails on the lth toss, in which case "$\overline{\phi x_l}$" signifies that it falls heads on the lth toss. Strictly speaking, "$\overline{\phi x_l}$" means that it is not the case that the coin falls tails on the lth toss. But we use "$\overline{\phi x_l}$" relative to a general condition g that implies the coin is tossed at least l times and does not land on its edge. Relative to these assumptions, "not (the coin falls tails on the lth toss)" is equivalent to "the coin falls heads on the lth toss."†

* The reader is referred to any standard text in probability theory for details and proofs; for example, Neyman's *First Course in Probability and Statistics* or Feller's *An Introduction to Probability Theory and Its Applications*, vol. 1.

Todhunter, *A History of the Mathematical Theory of Probability*, is a useful reference for the history of probability through Laplace.

† The status of a term like "the lth toss" when there is no lth toss is discussed in my "Icon, Index, and Symbol," p. 688. Note that "l" stands for "length."

A series of trials defines a set of sequences, each sequence being one of the possible outcomes of the trials. The symbolism "ϕx_1, ϕx_2, . . . , ϕx_l, . . ." is used to refer to such a set of sequences. If the series of trials is infinite, l ranges over all positive integers; while if the series of trials is of length L, then $l = 1, 2, 3, \ldots, L$. In the cases of interest to us, every finite subsequence of ϕx_1, ϕx_2, ϕx_3, . . . is logically independent in the sense of Section 2.3.2, either unconditionally or relative to some condition. Such a set of logically independent sequences is called a *process*, perhaps relative to some condition. Note that a process is a set of logically possible "worlds," either finite or infinite (cf. secs. 3.2 and 6.3).

We can now define the concept of an independent process of equiprobable events. A process $\phi x_1, \phi x_2, \phi x_3, \ldots, \phi x_l, \ldots$ is an **independent process of probability α on condition** g if and only if ϕx_1, ϕx_2, ϕx_3, . . . , ϕx_l, . . . are independent on condition g and $\mathbf{P}(\phi x_l, g) = \alpha$ for every l.

To say that a process is independent and of some given probability is to assign inductive probabilities to the logically possible sequences or worlds defined by the process. Consider a specific penny that is tossed three times, and let Tx_l mean that it falls tails on the lth toss. The assertion "Tx_1, Tx_2, Tx_3 is an independent process of probability α on condition g" says something about eight different possible sequences, namely that

$$\mathbf{P}(Tx_1Tx_2Tx_3, g) = \alpha^3$$

$$\mathbf{P}(\overline{Tx_1}Tx_2Tx_3, g) = \mathbf{P}(Tx_1\overline{Tx_2}Tx_3, g) = \mathbf{P}(Tx_1Tx_2\overline{Tx_3}, g) = (1-\alpha)\alpha^2$$

$$\mathbf{P}(\overline{Tx_1}\,\overline{Tx_2}Tx_3, g) = \mathbf{P}(\overline{Tx_1}Tx_2\overline{Tx_3}, g) = \mathbf{P}(Tx_1\overline{Tx_2}\,\overline{Tx_3}, g) = (1-\alpha)^2\alpha$$

$$\mathbf{P}(\overline{Tx_1}\,\overline{Tx_2}\,\overline{Tx_3}, g) = (1-\alpha)^3 \quad .$$

Observe that only one of these eight sequences is actual.

We next define two notions that are applicable to a specific finite or infinite sequence of events ϕx_1, ϕx_2, . . . , ϕx_L, ... For convenience of reference we say that an occurrence of ϕ is a "success" and an occurrence of $\bar{\phi}$ is a "failure." The **number of successes** $S_L(\phi)$ is defined to be the number of times "ϕx" is true in L trials. The **relative frequency of success** $\sigma_L(\phi)$ is defined to be $S_L(\phi)/L$. For example, if the outcome of tossing the penny three times is $Tx_1\overline{Tx_2}Tx_3$, then $S_3(T) = 2$ and $\sigma_3(T) = 2/3$. The values of S_L and σ_L for all the initial segments of the following sequence of ten tosses of the coin are

	Tx_1	$\overline{Tx_2}$	Tx_3	Tx_4	Tx_5	Tx_6	Tx_7	$\overline{Tx_8}$	$\overline{Tx_9}$	$\overline{Tx_{10}}$
L	1	2	3	4	5	6	7	8	9	10
$S_L(T)$	1	1	2	3	4	5	6	6	6	6
$\sigma_L(T)$	1	1/2	2/3	3/4	4/5	5/6	6/7	6/8	6/9	6/10

.

The functions $S_L(\phi)$ and $\sigma_L(\phi)$ are defined for any sequence of the form $\phi x_1, \phi x_2, \phi x_3, \ldots$. However, in this section we are interested only in sequences produced by an independent process of equiprobable events. For such a process, all outcomes (sequences) with S_L successes and $L - S_L$ failures are equiprobable. Later we shall study sequences that are not produced by independent processes of equiprobable events (secs. 2.5, 3.2, and 8.3).

Suppose $\phi x_1, \phi x_2, \ldots, \phi x_L$ is an independent process of probability α. We examine how the most likely number of successes depends on α and L. Look at the probability that the number of successes S_L is k, for $k = 0, 1, 2, \ldots, L$ in turn; that is, notice how $\mathbf{P}(S_L = k)$ changes as k varies but L is

TABLE 2

THE MOST LIKELY NUMBER OF SUCCESSES

	$\alpha = 0.3$ ($5\alpha = 1.5$)	$\alpha = 0.5$ ($5\alpha = 2.5$)	$\alpha = 0.6$ ($5\alpha = 3$)
$\mathbf{P}(S_5 = 0)$	0.168	0.031	0.010
$\mathbf{P}(S_5 = 1)$	0.360 (max)	0.156	0.077
$\mathbf{P}(S_5 = 2)$	0.309	0.312 (max)	0.230
$\mathbf{P}(S_5 = 3)$	0.132	0.312 (max)	0.346 (max)
$\mathbf{P}(S_5 = 4)$	0.028	0.156	0.259
$\mathbf{P}(S_5 = 5)$	0.002	0.031	0.078

An event of probability α is repeated five times. $\mathbf{P}(S_5 = k)$ is the probability that there are k successes in these five trials. Table 2 illustrates the fact that $\mathbf{P}(S_5 = k)$ is a maximum when k is near 5α.

fixed. It is clear on reflection (and true) that $\mathbf{P}(S_L = k)$ is a maximum when k is about αL, that is, when S_L equals approximately the length of the sequence L multiplied by the probability α. This fact is illustrated in Table 2, where rounded-off values of $\mathbf{P}(S_5 = k)$ are given for three values of α. The maxima have been indicated: there may be two maxima, as in the column for $\alpha = 0.5$. In each case $\mathbf{P}(S_5 = k)$ reaches its maximum when k is within one unit of αL, i.e., 5α. Of course, if αL is not an integer, the most probable number of successes S_L cannot be exactly αL. It can be proved that the most probable number of successes is an integer within one unit of αL; there may be two most probable numbers of successes, in which case each is within one unit of αL. For example, the most likely number of tails in 100 tosses of the penny is 50; while in 101 tosses there are two most likely numbers of tails, 50 and 51.

When the length L of the sequence is large there are many possible values for the number of successes S_L, and even the most likely of these is not very probable. We illustrate this point with the coin again. Since $\alpha = 1/2$, the most likely number of successes S_L, when L is even, is $L/2$. Table 3 (A1) gives the approximate probability that the number of successes (tails) is exactly $L/2$, for $L = 10$, 100, 1,000, and 10,000. But for any given percentage deviation from αL, the larger L becomes the greater the likelihood that the number of successes S_L will fall within this percentage of αL. Table 3 (A2) gives the approximate probabilities that S_L will fall within 20 percent of αL.*

We restate these facts in terms of the relative frequency of success σ_L. Since $\sigma_L = S_L/L$, to say that the most likely number of successes is very near αL is to say that the most likely relative frequency of success is very

TABLE 3

PROBABILITY AND FREQUENCY

(A) Probability that the number of successes S_L is			
(1) exactly αL:		(2) within 20% of αL:	
$\mathbf{P}(S_{10} = 5)$	$= 0.246$	$\mathbf{P}(4 \leqq S_{10} \leqq 6)$	$= 0.656$
$\mathbf{P}(S_{100} = 50)$	$= 0.080$	$\mathbf{P}(40 \leqq S_{100} \leqq 60)$	$= 0.965$
$\mathbf{P}(S_{1000} = 500)$	$= 0.025$	$\mathbf{P}(400 \leqq S_{1000} \leqq 600)$	$= 1 - 2.1\text{x}10^{-10}$
$\mathbf{P}(S_{10000} = 5000)$	$= 0.008$	$\mathbf{P}(4000 \leqq S_{10000} \leqq 6000)$	$= 1 - 4.5\text{x}10^{-90}$
(B) Probability that the relative frequency of success σ_L is			
(1) exactly α:		(2) within 20% of α:	
$\mathbf{P}(\sigma_{10} = 0.5)$	$= 0.246$	$\mathbf{P}(0.4 \leqq \sigma_{10} \leqq 0.6)$	$= 0.656$
$\mathbf{P}(\sigma_{100} = 0.5)$	$= 0.080$	$\mathbf{P}(0.4 \leqq \sigma_{100} \leqq 0.6)$	$= 0.965$
$\mathbf{P}(\sigma_{1000} = 0.5)$	$= 0.025$	$\mathbf{P}(0.4 \leqq \sigma_{1000} \leqq 0.6)$	$= 1 - 2.1\text{x}10^{-10}$
$\mathbf{P}(\sigma_{10000} = 0.5)$	$= 0.008$	$\mathbf{P}(0.4 \leqq \sigma_{10000} \leqq 0.6)$	$= 1 - 4.5\text{x}10^{-90}$

Probabilistic relations of S_L and σ_L to αL and α for the case $\alpha = 0.5$.

near α. Of course, if αL is not an integer, the most probable number of successes will not be exactly αL. The results of Table 3 (A1), converted to relative frequency, are given in Table 3 (B1). As before, when L is large the probability that σ_L will hit its most likely value is low. But also as before, the probability that σ_L will come close to this most likely value, and hence to α, is high. This fact is illustrated in Table 3 (B2), which contains the results of Table 3 (A2) converted to relative frequencies.

We may now outline the relations that hold, in an independent process, between probability and relative frequency. Let α be the probability of success on an arbitrary trial, σ_L the actual relative frequency of success in L trials, and β_L the most likely relative frequency of success in L trials.

* The first two probabilities in each part of Table 3 were obtained from *Tables of the Cumulative Binomial Probability Distribution*.

The last two probabilities in each part of Table 3 were obtained by using the normal integral as an approximation to cumulative binomial probabilities. Values of the normal density and integral functions are tabulated in *Tables of Probability Functions*, vol. 2.

Relative frequency β_L is very near probability α. It is unlikely that σ_L will be exactly β_L but likely that σ_L will be close to β_L and hence close to α.

Table 3 (B2) shows that as L becomes indefinitely large the probability that σ_L falls within a given range around α approaches closer and closer to unity. This is the famous "law of large numbers" in its classical form. To express it precisely we need the concept of the limit of an infinite sequence of numbers, which in turn involves the notion of the absolute value of a real number. The absolute value of x, written "$|x|$", is the positive number having the same magnitude as x. In other words, if $x \geqq 0$, then $|x| = x$, while if $x < 0$, then $|x| = -x$.

Let $\sigma_1, \sigma_2, \sigma_3, \ldots$ be an infinite sequence of real numbers. This sequence is said to have a limit σ if and only if: for any positive real number ϵ, there is a positive integer n such that for all positive integers m, if $m > n$ then $|\sigma - \sigma_m| < \epsilon$. "$\underset{n\to\infty}{\text{Limit}}\ \sigma_n$" denotes this limit if it exists; otherwise the expression "$\underset{n\to\infty}{\text{Limit}}\ \sigma_n$" is undefined. Roughly speaking, to say that a sequence has a limit is to say that it approaches closer and closer to a particular real number. For example, the sequence $1/2, 3/4, 15/16, \ldots, (2^n - 1)/2^n, \ldots$ has the limit one.

Consider next an infinite independent process of equiprobable events of probability α. Let σ_L be the relative frequency of success for the first L terms of this process. The *law of large numbers* is: for any positive real number ϵ,

$$\underset{L\to\infty}{\text{Limit}}\ \mathbf{P}(\alpha - \epsilon \leqq \sigma_L \leqq \alpha + \epsilon) = 1 \quad .$$

Roughly speaking, the law of large numbers says that the relative frequency σ_L of a type of event tends in the long run to the probability α of that type of event; that is, the relative frequency tends to equal the probability, and the longer the sequence the stronger the tendency.

We give some more examples to illustrate the relation of probability to frequency. The probability of a bridge hand having no aces is about 0.3. There is less than half a chance that out of three hands exactly one will have no aces, but over a long period of time a player should expect about 30 percent of his hands to be of this sort. Another example concerns the relation between *being* guilty of an act and being *declared* guilty by some process. Discounting biased judges, unfair trials, etc., the connection between the two is a matter of evidence and hence of probability. The degree of probability required for conviction is sometimes set high (as in the criterion "innocent until proven guilty beyond a reasonable doubt"), sometimes at a medium level (as when an overbalance of evidence is required for conviction), and sometimes low (as when every suspect is punished). The relation between probability and frequency is subtle here, but the following contrast is clear: The higher the strength of evidence required for conviction, the less often will an innocent person be convicted and the more often will a guilty person go free. Compare a judicial system that has many protections for the accused with one that does not. Other things being equal, the former punishes fewer innocent people and allows more guilty people to go unpunished than the latter. As Blackstone expressed the underlying principle of English law, "... all presumptive evidence of felony should be admitted cautiously; for the law holds that it is better that ten guilty persons escape than that one innocent suffer."* But whatever the degree of probability required for conviction, very probably some innocents will be punished while some of the guilty will not be.

Three important fallacies are associated with probability and frequency. The first can be stated briefly and dismissed quickly. It is sometimes said that one should be surprised every time he picks up a bridge hand, since the chance of getting *that* particular hand is very small; indeed, the probability of a particular bridge hand is about 0.64×10^{-12}, so that each hand is a rare event and its occurrence is almost miraculous! The fallacy here is to confuse two obviously different events: the occurrence of *this* particular hand (which is indeed rare) and the occurrence of *some* hand (which is as common as bridge).

The second fallacy is more subtle. A driver is criticized for his habitual recklessness. He replies, "But I am very much alive." His fallacy is to think that the way events turn out refutes or confirms a hypothesis in a very simple way. Let us estimate, conservatively, that the probability of an average driver dying from an automobile accident in a given year is 1/7,000. Suppose this driver is so reckless that his chance of dying is 1/2,000. But whether he is average or reckless it is highly unlikely that he will die from an automobile accident in any given year, and so the fact that he lives is only very slight evidence that his driving is relatively safe (see sec. 2.5).

The third fallacy, which we will analyze at some length, is called the *gambler's fallacy*. Suppose a coin has been tossed a number of times, with more heads than tails; for instance, 55 heads and 45 tails. Gamblers commonly think the next toss is more likely to be a tail than a head, on the ground that there is a tendency for the number of heads to equal the number of tails. But this is wrong. If the coin is weighted on one side, the observed number of successes $S_{100} = 55$ is evidence concerning the next toss, but it shows that a head is more likely, not a tail! And if the coin is fair, so that the tosses really are independent, the probability of a head on the next toss is 1/2, no matter what the actual frequency of heads on the previous tosses.

Here are some other instances of the gambler's fallacy. A card player who has had bad cards all evening reasons: I have had bad cards tonight; but by the law of averages things must eventually even out; therefore, I should have better cards tomorrow. In a state lottery a number from 1 to

* *Commentaries on the Laws of England* 4: 358.

100 was drawn each week; when number 67 did not come up for 125 successive weeks, the people placed so much money on it that had 67 come up the lottery would have suffered a large loss!

As the appeal to the "law of averages" shows, the source of the "gambler's fallacy" lies close to the law of large numbers. This law tells us that the relative frequency σ_L tends to α as L increases indefinitely. But it does not say that the number of successes S_L tends to αL as L increases. The opposite is in fact the case: The difference between S_L and αL tends to become larger and larger as L increases indefinitely.

Let us examine the matter closely. Consider an infinite process of independent and equiprobable events of probability α and relative frequency of success σ_L. Use the exchange principle [10] on the law of large numbers, multiplying through by L. Since $S_L = \sigma_L L$, we get: if $\epsilon > 0$, then

$$\operatorname*{Limit}_{L\to\infty} \mathbf{P}(\alpha L - \epsilon L \leqq S_L \leqq \alpha L + \epsilon L) = 1 \quad .$$

In words: The probability that the number of successes S_L falls within ϵL of αL approaches one as L becomes larger and larger. But notice that, since ϵ is fixed, the quantity ϵL becomes larger and larger as L goes to infinity.

Now consider in contrast the probability that the difference between S_L and αL will stay within *a fixed quantity m*. *This* probability tends to zero, for it is a theorem that for any $m \geqq 0$:

$$\operatorname*{Limit}_{L\to\infty} \mathbf{P}(\alpha L - m \leqq S_L \leqq \alpha L + m) = 0 \quad .$$

We call this theorem the *anti-gambler's-fallacy theorem!* Expressing this result in terms of the relative frequency of success σ_L we get: for any $m \geqq 0$,

$$\operatorname*{Limit}_{L\to\infty} \mathbf{P}(\alpha - m/L \leqq \sigma_L \leqq \alpha + m/L) = 0 \quad .$$

Though the anti-gambler's-fallacy theorem resembles the law of large numbers, it is essentially different; for since m is fixed, the ratio m/L goes to zero as L goes to infinity, while in the law of large numbers ϵ does not change as L changes.

The probability values given in Table 3 illustrate the difference between the anti-gambler's-fallacy theorem and the law of large numbers. For parts A1 and B1, $m = 0$, but the values given there also hold for $0 \leqq m < 1$. For parts A2 and B2, $\epsilon = 0.10$. The difference between the anti-gambler's-fallacy theorem and the law of large numbers may also be understood in terms of the absolute value $|S_L - \alpha L|$ of the difference between S_L and αL. The anti-gambler's-fallacy theorem states that $|S_L - \alpha L|$ tends to grow without limit. In contrast, the law of large numbers states that $|S_L - \alpha L|$ tends to grow more slowly than L, that is, the ratio $|S_L - \alpha L|/L$ tends to zero; and to say that $|S_L - \alpha L|/L$ tends to zero is to say that σ_L tends to α. Note that in these formulations the meaning of "tends" involves the concept of probability.

The reader who is puzzled by the fact that $|S_L - \alpha L|$ tends to grow without limit while the ratio $|S_L - \alpha L|/L$ tends to zero may find it helpful to consider an example. Let $Ax_1, Ax_2, Ax_3, \ldots$ be an infinite independent process of probability .5. We saw earlier that the concept of an independent process involves a set of possible specific sequences. For our purpose we shall choose a specific infinite sequence that illustrates the tendencies under consideration, though it is highly artificial in its structure. Imagine that the event A of probability .5 is repeated indefinitely, with the result

$$Ax_1, Ax_2; Ax_3, Ax_4, Ax_5, \overline{Ax_6}; Ax_7, Ax_8, Ax_9, Ax_{10}, \overline{Ax_{11}}, \overline{Ax_{12}};$$
$$Ax_{13}, Ax_{14}, Ax_{15}, Ax_{16}, Ax_{17}, \overline{Ax_{18}}, \overline{Ax_{19}}, \overline{Ax_{20}}; \ldots \qquad .$$

This sequence is composed of a succession of blocks separated by semicolons, the nth block containing $n + 1$ successes and $n - 1$ failures. The situation at the end of the nth block is this: $L = n(n + 1)$, $S_L = .5n(n + 3)$, $|S_L - .5L| = n$, $(|S_L - .5L|/L) = (n + 1)^{-1}$, and $\sigma_L = .5(n + 3)/(n + 1)$. As n increases, $|S_L - .5L|$ increases without limit, $|S_L - .5L|/L$ approaches zero as a limit, and σ_L approaches the probability .5 as a limit.

To sum up: Consider an independent process of equiprobable events of probability α. By the law of large numbers the relative frequency of success σ_L tends in the long run to the probability α. By the anti-gambler's-fallacy theorem the difference between the actual number of successes S_L and the most likely number of successes αL tends to grow without limit.

Let us apply these results to a gambler who is playing a purely chance, fair game with others. His *net* loss or *net* gain tends to increase indefinitely, while the *ratio* of his net loss or net gain to the amount gambled tends to decrease. But the gambler's wealth is governed by his net loss or gain, not by the amount of business he does, though these are of course related. Thus we arrive at an interesting corollary of the anti-gambler's-fallacy theorem. Suppose a number of gamblers, each with the same initial stakes, agree to play indefinitely with one another a purely chance game, each gambler's chance of winning being the same. Consider the probability that at a given time t some one gambler possesses all the wealth. Since the tendency is for each man's net loss or net gain to increase with time, the probability that at a given time t one gambler will possess all the wealth approaches unity as t increases indefinitely. That is, it is inevitable that all the gamblers but one will go broke. This might be called the "law of the gambler's ruin." The inevitable can be accomplished more quickly, but perhaps with less pleasure, by one play: All stakes are placed in a pot, and he who draws the highest card takes all! The choice between betting all one's money at once or in small amounts involves the concept of utility.

This discussion of gambling illustrates an important fact about chance: One can gain in surety by shifting attention from the individual case or small set to a sequence or larger set. Thus while we cannot be very sure that the relative frequency with which a fair coin falls tails will be near 0.5 in 10 tosses, we can be quite certain that it will be very near 0.5 in 10,000 tosses. An important practical application of this principle is that by treating a number of events together and developing policies for them one can reduce the incalculable and fortuitous element in human existence. A player is, for example, quite uncertain about how the next play at roulette will turn out, but he can be very sure that in the long run he will lose. My insurance company does not know when I will die, but it knows that the chance of its going broke is very slight. The relation of probability and chance to utility and policymaking will be discussed in Chapters 4 and 5.

2.5 Bayes' Theorem and Induction

2.5.1 Bayes' theorem

We shall now study some theorems of the calculus of inductive probability that have particular relevance to the process of verifying a hypothesis by testing its consequences. In the present subsection we prove and illustrate a prediction theorem ([19]), two forms of Bayes' theorem for calculating the probability of a hypothesis after a prediction of that hypothesis has been confirmed or disconfirmed ([20] and [21]), and a theorem stating a condition for confirmation ([22]). We shall then study the repeated use of Bayes' theorem for confirmation (sec. 2.5.2, Confirmation by repeated experimentation) and state a theorem concerning this use (sec. 2.5.3, The confirmation theorem). Finally, we shall discuss the applicability of the theorems of this section to actual cases of inductive reasoning.

Theorems [19] through [22] do not depend on the results about relative frequency that were offered without proof in the last section. The confirmation theorem does depend on these results, but this theorem is only stated, not proved.

We first prove a theorem for predicting a result r on the basis of a set of alternative hypotheses. Assume that hypotheses $h_1, h_2, \ldots, h_N$ are mutually exclusive and jointly exhaustive on condition g. Any event r may be divided into the subcases $h_1r, h_2r, \ldots, h_Nr$ that are the mutually exclusive and jointly exhaustive ways in which r may be true. Hence $g \rightarrow [r \equiv (h_1r \vee h_2r \vee \ldots \vee h_Nr)]$, and by theorem [9]

$$\mathbf{P}(r, g) = \mathbf{P}(h_1r \vee h_2r \vee \ldots \vee h_Nr, g) \quad .$$

Since $h_1r, h_2r, \ldots, h_Nr$ are mutually exclusive, the special addition principle [13] applies, giving

$$\mathbf{P}(h_1r \vee h_2r \vee \ldots \vee h_Nr, g) = \sum_{n=1}^{N} \mathbf{P}(h_nr, g) \quad .$$

Axiom [2] can be applied separately to each term of the summation, giving

$$\sum_{n=1}^{N} \mathbf{P}(h_n r, g) = \sum_{n=1}^{N} \mathbf{P}(h_n, g)\mathbf{P}(r, h_n g) \quad .$$

Combining all these results we have the *prediction theorem.*

[19] If $h_1, h_2, \ldots, h_N$ are mutually exclusive and jointly exhaustive on condition g, then

$$\mathbf{P}(r, g) = \sum_{n=1}^{N} \mathbf{P}(h_n, g)\mathbf{P}(r, h_n g) \quad .$$

For example, a suspicious-looking gambler approaches you with a coin. You estimate that the probability of the coin being fair (F) is only 1/4 and that the probability of its having two tails (U) is 3/4. Theorem [19] enables you to calculate the probability with which you should expect a tail (T): $\mathbf{P}(T) = \mathbf{P}(F)\mathbf{P}(T, F) + \mathbf{P}(U)\mathbf{P}(T, U) = (1/4)(1/2) + (3/4)(1) = 7/8.$

Suppose the coin is fairly tossed and falls tails. This would tend to confirm your belief that the coin is unfair, i.e., $\mathbf{P}(U, T)$ is greater than $\mathbf{P}(U)$. This "inverse probability" $\mathbf{P}(U, T)$ may be calculated in the case of just two hypotheses as follows. By the exchange principle

$$\mathbf{P}(rh, g) = \mathbf{P}(hr, g) \quad .$$

Application of the general multiplication principle to both sides gives

[α] $\mathbf{P}(r, g)\mathbf{P}(h, rg) = \mathbf{P}(h, g)\mathbf{P}(r, hg) \quad .$

By similar reasoning,

[β] $\mathbf{P}(r, g)\mathbf{P}(\bar{h}, rg) = \mathbf{P}(\bar{h}, g)\mathbf{P}(r, \bar{h}g) \quad .$

Using [α] alone we get

[γ] If $\mathbf{P}(r, g) > 0$, then $\mathbf{P}(h, rg) = \dfrac{\mathbf{P}(h, g)\mathbf{P}(r, hg)}{\mathbf{P}(r, g)}$

Using both [α] and [β] we get

[20[If $\mathbf{P}(\bar{h}, g) > 0$ and $\mathbf{P}(r, \bar{h}g) > 0$, then $\dfrac{\mathbf{P}(h, rg)}{\mathbf{P}(\bar{h}, rg)} = \dfrac{\mathbf{P}(h, g)\mathbf{P}(r, hg)}{\mathbf{P}(\bar{h}, g)\mathbf{P}(r, \bar{h}g)}.$

This is one form of **Bayes' theorem** for calculating inverse probabilities from direct probabilities.*

Applying Bayes' theorem to the coin that probably has two tails we get

$$\frac{\mathbf{P}(U, T)}{\mathbf{P}(F, T)} = \frac{\mathbf{P}(U)\mathbf{P}(T, U)}{\mathbf{P}(F)\mathbf{P}(T, F)} = \frac{(3/4)(1)}{(1/4)(1/2)} = 6$$

* "An Essay Towards Solving a Problem in the Doctrine of Chances." Actually theorems [γ], [20], [21], and [22] all derive from Bayes, though he stated none of them in the form given here.

Since U and F are mutually exclusive and jointly exhaustive, $\mathbf{P}(U, T) = 6/7$ and $\mathbf{P}(F, T) = 1/7$ by theorem [14].

Another form of **Bayes' theorem** is

[21] If $h_1, h_2, \ldots, h_N$ are mutually exclusive and jointly exhaustive on condition g, and $\mathrm{P}(r, g) > 0$, then

$$\mathbf{P}(h_n, rg) = \frac{\mathbf{P}(h_n, g)\mathbf{P}(r, h_n g)}{\sum_{m=1}^{N} \mathbf{P}(h_m, g)\mathbf{P}(r, h_m g)} \qquad \text{for } n = 1, 2, \ldots, N.$$

This theorem follows directly from [19] and [γ].

We may illustrate the prediction theorem and Bayes' theorem with an example involving three hypotheses, H_1, H_2, H_3. Suppose a bag is chosen from among three bags by a hidden mechanism in such a way that there is probability 1/6 that

H_1: It contains 25 wine and 75 yellow cubes,

probability 1/3 that

H_2: It contains 50 wine and 50 yellow cubes,

and probability 1/2 that

H_3: It contains 75 wine and 25 yellow cubes.

One is not allowed to examine the contents of the bag, but he is allowed to make random drawings from it with replacements. The question "What is the probability that two successive draws will both be wine (W)?" is answered by means of the prediction theorem,

$$\mathbf{P}(W_1W_2) = \mathbf{P}(H_1)\mathbf{P}(W_1W_2, H_1) + \mathbf{P}(H_2)\mathbf{P}(W_1W_2, H_2) + \mathbf{P}(H_3)\mathbf{P}(W_1W_2, H_3) = 3/8 \quad .$$

Suppose now that two drawings are made and both are wine. This is additional evidence for hypothesis H_3 and against the other hypotheses. The exact evidential weight it has can be computed by Bayes' theorem.

$$\mathbf{P}(H_1, W_1W_2) = \frac{\mathbf{P}(H_1)\mathbf{P}(W_1W_2, H_1)}{\sum_{n=1}^{3} \mathbf{P}(H_n)\mathbf{P}(W_1W_2, H_n)}$$

$$= \frac{1/6(1/4)^2}{1/6(1/4)^2 + 1/3(2/4)^2 + 1/2(3/4)^2} = 1/36$$

$$\mathbf{P}(H_2, W_1W_2) = \frac{\mathbf{P}(H_2)\mathbf{P}(W_1W_2, H_2)}{\sum_{n=1}^{3} \mathbf{P}(H_n)\mathbf{P}(W_1W_2, H_n)}$$

$$= \frac{1/3(2/4)^2}{1/6(1/4)^2 + 1/3(2/4)^2 + 1/2(3/4)^2} = 8/36$$

$$\mathbf{P}(H_3, W_1W_2) = \frac{\mathbf{P}(H_3)\mathbf{P}(W_1W_2, H_3)}{\sum_{n=1}^{3} \mathbf{P}(H_n)\mathbf{P}(W_1W_2, H_n)}$$

$$= \frac{1/2(3/4)^2}{1/6(1/4)^2 + 1/3(2/4)^2 + 1/2(3/4)^2} = 27/36 \quad .$$

These three probabilities sum to one, as they must since H_1, H_2, H_3 are assumed to be jointly exhaustive. Thus hypothesis H_3 was somewhat confirmed by the result W_1W_2, and the other two hypotheses were somewhat disconfirmed.

Viewed in this way the probabilities $\mathbf{P}(h_n, g)$ measure the evidential strength of each hypothesis relative to what is known prior to the test, and so they are called **prior probabilities.** The probabilities $\mathbf{P}(r, h_n g)$ express the extent to which each hypothesis favors the result r, which in some cases is a prediction, and they are called **degrees of prediction.** The probabilities $\mathbf{P}(h_n, rg)$ express the likelihood of each hypothesis being true after the result r is obtained and hence are called **posterior probabilities.** Bayes' theorem is a formula for calculating the posterior probabilities from the prior probabilities and degrees of prediction.

A good format for calculating posterior probabilities is shown in Table 4. It simplifies the computations to modify the prior probabilities by a

TABLE 4

CALCULATION FORMAT FOR BAYES' THEOREM

Hypothesis	(1) Prior probability (times a constant)	(2) Degree of prediction of W_1W_2 (times a constant)	(1)x(2)	Posterior probability
$H_1 \binom{25W}{75Y}$	1	1	1	$\frac{1}{36}$
$H_2 \binom{50W}{50Y}$	2	4	8	$\frac{8}{36}$
$H_3 \binom{75W}{25Y}$	3	9	27	$\frac{27}{36}$
			36	

common factor [column (1)] and similarly to modify the degrees of predictions [column (2)]; these constant factors appear in both the numerator and the denominator of theorem [21] and hence cancel out.

When there are only two hypotheses involved, the calculation of the posterior probabilities can best be done by means of the ratio form of Bayes' theorem ([20]). The concept of *odds* is useful here. If $\mathbf{P}(c, d) = x$, then given d, the *odds* in favor of c are x to $(1 - x)$. For example, the odds in favor of drawing a spade from a bridge deck are 1/4 to 3/4, or more simply 1 to 3. This is strictly classroom usage, but it is convenient for our purposes. The actual usage of gamblers is governed by a more complicated rule. The odds are always expressed in terms of integers, usually with the larger integer first. For example, if $\mathbf{P}(a) = .4$, the odds are 3 to 2 *against* a; while if $\mathbf{P}(b) = .8$, the odds are 4 to 1 *in favor of* b. The British would say, "The odds on a are 3 to 2, *against*" and "The odds on b are 4 to 1, *on*."

The ratio form of Bayes' theorem ([20]) can be stated verbally in terms of odds in this way: The posterior odds for any hypothesis are equal to the product of the prior odds and the ratio of the degrees of prediction. Given the posterior odds, one can easily calculate the posterior probabilities. Since $\mathbf{P}(h, rg) + \mathbf{P}(\bar{h}, rg) = 1$, if $\mathbf{P}(h, rg)/\mathbf{P}(\bar{h}, rg) = \alpha/\beta$, then $\mathbf{P}(h, rg) = \alpha/(\alpha + \beta)$ and $\mathbf{P}(\bar{h}, rg) = \beta/(\alpha + \beta)$.

We illustrate this method with an example. There are two boxes that look alike externally; the first contains six maize (M) and two blue (B) marbles, while the second contains two maize and six blue marbles. A box is chosen in such a way that the prior odds $\mathbf{P}(H_1)$ to $\mathbf{P}(H_2)$ are equal. The problem is to determine which box was chosen without looking inside it, by making random draws from it *with* replacement. The problem may be viewed as one of testing alternative hypotheses by their consequences. Let H_1 be the hypothesis that the box with six maize and two blue marbles was chosen and H_2 the alternative hypothesis. Relative to the general information given, H_1 and H_2 are mutually exclusive and jointly exhaustive. Suppose a test of eight drawings is made with the result (R): $BMMMMBBM$. By the ratio form of Bayes' theorem:

$$\frac{\mathbf{P}(H_1, R)}{\mathbf{P}(H_2, R)} = \frac{\mathbf{P}(H_1)\mathbf{P}(R, H_1)}{\mathbf{P}(H_2)\mathbf{P}(R, H_2)} = 1 \times \frac{(3/4)^5(1/4)^3}{(3/4)^3(1/4)^5} = \frac{9}{1}$$

Hence

$$\mathbf{P}(H_1, R) = \frac{9}{9+1} = 0.9 \text{ and } \mathbf{P}(H_2, R) = \frac{1}{9+1} = 0.1$$

The hypothesis H_1 was confirmed to a certain degree by the result R, and its alternative H_2 was simultaneously disconfirmed.

Of course the posterior probability of a hypothesis may be equal to its prior probability. If the result in the preceding example had been four blue and four maize marbles, then we would know no more about the box after the draw than we knew before. It is of interest to establish a general condition on which the verification process increases the probability of a hypothesis h. For this purpose it will suffice to lump all alternatives to h

into its negation $\bar{h}$. Bayes' theorem [21] then reduces to

$$\mathbf{P}(h, rg) = \frac{\mathbf{P}(h, g)\mathbf{P}(r, hg)}{\mathbf{P}(h, g)\mathbf{P}(r, hg) + \mathbf{P}(\bar{h}, g)\mathbf{P}(r, \bar{h}g)}$$

under the condition $\mathbf{P}(r, g) > 0$. If $\mathbf{P}(h, g)$ and $\mathbf{P}(r, hg)$ are both greater than zero we can divide through by these terms, obtaining

$$\frac{\mathbf{P}(h, rg)}{\mathbf{P}(h, g)} = \frac{1}{\mathbf{P}(h, g) + \mathbf{P}(\bar{h}, g)\dfrac{\mathbf{P}(r, \bar{h}g)}{\mathbf{P}(r, hg)}} .$$

By the subtraction principle [7], $\mathbf{P}(h, g) + \mathbf{P}(\bar{h}, g) = 1$. Hence if $\mathbf{P}(h, g) < 1$, the denominator of the right-hand side is less than one if and only if the ratio $\mathbf{P}(r, \bar{h}g)/\mathbf{P}(r, hg)$ is less than one. Consequently, the left-hand side $\mathbf{P}(h, rg)/\mathbf{P}(h, g)$ is greater than one if and only if $\mathbf{P}(r, \bar{h}g)/\mathbf{P}(r, hg)$ is less than one. This is under the conditions $\mathbf{P}(r, g) > 0$, $0 < \mathbf{P}(h, g) < 1$, and $\mathbf{P}(r, hg) > 0$. By theorem [19] the last two conditions imply the first. Combining and rearranging all these results, we get the corollary

[22] $\mathbf{P}(h, rg) > \mathbf{P}(h, g)$ if and only if $\mathbf{P}(r, hg) > \mathbf{P}(r, \bar{h}g)$,
provided that $0 < \mathbf{P}(h, g) < 1$ and $\mathbf{P}(r, hg) > 0$.

In words: The posterior probability of a hypothesis is larger than its prior probability if and only if the degree of prediction on the hypothesis is larger than the degree of prediction on its negation.

Let us review briefly the essential steps in an application of Bayes' theorem. One begins with a set of mutually exclusive and jointly exhaustive hypotheses $h_1, h_2, \ldots, h_N$, each having a prior probability $\mathbf{P}(h_n)$. One next considers a particular result r and determines, for each hypothesis h_n, the degree of prediction $\mathbf{P}(r, h_n)$, that is, the degree to which hypothesis h_n predicts r. Bayes' theorem then gives the posterior probability $\mathbf{P}(h_n, r)$ of each hypothesis being true if the result r is true.

Ideally one continues this confirmation process until the accumulated results are overwhelmingly in favor of a particular hypothesis. We shall study this situation in the next two subsections. Of course at any given time an investigator may not have sufficient evidence to make a definitive decision among alternative hypotheses. Such was the situation with respect to the geocentric and heliocentric hypotheses at the time of the famous controversy between Galileo and the Roman Catholic Church (pp. 19–21). Relevant experiments may be difficult to perform, or costly. In this case it may be best to suspend judgment and wait.

If a decision is forced on a person before he has conclusively confirmed one hypothesis, then he should take into account all the alternative hypotheses, each weighted according to its probability. He can do this by first using Bayes' theorem and then applying the prediction theorem. We illustrate the procedure with the maize and blue problem. The hypotheses are H_1 and H_2, the observed result is R (=$BMMMMMBBM$), and the posterior probabilities are

$$\mathbf{P}(H_1, R) = 0.9 \text{ and } \mathbf{P}(H_2, R) = 0.1 \quad .$$

Let the prediction be that the next draw will be maize (M_9). We now apply the prediction theorem, substituting "M_9" for "r" and including R in the general information:

$$\begin{aligned}\mathbf{P}(M_9, R) &= \mathbf{P}(H_1, R)\mathbf{P}(M_9, H_1R) + \mathbf{P}(H_2, R)\mathbf{P}(M_9, H_2R)\\ &= (.9)(.75) + (.1)(.25) = 0.7 \quad .\end{aligned}$$

That is, after drawing five maize and three blue marbles, the chance of getting a maize marble on the next draw is 7/10.

2.5.2 Confirmation by repeated experimentation

The materials of the last subsection can be taken as a formal model of the scientific process of verification and prediction. The investigator begins with a set of hypotheses and an assignment of prior probabilities to them, obtains a result by observation or experiment, calculates the posterior probabilities of the hypotheses by Bayes' theorem, and then makes a probabilistic prediction based on these posterior probabilities. This step can be iterated, and it is instructive to imagine that it is repeated indefinitely. We shall now study the process of verifying a hypothesis by repeatedly testing its consequences. This will involve combining Bayes' theorem with our earlier results about frequencies (sec. 2.4).

To begin with, we analyze our maize and blue example as a general process (p. 69). We stipulate that a maize (M) drawing is a "success" and a blue drawing ($\bar{M}$) is a "failure," and we relabel the two hypotheses H_1 and H_2 as $H_{.75}$ and $H_{.25}$ respectively, so that the subscript on each label shows the probability of success. The process under consideration is then Mx_1, Mx_2, Mx_3, ... Relative to $H_{.75}$ this is an independent process of probability 0.75, while relative to $H_{.25}$ it is an independent process of probability 0.25. Call a finite sequence of L events "an experiment of length L" and let s be the number of "successes" (maize drawings), f the number of "failures" (blue drawings). Hence, $S_L(M) = s$, $\sigma_L(M) = s/L$, and $s + f = L$.

We derive a formula for calculating the posterior odds after an experiment of length L. The first step is to obtain a formula for calculating the degrees of prediction for all possible outcomes of an experiment. The probability of one particular ordering, e.g., s maize followed by f blue, is $(3/4)^s(1/4)^f$ on $H_{.75}$ and $(1/4)^s(3/4)^f$ on $H_{.25}$. Since an ordering is completely characterized by a list of the positions of its maize drawings, the number of ways in which s maize and f blue drawings may be ordered is C_s^{s+f}, the number of combinations of $s+f$ things taken s at a time (p. 53). Note in this connection that $C_s^{s+f} = C_f^{s+f}$, since to draw s objects from a set of $s+f$ objects is to leave f objects. The degrees of prediction are, accordingly,

$$\mathbf{P}[S_L(M) = s, H_{.75}] = C_s^{s+f}(3/4)^s(1/4)^f$$

$$\mathbf{P}[S_L(M) = s, H_{.25}] = C_s^{s+f}(1/4)^s(3/4)^f \qquad ,$$

where brackets are used instead of parentheses after the probability operator to make the formulas more perspicuous. The prior probabilities are each 1/2. Applying the ratio form of Bayes' theorem we obtain

$$\frac{\mathbf{P}[H_{.75}, S_L(M) = s]}{\mathbf{P}[H_{.25}, S_L(M) = s]} = \frac{(1/2)[C_s^{s+f}(3/4)^s(1/4)^f]}{(1/2)[C_s^{s+f}(1/4)^s(3/4)^f]} = 3^{s-f} \qquad ;$$

that is, after s maize and f blue marbles have been drawn, the posterior odds in favor of $H_{.75}$ are 3^{s-f} to 1.

Thus the posterior odds in favor of $H_{.75}$ depend only on the *difference* between the number of successes and the number of failures. This is as we would expect; for because of the symmetry of the constitution of the two boxes, drawing an equal number of maize and blue marbles leaves the posterior probabilities the same as the prior probabilities (see condition [22], p. 70). Now no matter how long the experiment is there is some chance that $s-f$ will be small and the investigator will be uncertain as to which box he has. However, the longer the experiment the less likely it is that he will be uncertain. In other words, the longer the experiment the more likely it is that the difference $s-f$ will be substantial. Moreover, the difference $s-f$ will very probably be in the right direction: s larger than f if $H_{.75}$ is true, f larger than s if $H_{.25}$ is true.

Let us analyze this verification process in terms of relative frequency. By definition, the relative frequency $\sigma_L(M)$ equals the number of successes $S_L(M)$ divided by the number of events L. Hence our last equation becomes

$$\frac{\mathbf{P}[H_{.75}, \sigma_L(M) = s/L]}{\mathbf{P}[H_{.25}, \sigma_L(M) = s/L]} = 3^{s-f} \qquad .$$

The probability of a success is 0.75 on $H_{.75}$ and 0.25 on $H_{.25}$. Therefore, if $H_{.75}$ is true the most likely relative frequency of successes is very near 0.75, while if $H_{.25}$ is true the most likely relative frequency of successes is very near 0.25. By Bayes' theorem the posterior odds in favor of $H_{.75}$ are 3^{s-f}. If the observed relative frequency is near 0.75 the quantity 3^{s-f} is very large; e.g., for $s = 15$ and $f = 5$ it is 59,049. On the other hand, if the observed relative frequency is near 0.25, the quantity 3^{s-f} is very small; e.g., for $s = 5$ and $f = 15$, it is about 1.7×10^{-5}. Consequently, if the observed relative frequency is near 0.75 the posterior odds greatly favor $H_{.75}$ and the investigator accepts $H_{.75}$ as confirmed, while if the observed relative frequency is near 0.25 the posterior odds favor $H_{.25}$ and the investigator accepts

$H_{.25}$ as confirmed. In this case, then, where the prior odds are even, the investigator chooses the hypothesis that predicts a relative frequency close to the observed relative frequency, and this hypothesis is very probably the true hypothesis.

Consider next the more general case in which the prior odds are unequal. For this case Bayes' theorem gives

$$\frac{\mathbf{P}[H_{.75}, \sigma_L(M) = s/L]}{\mathbf{P}[H_{.25}, \sigma_L(M) = s/L]} = \frac{\mathbf{P}(H_{.75})}{\mathbf{P}(H_{.25})} 3^{s-f}$$

for the posterior odds after s successes and f failures. This formula shows that there are two factors determining which hypothesis is accepted as the more probable hypothesis: the prior odds and the observed relative frequency. We illustrate the relative weights of these two factors by some calculations.

Suppose an investigator, being almost certain that the marbles are mostly blue, assigns 99 to 1 odds in favor of $H_{.25}$. Compare the effects of the following two experiments. In the first experiment, five out of eight drawings are successes, so that 3^{s-f} is 9 and the posterior odds still favor $H_{.25}$ by 11 to 1. Thus the observed data favor $H_{.75}$ but are not strong enough to outweigh the effect of the prior odds, and at the end of the experiment hypothesis $H_{.25}$ is still accepted as the more likely hypothesis. In the second experiment, fifteen out of twenty drawings are successes, so that 3^{s-f} is 59,049 and the posterior odds now favor $H_{.75}$ by more than 596 to 1. Here the observed data not only favor $H_{.75}$ but are sufficiently strong to outweigh the effect of the prior odds, so that $H_{.75}$ is now accepted as the correct hypothesis. Thus in the longer experiment the observed data are more important and the prior probabilities less important than in the shorter experiment.

Let us carry this analysis of confirmation to the limit as the experiment gets longer and longer. By the law of large numbers (sec. 2.4): If $H_{.75}$ is true the relative frequency of successes will tend in the long run to 0.75, while if $H_{.25}$ is true the relative frequency of successes will tend in the long run to 0.25. By Bayes' theorem, assuming that neither prior probability is zero: If the observed relative frequency is close to 0.75, the posterior probability of $H_{.75}$ will tend to unity and the investigator will ultimately accept $H_{.75}$ as the correct hypothesis; while if the observed relative frequency is close to 0.25, the posterior probability of $H_{.25}$ will tend to unity and the investigator will ultimately accept $H_{.25}$ as the correct hypothesis. This will be so for any assignment of non-zero probabilities to the hypotheses. Combining the law of large numbers and Bayes' theorem: For any assignment of non-zero probabilities to the hypotheses, the posterior probabilities tend in the long run to the truth, and the investigator will ultimately accept the true hypothesis. This result is of fundamental importance for the logic of induction; in the next subsection we state it more rigorously as the "confirmation theorem."

The two hypotheses $H_{.75}$ and $H_{.25}$ concern the constitution of the box of marbles, each stating that the box contains a certain proportion of maize marbles. Viewed in these terms, the purpose of drawing marbles from the box is to ascertain the constitution of the box, and the posterior probabilities tend in the long run to tell us the constitution of the box. The drawing procedure is such that the probability of drawing a maize marble is the same as the proportion of maize marbles in the box. Each hypothesis, therefore, determines an inductive probability for the event of drawing a maize marble. From this point of view, the essential feature of $H_{.75}$ is that conditional on it the probability of a maize drawing is 3/4; and the essential characteristic of $H_{.25}$ is that conditional on it the probability of a maize drawing is 1/4. Likewise, the purpose of drawing marbles from the box is to ascertain the value of an unknown inductive probability, and the observed relative frequency tends in the long run to this unknown probability. Accordingly, we call this procedure "Bayes' method of finding an unknown probability."

As the posterior probabilities of the two hypotheses change, so does the probability of drawing a maize marble. Let "Mx_i" mean that a future drawing $(i > L)$ will be maize. The prediction theorem may be used to calculate the predicted probability of Mx_i prior to any observations. Substituting "Mx_i" for "r", "$H_{.75}$" for "h_1," and "$H_{.25}$" for "h_2," and letting "g" express the general information given above, we obtain

$$\begin{aligned}\mathbf{P}(Mx_i) &= \mathbf{P}(H_{.75})\mathbf{P}(Mx_i, H_{.75}) + \mathbf{P}(H_{.25})\mathbf{P}(Mx_i, H_{.25})\\ &= .75\mathbf{P}(H_{.75}) + .25\mathbf{P}(H_{.25}) \quad .\end{aligned}$$

The prediction theorem may also be used to calculate the predicted probability of drawing a maize marble conditional on the result $S_L(M) = s$ of an experiment. But in this case the posterior probability of each hypothesis is used instead of its prior probability. Note that the draws are independent on condition $H_{.75}$ so that $\mathbf{P}(Mx_i, H_{.75}\&[S_L(M) = s]) = .75$; likewise, $\mathbf{P}(Mx_i, H_{.25}\&[S_L(M) = s]) = .25$. The result is

$$\mathbf{P}[Mx_i, S_L(M) = s] = .75\mathbf{P}[H_{.75}, S_L(M) = s] + .25\mathbf{P}[H_{.25}, S_L(M) = s]$$

$$= \frac{.75\mathbf{P}(H_{.75})\mathbf{P}[S_L(M) = s, H_{.75}] + .25\mathbf{P}(H_{.25})\mathbf{P}[S_L(M) = s, H_{.25}]}{\mathbf{P}(H_{.75})\mathbf{P}[S_L(M) = s, H_{.75}] + \mathbf{P}(H_{.25})\mathbf{P}[S_L(M) = s, H_{.25}]}$$

We calculate some values for these formulas. Suppose the prior odds in favor of $H_{.25}$ are 99 to 1. Then

$$\begin{aligned}\mathbf{P}(Mx_i) &= .255\\ \mathbf{P}[Mx_i, S_8(M) = 5] &= .292\\ \mathbf{P}[Mx_i, S_{20}(M) = 15] &= .749 \quad .\end{aligned}$$

Let us examine next the evolution of these values as L increases, using the facts noted above concerning the evolution of posterior probabilities. For short experiments the predicted probability $\mathbf{P}[Mx_i, S_L(M) = s]$ is dominated by the prior probabilities. But as the experiments get longer the contribution of the prior probabilities diminishes, and the predicted probability $\mathbf{P}[Mx_i, S_L(M) = s]$ tends to approximate the observed relative frequency. Since the observed relative frequency tends in the long run to the unknown probability, it follows that this predicted probability $\mathbf{P}[Mx_i, S_L(M) = s]$ also tends in the long run to the unknown probability.

All of this makes clear that, relative to the general information given, the sequence of drawings $Mx_1, Mx_2, Mx_3, \ldots$ is not an independent process. For when a process is independent, information about some events of the process does not alter our probabilistic expectations about other events of the process, whereas the above examples show that $\mathbf{P}[Mx_i, S_L(M) = s]$ changes as $S_L(M) = s$ changes. Relative to hypothesis $H_{.75}$ the process $Mx_1, Mx_2, Mx_3, \ldots$ is independent, with $\mathbf{P}(Mx_i, H_{.75}) = \mathbf{P}(Mx_i, H_{.75}\&[S_L(M) = s])$ for all values of s; similarly for $H_{.25}$. In other words, if one knew the constitution of the box, the result of an experiment would never change his predictions. But since we do not know the constitution of the box, $\mathbf{P}(Mx_i) \neq \mathbf{P}[Mx_i, S_L(M) = s]$ in general. Thus $Mx_1, Mx_2, Mx_3, \ldots$ is an independent process conditional on each hypothesis; but conditional on the general information it is not independent. We call such a process a "mixture of independent processes."

A finite or infinite process $\phi x_1, \phi x_2, \ldots$ is a **mixture of independent processes of probabilities** $\alpha_1, \alpha_2, \ldots, a_{N-1}$ and α_N **on condition** g when there are hypotheses $h_{\alpha_1}, h_{\alpha_2}, \ldots, h_{\alpha_N}$ such that

(1) for each hypothesis h_{α_n} $(n = 1, 2, \ldots, N)$, the process $\phi x_1, \phi x_2, \ldots$ is an independent process of probability α_n relative to $h_{\alpha_n}g$,

(2) hypotheses $h_{\alpha_1}, h_{\alpha_2}, \ldots, h_{\alpha_N}$ are mutually exclusive and jointly exhaustive relative to g, and

(3) for at least one hypothesis h_{α_n}, $0 < \alpha_n < 1$.

This last clause is added to avoid certain cases of probability zero.

The concept of a mixture of independent processes is defined in terms of the concept of an independent process, which was earlier defined in terms of the concept of independence. Two points should be noted about this train of definitions. First, the only kind of probability used in these definitions is inductive probability (**P**). Second, all three concepts are defined relative to a condition g, though we do not always make explicit reference to this condition. Both of these facts are important for the dispositional theory of empirical probability (chap. 8).

In some applications of the concept of a mixture of independent processes, it is known that the true probability value is one of a given finite set of possible values. The maize and blue marble example is a case in point. In other applications, it may be known only that the unknown probability is a real number between zero and one. For these applications, it is more elegant to define the concept "mixture of independent processes" so that the unknown probability can have any value between zero and one. We will do this in the next chapter (p. 125), and later we will generalize the notion of a mixture of independent processes to the notion of a mixture of empirical probability theories (p. 511).

Actually, there is no real practical loss in limiting the possible values of the unknown probability to a finite set, for the continuous case can be approximated to any desired degree by choosing N to be large and spreading the values of α over the probability range of zero to one. Suppose, for example, an investigator knows that the box contains maize and blue marbles but does not know how many there are of each. As a first approximation he can consider the eleven hypotheses H_γ ($\gamma = 0, .1, .2, \ldots, .9, 1$) such that the probability of drawing a maize marble is γ on condition H_γ. After having found that the value of the unknown probability was close to one of these eleven values, he could refine his analysis to allow γ to range over the 101 values 0, .01, .02, . . . , .99, 1. This refinement can be extended as far as the circumstances warrant.

2.5.3 The confirmation theorem

A mixture of independent processes is an independent process of unknown probability, the possible values of this unknown probability being given by a set of alternative hypotheses. By repeated sampling, as in the maize and blue example, an investigator can make gradually improved estimates of the unknown probability and concomitantly make gradually improved predictions. We shall formulate this procedure, study it, and state a theorem about its limiting properties.

Consider an infinite process $\phi x_1, \phi x_2, \phi x_3, \ldots$ that is a mixture of independent processes of probabilities $\alpha_1, \alpha_2, \ldots, \alpha_{N-1}$, and α_N. Let h_{α_n} ($n = 1, 2, \ldots, N$) be the hypothesis that the probability is in fact α_n. Assume as given an assignment of non-zero prior probabilities $\mathbf{P}(h_{\alpha_n})$, for $n = 1, 2, \ldots, N$, summing to unity. **Bayes' method of finding an unknown probability** consists in performing successive experiments of length $L = 1, 2, 3, \ldots$, observing the outcomes, and carrying out the following three calculations for each value of L. Suppose that in an experiment of length L there are s successes [that is, $S_L(\phi) = s$] and f failures [that is, $S_L(\bar{\phi}) = f$], with $s + f = L$.

First, calculate the degree of prediction of each hypothesis by

$$\mathbf{P}[S_L(\phi) = s, h_{\alpha_n}] = C_s^{s+f}(\alpha_n)^s(1 - \alpha_n)^f \quad ,$$

where C_s^{s+f} is the number of combinations of $s+f$ things taken s at a time.
Second, calculate the posterior probability $\mathbf{P}[h_{\alpha_n}, S_L(\phi) = s]$ of each hypothesis by Bayes' theorem.
Third, calculate the predicted probability of some future event x_i being ϕ, where $i > L$, by the prediction theorem:

$$\mathbf{P}[\phi x_i, S_L(\phi) = s] = \sum_{n=1}^{N} \mathbf{P}[h_{\alpha_n}, S_L(\phi) = s]\mathbf{P}(\phi x_i, h_{\alpha_n}[S_L(\phi) = s])$$

$$= \sum_{n=1}^{N} \alpha_n \mathbf{P}[h_{\alpha_n}, S_L(\phi) = s] \quad .$$

Table 5 gives the results of applying Bayes' method to a mixture of independent processes of probabilities 0.25 and 0.75. This mixed process was obtained by starting with two outwardly identical boxes of marbles. Twenty-five percent of the marbles in one box and 75 percent of the marbles in the other box were of color ϕ. One of the boxes was chosen at random, so that the prior probabilities of the two hypotheses were equal. Random drawings with replacement were made from the chosen box. Next, the ratio of the degrees of prediction

$$\frac{\mathbf{P}[S_L(\phi) = s, H_{.75}]}{\mathbf{P}[S_L(\phi) = s, H_{.25}]} = 3^{s-f}$$

was calculated for each outcome. Finally, the successive posterior and predicted probabilities were calculated.

Consider now an investigator who applies Bayes' method of finding an unknown probability to a mixture of independent processes. He begins with a prior probability distribution and by successive experiments obtains a sequence of posterior probability distributions. In our earlier discussion of the maize and blue marble example, we observed that the posterior probability of the true hypothesis tends toward unity and the predicted probability tends to the actual probability. However, these are only probabilistic tendencies, not deterministic certainties, so that at any given stage there is some chance that the hypothesis accepted is false and that the predicted probability is wrong. Using the initially given prior probabilities, the investigator can calculate in advance the probability that his experiment will succeed. Let us see how this is done.

Some parameters are needed for measuring success. Of the given hypotheses, let h_β be the true hypothesis and β the actual probability. As noted before, since there are only N possible probability values, the actual probability of a process may not be among these. But if N is sufficiently large and the α's are suitably distributed over the range zero to one, β will approximate the actual value to a sufficient degree and h_β will similarly approximate the true hypothesis.

The second and third steps of Bayes' method give information about the unknown probability in two different forms. The posterior probability distribution tells what value of α_n is the most likely to be the true value β; in exceptional cases the posterior probabilities of two neighboring hypotheses h_{α_n}, $h_{\alpha_{n+1}}$ will be equal. The predicted probability is a probabilistic estimate of the unknown probability β. Consequently, there are two interdependent

TABLE 5

BAYES' METHOD OF FINDING AN UNKNOWN PROBABILITY APPLIED TO A MIXTURE OF INDEPENDENT PROCESSES OF PROBABILITIES .25 AND .75

Length of experiment	Observed result: Outcome	Observed result: $S_L(\phi)$	Observed result: $s - f$	Ratio of degrees of prediction	Prior and posterior probabilities: of $H_{.25}$	Prior and posterior probabilities: of $H_{.75}$	Predicted probability
—	—	—	—	—	.50000	.50000	.50000
1	ϕ	1	1	3	.25000	.75000	.62500
2	ϕ	2	2	9	.10000	.90000	.70000
3	ϕ	3	3	27	.03571	.96429	.73210
4	ϕ	4	4	81	.01220	.98780	.74390
5	$\bar{\phi}$	4	3	27	.03571	.96429	.73210
6	ϕ	5	4	81	.01220	.98780	.74390
7	$\bar{\phi}$	5	3	27	.03571	.96429	.73210
8	ϕ	6	4	81	.01220	.98780	.74390
9	ϕ	7	5	243	.00410	.99590	.74795
10	$\bar{\phi}$	7	4	81	.01220	.98780	.74390
11	$\bar{\phi}$	7	3	27	.03571	.96429	.73210
12	ϕ	8	4	81	.01220	.98780	.74390
13	ϕ	9	5	243	.00410	.99590	.74795
14	$\bar{\phi}$	9	4	81	.01220	.98780	.74390
15	ϕ	10	5	243	.00410	.99590	.74795
16	ϕ	11	6	729	.00137	.99863	.74932
17	ϕ	12	7	2187	.00046	.99954	.74977
18	$\bar{\phi}$	12	6	729	.00137	.99863	.74932
19	ϕ	13	7	2187	.00046	.99954	.74977
20	ϕ	14	8	6561	.00015	.99985	.74992

ways of measuring success: the closeness of the posterior probability of the true hypothesis h_β to unity, and the closeness of the predicted probability $\mathbf{P}[\phi x_i, S_L(\phi) = s]$ to β. Let us study these in turn.

Suppose an investigator decides to accept a hypothesis if its posterior probability is within ϵ_a of unity; that is, he accepts hypothesis h_{α_n} if $\mathbf{P}[h_{\alpha_n}, S_L(\phi) = s] > 1 - \epsilon_a$. The parameter ϵ_a will be called the "acceptance parameter." It is required that ϵ_a be less than one-half, so that at most one hypothesis can be accepted, and also that ϵ_a be positive, so that a hypothesis is sometimes accepted. There are three cases of interest. After any given experiment, the investigator may accept the true hypothesis, he may accept a false hypothesis, or he may accept no hypothesis. The probability of each of these three cases can be calculated in a straightforward way without knowing which hypothesis is in fact true. This is done in Table 6 for four different experiments on the hypotheses $H_{.25}$, $H_{.75}$, with the acceptance criterion $\epsilon_a = .02$.

The calculations are made as follows:
The statement

(a) The true hypothesis is accepted

is logically equivalent to

(b) $[(H_{.25})(H_{.25}$ is accepted) v $(H_{.75})(H_{.75}$ is accepted)].

Now $H_{.25}$ is accepted just in case the observed relative frequency has certain values; for $L = 6$, $H_{.25}$ is accepted if either $\sigma_6(\phi) = 0$ or $\sigma_6(\phi) = 2/12$. Let "$R_{.25}$" be the disjunction of those results leading to the acceptance of $H_{.25}$, and let "$R_{.75}$" be the disjunction of those results leading to the acceptance of $H_{.75}$. Statement (*b*) is then logically equivalent to

(c) $H_{.25}R_{.25} \text{ v } H_{.75}R_{.75}$.

Therefore, the probability that the true hypothesis will be accepted is given by

(d) $\mathbf{P}(H_{.25}R_{.25} \text{ v } H_{.75}R_{.75}) = \mathbf{P}(H_{.25})\mathbf{P}(R_{.25}, H_{.25}) + \mathbf{P}(H_{.75})\mathbf{P}(R_{.75}, H_{.75})$.

For the case of $L = 6$, we have from Table 6(A)

(e) $R_{.25} = (\sigma_6{=}0 \text{ v } \sigma_6{=}2/12)$ and $R_{.75} = (\sigma_6{=}10/12 \text{ v } \sigma_6{=}1)$.

Hence (d) becomes

(f) $$\begin{aligned}\mathbf{P}(H_{.25}R_{.25} \text{ v } H_{.75}R_{.75}) &= .5(.17798 + .35596) + .5(.17798 + .35596) \\ &= .53394 \quad .\end{aligned}$$

The probability that the false hypothesis will be accepted and the probability that no hypothesis will be accepted are calculated similarly. All of these probabilities are relative to the general information.

The second criterion of success is the nearness of the predicted probability $\mathbf{P}[\phi x_i, S_L(\phi) = s]$ to the true probability β. This predicted probability is based on the posterior probability distribution, and it is thus a probabilistic estimate of the unknown probability. A parameter is needed to measure the accuracy of the estimate. Let this be ϵ_a', so that an experiment is deemed successful if

$$|\mathbf{P}[\phi x_i, S_L(\phi) = s] - \beta| < \epsilon_a' \quad .$$

Thus ϵ_a' can be thought of as an "accuracy parameter." It is required that ϵ_a' be positive, in order that some experiments will be successful. Table 7 gives probabilities of success for the experiments of Table 6, using the accuracy criterion $\epsilon_a' = .001$.

TABLE 6

SUCCESS OF BAYES' METHOD IN FINDING THE TRUE HYPOTHESIS

(A) The prior probabilities of hypotheses $H_{.25}$ and $H_{.75}$ are equal.

Observed result R	Six observations ($L = 6$)				Twelve observations ($L = 12$)			
	Probability of R on		Posterior odds	Hypothesis accepted ($\epsilon_a = .02$)	Probability of R on		Posterior odds	Hypothesis accepted ($\epsilon_a = .02$)
	$H_{.25}$	$H_{.75}$	$\frac{P(H_{.25}, R)}{P(H_{.75}, R)}$		$H_{.25}$	$H_{.75}$	$\frac{P(H_{.25}, R)}{P(H_{.75}, R)}$	
$\sigma = 0$	.17798	.00024	729	$H_{.25}$	.03168	6×10^{-8}	3^{12}	
$\sigma = 1/12$					.12671	2×10^{-6}	3^{10}	
$\sigma = 2/12$	.35596	.00439	81	$H_{.25}$	.23229	.00004	3^{8}	$H_{.25}$
$\sigma = 3/12$					.25810	.00035	3^{6}	
$\sigma = 4/12$	.29663	.03296	9	None	.19358	.00239	3^{4}	
$\sigma = 5/12$					.10324	.01147	3^{2}	
$\sigma = 6/12$	.13184	.13184	1	None	.04015	.04015	1	None
$\sigma = 7/12$					.01147	.10324	3^{-2}	
$\sigma = 8/12$	.03296	.29663	9^{-1}	None	.00239	.19358	3^{-4}	
$\sigma = 9/12$					.00035	.25810	3^{-6}	
$\sigma = 10/12$	.00439	.35596	81^{-1}	$H_{.75}$	.00004	.23229	3^{-8}	$H_{.75}$
$\sigma = 11/12$					2×10^{-6}	.12671	3^{-10}	
$\sigma = 1$	.00024	.17798	729^{-1}	$H_{.75}$	6×10^{-8}	.03168	3^{-12}	
Probability of acceptance of			*true hypothesis*	.53394				.84236
			false hypothesis	.00463				.00278
			no hypothesis	.46143				.15486

(B) $\frac{\mathbf{P}(H_{.25})}{\mathbf{P}(H_{.75})} = 9.$

Observed result R	Six observations ($L = 6$): Probability of R on $H_{.25}$	Probability of R on $H_{.75}$	Posterior odds $\frac{\mathbf{P}(H_{.25}, R)}{\mathbf{P}(H_{.75}, R)}$	Hypothesis accepted ($\epsilon_a = .02$)	Twelve observations ($L = 12$): Probability of R on $H_{.25}$	Probability of R on $H_{.75}$	Posterior odds $\frac{\mathbf{P}(H_{.25}, R)}{\mathbf{P}(H_{.75}, R)}$	Hypothesis accepted ($\epsilon_a = .02$)
$\sigma = 0$	.17798	.00024	6561	$H_{.25}$	.03168	$6\text{x}10^{-8}$	3^{14}	
$\sigma = 1/12$					.12671	$2\text{x}10^{-6}$	3^{12}	
$\sigma = 2/12$	.35596	.00439	729	$H_{.25}$	.23229	.00004	3^{10}	$H_{.25}$
$\sigma = 3/12$					.25810	.00035	3^{8}	
$\sigma = 4/12$	.29663	.03296	81	$H_{.25}$	.19358	.00239	3^{6}	
$\sigma = 5/12$					.10324	.01147	3^{4}	
$\sigma = 6/12$	.13184	.13184	9	None	.04015	.04015	3^{2}	
$\sigma = 7/12$					.01147	.10324	1	None
$\sigma = 8/12$	.03296	.29663	1	None	.00239	.19358	3^{-2}	
$\sigma = 9/12$					.00035	.25810	3^{-4}	
$\sigma = 10/12$	.00439	.35596	9^{-1}	None	.00004	.23229	3^{-6}	$H_{.75}$
$\sigma = 11/12$					$2\text{x}10^{-6}$	.12671	3^{-8}	
$\sigma = 1$	.00024	.17798	81^{-1}	$H_{.75}$	$6\text{x}10^{-8}$	.03168	3^{-10}	
Probability of acceptance of			*true hypothesis*	.76531				.91591
			false hypothesis	.00398				.00178
			no hypothesis	.23071				.08231

TABLE 7

SUCCESS OF BAYES' METHOD IN ESTIMATING AN UNKNOWN PROBABILITY

(A) The prior probabilities of hypotheses $H_{.25}$ and $H_{.75}$ are equal.

Observed result R	Six observations ($L = 6$): Probability of R on $H_{.25}$	Probability of R on $H_{.75}$	Predicted probability $\mathbf{P}(\phi x_i, R)$	Accuracy of predicted probability ($\epsilon'_a = .001$)	Twelve observations ($L = 12$): Probability of R on $H_{.25}$	Probability of R on $H_{.75}$	Predicted probability $\mathbf{P}(\phi x_i, R)$	Accuracy of predicted probability ($\epsilon'_a = .001$)
$\sigma = 0$	.17798	.00024	.25068	Within ϵ'_a of .25	.03168	$6\text{x}10^{-8}$	.250001	
$\sigma = 1/12$					.12671	$2\text{x}10^{-6}$	.250008	Within ϵ'_a of .25
$\sigma = 2/12$	.35596	.00439	.25610	Failure	.23229	.00004	.250076	
$\sigma = 3/12$					.25810	.00035	.250685	
$\sigma = 4/12$	.29663	.03296	.30000	Failure	.19358	.00239	.256098	
$\sigma = 5/12$					.10324	.01147	.300000	
$\sigma = 6/12$	.13184	.13184	.50000	Failure	.04015	.04015	.500000	Failure
$\sigma = 7/12$					.01147	.10324	.700000	
$\sigma = 8/12$	.03296	.29663	.70000	Failure	.00239	.19358	.743902	
$\sigma = 9/12$					.00035	.25810	.749315	
$\sigma = 10/12$	.00439	.35596	.74390	Failure	.00004	.23229	.749924	
$\sigma = 11/12$					$2\text{x}10^{-6}$	.12671	.749992	Within ϵ'_a of .75
$\sigma = 1$	.00024	.17798	.74932	Within ϵ'_a of .75	$6\text{x}10^{-8}$	.03168	.749999	
Probability of success, i.e., that the predicted probability is within ϵ'_a (.001) of the true value				.17798				.64878

(B) $\frac{\quad}{\mathbf{P}(H_{.75})} = 9.$

Observed result R	Six observations ($L = 6$)				Twelve observations ($L = 12$)			
	Probability of R on		Predicted probability $\mathbf{P}(\phi x_i, R)$	Accuracy of predicted probability ($\epsilon'_a = .001$)	Probability of R on		Predicted probability $\mathbf{P}(\phi x_i, R)$	Accuracy of predicted probability ($\epsilon'_a = .001$)
	$H_{.25}$	$H_{.75}$			$H_{.25}$	$H_{.75}$		
$\sigma = 0$	.17798	.00024	.25008	Within ϵ'_a of .25	.03168	$6\text{x}10^{-8}$	$.25+10^{-7}$	
$\sigma = 1/12$					.12671	$2\text{x}10^{-6}$	.250001	
$\sigma = 2/12$	.35596	.00439	.25068	Within ϵ'_a of .25	.23229	.00004	.250008	Within ϵ'_a of .25
$\sigma = 3/12$					.25810	.00035	.250076	
$\sigma = 4/12$	.29663	.03296	.25610	Failure	.19358	.00239	.250683	
$\sigma = 5/12$					.10324	.01147	.256098	
$\sigma = 6/12$	.13184	.13184	.30000	Failure	.04015	.04015	.300000	
$\sigma = 7/12$					.01147	.10324	.500000	Failure
$\sigma = 8/12$	.03296	.29663	.50000	Failure	.00239	.19358	.700000	
$\sigma = 9/12$					.00035	.25810	.743902	
$\sigma = 10/12$	.00439	.35596	.70000	Failure	.00004	.23229	.749315	
$\sigma = 11/12$					$2\text{x}10^{-6}$	.12671	.749924	Within ϵ'_a of .75
$\sigma = 1$	.00024	.17798	.74390	Failure	$6\text{x}10^{-8}$	.03168	.749992	
Probability of success, i.e., that the predicted probability is within ϵ'_a (.001) of the true value				.48055				.79719

It is clear that the two criteria of success—acceptance of the true hypothesis and making an accurate estimate of the unknown probability—are interdependent. For example, had the accuracy criterion $\epsilon_a' = .01$ been chosen for Table 7, the probabilities of success in this table would have been the same as in Table 6.

Consider now an investigator who applies Bayes' method to a given process. He begins with certain general information, on the basis of which he decides that the process is a mixture of independent processes and makes an assignment of prior probabilities to the various alternatives. He then conducts a sequence of experiments of increasing lengths. It is intuitively clear that the longer the experiment, the more likely it is to succeed on either criterion of success. That is, the posterior probability of the true hypothesis will tend toward unity, and the predicted probability will tend toward the actual probability. The precise expression of this convergence is given by the confirmation theorem, which we now state. For this purpose we use a "success parameter" ϵ_s to measure the probability of success.

The **confirmation theorem** applies to an infinite process $\phi x_1, \phi x_2, \ldots, \phi x_L, \ldots$ that is a mixture of independent processes of probabilities $\alpha_1, \alpha_2, \ldots, \alpha_N$. Let h_{α_n} $(n = 1, 2, \ldots, N)$ assert that the unknown probability is α_n. Let β be the actual probability of the process, so that h_β is the true hypothesis. Then

(1) For each assignment of non-zero prior probabilities $\mathbf{P}(h_{\alpha_n})$ to the hypotheses and each positive ϵ_s and ϵ_a (with $\epsilon_a < .5$), there is a length of experiment l such that for every $L \geqq l$:

$$\mathbf{P}\{\mathbf{P}[h_\beta, S_L(\phi) = s] > 1 - \epsilon_a\} > 1 - \epsilon_s \qquad ,$$

i.e., the probability is at least $1 - \epsilon_s$ that the observed result will be such that the true hypothesis will be accepted.

(2) For each assignment of non-zero prior probabilities $\mathbf{P}(h_{\alpha_n})$ to the hypotheses and each positive ϵ_s and ϵ_a', there is a length of experiment l such that for every $L \geqq l$:

$$\mathbf{P}\{|\mathbf{P}[\phi x_i, S_L(\phi) = s] - \beta| < \epsilon_a'\} > 1 - \epsilon_s \qquad \text{for } i > L\,,$$

i.e., the probability is at least $1 - \epsilon_s$ that the predicted probability is correct to within ϵ_a'.

The confirmation theorem is the result of combining the law of large numbers for independent processes (sec. 2.4) with Bayes' theorem. The proof is beyond the scope of this work.*

Let us suppose that the investigator who is employing Bayes' method is aware of the confirmation theorem. If the posterior probability of the true

* For a proof and discussion of the more general, continuous case, see Savage, *The Foundations of Statistics*, pp. 46–50.

hypothesis is at least $1 - \epsilon_a$, we can say that the observer "knows the true hypothesis to degree $1 - \epsilon_a$" after performing the experiment. Looked at in this way, the confirmation theorem may be expressed as follows. For each assignment of non-zero prior probabilities to the hypotheses and for each positive ϵ_s and ϵ_a, there is a length of experiment l such that: after performing the experiment, the investigator will know the truth to degree $1 - \epsilon_a$ with a probability of at least $1 - \epsilon_s$.

It follows from Bayes' theorem that if the prior probability of a hypothesis is zero (or one) the posterior probability is also zero (or one). This is reasonable: If there is no chance of a hypothesis being correct (or wrong), then no amount of evidence is relevant to it. This explains why the condition that every hypothesis should have non-zero prior probability is inserted in the confirmation theorem. It also follows from Bayes' theorem that if the degree of prediction of a statement is zero conditional on a hypothesis, and the predicted statement is true, then the hypothesis has a posterior probability of zero. Except for such cases, no hypothesis can acquire a posterior probability of zero or one after a finite experiment. Hence, if "certainty" means a posterior probability of zero or one, certainty cannot be attained by Bayes' method except in some uninteresting special cases. But in practice a probability very close to zero or one suffices for "certainty." Consequently, when ϵ_a is sufficiently minute, we can drop the qualification "to degree $1 - \epsilon_a$" and speak simply of "knowing the true hypothesis." Similarly, when ϵ_s is sufficiently small, we can say that it is "certain" that the investigator will reach the truth. Using this terminology, we express the confirmation theorem informally as: An investigator who applies Bayes' method of finding an unknown probability to a mixture of independent processes will eventually know the truth.

Both Bayes' method of finding an unknown probability and the confirmation theorem are of fundamental importance for the logic of induction. Of course, many processes of interest to the scientist are not mixtures of independent processes (see sec. 8.3.2). But a mixture of independent processes is the simplest kind of case in which iterated confirmation is possible, and it can often serve as a model for more complicated confirmation situations. We shall use it as such a model in the next subsection.

2.5.4 *Applications to induction*

The examples and discussion of the two previous subsections show the relevance of Bayes' theorem to the confirmation process in artificial cases. This theorem is also relevant to the reasoning involved in many natural cases of confirmation, as we shall now see.

Let H_g and H_h be the geocentric and heliocentric hypotheses, respectively, as presented in Section 1.4.2. Let G_1 express the relevant information known at the time, *except* for the facts about stellar parallax. When H_g and H_h are interpreted as saying that the earth really does stand still while the sun moves, and vice versa, they are mutually exclusive. They are obviously not jointly exhaustive, but no other alternatives were considered at the time of Galileo; hence it is reasonable to say that, relative to G_1, the sum of the prior probabilities of H_g and H_h is almost one. This being so, we can, as a first approximation, treat H_g, H_h as jointly exhaustive.* Let R_p be the fact that no parallax was observed then; given the general information available at the time, the degree of prediction of R_p on the geocentric hypothesis H_g is considerably greater than the degree of prediction of R_p on the heliocentric hypothesis H_h. Applying theorem [22] we see that the posterior probability of H_g is greater than its prior probability; i.e., the geocentric hypothesis H_g is confirmed by R_p, which is the conclusion reached earlier.

There is an idealization involved in this application of Bayes' theorem, for the theorem is stated for quantitative probabilities, whereas the probabilities in the example are qualitative (see sec. 4.3.2). The conclusion drawn, however, is not vitiated by this idealization. Suppose it is agreed that the degree of prediction on H_g is considerably greater than that on H_h. Since theorem [22] involves only inequalities, it is legitimate in the present case to represent these degrees of prediction by real numbers. More generally, in many applications of Bayes' theorem and its corollaries, the conclusion is the same for a wide variety of assignments of real numbers to the probabilities; and in such instances it is useful to apply these theorems to probabilities that are not real numbers. The next example will also illustrate this point.

For several centuries there were two competing theories of light: the corpuscular theory (H_c) and the wave theory (H_w). Science and scientists oscillated back and forth in their support of these two theories. By about 1825, as a result of work by Thomas Young and Augustin Fresnel, the wave theory was pushed into the ascendancy, but the matter was by no means settled. Two important experiments played a decisive role in the controversy. The wave theory implied that Newton's rings should not appear if there is no reflection from the first surface of a thin plate, while the corpuscular theory implied they should still be seen in this circumstance; about 1831, G. B. Airy made the test with the result (R_a) that the rings did not appear. Second, the corpuscular theory held that light should travel more rapidly in water than in the less dense medium air, while the wave theory held that light should travel more rapidly in air; J. B. L. Foucault and A. H. L. Fizeau measured the two speeds experimentally in 1850 with the result (R_f) that light travels more rapidly in air than in water.†

* More precisely, we are considering the hypotheses H_g, H_h, and $\sim(H_g \vee H_h)$ and are assuming that both the prior and posterior probabilities of $\sim(H_g \vee H_h)$ are negligible.

† Whittaker, *A History of the Theories of Aether and Electricity*, vol. 1, particularly pp. 11–12, 96, 126–27.

As in the previous example we can, to an approximation, treat H_c and H_w as jointly exhaustive. Let G_2 summarize the relevant empirical evidence before these two experiments. Both theories were supported by G_2, but the wave theory much more than the corpuscular theory; that is, the prior probability of H_w was considerably greater than the prior probability of H_c. The degree of prediction of R_aR_f on H_w is very high, while on H_c it is very low. From these facts we conclude by Bayes' theorem that the posterior probability of the corpuscular theory H_c is very low, whereas that of the wave theory H_w is extremely high; that is, these two experiments decisively verified the wave hypothesis at that time. In this example, Bayes' theorem tells us that the posterior probability of the wave theory H_w is *strikingly* higher than its prior probability, not merely that it is higher as in the previous example of the geocentric hypothesis H_g. Thus, even though it is an idealization to assign real numbers to the probabilities involved, one may obtain rough quantitative information from an application of Bayes' theorem to a natural case of verification.

Since the corpuscular theory logically implies that light would travel faster in water than in air, it might seem that the degree of prediction of R_f on the corpuscular hypothesis H_c should be zero. By Bayes' theorem the posterior probability of H_c would then be zero, and the Foucault-Fizeau experiment would have shown the corpuscular theory to be definitely false. By the same reasoning, Airy's experiment would have earlier shown the corpuscular theory wrong, and the Foucault-Fizeau experiment would have been superfluous! This reasoning is clearly erroneous, but it is instructive to see why. First of all, the theories in question were not precisely defined and were subject to change and reformulation. Thus after Airy's experiment the corpuscular theory might have been revised to accommodate the new results. Indeed, the wave theory was in such a strong position at this time partly because Young had revised it to say that the vibrations of light are at right angles to the direction of propagation, rather than in the direction of propagation as had formerly been supposed. Both theories of light involved the concept of the ether, a highly "ethereal" concept. Traces of both theories of light are found in modern quantum theory.

Second, there is many a slip between the study and the laboratory, so that it was possible (though unlikely) that the experiments of Airy and Foucault-Fizeau did not really establish the results they thought they did. Foucault and Fizeau did not directly observe that light travels faster in air than in water. Rather, they made certain observations with a complicated apparatus composed of a rapidly revolving mirror and lens, stationary mirrors, etc., and these are the observations that should be summarized in the result R_f. Taken in this way $\sim R_f$ may not be deduced from $H_c \& G_2$; to deduce it we must use a specific formulation of the corpuscular theory together with certain other premises: the laws of refraction and reflection of light, the assumption that Foucault and Fizeau made no significant error in their experiment, etc. Consequently it is best to take the degrees of prediction of R_f and R_a on $H_c\&G_2$ to be non-zero, although they are close to zero.*

In many cases of inductive inference the probabilities needed for an application of Bayes' theorem can be ascertained much more precisely than in the two examples just discussed. Genetics provides some interesting instances. Suppose that the alternative hypotheses concern the genetic constitution of two parents, e.g., the presence of certain recessive and dominant genes. Mendel's laws of genetics being statistical rather than deterministic, we cannot predict the characteristics of the offspring with certainty, but only with probability. However, because these laws are quantitative, the degrees of prediction can be calculated more or less precisely. Precise statistical predictions may also be made in statistical mechanics and in quantum theory. The theory of evolution is essentially statistical in character, yielding probabilistic predictions: for example, that in a certain environment one population will probably predominate over another. The probabilities devised from the theory of evolution are not so precise as those obtained from Mendel's laws and quantum mechanics, but are more precise than those in our astronomical and theory-of-light examples. And the theory of evolution will undoubtedly be given a more quantitative formulation in the future.†

The confirmation theorem, though presented in terms of artificial examples (such as drawing balls from a box), can also be applied to natural examples of confirmation. We divide these into two groups, according to whether they do or do not involve the concept of empirical probability. In Chapter 8, we analyze those that do involve this concept. We discuss the others briefly here and then at length in the next chapter.

In artificial cases an investigator can in principle repeatedly apply the "same" set of hypotheses. Thus, in the maize and blue marble case one can repeatedly choose a box at random and make drawings from it, thereby repeatedly applying Bayes' method to a mixture of independent processes of probabilities .25 and .75. This usually cannot be done in natural cases of verification, however. A scientist cannot apply the wave theory of light to any universe other than the one that actually exists, let alone to an indefinite

* A number of interesting philosophical problems are connected with this example. See my "Justification in Science" and Will's "The Justification of Theories."

† See, for example, Fisher's *The Genetical Theory of Natural Selection*, Wright's *The Theory of Gene Frequencies*, Crow and Kimura, *An Introduction to Population Genetics Theory*, Kimura and Ohta, *Theoretical Aspects of Population Genetics*, and Holland's *Adaptation in Natural and Artificial Systems*.

Statistics books provide many examples of quantitative probability. See Neyman's *First Course in Probability and Statistics*, Raiffa and Schlaifer's *Applied Statistical Decision Theory*.

number of universes. As Peirce remarked, universes are not as plentiful as blackberries.*

Nevertheless, there is an analogy between the confirmation of a scientific hypothesis by repeated verification of its consequences, on the one hand, and finding the true hypothesis by Bayes' method, on the other. Because of this analogy, the confirmation theorem can be applied to inductive reasoning by treating Bayes' method as a formal model of the process of inquiry. We shall do this in the next chapter, where we show that the confirmation theorem is closely related to the traditional rule of induction by simple enumeration (sec. 3.2.4) and to the self-corrective character of scientific method (sec. 3.4.2).

Bayes' method of finding an unknown probability is a simple statistical procedure and hence is a very limited model of inductive reasoning. Because it is purely statistical, it does not model causal laws (see sec. 10.3). There are also statistical features of induction that it does not capture. For example, repetition sometimes plays a checking role; one may repeat an experiment to insure that he did not make a mistake in performing the experiment or in recording the result. Again, two experiments of a different kind constitute a better test of a hypothesis than two experiments of the same kind. Nevertheless, Bayes' method of finding an unknown probability does capture some basic features of induction: the interplay of hypotheses and their consequences, and the basic force of repeated verification. In the next chapter we shall discuss a number of philosophical problems of induction on the basis of Bayes' method and related statistical models.

In the meantime, let us examine some of the effects of repeated verification in terms of Bayes' method. Note first that the confirmatory value of sheer repetition decreases rapidly as a hypothesis becomes well-confirmed. For after the probability of a hypothesis is close to unity, the percentage change induced by repeated verification is very small. Table 5 illustrates how rapidly the posterior probability of one hypothesis converges to one. This limit to the value of repetition applies to natural cases as well. It would be silly to test the law of gravity by dropping a stone, just as it would be silly to draw another marble to test the hypothesis $H_{.75}$ of Table 5 after a billion drawings had been made with a relative frequency near 0.75.

On the other hand, when no hypothesis has yet been confirmed, or when there is a disagreement between investigators about which hypothesis has been confirmed, repeated testing of a hypothesis is important. Consider two investigators who agree that the process $\phi x_1, \phi x_2, \ldots$ is a mixture of independent processes of probabilities .25 and .75, but who start their inquiry with very different prior probability assignments. The character of the

* *Collected Papers*, 2.684. See pp. 533–34, below.

References to Peirce's *Collected Papers* are to volume and paragraph; e.g., 2.684 refers to vol. 2, par. 684.

observed sequence is, of course, a matter of chance, but as we saw in Section 2.4, there is a tendency for the observed relative frequency to be near the actual probability of the process. On the assumption that the observed relative frequency is .75, Table 8 traces the posterior probability of the hypothesis $H_{.75}$ for two radically different assignments of prior probabilities. The two investigators come to agree very rapidly.

TABLE 8

CONVERGENCE OF OPINION OF TWO INVESTIGATORS WHO START INQUIRY WITH DIFFERENT PRIOR ODDS

Observed result R	Posterior probability of $H_{.75}$	
	First investigator $\mathbf{P}(H_{.75}) = .01$ $\mathbf{P}(H_{.25}) = .99$	Second investigator $\mathbf{P}(H_{.75}) = .99$ $\mathbf{P}(H_{.25}) = .01$
—	.01000	.99000
$\sigma_4(\phi) = .75$	.08333	.99898
$\sigma_8(\phi) = .75$	.45000	.99988
$\sigma_{12}(\phi) = .75$	.88043	.999986
$\sigma_{16}(\phi) = .75$	.98514	.9999985
$\sigma_{20}(\phi) = .75$	.99833	.99999983
$\sigma_{24}(\phi) = .75$	.99991	.999999981
$\sigma_{28}(\phi) = .75$	.999979	.9999999979
$\sigma_{32}(\phi) = .75$	.9999976	.99999999977

It should be noted that the confirmation theorem holds for every nonzero prior probability assignment, so that in the limit the prior probability assignment makes no difference. In other words, an investigator who applies Bayes' method to a mixture of independent processes will eventually know the truth, no matter what his prior probability assignment is, provided only that no hypothesis is assigned a probability of zero. Similarly, if two investigators apply Bayes' method of finding an unknown probability to a mixture of independent processes, and they differ only in their prior probability assignments, they will ultimately come to agree on the true hypothesis. It is thus a corollary of the confirmation theorem that under repeated experimentation the effects of differences in prior probabilities ultimately disappear.

This is significant, for prior probabilities are philosophically puzzling, and these puzzles would not matter if in the end prior probabilities made no difference. Let us see if the confirmation theorem really has this implication.

In each application of Bayes' theorem it is fair to ask: What is the source of the prior probabilities? Usually they derive from previous empirical situations. They might be posterior probabilities just renamed. More typically they come from general experience. Thus in Table 5 we assigned equal prior probabilities to the hypotheses because the selected box was chosen by a certain procedure. We could in turn justify this by saying that objects selected by this procedure tend to occur with equal frequency. But this process of tracing back prior probabilities to earlier evidence must finally terminate, since the total available evidence is finite. And when it does terminate the same question arises: What is the epistemological basis of the prior probability assignment?

It is natural to appeal to the confirmation theorem at this point, asserting that in the limit the prior probability assignment does not matter anyhow. But this appeal fails, for at any given stage of inquiry there is only a finite amount of evidence, which may not be sufficient to bring different investigators into close agreement. Consider, for instance, the evidential effect of $\sigma_{100}(\phi) = .75$ on the pair of hypotheses $H_{.25}$ and $H_{.75}$. By the ratio form of Bayes' theorem,

$$\frac{\mathbf{P}[H_{.75}, \sigma_{100}(\phi) = .75]}{\mathbf{P}[H_{.25}, \sigma_{100}(\phi) = .75]} = \frac{\mathbf{P}(H_{.75})}{\mathbf{P}(H_{.25})}\, 3^{50}\;.$$

Suppose the first investigator's prior odds are even, while the second investigator's prior odds are 1 to 3^{100}. After observing the result $\sigma_{100}(\phi) = .75$, the first investigator is strongly convinced that $H_{.75}$ is true, while the second investigator is still strongly convinced that the opposite hypothesis ($H_{.25}$) is true.

The hypothesis that people sometimes communicate by mental telepathy may be made the basis of another example. A scientist can agree that there is some evidence for mental telepathy but still hold that the prior probability of this hypothesis is so low that, relative to this evidence, the mental telepathy hypothesis is too implausible to be taken seriously.

Thus it is clear from Bayes' theorem that insofar as two scientists who have the same data agree (or disagree) on the posterior probabilities of a hypothesis, they must agree (or disagree) on the prior probability of this hypothesis. Consequently, the confirmation theorem does not eliminate the problem of the epistemological status of prior probabilities. Since prior probabilities are expressed by atomic inductive probability statements, this problem is a special case of our first main question: What is the general nature of an atomic inductive probability statement? We shall discuss this problem at length in Chapter 3 (Alternative Inductive Logics and the Justification of Induction), Chapter 5 (The Pragmatic Theory of Inductive Probability), and Chapter 10 (The Presupposition Theory of Induction).

The epistemological status of prior probabilities will also be discussed in connection with empirical probabilities (sec. 8.3.4).

Let us now draw some general conclusions from this long discussion of the calculus of inductive probability. First, Bayes' theorem, Bayes' method of finding an unknown probability, and the confirmation theorem together give a good account of many artificial and natural cases of verifying a hypothesis by testing its observable consequences. Second, inductive probability plays a basic role in scientific inference, and the calculus of inductive probability is a good model of the ordinary use of "probable." Third, the axioms and theorems of the calculus of inductive probability are true. They are clearly not empirically true. The question remains: Are they logically true? Fourth, it is often desirable to model systems of interrelated probability statements rather than isolated probability statements. Thus in applying Bayes' theorem it was necessary to consider the prior probabilities, degrees of prediction, and posterior probabilities all together. And the notion of a mixture of independent processes involves a system of probability statements.

These last two conclusions lead us to revise our first and second main questions (sec. 1.6.1). The new formulations of these two questions are: (I) *What is the general nature of a system of atomic inductive probability statements?* (II) *Is an atomic inductive probability statement logically true-or-false, empirically true-or-false, or neither? Are the theorems of the calculus of inductive probability logically true?*

2.6 Unconditional Probability

The concept we have been treating axiomatically in this chapter is that of conditional inductive probability $\mathbf{P}(c, d)$. It is conditional because $\mathbf{P}(c, d)$ expresses the probability of c conditional on or relative to d. There is a closely related concept, unconditional probability, which we will discuss now.

In an atomic inductive probability statement $\mathbf{P}(c, d) = x$, the variables "c" and "d" range over all empirically true-or-false and all logically true-or-false statements, except that d cannot be logically impossible. Let $\mathbf{P}(c)$ abbreviate $\mathbf{P}(c, d)$ when d is logically true. Though logical truths play an important role in scientific evidence, a logical truth is not itself inductive evidence for any empirical statement c. Hence $\mathbf{P}(c)$ is in effect the probability of c not conditional on or relative to any evidence. Accordingly, we call $\mathbf{P}(c)$ an **unconditional probability,** and we call our original comparative notion $\mathbf{P}(c, d)$ a **conditional probability.** Atomic inductive probability statements may be either unconditional, as $\mathbf{P}(c) = x$, or conditional, as $\mathbf{P}(c, d) = x$.

Unconditional probabilities are sometimes called absolute, and conditional probabilities are sometimes called relative. The contrast between unconditional and conditional probability holds also for empirical probability

($\mathbf{P}_e$), frequency probability ($\mathbf{P}_f$), number of successes (S_L), and relative frequency of success (σ_L).

A useful formula relating conditional and unconditional probabilities may be derived from axiom [2]. Substituting a logical truth for e we get $\mathbf{P}(cd) = \mathbf{P}(c)\mathbf{P}(d, c)$, and hence

[23] If $\mathbf{P}(c) \neq 0$, then $\mathbf{P}(d, c) = \dfrac{\mathbf{P}(cd)}{\mathbf{P}(c)}$.

Since this result enables one to reduce conditional probabilities to unconditional probabilities, it is appropriately called the *reduction principle.*

We have taken conditional probability to be the primitive notion and have defined the unconditional probability $\mathbf{P}(c)$ to be a special case of the conditional probability $\mathbf{P}(c, d)$, namely, the case in which d is logically true. The reverse procedure is possible. One can take unconditional probability as primitive, state axioms for it, and then use the reduction principle to define conditional probability in terms of unconditional probability. A satisfactory set of axioms is

[1′] If $\sim\Diamond(cd)$, then $\mathbf{P}(c \vee d) = \mathbf{P}(c) + \mathbf{P}(d)$

[3′] If $\Box c$, then $\mathbf{P}(c) = 1$.

The following is a theorem.

[4′] If $c \leftrightarrow d$, then $\mathbf{P}(c) = \mathbf{P}(d)$.

Proof: Assume $c \leftrightarrow d$. By [1′], $\mathbf{P}(c \vee \bar{d}) = \mathbf{P}(c) + \mathbf{P}(\bar{d})$ and $\mathbf{P}(d \vee \bar{d}) = \mathbf{P}(d) + \mathbf{P}(\bar{d})$. By [3′], $\mathbf{P}(c \vee \bar{d}) = \mathbf{P}(d \vee \bar{d}) = 1$. Hence $\mathbf{P}(c) = \mathbf{P}(d)$.*

This new axiom system is logically equivalent to our earlier axiom system (pp. 40–41) except for a slight difference in scope. In the earlier systems $\mathbf{P}(c, e)$ is always defined if e is logically possible. Suppose we change this requirement to: $\mathbf{P}(c, e)$ is defined if $\mathbf{P}(e, d) \neq 0$, where d is a logical truth. It is not hard to show that this modified conditional system is equivalent to our new unconditional system.

Thus the calculus of inductive probability can be based on either conditional or unconditional probability. It was natural for us to choose conditional probability as primitive, since we began with actual inductive inference, found the notion of conditional probability in it, and then developed an abstract system (the calculus of probability) to model inductive inference. But if one wishes to begin with the abstract calculus and later apply it, it is better to choose unconditional probability as primitive because this notion and the axioms for it are formally simpler than the notion of conditional probability and the axioms for it.

* Soshichi Uchii pointed out to me that [4′] can be derived from [1′] and [3′] even though its conditional form [4] cannot be derived from [1], [2], and [3] of pp. 40-41.

The interpretation of unconditional inductive probability is generally more difficult and controversial than the interpretation of conditional inductive probability. Our specification of the meaning of conditional probability **P**(*c*, *d*) was in terms of an inductive argument from premise *d* to conclusion *c* (sec. 1.5.2). This explanation, of course, does not cover the case in which *d* is a logical truth and hence does not cover the concept of unconditional probability. In the next chapter we shall specify a concept of unconditional inductive probability by means of a formal model (sec. 3.2). On the interpretation to be given there, the unconditional probability **P**(*c*) means the inductive probability of *c* absolutely prior to any evidence, and it is the same for all rational people. There is, however, a strong element of idealization in this interpretation.

A second interpretation of unconditional inductive probability will emerge from Chapter 5, "The Pragmatic Theory of Inductive Probability." We introduce this interpretation now through a comparison of inductive with deductive inference (sec. 1.5). Consider first a person who accepts a premise Φ, the corresponding conditional "If Φ then θ," and on this basis accepts the conclusion θ. The premise Φ is the ground for his believing θ, as he would probably tell you if you asked him, but when he asserts θ he is not asserting Φ, nor "If Φ then θ," even implicitly. Consider next a person who accepts *g* and the conditional probability assertion **P**(*c*, *g*) = *x*. He further believes that *g* expresses all his relevant information, and using the rule of total evidence he accepts the unconditional probability assertion **P**(*c*) = *x*. Though *g* is the ground for his assertion that **P**(*c*) = *x*, when he makes this assertion he is not asserting *g*, nor **P**(*c*, *g*) = *x*, either directly or indirectly. It is natural to ask here: What does the unconditional probability statement **P**(*c*) = *x* express in this context? We answer this question in Chapter 5. Very briefly, the answer is that the unconditional probability statement **P**(*c*) = *x* has a pragmatic meaning in terms of the asserter's disposition to act in particular ways under conditions of uncertainty.

These two interpretations of unconditional probability should be distinguished from the following two applications of conditional probability. First, in Section 2.2.1 we introduced the convention of dropping a statement *g* that is common to all the probability terms under consideration, so that "**P**(*c*)" abbreviates "**P**(*c*, *g*)" and "**P**(*c*, *d*)" abbreviates "**P**(*c*, *d*&*g*)." Second, instead of explicitly presenting the condition of a conditional probability one may refer to this condition. Thus "**P**(*c*)" may mean "the probability of *c* conditional on my total evidence (or all the information available to me and my colleagues, or what is known in the present state of science)." For example, if a scientist says, "The general theory of relativity is well confirmed," he may mean, "Given what is known in science today, the general theory of relativity is highly probable." This implicit reference to general information will play a role in our analysis of empirical probability statements (sec. 8.2.1).

Our presentation of the calculus of inductive probability, its applications, and its relations to frequencies is now completed. In the next chapter, we shall extend this calculus and discuss the philosophical implications of the extension. Then in Chapters 4 and 5 we shall investigate the relation of probability to action.

2.7 Summary

As a preliminary to investigating the internal nature of atomic inductive probability statements, we have studied some interrelations among them. These interrelations are systematized by the calculus of inductive probability, which is an interpretation of the traditional calculus of probability. The calculus of inductive probability formalizes some of the actual rules governing probability in inductive reasoning. It is both a normative and a descriptive model. (Sec. 2.1)

The calculus of inductive probability is defined by four axioms. Arithmetic, truth-functional logic, and modal logic may be used to derive theorems. English is used as an informal metalanguage for defining the truth-functional connectives. Truth-functional logic captures some basic aspects of the functioning of natural language, and it is the core of modal logic. But modal logic is a better model of natural language than truth-functional logic. (Sec. 2.2)

Many basic theorems of the calculus of inductive probability were derived and illustrated. The subtraction principle says that the probability of a statement is one minus the probability of its negation. The exchange principle allows logically equivalent statements to be exchanged in probability contexts. Material equivalents cannot generally be exchanged in modal logic or the calculus of inductive probability. (Sec. 2.3.1)

The general multiplication principle states that the probability of a conjunction is the product of the probabilities of its conjuncts, the probability of each conjunct being taken conditionally on the truth of the prior conjuncts. When the conjuncts are probabilistically independent, the probability of a conjunction is simply the product of the probabilities of its conjuncts; this is the special multiplication principle. (Sec. 2.3.2)

The special addition principle applies to mutually exclusive statements; in this case the probability of a disjunction is the sum of the probabilities of its disjuncts. The principle of counting equiprobable cases applies to statements that are mutually exclusive, jointly exhaustive, and equally probable; here the probability of an event is the number of favorable cases divided by the total number of cases. The general addition principle does not require the disjuncts to be mutually exclusive. For a disjunction of two events it states that the probability of the disjunction is the sum of the probabilities of the disjuncts less the probability of their conjunction. The probability of a longer disjunction of nonexclusive statements is best calculated with De Morgan's law and the subtraction principle. (Sec. 2.3.3)

Inductive probability is closely related to relative frequency. An independent process of equiprobable events is the simplest and most basic probabilistic situation involving these two concepts. In an independent process of equiprobable events, the most probable relative frequency of success lies close to the inductive probability. By the law of large numbers, the relative frequency tends in the long run to the probability. In contrast, the anti-gambler's-fallacy theorem states that the actual number of successes tends to grow away from the most likely number of successes. (Sec. 2.4)

A group of theorems centering around Bayes' theorem is especially relevant to the confirmation process. Consider a set of mutually exclusive and jointly exhaustive hypotheses about a predicted event. The probability of a hypothesis relative to the background information is called its "prior probability." The extent to which a hypothesis predicts the event is called the "degree of prediction" of that hypothesis. The probability of a hypothesis given that the event occurred is called the "posterior probability" of that hypothesis.

The prediction theorem gives the probability of the event as a function of the prior probabilities and the degrees of prediction of the hypotheses. Bayes' theorem gives the posterior probability of each hypothesis also as a function of the prior probabilities and the degrees of prediction. The simplest version of Bayes' theorem is the ratio form, which states that the posterior odds of a hypothesis equal the product of these two factors: the prior odds and the ratio of the degrees of prediction. (Sec. 2.5.1)

Bayes' theorem can be combined with the law of large numbers to make a formal model of the scientific process of confirmation and prediction. A mixture of independent processes is an independent process of unknown probability. Take as given an assignment of prior probabilities to the different hypotheses about the value of this unknown probability. Bayes' method of finding an unknown probability consists in performing a sequence of experiments, observing the outcomes, and calculating the following for each experiment: the degrees of prediction of the observed result, the posterior probabilities of the hypotheses, and the predicted probability of some future event.

There are two criteria for the success of an experiment: acceptance of the true hypothesis on the basis of an acceptance parameter, and the closeness of the predicted probability to the true probability value (as measured by an accuracy parameter). When planning an experiment of some given length an investigator can calculate in advance the probability that the experiment will succeed, that is, that he will have accepted the true hypothesis or will have found the unknown probability at the end of the experiment. For fixed values of the acceptance and accuracy parameters, the probability of success increases as the length of the experiment increases. As the length of the experiment goes to infinity, the posterior probability of the true hypothesis tends toward unity and the predicted probability tends toward the actual probability. Thus an investigator who applies Bayes' method of finding an unknown probability to a mixture of independent processes will eventually know the truth. This fact is expressed precisely by the confirmation theorem, which results from combining the law of large numbers with Bayes' theorem. (Secs. 2.5.2–2.5.3)

Bayes' theorem is relevant to the reasoning involved in many natural cases of confirmation. This point was illustrated with the geocentric-heliocentric controversy, and later with the history of the conflict between the wave and corpuscular theories of light. The confirmation theorem is also relevant to natural examples of confirmation. There is an analogy between the confirmation of a scientific hypothesis by repeated verification of its consequences, and finding the true hypothesis by Bayes' method.

It is a corollary of the confirmation theorem that under repeated experimentation the effects of differences in prior probabilities ultimately disappear. But the confirmation theorem does not eliminate the problem of the epistemological status of prior probabilities. Consider two scientists who are investigating the same hypothesis and will observe the same experiment but who disagree on the prior probability of this hypothesis. After the experiment each can calculate the posterior probability of the hypothesis by Bayes' theorem. While the outcome of the experiment will probably bring their opinions closer together, a given amount of agreement on the posterior probability of the hypothesis requires a certain amount of agreement on the prior probability of the hypothesis.

We drew some general conclusions from this long discussion of the calculus of inductive probability. Bayes' theorem, Bayes' method of finding an unknown probability, and the confirmation theorem together give a good account of many artificial and natural cases of confirming a hypothesis by testing its observable consequences. Inductive probability plays a basic role in scientific inference, and the calculus of inductive probability is a good model of the ordinary use of "probable." The theorems of the calculus of inductive probability are true, but not empirically true. In applying Bayes' theorem it was necessary to consider a system of probability statements, rather than a single probability statement.

These last two conclusions led us to revise and extend our first two main questions: (I) What is the general nature of a system of atomic inductive probability statements? (II) Is an atomic inductive probability statement logically true-or-false, empirically true-or-false, or neither? Are the theorems of the calculus of inductive probability logically true? (Sec. 2.5.4)

The concept we have been studying is that of conditional probability, $\mathbf{P}(c, d)$. The calculus of probability can also be constructed in terms of unconditional probability, $\mathbf{P}(c)$. The reduction principle expresses a conditional probability as the ratio of two unconditional probabilities. The interpretation of the concept of unconditional inductive probability is generally more difficult and controversial than the interpretation of the concept of conditional inductive probability. (Sec. 2.6)

3 Alternative Inductive Logics and the Justification of Induction

We have said that all arguments concerning existence are founded on the relation of cause and effect; that our knowledge of that relation is derived entirely from experience; and that all our experimental conclusions proceed upon the supposition that the future will be conformable to the past. To endeavor, therefore, the proof of this last supposition by probable arguments, or arguments regarding existence, must be evidently going in a circle, and taking that for granted, which is the very point in question.*

3.1 Three Inductive Logics

In this section we shall discuss further the relation of the calculus of inductive probability (chap. 2) to inductive logic. We originally defined inductive logic in terms of inductive arguments (sec. 1.4.1), but later we reduced inductive arguments to atomic inductive probability statements (sec. 1.5.2). We begin, then, by examining the bearing of the calculus of inductive probability on the truth or falsity of an atomic inductive probability statement.

The calculus of inductive probability enables one to infer certain atomic inductive probability statements from others. The calculus does not, however, enable one to decide on the truth-status of an atomic inductive probability statement by itself, except in some limiting cases. Consider an example. Let E state that a deck of bridge cards is carefully shuffled and a card drawn from it in the usual manner; the card is then replaced and the whole process repeated. In addition, let E include the information that when cards have been drawn this way in the past each card has appeared with a relative frequency of about 1/52, each possible sequence of two cards has appeared with a relative frequency of about $(1/52)^2$, and in general, each possible sequence of n cards has appeared with a relative frequency of approximately $(1/52)^n$.

Let H_1 say that the first card drawn is a heart. The correct value of $\mathbf{P}(H_1, E)$ is clearly 1/4, that is, the atomic inductive probability statement

This chapter is based on my articles, "Reichenbach's Theory of Probability and Induction" and "The Presupposition Theory of Induction."

* Hume, *An Enquiry Concerning Human Understanding*, pp. 35-36.

$\mathbf{P}(H_1, E) = 1/4$ is true.* But neither this statement nor its negation can be deduced from the calculus of inductive probability, because for any number α between zero and one ($0 \leqq \alpha \leqq 1$), if the statement $\mathbf{P}(H_1, E) = \alpha$ is added to axioms [1] through [4] of Chapter 2, the result will be a consistent system. Axioms [1] and [2] may be satisfied by assigning probability values that are proper functions of α to all truth-functional compounds involving H_1 and E. The evidence statement E does not logically imply H_1, nor does it logically imply $\sim H_1$, and so [3] is inapplicable. When applied to $\mathbf{P}(H_1, E) = \alpha$, axiom [4] requires only that for any logically equivalent way E' of expressing the evidence E, $\mathbf{P}(H_1, E') = \alpha$. Thus axioms [1] through [4] are consistent with the assignment of any number α to $\mathbf{P}(H_1, E)$, and therefore no particular value for $\mathbf{P}(H_1, E)$ can be deduced from them alone.†

A similar result holds for an independence assertion, such as $\mathbf{P}(H_2, E) = \mathbf{P}(H_2, H_1E)$, where H_2 means that the second card drawn is a heart. The independence assertion is not itself an atomic probability statement, but it is a compound of such, being equivalent to: There is a number α such that $\mathbf{P}(H_2, E) = \alpha$ and $\mathbf{P}(H_2, H_1E) = \alpha$. Since the first card drawn is replaced and the deck is shuffled before the second card is drawn, this independence assertion is true. But neither it nor its negation is a theorem of the calculus of inductive probability.

Let us express more precisely the fact that the calculus of inductive probability does not in general determine the truth-status of a single atomic inductive probability statement. Here we employ the notion of logical independence (p. 50). Two propositions p, q are logically independent if and only if pq, $p\bar{q}$, $\bar{p}q$, and $\bar{p}\bar{q}$ are each logically possible. Note that when p and q are logically independent, it follows that p, q, "if p then q," and "if p then $\sim q$" are each empirically true-or-false; for if, e.g., p were logically necessary, $\bar{p}\bar{q}$ would not be logically possible.

Consider a pair of logically independent statements h, e and any number x between zero and one inclusive. The result of adding $\mathbf{P}(h, e) = x$ to the axioms of the calculus of inductive probability is a consistent system; this may be seen by considering each axiom in turn as we did in the case of $\mathbf{P}(H_1, E) = \alpha$. Hence, for any h, e, and x, if h and e are logically independent

* But it is not true by definition. We deliberately avoided using the words "fair" and "random" in describing the content of E to insure that $\mathbf{P}(H_1, E) = 1/4$ would not be true by definition.

The concepts of fairness and randomness play an important role in empirical probability statements (see sec. 8.2).

† One might justify the atomic inductive probability statement $\mathbf{P}(H_1, E) = 1/4$ on the ground that, conditional on E, each card is equally likely. From the premises that each card is equally likely and that there are 52 cards of which 13 are hearts, we can infer $\mathbf{P}(H_1, E) = 1/4$ by the principle of counting equiprobable cases. But there is nothing in the calculus of inductive probability to tell us that, conditional on E, each card is equally likely.

and $0 \leqq x \leqq 1$, the atomic inductive probability statement $\mathbf{P}(h, e) = x$ is not a theorem of the calculus of inductive probability.

The fact that this result holds even when $x = 0$ or $x = 1$ shows that the converse of axiom [3], namely,

$$\text{If } \mathbf{P}(c, d) = 1, \text{ then } d \rightarrow c \qquad ,$$

is not a theorem of the calculus of inductive probability. It is an interesting question whether or not this converse should be added to the system (cf. p. 147). But even if it is added, it will still be true that if h and e are logically independent and $0 < x < 1$, the atomic inductive probability statement $\mathbf{P}(h, e) = x$ is not a theorem of the system.

To say that the calculus of inductive probability does not determine the truth-status of an atomic inductive probability statement $\mathbf{P}(h, e) = x$ except when h and e are logically dependent, is to say that the calculus is incomplete in a certain sense. The following question naturally arises: Should it be completed? More specifically, are there rules of inductive logic that do determine the truth-status of at least some atomic inductive probability statements $\mathbf{P}(h, e) = x$ when h and e are logically independent?

Consider again the Semmelweis example (sec. 1.5.2),

[42″] $\mathbf{P}(C, D)$ is high,

where C contains Semmelweis' conclusion about puerperal fever and D expresses his data. This atomic inductive probability statement is true. But *how* do we know it is true? It seems plausible to say it is true, *at least in part,* because the data and the conclusion are connected by logical rules governing evidence. Of course, whether Semmelweis' data were correct is an empirical matter, but whether they constitute evidence for his conclusion seems to be at least partially a question of the *logic* of evidence.

This suggests that there are important logical rules for judging empirical evidence that are not encompassed by the calculus of inductive probability but should be included in an adequate logic of inductive probability. Inductive logicians have formulated many such rules, of which we will mention some of the most common. There are rules governing arguments by analogy: e.g., "The closer the analogy, the more likely the conclusion."* Other rules arise in connection with a basic method for showing that one property or event is the cause of another, namely, the method of altering the qualities that seem to be causally relevant while leaving other qualities fixed. For example, at one stage investigators considered two possible modes of transmission of yellow fever: infected mosquitoes and the excreta of yellow fever patients. They conducted carefully controlled experiments in which they varied these qualities one at a time: e.g., volunteers would contact the excreta but *not* mosquitoes, other volunteers would be bitten by

* Keynes, *A Treatise on Probability*, chap. 19, gives several rules for analogy.

infected mosquitoes but *not* contact the excreta, etc. Not every property of the situation was controlled, of course, but only those thought by the investigators to be causally relevant. Thus cleanliness, contact with mosquitoes, and food were controlled, but not the color of the men's dress.* Let us call this general procedure the *method of varying causally relevant qualities*. This is the essence of the controlled experiment; and of Bacon's tables of instances: the table of essence and presence, the table of deviation (or of absence in proximity), and the table of degrees (or comparison); and also of Mill's methods of experimental inquiry: the method of agreement, the method of difference, the joint method of agreement and difference, the method of residues, and the method of concomitant variations.† When the rules for the method of varying causally relevant qualities, for the controlled experiment, for Bacon's tables, and for Mill's methods are carefully and correctly formulated, some turn out to belong to the logic of empirical inquiry but others belong to inductive logic (sec. 1.4). These latter go beyond the calculus of inductive probability.

Another rule of evidence not included in the calculus of inductive probability is the following: If observations show many instances in which property ϕ has been accompanied by property ψ, with no counterinstances, then it is quite likely that the next instance of ϕ will be accompanied by ψ. We call this the *rule of induction by simple enumeration*. For an example, let ϕ be "is a swan" (or "S") and ψ be "is white" (or "W"). Many swans (S) were observed in England and all were white (W), and so it was probable that the next swan observed would be white. If the swans are labeled a, b, c, etc., the argument is

$SaWaSbWb \ldots$

Sz

$\therefore$ Probably Wz

Corresponding to this inductive argument there is an atomic probability statement

$\mathbf{P}(Wz, SzSaWaSbWb \ldots)$ is high.

The rule of induction by simple enumeration tells us that this atomic probability statement is true. The fact that black swans were later discovered in Australia does not show this statement to be false, of course, because even a high probability is compatible with exceptions (sec. 2.4). As in the case of the card example, this atomic probability statement is not decidable by means of the calculus of inductive probability. So far as this calculus is

* Hallock and Turner, *Walter Reed*, pp. 14-20. The original documents are in the Government Printing Office compilation, *Yellow Fever*.

† Bacon, *Novum Organum*, book 2. Mill, *A System of Logic*, book 3, chap. 8.

concerned we could assert that the probability of the next swan being white is infinitesimal.

Let us call the system of rules of inductive inference actually used and aspired to by the practicing scientists **standard inductive logic.** This will include the calculus of inductive probability together with rules for analogy, the method of varying causally relevant qualities, and induction by simple enumeration.

Our analysis of geometry (sec. 1.2.2) suggests the question: Are there systems of inductive logic alternative to standard inductive logic, systems having the calculus of inductive probability in common but varying with respect to other inductive rules such as analogy and induction by simple enumeration? In this chapter, we argue that there are such systems and discuss the epistemological implications of this fact.

A system of inductive rules that includes the calculus of inductive probability and at least partially specifies atomic probabilities by means of the standard rules of analogy, the method of varying causally relevant qualities, induction by simple enumeration, etc., *or alternatives thereto* will be called an **inductive logic.** We shall indicate the nature of two alternatives to standard inductive logic by discussing alternatives to the principle of induction by simple enumeration.

We first reformulate the rule of induction by simple enumeration in standard inductive logic in comparative terms: The probability that the next ϕ will have the property ψ *increases* as the number of instances in which ψ has accompanied ϕ increases, assuming that there are no counterinstances and that ϕx and ψx are logically independent.

Inverse inductive logic contains the rule: The probability that the next ϕ will be a ψ *decreases* as the number of instances in which ψ has accompanied ϕ increases, assuming no counterinstances and the logical independence of ϕ and ψ. For example, the probability that the next swan is white given that 100 swans have been observed and all were white is *less than* the probability that the next swan is white given that only 10 swans were observed and found to be white.

In both standard and inverse logic the probability of a prediction is generally affected by knowledge of the past, though in opposite ways in the two methods. But one could conceivably hold that what has happened in the past is inductively irrelevant to what will happen in the future. To do this is to employ **random inductive logic,** so-called because it treats the succession of states of the universe as a random, independent sequence (cf. p. 58). Random inductive logic includes the rule: The probability that the next ϕ will be ψ does not depend on the number of instances in which ψ has accompanied ϕ. For example, the probability that the next swan is white given that 100 swans have been observed and are white is the same as the probability that the next swan is white given that 100 swans were observed and all found to be black.

The foregoing will serve as an introduction to standard, inverse, and random inductive logic. In the next section we shall give rigorous definitions of these logics for some very limited models of reality. Later we shall discuss the causal aspects of standard inductive logic (sec. 10.3).

3.2 Inductive Logics for Simple Models of Reality

3.2.1 Simple models of reality

For some highly simplified models of reality, Rudolf Carnap has shown how to extend the calculus of inductive probability to attain complete systems in which every atomic inductive probability statement has a truth-value.* Carnap's procedure is quite complex; the essence of it is presented below and will suffice for our purposes. Our treatment and terminology differ considerably from his.

We describe the structure of these models in the present subsection, and in the next we convert them into models of standard, inverse, and random inductive logic by distributing probabilities over them. Then we discuss the relation of these inductive logics to statistical uniformity and entropy (sec. 3.2.3) and compare them with Bayes' method of finding an unknown probability (sec. 3.2.4).

Consider a model $\mathfrak{M}$ containing a finite number m of *basic individuals* and a finite number n of monadic *basic properties*, e.g., whiteness, circularity, where m and n are positive integers. Any logically possible universe constructible in this model $\mathfrak{M}$ may be completely described in an artificial language $\mathfrak{L}$ having the following primitive symbols: m *proper names* "a," "b," "c," . . . ; n monadic *predicates* "A," "B," "C," . . . ; the truth-functional connectives "and," "or," "not," etc. of Section 2.2.2; and parentheses for punctuation. An *atomic statement* of $\mathfrak{L}$ consists of a predicate followed by a proper name, e.g., "Ac." Every atomic statement and every truth-functional combination of atomic statements is a *formula* of $\mathfrak{L}$.

Each proper name is assigned to just one basic individual and each predicate is assigned to just one basic property. It is required that the predicates be logically independent; that is, for any two distinct predicates ϕ and ψ and any proper name, α, $\phi\alpha$ and $\psi\alpha$ are logically independent. The basic individuals may be thought of as individuals in the ordinary sense, individuals at specific times (e.g., this train now), events, or space-time points or regions (cf. sec. 9.2). But it is required that the individuals be nonoverlapping and logically disconnected entities: For any two distinct

* Our exposition is based on Carnap's *Logical Foundations of Probability* and *The Continuum of Inductive Methods*. In his "Replies and Systematic Expositions" Carnap develops his system somewhat differently.

proper names α and β, and any predicates ϕ and ψ (distinct or identical), $\phi\alpha$ and $\psi\beta$ are logically independent.

The models we are considering include only monadic properties, e.g., "is red," "is round," and not relations, e.g., "is heavier than," "is between." Many of the concepts and methods of this section also apply to models with relations. However, traditional probability theory has studied mainly the monadic case, and little is known about inductive logics for models with relations. Since monadic models are adequate for our purpose, we will concentrate on them.

An *individual state* of a model $\mathfrak{M}$ is described by a conjunction that tells, for each basic property, whether that property is present or absent. Since $\mathfrak{M}$ has n basic properties, it has 2^n individual states. A *universe description* of language $\mathfrak{L}$ is a conjunction that gives the individual state of each basic individual of $\mathfrak{M}$. A universe description is a basic conjunction of all the atomic statements of the language (p. 50). There are 2^{mn} different universe descriptions of language $\mathfrak{L}$.

A universe description tells, for each basic individual and basic property of a model, whether the individual has or lacks that property. A universe description is logically possible ($\Diamond$) in the sense of Section 1.2.3. Moreover, each *logically possible universe* based on the individuals and properties of a model $\mathfrak{M}$ is portrayed in full detail by one of the universe descriptions of language $\mathfrak{L}$. Because of the logical independence requirement on the proper names and predicates of $\mathfrak{L}$, each universe description is logically consistent and delineates a logically possible universe. There is thus a one-to-one correspondence between the universe descriptions of language $\mathfrak{L}$ and the logically possible universes of model $\mathfrak{M}$.

Designate one of the logically possible universes of $\mathfrak{M}$ as the *actual universe* of $\mathfrak{M}$. That universe description of $\mathfrak{L}$ that describes this actual universe is true, while all other universe descriptions of $\mathfrak{L}$ are false. Likewise, those sentences of $\mathfrak{L}$ that describe the actual universe, i.e., are logically implied by the true universe description, are true and all others are false. Note that if the basic individuals of $\mathfrak{M}$ are space-time regions, a universe description depicts the complete history of the universe, not merely its state at a particular time.*

An example may be helpful. Consider a model based on two individuals a and b, two basic properties S (swanness) and W (whiteness), and having the actual universe $SaWaSbWb$. For this model both m and n equal 2, and there are $2^{2\times2}$ or 16 universe descriptions. These are listed in two different ways in Table 9: by declaring which individuals have which individual states, and by writing the basic conjunction of the atomic statements "Sa," "Wa,"

* It is for this reason that I use "universe description" in preference to Carnap's "state-description." If the basic individuals of a model are successive moments of time, each individual state is a possible state of the universe at a given time.

"Sb," and "Wb." The sentences "$SaWaSbWb$" and "Sb" of $\mathfrak{L}$ are true, while the sentences "$\overline{Sa}$" and "$\overline{WaSb}$" are false.

Although our basic models are finite, we sometimes consider models with an infinite sequence of individuals and a corresponding infinite sequence of proper names. These models do not have "universe descriptions" in the usual sense, since an infinite conjunction is not a formula. To avoid this

TABLE 9

UNIVERSE DESCRIPTIONS OF A MODEL WITH TWO INDIVIDUALS AND TWO BASIC PROPERTIES

Universe description (u)	Individual states				Basic conjunction	Isomorphism measure $I(u)$
	SW	$S\overline{W}$	$\overline{S}W$	$\overline{S}\,\overline{W}$		
1	a, b				$Sa\ Wa\ Sb\ Wb$	1
2		a, b			$Sa\ \overline{Wa}\ Sb\ \overline{Wb}$	1
3			a, b		$\overline{Sa}\ Wa\ \overline{Sb}\ Wb$	1
4				a, b	$\overline{Sa}\ \overline{Wa}\ \overline{Sb}\ \overline{Wb}$	1
5 6	a b	b a			$Sa\ Wa\ Sb\ \overline{Wb}$ $Sa\ \overline{Wa}\ Sb\ Wb$	2
7 8	a b		b a		$Sa\ Wa\ \overline{Sb}\ Wb$ $\overline{Sa}\ Wa\ Sb\ Wb$	2
9 10	a b			b a	$Sa\ Wa\ \overline{Sb}\ \overline{Wb}$ $\overline{Sa}\ \overline{Wa}\ Sb\ Wb$	2
11 12		a b	b a		$Sa\ \overline{Wa}\ \overline{Sb}\ Wb$ $\overline{Sa}\ Wa\ Sb\ \overline{Wb}$	2
13 14		a b		b a	$Sa\ \overline{Wa}\ \overline{Sb}\ \overline{Wb}$ $\overline{Sa}\ \overline{Wa}\ Sb\ \overline{Wb}$	2
15 16			a b	b a	$\overline{Sa}\ Wa\ \overline{Sb}\ \overline{Wb}$ $\overline{Sa}\ \overline{Wa}\ \overline{Sb}\ Wb$	2

difficulty we treat infinite models as infinite sequences of finite models with ever increasing numbers of individuals and proper names, so that an infinite universe is completely described by a suitable infinite sequence of universe descriptions (pp. 119–20).

In summary: a finite *model* $\mathfrak{M}$-$\mathfrak{L}$ consists of two isomorphic structures, a model $\mathfrak{M}$ and the corresponding language $\mathfrak{L}$. The structure $\mathfrak{M}$ consists of (1) m basic individuals $\{m = 1,2,3, \ldots\}$, (2) n basic properties $\{n = 1,2,3, \ldots\}$, (3) 2^{mn} logically possible universes, and (4) an actual universe, which is one of the logically possible universes. The structure $\mathfrak{L}$ corresponding to $\mathfrak{M}$ contains, besides the truth-functional connectives and parentheses, (1′)

m proper names, (2′) n monadic predicates, (3′) 2^{mn} universe descriptions, and (4′) one true universe description. Each individual of $\mathfrak{M}$ has one name in $\mathfrak{L}$ and each property of $\mathfrak{M}$ is represented by one predicate of $\mathfrak{L}$. Infinite models are to be treated as infinite sequences of finite models.

The logical relation of isomorphism between formulas will be useful in defining inductive logics for these models. Two formulas Φ and Ψ are *isomorphic* if and only if Φ can be transformed into a formula that is logically equivalent to Ψ by renaming the individuals referred to in Φ. The renaming is understood to be done in such a way that different individuals still have different names. For example, "$\overline{Fb} \vee Fb(Fd \supset Fc)$" is isomorphic to "$Fc \supset (Fa \vee \overline{Fb})$," since the first formula becomes "$\overline{Fc} \vee Fc(Fb \supset Fa)$" when "$b$," "$c$," "$d$," are replaced by "$c$," "$a$," "$b$," respectively, and "$\overline{Fc} \vee Fc(Fb \supset Fa)$" is logically equivalent to "$Fc \supset (Fa \vee \overline{Fb})$." Again, when "$a$" and "$b$" are exchanged in "$SaWaSb\overline{Wb}$" we get "$SbWbSa\overline{Wa}$," which becomes "$Sa\overline{Wa}SbWb$" by commutation; hence the two universe descriptions "$SaWaSb\overline{Wb}$" and "$Sa\overline{Wa}SbWb$" are isomorphic. On the other hand, "$\overline{Sa}\overline{Wa}SbWb$" is not isomorphic to "$Sa\overline{Wa}SbWb$."

It is clear that two universe descriptions are isomorphic if and only if they agree on the number of individuals said to be in each individual state. The isomorphic universe descriptions of Table 9 are bracketed together. A disjunction of all the universe descriptions that are isomorphic to one another is called a *distribution description;* a distribution description says of each individual state how many individuals in the universe are in that state. For example, the distribution description "$SaWaSb\overline{Wb} \vee Sa\overline{Wa}SbWb$" says that one individual is a white swan and the other is a non-white swan.

The isomorphism of two formulas Φ and Ψ is symbolized by $\Phi \mathbf{I} \Psi$. It is sometimes convenient to have a measure of the number of formulas in a model that are isomorphic to a given formula. For this purpose logically equivalent formulas should be identified. The isomorphism measure $\mathbf{I}(\Phi)$ of a formula Φ of $\mathfrak{L}$ is defined to be the number of logical distinct formulas of $\mathfrak{L}$ that are isomorphic to Φ, including itself. For example, in the model of Table 9, $\mathbf{I}(SaWa\overline{Sb}\,\overline{Wb}) = 2$. The measure $\mathbf{I}(\Phi)$ is relative to a model, since different models have different sets of formulas.

This concludes our presentation of the models $\mathfrak{M}$-$\mathfrak{L}$, but we will discuss them and extend them later (secs. 3.3.3, 6.1, 6.3, 10.3).

3.2.2 Carnap's inductive logics

We shall use a model $\mathfrak{M}$-$\mathfrak{L}$ as a model of reality for defining standard, inverse, and random inductive logic. The actual universe of $\mathfrak{M}$ will correspond to our actual universe, and the logically possible universes of $\mathfrak{M}$ will correspond to the logically possible alternatives to our actual universe. The language $\mathfrak{L}$ will correspond to the language in which we reason about reality. The term *reality* is used here in the sense of the total system of all real entities or existences; it includes not only the actual universe in which we live, but the logically possible alternatives to our actual universe. Thus we take $\mathfrak{M}$ as a model of the nonlinguistic part of reality, the actual universe of $\mathfrak{M}$ as a model of the actual universe in which we live, $\mathfrak{L}$ as a model of actual language, and the pair $\mathfrak{M}$-$\mathfrak{L}$ as a model of reality as a whole.* The individuals of the model will be interpreted as things, events, or space-time regions and the properties of the model as properties of these individuals. Though these models are highly idealized, they are sufficiently realistic for our present purposes. We shall discuss the philosophical significance of these limitations in Section 3.3.3.

An *inductive logic for a model* $\mathfrak{M}$-$\mathfrak{L}$ is a set of rules determining a unique numerical value $\mathbf{P}(c)$ for each sentence c of the language $\mathfrak{L}$, such that these probability values satisfy the calculus of inductive probability. The probability $\mathbf{P}(c)$ is unconditional, but by the reduction principle

$$[23] \qquad \text{If } \mathbf{P}(c) \neq 0\text{, then } \mathbf{P}(d, c) = \frac{\mathbf{P}(dc)}{\mathbf{P}(c)} \quad ,$$

an assignment of unconditional probabilities to the sentences of $\mathfrak{L}$ determines a conditional probability for each pair of sentences h, e of $\mathfrak{L}$, except when $\mathbf{P}(e) = 0$. When $\mathbf{P}(e) = 0$, we say that the expression "$\mathbf{P}(h, e) = x$" is undefined and not an atomic inductive probability statement. Hence an inductive logic for a model $\mathfrak{M}$-$\mathfrak{L}$ is a complete probability calculus for that model, determining the truth-status of every atomic inductive probability statement about $\mathfrak{M}$. An inductive logic as a set of probability rules is, of course, to be distinguished from the subject of inductive logic described in Section 1.4.1.

A very important theorem about inductive logics for a model $\mathfrak{M}$-$\mathfrak{L}$ is this: Any assignment of non-negative real numbers to the universe descriptions of $\mathfrak{L}$ that sums to one determines an inductive logic for $\mathfrak{M}$-$\mathfrak{L}$. We prove this theorem in two steps.

(1) Each universe description of language $\mathfrak{L}$ is logically consistent, and the universe descriptions of $\mathfrak{L}$ are mutually exclusive and jointly exhaustive. The fact that each universe description is assigned a non-negative real number is in conformity with theorem [8] (p. 46), and the fact that these numbers sum to one is in conformity with theorem [14] (p. 52). Hence any assignment of non-negative real numbers to the universe descriptions of $\mathfrak{L}$ that sums to one constitutes an assignment of unconditional probabilities to these universe descriptions.

* Our use of "model" here conforms to our definition of it in Sec. 1.6.2, but differs from the usage of mathematical logic. There is a branch of mathematical logic called "model theory." In model theory $\mathfrak{M}$ is taken as a model of $\mathfrak{L}$, whereas we take the complex $\mathfrak{M}$-$\mathfrak{L}$ as a model of reality.

(2) We show next how to calculate the unconditional probability $\mathbf{P}(e)$, for any event e, from an assignment of unconditional probabilities to the universe descriptions of $\mathfrak{L}$. Any event e of model $\mathfrak{M}$ may be described by a disjunction $u_1 \vee u_2 \vee \ldots \vee u_\gamma$ of those universe descriptions in which e occurs; hence

$$e \leftrightarrow (u_1 \vee u_2 \vee \ldots \vee u_\gamma) \quad .$$

In the terminology of truth-function theory, this amounts to writing e in "disjunctive normal form." By the exchange principle,

$$\mathbf{P}(e) = \mathbf{P}(u_1 \vee u_2 \vee \ldots \vee u_\gamma) \quad .$$

These universe descriptions are mutually exclusive, and so the special addition principle applies, giving

$$\mathbf{P}(e) = \mathbf{P}(u_1) + \mathbf{P}(u_2) + \ldots + \mathbf{P}(u_\gamma) \quad .$$

In this way the unconditional probability of any event of model $\mathfrak{M}$ may be computed.

This completes our proof of the theorem, which leads in turn to a method of constructing a calculus of probability for a model $\mathfrak{M}$-$\mathfrak{L}$. Begin with an assignment of real numbers to possible universes that sums to unity. Then define the unconditional probability of a formula of $\mathfrak{L}$ to be the sum of the probabilities of the universes in which it is true. Finally, define the conditional probability of a pair of formulas of $\mathfrak{L}$ by the reduction principle. This method of constructing a calculus of probability is an alternative to using the axioms of conditional probability of Section 2.2.1 or the axioms of unconditional probability of Section 2.6. Note that this method also works for finite models containing relations.

Table 10 gives three inductive logics for a model having two individuals and two properties. As an example, we show how to compute $\mathbf{P}(Wb, SaWaSb)$ for standard inductive logic. The disjunctive normal form of "$SaWaSb$" is "$SaWaSbWb \vee SaWaSb\overline{Wb}$." Hence

$$\begin{aligned}\mathbf{P}(SaWaSb) &= \mathbf{P}(SaWaSbWb \vee SaWaSb\overline{Wb}) \\ &= \mathbf{P}(SaWaSbWb) + (SaWaSb\overline{Wb}) \\ &= 2/20 + 1/20 = 3/20 \quad .\end{aligned}$$

By the reduction principle,

$$\mathbf{P}(Wb, SaWaSb) = \frac{\mathbf{P}(SaWaSbWb)}{\mathbf{P}(SaWaSb)} = \frac{2/20}{3/20} = 2/3 \quad .$$

So in this model the probability that the next swan will be white, conditional on the observation that one swan was observed and was white, is 2/3.

The basic concept of an inductive logic is defined relative to some particular model $\mathfrak{M}$-$\mathfrak{L}$. However, we are often interested in rules that determine inductive logics for all finite models, and *inductive logic* will also be used in this broader sense. We proceed next to formulate axioms to define standard, random, and inverse inductive logic for all finite models.

We define *standard inductive logic for a model* $\mathfrak{M}$-$\mathfrak{L}$ as the system obtained by adding this axiom to the calculus of inductive probability:

[24] For each universe description u, $\mathbf{P}(u) = k/I(u)$.

The constant k, which depends on the parameters m, n of the model $\mathfrak{M}$-$\mathfrak{L}$, can be calculated in the following way. Let $u_1, u_2, \ldots, u_{2^{mn}}$ be the universe descriptions of the model. Since these universe descriptions are mutually exclusive and jointly exhaustive, these unconditional probabilities must total one, and so

$$k = \left\{\sum_{\gamma=1}^{2^{mn}} [\mathbf{I}(u_\gamma)^{-1}]\right\}^{-1} \quad .$$

Thus $k = 0.1$ in Table 10. Actually, k^{-1} is the number of distribution descriptions of the model, because standard inductive logic assigns equal probabilities to distribution descriptions. Each universe description u receives a probability $\mathbf{P}(u)$ inversely proportional to $\mathbf{I}(u)$, and $\mathbf{I}(u)$ measures the number of disjuncts in a distribution description.

The effect of adding axiom [24] to the calculus of inductive probability is to complete this calculus with respect to atomic inductive probability statements. Consider an atomic inductive probability statement $\mathbf{P}(h, e) = x$ and its negation $\sim[\mathbf{P}(h, e) = x]$, where h and e are logically independent and $0 \leqq x \leqq 1$. As we saw in Section 3.1, neither $\mathbf{P}(h, e) = x$ nor $\sim[\mathbf{P}(h, e) = x]$ is a theorem in the calculus of inductive probability. But for any model $\mathfrak{M}$-$\mathfrak{L}$, either $\mathbf{P}(h, e) = x$ is a theorem or $\sim[\mathbf{P}(h, e) = x]$ is a theorem in the system consisting of the calculus of inductive probability and axiom [24]. The calculus of inductive probability can also be completed by adding alternatives to axiom [24], such as axiom [24^i] or [24^r] below.

Consider the system consisting of the calculus of inductive probability and axiom [24].* We shall see in Section 3.2.4 (Inductive logics and Bayes' method) that the rule of induction by simple enumeration holds in this system. Accordingly, within the range of accuracy concerning us here, this system models standard inductive logic. We illustrate this fact by means of Table 10.

The formula "*SbWb*" is equivalent to the disjunction of universe description 1, 6, 8 and 10 of Table 10, and "*Sb*" is equivalent to the disjunc-

* This system defines Carnap's degree of confirmation function c^*, while the system consisting of the calculus of inductive probability and axiom [24^r] below defines his function $c\dagger$. Carnap's procedure is to define these functions explicitly, whereas we have defined them axiomatically.

tion of these together with descriptions 2, 5, 12 and 14. Hence

$$\mathbf{P}(Wb, Sb) = \frac{1/10 + 3(1/20)}{2(1/10) + 6(1/20)} = 1/2 \quad .$$

Thus in this model the probability that swan b is white is one-half. By the rules of standard inductive logic, the probability that swan b is white should increase if it is known that swan a is white. That is, it should be the case

TABLE 10

ALTERNATIVE INDUCTIVE LOGICS FOR A MODEL

Universe description (u)	Isomorphism measure $\mathbf{I}(u)$	Probability assignment $\mathbf{P}(u)$		
		Standard inductive logic	Inverse inductive logic	Random inductive logic
1. $Sa\ Wa\ Sb\ Wb$	1	2/20	1/28	1/16
2. $Sa\ \overline{Wa}\ Sb\ \overline{Wb}$	1	2/20	1/28	1/16
3. $\overline{Sa}\ Wa\ \overline{Sb}\ Wb$	1	2/20	1/28	1/16
4. $\overline{Sa}\ \overline{Wa}\ \overline{Sb}\ \overline{Wb}$	1	2/20	1/28	1/16
5. $Sa\ Wa\ Sb\ \overline{Wb}$	2	1/20	2/28	1/16
6. $Sa\ \overline{Wa}\ Sb\ Wb$	2	1/20	2/28	1/16
7. $Sa\ Wa\ \overline{Sb}\ Wb$	2	1/20	2/28	1/16
8. $\overline{Sa}\ Wa\ Sb\ Wb$	2	1/20	2/28	1/16
9. $Sa\ Wa\ \overline{Sb}\ \overline{Wb}$	2	1/20	2/28	1/16
10. $\overline{Sa}\ \overline{Wa}\ Sb\ Wb$	2	1/20	2/28	1/16
11. $Sa\ \overline{Wa}\ \overline{Sb}\ Wb$	2	1/20	2/28	1/16
12. $\overline{Sa}\ Wa\ Sb\ \overline{Wb}$	2	1/20	2/28	1/16
13. $Sa\ \overline{Wa}\ \overline{Sb}\ \overline{Wb}$	2	1/20	2/28	1/16
14. $\overline{Sa}\ \overline{Wa}\ Sb\ \overline{Wb}$	2	1/20	2/28	1/16
15. $\overline{Sa}\ Wa\ \overline{Sb}\ \overline{Wb}$	2	1/20	2/28	1/16
16. $\overline{Sa}\ \overline{Wa}\ \overline{Sb}\ Wb$	2	1/20	2/28	1/16
Sum of $\mathbf{P}(u)$ over all universes u:		1	1	1

that $\mathbf{P}(Wb, SaWaSb) > \mathbf{P}(Wb, Sb)$. And it is, since by our earlier calculation $\mathbf{P}(Wb, SaWaSb) = 2/3$. Hence in this example axiom [24] leads to a result in accordance with the rule of induction by simple enumeration. We are not claiming that these probability values are realistic, but only that they increase in the right way. More realistic values can be obtained by increasing the number of basic properties and modeling "white" and "swan" with complexes of basic properties.

To obtain *inverse inductive logic for a model*, replace axiom [24] by

[24^{i}] For each universe description u, $\mathbf{P}(u) = k^{\mathrm{i}}\mathbf{I}(u)$.

This axiom assigns each universe description a probability in proportion to the number of universe descriptions isomorphic to it. The constant k^{i} can be calculated by the formula

$$k^{\mathrm{i}} = \left\{ \sum_{\gamma=1}^{2^{mn}} \mathbf{I}(u_{\gamma}) \right\}^{-1} \quad .$$

In Table 10, $k^{\mathrm{i}} = 1/28$. As before, axiom [24^{i}] plus the calculus of inductive probability determines the truth value of every atomic inductive probability statement about the model $\mathfrak{M}$. For example, using the column of Table 10 for inverse inductive logic we obtain

$$\mathbf{P}(Wb, Sb) = \frac{\mathbf{P}(SbWb)}{\mathbf{P}(Sb)} = \frac{1/28 + 3(2/28)}{2(1/28) + 6(2/28)} = 1/2$$

$$\mathbf{P}(Wb, SaWaSb) = \frac{\mathbf{P}(SaWaSbWb)}{\mathbf{P}(SaWaSb)} = \frac{1/28}{1/28 + 2/28} = 1/3 \quad .$$

Hence axiom [24^{i}] implies that $\mathbf{P}(Wb, SaWaSb) < \mathbf{P}(Wb, Sb)$, i.e., in inverse inductive logic the chance that the next swan is white is reduced by the information that the only swan observed is white. Anyone who has worked much with this system will see that the calculus of inductive probability and [24^{i}] imply that when ϕ and ψ are logically independent, the probability that the next ϕ will be ψ decreases as the number of instances in which ψ has accompanied ϕ increases.

To obtain *random inductive logic for a model* $\mathfrak{M}$-$\mathfrak{L}$, replace axiom [24] by

[24^{r}] For each universe description u, $\mathbf{P}(u) = k^{\mathrm{r}}$.

According to this axiom each logically possible universe is equally likely. The constant k^{r} is thus the reciprocal of the number of universe descriptions of $\mathfrak{L}$ and equals 2^{-mn}; in Table 10, $k^{\mathrm{r}} = 1/16$. As before, the system consisting of axiom [24^{r}] plus the calculus of inductive probability determines all atomic inductive probabilities. In this case, calculating the unconditional probability of an event e reduces to counting the number of universe descriptions in which e holds and dividing by the total number of universe descriptions. For example, using the random inductive logic column of Table 10 we obtain

$$\mathbf{P}(Wb, SaWaSb) = \frac{\mathbf{P}(SaWaSbWb)}{\mathbf{P}(SaWaSb)} = \frac{1/16}{2/16} = 1/2$$

$$\mathbf{P}(Wb, Sb) = \frac{\mathbf{P}(SbWb)}{\mathbf{P}(Sb)} = \frac{4/16}{8/16} = 1/2 \quad .$$

Hence axiom [24^{r}] implies that $\mathbf{P}(Wb, SaWaSb) = \mathbf{P}(Wb, Sb)$, i.e., in random inductive logic the chance that the next swan will be white is not affected by the observation of a white swan. More generally, the calculus of inductive probability and [24^r] yield the result that when ϕ and ψ are logically independent, the probability that the next ϕ will be ψ does not depend on the number of instances in which ψ has accompanied ϕ. For axiom [24^r] is equivalent to treating the basic individuals of model $\mathfrak{M}$ as independent and regarding each individual state as equally likely (pp. 50, 58). Hence, if the individuals referred to in data d are not referred to in hypothesis h, $\mathbf{P}(h, de) = \mathbf{P}(h, e)$.

This last fact distinguishes random inductive logic from the other two inductive logics. We so constructed our models $\mathfrak{M}$-$\mathfrak{L}$ that a statement about one basic individual is *logically* independent of a statement about another. Now in both standard and inverse inductive logics these statements are *inductively* (probabilistically) dependent, but in random inductive logic they are inductively independent.

Thus we see that axioms [24], [24^i] and [24^r] assign unconditional probabilities to possible universes in such a way that instances of one property ψ accompanying another property ϕ raise, lower, or leave unchanged, respectively, the probability that ψ will accompany the next instance of ϕ. It is for this reason that these axioms are taken as definitive of standard, inverse, and random inductive logic for a model universe. In the next subsection we look at these axioms from the point of view of uniformity.

This shows how standard, inverse, and random inductive logic are defined for finite models. It should be pointed out that these definitions actually cover finite models that include relations as well as monadic properties. Each of the axioms [24], [24^i], [24^r] determines a probability assignment to the universe descriptions of such an enriched model, and each of these assignments then determines an inductive logic for the model.

Two further matters deserve comment. The first concerns the assignment of zero probability to a universe description. As was noted in the discussion of Bayes' theorem, a statement with zero probability can never be confirmed, that is, its posterior probability will always be zero. This fact suggests the question: Should we require that every universe description be assigned a positive probability so that it will be confirmable at least in principle? In using inductive logic, we have relatively direct information about only a small fragment of the actual universe, and we make probabilistic inferences from this information to conclusions about the nonobserved portion of the actual universe and to certain pervasive features of the whole universe. Why should we exclude any logical possibility by this prior probability assignment?

While this argument has considerable force, it is not compelling. It is obviously beyond man's capacity to learn *everything* about the actual universe. The most he can do is say that a certain partial description is true of the actual universe. An inductive logic must make this epistemologically possible, but to do so it need not assign a positive probability to every universe description (see further pp. 593, 631).

The second comment concerns the relation of modal logic to inductive logic. They have some important features in common. Both deal with possible worlds, and both restrict exchange to logical equivalents (sec. 2.3.1). Modal logic treats the deductive relations of statements about possible worlds, while inductive logic treats assignments of probability to possible worlds.

3.2.3 Induction and statistical uniformity

Standard, inverse, and random inductive logic differ on the rule of induction by simple enumeration. On standard logic the repeated coincidence of two properties increases the probability that one of the properties will be accompanied by the other in the future. But on inverse logic increased repetition decreases the probability of the prediction, while on random logic it has no effect.

It is clear from axioms [24], [24^i], and [24^r] that these differences are connected to the role played by the isomorphism measure $\mathbf{I}(u)$ in assigning probabilities to universes. The isomorphism measure $\mathbf{I}(u)$ is in turn related to statistical uniformity. A universe in which all individuals have the same properties (a rather dull universe!) is more uniform and regular (has less variety and irregularity) than a universe in which individuals differ. The former universe has the minimal isomorphism measure of one, while the latter universe has a larger isomorphism measure. This suggests that the isomorphism measure $\mathbf{I}(u)$ is also a measure of the irregularity of u, a suggestion confirmed by the close connection between $\mathbf{I}(u)$ and the notion of entropy in classical thermodynamics. Let us examine this connection.

Two universe descriptions were defined to be isomorphic when one could be transformed into the other by a succession of interchanges of individual constants. Then clearly, two universe descriptions are isomorphic if and only if they agree on the number of individuals said to be in each individual state. A distribution description is a disjunction of all the universe descriptions that are isomorphic to one another; a distribution description says of each individual state how many individuals in the universe are in that state. For example, the distribution description "$SaWaSb\overline{Wb} \vee Sa\overline{Wa}SbWb$" says that one individual is a white swan and the other is a nonwhite swan. Further, let us extend the isomorphism measure $\mathbf{I}$ to cover a distribution description d; $\mathbf{I}'(d)$ is the isomorphism measure of any disjunct of d, that is, the number of disjuncts of d. For example, $\mathbf{I}'(SaWaSb\overline{Wb} \vee Sa\overline{Wa}SbWb) = 2$.

Now, a gas is composed of particles. At each moment of time a particle is in one of many possible particle states (sometimes called "elements of state space"). A description giving the particle state of every particle of the gas at a given time gives the "complexion" or "microscopic state" of the gas as a whole at that time. A "macroscopic state" tells how many particles are in each particle state. Two complexions belong to the same macroscopic state if and only if they agree on the number of individuals said to be in each particle state. The "thermodynamic probability" ("configuration number") **W**(*s*) of a macroscopic state *s* is the number of complexions

TABLE 11

PARALLELISM BETWEEN SOME CONCEPTS OF CLASSICAL THERMODYNAMICS AND SOME CONCEPTS OF INDUCTIVE LOGIC

	Gas	Model 𝔐-𝔏
Correlation of primitive terms	Particle Particle state, or element of state space Complexion, or microscopic state Macroscopic state Two complexions belonging to the same macroscopic state	Individual Individual state Universe description Distribution description Two universe descriptions belonging to the same distribution description, i.e., two universe descriptions being isomorphic
Correlation of entropy and irregularity	Thermodynamic probability ***W***(*s*) (or configuration number) of a macroscopic state *s* Entropy Reciprocal of entropy	Isomorphism measure ***I***′(***d***) of a distribution description ***d*** Irregularity Uniformity
Correlation of second law of thermodynamics and random inductive logic	Each microscopic state has the same prior probability The macroscopic state of highest entropy is the most probable Second law of thermodynamics	Each universe description has the same prior probability The distribution description of greatest irregularity is the most probable Random inductive logic

belonging to the macroscopic state *s*. These definitions make obvious the close parallelism between the concepts used in gas theory (classical thermodynamics) and the concepts introduced in this section. This parallelism is displayed in Table 11.

In random inductive logic each universe description is assigned the same unconditional probability. Similarly, classical thermodynamics assigns the same probability to each microscopic state of a gas. Hence the thermodynamic probability **W**(*s*) has the following physical significance: It is proportional to the probability of this state *s* actually occurring. This result leads directly to the famous second law of thermodynamics: The macroscopic state of maximum entropy is the most probable macroscopic state of a gas. The entropy $\mathbf{E}(s)$ of a macroscopic state s is defined to be proportional to the logarithm of the thermodynamic probability $\mathbf{W}(s)$, except for an additive constant; that is,

$$\mathbf{E}(s) = c_1 \log \mathbf{W}(s) + c_2 \quad ,$$

where c_1 and c_2 are constants. Clearly, the macroscopic state s_1 that has the highest thermodynamic probability (and is the most likely to occur) will have the highest entropy. Hence an assignment of the same probability to every microscopic state of a gas yields the law: The macroscopic state of maximum entropy is the most probable macroscopic state.*

Thus the thermodynamic probability $\mathbf{W}(s)$ parallels the isomorphism measure $\mathbf{I}'(d)$. It is therefore natural to define the *entropy* of a distribution description in exactly the same way the entropy of a macroscopic state is defined:

$$\mathbf{E}(d) = c_3 \log \mathbf{I}'(d) + c_4 \quad .$$

Entropy measures randomness, disorder, and irregularity. Since uniformity is the opposite of irregularity, uniformity may be measured by the reciprocal of entropy $[\mathbf{E}(d)]^{-1}$, provided the constants c_3 and c_4 are chosen to avoid division by zero. Moreover, the isomorphism measure of a distribution description is by definition equal to the isomorphism measure of each universe description that is a disjunct of it, so it is natural to define the entropy of a universe description by

$$\mathbf{E}(u) = c_3 \log \mathbf{I}(u) + c_4 \quad .$$

It follows that for any universe description u, $\mathbf{E}(u)$ measures its irregularity while $[\mathbf{E}(u)]^{-1}$ measures its *statistical uniformity*. This measure is, of course, relative to a particular model $\mathfrak{M}$-$\mathfrak{L}$; no comparison is intended between universe descriptions of different models.

Looked at in this light, standard inductive logic (axiom [24]) assigns higher probabilities to uniform universes than to irregular ones, while inverse inductive logic (axiom [24^{i}]) does the reverse. Random inductive logic (axiom [24^{r}]) assigns equal probabilities to all possible universes, ignoring their uniformity or irregularity. These three ways of treating uniformity are expressed by the conditions

[25] $\{\mathbf{I}(u_1) > \mathbf{I}(u_2)\} \supset \{\mathbf{P}(u_1) < \mathbf{P}(u_2)\}$

* We have analyzed the equilibrium state of a gas. The situation is more complicated when two different gas systems are mixed. Suppose, for example, two chambers containing gases at different temperatures are separated by a removable partition. The state of the whole system "immediately after" the partition is withdrawn will not have the probability characteristics of random inductive logic. But by the second law of thermodynamics, the succession of microscopic states of the system tends to an equilibrium state that does have the probability characteristics of random inductive logic.

See, for example, Page, *Introduction to Theoretical Physics*, pp. 288-92 and 317-24.

[25^{i}] $\{\mathbf{I}(u_1) > \mathbf{I}(u_2)\} \supset \{\mathbf{P}(u_1) > \mathbf{P}(u_2)\}$

[25^{r}] $\mathbf{P}(u_1) = \mathbf{P}(u_2)$ for all u_1, u_2.

The bearing of each of these conditions on the rule of induction by simple enumeration is illustrated in the following example.

Consider a model with one property Q and three individuals a, b, c. By symmetry considerations, $\mathbf{P}(Qb) = 1/2$ in all three logics. Now consider $\mathbf{P}(Qb, Qa)$, that is, the ratio $\mathbf{P}(QaQb)/\mathbf{P}(Qa)$. This reduces, by [$24^{r}$], to the ratio: (the number of universe descriptions in which "$QaQb$" is true) $\div$ (the number of universe descriptions in which "Qa" is true). This ratio equals one-half, since for each universe in which "$QaQb$" is true there are two with "Qa" true (one in which "Qb" is true and one in which "Qb" is false). By comparison, according to axiom [24], $\mathbf{P}(Qb, Qa)$ is greater than one-half, because, on the average, universes in which "$QaQb$" is true are more uniform (and hence by [24] more likely) than universes in which "Qa" is true. Conversely, by axiom [24^{i}], $\mathbf{P}(Qb, Qa)$ is less than one-half; for, on the average, universes in which "Qa" is true are more irregular (and hence by [24^{i}] more probable) than universes in which "$QaQb$" is true. These considerations show that in this model assigning higher probabilities to uniform universes than to irregular ones leads to the rule of induction by simple enumeration.

We see from the foregoing that statistical uniformity plays an essential role in the three inductive logics. We have called it "statistical" uniformity to contrast it with a kind of causal uniformity to be studied later (sec. 9.3.1; see also sec. 9.4.3, Determinism and randomness).

The statistics of classical thermodynamics is sometimes called Maxwell-Boltzmann statistics. It may be contrasted with two statistics of quantum mechanics: Bose-Einstein statistics and Fermi-Dirac statistics. The analogy between Maxwell-Boltzmann statistics and random inductive logic is paralleled by an analogy between Bose-Einstein statistics and standard inductive logic and also by an analogy between Fermi-Dirac statistics and inverse inductive logic. We discuss these analogies later in connection with empirical probability (sec. 8.3.1).

While there are these important similarities between the concepts of classical thermodynamics and the concepts of inductive logics for model universes and languages, there is also a very important difference. In thermodynamics, probabilities are assigned to the microscopic states of a gas on the basis of empirical information about the gas, so that the second law of thermodynamics is an empirical truth. In contrast, the unconditional probabilities assigned to universe descriptions are assigned prior to any empirical information. Since empirical evidence is evaluated by means of an inductive logic, and since an inductive logic is based on an assignment of unconditional probabilities to universe descriptions, it would seem to be circular to base an assignment of unconditional probabilities to universe descriptions on empirical evidence. We shall discuss this point at length in the next section (Hume's Thesis on the Justification of Induction), after first relating standard and random inductive logic to Bayes' method of finding the unknown probability of a mixture of independent processes.

3.2.4 Inductive logics and Bayes' method

There are close similarities between some of the probabilistic systems presented in this section and those developed in the last chapter. Random inductive logic treats the events of a model $\mathfrak{M}$-$\mathfrak{L}$ as an independent sequence. In both standard inductive logic and Bayes' method of finding an unknown probability, repeated success has a positive effect. We will show now that from a formal point of view an inductive logic and a probability assignment to a process are fundamentally the same and also that standard inductive logic is a special case of Bayes' method.

Inductive logics were defined for models $\mathfrak{M}$-$\mathfrak{L}$. Each model has n monadic properties and hence 2^n individual states. Let $\kappa = 2^n$, and let the individual states be $\phi_1, \phi_2, \ldots, \phi_\kappa$. Order the individuals of the model so they will constitute a finite or infinite sequence $x_1, x_2, x_3, \ldots$. If the model has a finite number (m) of individuals, a universe description is equivalent to a sequence of the form $\phi x_1, \phi x_2, \ldots, \phi x_m$, with each ϕ being $\phi_1, \phi_2, \ldots,$ or ϕ_κ. If the model has an infinite number of individuals, then a particular outcome or universe is described by a succession of universe descriptions equivalent to an infinite sequence of the form $\phi x_1, \phi x_2, \phi x_3, \ldots$, with each ϕ being $\phi_1, \phi_2, \ldots,$ or ϕ_κ. An inductive logic is thus concerned with a process in a somewhat more general sense than was considered in the last chapter: each individual x_l ($l = 1, 2, 3, \ldots$) can have any of κ properties $\phi_1, \phi_2, \phi_3, \ldots, \phi_\kappa$, whereas earlier an individual event of a process had just one of two properties ϕ and $\bar{\phi}$ (cf. pp. 58, 503–4).

Let us extend our notion of *process* to cover the multistate case. Our original definition of an independent process is easily extended to multistate processes, as is the notion of a mixture of independent processes. Where many states are allowed, a process $\phi x_1, \phi x_2, \phi x_3, \ldots$ and a model $\mathfrak{M}$ are basically the same. The number of states of a model is always a power of two, the model has a designated actual universe while a process does not, and the individuals of a model are not ordered while those of a process are, but these differences are not crucial in the present context.

An inductive logic assigns a probability to every truth-function about the events of a model. Similarly, to say that a process is an independent process in which each state $\phi_1, \phi_2, \ldots, \phi_\kappa$ has a certain designated probability is to assign a probability to every truth-function of the events of that process. The completeness of these assignments suggests the following definition.

Let $\phi x_1, \phi x_2, \phi x_3, \ldots$ be a sequence of events, finite or infinite, with each occurrence of ϕ being $\phi_1, \phi_2, \ldots,$ or ϕ_κ. Let $\mathcal{R}$ be a truth-function of a finite number of the events $\phi x_1, \phi x_2, \phi x_3, \ldots$. An assignment of a probability to each $\mathcal{R}$ conditional on $\mathcal{G}$ constitutes a **complete probability assignment to the process $\phi x_1, \phi x_2, \phi x_3, \ldots$ on condition $\mathcal{G}$**. In other words, a complete probability assignment to the process $\phi x_1, \phi x_2, \phi x_3, \ldots$ is defined by a function $\mathbf{P}(\mathcal{R}, \mathcal{G})$ that, for given $\mathcal{G}$, assigns a real number to each truth-function $\mathcal{R}$ of a finite number of the events $\phi x_1, \phi x_2, \phi x_3, \ldots$ and satisfies the axioms for unconditional probability of Section 2.6.

Any property ψ of an individual can be expressed as a disjunction of individual states. Let $\psi_1, \psi_2, \ldots, \psi_q$ be mutually exclusive and jointly exhaustive disjunctions of $\phi_1, \phi_2, \ldots, \phi_\kappa$. Then a complete probability assignment to the basic process $\phi x_1, \phi x_2, \phi x_3, \ldots$ (where each occurrence of ϕ is $\phi_1, \phi_2, \ldots,$ or ϕ_κ) yields a complete probability assignment to the derived process $\psi x_1, \psi x_2, \psi x_3, \ldots$ (where each occurrence of ψ is $\psi_1, \psi_2, \ldots,$ or ψ_q).

It is clear that an inductive logic for a process is a complete probability assignment for that process. To say that a process is an independent process with specified probabilities for each state is to make a complete probability assignment to the process. The concept of a mixture of independent processes does not define a complete probability assignment, however, for that concept leaves open the assignment of prior probabilities to the alternatives. But the concept of a mixture of independent processes of specified probabilities together with an assignment of prior probabilities to the alternatives defines a complete probability assignment.

The notion of a complete probability assignment to a process is defined relative to a condition $\mathcal{G}$. The condition is not used in an inductive logic, since an assignment to possible universes is unconditional or absolutely prior. The condition does play an important role in the analysis of empirical probability (chap. 8).

A complete probability assignment to an infinite process or model determines a complete probability assignment to every subprocess or submodel. The converse is not the case, since the probability assignments to overlapping subprocesses or submodels may not agree. The inductive logics of Section 3.2.2 were defined for finite models only. However, inductive logics can be defined for infinite models by treating them as infinite sequences of nested finite models.

Let $\phi x_1, \phi x_2, \phi x_3, \ldots$ be an infinite process with each ϕ being $\phi_1, \phi_2, \ldots, \phi_\kappa$. Let $\mathfrak{M}_i$ be the initial subprocess containing the individuals $x_1, x_2, \ldots, x_i$. Consider any rule that defines an inductive logic for each $\mathfrak{M}_i$; such a rule determines a complete probability assignment $\mathcal{A}_i$ for each $\mathfrak{M}_i$. Now, for each $i > j$, the process $\mathfrak{M}_i$ contains the process $\mathfrak{M}_j$, and so the assignment $\mathcal{A}_i$ determines a complete probability assignment for $\mathfrak{M}_j$; call this derived assignment $\mathcal{A}_j^i$. There are two cases of interest. The assignments $\mathcal{A}_j^i$ and $\mathcal{A}_j$ may be the same, that is, the probability of every statement about the individuals $x_1, x_2, x_3, \ldots, x_j$ is the same in both assignments. Alternatively, the assignments $\mathcal{A}_j^i$ and $\mathcal{A}_j$ may be different, i.e., at least one statement about model $\mathfrak{M}_j$ is assigned different probabilities by $\mathcal{A}_j^i$ and $\mathcal{A}_j$. If for every j, the assignments $\mathcal{A}_j^i$ and $\mathcal{A}_j$ are the same for all i such that $i > j$ $(i, j = 1, 2, 3, \ldots)$, then the given rule determines a complete probability assignment to the infinite process $\phi x_1, \phi x_2, \phi x_3, \ldots$.

It is evident from the essential identity of random inductive logic and an independent process that random inductive logic is defined for infinite as well as finite models. Carnap has shown that standard inductive logic also determines a complete probability assignment for infinite models.* In other words, for both standard and random inductive logic, the probability of a statement in a given model is unchanged when more individuals and proper names (but not more properties or predicates) are added to that model. In contrast, inverse inductive logic does not give a complete probability assignment for the infinite process $\phi x_1, \phi x_2, \ldots$, as the following example shows. Apply inverse inductive logic (axiom [24^{i}]) to models with two individual states "B" and "$\bar{B}$." The probability $\mathbf{P}(Bx_1Bx_2)$ equals 1/6 in the model with two individuals but 1/5 in a model with three individuals. Thus standard and random inductive logic are defined for both finite and infinite models, whereas inverse inductive logic is defined only for finite models.

It will be fruitful to study the standard inductive logic of an infinite model and to relate it to similar inductive logics for the same model. It was shown in Section 3.2.3 that, for any finite submodel, standard inductive logic assigns higher probabilities to uniform universe descriptions than to irregular ones. Obviously, there are many inductive logics favoring uniformity. Carnap has constructed a continuum of inductive logics of this sort, which is of interest because of its organizing principle and its relation to Bayes' method of finding an unknown probability.† We will describe the main features of this continuum without proofs.

Consider an infinite model $\phi x_1, \phi x_2, \phi x_3, \ldots$. Let n be the number of monadic predicates of the model, so that there are 2^n individual states. Let $\kappa = 2^n$. Any property ψ can be expressed as a disjunction of individual states; let ω be the number of disjuncts of this disjunction. The ratio ω/κ is called the *relative width* of ψ; it runs from zero (for a contradictory property)

* *The Continuum of Inductive Methods,* pp. 13 and 45. See also *Logical Foundations of Probability,* p. 291.

† *The Continuum of Inductive Logics.* See p. 30 for formula [A], below.

to one (for a tautological property). For a model with two properties S and W, there are four individual states, and so $\kappa = 4$. $Sx \leftrightarrow (SxWx \vee Sx\overline{Wx})$, and so $\omega = 2$ for the property S.

Carnap's continuum of inductive logics is defined by the recursive rule,

$$[A](1) \quad \mathbf{P}(\psi x_i) = \frac{\omega}{\kappa} \qquad \text{for } i = 1, 2, 3, \ldots$$

$$(2) \quad \mathbf{P}[\psi x_i, \sigma_L(\psi) = s/L] = \frac{s}{L}\left(\frac{L}{L+\lambda}\right) + \frac{\omega}{\kappa}\left(\frac{\lambda}{L+\lambda}\right) \qquad \text{for } i > L,$$

where λ is any non-negative real number.* We shall see later how the continuum of inductive logics is generated by varying the parameter λ.

To obtain an example of this rule, let $\lambda = 2$, $\kappa = 2$, and let ψ be either of the two individual states F or $\bar{F}$. Rule [A] reduces to

$$\left.\begin{aligned} &[A^*](1) \quad \mathbf{P}(\psi x_i) = \tfrac{1}{2} \\ &(2) \quad \mathbf{P}[\psi x_i, \sigma_L(\psi) = s/L] = \frac{s+1}{L+2} \qquad \text{for } i > L \end{aligned}\right\} \psi \text{ is either } F \text{ or } \bar{F}.$$

Consider in turn the submodels

Fx_1

Fx_1, Fx_2

Fx_1, Fx_2, Fx_3

etc.

The probability of each universe description of each of these finite models can be calculated by the general multiplication theorem and the repeated use of rule [A*]. Thus the probabilities for the sub-model Fx_1, Fx_2, Fx_3, are given by:

$$\begin{aligned} \mathbf{P}[Fx_1Fx_2Fx_3) &= \mathbf{P}(Fx_1)\mathbf{P}(Fx_2, Fx_1)\mathbf{P}(Fx_3, Fx_1Fx_2) \\ &= \mathbf{P}(Fx_1)\mathbf{P}[Fx_2, \sigma_1(F) = 1]\mathbf{P}(Fx_3, \sigma_2(F) = 1] = 1/4 \\ \mathbf{P}(\overline{Fx_1}Fx_2Fx_3) &= \mathbf{P}(\overline{Fx_1})\mathbf{P}[Fx_2, \sigma_1(F) = 0]\mathbf{P}[Fx_3, \sigma_2(F) = 1/2] = 1/12 \\ \mathbf{P}(Fx_1\overline{Fx_2}Fx_3) &= \mathbf{P}(Fx_1)\mathbf{P}[\overline{Fx_2}, \sigma_1(F) = 1]\mathbf{P}[Fx_3, \sigma_2(F) = 1/2] = 1/12 \end{aligned}$$

etc.

This assignment turns out to be that of standard inductive logic.

* More strictly, the recursive definition should give the unconditional probability of the first event x_1 and the conditional probability of the "next" event x_{L+1}:

$$\mathbf{P}(\psi x_1) = \frac{\omega}{\kappa}$$

$$\mathbf{P}[\psi x_{L+1}, \sigma_L(\psi) = s/L] = \frac{s}{L}\left(\frac{L}{L+\lambda}\right) + \frac{\omega}{\kappa}\left(\frac{\lambda}{L+\lambda}\right).$$

Rule [A] follows from this definition.

The continuum of inductive logics is best viewed relative to an infinite process with some fixed number of individual states (κ). Since formula [A] is of interest only when ψ is empirical, we restrict ω by the condition $0 < \omega < \kappa$. By setting λ equal to a non-negative real number we define a particular inductive logic of the continuum.

The inductive logics of the continuum are ordered according to the relative role played by empirical data and prior probability in induction by simple enumeration. To see how these factors operate, consider a particular inductive logic (that is, a fixed value of λ). The right-hand side of formula [A](2) is now best thought of as a sum of the two factors s/L and ω/κ, combined in the proportion L to λ. The factor s/L is the observed relative frequency, and the factor ω/κ is the relative width of the predicate ψ. The observed relative frequency is clearly an "empirical factor." The relative width is based on the logical structure of the model and hence is fixed in advance of any observations. As is evident from [A](1), the relative width of ψ gives the prior probability of ψx_i. For this reason we will call ω/κ the "prior probability factor."

Let us observe how the conditional probability $\mathbf{P}[\psi x_i, \sigma_L(\psi) = s/L]$ changes as the length L of the experiment increases. Before the experiment begins, $\mathbf{P}(\psi x_i) = \omega/\kappa$. As L increases, $\mathbf{P}[\psi x_i, \sigma_L(\psi) = s/L]$ moves from ω/κ towards the empirical factor s/L, approaching it in the limit:

$$\lim_{L\to\infty} \mathbf{P}[\psi x_i, \sigma_L(\psi) = s/L] = s/L \qquad \text{for } i > L\,.$$

Thus the predicted probability depends initially on the prior probability factor, then on both factors, and ultimately on the empirical factor. This behavior of the predicted probability is similar to its behavior when Bayes' method of finding an unknown probability is applied to a mixture of independent processes. We shall see the reason for this later in the current section.

Rule [A] is closely related to the rule of induction by simple enumeration introduced in the first section of this chapter and subsequently modeled by means of standard inductive logic. The earlier rule treated a correlation of two properties, whereas rule [A] treats only a single property ψ. Except for this, the earlier rule is a special case of rule [A], the case in which there are no counterinstances ($s = L$). When $s = L$, rule [A] reduces to

$$\text{[B](1)} \quad \mathbf{P}(\psi x_i) = \frac{\omega}{\kappa}$$

$$\text{(2)} \quad \mathbf{P}[\psi x_i, \sigma_L(\psi) = 1] = \frac{L}{L+\lambda} + \frac{\omega}{\kappa}\left(\frac{\lambda}{L+\lambda}\right) \qquad \text{for } i > L$$

Hence

$$\lim_{L\to\infty} \mathbf{P}[\psi x_i, \sigma_L(\psi) = 1] = 1 \qquad .$$

Thus the probability of ψx_i tends to unity as the number of confirming instances (L) tends to infinity, just as in the earlier version of induction by simple enumeration.

Let us now compare different inductive logics of Carnap's continuum. For positive L, the probability of ψx_i depends on both the empirical factor s/L and the prior probability factor ω/κ, the relative contribution of these two factors depending on the ratio L to λ. To compare the different inductive logics of the continuum, imagine L fixed at some positive value and vary λ.

The logic defined by $\lambda = \kappa$ is an interesting representative of the continuum and, as it turns out, is one we have already studied. For $\lambda = \kappa$, rule [A] becomes

$$[A_\kappa](1)\quad \mathbf{P}(\psi x_i) = \frac{\omega}{\kappa}$$

$$(2)\quad \mathbf{P}[\psi x_i, \sigma_L(\psi) = s/L] = \frac{s + \omega}{L + \kappa} \qquad \text{for } i > L\,.$$

This rule actually defines standard inductive logic for the models $\mathfrak{M}$-$\mathfrak{L}$. That is, rule [A_κ] is equivalent to axiom [24] (p. 110).

As the value of λ is increased from κ, the prior probability factor becomes more important (and the empirical probability factor less important) in determining the conditional probability $\mathbf{P}[\psi x_i, \sigma_L(\psi) = s/L]$. As λ goes to infinity, rule [A] approaches random inductive logic as a limit.

$$[A_\infty](1)\quad \mathbf{P}(\psi x_i) = \frac{\omega}{\kappa}$$

$$(2)\quad \mathbf{P}[\psi x_i, \sigma_L(\psi) = s/L] = \frac{\omega}{\kappa} \qquad \text{for } i > L\,.$$

The empirical factor has now disappeared, so that the prediction of an event is independent of the outcome of preceding events. Each individual state $\phi_1, \phi_2, \ldots, \phi_\kappa$ has a probability of $1/\kappa$. Note that random inductive logic is not in the continuum, but is only a limit point of it (as λ goes to infinity).

Conversely, as the value of λ is decreased from κ the empirical probability factor becomes more important and the prior probability factor less important. For $\lambda = 0$, [A] becomes

$$[A_0](1)\quad \mathbf{P}(\psi x_i) = \frac{\omega}{\kappa}$$

$$(2)\quad \mathbf{P}[\psi x_i, \sigma_L(\psi) = s/L] = s/L \qquad \text{for } i > L\,.$$

Here the empirical factor completely dominates the conditional probability $\mathbf{P}[\psi x_i, \sigma_L(\psi) = s/L]$ and the prior probability factor makes no contribution. The second part of this rule {[A_0](2)} simply extrapolates the observed relative frequency and is closely related to the "straight rule of induction" of the frequency theory of probability (p. 153). Note that by itself $[A_0](2)$ makes no prediction prior to an experiment, and hence it does not define a complete probability assignment or an inductive logic.

Let us pause a moment to summarize the main features of Carnap's continuum of inductive logics. For each infinite process or model, rule [A] defines a continuum of inductive logics obtained by varying λ over the non-negative real numbers. Each inductive logic of the continuum predicts future events in an infinite model by a rule of induction by simple enumeration. An initial prediction is given by a prior probability factor; after an outcome of the process is observed, the predicted probability depends also on an empirical factor, the observed relative frequency; in the long run the predicted probability approaches the observed relative frequency as a limit. The logics of the continuum differ from each other with respect to the relative weights they assign to the two factors. As λ goes from zero to infinity, the following change takes place. At $\lambda = 0$, the conditional probability $\mathbf{P}[\psi x_i, \sigma_L(\psi) = s/L]$ depends entirely on the empirical factor s/L. For positive λ, this conditional probability depends on both factors. As λ increases, the prior probability factor becomes more important and the empirical factor less important. The value $\lambda = \kappa$ gives standard inductive logic. In the limit, as λ goes to infinity, the conditional probability $\mathbf{P}[\psi x_i, \sigma_L(\psi) = s/L]$ depends entirely on the prior probability factor; this is random inductive logic.

Because our models $\mathfrak{M}$-$\mathfrak{L}$ are such simple models of reality, it is inappropriate to consider whether the particular value of $\lambda = \kappa$ gives the best model of standard inductive logic as it is employed by the practicing scientist (sec. 3.1), or some other value of λ is better. We are interested mainly in the qualitative behavior of induction by simple enumeration, not in the exact rate at which the predicted probability converges to the observed relative frequency. For our purposes, the inductive logic defined by rule $[A_\kappa]$ gives a convenient formulation of the rule of induction by simple enumeration, and so we have chosen it to represent the continuum of inductive logics in our philosophical discussion.

We turn now to the similarity noted a few paragraphs back between the inductive logics of Carnap's continuum and Bayes' method of finding the unknown probability of a mixture of independent processes (sec. 2.5.3). The qualitative behavior of the predicted probability $\mathbf{P}[\psi x_i, \sigma_L(\psi) = s/L]$ is the same in both cases, with the prior probability assignment in Bayes' method playing the role of the prior probability factor in the inductive logics. Moreover, an independent process is a limiting case of a mixture of independent processes, just as random inductive logic is a limit point of the continuum of inductive logics. This suggests that an inductive logic of the continuum is equivalent to a complete probability assignment of some mixture of independent processes. It follows from a theorem of de Finetti that this is in fact the case.

De Finetti's theorem is about complete probability assignments to infinite processes. Before stating this theorem we need to extend the scope of our concept of "mixture of independent processes" and define a new concept of "exchangeability." Our original definition of "mixture of independent processes" limited the possible values of the unknown probability to the finite set of values $\alpha_1, \alpha_2, \ldots, \alpha_N$ (sec. 2.5.2). Let us now generalize the concept of ***mixture of independent processes*** so that the unknown probability α can be any real number between zero and one inclusive. The corresponding distribution of prior probabilities is a continuous distribution.

A complete probability assignment to a finite or infinite model or process $\phi x_1, \phi x_2, \ldots$ is *exchangeable* if and only if it assigns equal probabilities to isomorphic truth-functions of the formulas "ϕx_1," "ϕx_2," .... Intuitively, exchangeability means that the probability of a formula does not depend on what particular individuals that formula is about. Since any truth-functional formula can be expressed as a disjunction of universe descriptions (disjunctive normal form), an inductive logic that assigns equal probabilities to isomorphic universe descriptions assigns equal probabilities to isomorphic truth functions, and is exchangeable. In symbols,

$$\text{If } (u_1)(u_2)[u_1\mathbf{I}u_2 \supset \mathbf{P}(u_1) = \mathbf{P}(u_2)], \text{ then}$$
$$(\Phi)(\Psi)[\Phi\mathbf{I}\Psi \supset \mathbf{P}(\Phi) = \mathbf{P}(\Psi)] \qquad ,$$

where u_1 and u_2 range over the universe descriptions, and Φ and Ψ range over the truth-functions, of the model. It is clear from axioms [24], [24^i], and [24^r] (pp. 110–12) that standard, inverse, and random inductive logics all assign equal probabilities to isomorphic universe descriptions. It is in fact the case that every inductive logic of Carnap's continuum is exchangeable. Thus all these inductive logics are exchangeable: standard, inverse, random, and every logic of the continuum of inductive logics.

An independent process of probability α is also exchangeable, for the probability of a truth-functional statement about the process does not depend on which individuals are referred to in that statement. Likewise, a mixture of independent processes together with a prior probability assignment is exchangeable. To see this, consider any two isomorphic truth-functions about the process. They will have the same probability in each of the independent processes of which the mixture is composed, and hence they will have the same probability in the mixture itself.

An example of a complete probability assignment that is not exchangeable is provided by a Markov chain. A *Markov chain* is a finite or infinite process $\phi x_1, \phi x_2, \phi x_3, \ldots$ in which the probability of ϕx_{i+1} depends on ϕx_i but not directly on earlier terms of the sequence. Consider, for example, a two-state Markov chain $Sx_1, Sx_2, Sx_3, \ldots$ defined by the equations

$$\mathbf{P}(Sx_1) = .5$$

$$\mathbf{P}(Sx_{i+1}, Sx_i) = .9 \qquad \mathbf{P}(Sx_{i+1}, Sx_iQ_i) = .9$$

$$\mathbf{P}(Sx_{i+1}, \overline{Sx_i}) = .1 \qquad \mathbf{P}(Sx_{i+1}, \overline{Sx_i}Q_i) = .1 \quad ,$$

where $i = 1, 2, 3, \ldots$ and Q_i is any noncontradictory truth-function of Sx_1, $Sx_2, \ldots, Sx_{i-1}$ (see sec. 8.3.1). In this Markov chain the following two isomorphic truth-functions have different probabilities:

$$\mathbf{P}(Sx_1\overline{Sx_2}\overline{Sx_3}) = (.5)(.1)(.9) = .045$$

$$\mathbf{P}(\overline{Sx_1}Sx_2\overline{Sx_3}) = (.5)(.1)(.1) = .005 \quad .$$

It is clear from this example that the complete probability assignment of a Markov chain is not exchangeable.

With this background we can now state *de Finetti's theorem* about complete probability assignments to infinite processes:

> A complete probability assignment to an *infinite* process is exchangeable if and only if that process is a mixture of independent processes.

The "if" clause of this theorem is self-evident. The proof of the "only if" clause requires mathematical tools beyond the scope of the present work.*

We conclude this section by using de Finetti's theorem to relate various inductive logics to mixtures of independent processes. De Finetti's theorem applies directly to Carnap's continuum of inductive logics. These logics were defined for infinite processes, so that each logic of the continuum defines a complete probability assignment to an infinite process. Moreover, this assignment is exchangeable. By de Finetti's theorem, an inductive logic of the continuum is equivalent to the complete probability assignment of some mixture of independent processes. In short, every inductive logic of the continuum of inductive logics, including standard inductive logic, is a mixture of independent processes. Accordingly, Bayes' method of finding an unknown probability and the confirmation theorem apply to every inductive logic of the continuum, and the rule of induction by simple enumeration makes the same probabilistic predictions of future events as does Bayes' method.

Thus by de Finetti's theorem, an inductive logic of the continuum is formally or mathematically equivalent to a mixture of independent processes. Nevertheless, the way we are interpreting an inductive logic in the present chapter is quite different from the way we applied the notion of a mixture of independent processes in the last chapter. In the first place, inductive

* De Finetti, "La Prévision: ses lois logiques, ses sources subjectives," chap. 4. Savage, *The Foundations of Statistics*, p. 53. The term "exchangeable" is taken from the English translation of de Finetti's article. The original French article uses "équivalent," while Savage uses "symmetric."

logics are defined for models of the whole universe, while the concept of "mixture of independent processes" was applied to empirical or inferential processes taking place within the universe. Second, the inferential objectives differ in the two cases. An inductive logic is used to make probabilistic predictions about individual events of the universe. Bayes' method of finding an unknown probability is also used for this purpose, but its primary use is to find the unknown probability of a statistical process. When using an inductive logic of Carnap's continuum, we are not interested in the unknown probability of the corresponding mixture of independent processes.

Let us next apply de Finetti's theorem to inverse inductive logic. Standard inductive logic was introduced as a representative of those logics that have a rule of induction by simple enumeration, under which the predicted probability of the next event tends toward the observed relative frequency (e.g., rule [A_κ]). Similarly, inverse inductive logic was introduced as a representation of those logics that have a contrary rule: The predicted probability of the next event tends away from the observed relative frequency. Let us call this the "anti-enumeration rule." Now by de Finetti's theorem, if an inductive logic is (1) exchangeable and (2) defined for an infinite process, then it is a mixture of independent processes. By the confirmation theorem, in a mixture of independent processes the predicted probability of the next event tends toward the observed relative frequency, and the rule of induction by simple enumeration holds. Consequently, in an exchangeable inductive logic for an infinite model the anti-enumeration rule cannot hold. Thus inverse logic and the anti-enumeration rule are limited to finite models, whereas standard inductive logic and the rule of induction by simple enumeration are applicable to both finite and infinite models.

This difference seems rooted in the way these inductive logics treat statistical uniformity (see sec. 3.2.3). I offer some intuitive reflections on the relation of uniformity to enumerative induction. Consider only inductive logics satisfying the following condition for each finite submodel:

[C] $\{\mathbf{I}(u_1) = \mathbf{I}(u_2)\} \supset \{\mathbf{P}(u_1) = \mathbf{P}(u_2)\}$.

This condition is satisfied by all the inductive logics of Carnap's continuum as well as by inverse and random inductive logic. Recall that for a given submodel, the irregularity of a universe description varies directly (and its uniformity varies inversely) as its isomorphism measure. Every inductive logic of Carnap's continuum favors uniform universes, and so satisfies the condition

[25] $\{\mathbf{I}(u_1) > \mathbf{I}(u_2)\} \supset \{\mathbf{P}(u_1) < \mathbf{P}(u_2)\}$.

Every mixture of independent processes with a prior probability assignment satisfies [25], except for the limiting case of a single independent process (random inductive logic), which satisfies

$$[25^r] \quad \mathbf{I}(u_1) = \mathbf{I}(u_2) \qquad \text{for all } u_1, u_2.$$

Every inductive logic in which the anti-enumeration rule holds favors irregular universes, and so satisfies the condition

$$[25^i) \quad \{\mathbf{I}(u_1) > \mathbf{I}(u_2)\} \supset \{\mathbf{P}(u_1) > \mathbf{P}(u_2)\} \quad .$$

Moreover, among all inductive logics satisfying condition [C], condition $[25^i]$ is satisfied if and only if the anti-enumeration rule holds. There are inductive logics for infinite models that satisfy [25] and $[25^r]$, but no inductive logics for infinite models that satisfy $[25^i]$.

This last difference seems connected to uniformity and the law of large numbers in the following intuitive way. In an inductive logic for an infinite model, the probability assigned to a possible universe with L individuals must equal the sum of the probabilities of the extension of this universe to $L + 1$ individuals. By the law of large numbers, random universes become relatively more frequent as the number of individuals increases, and in the long run random universes prevail. Hence a logic such as inverse inductive logic, which assigns higher probabilities to random universes than to uniform universes of a given size, is forced to reduce the assignment to random universes when they are part of a larger model.

This concludes our discussion of inductive logics for models. We have defined some simple models, both finite and infinite, and defined inductive logics for them. We have studied the relation of these logics to statistical uniformity, to Bayes' method of finding the unknown probability of a mixture of independent processes, and to the rule of induction by simple enumeration. While much more can be said about inductive logics for models, the material we have covered will be sufficient for our philosophical purposes. We shall next use this material to discuss Hume's traditional problem of the justification of induction.

3.3 Hume's Thesis on the Justification of Induction

3.3.1 Alternative inductive logics and Hume's thesis

The preceding two sections of this chapter contain informal characterizations of standard, inverse, and random inductive logic; and formal definitions of each for some limited models of reality. We may now use these models to draw some philosophical conclusions about induction.

Here is a basic fact about the logic of inductive argument: *There are different deductively consistent inductive logics applicable to reality.*

The existence of alternative inductive logics is analogous to the existence of alternative geometries: Euclidean, Lobachevskian, and Riemannian (sec. 1.2.2). In both cases there is a common core that justifies speaking of "alternatives"; in induction this core is the calculus of inductive probability; in geometry it consists of the common concepts of point, line, parallel, etc., and certain common axioms. In both cases there are alternatives: the axioms [24], [24^i], [24^r] in inductive logic, various parallel postulates in geometry. And in both cases the existence of alternatives can be used to establish that certain propositions are not logically true-or-false. Let us see how this is done.

The three geometries may be interpreted in terms of the actual world, as when "straight line" is interpreted to mean "the path of a beam of light." They may also be given idealized interpretations in terms of models. Three models are commonly used for two-dimensional geometry: the ordinary infinite plane (usually called the "Euclidean plane"), a surface of a sphere, and a surface of a "pseudosphere." A surface of a sphere or pseudosphere has constant curvature; the spherical surface is *convex* when viewed from outside, while the surface of a pseudosphere is *concave* when viewed from outside. In all of these interpretations "straight line" is defined to mean "geodesic," or the path of shortest distance between two points. In the case of the plane, a geodesic is the ordinary straight line. In the case of a sphere, a geodesic is a "great circle," or circle made by the intersection of a plane passing through the center of the sphere with the surface of the sphere. Geodesics are infinite on the plane and pseudosphere, but finite on the sphere.

Under these interpretations each geometry is true in one model and false in the others. Lobachevskian, Euclidean, and Riemannian geometries are true of the pseudosphere, the plane, and the sphere, respectively. Now a statement with uninterpreted terms is logically true if and only if it is true under all interpretations, and logically false if and only if it is false under all interpretations (secs. 1.2.2, 6.3). Consequently, the axioms of Euclidean geometry are not logically true-or-false.

Just as the existence of alternative geometries shows that the axioms of Euclidean geometry are not logically true-or-false, so does the existence of alternative inductive logics show that atomic inductive probability statements are not logically true-or-false. An atomic inductive probability statement is of the form $\mathbf{P}(c, d) = x$. The meaning of "**P**" (inductive probability) was originally specified in terms of ordinary inductive reasoning (sec. 1.5.2). "Standard inductive logic" consists of the rules governing ordinary inductive reasoning (sec. 3.1). Consequently, atomic inductive probability statements are statements of standard inductive logic.

As modeled in the preceding section, atomic inductive probability statements satisfy axiom [24] (p. 110). But this axiom is true for some probability assignments to possible universes and false for others; see, for example, Table 10. Consequently, *atomic inductive probability statements are not logically true-or-false.* This partially answers our second main question

(p. 92). Later we will explicate the pragmatic content of atomic inductive probability statements and show that this result still holds when the pragmatic content is taken into account (sec. 5.6.3).

Our original classification of statements into logical and empirical left open the possibility of a third kind (sec. 1.2.1). Hence to show that a statement is not logically true-or-false is not to show that it is empirically true-or-false. Here there is an important difference between alternative geometries and alternative inductive logics. In principle, it can be decided on empirical grounds which physical geometry describes actual space. But to make any such empirical decision presupposes the use of inductive logic. Thus the existence of alternatives in induction is epistemologically much more fundamental than in geometry. This suggests that atomic inductive probability statements are not empirical. We argue for this position in the current chapter, the conclusion being drawn at the end of Section 3.4.2 (The frequency theory of inductive probability).

To bring into view the basic role of standard inductive logic in scientific knowledge, we analyze our three alternatives further. An inductive logic provides standards for reasoning, and insofar as a man is rational he acts on the conclusions obtained by reasoning. Clearly what conclusions one reaches will depend on the inductive logic he employs. Thus to use an inductive logic is to behave in a certain way (see sec. 5.6). Since there are alternative inductive logics, there are, theoretically, alternative inductive patterns of behavior: Were one to use inverse or random inductive logic, he would behave differently from one who uses standard inductive logic. Now in fact we all employ standard inductive logic and no one has ever seriously considered using any other. But these others exist, and so we can contemplate theoretically the possibility of using them and ask whether our use of standard inductive logic can be justified.

Since inverse inductive logic and random inductive logic are each deductively consistent, there is no deductive justification for using standard inductive logic instead of one of these alternatives. To see if there is any other kind of justification, let us consider how one should make or justify a choice among alternative courses of action. The basic procedure will be analyzed later in terms of the rule of maximizing utility (chaps. 4–5). To determine the utility of an action, one must consider its consequences, evaluate each, and estimate the probability that it will occur. But chances are estimated by means of inductive logic.

This last fact becomes very significant when one attempts to apply the procedure just described to the choice of an inductive logic. Here the consequences are the successes and failures that result from using that logic. These results cannot be known before the event by direct observation, but can only be predicted; and predictions are made by means of inductive logic. One starts with relatively direct information about a very small fragment of the actual world. He then gathers data about the past and with this data makes predictions about the future; inductive reasoning is employed in both steps. After the event, it may be known which inductive logic did in fact predict best, but an inductive logic is needed to decide whether this result was a matter of chance and whether it will continue into the future. Hence the usual process of choice presupposes an inductive logic. And if this process is applied to the choice of an inductive logic, the judge and the judged are both inductive logics. Therefore, any attempt to show that man's use of standard inductive logic is at least as beneficial as the use of random or inverse inductive logic is question-begging and circular.

Man's propensity to pull himself up by his standard-inductive bootstraps is so strong that our contrary result needs amplification. Let the ordinary man, who employs standard inductive logic, be represented by *Mr. Standard.* Mr. Standard uses axiom [24]. Imagine a hypothetical *Mr. Inverse* who reasons in accord with and defends inverse inductive logic; he employs axiom [24^i]. Similarly, a hypothetical *Mr. Random* reasons according to and defends random inductive logic; he uses axiom [24^r]. All three, of course, employ the calculus of inductive probability.

Moreover, all three are interested in predictive success over some finite range of space-time. Some philosophers have attempted to justify the use of standard inductive logic over an infinite span of time ("in the long run"—see sec. 3.4.2). I personally am doubtful that any human interest really has an eternal scope. A sufficiently large period, e.g., a trillion trillion trillion years, and a corresponding distance, e.g., a trillion trillion trillion light-years, would certainly encompass anything I am interested in, and I suspect this is the case for most people. As Keynes said, "*In the long run* we are all dead."* Whether or not there is a bona fide problem of justifying induction over an infinite span depends on questions of immortality and theology beyond the scope of this work (see sec. 4.3.3 also). But we are finite creatures with finite lives, and so there is a significant finite problem of success. This is the problem that concerns us here.

It should be recalled in this connection that inverse inductive logic is defined only for finite models and hence cannot be used for the problem of justifying induction over an infinite space-time span. By de Finetti's theorem, no exchangeable inductive logic with an anti-enumeration rule can be defined for an infinite model (sec. 3.2.4). But all the logics of Carnap's continuum of inductive logics (including standard and random inductive logic) and nonexchangeable complete probability assignments to infinite models (such as Markov chains) can be used as possible models in the problem of justifying induction over an infinite span.

We will state some of the traditional arguments for the justification of

* Keynes said this in criticizing the quantity theory of money. *Monetary Reform*, p. 88.

induction in the form of an imaginary discussion between Mr. Standard, Mr. Inverse, and Mr. Random.

Mr. Standard might argue for the superiority of his inductive logic in the following way. In the past, he has made predictions of what would happen and by and large these predictions have been successful. Since the predictions made by an inductive logic are probabilistic, their success cannot be measured by comparing a single prediction with its outcome, but only by making a statistical comparison. A reasonably large number of probabilistic predictions can be compared with their outcomes. Suppose a set of probability assignments is made, each with probability α, and they turn out to be true with relative frequency σ (see sec. 2.4). The statistical degree of success of this set of assignments is measured by the closeness of α to σ. Consider, for example, 100 events, each of which is assigned a probability of 0.9 by one man and 0.1 by another; if there are in fact 85 successes ($\sigma = 0.85$) the first man has been a more successful prophet than the second. Mr. Standard would contend that, had the hypothetical Mr. Inverse and Mr. Random made predictions, these would have been wrong for the most part, so wrong that the two gentlemen would not even have survived.

But this line of argument would not convince or frighten his opponents, who would counter: "The past is known at the time of the controversy by making inductive inferences from available records and data. You, Mr. Standard, used standard inductive logic in constructing your picture of the past from these records and data, while we used *our* inductive logics. Memory in the ordinary sense requires uniformity of records, so that the 'record,' whether on paper or in the nervous system, is an accurate copy of the original. Since random inductive logic treats history as an independent process, on this logic the highly organized view of the universe that one has at any moment is not an accumulation from the past but is the result of chance. On inverse inductive logic, the past is likely to have been different from the way it appears to us now. Consequently, the descriptions given of the past by the three of us differ, and according to our accounts of the past your predictions were not successful. This shows very clearly, Mr. Standard, that you used standard inductive logic in evaluating the success of standard inductive logic. Memory and written records as you conceive them presuppose standard inductive logic."

But suppose, for purposes of argument, that Mr. Inverse and Mr. Random accept Mr. Standard's account of the past. This account describes one possible past universe from among many. The probability of this universe is in any case low, but it is lower for Mr. Random than for Mr. Standard, and lower still for Mr. Inverse. Now probability and frequency are connected only probabilistically, as we saw in Section 2.4. Hence Messrs. Random and Inverse would say: "For a proposition with very low nonrelative probability to come true shows only that the extremely improbable does happen, not that our inductive logic is wrong. Any attempt to justify standard inductive logic on the ground that it maximizes the unconditional probability of our present information is question-begging. Even if it were true that we would have perished, this would show only that Mr. Standard was luckier than we. The proper standard of success is not what actually did happen, but what was likely to happen, and the latter can be decided only by means of an inductive logic." Moreover, the fact that Mr. Standard was successful does not show that he will be successful in the future. Mr. Random would say that the past has no evidential bearing on the future. Mr. Inverse would say that the more often an inductive logic has been successful in the past, the less likely it is to succeed in the future.

Two other lines of argument have been used in an attempt to justify standard inductive logic. First, suppose one wishes to learn inductively about some individuals or events that cannot be observed directly. Science assumes that in these circumstances it is worthwhile to collect data concerning other individuals and events; whereas, according to random inductive logic, there is no evidential value to this data with respect to the unobserved individuals or events. Does this not justify the use of some inductive logic other than random logic? No, it merely shows that science as we know it is actually based on an inductive logic other than random logic; and this fact is not at issue, since standard inductive logic was introduced as the logic actually used by the practicing scientist. Thus scientific reasoning presupposes standard inductive logic.

Second, it has been argued that our use of language, our reasoning, our actions, indeed, our very existence, all presuppose standard inductive logic. Language, thought, action, and evolution all presuppose a great amount of uniformity, regularity, and lawlikeness in the universe, it is said. How could man learn to talk if the uses of words were not highly invariant? How could one think if he could not hold his ideas steady? How could man act successfully and survive in the evolutionary process if what he learned through experience were not a reliable guide to the future? Our very concepts of causality and substance rest on standard inductive logic. In short: Standard inductive logic is built into our minds, nerves, muscles, and bones, and its use is accordingly justified.

Three claims seem to be implicit in this line of reasoning. First, that man would never have come into existence in a world in which standard inductive logic was not the correct logic to use. Second, that man is so constituted that he cannot use any inductive logic other than the standard one. And, third, that even if man could employ a different inductive logic there would be no point to it, for man's only chance to survive is to use standard inductive logic. Another inductive logic might predict the future more successfully, but this could happen only in a world so different from the one we are accustomed to that we would not survive anyhow.

The answer to the first claim is: Any present state of the world is possible on any inductive logic. Inductive logics differ only on the likelihood of that state, and hence only with respect to whether the occurrence of man in the universe is accidental. The second claim is not at issue, since no one is proposing that we use any logic other than standard inductive logic. The third claim presupposes that for each inductive logic there is a corresponding type of world best suited to that logic, and that an organism adapted to one type of world could not survive in a different type of world. Note here the passage from characteristics of an inductive logic to characteristics of a world in which it works best. This line of reasoning has not been worked out sufficiently to make detailed criticism possible; but it seems to this writer that if it were it would involve an inductive argument employing standard inductive logic and hence would be question-begging.

The conclusions we have reached in this section are a reformulation in terms of modern probability theory of Hume's skeptical views about the justification of induction. For future reference we shall combine our conclusions into a single thesis named after Hume.

Hume's thesis that there is no noncircular justification of induction: There are different deductively consistent inductive logics applicable to reality. Consequently, atomic inductive probability statements are not logically true-or-false, and there is no deductive justification for using standard inductive logic instead of an alternative. Moreover, the usual procedure for showing that one behavior pattern is more beneficial than any other involves the use of standard inductive logic. Any attempt, then, to justify the use of an inductive logic in this way is circular and question-begging. An inductive logic constitutes a standard of evidence and of probable predictive success, and a person who uses it can never find empirical grounds for modifying or abandoning it.

3.3.2 Historical comment

Though Hume deserves the credit for the thesis that there is no noncircular justification of induction, it should be emphasized that both my formulation of his result and my argument differ considerably from Hume's. The mathematics of probability was very rudimentary in Hume's time, and he did not use it.

Very briefly, Hume's argument went like this.* Statements are of two kinds: relations of ideas and matters of fact. This corresponds to our classification of statements into the logical and the empirical (sec. 1.2.1). Induction takes past conjunctions of events as evidence of causal connections and on this basis makes predictions of future conjunctions. Thus all reasonings

* *A Treatise of Human Nature*, book 1, part 3, secs. 6 and 12. *An Enquiry Concerning Human Understanding*, secs. 4 and 5.

concerning matters of fact rest on what Hume calls "the relation of cause and effect," or "the supposition, *that the future resembles the past.*"* He also expresses this as the

> principle *that instances, of which we have had no experience, must resemble those, of which we had had experience, and that the course of nature continues always uniformly the same.*
>
> From causes which appear *similar* we expect similar effects.†

Hume had no single name for this principle. For future reference we will call it "Hume's uniformity of nature principle."

This principle is not logically true. As Hume said,

> We can at least conceive a change in the course of nature. . . .
>
> *That the sun will not rise to-morrow* is no less intelligible a proposition, and implies no more contradiction than the affirmation, *that it will rise.*‡

To argue for it from past experience is to assume it, which is circular. See the epigraph of the current chapter. Hume concluded that inductive inference is a matter of "habit" and "custom," not of reasoning.

> . . . it is not reasoning which engages us to suppose the past resembling the future, and to expect similar effects from causes which are, to appearance, similar.
>
> All inferences from experience, therefore, are effects of custom, not of reasoning.
>
> Custom, then, is the great guide of human life. It is that principle alone which renders our experience useful to us, and makes us expect, for the future, a similar train of events with those which have appeared in the past. Without the influence of custom, we should be entirely ignorant of every matter of fact beyond what is immediately present to the memory and senses.§

Our argument for Hume's thesis does not make explicit use of a uniformity-of-nature principle, though a concept of uniformity is involved in standard inductive logic (sec. 3.2.3; see also secs. 9.3 and 10.3). A much more important difference is the fact that our formulation of Hume's result neither states nor implies that inductive inference is not reasoning. When Hume says this, he is simply wrong and is failing to express what his argument has in fact shown, with consequent misleading and skeptical effects.||

* *Enquiry*, p. 26, and *Treatise*, p. 134, respectively.

† *Treatise*, p. 89; *Enquiry*, p. 36.

‡ *Treatise*, p. 89; *Enquiry*, pp. 25-26.

§ *Enquiry*, pp. 39 and 43-45, respectively. See also *Treatise*, p. 139.

|| In discussing induction and causality, Hume does refer to inductive inference as "reasoning from causation," "reasoning concerning matters of fact," "moral reasoning," "probable reasoning," and "reasoning from conjecture" (*An Enquiry Concerning Human Understanding*, sec. 4, and part 3 of sec. 12; *A Treatise of Human Nature*, book 1, part 3, secs. 11 and 12). But *after* analyzing the foundations of inductive inference, he concludes that inductive inference is not reasoning.

As the name implies, everyone accepts standard inductive logic and employs the word "probability" in conformity with that logic. Hence, taken as assertions of ordinary language, such atomic inductive probability statements as the following are true: "The probability that the next swan is white, relative to the fact that many swans have been observed and all were white, is high." Similarly, standard inductive logic is a norm underlying the ordinary use of inductive expressions such as: chance, probable, likely, fate, luck, accident, plausible, confirm, verify, doubt, valid, support, substantiate, corroborate, explain, reliable, justify, evidence, rational, correct betting odds, correct inductive reasoning, etc. For example, the fact that the sun has risen many times *is* a good *reason* for believing that it will rise tomorrow.

Bertrand Russell has presented Hume's result in the same misleading way. He asks: "Do *any* number of cases of a law being fulfilled in the past afford evidence that it will be fulfilled in the future?" He reduces the question to one concerning the principle of induction by simple enumeration and finally concludes that we must either accept this principle "on the ground of its intrinsic evidence, or forego all justification of our expectation about the future."* Now, as "evidence" is normally used, the answer to Russell's question is an obvious "yes"; and as "justify" is normally used some expectations are justifiable while others are not, the decision in each case being made by the rules of standard inductive logic. When these rules are applied to themselves the result is not a lack of justification, but a circularity. This difference is important, because our formulation of Hume's thesis that there is no noncircular justification of induction does not imply that standard inductive logic stands in need of justification, whereas Russell's formulation does.

Another way of looking at the matter is this. To justify a system, procedure, practice, or decision, one must appeal to another system, procedure, or set of rules that needs justification less than the given system. Now the fact that there are alternative inductive logics shows that inductive logic is not a branch of deductive logic and that standard inductive logic cannot be justified by an appeal to deductive logic. Hence there is no system of rules that can be used legitimately to justify standard inductive logic. But standard inductive logic needs no justification. Indeed, our faith in it is so strong that no argument could cause us to abandon it. Hume's thesis that there is no noncircular justification of induction is thus a purely theoretical result: It tells us that if we were to seek for a justification we would move in a circle.

The conclusion of our criticism of the formulations of Hume and Russell is that to express the essence of Hume's result we must speak about ordinary

* *The Problems of Philosophy*, pp. 96 and 106.

language, not use ordinary language in extraordinary ways. The effect of doing the latter is to give the false appearance of seriously considering a change in the inductive rules we employ. Often, if there is no reason for something, we will have doubts about it and, perhaps, fail to act. Thus Russell raises "the interesting doubt . . . as to whether the laws of motion will remain in operation until tomorrow," and Hume expresses his skeptical mood by saying

> The *intense* view of these manifold contradictions and imperfections in human reason has so wrought upon me, and heated my brain, that I am ready to reject all belief and reasoning, and can look upon no opinion even as more probable or likely than another.*

There is an implication here that astrology is as scientific as astronomy and that witchcraft is as reliable as scientific method. Yet no one who has ever discussed this matter has seriously considered altering his commitment to standard inductive logic. The Greek skeptic Pyrrho of Elis asserted he did not trust his senses, and started to walk over a cliff, as if it could not matter. But since he did this in the presence of his friends, and after sufficient indoctrination of them to insure his safety, we can write this off as a pedagogical and publicity-seeking device.

> And so, universally, he held that there is nothing really existent, but custom and convention govern human action; for no single thing is in itself any more this than that.
>
> He led a life consistent with this doctrine, going out of his way for nothing, taking no precaution, but facing all risks as they came, whether carts, precipices, dogs or what not, and generally, leaving nothing to the arbitrament of the senses; but he was kept out of harm's way by his friends who, as Antigonus of Carystus tells us, used to follow close after him. But Aenesidemus says that it was only his philosophy that was based upon suspension of judgement, and that he did not lack foresight in his everyday acts. He lived to be nearly ninety.†

3.3.3 Speculative character of Hume's thesis

Hume's thesis that there is no noncircular justification of induction is of great philosophic importance and underlies many of the philosophic conclusions of this book. Before proceeding further, therefore, it is desirable to assess its speculative status and its limitations.

Since the thesis rests on the existence of the three inductive logics, let us examine the way we introduced them. It is a commonplace to say that

* Russell, *The Problems of Philosophy*, p. 95. Hume, *A Treatise of Human Nature*, pp. 268-69.

† Diogenes Läertius, *Lives of Eminent Philosophers* 2: 475.

definitions are arbitrary, that one can define his terms as he pleases. Lewis Carroll expressed it best in *Through the Looking Glass:*

"I don't know what you mean by 'glory,' " Alice said.

Humpty Dumpty smiled contemptuously. "Of course you don't—till I tell you. I meant 'there's a nice knock-down argument for you!' "

"But 'glory' doesn't mean 'a nice knock-down argument,' " Alice objected.

"When *I* use a word," Humpty Dumpty said, in rather a scornful tone, "it means just what I choose it to mean—neither more nor less."

"The question is," said Alice, "whether you *can* make words mean so many different things."

"The question is," said Humpty Dumpty, "which is to be master—that's all."

But defining and specifying the meanings of terms, like all other activities, should be subject to rules. For example: The same term should not be defined twice in incompatible ways, and a definition that presupposes something that is not the case is clearly unacceptable. Both of these rules are relevant to our characterizations of standard inductive logic and its alternatives. We defined each of these twice, once in Section 3.1 and once in Section 3.2.2. And the second definition presupposes that the models of Section 3.2.1 do not differ from reality in any respects essential to Hume's thesis.

Consider first our specification of standard inductive logic in terms of the inductive precepts scientists actually use. As we noted earlier (sec. 1.4.2), inductive rules are harder to state precisely and in an easily applicable form than deductive rules. We may illustrate this by pointing out an incompleteness in our formulation of the standard rule of induction by simple enumeration. Compare the following three arguments. First, the swan argument of Section 3.1. Second, the argument: this wire has been bent many times and has not broken yet, therefore it will probably break soon. Third, the argument: though this normal, i.e., symmetrical and homogeneous, coin has turned up heads more often than tails when tossed in the normal way, the probability that it will fall heads next time is still one-half. As stated, these three arguments are in accord with standard, inverse, and random inductive logic, respectively.* But when relevant background information is added to the premises, all can be accounted for by standard inductive logic. For we know

* Quantum-mechanical and thermodynamical distribution laws constitute a similar example, with Einstein-Bose, Fermi-Dirac, and Maxwell-Boltzmann statistics corresponding to standard, inverse, and random inductive logic, respectively. In this connection the use of standard inductive logic to verify the second law of thermodynamics is of special philosophical interest. See sec. 3.2.3, above, and sec. 8.3.1, below.

from past experience that bird coloration tends to be uniform, that wires wear out when bent repeatedly, and that the normal tosses of a normal coin are independent. Let us examine the role played by this information in induction.

In each case this background knowledge constitutes the premise for a standard induction by simple enumeration, but here the inference concerns properties (or sets of individuals or events) rather than single individuals or events, and thus takes place on a higher level. We infer that bird coloration tends to be uniform from the fact that this tendency is found in many species; we conclude that the more often this wire is bent the more likely it is to break from our past experience with many wires; and we extrapolate the probabilistic notion of independence on a similar basis. Thus we know that bird coloration is a property that should be extrapolated, frequency of heads (for a fair coin) is not, and bending a wire without breaking should be extrapolated inversely; we know all this on the basis of higher order standard inductions by simple enumeration. And according to standard inductive logic, in the *absence* of this background information, the more often a wire bends without breaking the *less* likely it is to break, and the more often a normal coin comes up heads, the *more* likely it is to fall heads next time. These probability judgments all seem correct to me, but it must be admitted that there is a difficulty here.

The difficulty arises from the fact that when making a probability assertion one always has a great deal of information, and it is hard to decide what he would judge if, contrary to fact, he did not have all this information. Insofar as this information affects his probability evaluation implicitly, he cannot in fact abstract from it. Moreover, evolutionary considerations suggest that there is a great deal of inductive information built into ordinary and scientific language. The theory of evolution, applied to language, implies that words and terms have developed, generally speaking, in ways that facilitate inductive inference.

As this discussion makes clear, scientific knowledge is a hierarchical, complex structure, with the laws and knowledge of one level supporting those of the next. Our formulation of induction by simple enumeration applies only within one level and so does not do justice to the complexity of inductive knowledge. Since no inductive logic does, there are several important unanswered questions, of which we will mention a few in passing.

We have shown how to accommodate the swan, wire, and coin arguments within standard inductive logic. Can this also be done within inverse and random inductive logics? Note that if this cannot be done in either logic there would be an important formal characteristic distinguishing standard inductive logic from the nonstandard inductive logics. Another formal property that distinguishes standard inductive logic from the others was established in the last section: standard inductive logic is the only one of the three that is exchangeable, makes the past relevant to the future, and also applies to infinite models (pp. 125–27). Mr. Standard might argue that his inductive logic is to be preferred to the others because it has these formal properties, but Mr. Inverse and Mr. Random would say that this begs the question. Moreover, there are nonexchangeable inductive logics that make the past relevant to the future and apply to infinite models, so that any appeal to exchangeability can be challenged.

The reader can see, then, that our specification of standard inductive logic by reference to the rules scientists use is not as formal and complete as we would like. We are, in effect, taking the existing formulations of inductive rules as simplified representatives of a more precise and complete hypothetical set. This idealization again raises the problem of our use of model universes to draw philosophical conclusions. We shall discuss this problem now, beginning with a review of the main features of the models $\mathfrak{M}$-$\mathfrak{L}$.

A finite model $\mathfrak{M}$ contains a finite number each of monadic properties, individuals, and logically possible universes, together with a designated actual universe. Correspondingly, the language $\mathfrak{L}$ contains a finite number each of monadic predicates, proper names, and universe descriptions, together with a designated true universe description. Infinite models are treated as infinite sequences of finite models with ever-increasing numbers of individuals and proper names. It is obvious that these models are extreme idealizations of reality. The models $\mathfrak{M}$ are qualitative and discrete, while reality is quantitative and continuous. And the languages $\mathfrak{L}$ are very much weaker than ordinary scientific language.

Actually Carnap's system of inductive logic has been extended to somewhat stronger models and it has been improved in several respects.* As noted early in Section 3.2.1, it covers relations of any degree (e.g., the dyadic relation "is taller than," the triadic relation "the temperature of x is between that of y and z"). The logical independence requirement on the proper names and predicates may be dropped, and universe descriptions that are not logically possible assigned a probability of zero (see the models of sec. 6.3). Quantifiers over individuals ("for all x," "for some y") and a symbol for equality ("$x = y$") may be included in a language $\mathfrak{L}$. Inductive logics in which induction by simple enumeration holds have been defined for models with an infinite number of properties in such a way that the probability of a statement does not change when new predicates not contained in that statement are added to the model. Note that random inductive logic possesses

* Carnap, "Replies and Systematic Expositions," sec. 26.

See also Hintikka's papers "On a Combined System of Inductive Logic," "Induction by Enumeration and Induction by Elimination," and "Towards a Theory of Inductive Generalization"; *Aspects of Inductive Logic* (edited by Hintikka and Suppes); and *Studies in Inductive Logic and Probability* (edited by Carnap and Jeffrey).

this last property. Basically, Carnap's system covers first-order quantification theory with equality (see sec. 6.2.3).

For our purposes the simpler models we are using will do about as well as these stronger models, since the differences between the two types of models are slight compared to the differences between the models and reality. We will list the most important differences. It is not possible in first-order quantification theory to quantify predicates and hence it is not possible, for example, to express causal dispositions (sec. 7.3.2) or empirical probability statements (sec. 8.3). First-order quantification theory does not have predicates that apply to predicates, i.e., symbols for classes of classes, or predicates of predicates of predicates, etc., etc. Consequently, algebra, the calculus, differential equations, etc., cannot be formulated in it. Clearly all these things are essential for the language of science, particularly for well-developed, quantitative sciences such as physics and biochemistry. Moreover, first-order quantification theory is an idealization of ordinary language with respect to the "proper names" $a, b, c, \ldots$. For a proper name actually to function in natural language there must be a means of establishing a connection between the name and the individual it represents. This is a complex process involving indexical terms* and reflects the fact that real substances and events are much more complex and interrelated than the individuals of our models. Finally, first-order quantification theory, as it stands, is not adequate for formulating modal concepts, such as the concept of causal necessity (see chap. 7 and sec. 10.2).

There is thus a substantial gap between our models and reality, the latter being of a much higher order of complexity than the former. This gap is particularly noticeable when one considers the unconditional probability $\mathbf{P}(u)$ in axioms [24], [24^{i}], and [24^{r}] of Section 3.2.2. In these axioms $\mathbf{P}(u)$ means the probability that the universe description u is true, absolutely prior to any evidence. Now a universe description of the actual universe would be too complex for man to comprehend (cf. pp. 113–14). Apart from this is the aforementioned difficulty of abstracting from the empirical evidence one already has. This difficulty is extreme in the case of the unconditional probability $\mathbf{P}(u)$, for in this case one needs to decide on a probability for u on the contrary-to-fact assumption that his mind is entirely void of empirical information.

Another important respect in which these models differ from reality is very deep-rooted. The model languages are rigorous, formal, and precise. In contrast, actual scientific inductive reasoning is strongly intuitive, and while it employs rigorous mathematics, it is frequently vague at the general conceptual level (see sec. 7.1). Ordinary probability assessments are often qualitative rather than quantitative (see sec. 4.3.2). Note in this connection that it is not necessary to Hume's thesis that alternative inductive logics

* See my "Icon, Index, and Symbol" and "A Theory of Proper Names."

specify values for *all* atomic probabilities. Hume's thesis will still hold if there are some probability statements on which Mr. Standard, Mr. Inverse, and Mr. Random systematically disagree.

This concludes our survey of the models on which Hume's thesis is based. It is clear that they are highly idealized and unrealistic. In my opinion, actual inductive reasoning is so complex that realistic models can be developed only with the assistance of electronic computers (see sec. 10.2.1). While it is difficult to make accurate predictions, I believe there will be good computer models of many human processes, including inductive reasoning, by the end of this century. In the meantime, of course, we must employ the models that are presently available.

When using models as a tool of investigation one reasons about them analogically: It is thus and so in the model, hence it is thus and so in reality. We have given this same argument in the current chapter: There are alternative inductive logics for these models of reality, hence there are alternative inductive logics applicable to reality. This conclusion is the main premise of our argument for Hume's thesis that there is no noncircular justification of induction.

Now a conclusion by analogy is true only if the model is similar to reality in the relevant respects; therefore, we must consider whether our conclusion depends on the limitations of our models. How do we know that if these inductive logics were given full and precise statements each would be consistent and empirically irrefutable? The answer is that we do not know, we can only speculate (see sec. 1.6.3). But there is no reason to think these alternative inductive logics should cease to be consistent and empirically irrefutable when they are developed to cover more realistic models. Hence I shall assume Hume's thesis that there is no noncircular justification of induction for the remainder of this book.

3.4 Frequency Theories of Probability

3.4.1 The frequency theory of empirical probability

In Section 1.5.2 we introduced the concepts of inductive probability (**P**) and empirical probability ($\mathbf{P}_e$) and stated that, prima facie, they are quite different. In this section we shall argue for this difference in some detail. It will turn out that Hume's thesis that there is no noncircular justification of induction plays an important role in this argument.

The argument will be carried out in two stages. In the present subsection we refine our third main question, which is about empirical probability, and present a partially satisfactory answer to it. In the next subsection we evaluate an attempt to identify inductive probability and frequency probability.

Our third main question was: What is the general nature of an atomic empirical probability statement, and how are empirical and inductive probability related? (sec. 1.6.1). In Section 2.5.4 we saw that, with respect to atomic inductive probability statements, it is desirable to focus attention on interrelated sets or systems of such statements rather than on isolated statements. The same conclusion holds for atomic empirical probability statements, and for the same reasons we saw then.

Let us begin with an example. I have on my desk at this moment a single coin and a single die. The coin is a 500-lira piece, dated 1861 and 1961, commemorating one hundred years of Italian unity. The die is red, with gold spots and rounded corners. Let us imagine that the coin and the die are to be tossed repeatedly and simultaneously by a certain process. The atomic empirical probability statements

(*A*) The empirical probability of this coin falling tails is 1/2

(*B*) The empirical probability of this die rolling deuce is 1/6

are symbolized

(*A'*) $\mathbf{P}_e(T) = 1/2$

(*B'*) $\mathbf{P}_e(D) = 1/6$,

where "*T*" means that the coin falls tails and "*D*" means that the die rolls deuce. The independence condition

(*C*) The tosses of the coin and throws of the die are independent

is symbolized

(*C'*) $\mathbf{P}_e(D, T) = \mathbf{P}_e(D)$.

This independence condition is not an atomic empirical probability statement but a compound of such, for it may be expressed "For some number β, $\mathbf{P}_e(D, T) = \beta$ if and only if $\mathbf{P}_e(D) = \beta$." It is, however, empirical, for it will be rejected if a long sequence of tosses shows a statistically significant correlation of tails and deuces (see sec. 8.2). Thus all three of the statements *A'*, *B'*, *C'* are empirically true-or-false. One or more of them will be abandoned if the coin or die is loaded or if the tossing procedure shows bias.

Observe now that empirical probabilities obey the laws of the traditional calculus of probability (sec. 2.1). Consider, for example, the empirical probability statement

(*E*) The empirical probability of the coin falling tails and the die falling deuce is 1/12,

which is symbolized

(*E'*) $\mathbf{P}_e(TD) = 1/12$

It is clear that statements A', B', and C' imply statement E' by any of the multiplication principles of Chapter 2, when the symbol "**P**" is interpreted to mean empirical probability ($\mathbf{P}_e$). More generally, if "$\mathbf{P}_e$" is substituted for "**P**" throughout the axioms and theorems of Chapter 2, the resultant axioms and theorems are true statements about empirical probabilities. This fact leads directly to the question: Why is the traditional calculus of probability applicable to empirical probabilities? This is an important question, for the traditional calculus of probability is widely applied to natural sequences of events; for example, to successive generations of animals, the states of a nuclear process, the output of a production line, calls on a telephone trunk line, and gas diffusion.

Hence we revise our third main question to read: *What is the general nature of a system of atomic empirical probability statements? How are empirical* ($\mathbf{P}_e$) *and inductive probability* (**P**) *related? Why is the traditional calculus of probability applicable to empirical probabilities?*

One of the best known theories of probability is the frequency theory. A particular version of it, which we call the "frequency theory of empirical probability," offers an answer to our third main question. This answer is based on the identification of empirical probability with relative frequency in the long run.

Consider an infinite sequence of events, with the Lth event x_L being characterized by either ϕ or $\bar{\phi}$ as well as by either ψ or $\bar{\psi}$. Let $\sigma_L(\psi\phi)$ be the relative frequency of the occurrence of $\psi\phi$ in L events, and let $\sigma_L(\psi)$ be the relative frequency of the occurrence of ψ in L events (sec. 2.4). Define

$$(F) \qquad \sigma_L(\phi, \psi) = \frac{\sigma_L(\psi\phi)}{\sigma_L(\psi)} \qquad ;$$

compare the reduction principle (sec. 2.6). Note that $\sigma_L(\phi, \psi)$ is not defined if the first L events are all $\bar{\psi}$. The **frequency probability** of ϕ conditional on ψ is defined by

$$(G) \qquad \mathbf{P}_f(\phi, \psi) = \operatorname*{Limit}_{L\to\infty} \sigma_L(\phi, \psi)$$

if this limit exists; otherwise this probability is undefined. If all events are $\bar{\psi}$, then $\mathbf{P}_f(\phi, \psi)$ is not defined. If the first L events are $\bar{\psi}$ but the $(L + 1)$st event is ψ, then the first L terms are to be ignored in applying definition (*G*). When every event is ψ, definition (*G*) reduces to

$$(J) \qquad \mathbf{P}_f(\phi) = \operatorname*{Limit}_{L\to\infty} \sigma_L(\phi) \qquad ;$$

in words: $\mathbf{P}_f(\phi)$ is the limit of $\sigma_L(\phi)$ as L goes to infinity. This last definition should be compared with the law of large numbers, according to which the relative frequency σ_L of a type of event tends in the long run to the probability α of that type of event (sec. 2.4).

Some simple examples may be useful. In the sequence Bx_1, Bx_2, Bx_3, Bx_4, Bx_5, $\overline{Bx_6}$, Bx_7, $\overline{Bx_8}$, Bx_9, $\overline{Bx_{10}}$, Bx_{11}, $\overline{Bx_{12}}$, . . . the type of event B occurs four times in succession and then alternates with its contradictory forever after. The relative frequency $\sigma_L(B)$ is 1, 1, 1, 1, 1, 5/6, 6/7, 6/8, 7/9, 7/10, . . . and clearly approaches 1/2 as a limit, so that $\mathbf{P}_f(B) = 1/2$. In the sequence 1, 2, 3, 4, 5, 6, . . . the ratio of odd numbers divisible by three to odd numbers approaches 1/3 as a limit, so that the probability of an odd number being divisible by three is 1/3. The probability of a positive integer being even is 1/2 in the sequence 1, 2, 3, 4, 5, . . . , but 1/3 in the sequence 1, 3, 2; 5, 7, 4; 9, 11, 6; 13, 15, 8; . . . , though both sequences contain all positive integers. This illustrates the fact that the frequency probability of a type of event depends on the order of the items in the sequence. It is easy to define a sequence in which the relative frequency of success oscillates back and forth and never reaches a limit. Let Cx_1 be followed by 10 occurrences of $\bar{C}$, 100 occurrences of C, 1,000 of $\bar{C}$, 10,000 of C, etc., etc. In this series the relative frequency of success oscillates between 1/11 and about 10/11, and hence $\mathbf{P}_f(C)$ is undefined.

The reader should keep in mind that most of the statements about frequency probability that follow presuppose that "$\mathbf{P}_f$" is defined.

The traditional calculus of probability was defined in Chapter 2 as a formal, uninterpreted system, and the interpretation of it in terms of inductive probability was called the calculus of inductive probability. The traditional calculus of probability may also be applied to frequency probability; we will call this interpreted system the "calculus of frequency probability." The axioms of this calculus are obtained from the axioms of Section 2.2.1 in two steps. First, rewrite axioms [1]–[4], substituting "$\mathbf{P}_f$" for "$\mathbf{P}$" throughout and replacing the statement variables "c," "d," etc., by the predicate variables "ϕ," "ψ," etc. Second, replace the modal conditions in the antecedents of axioms [1], [3], [4] by the corresponding universally quantified conditions. Thus the **calculus of frequency probability** is defined by the axioms

[1_f] If $(x)[\theta x \supset \sim(\phi x \psi x)]$, then $\mathbf{P}_f(\phi \vee \psi, \theta) = \mathbf{P}_f(\phi, \theta) + \mathbf{P}_f(\psi, \theta)$

[2_f] $\mathbf{P}_f(\phi\psi, \theta) = \mathbf{P}_f(\phi, \theta)\mathbf{P}_f(\psi, \phi\theta)$

[3_f] If $(x)(\psi x \supset \phi x)$, then $\mathbf{P}_f(\phi, \psi) = 1$

[4_f] If $(x)(\phi x \equiv \psi x)$, then $\mathbf{P}_f(\theta, \phi) = \mathbf{P}_f(\theta, \psi)$

The calculus of frequency probability may be applied to a set of probability statements concerning a particular infinite sequence. Consider, for example, the sequence of tosses of the coin and die mentioned at the beginning of this section, and imagine it to be infinite. This sequence is of the form ϕx_1, ϕx_2, ϕx_3, . . . , where ϕ is TD, $T\bar{D}$, $\bar{T}D$, or $\bar{T}\bar{D}$. According to the frequency theory of empirical probability, the argument from the premises A, B, and C to the conclusion E is to be analyzed into the argument from the premises

(A'') $\mathbf{P}_f(T) = 1/2$

(B'') $\mathbf{P}_f(D) = 1/6$

(C'') $\mathbf{P}_f(D, T) = \mathbf{P}_f(D)$

to the conclusion

(E'') $\mathbf{P}_f(TD) = 1/12$.

The premises of this argument imply the conclusion by the general multiplication principle [2_f].

Since the calculus of frequency probability is an interpreted system, its axioms and theorems are either true or false. These axioms and theorems concern the limits of sequences, and they turn out to be logically true statements of conventional mathematics.

Before proceeding further, we need to contrast the concepts of frequency probability ($\mathbf{P}_f$) and inductive probability ($\mathbf{P}$). A frequency probability statement refers to a particular infinite sequence of events. In contrast, an inductive probability statement refers to a process, which is a set of possible sequences. Fundamentally, inductive probabilities apply to finite processes, but derivatively (via limits, as in the law of large numbers) they apply to infinite processes also. A single event may be regarded as a special case of a finite process, a process of length one. Hence frequency probabilities are defined only for infinite sequences of events, whereas inductive probabilities are not so limited.

Three subsidiary differences between frequency and inductive probability flow from this main difference. The first concerns the "arguments" (independent variables) of $\mathbf{P}_f(\phi, \psi)$ and $\mathbf{P}(c, d)$. The arguments ϕ, ψ of $\mathbf{P}_f(\phi, \psi)$ are predicates applicable to the individual events of an infinite sequence. In contrast, the arguments c and d of $\mathbf{P}(c, d)$ are any empirical or logical statements, except that d must be logically possible. The statements c and d may be about single events, finite processes, or infinite processes. The arguments of an inductive probability operator may be statement forms applying to an arbitrary term of an infinite process. Consider an independent process $\phi x_1, \phi x_2, \phi x_3, \ldots$ of probability α. Here $\mathbf{P}(\phi x_i) = \alpha$ for $i = 1, 2, 3, \ldots$. Note the close connection of inductive and frequency probability in this independent process. By the law of large numbers, any infinite sequence of this process is likely to be such that $\mathbf{P}_f(\phi) = \alpha$.

Second, since frequency probability statements refer to single infinite sequences, rather than to sets of possible sequences, the modal restrictions on the axioms of the calculus of inductive probability [1]–[4] are not needed in the axioms of the calculus of frequency probability [1_f]–[4_f].

The third respect in which frequency probability differs from inductive probability concerns the converses of axioms [3] and [3_f]. The converse of [3] is

$$\text{If } \mathbf{P}(c, d) = 1, \text{ then } d \rightarrow c .$$

We saw in Section 3.1 that this converse is not a theorem of the calculus of inductive probability. And we can easily show that for the finite models of Section 3.2 this converse is equivalent to the condition that every universe description has a positive unconditional probability. Note that by Bayes' theorem, if the prior probability of a statement is zero (or one) then the posterior probability is also zero (or one). The question as to whether the converse of axiom [3] is true is a difficult one that we need not settle here (see pp. 113–14). But the corresponding question for frequency probability is easily answered.

The converse of [3_f] is

$$\text{If } \mathbf{P}(\phi, \psi) = 1, \text{ then } (x)(\psi x \supset \phi x) \quad .$$

This converse is false, as is shown by a sequence that has exactly one occurrence of $\psi\bar{\phi}$ and infinitely many occurrences of $\psi\phi$. A more revealing sequence is the following, every element of which is D.

(K) $\overline{Cx_1}$; Cx_2, $\overline{Cx_3}$; Cx_4, Cx_5, Cx_6, $\overline{Cx_7}$; Cx_8, Cx_9, Cx_{10}, Cx_{11}, Cx_{12}, Cx_{13}, Cx_{14}, $\overline{Cx_{15}}$; . . . .

This sequence consists of successive blocks of length 1, 2, 4, 8, 16, . . . , each block containing exactly one failure $\bar{C}D$. The ratio $\sigma_L(CD)/\sigma_L(D)$ approaches one as a limit, so that $\mathbf{P}_f(C, D) = 1$, though there are infinitely many failures $\bar{C}D$. Symmetrically, a frequency probability of zero is compatible with infinitely many successes.

The calculus of frequency probability is a theory of *all* infinite sequences of events with limiting relative frequencies. In contrast, von Mises held that probability theory should be restricted to random sequences with limiting relative frequencies, or what he called "collectives."* There is an apparent reason for some limitation of this kind. For example, when one recognizes the simple, deterministic rule governing sequence (K) of the preceding paragraph, he does not need probability theory to make predictions about the events of this sequence. A calculus that covers just the sequences for which probability theory is needed would be superior to the calculus of frequency probability, because it would fit its domain of application more closely. Unfortunately, there is no satisfactory way of distinguishing those sequences for which probability theory is useful from those for which it is not. It is doubtful that there is a single notion of randomness suitable for all purposes, but even if there were, we would not want to restrict the calculus

* *Probability, Statistics, and Truth*, lectures 1 and 2.

of frequency probability to random sequences. Often we do not know whether the sequence at hand is or is not random. Moreover, the calculus is useful in studying sequences that are known to be nonrandom, such as pseudorandom sequences. Randomness is of great interest in its own right (see secs. 3.2.3 and 9.4), but the calculus of frequency probability should not be limited to random sequences.

Having explained the concept of and calculus of $\mathbf{P}_f$, we can now formulate the frequency theory of empirical probability. We originally characterized an empirical probability statement as one that is accepted or rejected on the basis of observed relative frequencies (sec. 1.5.2). The frequency theory analyzes an empirical probability statement in terms of its evidence by equating it to a frequency probability statement. Thus this theory analyzes "$\mathbf{P}_e(\phi, \psi) = \alpha$" into "$\mathbf{P}_f(\phi, \psi) = \alpha$." The question of whether "$\mathbf{P}_f(\phi, \psi) = \alpha$" is true of the sequence to which it refers is an empirical question, and so this analysis preserves the empirical status of empirical probability statements. The calculus of frequency probability is an interpretation of the traditional calculus of probability, and it consists of logically true statements that may be used to make deductive inferences from some frequency probability statements to others.

In sum, the **frequency theory of empirical probability** is the theory that *atomic empirical probability statements should be analyzed into frequency probability statements and reasoned about by means of the calculus of frequency probability, which is an interpretation of the traditional calculus of probability.* This theory originated with Leslie Ellis. It was developed by John Venn and Charles S. Peirce. More recently, it was further developed by Richard von Mises and Hans Reichenbach.* Peirce and Reichenbach also advocated the stronger frequency theory of *inductive* probability, which we will present in the next subsection.

By thus identifying empirical probability ($\mathbf{P}_e$) with frequency probability ($\mathbf{P}_f$), the frequency theory of empirical probability gives partially satisfactory answers to the first and last parts of our third main question. Briefly put, its account of the nature of empirical probability holds that an atomic empirical probability statement concerns the limit of a relative frequency in an infinite sequence of events. The frequency theory of empirical probability interprets the traditional calculus of probability to be the calculus of frequency probability and thereby explains, at least partially, why the

* Ellis, "On the Foundations of the Theory of Probabilities." Venn, *The Logic of Chance.* Von Mises, *Probability, Statistics, and Truth.* Reichenbach, *The Theory of Probability.*

Peirce, *Collected Papers.* Peirce adopted this theory in an 1867 review of Venn's *The Logic of Chance,* 8.1-6; see also 3.19 (1867). Peirce's presentation of his theory of probability is scattered throughout the *Collected Papers,* but it is found principally in book 3 of vol. 2 and book 2 of vol. 7.

traditional calculus applies to empirical probability. These are important contributions, though later we will offer what we think is a better account of empirical probability (chap. 8). At the moment we wish only to argue that the frequency theory of empirical probability does not explain how empirical probability and inductive probability are related and hence does not give a complete answer to our third main question.

Frequencies and relative frequencies can be directly observed in the finite case. But this does not mean that a frequency probability statement can be verified by direct observation. A frequency probability statement such as "$\mathbf{P}_f(T) = 1/2$" refers to a completely hypothetical infinite sequence of events, since no one will toss this coin infinitely many times. It is even questionable whether there will be infinitely many tosses of coins in general; but that is irrelevant here, for "$\mathbf{P}_f(T) = 1/2$" is not about all coins but about one particular coin, the 500-lira piece on my desk. Thus a frequency probability statement transcends any possible observation or finite set of observations. To verify it, then, one must use inductive inference, as a detailed consideration of the matter will confirm.

The statement that the frequency probability $\mathbf{P}_f(T)$ is $1/2$ is meant as an approximation, for exactly what is intended depends on the alternatives under consideration. To simplify the discussion let us assume that there are only two other possibilities, namely probabilities of $1/4$ and $3/4$, so that we have three alternatives under consideration.

($A''_{.25}$) $\mathbf{P}_f(T) = .25$

($A''_{.50}$) $\mathbf{P}_f(T) = .50$

($A''_{.75}$) $\mathbf{P}_f(T) = .75$

Suppose that to decide among these alternatives the coin is thrown 1,000 times (by the usual process), with the result

(*R*) Of 1,000 tosses, 738 are tails and 262 are heads.

There is clearly no deductive connection between the observed result *R* and any of the alternatives; for the alternatives refer to an infinite sequence while *R* refers to only a finite part of it, and *any* character of a finite part of an infinite sequence is logically compatible with any limit of the whole sequence. On the other hand, there is clearly an inductive connection between *R* and each of the alternatives: *R* is overwhelming evidence for $A''_{.75}$ and against $A''_{.25}$ and $A''_{.50}$, and so we may inductively infer $A''_{.75}$ from *R*. Thus the empirical verification of a frequency probability statement presupposes rules of inductive inference and the concept of inductive probability. It is a shortcoming of the frequency theory of empirical probability that it does not say what rules are used in the inductive inference of $A''_{.75}$ from *R*. This inference looks like an application of Bayes' theorem (sec. 2.5), and

I think it really is, but more needs to be said about the nature of empirical probability and its relation to frequency before we can show that this is so (see sec. 8.2).

The frequency theory of empirical probability analyzes empirical probability into relative frequency in the long run. A variant of this theory analyzes empirical probability into approximate relative frequency in a finite but very long sequence. When frequency probability (**P**$_f$) is taken in the finitistic sense, "**P**$_f$(T) = .50" means that approximately half of the tosses in a finite but very long sequence are tails. However, this finitistic version of frequency probability does not avoid the conclusion reached with respect to the "long run" version of frequency probability, namely, that the empirical verification of a frequency probability statement presupposes rules of inductive inference and the concept of inductive probability. To see this, consider a sequence of one million tosses of the coin. According to the finitistic version of the frequency theory of empirical probability, alternative $A''_{.25}$ implies that about 250,000 of these tosses will be tails, $A''_{.50}$ implies that about 500,000 of them will be tails, and $A''_{.75}$ implies that about 750,000 of them will be tails. Observation R is logically compatible with all three alternatives, for it merely limits the number of tails to the range 738 to 999,738. To argue that R is strong evidence for $A''_{.75}$, one still needs to use inductive rules.

We have shown that the empirical verification of a frequency probability statement presupposes rules of inductive inference and that the frequency theory of empirical probability does not say what these rules are. In other words, the frequency theory of empirical probability gives no account of the verification of empirical probability statements, and it does not explain the relation of empirical probability to inductive probability. Consequently, this theory does not give a complete answer to our third main question. We shall develop a complete answer in Chapter 8, "The Dispositional Theory of Empirical Probability."

3.4.2 The frequency theory of inductive probability

There is a version of the frequency theory of probability that does attempt to give an account of the relation between empirical and inductive probability. The **frequency theory of inductive probability** proposes to analyze both atomic empirical probability statements and atomic inductive probability statements into frequency probability statements. Hence according to this theory empirical probability (**P**$_e$), inductive probability (**P**), and frequency probability (**P**$_f$) are all identical, and the calculus of inductive probability should be interpreted as the calculus of frequency probability. It follows that atomic inductive probability statements are empirically true-or-false, excluding, of course, those that are logically true-or-false by virtue of axiom [3]. It also follows that the axioms and theorems of the calculus of inductive probability are logical truths of conventional mathematics. Thus the frequency theory of inductive probability offers answers to our first three main questions (pp. 92, 144).

The frequency theory of inductive probability was first advanced by Peirce and more recently by Reichenbach. Their formulations differ somewhat, the main difference being that Reichenbach gives an explicit argument for his theory, whereas Peirce's argument tends to be hidden in his definition of truth.* Rather than attempt a historical analysis here, I present what I think is the core of the frequency theory of inductive probability and criticize it. Late in life Peirce proposed a somewhat different theory of probability, which I call "Peirce's dispositional-frequency theory of probability"; this is discussed in Section 8.4.2, below.†

The first problem in identifying inductive and frequency probability is to identify the arguments of the operators **P** and $\mathbf{P}_f$. Peirce accomplished this in the following way.

As we noted earlier (p. 15), the essence of an argument is its generality. In arguing, one passes from premises to conclusion in conformity with some rule that, in the nature of the case, is applicable to many other arguments. An essential characteristic of a good deductive rule is that when the premises are true, the conclusion will always be true. Peirce made this the defining property of a valid deductive argument, and he extended it to cover valid inductive arguments as well.

> . . . the validity of an inference . . . consists in the real fact that, when premises like those of the argument in question are true, conclusions related to them like that of this argument are also true. . . . in a logical mind an argument is always conceived as a member of a *genus* of arguments all constructed in the same way, and such that, when their premises are real facts, their conclusions are so also. If the argument is demonstrative, then this is always so; if it is only probable, then it is for the most part so.
>
> . . . in the long run, there is a real fact which corresponds to the idea of probability, and it is that a given mode of inference sometimes proves successful and sometimes not, and that in a ratio ultimately fixed. As we go on drawing inference after inference of the given kind, during the first ten or hundred cases the ratio of successes may be expected to show considerable fluctuations; but when we come into the thousands and millions, these fluctuations become less and less; and if we continue long enough, the ratio will approximate toward a fixed limit. We may, therefore, define the probability of a mode of argument as the proportion of cases in which it carries truth with it.‡

* See John Lenz, "Induction as Self-Corrective," my "Reichenbach's Theory of Probability and Induction," and my "Peirce's Two Theories of Probability."

† Peirce's "early" (before 1890) views on pragmatism and laws of nature also differ from his later views (see pp. 172–74). When quoting Peirce on these topics we will give the original date of his text in parentheses.

‡ *Collected Papers* 2.649 and 2.650 (1878).

Peirce is saying that any given argument form

$$\psi \quad \therefore \text{ Probably } \Phi$$

should be considered in terms of an infinite sequence of applications of it

$$\psi x_1 \quad \therefore \text{ Probably } \phi x_1$$

$$\psi x_2 \quad \therefore \text{ Probably } \phi x_2$$

$$\psi x_3 \quad \therefore \text{ Probably } \phi x_3$$

$$\vdots$$

Hence the atomic inductive probability statement

$$\mathbf{P}(\phi x_i, \psi x_i) = \alpha$$

may be replaced by the corresponding frequency probability statement

$$\mathbf{P}_f(\phi, \psi) = \alpha \qquad .$$

We have already noted the difficulty in formulating a general rule governing an inductive argument (secs. 1.5.2, 3.3.3), but this is a problem for the subject of inductive logic and not an objection to Peirce's definition of inductive validity.

It is appropriate to recall here the conclusion of our recent discussion of the frequency theory of empirical probability: Since frequency probability statements are empirically true-or-false, an inductive logic is needed for their verification. The crucial point to examine next is whether this inductive logic can be accounted for in terms of frequency probability, as the frequency theory of inductive probability claims. Now to reason inductively one must assign a probability to the relation of premises ψx_i to conclusion ϕx_i. This probability is defined (in the frequency theory of inductive probability) to be the relative frequency with which true premises of the form ψ lead to true conclusions of the form ϕ in the long run. But at the time one uses an inductive argument he does not know what this long run frequency is. Past successes of the argument form are evidence as to what the probability is, but to assess their weight as evidence one needs an inductive argument. Hence the frequency theory of inductive probability seems trapped in a circle: Reasoning inductively involves assigning a probability to the relation of premises to conclusion, but to choose this probability rationally one must first reason inductively. This charge of circularity is serious; for if it is sound, science cannot really avoid using inductive probability in a nonfrequency sense, and the analysis of inductive probability ($\mathbf{P}$) into frequency probability ($\mathbf{P}_f$) fails.

The frequency theory of inductive probability attempts to avoid this difficulty by presenting a method of scientific inference along with a putative justification of the use of this method. We call the proposed method the "self-corrective inductive method" and the proffered justification of it the "Peirce-Reichenbach justification of induction"; though it should be repeated that we are not attempting to reproduce the exact views of Peirce and Reichenbach, but only what we think is the essence of them.

Consider an infinite sequence $x_1, x_2, \ldots, x_L, \ldots$ of applications of the argument form "ψ, therefore probably ϕ." $\mathbf{P}_f(\phi, \psi)$ is the correct probability to assign to this argument form, though of course the investigator does not know the value of $\mathbf{P}_f(\phi, \psi)$ when he uses the argument form. The self-corrective inductive method tells him how to proceed. Since every term of the sequence $x_1, x_2, x_3, \ldots$ is a case of ψ, it will suffice to study $\mathbf{P}_f(\phi)$. That is, since conditional probability may be defined in terms of unconditional probability (by the reduction principle of sec. 2.6 and definition (F) of sec. 3.4.1), the method may be defined in terms of the unconditional probability $\mathbf{P}_f(\phi)$. The *self-corrective inductive method* consists in an indefinite repetition of the following basic step: Observe the sequence up to x_L to determine the relative frequency $\sigma_L(\phi)$, accept this *tentatively* as the correct value of the probability $\mathbf{P}_f(\phi)$, and extrapolate it by making predictions as if it were true.

In the terminology of Section 2.5.2 (Confirmation by repeated experimentation) one performs an experiment of length L, asserts that the limit of the sequence is $\sigma_L(\phi)$, and acts as if an arbitrary future event ϕx_i $(i > L)$ will occur with probability $\sigma_L(\phi)$. This rule of prediction is called the *straight rule of induction.*

As Peirce noted, there is a close analogy between the self-corrective inductive method and the general evolutionary process. If a tentative value of $\mathbf{P}_f(\phi)$ is wrong, it will not survive but will eventually be replaced by another value. To put the matter in epistemological terms: This erroneous value will be corrected. If this new value is also in error, it will ultimately be corrected too. Thus the procedure is self-corrective, producing a succession of values $\sigma_1(\phi), \sigma_2(\phi), \ldots, \sigma_L(\phi), \ldots$ that evolves toward the limit $\mathbf{P}_f(\phi)$, i.e., the "truth."

The *Peirce-Reichenbach justification of induction* is divided into two parts, according to whether the relative frequency $\sigma_L(\phi)$ does or does not have a limit. It is argued in the latter case that there is nothing to find. As Reichenbach expressed it, our only chance for success is to assume that the limit exists and to follow the recommended inductive method. Peirce embodied this argument in his definition of truth as "the opinion which is fated to be ultimately agreed to by all who investigate."* According to Peirce's definition, there is no truth insofar as a limit does not exist, and since scientific inquiry is directed toward the truth, science presupposes

* Reichenbach, *The Theory of Probability*, pp. 475, 482. Peirce, *Collected Papers* 5.407 (1878).

that the limit exists. The problem is then to justify the use of the self-corrective inductive method for the case where there is a limit. This seems easy, for it follows directly from the definition of limit that if $\sigma_L(\phi)$ has a limit, this method will find it sometime. Putting the matter more formally, to say that the sequence $\sigma_1(\phi), \sigma_2(\phi), \ldots, \sigma_L(\phi), \ldots$ has a limit is to say that for any amount of error ϵ, no matter how small, there is an L such that for any $m \geqq L$, the observed relative frequency $\sigma_m(\phi)$ is to within ϵ of $\mathbf{P}_f(\phi)$. The conclusion is then drawn that the use of the self-corrective inductive method is justified.

We devote the rest of this section to a criticism of the Peirce-Reichenbach justification of induction. Prima facie, this putative justification is refuted by Hume's thesis that there is no noncircular justification of induction, and in the end we will conclude that this is in fact the case. However, since Peirce and Reichenbach were aware of Hume and nevertheless attempted to justify induction in a noncircular manner, their argument deserves detailed criticism.

It should be noted first that a given argument form "ψ, therefore probably ϕ" may not in fact be used infinitely many times. Suppose that during the entire history of the universe this argument form is used only L times. Because a frequency probability is defined only for an infinite sequence, $\mathbf{P}_f(\phi, \psi)$ would then be undefined. Peirce met this difficulty by assuming that there will actually be an infinite sequence of applications of the argument form "ψ, therefore probably ϕ." As he expressed the matter, a belief in the existence of an unlimited community of scientific investigators is an indispensable requirement of inductive logic.*

Another way of meeting the difficulty would be to extend the definition of $\mathbf{P}_f(\phi, \psi)$ so that if the sequence is of finite length L, $\mathbf{P}_f(\phi, \psi) = \sigma_L(\phi, \psi)$. Because the frequency theory of inductive probability identifies all three kinds of probability ($\mathbf{P}$, $\mathbf{P}_f$, and $\mathbf{P}_e$), the inductive probability $\mathbf{P}(\phi x_l, \psi x_l)$ would then equal $\sigma_L(\phi, \psi)$ for $l \leqq L$, and the empirical probability $\mathbf{P}_e(\phi, \psi)$ would also equal the relative frequency $\sigma_L(\phi, \psi)$. This is very odd and conflicts with our intuition that an event of probability α does not necessarily occur exactly αL times in L trials, though αL is close to or equal to the most likely number of occurrences of the event in L trials (sec. 2.4). To take an extreme example, imagine that in the entire history of the universe there were only two instances of a coin being tossed, both cases resulting in heads. Then on the frequency theory of inductive probability the probability of a tail would have been zero! Since this oddity is less noticeable for large L, one might assume only that the sequence of applications of the argument form "ψ, therefore probably ϕ" is very long.

* *Collected Papers* 2.655-56 (1878). Cf. 5.357 (1869).

An alternative to strictly equating frequency probability and relative frequency in the finite case is to say that they are approximately equal, the approximation being better for longer than for shorter sequences. How might these approximations be dealt with? One possibility is to construct a calculus for them. Since approximations are a matter of degree, such a calculus would be complex and unwieldly; moreover, this calculus might well involve a nonfrequency concept of probability. Another possibility is to use the frequency calculus of infinite sequences in dealing with finite sequences, on the ground that in doing so one is making a normal scientific idealization. But this particular idealization hides the problem at issue: how to make inferences between statements about finite sequences and statements about infinite sequences without using a nonfrequency concept of probability.*

But I do not see why inductive logic needs to make any assumption about how often an inductive argument is used. The validity of a deductive argument was defined in terms of the *logical* truth of the corresponding conditional, not in terms of the *actual* truth of that conditional (sec. 1.5.1). Similarly, inductive validity should be defined in terms of *possible* sequences, not in terms of *actual* sequences. When this is done, the use of an inductive argument form does not presuppose anything about the number of times that argument form will actually be employed. It is a basic objection to the frequency theory of inductive probability that it requires an assumption about the number of times an inductive argument form will actually be used.

The remainder of our critical discussion of the Peirce-Reichenbach justification of induction will be based on a comparison of the self-corrective inductive method with standard inductive logic and also with Bayes' method of finding an unknown probability. The self-corrective method and standard inductive logic differ in their treatment of inductive probability. Standard inductive logic distinguishes inductive probability from relative frequency and uses such notions as "assignment of unconditional probabilities to alternative possible universe descriptions." In contrast, the self-corrective inductive method identifies inductive probability with frequency probability and uses such notions as "tentative acceptance of a relative frequency." Nevertheless, the predictions made by the self-corrective inductive method are very similar to those made by standard inductive logic. To bring out the similarities and differences in more detail, we compare the straight rule of induction with the inductive logics of Carnap's continuum (pp. 120–25).

The logics of Carnap's continuum are characterized by a rule of induction by simple enumeration that has an unconditional probability part and a conditional probability part.

* These criticisms are elaborated in my "Reichenbach's Theory of Probability and Induction," pp. 380-82. See also Salmon's *The Foundations of Scientific Inference*, pp. 83-96.

$$[\text{A}](1)\quad \mathbf{P}(\phi x_i) = \frac{\omega}{\kappa}$$

$$(2)\quad \mathbf{P}[\phi x_i, \sigma_L(\phi) = s/L] = \frac{s}{L}\left(\frac{L}{L+\lambda}\right) + \frac{\omega}{\kappa}\left(\frac{\lambda}{L+\lambda}\right) \qquad \text{for } i > L\,,$$

where s/L is the observed relative frequency (the empirical factor), ω/κ is the relative width of the predicate ϕ (the prior probability factor), and λ is a non-negative real number. Standard inductive logic is a special case of rule [A], obtained by setting $\lambda = \kappa$.

$$[\text{A}_\kappa](1)\quad \mathbf{P}(\phi x_i) = \frac{\omega}{\kappa}$$

$$(2)\quad \mathbf{P}[\phi x_i, \sigma_L(\phi) = s/L] = \frac{s+\omega}{L+\kappa} \qquad \text{for } i > L\,.$$

As far as its quantitative probabilistic predictions are concerned, the straight rule of induction is also a special case of rule [A]. For $\lambda = 0$, [A] becomes

$$[\text{A}_0](1)\quad \mathbf{P}(\phi x_i) = \frac{\omega}{\kappa}$$

$$(2)\quad \mathbf{P}[\phi x_i, \sigma_L(\phi) = s/L] = \frac{s}{L} \qquad \text{for } i > L\,.$$

The frequentist denies the intelligibility of prior probabilities and hence of $[\text{A}_0](1)$; he will make no predictions in the absence of observations. However, rule $[\text{A}_0](2)$ is very similar to the straight rule in that both predict a future event with probability s/L on the basis of an observed relative frequency of s/L. There are these differences. The frequentist employs the straight rule to predict the limit of a sequence as well as to predict an arbitrary event. Moreover, he considers a prediction of the latter kind a matter of action, not thought, and denies that he needs any probability concept other than frequency probability. Also, there is a quantitative difference between the predicted probability s/L assigned by the straight rule and the predicted probability $(s+\omega)/(L+\kappa)$ given by standard inductive logic.

This last difference is not important here, for the inductive logic defined by $\lambda = \kappa$ was chosen as a convenient model of standard inductive logic as this logic is used in actual human inference, and many other logics of Carnap's continuum would do just as well. Indeed, in evaluating the attempt of Peirce and Reichenbach to justify the use of the straight rule, we can accept their claim that the straight rule is a quantitatively adequate model of standard inductive logic. The crucial point is that the straight rule partly specifies an inductive logic to which there are alternatives, and these alternatives must be considered in attempting to justify the straight rule. This being so, Hume's thesis that there is no noncircular justification of induction applies to the self-corrective inductive method as well as to standard inductive logic. Since the Peirce-Reichenbach justification of induction is an attempt to justify induction in a noncircular manner, this putative justification contradicts Hume's thesis. We shall show that the self-corrective inductive method employs standard inductive logic at three places and hence that the Peirce-Reichenbach justification of induction fails.

Each step of the self-corrective inductive method contains two stages: a description $\sigma_L(\phi)$ of that part of the sequence already observed, and a projection of this observed relative frequency into the future by means of the straight rule of induction. The description $\sigma_L(\phi)$ is inferred from accumulated memories and records of observations by means of standard inductive logic. If one used a different inductive logic, his knowledge of the past could be wrong in such a way that he would not approach the limit $\mathbf{P}_f(\phi)$ even if it existed. Thus standard inductive logic is employed in the first stage of the self-corrective inductive method.

The second stage of the self-corrective inductive method uses the straight rule of induction. This rule is actually applied in two very different ways: (1) to a finite portion of the future sequence, and (2) to the whole infinite sequence. Both types of application turn out on analysis to involve standard inductive logic, though in somewhat different ways.

(1) One may apply the straight rule of induction to some finite part of the sequence, such as a single event or the next million events. This use of the straight rule is required whenever probability is to serve as a guide to action (see chaps. 4 and 5). We can confine our discussion, without the loss of generality, to the case of predicting an arbitrary future event. One then acts (bets) *as if* some future event ϕx_i $(i > L)$ will occur with probability $\sigma_L(\phi)$. But as we have just seen, the straight rule is a kind of rule of induction by simple enumeration; and so when the self-corrective inductive method is applied to a single case, it is similar to standard inductive logic. Since there are alternative inductive logics, there are alternatives to this finitistic use of the straight rule. Appealing to Hume's thesis that there is no noncircular justification of induction, we conclude that the Peirce-Reichenbach "justification" of induction fails to justify the finitistic use of the straight rule.

Before turning to discuss the application of the straight rule of induction to the infinite case, we wish to make another point about the application of the rule to the finite case. The Peirce-Reichenbach justification of induction contains the claim that if there is no limit $\mathbf{P}_f(\phi)$ there is nothing to find and the investigator has no chance for success. But this claim is wrong with respect to the application of the straight rule to a single case, for one can be successful over a finite span even if the infinite sequence has no limit.

Actually it is a mystery, on the frequency theory of inductive probability, why one should act as if the next event or a finite sequence of events would occur with a certain probability; for according to this theory "probability" refers to the occurrence of properties in an infinite sequence of events and is therefore meaningless when applied to a single case or to any finite sequence. The time-honored illustration of this difficulty for the frequency theory of inductive probability is the story of a medical doctor who performs a risky operation. "The probability that you will survive this operation," he tells a prospective patient, "is three-quarters." According to the frequency theory of inductive probability this is an assertion about the limit of an infinite sequence of such operations and says nothing about this particular patient's operation. Hence the frequency theory implies that the doctor has given no information of value to a patient whose only interest is in his own survival. It might seem that the statement made by the doctor conveys information of value to himself, since the doctor is interested in his overall success; but even this is not so, because the doctor is interested in a finite number of cases, not an infinite number. Hence the frequency theory of inductive probability should say nothing about the application of probabilities to single cases or finite sets of cases. That most proponents of this theory are inconsistent and talk about finite applications is a tribute to their realism.

The inapplicability of the frequency theory of inductive probability to single cases or finite sets of cases is clearly a fatal defect in the theory, for all applications of science are finitistic and most applications are to single events. In contrast, an inductive probability $\mathbf{P}(c)$ is applicable to a single case, since "c" can be a singular statement. This is a clinching argument against analyzing inductive probability ($\mathbf{P}$) into frequency probability ($\mathbf{P}_f$).

The preceding argument against the frequency theory of inductive probability is also relevant to the frequency theory of empirical probability, for it shows that the frequency theory of empirical probability cannot explain how an empirical probability statement is relevant to a single event. Frequency probability is defined for infinite sequences, and rules are needed to pass from the limiting characteristics of an infinite sequence to the properties of a finite portion of that sequence. Thus the frequency theory of inductive probability not only fails to explain how empirical probability statements are verified, but it also fails to explain how empirical probability statements are applied. We shall see later how inferences from empirical probability statements to finite applications, and inversely, from finite observations to empirical probability statements, can be made by means of the calculus of inductive probability (sec. 8.3.2).

(2) The self-corrective method is defined in terms of an infinite sequence $x_1, x_2, \ldots, x_L, \ldots$ of uses of the argument form "ψ, therefore probably ϕ." The second application of the straight rule of induction is to this whole sequence. In this application the investigator says, tentatively, that the

limit of the sequence, i.e., $\mathbf{P}_f(\phi)$, is approximately $\sigma_L(\phi)$. We will show that the Peirce-Reichenbach justification of this use of the straight rule of induction does not succeed. It is clearly true that if the sequence has a limit, at some time the description $\sigma_L(\phi)$ will become and remain approximately equal to this limit. This gives true opinion, but it does not give grounded opinion or knowledge, and it is not epistemologically sufficient. The scientist holds at some stage of an inquiry that the description $\sigma_L(\phi)$ is good evidence for the claim that $\mathbf{P}_f(\phi)$ is approximately $\sigma_L(\phi)$. For the reasons given in connection with the first use (1) of the straight rule, this appeal to evidence employs standard inductive logic or an inductive logic very similar to it.

This completes our comparison of the self-corrective inductive method and standard inductive logic. We will make a similar comparison of the self-corrective method and Bayes' method of finding the unknown probability of a mixture of independent processes. Note that both the self-corrective method and Bayes' method involve repeated observations and probabilistic predictions based on these observations. In following this next comparison, the reader should keep in mind that standard inductive logic and all the other inductive logics of Carnap's continuum are complete probability assignments to mixtures of independent processes (p. 126). As before, we will consider both (1′) the finite application and (2′) the infinite application of the straight rule.

(1′) On Bayes' method, the predicted probability $\mathbf{P}[\psi x_i, \sigma_L(\psi) = s/L]$ depends on both the prior probability assignment and the observed relative frequency. At any given stage of inquiry, there is only a finite amount of evidence, and this evidence may not be sufficient to bring different investigators into close agreement. It is clear from Bayes' theorem that insofar as two scientists who have the same data agree (or disagree) on a prediction, they must agree (or disagree) on the prior probability assignment (see pp. 90–92). Exploiting the parallelism between alternative inductive logics and alternative prior probability assignments, we can now argue as we argued in (1) above. To justify an inductive logic, one must show its superiority to the alternatives. Similarly, to justify the straight rule one must show its superiority to other rules. Each prior probability assignment to a mixture of independent processes yields a set of probability predictions and hence constitutes an alternative to the straight rule. The Peirce-Reichenbach justification of induction fails to show that the straight rule is superior to these other rules and so does not justify the finite use of the straight rule.

(2′) The second application of the straight rule is to the whole infinite sequence. The fact that the self-corrective inductive method gives only true opinion, not grounded opinion, should be contrasted with the confirmation theorem. This theorem states that an investigator who applied Bayes' method of finding an unknown probability to a mixture of independent processes will eventually know the truth. Thus the confirmation theorem justifies the use of Bayes' method of finding an unknown probability, but *only* on the assumption that the process to which Bayes' method is applied is a mixture of independent processes.* The need for this assumption parallels Hume's thesis that there is no noncircular justification of induction and contrasts with the attempt of Peirce and Reichenbach to avoid all assumptions about induction.

We have now concluded our criticism of the Peirce-Reichenbach justification of the self-corrective inductive method. We have shown that this putative justification rests on standard inductive logic or a closely similar inductive logic. Since Peirce and Reichenbach wished to justify the use of the self-corrective inductive method without an appeal to any inductive logic, the attempt fails. Thus the Peirce-Reichenbach justification of induction founders on the rock of Hume's thesis that there is no noncircular justification of induction. We conclude that *the frequency theory of inductive probability is wrong, that inductive probability cannot be analyzed into frequency probability, and that empirical probability and inductive probability are substantially different.*

Let us see how this conclusion bears on the question: Are atomic inductive probability statements empirically true-or-false? According to the frequency theory of inductive probability, they are. Moreover, this theory is the only existing theory to take this position. The fact that this theory turns out to be wrong is certainly good evidence that the answer to the question is negative. There is, of course, the possibility that a nonfrequency theory answering the question positively might be developed. But if it were, much of the argument of the present subsection could probably be used against it. Any theory that holds atomic inductive probability statements to be empirically true-or-false faces the charge of vicious circularity or vicious infinite regress. For the verification of an empirically true-or-false statement involves the use of atomic inductive probability statements; and if these were empirically true-or-false, their verification would in turn involve an appeal to atomic inductive probability statements. We conclude from all this that *atomic inductive probability statements are not empirically true-or-false.*

The existence of alternative inductive logics shows that these statements are not logically true-or-false. Hence atomic inductive probability statements are neither logically nor empirically true-or-false. This partly answers our second main question (p. 144; cf. p. 129).

* The confirmation theorem may be generalized to cover processes that are not mixtures of independent processes; such processes are discussed in sec. 8.3.1. But the argument of the present section shows that some condition on a process is needed to ground inductive inference from one part to another part of the process.

3.5 Summary

The calculus of inductive probability relates atomic inductive probability statements to each other, but, except in some uninteresting cases, it does not determine the truth-status of any atomic inductive probability statement. Some important logical rules for judging empirical evidence are not included in the calculus of inductive probability, such as rules of analogy, the method of varying causally relevant qualities, and the rule of induction by simple enumeration. These rules need to be added to the calculus of inductive probability to obtain a complete system.

An inductive logic is a system that includes the calculus of inductive probability and at least partially specifies atomic inductive probabilities. Standard inductive logic is the system of rules actually used and aspired to by the practicing scientist, including the rule of induction by simple enumeration. Two other inductive logics are useful as hypothetical alternatives to standard inductive logic. Inverse inductive logic is characterized by an anti-enumeration rule, while random inductive logic treats the successive states of the universe as an independent process.

Inductive logics for simple models of reality (sec. 3.2). For some highly simplified models of reality, Carnap has shown how to extend the calculus of inductive probability to attain complete systems in which every atomic inductive probability statement has a truth-value. Each model consists of a finite number of basic individuals and a finite number of basic properties. Logically possible universes are constructed from these individuals and properties, and one of the universes is designated as the actual universe. There is a corresponding linguistic structure of proper names, monadic predicates, universe descriptions, and a true universe description. Models with an infinite number of individuals are treated as infinite sequences of finite models. Both finite and infinite models may be used as models of reality for defining inductive logics.

An assignment of non-negative numbers to the universe descriptions of a finite model that sums to one determines an inductive logic for that model. Standard, inverse, and random inductive logic are defined for all finite models by means of axioms expressed in terms of the isomorphism measure of a universe description. The isomorphism measure of a universe description varies inversely with its statistical uniformity. Standard inductive logic assigns higher probabilities to uniform universes than to irregular ones, inverse inductive logic does the reverse, while random inductive logic assigns equal probabilities to all possible universes. There are interesting connections between concepts of inductive logic and concepts of thermodynamics.

The notion of a complete probability assignment to a process, finite or infinite, encompasses the probabilistic processes of Chapter 2 as well as the inductive logics of the present chapter. Carnap has arranged an infinite number of inductive logics into a continuum by means of a generalized rule of induction by simple enumeration. On this rule the predicted probability of a future event depends on two factors: a prior probability factor and an empirical factor (the observed relative frequency). The logics of Carnap's continuum vary in the relative weights they assign to these two factors. Standard inductive logic is a representative logic of the continuum.

De Finetti proved that a complete probability assignment to an infinite process is exchangeable if and only if that process is a mixture of independent processes. Every inductive logic of Carnap's continuum is defined for infinite models and is exchangeable and hence is a mixture of independent processes. Inverse inductive logic is exchangeable, but it is definable only for finite models.

Hume's thesis on the justification of induction (sec. 3.3). The meanings of "inductive logic," "standard inductive logic," "inverse inductive logic," and "random inductive logic" were specified both by informal considerations and by formal definitions of them for these limited models. There are different deductively consistent inductive logics applicable to reality, and hence atomic inductive probability statements are not logically true-or-false.

The possibility of justifying the use of standard inductive logic over a finite span was considered. The conclusions reached were formulated as Hume's thesis that there is no noncircular justification of induction. According to Hume's thesis, there are alternative deductively consistent inductive logics. Consequently, atomic inductive probability statements are not logically true-or-false, and there is no deductive justification for using standard inductive logic instead of an alternative. Moreover, the usual procedure for showing that one behavior pattern is more beneficial than any other involves the use of standard inductive logic. Therefore any attempt to justify the use of an inductive logic in this way is circular and question-begging. An inductive logic constitutes a standard of evidence and of probable predictive success, and so a person who uses it can never find empirical grounds for modifying or abandoning it.

Though the preceding thesis is rightfully named after Hume, his own formulation and argument were quite different from ours. His formulation centered on a uniformity of nature principle: the future will resemble the past. This principle is empirical, he said, and therefore any attempt to obtain evidence for it is necessarily circular. He further concluded that inductive inference is not reasoning. This last conclusion is incorrect, for everyone accepts standard inductive logic and employs words like "probability" in conformity with that logic.

The formal models of this chapter are extreme idealizations of reality. They are limited to first-order quantification theory and therefore do not cover the continuous mathematics used by science. Moreover, causal dispositions, empirical probability statements, and the concept of causal necessity cannot be expressed in first-order quantification theory. Consequently, Hume's thesis that there is no noncircular justification of induction is speculative.

Frequency theories of probability (*sec. 3.4*). The concept of frequency probability applies to an infinite sequence of events. The frequency probability of a property is the limit of the relative frequency with which that property occurs in the sequence, if the limit exists. There are two distinct frequency theories of probability. The frequency theory of *empirical* probability analyzes empirical probability into frequency probability. The frequency theory of *inductive* probability accepts this analysis and also analyzes inductive probability into frequency probability. Hume's thesis that there is no noncircular justification of induction is useful in evaluating the latter theory.

Our third main question is: What is the general nature of a system of atomic empirical probability statements? How are empirical and inductive probability related? Why is the traditional calculus of probability applicable to empirical probabilities? The answer offered by the frequency theory of empirical probability is that atomic empirical probability statements should be analyzed into frequency probability statements and reasoned about by means of the calculus of frequency probability. This calculus is an interpretation of the traditional calculus of probability; its theorems refer to the limits of sequences, and they are all logically true.

The frequency theory of empirical probability gives partially satisfactory answers to the first and last parts of the third main question, but it gives no account either of the verification of empirical probability statements or of their application. Frequencies can be observed only in the finite case, whereas frequency probability statements concern infinite sequences, and rules of inductive inference are needed to make the connection. Conversely, though empirical probability statements concern sequences of events, they are often applied to single events, and rules of inductive inference are needed to make the connection in this direction also. Hence the frequency theory of empirical probability fails to explain how empirical probability and inductive probability are related (pp. 149–50, 156–60).

The frequency theory of inductive probability proposes to analyze inductive as well as empirical probability into frequency probability, and so it also offers answers to the first and second main questions (sec. 2.5.4). On this theory, atomic inductive probability statements refer to limiting relative frequencies. With unimportant exceptions, atomic inductive probability statements are empirically true-or-false. The theorems of the calculus of inductive probability are logical truths about limits of sequences.

The frequency theory of inductive probability seems beset with circularity from the beginning, for if inductive probability statements are empirical an inductive logic is needed for their verification. The Peirce-Reichenbach justification of induction is designed to avoid this circle; it attempts to justify the self-corrective inductive method without employing any assumptions.

The self-corrective inductive method consists of the repeated use of the straight rule of induction to predict both a single event and the limit of the sequence. When the straight rule is used to predict a single event it is similar to standard inductive logic, so that Hume's thesis that there is no noncircular justification of induction applies to it. When the straight rule is used to predict the limit of the sequence, it gives at best true opinion, not grounded opinion. Standard inductive logic is needed to obtain grounded opinion, and Hume's thesis is again applicable.

Thus the Peirce-Reichenbach justification of induction fails, and with it the frequency theory of inductive probability. It follows that inductive probability cannot be analyzed into frequency probability and that empirical and inductive probability are fundamentally different.

Conclusion. The arguments used against the frequency theory of inductive probability show also that atomic inductive probability statements are not empirical. The existence of alternative inductive logics shows that these statements are not logically true-or-false. Hence atomic inductive probability statements are neither logically nor empirically true-or-false. This partially answers our second main question. (P. 160)

4 Probability and Action

. . . what we think is to be interpreted in terms of what we are prepared to do. . . .
. . . the intellectual purport of a concept consists in the truth of certain conditional propositions asserting that if the concept be applicable, and the utterer of the proposition or his fellow have a certain purpose in view, he would act in a certain way.

But, to us, probability is the very guide of life.*

4.1 Introduction

We shall study the relation of probability to action in this and the following chapter. Our investigation will culminate in my "pragmatic theory of inductive probability," which explains probability in terms of rules for acting in uncertain situations.

The idea of grounding the concept of probability on its uses in action is a special case of C. S. Peirce's pragmatism. For this reason we first present and criticize this doctrine (sec. 4.2). Peirce's pragmatism is of interest not only because it is closely related to the pragmatic theory of inductive probability; it is also an important doctrine about the nature of scientific knowledge.

Since traditionally the concept of probability has been connected to action via the concept of utility, we discuss utility next (sec. 4.3). We present the concept, derive some obvious implications from it, raise some problems concerning it, and discuss its relation to the simple ordering of preferences and uncertainties. Finally, we state a theorem about gambling that shows a value to be gained from using the calculus of probability in conditions of uncertainty (sec. 4.4).

Though the pragmatic theory of inductive probability is an application of Peirce's pragmatism, Peirce did not himself originate or advocate a theory of this kind. Rather, he based inductive probability on frequencies (secs. 3.4, 8.4.2). The historical background of the pragmatic theory will be discussed in the next chapter (sec. 5.1.2).

* Peirce, *Collected Papers* 5.35 and 5.528. Butler, *The Analogy of Religion,* from the third paragraph of the "Introduction." Butler is contrasting man with God, who does not need to use induction since he knows everything directly.

4.2 Peirce's Pragmatism*

4.2.1 The pragmatic principle of meaning

Peirce expressed his pragmatism in the form of a principle of meaning that we will call "Peirce's pragmatic principle of meaning." He developed this principle to account for the meaning of nonprobability statements, handling probability statements by means of the frequency theory of probability. In the present section we describe and criticize Peirce's pragmatic principle of meaning, concluding that while it contains some valuable insights it needs to be revised in a number of respects, particularly to take better account of inductive probability.

Peirce characterized a belief as a conscious, deliberate habit of action: ". . . what we think is to be interpreted in terms of what we are prepared to do. . . ." † Suppose you believe that there is a dumbbell on the floor. Your belief is a rule of action in the following way: If you walk across the room you go around the dumbbell in order not to trip over it; if you reach to pick it up you adjust the tension of your muscles in accordance with your expectation that it is heavy; if you drop a book on it you expect that the dumbbell will not be crushed. All these conditional (if . . . then . . .) statements involve action; we call them "practical conditionals." ‡ According to Peirce, your belief that there is a dumbbell on the floor consists of a system of such practical conditionals, and similarly for all nonmathematical beliefs.

Peirce's famous pragmatic principle or theory of meaning follows quite directly from his account of belief. This is

> the theory that a *conception*, that is, the rational purport of a word or other expression, lies exclusively in its conceivable bearing upon the conduct of life; so that, since obviously nothing that might not result from experiment can have any direct bearing upon conduct, if one can define accurately all of the conceivable experimental phenomena which the affirmation or denial of a concept could imply, one will have therein a complete definition of the concept, and *there is absolutely nothing more in it.*
>
> *In order to ascertain the meaning of an intellectual conception one should consider what practical consequences might conceivably result by necessity from the truth of that conception; and the sum of these consequences will constitute the entire meaning of the conception.*

* This section draws from my introduction to the Peirce selections in *Classic American Philosophers*.

†*Collected Papers* 5.35.

‡ "If *p* then *q*" has the antecedent condition *p* and the consequent *q*. The whole is called a "hypothetical" or a "conditional." Peirce called the whole a "consequence," and so for him "practical consequence" refers to the whole conditional (to what we call a "practical conditional"), and not just to its consequent. His usage is now archaic.

The idea which the word force excites in our minds has no other function than to affect our actions, and these actions can have no reference to force otherwise than through its effects. Consequently, if we know what the effects of force are, we are acquainted with every fact which is implied in saying that a force exists, and there is nothing more to know.*

For example, the meaning of the statement

[1] This diamond is harder than any known metal

consists of all the practical conditionals logically implied by it, one of which is

[2] If this diamond were rubbed with the point of a metal knife in normal circumstances, it would not be scratched.

Note that a *practical conditional* takes the form

[3] If the experiment θ should be performed in circumstances ψ, the observed result would be χ.

Thus a practical conditional is a hypothetical whose antecedent describes an experiment or action and whose consequent describes an observable result.

Peirce's pragmatic principle of meaning states that the meaning of a statement consists in the set of those practical conditionals that are logically implied by the statement. This principle is intended to clarify the meaning of any general statement that is not logically true-or-false in terms of statements of a different kind, namely, practical conditionals. It thus presupposes a sharp distinction between general statements and practical conditionals. It is a weakness of Peirce's pragmatism that it does not tell us how to draw a sharp line between these two kinds of statements.

Essentially the same principle of meaning is found in the later doctrine of operationalism (scientific concepts are to be specified in terms of operations for applying them) and the verifiability principle of meaning (the meaning of a statement consists in its mode of verification).† Differences exist between these two doctrines and Peirce's pragmatic principle of meaning, but most of what we shall say about the latter applies, with appropriate modifications, to the former. In particular, the fact that practical conditionals cannot themselves be tested by direct observation (p. 174, below) is an objection to these doctrines as well as to Peirce's pragmatism.

* These three quotations are from *Collected Papers* 5.412, 5.9, and 5.404, respectively. See also 5.197, 5.467. Peirce first published his pragmatism in 1878 (5.388-410) but he had developed it in the early seventies (8.33 and 7.360).

† For operationalism see Bridgman, *The Logic of Modern Physics*. For the verifiability theory see Schlick, "Meaning and Verification," and Ayer, *Language, Truth and Logic*.

Sometimes verificationists make a weaker claim: A statement is meaningful if and only if it is verifiable. This "verification criterion of meaningfulness" is analogous to principle [6] below.

The word "meaning" itself has several meanings, and so the sense in which the practical conditionals implied by a proposition are said to constitute the meaning of that proposition needs further specification. In the next four subsections, we shall discuss, in turn, the criterion of sameness of meaning involved in Peirce's pragmatic principle of meaning, the notion of analysis involved in this principle, the descriptive component of the analysis, and the normative component of the analysis.

4.2.2 Sameness of meaning

Consider now two apparently different statements that in fact imply the same practical conditionals. According to Peirce's pragmatic principle of meaning, these two statements have the same meaning. An example is

[4] There are 1,591 grains of wheat in the box

[5] There are 37 x 43 grains of wheat in the box.

In this sense of "meaning," any two logically equivalent statements have the same meaning. But "meaning" is tricky; only in a very broad sense of this word can we identify the meanings of any two logically equivalent statements. In a stricter sense of "meaning," statements [4] and [5] differ in meaning, for a person might understand one of them and not the other. A person who did not know how to multiply could not understand [5], and yet if he knew how to count he might understand [4] and be able to verify it.

Such differences are important for the logic of empirical inquiry because two logically equivalent theories may have very different heuristic effects. The geocentric-heliocentric controversy is an illustration. Regarded as alternative ways of calculating the apparent motions of the planets, the geocentric and heliocentric hypotheses were essentially logically equivalent. But the paths of the planets are simpler when referred to the sun as origin than when plotted with the earth as origin. This difference in simplicity was historically important, for Kepler would not have discovered his three laws of planetary motion had he been using the geocentric rather than the heliocentric theory (sec. 1.4.2).

The contrast between "causal" and "minimizing" theories provides other examples of logically equivalent theories having different heuristic effects.* A causal theory gives the next state of the system as a function of its present state, whereas a minimizing theory asserts that over any finite history of the system, a certain quantity is minimized or maximized. Consider, for example, light moving from point *A* to a mirror, being reflected,

* This point is taken from von Neumann, "Method in Physical Sciences," but he calls the second type of theory "teleological."

and going to point *B*. The laws that the light will travel in a straight line and that the angle of reflection will equal the angle of incidence together constitute a causal theory. The law of least time, which says that the path from *A* to *B* must be such that the time of transit is a minimum,* is a minimizing theory. These two theories of light are very different, and yet they are logically equivalent.

The contrast between mechanical and teleological explanations is common in biology. Mechanical explanations are clearly causal in the sense just defined; and it seems likely that teleological explanations can be formulated as minimizing theories, though the particular functions that are minimized have not yet been characterized mathematically.

It should be noted in connection with the foregoing that a definition of a class term may contain two criteria: an applicability criterion for deciding whether the term is applicable to a given entity, and a counting criterion for deciding whether two entities to which the term is applicable are identical. Compare, for example, the term "word" in "There are 250 words on that page" with the term "word" in "He has a vocabulary of 2,000 words"; these two terms have the same applicability criteria but different counting criteria. I classified, or counted, the causal theory of light and the law of least time as two *different* theories, but they might also be counted as two different formulations of the *same* theory.

Now pragmatism wishes to account for the meaning of statements that are not logically true-or-false; hence logical equivalence is the criterion of sameness to be employed here. The proposition

[6] If two statements or theories logically imply the same practical conditionals, ultimately and in principle, they should be treated as logically equivalent

expresses this aspect of Peirce's pragmatic principle of meaning.

4.2.3 Analysis

On any view, the practical conditionals implied by a statement are intimately related to the meaning of that statement. What is distinctive in pragmatism (and operationalism and the verifiability principle of meaning as well) is the assertion that the entire meaning of a statement is, or should be, constituted by the practical conditionals implied by it. This assertion can be expressed technically in terms of the notion of *analysis*.† The term, statement, or argument analyzed is called the *analysandum;* that which is to be substituted for the analysandum is called the *analysans*. That is, the

* This and other minimal principles are discussed in Courant and Robbins, *What is Mathematics?*, chap. 7.

† See Langford, "The Notion of Analysis in Moore's Philosophy."

analysandum is analyzed into the analysans. In giving an analysis one asserts that the analysans has approximately the same meaning as the analysandum, that the analysans is superior to the analysandum in clarity and precision, and that for certain purposes one should think in terms of the analysans rather than the analysandum. In the case of Peirce's pragmatic principle of meaning, the analysandum is a sentence like "This diamond is harder than any known metal," while the corresponding analysans is the set of practical conditionals logically implied by this sentence.

An analysis has both a descriptive and a normative component. The descriptive component consists in the claim that, to a first approximation, the analysans has the same meaning as the analysandum in actual usage and that to this degree the analysans and analysandum are logically equivalent. The normative component consists in the assertion that insofar as there are differences in meaning between the analysandum and the analysans, these differences are in favor of the latter; i.e., for certain purposes the analysans is a better term to use than the analysandum. Peirce's pragmatic principle of meaning had both components, as the following quotation shows:

> But when you *have found*, or *ideally constructed* upon a basis of observation, the typical experimentalist, you will find that whatever assertion you make to him, he will either understand as meaning that if a given prescription for an experiment ever can be and ever is carried out in act, an experience of a given description will result, or else he will see no sense at all in what you say.*

The descriptive and normative components of the pragmatic principle of meaning will be discussed in Sections 4.2.4 and 4.2.5 after we have made some further remarks about analysis in general.

The unit of discourse analyzed may be larger than a single term, statement, or argument; it may be an interrelated set of these or a certain portion of a language. For example, the frequency theory of empirical probability analyzes sets of empirical probability statements into sets of frequency probability statements (sec. 3.4). How large the unit to be analyzed should be depends upon the amount of contextual interdependency relevant to the particular analysis being made.

Analysis is closely related to language modeling (sec. 1.6.3). Some cases of one are cases of the other, as in the example of the frequency theory cited in the preceding paragraph. But not all cases of the one are cases of the other, and the two notions have basic differences. Language modeling requires the use of a formal or artificial language, with the consequence that the pragmatic analysis of a statement into practical conditionals is not a case

* *Collected Papers* 5.411; italics added. That Peirce intended his pragmatic maxim to be normative as well as descriptive follows from his insistence that logic is a normative science. See my "Peirce's Conception of Logic as a Normative Science."

of language modeling. Analysis requires that the analysans have approximately the same meaning as the analysandum, whereas a formula used as a model may differ significantly in meaning from the statement it models; therefore, most of the cases of language modeling in the present book are not cases of analysis. See particularly Chapter 7, "The Logic of Causal Statements as a Model of Natural Language."

4.2.4 The descriptive component

We consider now the descriptive component of a pragmatic analysis. Peirce's pragmatic principle of meaning makes two claims here. The first is that the set of practical conditionals logically implied by a statement has approximately the same meaning as the statement. The second is that these practical conditionals are clearer and more precise than the original statement and hence are less in need of analysis than the original statement. We evaluate these two claims in turn.

With respect to the first claim, it is a mistake to limit the meaning of a statement that is not logically true-or-false to its deductive consequences. As we saw in our discussion of Bayes' theorem, some of the testable consequences of a statement are not logically implied by the statement but are only implied by it with probability (sec. 2.5). In excluding these probabilistic consequences, Peirce is excluding an important part of the meaning of a statement. And the fault is inherent in analysis itself, since the analysans is required to be logically equivalent to the analysandum and is not allowed to be merely probabilistically equivalent. In Section 4.2.6 we revise Peirce's pragmatic principle of meaning to take account of these probabilistic, nondeductive consequences of a statement.

Consider next the claim that practical conditionals are clearer and more precise than the statement they are used to analyze. The pragmatist thinks that practical conditionals clarify because they are so closely connected to action, observation, and experimentation. Now, by relating a statement to its empirical tests one often clarifies the statement, and in pointing this out Peirce made a very important contribution to philosophy. But his pragmatic principle of meaning leads to two basic problems that it fails to solve, and hence it gives an incomplete account of the meaning of a statement.

One of the two problems concerns the relation of a statement to its practical consequences. We enumerate five facts about meaning that are relevant here. First, one must understand the meaning of a statement, at least vaguely or imperfectly, before he can derive its practical conditionals, else he could not even identify them. Second, one may understand a scientific statement and still not be able to derive testable consequences from it. We gave examples in Section 1.2.1. Another example is Einstein's field theory, of which he said "we cannot at present compare the content of a nonlinear field theory with experience. Only a significant progress in the mathematical method can help here." * A third fact concerns the extent to which a practical conditional is explicitly part of the meaning of a statement. Consider the dispositional statement "That lump of sugar is soluble in coffee," which clearly implies the practical conditional "If that lump of sugar should be placed in coffee it would dissolve" (see sec. 7.3.2). But sometimes it is not clear whether a practical conditional follows from a given statement alone or from that statement together with other (assumed) statements. Fourth, a statement may be so highly theoretical that it does not imply any practical conditionals by itself, but only in conjunction with other statements (see pp. 87–88). Finally, any single statement or theory implies so many practical conditionals that it cannot be replaced in discourse by the conjunction of all of them.

Thus we see that the relation of a statement to its practical conditionals is generally subtle and indirect. One who understands a statement or theory must have some criterion or rule in mind whereby he can sometimes recognize that certain practical conditionals do belong to that statement or theory. What is the nature of this rule or criterion? This is a basic problem about meaning raised by, but not answered by, Peirce's pragmatic principle of meaning.

The other problem concerns the nature of a practical conditional. When we used the subjunctives "were . . . would" and "should . . . would" in formulating Peirce's practical conditionals, we were not complying with his original version of pragmatism, which was explicitly nominalistic rather than realistic.† On this version the sentence

[1] This diamond is harder than any known metal

asserts only that this diamond never has been and never will be scratched by a piece of metal, and it does not logically imply such subjunctive conditionals as

[2] If this diamond were rubbed with the point of a metal knife in normal circumstances, it would not be scratched.

Rather, sentence [1] implies only such material conditionals as

[2′] (This diamond is rubbed with the point of a metal knife in normal circumstances at time t) $\supset$ (it will not be scratched at time t),

* *Meaning of Relativity*, p. 165.

† I follow Peirce in this use of "nominalism" and "realism," which differs from the traditional use. The traditional nominalist-realist controversy concerns the ontological status of general properties (universals). The present issue is an analogous one concerning certain universal propositions, namely, those expressing general laws of nature. Does a law of nature cover only actualities, or does it cover causal possibilities as well? In his later period, Peirce was a realist on both issues.

where the horseshoe "$\supset$" is the symbol for material implication defined in Section 2.2.2. Since "$p \supset q$" is true whenever p is false, the material conditional [2′] is true whenever its antecedent is false, i.e., whenever the diamond is not rubbed by a knife. But for the same reason, the material conditional

[2″] (This diamond is rubbed with the point of a metal knife in normal circumstances at time t) $\supset$ (it *will be* scratched at time t)

is also true for each time t at which the diamond is not rubbed by a knife. As Peirce expressed it, "There is absolutely no difference between a hard thing and a soft thing so long as they are not brought to the test." *

So far as his pragmatism and his views on probability are concerned, Peirce's thought falls into two periods, an earlier and a later, the year 1890 being an approximate dividing line between the two periods. In his later period he saw that his nominalistic interpretation of practical conditionals was incorrect and he thereafter interpreted them realistically, as logically implying subjunctive conditionals.

For to what else does the entire teaching of chemistry relate except to the "behavior" of different possible kinds of material substance? And in what does that behavior consist except that if a substance of a certain kind should be exposed to an agency of a certain kind, a certain kind of sensible result *would* ensue according to our experiences hitherto.

Whereas Peirce had held earlier that practical conditionals and causal laws concern only what actually was, is, and will be, he now held that practical conditionals and causal laws concern "would be's" as well.

. . . the *will be's*, the actually *is's*, and the *have beens* are not the sum of the reals. They only cover actuality. There are besides *would be's* and *can be's* that are real. . . .

It certainly can be proved very clearly that the Universe does contain both *would be's* and *can be's*.

Peirce also saw that material implication is not adequate for symbolizing causal and subjunctive conditionals.

Some years ago, however, when in consequence of an invitation to deliver a course of lectures in Harvard University upon Pragmatism, I was led to revise that doctrine, in which I had already found difficulties, I soon discovered, upon a critical analysis, that it was absolutely necessary to insist upon and bring to the front, the truth that a mere possibility may be quite real. That admitted, it can no longer be granted that every conditional proposition whose antecedent does not happen to be realized is true. . . .†

* *Collected Papers* 5.403, originally published in 1878.

† The first quotation is from *Collected Papers* 5.457, originally published in 1905. The second quotation is from 8.216–17 and was written about 1910. The third quotation is

The difference between Peirce's earlier, nominalistic, and later, realistic, interpretation of practical conditionals may be expressed in the terminology of the logic of causal statements of Chapters 6 and 7. The nominalistic interpretation was in terms of material implication and nonmodal logic, while the realistic interpretation was in terms of causal implication and modal logic. It will be seen later that causal implication involves causal necessity. Hence Peirce's pragmatism employs the notion of causal necessity in the analysans of a statement. Now the concept of causal necessity is itself in need of analysis or explanation. Indeed, our fourth main question was: What is the nature of causal necessity, and how is it related to inductive probability? Since Peirce's pragmatic principle of meaning uses the notion of causal necessity, it does not help to answer this question.

A closely related point is: By reducing general and theoretical statements to practical conditionals, pragmatism *seems* to reduce them to statements verifiable by direct observation. While this is so on the nominalistic interpretation of practical conditionals, it is not so on the realistic interpretation. The antecedent of a practical conditional describes an experiment or action and the consequent describes an observable result. Hence, in principle, the antecedent and consequent of a practical conditional can be verified or falsified by direct observation, though in reality they cannot always be so verified; e.g., a practical conditional may refer to a past event that was not observed. But since a practical conditional involves causal necessity, its truth cannot be established by direct observation, even in principle. For direct observation is limited to the actual universe, whereas a causally necessary statement holds for all causally possible universes as well as for the actual universe (see pp. 341–42, 426, 622, and 627). Therefore, pragmatism does not in fact reduce general and theoretical statements to statements verifiable by direct observation.

This failure of pragmatism is similar to the failure of the frequency theory of empirical probability, which seems to analyze empirical probability statements into directly verifiable statements about relative frequencies. But while relative frequencies can be directly observed in the finite case, frequency probability statements concern the limits of infinite sequences and are never directly confirmable (p. 149).

Thus Peirce's pragmatic principle of meaning leads to two questions it does not answer: What is the nature of the rule or criterion connecting a statement to its practical conditionals? and, What is the nature of causal necessity? These are difficult questions, and, as Peirce himself recognized in his later period, a fully adequate theory of meaning must contain answers to both of them.

---

from 4.580 and was written about 1906; the Harvard lectures on pragmatism were delivered in 1903. See also the quotations on p. 421 below.

4.2.5 The normative component

We consider finally the normative component of Peirce's pragmatic principle of meaning. This principle sets forth two closely related maxims for guiding one's thinking in nonmathematical matters. First, to clarify a statement we should analyze it into its practical conditionals. Second, the pragmatic principle of meaning should be taken as definitive: If two statements imply the same practical conditionals, they should be treated as logically equivalent, even though one may have a logical consequence (which is not a practical conditional) that the other does not have.

We illustrate the force of this advice by applying Peirce's pragmatic principle of meaning to a metaphysical dispute, the controversy between the Cartesian dualist and the subjective idealist over the nature of physical objects. According to the dualist, a physical object exists independently of the knowing mind, possessing intrinsically the primary qualities of size, shape, solidity, etc., along with various causal properties (e.g., obeying the laws of gravitation). The secondary qualities of an object (e.g., looking brown, feeling smooth, tasting salty) are not properties of the object itself but only of the appearances of it (sense data) in the observer's mind. The subjective idealist, on the other hand, holds that these mental appearances or sense data (past, present, future), together with the laws connecting them, are all there is to a physical object. For him, physical objects are really mental in character and have no existence apart from minds. Thus Cartesian dualism and subjective idealism are very different doctrines, and they seem to be logically inequivalent.

To apply Peirce's pragmatic principle of meaning to this disagreement, we consider whether the dualist and the idealist react to physical objects in different ways or have basically different expectations about physical objects. They clearly do not: the Cartesian dualist and the subjective idealist infer the same practical conditionals from statements about physical objects. It follows from Peirce's pragmatic principle of meaning that we should treat Cartesian dualism and subjective idealism as logically equivalent, even though most metaphysicians hold that they are not.

Of course it is possible that there is some yet unthought-of practical conditional implied by one doctrine and not the other. But few if any metaphysicians base their belief that Cartesian dualism and subjective idealism are not logically equivalent on the assumption that this is so.

This consequence of Peirce's pragmatic principle of meaning, that Cartesian dualism and subjective idealism are logically equivalent doctrines, has been taken as an argument against metaphysics. But it also can be taken as an objection to the pragmatic principle of meaning, on the ground that this principle is not true to the way people actually use language.*

* See Henle, "Meaning and Verifiability."

And to this it can be retorted that people should not use language in this way.

There is not space to argue the issue here, but I will state my own opinion. In his pragmatism Peirce is setting up norms of significance for scientific discourse and then extending these norms to all inquiry. I personally see no reason to take science as the ideal of all cognitive endeavors, and I argue later that inductive logic rests on statements that are not verifiable (secs. 5.6.3, 10.4.2). Hence I think that Peirce's pragmatic principle of meaning should be restricted to empirically true-or-false statements.

4.2.6 Probability and pragmatism

The basic intent of Peirce's pragmatism was to find the meaning of a theory in its observable and experimental consequences. Now, we saw in Chapter 2 that a theory is often related to its empirical tests probabilistically rather than deductively. For example, relative to the corpuscular theory of light, Foucault's observations were highly unlikely; but these observations were not logically incompatible with the corpuscular theory of light (p. 87). Another example is

[7] **P**(40 to 60 tosses are heads, this symmetrical homogeneous balanced coin is thrown 100 times in the usual way) = 0.965.

Atomic inductive probability statement [7] relates a possible observation to a nonprobabilistic proposition about the coin. These probabilistic consequences of a theory are clearly important to its meaning. Hence the meaning of a theory consists not only in its empirical consequences, but in its probabilistic relations to these consequences as well. In the terminology associated with Bayes' theorem: One must take into account the prior and posterior probabilities and the degrees of prediction of the theory and its alternatives.

Peirce's frequency theory of probability gives a pragmatic analysis of inductive probability in terms of practical conditionals.

> . . . that real and sensible difference between one degree of probability and another, in which the meaning of the distinction lies, is that in the frequent employment of two different modes of inference, one will carry truth with it oftener than the other. It is evident that this is the only difference there is in the existing fact.*

Our criticism of the frequency theory shows this analysis of inductive probability to be unsatisfactory (sec. 3.4.2). Peirce himself later recognized this and proposed a somewhat different theory of probability, but it does not give a satisfactory analysis of inductive probability either (sec. 8.4.2).

* *Collected Papers* 2.650 (1878). This quotation falls between the two paragraphs quoted on p. 151. See also 5.20–21 (1903).

We therefore revise Peirce's pragmatic principle of meaning to take account of the probabilistic relations between theory and evidence as well as the deductive relations, at the same time restricting the scope of the principle to empirically true-or-false statements and avoiding explicit dependence on the notion of causal necessity. The revised principle reads: If, in all contexts, two empirically true-or-false statements h_1 and h_2 imply the same predictions to the same degree and are supported in the same way by the same observation statements, then h_1 and h_2 should be treated as logically equivalent. More formally,

[8] Let h_1 and h_2 be two empirically true-or-false statements, g the general information, and o a report on an observation or experiment. If, for all general information statements g and all observation statements o, $\mathbf{P}(h_1, og) = \mathbf{P}(h_2, og)$ and $\mathbf{P}(o, h_1g) = \mathbf{P}(o, h_2g)$, then h_1 and h_2 should be treated as logically equivalent.

We call this the ***probabilistic version of the pragmatic principle of meaning***. Note that this principle is a partial converse of the exchange principle of p. 47, which implies that if h_1 and h_2 are logically equivalent, then for any statement q, $\mathbf{P}(h_1, q) = \mathbf{P}(h_2, q)$ and $\mathbf{P}(q, h_1) = \mathbf{P}(q, h_2)$.

The probabilistic version of the pragmatic principle of meaning makes explicit what is implicit in the very notion of "empirically true-or-false" as we specified it in Section 1.2.1. And for this reason the principle is true. But still, even as far as empirically true-or-false statements are concerned, the probabilistic version does not solve the problem that Peirce's pragmatic principle was put forward to solve. His pragmatic principle analyzes a theory (taken as an analysandum) into a set of practical conditionals (the analysans), and it claims that the important content of the analysans is logically equivalent to the analysandum and hence that the theory is "reduced" to its practical conditionals. Such a reduction, if correct, would show us a great deal about the nature of scientific knowledge. Indeed the historical appeal of pragmatism, operationalism, and the verifiability principle of meaning rests mainly on this claim. But the probabilistic version of the pragmatic principle shows clearly that the claim is false; for the pragmatic principle does not analyze a theory into or reduce a theory to nontheoretical consequences. Rather, the probabilistic version of the pragmatic principle makes it manifest that the probability relations between a theory and its testable consequences are as basic epistemologically as either the consequences themselves or the deductive relations between the theory and its consequences. Since there are important philosophical questions about inductive probability—in particular, our first and second main questions (p. 92)—the probabilistic version of the pragmatic principle does not give a final solution to the problem of the nature of scientific knowledge, as Peirce's pragmatic principle was supposed to do. On the contrary, the probabilistic version of the pragmatic principle of meaning shows that an answer to the question, "What is the nature of scientific knowledge?" presupposes an answer to the question, "What is the nature of inductive probability?"

It will be recalled that a practical conditional is of the form

[3] If the experiment θ should be performed in circumstances ψ, the observable result would be χ.

In his later period, Peirce also used another form of conditional for analyzing nonprobability statements, namely

[9] If one wants ϕ and should be in circumstances ψ, then he would act in manner θ.

When this form is used, the analysis takes explicit account of the dependency of action on valuations as well as beliefs.

> . . . the intellectual purport of a concept consists in the truth of certain conditional propositions asserting that if the concept be applicable, and the utterer of the proposition or his fellow have a certain purpose in view, he would act in a certain way.*

The use of pattern [9] in place of pattern [3] does not save Peirce's pragmatic principle of meaning, however. That is, all of our objections to his pragmatic principle of meaning apply also to a reformulation of the principle in terms of conditionals of type [9] instead of practical conditionals, i.e., conditionals of type [3].

On the other hand, pattern [9] is much better than pattern [3] for analyzing atomic inductive probability statements. As Peirce recognized, partial belief is closely related to betting behavior.

> Belief and doubt may be conceived to be distinguished only in degree.
>
> Doubt has degrees and may approximate indefinitely to belief, but when I doubt, the effect of the mental judgment will not be seen in my conduct as invariably or to the full extent that it will when I believe. Thus, if I am perfectly confident that an insurance company will fulfill their engagements I will pay them a certain sum for a policy, but if I think there is a risk of their breaking, I shall not pay them so much.†

This connection between partial belief and betting behavior may be explicated by conditionals of form [9]. Compare the effect of a rational person's believing

[10] $\mathbf{P}(h, e) = 0.9$

as against his believing

[11] $\mathbf{P}(h, e) = 0.1$,

* *Collected Papers* 5.528 (c. 1905). See 5.212, 5.428. 5.438, 5.548.

† *Collected Papers* 7.314 (c. 1873).

where e expresses his total evidence concerning h. Assume that he is not opposed on principle to betting. Suppose, now, that he is offered a choice between the two acts

(A) $90 if h is true, nothing otherwise

(A') $90 if h is false, nothing otherwise.

If he wants $90, he will choose Act A if he believes [10], act A' if he believes [11]. Hence for this person a belief in atomic inductive probability statement [10] implies a commitment to the type [9] conditional "If I should want $90 and should be offered my choice of A and A', I would choose A."

Thus a person's belief in an atomic inductive probability statement commits him, under certain conditions, to choose in certain specifiable ways, which suggests that atomic inductive probability statements should be analyzed into conditionals of form [9]. Although this pragmatic insight into probability is valuable, it is only a suggestion and needs development. A satisfactory pragmatic theory of inductive probability must characterize the sets of conditionals associated with particular atomic inductive probability statements and also explain the role of the calculus of inductive probability in pragmatic terms. Moreover, it must distinguish the content of a partial belief from the partial belief itself.

A pragmatic theory of inductive probability will be developed in the next chapter. We devote the remainder of this chapter to background materials. In the next section we shall see what can be learned about the relation of probability to action from a study of the principle of maximizing utility as it was traditionally conceived. And in Section 4.4 we shall present the "book" theorem, which connects systematic betting behavior to the calculus of probability.

4.3. The Traditional Theory of Utility

4.3.1 Utility and choice

Many actions involve uncertainty and probability, a factor often taken into account in evaluating them. One man seeks security in his job, another a chance for advancement. An investor can either speculate in the stock market or buy "blue chips." One can insure his auto against collision or take the risk himself. Some like to gamble, others think it immoral.

From the beginning, probability theory has been used to guide action in conditions of uncertainty. It was originally applied mainly to a limited kind of life situation, namely games of chance, though Pascal in his famous "wager" applied it to what was for him the most important decision in life (see p. 189). This tendency to treat life itself as a "gamble and a game" and to use probability as an aid to making choices when the outcomes are uncertain has become more and more pronounced as probability theory has developed. Economists, statisticians, and psychologists are now very actively applying probability and utility theory to individual, social, and managerial choices made under conditions of uncertainty.

Probability theory may be applied to action by maximizing a certain quantity, originally called "moral expectation" and now called "utility." Actually there are two quite different conceptions of the process of maximizing utility: the traditional one and a more recent one. The former, which we call the "traditional theory of utility," provides a good introduction to the subject of utility, and it will be studied in the present section. The more recent view of utility is discussed in the next chapter: it is axiomatized in the calculus of choice and is expressed by the personalistic and pragmatic theories of probability.

The traditional theory of utility is based on a procedure of this type. A person is to make a choice in a situation involving uncertainty. He analyzes it into a finite number of alternative *acts* $a, a', a'', \ldots$. His choice should be guided by an evaluation of the *consequences* of each act and an assessment of the probability that each of these consequences will occur. He therefore calculates the utility of each act in the following way. He "divides" act a into a finite number of mutually exclusive and jointly exhaustive states $p_1, p_2, \ldots, p_N$ such that each state p_n has consequence c_n ($n = 1, 2, \ldots, N$). He assesses the probability $\mathbf{P}(p_n, g)$ that consequence c_n will obtain, where "g" expresses his general information. To each consequence c_n he assigns a real number (positive or negative) representing its value or utility. Let $\mathbf{U}(c_n)$ be the **utility** of consequence c_n, that is, the value the person making the choice believes will be realized if "p_n" is true and consequence c_n obtains. The utility of a consequence is the net return, that is, the prize less the cost.

Since the utility $\mathbf{U}(c_n)$ of a consequence is a real number, it may be multiplied by a probability. When these products are added for all the consequences of an act a, the result is the utility of the act relative to the circumstances g. Thus the utility $\mathbf{U}(a, g)$ of an act a is defined by

[12] Let $p_1, p_2, \ldots, p_N$ be mutually exclusive and jointly exhaustive on g, and let c_n be the consequence of act a that obtains if p_n is true ($n = 1, 2, \ldots, N$). Then

$$\mathbf{U}(a, g) = \sum_{n=1}^{N} \mathbf{P}(p_n, g)\mathbf{U}(c_n) \quad .$$

(The right-hand side of the equation abbreviates the sum "$\mathbf{P}(p_1, g)\mathbf{U}(c_1) + \ldots + \mathbf{P}(p_N, g)\mathbf{U}(c_N)$.") The utilities $\mathbf{U}(a', g)$, $\mathbf{U}(a'', g), \ldots$ are calculated similarly. The *rule of maximizing utility* states that the person *should* choose an act with a maximum utility, i.e., an act a with $\mathbf{U}(a, g)$ such that there is no alternative act a' with $\mathbf{U}(a', g)$ greater than $\mathbf{U}(a, g)$.

A simple example will illustrate the principle of maximizing utility and will also reveal its problematic character. The choice is between betting a dollar on red in roulette (act A) and not betting (act A'). Act A divides into two possibilities: gain one dollar (C_1) if the pointer of the wheel comes to rest on red (P_1); and lose one dollar (C_2) otherwise (P_2). Assume that the utility of these consequences is reasonably measured by their dollar value. The utilities of the two acts are then computed as follows:

$$\begin{aligned} \mathbf{U}(A) &= \mathbf{P}(P_1)\mathbf{U}(C_1) + \mathbf{P}(P_2)\mathbf{U}(C_2) \\ &= (18/38)\ (\$1) + (20/38)\ (-\$1) = -\$1/19 \\ \mathbf{U}(A') &= 0 \end{aligned}$$

The alternative A' of not playing has a utility of zero (nothing ventured, nothing lost), which is greater than the utility of betting one dollar on red. Hence by the principle of maximizing utility one should not bet in this case!

Yet it is in many respects a typical betting case and, prima facie, a reasonable one on which to gamble. Thus this example illustrates the need for further analysis of the principle of maximizing utility. There are indeed many questions to ask. How is utility related to money? What units should be used for measuring utilities? Under what conditions should one follow the procedure of maximizing utility? What is the justification for the principle of maximizing utility? To what extent do people apply this normative principle? Is it reasonable always to make quantitative estimates of chances and values in real-life situations? We shall discuss these questions and offer answers to them in due course. But first we wish to introduce some diagrams representing choice situations of the kind envisaged in the principle of maximizing utility. (All of the diagrams for utility theory, figs. 1–34, appear as a unit between this chapter and chap. 5.)

The choice example just discussed is represented by the *choice tree* of Figure 1. Point R is the *root* of the tree; it is a *choice point* because the subject can choose to go down either solid line. Point A is a *chance point*, since the outcome of a chance event determines a passage along a dashed line. The dashed lines emanating from a chance point are labeled with a mutually exclusive and jointly exhaustive set of propositions. The terminal points C_1 and C_2 are *consequence points*, labeled with names or descriptions of the consequences of act A. Act A' consists of the single consequence "status quo," and is represented by the consequence point A'.

A person's choice of an act may be symbolized by placing an arrowhead on the solid line leading to the corresponding chance point. Thus Figure 2 symbolizes the choice of a play at roulette. The subject's choice combined with the outcome of the chance event (sometimes called "the state of nature") determines which consequence he receives. For example, if the pointer stops on red, the path R-A-C_1 is traced and the subject receives one dollar. A marked choice tree will be called an *act tree*, since it symbolizes the subject's choice of one act from among many.

One special case, that of *indifference* or equal utility, needs consideration. There may be two or more acts to which the subject assigns equal utilities. Then he can choose only one act, but to symbolize that certain acts are equally valuable to him, all of them should be marked with arrowheads. An example is shown in Figure 3. A guilder and a shilling are to be tossed. The subject may choose between

(A_1) Receiving Sir Richard Burton's edition of *The Arabian Nights* if the guilder falls heads, nothing otherwise,

and

(A_2) Receiving one hundred dollars if both guilder and shilling fall heads, nothing otherwise.

The fact that both solid lines of Figure 3 are marked with arrowheads indicates that he is indifferent (attaches the same utilities) to these two acts.

The general form of a choice tree is displayed in Figure 4a. In this example there are three acts (a, a', and a'') to choose from, and each is divided into the mutually exclusive and jointly exhaustive consequences indicated. It is important to keep in mind that the symbolic content of each such tree is relative to the general information g. The statements on the dashed lines emerging from a chance point are not necessarily mutually exclusive and jointly exhaustive in themselves, but only relative to g. The probabilities of these statements are also relative to g, and hence how a choice tree is marked (converted into an act tree) will usually depend on g.

Reference to this general information g may be dropped under any of the circumstances discussed in Section 2.6 (Unconditional Probabilities). Omitting g, the utilities of the acts represented in Figure 4a are given by the formulas

$$\mathbf{U}(a) = \sum_{n=1}^{3} \mathbf{P}(p_n)\mathbf{U}(c_n)$$

$$\mathbf{U}(a') = \sum_{n=1}^{2} \mathbf{P}(p'_n)\mathbf{U}(c'_n)$$

$$\mathbf{U}(a'') = \sum_{n=1}^{4} \mathbf{P}(p''_n)\mathbf{U}(c''_n) \quad .$$

If Figure 4b is marked in accord with the principle of maximizing utility, then $\mathbf{U}(a) > \mathbf{U}(a')$ and $\mathbf{U}(a) > \mathbf{U}(a'')$.

Note that a set of mutually exclusive and jointly exhaustive empirical statements can be viewed as a set of descriptions of logically possible universes (secs. 3.2.1 and 6.3). Thus in calculating the utility of an act one "divides" that act into parts, each of which is a logically possible universe containing a consequence, and assigns a probability to each universe and a utility to its consequence. It is often convenient to refer to these parts as "partial acts." For example, act a of Figure 4 is composed of the three partial acts

If p_1, then c_1 obtains

If p_2, then c_2 obtains

If p_3, then c_3 obtains.

Each of these partial acts is represented in the figure by a labeled dotted line with labeled terminal point.

The act symbols "a," "a'," etc., and the consequence symbols "c_1," "c_2," "c_1'," etc., were introduced as variables ranging over acts and consequences. It is sometimes convenient to let them be statement variables, with the interpretation that "a" means "act a is chosen" and "c" means "consequence c obtains." No ambiguity need result from this multivocality of the symbols, since the context will always make clear which interpretation is intended.

When these symbols are used as statement variables, acts can be represented in terms of their parts by means of truth-functional formulas. For the first act of Figure 4 we have

[13] $$a \equiv [(p_1 \supset c_1)(p_2 \supset c_2)(p_3 \supset c_3)] \quad .$$

It is clear from Figure 4 that this formula is equivalent to

[14] $$a \equiv (p_1c_1 \vee p_2c_2 \vee p_3c_3) \quad .$$

This disjunctive representation of acts is more convenient than the preceding conjunctive representation. Relative to the fact that p_1, p_2, and p_3 are mutually exclusive and jointly exhaustive, formulas [13] and [14] are tautologically equivalent. This can be seen from Figure 4, or shown by truth-functional logic. Of course, if they are mutually exclusive and jointly exhaustive relative to the general information g, then the tautological equivalence of [13] and [14] is relative to this same general information.

While acts are ordinarily constructed from several consequences, an act may consist of or reduce to a single consequence. For example, act A' of Figure 1 consists of the single consequence "status quo," and the act $PC \vee \bar{P}C$ reduces to the single consequence C. Hence statements we make about acts will apply automatically to consequences as special cases. An act containing more than one consequence, i.e., not logically equivalent to some consequence, is called a *mixed act*.

It may be helpful to restate the definition of utility in terms of partial acts. For this purpose we introduce two symbolic conventions. First, the truth-functional operation of disjunction is analogous to the arithmetic operation of addition, and we represent it with a capital sigma also. For example,

$$\sum_{n=1}^{N} p_n c_n \equiv (p_1 c_1 \vee p_2 c_2 \vee \ldots \vee p_N c_N) \quad .$$

Second, we define the utility $\mathbf{U}(pc)$ of a partial act pc thus:

$$\mathbf{U}(pc) = \mathbf{P}(p)\mathbf{U}(c) \quad .$$

Now, to calculate the utility of an act one divides it into its parts $p_1c_1, p_2c_2, \ldots, p_Nc_N$, multiplies the probability $\mathbf{P}(p_n)$ of each part by the utility $\mathbf{U}(c_n)$ of its consequence to obtain the utility $\mathbf{U}(p_nc_n)$ of that part, and sums these products. More formally,

[12′] Let $a = \sum_{n=1}^{N} p_n c_n$, where $p_1, p_2, \ldots, p_N$ are mutually exclusive and jointly exhaustive on g, and c_n is the consequence of $p_n (n = 1, 2, \ldots, N)$.

$$\text{Then } \mathbf{U}(a, g) = \mathbf{U}\left(\sum_{n=1}^{N} p_n c_n, g\right) = \sum_{n=1}^{N} \mathbf{U}(p_n c_n, g) = \sum_{n=1}^{N} \mathbf{P}(p_n, g)\mathbf{U}(c_n) \quad .$$

In mathematical terms, the utility of an act is the *mathematical expectation* (expected value, mean) of the utilities $\mathbf{U}(c_n)$ of its consequences. That is, $\mathbf{U}\left(\sum_{n=1}^{N} p_n c_n\right)$ is the weighted average of the utilities $\mathbf{U}(c_n)$, each utility $\mathbf{U}(c_n)$ being weighted by the probability $\mathbf{P}(p_n)$ with which the consequence c_n is expected. For this reason the utility of an act is sometimes called "expected utility," the term "utility" then being reserved for the utilities of consequences. The term "utility," however, is so well established for both concepts that we too shall use it for both.

It is important, nevertheless, to distinguish the utility of a consequence from the utility of a mixed act, for the latter involves uncertainty while the former does not. The utility $\mathbf{U}(c_n)$ of a consequence c_n is a measure of the value of a thing or event without any uncertainty in it, that is to say, on the assumption that the thing will be possessed or the event will occur. In contrast, a mixed act a has more than one consequence and it is uncertain which of these will ensue, so that its utility $\mathbf{U}(a, g)$ is a kind of probabilistic value or amalgam of the "probably true" and the good. This difference is reflected in the fact that the expression "$\mathbf{U}(c_n)$" contains no reference to the general information g, whereas the expression "$\mathbf{U}(a, g)$" does.

With this background we can state the *traditional theory of utility*: to choose an act from a set of alternatives, one should analyze each act into its consequences, evaluate the utility of each consequence and the probability that it will occur, calculate the utility of each act by means of the formula

$$\mathbf{U}\left(\sum_{n=1}^{N} p_n c_n, g\right) = \sum_{n=1}^{N} \mathbf{P}(p_n, g)\mathbf{U}(c_n) \quad ,$$

and then select an act of maximum utility.

In following the procedure recommended by the traditional theory, one must estimate the utilities and probabilities of consequences to a certain degree of precision; if he cannot do this the procedure is inapplicable and of no help in deciding what choice to make. Other problems concerning the nature of probability and utility arise in connection with the traditional theory. We formulate some of these in the current chapter and solve them in the next (sec. 5.6.2).

4.3.2 Quantitative probabilities and valuations

The first questions concern the quantitative nature of probability and utility. We shall state them after a brief presentation of utility scales.

There are many different measuring scales for utility. Suppose several acts have been ranked by the formula

$$\mathbf{U}(a) = \sum_{n=1}^{N} \mathbf{P}(p_n)\mathbf{U}(c_n) \quad .$$

This ranking will not be altered by what is called a linear change of scale: a shift of the origin (adding a constant to the utility of every consequence), a change of scale (multiplying the utility of every consequence by a constant factor), or both. In other words, any two utility scales U and U′ that are related by the linear equation

$$\mathrm{U} = \rho \mathrm{U}' + \sigma \qquad \text{for } \rho > 0$$

give the same ranking of acts.

Thus both the origin and the unit of a utility scale are arbitrary. In any application of the rule of maximizing utility, the scale may be specified by choosing two consequences c_z and c_u such that $\mathbf{U}(c_u) > \mathbf{U}(c_z)$ and assigning $\mathbf{U}(c_z) = 0$ *utiles* and $\mathbf{U}(c_u) = 1$ *utile*. Whenever acts are being compared with respect to their utilities, the same scale must be used for the comparison to be valid. Sometimes there is a "natural" zero for a utility scale, e.g., the status quo, or the difference between what we want and what we want to get rid of, or the difference between pleasure and pain.

It is important to realize that utiles are not monetary units but units of personal and social values (including, of course, relevant monetary values). That the utility of money is not proportionate to its quantity is shown by the following example. I like to imagine someone offering me a choice between: (A) one million dollars tax free (C_1) if a coin falls heads, nothing (C_2) otherwise; and (A') ten million dollars tax free (C'_1) if two coins fall heads, nothing (C'_2) otherwise. Assume for the moment that each dollar is worth one utile. The utilities of A and A' are then

$$\begin{aligned}\mathbf{U}(A) &= \mathbf{P}(C_1)\mathbf{U}(C_1) + \mathbf{P}(C_2)\mathbf{U}(C_2)\\ &= 1/2(1{,}000{,}000) + 1/2(0) = 500{,}000 \text{ utiles}\\ \mathbf{U}(A') &= \mathbf{P}(C'_1)\mathbf{U}(C'_1) + \mathbf{P}(C'_2)\mathbf{U}(C'_2)\\ &= 1/4(10{,}000{,}000) + 3/4(0) = 2{,}500{,}000 \text{ utiles.}\end{aligned}$$

This calculation shows $\mathbf{U}(A')$ to be greater than $\mathbf{U}(A)$, a conclusion that is simply incorrect for me and for most others who have not yet acquired their first million. Ten million dollars is not worth ten times one million to me, since ten million would not make ten times as much difference in the welfare and happiness of my family as one million dollars would. It is hard to estimate here, but as in many applications of Bayes' theorem (sec. 2.5.4) exact figures are not necessary. It is not too far off to say that $\mathbf{U}(C_1) =$ 1,000,000 utiles and $\mathbf{U}(C'_1) = 1{,}200{,}000$ utiles. Recalculating, we find $\mathbf{U}(A) = 500{,}000$ utiles and $\mathbf{U}(A') = 300{,}000$ utiles, so that $\mathbf{U}(A) > \mathbf{U}(A')$, which accords with the actual situation.

The principle just illustrated is that of the diminishing marginal utility of money: the value of money does not increase in proportion to its quantity, but at a slower rate. This principle looks plausible. For example, it seems that a dollar should be worth less to a millionaire than to a pauper.

The diminishing marginal utility principle may be used to justify the purchase of fire insurance. Suppose a man's only possession is his home, worth \$27,000. Fires can be of varying severity, but to simplify matters we will consider only total loss and assume that the probability of it in any year is 0.001. The insurance company must charge *more* than the expected loss in dollars to cover operating costs and profits; suppose its rate is 0.0015. The owner has two alternatives: (A) not to insure, with consequence (C_1) total loss, which has a probability of 0.001, and consequence (C_2) worth \$27,000 with probability 0.999; and (A') to insure, in which case he is worth \$27,000 less \$40.50 at the end of the year. Depreciation is disregarded on both alternatives. Assuming that one dollar is worth one utile, the utilities of these alternatives are

$$\begin{aligned}\mathbf{U}(A) &= 0.001(0) + 0.999(27{,}000) = 26{,}973 \text{ utiles}\\ \mathbf{U}(A') &= 27{,}000 - 40.50 = 26{,}959.50 \text{ utiles.}\end{aligned}$$

This makes it appear that insurance never pays, except for the insurance company. But, as before, the utility should be calculated in units of satisfaction, not in dollars. To show how this can make a difference, let us assume that the utility of money is equal to the cube root of the number of dollars. Recalculating, we get

$$\mathbf{U}(A) = 0.001(0) + 0.999(27{,}000)^{1/3} = 29.970 \text{ utiles}$$

$$\mathbf{U}(A') = (27{,}000 - 40.50)^{1/3} = 29.985 \text{ utiles.}$$

According to this new calculation, fire insurance does pay.

We use the cube root function here because it is a simple function illustrating the diminishing marginal utility of money, though we do not claim it is a particularly good utility function, either descriptively or normatively. The shape of utility functions will be discussed in Section 4.3.5 (Insurance and gambling).

After this brief introduction to utility scales, we can present a major problem concerning the quantitative nature of probability and utility. The calculus of inductive probability (chap. 2) treats probabilities as real numbers. It is easy to accept the notion that probabilities are quantitative for most gambling and gaming situations (cards, dice, roulette wheels, pinball machines, etc.) and for some applications of probability theory to empirical science (e.g., the statistics of particles—see pp. 506–7). But it is a distortion to use real numbers in all applications of the concept of probability. The evidence in favor of the heliocentric hypothesis in Galileo's time (pp. 19–21) does not have an exact weight, and one cannot significantly assign a precise value to the probability that Semmelweis' conclusion was correct, given his data (pp. 23–24). No scientist would assign a precise number to such a speculation as the theory of the continuous creation of matter* on the basis of his present information. Exactly what probability do you attach to the statement "There was once a battle at Birdum"? Clearly, many real-life situations of uncertainty are not quantitative in nature.

Our original specification of the conception of inductive probability allowed probabilities to be either qualitative, e.g., "high," "low," or quantitative (p. 26). The foregoing remarks show that there is a difference, though perhaps not a sharp one, between qualitative and quantitative probabilities. Any adequate theory of inductive probability must accommodate or explain this difference.

A similar objection applies to the quantitative valuations assumed by the rule of maximizing utility. Indeed, it has even more force here, because valuations are more subjective than conditional probabilities: the latter are relative to the evidence, while the former seem relative to the individual. Since the time of the Greeks, philosophers have been aware of the difficulties

* The theory of H. Bondi and T. Gold. Bondi, *Cosmology*, chap. 12.

in defining and measuring the quantitative values of consequences, particularly in cases where more than one individual is affected. Shall all individuals be treated the same? This is the issue of egoism versus altruism, an important issue for utilitarianism. In our treatment of utility we will bypass these problems, assuming that only one individual is involved. Even so, the principle of maximizing utility would seem to have very limited applicability. How can one assign numerical weights to his most important goals in life, except in an arbitrary manner? Are not preferences fundamentally qualitative?

It might seem that where the market and money are involved, quantification of acts and consequences would be easy. This is true for corporations, which handle many cases and can average their gains and losses. An insurance company or gambling house can adopt a simple utility function equating utiles to dollars. But generally this will not do for individuals, where single cases are preeminent. Nevertheless, utility theory does have relevance to an individual's decisions. As Bishop Butler said, "Probability is the very guide to life" (p. 165 above).

One must be careful in his terminology here. "Utility," as we have defined it, is quantitative only, and so it would be a contradiction to speak of "qualitative utility." In this we are following mathematicians and economists; philosophers often use "utility" nonquantitatively, as in "Mill's utilitarianism." Standard usage of the term probability is freer on this point. "Probability" is generally used quantitatively but may be used qualitatively, and we have employed it both ways. Later we will also use "uncertainties" for qualitative probabilities.

We conclude that there is an important distinction between quantitative and qualitative probabilities and an even more significant distinction between quantitative and qualitative valuations. An adequate theory of probability and utility must accommodate or explain both of these distinctions. I shall give my solution later (pp. 311–12).

4.3.3 *Infinite utilities*

The question naturally arises as to whether there are any acts or consequences of infinite utility. It is sometimes said that the value of life is infinite. If there is a life after death, and it is eternal and generally happy, it seems reasonable to say that it has infinite utility. But life on earth is finite and is therefore probably of finite utility.

It is hard to see how a finite life span could have infinite value. A good example concerns the choice of mode of travel when the railroads provided both the safest transportation and relatively good service. Suppose a man had to choose a way of traveling from Chicago to New Orleans in 1958. He could go by auto, plane, bus, or train. His chance of death was about 24 millionths by auto, 3.6 millionths by plane, 1.9 millionths by bus, and 1.2 millionths by train.* If life on earth were of infinite value, each of these acts would have infinite utility, and the rule of maximizing utility would justify them all equally. This seems paradoxical. Perhaps a defender of the view that life on earth is of infinite value would argue that one should not maximize utility in this case; rather, he should choose the act that maximizes life expectancy and so go by train. On this interpretation, people generally did not act as if life on earth were of infinite value, for most people used bus, plane, or auto.

The appeal to maximum utility is about as old as the theory of probability itself, and one of the first appeals involved the presumed infinite utility of life in heaven. This occurs in an ingenious argument to persuade nonbelievers to become Roman Catholics, advanced by Blaise Pascal, one of the founders of the theory of probability. If you believe in God and join the Roman Catholic Church, Pascal said, your soul may be saved and you then will gain infinite utility. There is surely a finite probability that Christianity is true, and a finite probability that if you become a believing Catholic you will be saved. Thus the chance of success is finite, the utility of salvation is infinite, and hence the utility of adopting Christianity is infinite. Therefore, to maximize your utility, believe in God and join the Roman Catholic Church.

> Let us weigh the gain and the loss in wagering that God is. Let us estimate these two chances. If you gain, you gain all; if you lose, you lose nothing. Wager, then, without hesitation that He is. . . . there is an eternity of life and happiness. . . . there is here an infinity of an infinitely happy life to gain, a chance of gain against a finite number of chances of loss, and what you stake is finite.†

Pascal made no reference to joining the Church, but he was a Jansenist, and the Jansenists believed that there was no salvation outside the Roman Catholic Church.

Made more explicit, Pascal's argument seems to be the following. The act "believe in God and join the Roman Catholic Church" has infinite utility, the utility of any other act is finite or negatively infinite (because of the possibility of eternal damnation); therefore, by the rule of maximizing utility, one should believe in God and join the Roman Catholic Church. This argument is of historical interest as a very early application of utility theory outside of gambling games. We shall analyze it and show that it begs

* Based on 1957–59 death rates in the *Information Please Almanac.* Of course, one had considerable control over the probability if he traveled by auto; even so, an auto was not as safe as a train.

† Pascal, *Pensées*, no. 233.

John Locke used a similar argument to show that one should be good in this life; *An Essay Concerning Human Understanding*, vol. 1, book 2, chap. 21, par. 72.

some debatable questions, such as the truth of some versions of Protestantism.

As the definition of utility makes explicit, the utility $\mathbf{U}(a, g)$ of act a is relative to the general information g, which must be assumed as a premise in any appeal to maximizing utility. Let us see what must be included in Pascal's general information for his calculations to be correct.

The dotted lines emerging from a chance point must be labeled with statements that are mutually exclusive and jointly exhaustive relative to the general information. Now there are many logically possible alternatives to the Jansenist version of Christianity that have payoffs of positive infinity or negative infinity according to whether one does or does not believe in them. Consider, for example, some religious faith other than Catholicism that holds salvation to be possible only within that faith and further holds anyone not saved by allegiance to that faith likely to be damned. Some versions of Protestantism fit this description. If such a doctrine has nonzero probability, it contributes a negative infinity to the act of believing in God and joining the Catholic Church and contributes a positive infinity to some alternative acts.

Hence Pascal's calculation assumes that all such doctrines have zero probability relative to his general information. But to say a statement has zero probability is to say it is definitely false. This shows that Pascal assumed the falsity of all faiths (other than Catholicism) that hold salvation to be possible inside the faith and damnation likely outside. Clearly, the premises of Pascal's argument contain implicitly much debatable material. When this is realized, the force of Pascal's wager is greatly diminished.

Pascal's wager involves an act that has infinite utility because one consequence (salvation) has infinite utility. Even if every consequence of an act had finite utility, the act might have infinite utility if it had infinitely many consequences. This possibility was excluded by our definition of "act" (p. 180), but it is instructive to consider the effect of allowing acts with infinitely many consequences. The famous Saint Petersburg paradox is based on such an act.

A single play of the Saint Petersburg game consists in tossing a fair coin until a head comes up and then stopping. Let n ($= 1, 2, 3, \ldots$) be the number of the last toss, that is, the toss on which the first head occurs. The player will be paid 2^n utiles. How many utiles is a single play of the Saint Petersburg game worth? Our definition of utility was for an act with a finite number of consequences, but a similar definition can be given for an act with an infinite number of consequences. A single play of the Saint Petersburg game is such an act, with infinitely many jointly exhaustive and mutually exclusive consequences, according to whether $n = 1, 2, 3, \ldots$. The probability $\mathbf{P}(C_n)$ of the nth consequence is $1/2^n$, its utility $\mathbf{U}(C_n)$ is 2^n utiles, and so its expected utility is one utile. Since there are an infinite number of possible consequences, each worth one utile, the utility of a *single* play is infinite! This result is paradoxical because a single play does not appear to be worth so much.

Note that the utility of a single play is still infinite when a finite number of consequences (e.g., the first quadrillion) have zero utility, and for every other consequence C_n, $\mathbf{U}(C_n) = \epsilon \cdot 2^n$, where ϵ is any positive real number, no matter how small.

It is essential that the paradox be expressed in utiles rather than in monetary units. Daniel Bernoulli proposed to resolve the paradox by the principle of diminishing marginal utility (p. 186). Specifically, Bernoulli suggested taking the logarithm of the amount of money as the utility.* Suppose the utility of money is the logarithm to the base two of the number of dollars. Then if the payoff for the nth consequence were 2^n dollars, the utility of a play of the Saint Petersburg game would be $1/2 + 2/4 + 3/8 + \ldots + n/2^n + \ldots$, which is only two utiles. But the paradox can be reinstated by letting the payoff for the nth consequence be 2^{2^n} dollars. Then the utility of the nth outcome would be $(2^{-n})(\log_2 2^{2^n})$, or one utile, and the utility of a play would be infinite.

No paradox exists if there is a consequence of greatest utility and this greatest utility is finite. Suppose, for example, that the Saint Petersburg game is played at a gambling house. Let 4.3 billion dollars be the wealth of the gambling house and hence the most the gambling house can pay. Suppose the payoff for the nth consequence is 2^{2^n} dollars and the utility of money is the logarithm (to the base two) of the number of dollars. Then the utility of a single play of the game is only five utiles! Hence the Saint Petersburg paradox assumes that utility is not bounded from above. Utility might be bounded from above but not from below, that is, there might be no consequence of greatest negative utility. For this case one can construct a kind of reverse Saint Petersburg paradox, in which a single play has infinite negative utility.

But if there is no greatest utility, the Saint Petersburg paradox remains. Let us express it more concretely. Imagine a person who knows that if he does not gamble he will live 60 more years, enjoying one utile per hour, or approximately 526,000 utiles altogether. Now a devil of infinite power offers him a single play of the Saint Petersburg game at the cost of his present life span, with a payoff of 2^n utiles for the nth consequence. If each possible hour were worth one utile, this would mean that with probability

* The Saint Petersburg paradox was discussed by Daniel Bernoulli in "Specimen Theoriae Novae de Mensura Sortis," published by the Saint Petersburg Academy of Science, whence its name. For a historical account of the paradox and proposed resolutions see Savage, *The Foundations of Statistics*, pp. 91–95.

1/2 the man would live only two more hours, with probability 1/4 he would live four hours, etc. The odds against his living more than 120 years are about one million to one. The chance of his living 240 million years or more is about 1 in 10^{12}, etc. Of course, the law of diminishing marginal utility may apply to life, so that the millionth year may not be worth as much as the first year of life, and if so the devil must offer more than 2^n hours for the nth consequence to make the utility of the nth consequence 2^n utiles. But if utility is not bounded, the utility of the devil's offer is infinite, and by the rule of maximizing utility it should be accepted. This is paradoxical, because it does not seem unreasonable to prefer a guaranteed 60 years of happiness to a single play of the Saint Petersburg game.

Actually, I think the paradox here derives in part from the feeling that the partial acts "a consequence worth 2^n utiles with probability 2^{-n}" for $n = 0, 1, 2, 3, \ldots$ are not all of equal value, because they vary so widely with respect to the likelihood that one will get a consequence of value. One traditional suggestion for resolving the paradox is to neglect sufficiently small probabilities. This does not seem reasonable if utilities are unbounded, but it might be reasonable to value partial acts with small probabilities less than utility theory does. The variance paradox of pp. 195–96 is constructed to bring out this feature of the Saint Petersburg paradox without assuming unbounded utilities.

A play of the Saint Petersburg game is an act having an infinite number of consequences; each consequence has a finite utility, but there is no bound on these utilities. One can also imagine a choice situation having an infinite number of acts, each act having a finite utility, there being no bound on these utilities. For example, the devil might offer you a choice from among acts $a_1, a_2, \ldots, a_m, \ldots$, act a_m having a utility of m utiles ($m = 1, 2, 3, \ldots$). In this choice situation there is no act of maximum utility, and so the rule of maximizing utility is inapplicable.

Our discussion of infinite utilities has raised a number of interrelated questions. Do infinite utilities actually exist; for example, an infinite amount of pain or an infinite amount of pleasure? If all utilities are finite, are they bounded either from above or from below? Do any real acts have infinitely many consequences? Are human beings ever really faced with a choice from among infinitely many alternative acts? These are questions belonging to theology, metaphysics, and ethics, and they are beyond the scope of this book. So far as the philosophy of science is concerned, we may assume: Each consequence has a finite utility, each act has a finite number of consequences, and each choice situation contains a finite number of acts. It follows from these assumptions that every act has a finite utility and that every choice situation has an act of maximum utility, so that the rule of maximizing utility is applicable in every choice situation. Whether utilities are bounded from above, from below—or both or neither—we leave as open questions.

4.3.4 Two paradoxes of utility

We shall next present two paradoxes of utility, which I call the "sure-thing paradox" and the "variance paradox." These constitute challenges to the rule of maximizing utility, for if this rule is correct both paradoxes are merely disguised fallacies.

The sure-thing paradox is constructed as follows. Two regular icosahedra are to be thrown in the usual fashion. One is red, the other is blue, and each is labeled twice with the digits 0 through 9. The digits on the red die are interpreted as units and those on the blue die as tens, so the numbers 00 through 99 may come up. A subject would normally regard these as equiprobable.

Let

P_1 = One of the numbers 00 through 78 comes up

P_2 = The number 79 comes up

P_3 = One of the numbers 80 through 99 comes up

C_0 = The subject receives nothing

C_1 = The subject receives $1,000,000

C_{10} = The subject receives $10,000,000.

Note that P_1, P_2, and P_3 are mutually exclusive and jointly exhaustive.

I would choose act

(A_1) $10,000,000 if P_3, nothing otherwise,

over act

(A_2) $1,000,000 if P_2 or P_3, nothing otherwise,

on the ground that success is unlikely in either case but nearly equiprobable in the two cases, and the prize in act A_1 is much larger than the prize in A_2. But I would choose act

(B_1) $1,000,000 with certainty

over act

(B_2) $1,000,000 if P_1, nothing if P_2, $10,000,000 if P_3,

because act B_1 gives me a considerable fortune with certainty. In other words, the fortune of act B_1 is a "sure-thing," while in B_2 there is a chance I will receive nothing. These preferences are symbolized in Figure 5.

My preference of A_1 over A_2 may be expressed in terms of utility as

[15] $$\{\mathbf{U}(P_1C_0) + \mathbf{U}(P_2C_0) + \mathbf{U}(P_3C_{10})\} > \{\mathbf{U}(P_1C_0) + \mathbf{U}(P_2C_1) + \mathbf{U}(P_3C_1)\} .$$

Subtracting $\mathbf{U}(P_1C_0)$ from each side we obtain

[16] $$\{\qquad \mathbf{U}(P_2C_0) + \mathbf{U}(P_3C_{10})\} > \{\qquad \mathbf{U}(P_2C_1) + \mathbf{U}(P_3C_1)\} .$$

The addition of $\mathbf{U}(P_1C_1)$ to both sides gives

[17] $$\{\mathbf{U}(P_1C_1) + \mathbf{U}(P_2C_0) + \mathbf{U}(P_3C_{10})\} > \{\mathbf{U}(P_1C_1) + \mathbf{U}(P_2C_1) + \mathbf{U}(P_3C_1)\} .$$

But this is a preference for B_2 over B_1. Hence, by the rule of maximizing utility, my preference of A_1 over A_2 contradicts my preference of B_1 over B_2.

This is paradoxical. I gave good *reasons* for my preferences of A_1 over A_2 and of B_1 over B_2. And yet the principle of maximizing utility also seems reasonable. We call this paradox the *sure-thing paradox*.* Note that it results from adding the utilities of partial acts and does not depend on the equation $\mathbf{U}(p_nc_n) = \mathbf{P}(p_n)\mathbf{U}(c_n)$ or on the particular values of utility assigned.

The source of the paradox is the putative reason given for preferring act B_1 to act B_2, namely, that with act B_1 the subject is certain to succeed. By the rule of maximizing utility, this kind of appeal to a "sure-thing" is illegitimate. Let us see why. Consider again

[15] $$\{\mathbf{U}(P_1C_0) + \mathbf{U}(P_2C_0) + \mathbf{U}(P_3C_{10})\} > \{\mathbf{U}(P_1C_0) + \mathbf{U}(P_2C_1) + \mathbf{U}(P_3C_1)\} .$$

Since the utility of an act is the sum of the utilities of its parts (formula [12′] of sec. 4.3.1), preference [15] implies a commitment to

[18] $$\{\mathbf{U}(P_1c) + \mathbf{U}(P_2C_0) + \mathbf{U}(P_3C_{10})\} > \{\mathbf{U}(P_1c) + \mathbf{U}(P_2C_1) + \mathbf{U}(P_3C_1)\}$$

for *any consequence* c. But if c is C_1, the right-hand act guarantees a prize while the left-hand act does not. Hence the reason "The fortune of B_1 is a sure-thing, while in B_2 there is a chance I will receive nothing" adduced in justifying my preference of act B_1 over act B_2, is incompatible with the rule of maximizing utility. More generally, the rule of maximizing utility does not allow one to attach *any* utility to the consideration "On this alternative I am sure to get at least this much, whereas on the other I may get nothing."

Our second paradox of utility is a statistical generalization of the sure-

* The paradox is from Allais, "Le comportement de l'Homme Rationnel devant le Risque: Critique des Postulats et Axioms de l'Ecole Americaine," p. 527.

thing paradox. It employs the concept of variance and is called the "variance paradox." As before, let $p_1, p_2, \ldots, p_N$ be mutually exclusive and jointly exhaustive, and let c_n be the consequence of an act a that obtains if p_n is true ($n = 1, 2, \ldots, N$). Then

$$[19] \qquad \textit{Variance of act } a =_{df} \sum_{n=1}^{N} \mathbf{P}(p_n)[\mathbf{U}(c_n) - \mathbf{U}(a)]^2 \quad .$$

For the sake of completeness we define a closely related statistical concept,

$$[20] \qquad \textit{Standard deviation: } \sigma(a) = [\text{Variance of } a]^{1/2} \quad .$$

These concepts measure the variation in the utilities of the different consequences of an act. An act consisting of a single consequence (a "sure-thing")

TABLE 12

VARIANCE OF ACTS

Act	Utility U	Variance
(A_0) Consequence worth 1 utile (C_u)	1	0
(A_1) Consequence worth 2 utiles (C_1) with probability 1/2, nothing (C_z) otherwise	1	1
(A_2) Consequence worth 4 utiles (C_2) with probability 1/4, nothing (C_z) otherwise	1	3
(A_3) Consequence worth 8 utiles (C_3) with probability 1/8, nothing (C_z) otherwise	1	7
⋮		
(A_n) Consequence worth 2^n utiles (C_n) with probability 2^{-n}, nothing (C_z) otherwise	1	$2^n - 1$
⋮		

has a variance of zero, while an act whose consequences have different utilities has positive variance. The acts $A_0, A_1, A_2, \ldots, A_n, \ldots$ of Table 12 all have the same utility, but their variances increase as n increases.

The variance paradox concerns a sequence of acts $A_0, A_1, A_2, \ldots$ constructed as follows. Stipulate that some consequence C_z is of zero utility and that some preferred consequence C_u is of unit utility. Act A_0 consists of the consequence C_u, and hence has unit utility and zero variance. Next, find a consequence C_1 such that the subject is indifferent between A_0 and the mixed act

(A_1) $\quad C_1$ with probability 1/2, C_z otherwise,

and call this act "A_1" as indicated. Proceed in this manner indefinitely, so that at each step the subject is indifferent between act

(A_n) C_n with probability 2^{-n}, C_z otherwise

and act

(A_{n+1}) C_{n+1} with probability $2^{-(n+1)}$, C_z otherwise.

These indifferences seem to establish that each of the acts $A_0, A_1, \ldots, A_n, A_{n+1}, \ldots$ has the same utility as A_0, namely, one utile. By the rule of maximizing utility the subject should be indifferent between any two acts of the sequence $A_0, A_1, A_2, \ldots$.

But suppose the subject compares an act early in the sequence with one very far out. Let the two acts be A_S and A_L, where S is a small integer and L a very large integer, perhaps a trillion. The variance of A_L is many orders of magnitude greater than that of A_S, and the subject might reasonably prefer A_S on that ground. He could say: "I never compared A_S and A_L before. In comparing them now I see that if I choose A_S I have a reasonable chance of getting a prize, whereas if I choose A_L the chance of winning a prize is negligible. Therefore I prefer A_S to A_L."

This is the *variance paradox.* It arises from a conflict of two apparently reasonable criteria for choice: The rule of maximizing utility, and the principle that the variance of an act is sometimes relevant to its value. By the rule of maximizing utility the subject should be indifferent between A_S and A_L, but because of a difference in variance it is reasonable for him to prefer A_S to A_L.

Of course the rule of maximizing utility does take into account some differences in variance. The sequence $A_0, A_1, \ldots, A_n, A_{n+1}, \ldots$ was designed to do just that. Given each act A_n, consequence C_{n+1} is so chosen that the subject is indifferent between A_n and act

(A_{n+1}) C_{n+1} with probability $2^{-(n+1)}$, C_z otherwise.

The subject can express a fear of risk or a love of gambling by choosing the consequence C_{n+1} (e.g., the number of dollars) so that A_{n+1} has for him the same utility as A_n. By construction, each successive act of the sequence $A_0, A_1, A_2, \ldots$ has the same utility but more than twice the variance of its predecessor. Nevertheless, the subject has good reason to reject the transitivity of indifference and to prefer A_S to A_L. Thus in the variance paradox, each single step from A_n to A_{n+1} is acceptable but the whole journey from A_S to A_L is not.

It may be objected that by employing a different sequence of indifferences, we can in some sense make the whole journey from A_S to A_L in a single step. As before, let act A_0 consist of consequence C_u. For each value of $n = 1, 2, 3, \ldots$ find a consequence C'_n such that the subject is indifferent between A_0 and

(A'_n) C'_n with probability 2^{-n}, C_z otherwise.

According to the traditional theory of utility, each act A'_n has the same utility as A_0, namely one utile, and the subject should therefore be indifferent between any two acts of the sequence $A_0, A'_1, \ldots, A'_n, A'_{n+1}, \ldots$. Thus this new use of the method of comparison employed in constructing the variance paradox directly establishes indifference between two acts of widely different variance.

However, the subject might reasonably balk at extending this sequence indefinitely. Let L be one trillion, as before. The subject could properly refuse to compare A_0 and any act

(A'_L) C'_L with probability 2^{-L}, C_z otherwise

on the ground that the likelihood of obtaining C'_L is so small that he does not know how to evaluate the worth of A'_L. And even if the subject makes enough comparisons to establish the equivalence of A_0 to $A'_1, A'_2, \ldots, A'_L$, respectively, he need not be indifferent between successive terms of the sequence $A'_1, A'_2, \ldots, A'_L$. Thus when indifference is established directly between A_0 and A'_L, the equivalence between A'_{L-1} and A'_L may become suspect.

The sequence $A_0, A_1, A_2, \ldots$ of the variance paradox and the last sequence of acts $A_0, A'_1, A'_2, \ldots$ show that the theory of utility imposes a much more interdependent structure on choices than can be captured by a simple chain of definitions. It is this structure that needs analysis.

Let us next compare the variance paradox with the sure-thing paradox and the earlier Saint Petersburg paradox (pp. 190–92). Each consequence C_n of Table 12 has utility $\mathbf{U}(C_n) = 2^{-n}$. Hence the variance and the Saint Petersburg paradoxes are both based on acts constructed from the partial acts "a consequence worth 2^n utiles with probability 2^{-n}," for $n = 1, 2, 3, \ldots$. In the Saint Petersburg paradox this infinite set of partial acts is combined into one act to make a single play of the game. For the variance paradox each of these partial acts is combined with the partial act "nothing otherwise" to make an act worth one utile. The resultant acts are finite, and a finite sequence of them is sufficient to generate the variance paradox; so clearly this paradox does not assume that utility is unbounded as the Saint Petersburg paradox does.

The variance paradox is a probabilistic generalization of the sure-thing paradox. An act consisting of a "sure-thing" or single consequence has a variance of zero. Act B_1 of the sure-thing paradox is an example.

The sure-thing and variance paradoxes suggest that the best choice may not always maximize utility. We saw in Section 4.3.2 that choice situations cannot always be handled quantitatively. But let us grant for a moment that every act has a quantitative value and that the best choice maximizes this quantity. The question we have been discussing in this subsection then becomes: Is utility the quantity to be maximized? This question can be made more precise by introducing a quantitative concept of value that does not prejudge the issue.

Assume every act a has a numerical value $V(a)$ that can be expressed by a real number and that should be maximized in choice situations involving uncertainty. An act $\sum_{n=1}^{N} p_n c_n$ is constructed from possible states of affairs $p_1, p_2, \ldots, p_N$ and corresponding consequences $c_1, c_2, \ldots, c_N$. It seems clear that the probabilities of these states of affairs and the values of these consequences are the only intrinsic factors relevant to the value of the act. Therefore,

$$[21] \qquad V\left(\sum_{n=1}^{N} p_n c_n\right) = \Phi\{\mathbf{P}(p_1), \ldots, \mathbf{P}(p_N); V(c_1), \ldots, V(c_N)\} \qquad ,$$

where Φ is some function of the quantities inside the bracket. The question at issue between the paradoxes of utility and the rule of maximizing utility concerns the nature of this mathematical function Φ.

According to the rule of maximizing utility, Φ is the utility function. In other words, $V(a) = \mathbf{U}(a)$ for all acts a, or equivalently

$$[22] \qquad V\left(\sum_{n=1}^{N} p_n c_n\right) = \sum_{n=1}^{N} \mathbf{P}(p_n) V(c_n) \qquad .$$

The utility of a mixed act is a linear combination of the utilities of its consequences. Therefore, variations in part of an act that change the variance of the total or, in the limit, convert an act with some uncertainty into one with none cannot change the contributions of the other parts of the act.

In contrast, the sure-thing and variance paradoxes seem to show that $V(a) \neq \mathbf{U}(a)$ for at least some acts a, so that the function Φ requiring maximization is not the utility function but some other function. On the positive side, both these paradoxes and common sense suggest a "holistic view" of the value of a mixed act. This is the view that security and risk are properties of the whole act rather than of its parts taken distributively. On this holistic view, the value of an act need not be equal to the sum of the values of its parts but may be more or less than this sum. For example, a gambler gains satisfaction from a certain kind of risk-taking and insecurity per se, whereas one who thinks gambling is immoral does not.

Sometimes the phrase "utility of risk" is used to refer to the putative value of risk over and above the values of the parts of an act taken separately. Such a phrase is misleading, however, for in the technical sense of "utility" there can be no utility of risk per se. It was for this reason that we introduced the notion of the "value" $V(a)$ of an act. By definition, the quantity $V(a)$ is to be maximized in a choice situation, but it is left open as to whether the value $V(a)$ of an act always equals its utility $\mathbf{U}(a)$. The sure-thing and variance paradoxes provide examples of acts whose values $V(a)$ *seem* to differ from their utilities $\mathbf{U}(a)$.

4.3.5 *Insurance and gambling*

The factors of security and risk are predominant in the activities of insuring and gambling, and so it will be instructive to study these activities in terms of the traditional theory of utility. Insuring and gambling involve monetary transactions; to see whether one who engages in these activities is maximizing utility, we must consider his "utility function," i.e., the function relating his monetary wealth to utility.

One insures to gain security. Perhaps a property owner cannot tolerate total loss; by insurance he avoids risk and is guaranteed a minimum level of wealth. Thus he uses insurance to replace chance by certainty. For him, "A bird in the hand is worth two in the bush." In contrast, a gambler chooses to risk some of his wealth in the hope of a greater gain. Thus insuring and gambling are complementary: one insures to reduce risk and gambles to increase risk. To see this complementarity more clearly, imagine that one man insures his house with another, and that neither is involved in any other chance event. Then the first man has increased his security while the second has accepted a gamble.

Though insurance and gambling are complementary, some people do both. It is natural to ask whether this is rational, and if so, what kind of utility function justifies it. In Section 4.3.2 we saw how the rule of maximizing utility justified the purchase of insurance for one who values money according to the utility function $\mathbf{U}(x) = x^{1/3}$. We now generalize this justification of insurance, construct a corresponding justification for gambling, and then consider simultaneous insuring and gambling. Figures 6–8 will be used for this purpose. The reader should keep in mind that the curves and parameters used in these figures were chosen for their illustrative merits, not for their realism.

Because of operating costs and profits, an insurance company must charge a premium in excess of its expected loss. This additional amount is called the "loading." Similarly, the payoffs of games in casinos are adjusted to cover the costs and profits of the "house." In deciding whether the utility of any particular act of insuring or gambling is maximal, one must take quantitative account of the loading charge. However, to make a general comparison of insuring and gambling it is best to concentrate on the case in which there is no loading, for in this case there is a sharp contrast between utility functions that always justify insurance and utility functions that always justify gambling.

The particular utility function $\mathbf{U}(x) = x^{1/3}$ that was used earlier to justify one example of insurance was actually chosen to illustrate the principle of the decreasing marginal utility of money (pp. 186–87). Now to say, as this principle does, that the value of a dollar decreases with increasing wealth is to say that the curve of utility versus money has a certain shape, namely, that it curves downward. In mathematical parlance, it is everywhere convex from above. We shall show that insurance is always justified when the utility function has this shape.

The solid curve of Figure 6 is a plot of the utility function $\mathbf{U}(x) = d_1x^{1/4}$, where x is monetary wealth, for the case $d_1 = 1$ and the range $0 \leqq x \leqq 1$. It is easy to reinterpret this curve for different units of utility and wealth. For example, if $d_1 = 1{,}000$ and the money scale is changed so that $x = 1$ corresponds to \$10,000, the top of the utility scale $[\mathbf{U}(x) = 1]$ will then correspond to 10,000 utiles. On this change of scale, \$7,000 will be worth 9,147 utiles and \$1,000 will be worth 5,623 utiles. A dollar added to \$1,000 is worth 1.4 utiles, while a dollar added to \$7,000 is worth only 0.3 utiles. Thus the utility function $\mathbf{U}(x) = d_1x^{1/4}$ is an example of diminishing marginal utility.

Let a man's total wealth consist of two parts: cash (W units) and a house (worth Δ units). Assume that the cash is securely banked and that the only risk to the house is from fire. Simplify all the alternatives down to two: total loss and no loss. Let α be the probability of total loss so that $\alpha\Delta$ is the unloaded fire insurance premium, and let "$\bar{\alpha}$" symbolize "1-α." If the owner insures his house (I) his net monetary worth will be $W + \bar{\alpha}\Delta$, and so

$$[23a] \quad \mathbf{U}(I) = \mathbf{U}(W + \bar{\alpha}\Delta) \quad .$$

This utility is represented in Figure 6 by the point marked "$\mathbf{U}(I)$". If the owner does not insure ($\bar{I}$), the probability is α that there will be a fire and his wealth will be reduced to W, while the probability is $\bar{\alpha}$ that there will be no fire and his wealth will be $W + \Delta$. The utility of not insuring is thus

$$[23b] \quad \mathbf{U}(\bar{I}) = \alpha\mathbf{U}(W) + \bar{\alpha}\mathbf{U}(W + \Delta)$$
$$= \mathbf{U}(W) + \bar{\alpha}[\mathbf{U}(W + \Delta) - \mathbf{U}(W)] \quad .$$

Since corresponding sides of similar triangles are proportional, $\mathbf{U}(\bar{I})$ is represented by the intersection of these two lines: the vertical dotted line at $x = W + \bar{\alpha}\Delta$ and the dashed line from point $\mathbf{U}(W)$ to point $\mathbf{U}(W + \Delta)$.

Equations [23a] and [23b] hold for any utility function. The utility function of Figure 6 is $\mathbf{U}(x) = x^{1/4}$, and the parameter values illustrated there are $W = 0.1$, $\Delta = 0.6$, and $\alpha = 0.25$. For this case

$$[23a'] \quad \mathbf{U}(I) = \mathbf{U}(.55) \qquad = 0.861$$

$$[23b'] \quad \mathbf{U}(\bar{I}) = .25\mathbf{U}(.1) + .75\mathbf{U}(.7) = 0.827 \quad ,$$

so that the utility of insuring is greater than the utility of not insuring. Moreover, since the dashed line lies below the utility curve of Figure 6, it is evident that $\mathbf{U}(I)$ is greater than $\mathbf{U}(\bar{I})$ for all values of the parameters W, Δ, α such that $0 < (W + \Delta) \leqq 1$, $0 < \Delta$, and $0 < \alpha < 1$. In other words, if one applies the rule of maximizing utility to the utility function $\mathbf{U}(x) = d_1x^{1/4}$ and ignores loading, then he should insure against every risk.

This argument clearly holds for any utility function that is everywhere convex from above (in the interval under consideration). Therefore, if the curve representing utility as a function of monetary wealth is everywhere convex from above in a given range, the rule of maximizing utility implies that whenever one can insure against risk without paying a loading charge he should do so. In other words, in the absence of loading, the principle of decreasing marginal utility of money justifies insurance. When a loading charge is made, whether one should insure or not depends on the amount of loading.

We next analyze gambling, using a notation similar to that just used for insurance to facilitate comparison of the two cases. In the analysis of insurance, W was the minimum wealth on any outcome, Δ was the wealth subject to risk (the value of the house), $W + \Delta$ was the maximum wealth of any outcome, and α was the probability that Δ would be *lost*. For the analysis of gambling, let W be the minimum wealth, Δ the wealth subject to risk (the lottery prize), $W + \Delta$ the maximum wealth, and α the probability that Δ will be *won*. The unloaded insurance premium is $\alpha\Delta$ and the unloaded cost of the lottery ticket is $\alpha\Delta$, the probability α typically being small in both cases. The initial wealth is $W + \Delta$ in the insurance case and $W + \alpha\Delta$ in the gambling case.

The principle of *decreasing* marginal utility of money justifies insurance. A complementary condition, the principle of *increasing* marginal utility of money justifies gambling. To say that a unit of money (e.g., a dollar) increases with increasing wealth is to say that the curve of utility versus money is everywhere concave from above. The solid curve of Figure 7 is a plot of the utility function $\mathbf{U}(x) = d_2x^3$ for the case of $d_2 = 1$ and the range $0 \leqq x \leqq 1$. This function is representative of the class of functions that are everywhere concave from above.

Consider a man worth $W + \alpha\Delta$ who is offered a fair bet or lottery ticket for $\alpha\Delta$, where α is the probability of winning prize Δ. If he gambles (G), the probability is $\bar{\alpha}$ that he will lose and be worth W, while the probability is α that he will win and be worth $W + \Delta$. The utility of gambling is thus

$$\text{[24a]} \quad \begin{aligned} \mathbf{U}(G) &= \bar{\alpha}\mathbf{U}(W) + \alpha\mathbf{U}(W + \Delta) \\ &= \mathbf{U}(W) + \alpha[\mathbf{U}(W + \Delta) - \mathbf{U}(W)] \quad , \end{aligned}$$

where $\bar{\alpha} = 1 - \alpha$ as before. Corresponding sides of similar triangles are proportional, and hence $\mathbf{U}(G)$ is represented by the intersection of these two lines: the vertical dotted line at $x = W + \alpha\Delta$ and the dashed line from $\mathbf{U}(W)$ to $\mathbf{U}(W + \Delta)$. If he does not gamble, his net worth will be $W + \alpha\Delta$, and so

$$\text{[24b]} \quad \mathbf{U}(\bar{G}) = \mathbf{U}(W + \alpha\Delta) \quad .$$

This utility is represented in Figure 7 by the point marked "$\mathbf{U}(\bar{G})$".

Equations [24a] and [24b] hold for any utility function. The utility function of Figure 7 is $\mathbf{U}(x) = x^3$, and the parameter values illustrated there are $W = 0.6$, $\Delta = 0.3$, and $\alpha = 1/3$. For this case

$$[24a'] \quad \mathbf{U}(G) = (2/3)\mathbf{U}(.6) + (1/3)\mathbf{U}(.9) = 0.387$$

$$[24b'] \quad \mathbf{U}(\bar{G}) = \mathbf{U}(.7) = 0.343 \quad ,$$

so that the utility of gambling is greater than the utility of not gambling. Since the dashed line lies above the utility curve in this figure, $\mathbf{U}(G)$ is greater than $\mathbf{U}(\bar{G})$ for all W, Δ, α such that $0 < (W + \Delta) \leqq 1$, $0 < \Delta$, and $0 < \alpha < 1$. Thus if one applies the rule of maximizing utility to the function $\mathbf{U}(x) = d_2x^3$ and ignores loading, he should gamble at every opportunity.

This argument clearly holds for any utility function that is everywhere concave from above in the interval under consideration. Hence if the curve representing utility as a function of monetary wealth is everywhere concave from above in a given range, the rule of maximizing utility implies that whenever one can gamble without paying a loading charge he should do so. In other words, the principle of *increasing* marginal utility of money justifies gambling, when loading is neglected. When loading is included, whether one should gamble or not depends on the amount of loading.

The complementarity of insuring and gambling is manifest in the similarity of equations [23] and [24] and of the constructions of Figures 6 and 7. The minimum wealth W and the maximum wealth $W + \Delta$ determine two points on the utility curve: $\mathbf{U}(W)$ and $\mathbf{U}(W + \Delta)$. These two points are connected by a dashed line. The risk α determines a vertical line, at $x = W + \bar{\alpha}\Delta$ for insurance and $x = W + \alpha\Delta$ for gambling, which intersects the dashed line and the solid utility curve. The relative positions of these intersections show which alternative has maximum utility. Note that the intersection with the dashed line represents the alternative with risk (don't insure, gamble), while the intersection with the utility curve represents the alternative with security (insure, don't gamble). Consequently, if "α" and "$\bar{\alpha}$" are exchanged in Figure 6 (and some relabeling is done), the result will show that one whose utility function is everywhere convex from above should never gamble. Similarly, Figure 7 may be used to show that if one's utility is everywhere concave from above he should never insure.

The result of this analysis of insurance and gambling, in which loading is neglected, is as follows. According to the rule of maximizing utility, a person whose utility curve is everywhere *convex* from above should always insure and never gamble, while a person whose utility curve is everywhere *concave* from above should always gamble and never insure. Thus gambling and insuring are incompatible for a person whose utility function always curves in the same direction (is everywhere convex or everywhere concave). Moreover, this incompatibility remains when loading is taken into consideration, since loading makes both insuring and gambling less attractive.

We are now prepared to consider the question: Should a person who maximizes utility ever both insure and gamble? The preceding result suggests that he should, if his utility function is convex in one region and concave in another.* This is indeed the case, as we now show by means of Figure 8. The utility curve of this figure is a cubic.

$$[25] \qquad \mathbf{U}(x) = .5 + 4(x - .5)^3 \quad .$$

This utility function is convex from above in the region $0 \leqq x \leqq 0.5$ and concave from above in the region $0.5 \leqq x \leqq 1$. Convexity favors insuring and concavity favors gambling, so that one who uses this utility curve should sometimes insure and sometimes gamble. Should he ever do both simultaneously? We can construct an example to show that he should.

Consider a man with cash wealth W and a house worth Δ, who is presented with two independent options. For a premium $\alpha\Delta$ he may insure his house against total loss from fire, the probability of this event being α. Independently, he may buy a lottery ticket for $\alpha\Delta$ that gives him a chance α of winning a prize Δ. Let "I" mean that he insures and "G" that he gambles. He thus has a choice of one of four acts: IG, $I\bar{G}$, $\bar{I}G$, and $\bar{I}\bar{G}$.

Consider first the choice between acts $I\bar{G}$ and $\bar{I}\bar{G}$. This is the insurance choice analyzed in connection with Figure 6, with minimum wealth W, wealth Δ subject to risk, and probability of loss α. If the man insures, his net wealth is $W + \bar{\alpha}\Delta$, and so

$$[26a] \qquad \mathbf{U}(I\bar{G}) = \mathbf{U}(W + \bar{\alpha}\Delta) \quad .$$

If he does not insure, his wealth will be W if there is a fire (probability α) and $W + \Delta$ if there is no fire (probability $\bar{\alpha}$), and so

$$[26b] \qquad \mathbf{U}(\bar{I}\bar{G}) = \alpha\mathbf{U}(W) + \bar{\alpha}\mathbf{U}(W + \Delta)$$
$$= \mathbf{U}(W) + \bar{\alpha}[\mathbf{U}(W + \Delta) - \mathbf{U}(W)] \quad .$$

The quantity $\mathbf{U}(\bar{I}\bar{G})$ is represented in Figure 8 by the intersection of these two lines: the vertical solid line at $x = W + \bar{\alpha}\Delta$ and the dotted line from $\mathbf{U}(W)$ to $\mathbf{U}(W + \Delta)$.

Consider next the choice between acts IG and $I\bar{G}$. After insuring his house the man has net wealth $W + \bar{\alpha}\Delta$. He is then in the gambling situation analyzed in connection with Figure 7, with an initial wealth of $W + \bar{\alpha}\Delta$ and minimum wealth of $W + \bar{\alpha}\Delta$ less the cost $\alpha\Delta$ of a lottery ticket. Call this minimum wealth W' to distinguish it from W. Then

$$[27] \qquad W' = W + \bar{\alpha}\Delta - \alpha\Delta \quad .$$

If the man does not gamble, his wealth will be $W' + \alpha\Delta$; so

$$\mathbf{U}(I\bar{G}) = \mathbf{U}(W' + \alpha\Delta) \quad .$$

* See Friedman and Savage, "The Utility Analysis of Choices Involving Risk," pp. 294–95.

This is equivalent to [26a] by virtue of equation [27]. If the man gambles, his wealth will be W' if he loses (probability $\bar{\alpha}$) and $W' + \Delta$ if he wins (probability α); so

$$[26c] \quad \mathbf{U}(IG) = \alpha \mathbf{U}(W' + \Delta) + \bar{\alpha}\mathbf{U}(W') = \mathbf{U}(W') + \alpha[\mathbf{U}(W' + \Delta) - \mathbf{U}(W')] \quad .$$

The point $\mathbf{U}(IG)$ is represented in Figure 8 by the intersection of these two lines: the vertical solid line at $x = W' + \alpha\Delta$ and the dashed line from $\mathbf{U}(W')$ to $\mathbf{U}(W' + \Delta)$.

Act $\bar{I}G$ remains. It is the most complicated of the four acts because it involves a double risk: if the man chooses $\bar{I}G$ he may lose both his house and the gamble. The man's initial wealth is $W + \Delta$. From this he pays $\alpha\Delta$ for a lottery ticket, leaving $W + \Delta - \alpha\Delta$ or $W + \bar{\alpha}\Delta$. Δ is subtracted from this if there is a fire (probability α), while Δ is added to this if he wins the lottery (probability $\bar{\alpha}$); these two events are independent. Act $\bar{I}G$ thus consists of the four partial acts:

(Lose house and lottery)	Net worth $W - \alpha\Delta$, with probability $\alpha\bar{\alpha}$
(Lose house, win lottery)	Net worth $W + \bar{\alpha}\Delta$, with probability $\alpha\alpha$
(Keep house, lose lottery)	Net worth $W + \bar{\alpha}\Delta$, with probability $\bar{\alpha}\bar{\alpha}$
(Keep house, win lottery)	Net worth $W + \Delta + \bar{\alpha}\Delta$, with probability $\bar{\alpha}\alpha$.

Hence

$$[26d] \quad \mathbf{U}(\bar{I}G) = \alpha\bar{\alpha}\mathbf{U}(W - \alpha\Delta) + (\alpha^2 + \bar{\alpha}^2)\mathbf{U}(W + \bar{\alpha}\Delta) + \bar{\alpha}\alpha\mathbf{U}(W + \Delta + \bar{\alpha}\Delta) \quad .$$

Equations [26a]–[26d] give the utilities of the four acts $I\bar{G}$, $\bar{I}\bar{G}$, IG, $\bar{I}G$ for any utility function and any values of the parameters W, Δ, and α. The utility function shown in Figure 8 is $\mathbf{U}(x) = .5 + 4(x - .5)^3$. The parameter values illustrated there are $W = 0.2$, $\Delta = 0.4$, and $\alpha = 0.25$; W' equals 0.4 by equation [27]. For this example the utilities of the four acts are

$$[26a'] \quad \mathbf{U}(I\bar{G}) = \mathbf{U}(.5) = 0.5$$

$$[26b'] \quad \mathbf{U}(\bar{I}\bar{G}) = .25\mathbf{U}(.2) + .75\mathbf{U}(.6) = 0.476$$

$$[26c'] \quad \mathbf{U}(IG) = .75\mathbf{U}(.4) + .25\mathbf{U}(.8) = 0.524$$

$$[26d'] \quad \mathbf{U}(\bar{I}G) = .1875\mathbf{U}(.1) + .625\mathbf{U}(.5) + .1875\mathbf{U}(.9) = 0.5 \quad .$$

The act IG has maximum utility, so that by the rule of maximizing utility the man should both insure and gamble. This result was derived on the assumption there is no loading, but it is clear that it also holds for suitably small loadings.

This example shows that the rule of maximizing utility sometimes justifies simultaneous gambling and insuring. The essential condition concerns the shape of the utility function: the curve giving utility as a function of increasing wealth is first convex from above and then concave from above. By reversing the order of convexity and concavity we can produce a situation in which the best choice is neither to insure nor to gamble. Let

$$[28] \quad \mathbf{U}'(x) = .5 + \left(\frac{x - .5}{4}\right)^{1/3} \quad .$$

For the case $W = 0.2$, $\Delta = 0.4$, $\alpha = 0.25$ (and hence $W' = 0.4$) the utilities of the four acts can be determined by substituting $\mathbf{U}'$ for $\mathbf{U}$ in equations [26a′]–[26d′] and evaluating the results.

$$[29a] \quad \mathbf{U}'(I\bar{G}) = \mathbf{U}'(.5) = 0.5$$

$$[29b] \quad \mathbf{U}'(\bar{I}\bar{G}) = .25\mathbf{U}'(.2) + .75\mathbf{U}'(.6) = 0.614$$

$$[29c] \quad \mathbf{U}'(IG) = .75\mathbf{U}'(.4) + .25\mathbf{U}'(.8) = 0.386$$

$$[29d] \quad \mathbf{U}'(\bar{I}G) = .1875\mathbf{U}'(.1) + .625\mathbf{U}'(.5) + .1875\mathbf{U}'(.9) = 0.5 \quad .$$

The act $\bar{I}\bar{G}$ has maximum utility.

It follows from our earlier discussion that act $I\bar{G}$ will have maximum utility if the utility curve is everywhere convex from above, while act $\bar{I}G$ will have maximum utility if the utility curve is everywhere concave from above. Hence for insurance and gambling considered together, we have the following result concerning the set of acts IG, $I\bar{G}$, $\bar{I}G$, $\bar{I}\bar{G}$: For each of these acts there are a utility function and values for W, Δ, and α such that by the rule of maximizing utility that act should be chosen over the others.

Since insuring and gambling are complementary, it is of interest to see when they cancel each other. The acts IG, $I\bar{G}$, $\bar{I}\bar{G}$, $\bar{I}G$ were defined so that the wealth subject to risk is the same for both options: the house is worth Δ and the lottery prize is also worth Δ. The risk α is the same for both options, but α is the probability of *losing* Δ by fire while it is the probability of *winning* Δ in the lottery. Therefore, when $\alpha = \bar{\alpha}$, the insurance policy and the lottery ticket cancel, and act IG becomes logically equivalent to act $\bar{I}\bar{G}$. This conclusion can also be derived directly from equations [26b], [26c], and [27]. If $\alpha = \bar{\alpha}$, then $\alpha = 0.5$ and $W = W'$. Under these conditions

$$[26b''] \quad \mathbf{U}(\bar{I}\bar{G}) = .5\mathbf{U}(W) + .5\mathbf{U}(W + \Delta)$$

$$[26c''] \quad \mathbf{U}(IG) = .5\mathbf{U}(W + \Delta) + .5\mathbf{U}(W) \quad .$$

Therefore, $\mathbf{U}(\bar{I}\bar{G}) = \mathbf{U}(IG)$ when $\alpha = \bar{\alpha}$.

This completes our study of the utility functions that justify a person's choosing to insure and/or gamble under the rule of maximizing utility. The crucial property is the shape of the utility curve in the region where the alternatives lie. There are three cases. (1) The principle of decreasing marginal utility of money holds; that is, the utility curve is everywhere convex from above. In this case, one should never gamble. If there is no loading, he should always insure; if there is loading, whether or not he should insure depends on the exact conditions. (2) The principle of increasing marginal utility of money holds; that is, the utility curve is everywhere concave from above. In this case, one should never insure. If there is no loading, he should always gamble; if there is loading, he should gamble or not according to the exact conditions. (3) The utility curve is both convex and concave. In this case, any of the four acts, insure and gamble, insure and do not gamble, do not insure but gamble, and neither insure nor gamble, may have maximum utility, depending on the exact circumstances. In general, convexity favors insurance, concavity favors gambling, and loading makes both insurance and gambling less attractive.

Let us now consider this analysis of insurance and gambling in relation to the paradoxes of the preceding subsection. The sure-thing and variance paradoxes suggested a "holistic" view of a mixed act. This is the view that the values of security and risk-taking are characteristics of the whole act rather than of its parts taken distributively, and hence they are not completely captured by the concept of utility. Now since security and risk are the essence of insuring and gambling, it is natural to ask whether our analysis of them confirms the holistic view. It does not, for we have seen that there are utility functions (relating the subject's wealth to his utilities) on which insurance and gambling maximize utility. Thus the holistic view finds no support in insurance and gambling, as far as we have analyzed them.

This result is not conclusive, however, because of the limitations of our present study. We have considered only single choices in a static situation, whereas in life one makes a series of choices in a dynamic situation. For instance, a complete analysis of gambling must explain why a person stops gambling as well as why he started. Sequences of choices are, of course, much more complicated than single choices. An example will illustrate the kind of considerations involved.

Suppose Mr. Gamble's utility function is $\mathbf{U}_g(x) = x^2$ utiles, where x is measured in units of one thousand dollars (kilobucks!). Mr. Gamble has a chance to invest 10 kilobucks in a wildcat oil well, with the probability .06 that he will receive 100 kilobucks, otherwise nothing. Suppose his initial capital is $10,000. The utilities of the alternatives are

[30] $\mathbf{U}(\text{Investing}) = .06\mathbf{U}(100) + .94\mathbf{U}(0) = 600$ utiles

$\mathbf{U}(\overline{\text{Investing}}) = \mathbf{U}(10) = 100$ utiles.

Clearly, he would invest in the oil well. Assume that he strikes oil and then has an opportunity to make another investment on the same terms. The utilities of the alternatives are now

[31] $$\mathbf{U}(\text{Investing*}) = .06\mathbf{U}(190) + .94\mathbf{U}(90) = 9{,}780 \text{ utiles}$$
$$\mathbf{U}(\overline{\text{Investing*}}) = \mathbf{U}(100) = 10{,}000 \text{ utiles.}$$

This time he does not take a chance on the oil well. (It may be helpful to recall that neither investment would be wise if $\mathbf{U}(x) = x$.)

The subject of sequential behavior in relation to utility functions is beyond the scope of this book, and we shall say no more about it. The analysis of strategies in the next chapter is, however, relevant to it.

4.3.6 Simple ordering of preferences and uncertainties

In this subsection we shall look beneath the quantitative nature of utility and probability and raise some questions about their qualitative nature. These questions concern the transitivity and comparability of the subject's qualitative preferences for acts and assessments of likelihoods.

Consider the choice and act trees shown in the figures. Imagine that a subject is presented with a set of choice trees and given an opportunity to make choices by marking them and converting them into act trees. If the subject does not know the truth-values of the propositions on the dotted lines when he marks a choice tree, his act of marking constitutes a behavioral or pragmatic manifestation of his preferences under conditions of uncertainty. The subject might, of course, choose an act he did not really prefer, e.g., if he wanted to upset an experiment; but this would occur only under unusual circumstances.

Three different relations between acts are represented in Figure 9. If two acts are both chosen, the subject is "indifferent" between them (sec. 4.3.1). Thus, the fact that the subject placed arrows on the lines leading to a_1 and a_2 shows that he is indifferent between a_1 and a_2. If one act is chosen and the other is not, we say that the subject *prefers* the former to the latter. In Figure 9 the subject prefers a_1 to b_1. A subject *likes* one act *at least as much as* another if and only if he either prefers it to the other or is indifferent between them. For example, he likes a_1 at least as much as a_2 and at least as much as b_1, but he does not like b_1 at least as much as a_1. Note that indifference and preference exclude one another. Note also that when two acts are unmarked nothing is implied about their relative merits. Thus Figure 9 does not say whether indifference or preference holds between b_1 and b_2 in either direction. This is settled by how the subject marks a choice tree having b_1 and b_2 as the only acts.

The relations "the subject is indifferent between acts a and b," "the subject prefers act a to act b," and "the subject likes act a at least as much as act b" are all binary relations. We consider next the general properties of these three relations.

The following properties of a binary relation R over a set of objects are of interest:

Reflexive: Rxx
Irreflexive: Not-Rxx
Symmetrical: If Rxy then Ryx
Asymmetrical: If Rxy then not-Ryx
Comparable: Either Rxy or Ryx
Transitive: If Rxy and Ryz then Rxz,

where x, y, and z are objects of the set in question. A relation that is both comparable and transitive is said to be *simply ordered.* A relation that is transitive, reflexive, and symmetrical is said to be an *equivalence relation.*

Consider now "indifference," "preference," and "likes at least as much as," taken as relations over the set of acts. Assume that the subject assigns a utility to every consequence and a quantitative probability to every statement on a choice tree, and makes his choices by the rule of maximizing utility. The three relations will then have the following properties. "Indifference" is transitive, symmetrical, and reflexive and hence is an equivalence relation. "Preference" is transitive and irreflexive. The relation "likes at least as much as" is comparable and transitive and hence is simply ordered. Accordingly, it is appropriate to symbolize these relations by "$=$", "$>$", and "$\geqq$", respectively.

Of the three relations, "$a_1 \geqq a_2$" is the most convenient to work with; the others can be defined in terms of it. The simple ordering of the subject's preferences is then expressed as

[32a] Either $a_1 \geqq a_2$ or $a_2 \geqq a_1$ (comparable)

[32b] If $a_1 \geqq a_2$ and $a_2 \geqq a_3$, then $a_1 \geqq a_3$ (transitive).

Since a consequence is by definition an act, the simple ordering of the subject's choices of consequences follows immediately from the simple ordering of his choices of acts. When consequence symbols are substituted for act symbols in [32a] and [32b], the result is

[33a] Either $c_1 \geqq c_2$ or $c_2 \geqq c_1$ (comparable)

[33b] If $c_1 \geqq c_2$ and $c_2 \geqq c_3$, then $c_1 \geqq c_3$ (transitive).

If the subject marks his choice trees thoughtfully, his choice of one act over another is a pragmatic manifestation of his judgment of the values of the acts. These judgments are, of course, relative to the subject and to the context in which he marks the choice trees. Acts are composed of consequences and statements, requiring the subject to take into account both the values of the consequences and the probabilities of the statements. Two special cases are of interest: the one in which all the acts are consequences and the one in which two acts have the same consequences but involve different statements. In the first case the subject's choices give his ordering of preferences for consequences. In the second case his choice is a pragmatic manifestation of his estimate of the relative probabilities of the statements. This point is illustrated in Figures 10 and 11.

Act tree 1 of Figure 10 shows that the subject prefers C_1 to C_2. Therefore, he would choose act 3 if he thought P more likely than Q, act 4 if he thought Q more likely than P, and both acts 3 and 4 if he thought P and Q equally likely. Since he chose act 3 over act 4, he must have thought that P was more likely than Q. Similarly, Figure 11 is a pragmatic manifestation of the subject's belief that the four tail-head sequences T_1T_2, $T_1\bar{T}_2$, $\bar{T}_1T_2$, and $\bar{T}_1\bar{T}_2$ were equally probable, assuming that he prizes a Polish gold ducat.

Consider now the relations "p and q are equally likely," "p is more likely than q," and "p is at least as likely as q." In the process of applying the rule of maximizing utility, the subject assigns a quantitative probability to every statement in a choice tree. Clearly then, the relation of equal likelihood is an equivalence relation, the relation of "is more likely than" is transitive and irreflexive, and the relation "is at least as likely as" is simply ordered. Hence it is appropriate to symbolize these relations by "$=$", "$>$", and "$\geqq$" as before. The simple ordering of uncertainties is expressed by

[34a] Either $(p \geqq q)$ or $(q \geqq p)$ (comparable)

[34b] If $(p \geqq q)$ and $(q \geqq r)$, then $(p \geqq r)$ (transitive).

It should be emphasized that our use of "$=$", "$>$", and "$\geqq$" to express preferences for acts and estimates of likelihood is not necessarily numeric or quantitative. Thus "$a_1 > a_2$" says that the subject prefers a_1 to a_2, and not that the utility of a_1 is greater than the utility of a_2. Similarly, "$p_1 > p_2$" says that the subject thinks that p_1 is more likely to be true than is p_2, and this may be so without his assigning quantitative probabilities to p_1 and p_2. We shall often use the term "uncertainty" rather than "probability" when we wish to leave open the question as to whether the probability involved is quantitative or qualitative.

The foregoing discussion shows that the quantitative notions of utility and probability are related to their qualitative counterparts, preference and uncertainty, in the following way: the rule of maximizing utility implies that preferences and uncertainties should be simply ordered. It is intuitively clear that the reverse does not hold: one who simply orders his preferences and uncertainties is not committed to use the quantitative machinery of the traditional theory of utility. In the next chapter, we shall analyze this difference axiomatically and see that it is not as large as it appears to be (pp. 310–12).

But at the moment I am interested in the fact that the rule of maximizing utility implies that preferences and uncertainties should be simply ordered. For I wish to object to the latter, and thereby to the former. More specifically, I shall argue that some uncertainties are not comparable and that some preferences are neither transitive nor comparable.

The incomparability of uncertainties or probabilities is best brought out by examining the difference between a quantitative and a qualitative probability in a specific case. Consider the conclusion

(C_1) This die will fall deuce the next time it is thrown in the usual way

and the evidence

(E_1) This die is symmetrical, and most symmetrical dice have fallen deuce about one-sixth of the time.

Most people would agree right off that $\mathbf{P}(C_1, E_1) = 1/6$. Contrast this with the nonquantitative case. Let the conclusion be

(C_2) It snowed in Jackfield during the first week in January 1817,

and let E_2 express all the information of a person who knows nothing about the town of Jackfield. Clearly, the nonquantitative probability $\mathbf{P}(C_2, E_2)$ cannot really be compared with certain other probabilities. Under suitable conditions one can force the subject to assign a quantitative value to $\mathbf{P}(C_2, E_2)$, but one is only forcing him to guess. Suppose a subject, under such pressure, simply orders his uncertainties and assigns the probability 1/6 to the pair C_2, E_2 so that for him $\mathbf{P}(C_2, E_2) = 1/6$. In contrast to the quantitative case, $\mathbf{P}(C_2, E_2) = 1/6$ is here highly hypothetical and arbitrary. It is hypothetical because it refers to the guesses a subject would make if he were forced to. The particular probability value 1/6 the subject assigned is arbitrary. He might reasonably have chosen a different value, such as 1/10, and two people can properly assign quite different values. There is a limit to reasonable variations here, however; for example, it does not seem reasonable to say in this case that $\mathbf{P}(C_2, E_2) = 10^{-10}$.

Thus the principle of comparability holds for all quantitative probabilities but not for all qualitative probabilities. The distinction between the quantitative probability $\mathbf{P}(C_1, E_1)$ and the qualitative probability $\mathbf{P}(C_2, E_2)$ is related to the nature, quantity, and quality of the evidence expressed by E_1 and E_2, respectively. The data available must satisfy certain minimal conditions before one can reasonably assign a quantitative value to a probability or compare two qualitative probabilities. Since the calculus of inductive probability assigns a single real number to $\mathbf{P}(c, e)$, it does not possess a formal means for expressing the difference between quantitative and qualitative probabilities.*

* See sec. 4 (Indeterminate Probabilities) of my "A Pragmatic-Humean Theory of Probability and Lewis's Theory."

The simple ordering of uncertainties or probabilities has been challenged before. Keynes and Koopman developed systems in which transitivity holds but comparability does not, so that probabilities are not simply ordered but only partially ordered.* These systems are better models of nonquantitative probabilities than is the calculus of inductive probability, though the latter is a better model of quantitative probabilities.

We argue next that the principles of transitivity and comparability sometimes fail for preferences. Take transitivity first. A subject may prefer act a_1 to act a_2 on the basis of one criterion, a_2 to a_3 on the basis of another criterion, a_3 to a_1 on the basis of a third, and yet be unable to measure the relative strength of his desire for each act in terms of each criterion or to weigh the relative merits of the three criteria. For example, he may prefer a Volkswagen (a_1) to a Ford (a_2) on the basis of size, a Ford to a Plymouth (a_3) on the basis of safety, a Plymouth to a Volkswagen on the basis of speed, and yet be unable to rank the criteria of size, safety, and speed. In this case it seems reasonable for his preferences to be intransitive.

But suppose the subject is forced to choose one of the three acts a_1, a_2, a_3 and in fact chooses a_1. Suppose further that he clings to his original preferences: a_1 over a_2, a_2 over a_3, but a_3 over a_1. Is he unreasonable? While a subject who makes these choices is not illogical in the deductive sense, it seems irrational for him to make both of these choices:

a_3 over a_1 when presented with the pair a_1, a_3

a_1 over a_3 when presented with the triplet a_1, a_2, a_3.

Why should the choice he makes between a_1 and a_3 depend on whether he is forced to consider a_2 at the same time?

The answer to this question can be found by examining the decision process. In some cases of comparison, a subject need not make up his mind; he knows immediately that he prefers one act to another. But in other cases he is uncertain. He may then analyze the alternative acts and look for reasons to prefer one to the other. In doing this, he may consider certain factors or characteristics and evaluate each act with respect to each of these. In the typical case, one act will be superior to another in certain respects but inferior to it in other respects. In order to make a choice the subject must then evaluate the relative importance of each factor. This he may find hard to do. If he does carry the decision process far enough to rank all three acts "at once" (e.g., in the order: a_1 first, a_2 second, and a_3 third), then by the reasoning that led to this ranking he should rank these acts taken pairwise in the corresponding order (a_1 over a_2, a_2 over a_3, and a_1 over a_3). But the reverse does not hold. He may carry the process far enough to prefer a_1 to a_2, a_2 to a_3, and a_3 to a_1, but not far enough to consider the three acts a_1, a_2, a_3 together. In this connection, see the subset axiom of page 266.

* Keynes, *A Treatise on Probability*, chap. 3; Koopman, "The Bases of Probability."

The objection to comparability is along similar lines. Comparability requires the subject to compare *any* two acts and choose one of them. When he is actually forced to make a choice or is sufficiently rewarded for choosing, as we assumed earlier in this subsection, then clearly he should choose. But why should one always compare hypothetical acts and decide which he prefers? The act of choosing may itself have a price, and so the subject must make a second-order decision whether to choose and, if so, how extended his study of the alternatives should be. Choices do require reflection, and not only do people often find it very hard to choose from among acts, but they sometimes regret their choices subsequently. It is a mark of a good administrator that he judge successfully which decisions to make and which decisions to avoid or postpone.

Let us summarize our conclusions concerning the simple ordering of uncertainties and preferences. When the available evidence is weak, it is reasonable not to compare uncertainties. Also, in some situations it is reasonable to leave the decision process incomplete, with the result that the preferences involved may be incomparable or intransitive. Thus, not all uncertainties and preferences are simply ordered, and the distinctions between quantitative and qualitative probabilities and between utilities and qualitative valuations are both valid.

Much more needs to be said about the circumstances under which one should complete the decision process, either by simply ordering one's preferences or by assigning utilities to all acts. The theorem of the next section bears on this problem, and more will be said in the next chapter (sec. 5.6.2).

This completes our introduction to the subject of utility, which was by way of the traditional theory of utility. On this theory, to choose an act from among alternatives one should estimate the utilities and probabilities of all the consequences involved, calculate the utility of each act, and then apply the rule of maximizing utility. The traditional theory gives good insight into utility and choice, and it accounts for insurance and gambling, at least as far as single choices are concerned. However, the theory does give rise to some problems about the concept of utility. The distinction between quantitative and qualitative probability and that between utility and qualitative valuation need to be explained. Two paradoxes need to be resolved: the sure-thing paradox and the variance paradox. Finally, our objections to the simple ordering of preferences and uncertainties should be met.

In the next section we shall state a classical theorem relating probability and utility to systematic betting behavior. Then in the next chapter we shall present a pragmatic analysis of probability and utility, in terms of which we can solve the problems raised by the traditional theory of utility.

4.4 The "Book" Theorem

We saw in studying the calculus of inductive probability that this calculus is concerned with systems of probability statements (p. 92). It is now equally clear that utility theory is concerned with systems of choices made under conditions of uncertainty. The systematic character of the concepts of probability and utility is revealed by a theorem of Ramsey and of de Finetti that relates the calculus of probability to the gambling notion of a "book." Their theorem provides a good transition to the calculus of choice of the next chapter, for in both cases the rules of the calculus of probability are derived from rules for playing a certain type of "game."

In gambling terminology, a bettor who makes a set of bets such that he will lose on every outcome has had a book made against him. A book is made against him in a single play of roulette, for instance, if he places a dollar on every number (00, 0, 1, 2, . . . , 35, 36). No matter where the ball stops he will pay $38 and receive $36 for a net loss of $2. Note the subtle difference: these bets are reasonable enough if placed in sequence (they might even make his fortune!), but, made simultaneously, they are foolish. This difference is connected to the incompleteness of the calculus of probability (pp. 99–101): the statement "the probability of drawing a heart is one in a million" is consistent with the calculus, but it is not consistent with the calculus and also the statement "each card is equally likely."

A "bookie" has made a "book" when he sells a set of bets such that he will win on every outcome. Since a bookie has many customers, he can make a book without making a book against any customer. A bookie often sets his odds and tries to attract bets in such a way as to make a book or come close to it. The parimutuel betting system used at race tracks guarantees the house a book.

The book theorem relates inductively consistent or "coherent" sets of partial beliefs to the calculus of probability. See the epigraph of the next chapter (p. 247). "Coherence" is defined in terms of a book, which is a specific kind of "system of bets." All of these concepts rest on the notion of inductive probability and can therefore be defined in either conditional or unconditional form. We use the unconditional forms, which are easier for us to work with, but the book theorem applies to the conditional forms as well.

The concepts of "book" and "coherent" are best presented in terms of an imaginary game between a subject and his opponent, whom we call "the devil." The game starts with a set of statements Λ. The subject assigns a degree of belief to each statement, hoping to avoid a book. The devil then assigns a stake to each statement, trying to make a book against the subject.

In more detail, the subject's move in the game is to assign a number $P(c)$ to each statement c of Λ. This assignment is called a *set of partial beliefs*, the quantity $P(c)$ being interpreted as the subject's degree of belief in c. A set of partial beliefs need not satisfy the calculus of probability; the use of the italic P instead of the boldface **P** leaves this possibility open.

The devil's move in the game is to assign a real number $S(c)$ to each c of Λ. The quantity $S(c)$ is the *stake* of the gamble, and a payoff is made according to the following natural rule:

If c is true, the subject receives $\overline{P(c)}S(c)$

If c is false, the subject receives $-P(c)S(c)$,

where a negative quantity means that the subject actually pays (loses) rather than receives (wins), and "$\overline{P(c)}$" means "$1 - P(c)$" as before. By choosing whether the stake $S(c)$ is positive or negative the devil chooses whether the subject is betting on c or against c. If $S(c) = 0$, the statement c is in effect excluded from the system of bets.

We can now offer three more definitions. A *system of bets* is a set of partial beliefs together with an assignment of stakes to these beliefs. A *book* against the subject is a system of bets such that the subject will lose (his net "receipts" will be negative) on every outcome. A set of partial beliefs is *incoherent* if it allows the devil to make a book against the subject, otherwise it is *coherent.*

The *"book" theorem* of Ramsey and of de Finetti is: *A set of partial beliefs is coherent if and only if it satisfies the calculus of inductive probability.*

For a proof, the reader is referred to the literature.* The theorem is usually restricted to truth-functionally complete sets of beliefs, but it holds for incomplete sets of partial beliefs as well. The latter, stronger, version is much more interesting philosophically, because in actual choice situations one's sets of partial beliefs are often incomplete.

The book theorem can be illustrated with a simple example. Since the probability of a disjunction cannot exceed the sum of the probabilities of its disjuncts, the set of partial beliefs $\{P(a) = .25,\ P(b) = .25,\ P(a \vee b) = .75\}$ violates the calculus of probability. Hence by the book theorem this

* Ramsey, "Truth and Probability," pp. 182–83; de Finetti, "Sul Significato Soggetivo della Probabilità"; de Finetti, "La Prevision: Ses Lois Logiques, Ses Sources Subjectives" (English translation, pp. 103–11).

See also Shimony, "Coherence and the Axioms of Confirmation"; Lehman, "On Confirmation and Rational Betting"; and Kemeny, "Fair Bets and Inductive Probabilities."

In these references the theorem is stated for truth-functionally complete sets of statements (if c and d belong to the set, every truth-function of c and d is expressed by some formula of the set), but as Lehman shows (pp. 261–62) the proofs also cover incomplete sets.

set of partial beliefs is incoherent and permits a book. The payoffs to the subject for the different cases are:

If ab, the payoff is $.75S(a) + .75S(b) + .25S(a \vee b)$

If $a\bar{b}$, the payoff is $.75S(a) - .25S(b) + .25S(a \vee b)$

If $\bar{a}b$, the payoff is $-.25S(a) + .75S(b) + .25S(a \vee b)$

If $\bar{a}\bar{b}$, the payoff is $-.25S(a) - .25S(b) - .75S(a \vee b)$.

To make all these negative the devil assigns $S(a) = S(b) = -1$ and $S(a \vee b) = 1$. This system of bets is a book, confirming that the given set of partial beliefs is incoherent.

We can also illustrate the book theorem by applying it to the roulette example mentioned earlier. Let C_i assert that the ball stops on number i, for $i = 00, 0, 1, 2, \ldots, 35, 36$. If the player is willing to bet on every number, his set of partial beliefs consists of $P(C_i) = 1/36$ for every i. Since the sum of the $P(C_i)$ is 38/36, this set of partial beliefs violates the calculus of inductive probability. Placing a dollar on a number is equivalent to accepting the stake $S(C_i) = \$36$, for $\overline{P(C_i)}S(C_i) = \$35$ and $-P(C_i)S(C_i) = -\$1$. If a bettor places a dollar on each of the 38 numbers he suffers a net loss of \$2, and so the system of bets is a book and his set of partial beliefs is incoherent.

The book theorem can be formulated in such a way that it equates two different kinds of consistency. Coherence is "gambling consistency." A set of partial beliefs that satisfies the calculus of inductive probability is "inductively consistent." Thus the book theorem equates gambling consistency to inductive consistency.

There is a weaker concept of a book, according to which the bettor cannot win but might lose. A set of beliefs is "strictly coherent" if no assignment of stakes permits a book in this weaker sense. There is a modified book theorem based on these concepts: A set of partial beliefs is strictly coherent if and only if it satisfies the calculus of inductive probability and also the principle "If $\mathbf{P}(c) = 1$, then $\Box c$." The original book theorem holds for infinite sets of statements, but this modified book theorem does not.

The book theorem shows a value to be gained in making one's partial beliefs satisfy the calculus of inductive probability. If one's set of partial beliefs always satisfies the calculus, he can never have a book made against him, even though he sometimes allows his opponent to set a stake for every partial belief. Conversely, if a set of partial beliefs does not satisfy the calculus, *and* the subject allows his opponent to set all the stakes, he may have a book made against him.

It has been said that the book theorem justifies the use of the calculus of probability in making choices; this justification is valid only to the extent that a person's use of utility theory is analogous to playing the "book-theorem game." In that game one first makes an assignment of partial beliefs and then allows his opponent to set the stakes, but one rarely follows such a procedure when actually using utility theory. The idea of deriving the calculus of probability from a game is nevertheless an important one; we shall develop it further in the next chapter (secs. 5.2–5.5). The book theorem is also of interest because it relates uncertainties (probabilities) to certainties (a book means a loss will certainly occur) and thereby reveals a parallelism between inductive consistency (coherence) and deductive consistency.

4.5 Summary

This and the following chapter are devoted to the study of probability and action. The idea of grounding the concept of probability on its uses in action is a special case of Peirce's pragmatism, and so we studied this doctrine first. The pragmatic theory of the nature of scientific knowledge is also of interest in its own right.

Peirce's pragmatism (*sec. 4.2*). A conditional whose antecedent describes an experiment or action and whose consequent describes an observable result is called a "practical conditional." Pragmatism treats beliefs as systems of practical conditionals. Accordingly, the meaning of a nonlogical statement consists in the set of those practical conditionals that are logically implied by the statement. This is Peirce's famous pragmatic principle of meaning. The criterion of sameness of meaning involved here is logical equivalence. Hence, according to pragmatism, if two statements or theories logically imply the same practical conditionals, ultimately and in principle, they should be treated as logically equivalent, even though they seem to be logically inequivalent when all their logical consequences are considered. Peirce's pragmatic principle gives an analysis of meaning that has both a descriptive and a normative component. Analysis is closely related to, but distinct from, language modeling.

Pragmatism makes two descriptive claims: the set of practical conditionals logically implied by a statement has approximately the same meaning as the statement, and the practical conditionals used in the analysis are clearer and more precise than the original statement. However, it is a mistake to limit the meaning of a statement that is not logically true-or-false to its deductive consequences; probabilistic consequences should also be included. Moreover, while statements are sometimes clarified by being related to their empirical tests, the pragmatic principle of meaning leads to two basic problems it does not solve. First, a rule is needed to identify the practical conditionals implied by a statement, and pragmatism does not explain the nature of this rule. Second, practical conditionals involve causal necessity, and pragmatism does not explain this notion, either.

Normatively, pragmatism holds that if two statements imply the same practical conditionals they should be treated as logically equivalent. This principle renders meaningless certain metaphysical disputes and constitutes an unwarranted extension of scientific norms to all inquiry.

The probabilistic version of the pragmatic principle of meaning takes into account the probabilistic relations between a theory and evidence, as well as the deductive relations. This principle shows that an answer to the question "What is the nature of scientific knowledge?" presupposes an answer to the question "What is the nature of inductive probability?" A person's belief in an atomic inductive probability statement will generally affect his choice of a course of action. This in turn suggests that atomic inductive probability statements are closely related to conditionals of the form "If one wanted ϕ and were in circumstances ψ, he would act in manner θ." We develop this suggestion in the next section and in the next chapter.

The traditional theory of utility (*sec. 4.3*). The pragmatic content of the concept of probability involves the notion of utility, which is explicated by the traditional theory of utility in the following way. A person is to make a choice in a situation involving uncertainty. He analyzes it into alternative acts, and he analyzes each of these into its possible consequences. He then evaluates the utility of each consequence, estimates the probability it will occur, and calculates the utility of each act. Finally, he chooses an act of maximum utility. Choice situations may be represented by choice trees containing choice, chance, and consequence points. A marked choice tree is an act tree.

Any two utility scales are linearly related, so that both the origin and the unit of a utility scale are arbitrary. Utiles are not monetary units but units of personal and social values. The distinctions between quantitative and qualitative probabilities and between utilities and qualitative valuation need to be explained. Pascal's wager is a question-begging argument involving an infinite utility. The Saint Petersburg paradox is a bona fide paradox if there is no greatest utility and if there are acts with infinitely many consequences. But we shall assume that every consequence has a finite utility, each act has a finite number of consequences, and each choice situation contains a finite number of acts.

Two paradoxes constitute challenges to the rule of maximizing utility. The sure-thing paradox attaches weight to the consideration "On this alternative I am sure to get at least this much, whereas on the other alternative I may get nothing." The variance paradox stems from the belief that the variance and standard deviation of an act ought sometimes to be relevant to its desirability. These paradoxes suggest that security and risk are properties of the whole act rather than of its parts taken distributively, and also that the quantity maximized by the best choice may not be utility.

Security and risk are predominant in insurance and gambling, and so it was instructive to study the shape of a utility function (a function from monetary wealth to utility) that justifies one of these activities. The crucial property is the shape of the utility curve in the region where the alternatives lie. In general, convexity (the principle of *decreasing* marginal utility of money) favors insurance, concavity (the principle of *increasing* marginal utility of money) favors gambling, and loading makes both insurance and gambling less attractive. The rule of maximizing utility sometimes justifies simultaneous gambling and insuring.

A relation that is both comparable and transitive is simply ordered. A person who applies the rule of maximizing utility simply orders his preferences and uncertainties. But when the available evidence is weak, it is reasonable not to compare uncertainties. And in some situations it is reasonable to leave the decision process incomplete, in which case the preferences involved may be incomparable or intransitive.

Thus the traditional theory of utility gives a good account of many aspects of utility and choice, but it is nevertheless open to several objections. These will be resolved in the next chapter (sec. 5.6.2).

The "book" theorem (sec. 4.4). A set of partial beliefs is incoherent (inductively inconsistent) if it allows an assignment of stakes that constitutes a book against the subject. The book theorem states that a set of partial beliefs is coherent if and only if it satisfies the calculus of inductive probability. This theorem brings out the systematic character of probability and utility and shows a value to be gained by using the calculus of inductive probability to guide one's behavior in conditions of uncertainty. The idea of deriving the calculus of probability from a game is important and will be developed further in the next chapter.

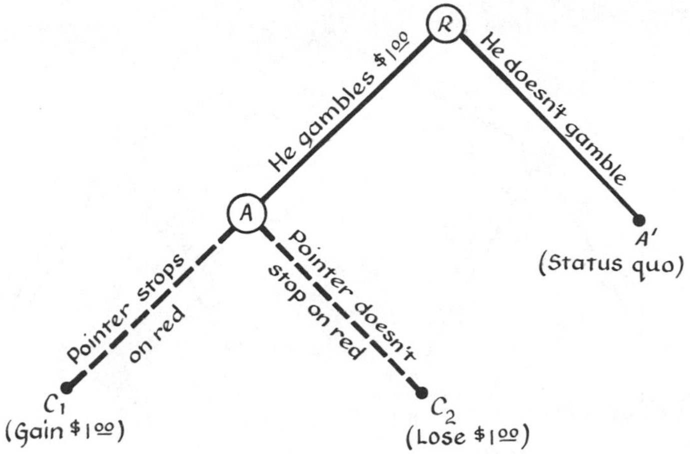

Fig. 1. Choice tree for gambling

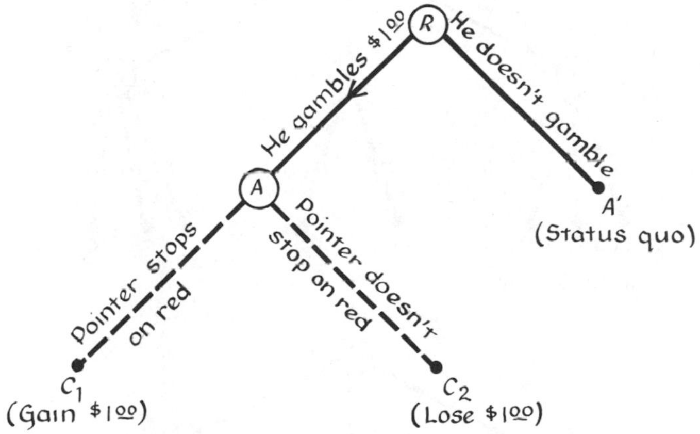

Fig. 2. Act tree for Fig. 1

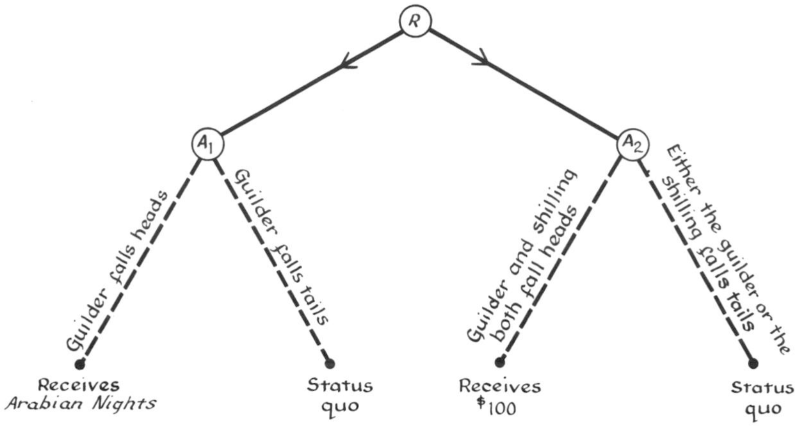

Fig. 3. Act tree for indifference

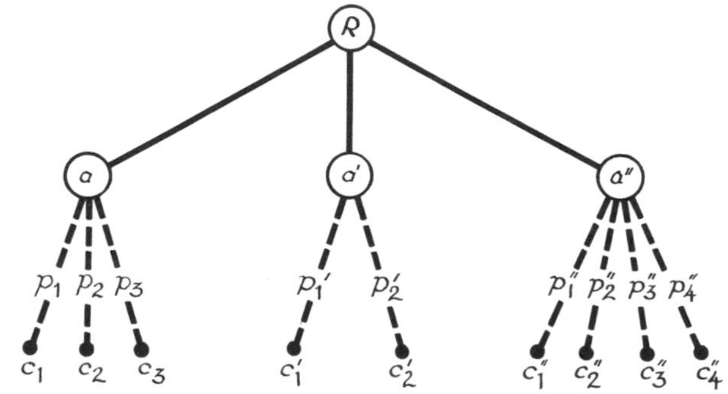

a. Choice tree

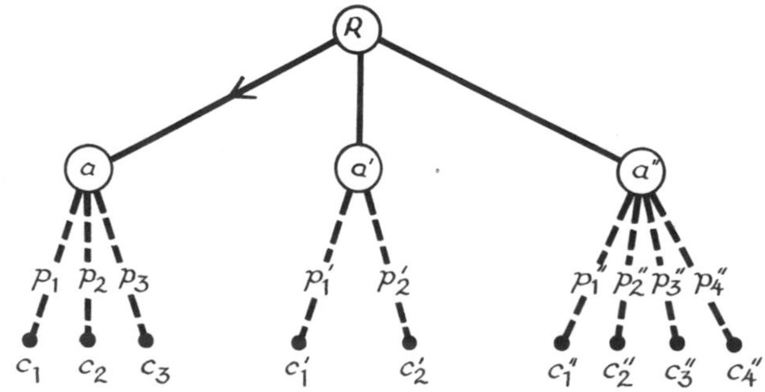

b. Corresponding act tree

Fig. 4. General form of choice and act trees

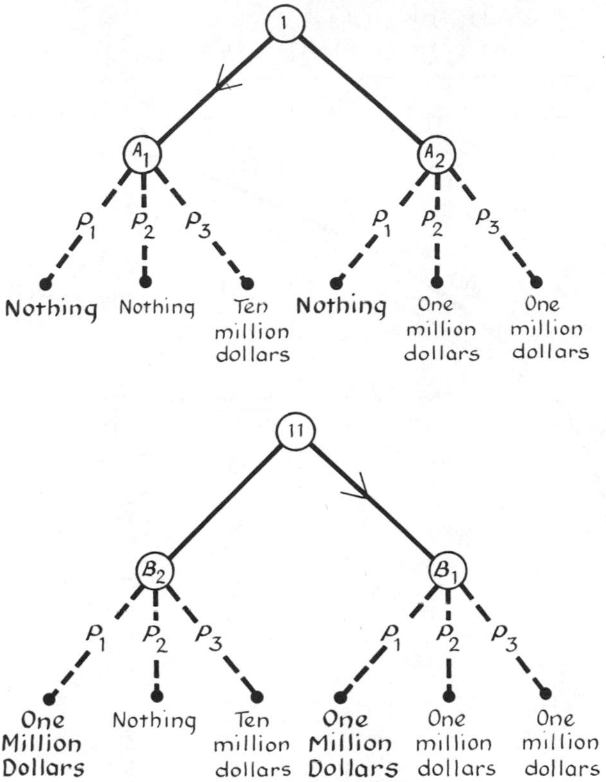

Fig. 5. The sure-thing paradox

By the rule of maximizing utility, these two act trees are incompatible.

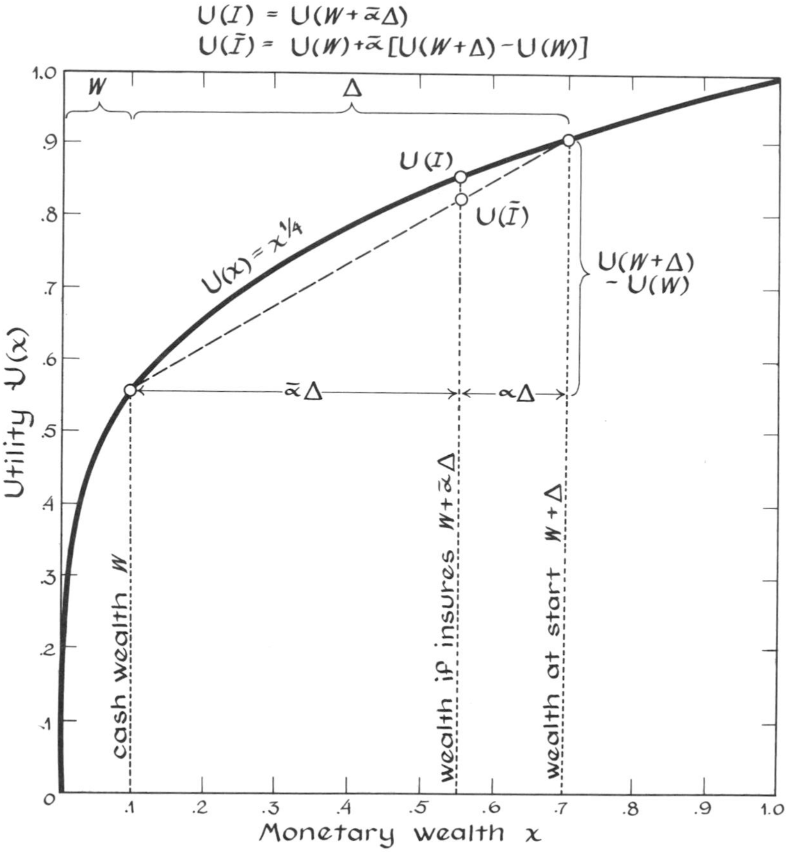

Fig. 6. Utility function that justifies insuring (I)

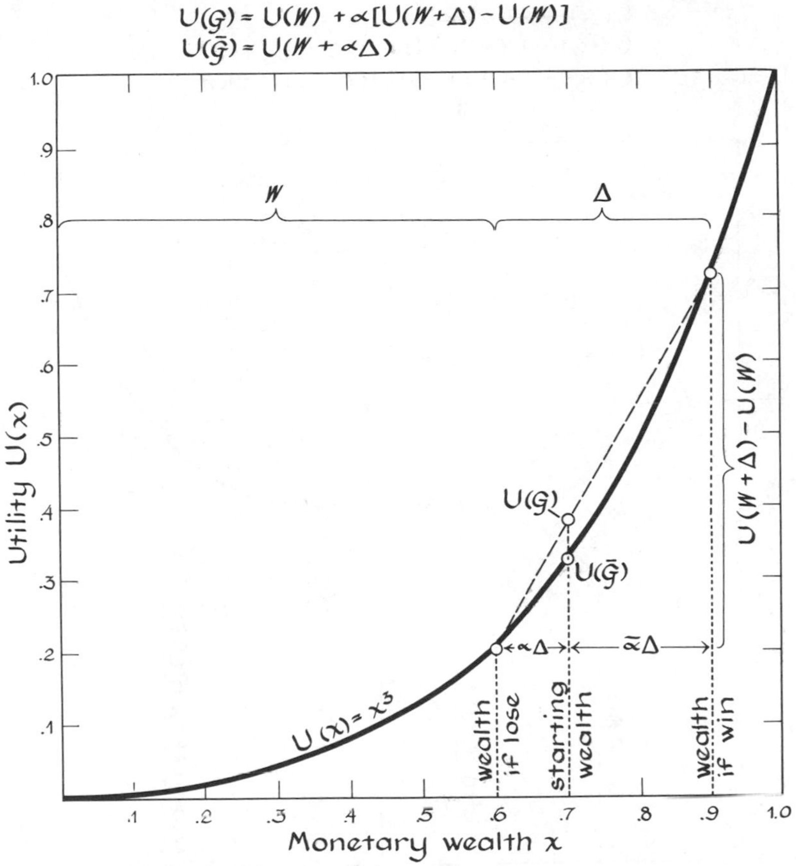

Fig. 7. Utility function that justifies gambling (G)

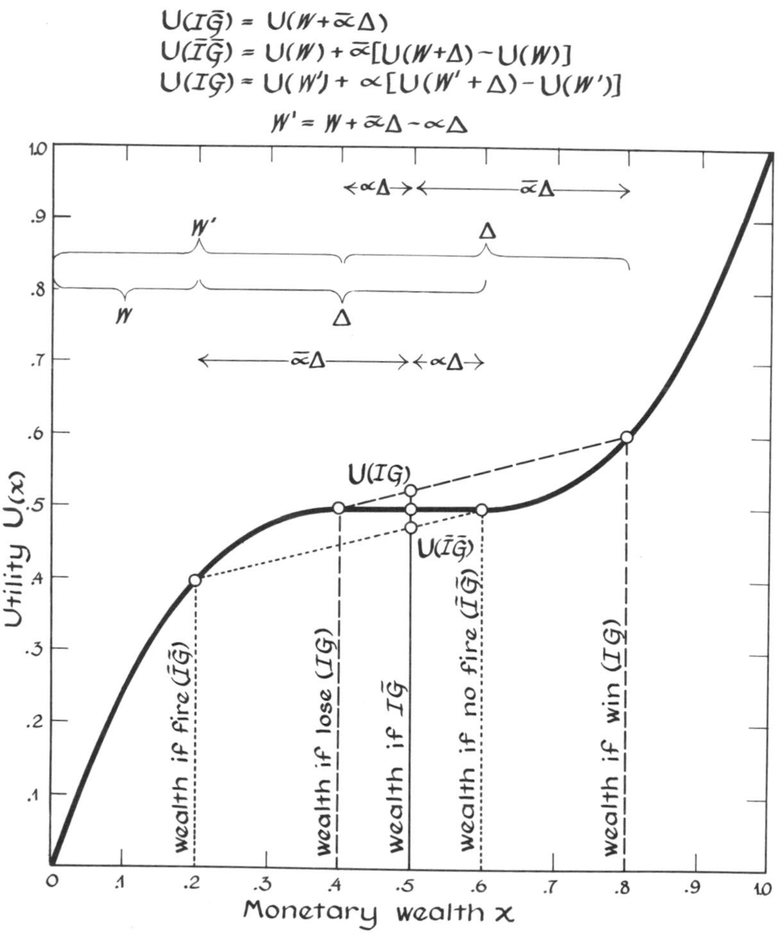

Fig. 8. Utility function that justifies simultaneous insuring (I) and gambling (G)

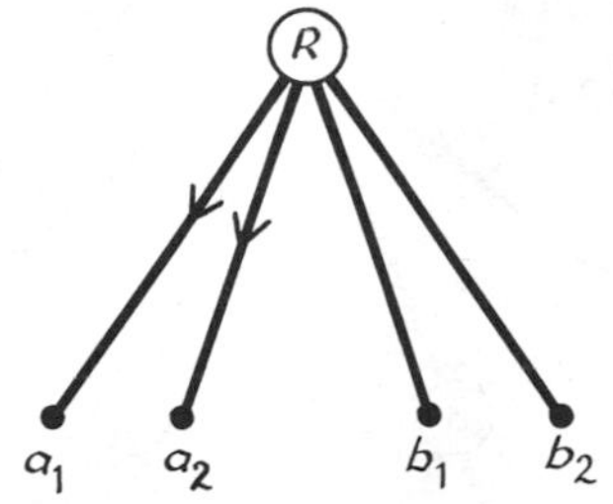

Fig. 9. Preference relations among acts

The subject is indifferent between a_1 and a_2 [$a_1 = a_2$]
He prefers a_1 to b_1 [$a_1 > b_1$]
He likes a_1 at least as much as a_2 [$a_1 \geqq a_2$] and at least as much as b_1 [$a_1 \geqq b_1$]

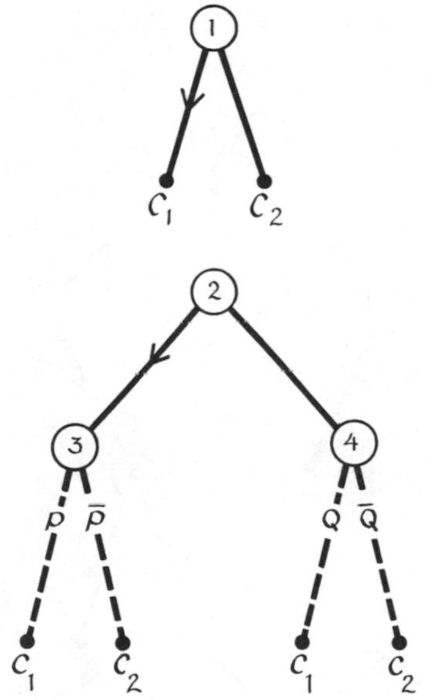

Fig. 10. Pragmatic manifestation of "P is more likely than Q" [$P > Q$]

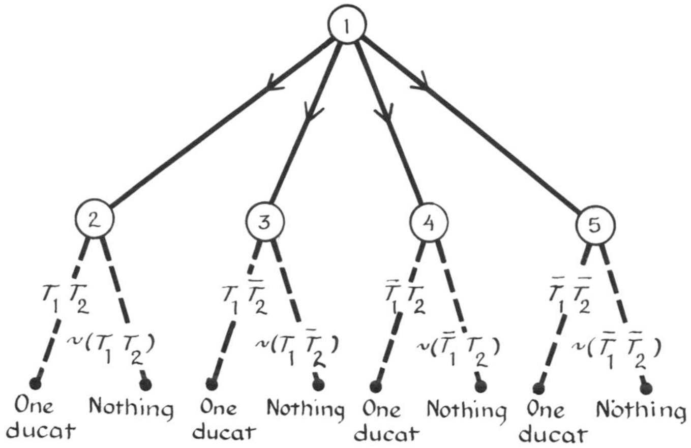

Fig. 11. Pragmatic manifestation of equal probabilities: $\mathbf{P}(T_1T_2) = \mathbf{P}(T_1\bar{T}_2) = \mathbf{P}(\bar{T}_1T_2) = \mathbf{P}(\bar{T}_1\bar{T}_2) = 1/4$

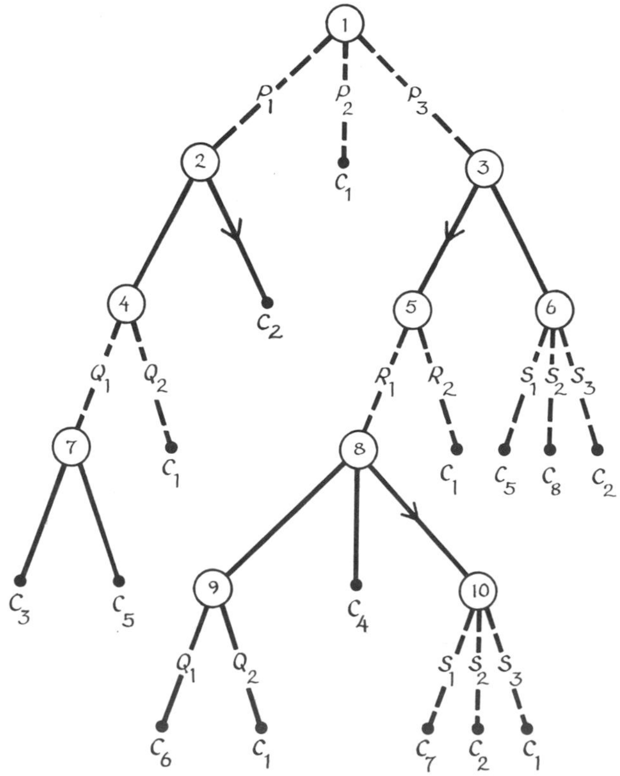

Fig. 12. An extended act tree

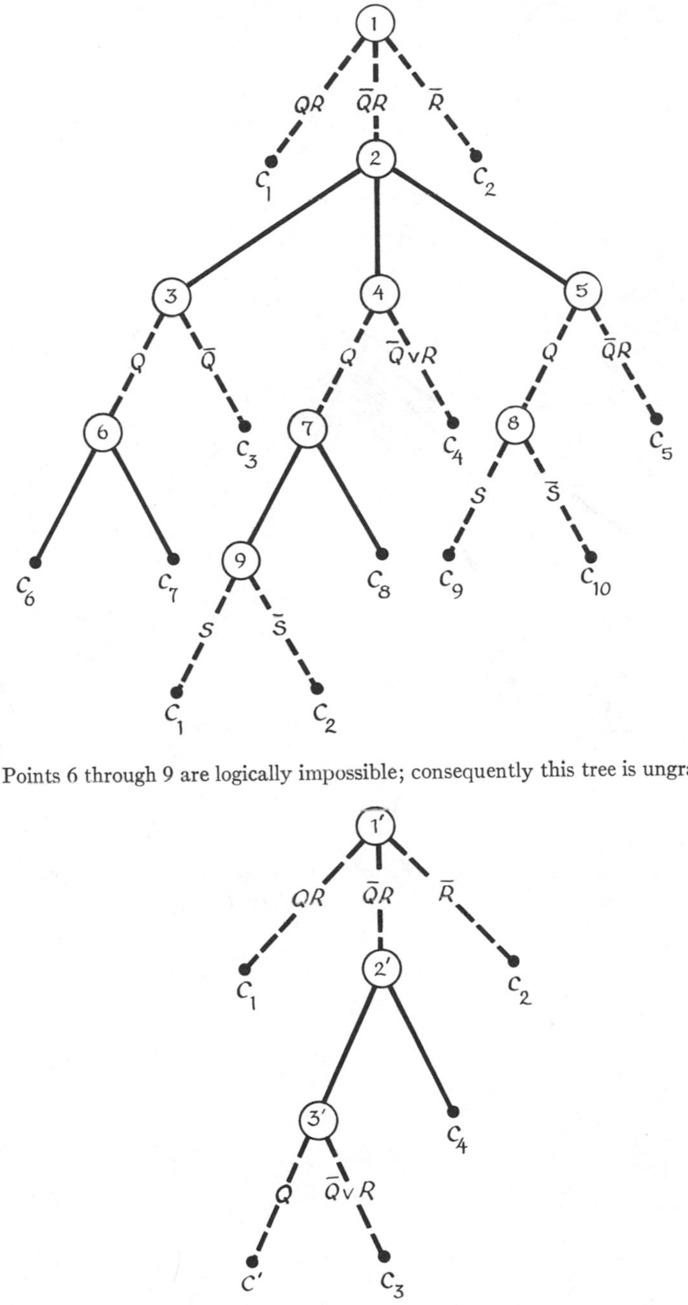

a. Points 6 through 9 are logically impossible; consequently this tree is ungrammatical.

b. This tree is grammatical. But because consequence point C' is logically impossible, C' contributes nothing to the value of act 3′.

Fig. 13. Ungrammatical and grammatical trees

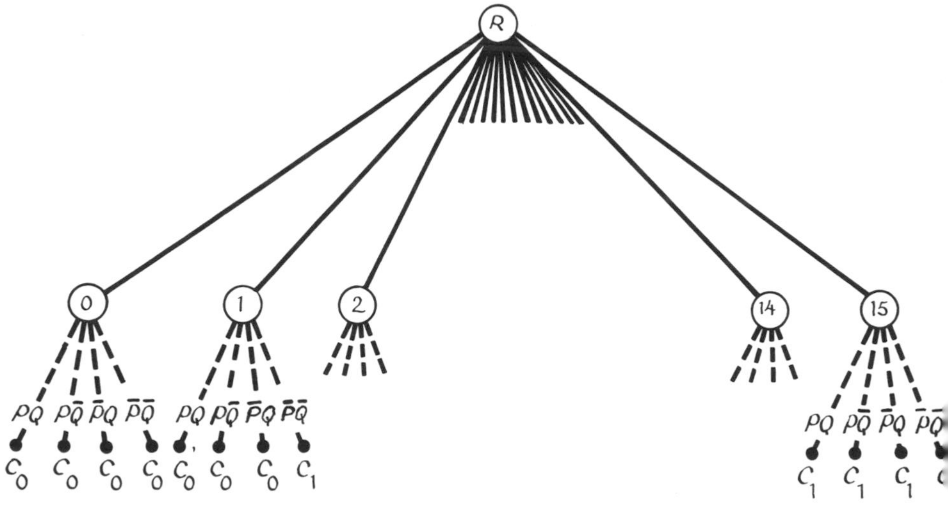

Fig. 14. Normal-form choice tree for all normal-form acts constructed from the choice basis $\langle\langle C_0, C_1\rangle, \langle\langle P, \bar{P}\rangle, \langle Q, \bar{Q}\rangle\rangle\rangle$

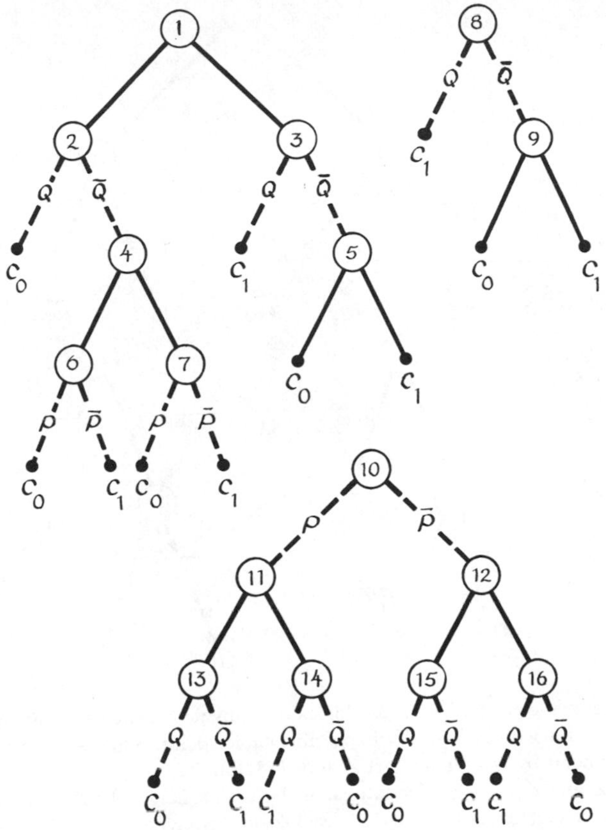

Fig. 15. Non normal-form choice trees based on $\langle\langle C_0, C_1\rangle, \langle\langle P, \bar{P}\rangle, \langle Q, \bar{Q}\rangle\rangle\rangle$

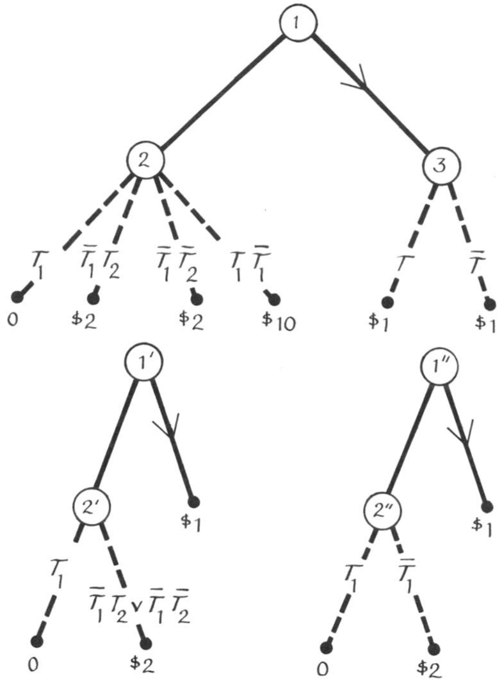

a. Subtree 2 is converted into the logically equivalent subtree 2′ by combining two partial acts and deleting a logically impossible choice point. Subtree 3 is converted into a consequence point by combining partial acts T($1) and $\bar{T}$($1).

Subtrees 2′ and 2″ are logically equivalent by the exchange of "$\bar{T}_1$" for "$\bar{T}_1 T_2 \vee \bar{T}_1 \bar{T}_2$".

Hence choice (act) trees 1, 1′, and 1″ are logically equivalent, and if any belong to the marked set, so do the others.

Fig. 16. Examples of the logical equivalence axiom

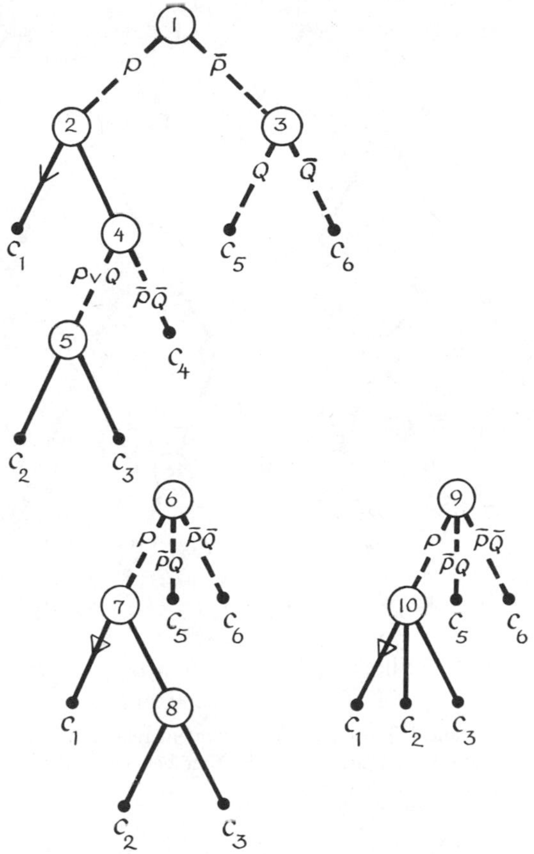

b. Choice (act) trees 1 and 6 are logically equivalent by virtue of these two operations: the logically impossible consequence point C_4 is deleted (and points 4 and 5 are combined into point 8); chance points 1 and 3 are merged.

Choice (act) trees 6 and 9 are logically equivalent by the operation of merging the successive choice points 7 and 8.

Hence if the subject marks tree 1 as shown, he must mark trees 6 and 9 as shown.

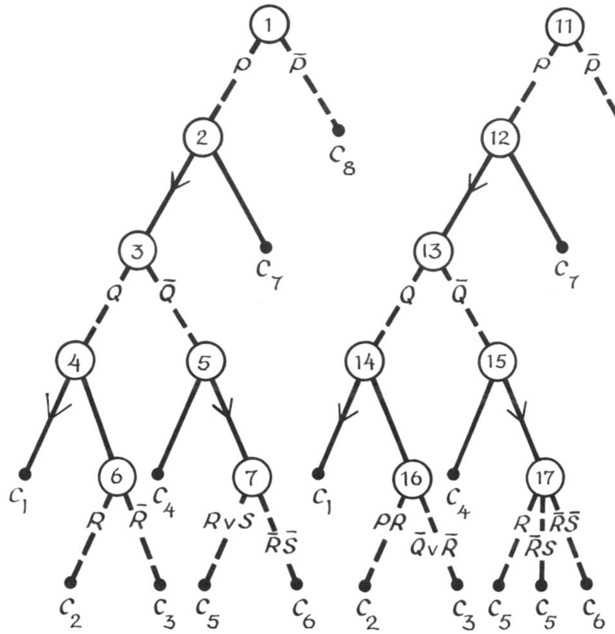

Fig. 17. Illustration of the first part of the logical equivalence axiom

Subtrees 6 and 16 {7 and 17} are logically equivalent relative to PQ $\{P\bar{Q}\}$. Hence act trees 1 and 11 are logically equivalent, and if either belongs to the marked set, so does the other.

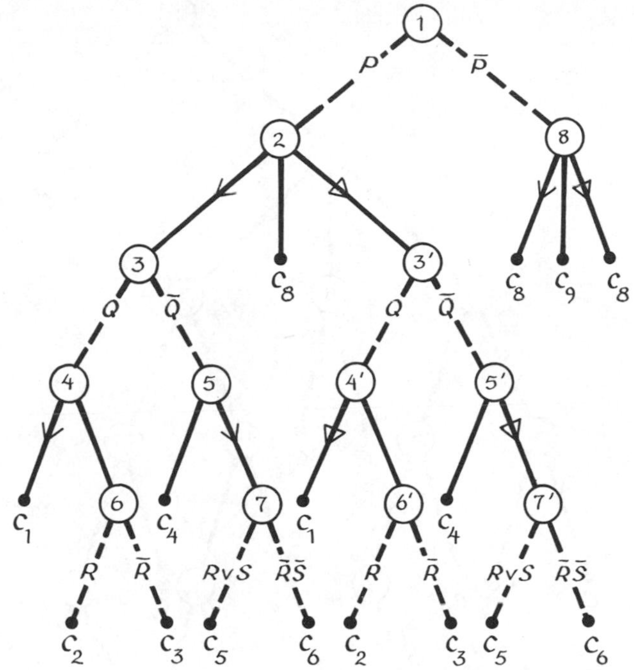

Fig. 18. Illustration of the second part of the logical equivalence axiom

Subtrees 3 and 3′ are of the same type; so if the subject chooses one, he must choose the other and mark both the same.

Likewise, if the subject chooses one token of C_8 at point 8, he must choose the other.

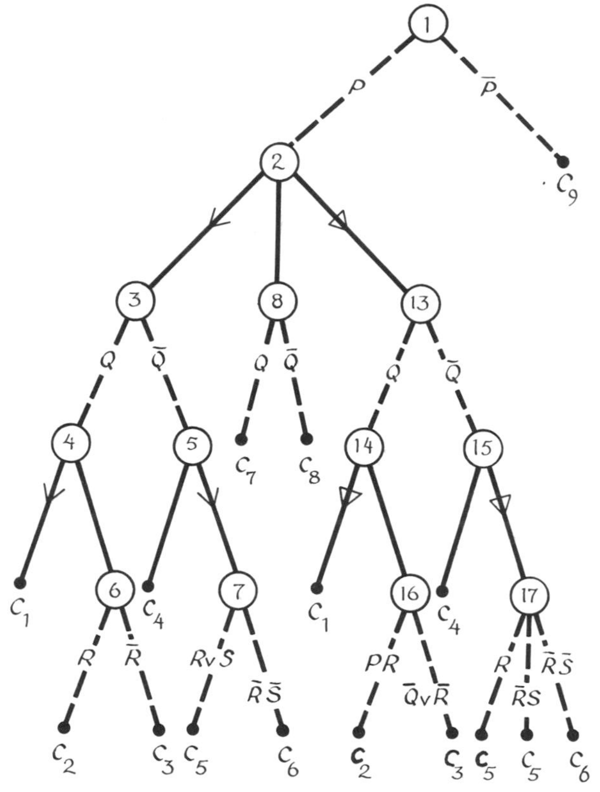

Fig. 19. Example involving both parts of the logical equivalence axiom

Subtrees 3 and 13 are logically equivalent on condition P. Hence if the subject places V-shaped arrowheads as indicated, he must also place triangular arrowheads as indicated.

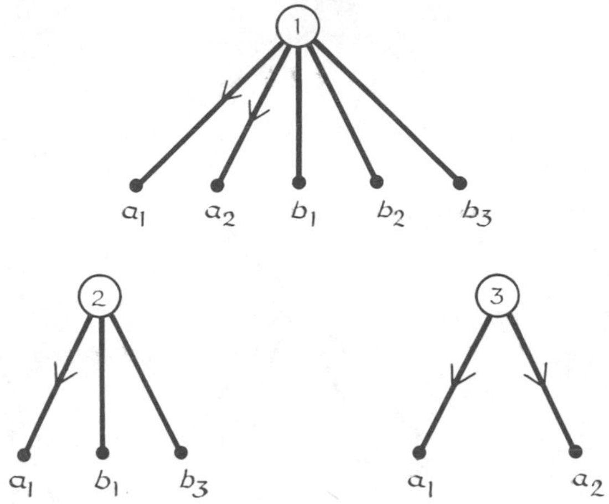

Fig. 20. Example of the subset axiom

If the upper act tree belongs to the marked set, so do the lower act trees.

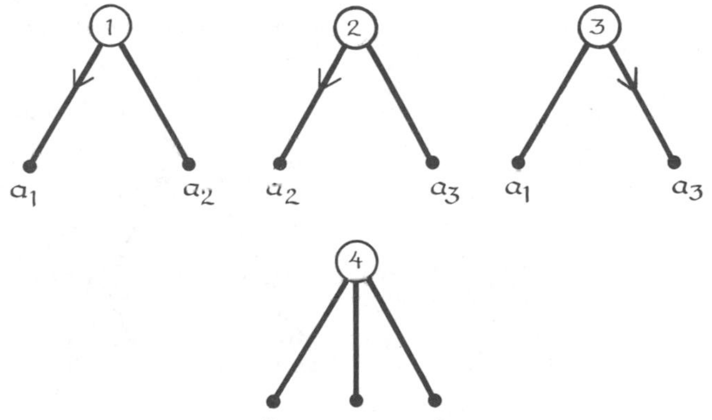

Fig. 21. Transitivity of preference

The intransitivity of the upper set of trees is compatible with the subset axiom by itself. But there is no way of marking the lower tree so that all four trees are compatible with the subset axiom. Hence the marking and subset axioms together entail that preferences are transitive.

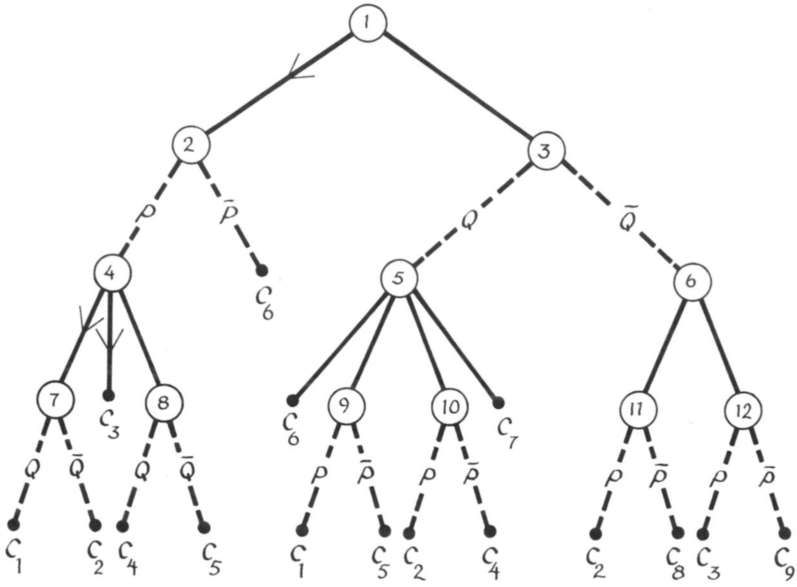

Fig. 22. Subset axiom applied to an extended tree

If this act tree is in the marked set, so are the act trees formed by deleting one of the lines from choice point 4 and/or either one or two of the lines from choice point 5.

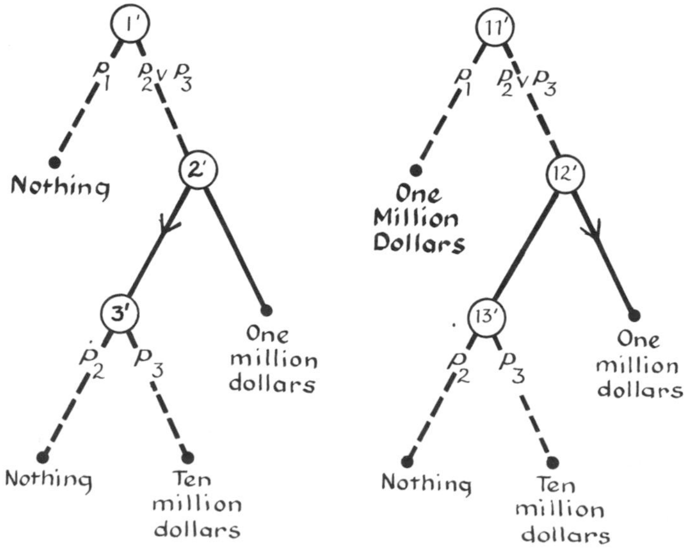

Fig. 23. Violation of the invariance axiom

Choice trees 2′ and 12′ are of the same type and have the same information ($P_2 \vee P_3$) at their roots. Since they are marked differently, they violate the invariance axiom.

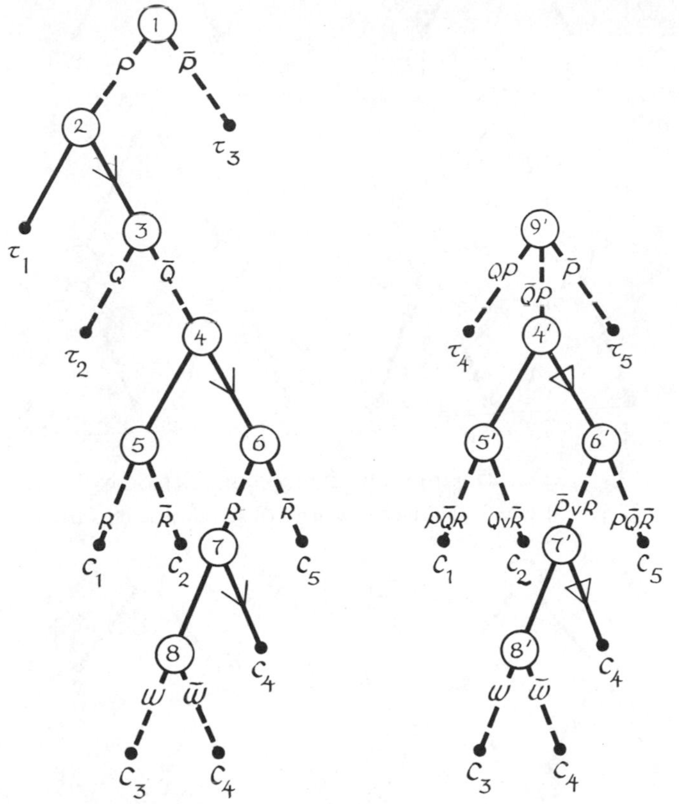

Fig. 24. Joint example of logical equivalence and invariance axioms

The choice trees underlying subtrees 4 and 4′ are logically equivalent on condition $P\bar{Q}$. If the subject marks tree 1 as indicated, then he must mark tree 9′ as indicated.

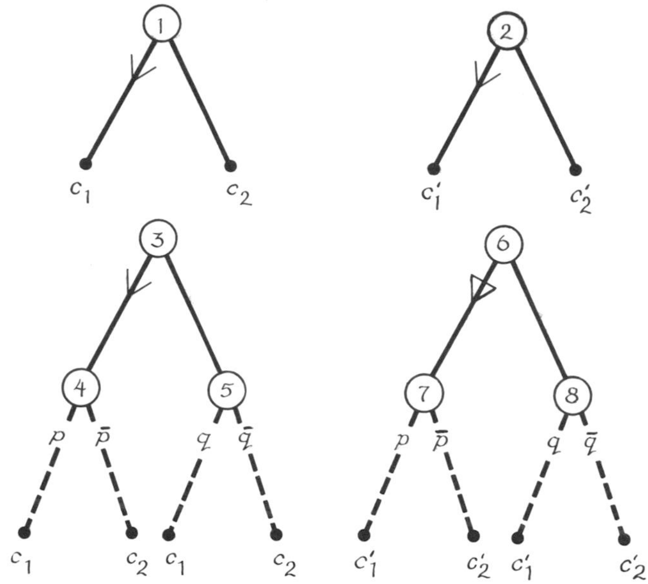

Fig. 25. Ordering of uncertainties axiom

If trees 1, 2, and 3 belong to the marked set, then so does tree 6.

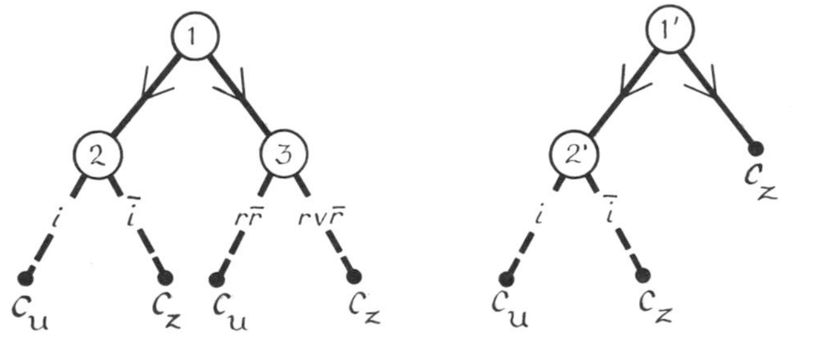

a. By tree 1, $i = r\bar{r}$ and so i is probabilistically impossible. Note that tree 1′ is logically equivalent to tree 1.

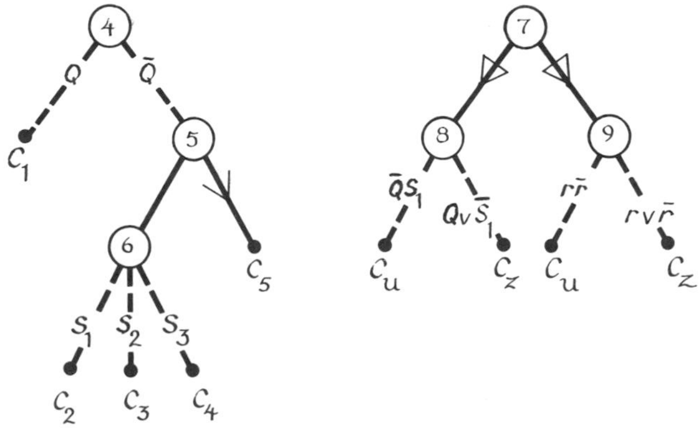

b. By definition, consequence point C_2 is probabilistically impossible if and only if the subject marks tree 7 as indicated ($\bar{Q}S_1 = r\bar{r}$).

Fig. 26. Probabilistic impossibilities

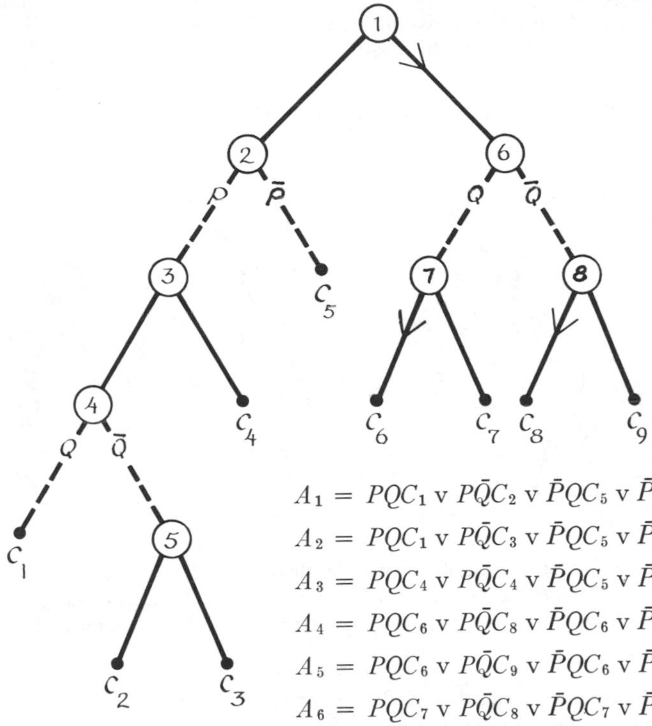

$$A_1 = PQC_1 \text{ v } P\bar{Q}C_2 \text{ v } \bar{P}QC_5 \text{ v } \bar{P}\bar{Q}C_5$$
$$A_2 = PQC_1 \text{ v } P\bar{Q}C_3 \text{ v } \bar{P}QC_5 \text{ v } \bar{P}\bar{Q}C_5$$
$$A_3 = PQC_4 \text{ v } P\bar{Q}C_4 \text{ v } \bar{P}QC_5 \text{ v } \bar{P}\bar{Q}C_5$$
$$A_4 = PQC_6 \text{ v } P\bar{Q}C_8 \text{ v } \bar{P}QC_6 \text{ v } \bar{P}\bar{Q}C_8 \quad \text{[chosen]}$$
$$A_5 = PQC_6 \text{ v } P\bar{Q}C_9 \text{ v } \bar{P}QC_6 \text{ v } \bar{P}\bar{Q}C_9$$
$$A_6 = PQC_7 \text{ v } P\bar{Q}C_8 \text{ v } \bar{P}QC_7 \text{ v } \bar{P}\bar{Q}C_8$$
$$A_7 = PQC_7 \text{ v } P\bar{Q}C_9 \text{ v } \bar{P}QC_7 \text{ v } \bar{P}\bar{Q}C_9$$

a. The acts implicit in an extended tree

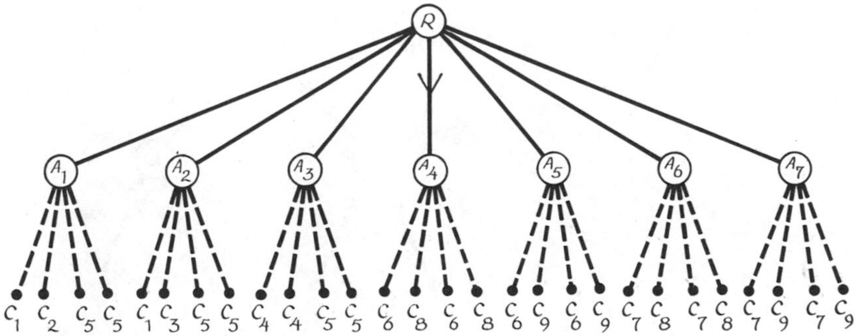

b. The normal form of tree 1. The labels on the dashed lines from each chance point are, from left to right, PQ, $P\bar{Q}$, $\bar{P}Q$, $\bar{P}\bar{Q}$.

Fig. 27. Normal form of an extended tree

The following are given:
C_1 is prized over C_2 and C_2 is prized over C_3.
All points of the trees are logically possible.

a. If P and $\bar{P}$ are both probabilistically possible,

then the normal form of

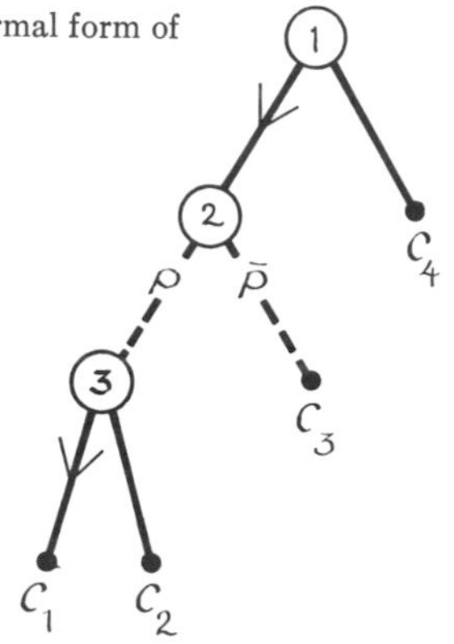

is

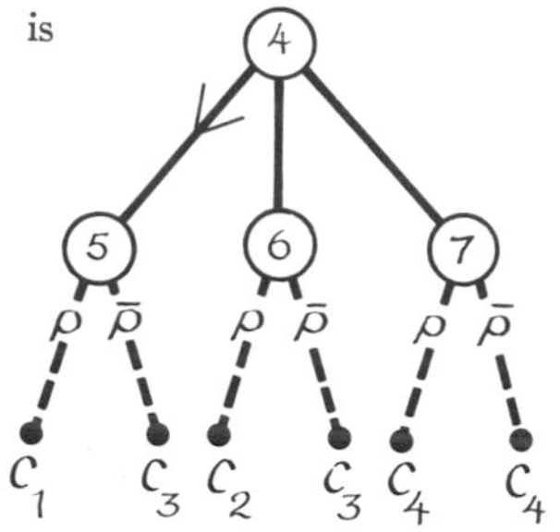

However, if P is probabilistically impossible, then $PC_1 \text{ v } \bar{P}C_3 = C_3$, $PC_2 \text{ v } \bar{P}C_3 = C_3$, and hence $PC_1 \text{ v } \bar{P}C_3 = PC_2 \text{ v } \bar{P}C_3$, which contradicts tree 4. This shows that probabilistically impossible choice points require special handling when the normal form of a tree is constructed.

b. By the trimming algorithm, if P is probabilistically impossible, point 3 is replaced by C_z. Thus the trimmed form of tree 1 is

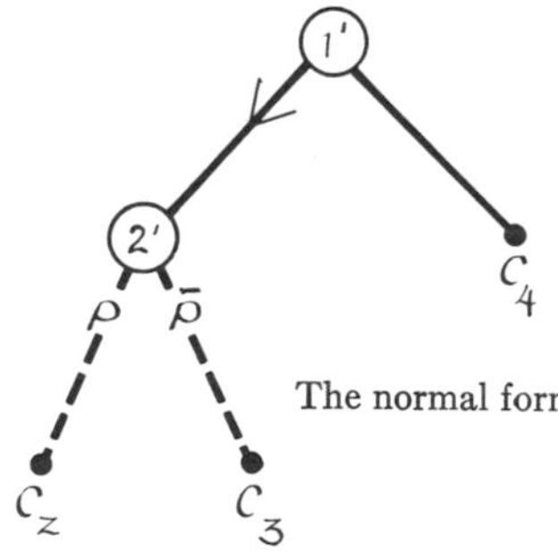

The normal form of tree 1 is then

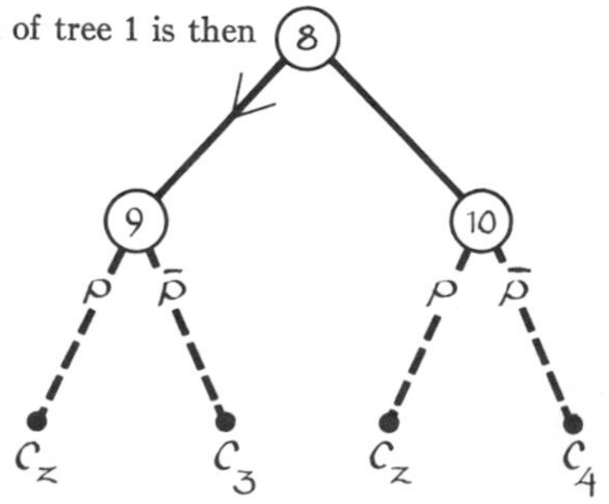

There is no contradiction in tree 8. Moreover, when P is probabilistically impossible, trees 1′ and 8 preserve the essence of the preferences expressed by tree 1. This resolves the contradiction of Fig. 28a.

Fig. 28. Probabilistic impossibilities and normal form

It is given that all logically possible universes are also probabilistically possible except for PQ_2, and hence all points in tree 1 are probabilistically possible except C_3, C_6, and C_7.

a. To trim tree 1, remove logically impossible consequence point C_3 and trim the paths which contain probabilistically impossible points at the highest such point (point 5), labeling that point "C_z." Thus tree

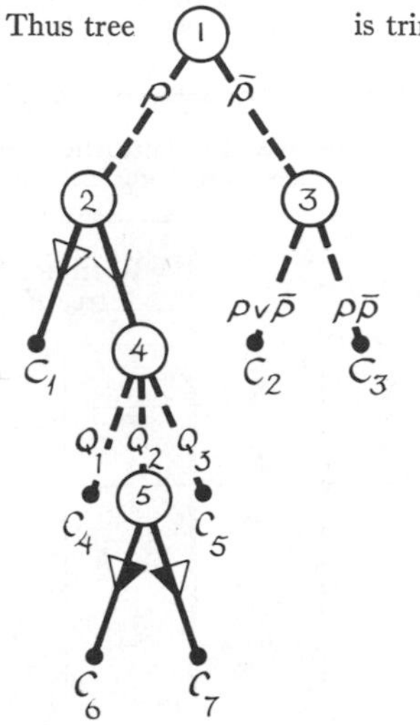

is trimmed to

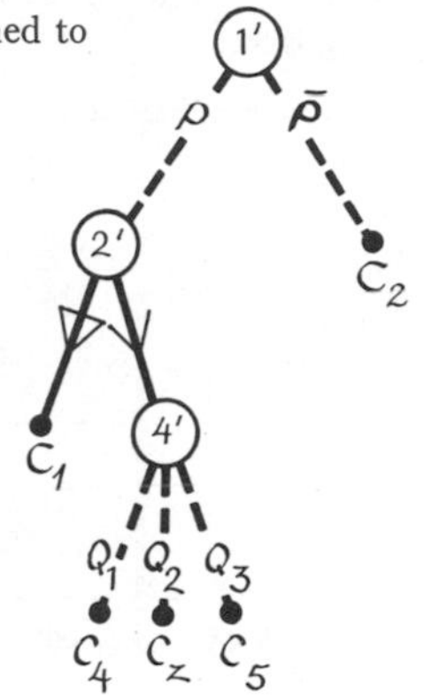

b. To construct the normal form of tree 1, first trim it. Then find the (two) acts of trimmed tree 1′, replace each probabilistically impossible consequence by C_z, and represent these modified acts in a normal form tree. Finally, choose those acts that were chosen in the trimmed tree. The normal form of tree 1 is thus

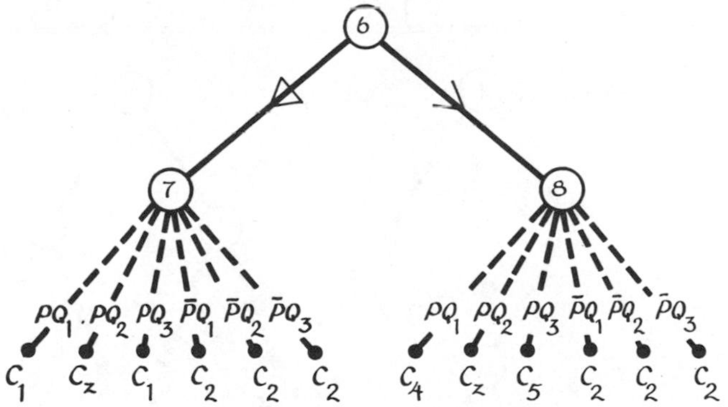

Fig. 29. Illustration of the trimming and normal form algorithms

Fig. 29. (*Continued*)

c. For each act a in extended tree 1, there is an act a_t in trimmed tree 1′ (and an act a_n in normal form tree 6) that agrees with a on all probabilistically possible universes. In the table below, the acts are named by means of the arrowheads used to select them in the preceding trees.

Logically possible universes	Acts (assignments of consequences to logically possible universes), represented by arrowheads						
	In extended tree 1			In trimmed tree 1′		In normal form tree 6	
	▽	V ▼	V ▼	▽	V	▽	V
PQ_1	C_1	C_4	C_4	C_1	C_4	C_1	C_4
Probabilistically impossible PQ_2	C_1	C_6	C_7	C_1	C_z	C_z	C_z
PQ_3	C_1	C_5	C_5	C_1	C_5	C_1	C_5
$\bar{P}Q_1$	C_2	C_2	C_2	C_2	C_2	C_2	C_2
$\bar{P}Q_2$	C_2	C_2	C_2	C_2	C_2	C_2	C_2
$\bar{P}Q_3$	C_2	C_2	C_2	C_2	C_2	C_2	C_2

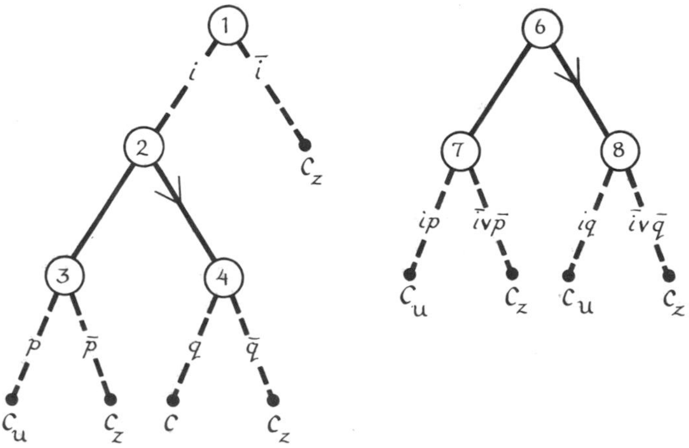

Fig. 30. Proof of a reduction theorem

If i is probabilistically possible, then by the normal form and logical equivalence axioms, tree 1 belongs to the marked set if and only if tree 6 does. Hence $(i \neq r\bar{r}) \supset [(q >_i p) \equiv (qi > pi)]$.

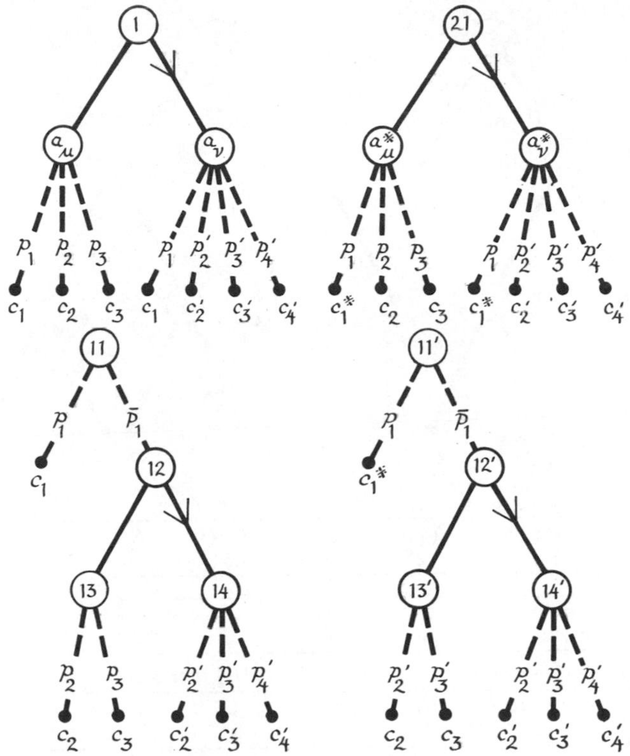

Fig. 31. Proof of the partial act theorem

Act tree 1 belongs to the marked set if and only if act tree 21 does.

It is given that p is probabilistically possible ($p \neq r\bar{r}$).

If $\bar{p} \neq r\bar{r}$, then tree 1 has the normal form 3

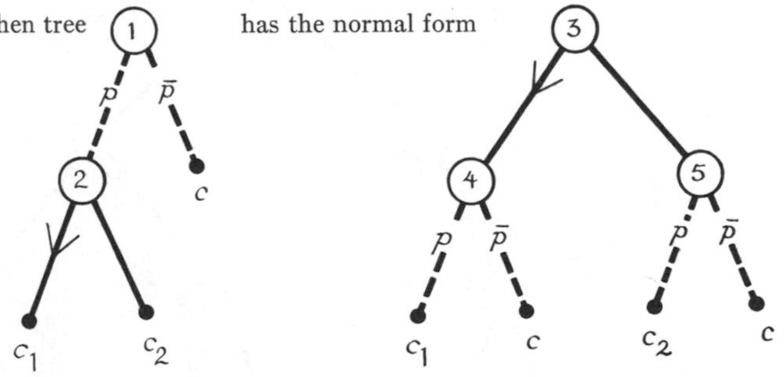

If $\bar{p} = r\bar{r}$, tree 3 is equivalent to the normal form of tree 1 by corollary [8]. This proves $(p \neq r\bar{r}) \supset \{(c_1 >_p c_2) \equiv [(pc_1 \vee \bar{p}c) > (pc_2 \vee \bar{p}c)]\}$. The result $(p \neq r\bar{r}) \supset \{(c_1 > c_2) \equiv [(pc_1 \vee \bar{p}c) > (pc_2 \vee \bar{p}c)]\}$ then follows by the invariance axiom [IVB].

Fig. 32. Proof of a lemma on comparative values

a. A trimmed tree is given:

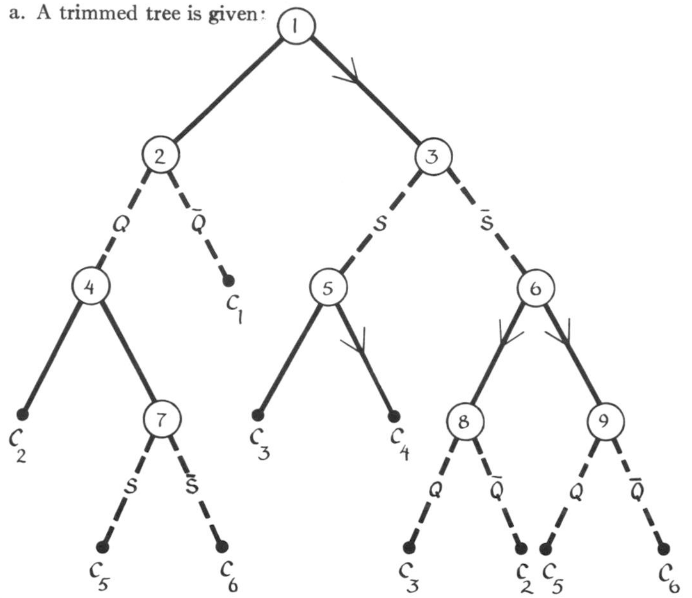

b. The following degree-of-belief function $P^*(q, i)$ is given:

Statement pair	$\langle Q, \bar{S}\rangle$	$\langle \bar{Q}, \bar{S}\rangle$	$\langle S, Q\rangle$	$\langle \bar{S}, Q\rangle$
$P^*(q, i)$	.25	.75	.625	.375

and

Statement	Q	$\bar{Q}$	S	$\bar{S}$
$P^*(q, r \vee \bar{r})$	.6	.4	.5	.5

The following consequence valuation function $U^*(c)$ is also given:

Consequences	C_1	C_2	C_3	C_4	C_5	C_6
$U^*(c)$	0	4	2	5	8	2

c. The result of applying the functions $P^*(q, i)$ and $U^*(c)$ to tree 1 is shown as tree 1′ below. The number in the box attached to a chance point is $\Sigma_{n=1}^{N} P^*(q_n, i)U^*(a_n, iq_n)$. The number in the box attached to a choice point is the maximum of the values of the alternatives. Since the alternatives of maximum value are selected by arrows at each marked choice point (1′, 5′, and 6′) of act tree 1, every choice of this tree maximizes the utility function $\Sigma_{n=1}^{N} P^*(q_n, i)U^*(a_n, iq_n)$.

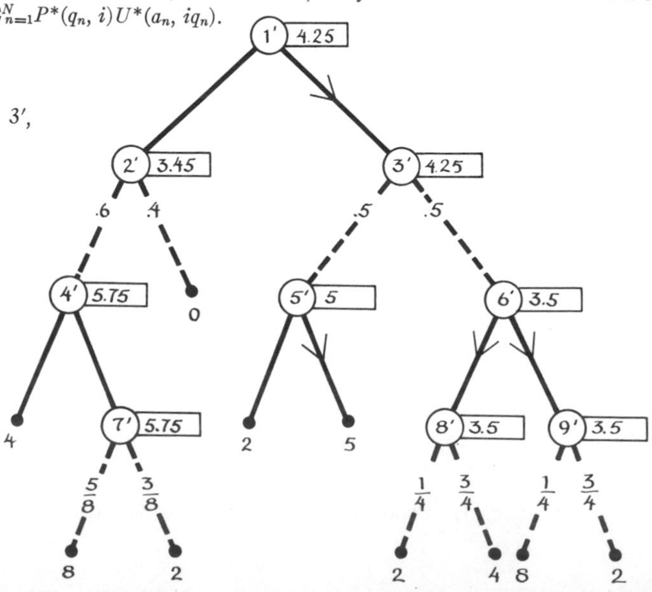

Fig. 33. An act tree in which every choice maximizes a utility function

a. It is given that pq, $p\bar{q}$, $\bar{p}q$, $\bar{p}\,\bar{q}$ is an equipartition and that $c = pC_u \text{ v } \bar{p}C_z$. Consider the choice tree underlying the following act tree:

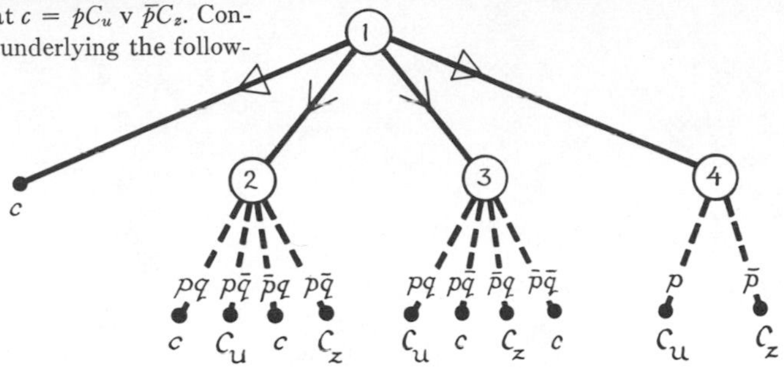

The subset axiom and $c = pC_u \text{ v } \bar{p}C_z$ imply that c is chosen if and only if act 4 is chosen. The subset axiom and theorem [17] imply that act 2 is chosen if and only if act 3 is chosen. Hence there are only three allowable markings of tree 1: the triangular arrowheads, the V-shaped arrowheads, or both.

b. Now, the choice tree underlying tree 1 is the normal form of the choice tree underlying the following tree:

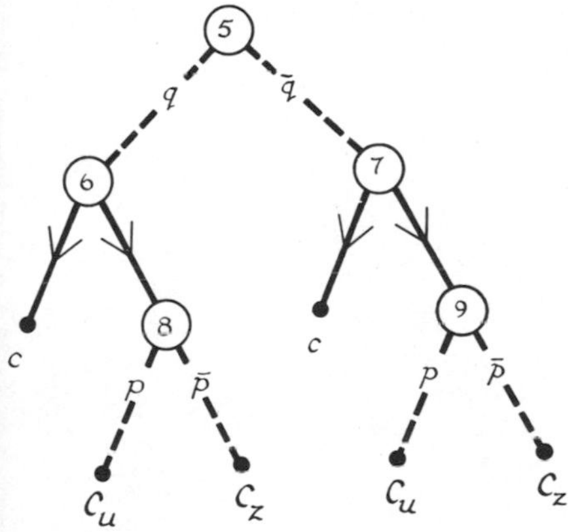

Consider the four markings of this tree, not including cases of indifference.

Choice at point 6	Choice at point 7	Corresponding act of tree 1
c	c	c
c	$pC_u \text{ v } \bar{p}C_z$	2
$pC_u \text{ v } \bar{p}C_z$	c	3
$pC_u \text{ v } \bar{p}C_z$	$pC_u \text{ v } \bar{p}C_z$	4

By the normal form axiom, none of these four markings taken alone is compatible with the allowable markings of tree 1. A review of the remaining ways of marking tree 5, involving indifferences, shows that tree 5 is now marked in the only way compatible with the allowable markings of tree 1. Hence all acts of tree 1 must be chosen.

c. By the invariance axiom, this tree must then be marked as shown:

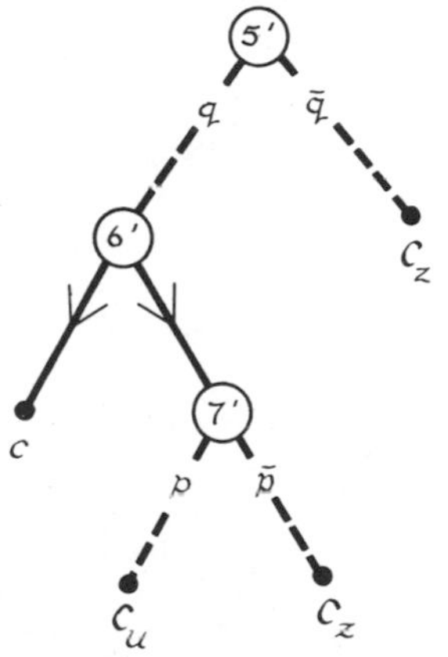

d. The normal form of tree 5′ is

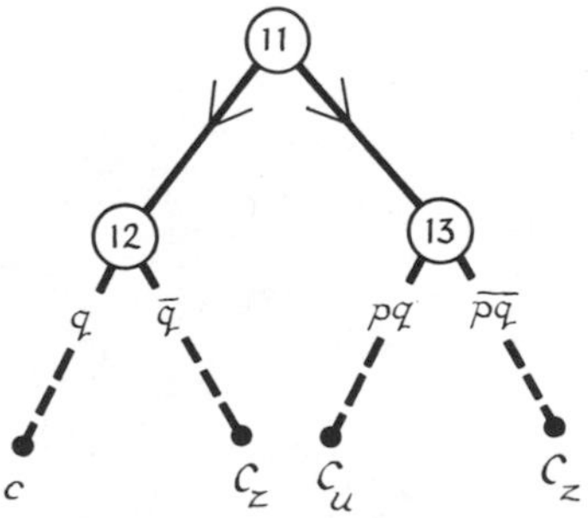

Hence $(qc \text{ v } \bar{q}C_z) = (pqC_u \text{ v } \overline{pq}C_z)$, which is what was to be proved.

Fig. 34. Proof of theorem [18]

5 The Pragmatic Theory of Inductive Probability

> These are the laws of probability, which we have proved to be necessarily true of any consistent set of degrees of belief. Any definite set of degrees of belief which broke them would be inconsistent in the sense that it violated the laws of preference between options, such as that preferability is a transitive asymmetrical relation. . . . If anyone's mental condition violated these laws, his choice would depend on the precise form in which the options were offered him, which would be absurd. He could have a book made against him by a cunning better and would then stand to lose in any event.*

5.1 Introduction

5.1.1 Preview

In this chapter we shall conclude our analysis of the relation of probability to action, begun in the last chapter.

We saw there that probability theory may be used explicitly to guide action in choice situations involving uncertainty. Suppose a subject is presented with a set of acts, each consisting of an assignment of consequences to the possible outcomes of some chance situation, and is allowed to choose one of them. According to the traditional theory of utility, he should proceed as follows: assign a utility to each consequence, estimate the likelihood that each consequence will obtain, calculate the utility of each act, and choose an act of maximum utility.

The traditional theory gives a good account of many phenomena such as gambling and insuring. But it does not explain the quantitative-qualitative distinction for probabilities and valuations, and it is subject to the sure-thing and variance paradoxes. Moreover, it implies that preferences and uncertainties should always be simply ordered, and this does not seem to be the case. My "pragmatic theory of inductive probability," presented in this chapter, is designed to solve these problems.

The traditional theory of utility is based on a mathematical structure consisting of the calculus of probability and a formula for calculating the

* Ramsey, *The Foundations of Mathematics*, p. 182. Note that Ramsey's "consistent" is synonymous with our word "coherent" (sec. 4.4).

utility of a mixed act. The pragmatic theory of inductive probability is also based on a mathematical structure, which we call "the calculus of choice." We present this calculus as a quasiformal system in the next four sections. It consists of a grammar, eight axioms, and some theorems. For convenience of reference, all the axioms and theorems are listed in the summary (pp. 329–33).

The "grammar" contains definitions of the entities to be interpreted, the most important of which are the following: choice trees, act trees (marked choice trees), a basis of statements and consequences, a set of choice trees complete with respect to this basis, and a marked set of trees (which results from marking one or more of a complete set of choice trees).

The trees of the last chapter were all "normal form trees," having a single choice point leading to alternate chance points. The calculus of choice also covers extended trees, which have many levels of choice and chance points. In marking an extended tree, a subject expresses his conditional probability judgments, for a choice point may be reached only if certain statements are true. (Sec. 5.2)

The axioms of the calculus of choice restrict how a subject marks a complete set of choice trees. The first six axioms are [I] marking, [II] logical equivalence, [III] subset, [IV] invariance, [V] existence, and [VI] ordering of uncertainties. These axioms yield the simple ordering of preferences and uncertainties, both conditional and unconditional. (Sec. 5.3)

The normal form axiom [VII] reduces choices made in an extended tree to choices made in its normal form equivalent. This axiom completes the comparative structure of preferences and uncertainties (sec. 5.4). Finally, the quantitative axiom [VIII] converts this comparative structure into a quantitative structure.

The main theorem of the calculus of choice shows that choices made in accordance with axioms [I]–[VIII] do in fact maximize utility and satisfy the calculus of probability. But the axioms are rules for marking choice trees and do not make any explicit reference to the concepts of probability and utility. Hence, a subject whose choices satisfy the calculus of choice acts as if he were using the calculus of probability and the rule of maximizing utility even if he is not explicitly doing so. (Sec. 5.5)

The pragmatic theory of probability resolves the difficulties of the traditional theory of utility by placing limits on the normative application of the calculus of choice. While the axioms are stated in factual terms for reasons of convenience, their normative interpretation is more important. An analysis of the individual axioms shows that one should generally choose in accordance with them, though there are important exceptions. In some circumstances it is reasonable to violate the marking axiom [I] or invariance axiom [IV], and the quantitative axiom [VIII] is only a convenient idealization. (Sec. 5.6.2)

The pragmatic theory answers our first main question and helps to answer the second. According to this theory, a system of inductive probability statements has both an a priori aspect and a pragmatic aspect. The former concerns the assignment of probability values to statements by the rules of the calculus of probability and standard inductive logic, while the latter concerns the action implications of these probability assignments. On account of its a priori aspect, an atomic inductive probability statement has a logically true-or-false component. But because of its pragmatic aspect, a true atomic inductive probability statement is not logically true. (Sec. 5.6)

Finally, we compare the pragmatic theory with two closely related theories of inductive probability: the a priori theory and the personalistic theory. (Sec. 5.7)

5.1.2 Historical remarks

The pragmatic theory of inductive probability and the underlying calculus of choice have many facets. We shall trace their historical development in the present subsection. The reader who is not interested in this account can proceed directly to the calculus of choice (p. 254).

As we saw in the last chapter, the use of probability theory to guide action is as old as the theory itself. Likewise, it has long been recognized that there are subjective probabilities or degrees of partial belief. But it is one thing to use probability as a guide to life and quite another to ground or define probability and utility in terms of their applications to action. The pragmatic theory of inductive probability does just that; it explains probability in terms of rules for acting in uncertain situations.

In his "Truth and Probability," written in 1926 and published posthumously in 1931, F. P. Ramsey showed how to specify the meanings of "probability" and "utility" in terms of rules for acting in the face of uncertainty.* He summarizes his own position nicely in the epigraph of this chapter and continues as follows:

> We find, therefore, that a precise account of the nature of partial belief reveals that the laws of probability are laws of consistency, an extension to partial beliefs of formal logic, the logic of consistency. They do not depend for their meaning on any degree of belief in a proposition being uniquely determined as the rational one; they merely distinguish those sets of beliefs which obey them as consistent ones.
>
> Having any definite degree of belief implies a certain measure of consistency, namely willingness to bet on a given proposition at the same odds for any stake, the stakes being measured in terms of ultimate values. Having degrees of belief obeying the laws of probability implies a further measure of consistency, namely such a consistency between the

* Ramsey, *The Foundations of Mathematics*, pp. 156–98; see also pp. 199–211, 256–57. The ensuing quotation comes from pp. 182–83.

odds acceptable on different propositions as shall prevent a book being made against you.

[This analysis] is based fundamentally on betting, but this will not seem unreasonable when it is seen that all our lives we are in a sense betting.

Independently of Ramsey, Bruno de Finetti developed a subjective theory of probability similar to, but less pragmatic than, Ramsey's theory.*

. . . the degree of probability attributed by an individual to a given event is revealed by the conditions under which he would be disposed to bet on that event.

This being granted, once an individual has evaluated the probabilities of certain events, two cases can present themselves: either it is possible to bet with him in such a way as to be assured of gaining, or else this possibility does not exist. In the first case one clearly should say that the evaluation of the probabilities given by this individual contains an incoherence, an intrinsic contradiction; in the other case we will say that [his probability evaluations are coherent (consistent)]. It is precisely this condition of coherence which constitutes the sole principle from which one can deduce the whole calculus of probability: this calculus then appears as a set of rules to which the subjective evaluation of probability of various events by the same individual ought to conform if there is not to be a fundamental contradiction among them.

. . . probability theory is not an attempt to describe actual behavior; its subject is coherent behavior, and the fact that people are only more or less coherent is inessential.

Both Ramsey and de Finetti base their subjective accounts of probability on the relation between coherence and the calculus of probability stated by the "book" theorem (sec. 4.4). As Ramsey indicates in the epigraph, and as we saw in Section 4.3.6 (Simple ordering of preferences and uncertainties), there is also an intimate connection between rules governing choice and the calculus of probability. We will devote the present chapter to this connection, a deeper and philosophically more important one than that between coherence and the calculus.

Ramsey started but did not finish an axiomatic analysis of utility and probability in terms of rules of choice. Influenced by Ramsey, but more especially by de Finetti, L. J. Savage developed a much better axiomatic system for choice in *The Foundations of Statistics*. He started with a set of choice situations and stipulated that the choices be made according to certain rules such as the simple ordering of preferences. He then showed that choices made this way both maximize utility and satisfy the calculus of probability. In effect, he replaced the calculus of inductive probability, the definition of utility, and the single bare rule "maximize utility" by a rich set of rules concerning how choices should be made.

* De Finetti, "La prévision: ses lois logiques, ses sources subjectives." The three quotations are from pp. 101, 103, and 111, respectively, of the English translation.

This reveals a content in the rule of maximizing utility that is not evident on the traditional theory of utility (sec. 4.3). For on this theory, the rule of maximizing utility *sounds* empty. The rule states that one should choose an act of maximum utility. But what does it mean to say an act has maximum utility other than to say it is an act that should be chosen? Savage's axiomatic system shows that the rule "choose an act of maximum utility" is equivalent to a certain set of rules, of which the rule "make your preferences transitive" is typical.

An axiomatic system constructed to provide a foundation for a subject should analyze that subject into logical elements (definitions, axioms, rules) to be studied separately. Consequently, a foundational system for utility should divide the decision process into rules that can be evaluated separately. Since these rules concern our own choices, they should have a certain "self-evident" character: it should be fairly evident whether a given rule should be used under specified conditions. Moreover, these rules should help solve the problems of the traditional theory of utility: they should enable us to account for the distinction between quantitative and qualitative probabilities (or valuations) and for the fact that preferences and uncertainties are not always simply ordered, and they should help us resolve the two paradoxes of utility (secs. 4.3.2, 4.3.4, 4.3.6).

While Savage's axiomatic system goes a long way toward fulfilling these desiderata, I do not find it completely satisfactory. I have therefore modified it in two respects. The first involves a change in the universe of discourse: the rules are stated in terms of the choice trees introduced in the last chapter and extensions of them to an arbitrary number of levels (see, e.g., fig. 12). Second, I have replaced some of Savage's axioms by others that seem to me more basic or perspicuous. The resultant axiomatic system is called the "calculus of choice." It is presented in Sections 5.2 to 5.5, below.*

The trees of the last chapter had only a single choice point. But more extended trees are needed to represent the structure of sequential choice situations and decisions concerning them. For example, to go to a Philadelphia meeting and back, a person must choose his mode of transportation to Philadelphia and from the station or airport to the meeting, then repeat all this in reverse; each mode has its attendant costs and risks. There are obviously several choice and chance points in this situation, necessitating a multilevel tree to represent it. The person can make his decisions as he passes down the successive levels of the tree, or he can make them all in advance. In the latter case he has adopted a plan of action or "strategy."

* I originally developed my calculus of choice in the early 1960s, but I have modified it somewhat since then. I benefited from general discussions with my friend Jimmie Savage, now deceased, as well as from his book.

Another variant of Savage's system is given in Luce and Krantz's "Conditional Expected Utility." This paper came to my attention after the present chapter was completed.

Thus the act trees of the calculus of choice express strategies in the game-theoretic sense, and the calculus of choice is closely related to game theory. This connection is a generalization of the "book" theorem, which is in turn a phase in the long historical connection between probability theory and gambling.

Differences exist, of course, between the trees of the calculus of choice and the more typical trees of game theory. There are generally two or more participants in a game, and the corresponding tree diagrams must have choice points associated with each player. In games of pure skill, e.g., chess, the game trees have no chance points. Our choice trees could be used to represent a game of solitaire in which the subject alternately makes choices and throws a die. Games of this sort are sometimes called "games against nature," but it is not always the case that "nature" acts as an opponent, as we assumed in presenting the "book" theorem (sec. 4.4).

Emile Borel and John von Neumann advanced the idea of a formalized and abstract strategy. Von Neumann built a theory of games based on strategies and in the *Theory of Games and Economic Behavior* (written jointly with Oscar Morgenstern) related game theory to utility theory and economics.* The theory of games and economic behavior continues and extends the close connection that probability theory has had with games of chance and monetary matters from the very beginning.

Earlier than either Ramsey or de Finetti, Borel suggested that probability should be analyzed in terms of its applications and also that it should be related to the theory of games and to economics. In a 1924 review of Keynes' *Treatise on Probability* he wrote:

> The applications [of the theory of probability] are the true realities: the realities are insurance premiums, samples obtained by biologists and agronomists, phenomena observed and predicted by physicists.
>
> . . . the method of betting permits us in the majority of cases a numerical evaluation of probability that has exactly the same characteristics as the evaluation of prices by the methods of exchange.
>
> The deep study of certain games will perhaps lead to a new chapter of the theory of probabilities, a theory whose origins go back to the study of games of chance of the simplest kind. It will be a new science where psychology will be no less useful than mathematics. . . .†

* The earliest papers are Borel's "La théorie du jeu et les équations intégrales à noyau symétrique" (1921) and von Neumann's "Zur Theorie der Gesellschaftsspiele" (1928).

For further references on utility theory and game theory see Thrall, Coombs, and Davis, *Decision Processes;* Arrow's "Alternative Approaches to the Theory of Choice in Risk-taking Situations"; Luce and Raiffa, *Games and Decisions;* and references cited therein.

† "Apropos of a Treatise on Probability," pp. 49, 57, and 58–59, respectively.

In this review Borel comes close to suggesting a subjective theory of probability, but he does not mention an essential element of the theory, its normative character. Taken only descriptively, the subjective theory of probability is a psychological theory of partial belief and not a theory of inductive probability.*

Utility theory was presented in the preceding chapter via the traditional theory of utility, according to which one first assigns real number probabilities to statements and real number utilities to consequences, then calculates the utility of each act and applies the rule of maximizing utility to obtain a preference ordering of acts. Thus the traditional theory proceeds from the utilities and probabilities of consequences, through the utilities of acts, to choices. The calculus of choice proceeds in the opposite direction. It starts with a large set of choice situations and stipulates that choices are to be made by certain rules, like the rule that preferences should be transitive. It follows as a theorem that choices made in accordance with these rules do in fact maximize utility and satisfy the calculus of inductive probability. Thus the calculus of choice proceeds from rules for choices to the calculi of utility and probability.

The two approaches also differ in the depth of their pragmatic analyses. The traditional theory does relate probability to action. However, it does not give a pragmatic analysis of the meanings of "utility" and "probability," for these concepts are presupposed by the theory. In contrast, the calculus of choice derives the rule of maximizing utility and the calculus of probability from rules of choice, thereby giving pragmatic analyses of the concepts of utility and probability.

These pragmatic analyses constitute the essence of the theories of Ramsey, de Finetti, Savage, as well as my own. De Finetti called his theory "subjective" while Savage called his more complete development "the personalistic view of probability." We use the name "personalistic theory of inductive probability" for the theory of Ramsey, de Finetti, and Savage. My own theory is somewhat different, and I call it the "pragmatic theory of inductive probability." But it should be kept in mind that the personalistic theory of inductive probability is equally pragmatic.

The main difference between the pragmatic and personalistic theories of probability concerns the status of standard inductive logic. Ramsey, de Finetti, and Savage are all concerned with the foundations of the calculus of inductive probability (chap. 2) and not with alternative inductive logics. They hold that people should agree on the calculus of inductive probability, but they do not hold that people should agree on the truth-status of atomic inductive probability statements. In contrast, the pragmatic theory of inductive probability provides an epistemological foundation for standard inductive logic, which was defined in the models of Section 3.2 by the

* These remarks also apply to Koopman's "The Bases of Probability."

calculus of probability *plus* axiom [24]. Thus the pragmatic theory is less relative and subjective than the personalistic theory. This difference will be discussed further near the end of the chapter (sec. 5.7.2).

We have already seen that Peirce, the founder of pragmatism, did not advocate a pragmatic theory of probability (sec. 4.2.6).* But through his pragmatism he contributed to the development of the personalistic and pragmatic theories of probability. Ramsey was affected directly by Peirce's writings. I asked de Finetti if he was influenced by pragmatism, and he replied:

> Pragmatism has influenced me very much, and if I had to choose a philosophical epithet for myself, I would say that I was a pragmatist. But the words frighten me; everyone uses them so differently. I do not know whether I have read Peirce's writings, but certainly I have read those of others who speak of him, the writings of James and of Italians like Papini and, above all, Vailati (a mathematical historian of science and philosophy, too little known for his worth).†

This concludes our historical introduction to the pragmatic theory of inductive probability. We proceed now to my **calculus of choice**: the next section contains the grammar of the calculus, while Sections 5.3, 5.4, and 5.5 contain the axioms and theorems. (All the figures for the calculus appear together, preceding this chapter.)

5.2 The Calculus of Choice—Grammar

5.2.1 The marking "game"

Borrowing an idea from the "book theorem" (sec. 4.4), we shall present the calculus of choice in the context of a game, to be called "the marking game."

Each instance or play of the marking game starts from a given "choice basis" consisting of a set of "consequence names," a sequence of sequences of statements, and some general information Γ. From this choice basis is constructed a "complete set of choice trees," which gives the subject all possible choices among all possible strategies involving the statements and the consequence names of the choice basis.

Consider, for example, a basis consisting of the consequence names "C_1" through "C_8" and the four sequences of statements $\langle P_1, P_2, P_3\rangle$, $\langle Q_1, Q_2\rangle$, $\langle R_1, R_2\rangle$, and $\langle S_1, S_2, S_3\rangle$. Relative to the general information Γ: (a)

* The same is true of C. I. Lewis, whose pragmatic epistemology is very much the same as Peirce's. Lewis espoused a mixed a priori, empirical theory of probability. See secs. F1 and F2 of my "A Pragmatic-Humean Theory of Probability and Lewis's Theory."

† Translated from a letter to Savage of 18 March 1961, written in response to a letter from me. This quotation is reproduced with Professor de Finetti's kind permission. Peirce influenced William James, who in turn influenced G. Vailati and G. Papini.

the statements of each sequence are mutually exclusive and jointly exhaustive, and (b) each statement of a sequence is logically independent (but not necessarily probabilistically independent) of the statements of the other sequences. The complete set of choice trees that is constructed from this basis is exceedingly large. Some are of the form used in Chapter 4, which give the subject a choice from mixed acts composed of the consequences and statements of the basis. Beyond this, there are many extended trees, which have several different levels of choice and chance points; Figure 12 is an example.

The *marking game* consists of four moves. First, the subject is presented with the complete set of choice trees and is requested to convert them into act trees by indicating his choices with arrowheads. He does not know the truth-values of the statements on the trees, though his general information Γ is inductively relevant to these statements. So far as the rules of the game are concerned, the subject may mark any or all of the trees, provided he marks at least one. The result is called a "marked set of trees."

In the second move, a single act tree is selected from the marked set to serve as a basis for the payoff at the end of the game. There are different possible procedures for this selection. It could be made by an opponent who is motivated to choose a tree (if there is one) that is particularly unfavorable to the subject. The devil plays this role in the "book" theorem. Alternatively, the tree might be selected by a chance mechanism, so that the marking game would be partly a game of chance. Whatever procedure is used, it is essential that the subject believe in advance that any act tree of the marked set might be used to determine the payoff, so that he will be motivated to mark each choice tree he does mark in such a way that it reflects his real preferences.

This same procedure should be used to choose between cases of indifference in the act tree selected for the payoff. Otherwise, such cases may lead to more than one consequence, whereas each consequence defines the total of what the subject is to receive in the payoff, the prize less the cost.

In the third move of the marking game, the truth-value of each statement that occurs in the act tree selected for payoff is ascertained. Since there are no cases of indifference, there will then be a unique path from root to consequence point traversing only "true" dashed lines and only marked (chosen) solid lines. This is the *payoff path.*

The subject then receives the consequence named at the end of the payoff path. This is the fourth and final move of the game. The payoff resulting from the possible outcomes of Figure 12 are:

P_1: C_2
P_2: C_1
$P_3R_1S_1$: C_7

$P_3R_1S_2: C_2$
$P_3R_1S_3: C_1$
$P_3R_2: C_1$.

The structure of the marking game is very similar to that of the "book" theorem game. The latter is based on a set of statements and consists of four moves: (1) the subject assigns a partial belief to each statement, (2) the devil assigns a stake to each statement, (3) the truth-values of the statements are ascertained, and (4) a payoff is made according to the outcome. There is also a similarity between the theories built on these two games: the "book" theorem connects a property of partial beliefs (coherence) to the calculus of probability, while the calculus of choice connects a property of choices (satisfying the axioms of the calculus) to the calculus of probability and the rule of maximizing utility.

5.2.2 Choice and act trees

Here we will be precise about the structure of choice and act trees. This enterprise is grammatical, since it distinguishes those tree expressions that are to be interpreted from those that are not. Compare the definition of "formula" in the logic of causal statements (p. 343).

Each *tree* of the calculus of choice has a distinguished point called the *root.* The root can be either a choice point or a chance point. The trees are normally drawn "upside down," with the root at the top and the lines going down. By definition, a tree has no cycles or looped paths.

There are three kinds of points in a tree: choice points, chance points, and consequence points. Two or more solid lines emanate from a *choice point;* there is at least one such point in a tree. In an act tree a solid line may have an arrowhead on it. Two or more dashed lines emanate from a *chance point;* these lines are labeled with formulas satisfying a condition to be stated soon. While choice and chance points generally alternate down a tree, they need not do so. A terminal or bottom point is a *consequence point*, and it is labeled with a consequence name.

In marking an extended tree, a subject should estimate probabilities conditional on the information available at a choice point. For example, in marking choice point 8 of Figure 12, he should assess the probabilities of Q_1, Q_2, S_1, S_2, and S_3 conditional on P_3R_1. For in the payoff process, point 8 will be reached only if "P_3R_1" is true. Now the conditional probability term "$\mathbf{P}(c, d)$" is not defined in the calculus of probability when d is contradictory (pp. 40, 92), and it is natural to restrict the grammatical trees of the calculus of choice analogously. We next define some terms needed for this restriction.

Consider a tree with general information Γ. Let π be some point of the tree and let Φ be a conjunction of all the statements on the path from the root to π. The *information at point* π is expressed by $\Phi\Gamma$. More technically, the information at π consists of the class of statements logically equivalent to $\Phi\Gamma$. Note the counting criterion implicit in this concept (p. 169): If $\Phi_1\Gamma$ and $\Phi_2\Gamma$ express the information at points π_1 and π_2 (respectively), then the information at these two points is the same just in case $\Box(\Phi_1\Gamma \equiv \Phi_2\Gamma)$.

A *choice, chance,* or *consequence point* is *logically impossible* when a formula expressing the information at that point is logically impossible. One natural way to mark a tree is to start at the bottom and work up, estimating the likelihoods of the statements below a point conditional on the information at that point. Such estimates are meaningless if the information is contradictory, just as a probability conditional on a contradiction is unintelligible. Moreover, since a subject knows that a payoff path will never reach a contradictory point, he has no motive to make a choice at this point. For these reasons, logically impossible choice and chance points are not allowed in grammatical trees. (See fig. 13a.)

On the other hand, a logically impossible consequence point has a natural interpretation: its consequence contributes nothing to the value of the strategy that includes it. For this reason, we allow logically impossible consequence points to be grammatical. (See fig. 13b.)

A tree is either a choice tree or an act tree. A **choice tree** is a rooted tree with one or more logically possible choice points, zero or more logically possible chance points, and consequence points. Two or more solid lines emanate from each choice point. Two or more dashed lines emanate from each chance point; these lines are labeled with formulas that are mutually exclusive and jointly exhaustive relative to the information at that point.

To "mark" a choice point is to put an arrowhead on one or more lines emanating from that choice point. An **act tree** is derived from a choice tree by marking certain of its choice points according to the following inductive rule. The root is marked if it is a choice point, otherwise all the choice points connected to it by dashed lines are marked. If every solid line on a path from a root to a choice point is marked with an arrowhead, then that choice point is also marked.

The arrowheads will usually be plain or V-shaped, but other kinds of arrowheads will be employed to express contingent markings (figs. 16b, 18, 19, 24, 25, and 26b; see p. 265) and alternative markings (figs. 29 and 34a; see pp. 275, 296).

The statement component of a choice basis defines a set of logically possible universes (see p. 260). An *act* in the most general sense is an assignment of consequences to logically possible universes. A choice tree represents a set of acts. In marking a choice tree by the rule just stated, a subject chooses one or more acts from this set. If there are no cases of indifference (more than one arrowhead at a choice point), he chooses exactly one act.

The consequence it assigns to a logically possible universe is found by tracing the payoff path for that universe.

The following alternate marking rule could also be used to define an act tree: the subject marks every choice point of a tree. This rule is not as good as the one adopted, because it requires the subject to mark choice points that will not occur in any payoff path and hence will provide him no motive to express his real preferences.

Because the act expressions and trees studied in the last chapter are of special interest, let us characterize them precisely. For this we need the following notion. A *subtree* of a given tree is defined by a point (other than the root) and what lies beneath it. Note that a consequence point (and its label) is a subtree by this definition. Note also that a subtree may not be grammatical by itself; for the statement labels at a chance point may not be mutually exclusive and jointly exhaustive relative to the general information Γ of the basis, but only relative to the information at that chance point. Subtree 5 of Figure 13 and subtree 3′ of Figure 23 are examples.

Consider now the expressions used to represent acts in the last chapter. The linear expressions are of two kinds: consequence names and expressions for mixed acts. The latter are of the form $\Sigma_{n=1}^{N} p_n c_n$, with $N \geqq 2$, where p_1, $p_2, \ldots, p_N$ are mutually exclusive and jointly exhaustive and no p_n is contradictory (all relative to the general information). The subtrees corresponding to these two kinds of linear expressions are: consequence points, and chance points that lead directly to consequence points via dashed lines labeled with a partition (pp. 52, 287). An expression of any of these forms (one-dimensional or two-dimensional) is a *normal form act expression.*

Here are some examples. "C_1," "$PC_1 \text{ v } \bar{P}C_2$," "$PQC_1 \text{ v } \bar{P}QC_2 \text{ v } P\bar{Q}C_3 \text{ v } \bar{P}\bar{Q}C_4$" are normal form act expressions, as are all the subtrees of the figures of Chapter 4. The following are not normal form act expressions: formulas "$(P \text{ v } \bar{P})C_1$" and "$PC_1 \text{ v } PC_2 \text{ v } P\bar{P}C_3$," and subtrees 2, 3, 4, 5, 7, and 8 of Figure 12.

A *normal form choice* (*act*) *tree* is a choice (act) tree containing a single choice point, the root, from which the solid lines lead to subtrees that are normal form act expressions. All the trees of Chapter 4 are normal form trees, so that the concepts of choice tree and act tree defined there (pp. 181–82) are the normal form versions. The trees of Figures 12, 13, and 15 are not normal form trees. We will refer informally to non-normal form trees as "extended trees," though in this sense an "extended" tree may have no more levels than a normal form tree (see tree 8 of fig. 15).

There are many logically equivalent normal form expressions that represent the same act, and hence there are many logically equivalent normal form trees that represent the same set of acts. For example, "$PQC_1 \text{ v } P\bar{Q}C_1 \text{ v } \bar{P}QC_2 \text{ v } \bar{P}\bar{Q}C_3$," "$PC_1 \text{ v } \bar{P}QC_2 \text{ v } \bar{P}\bar{Q}C_3$," and the corresponding subtrees are logically equivalent. The operation of exchanging these subtrees in normal form trees preserves logical equivalence. Later we will define a unique normal form for each given tree and relate the choices made in the given tree to the choices made in its normal form by the normal form axiom (sec. 5.4.1).

In the next subsection we will consider sets of choice and act trees. For this purpose we need to make explicit our counting criterion for trees and subtrees (p. 169). Actually, there are two related concepts, with the same applicability criteria but different counting criteria: "token" and "type." Two tree tokens (copies, occurrences, instances) are of the same tree type when there is an isomorphism under which point corresponds to point and line to line and the following are preserved: unmarked solid lines, marked solid lines, dashed lines and formulas, and consequence point labels. Subtrees 11 and 12 of Figure 15 are tokens of the same type, as are subtrees 3 and 3′ of Figure 18. Notice that the labels placed "inside" choice and chance points are not counted as parts of a tree.

5.2.3 *Complete sets of trees*

Each set of grammatical trees of the calculus of choice is constructed from a given "choice basis" of consequences and statements. The question arises: How large should we allow a choice basis to be? In most situations a subject considers only a few consequences and statements. But the calculus of choice will be a simpler theory if we set no finite bound on the size of a choice basis. This also insures that our theory will not be inapplicable because of an arbitrary restriction on size.

Obviously, a subject cannot mark infinitely many choice trees. Yet once we have arbitrarily large sets of trees, we can consider consequences of sets of trees that grow larger and larger without limit. Therefore, it is simpler to allow infinite sets of trees from the start. Moreover, in using real numbers for probabilities and utilities, one is in effect considering an infinite marked set of trees; for rational numbers are adequate for any finite marked set. An infinite marked set of trees is a fiction, but it is a convenient one (see pp. 309–12).

A *choice basis* is a pair of sequences: a sequence of two or more distinct consequence names and a sequence (possibly null) of sequences of statements. Each consequence has exactly one consequence name. The statements within each (lower level) sequence are mutually exclusive and jointly exhaustive, relative to the subject's general information. Moreover, each statement of a sequence is logically independent of all the statements in the other sequences, relative to the subject's general information. This last restriction could be removed at the cost of a little complexity (cf. pp. 354–56).

We use uppercase letters with subscripts or superscripts as constant symbols for consequence names and statements. The choice basis of Figure 12 is written as $\langle C_1, C_2, \ldots, C_8\rangle$ and $\langle \langle P_1, P_2, P_3\rangle, \langle Q_1, Q_2\rangle, \langle R_1, R_2\rangle, \langle S_1, S_2, S_3\rangle \rangle$, while the choice basis of Figure 14 is $\langle \langle C_0, C_1\rangle, \langle \langle P, \bar{P}\rangle, \langle Q, \bar{Q}\rangle \rangle \rangle$.

It is clear that the statement component of a choice basis defines a set of logically possible universes. A universe description is a conjunction containing exactly one statement from each sequence. For example, the choice basis $\langle \langle C_0, C_1\rangle, \langle \langle P, \bar{P}\rangle, \langle Q, \bar{Q}\rangle \rangle \rangle$ gives rise to four universe descriptions: PQ, $P\bar{Q}$, $\bar{P}Q$, and $\bar{P}\bar{Q}$. Thus the calculus of choice is based on formal models similar to those used for studying inductive logic (sec. 3.2). However, the interpretation of these models differs in the two cases. The universe descriptions of the calculus of choice describe those possible future partial states of the universe that are under consideration in a certain choice situation, whereas the universe descriptions of inductive logic describe alternative complete universes.

Only constants (capital letters) are used as symbols on choice and act trees in the strict sense. However, we sometimes employ tree-forms or tree schemata, which show the general form of trees or portions of trees of different types. Figures 20, 21, 25, and 26 are examples. For these we use lowercase letters as variables: "c," "c_1," etc., for consequences, "a," "a_1," etc., for normal form acts, and "p," "q," "r," and "p_1," etc., for statements.

We want the sets of choice trees presented to a subject to be complete in the sense of giving him all possible choices from among acts and strategies that can be made from a given choice basis. To give an intuitive idea of a "typical" complete set and of its tremendous size, we start with the choice basis $\langle \langle C, C_1\rangle, \langle \langle P, \bar{P}\rangle, \langle Q, \bar{Q}\rangle \rangle \rangle$. There are four possible universes. A total of $2^4(= 16)$ normal form acts can be constructed from two consequences and four universes, since any consequence can be assigned to any universe; see Table 13. Figure 14 is the corresponding choice tree.

The complete set of choice trees constructed on this basis also includes the 65,518 choice trees that result from deleting one to fourteen of the branches of Figure 14, as well as the variations of these that result from replacing any normal form subtree by a logically equivalent subtree. Furthermore, there are very many extended trees constructed on this choice basis, giving the subject a choice from among alternative strategies involving the consequences and statements of the basis.

Actually, infinitely many different types of choice trees can be constructed from a finite choice basis. For in defining our classes of grammatical (interpreted) trees we have allowed unlimited repetitions and variations of certain kinds. Any number of tokens of a subtree can be connected to a choice point, and the subject could mark these differently. Also, there is no limit to the number of logical variants of a given tree type, and the subject need not mark them in logically equivalent ways. These markings are excluded by the logical equivalence axiom, which is discussed in the next subsection.

Though these variants are needed, only a finite number of them are of interest for any given choice basis, and beyond a certain point they will be excluded. For this purpose we assume that a maximum height (number of levels) and a maximum width (number of points allowed on any level) are set for each finite choice basis. These maxima depend on the size (the number

TABLE 13

NORMAL FORM ACTS FOR TWO CONSEQUENCES AND FOUR POSSIBLE UNIVERSES

Acts	Assignment of consequences to universes				Normal form act expressions
	PQ	$P\bar{Q}$	$\bar{P}Q$	$\bar{P}\bar{Q}$	
A_0	C_0	C_0	C_0	C_0	C_0
A_1	C_0	C_0	C_0	C_1	$(P \vee Q)C_0 \vee \bar{P}\bar{Q}C_1$
A_2	C_0	C_0	C_1	C_0	$(P \vee \bar{Q})C_0 \vee \bar{P}QC_1$
A_3	C_0	C_0	C_1	C_1	$PC_0 \vee \bar{P}C_1$
A_4	C_0	C_1	C_0	C_0	$(\bar{P} \vee Q)C_0 \vee P\bar{Q}C_1$
A_5	C_0	C_1	C_0	C_1	$QC_0 \vee \bar{Q}C_1$
A_6	C_0	C_1	C_1	C_0	$(P \equiv Q)C_0 \vee (P \not\equiv Q)C_1$
A_7	C_0	C_1	C_1	C_1	$PQC_0 \vee (\bar{P} \vee \bar{Q})C_1$
A_8	C_1	C_0	C_0	C_0	$PQC_1 \vee (\bar{P} \vee \bar{Q})C_0$
A_9	C_1	C_0	C_0	C_1	$(P \equiv Q)C_1 \vee (P \not\equiv Q)C_0$
A_{10}	C_1	C_0	C_1	C_0	$QC_1 \vee \bar{Q}C_0$
A_{11}	C_1	C_0	C_1	C_1	$(\bar{P} \vee Q)C_1 \vee P\bar{Q}C_0$
A_{12}	C_1	C_1	C_0	C_0	$PC_1 \vee \bar{P}C_0$
A_{13}	C_1	C_1	C_0	C_1	$(P \vee \bar{Q})C_1 \vee \bar{P}QC_0$
A_{14}	C_1	C_1	C_1	C_0	$(P \vee Q)C_1 \vee \bar{P}\bar{Q}C_0$
A_{15}	C_1	C_1	C_1	C_1	C_1

of consequence names and the number of statements) of the choice basis. It is obvious that there are suitable formulas for determining these maxima. We need not bother to state one explicitly.

The notion of a **complete set of choice trees** is defined for two cases. (1) A finite complete set of choice trees consists of all choice trees of allowed height and width that can be constructed from a given finite choice basis. (2) An infinite complete set of choice trees is constructed from a given infinite choice basis as follows: (a) The two sequences of the basis are merged to form a single infinite sequence of alternating consequence names and sequences of statements. (b) Each finite initial segment of the merged sequence is used as a basis for a finite complete set of choice trees. (c) All the finite complete sets so obtained are combined to obtain the desired infinite complete set of choice trees.

The first seven axioms of the calculus of choice apply to all complete sets of choice trees. But the last axiom, the quantitative axiom, applies only to infinite complete sets of choice trees.

If one or more of the trees of a complete set of choice trees is converted into an act tree, the resultant set of trees is a **marked set of trees.**

Having completed the grammar of the calculus of choice, we turn to the axioms. We shall evaluate them after presenting the whole system.

5.3 The Calculus of Choice—Simple Ordering

5.3.1 Marking and logical equivalence axioms

The rules of the marking game allow a subject to mark the trees of a given complete choice set in any way he pleases, provided he marks at least one tree. The function of the eight axioms of the calculus of choice is to place substantial restrictions on how he marks trees.

The axioms will be interpreted both descriptively and normatively. For reasons of convenience we have formulated them as statements about how a subject marks the trees of a complete choice set—equivalently, as facts about the marked set. The axioms could also be formulated as normative rules for marking trees, and this interpretation actually proves more important (see sec. 5.6.2). The axioms have been chosen to express fundamental rules of choice in simple terms. Some of these could be weakened without changing the content of the system.

The first axiom requires the subject to mark every choice tree of the given complete set, thereby guaranteeing that every tree of the resultant marked set is an act tree. The *marking axiom* is

[I] The subject converts every choice tree into an act tree.

In other words, the subject adopts a complete set of strategies for the possible sequences of choices that can be constructed on the given choice basis.

Many of the choices and acts of a marked set of trees are deductively related; the second axiom covers these relations. We will motivate it by discussing the relation of inductive to deductive logic.

Since we specified inductive probability as an evidential relation between statements (pp. 24–25), it was natural to treat the deductive relations between these same statements explicitly by building the calculus of inductive probability and formal inductive logic around a core of deductive logic (secs. 2.2.1, 3.2). This approach leads to the exchange principle, which allows logically equivalent statements to be exchanged in probability contexts (p. 47).

Mathematicians generally use a more extensional approach to probability, predicating probability of "events." On this approach an event functions similarly to a class of logically equivalent statements, so that the exchange principle is implicit rather than explicit. Other logical relations are treated explicitly—for example, those obtaining among mutually exclusive and jointly exhaustive events. This second approach is simpler than the first and hence is preferable for anyone not interested in making explicit the relation of deductive to inductive logic.

But the second approach is ill-suited to a subjective or pragmatic theory of probability, in which the subject's reasoning processes, including deductive reasoning, play a central role. We therefore continue the first approach, building the calculus of choice around a core of deductive logic. This is accomplished by our next axiom, the logical equivalence axiom. It should be noted that Savage uses the second approach in *The Foundations of Statistics*, so that there is nothing equivalent to our second axiom in his system.

Since the trees of the calculus of choice are signs or symbols in the most general sense, the notions of deductive logic apply to them. A choice tree gives the content of a choice offered to a subject, and an act tree signifies the act (or strategy) he chooses. The choices involved can be described in different but logically equivalent ways, so that trees can be logically equivalent to one another. Examples are given in Figures 16–19.

We proceed now to define the notion of two trees or subtrees being logically equivalent, relative to a statement i. Generally, i expresses the information at the roots of the trees or subtrees. When this is the general information Γ of the choice basis, we will simply say that the trees are logically equivalent. This parallels our practice of dropping the general condition G in a probability statement (pp. 41, 94).

Two *trees* or *subtrees* are *logically equivalent on condition i* if and only if one can be converted into the other by a sequence of the following four operations and their converses.

(1) *Exchange of logically equivalent formulas.* A formula p may be replaced by another formula q that is logically equivalent to it conditional on i, that is, when $\Box\{i \supset (p \equiv q)\}$. By this rule, subtrees 2′ and 2″ of Figure 16a are logically equivalent, and subtrees 6 and 16 of Figure 17 are logically equivalent on condition PQ.

Note here the force of the restriction that a consequence has only one name (p. 259). Two subtrees that are consequence points are logically equivalent if and only if they have the same consequence label.

(2) *Combining partial acts.* Consider a chance point with two dashed lines terminating in the same consequence and hence representing two partial acts involving the same consequence. These two lines may be replaced by a single dashed line leading to the consequence and having as its label the disjunction of the labels of the two lines. For an example, compare subtrees 2 and 2′ of Figure 16a. Trees 1 and 11 of Figure 17 are logically equivalent by this and the preceding operation.

As so far described, this operation may result in there being a single dashed line from the chance point terminating in a consequence, which line will be labeled with a formula that is logically necessary relative to information at that chance point. If this happens, the chance point is to be replaced by the consequence to preserve the grammaticality of the tree. The passage from subtree 3 to the consequence point "$1" in Figure 16a is an example.

(3) *Deleting a logically impossible consequence point.* Since a logically impossible consequence point cannot occur in any payoff path, it and the dashed line leading to it may be deleted. The deletion of the partial act "$T_1\bar{T}_1$($10)" from subtree 2 of Figure 16a is an example.

This operation may produce a chance point ρ having a single dashed line (with a formula that is logically necessary on the information at ρ). If so, the line is to be collapsed; that is, both end points should be identified or merged into a single point. For example, points 4 and 5 of Figure 16b become point 8 by this rule.

(4) *Merging successive choice (chance) points.* Two successive choice points may be merged, provided the original options and the original choices (if there are arrows) are preserved. In Figure 16b, choice points 7 and 8 become choice point 10 by this rule. Directly successive chance points may be combined similarly, but then the logical structure of the alternatives must be preserved. For example, the right branch of tree 1 of Figure 16b becomes the two partial acts $(\bar{P}Q)C_5$ and $(\bar{P}\bar{Q})C_6$ in tree 6.

The operation of merging successive choice (chance) points can be used to convert any tree into a logically equivalent tree in which choice and chance points alternate on every path from root to consequence point.

This concludes our presentation of the four operations used to extend the concept of conditional logical equivalence to cover trees and subtrees. Further examples occur in Figure 19. Subtrees 3 and 13 {4 and 14} [5 and 15] are logically equivalent on condition P $\{PQ\}$ $[P\bar{Q}]$.

The exchange principle of the calculus of probability allows the exchange in probability contexts of statements that are logically equivalent relative to a condition (p. 47). One who follows this principle treats logically equivalent statements in the same way when assigning probabilities. Analogously, a subject should mark logically equivalent trees the same when making choices, since these present the subject with essentially the same choices expressed in different ways. Moreover, the subject should be indifferent between two tokens of the same subtree and should mark them the same also. These considerations lead to the second axiom of the calculus of choice.

The *logical equivalence axiom* is

[II] (A) The subject converts logically equivalent choice trees into logically equivalent act trees.

(B) Suppose the alternatives at a choice point include two or more tokens of the same subtree. The subject treats them all the same (choosing all if he chooses one, and marking them the same if marking is required).

We will comment on the two parts separately and then state a corollary that depends on both of them.

The first part of the axiom applies to distinct trees of the choice set. It is illustrated by Figures 16 and 17. Here are two alternative formulations of it: (1) If an act tree belongs to the marked set, so do all act trees logically equivalent to it. (2) Let τ and τ' be trees that are logically equivalent on condition i; if they are exchanged in an act tree of the marked set at a point where the information is (or logically implies) i, the resulting tree also belongs to the marked set, assuming that the exchange preserves grammaticality.

(Here is an opportune place to explain the triangular arrowheads used to express contingency in Figures 16b, 18, 19, 24, 25, and 26b. Figure 16b may be construed as an argument, governed by the rule of inference corresponding to the logical equivalence axiom; compare the deductive rules and the corresponding conditionals of p. 22. Tree 1 of Figure 16b is the premise of the argument, and trees 6 and 9 constitute the conclusion. Plain arrowheads are used in the premise, and triangular arrowheads in the conclusion. Interpreted as an argument, Figure 16b may be read: the plain arrowheads are placed in tree 1 as indicated; *therefore* the triangular arrowheads must be placed in trees 6 and 9 as indicated.)

The second part of the axiom applies to a single tree. When two or more tokens of a subtree are directly beneath a choice point, the subject chooses all or none of them. In Figure 18 this rule is illustrated both for consequences (see subtree 8) and for subtrees having choice points themselves (see subtrees 3 and 3′, directly below choice point 2). When the selected subtrees contain choice points, the marking rule requires that they be marked; and the logical equivalence axiom requires that they be marked the same, i.e., converted into act trees of the same type.

The following corollary is about a single tree, but depends on both parts of the logical equivalence axiom.

[1] Let i be the information at a choice point whose alternatives include two or more subtrees that are logically equivalent on condition i. If the subject chooses one of these subtrees, then
(a) he chooses all of them
(b) if the subtrees have any choice points, he converts them all into act trees that are logically equivalent on condition i.

Corollary [1] is illustrated in Figure 19.

This concludes our discussion of the logical equivalence axiom. As noted earlier, we have included it in the calculus of choice so that this system will treat the relation of deductive to inductive reasoning explicitly. The calculus of choice is now a more realistic model of actual reasoning than it would otherwise be. The exchange principle makes a similar contribution to the calculus of probability.

Nevertheless, the calculi of probability and choice are idealized models of natural reasoning in this respect: they assume that the subject is deductively omniscient. Now while one who is reasoning should *try* to avoid deductive error, he may in fact be unable to apply the exchange principle or the logical equivalence axiom because he is ignorant of the relevant logical truths.

Thus if a subject does not know that two acts are logically equivalent, his preference for one over the other may be reasonable. Also, a subject may have cause to estimate the probability of a statement he knows to be logically true-or-false. For example, when one is close to proving a mathematical conjecture he may reasonably say "This conjecture is *probably* true, though I don't yet have a proof of it." Again, forced to bet with my present information I would assign a probability of one-half to the proposition that the millionth decimal digit of π is even. Neither of these probability claims makes sense in the calculus of probability, for in it a logically true-or-false statement has a probability of either one or zero.

But though such probability claims are intelligible, it is not worthwhile to extend our formal inductive logic to encompass them. The rational considerations relevant to them are highly subjective and relative; formalizing them would only increase the complexity of inductive logic without commensurate gain. Thus we elect to accept the idealization involved in the exchange principle and the logical equivalence axiom.

5.3.2 Simple ordering of preferences

We now add two more axioms and derive the simple ordering of preferences as a theorem.

The *subset axiom* is so called because it states that the choices made from a set of acts determine the choices made from some subsets of that set.

[III] If an act tree belongs to the marked set, so does every *act* tree obtained from it by deleting one or more solid lines and their subtrees.

In other words, if an act tree belongs to the marked set and the result of deleting solid lines and their subtrees from it is an act tree, that also belongs to the marked set.

Let us study the implications of the subset axiom for normal form trees first. Figures 20 and 21 give examples. The subset axiom goes from set to subset, but not vice-versa. Thus the intransitive pairwise choices of a_1 over a_2, a_2 over a_3, but a_3 over a_1, are compatible with this axiom, provided the subject does not mark any normal form tree containing all of the acts a_1, a_2, a_3. However, the marking and subset axioms together exclude intransitive choices, as may be seen by examining all the ways a subject might choose from three acts, taken both as a group and pairwise. In other words, the marking and subset axioms together imply that preferences for normal form acts are transitive.

Consider now "indifference," "preference," and "likes at least as much as," taken as binary relations over the set of normal form acts. The marking axiom requires the subject to compare any two acts and state his preferences with respect to them. By the subset axiom he cannot change these preferences when these acts are presented in a larger context. Hence the relation "likes at least as much as" is comparable. We have just shown that the marking and subset axioms together imply that "preference" is transitive, and a similar argument shows that they imply the transitivity of "indifference" and "likes at least as much as." The relation of indifference is obviously symmetrical, and the logical equivalence axiom implies that it is reflexive. The relation of "preference" is obviously asymmetrical and thus irreflexive.

Hence the first three axioms imply that "indifference" is an equivalence relation, "preference" is transitive and asymmetrical, and "likes at least as much as" is simply ordered. All this being so, it is appropriate to symbolize these three relations by "$=$," "$>$," and "$\geqq$," respectively, though it should be remembered that they connect normal form acts rather than numbers. In this notation, the simple ordering of "the subject likes act a at least as much as act b" becomes

[2a] $$(a_1 \geqq a_2) \vee (a_2 \geqq a_1)$$ (comparable)

[2b] $$[(a_1 \geqq a_2)(a_2 \geqq a_3)] \supset (a_1 \geqq a_3)$$ (transitive).

The simple ordering of the subject's preferences for consequences obviously follows as a special case.

We showed in the last chapter that a subject who uses the traditional theory of utility simply orders his preferences (see [32] and [33] of sec. 4.3.6). Likewise, if a subject assigns utilities to the consequences and probabilities to the statements of a set of normal form choice trees and then marks them to maximize utility, his preferences will be simply ordered. We see now that a system as strong as the traditional theory of utility is not needed for this simple ordering, which follows from the much weaker system of axioms [I]–[III]. These axioms, however, do not require that a subject simply order his uncertainties; two further axioms will be added in the next subsection to extend this requirement to uncertainties.

Let us now generalize the simple ordering of preferences to extended trees. The subset axiom applies to extended trees as well as to normal form trees. An example is given in Figure 22. Not counting cases of indifference, each of the eleven possible markings of choice tree 1 represents a different act that the subject may select. The subject has chosen two of these eleven extended acts. If he follows the subset axiom, he cannot change any of his preferences when presented with a subset of these eleven acts that contains at least one of the two chosen acts.

Despite the fact that the subset axiom covers extended trees, axioms [I]–[III] do not require that the subject simply order his conditional choices, because these three axioms do not require the subject to make the same choices in two subtrees of the same type having the same information at their roots and occurring in two distinct choice trees of the complete set.* Thus in Figure 23, which satisfies axioms [I]–[III], the subject has made one choice at point 2′ and the opposite choice at point 12′. We next state an axiom to preclude this.

The *invariance axiom* is

[IV] (A) No two tokens of a choice tree that occur as subtrees with the same information are marked differently.
(B) The subject's preferences for consequences are the same in all contexts.

This is called the invariance axiom because it requires the subject's choices in a subtree to be invariant through certain kinds of changes of the context of that subtree, i.e., changes in the rest of the tree of which it is a subtree. Considering only subtrees that are marked, we can reformulate the axiom in the following way. By [IVA], a subtree with chance points should be marked the same in all contexts having the same information. By [IVB] a subtree *without* chance points should be marked the same in every context.

As stated, part [IVA] covers only tokens of the same tree type, but it can be combined with the logical equivalence axiom to yield a theorem covering logically equivalent trees with the same information at their roots.

[3] Let τ and τ' be choice trees that are logically equivalent on condition i and occur as subtrees with information i. If the subject marks both τ and τ', then he converts them into act trees that are logically equivalent on condition i.

Figure 24 will be used in the proof of this theorem. Subtrees τ_1, τ_2, τ_3, τ_4, and τ_5 may be any subtrees that make the main trees grammatical. Assume

* If the two subtrees in question occur in the *same* tree (as do subtrees 3 and 3′ of fig. 18), then by the logical equivalence axiom, if they are marked they must be marked the same way. In these cases the invariance axiom [IVA] overlaps the logical equivalence axiom.

the subject marks tree 1 as indicated; we will prove that he must mark tree 9′ as indicated. The choice trees underlying subtrees 4 and 4′ are logically equivalent on the available information ($P\bar{Q}$, or $\bar{Q}P$). Define tree 9 to be the result of replacing subtree 4′ by subtree 4. By the first part of the invariance axiom, tree 9 must be marked as indicated. But tree 9 is logically equivalent to tree 9′; so by the first part of the logical equivalence axiom the subject must mark tree 9′ as indicated.

The second part of the invariance axiom, [IVB], states that the subject's preferences for consequences should be the same in *all* contexts. Taken normatively, [IVB] expresses the requirement that the subject's preferences for consequences should depend only on their intrinsic values and should not be influenced by his estimates of the chances that he will receive them. Such a requirement presupposes that the statements of a tree contain no information relevant to the subject's evaluations of the consequences of that tree. Suppose, for example, that one of the consequences is a trout dinner, that the subject has eaten cod but knows nothing about the taste of fish beyond this, and that he prefers some consequence C to a cod dinner. He then chooses C over the trout dinner at a choice point that is a root. It would be reasonable for him to reverse this choice at a choice point whose information included the statement "Trout tastes very much better than cod." Hence [IVB] presupposes that no statements of this sort occur in the choice basis.

We established earlier in this section that preference relations between normal form acts have certain properties such as comparability and transitivity, and on this basis we introduced the symbols "$a_1 \geqq a_2$," "$a_1 > a_2$," and "$a_1 = a_2$." Our discussion of the invariance axiom shows that preference relations between normal form acts *conditional on fixed information* have the same general properties as their unconditional counterparts. In particular, consider all marked normal form trees occurring as subtrees in the marked set with information i. Taken over these subtrees, the relation "likes a_1 at least as much as a_2 on condition i" is simply ordered.

These facts justify the following symbolism for conditional preferences between normal form acts. The expression "$a_1 \geqq_i a_2$" means that, in marked normal form subtrees with available information i, the subject likes a_1 at least as much as a_2. The symbols "$>_i$" and "$=_i$" are defined in terms of "$\geqq_i$" in the usual manner. The simple ordering of "conditional preferences" is expressed by

[4a] $(a_1 \geqq_i a_2) \vee (a_2 \geqq_i a_1)$

[4b] $[(a_1 \geqq_i a_2)(a_2 \geqq_i a_3)] \supset (a_1 \geqq_i a_3)$.

Since the information i can be the general information common to all trees of a complete set, [4] subsumes [2] as a special case.

5.3.3 *Simple ordering of uncertainties*

Nothing in our axioms so far precludes the subject from marking all the solid lines of every choice tree with arrowheads, thereby reducing everything to complete indifference and reducing the simple ordering of preferences to a single point. This, of course, is what he should do if he values all consequences equally; but then there is no need for him to use utility theory in making his choices, and the pragmatic analysis of probability collapses. The next axiom prevents such an occurrence.

The *existence axiom* is

[V] There are two consequences, one of which is preferred to the other.

We assume that the two consequences of the choice basis are named C_u and C_z (with $C_u > C_z$) and are used to define the unit and zero of a utility scale (p. 185).

A "prize" in ordinary usage is a single (preferred) consequence, but it is prized only because it is preferred to the status quo, which is another consequence. In discussing our formal system, it is convenient to use "prize" to mean a preference for one consequence over another. The existence axiom then states that there is at least one prize.

We showed earlier how to use a prize to obtain a pragmatic manifestation of a subject's belief that one statement is more likely than another; a subject will normally stake a prize on the statement he thinks is most likely to come true (p. 209 and fig. 10). But nothing in axioms [I]–[V] requires a subject's preferences of this kind to be independent of the prize. As far as these axioms go, the subject could stake one prize on p over q and another prize on q over p. For example, in Figure 25 the subject could stake c_1 over c_2 on p instead of on q but stake c_1' over c_2' on q rather than on p. The next axiom excludes such choices, conditionally as well as unconditionally. It thereby causes the simple ordering of values or preferences [4] to induce a simple ordering of uncertainties or likelihoods ([7], below).

The *ordering of uncertainties* axiom is

[VI] If for some prize $c_1 > c_2$, $(pc_1 \vee \bar{p}c_2) \geqq_i (qc_1 \vee \bar{q}c_2)$,

then for any prize $c_1' > c_2'$, $(pc_1' \vee \bar{p}c_2') \geqq_i (qc_1' \vee \bar{q}c_2')$.

Suppose a subject, given information i, likes to stake some prize at least as much on p as on q. Then, given the same information and any other prize, he wishes to stake it at least as much on p as on q.

The converse follows easily, since what is true in every case is true in some case, it being guaranteed by the existence axiom that there is a prize. Hence axiom [VI] has the corollary

[5] $$(\exists c_1)(\exists c_2)[\{c_1 > c_2\}\{(pc_1 \vee \bar{p}c_2) \geqq_i (qc_1 \vee \bar{q}c_2)\}] \equiv (c_1')(c_2')[\{c_1' > c_2'\} \supset \{(pc_1' \vee \bar{p}c_2') \geqq_i (qc_1' \vee \bar{q}c_2')\}] ,$$

where the existential quantifier "$(\exists c)$" symbolizes "for some consequence c" and the universal quantifier "(c)" symbolizes "for each consequence c." A more formal proof of [5] from [IV] and [VI] may be given by means of truth-function theory (sec. 2.2.2), the rule of universal instantiation (p. 348), and the rule of existential generalization (p. 411).

Hence, for fixed information i, the subject's ranking of the relative chances of p and q being true is independent of the prize. It is natural, therefore, to define the probability relation "$p \geqq_i q$" as follows.

[6a] $(p \geqq_i q) =_{df} (c_1)(c_2)[\{c_1 > c_2\} \supset \{(pc_1 \vee \bar{p}c_2) \geqq_i (qc_1 \vee \bar{q}c_2)\}]$.

The relations "$p >_i q$" and "$p =_i q$" can then be defined in terms of "$p \geqq_i q$" in the standard way. The following two theorems complement [6a].

[6b] $(p >_i q) \equiv (\exists c_1)(\exists c_2)[\{c_1 > c_2\}\{(pc_1 \vee \bar{p}c_2) >_i (qc_1 \vee \bar{q}c_2)\}]$

[6c] $(p =_i q) \equiv (c_1)(c_2)[\{c_1 > c_2\} \supset \{(pc_1 \vee \bar{p}c_2) =_i (qc_1 \vee \bar{q}c_2)\}]$.

These theorems may be derived from the definitions by truth-function theory and some rules for manipulating quantifiers.

The simple ordering of "$\geqq_i$" as a relation between statements now follows from the simple ordering of "$\geqq_i$" as a relation between normal form acts ([4]).

[7a] $(p \geqq_i q) \vee (q \geqq_i p)$

[7b] $[(p \geqq_i q)(q \geqq_i r)] \supset (p \geqq_i r)$.

Likewise, "$p >_i q$" is asymmetrical and transitive, and "$p =_i q$" is an equivalence relation. After the next axiom is introduced, we shall prove enough about these three relations to justify calling them conditional probability relations (sec. 5.4.3). It will be convenient to anticipate this result and read "$p \geqq_i q$" as "conditional on i, p is at least as likely (probable) as q," and correspondingly for "$p >_i q$" and "$p =_i q$." We should keep in mind that all these likelihoods or probabilities are relative to a given person at a given time, and are not necessarily quantitative (sec. 5.5).

As we observed above, in the absence of the existence axiom the subject could mark all solid lines with arrowheads, thereby reducing everything to complete indifference. If he did this, the right-hand side of [6c] would hold vacuously, and in the calculus of choice all statements would be equally likely. Thus value differences are required for a pragmatic manifestation of probability differences.

We conclude this section with a discussion of the pragmatic analogs of probability zero and one. In the calculus of inductive probability a logical truth has probability one and a logical falsehood has probability zero, but the calculus also allows an empirically true-or-false statement to have a probability of zero or one (p. 101). Clearly, an empirical statement with probability zero can never be inductively confirmed, and an empirical statement with probability one can never be disconfirmed (p. 85). Hence it is appropriate to say that the former is "probabilistically impossible" and that the latter is "probabilistically necessary."

Similarly, in marking choice trees a subject can treat an empirical statement and a logical falsehood as equally likely, and he can treat an empirical statement and a logical truth as equally likely. This is so for conditional, as well as for unconditional, likelihoods or probabilities. These considerations suggest the following terminology for the calculus of choice:

$$p \text{ is probabilistically necessary on condition } i =_{\mathrm{df}} (p =_i r \vee \bar{r})$$

$$q \text{ is probabilistically impossible on condition } i =_{\mathrm{df}} (q =_i r\bar{r}) \quad .$$

For example, in tree 1 of Figure 26 the subject is indifferent between staking the prize "C_u over C_z" on i and staking it on $r\bar{r}$. Since he holds that $C_u > C_z$, he is treating i as probabilistically impossible.

Probabilistic impossibilities and necessities are limit points in the simple ordering of uncertainties (p. 282). Probabilistic impossibilities require special handling when the normal form of an extended tree is constructed (pp. 275–76). The notion of a "probabilistically impossible *point*" will be useful in explaining this construction. A *choice*, *chance*, or *consequence point* is *probabilistically impossible* if and only if a formula expressing the information at that point is probabilistically impossible. This definition is illustrated in Figure 26. The information at consequence point C_2 of tree 4 is expressed by "$\bar{Q}S_1$." If tree 7 is marked as shown, $\bar{Q}S_1$ is probabilistically impossible, and so point C_2 is probabilistically impossible. Conversely, if statement "$\bar{Q}S_1$" and hence consequence point C_2 are probabilistically impossible, the subject must mark tree 7 as indicated. Clearly, every *logically* impossible point is *probabilistically* impossible, but not conversely (p. 257).

We have now presented six of the eight axioms of the calculus of choice. The first four (marking, logical equivalence, subset, and invariance) yielded the simple ordering of conditional preferences. These and the next two axioms (existence, ordering of uncertainties) yielded the simple ordering of conditional uncertainties.

5.4 The Calculus of Choice—Normal Forms

5.4.1 Normal form axiom

Axioms [VII] and [VIII] of the calculus of choice are the normal form axiom and the quantitative axiom, respectively. Axiom [VII] reduces choices made in an extended tree to the choices made in that tree's normal form equivalent; it completes the comparative structure of both preferences (sec. 5.3.2) and uncertainties (sec. 5.3.3). Axiom [VIII] will convert this comparative structure into a quantitative structure (sec. 5.5).

The normal form axiom states that if an act tree belongs to the marked set, so does its normal form. Though we have defined the notion of a normal form tree (p. 258), we have yet to explain how to construct the normal form of an extended tree. Two algorithms are used in the construction. The "trimming algorithm" handles the probabilistically impossible points of an extended tree. The "normal form algorithm" produces a normal form tree containing the same choices (in a certain sense) as the given tree. But before stating these algorithms we must discuss the basic concepts and illustrate the essence of the normal form algorithm.

An act is an assignment of consequences to logically possible universes. The assignments are explicit in a normal form tree, implicit in other trees. Each normal form act expression (subtree) of a normal form tree represents one such assignment, with each dashed line corresponding to one or more possible universes. In an extended tree a universe description is distributed over different dashed segments or paths. Nevertheless, in marking an extended tree the subject is choosing one or more acts from a proffered set. The normal form axiom requires him to make essentially the same choice in the normal form of that extended tree.

Consider the extended tree of Figure 27a, under the assumption that every point is probabilistically possible. The underlying choice tree gives the subject a choice from among seven acts, for there are seven different ways to mark this choice tree, excluding cases of indifference. The assignment of consequences to universes made by one of these act trees can be found by tracing the payoff path for each universe to the consequence the subject receives in that universe. In a grammatical act tree without any cases of indifference, there will be exactly one payoff path for each logically possible universe (see p. 255).

As noted earlier, many logically equivalent normal form act expressions represent the same act (p. 258), and hence a normal form tree generally has many logically equivalent normal forms. But in constructing *the* normal form *of* a given tree, we will use the "expanded" normal form act expressions explicitly containing all the universe descriptions that can be constructed from the statements of the tree. In Figure 27, for example, the act selected in tree 1 is represented by "$PQC_6 \vee P\bar{Q}C_8 \vee \bar{P}QC_6 \vee \bar{P}\bar{Q}C_8$" in the normal form tree R, rather than by "$QC_6 \vee \bar{Q}C_8$."

The normal form of *choice* tree 1 is constructed by placing the seven expanded normal form act expressions derivable from tree 1 in one normal form tree, as in the choice tree underlying Figure 27b. The normal form of *act* tree 1 is obtained by indicating with an arrowhead the act selected in tree 1. Under obvious alphabetic conventions the normal form of a given tree will always be unique.

By the normal form axiom, if act tree 1 belongs to the marked set, then its normal form R also belongs to the marked set. The converse is also the case, as the following considerations demonstrate. By the marking axiom [I] the subject must mark choice tree 1. If he marks it other than as shown, then he must mark the normal form tree R other than as shown. Thus the normal form axiom requires the subject to choose the same acts in an extended choice tree and in its normal form.

All the probabilities involved in a complete set of choice trees are conditional on the subject's general information. For convenience we call a probability "unconditional" or "conditional" according to whether it depends on further information (cf. p. 94). In marking the choice point of a normal form tree the subject considers only unconditional probabilities. But when marking the choice points of an extended tree the subject should estimate the probabilities conditional on the information available at these points. For example, the subject should base his choice of act 10 over act 9 in Figure 12 on the probabilities of Q_1, Q_2, S_1, S_2, and S_3 conditional on the information P_3R_1 of choice point 8.

Hence extended trees are to normal form trees as conditional probabilities are to unconditional probabilities. The normal form axiom operates on trees somewhat analogously to the way the reduction principle [23] of Section 2.6 operates on probabilities: the former reduces conditional choices to unconditional choices, while the latter reduces conditional probabilities to unconditional probabilities. Probabilistic impossibilities (statements of zero probability) are treated specially in the reduction principle, and they also require special treatment when the normal form of a tree is constructed, as Figure 28a shows.

Suppose the subject prefers C_1 to C_2 and C_2 to C_3. By the invariance axiom he must prefer C_1 to C_2 at choice point 3. Suppose further that he marks choice point 1 as shown; this is reasonable if, for example, he prefers C_3 to C_4. Thus in tree 1 he has chosen $PC_1 \vee \bar{P}C_3$ over both $PC_2 \vee \bar{P}C_3$ and C_4. If neither P nor $\bar{P}$ is probabilistically impossible, he should make the same choice in the normal form tree 4. But if P is probabilistically impossible, this choice leads to a contradiction; for by applying the definition of "probabilistically impossible" and [6c] we get

(a) $PC_1 \vee \bar{P}C_3 = (r\bar{r})C_1 \vee (r \vee \bar{r})C_3 = C_3$

(b) $PC_2 \vee \bar{P}C_3 = (r\bar{r})C_2 \vee (r \vee \bar{r})C_3 = C_3$

and hence by the transitivity of indifference

(c) $PC_1 \vee \bar{P}C_3 = PC_2 \vee \bar{P}C_3$,

contradicting tree 4, which is marked

(d) $(PC_1 \vee \bar{P}C_3) > (PC_2 \vee \bar{P}C_3)$.

Equality (c) is intuitively correct, for if P is probabilistically impossible the value difference between C_1 and C_2 should not matter in tree 4. This shows that probabilistically impossible choice points require special handling when the normal form tree is constructed.

Probabilistically impossible points that are also logically impossible are easily eliminated from a tree by means of the logical equivalence axiom (p. 264). But probabilistically impossible points that are *not* logically impossible cannot be handled in this fashion, because the resultant tree may be ungrammatical. For example, if the dashed line Q_2 and subtree 5 were deleted in Figure 29a, the labels left at point 4 (namely, Q_1 and Q_3) would not be jointly exhaustive. Instead of making these deletions we will "trim" the payoff paths from the root to points C_6 and C_7 at point 5, attaching a standard consequence label to this point. See Figures 28b and 29a for examples.

The general procedure is given by the *trimming algorithm.*

(A) Remove logically impossible consequence points by operation (3) of p. 264.

(B) Trim every payoff path that contains probabilistically impossible points at the highest such point and label that point "C_z."

The result is called the *trimmed form* of the given tree. The only impossible points of a trimmed tree are probabilistically impossible consequence points. The trimming algorithm applies to every tree, but if a tree has no probabilistically possible choice point then it has no trimmed form.

The trimming algorithm is a part of the normal form algorithm, which may be applied to any tree having at least one probabilistically possible choice point. The *normal form algorithm* is

(A) Let the given tree be Υ. The trimming algorithm is applied to Υ to obtain its trimmed form τ.

(B1) If τ is a choice tree, form all possible act trees from it, excluding cases of indifference. Let these be $\tau_1, \tau_2, \ldots, \tau_M$. Construct the universe descriptions based on the statements that occur in τ. For each $\tau_m (m = 1, 2, \ldots, M)$ find the act represented by τ_m, assign C_z to every probabilistically impossible universe, and express the result as an expanded normal form act expression (subtree) a_m. The normal form choice tree containing the expressions $a_1, a_2, \ldots, a_M$ is the *normal form of* the given choice tree Υ.

(B2) If τ is an act tree, use (B1) to construct the normal form of the choice tree underlying it. In this normal form tree, mark with an arrowhead each act that agrees on all probabilistically possible universes with an act selected in τ. The result is the *normal form of* the given act tree Υ.

This algorithm and the next axiom are illustrated in Figures 27–32. Notice that different kinds of arrowheads are used in Figure 29 to distinguish different acts.

A given choice tree, its trimmed form, and its normal form all present the subject with essentially the same set of acts to choose from. More precisely, for each act a of the given tree, there is an act a_t of the trimmed tree that agrees with a over all probabilistically possible universes. Again, for each act a_t of the trimmed tree, there is a corresponding act a_n of the normal form tree that agrees with it over all probabilistically possible universes. This correspondence is illustrated in Figure 29 (pp. 241–42).

Act a of the given tree, act a_t of its trimmed version, and act a_n of its normal form version may differ in their assignments of consequences to probabilistically impossible universes. But such differences should have no influence on the subject's choices, since in treating a universe as probabilistically impossible he has acted as if he believes that it will never obtain. In other words, it should not matter to a subject how he chooses at a probabilistically impossible choice point, for he believes that this point will never be reached in the payoff process. The foregoing constitutes the rationale behind the next axiom.

The *normal form axiom* is

[VII] If an act tree belongs to the marked set, so does its normal form.

The following corollary is obvious.

[8] Let Υ be an act tree whose only probabilistically impossible points are consequence points. If Υ belongs to the marked set, so does any tree obtained from Υ by changing a consequence name at a probabilistically impossible consequence point.

In other words, consequences attached to probabilistically impossible consequence points do not affect the subject's choices.

The normal form axiom should be compared and contrasted with the logical equivalence axiom. The former incorporates one of the deductive operations permitted by the latter: the elimination of logically impossible consequence points. But the normal form algorithm modifies trees in a way that the logical equivalence operations cannot. For example, the normal form of the extended tree of Figure 27a is not logically equivalent to it, for none of the logical equivalence operations can be used to reduce it to a two-level tree.

We have already noted the strong analogy between the normal form axiom (of the calculus of choice) and the reduction principle (of the calculus of probability). This analogy is made explicit by the following reduction theorem of the calculus of choice.

[9] $(i \neq r\bar{r}) \supset [(p \geqq_i q) \equiv (pi \geqq qi)]$.

The proof of this theorem is based on Figure 30.

It is given that i is probabilistically possible ($i \neq r\bar{r}$). Assume for a moment that all eight universe descriptions "ipq," "$ip\bar{q}$," . . . , "$\bar{i}\bar{p}\bar{q}$" are probabilistically possible. Expand points 3 and 4 to pqC_u v $p\bar{q}C_u$ v $\bar{p}qC_z$ v $\bar{p}\bar{q}C_z$ and pqC_u v $p\bar{q}C_z$ v $\bar{p}qC_u$ v $\bar{p}\bar{q}C_z$, respectively, and call the result tree 1′. Trees 1 and 1′ are logically equivalent. Construct the normal form of 1′ and call it tree 6′. Tree 6′ reduces to tree 6 of Figure 30 by the logical equivalence axiom. Hence, act tree 1 belongs to the marked set if and only if act tree 6 does, and so $(q >_i p) \equiv (qi > pi)$.

Suppose next that some universe description ν is probabilistically impossible. If ν leads to "C_z" in tree 1′, nothing changes. If ν leads to "C_u" in tree 1′, the trimming algorithm replaces "C_u" by "C_z" in normal form tree 6′, but "C_u" can be put back by means of corollary [8]. Hence, in this case also, act tree 1 belongs to the marked set if and only if act tree 6 does. Therefore,

$$(i \neq r\bar{r}) \supset [(q >_i p) \equiv (qi > pi)] \quad .$$

A truth-functional modification of the consequent gives [9]. This completes the proof.

Note that if i is logically possible ($\Diamond i$) but probabilistically impossible ($i = r\bar{r}$), the expression "$q >_i p$" is still defined (well-formed). But in this case, tree 1 is trimmed to iC_z v $\bar{i}C_z$ (or C_z) and theorem [9] is inapplicable. Compare the expression "$\mathbf{P}(q, i) = x$" of the calculus of probability (p. 40). If $\Diamond i$, then "$\mathbf{P}(q, i) = x$" is well-formed even though $\mathbf{P}(i, r \text{ v } \bar{r}) = 0$; but in the latter case "$\mathbf{P}(q, i)$" cannot be reduced to unconditional probabilities by the reduction principle (p. 93).

5.4.2 Comparative values

The dyadic preference relation "$a_1 \geqq a_2$" is a comparative value relation, expressing how the subject values one act or consequence in relation to another. In contrast, the monadic utility function $\mathbf{U}(a)$ expresses the subject's numerical valuation of a single act or consequence. Using the first seven axioms, we shall prove several more theorems about the preference relation "$a_1 \geqq a_2$." When the eighth axiom is added it will convert the dyadic relation "$a_1 \geqq a_2$" into the monadic function $\mathbf{U}(a)$ (sec. 5.5).

The theorems proved in the remainder of this section are for unconditional choices (normal form trees), though their proofs depend on the normal form axiom and hence involve extended trees as well. Moreover, these theorems may be generalized to cover the conditional case. For conditional choices can be reduced to unconditional choices by means of the normal form axiom, except for choices made at probabilistically impossible choice points, which are irrelevant anyhow.

We begin with the sure-thing paradox (sec. 4.3.4). The choices of Figure 5 are contradictory in the theory of utility, and we will show that they are contradictory in the calculus of choice. For this purpose we will employ Figure 23 and assume that P_1, P_2, and P_3 are all probabilistically possible. Trees 1 and 11 (of Fig. 5) are the normal forms of trees 1′ and 11′ (of Fig. 23). Now subtrees 2′ and 12′, without their arrowheads, are of the same type and have the same information at their roots. Hence act trees 1′ and 11′ violate the invariance axiom, and trees 1 and 11 cannot both be in the marked set. This shows that the choices of the sure-thing paradox violate the calculus of choice.

The principle of this proof may be generalized to give a proof of the following basic theorem. The *partial act theorem* is

[10] Let $a_\mu = p_1c_1 \text{ v } \sum_{m=2}^{M} p_m c_m \qquad a_\nu = p_1c_1 \text{ v } \sum_{n=2}^{N} p'_n c'_n$

$$a^*_\mu = p_1c^*_1 \text{ v } \sum_{m=2}^{M} p_m c_m \qquad a^*_\nu = p_1c^*_1 \text{ v } \sum_{n=2}^{N} p'_n c'_n \quad ,$$

where $p_1, p_2, \ldots, p_M$ ($p_1, p'_2, \ldots, p'_N$) are mutually exclusive and jointly exhaustive.

Then $(a_\mu \geqq a_\nu) \equiv (a^*_\mu \geqq a^*_\nu)$.

We will interpret the theorem and then prove it.

A mixed act $\Sigma_{i=1}^{I} p_i c_i$ is a disjunctive sum of the "partial acts" p_1c_1, $p_2c_2, \ldots, p_Ic_I$ (p. 183). The acts a_μ and a_ν of the theorem contain the same partial act p_1c_1. When this is replaced by the partial act $p_1c^*_1$, acts a_μ and a_ν become acts a^*_μ and a^*_ν respectively. The partial act theorem states that the preference relation between a^*_μ and a^*_ν is the same as that between a_μ and a_ν. In other words, the contribution of the partial act $\Sigma_{m=2}^{M} p_m c_m$ to the mixed act a_μ (and likewise of $\Sigma_{n=2}^{N} p'_n c'_n$ to a_ν) is invariant through change of context (from p_1c_1 to $p_1c^*_1$). This establishes that the value of a mixed act is, in a sense, the sum of the values of its partial acts.

To prove the partial act theorem, we first prove that act tree 1 of Figure 31 belongs to the marked set if and only if act tree 21 does. Stated differently, we prove that act trees 1 and 21 are "marked-set equivalent." The proof is divided into two cases.

Case 1: $\bar{p}_1$ is probabilistically impossible.

(a) The following transformations show that tree 1 is marked-set equivalent to the tree expressing $c_1 > c_1$. Using the logical equivalence axiom, replace the compound partial act $p_2c_2 \text{ v } p_3c_3$ of tree 1 by $\bar{p}_1(p_2c_2 \text{ v } p_3c_3)$, i.e. by a subtree $p_2c_2 \text{ v } p_3c_3$ connected to point a_μ via a dashed line $\bar{p}_1$. Using theorem [8] and the fact that $\bar{p}_1$ is probabilistically impossible, replace this subtree $p_2c_2 \text{ v } p_3c_3$ by c_1. Act a_μ then becomes $p_1c_1 \text{ v } \bar{p}c_1$, which is logically equivalent to c_1. Act a_ν can be transformed into c_1 in the same way. Hence, tree 1 is marked-set equivalent to the tree $c_1 > c_1$.

(b) Tree 21 is marked-set equivalent to the tree $c_1^* > c_1^*$ by a similar argument.
(c) By the logical equivalence axiom, neither of the trees $c_1 > c_1$ and $c_1^* > c_1^*$ belongs to the marked set, and so they are marked-set equivalent.
(d) Trees 1 and 21 are thus marked-set equivalent by (a), (b), and (c).

Case 2: $\bar{p}_1$ is probabilistically possible.

(e) Trees 1 and 11 are marked-set equivalent by the normal form and logical equivalence axioms. If there are no probabilistically impossible universe descriptions, this is so because tree 1 is a logical simplification of the normal form of tree 11. If there are probabilistically impossible universe descriptions, corollary [8] must also be used. Note that this proof that trees 1 and 11 are marked-set equivalent is very similar to the proof of the reduction theorem [9] (p. 276).
(f) Trees 21 and 11′ are likewise marked-set equivalent by the normal form and logical equivalence axioms.
(g) Since trees 12 and 12′ are of the same type, trees 11 and 11′ are marked-set equivalent by the invariance axiom.
(h) Trees 1 and 21 are thus marked-set equivalent by (e), (f), and (g).

Combining these two cases we have: Trees 1 and 21 of Figure 31 are marked-set equivalent. Though $M = 3$ and $N = 4$ in these trees, the same proof applies to any M and N, with minor modifications if either is 1. Hence $(a_\nu > a_\mu) \equiv (a_\nu^* > a_\mu^*)$. But this is truth-functionally equivalent to theorem [10], which was to be proved.

Our next theorem states how the comparative value of two consequences c_1 and c_2 is related to the comparative value of the mixed acts $pc_1 \vee \bar{p}c$ and $pc_2 \vee \bar{p}c$, where c is any consequence.

[11a] $[(p \neq r\bar{r})(c_1 > c_2)] \equiv [(pc_1 \vee \bar{p}c) > (pc_2 \vee \bar{p}c)]$

[11b] $[(p = r\bar{r}) \vee (c_1 = c_2)] \equiv [(pc_1 \vee \bar{p}c) = (pc_2 \vee \bar{p}c)]$.

The essential content of this theorem may be seen by considering the following application of it. Suppose that a subject prefers c_1 to c_2 and that p is probabilistically possible. Then by [11a] he "prefers" the partial act pc_1 to the partial act pc_2.

The proof of [11a] is as follows. We first prove the lemma

(a) $(p \neq r\bar{r}) \supset \{(c_1 > c_2) \equiv [(pc_1 \vee \bar{p}c) > (pc_2 \vee \bar{p}c)]\}$.

The complete proof is given in Figure 32. Now formula (a) truth-functionally implies

(b) $[(p \neq r\bar{r})(c_1 > c_2)] \supset [(pc_1 \vee \bar{p}c) > (pc_2 \vee \bar{p}c)]$.

This establishes [11a] from left to right. To prove it in the opposite direction we use the lemma

(c) $[p = r\bar{r}] \supset [(pc_1 \vee \bar{p}c) = (pc_2 \vee \bar{p}c)]$.

This follows directly from corollary [8]. Now assume

(d) $(pc_1 \vee \bar{p}c) > (pc_2 \vee \bar{p}c)$.

This implies a denial of the consequent of (c), and hence we have

(e) $p \neq r\bar{r}$.

But (d), (e), and (a) yield

(f) $c_1 > c_2$.

Steps (d), (e), and (f) establish, by conditional proof,

(g) $[(pc_1 \vee \bar{p}c) > (pc_2 \vee \bar{p}c)] \supset [(p \neq r\bar{r})(c_1 > c_2)]$.

Theorem [11a] is a simple truth-functional combination of (b) and (g).

Theorem [11b] is a truth-functional and substitutional variant of [11a]. Negate both sides of [11a], obtaining

(h) $[(p = r\bar{r}) \vee (c_2 \geqq c_1)] \equiv [(pc_2 \vee \bar{p}c) \geqq (pc_1 \vee \bar{p}c)]$.

Interchange "c_2" and "c_1" in (h), to get

(i) $[(p = r\bar{r}) \vee (c_1 \geqq c_2)] \equiv [(pc_1 \vee \bar{p}c) \geqq (pc_2 \vee \bar{p}c)]$.

Conjoin the left-hand sides of (h) and (i), reduce, and conjoin the right-hand sides of (h) and (i). The result is

(j) $[(p = r\bar{r}) \vee (c_1 = c_2)] \equiv [(pc_1 \vee \bar{p}c) = (pc_2 \vee \bar{p}c)]$,

or theorem [11b]. This completes the proof of theorem [11].

This theorem and its proof are easily extended to cover a partition of the partial act $\bar{p}c$ into further partial acts.

[11a′] $[(p \neq r\bar{r})(c_1 > c_1^*)] \equiv \left[\left(p_1c_1 \vee \sum_{n=2}^{N} p_nc_n\right) > \left(p_1c_1^* \vee \sum_{n=2}^{N} p_nc_n\right)\right]$

[11b′] $[(p = r\bar{r}) \vee (c_1 = c^*{}_1)] \equiv$

$$\left[\left(p_1c_1 \vee \sum_{n=2}^{N} p_nc_n\right) = \left(p_1c_1^* \vee \sum_{n=2}^{N} p_nc_n\right)\right] .$$

But for our purposes the simpler form [11] will suffice.

The next theorem shows how a mixture of two consequences is valued in comparison to these consequences.

[12a] $[c_1 \geqq c_2] \supset [c_1 \geqq (pc_1 \vee \bar{p}c_2) \geqq c_2]$

[12b] $[(p \neq r\bar{r})(\bar{p} \neq r\bar{r})(c_1 > c_2)] \supset [c_1 > (pc_1 \vee \bar{p}c_2) > c_2]$.

Thus the value of the mixture of two consequences is bounded by the values of the consequences, and if each alternative is probabilistically possible, the value of the mixture falls between the values of the consequences.

To prove [12a], start with formula (i) of the proof of theorem [11] above. By truth-function theory, formula (i) yields

(a) $(c_1 \geqq c_2) \supset [(pc_1 \vee \bar{p}c) \geqq (pc_2 \vee \bar{p}c)]$.

Substitute "c_2" for "c" and reduce by logical equivalence to get

(b) $(c_1 \geqq c_2) \supset [(pc_1 \vee \bar{p}c_2) \geqq c_2]$.

Substitute "$\bar{p}$" for "p" and "c_1" for "c" in (a) and reduce by logical equivalence to obtain

(c) $(c_1 \geqq c_2) \supset [c_1 \geqq (pc_1 \vee \bar{p}c_2)]$.

Theorem [12a] is a combination of (b) and (c). Now substitute "c_2" for "c" in [11a] and use the logical equivalence axiom and truth-function theory to obtain

(d) $[(p \neq r\bar{r})(c_1 > c_2)] \supset [(pc_1 \vee \bar{p}c_2) > c_2]$.

Finally, substitute "$\bar{p}$" for "p" and "c_1" for "c" in [11a] and use logical equivalence and truth-function theory to obtain

(e) $[(\bar{p} \neq r\bar{r})(c_1 > c_2)] \supset [c_1 > (pc_1 \vee \bar{p}c_2)]$.

Theorem [12b] is a combination of (d) and (e). This completes the proof of theorem [12].

5.4.3 Comparative probabilities

The dyadic preference relation "$p \geqq q$" is a comparative probability relation, expressing the subject's estimate that p is at least as likely as q. In contrast, the monadic function $\mathbf{P}(r)$ expresses the subject's numerical estimate of the likelihood of a single statement. We shall prove several more theorems about "$p \geqq q$" in the present subsection. When the eighth axiom is added, it will convert the dyadic relation "$p \geqq q$" into the monadic function $\mathbf{P}(r)$ (sec. 5.5).

The next theorems, [13], [14], and [15], contain comparative versions of some theorems of the calculus of probability.

[13a] $(p \geqq q) \equiv (\bar{q} \geqq \bar{p})$

[13b] $[p = (r \vee \bar{r})] \equiv [\bar{p} = (r\bar{r})]$.

Statement [13a] is a comparative form of the subtraction principle (p. 46), while [13b] is the comparative analog of the theorem $[\mathbf{P}(q) = 1] \equiv [\mathbf{P}(\bar{q}) = 0]$.

To prove [13a] from left to right we assume $p \geqq q$. By definition [6a], instantiation, and the fact that $C_u > C_z$, we have

(a) $(pC_u \vee \bar{p}C_z) \geqq (qC_u \vee \bar{q}C_z)$.

Exchange of logical equivalents by [II] gives

(b) $[pqC_u \vee p\bar{q}C_u \vee \bar{p}qC_z \vee \bar{p}\bar{q}C_z] \geqq [pqC_u \vee \bar{p}qC_u \vee p\bar{q}C_z \vee \bar{p}\bar{q}C_z]$.

Now apply the partial act theorem [10] twice, first replacing "pqC_u" by "pqC_z" and then replacing "$\bar{p}\bar{q}C_z$" by "$\bar{p}\bar{q}C_u$," to get

(c) $[pqC_z \vee p\bar{q}C_u \vee \bar{p}qC_z \vee \bar{p}\bar{q}C_u] \geqq [pqC_z \vee \bar{p}qC_u \vee p\bar{q}C_z \vee \bar{p}\bar{q}C_u]$.

Exchanging logical equivalents again gives

(d) $(\bar{q}C_u \vee \bar{\bar{q}}C_z) \geqq (\bar{p}C_u \vee \bar{\bar{p}}C_z)$.

Combining this with $C_u > C_z$ and using existential quantification, we obtain

(e) $(\exists c_1)(\exists c_2)\{(c_1 > c_2)[(\bar{q}c_1 \vee \bar{\bar{q}}c_2) \geqq (\bar{p}c_1 \vee \bar{\bar{p}}c_2)]\}$.

The formula $\bar{q} \geqq \bar{p}$ now follows by the ordering of uncertainties axiom and definition [6a]. A similar argument can be repeated going from right to left. This completes the proof of [13a]. Part [13b] follows as a corollary.

The next theorem states that a probabilistic necessity is more likely than a probabilistic impossibility and that every other likelihood falls in between.

[14a] $(r \vee \bar{r}) > (r\bar{r})$

[14b] $(r \vee \bar{r}) \geqq p \geqq (r\bar{r})$.

This is analogous to the principle that every probability is in the range one to zero.

To prove the first part, we start with

(a) $C_u > C_z$.

By axiom [II] this is logically equivalent to

(b) $[(r \vee \bar{r})C_u \vee (r\bar{r})C_z] > [(r\bar{r})C_u \vee (r \vee \bar{r})C_z]$.

Formulas (a) and (b) can be conjoined and existentially quantified with respect to "C_u" and "C_z" to give [14a] by definition [6b]. To prove the second part we first substitute "C_u" for "c_1" and "C_z" for "c_2" in [12a], obtaining

(c) $[C_u \geqq C_z] \supset [C_u \geqq (pC_u \vee \bar{p}C_z) \geqq C_z]$.

The antecedent is implied by (a), and so we have

(d) $C_u \geqq (pC_u \vee \bar{p}C_z) \geqq C_z$.

This is logically equivalent to

(e) $[(r \vee \bar{r})C_u \vee (r\bar{r})C_z] \geqq (pC_u \vee \bar{p}C_z) \geqq [(r\bar{r})C_u \vee (r \vee \bar{r})C_z]$.

This can be conjoined with (a) and existentially quantified with respect to "C_u" and "C_z" to give [14b] by the ordering of uncertainties axiom and definition [6a].

The next theorem contains a comparative analog of the special addition principle of the calculus of probability (pp. 51, 93), and two corollaries.

[15a] $\{\sim\Diamond(ps)\sim\Diamond(qs)\} \supset \{(p \geqq q) \equiv [(p \vee s) \geqq (q \vee s)]\}$

[15b] $[\sim\Diamond(qs)(q \neq r\bar{r})] \supset [(q \vee s) > s]$

[15c] $p \geqq pq$.

The last part is a comparative analog of $\mathbf{P}(p) \geqq \mathbf{P}(pq)$, which follows from the multiplication axiom of the calculus of probability and the fact that probabilities fall in the range zero to one (pp. 40, 46).

The proof of [15a] is as follows. We first assume $\sim\Diamond(ps)$, $\sim\Diamond(qs)$, and $p \geqq q$ and show that $(p \vee s) \geqq (q \vee s)$. From definition [6a] and $C_u > C_z$ we obtain

(a) $(pC_u \vee \bar{p}C_z) \geqq (qC_u \vee \bar{q}C_z)$.

The first two assumptions are equivalent to

(b) $\Box\{\bar{p} \equiv (s \vee \bar{p}\bar{s})\}$

(c) $\Box\{\bar{q} \equiv (s \vee \bar{q}\bar{s})\}$,

respectively. Exchanging logical equivalents (b) and (c) in (a) gives

(d) $[pC_u \vee sC_z \vee \bar{p}\bar{s}C_z] \geqq [qC_u \vee sC_z \vee \bar{q}\bar{s}C_z]$.

By the partial act theorem, "sC_z" may be replaced by "sC_u" on both sides.

(e) $[pC_u \vee sC_u \vee \bar{p}\bar{s}C_z] \geqq [qC_u \vee sC_u \vee \bar{q}\bar{s}C_z]$.

This is logically equivalent to

(f) $[(p \vee s)C_u \vee \sim(p \vee s)C_z] \geqq [(q \vee s)C_u \vee \sim(q \vee s)C_z]$.

This, conjoined with $C_u > C_z$, yields

(g) $(p \vee s) \geqq (q \vee s)$

by theorem [5] and definition [6a]. Thus, steps (a) to (g) establish

(h) $\{\sim\Diamond(ps)\sim\Diamond(qs)(p \geqq q)\} \supset \{(p \vee s) \geqq (q \vee s)\}$.

The preceding argument can be reversed to give

(i) $\{\sim\Diamond(ps)\sim\Diamond(qs)[(p \vee s) \geqq (q \vee s)]\} \supset (p \geqq q)$.

Theorem [15a] is a truth-functional combination of (h) and (i).

To prove [15b], substitute "$r\bar{r}$" for "p" in [15a], getting

(j) $\{\sim\Diamond(r\bar{r}s)\sim\Diamond(qs)\} \supset \{(r\bar{r} \geqq q) \equiv [(r\bar{r} \vee s) \geqq (q \vee s)]\}$.

Now

(k) $\sim\Diamond(r\bar{r}s)$.

Moreover, it follows from [14b] that

(m) $(q \neq r\bar{r}) \supset \sim(r\bar{r} \geqq q)$.

Combining (j), (k), and (m) truth-functionally we obtain

(n) $[\sim\Diamond(qs)(q \neq r\bar{r})] \supset [(q \vee s) > (r\bar{r} \vee s)]$.

Drop the rightmost occurrence of "$r\bar{r}$" by the logical equivalence axiom, and the result is theorem [15b].

To prove [15c], substitute "pq" for "q" and "$\bar{p}$" for "s" in [15a].

(t) $\{\sim\Diamond(p\bar{p})\sim\Diamond(pq\bar{p})\} \supset \{(p \geqq pq) \equiv [(p \vee \bar{p}) \geqq (pq \vee \bar{p})]$.

The antecedent is obviously true, and so

(u) $(p \geqq pq) \equiv [(p \vee \bar{p}) \geqq (pq \vee \bar{p})]$.

The right-hand side of this equivalence is true by [14b], and so

(v) $p \geqq pq$.

This completes the proof of theorem [15].

Our final theorem in this section shows that the value of a mixed act depends on both the likelihoods of the component statements and the values of the component consequences.

[16a] $[(p > q)(c_1 > c_2) \vee (q > p)(c_2 > c_1)] \equiv [(pc_1 \vee \bar{p}c_2) > (qc_1 \vee \bar{q}c_2)]$

[16b] $[(p = q) \vee (c_1 = c_2)] \equiv [(pc_1 \vee \bar{p}c_2) = (qc_1 \vee \bar{q}c_2)]$.

The first part says that for a mixed act $pc_1 \vee \bar{p}c_2$ to be more valuable than $qc_1 \vee \bar{q}c_2$, it is necessary and sufficient that the prize be staked on the more likely proposition. The second part states that the subject is indifferent between $pc_1 \vee \bar{p}c_2$ and $qc_1 \vee \bar{q}c_2$ if and only if he is indifferent either between p and q or between c_1 and c_2.

We first prove [16a] from left to right. By definition [6b] and theorem [5], we have

(a) $[(p > q)(c_1 > c_2)] \supset [(pc_1 \vee \bar{p}c_2) > (qc_1 \vee \bar{q}c_2)]$

(b) $[(\bar{p} > \bar{q})(c_2 > c_1)] \supset [(\bar{p}c_2 \vee \bar{\bar{p}}c_1) > (\bar{q}c_2 \vee \bar{\bar{q}}c_1)]$.

By [13a] and the logical equivalence axiom (the law of double negation), (b) becomes

(c) $[(q > p)(c_2 > c_1)] \supset [(pc_1 \vee \bar{p}c_2) > (qc_1 \vee \bar{q}c_2)]$.

Combining (a) and (c) we obtain

(d) $[(p > q)(c_1 > c_2) \vee (q > p)(c_2 > c_1)] \supset [(pc_1 \vee \bar{p}c_2) > (qc_1 \vee \bar{q}c_2)]$.

To prove [16a] from right to left we first derive a corollary of [11b]. Substituting "c_2" for "c" and making some truth-functional manipulations, we get

(e) $[c_1 = c_2] \supset [(pc_1 \vee \bar{p}c_2) = c_2]$.

Replacing "p" by "q" gives

(f) $[c_1 = c_2] \supset [(qc_1 \vee \bar{q}c_2) = c_2]$.

Combining (e) and (f) gives

(g) $[c_1 = c_2] \supset [(pc_1 \vee \bar{p}c_2) = (qc_1 \vee \bar{q}c_2)]$.

This is the corollary we need. Now assume the right-hand side of [16a].

(h) $(pc_1 \vee \bar{p}c_2) > (qc_1 \vee \bar{q}c_2)$.

This contradicts the consequent of corollary (g), and hence

(i) $(c_1 > c_2) \vee (c_2 > c_1)$.

Using (h), one can establish

(j) $(c_1 > c_2) \supset (p > q)$

by existential quantification and definition [6b]. Following the same procedure and also using the law of double negation, we can obtain

(k) $(c_2 > c_1) \supset (q > p)$.

It follows from (i), (j), and (k) that

(m) $(p > q)(c_1 > c_2) \vee (q > p)(c_2 > c_1)$.

Since (m) has been derived from (h), we have proven

(n) $[(pc_1 \vee \bar{p}c_2) > (qc_1 \vee \bar{q}c_2)] \supset$
$[(p > q)(c_1 > c_2) \vee (q > p)(c_2 > c_1)]$.

Theorem [16a] follows directly from (d) and (n).

Theorem [16b] is a truth-functional and substitutional corollary of [16a]. Negating both sides of [16a] and performing some truth-functional operations, we obtain

(t) $[\sim\{(p > q)(c_1 > c_2)\} \,\&\, \sim\{(q > p)(c_2 > c_1)\}] \equiv$
$\sim[(pc_1 \vee \bar{p}c_2) > (qc_1 \vee \bar{q}c_2)]$.

Exchanging "p" and "q" in (t) gives

(u) $[\sim\{(q > p)(c_1 > c_2)\} \,\&\, \sim\{(p > q)(c_2 > c_1)\}] \equiv$
$\sim[(qc_1 \vee \bar{q}c_2) > (pc_1 \vee \bar{p}c_2)]$.

The conjunction of the left-hand sides of (t) and (u) is logically equivalent to

(v) $(p = q) \vee (c_1 = c_2)$.

The conjunction of the right-hand sides of (t) and (u) is logically equivalent to

(w) $(pc_1 \vee \bar{p}c_2) = (qc_1 \vee \bar{q}c_2)$.

Hence

(x) $[(p = q) \vee (c_1 = c_2)] \equiv [(pc_1 \vee \bar{p}c_2) = (qc_1 \vee \bar{q}c_2)]$,

which is what was to be proved.

We have derived sufficient theorems from axioms [I]–[VII] to give the reader an intuitive grasp of the comparative structure for preferences (values) and uncertainties (probabilities) that these axioms yield. Many of these theorems will be used in the next section.

5.5 The Calculus of Choice—Quantitative

5.5.1 Utilities and quantitative probabilities

In this section we shall formulate and discuss the last axiom and the main theorem of the calculus of choice. The last axiom converts the qualitative, comparative structure of the previous axioms into a quantitative structure, and is therefore called the "quantitative axiom." It will be presented in two forms: a symmetrical form [VIII] and a weaker, nonsymmetrical form [VIII′]. The main theorem is numbered [IX] or [IX′] according to whether [VIII] or [VIII′] is used. This theorem states that a subject whose choices conform to the calculus of choice is in effect maximizing utility and using the calculus of probability.

The symmetrical [VIII] is much simpler than the nonsymmetrical [VIII′], and the proof of [IX] is correspondingly simpler than the proof of [IX′]. Indeed, the proof of [IX′] is highly technical, requiring mathematics beyond the scope of this book. On the other hand, [VIII] is philosophically objectionable because it postulates an unlimited amount of symmetry in the universe (see p. 311), and so it is important for the reader to be convinced that [IX′] holds.

To resolve this dilemma, we shall discuss both the symmetrical and the nonsymmetrical approaches. We state and explain [VIII] and [IX] in the present subsection and prove [IX] in the next. In the last subsection we explain [VIII′] and reduce [IX′] to the main theorem of Savage's axiomatic system for probability and utility.

The symmetrical form of the quantitative axiom uses the notion of an "equipartition": a division of the realm of logical possibilities into mutually exclusive, jointly exhaustive, and "equally likely" alternatives (cf. theorem [15] of p. 52). This concept is defined in terms of the qualitative notion of "equally likely" of definition [6c] (p. 271): "$p =_i q$" means that given information i, the subject is indifferent between staking a prize on p and on q.

A sequence of statements $p_1, p_2, \ldots, p_M$ is a *partition of size M* ($M \geqq 2$) conditional on i if and only if (1) $p_1, p_2, \ldots, p_M$ are mutually exclusive and jointly exhaustive on i, and (2) no p_m is contradictory relative to i. A partition $p_1, p_2, \ldots, p_M$ is an *equipartition* on condition i if and only if $p_m =_i p_n$ for every m, n from 1 to M. The condition i may be the general information Γ of the choice basis, as in the next theorem. Figure 11 expresses an equipartition of size 2^2, assuming that the subject prizes a Polish gold ducat.

A normal form act is an assignment of consequences to the alternatives of the partition. If the partition is also an equipartition, then these consequences can be permuted without changing the value of the act.

[17] Let $p_1, p_2, \ldots, p_M$ be an equipartition, $c_1, c_2, \ldots, c_M$ a sequence of consequence names, and $c'_1, c'_2, \ldots, c'_M$ a permutation of this sequence. Then

$$\sum_{m=1}^{M} p_m c_m = \sum_{m=1}^{M} p_m c'_m \quad .$$

Proof: The act $\Sigma_{m=1}^{M} p_m c_m$ can be transformed into the act $\Sigma_{m=1}^{M} p_m c'_m$ by a succession of exchanges according to the following lemma.

Lemma: Consider two normal form acts $a =_{df} \Sigma_{m=1}^{M} p_m c_m$ and $b =_{df} \Sigma_{m=1}^{M} p_m c'_m$ that make the same assignment of consequences to the partition $p_1, p_2, \ldots, p_M$ except that for some i and j ($1 \leqq i, j \leqq M$) the consequences assigned to p_i and p_j in a are exchanged in b. If $p_i = p_j$, then $a = b$. (Two kinds of equality are used in this lemma and its proof and are distinguished symbolically. Definitional identity is symbolized by "$=_{df}$" and indifference between acts, consequences, and statements is symbolized by "$=$".)

Proof of lemma. For notational simplicity we will assume that $i = 1$ and $j = 2$, so that $p_1 = p_2$. Since acts a and b then make the same assignment of consequences to the partition $p_1, p_2, \ldots, p_M$ except that c_1 and c_2 are interchanged, the following definitional identities will hold.

(α)
$$a =_{df} p_1 c_1 \vee p_2 c_2 \vee \sum_{m=3}^{M} p_m c_m$$

$$b =_{df} p_1 c_2 \vee p_2 c_1 \vee \sum_{m=3}^{M} p_m c_m \quad .$$

We are to prove that if $p_1 = p_2$, then $a = b$. The proof is divided into three cases.

Case 1: $c_1 > c_2$. Let $a^* =_{df} p_1c_1 \vee \bar{p}_1c_2$ and let $b^* =_{df} p_2c_1 \vee \bar{p}_2c_2$. Since $p_1 = p_2$ and c_1 is prized over c_2, $a^* = b^*$ by theorem [6c]. By the logical equivalence axiom

$$(\beta) \qquad a^* = p_1c_1 \vee p_2c_2 \vee \sum_{m=3}^{M} p_mc_2$$

$$b^* = p_1c_2 \vee p_2c_1 \vee \sum_{m=3}^{M} p_mc_2 \quad .$$

Apply the partial act theorem to a^* and b^* for each $m = 3, 4, \ldots, M$, replacing "p_mc_2" of a^* and b^* by "p_mc_m." Each application preserves indifference ($=$), and at the end the subject is indifferent between a and b by (α) above. This establishes $a = b$.

Case 2: $c_1 < c_2$. The proof is the same as for case 1, with "c_1" and "c_2" exchanged throughout.

Case 3: $c_1 = c_2$. The lemma follows by theorem [11b].

These three cases are exhaustive, and so the lemma is proved.

The *symmetrical form of the quantitative axiom* postulates an infinite sequence of equipartitions of ever-increasing size and fineness.

[VIII] There is an integer b ($b \geqq 2$) such that for every integer d ($d \geqq 1$) there is an equipartition of size b^d.

Suppose, for example, the subject believes that a certain coin and tossing procedure are fair in the sense that all tail-head sequences of length n are equally likely. Then the axiom is satisfied, with $b = 2$. Axiom [VIII] will be compared with the nonsymmetrical form [VIII′] later (pp. 299–302). Both forms of the quantitative axiom require that the marked set of trees be infinite.

There are now sufficient axioms to establish the *main theorem.* Roughly put, this theorem states that if a complete set of choice trees is marked according to the rules of the calculus of choice, every choice so made will in fact maximize utility. Since the consequent of the theorem is long and involved, it is presented separately from the antecedent.

[IX] *Antecedent*: A marked set of trees satisfies axioms [I]–[VIII].

Consequent: There exist two functions

(1) a unique degree-of-belief function $P(q, i)$

(2) a consequence valuation function $U(c)$, unique up to an increasing linear transformation,

such that

(a) $P(q, i)$ satisfies the calculus of probability

(b) every choice made at a probabilistically possible choice point with information i maximizes the function

$$\sum_{n=1}^{N} P(q_n, i)U(a_n, iq_n) \quad .$$

We next explain the technical terms of the consequent.

A *degree-of-belief function* $P(q, i)$ assigns a real number to each pair $\langle q, i\rangle$ of statements of the choice basis *in which i is probabilistically possible.* A degree-of-belief function $P(q, i)$ "satisfies" the calculus of probability if and only if it is compatible with the axioms of the calculus (pp. 40–41). If there are finitely many statements in the choice basis, a degree-of-belief function $P(q, i)$ can be expressed as a conjunction $\mathcal{P}$ of atomic probability statements. Then $P(q, i)$ "satisfies the calculus of probability" if and only if the conjunction of $\mathcal{P}$ with the axioms of the calculus is logically possible. A degree-of-belief function $P(q, i)$ is not defined when i is probabilistically impossible. Consequently, the main theorem does not say anything about the choices made by the subject at probabilistically impossible choice points. This does not matter, since the subject feels sure that these points will never be reached in the payoff process.

A *consequence valuation function* $U(c)$ is a function that assigns a real number to every consequence of the choice basis. Any two consequence valuation functions $U(c)$ and $U'(c)$ that are related by the equation

$$U(c) = \rho U'(c) + \sigma \qquad \text{for } \rho > 0$$

are said to be the same "to within an increasing linear transformation" (see p. 185).

These functions $P(q, i)$ and $U(c)$ appear in the "book" theorem under different names (p. 214). In adopting a set of partial beliefs, the subject is, in effect, choosing a degree-of-belief function. And in assigning a stake $S(c)$ to each possible outcome c, the devil is, in effect, choosing a consequence valuation function. Moreover, the "utility" function $\Sigma_{n=1}^{N} P(q_n, i)U(a_n, iq_n)$ plays a key role in the theory of each game. For the marking game, this is clear from the main theorem [IX]. In the "book" theorem game, let $c_1, c_2, \ldots, c_m$ be the statements of set Λ. The subject's payoff in any universe u turns out to be the sum of the stakes $S(c')$ over all statements c' of Λ that are true in u, less the quantity $\Sigma_{m=1}^{M} P(c_m)S(c_m)$. To avoid his payoffs being negative in every universe, the subject must make his set of partial beliefs conform to the calculus of probability. Thus the "book" theorem can be expressed as a maximizing-minimizing theorem: Assume that the devil will seek to maximize his gain; then, a set of partial beliefs will minimize the subject's loss (to the extent of avoiding a negative payoff) if and only if that set of partial beliefs satisfies the calculus of inductive probability.

The last clause of our main theorem states that every choice of the marked set maximizes the function $\Sigma_{n=1}^{N} P(q_n, i)U(a_n, iq_n)$. Since $P(q, i)$ satisfies the calculus of probability, this last function *is* a utility function, and so the subject is behaving as if he were maximizing utility. To show that the concept of utility is not presupposed by the theorem, we give an algorithm (see p. 388) for assigning the utility function $\Sigma_{n=1}^{N} P(q_n, i)U(a_n, iq_n)$ to every point of a tree in such a way that this function is maximized at each choice point. See Figure 33.

But first, note the presence of condition i in $P(q_n, i)$ and of condition iq_n in $U(a_n, iq_n)$. The need for those conditions may be seen by calculating the utility of a subtree of the form $q_1a_1 \vee q_2a_2 \vee \ldots \vee q_na_n$, where the information at the root of the subtree is i. The utility of each a_n clearly depends on both i and q_n, and the probability that point a_n will be reached in the payoff process clearly depends on i.

The algorithm for assigning a utility function to every part of a tree so that this function is maximized at each choice point starts with the given functions $P(q, i)$ and $U(c)$. First, trim the tree (p. 275) and convert it into a logically equivalent tree in which choice and chance points alternate (p. 264). Second, apply the given functions to the tree by substituting the value of each statement and consequence in the trimmed tree, as in Figure 33c. Third, proceeding from the bottom of the tree to the root, assign a value of $U(a, i)$ to every point a of the tree as follows. The value of $U(a, i)$ at consequence point c is $U(c)$. If a' is a chance point (with information i) whose dashed lines $q_1, q_2, \ldots, q_N$ terminate in points $a_1, a_2, \ldots, a_N$, respectively, assign

$$U(a', i) = \sum_{n=1}^{N} P(q_n, i)U(a_n, iq_n) \quad .$$

Finally, if a' is a choice point (with information i) whose solid lines terminate in points $a_1, a_2, \ldots, a_N$, assign

$$U(a', i) = \text{Max}\,\{U(a_1, i), U(a_2, i), \ldots, U(a_N, i)\} \quad ,$$

or the maximum of the values of the $U(a_n, i)$. This completes the algorithm. In Figure 33c the value of $U(a, i)$ at each non-consequence point is written in the box attached to that point.

The last clause of the main theorem can now be explained in terms of this algorithm. *Every choice of the act tree maximizes the function*

$$\sum_{n=1}^{N} P(q_n, i)U(a_n, iq_n)$$

if and only if, at each marked choice point of the act tree with information i, all alternatives of the maximum value $U(a, i)$ are selected by arrows.

This concludes our exegesis of the main theorem [IX]. Very briefly, the theorem states that if a subject obeys the rules of the calculus of choice, he is behaving as if he were using the calculus of probability and the rule of maximizing utility, whether or not he is doing so consciously. Notice that by this theorem, the calculus of inductive probability is, in a certain sense, a subsystem of the calculus of choice.

We turn next to the proof of the main theorem. The reader who accepts this theorem on faith can proceed directly to Section 5.6 (The Pragmatic Theory of Inductive Probability).

5.5.2 *Proof of the main theorem*

In this subsection we present a proof of the main theorem [IX]. The proof is sometimes sketchy and informal, though it could be filled out to make a rigorous proof. Sufficient detail is offered to convince the general reader and also to give him some insight into the mathematical structure of a marked set that satisfies the axioms of the calculus of choice. Our philosophical interest is in the main theorem, rather than its proof, and in the calculus of choice as an interpreted, rather than formal, system.

Let $\mathfrak{M}$ be a marked set of trees satisfying the antecedent of theorem [IX] (p. 288), that is, all the axioms and theorems of the calculus of choice. We will show that $\mathfrak{M}$ satisfies the consequent of [IX].

Assume without loss of generality that axiom [VIII] is satisfied for the binary case ($b = 2$), and let E_d be an equipartition of size 2^d ($d = 1, 2, 3, \ldots$). Form the sequence

(1) $E_\infty = \langle E_1, E_2, E_3, \ldots \rangle$.

Each equipartition E_d is a refinement of its predecessors in the following sense. Let

(2) $E_d = \langle Q_1^d, Q_2^d, \ldots, Q_M^d \rangle$ for $d = 1, 2, \ldots$ and $M = 2^d$.

Define a new partition by successively disjoining the alternatives of E_d pairwise, obtaining

(3) $Q_m^{d-1} = Q_n^d \vee Q_{n+1}^d$ where $n = 2m - 1$, for $m = 1, 2, \ldots, 2^{d-1}$ and $d > 1$.

It follows from theorems [10] and [17] that (3) is the equipartition E_{d-1}, and so E_d is a refinement of E_{d-1}. Hence the sequence of equipartitions E_∞ is a structure of ever-increasing fineness.

The proof of the main theorem [IX] will be divided into two parts: a long part [[A]], which establishes [IX] for normal form trees, and a short part [[B]], which extends this result to the marked set $\mathfrak{M}$.

[[A]] Let $\mathfrak{M}_{nf}$ be the subset of all normal form trees of the marked set $\mathfrak{M}$. We will show that since the antecedent of [IX] holds for $\mathfrak{M}$, the consequent holds for $\mathfrak{M}_{nf}$.

We extend every consequence valuation function $U(c)$ to cover the normal form acts of $\mathfrak{M}_{nf}$ by defining

(4) If $a = \sum_{n=1}^{N} p_n c_n$, then $U(a) = \sum_{n=1}^{N} P(p_n)U(c_n)$.

The choices of $\mathfrak{M}_{nf}$ reduce to pairwise comparisons by the subset axiom [III], and the last clause (b) of [IX] then reduces to

(5) $(a \geqq b) \equiv [U(a) \geq U(b)]$.

We express this more briefly as "maximizing the function $U(a)$."

The relation symbol "$\geqq$" is used in two different senses in formula (5). On the left it represents a preference relation between acts ("likes at least as much as"). On the right it represents a relation between real numbers ("is at least as large as"). It is clear from the kind of symbol flanking "$\geqq$" which sense is intended. The relation symbols "$>$" and "$=$" will also be used in these two ways.

To prove that the consequent of [IX] holds for $\mathfrak{M}_{nf}$, we will define a degree-of-belief function $P^*(q)$ and a consequence valuation function $U^*(c)$ for statements and consequences of $\mathfrak{M}_{nf}$ and show that

(a) $P^*(q)$ satisfies the calculus of probability

(b) every choice of $\mathfrak{M}_{nf}$ maximizes $U^*(a)$

(c) $P^*(q)$ and $U^*(c)$ are the only functions satisfying these conditions, except for increasing linear transformations of $U^*(c)$.

The proof is in three parts. In [[A-1]] we consider all trees of $\mathfrak{M}_{nf}$ constructed from two consequences C_u and C_z and the structure of equipartitions E_∞; in [[A-2]] we consider all trees of $\mathfrak{M}_{nf}$ constructed from C_u, C_z, and the statements of $\mathfrak{M}_{nf}$; and in [[A-3]] we consider the set of trees $\mathfrak{M}_{nf}$ itself.

[[A-1]] Let $\mathfrak{M}_1$ consist of all trees of $\mathfrak{M}_{nf}$ constructed from the choice basis consisting of two consequences C_u and C_z ($C_u > C_z$) and the structure of equipartitions E_∞.

The functions $U^*(c)$ and $P^*(q)$ are defined for $\mathfrak{M}_1$ as follows.

(6) $U^*(C_u) = 1$ and $U^*(C_z) = 0$.
$P^*(s\bar{s}) = 0$. If q_μ is logically equivalent to a disjunction of μ elements of E_d, then $P^*(q_\mu) = \mu/M$ (for $\mu = 1, 2, \ldots, M$; $M = 2^d$, $d = 1, 2, 3, \ldots$) .

Since each E_d is a refinement of its predecessors, the function $P^*(q)$ satisfies the calculus of probability (see p. 289).

We next construct from C_u, C_z, and E_∞ two further sequences S_∞ and A_∞ that will be useful as reference frames.

(7) $p_0^d = s\bar{s}$. $p_\mu^d = (Q_1^d \vee Q_2^d \vee \ldots \vee Q_\mu^d)$ for $\mu = 1, 2, \ldots, M$; $M = 2^d$
$S_d = \langle p_M^d, p_{M-1}^d, \ldots, p_1^d, p_0^d \rangle$ for $d = 1, 2, 3, \ldots$; $M = 2^d$
$S_\infty = \langle S_1, S_2, S_3, \ldots \rangle$.

(8) $a^d_\mu = p^d_\mu C_u \text{ v } \bar{p}^d_\mu C_z \quad \text{for } \mu = 0, 1, 2, \ldots, M; M = 2^d$

$$A_d = \langle a^d_M, a^d_{M-1}, \ldots, a^d_1, a^d_0 \rangle \quad \text{for } d = 1, 2, 3, \ldots; M = 2^d$$

$$A_\infty = \langle A_1, A_2, A_3, \ldots \rangle \quad .$$

For each d, S_d is a sequence of statements of decreasing likelihood and A_d is a sequence of acts of decreasing value. Since each E_d is a refinement of its predecessors, the same is true in an appropriate sense for each S_d and each A_d. Consequently, S_∞ and A_∞ are structures of ever-increasing fineness.

We show by means of A_∞ that every choice of $\mathfrak{M}_1$ maximizes $U^*(a)$. It will suffice to show this for arbitrary A_d.

It follows from definitions (4), (6), and (8), above, that $U^*(a^d_\mu) = \mu/M$ for $\mu = 0, 1, 2, \ldots, M$ ($M = 2^d$). By theorem [15b] and definition [6b], the subject prefers an earlier act of A_d to a later act, so that he is maximizing the function $U^*(a)$ with respect to these acts. By the equipartition theorem [17], the subject is indifferent, for fixed M, between any two acts of the form $\Sigma^M_{m=1} Q^d_m c_m$ that have the same number of occurrences of C_u (and the same number of occurrences of C_z). Hence every choice of $\mathfrak{M}_1$ maximizes $U^*(a)$.

It remains to show that, as so far defined, $P^*(q)$ and $U^*(c)$ satisfy the uniqueness conditions of theorem [IX]. Any values may be assigned to $U(C_u)$ and $U(C_z)$ provided that $U(C_u) > U(C_z)$, but the resultant function $U(c)$ will differ from $U^*(c)$ only in unit and origin. Hence $U^*(c)$ is unique up to an increasing linear transformation. The calculus of probability requires that $P^*(s\bar{s}) = 0$ and $P^*(s \text{ v } \bar{s}) = 1$. How, now, shall the unit interval be divided among the alternatives of E_d? $P^*(q)$ assigns the same value to every alternative. Suppose some other assignment $P'(q)$ were made. There would then be a Q^d_μ and a Q^d_ν such that $P'(Q^d_\mu) > P'(Q^d_\nu)$. To maximize the function $\Sigma^M_{m=1} P'(Q^d)U^*(c_m)$ the subject would then have to choose $Q^d_\mu C_u \text{ v } \bar{Q}^d_\mu C_z$ over $Q^d_\nu C_u \text{ v } \bar{Q}^d_\nu C_z$. But this contradicts the fact that $\langle Q^d_1, Q^d_2, \ldots, Q^d_M \rangle$ is an equipartition. Hence $P^*(q)$ is the only function $P(q)$ satisfying the consequent of [IX] with respect to $\mathfrak{M}_1$.

This shows that the consequent of [IX] holds for $\mathfrak{M}_1$.

[[A-2]] Let $\mathfrak{M}_2$ consist of all trees of $\mathfrak{M}_{nf}$ constructed from C_u, C_z, E_∞, and an arbitrary statement r. We will show that the consequent of [IX] holds for $\mathfrak{M}_2$.

By theorem [15b] the subject ranks the statements of each S_d in decreasing order of likelihood. By [14b] and the simple ordering of uncertainties [7], he must fit r into each S_d. Hence for each d (= 1, 2, 3, . . .) there is an integer μ (= M, $M - 1$, . . . , 2, or 1) such that

(9) $p^d_\mu \geqq r \geqq p^d_{\mu-1} \qquad (M = 2^d) \quad .$

There are two subcases to consider, one finite in character and easily handled, the other infinite and requiring the use of a limiting process.

Finite subcase: For some S_d one of the equalities in (9) holds. Then there are integers d ($d \geqq 1$) and μ ($0 \leqq \mu \leqq 2^d$) such that

$$(10) \qquad r = p^d_\mu \qquad .$$

By theorem [16b] the subject treats r and p^d_μ as exchangeable in normal form acts. Hence, to extend the consequent of [IX] from $\mathfrak{M}_1$ to $\mathfrak{M}_2$ (i.e., to ensure that the statements and consequences of $\mathfrak{M}_2$ satisfy the uniqueness and existence conditions of [IX]) it is necessary and sufficient to extend $P^*(q)$ by setting

$$(11) \qquad P^*(r) = P^*(p^d_\mu) = \mu/M \qquad .$$

Infinite subcase: For every S_d ($d = 1, 2, 3, \ldots$) there is a μ ($= M, M - 1, \ldots, 2$, or 1) such that

$$(12) \qquad p^d_\mu > r > p^d_{\mu-1} \qquad (1 \leqq \mu \leqq 2^d) \qquad .$$

Then for the function $U^*(a)$ to be maximized, $P^*(r)$ must satisfy the condition

$$(13) \qquad \frac{\mu}{M} > P^*(r) > \frac{\mu - 1}{M} \qquad ,$$

where, for each d ($= 1, 2, 3, \ldots$), μ and M have the values given by (12). Since each S_d is a refinement of its predecessors, condition (13) places narrower and narrower limits on $P^*(r)$ as d increases. To obtain a unique value for $P^*(r)$ we need to carry this condition to the limit. We do this in one fell swoop by defining, for each real number α ($0 \leqq \alpha \leqq 1$), a "pseudostatement" q_α such that $P^*(q_\alpha) = \alpha$. These q_α are limit points of sequences implicit in the structure S_∞.

Since each equipartition E_d is a refinement of its predecessors, there is a single process $T_1, T_2, T_3, \ldots, T_d, \ldots$ that generates all these equipartitions. For example, if "T_d" means that a coin falls tails on the dth toss, then E_d is the set of all tail-head sequences of length d. Using the process $T_1, T_2, T_3, \ldots$ we generate a single infinite partition $\langle B_1, B_2, B_3, \ldots \rangle$ such that $P^*(B_n) = 2^{-n}$ as follows.

(B_1)	$\bar{T}_1$	0.1
(B_2)	$T_1\bar{T}_2$	0.01
(B_3)	$T_1T_2\bar{T}_3$	0.001
	$\vdots$	
(B_n)	$T_1T_2 \ldots T_{n-1}\bar{T}_n$	2^{-n}
	$\vdots$	

The P^*-values are written on the right in binary notation. The partition $\langle B_1, B_2, B_3, \ldots \rangle$ happens to be the sequence of statements on which the Saint Petersburg paradox is based (p. 190). A similar sequence in decimal notation can be defined with reference to the throws of a regular icosahedron.

A "pseudostatement" is any disjunction (finite or infinite) of the B's (see p. 357). We define the P^*-value of a pseudostatement to be the sum of the P^*-values of its disjuncts. Let α be a real number such that $0 \leqq \alpha \leqq 1$, and let $0.\alpha_1\alpha_2\alpha_3 \ldots$ be its binary form. The pseudostatement q_α is defined by the rule: if $\alpha \neq 0$, then B_n is a disjunct of q_α if and only if $\alpha_n = 1$; $q_0 = s\bar{s}$. Clearly $P^*(q_\alpha) = \alpha$.

Let S^*_∞ be the set of q_α ranked in order of decreasing α $(1 \geqq \alpha \geqq 0)$. By [15b] this is also the subject's preference ranking of the q_α. By [14b] and the simple ordering of uncertainties [7], he must fit r into S^*_∞. Since there is a q_α for every real number α $(1 \geqq \alpha \geqq 0)$, there is a pseudostatement q_β such that $r = q_\beta$. To extend the consequent of [IX] from $\mathfrak{M}_1$ to $\mathfrak{M}_2$, it is necessary and sufficient to extend $P^*(q)$ by setting

(14) $$P^*(r) = P^*(q_\beta) = \beta \quad .$$

Thus S^*_∞ is a continuous reference frame of pseudostatements whose quantitative probabilities cover the range from 1 to 0. By the rule of simple ordering, each statement of the marked set fits into S^*_∞ exactly, and thereby acquires a quantitative probability.

This completes the proof that the consequent of [IX] holds for $\mathfrak{M}_2$. Let $\mathfrak{M}'_2$ consist of all trees of $\mathfrak{M}_{nf}$ constructed from the choice basis consisting of C_u, C_z, and the statements occurring in $\mathfrak{M}_{nf}$. Since r is an arbitrary statement of $\mathfrak{M}_{nf}$, the consequent of [IX] also holds for $\mathfrak{M}'_2$.

⟦A-3⟧ Let $\mathfrak{M}_3$ consist of all trees of $\mathfrak{M}_{nf}$ constructed from C_u, C_z, the statements of $\mathfrak{M}_{nf}$, and some arbitrary consequence c. This case divides into three, according to how the subject ranks c in comparison to C_u and C_z.

⟦A-3a⟧ $C_u \geqq c \geqq C_z$

⟦A-3b⟧ $c > C_u > C_z$

⟦A-3c⟧ $C_u > C_z > c$.

⟦A-3a⟧ Consider A_∞ as defined in (8). It was shown earlier that the subject maximizes $U^*(a)$ in choosing among the acts of A_∞.

Now a_0^d is logically equivalent to C_z, and for $M = 2^d$, a_M^d is logically equivalent to C_u. By the simple ordering of consequences, the subject must fit c into each A_d. Hence, for each d $(= 1, 2, 3, \ldots)$ there is an integer μ $(= M, M-1, \ldots, 2, 1)$ such that

(15) $$a_\mu^d \geqq c \geqq a_{\mu-1}^d \qquad (M = 2^d).$$

As in dealing with (9), we consider two subcases.

Finite subcase: For some A_d one of the equalities in (15) holds. Then there are integers d ($d \geqq 1$) and μ ($0 \leqq \mu \leqq 2^d$) such that

(16) $$c = a^d_\mu \quad .$$

For $U^*(a)$ to be maximized it must have the same value for acts between which the subject is indifferent; so we extend the function $U^*(a)$ to cover c by setting

(17) $$U^*(c) = U^*(a^d_\mu) = \mu/M \quad .$$

This fits the consequence c into $\mathfrak{M}'_2$ in such a way that the subject's choices among c and the acts of $\mathfrak{M}'_2$ maximize $U^*(a)$.

This does not extend the consequent of [IX] to cover all choices of $\mathfrak{M}_{nf}$ involving c, C_u, and C_z, however, for not all of these choices are of form (15). There are other choices involving mixed acts of the forms $rc \vee \bar{r}C_z$ and $rc \vee \bar{r}C_u$, and we must consider whether these clauses satisfy the consequent of [IX]. Case ⟦A-2⟧ also relates every statement r of $\mathfrak{M}_{nf}$ to S_∞, and so it suffices to consider the set of acts constructed from c, C_u, C_z, and the elements of an arbitrary equipartition E_d.

The details of this are rather complicated; we will limit ourselves to a simple, but typical, case. Let pq, $p\bar{q}$, $\bar{p}q$, $\bar{p}\bar{q}$ be an equipartition and let $c = pC_u \vee \bar{p}C_z$. Consider the mixed acts $qc \vee \bar{q}C_z$ and $pqC_u \vee \overline{pq}C_z$. The U^*-values of these acts are:

$$U^*(c) = U^*(pC_u \vee \bar{p}C_z) = P^*(p)U^*(C_u) + P^*(\bar{p})U^*(C_z) = .5$$
$$U^*(qc \vee \bar{q}C_z) = P^*(q)U^*(c) + P^*(\bar{q})U^*(C_z) = .25$$
$$U^*(pqC_u \vee \overline{pq}C_z) = P^*(pq)U^*(C_u) + P^*(\overline{pq})U^*(C_z) = .25 \quad .$$

Hence if the subject's choices are to maximize the function $U^*(a)$, the subject must be indifferent between $qc \vee \bar{q}C_z$ and $pqC_u \vee \overline{pq}C_z$. The following theorem shows that he is.

[18] Let pq, $p\bar{q}$, $\bar{p}q$, $\bar{p}\bar{q}$ be an equipartition. If $c = pC_u \vee \bar{p}C_z$, then $$(qc \vee \bar{q}C_z) = (pqC_u \vee \overline{pq}C_z) \quad .$$

The proof is given in Figure 34; note that different kinds of arrowheads are used in this figure to distinguish different acts.

Infinite subcase: For every A_d ($d = 1, 2, 3, \ldots$) there is a μ ($= M, M - 1, \ldots, 2$, or 1) such that

(18) $$a^d_\mu > c > a^d_{\mu-1} \qquad (1 \leqq \mu \leqq 2^d).$$

For the function $U^*(a)$ to be maximized, $U^*(c)$ must satisfy the condition

(19) $$\frac{\mu}{M} > U^*(c) > \frac{\mu - 1}{M} \quad ,$$

where, for each d (= 1, 2, 3, . . .), μ and M have the values given by (12). Since each S_d is a refinement of its predecessors, condition (19) places narrower and narrower limits on $U^*(c)$ as d increases. To obtain a unique value for $U^*(c)$ we carry this to the limit by means of the pseudostatements q_α introduced in case (A-2).

Let A^*_∞ be the set of "pseudo-acts" $q_\alpha C_u \text{ v } \bar{q}_\alpha C_z$ ranked in order of decreasing α $(1 \geqq \alpha \geqq 0)$. By [6b] and [15b], this is also the subject's ranking of preference. $U^*(q_\alpha C_u \text{ v } \bar{q}_\alpha C_z) = P^*(q_\alpha) = \alpha$, and so the subject's ranking maximizes $U^*(a)$. By the simple ordering of preferences [4], the subject must fit the consequence c into A^*. Since there is a q_α for every real number α $(1 \geqq \alpha \geqq 0)$, there is a pseudostatement q_β such that $c = q_\beta C_u \text{ v } \bar{q}_\beta C_z$. To extend the consequent of [IX] from $\mathfrak{M}'_2$ to $\mathfrak{M}_3$, it is necessary and sufficient to define

$$(20) \qquad U^*(c) = U^*(q_\beta C_u \text{ v } q_\beta C_z) = \beta \quad .$$

Thus A^*_∞ is a continuous reference frame of pseudo-acts whose utility values (quantitative valuations) cover the range from 1 to 0. By the rule of simple ordering, each consequence c (such that $C_u \geqq c \geqq C_z$) fits into A^*_∞ exactly and thereby acquires a numerical utility.

This concludes the proof, for case [[A-3a]], that the consequent of [IX] holds for $\mathfrak{M}_3$.

[[A-3b]] In this case $c > C_u$, so that c is preferred to each act of A_∞. Hence we need some new reference frames of acts and pseudo-acts to play the roles of A_∞ and A^*_∞, respectively. Let $\dot{A}_\infty$ be the result of substituting "c" for "C_u" in A_∞. Since $c > C_u > C_z$, the consequence C_u must fit into each $\dot{A}_d$ of $\dot{A}_\infty$. The procedure of case [[A-3a]] can then be used to establish the following relations. In the finite subcase, there are a d (= 1, 2, 3, . . .) and a μ (= M, $M - 1$, . . . , 2, or 1; $M = 2^d$) such that $C_u = \dot{a}^d_\mu = p^d_\mu c \text{ v } \bar{p}^d_\mu C_z$, and hence we set

$$(21) \qquad U^*(C_u) = U^*(\dot{a}^d_\mu) = \frac{\mu}{M}\, U^*(c) \quad ,$$

and so $U^*(c) = M/\mu$. In the infinite subcase, let $\dot{A}^*_\infty$ be the set of pseudo-acts $q_\alpha c \text{ v } \bar{q}_\alpha C_z$ ranked in order of decreasing α $(1 \geqq \alpha \geqq 0)$. By the rule of simple ordering, there is a pseudostatement q_β such that $C_u = q_\beta c \text{ v } \bar{q}_\beta C_z$, and hence we set $U^*(c) = \beta^{-1}$ so that $U^*(q_\beta c \text{ v } \bar{q}_\beta C_z)$ will equal one. The proof that the consequent of [IX] holds for $\mathfrak{M}_3$ is essentially the same as for case [[A-3a]].

[[A-3c]] Here $C_z > c$. A similar procedure is followed for this case, with $\ddot{A}_\infty$ resulting from the substitution of "c" for "C_z" in A_∞. In the finite subcase there are a d (= 1, 2, 3, . . .) and a μ (= M, $M - 1$, . . . , 2, or 1; $M = 2^d$) such that $C_z = \ddot{a}^d_\mu = p^d_\mu C_u \text{ v } \bar{p}^d_\mu c$, and hence we set

$$(22) \qquad U^*(C_z) = U^*(\ddot{a}^d_\mu) = \frac{\mu}{M}\, U^*(C_u) + \frac{M - \mu}{M}\, U^*(c) \quad ,$$

so that $U^*(c) = \mu/(\mu - M)$. In the infinite subcase, $\ddot{A}_\infty$ is the set of pseudoacts $q_\alpha C_u \vee q_\alpha c$ ranked in order of decreasing α $(1 \geqq \alpha \geqq 0)$. By the rule of simple ordering there is a pseudostatement q_β such that $C_z = q_\beta C_u \vee \bar{q}_\beta c$, and hence we set $U^*(c) = \beta/(\beta - 1)$ so that $U^*(q_\beta C_u \vee \bar{q}_\beta c)$ will equal zero. The proof that the consequent of [IX] holds for $\mathfrak{M}_3$ is similar to those of cases ⟦A-3a⟧ and ⟦A-3b⟧.

This completes the proof that the consequent of [IX] holds for M_3. Since c is an arbitrary consequence of $\mathfrak{M}_{nf}$, the consequent of [IX] holds for $\mathfrak{M}_{nf}$. This finishes case ⟦A⟧.

⟦B⟧ We indicate finally how to extend this result from the set $\mathfrak{M}_{nf}$ to the marked set $\mathfrak{M}$, using the normal form axiom [VII] (p. 276).

Every consequence of $\mathfrak{M}$ occurs in $\mathfrak{M}_{nf}$, so that the function $U^*(c)$ is already defined for $\mathfrak{M}$. However, the unconditional function $P^*(q)$ of $\mathfrak{M}_{nf}$ needs to be extended to a conditional function $P^*(q, i)$ of $\mathfrak{M}$. This is essentially the extension of unconditional probabilities to conditional probabilities, and we use the reduction principle (p. 93):

$$\text{If } P^*(i) \neq 0\,,\ \text{then } P^*(q, i) = \frac{P^*(qi)}{P^*(i)}\,.$$

Recall that a degree-of-belief function $P(q, i)$ is not defined when i is probabilistically impossible (p. 289).

In the most general sense, an act is an assignment of consequences to logically possible universes. The acts represented in an extended tree are all represented in its normal form, and by [VII] the subject makes the same choices in both trees. Moreover, the normal form of every tree of $\mathfrak{M}$ is in $\mathfrak{M}_{nf}$. Thus the whole structure of the acts of $\mathfrak{M}$ and of the choices the subject makes from them is reflected in the structure of the acts of $\mathfrak{M}_{nf}$ and the choices the subject makes from these. Consequently, every choice of $\mathfrak{M}$ maximizes the function $\Sigma_{n=1}^{N} P^*(q_n, i)U^*(a_n, iq_n)$ if and only if every choice of $\mathfrak{M}_{nf}$ maximizes the function $U^*(a, i)$. Since the consequence of [IX] holds for $\mathfrak{M}_{nf}$ by case ⟦A⟧, it must also hold for $\mathfrak{M}$.

In this subsection we started from the assumption that a marked set $\mathfrak{M}$ satisfies the antecedent of the main theorem [IX] and showed that $\mathfrak{M}$ then satisfies the consequent of [IX]. This proves [IX].

We note in closing that the comparison technique used in part ⟦A-3⟧ of the proof enables one to measure the utility of any consequence c. If $C_u \geqq c \geqq C_z$, find a pseudostatement p such that the subject is indifferent between c and the mixed act $pC_u \vee \bar{p}C_z$; then $U(c) = U(pC_u \vee \bar{p}C_z) = P(p)$. If $c > C_u > C_z$, the comparison is between $pc \vee \bar{p}C_z$ and C_u; while if $C_u > C_z > c$, then $pC_u \vee pc$ is to be compared with C_z. The quantitative axiom guarantees that the requisite pseudostatement p exists. The same technique may be used to measure the utility of an arbitrary act a, but the pseudostatements used in the comparison must be probabilistically independent of the statements contained in act a.

5.5.3 Savage's axiomatic system

My calculus of choice is based on Savage's axiomatic system for probability and utility, presented in *The Foundation of Statistics* (chap. 2, secs. 1–3 of chap. 3, and secs. 1–3 of chap. 5). This system uses the nonsymmetrical quantitative axiom [VIII′]. We shall describe the system and explain how it is related to the calculus of choice.

Savage's universe of discourse is more restricted than ours. His acts are based on events rather than statements (see p. 262, above), and he considers only pairwise comparisons between normal form acts. His system has six postulates. The first five are theorems of the calculus of choice; we adopt the sixth as axiom [VIII′] of this calculus.

Savage's postulate P1 is the simple ordering of preferences [2]. Postulate P2 is the partial act theorem [10]. The third postulate is

(P3) $(i \neq s\bar{s}) \supset [\{ic_1 \vee \bar{i}c) \geqq (ic_2 \vee \bar{i}c)\} \equiv (c_1 \geqq c_2)]$.

This follows easily from theorem [11]. Postulate P4 is the ordering of uncertainties axiom [VI] in unconditional form. Postulate P5 is the existence axiom [V].

It is noteworthy that Savage uses extended trees implicitly in justifying two of these postulates. He argues that P2 should be accepted because it merely formalizes the noncontroversial "sure-thing principle"

($P2_i$) If $a_1 \geqq a_2$ given p and $a_1 \geqq a_2$ given $\bar{p}$, then $a_1 \geqq a_2$.

Informally, he treats "$a_1 \geqq a_2$ given p" as a fact about extended trees: given information p, the subject would like a_1 at least as much as a_2. Formally, he treats "$a_1 \geqq a_2$ given p" as a relation between normal form acts: for any act b, $(pa_1 \vee \bar{p}b) \geqq (pa_2 \vee \bar{p}b)$.* The informal $P2_i$ can be formulated and proved in the calculus of choice. It is a noncontroversial principle, as Savage says. But $P2_i$ is too weak to justify the more controversial P2, which is the partial act theorem [10] that leads to the sure-thing paradox (p. 278).

Savage defends P3 in the same way. It formalizes the noncontroversial principle

($P3_i$) If $p \neq s\bar{s}$, then $c_1 \geqq c_2$ given p if and only if $c_1 \geqq c_2$.

$P3_i$ can be formulated in the calculus of choice and P3 derived from it by the normal form axiom, and so his argument here is more successful.

This brings us to Savage's last axiom, P6, which we shall adopt as the nonsymmetrical form of the quantitative axiom [VIII′]. To motivate it and relate it to its symmetrical variant [VIII] (p. 288), we first prove the following corollary to the main theorem [IX].

* "$pa_1 \vee \bar{p}b$" and "$pa_2 \vee \bar{p}b$" are not themselves normal form act expressions, but each reduces easily to a logically equivalent normal form act expression.

[19] Assume $a > b$. Then for any consequence c, there exists an equipartition $q_1, q_2, \ldots, q_N$ such that, for each $n = 1, 2, \ldots, N$, both $a > (q_n c \vee \bar{q}_n b)$ and $(q_n c \vee \bar{q}_n a) > b$.

Proof: Since $a > b$, the main theorem [IX] implies the existence of a utility function $\mathbf{U}$ such that

$$(1) \qquad \mathbf{U}(a) > \mathbf{U}(b) \quad .$$

From this let us derive the two inequalities $\mathbf{U}(a) > \mathbf{U}(q_N c \vee \bar{q}_N b)$ and $\mathbf{U}(q_N c \vee \bar{q}_N a) > \mathbf{U}(b)$; the main theorem will then imply $a > (q_N c \vee \bar{q}_N b)$ and $(q_N c \vee \bar{q}_N a) > b$, respectively. Since the elements of an equipartition must be assigned equal probabilities (p. 293), this will show that $a > (q_n c \vee \bar{q}_n b)$ and $(q_n c \vee \bar{q}_n a) > b$ for each $n = 1, 2, \ldots, N$. For convenience, let $\mathbf{U}(rc) =_{\text{df}} \mathbf{P}(r)\mathbf{U}(c)$ for any statement r and any consequence c. The inequalities to be proved then become $\mathbf{U}(a) > [\mathbf{U}(q_N c) + \mathbf{U}(\bar{q}_N b)]$ and $[\mathbf{U}(q_N c) + \mathbf{U}(\bar{q}_N a)] > \mathbf{U}(b)$.

Axiom [VIII] and the fact that the elements of an equipartition must be assigned equal probabilities imply

$$(2) \qquad \operatorname*{Limit}_{N \to \infty} \mathbf{P}(q_N) = 0 \quad .$$

Hence, for any consequence c,

$$(3) \qquad \operatorname*{Limit}_{N \to \infty} \mathbf{P}(q_N)\mathbf{U}(c) = 0 \quad .$$

By the definition of "$\mathbf{U}(q_N c)$" this becomes

$$(4) \qquad \operatorname*{Limit}_{N \to \infty} \mathbf{U}(q_N c) = 0 \quad .$$

Since a and b are normal form acts, they are of the form

$$(5) \qquad a = \sum_{i=1}^{I} p_i c_i \quad \text{and} \quad b = \sum_{j=1}^{J} p'_j c'_j \quad .$$

Choose the utility function $\mathbf{U}$ so that the utility of every consequence in a and in b is non-negative. It is clear from the reduction principle [23] (p. 93) and theorem [15c] above that for any statements r and s, $\mathbf{P}(r) \geqq \mathbf{P}(rs)$. Consequently,

$$(6) \qquad \mathbf{P}(q_N)\sum_{j=1}^{J} \mathbf{U}(c'_j) = \sum_{j=1}^{J} \mathbf{P}(q_N)\mathbf{U}(c'_j) \geqq \sum_{j=1}^{J} \mathbf{P}(q_N p'_j)\mathbf{U}(c'_j) \geqq \mathbf{U}(q_N b) \geqq 0$$

$$\mathbf{P}(q_N)\sum_{i=1}^{I} \mathbf{U}(c_i) = \sum_{i=1}^{I} \mathbf{P}(q_N)\mathbf{U}(c_i) \geqq \sum_{i=1}^{I} \mathbf{P}(q_N p_i)\mathbf{U}(c_i) = \mathbf{U}(q_N a) \geqq 0 \quad .$$

Formulas (2) and (6) together imply

(7) $\lim_{N\to\infty} \mathbf{U}(q_N b) = 0$ and $\lim_{N\to\infty} \mathbf{U}(q_N a) = 0$.

By the logical equivalence axiom,

(8) $\mathbf{U}(b) = \mathbf{U}(q_N b) + \mathbf{U}(\bar{q}_N b)$ and $\mathbf{U}(a) = \mathbf{U}(q_N a) + \mathbf{U}(\bar{q}_N a)$.

Hence

(9) $\lim_{N\to\infty} \mathbf{U}(\bar{q}_N b) = \mathbf{U}(b)$ and $\lim_{N\to\infty} \mathbf{U}(\bar{q}_N a) = \mathbf{U}(a)$.

Combining (4) and (9) we obtain

(10) $\lim_{N\to\infty} [\mathbf{U}(q_N c) + \mathbf{U}(\bar{q}_N b)] = \mathbf{U}(b)$ and

$\lim_{N\to\infty} [\mathbf{U}(q_N c) + \mathbf{U}(\bar{q}_N a)] = \mathbf{U}(a)$.

Consider the first of these equalities. It says that by choosing N sufficiently large we can make the quantity $\mathbf{U}(q_N c) + \mathbf{U}(\bar{q}_N b)$ as close to $\mathbf{U}(b)$ as we want. Since $\mathbf{U}(a) > \mathbf{U}(b)$, there must be an N such that

(11a) $\mathbf{U}(a) > [\mathbf{U}(q_N c) + \mathbf{U}(\bar{q}_N b)]$.

By similar reasoning, there is an N such that

(11b) $[\mathbf{U}(q_N c) + \mathbf{U}(\bar{q}_N a)] > \mathbf{U}(b)$.

Using the definition of "$\mathbf{U}(rc)$" on both parts of (11), we obtain

(12) $\mathbf{U}(a) > \mathbf{U}(q_N c \vee \bar{q}_N b)$ and $\mathbf{U}(q_N c \vee \bar{q}_N a) > \mathbf{U}(b)$.

By the main theorem [IX] the subject's choices maximize utility, so that

(13) $a > (q_N c \vee \bar{q}_N b)$ and $(q_N c \vee \bar{q}_N a) > b$.

This completes the proof of theorem [19].

Axiom [VIII] asserts the existence of equipartitions of ever-increasing size and fineness, with no bound on the fineness. Theorem [19] does this also, but in a different way. Let a be preferred to b but very close to it in value. If c is much more valuable than b, then each q_n must be unlikely for $a > q_n c \vee \bar{q}_n b$ to hold; and if c is much less valuable than a, then each q_n must be unlikely for $q_n c \vee \bar{q}_n a > b$ to hold. Starting with the consequences C_u and C_z, we can by iterated use of theorem [19] build an infinite sequence of equipartitions of ever increasing size and fineness.

Consider finally Savage's last postulate P6, which we adopt as the *nonsymmetrical form of the quantitative axiom*

[VIII′] Assume $a > b$. Then for any consequence c, there exists a partition $q_1, q_2 \ldots, q_N$ such that, for each $n = 1, 2, \ldots, N$, both $a > (q_n c \vee \bar{q}_n b)$ and $(q_n c \vee \bar{q}_n a) > b$.

This is [19] weakened by dropping the requirement that the postulated partitions be equipartitions. It turns out that [VIII′] can be used in place of [VIII] and the main theorem [IX] still holds. In other words, it is sufficient to postulate an infinite sequence of partitions of ever-increasing size and fineness, with no bound on the fineness, without requiring that these partitions be equipartitions. This result follows directly from Savage's conclusions.

Savage proves the following main theorem for normal form acts based on events

[IX_s] If the subject's choices from pairs of normal form acts satisfy Savage's postulates P1–P6, then there exist a unique function $P(q)$ and a function $U(c)$, unique up to an increasing linear transformation, such that

(a) $P(q)$ satisfies the calculus of probability

(b) $$\left(\sum_{n=1}^{N} p_n c_n \geqq \sum_{m=1}^{M} p'_m c'_m\right) \equiv$$

$$\left(\sum_{n=1}^{N} P(p_n) U(c_n) \geqq \sum_{m=1}^{M} P(p'_m) U(c'_m)\right) .$$

The probabilistic part of his proof is given in Section 3.3 (Theorems 2-4) and the utility part in Section 5.3 (Theorems 3-4) of *The Foundations of Statistics.**

Since Savage's postulates P1–P6 imply [IX_s], and these postulates are theorems of the calculus of choice, [IX_s] is also a theorem of the calculus of choice. Let [IX′] be the same as [IX] (p. 286) except that [VIII′] replaces [VIII]. Savage's theorem [IX_s] is our main theorem [IX′] cut down to fit Savage's system. Hence his proof of [IX_s] may be extended to make a proof of [IX′] by bridging the gap between the subject matters of the two systems. We will indicate how this can be done.

The subject matter of the calculus of choice is richer than that of Savage's system in three basic respects. First, Savage's system is based on events, whereas our system is based on statements. Since an event is a class of logically equivalent statements, this difference is covered by the logical

* Savage builds on de Finetti's "La prévision: ses lois logiques, ses sources subjectives" and on von Neumann's proof in "The Axiomatic Treatment of Utility," an appendix added in the second edition of *Theory of Games and Economic Behavior.*

The general technique is that of sec. 5.5.2, but the proof is much more difficult. Let $\hat{E}_\infty$ be the infinite sequence of partitions of ever-increasing size and fineness postulated by [VIII′]. From $\hat{E}_\infty$, C_u, and C_z we can construct nonsymmetrical reference frames $\hat{S}_\infty$, $\hat{S}^*_\infty$, $\hat{A}_\infty$, $\hat{A}^*_\infty$, etc. These perform functions in the proof of [IX_s] that are similar to the functions performed in the proof of [IX] by the symmetrical reference frames S_∞, S^*_∞, A_∞, A^*_∞, etc.

equivalence axiom [II] (p. 264). Second, Savage considers only pairwise comparisons of acts, whereas the calculus of choice treats choices made from arbitrary sets of acts. This gap is bridged by the subset axiom [III] in conjunction with the marking axiom [I]. Third, Savage's system deals only with normal form acts, whereas the calculus of choice covers extended acts (represented by extended trees) as well. All axioms of the calculus directly restrict the extended trees of a marked set except the existence and quantitative axioms. Savage's proof of the main theorem [IX_s] for normal form acts may be extended to a proof of [IX′] for all acts by means of the normal form axiom [VII] (see pp. 276, 298).

This shows that theorem [IX′] follows from axioms [I]–[VII] and [VIII′]; it completes our discussion of the main theorem of the calculus of choice.

The main theorem has shown that in marking an infinite complete set of choice trees according to the axioms of the calculus of choice, the subject implicitly follows the calculus of probability and maximizes utility, whether or not he explicitly does so. Hence the calculus of choice implies, in a foundational sense, the traditional theory of utility (sec. 4.3.1). It is natural to ask about the converse implication.

Suppose a subject is presented with an infinite complete set of choice trees and makes his choices according to the traditional theory of utility. He assigns probabilities to statements and utilities to consequences, calculates the utilities at each choice point, and applies the rule of maximizing utility. Will he have satisfied the axioms of the calculus of choice?

Whether the existence axiom [V] is satisfied depends on the consequences and his valuation of them. Whether the quantitative axiom in form [VIII] or form [VIII′] is satisfied depends on the statements of the choice basis and his partial beliefs concerning them. But all the other axioms ([I]–[IV], [VI], [VII]) will be satisfied except for choices made at probabilistically impossible choice points. Thus in a pragmatic sense the calculus of choice is equivalent to traditional utility theory, though foundationally it is much deeper.

Finally, we draw a corollary to the main theorem that concerns marked sets only partially satisfying the axioms. This corollary connects the calculus of choice to the "book" theorem (sec. 4.4) and bears on the normative use of the calculus of choice (pp. 308–11).

The following two concepts are generalizations of the notion of a coherent set of partial beliefs (p. 214). A marked set that satisfies axioms [I]–[VII], i.e., all the axioms except the quantitative axiom, is *coherent*. A partially marked set that can be completely marked to satisfy axioms [I]–[VII] is *potentially coherent*. For simple examples of these concepts, consider a choice basis consisting of only three consequences. Transitive pairwise choices yield a potentially coherent marked set, since the subject can choose that consequence that he prefers to the other two. But intransitive pairwise choices yield a marked set that is not potentially coherent, for there is no coherent way of choosing from all three consequences at once (see Fig. 21).

The corollary to the main theorem is

[X] If a marked set of trees is coherent or potentially coherent, then there exists a degree-of-belief function $P(q, i)$ and a consequence valuation function $U(c)$ such that
(a) $P(q, i)$ satisfies the calculus of probability
(b) every choice made at a probabilistically possible choice point with information i maximizes the utility function

$$\sum_{n=1}^{N} P(q_n, i)U(a_n, iq_n) \quad .$$

Proof. Let $\mathfrak{M}$ be a marked set that is coherent or potentially coherent. If $\mathfrak{M}$ is coherent, call it $\mathfrak{M}'$. If $\mathfrak{M}$ is only potentially coherent, mark it so that it becomes a coherent marked set $\mathfrak{M}'$. The set $\mathfrak{M}'$, being coherent, satisfies axioms [I]–[VII]. If $\mathfrak{M}'$ does not also satisfy the quantitative axiom [VIII], extend it to a marked set $\mathfrak{M}''$ that does. Since $\mathfrak{M}''$ satisfies axioms [I]–[VIII], the main theorem [IX] applies to it. Therefore, there are functions $P(q, i)$ and $U(c)$ such that all choices made at probabilistically possible choice points of $\mathfrak{M}''$ with information i maximize the utility function $\Sigma_{n=1}^{N} P(q_n, i)U(a_n, iq_n)$. But $\mathfrak{M}''$ is an extension of $\mathfrak{M}$, containing all the choices of $\mathfrak{M}$, and so the choices of $\mathfrak{M}$ also maximize this same utility function. Q.E.D.

The consequent of the main theorem requires uniqueness of the functions $P(q, i)$ and $U(c)$. This uniqueness requirement does not occur in the consequent of corollary [X], because when $\mathfrak{M}$ is extended to $\mathfrak{M}'$ and $\mathfrak{M}''$ further choices are made. These choices can be made in different ways, reflecting different functions $P(q, i)$ and $U(c)$. Thus in general there are many functions $P(q, i)$ and $U(c)$ for which corollary [X] holds of $\mathfrak{M}$. For example, the preferences $C_u > C_1 > C_z$ and $C_u > C_2 > C_z$ are maximized by any utility function satisfying the constraints $1 > U(C_1) > 0$ and $1 > U(C_2) > 0$. This shows that corollary [X] does not imply comparability of preferences. On the other hand, corollary [X] does imply transitivity, for there is no maximizing utility function for an intransitive set of preferences. In sum, [X] implies transitivity but not comparability (see sec. 4.3.6).

We have now completed our presentation of the calculus of choice. It consists of a grammar, eight axioms ([I]–[VII] and either [VIII] or [VIII′]), a number of auxiliary theorems ([1]–[19]), the main theorem ([IX] or [IX′]), and corollary [X]. We turn next to a consideration of the truth and applicability of the calculus of choice.

5.6 The Pragmatic Theory of Inductive Probability*

5.6.1 Introduction

My pragmatic theory of inductive probability will be developed in the present section. This theory gives an answer to the first of our four main questions, and it helps to answer the second (see sec. 5.6,3).

The first main question was: What is the general nature of a system of atomic inductive probability statements? (P. 92) We have explicated such systems of statements by means of three axiomatic systems: the calculus of inductive probability (chap. 2); and two extensions of it, standard inductive logic for simple models of reality (chap. 3) and the calculus of choice (secs. 5.2–5.5). The pragmatic theory makes both descriptive and normative claims concerning the adequacy of these axiomatic systems as models of inductive reasoning and decision-making in conditions of uncertainty.

Consider a system of atomic inductive probability statements asserted by a subject. The **pragmatic theory of inductive probability** holds that this system of statements has two interrelated but coequal aspects, an *a priori aspect* and a *pragmatic aspect. The a priori aspect concerns the assignment of probability values to statements by formal rules. Probability values are and should be assigned according to the rules of the calculus of probability and standard inductive logic. Consequently, both individual atomic probability statements and systems of them have logically true-or-false components.*

The pragmatic aspect concerns the action implications of these probability assignments. An atomic inductive probability statement does and should express a disposition to act or "bet" in certain ways under conditions of uncertainty; in a generalized sense of "betting," the subject's belief in $\mathbf{P}(c, d) = x$ *expresses a commitment to bet on the pair* $\langle c, d\rangle$ *with odds* x *to* $1 - x$*. A system of atomic inductive probability statements does and should express a commitment to make one's probability assignments conform to the calculus of probability and standard inductive logic. Because of their pragmatic aspect, true atomic inductive probability statements and the theorems of the calculus of inductive probability are not logically true.*

Since the rule of maximizing utility plays a dominant role in the application of probability theory to action, the pragmatic aspect of inductive probability involves the concept of utility. The calculus of choice explicates the concepts of probability and utility as they are and should be reflected in the choices of a single subject.

Both the descriptive and the normative claims of the pragmatic theory are subject to certain qualifications. Descriptively, the calculus of probability,

* This section is based on my papers "On the Significance of Carnap's System of Inductive Logic for the Philosophy of Induction" and "A Pragmatic-Humean Theory of Probability and Lewis's Theory."

standard inductive logic, and the calculus of choice are only fair models of actual inductive reasoning and decision-making. Normatively, one should generally follow these three axiomatic systems when reasoning inductively and making decisions. But the difficulties we found in the traditional theory of utility show that there are important exceptions to this general rule. These difficulties are resolved by limiting the range of application of the marking and invariance axioms, and by recognizing that the quantitative axiom is a convenient idealization.

These are the essential features of the pragmatic theory. We shall elaborate the descriptive and normative claims in the next subsection, then discuss the interplay of the a priori and pragmatic aspects with respect to logical truth, thereby completing the answer to our second main question (sec. 5.6.3).

5.6.2 The normative use of the calculus of choice

The pragmatic theory makes two kinds of claims concerning inductive probability: descriptive claims about how human beings *do* choose and reason, and normative claims about how they *should* choose and reason (pp. 33–34, 175). Let us look at these claims in more detail.

As far as it goes, the calculus of inductive probability is a good model of actual inductive reasoning or argumentation (secs. 1.4.1, 2.1). The chief limitations of the model are its purely quantitative character and the requirement that all uncertainties be comparable (secs. 4.3.2, 4.3.6). By definition, standard inductive logic consists of the rules governing ordinary inductive reasoning, but our simple models of reality are highly idealized (secs. 3.1–3.3). The calculus of choice is a moderately good model of actual choice behavior; its main weaknesses are those we found in the traditional theory of utility (p. 212). Psychological experiments have confirmed that the calculus of choice is an approximate model of decision behavior; these results* are of limited value, though, because it is impossible to conduct controlled experiments with large utilities, e.g., a million dollars, life itself. Nevertheless, people generally behave in accordance with the axioms of the calculus of choice, and so this calculus and standard inductive logic constitute a rough model of how people behave and reason.

The normative claims of the pragmatic theory are more important and much more complex than the descriptive claims. The normative status of standard inductive logic was discussed in connection with Hume's thesis that there is no noncircular justification of induction (sec. 3.3). The calculus of choice was constructed to facilitate the evaluation of normative utility theory (sec. 5.1.1); we shall now use it for this purpose by evaluating its axioms. We judge the axioms in terms of the difficulties we found with the

* See, for example, Davidson and Suppes' *Decision Making* and Ward Edwards' review article "Behavioral Decision Theory."

traditional theory of utility (p. 212). Each of these difficulties will be resolved by transforming it into a normative challenge to a specific axiom of the calculus of choice, such resolutions becoming part of the pragmatic theory of inductive probability. Since the calculus of inductive probability is a subsystem of the calculus of choice (pp. 290–91), our evaluation will cover it also.

The existence axiom [V] requires the choice basis to contain at least two consequences of different value; it states a minimal condition for applying utility theory, for if it is false all acts are equally valuable (p. 270).

The marking axiom [I] requires a subject to mark completely a set of choice trees. Our discussion of it is best postponed until after we have evaluated the axioms that constrain *how* a subject marks his trees, insofar as he does mark them. There are five of these axioms, and they fall into two classes. We have found reasons to accept, and no reason to question, axioms

[II] Logical equivalence

[III] Subset

[VI] Ordering of uncertainties.

The logical equivalence axiom builds inductive logic around a core of deductive logic; the idealization involved in doing so is not relevant here (pp. 262–63, 265–66). The subset axiom is correct, for if an act is more valuable than another in a given context, it is more valuable than the other in a narrower context. Under the intended interpretation of the calculus of choice, the ordering of uncertainties axiom does seem reasonable (p. 270).

On the other hand, axioms

[IV] Invariance

[VII] Normal form

lead to the sure-thing and variance paradoxes, which constitute objections to the traditional theory of utility (sec. 4.3.4). Since the variance paradox is a statistical generalization of the sure-thing paradox, it will suffice to resolve the former.

The sure-thing paradox is presented in Figures 5 and 23. The only axioms at issue are part [IVA] of invariance (concerning tokens of a choice tree that occur as subtrees in the context of the same information) and normal form. The choices of Figure 5 are reasonable (pp. 193–94); so, in this situation, it is reasonable to reject either [IVA] of invariance or the normal form axiom, and hence to reject the rule of maximizing utility.

The choices of Figure 23 appear reasonable to me; in this instance I reject invariance [IVA] rather than the normal form axiom. My rationale is as follows. The information available at choice points 2′ and 12′ is "P_2 v P_3." If I really knew that "P_2 v P_3" was true when I made my choices, I should obey [IVA] and mark subtrees 2′ and 12′ the same. But by the rules of the marking game, when I mark these subtrees I do not know whether or not "P_2 v P_3" is true. Since I want to use the holistic reason "This choice will give me a sure-thing," I must go beyond the subtrees 2′ and 12′ to the wider context of the whole trees 1′ and 11′ in making my decision. In other words, if I knew the information at the choice points when I made my decision, I should obey [IVA]; but since I am uncertain about this information, it is reasonable for me to violate [IVA].

Moreover, the normal form axiom is basic to the very idea of a strategy and so seems acceptable. By the rules of the marking game, a subject must mark an extended tree on the basis of his general information, without knowing the outcomes of the contingencies represented by the statements on the tree (sec. 5.2.1). In doing this, he adopts a plan or strategy in advance for meeting these contingencies if they materialize. Now the value of an act or strategy should depend only on its assignment of consequences to possible universes, not on how the content of a universe description is distributed along a path through the tree. Hence a subject should make the same selection of assignments of consequences to universes when he marks the normal form of a tree as when he marks the tree itself. For this reason, I am strongly inclined to accept the normal form axiom in all cases.

Thus the pragmatic theory of inductive probability resolves the sure-thing and invariance paradoxes by showing that in these situations it may be reasonable for one to make a choice that violates part [IVA] of the invariance axiom, and thereby reject the rule of maximizing utility.

This finishes our evaluation of axioms [II] through [VII]; we shall assume in the remainder of this subsection that these axioms are satisfied. The evaluation of the marking [I] and quantitative [VIII] axioms is best done by considering three cases that illustrate the most important ways in which they can be violated.

(1) The subject is presented a complete set of choice trees that is finite; he partially marks them in such a way that the marked set $\mathfrak{M}$ is not potentially coherent. Axiom [VIII] is violated because the choice set is finite. Axiom [I] is violated because $\mathfrak{M}$ is only partly marked; furthermore, by the definition of "potentially coherent" (p. 303), if the marking should be completed, axioms [II] – [VII] would no longer be satisfied.

This case includes that of intransitive preferences, and we have argued that these are sometimes reasonable (p. 211). When pairwise comparisons are made of three acts, the subject may reasonably prefer a_1 to a_2, a_2 to a_3, but a_3 to a_1. Decision-making is sometimes costly, and an incomplete decision process yielding intransitive preferences may be preferable to a complete decision process. Of course, if the subject later completes the decision process and compares a_1, a_2, and a_3 all at once, his preferences should be transitive (see fig. 20).

This completes our study of the first case of axiom violation. The second and third cases involve a rather complex structure of sets $\mathcal{C}$, $\mathfrak{I}$, $\mathfrak{M}$, and $\mathfrak{M}'$. Set $\mathcal{C}$ is a finite choice basis of statements and consequences, including consequences C_u and C_z. We assume $U(C_u) = 1$ and $U(C_z) = 0$, so that a marked set of trees satisfying axioms [I] — [VIII] will specify unique consequence-valuation and utility functions. Set $\mathfrak{I}$ is the complete set of choice trees constructed on choice basis $\mathcal{C}$ (pp. 259–61). The richness of $\mathcal{C}$ is manifest by the following two alternative markings of $\mathfrak{I}$. The first is a completely marked set $\mathfrak{M}'$ satisfying axioms [I] – [VII]; moreover, any utility function $\Sigma_{n=1}^{N} P(q_n, i)U(a, iq_n)$ maximized by the choices of $\mathfrak{M}'$ specifies $P(q, i)$ and $U(c)$ with a fair degree of precision, e.g., to within one per cent. The second marking of $\mathfrak{I}$ is a partially marked set $\mathfrak{M}$ that is contained in $\mathfrak{M}'$, is potentially coherent, but specifies $P(q, i)$ and $U(c)$ only roughly; e.g., for some statement Q, $P(Q)$ is determined only to within $1 > P(Q) > .8$, and for some consequence C, $U(C)$ is determined only to within $.3 > U(C) > 0$. We can now formulate our second case of axiom violation.

(2) The subject accepts marked set $\mathfrak{M}$ and rejects marked set $\mathfrak{M}'$. In other words, he elects to violate the marking axiom and specify his degrees of belief and consequence valuations only roughly, rather than to satisfy the marking axiom and specify them with a fair degree of precision, e.g., to within one per cent.

Since $\mathfrak{M}$ is potentially coherent, corollary [X] applies and the preferences expressed by $\mathfrak{M}$ are transitive but not comparable (see p. 304). Hence the central issue here is that of justifying comparability. Now why should the subject not adopt the marking axiom and make a complete set of choices? This question may be answered by viewing the calculus of choice as a tool for organizing and guiding behavior. Insofar as the subject does not follow the marking axiom, he is not using the calculus of choice, and whether a tool should be used depends on the costs as well as the benefits.

There are two main tasks in applying the calculus of choice, both of which are difficult and time-consuming: making choice trees and applying the marking axiom. To construct a choice tree, one divides his actual environmental situation into acts and ascertains the consequences of each act. It is not possible to consider all circumstances and alternatives, so that one must simplify and idealize. Making the higher-order choice of alternatives to be analyzed can be especially trying. After the choice trees have been constructed, it may be difficult to make all the decisions required by the marking axiom. Thus the cost of formulating and choosing a strategy is considerable. Moreover, the subject may need to revise his chosen strategy subsequently, either because new information renders his analysis inadequate or because his preferences have changed. The economic considerations involved in applying the calculus of choice will be illustrated in connection with the rule of total evidence (p. 20). One should use all the information "available" to him when making a decision. But information is "available" in varying degrees and at different costs. How carefully should one reflect on what he knows? Should he do library research? Should he pay the cost of further experiments?

In conclusion, the pragmatic theory of inductive probability gives this explanation of preferences and uncertainties that are potentially coherent (and hence transitive) but incompletely specified (and hence not comparable): The calculus of choice is a tool, and in some cases it is economic and rational not to make full use of this tool.

Our third and last case of axiom violation focuses on the quantitative axiom [VIII] but involves the marking axiom [I] as well. We enrich the structure $\mathfrak{C}$, $\mathfrak{J}$, $\mathfrak{M}$, and $\mathfrak{M}'$ of the second case as follows. Extend the choice basis $\mathfrak{C}$ to $\mathfrak{C}^*$ by adding all the statements of the fair-coin assumption (p. 288), and let $\mathfrak{J}^*$ be the complete set of choice trees based on $\mathfrak{C}^*$. Let $\mathfrak{M}^{**}$ range over all markings of $\mathfrak{J}^*$ that satisfy axioms [I] – [VIII] and contain $\mathfrak{M}'$. By the main theorem [IX], for each $\mathfrak{M}^{**}$ there is a unique utility function maximizing the choices of $\mathfrak{M}^{**}$; since $\mathfrak{M}^{**}$ contains $\mathfrak{M}'$, this utility function also maximizes the choices of $\mathfrak{M}'$.

We next construct a marking of $\mathfrak{J}^*$ alternative to $\mathfrak{M}^{**}$ that satisfies the quantitative axiom but does not specify a unique utility function. Let $\mathfrak{J}_{\text{VIII}}$ consist of all trees based on C_u, C_z, and the statements of the fair coin assumption, and let $\mathfrak{M}_{\text{VIII}}$ be a marking of these that renders the quantitative axiom true. The marked set $\mathfrak{M}^*$ is a marking of $\mathfrak{J}^*$ whose marked trees consist of $\mathfrak{M}_{\text{VIII}}$ and of the marked trees of $\mathfrak{M}'$. Since $\mathfrak{M}^*$ contains $\mathfrak{M}_{\text{VIII}}$, $\mathfrak{M}^*$ satisfies the quantitative axiom. Because the only other marked trees of $\mathfrak{M}^*$ are those of $\mathfrak{M}'$, $\mathfrak{M}^*$ does not satisfy the marking axiom, and any utility function that maximizes the choices of $\mathfrak{M}'$ maximizes the choices of $\mathfrak{M}^*$, and vice-versa. In other words, so far as the statements and consequences of $\mathfrak{C}$ are concerned, $\mathfrak{M}^*$ and $\mathfrak{M}'$ specify the functions $P(q, i)$ and $U(c)$ to the same degree of precision, e.g., to within one per cent. In contrast, each marked set $\mathfrak{M}^{**}$ specifies $P(q, i)$ and $U(c)$ uniquely. This brings us to our third and last case of axiom violation.

(3) The subject chooses $\mathfrak{M}^*$ and rejects every $\mathfrak{M}^{**}$. Thus the subject accepts the quantitative axiom, but he refuses to use its equipartitions to specify uniquely his degrees-of-belief and consequence-valuation functions. Rather, he deliberately elects to leave these functions partially specified, thereby violating the marking axiom and comparability. Is this election justifiable?

Suppose that in choosing marked set $\mathfrak{M}'$ the subject has already specified his degrees of belief and consequence valuations to the precision needed in practice and as far as it is economic to do. He might then correctly say that any further specification of his degrees of belief and consequence valuations would be arbitrary. Accepting the quantitative axiom, he can accept $\mathfrak{M}^*$, but he does not want to accept arbitrarily any $\mathfrak{M}^{**}$ and thereby uniquely specify his degrees of belief and consequence valuations.

The chief reply to this is that acceptance of an $\mathfrak{M}^{**}$ is a convenient and simplifying idealization that enables him to treat uncertainties and valuations quantitatively. The mathematics of the continuum of real numbers is generally simpler and more powerful than the mathematics of discrete processes. For example, the principles of the calculus of probability (chap. 2) are simpler than their comparative counterparts of the calculus of choice (sec. 5.4.3). Also, quantitative functions often have useful properties, such as continuity and differentiability, that their discrete counterparts lack.

Axioms [I] – [VII] yield a rich structure of comparative relations on likelihoods and valuations, so rich that these axioms imply the main theorem [IX] except for the uniqueness of $P(q, i)$ and $U(c)$ (sec. 5.4.2, sec. 5.4.3, and p. 304). What does the quantitative axiom [VIII] or [VIII′] add to this structure? Both forms of this axiom postulate an infinite sequence of partitions of ever-increasing size and fineness, with no bound on the fineness. One can construct from this sequence and the consequences C_u and C_z a continuous reference frame of pseudostatements whose quantitative probabilities cover the range from one to zero. By the rule of simple ordering, each statement of the marked set fits exactly into this framework and thereby acquires a quantitative probability. Utilities are assigned to consequences and acts in a similar way (sec. 5.5.2 and p. 302n).

The partitions postulated by the symmetrical form of the quantitative axiom [VIII] are equipartitions. The subject might reject this axiom on the ground that nature does not possess that much symmetry. He can then use the nonsymmetrical form of the axiom [VIII′], which comes much closer to being true. To illustrate: One can mint nearly-fair coins and toss them by an almost-random method until they wear out, and in principle this procedure could be continued forever. Since probability is modal (secs. 2.2.2, 3.2), this hypothetical example establishes the existence of an infinite process Tx_1, Tx_2, Tx_3, . . . that is approximately an independent process of probability one-half. In turn, this process generates an infinite sequence of partitions of ever-increasing size and fineness, with no bound on the fineness (see pp. 293–95).

However, the symmetry difference between [VIII] and [VIII′] does not seem very important, since the use of infinite partitions is already an idealization. For any desired degree of accuracy, the comparison process can in principle be carried far enough to determine numerical values for probabilities and utilities to that degree of accuracy. Hence both forms of the quantitative axiom are true as idealizations.

Thus the pragmatic theory of inductive probability gives the following explanation of the distinction between qualitative and quantitative probabilities and valuations. The distinction reduces to the difference between carrying the comparison process finitely far and imagining that it is carried to the limit. Utilities and quantitative probabilities are accepted as convenient idealizations that can be approximated as much as desired. The calculus of choice is a model of decision-making, and it is generally simpler to handle the quantitative-qualitative distinction outside the model than inside it (see pp. 31–32).

We have now completed our evaluation of the axioms of the calculus of choice taken as normative rules. Overall, the pragmatic theory of inductive probability answers our objections to the traditional theory of utility by placing limits on the normative application of the calculus of choice. The quantitative axiom [VIII] is a convenient idealization. In some cases it is reasonable to violate the marking axiom [I] or part [IVA] of invariance. When using the complete calculus of choice, one is treating life as a gamble and a game. Whether or not we should regard life in this way and employ the calculus depends on the circumstances in each particular case. Life is a gamble, certainly, but in many cases the gamble is vague and ill-defined, and this takes away much of the sting.

Subject to these qualifications, one should follow the calculus of choice and the calculus of inductive probability.

5.6.3 Probability statements and logical truth

Our second main question was: Is an atomic inductive probability statement logically true-or-false, empirically true-or-false, or neither? Are the theorems of the calculus of inductive probability logically true? (pp. 29, 92). In this subsection, we shall modify this question slightly and answer it by means of the pragmatic theory of inductive probability, together with our earlier result that there are alternative inductive logics (sec. 3.3.1) and our refutation of the frequency theory of inductive probability (sec. 3.4.2). Our answer will delineate the limits of the a priori aspect of inductive probability.

We have analyzed deductive, inductive, and empirical truth hierarchically. The calculus of probability and formal inductive logic were built around a core of deductive logic (pp. 262–63). The verification or disverification of empirical statements and theories generally requires both deductive and inductive reasoning. Because of this hierarchical structure, the classification of compound statement forms according to how their truth values are ascertained may not be neat and simple. For example, the conjunction "$(3 + 5 = x)$&(there are x apples)" is logically false if $x \neq 8$ but empirically true-or-false if $x = 8$. Since an atomic inductive probability statement has a pragmatic aspect superimposed on an a priori aspect, its classification is complicated in a similar manner.

To avoid this bothersome complication we limit our discussion to *true* atomic inductive probability statements. These are, after all, the statements we wish to employ in inductive inference. The first part of our second question then becomes: *Is a true atomic inductive probability statement logically true, empirically true, or neither?* We eliminated the second alternative at the end of Chapter 3 (p. 160). We now establish the third alternative, showing that while $\mathbf{P}(h, e) = x$ has a logical component it also has a non-logical component. Our argument will be an extension of the argument from alternative inductive logics of Chapter 3 (pp. 128–30) to take explicit account of the pragmatic aspect of inductive probability.

We need consider only two inductive logics: the standard inductive logic of Mr. Standard, and the inverse inductive logic of the hypothetical Mr. Inverse. For the sake of concreteness we will work with the simplified example of pp. 109–12 in which it is assumed that *a* is a white swan and *b* is a swan, and it is predicted that *b* is white. The two inductive logics assign different conditional probabilities to this prediction, and correspondingly Mr. Standard and Mr. Inverse have different probabilistic beliefs. Mr. Standard believes that

(1) $\mathbf{P}(Wb, SaWaSb) = 2/3$,

while Mr. Inverse believes that

(1^i) $\mathbf{P}(Wb, SaWaSb) = 1/3$.

To explicate the contents of (1) and (1^i) we ascertain the commitments made by Mr. Standard and Mr. Inverse, respectively, when they assert these atomic probability statements.

According to the pragmatic theory of inductive probability, believing an atomic inductive probability statement implies having a disposition to behave in certain ways. Statement (1) expresses a commitment to bet on the pair $\langle Wb, SaWaSb\rangle$ with odds 2 to 1, while statement (1^i) expresses a commitment to bet on the same pair with odds 1 to 2. Now each man thinks the inductive logic he uses is the correct one. Hence the statement "The correct inductive logic assigns the number x to the pair $\langle c, d\rangle$" comes close enough in meaning to "The probability of c on d is x" to serve as a model of it in the present argument. Under this transformation the two atomic probability statements (1) and (1^i) become, respectively,

(2) The correct inductive logic assigns the number 2/3 to the pair $\langle Wb, SaWaSb\rangle$

(2^i) The correct inductive logic assigns the number 1/3 to the pair $\langle Wb, SaWaSb\rangle$.

The transformation from "probable" to "the correct inductive logic" treats "probable" as if it were used in the same sense by both Mr. Standard and Mr. Inverse, but there is an important respect in which these two men use the term differently. Mr. Standard uses "probable" in the ordinary sense, governed by axiom [24], whereas Mr. Inverse uses it in a hypothetical sense, governed by axiom [24^i] (pp. 110–11). We render this difference explicit by replacing the original probability statements with statements in which the inductive logic that is employed is explicitly referred to. Under this transformation Mr. Standard's statement (1) becomes

(3a) Standard inductive logic assigns the number 2/3 to the pair ⟨*Wb*, *SaWaSb*⟩, and

(3b) The correct odds for betting on the pair ⟨*Wb*, *SaWaSb*⟩ are 2 to 1,

while Mr. Inverse's statement (1^i) becomes

(3^ia) Inverse inductive logic assigns the number 1/3 to the pair ⟨*Wb*, *SaWaSb*⟩, and

(3^ib) The correct odds for betting on the pair ⟨*Wb*, *SaWaSb*⟩ are 1 to 2.

The two halves of these last two statements correspond respectively to the two aspects of inductive probability: (3a) and (3^ia) to the a priori aspect, (3b) and (3^ib) to the pragmatic aspect (sec. 5.6.1). The following should be observed about (3a) and (3^ia): They are concerned with different subject matters, are logically compatible, are both true, and are both believed by both Mr. Standard and Mr. Inverse; moreover, neither (3a) nor (3^ia) says or implies anything about the correctness of any inductive logic. In contrast, (3b) and (3^ib) are logically incompatible, for they commit a person to different betting odds for the same situation; Mr. Standard believes the first but not the second, and conversely for Mr. Inverse. Thus Mr. Standard and Mr. Inverse agree within the a priori dimension of inductive probability but disagree within the pragmatic dimension of inductive probability.

The crucial difference between the pragmatic and a priori aspects of inductive probability involves a commitment to use an inductive logic. We say that a term or statement is *inductive-method committive* if it expresses a commitment to use an inductive logic. Statements (3b) and (3^ib), and hence (1), (1^i), (2), and (2^i), are inductive-method committive, but statements (3a) and (3^ia) are not.

Paralleling the a priori and pragmatic aspects of inductive probability are two modes of rationality. We built the calculi of inductive probability and choice around a core of deductive logic (secs. 2.2.1, 3.2, 5.3.1). Correspondingly, we have assumed that Mr. Standard and Mr. Inverse are rational in the following core sense, which we call *deductively rational*. A person who is deductively rational has some training in mathematics and deductive logic, and he believes many propositions in these subjects (see secs. 1.4 and 1.5). He acts in accordance with all the propositions of these subjects that he believes.* Thus if he believes that the library is closed on holidays and that today is a holiday, when he recognizes that these two propositions logically entail that the library is closed today, he will accept this conclusion. When he combines 143 groups of 27 objects and no objects split, merge, or disappear, he expects a group of 3,861 objects. Finally, we stipulate that a person who is deductively rational is familiar with the formal properties of the system of inductive logic we have studied thus far: the calculus of inductive probability (chap. 2), Carnap's systems of inductive logic (sec. 3.2), and the calculus of choice (secs. 5.2–5.5).

A formal understanding of these systems does not carry with it a commitment to use them, of course. Let us imagine a modern Pyrrho who is deductively rational but whose rationality does not go beyond this (see sec. 3.2.2). Being deductively rational, he believes both (3a) and (3^ia). But belief in (3a) does not commit him to believe (3b), for he does not accept

(4) Standard inductive logic is the correct inductive logic to use.

Likewise rejecting

(4^i) Inverse inductive logic is the correct inductive logic to use,

he can accept (3^ia) without accepting (3^ib). This modern Pyrrho does not make any inductive-method committive statements at all. Indeed, he does not even use the calculus of inductive probability or the calculus of choice.

We saw earlier that one of the criteria of rationality, in the ordinary sense of that term, is the use of standard inductive logic (sec. 3.3.2). This criterion is not part of our definition of deductive rationality; moreover, the preceding argument shows that it is not implied by that definition. Since using deductive logic is the criterion for deductive rationality, it follows that inductive logic goes beyond and is not reducible to deductive logic. Thus rationality has at least two modes: deductive rationality, and reasoning and acting in accord with standard inductive logic. There may also be an ethical mode of rationality, but we need not consider it here.

Mr. Standard is not only rational in the core sense of deductively rational; his very use of standard inductive logic is rational in the ordinary sense. We shall say he is *rational*$_s$. Since the hypothetical Mr. Inverse does not use standard inductive logic, he is not rational$_s$. But he is much closer to being rational in this sense than the modern Pyrrho, who is only deductively rational. Mr. Inverse uses the calculus of inductive probability and the calculus of choice. Moreover, he uses that inductive logic that he believes to be correct, namely, inverse inductive logic. We shall say Mr. Inverse is *rational*$_i$. Rationality$_s$ and rationality$_i$ are both kinds of "rationality" in a

* Thus deductive rationality also has a pragmatic aspect. We are not arguing that inductive probability is unique in having a pragmatic aspect, but that the pragmatic aspect of inductive probability goes beyond the pragmatic aspect of deductive rationality.

generalized sense. Both contain deductive rationality and a commitment to use some inductive logic; they differ as to the particular inductive logic to be used.

Thus there are the following modes of deductive and inductive rationality, each including its predecessors: deductive rationality; using the calculus of inductive probability; using some inductive logic; and using standard inductive logic (rationality$_s$).

As ordinarily employed, the term "correct" belongs to the family of words that connote an appeal to standard inductive logic. "Probability," "evidence," and "rational" also belong to this family (pp. 135–36). Hence to formulate our theory, we need to use technical extensions of these terms that are not question-begging with respect to standard inductive logic. Our use of "correct" in statements (2), (2^i), (3b), (3^ib), (4), and (4^i) is to be taken in such an extended and technical sense. Enough has been said to make clear the meaning intended there.

We originally specified the meaning of "logically true-or-false" by giving examples and stating that a logically true-or-false statement is one that, in principle, can be decided by reasoning alone without the use of observation and experiment (sec. 1.2.1). We now see that there are different senses of "reason." Hence there are different senses of "logically true-or-false," and the answer to our second main question depends on which sense of "logically true-or-false" is taken. If "reasoning" is taken in the ordinary sense (which includes rational$_s$), atomic inductive probability statements are logically true-or-false. Then (1) is logically true and (1^i) is not. If reasoning is taken in the sense of rational$_i$, atomic inductive probability statements are logically true-or-false, but now (1) is not logically true while (1^i) is! Finally, if reasoning is taken in the sense of deductive rationality, neither (1) nor (1^i) is logically true, as we will see shortly.

Since we want "logically true-or-false" to be an unambiguous technical term, we must further specify its meaning (sec. 1.3). We do this by stipulating that "reasoning," as it is used in the specification of "logically true-or-false" in Section 1.2.1, be taken in the core sense of deductive rationality. Hence, as we employ the term, a **logically true-or-false statement** is one whose truth-value, in principle, can be decided by deductive reasoning alone without the use of observation and experiment and without appeal to the rules of inductive reasoning.

Let us look once again at the two aspects of the meaning of inductive probability: the a priori and the pragmatic. The a priori aspect corresponds to statements (3a) and (3^ia), and anyone who is deductively rational accepts both of these statements. So statements (3a) and (3^ia) are both logically true in any sense of this term. The pragmatic aspect corresponds to (3b) and (3^ib). Anyone who is rational in the ordinary sense (and hence rational$_s$) accepts (3b) but rejects (3^ib); while Mr. Inverse, who is rational$_i$, accepts

(3^{i}b) and rejects (3b). Statement (3b) is true but not logically true, while (3^{i}b) is false but not logically false. We conclude that true atomic inductive probability statements are not logically true.

Clearly, then, the a priori component (3a) does not logically imply the pragmatic component (3b), nor does (3^{i}a) imply (3^{i}b). Consequently, the a priori aspect of inductive probability is formal and empty of pragmatic content, and it does not entail or imply the pragmatic aspect. This conclusion is further supported by our earlier line of argument that culminated in Hume's thesis that there is no noncircular justification of induction (sec. 3.3).

It may be helpful to review the general steps of our argument that true atomic inductive probability statements are not logically true. Mr. Standard, who represents the ordinary user of standard inductive logic, asserts truly that

(1) $\mathbf{P}(Wb, SaWaSb) = 2/3$,

two-thirds being the value assigned to the pair $\langle Wb, SaWaSb\rangle$ by standard inductive logic. We modeled (1) by

(2) The correct inductive logic assigns the number 2/3 to the pair $\langle Wb, SaWaSb\rangle$

and then by

(3a) Standard inductive logic assigns the number 2/3 to the pair $\langle Wb, SaWaSb\rangle$, and

(3b) The correct odds for betting on the pair $\langle Wb, SaWaSb\rangle$ are 2 to 1.

The example was chosen so that (3a) is logically true. Because of the pragmatic aspect of inductive probability, statement (3b) is not logically true. We claim that statement (3a)&(3b) is a sufficiently good model of (2) to show that (2) is not logically true. We further claim that (2) models (1) in the respects needed for showing that (1) is not logically true.

Though we have limited our second question to true atomic inductive probability statements (p. 313), a comment on false ones is in order. Suppose Mr. Standard makes a logical error of some kind and as a result asserts the false statement.

(1*) $\mathbf{P}(Wb, SaWaSb) = 1/3$.

We model this as before by

(3* a) Standard inductive logic assigns the number 1/3 to the pair $\langle Wb, SaWaSb\rangle$, and

(3* b) The correct odds for betting on the pair $\langle Wb, SaWaSb\rangle$ are 1 to 2.

Statement (3*a) is logically false; hence (3*a)&(3*b) is, and (1*) is also. But suppose Mr. Standard only guessed at the probability in arriving at the erroneous value 1/3? Then it might be misleading to say that (1*) is logically false. This case shows that the models (3a)&(3b) and (3*a)&(3*b) make the a priori aspect of inductive probability more explicit than it sometimes is. The a priori aspect is nevertheless present at least implicitly, since the rules of standard inductive logic are a normative standard to which one can appeal in judging the truth of a statement of the form $\mathbf{P}(h, e) = x$. Clearly, Mr. Standard accepts this norm.

We are modeling $\mathbf{P}(h, e) = x$ as a conjunction of two statements, one logically true-and-false, and one not, to show that inductive probability has both an a priori aspect and a pragmatic aspect. We are not saying that these two aspects interact in a simple conjunctive fashion, but only that they are both present. In the next section we will argue that two traditional theories of probability fail to do justice to both aspects. The a priori theory recognizes only the a priori aspect (sec. 7.1). The personalistic theory recognizes both, but has an incomplete concept of the a priori aspect (sec. 7.2).

This completes our answer to the first part of our second main question. Consider finally the theorems of the calculus of inductive probability. This calculus has an a priori aspect, for a claim of the form "The axioms of this calculus imply Φ" is logically true-or-false. But what about the theorems themselves, construed as interpreted statements? (Cf. secs. 1.2.2, 2.1.)

It is evident from our normative evaluation of the calculus of choice that its subsystem, the calculus of inductive probability, has a pragmatic force beyond deductive rationality. A set of partial beliefs that does not satisfy the calculus of inductive probability is "inconsistent" in some sense, but it is not deductively inconsistent. In the terminology of the "book" theorem (sec. 4.4), it is "incoherent." Our modern Pyrrho, whose rationality is limited to deductive rationality, can legitimately hold and act upon a set of partial beliefs that is incoherent. He refuses to ground his partial beliefs on the assumption that he is playing a game against a malevolent nature. Coherence is thus a kind of inductive consistency that goes beyond deductive consistency. Since the theorems of the calculus of inductive probability have this pragmatic implication, they are not logically true.

Thus, because of their pragmatic aspect, true atomic inductive probability statements and the theorems of the calculus of inductive probability are not logically true. They are not empirically true, either (pp. 92, 160). Combining all this, we obtain the answer to our second main question: *True atomic inductive probability statements and the theorems of the calculus of inductive probability are neither logical nor empirical truths.*

5.6.4 Conclusion

Let us now summarize the pragmatic theory of inductive probability in terms of its contributions to our first two main questions.

(I) What is the nature of a system of atomic inductive probability statements?

(II) Is a true atomic inductive probability statement logically true, empirically true, or neither? Are the theorems of the calculus of inductive probability logically true?

The pragmatic theory provides an answer to question (I), and it contributes to answering question (II).

According to the pragmatic theory, a system of atomic inductive probability statements has two interrelated but coequal aspects, an a priori aspect and a pragmatic aspect. The a priori aspect concerns the assignment of probability values to statements by formal rules. Probability values are and should be assigned according to the rules of the calculus of probability and standard inductive logic. Consequently, both individual atomic probability statements and systems of them have logically true-or-false components.

The pragmatic aspect of inductive probability concerns the application of these probability assignments. An atomic inductive probability statement does and should express a disposition to act in certain ways in conditions of uncertainty. A system of such statements does and should express a commitment to make one's probability assignments conform to the calculus of probability and standard inductive logic. The calculus of choice explicates the concepts of probability and utility as they are and should be reflected in the choices of a single subject.

Because of their pragmatic aspect, true atomic inductive probability statements and the theorems of the calculus of probability are not logically true in our technical sense of that term (p. 317). These statements are clearly not empirically true, either (p. 160). They belong, then, to a third category of statements (cf. p. 7). We will later call them "inductive statements" and argue that the presuppositions of induction belong to this category (p. 638). Positive information as to the nature of inductive statements is contained in our answers to the first and fourth main questions.

We can throw further light on the a priori and pragmatic aspects of inductive probability by comparing Mr. Standard's and Mr. Inverse's uses of "probable." These uses agree in pragmatic aspect, for both are inductive method committive. They differ in a priori aspect, for Mr. Standard and Mr. Inverse employ different rules in assigning probabilities. The logically true-or-false statements that each employs in induction differ significantly.

The pragmatic theory makes both descriptive and normative claims about inductive probability. Descriptively, the calculus of probability, standard inductive logic, and the calculus of choice are fair models of actual reasoning and decision-making. Normatively, one should generally follow these three axiomatic systems when reasoning inductively and making decisions. But the difficulties we found in the traditional theory of utility show that there are important exceptions to this general rule. In some cases it is reasonable to violate the marking axiom [I] or part [IVA] of invariance. The quantitative axiom [VIII] should be treated as a convenient idealization (pp. 310–12).

This completes the summary of my pragmatic theory of inductive probability. The pragmatic theory, together with our earlier findings on inductive logics, answers the second main question of this treatise. And, as we have seen, it provides *an* answer to the first main question. But now we wish to show that this answer is incomplete, for it leads inevitably to our fourth main question, which it fails to answer.

Consider a system of atomic inductive probability statements asserted by a subject. The pragmatic content of these statements consists in his disposition to behave in certain ways under certain conditions. The very idea of a strategy or plan of action is to make choices before one is forced by circumstances to do so, and this involves deciding how one would act in various situations. Hence, to describe the pragmatic content of an inductive probability statement one must use subjunctives of the form "If he wants ϕ and should be in circumstances ψ, he would act in manner θ" (p. 178).

When discussing Peirce's practical conditionals we saw that such subjunctives express causal necessities (p. 174). Hence the concept of inductive probability is grounded on the notion of causal necessity, in the sense that one must employ the latter concept in describing the pragmatic content of the former concept. Thus the two concepts are interrelated, and a complete account of inductive probability must include some account of causal necessity.

Our fourth main question was: What is the nature of causal necessity and how is it related to inductive probability? (P. 30) So, in answering our first main question, the pragmatic theory of inductive probability leads us to our fourth main question. We deal with this fourth question in later chapters. In Chapters 6 and 7 we develop and interpret the logic of causal necessity, while in Chapters 9 and 10 we present the presupposition theory of induction, which answers this fourth question and thus gives a more complete answer to the first question.

5.7 Closely Related Theories of Inductive Probability

5.7.1 The a priori theory

I shall conclude this chapter by comparing and contrasting my pragmatic theory of inductive probability with two closely related theories, the a priori theory and the personalistic theory.

Traditionally, the a priori theory has been the chief competitor of the frequency theory (sec. 3.4). All a priorists agree that inductive probability

(**P**) is fundamentally a priori in character and cannot be analyzed into frequency probability ($\mathbf{P}_f$). Beyond this, the views of a priorists vary considerably. In my opinion, the best formulations and defenses are those in John Maynard Keynes' *A Treatise on Probability* (1921) and Rudolf Carnap's *Logical Foundations of Probability* (1950).* I shall discuss these works after first analyzing the a priori theory in my own terms.

The essential core of the *a priori theory of inductive probability* consists of two interrelated theses. (*1*) True atomic inductive probability statements are "logically true" in some sense. (*2*) There is an a priori justification for using standard inductive logic, so that the pragmatic aspect of inductive probability is derivable from the a priori aspect. However, both theses are ambiguous, because "logically-true" has a broad sense (inclusive of standard inductive logic) as well as a narrow sense (limited to deductive logic) (p. 316).

We therefore distinguish two versions of the a priori theory. The "deductive version" of the a priori theory of inductive probability consists of these essentially equivalent theses

(***1d***) True atomic inductive probability statements are logically true in the narrow sense.

(***2d***) There is a deductive justification for using standard inductive logic, so that the pragmatic aspect of inductive probability is deductively derivable from the a priori aspect.

The "nondeductive version" of the a priori theory of inductive probability is

(***1n***) True atomic inductive probability statements are logically true in the broad sense.

(***2n***) There is an a priori (but nondeductive) justification for using standard inductive logic, so that the pragmatic aspect is derivable (but not deductively derivable) from the a priori aspect.

Quite clearly, the deductive version makes much stronger claims than the nondeductive version. The deductive version contradicts both Hume's thesis that there is no noncircular justification of induction and our conclusion that true atomic inductive probability statements are not logically true (in the narrow sense). In contrast, the nondeductive version is consistent with both Hume's thesis and our conclusion. Despite these differences, both versions are incompatible with the pragmatic theory of inductive probability, because both make the pragmatic aspect of inductive probability subordinate to and derivable from the a priori aspect, albeit in different ways.

* See also von Kries, *Die Principien der Wahrscheinlichkeitsrechnung;* Broad, *Induction, Probability, and Causation;* Jeffreys, *Theory of Probability;* and Nicod, *Foundations of Geometry and Induction.*

Our line of criticism of the a priori theory of probability will be that the pragmatic aspect of inductive probability cannot be derived from the a priori aspect. Consider some true statement of standard inductive logic. While in the broad sense of "logically true" it is built into such a statement that one should employ standard inductive logic, citing this fact provides no justification for doing so. And in the narrow sense of "logically true" there is a pragmatic gap between assigning a probability value by the rules of standard inductive logic and using that probability value in inductive inference.

We turn now to Keynes' *A Treatise on Probability*. Keynes did not explicitly distinguish between the two versions of thesis (*1*), but his remarks on the relation of probability to certainty show that he held only the weaker version (***1n***). He maintained that deduction is a limiting case of induction.

> Of probability we can say no more than that it is a lower degree of rational belief than certainty; and we may say, if we like, that it deals with degrees of certainty. Or we may make probability the more fundamental of the two and regard certainty as a special case of probability, as being, in fact, the *maximum probability*. Speaking somewhat loosely we may say that, if our premisses make the conclusion certain, then it *follows* from the premisses; and if they make it very probable, then it very nearly follows from them.*

Also, he believed that probability is an indefinable relation between statements.

> A *definition* of probability is not possible, unless it contents us to define degrees of the probability-relation by reference to degrees of rational belief. We cannot analyze the probability-relation in terms of simpler ideas. As soon as we have passed from the logic of implication and the categories of truth and falsehood to the logic of probability and the categories of knowledge, ignorance, and rational belief, we are paying attention to a new logical relation in which, although it is logical, we were not previously interested, and which cannot be explained or defined in terms of our previous notions.

These views imply that true atomic inductive probability statements are not logically true in the narrow sense but only in the broad sense; this agrees with our conclusion (pp. 316, 318).

Keynes suggested an a priori, nondeductive justification for standard inductive logic and hence advocated thesis (***2n***). Since this justification is closely related to the presupposition theory of Chapter 10, it will be discussed there (pp. 641–42).

We consider next Carnap's *Logical Foundations of Probability*. Carnap said that a true atomic inductive probability statement is L-true (his pp. 29–31), and he defined "L-true" (p. 83) so that it is approximately

* *A Treatise on Probability*, p. 15, with a footnote reference deleted. The next quotation is from p. 8.

synonymous with "logically true" in our narrower technical sense. Thus he advocated the stronger thesis (***1d***), which makes inductive reasoning a species of deductive reasoning and so implies thesis (***2d***). If an atomic inductive probability statement were logically true in the narrow sense, we would have the same justification for using it that we have for using any deductive or mathematical truth. To deny a true atomic inductive probability statement would be to assert a deductive contradiction.

Carnap develops this theme in his Section 41F ("Presuppositions of Induction"). He considers the traditional problem of justifying the assumption that nature is uniform.

> . . . many philosophers have asserted that the assumption of the uniformity of the world is a necessary presupposition for the validity of inductive inferences. . . . There is no doubt that the principle is synthetic, that it makes a factual assertion about the world; it is conceivable that it is false, that is, that the world is chaotic or at least has a low degree of uniformity. Many philosophers maintain that the principle is fundamentally different from other factual hypotheses about the world, e.g., physical laws. The latter hypotheses can be empirically tested on the basis of observational evidence and thereby either confirmed or disconfirmed inductively. But any attempt to confirm inductively the principle of uniformity would contain a vicious circle, according to these philosophers, because the inductive method presupposes this principle.*

Carnap then offers the following solution to this justification problem. Let U be the statement "The degree of statistical uniformity of the world is high" and let E express the total available evidence concerning the statistical uniformity of the actual universe. Consider

(5) $\mathbf{P}(U, E)$ is high,

which asserts that on the basis of the available evidence it is very *probable* that the actual universe has a high degree of statistical uniformity. Statement (5) implies that one who uses standard inductive logic will *probably* succeed.

As Carnap points out, (5) is a true atomic inductive probability statement. By thesis (***1d***), statement (5) is logically true in the narrow sense of the term (L-true). In Carnap's words:

> What is needed as a presupposition for the validity of the inductive method and the justification of its application in determining practical decisions is not the principle of the uniformity of the world but only the statement that the uniformity is probable on the basis of the available evidence. This statement is an analytic statement [L-true or logically true] in inductive logic and hence not in need of empirical confirmation. Thus the apparent vicious circle, which many philosophers believe to be involved in the validation of the inductive method, disappears.

* *Logical Foundations of Probability*, pp. 178–79. He refers to chaps. 5 and 6 of part 6 of Russell's *Human Knowledge, Its Scope and Limits*. He could have referrred equally well to chap. 22 of Keynes' *A Treatise on Probability*.

The next quotation is Carnap's own summary of sec. 41F, p. 163; see also p. v.

Since it is a truth of deductive logic that one who uses standard inductive logic is *likely* to succeed, the use of standard inductive logic is justified on a priori grounds.

My earlier arguments for Hume's thesis that there is no noncircular justification of induction (sec. 3.3.1) and for the pragmatic theory of probability (sec. 5.6.3) show that Carnap's putative justification of induction fails. Statement (5) is an atomic inductive probability statement and hence has both an a priori component and a pragmatic component.

(5a) Standard inductive logic assigns a high value to the pair $\langle U, E\rangle$

(5b) The correct odds for betting on the pair $\langle U, E\rangle$ are high.

Component (5a) is an internal expression of the fact that standard inductive logic assigns higher probabilities to statistically uniform universes than to irregular ones; it has basically the same content as formula [25] of page 116. Hence (5a) is logically true in the narrow sense. But (5a) is not inductive-method committive. On the other hand, component (5b) is inductive-method committive, but it is not logically true in the narrow sense. Since (5b) is a component of (5), statement (5) is not logically true in the narrow sense. Therefore, Carnap's putative justification of induction fails.

I have thus refuted the deductive version of the a priori theory of inductive probability, which Carnap advocated in his *Logical Foundations of Probability*. For the sake of completeness I will comment on Carnap's later views before turning to the personalistic theory. The arguments I have just given against Carnap employ his formal models of induction (see sec. 3.2.1), so that the philosophical conclusions I draw from these models are diametrically opposed to those he drew. I presented the essentials of my position on the justification of induction (see secs. 3.3.1, 5.6.3) in my paper for *The Philosophy of Rudolf Carnap* (1963), and Carnap replied to me in the same volume.* I will here analyze his reply in terms of the deductive and nondeductive versions of the a priori theory of inductive probability.

Carnap wavers between the stronger (***1d***) and the weaker (***1n***). He agrees that an atomic inductive probability statement is inductive-method committive (pp. 980–81) and says "it is impossible to give a purely deductive justification of induction" (p. 978). On the other hand, he says that the proper explication of an atomic inductive probability statement is L-determinate [logically true-or-false in my narrow sense], and in arguing for

* My paper, "On the Significance of Carnap's System of Inductive Logic for the Philosophy of Induction," was written in 1954. Earlier I expressed similar opinions in my review of *Logical Foundations of Probability* and my "The Presupposition Theory of Induction."

The Philosophy of Rudolph Carnap contains several articles on Carnap's work in probability and induction. Carnap replied to all of these at pp. 966–98 of "Replies and Systematic Expositions." His comments on my paper are at pp. 980–83.

this he assumes that a cognitive statement that is not empirically true-or-false must be logically true-or-false in the narrow sense (p. 981).

Carnap now advocates the weaker thesis (***2n***), claiming there are a priori reasons (but not deductive reasons) for using standard inductive logic (p. 978). However, he gives no arguments for this claim. He agrees that his arguments in Section 41F of *Foundations of Probability* (discussed on pp. 322–24, above) do not justify the use of standard inductive logic (p. 982).* But he neither offers a new a priori justification for the use of standard inductive logic, nor gives any explanation of the nature of a statement that is logically true in the broad sense but not in the narrow sense (not L-true).

This concludes, for the present, our discussion of the a priori theory of inductive probability. We have seen that there are two, substantially different, versions of this theory. Keynes advocated the weaker, non-deductive version; we discuss this further in Section 10.5.1. In his *Logical Foundations of Probability* Carnap advocated the stronger, deductive version, but wavered between the two versions in his later writings; in both cases he failed to establish the a priori theory of probability.

5.7.2 The personalistic theory

We have already said a good deal about the personalistic theory of Ramsey, de Finetti, and Savage (sec. 5.1.2). Savage gives a good summary statement.

> **Personalistic** views hold that probability measures the confidence that a particular individual has in the truth of a particular proposition, for example, the proposition that it will rain tomorrow. These views postulate that the individual concerned is in some ways "reasonable," but they do not deny the possibility that two reasonable individuals faced with the same evidence may have different degrees of confidence in the truth of the same proposition.†

According to the *personalistic theory of inductive probability*, probability measures the "degree of rational belief or confidence" a person has in a proposition. "Degree of rational belief" is explicated pragmatically, in terms

* Surprisingly, Carnap says that these arguments were not intended as a justification of induction (p. 982). It still seems to me natural to interpret them as a putative justification, and I think that on his 1963 interpretation sec. 41F is otiose, being directed against a straw man. Moreover, if atomic inductive probability statements *were* L-determinate, as Carnap claimed in *Logical Foundations of Probability* (p. 83), the justification of induction in sec. 41F *would be* valid.

Personally, I think the philosophy of induction in *Logical Foundations of Probability* (1950) is clearer, better argued, and more substantial than the philosophy of induction in "Replies and Systematic Expositions" (1963).

† *The Foundations of Statistics*, p. 3.

of hypothetical betting behavior, and it is both descriptive and normative. The criteria of rationality are those of the calculus of probability and the calculus of choice. Thus a system of atomic inductive probability statements has both a pragmatic aspect (expressing the speaker's commitment to behave in a certain way) and an a priori aspect (conformity to the calculus of probability). However, the rules of standard inductive logic are not included in the criteria of rationality recognized by the personalistic theory. Consequently, the personalistic theory views the a priori aspect of inductive probability much more narrowly than does the pragmatic theory.

The pragmatic theory was derived from the personalistic theory, of course, and the two are similar in some respects but differ basically in others. Though the particular account of the normative use of the calculus of choice given in Section 5.6.2 is my own, there is no fundamental reason why a personalist could not accept it. On the other hand, most of my discussion of probability and logical truth in Section 5.6.3 would be unacceptable to the personalist, for this discussion is based on the existence of alternative inductive logics, which the personalist does not include in his underlying formalism.

This difference in the treatment of inductive logic is an important one. The calculus of inductive probability does not in general determine the value of an atomic probability. More precisely, if h and e are logically independent and $0 \leqq x \leqq 1$, neither the atomic probability statement $\mathbf{P}(h, e) = x$ nor its negation is a theorem of the calculus of inductive probability (sec. 3.1). Hence if the criteria of inductive rationality are limited to the calculus of inductive probability and do not include the rules of standard inductive logic, any value of $\mathbf{P}(h, e)$ in the range zero to one is inductively reasonable. Likewise, Mr. Standard, Mr. Inverse, and Mr. Random are all reasonable in this sense of "reasonable" (secs. 3.3.2, 5.6.3). In other words, the personalistic theory of inductive probability holds that two "rational" individuals who have the same total evidence e may differ without limit in their degrees of belief in h. If this be granted, I see no reason why an individual should not have the same privilege and change his degree of belief in the pair $\langle h, e \rangle$ from time to time, provided his probability assignments are always coherent (sec. 4.4).

We have argued in this book that the ordinary criteria of rationality include the rules of standard inductive logic, and this claim is incorporated in the pragmatic theory of inductive probability. The probability values determined by these rules may be only qualitative. The rules of standard inductive logic determine numerical probability values in our formal models, but these are idealizations of the actual world of induction. We are claiming against the personalistic theory only that the rules of standard inductive logic set limits on what atomic probability values are reasonable (secs. 4.3.2 and 5.6.2).

We may illustrate this point with an example. Let E say that a card is to be drawn from a bridge deck in the usual way and that in the past each card has been drawn with about the same relative frequency. Let H_1 state that the first card drawn is a heart. If the criteria of inductive rationality are limited to the calculus of inductive probability, any value for $\mathbf{P}(H_1, E)$ in the range zero to one is reasonable. But it seems to me that the correct value for $\mathbf{P}(H_1, E)$ is about 1/4 and that 10^{-10} and $1-10^{-10}$ are unreasonable values for $\mathbf{P}(H_1, E)$. In other words, $\mathbf{P}(H_1, E) \doteq 1/4$ is true on a priori grounds, while $\mathbf{P}(H_1, E) \doteq 10^{-10}$ and $\mathbf{P}(H_1, E) \doteq 1-10^{-10}$ are both false on a priori grounds, where "$\doteq$" symbolizes approximate equality. It follows that any two rational individuals who have the same total information E should believe in H_1 to approximately degree 1/4.

Thus the personalistic and the pragmatic theories of probability give different answers to the question: To what extent should two rational individuals who possess the same information agree on their atomic inductive probability assignments? Bayes' theorem and the confirmation theorem have a bearing on this issue, because these theorems show that disagreement over the probability of a hypothesis tends to be reduced by repeated experimentation (sec. 2.5.3).* However, these are theorems of the calculus of probability; as such they merely restrict systems of atomic probability statements. Consider two investigators who possess the same data and who make their partial beliefs conform to Bayes' theorem. Insofar as they agree (or disagree) on the posterior probability of a hypothesis, they must agree (or disagree) to a certain calculable extent on the prior probability of that hypothesis. But Bayes' theorem and the confirmation theorem allow this prior probability to have any value from zero to one (pp. 90–91 and sec. 8.3.4).

The question of whether the rules of standard inductive logic are to be included among the norms governing "probable" has a bearing on the extent to which probability is personal and subjective. Since the personalistic theory does not include the rules of standard inductive logic among the norms governing "probable," it makes probability more subjective and relative to the individual, more a matter of personal taste or preference, than the pragmatic theory does. From this point of view, the pragmatic theory could appropriately be called "the interpersonal theory" or "the intersubjective theory" of probability. We will see later that this difference between the personalistic and pragmatic theories has important implications concerning the nature of empirical probability (secs. 8.3.4 and 8.4.3).

5.8 Summary

The aim of this chapter is philosophical: to present my pragmatic theory of inductive probability. The pragmatic theory is based on an axiomatic

* De Finetti, "Recent Suggestions for the Reconciliation of Theories of Probability," p. 220.

system, the calculus of choice, and much of the chapter is devoted to the development of that system.

The pragmatic theory is a modification and extension of the personalistic theory of Ramsey, de Finetti, and Savage. Ramsey and de Finetti took gambling games to be the paradigmatic case of how probability theory is and should be applied. They based their personalistic account of probability on the relation between coherence and the calculus of probability expressed by the "book" theorem. Probability measures the strength of a partial belief, and one's partial beliefs should satisfy the calculus of probability so that no book can be made against him.

Savage also based his formulation of the personalistic theory on a mathematical theorem. Building on the work of Ramsey and de Finetti, he developed an axiomatic system for choice. His axioms are rules governing choice, such as the simple ordering of preferences [2], the partial act theorem [10], and the ordering of uncertainties axiom [VI] in unconditional form. Savage's main theorem states that choices made in accordance with these rules both maximize utility and satisfy the calculus of probability. (Secs. 5.1.2, 5.5.3)

My calculus of choice is a modification and extension of Savage's system. The "grammar" of the system has been modified and enlarged: rules of choice are stated in terms of trees, and extended trees are included as well as normal form trees. Some of Savage's axioms have been replaced by more basic ones that can be used to resolve the difficulties we found with the traditional theory of utility.

The grammar of the calculus of choice contains definitions of the entities to be interpreted. The most important of these are the following: choice trees and act trees (marked choice trees), a basis of statements and consequences, a set of choice trees complete with respect to this basis, and a marked set of trees (which results from marking one or more of a complete set of choice trees). The trees of Chapter 4 are all "normal form trees," having a single choice point leading to alternate chance points. The calculus of choice also covers extended trees, which have many levels of choice and chance points. In marking an extended tree, a subject expresses his conditional probability judgments, for a choice point may be reached only if certain statements are true. (Sec. 5.2)

The axioms of the calculus of choice restrict how a subject marks a complete set of choice trees. The first six axioms [I]–[VI] yield the simple ordering of preferences and uncertainties, for conditional as well as unconditional preferences and uncertainties. The normal form axiom [VII] reduces choices made in an extended tree to choices made in its normal form equivalent and completes the comparative structure of preferences and uncertainties. The quantitative axiom [VIII] converts this comparative structure into a quantitative structure.

The axioms and theorems of the calculus of choice are summarized below, by subsection.

5.3.1 *Marking and logical equivalence axioms*

[I] (Marking axiom) The subject converts every choice tree into an act tree.

[II] (Logical equivalence axiom)
(A) The subject converts logically equivalent choice trees into logically equivalent act trees.
(B) Suppose the alternatives at a choice point include two or more tokens of the same subtree. The subject treats them all the same (choosing all if he chooses one and marking them the same if marking is required).

[1] Let i be the information at a choice point whose alternatives include two or more subtrees that are logically equivalent on condition i. If the subject chooses one of these subtrees, then
(a) he chooses all of them
(b) if the subtrees have any choice points, he converts them all into act trees that are logically equivalent on condition i.

5.3.2 *Simple ordering of preferences*

[III] (Subset axiom) If an act tree belongs to the marked set, so does every *act* tree obtained from it by deleting one or more solid lines and their subtrees.

[2] (Simple ordering of preferences)
(a) $(a_1 \geqq a_2) \vee (a_2 \geqq a_1)$ (comparable)
(b) $[(a_1 \geqq a_2)(a_2 \geqq a_3)] \supset (a_1 \geqq a_3)$ (transitive).

[IV] (Invariance axiom)
(A) No two tokens of a choice tree that occur as subtrees with the same information are marked differently.
(B) The subject's preferences for consequences are the same in all contexts.

[3] Let τ and τ' be choice trees that are logically equivalent on condition i and occur as subtrees with information i. If the subject marks both τ and τ', then he converts them into act trees that are logically equivalent on condition i.

[4] (Simple ordering of conditional preferences)
(a) $(a_1 \geqq_i a_2) \vee (a_2 \geqq_i a_1)$
(b) $[(a_1 \geqq_i a_2)(a_2 \geqq_i a_3)] \supset (a_1 \geqq_i a_3)$.

5.3.3 *Simple ordering of uncertainties*

[V] (Existence axiom) There are two consequences, one of which is preferred to the other.

[VI] (Ordering of uncertainties axiom)
If for some prize $c_1 > c_2$, $(pc_1 \text{ v } \bar{p}c_2) \geqq_i (qc_1 \text{ v } \bar{q}c_2)$,
then for any prize $c'_1 > c'_2$, $(pc'_1 \text{ v } \bar{p}c'_2) \geqq_i (qc'_1 \text{ v } \bar{q}c'_2)$

[5] $$(\exists c_1)(\exists c_2)[\{c_1 > c_2\}\{(pc_1 \text{ v } \bar{p}c_2) \geqq_i (qc_1 \text{ v } \bar{q}c_2)\}] \equiv (c'_1)(c'_2)[\{c'_1 > c'_2\} \supset \{(pc'_1 \text{ v } \bar{p}c'_2) \geqq_i (qc'_1 \text{ v } \bar{q}c'_2)\}] .$$

[6] ("$p \geqq_i q$" means "given i, p is at least as likely as q")
(a) $(p \geqq_i q) =_{\text{df}} (c_1)(c_2)[\{c_1 > c_2\} \supset \{(pc_1 \text{ v } \bar{p}c_2) \geqq_i (qc_1 \text{ v } \bar{q}c_2)\}]$
(b) $(p >_i q) \equiv (\exists c_1)(\exists c_2)[\{c_1 > c_2\}\{(pc_1 \text{ v } \bar{p}c_2) >_i (qc_1 \text{ v } \bar{q}c_2)\}]$
(c) $(p =_i q) \equiv (c_1)(c_2)[\{c_1 > c_2\} \supset \{(pc_1 \text{ v } \bar{p}c_2) =_i (qc_1 \text{ v } \bar{q}c_2)\}]$

[7] (Simple ordering of conditional uncertainties)
(a) $(p \geqq_i q) \text{ v } (q \geqq_i p)$
(b) $[(p \geqq_i q)(q \geqq_i r)] \supset (p \geqq_i r)$

5.4.1 *Normal form axiom*

[VII] (Normal form axiom) If an act tree belongs to the marked set, so does its normal form.

[8] Let Υ be an act tree whose only probabilistically impossible points are consequence points. If Υ belongs to the marked set, so does any tree obtained from Υ by changing a consequence name at a probabilistically impossible consequence point.

[9] (Reduction theorem) $(i \neq r\bar{r}) \supset [(p \geqq_i q) \equiv (pi \geqq qi)]$

5.4.2 *Comparative values*

[10] (Partial act theorem)

$$\text{Let } a_\mu = p_1c_1 \text{ v } \sum_{m=2}^{M} p_mc_m \qquad a_\nu = p_1c_1 \text{ v } \sum_{n=2}^{N} p'_nc'_n$$

$$a^*_\mu = p_1c^*_1 \text{ v } \sum_{m=2}^{M} p_mc_m \qquad a^*_\nu = p_1c^*_1 \text{ v } \sum_{n=2}^{N} p'_nc'_n ,$$

where $p_1, p_2, \ldots, p_M$ $(p_1, p'_2, \ldots, p'_N)$ are mutually exclusive and jointly exhaustive.

Then $(a_\mu \geqq a_\nu) \equiv (a^*_\mu \geqq a^*_\nu)$

[11a] $[(p \neq r\bar{r})(c_1 > c_2)] \equiv [(pc_1 \text{ v } \bar{p}c) > (pc_2 \text{ v } \bar{p}c)]$

[11b] $[(p = r\bar{r}) \vee (c_1 = c_2)] \equiv [(pc_1 \vee \bar{p}c) = (pc_2 \vee \bar{p}c)]$

[12a] $[c_1 \geqq c_2] \supset [c_1 \geqq (pc_1 \vee \bar{p}c_2) \geqq c_2]$

[12b] $[(p \neq r\bar{r})(\bar{p} \neq r\bar{r})(c_1 > c_2)] \supset [c_1 > (pc_1 \vee \bar{p}c_2) > c_2]$

5.4.3 *Comparative probabilities*

[13a] $(p \geqq q) \equiv (\bar{q} \geqq \bar{p})$

[13b] $[p = (r \vee \bar{r})] \equiv [\bar{p} = (r\bar{r})]$

[14a] $(r \vee \bar{r}) > (r\bar{r})$

[14b] $(r \vee \bar{r}) \geqq p \geqq (r\bar{r})$

[15a] $\{\sim\Diamond(ps)\sim\Diamond(qs)\} \supset \{(p \geqq q) \equiv [(p \vee s) \geqq (q \vee s)]\}$

[15b] $[\sim\Diamond(qs)(q \neq r\bar{r})] \supset [(q \vee s) > s]$

[15c] $p \geqq pq$

[16a] $[(p > q)(c_1 > c_2) \vee (q > p)(c_2 > c_1)] \equiv [(pc_1 \vee \bar{p}c_2) > (qc_1 \vee \bar{q}c_2)]$

[16b] $[(p = q) \vee (c_1 = c_2)] \equiv [(pc_1 \vee \bar{p}c_2) = (qc_1 \vee \bar{q}c_2)]$

5.5.1 *Utilities and quantitative probabilities*

[17] (Permutation theorem)
Let $p_1, p_2, \ldots, p_M$ be an equipartition, $c_1, c_2, \ldots, c_M$ a sequence of consequence names, and $c'_1, c'_2, \ldots, c'_M$ a permutation of this sequence. Then

$$\sum_{m=1}^{M} p_m c_m = \sum_{m=1}^{M} p_m c'_m$$

[VIII] (Quantitative axiom, symmetrical form)
There is an integer b ($b \geqq 2$) such that for every integer d ($d \geqq 1$), there is an equipartition of size b^d.

[IX] (Main theorem of the calculus of choice)
Antecedent: A marked set of trees satisfies axioms [I]–[VIII].
Consequent: There exist two functions

(1) a unique degree-of-belief function $P(q, i)$
(2) a consequence valuation function $U(c)$, unique up to an increasing linear transformation,

such that

(a) $P(q, i)$ satisfies the calculus of probability

(b) every choice made at a probabilistically possible choice point with information i maximizes the function

$$\sum_{n=1}^{N} P(q_n, i)\, U(a_n, iq_n) \quad .$$

5.5.2 Proof of the main theorem

[18] Let pq, $p\bar{q}$, $\bar{p}q$, $\bar{p}\bar{q}$ be an equipartition. If $c = pC_u \vee \bar{p}C_z$, then $(qc \vee \bar{q}C_z) = (pqC_u \vee \overline{pq}C_z)$.

5.5.3 *Savage's axiomatic system*

[19] Assume $a > b$. Then, for any consequence c, there exists an equipartition $q_1, q_2, \ldots, q_N$ such that, for each $n = 1, 2, \ldots, N$, both $a > (q_n c \vee \bar{q}_n b)$ and $(q_n c \vee \bar{q}_n a) > b$.

[VIII′] (Quantitative axiom, nonsymmetrical form)
Assume $a > b$. Then, for any consequence c, there exists a partition $q_1, q_2, \ldots, q_N$ such that, for each $n = 1, 2, \ldots, N$, both $a > (q_n c \vee \bar{q}_n b)$ and $(q_n c \vee \bar{q}_n a) > b$.

[IX$_s$] (Main theorem of Savage's axiomatic system)
If the subject's choices from pairs of normal form acts satisfy Savage's postulates P1–P6, then there exist a unique function $P(q)$ and a function $U(c)$, unique up to an increasing linear transformation, such that

(a) $P(q)$ satisfies the calculus of probability

(b) $$\left(\sum_{n=1}^{N} p_n c_n \geqq \sum_{m=1}^{M} p'_m c'_m\right) \equiv$$
$$\left(\sum_{n=1}^{N} P(p_n) U(c_n) \geqq \sum_{m=1}^{M} P(p'_m) U(c'_m)\right) \quad .$$

[IX′] (Main theorem, alternative version)
This is the same as [IX], with [VIII′] replacing [VIII].

[X] (Corollary to the main theorem)
If a marked set of trees is coherent or potentially coherent, then there exist a degree-of-belief function $P(q, i)$ and a consequence valuation function $U(c)$ such that

(a) $P(q, i)$ satisfies the calculus of probability

(b) every choice made at a probabilistically possible choice point with information i maximizes the utility function

$$\sum_{n=1}^{N} P(q_n, i)\,U(a_n, iq_n) \quad .$$

Note that the consequent of this corollary is the same as the consequent of the main theorem except for the uniqueness conditions on the functions P and U.

The main theorem of the calculus of choice shows that choices made in accordance with axioms [I]–[VIII] (or axioms [I]–[VII] and [VIII′]) do in fact maximize utility and satisfy the calculus of probability. The axioms of the calculus of choice are rules for marking choice trees, and they do not make any explicit reference to the concepts of probability and utility. Hence, a subject whose choices satisfy the calculus of choice acts as if he were using the calculus of probability and the rule of maximizing utility, whether or not he is doing so consciously. This fact plays an important role in the pragmatic theory of inductive probability. (Sec. 5.5)

The Pragmatic Theory of Inductive Probability

According to the pragmatic theory, a system of atomic inductive probability statements has two interrelated but coequal aspects, an a priori aspect and a pragmatic aspect. The a priori aspect concerns the assignment of probability values to statements by formal rules. Probability values are and should be assigned according to the rules of the calculus of probability and standard inductive logic. Consequently, both individual atomic probability statements and systems of them have logically true-or-false components.

The pragmatic aspect of inductive probability concerns the application of these probability assignments. An atomic inductive probability statement does and should express a disposition to act or "bet" in certain ways under conditions of uncertainty; in a generalized sense of "betting," the subject's belief in $\mathbf{P}(c, d) = x$ expresses a commitment to bet on the pair $\langle c, d\rangle$ with odds x to $1 - x$. A system of atomic inductive probability statements does and should express a commitment to make one's probability assignments conform to the calculus of probability and standard inductive logic. Since the rule of maximizing utility plays a dominant role in the application of probability theory to action, the pragmatic aspect of inductive probability involves the concept of utility. The calculus of choice explicates the concepts of probability and utility as they are and should be reflected in the choices of a single subject.

The pragmatic theory makes both descriptive and normative claims about inductive probability. Descriptively, the calculus of probability, standard inductive logic, and the calculus of choice are fair models of actual reasoning and decision-making. Normatively, one generally should follow these three axiomatic systems when reasoning inductively and making decisions. But the difficulties we found in the traditional theory of utility show that there are important exceptions to this general rule. In some cases it is reasonable to violate the marking axiom [I] or part [IVA] of invariance. The quantitative axiom [VIII] should be treated as a convenient idealization. (Sec. 5.6.2)

As we employ the term, a logically true-or-false statement is one whose truth-value, in principle, can be decided by deductive reasoning alone, without the use of observation and experiment and without appeal to the rules of inductive reasoning. Because of their pragmatic aspect, neither true atomic inductive probability statements nor the theorems of the calculus of inductive probability are logically true in this sense of the term. This part of the pragmatic theory, together with earlier results, provides an answer to our second main question. True atomic inductive probability statements and the theorems of the calculus of inductive probability are neither logical nor empirical truths. (Sec. 5.6.3)

The pragmatic theory is an answer to the first main question: What is the general nature of a system of atomic inductive probability statements? The theory is correct as far as it goes, but it is incomplete. To describe the pragmatic content of an inductive probability statement one must use subjunctives, which express causal necessities. Hence the concept of inductive probability is grounded on the notion of causal necessity, and in answering our first main question the pragmatic theory leads us to the fourth main question: What is the nature of causal necessity and how is it related to inductive probability? We develop and interpret my logic of causal necessity in the next two chapters. Chapter 10 presents my presupposition theory of induction, which answers this fourth question and thus gives a more complete answer to the first question. (Sec. 5.6.4)

My pragmatic theory is closely related to the a priori and personalistic theories of inductive probability. There are two, substantially different, versions of the a priori theory. Keynes advocated the nondeductive version in his *A Treatise on Probability*, while Carnap advocated the deductive version in his *Logical Foundations of Probability*. Both versions agree with the pragmatic theory that the a priori aspect of inductive probability is very important and cannot be analyzed in terms of frequency probability. But the pragmatic theory holds the a priori and pragmatic aspects of inductive probability to be coequal, whereas the a priorist thinks that the pragmatic aspect is derivable from the a priori aspect by means of an a priori justification for using standard inductive logic. (Sec. 5.7.1)

According to the personalistic theory, probability measures the "degree of rational belief or confidence" a person has in a proposition. "Degree of rational belief" is explicated in terms of potential betting behavior, and it is both descriptive and normative. The criteria of rationality are those of the calculus of probability and the calculus of choice. Thus a system of atomic inductive probability statements has both a pragmatic aspect (expressing the speaker's commitment to behave in a certain way) and an a priori aspect (conformity to the calculus of probability).

The main difference between the personalistic and pragmatic theories concerns the rules of standard inductive logic. The pragmatic theory includes them in the criteria of inductive rationality, while the personalistic theory does not. For this reason, probability is more subjective and relative to the individual on the personalistic theory than on the pragmatic theory. (Secs. 5.1.2, 5.7.2)

6 The Logic of Causal Statements as a Formal Language

All our reasoning is nothing but the joining and substituting of characters, whether these characters be words or symbols or pictures.

. . . if we could find characters or signs appropriate for expressing all our thoughts as definitely and as exactly as arithmetic expresses numbers or geometric analysis expresses lines, we could in all subjects *in so far as they are amenable to reasoning* accomplish what is done in Arithmetic and Geometry.

For all inquiries which depend on reasoning would be performed by the transposition of characters and by a kind of calculus, which would immediately facilitate the discovery of beautiful results. . . .

Moreover, we should be able to convince the world what we should have found or concluded, since it would be easy to verify the calculation either by doing it over or by trying tests similar to that of casting out nines in arithmetic. And if someone would doubt my results, I should say to him: "Let us calculate, Sir," and thus by taking to pen and ink, we should soon settle the question.

Fundamental Features of a Universal Language

Following is the rule for constructing the characters: to any given term (that is, the subject or predicate of a statement), let there be assigned a number, but with this one reservation, that a term consisting of a combination of other terms shall have as its number the product of the numbers of those other terms multiplied together. For example, if the term for an "animate being" should be imagined as expressed by the number 2 (or, more generally, *a*), and the term for "rational" by the number 3 (or, more generally, *r*), the term for "man" will be expressed by the number, 2 x 3, that is, 6, or as the product obtained by multiplying 2 and 3 together (or more generally by the number *ar*).*

6.1 Introduction

Our fourth main question was: What is the nature of causal necessity, and how are causal necessity and inductive probability related? (Sec. 1.6.1)

This chapter and the next one are based on my articles "Laws of Nature and Reasonableness of Regret," "The Logic of Causal Propositions," and "Dispositional Statements."

* All three quotations are from Leibniz. The first is from his *Philosophische Schriften*, vol. 7, p. 31; the second, dated 1677, is from Couturat's *Opuscles*, pp. 155–56, as translated in Wiener's *Selections*, p. 15; and the third quotation, dated 1679, is from Couturat's *Opuscles*, p. 42. The first and third quotations were translated from the Latin by Frank O. Copley.

This question will be answered in two stages. Chapters 6 and 7 will develop my logic of causal statements and will use it as a formal model of ordinary and scientific discourse involving causality, thereby establishing the formal properties of causal necessity. Chapters 9 and 10 will present my presupposition theory of induction, which relates causal necessity to inductive probability and also gives the final answer to our first main question: What is the nature of inductive probability?

Since we shall use the logic of causal statements as a model of natural language, we are interested also in the general characteristics of formal languages and in the scope and limits of formalization. We therefore present the logic of causal statements as an example of a formal language and discuss the essential properties of formal languages.

The possibility of formalizing natural language was first envisioned by Gottfried Wilhelm von Leibniz (1646–1716), who conceived of a purely rigorous, mechanical, and mathematical treatment of reasoning; see the epigraph of the current chapter. This possibility has been realized only in the last one hundred and twenty-five years, which have seen the development of a full-blown theory of formal languages, recursive functions, and computability. While Leibniz perceived that logic was potentially mechanical, he did not realize that there were logical questions that could not be settled by calculation (see pp. 392–95).

This chapter will emphasize the formal structure of the logic of causal statements. After demonstrating the need for that system (sec. 6.1), we present it as an example of a formal language (sec. 6.2), give an abstract interpretation of it (sec. 6.3), develop some of the mechanical properties of formal languages (sec. 6.4), and prove some theorems useful in interpreting it (sec. 6.5).

The next chapter will emphasize the use of the logic of causal statements as a formal model of natural language. Though some further theorems will be established, the chapter will be devoted mainly to a concrete interpretation of the system. It will turn out that Leibniz was naïvely optimistic about what formalization could accomplish. Besides the fact that not all logical questions can be settled by calculation, there is the difficulty of knowing whether a formal language is a good model of a natural language in the relevant respects.

We begin with an example of a causal statement. A chemist remarks truly of his laboratory assistant's ring

[A] If this ring (r) is gold (G) and *should* be placed in aqua regia (A), then it *would* dissolve (D).*

* It is assumed, of course, that the aqua regia is in a certain temperature range, e.g., is not a solid. As stated, [A] covers only the future, but we want it to cover the past as well. Since it is clumsy to write this all out we do not do so. We often leave such things implicit in our examples, in the interest of brevity.

We call this a "causal subjunctive." How shall we symbolize it and similar conditionals? Let us try each of the four kinds of implication introduced so far: logical and material implication, and conditional inductive and empirical probability (secs. 1.2.3, 1.5.2, and 2.2.2).

Note that [A] is a true statement of chemistry and hence an empirically true statement. Symbolizing it with logical implication, we get "$GrAr \rightarrow Dr$," which is equivalent to "$\Box(GrAr \supset Dr)$." Since "$GrAr \supset Dr$" is not logically true, "$GrAr \rightarrow Dr$" is false and is therefore not a good symbolization of the true statement [A]. Material implication gives "$GrAr \supset Dr$." Now "$\sim Ar \supset (GrAr \supset Dr)$" is a tautology, and so "$GrAr \supset Dr$" can be inferred from the assumption that the ring was not placed in aqua regia ("$\sim Ar$"). But [A] cannot be inferred from "$\sim Ar$" alone, and so "$GrAr \supset Dr$" is not a good symbolization of [A]. Consider next the symbolization "$\mathbf{P}(Dr, GrAr) = x$," where x has the value "very high" or the value "1." Since no atomic inductive probability statement is empirically true-or-false (p. 160), this atomic probability statement is not empirically true-or-false. But statement [A] is empirically true, and so "$\mathbf{P}(Dr, GrAr)$ is very high" is not a good symbolization of it.

Consider finally the symbolization "$\mathbf{P}_e(D, GA) = x$," where x has the value "very high" or the value "1." Statement [A] does not *seem* to be an empirical probability statement, and we shall confirm later that it actually is not. A detailed comparison of the deductive and inductive properties of causal statements and empirical probability statements will show that these two kinds of statements are fundamentally different, even though there are important similarities (sec. 8.2.2).

We conclude that the implication expressed in causal subjunctive [A] is not any of the traditional kinds of implication (logical, material, or probability), but is a new kind of implication, which we call "causal implication." The word "causal" is appropriate here because this new kind of implication is intimately related to causality. The logic of causal statements is a formal language in which causal implication can be symbolized.

The problem of symbolizing causal subjunctives is an old one. Early in this century, Peirce argued that material implication is inadequate for this purpose on the ground that causal subjunctives are modal. See the quotations on page 173, above, and page 421, below, as well as the many discussions throughout the *Collected Papers* under the headings of "possibility" and "would be." The gamma part of Peirce's system of existential graphs (bk. 2 of vol. 4) was an attempt to formalize modal logic. C. I. Lewis, Frank Ramsey, and C. H. Langford also pointed out the inadequacy of material implication for symbolizing causal subjunctives.*

Originally my logic of causal statements was developed out of an

* Lewis, *Mind and the World Order*, p. 142. Ramsey, *The Foundations of Mathematics*, pp. 246–53. C. H. Langford, a review in *The Journal of Symbolic Logic* 6 (1941): 67–68.

analysis of arguments containing causal statements. We do not proceed from natural language to artificial language here, however, but in the reverse direction, describing the logic of causal statements first and then applying it to causal inferences.

There are two basic aspects to the **logic of causal statements**: its formal structure and its interpretation. The interpretation, built on the formal structure, is much more complex. For the most part, the present chapter will be devoted to the formal structure and the next chapter to the interpretation. The formal structure could be given entirely independently of the interpretation, but it is easier for one to grasp the formal structure if he knows something about its intended interpretation. For this reason, we explain the interpretation of the logic of causal statements in a preliminary way now.

The logic of causal statements consists of a nonmodal logic, called "first-order quantification theory" (or, "the first-order function calculus without identity"), augmented by a logical apparatus for the logical modalities and for the causal modalities. The chief symbols of the nonmodal part are "$\sim$", "v", "&", "$\supset$", "$\equiv$", "$\not\equiv$", "(x)," and "$(\exists x)$." The first six of these are to be interpreted in the strictly truth-functional way of Section 2.2.2. The *universal quantifier* "(x)" means "for every individual x," and the *existential quantifier* "$(\exists x)$" means "there is at least one individual x." As an example, take

[B] Every girl danced with some boy.

Expressed in terms of the individual variables "x" and "y" this is

[B′] For every x, if x is a girl then
there is a y such that y is a boy and x danced with y.

Abbreviating the monadic predicates "girl" and "boy" by "G" and "B" respectively and the dyadic predicate "danced with" by "D," we obtain

[B′] $(x)[Gx \supset (\exists y)(By \& Dxy)]$

There are four logically modal symbols: *logical necessity* "$\Box$", *logical possibility* "$\Diamond$", *logical implication* "$\rightarrow$", and *logical equivalence* "$\leftrightarrow$". The meanings of these symbols were explained originally in terms of modes of verification, a statement being logically true if and only if in principle it can be certified as true by reasoning alone (pp. 6, 316). These notions are closely related to the notion of a logically possible universe; for present purposes it is best to view them in terms of this relation.

We introduced logically possible universes in connection with our highly simplified models of reality (sec. 3.2.1). A model $\mathfrak{M}$-$\mathfrak{L}$ consisted of a model $\mathfrak{M}$ and the corresponding language $\mathfrak{L}$. The model $\mathfrak{M}$ contained basic individuals and properties, all the logically possible universes composed of these individuals and properties, and an actual universe. The language $\mathcal{L}$ had a proper name for each individual, a predicate for each basic property, truth-functional connectives, and parentheses. Only monadic properties and predicates were allowed in these models; we now extend them to encompass relations of all degrees and the corresponding relational predicates.

We saw in discussing the distinction between an interpreted and an uninterpreted system that a statement form is logically true just in case it is true in all interpretations (p. 8). This principle leads directly to the following equivalences.

[C] $\Box\Phi$ is true if and only if
Φ is true in every logically possible universe of $\mathfrak{M}$

[D] $\Diamond\Phi$ is true if and only if
Φ is true in some logically possible universe of $\mathfrak{M}$

[E] $\Phi \rightarrow \Psi$ is true if and only if
$\Phi \supset \Psi$ is true in every logically possible universe of $\mathfrak{M}$

[F] $\Phi \leftrightarrow \Psi$ is true if and only if
$\Phi \equiv \Psi$ is true in every logically possible universe of $\mathfrak{M}$,

where Φ and Ψ are sentences of $\mathcal{L}$. These equivalences are illustrated in Section 6.3.1.

The four logically modal symbols are paralleled by four causally modal symbols: *causal necessity* "$\Box^c$", *causal possibility* "$\Diamond^c$", *causal implication* "$\underset{c}{\rightarrow}$", and *causal equivalence* "$\underset{c}{\leftrightarrow}$". The formal behavior of these causal modalities is similar to the formal behavior of the logical modalities. Likewise, the interpretation of the causal modalities parallels that of the logical modalities.

We therefore extend our earlier definition of a model $\mathfrak{M}$-$\mathcal{L}$ to include a designated subset of the logically possible universes that includes the actual universe. The universes of this designated subset are called "causally possible universes," a notion to be interpreted in the following way. The model $\mathfrak{M}$ is governed by a set of causal laws. The causally possible universes are all those logically possible universes in which these causal laws all hold. The following relations clearly hold between the causally possible universes of $\mathfrak{M}$ and the sentences of $\mathcal{L}$. For any sentences Φ and Ψ of $\mathcal{L}$,

[C′] $\Box^c\,\Phi$ is true if and only if
Φ is true in every causally possible universe

[D′] $\Diamond^c\,\Phi$ is true if and only if
Φ is true in some causally possible universe

[E′] $\Phi \underset{c}{\rightarrow} \Psi$ is true if and only if
$\Phi \supset \Psi$ is true in every causally possible universe

[F′] $\Phi \underset{c}{\leftrightarrow} \Psi$ is true if and only if
$\Phi \equiv \Psi$ is true in every causally possible universe.

These four relations parallel the four relations [C], [D], [E], and [F], respectively.

The foregoing interpretation of the logical and causal modalities is in terms of our simplified models $\mathfrak{M}$-$\mathfrak{L}$. Using these as models of reality, let us return to and symbolize the causal subjunctive

[A] If this ring (r) is gold (G) and *should* be placed in aqua regia (A), then it *would* dissolve (D).

The use of the subjunctive "should . . . would" signifies this is a statement about causally possible worlds as well as the actual world. Part, at least, of what is asserted is that "$GrAr \supset Dr$" is true in all causally possible universes. Therefore "$GrAr \underset{c}{\rightarrow} Dr$" is a better symbolization of [A] than formulas using logical, material, or probabilistic implication. After presenting and studying the formal structure of the logic of causal statements in the current chapter, we pursue its interpretation in depth in the next chapter, arriving at a better symbolization of the causal subjunctive [A] (sec. 7.3).

6.2 The Structure of the Logic of Causal Statements*

6.2.1 Grammar

A formal axiomatic language is a system or structure composed of primitive symbols, formulas, axioms, rules of inference, proofs, and theorems. Though a formal language may be interpreted, it is essential that these notions be defined without reference to the interpretation. A mechanical procedure of calculation that refers to the form of the symbols alone (and not to their interpretation) is called an "algorithm" (see sec. 6.4.3). A formal language should be so constructed that there are algorithms to answer each of these three questions in a finite amount of time: Is this sequence of symbols a formula? Is this formula an axiom? Is this sequence of formulas a proof? It follows from the existence of these algorithms that there is also an algorithm that will enumerate one by one all the theorems of the system (p. 369).

The *primitive symbols* of the logic of causal statements fall into two classes, constants and variables, according to whether their interpretation is fixed or varies from context to context. The *logical constants* are the truth-functional "$\sim$" and "v", left and right parentheses (used for punctuation and for quantification), and the modal symbols "$\Box$" and "$\Box^c$". There are infinitely many *variables* of each of the following kinds:

* This presentation is self-contained. However, the reader who has little knowledge of nonmodal logics may need to consult a text on the subject.

Statement: A, B, P, Q, A_1, B_1, etc.
Individual: a, b, x, y, x_1, x_2, etc.
Predicate: A, B, C, A_1, A_2, etc.

The primitive symbols of the language are to be interpreted in the standard way. For example, the symbol "v" means "or" in the inclusive sense, and the variable "x" ranges over individuals. The modal symbols are interpreted in terms of models that have logically possible universes, causally possible universes, and an actual universe (pp. 341–42). The truth of a non-modal formula Φ is determined with respect to the actual universe. If Φ contains no modal symbols, then $\Box\Phi$ is true if and only if Φ is true in all logically possible universes, and $\Box^c \Phi$ is true if and only if Φ is true in all causally possible universes.

This interpretation of the modalities does not cover expressions containing "iterated modalities," or modalities applied to modalities, such as "$\Box(\Box^c P \supset P)$" and "$\sim\Box\Box^c (x)(GxAx \supset Dx)$." Iterated modalities play only a minor role in causality and induction, and we make little use of them. Moreover, there are problems concerning iterated modalities that are best postponed (sec. 7.5). For these reasons we exclude iterated modalities from the logic of causal statements.

Some finite sequences of primitive symbols are intelligible or meaningful on the standard interpretation, e.g., "$(x)(Ax \text{ v } \sim Ax)$," while others are not, e.g., "x v v$\sim A$." The intelligible sequences of symbols are called "well-formed formulas" in mathematical logic, but we call them simply "formulas" because this term is shorter and closer to ordinary usage. The formulas of a formal language correspond to the grammatical sentences of a natural language. The formulas of the logic of causal statements will be interpreted systematically in Section 6.3.2.

The class of *formulas* is defined mechanically and without reference to the interpretation, by the rule below. This is a *recursive definition*, with an initial step specifying an initial set of formulas and a general step generating further formulas from given formulas.

[Initial step] A statement variable alone is a formula. If $\alpha_1, \alpha_2, \ldots, \alpha_N$ are individual variables ($N = 1, 2, 3, \ldots$) and θ is a predicate variable, then $\theta\alpha_1\alpha_2 \ldots \alpha_N$ is a formula.

[General step] If Φ and Ψ are formulas and α is an individual variable, then $\sim\Phi$, $(\Phi \text{ v } \Psi)$, and $(\alpha)\Phi$ are formulas. If Φ is a formula containing no occurrences of $\Box$ or $\Box^c$, then $\Box\Phi$ and $\Box^c \Phi$ are formulas.

For example, "Ax" and "Bxy" are formulas by the initial step. Application of the general step gives first "$\sim Ax$" and "$(y)Bxy$," next "$(\sim Ax \text{ v } (y)Bxy)$," and finally the formula "$(x)(\sim Ax \text{ v } (y)Bxy)$." Note that each application of the general step increases the length of the formula. Consequently, there is an algorithm for deciding whether or not a finite sequence of primitive symbols is a formula: repeatedly dissect the sequence by means of the general step to see if it is properly constructed from formulas defined by the initial step. This algorithm is the *decision algorithm for formulahood.*

Note that we are now using capital letters for statement variables, whereas earlier we used lowercase letters for this purpose, e.g., in Sections 1.2.3 and 2.1; these same capital letters are also used for predicate variables. This dual usage is natural, since a statement variable can be regarded as a predicate variable with no individual variables following it. The interpretation of a variable will depend upon its context. Consider, for example, the formulas "$D \vee E$" and "Dxy." In the former "D" must be interpreted as a statement while in the latter it must be interpreted as a dyadic relation, e.g., as "x danced with y."

While Greek letters were used as variables in the definition of "formula," they do not belong to the formal language itself but to the *metalanguage* in which we discuss the formal language. We will use capital Greek letters for formulas and lowercase Greek letters for individual and predicate variables. The logical constants are used in the metalanguage to represent themselves and hence belong to both the formal language and its metalanguage.

We will systematically restrict the range of capital Greek letters to exclude iterated modalities. For example, rather than writing "If Φ is a formula *with no modal operators*, then $\Box\Phi$ is a formula," we will write "If Φ is a formula, then $\Box\Phi$ is a formula." In such a context capital Φ is understood as ranging over formulas without modal operators, rather than over all formulas.

Only the individual variables may be quantified. But no fixed meaning is assigned to any of the variables in the original interpretation of the system, so that all three kinds of variables are variables in the sense that their meanings vary from application to application. In Chapter 7, we will sometimes need to quantify predicates and statements. This will be done informally, however, it being clear in each case that the predicate or statement quantifier behaves analogously to an individual quantifier. We have two reasons for not handling the quantification of predicates and statements formally: simplicity, and the fact that there are many unsolved problems about the quantification of predicates and statements in modal logic (see sec. 7.5).

The following definitions, [1], allow us to use other logical constants as abbreviations.

[1a] $\Phi \& \Psi =_{df} \sim(\sim\Phi \vee \sim\Psi)$

[1b] $(\exists\alpha)\Phi =_{df} \sim(\alpha)\sim\Phi$

[1c] $\Diamond\Phi =_{df} \sim\Box\sim\Phi$ (*Logical possibility*)

[1d] $\Diamond^{c}\Phi =_{df} \sim\Box^{c}\sim\Phi$ (*Causal possibility*)

[1e] $\Phi \supset \Psi =_{\mathrm{df}} \sim\Phi \vee \Psi$ *(Material implication)*

[1f] $\Phi \rightarrow \Psi =_{\mathrm{df}} \Box(\Phi \supset \Psi)$ *(Logical implication)*

[1g] $\Phi \underset{c}{\rightarrow} \Psi =_{\mathrm{df}} \Box^{c}(\Phi \supset \Psi)$ *(Causal implication)*

[1h] $\Phi \equiv \Psi =_{\mathrm{df}} (\Phi \supset \Psi)\&(\Psi \supset \Phi)$ *(Material equivalence)*

[1i] $\Phi \leftrightarrow \Psi =_{\mathrm{df}} \Box(\Phi \equiv \Psi)$ *(Logical equivalence)*

[1j] $\Phi \underset{c}{\leftrightarrow} \Psi =_{\mathrm{df}} \Box^{c}(\Phi \equiv \Psi)$ *(Causal equivalence)*

[1k] $\Phi \not\equiv \Psi =_{\mathrm{df}} \sim(\Phi \equiv \Psi)$.

Braces and brackets will also be used, and parentheses will be dropped when the context makes it clear how to replace them. $\sim\Phi$ will also be written $\bar{\Phi}$, and $\Phi\&\Psi$ as $\Phi\Psi$. $((\Phi_1 \vee \Phi_2) \vee \Phi_3)$ will be abbreviated $(\Phi_1 \vee \Phi_2 \vee \Phi_3)$, $((\Phi_1\&\Phi_2)\&\Phi_3)$ will be abbreviated $(\Phi_1\&\Phi_2\&\Phi_3)$ or $(\Phi_1\Phi_2\Phi_3)$, and so on for any number of disjunctions or conjunctions. $(\Phi\Psi \vee \Theta)$ abbreviates $((\Phi\Psi) \vee \Theta)$ and $(\Phi\Psi \supset \Theta)$ abbreviates $((\Phi\Psi) \supset \Theta)$. Expressions containing defined symbols are not formulas in the technical sense defined a moment ago, but abbreviations for such. For example, "$\Diamond(AxBx) \vee \Box\{Cy \supset (\exists x)(Ax \vee Bx)\}$" abbreviates "$(\sim\Box\sim\sim(\sim Ax \vee \sim Bx) \vee \Box(\sim Cy \vee \sim(x)\sim(Ax \vee Bx)))$."

6.2.2 *Axioms*

The usual formal language combines rigor of formulation with a relatively simple and minimal set of axioms. But the latter characteristic makes derivation of the initial theorems somewhat slow and unintuitive. While we want a rigorous formal language, we also want one in which the theorems we need can be quickly and easily derived. Consequently, our axioms and axiom types are stronger and more numerous than required. For example, we take as axioms all truth-functional tautologies, whereas in the usual axiomatic approach only some of these are taken as axioms with the remaining ones derived as theorems.*

The class of axioms will be defined recursively. As the initial step of the recursive definition, we define three classes of axioms: (I) Truth-functional axioms; (II) Quantificational axioms; and (III) Modal axioms. The general step (IV) of the recursive definition generates more axioms from these by prefixing the universal quantifier and logical necessity operator to axioms.

(I) *Truth-functional axioms*. Any formula composed only of "$\sim$", "v", statement variables, and parentheses is a *truth-functional formula*. The *height* of a truth-functional formula is defined recursively.

[Initial step] Every statement variable is of height zero.

* A more minimal formulation of the logic of causal statements, with iterated modalities, is given in sec. 3 of my paper "The Logic of Causal Propositions."

[General step] The height of $\sim\Phi$ is one greater than the height of Φ.
Let h be the maximum of the separate heights of Φ and Ψ; then the height of $(\Phi \text{ v } \Psi)$ is $h + 1$.

Examples are given in Table 14. Note that the height of a formula measures, in a certain sense, the number of times the general step of the rule defining "formula" is applied when the formula is generated.

The concept of height leads directly to an algorithm for calculating the truth-value of a truth-functional formula for each assignment of truth-values to its variables. This calculation is arranged in a truth-table, of which an example is shown in Table 14. The truth-table for a truth-functional formula Φ with N variables is constructed as follows. Make a column for each subformula of Φ, including the variables, arranging these in ascending height. Make 2^N rows, and fill in the columns for the variables with all

TABLE 14

Truth-table for "$(P \text{ v } Q) \text{ v } (\sim P \text{ v } Q)$"

Subformulas of height zero		Subformulas of height one		Subformulas of height two	Formula of height three
P	Q	$\sim P$	$P \text{ v } Q$	$\sim P \text{ v } Q$	$(P \text{ v } Q) \text{ v } (\sim P \text{ v } Q)$
False	False	True	False	True	True
False	True	True	True	True	True
True	False	False	True	False	True
True	True	False	True	True	True

2^N possible assignments of truth-values to the variables. Then fill in the truth-values of all other columns in order of height, using the truth-functional definitions of Section 2.2.2. Since any compound formula Φ is composed of formulas of lesser heights, the truth-value of Φ can be computed from the values given in earlier columns.

A truth-functional formula is a *tautology* if and only if it is true for all assignments of truth-values to its variables. One can decide of any truth-functional formula whether or not it is a tautology by constructing its truth-table. Table 14 shows that "$(P \text{ v } Q) \text{ v } (\sim P \text{ v } Q)$" is a tautology. A *substitution instance* of a truth-functional formula Φ is the result of substituting formulas for one or more of the statement variables of Φ, under the condition that when Ψ is substituted for a statement variable Ψ is substituted for every occurrence of that variable. For example, "$\sim\Box Rc \text{ v } [\Box Rc \text{ v } (x)(\sim Ax \text{ v } Bx)]$" is a substitution instance of "$\sim P \text{ v } (P \text{ v } Q)$."

The class of *truth-functional axioms* is defined by the rule

[2] Every tautology and every substitution instance thereof is an axiom.

There is a simple algorithm for deciding whether an arbitrary formula Φ is or is not a truth-functional axiom. If the formula is a truth-functional formula, it can be tested in a truth-table. If the formula is not a truth-functional formula, a truth-functional formula expressing its truth-functional form can be tested in a truth-table. For example, the question of whether "$[\sim(x)Bx \& (x)Ax] \supset \sim[(x)Ax \supset (x)Bx]$" is a truth-functional axiom reduces to the question of whether "$[\sim Q \& P] \supset \sim[P \supset Q]$" is a tautology.

A formal language that has the set of truth-functional formulas as its set of formulas and the set of tautologies as its set of theorems is a version of *truth-function theory*. It is also called "the propositional calculus," "the statement calculus," and the "sentential calculus." By rule [2] we are taking as axioms all the theorems of truth-function theory and all their substitution instances. We do so in keeping with our preference for a system in which theorems are easily derived over a system with a minimal set of axioms. We may take all these formulas as axioms because we have an algorithm for deciding whether or not a formula is a truth-functional axiom.

(II) *Quantificational axioms*. While a truth-functional axiom may contain quantifiers and modal operators, the logical properties of these quantifiers and operators are clearly irrelevant to its being a truth-functional axiom. We next describe axioms that express some of the essential properties of quantifiers.

Such axioms are formulated in terms of the ideas of *free occurrence* and *bound occurrence* of an individual variable, where the binding is done by a quantifier covering the occurrence of a variable. These terms are defined recursively.

[Initial step] The individual variable occurrences $\alpha_1, \alpha_2, \ldots, \alpha_N$ are all free in $\theta\alpha_1\alpha_2 \ldots \alpha_N$ (where θ is a predicate variable).

[General step] The formation of $\sim\Phi$, $(\Phi \vee \Psi)$, $(\alpha)\Phi$, $\Box\Phi$, or $\Box^c\Phi$ from Φ and Ψ does not change the freedom status of any occurrence of a variable except that *every* occurrence of α in $(\alpha)\Phi$ is bound.

For example, in the formula "$(x)(Ax \supset Bx) \supset (Ax \supset Bx)$," the first three occurrences (tokens) of the individual (type) variable "x" are bound, while the last two occurrences are free.

The concepts of "free" and "bound" apply to predicate and statement variables also, but as noted earlier we never quantify (bind) any of these variables within our formal system.

The next rule defines three forms of quantificational axioms, each of which has been given a name for future reference.

[3a] (*Elimination of irrelevant quantifier*) If α does not occur free in Φ, then $\Phi \equiv (\alpha)\Phi$ is an axiom

[3b] (*Quantifier distribution*) $(\alpha)(\Phi \supset \Psi) \supset [(\alpha)\Phi \supset (\alpha)\Psi]$ is an axiom

[3c] (*Universal instantiation*) Let Ψ be the result of substituting the individual variable β for all free occurrences of α in Φ. If Ψ has exactly as many occurrences of free individual variables as Φ, then $(\alpha)\Phi \supset \Psi$ is an axiom.

The rule "elimination of irrelevant quantifier" enables one to eliminate (or add) a quantifier that does not bind a variable. The restriction that α not occur free in Φ is needed to exclude such a formula as "$Mx \equiv (x)Mx$" from being an axiom. When the monadic predicate variable "M" is interpreted as "man" and the free occurrence of the individual variable "x" is interpreted as "Socrates," this formula becomes the false statement "Socrates is a man if and only if everything is a man."

An example of quantifier distribution is "$(x)(Hx \supset Ox) \supset [(x)Hx \supset (x)Ox]$" or "If every horse is one-toed, then if everything is a horse everything is one-toed." An example of universal instantiation is

$$\stackrel{(\alpha)}{(x)}\ \overbrace{(Mx \supset Kx)}^{\Phi} \supset \overbrace{(Mt \supset Kt)}^{\Psi} \quad ,$$

or "If every mule kicks then if this is a mule it will kick." To see the role of the restriction on universal instantiation, consider

$$\stackrel{(\alpha)}{(x)}\ \overbrace{(\exists y)Dxy}^{\Phi} \supset \overbrace{(\exists y)Dyy}^{\Psi} \quad ,$$

where Ψ results from Φ by substituting "y" for every free occurrence of "x" in Φ. Now Ψ has no occurrences of free variables while Φ has one, so "$(x)(\exists y)Dxy \supset (\exists y)Dyy$" is not an axiom by universal instantiation. This is as it should be, for if we interpret the dyadic predicate variable "D" to mean "danced with" and consider a dance where each guest dances only with his or her date, the formula "$(x)(\exists y)Dxy \supset (\exists y)Dyy$" becomes the false sentence "If everyone danced with someone, someone danced with himself."

(III) *Modal axioms.* The logic of causal statements is constructed from a nonmodal system, called first-order quantification theory (without identity), by adding to this system the modal symbols "$\Box$" and "$\Box^c$" and rules governing these symbols. We describe next some axioms that give the essential properties of modal operators.* Every formula of each of the following forms, [4], is a modal axiom.

* Propositional calculi for the logical modalities originated with C. I. Lewis; see Lewis and Langford, *Symbolic Logic.* Quantifiers were first combined with the logical modalities by Barcan, "A Functional Calculus of First Order Based on Strict Implication" and "The Deduction Theorem in a Functional Calculus of First Order Based on Strict Implication"; and by Carnap, "Modalities and Quantification." There is now a large literature in modal logic, which is reviewed and indexed in *The Journal of Symbolic Logic.*

Some of the features of the logic of causal statements are adapted from Fitch, "Intuitionistic Modal Logic with Quantifiers."

[4a] $\Box\Phi \supset \Box^c\Phi$
[4b] $\Box^c\Phi \supset \Phi$ — *Modal ordering*

[4c] $\Box(\Phi \supset \Psi) \supset \{\Box\Phi \supset \Box\Psi\}$
[4d] $\Box^c(\Phi \supset \Psi) \supset \{\Box^c\Phi \supset \Box^c\Psi\}$ — *Modal distribution*

[4e] $(\alpha)\Box\Phi \equiv \Box(\alpha)\Phi$
[4f] $(\alpha)\Box^c\Phi \equiv \Box^c(\alpha)\Phi$ — *Modal-quantifier commutation.*

An interesting formal parallelism exists between (α), $\Box$, and $\Box^c$ on the one hand and $(\exists\alpha)$, $\Diamond$, $\Diamond^c$ on the other. (α) equals $\sim(\exists\alpha)\sim$, $\Box$ equals $\sim\Diamond\sim$, and $\Box^c$ equals $\sim\Diamond^c\sim$. The rules for modal ordering parallel the rule for universal instantiation: [4a] and [4b] together imply that if a formula is true in every logically possible universe, it is true in the actual universe; by [4b], if a formula is true in every causally possible universe, it is true in the actual universe; and by [3c], if a formula is true of all individuals, it is true of some particular individual. Likewise, the rules for modal distribution parallel the rule for quantifier distribution. This formal parallelism of the universal quantifier with a necessity operator and of the existential quantifier with a possibility operator results from the similarity of interpretation of the corresponding symbols. (α) means "for *every* individual α," $\Box$ means "in *every* logically possible universe," and $\Box^c$ means "in *every* causally possible universe." Similarly, $(\exists\alpha)$ means "for *at least one* individual α," $\Diamond$ means "in *at least one* logically possible universe," and $\Diamond^c$ means "in *at least one* causally possible universe." See equivalences [C], [D], [C′], and [D′] above (p. 341).

(IV) *Axiom generation.* The class of axioms of the logic of causal statements is defined recursively. Rules [2], [3], and [4] constitute the initial step. The general step is given by the rule

[5] If Φ is an axiom, so is $(\alpha)\Phi$. If Φ is an axiom containing no occurrences of $\Box$ or $\Box^c$, then $\Box\Phi$ is an axiom.

For example, since "$Px \vee \sim Px$" is an axiom, "$(x)(Px \vee \sim Px)$" and "$\Box(Px \vee \sim Px)$" are axioms. Again, "$(x)Ax \supset Ay$" is an axiom by universal instantiation, "$\Box\{(x)Ax \supset Ay\}$" is then an axiom by axiom generation, and "$(y)\Box\{(x)Ax \supset Ay\}$" is also an axiom by axiom generation.

The following *decision algorithm for axiomhood* may be applied to any finite sequence of primitive symbols to ascertain whether or not this sequence of primitive symbols is an axiom. Use the decision algorithm for formulahood to see if the sequence is a formula. If it is, use rule [5] in reverse to strip off all the initial quantifiers and the necessity operator. Then check the residue formula against each of the rules [2], [3], and [4] to see if it is an axiom by one of these rules.

6.2.3 *Proofs and theorems*

In Section 1.5.1 we introduced the idea of a conditional corresponding to a given argument, defining a deductive argument to be valid if its corresponding conditional is logically true. This approach to validity, restricted to axioms, is the basis of our sole *primitive rule of inference.*

[6] If $(\Phi_1\Phi_2 \ldots \Phi_N) \supset \Psi$ is an axiom,
then Ψ may be inferred from $\Phi_1, \Phi_2, \ldots, \Phi_N$.

Ψ is then called the *immediate consequence* of $\Phi_1, \Phi_2, \ldots, \Phi_N$. When the decision algorithm for axiomhood is applied to a formula $(\Phi_1\Phi_2 \ldots \Phi_N) \supset \Psi$, it will tell us whether or not Ψ is an immediate consequence of $\Phi_1, \Phi_2, \ldots, \Phi_N$. It is common in mathematical logic to take as primitive the rule of *modus ponens,* which is: from Φ and $\Phi \supset \Psi$ to infer Ψ. Since $[\Phi(\Phi \supset \Psi)] \supset \Psi$ is a truth-functional axiom, modus ponens is a special case of our primitive rule.

The notions of "proof" and "theorem" are defined in terms of the relation of immediate consequence, a proof involving repeated applications of the primitive rule of inference. We distinguish two kinds of *proofs,* according to whether or not there are formulas designated as premises.

A *categorical proof* is a finite sequence of formulas such that each formula is an axiom or an immediate consequence of preceding formulas of the sequence. A formula is a *theorem* if and only if it is the last formula of a categorical proof. We use $\vdash \Psi$ to assert that Ψ is a theorem, i.e., that there is a categorical proof of Ψ. The metalinguistic sign "$\vdash$" is read "yields." An example of a categorical proof is

(a)	$\vdash \Box(PQ \supset P)$	This is an axiom by axiom generation operating on a truth-functional axiom
(b)	$\vdash \Box^c (PQ \supset P)$	This is an immediate consequence of (a) by modal ordering
(c)	$\vdash \Box^c (PQ) \supset \Box^c P$	This is an immediate consequence of (b) by modal distribution.

A *proof from premises* is a finite sequence of formulas such that each formula of the sequence is a *premise,* an axiom, or an immediate consequence of preceding formulas of the sequence. To assert that there is a proof of Ψ from premises $\Phi_1, \Phi_2, \ldots, \Phi_N$, we use the notation, $\Phi_1, \Phi_2, \ldots, \Phi_N \vdash \Psi$. An example of a proof from premises is

(a)	$\Box^c (x)(GxAx \supset Dx)$	This is stipulated to be a premise
(b)	$(x)\Box^c (GxAx \supset Dx) \equiv \Box^c (x)(GxAx \supset Dx)$	This is an axiom by modal-quantifier commutation

(c) $(x)\Box^c(GxAx \supset Dx)$ — This is an immediate consequence of (a) and (b) by a truth-functional axiom

(d) $\Box^c(GrAr \supset Dr)$ — This is an immediate consequence of (c) by universal instantiation.

Hence: $\Box^c(x)(GxAx \supset Dx) \vdash \Box^c(GrAr \supset Dr)$. Note that the ordinary notion of a deductive argument (p. 22) is modeled in our formal language by the concept of a proof from premises.

Viewed in terms of primitive symbols, a proof is a finite sequence of finite sequences of primitive symbols. The following *decision algorithm for proofhood* may be applied to any finite sequence of finite sequences of primitive symbols to find out whether or not it is a proof. To begin with, apply the decision algorithm for formulahood to each sequence of primitive symbols. If any sequence is not a formula, then the sequence of sequences is not a proof. Suppose all sequences of symbols are formulas, and let the resultant sequence of formulas be $\Theta_1, \Theta_2, \ldots, \Theta_N$. Apply these three steps to each formula Θ_n $(n = 1, 2, \ldots, N)$. First, see if Θ_n is one of the given premises (if there are any). If it is not, apply the decision algorithm for axiomhood. Finally, if Θ_n is not an axiom, see if it is an immediate consequence of any subset of the set of preceding formulas. If each Θ_n is a premise, an axiom, or an immediate consequence of preceding formulas of the sequence, then the sequence $\Theta_1, \Theta_2, \ldots, \Theta_N$ is a proof, otherwise not.

This completes our specification of the **logic of causal statements** as a formal language. In brief, it is a system or structure composed of symbols, formulas, axioms, rule of inference, proofs, and theorems so constructed that there are decision algorithms for formulahood, axiomhood, and proofhood.

We have already defined one sublanguage of the logic of causal statements, namely, truth-function theory (p. 347). Another important, standard sublanguage of it is *first-order quantification theory*, which is obtained from the logic of causal statements by deleting all occurrences of $\Box$ and $\Box^c$ from the definitions of "primitive symbol," "formula," and "axiom." First-order quantification theory is also called the "restricted predicate calculus (without identity)" and the "first-order function calculus (without identity)." Obviously, every theorem, proof, axiom, etc., of first-order quantification theory is a theorem, proof, axiom, etc., of the logic of causal statements, but not conversely.

6.3 An Abstract Interpretation

6.3.1 Examples

The structure of the logic of causal statements is specified completely formally, with no reference being made to the meanings of the symbols of the language. Moreover, this language is constructed so that there are decision algorithms for formulahood, axiomhood, and proofhood. By constructing the logic of causal statements in this way, we can sharply distinguish its formal structure from its interpretation; an interpretation can be added later without destroying the formal character of the language.

Formal language interpretations are of two quite different kinds, which we shall call "abstract" and "concrete." In the present section we give an idealized, *abstract interpretation* of the logic of causal statements by means of simple models. This interpretation will be useful in supplying a model of our final concrete interpretation, and also in establishing certain results about the formal language itself such as proving its consistency and showing that certain formulas are not theorems.

The *concrete interpretation* of a formal language relates it to ordinary and scientific language and reasoning. We have already discussed the concrete interpretation of the logic of causal statements with respect to truth-function theory and the logical modalities (secs. 1.2.3, 1.5.1, 2.2.2, and 2.3.1; see also 6.5.3). In the next chapter we shall give a concrete interpretation of the causal modalities in terms of natural language statements of causality.

An abstract interpretation is a relation between two idealized systems: a formal language and a set of models. A formula is interpreted in a model by means of rules that assign a truth-value to the formula in that model. The models used to interpret the logic of causal statements will be called "modal models"; they are extensions of the simple models $\mathfrak{M}$-$\mathfrak{L}$ used earlier to model inductive logics (sec. 3.2.1). We extend them here to model causal necessity ($\Box^c$) without inductive probability (**P**); later we will extend them further to model causal necessity and inductive probability together (sec. 10.3).

A modal model $\mathfrak{M}$-$\mathfrak{L}$ is a very simple model of reality as a whole. It contains a model language $\mathfrak{L}$ and a corresponding model $\mathfrak{M}$ of the non-linguistic part of reality. As in our earlier modal models, $\mathfrak{L}$ contains symbols for describing $\mathfrak{M}$: individual constants to name the individuals, predicate constants to represent the basic properties, and truth-functional connectives. In our new models $\mathfrak{L}$ may contain predicate constants of any degree and it may contain infinitely many individual constants; correspondingly $\mathfrak{M}$ may contain relations of any degree and it may contain infinitely many individuals. Also, in our new models $\mathfrak{L}$ includes the logic of causal statements, and hence variables of three kinds (individual, predicate, and statement), quantifiers on individual variables, and the modal symbols "$\Box$" and "$\Box^c$". Corresponding to causal necessity, $\mathfrak{M}$ includes causally possible universes as well as logically possible universes and the actual universe (cf. pp. 341–42). The definitions and rules of the logic of causal statements (definitions of "formula" and "axiom" and the rule of inference) are extended to cover the individual and predicate constants of our new modal models, though individual constants cannot be quantified.*

In the models of Chapter 3, $\mathfrak{L}$ had individual and predicate constants but no variables. In the present models, $\mathfrak{L}$ has variables as well as constants, and a comment is needed on how they are symbolized. Upper case letters will be used for both predicate variables and predicate constants, and lower case letters for both individual variables and individual constants. In any specific case, the context (including informal explanations) will tell whether a letter is functioning as a variable or as a constant.

The new models will be defined rigorously in the next subsection. But first we will explain and illustrate the most important new concepts. These are, in the order in which they will be discussed: quantifiers, modalities, quantifiers and modalities, logical dependence between atomic statements, infinite models, and the distinction between variables and nonlogical constants.

Consider as an example the following model $\mathfrak{M}_1$-$\mathfrak{L}_1$. There are two individuals *a* and *b* and two monadic properties *S* (swan) and *W* (white). There are sixteen logically possible universes; see Table 9 (p. 106). Let there be three causally possible universes: $\overline{Sa}WaSbWb$, $\overline{Sa}\ \overline{Wa}\ \overline{Sb}\ \overline{Wb}$, and $SaWaSbWb$, of which the last is designated as the actual universe.

The universal quantifier means "for every individual" and the existential quantifier "for at least one individual." Hence "$(x)(Sx \supset Wx)$" is interpreted in this model to mean the conjunction "$(Sa \supset Wa)(Sb \supset Wb)$," and "$(\exists x)(SxWx)$" is interpreted to mean the disjunction "$(SaWa \vee SbWb)$." Both statements are true of the actual world $SaWaSbWb$ and hence true in the model $\mathfrak{M}_1$-$\mathfrak{L}_1$.

Logical necessity means "in every logically possible universe," and logical possibility means "in at least one logically possible universe." The statement "$Sa \vee \overline{Sa}$" is true in every logically possible universe of $\mathfrak{M}_1$-$\mathfrak{L}_1$, and hence "$\Box(Sa \vee \overline{Sa})$" is true. The statement "$\overline{Sa}$" is false in some logically possible universes and true in others; hence "$\Box\,\overline{Sa}$" is false but "$\Diamond\overline{Sa}$" is true.

Causal necessity means "in every causally possible universe," and causal possibility means "in at least one causally possible universe." The formula "$(x)(Sx \supset Wx)$" is true in each of the three causally possible universes of $\mathfrak{M}_1$-$\mathfrak{L}_1$, and hence "$\Box^c\,(x)(Sx \supset Wx)$" is true. That is, "All swans are white" is a causal law in this simple model. Consider the converse, "$(x)(Wx \supset Sx)$."

* These modal models are obtained from the standard models for first-order quantification theory by adding sets of possible universes. Our treatment of models is different from the usual one, in that we start with both properties and individuals rather than starting with individuals only and constructing properties as sets of sequences of individuals.

This is true in the actual universe $SaWaSbWb$ but false in the causally possible universe $\overline{Sa}WaSbWb$, so that "$\Box^c (x)(Wx \supset Sx)$" is false. Hence "All white objects are swans" is contingently true (true but not causally necessary) in model $\mathfrak{M}_1$-$\mathfrak{L}_1$.

The modal-quantifier axiom forms are probably the least intuitive of all the axiom forms, and so let us illustrate them (p. 349). The formula

$$(x)\Box^c (Sx \supset Wx) \equiv \Box^c (x)(Sx \supset Wx)$$

demonstrates the commutativity of the universal quantifier and the causal necessity operator. When the quantifiers are interpreted it becomes

$$\{\Box^c (Sa \supset Wa)\Box^c (Sb \supset Wb)\} \equiv \Box^c \{(Sa \supset Wa)(Sb \supset Wb)\} \quad .$$

Both of the formulas "$Sa \supset Wa$" and "$Sb \supset Wb$" are true in all three causally possible universes, so that both sides of the equivalence (and hence the equivalence itself) are true.

The universal quantifier and the logical necessity operator also commute. Consider the form

$$(\alpha)\Box\phi(\alpha) \equiv \Box(\alpha)\phi(\alpha) \quad ,$$

where $\phi(\alpha)$ is any formula containing free occurrences of the individual variable α. When interpreted in $\mathfrak{M}_1$-$\mathfrak{L}_1$ this becomes

$$\{\Box\phi(a)\}\&\{\Box\phi(b)\} \equiv \Box\{\phi(a)\&\phi(b)\} \quad .$$

The truth conditions of both sides of this equivalence are the same: $\phi(a)$ and $\phi(b)$ must both be true in all logically possible universes. Note the close connection of modal-quantifier commutation to the distribution of necessity over conjunction; see metatheorem [10] below.

The preceding examples, as well as the materials of Section 6.1, explain the interpretation of the modal operators when they apply to nonmodal formulas. In carrying out the interpretation of formulas containing modalities, it is convenient to represent "true" by "1" and "false" by "0." These symbols can be manipulated as in a truth-table: "0 v 1 " equals "1," "0 & 1" equals "0," and "0 v Sa" has the same truth-value as "Sa." The use of these symbols is illustrated in the following evaluation of "$\{Wb \& \Box(Sa \vee \overline{Sa})\} \vee \overline{Sb}$" in the model $\mathfrak{M}_1$-$\mathfrak{L}_1$. Since "$Sa \vee \overline{Sa}$" is true in every logically possible universe, "$\Box(Sa \vee \overline{Sa})$" should be replaced by "1," giving "$\{Wb\&1\} \vee \overline{Sb}$," which reduces to "$Wb \vee \overline{Sb}$." The last formula is true in the actual universe $SaWaSbWb$, and so the original formula is true in the model $\mathfrak{M}_1$-$\mathfrak{L}_1$.

Earlier we took every basic conjunction to be a description of a logically possible universe. The assumption underlying this choice was that any two distinct atomic statements are logically independent. But a model that permits logical connections between atomic statements is more general and better fits actual language. For example, if a relation is transitive, a basic conjunction in which transitivity is violated is contradictory and does not really describe a logically possible universe. We will illustrate this with a model of the ancestral relation.

The model $\mathfrak{M}_2$-$\mathfrak{L}_2$ is based on the dyadic relation A (ancestor of) and the three individuals 1, 2, and 3. There are nine atomic statements and hence 2^9 (or 512) basic conjunctions, of which some examples are shown in Table 15. But since the ancestral relation is irreflexive, transitive, and hence asymmetrical (p. 208), not all of these represent logically possible universes. Indeed, irreflexivity and asymmetry imply that at most three of the nine atomic statements can be jointly true. Accordingly, it is best not to take all 512 basic conjunctions as universe descriptions, but only those satisfying irreflexivity and transitivity. In $\mathfrak{M}_2$-$\mathfrak{L}_2$ there are just nineteen of these: one in which all atomic statements are false (number 5 of Table 15), and six basic conjunctions with one, six with two, and six with three true atomic statements. More generally, the universe descriptions of a model consist of any nonempty subset of basic conjunctions.

Whatever universes are designated as actual and causally possible in $\mathfrak{M}_2$-$\mathfrak{L}_2$, the following are clearly true.

[G] $\Box(x){\sim}Axx$ (irreflexive)

[H] $\Box(x)(y)(z)(AxyAyz \supset Axz)$ (transitive)

[I] $\Box(x)(y)(Axy \supset {\sim}Ayx)$ (asymmetrical).

To complete the model we stipulate that "$A12$" and "$A23$" (and hence "$A13$") are true of the actual universe and that every logically possible universe is causally possible. Then "$(x)(y)\{\Box Axy \equiv \Box^c Axy\}$" and "$(x)(\exists y)(Axy \vee Ayx)$" are both true in this model, while "$\Box(x)(\exists y)(Axy \vee Ayx)$" and "$(x)(\exists y)Axy$" are both false.

It is clear that the last formula is also false in any finite model satisfying the irreflexivity and transitivity of the ancestral relation. We will extend $\mathfrak{M}_2$-$\mathfrak{L}_2$ to an infinite model in which "$(x)(\exists y)Axy$" is true, after first discussing how to handle infinitely large universes.

Inductive logics were originally defined for finite models, and when infinite models were needed they were treated as infinite sequences of finite models (p. 119). It was desirable in that connection to have only a finite number of universes in each model, to simplify the assignment of probabilities to universes. But since we will not assign probabilities to the universes of the modal model $\mathfrak{M}$-$\mathfrak{L}$, infinite models can be handled directly. We will allow a denumerable (countable) number of individual constants (proper names), though still only a finite number of predicates and relations. Models with more than a denumerable number of individuals could be used, but they are not needed for our purposes.

TABLE 15

SOME BASIC CONJUNCTIONS OF A MODEL OF THE ANCESTRAL RELATION

	Basic conjunctions	Comments	
1	$A11\ A22\ A33\ A12\ A23\ \overline{A13}\ A21\ A32\ A31$	Violates irreflexivity, transitivity, asymmetry	These basic conjunctions ARE NOT universe descriptions
2	$A11\ A22\ A33\ \overline{A12}\ \overline{A23}\ \overline{A13}\ \overline{A21}\ \overline{A32}\ \overline{A31}$	Violates irreflexivity	
3	$\overline{A11}\ \overline{A22}\ \overline{A33}\ A12\ A23\ \overline{A13}\ \overline{A21}\ \overline{A32}\ \overline{A31}$	Violates transitivity	
4	$\overline{A11}\ \overline{A22}\ \overline{A33}\ A12\ \overline{A23}\ \overline{A13}\ A21\ \overline{A32}\ \overline{A31}$	Violates asymmetry	
5	$\overline{A11}\ \overline{A22}\ \overline{A33}\ \overline{A12}\ \overline{A23}\ \overline{A13}\ \overline{A21}\ \overline{A32}\ \overline{A31}$	All atomic statements are false	These basic conjunctions ARE universe descriptions
6	$\overline{A11}\ \overline{A22}\ \overline{A33}\ A12\ \overline{A23}\ \overline{A13}\ \overline{A21}\ \overline{A32}\ \overline{A31}$	One atomic statement is true	
7	$\overline{A11}\ \overline{A22}\ \overline{A33}\ A12\ \overline{A23}\ A13\ \overline{A21}\ \overline{A32}\ \overline{A31}$	Two atomic statements are true	
8	$\overline{A11}\ \overline{A22}\ \overline{A33}\ A12\ A23\ A13\ \overline{A21}\ \overline{A32}\ \overline{A31}$	Three atomic statements are true	

Let $\mathfrak{M}_3$-$\mathfrak{L}_3$ contain the dyadic relation A and the infinite sequence of individuals 1, 2, 3, 4, ... There are infinitely many atomic statements:

$$\begin{array}{l} A11\ A12\ A13 \ldots \\ A21\ A22\ A23 \ldots \\ A31\ A32\ A33 \ldots \\ \cdot \\ \cdot \\ \cdot \end{array}$$

These can be rearranged in simple order:

$$A11;\ A12,\ A21;\ A13,\ A22,\ A31;\ A14,\ A23,\ A32,\ A41;\ \ldots \qquad ,$$

where Axy precedes $Ax'y'$ if $(x + y) < (x' + y')$ or if $(x + y) = (x' + y')$ and $x < x'$.

For the sake of convenience, we extend the concepts "basic conjunction" and "universe description" to cover infinite conjunctions. Each term of the preceding sequence or its negation is a conjunct of a basic conjunction of $\mathfrak{M}_3$-$\mathfrak{L}_3$. Infinite conjunctions are not formulas as that term was defined, and so we will call them *pseudoformulas*. Pseudoformulas also result from interpreting quantifiers in infinite models, a universal quantifier being interpreted as an infinite conjunction and an existential quantifier as an infinite disjunction. For example, the formula "$(x)(\exists y)Axy$" is interpreted in $\mathfrak{M}_3$-$\mathfrak{L}_3$ by the pseudoformula

$$(A11 \vee A12 \vee A13 \vee \ldots)\&(A21 \vee A22 \vee A23 \vee \ldots)\& \\ (A31 \vee A32 \vee A33 \vee \ldots)\&\ldots \qquad .$$

To complete the specification of model $\mathfrak{M}_3$-$\mathfrak{L}_3$, we take as universe descriptions those basic conjunctions satisfying the irreflexivity and transitivity of the ancestral relation. Every logically possible universe is also causally possible. The actual universe is specified by the condition

$$Axy \text{ if and only if } x < y \qquad .$$

The statement "$(x)(\exists y)Axy$" is true, since every individual has a descendant. But the statement "$(x)(\exists y)Ayx$" is false, since the first individual (1) has no ancestor.

Consider finally the variables and nonlogical constants of a model language $\mathfrak{L}$. Since $\mathfrak{L}$ includes the logic of causal statements it contains individual, predicate, and statement variables. It also contains individual constants, which name individuals of $\mathfrak{M}$, and predicate constants, which represent basic properties and relations of $\mathfrak{M}$. Individual constants behave syntactically like individual variables, except that individual constants cannot be quantified. Predicate constants behave syntactically like predicate variables, except that each predicate constant has a preassigned degree, whereas the degree of a predicate variable is determined by its context in a formula.

These syntactic differences between constants and variables are less important than their semantic differences. In a model $\mathfrak{M}$-$\mathfrak{L}$ each constant of $\mathfrak{L}$ has a fixed interpretation in $\mathfrak{M}$, while each variable ranges over a certain class of entities of $\mathfrak{M}$. An individual constant designates a specific individual, whereas an individual variable ranges over all individuals. Likewise, a predicate constant is associated with a specific property or relation, while a predicate variable occurring in a certain context ranges over all relations of a certain degree. Sometimes superscripts are placed on predicate variables to signify their degrees, but we have chosen to use the context to convey this information. For example, in the formula "$(\exists y)(ByDxy)$," "B" is clearly monadic and "D" is clearly dyadic. As we already noted, we also employ the context to tell whether an upper case letter is a predicate variable or predicate constant, and whether a lower case letter is an individual variable or an individual constant.

A formula is *open* if it contains at least one free variable occurrence; otherwise it is *closed*. On the given interpretation of the symbols of $\mathfrak{L}$, every closed formula is completely interpreted and hence has a definite truth-value in the model $\mathfrak{M}$-$\mathfrak{L}$. In contrast, an open formula is only partly interpreted and so does not (in general) have a definite truth-value. We shall explain later how its interpretation is completed (p. 363). It should be noted that the distinction between an open and a closed formula models our earlier distinction between statement forms and statements (p. 8). An open formula is a statement form, and each interpretation of it is a statement of that form.

The fact that our model languages contain individual and predicate constants but no statement constants needs explanation. There are no natural entities in a model to which statement constants might correspond. We could add the truth-values "true" and "false" to each model and then in an interpretation correlate each statement constant to one of these truth values. But we will achieve the same practical effect in a less artificial way by a definitional procedure. Statement constants may be used as external, informal abbreviations for closed formulas (for examples, see pp. 447 and 461). Compare the use of the ampersand as an abbreviation (p. 344).

This finishes our exposition of the most important new concepts involved in modal models. We will now give a rigorous definition of these models.

6.3.2 *Modal models*

A *modal model* $\mathfrak{M}$-$\mathfrak{L}$ has the following structure.

Each language $\mathfrak{L}$ is built on the logic of causal statements, to which are added a finite or infinite sequence of *individual constants* and a finite sequence of *predicate constants* of specified degrees. The definition of "formula"

(p. 343) is then extended to include these new symbols, and the axioms and the rule of inference are construed as covering the new formulas. Note that individual constants cannot be quantified, and that universal instantiation (p. 348) now applies to individual constants as well as to individual variables.

There is a one-to-one correspondence between the nonlogical constants of $\mathfrak{L}$ and the basic entities of $\mathfrak{M}$. Each individual constant of $\mathfrak{L}$ names a *basic individual* of $\mathfrak{M}$ and each predicate of degree N corresponds to a *basic property* of degree N. If $N = 1$ the property is monadic, while if $N > 1$ the property is relational.

The language $\mathfrak{L}$ contains a nested structure of universe descriptions of various modalities constructed as follows. Any formula formed by prefixing a predicate constant of degree N to a sequence of N individual constants ($N = 1, 2, 3, \ldots$) is an *atomic statement* of $\mathfrak{L}$. Consider now the sequence composed of all atomic statements of $\mathfrak{L}$ arranged in some order. For each atomic statement, choose either the statement or its negation and conjoin all the statements so obtained. The result is called a *basic conjunction*. If there are infinitely many basic individuals in $\mathfrak{L}$, its basic conjunctions are infinitely long and are pseudoformulas rather than formulas.

The set of *universe descriptions* of a model $\mathfrak{M}$-$\mathfrak{L}$ is any designated nonempty set of basic conjunctions of $\mathfrak{L}$. A nonempty set of universe descriptions is designated as the set of *causally possible universe descriptions* and one of these is stipulated to be the *true universe description* of the language $\mathfrak{L}$. The model $\mathfrak{M}$ has a corresponding nested structure of universes. Each universe description of $\mathfrak{L}$ describes a *logically possible universe* of $\mathfrak{M}$, each causally possible universe description describes a *causally possible universe*, and the true universe description describes the *actual universe*.

To interpret a language $\mathfrak{L}$ in terms of its model $\mathfrak{M}$, we need to interpret the grammatical expressions or formulas of $\mathfrak{L}$. We do this by defining "Φ *is true in* $\mathfrak{M}$-$\mathfrak{L}$" for any closed formula Φ. Our definition will state how to evaluate the truth-value of Φ in terms of the symbols of Φ and facts about $\mathfrak{M}$. Rules for interpreting the following kinds of symbols need to be formulated: (1) bound occurrences of individual variables, (2) individual and predicate constants, (3) truth-functional connectives, and (4) modal operators. Let "1" represent "true" and "0" represent "false," and add these symbols to the language $\mathfrak{L}$ for the evaluation process.

(1) Quantifiers are interpreted by translating them into their truth-functional equivalents (possibly infinite) covering all the instances of the model. Let $\beta_1, \beta_2, \ldots, \beta_n, \ldots$ be the individual constants of $\mathfrak{L}$. $(\alpha)\Psi$ is translated into the conjunction

$$\Psi_{\beta_1} \cdot \Psi_{\beta_2} \cdot \ldots \cdot \Psi_{\beta_n} \cdot \ldots \quad ,$$

where Ψ_{β_n} is the result of substituting β_n for all free occurrences of α in Ψ. Existential quantifiers may be replaced by their defining expressions or, more directly, translated into truth-functional disjunctions. This process of translating out the quantifiers of a formula is to be repeated until all quantifiers are replaced by truth-functions. If the model $\mathfrak{M}$-$\mathfrak{L}$ has infinitely many individuals, the result of this translation will be infinitely long and hence will be a pseudoformula rather than a formula.

(2) The interpretation of individual and predicate constants is expressed by the following definition of truth for an atomic statement of $\mathfrak{L}$ relative to a given universe of $\mathfrak{M}$. An atomic statement $\phi\alpha_1 \ldots \alpha_N$ is true in the given universe of $\mathfrak{M}$ just in case the sequence of individuals $\alpha_1, \ldots, \alpha_N$ possesses the relational property ϕ.

(3) The interpretation of truth-functional constants occurring in formulas (finite expressions) is given by their truth-table definitions (sec. 2.2.2). An infinite disjunction {conjunction} is true (has the value "1") if and only if some disjunct {every conjunct} is true (has the value "1"); otherwise it is false (has the value "0"). Since each atomic statement has a definite truth-value in each universe, this also defines the truth-value in each universe of $\mathfrak{M}$ of each formula or pseudoformula of $\mathfrak{L}$ composed of atomic statements, truth-functional constants, and parentheses.

Note now the effect of applying the preceding three rules to a formula Φ. Rule (1) produces a closed formula or pseudoformula Φ' with no quantifiers. Rule (2) defines a truth-value for each atomic statement of Φ' in each universe of $\mathfrak{M}$. Rule (3) then defines the truth-value of every nonmodal formula or pseudoformula that occurs in Φ', with respect to each universe of $\mathfrak{M}$. We next interpret the modal symbols of Φ' and thereby complete the definition of "Φ is true in $\mathfrak{M}$-$\mathfrak{L}$."

(4) Since modal operators are not iterated and quantifiers have been eliminated, Φ' is a truth-functional compound of three forms: $\Box\Psi$, $\Box^c\Psi$, and Ψ, where Ψ is non-modal. For the third, non-modal form, replace Ψ by "1" or "0" according to whether or not Ψ is true in the actual universe. The modal forms are evaluated with respect to the corresponding sets of possible universes. Replace $\Box\Psi$ by "1" or "0" according to whether or not Ψ is true in all logically possible universes of $\mathfrak{M}$. Similarly, replace $\Box^c\Psi$ by "1" or "0" according to whether or not Ψ is true in all causally possible universes of $\mathfrak{M}$. The possibility operators may be evaluated by replacing them with their defining expressions or, more directly, by replacing $\Diamond\Psi$ by "1" or "0" according to whether or not Ψ is true in at least one logically possible universe of $\mathfrak{M}$ and replacing $\Diamond^c\Psi$ by "1" or "0" according to whether or not Ψ is true in at least one causally possible universe.

This completes the definition of "Φ is true in $\mathfrak{M}$-$\mathfrak{L}$" for closed formulas. If $\mathfrak{M}$ has finitely many individuals, the definition constitutes an algorithm for calculating the truth-value of any closed formula from the formula itself and a description of the model. This definition does not constitute such an algorithm for the class of all models; indeed, there is no such algorithm.*

We will illustrate the operation of this truth evaluation algorithm. Let the model $\mathfrak{M}_4$-$\mathfrak{L}_4$ contain the two individual constants "*i*" and "*j*," the monadic predicate constants "*A*" and "*B*," and the dyadic predicate constant "*C*." The atomic statements of $\mathfrak{L}_4$ are then

$$Ai,\ Aj,\ Bi,\ Bj,\ Cii,\ Cij,\ Cji,\ Cjj.$$

There are 256 basic conjunctions; let the 64 of these in which "*CiiCjj*" is true be designated as the universe descriptions of $\mathfrak{L}_4$. Let the causally possible universe descriptions be

$$Ai\overline{Aj}BiBjCiiCijCjiCjj$$

$$\overline{Ai}AjBiBjCiiCijCjiCjj \quad ,$$

and let the last of these be the true universe description.

Consider now the closed formula

$$[\Phi] \qquad \Box^c [(x)(Ax \supset Bx)] \vee [(x)Ax\Diamond(\exists y)Ciy] \quad .$$

The result of translating out its quantifiers is

$$[\Phi'] \qquad \Box^c [(Ai \supset Bi)(Aj \supset Bj)] \vee [AiAj\Diamond(Cii \vee Cij)] \quad ,$$

where each nonmodal subformula of Φ' has a truth-value in each possible universe. To evaluate Φ' in the model $\mathfrak{M}_4$-$\mathfrak{L}_4$ we evaluate the nonmodal component "$AiAj$" with respect to the actual universe (the result is "0"), we evaluate the modal component "$\Diamond(Cii \vee Cij)$" with respect to the set of logically possible universes (the result is "1"), and we evaluate the modal component "$\Box^c [(Ai \supset Bi)(Aj \supset Bj)]$" with respect to the set of causally possible universes (the result is "1"). This process yields "1 v (0 &1)," which reduces to "1" or "true." Hence the original formula Φ is true in the model $\mathfrak{M}_4$-$\mathfrak{L}_4$.

This completes the definition of a modal model $\mathfrak{M}$-$\mathfrak{L}$. In brief, each language $\mathfrak{L}$ consists of the logic of causal statements enriched by individual and predicate constants and having specified universe descriptions, causally possible universe descriptions, and a true universe description. The corresponding model $\mathfrak{M}$ has a similar structure of individuals and properties, with logically possible universes, causally possible universes, and an actual universe. The truth-value of a closed formula is defined in terms of its constituent symbols and facts about the model $\mathfrak{M}$-$\mathfrak{L}$.

* There is none because there are more infinite models than finite descriptions. The cardinality of the class of models $\mathfrak{M}$-$\mathfrak{L}$ is that of the continuum (*c*), while there are only a denumerable (countable) number ($\aleph_0$) of finite expressions. Hence most models cannot be finitely described.

6.3.3 Logical truth

We discuss the notion of logical truth as it appears in these models and prove some theorems about the logic of causal statements by means of it.

The distinction between logical and empirical statements is reflected in these models (sec. 1.2). For example, in the white swan model $\mathfrak{M}_1$-$\mathfrak{L}_1$ (p. 353), there are

Logically true statements: $Sa \vee \overline{Sa}$, $(x)(Sx \vee \overline{Sx})$, $\square(x)(Sx \vee \overline{Sx})$

Empirically true statements: Sa, $(x)(Wx \supset Sx)$, $\square^c (x)(Sx \supset Wx)$

Empirically false statements: $\overline{Sa}$, $(\exists x)(Sx\overline{Wx})$, $\square^c (x)(Wx \supset Sx)$

Logically false statements: $Sa\overline{Sa}$, $(x)(Sx\overline{Sx})$, $\diamond(\exists x)(Sx\overline{Sx})$.

The presence of empirically true-or-false statements in these models is connected to the fact that the individuals of the model are concrete things or events with contingent properties, such as swans, electrons, explosions, and magnetic fields. Equivalently, there are universes that are logically possible alternatives to the actual universe. Thus while the models $\mathfrak{M}$-$\mathfrak{L}$ are abstract in the sense of being idealized and simplified, they are conceived as models of concrete reality. In contrast, the standard model for arithmetic contains abstract entities (integers) with noncontingent properties (odd, greater than), contains only one universe, and has all its closed formulas logically true-or-false (pp. 369–71). But for our studies of induction and causality we need models with empirically true-or-false statements.

This modeling of the logical-empirical distinction in the modal models $\mathfrak{M}$-$\mathfrak{L}$ is very crude because of the extreme simplicity of the models. Some of these limitations were mentioned earlier (sec. 3. 3. 3). Two further limitations should be noted. First, if the class of logically possible universes has only one member, actuality becomes logical necessity. Second, statements reflecting the cardinality of a model may be logically true (or logically false) in one model but not another. For example, if a model with the monadic predicate "S" contains a single individual i, "$Si \equiv (x)Sx$" is true in all universes, and hence "$\square\{Si \equiv (x)Sx\}$" is true. Again,

$$\square\sim\{[(x)\sim Axx][(x)(y)(z)(AxyAyz \supset Axz)][(x)(\exists y)Axy]\}$$

is true in every finite model in which it occurs, but it may be false in an infinite model; compare $\mathfrak{M}_2$-$\mathfrak{L}_2$ and $\mathfrak{M}_3$-$\mathfrak{L}_3$ of Section 6.3.1, above.

The first limitation could be removed quite simply by stipulating that a model must contain at least two logically possible universes. The second defect could be removed by allowing universes with different numbers of individuals and thereby distinguishing actual from fictional individuals. However, to do this would be to make modal logic unnecessarily complex for our purposes. Moreover, these objections do not apply to the notion of logical truth implicit in our intended interpretation of the logic of causal statements.

We constructed our formal language with the following goal in mind: each theorem should express a general principle of logic applicable to many cases. The expression takes the form of an open formula; since the logic of causal statements contains no predicate or statement constants or quantifiers, it contains no closed formulas. For example, the theorem "$\Box P \supset P$" is an open formula expressing the principle: if a statement is necessary it is true. Thus we interpret formulas that are theorems as if all their variables were universally quantified. This procedure shows that the kind of truth appropriate to the formulas of the logic of causal statements is logical truth, and it motivates the following definitions.

Consider some formula Φ of the logic of causal statements and some modal model $\mathfrak{M}$-$\mathfrak{L}$. Let Φ^c be a closed formula of $\mathfrak{L}$ resulting from substitutions of the appropriate kinds in Φ: an individual constant for an individual variable, a predicate constant of degree N for a predicate variable of the same degree, and a closed formula of $\mathfrak{L}$ for a statement variable. It is understood that whenever a constant or closed formula of $\mathfrak{L}$ is substituted for a variable of Φ, it is substituted for all free occurrences of that variable in Φ. We call the closed formula Φ^c an "interpretation" of Φ in the model $\mathfrak{M}$-$\mathfrak{L}$.

The notion of logical truth is now defined as follows. A formula Φ of the logic of causal statements is *logically true* if and only if every interpretation of Φ in every modal model is true. This definition covers those formulas of a modal model that are also formulas of the logic of causal statements. We extend it to cover the remaining formulas of a modal model $\mathfrak{M}$-$\mathfrak{L}$ as follows. A formula Ψ with some individual or predicate constants is *logically true* if and only if there is a logically true formula Φ of the logic of causal statements such that Ψ results from substituting constants of $\mathfrak{L}$ in Φ.

We have completed our abstract, idealized interpretation of the logic of causal statements. Now it is desirable that every theorem of this system be logically true. We show next that such is indeed the case. Our proof makes double use of mathematical induction (p. 49), first to show that every axiom is logically true, and then to show that every formula of a categorical proof is logically true.

A detailed examination of the axiom schemes [2]–[4] reveals that every formula having one of these forms is logically true. Here are three examples. Every truth-functional axiom is logically true, as is demonstrated by its truth-table. The formula "$(x)(\exists y)Rxy \supset (\exists y)Rzy$" is an instance of universal instantiation: if the antecedent is true in a universe, then the consequent is also, no matter what individual constant is substituted for "z." Lastly, any formula of the form $\Box(\Phi \supset \Psi) \supset \{\Box\Phi \supset \Box\Psi\}$ is true on every interpretation. For suppose the consequent is false on some interpretation in some model, so that Φ is true in every universe but Ψ is false in at least one; then $\Phi \supset \Psi$ is false in that universe, and therefore $\Box(\Phi \supset \Psi)$ is false.

Hence all the axioms defined by rules [2]–[4] are logically true. Further axioms may be generated by applying rule [5], and so we need to show that this rule preserves logical truth. The first case is $(\alpha)\Phi$. If α does not occur free in Φ, $(\alpha)\Phi$ and Φ clearly have the same truth value. Let $\phi(\alpha)$ be a logically true formula with free occurrences of the individual variable α. Pick a model in which $\phi(\alpha)$ may be interpreted, and let $\phi^c(\alpha)$ be the result of substituting constants for all free variables other than α. Substitute the individual constants $a_1, a_2, a_3, \ldots$ of the model for α, obtaining the closed formulas $\phi^c(a_1)$, $\phi^c(a_2)$, $\phi^c(a_3)$, ... Each of these formulas is true, and therefore $(\alpha)\phi^c(\alpha)$ is true in the model. Since this argument holds for any model, $(\alpha)\phi(\alpha)$ is logically true.

The second case is $\Box\Phi$. Let Φ be a non-modal, logically true formula and Φ^c an interpretation of it in a model $\mathfrak{M}$-$\mathfrak{L}$. Because Φ^c is logically true, Φ^c is true in the actual universe of $\mathfrak{M}$-$\mathfrak{L}$. Now for each logically possible universe u of $\mathfrak{M}$-$\mathfrak{L}$, consider the variant of $\mathfrak{M}$-$\mathfrak{L}$ obtained by making u the actual universe and also, if necessary, making u causally possible. Since Φ is logically true, Φ^c is true of u in this variant model. And since this variant model differs from $\mathfrak{M}$-$\mathfrak{L}$ only in the designation of actual and causally possible universes, Φ^c is also true of u in the original model $\mathfrak{M}$-$\mathfrak{L}$. In other words, Φ^c is true of every logically possible universe of $\mathfrak{M}$-$\mathfrak{L}$, and $\Box\Phi^c$ is true in $\mathfrak{M}$-$\mathfrak{L}$. Therefore, if Φ is logically true, $\Box\Phi$ is logically true. This completes the proof that all axioms of the logic of causal statements are logically true.

Consider finally the rule of inference [6]. If $(\Phi_1\Phi_2 \ldots \Phi_N) \supset \Psi$ is logically true and $\Phi_1, \Phi_2, \ldots, \Phi_N$ are also, then Ψ is logically true; in other words, an immediate consequence of logical truths is itself a logical truth. Every formula of a categorical proof is either an axiom or an immediate consequence of preceding formulas of the proof; therefore, every formula of a categorical proof is logically true. It follows that *every theorem of the logic of causal statements is logically true.*

The consistency of the logic of causal statements is a corollary. A formal language $\mathfrak{L}$ is *consistent* if and only if $\mathfrak{L}$ does not contain a formula Φ such that both Φ and $\sim\Phi$ are theorems. Consider any theorem of the logic of causal statements. By the previous result, Φ is logically true. Hence $\sim\Phi$ is not logically true and by the previous result is not a theorem. Accordingly, *the logic of causal statements is consistent.* This is an important corollary; for if the logic of causal statements were inconsistent, every formula would be a theorem and the system would be useless (see sec. 6.5.3).

Because every theorem of the logic of causal statements is logically true, we can demonstrate that a formula is not a theorem by producing an interpretation under which the formula is false. For example, since "$\square^c (Pa \vee Qa) \supset (\square^c Pa \vee \square^c Qa)$" is false in a model in which "$Pa\overline{Qa}$" and "$\overline{Pa}Qa$" describe causally possible universes but "$PaQa$" and "$\overline{Pa}\,\overline{Qa}$" do not, the converse of metatheorem [10c], below, is not a metatheorem (p. 408). This method of showing that formulas are not theorems is a useful one.

We have just seen that every theorem of the logic of causal statements is logically true on the abstract interpretation given in the present section. Is that also the case for its concrete interpretation? Since this logic was constructed as a model language, the answer to that question is partly factual and partly stipulative (see secs. 1.6.3, 4.2.3). The logic of causal statements is of interest here mainly for the causal modalities, and we shall see in the next chapter that it provides a good model of ordinary and scientific deductive reasoning about causal laws and causal subjunctives. Insofar as the logic of causal statements is a good model of natural language deduction, its theorems express logical truths of natural language. And insofar as the logic of causal statements deviates from natural language, we stipulate that the theorems of the system are logically true. Thus we have accomplished part of our aim in constructing the logic of causal statements, namely, to have a formal language whose theorems express logical truths about the causal and logical modalities.

The logic of causal statements clearly does not contain all logical truths about the modalities and, a fortiori, does not contain all logical truths. Being a modal extension of first-order quantification theory, it is subject to many of the limitations of that theory. The truths of arithmetic and of mathematical analysis, for example, cannot even be expressed in the logic of causal statements. This system is limited by its symbolism to a small part of the domain of logical truth.

Much is known about stronger systems of logic, especially those of the nonmodal variety, but rather than consider other specific systems we will ask and answer one very basic question about formal languages: Is there a consistent formal language that is complete in the sense of containing *all* logical truths as theorems? This question presupposes the existence of a formal language in which every statement can be expressed. As the quotations that head the present chapter indicate, Gottfried Leibniz raised the possibility of such a "universal language" about three-hundred years ago; it is worthwhile to explore Leibniz's ideas further.

A careful formulation of the general completeness question requires a definition of "formal language." We established earlier that there are decision algorithms for formulahood, axiomhood, and proofhood in the logic of causal statements; indeed, we constructed this system in such a manner that these algorithms would exist and would be simple (sec. 6.2). From the point of view of the applications one makes of a formal language, the formulahood and proofhood algorithms are most fundamental, the axiomhood algorithm serving as a part of the latter. One needs to decide of a sequence of symbols whether it is a formula and hence has an interpretation. And one needs to decide of a sequence of formulas whether it is a proof, i.e., whether it establishes that its last formula is a theorem. If the design of an interpreted formal language is successful, all of its theorems are true. Thus the notions of "formula" and "proof" lie at the heart of a formal language, so that it is reasonable to say: a *formal language* is defined by specifying decision algorithms for formulahood and proofhood.

While it would be a prolepsis to attribute the precise concept of a formal language to Leibniz, his remarks make clear that if the universal language he envisioned were developed it would be a formal language. He proposed to represent linguistic expressions arithmetically so that reasoning could be done computationally. We should note in this connection that the common arithmetic procedures of addition, multiplication, etc., and of checking an addition or subtraction by casting out nines are all algorithmic.

A formal language per se has no interpretation, but Leibniz's universal language was to be an interpreted language of "complete" expressive power. Now there are many different languages, and information or content expressed in one may not be expressible in another. But a universal language would be universal in expressive power: any "information" expressible in language could be expressed in it. Empirical statements can be formed from the terms Leibniz used as examples; moreover, he repeatedly claimed that a universal language would have important practical applications. These facts together indicate that he thought his formal language would be complete with respect to empirical content as well as logical content, though he did not expect empirical questions to be settled by computation. Let us say, then, that an interpreted formal language $\mathfrak{L}$ has "complete expressive power" if and only if every statement can be expressed in $\mathfrak{L}$.

Leibniz's unqualified and oft-repeated claim that rational disputes could be settled by calculation presupposes an algorithm for calculating whether or not a formula is logically true. Leibniz was not thinking of an axiomatic language for arithmetic, but, as we shall see later, a calculating procedure for truth in a formal language can be converted into an axiomatic system (p. 393). Furthermore, the two questions "Is there an algorithm for deciding logical truth?" and "Is every theorem logically true, and conversely?" are intimately related. For this reason it will be convenient to lump together these two questions.

The following conjecture raises some basic questions about the relation of formal languages to logical truth. While it is framed in terms of modern notions, it contains the basic claims Leibniz made for his universal language and expresses the goal he sought, and so it is appropriately named after him. *Leibniz's conjecture:* There is an interpreted formal language $\mathfrak{L}$ of complete expressive power having these properties

(1) every theorem is logically true and every formula that is logically true is a theorem

(2) there is an algorithm for calculating whether or not a formula is logically true.

Gödel's famous incompleteness theorem of 1931 showed Leibniz's conjecture to be false. Besides having that important consequence, Gödel's theorem also revealed some of the essential properties of a formal language. For these reasons we will formulate his theorem, describe the main features of its proof, and then apply it to Leibniz's conjecture. The reader who is interested only in the specific properties of the logic of causal statements may proceed directly to Section 6.5.

6.4 The Mechanical Character of a Formal Language

*6.4.1 Arithmetization of a formal language**

We discuss first Gödel's method for arithmetizing a formal language (that is, treating it as an arithmetic system) and the formal language for arithmetic to which he applied this method.

Any formal language can be arithmetized by Gödel's coding technique, which uses positive integers to represent the symbols, sequences of symbols, and sequences of sequences of symbols of a language in such a way that the representation of each is unique. We illustrate the procedure with the logic of causal statements, applying Gödel's technique at three successive levels, as illustrated in Table 16. At the first level, each primitive symbol is repre-

TABLE 16

GÖDEL NUMBERS

Gödel number of sequence of formulas	$2^{2^5 3^{17} 5^7 7^{15} 11^{17}} \times 3^{2^{15} 3^{21}}$
Gödel numbers of formulas	$2^5 \times 3^{17} \times 5^7 \times 7^{15} \times 11^{17}$, $2^{15} \times 3^{21}$
Gödel numbers of symbols	5 17 7 15 17 , 15 21
Sequence of formulas	(*b*) *A* *b* , *A* *c*

sented by a single positive integer under the coding

~	v	(	)	□	□^{c}	*a*	*A*	*b*	*B*	*c*	*C*	. . .
1	3	5	7	9	11	13	15	17	19	21	23	. . .

,

* Gödel, "Über formal unentscheidbare Sätze der Principia Mathematica und Verwandter Systeme I" and "On Undecidable Propositions of Formal Mathematical Systems." See also Rosser, "Extensions of Some Theorems of Gödel and Church," and Kleene, *Introduction to Metamathematics*, chaps. 8-11.

the individual variables being represented by the integers 13, 17, 21, . . . and the symbols used as statement and predicate variables being represented by the integers 15, 19, 23, ... A finite sequence of primitive symbols is thus represented at the first level by a finite sequence of integers; for example, "$(b)Ab$" is represented by the sequence 5, 17, 7, 15, 17.

At the second level, a finite sequence of symbols is represented by a single integer, as follows. If the symbols $s_1, s_2, s_3, \ldots, s_N$ are represented by $\alpha_1, \alpha_2, \alpha_3, \ldots, \alpha_N$, respectively, then the sequence of symbols $s_1 s_2 s_3 \ldots s_N$ is represented by

$$2^{\alpha_1} \times 3^{\alpha_2} \times 5^{\alpha_3} \times \ldots \times \rho_N{}^{\alpha_N} \quad ,$$

where ρ_N is the Nth prime in order of magnitude. For example, the formula "$(b)Ab$" is represented by the integer $2^5 3^{17} 5^7 7^{15} 11^{17}$.

A sequence of sequences of symbols is represented on the second level by a sequence of integers. It is represented on the third level by a single integer, the passage from the second to the third level being made in the same way as the passage from the first to the second level. If the sequences of symbols $t_1, t_2, t_3, \ldots, t_N$ are represented by $\beta_1, \beta_2, \beta_3, \ldots, \beta_N$, respectively, then the sequence of sequences $t_1, t_2, t_3, \ldots, t_N$ is represented by

$$2^{\beta_1} \times 3^{\beta_2} \times 5^{\beta_3} \times \ldots \times \rho_N{}^{\beta_N} \quad .$$

For example, the proof "$(b)Ab$, Ac" is represented by the integer

$$2^{2^5 3^{17} 5^7 7^{15} 11^{17}} \times 3^{2^{15} 3^{21}} \quad .$$

Now each integer is uniquely decomposable into its prime factors, and the exponents so obtained can again be factored into their prime factors. Moreover, one can tell by analyzing an integer what, if anything, it represents. Integers representing symbols are odd; integers representing sequences of symbols are even, with the first factor of their prime decomposition being an odd power of two; integers representing sequences of sequences of symbols are even, with the first factor of prime decomposition being an even power of two. An integer representing a symbol, formula, or proof is said to be the *Gödel number* of that symbol, formula, or proof. We let $\mathbf{g}[\Phi]$ be the Gödel number of formula Φ. Thus $\mathbf{g}[Ac] = 2^{15} 3^{21}$ and $\mathbf{g}[(b)Ab] = 2^5 3^{17} 5^7 7^{15} 11^{17}$.

The foregoing shows how Gödel's coding technique can be used to convert or translate any formal language into a system of arithmetic in which each symbol, formula, and proof is uniquely expressed by a positive integer.

It is of historical interest that in his use of prime numbers for the arithmetic coding of non-numerical symbols, Gödel was anticipated by Leibniz. Leibniz proposed to represent the compound-atom distinction for concepts by the composite-prime distinction for integers (p. 337 above). For example, he analyzed the definition "man is a rational animal" into an arithmetical equation:

man = rational animal
6 = 3 x 2 .

Since an integer is uniquely decomposable into its prime factors, a concept represented in this way can be analyzed arithmetically into its constituent parts. Gödel's coding technique is much more powerful than Leibniz's, however, because it distinguishes one ordering of a set of symbols (or formulas) from another, and it distinguishes among symbols, sequences of symbols, and sequences of sequences of symbols.

We defined a formal language as a language with decision algorithms for formulahood and proofhood (p. 366). It is clear from Gödel's coding technique that these algorithms can work with Gödel numbers as well as with the symbols of the formal language.

Moreover, Gödel's coding technique can be made the basis of arithmetic procedures for enumerating the formulas and theorems of a formal language. The *theorem enumeration algorithm* works as follows. The even integers are enumerated 2, 4, 6, ... Each is treated as on the third level and factored twice to see whether or not it represents a sequence of sequences of primitive symbols. If it does, the decision algorithm for proofhood is applied to this sequence of sequences. If the sequence of sequences is a categorical proof, the last sequence (formula) is enumerated as a theorem. In this way an indefinite sequence of theorems is enumerated. Furthermore, every theorem occurs in this enumeration; for by definition every theorem has a categorical proof, and that proof is represented on the third level by some integer. The *formula enumeration algorithm* is constructed similarly, with two variations: the integers are treated as on the second level, and the decision algorithm for formulahood is employed.

Gödel applied his arithmetic coding technique to a formal language capable of expressing arithmetic, and he was thereby able to construct statements in that language referring to the language's own formal properties. Let us explain in a general way how Gödel accomplished this result. As a first step, we will describe a formal language, to be called *Peano arithmetic*, in terms of its interpretation. Peano arithmetic is simpler than the language Gödel used, but it is still adequate for the purpose.*

* What we call "Peano arithmetic" is a form of first-order quantification theory. For a full exposition of these systems and proofs of Gödel's incompleteness theorem and related theorems, see Mendelson, *Introduction to Mathematical Logic*, chap. 3. In his original proofs Gödel used a higher order language in which statement and function variables were quantified.

Peano arithmetic is based on five axioms traditionally called "Peano's axioms," after Giuseppe Peano. Actually, the axioms are not accurately named, for they came originally from Dedekind's *Was Sind und was Sollen die Zahlen?* Wang, "The Axiomatization of Arithmetic," discusses the history and a letter by Dedekind in which Dedekind explains how he arrived at these axioms.

Peano arithmetic is formed by modifying first-order quantification theory (p. 351) in the following ways. The statement and predicate variables are deleted, but one dyadic predicate constant ("=" for "equals") is added. There are infinitely many individual variables, w, x, y, z, . . . , etc. These individual variables are interpreted as ranging over the natural numbers zero, one, two, three, ... An individual constant 0 is added, as are three function constants: the monadic $'$ (for successor or "add one"), the dyadic $+$ (for addition), and the dyadic $\cdot$ (for multiplication). We will allow the symbols of Peano arithmetic to name themselves in the metalanguage, so that we can name a formula by writing it without quotes (cf. pp. 42–43).

The well-formed expressions of Peano arithmetic are of two types: "terms," which designate or range over natural numbers, and "formulas." Every individual variable is a term. The constant 0, which designates zero, is a term. Suffixing the successor symbol repeatedly to the symbol for zero gives terms that designate the remaining natural numbers: $0'$ designates one, $0''$ designates two, $0'''''$ designates five, etc. Still other terms can be formed by combining $'$, 0, $+$, $\cdot$, and individual variables in natural ways. Examples are: $x + y$, $y \cdot z'$, $(z + w')'$, $0' + 0'$ [one plus one], and $0'' \cdot 0'''$ [two times three].

There are no statement symbols in Peano arithmetic, and $=$ is the only predicate symbol. Hence atomic formulas are made by equating terms, as in $y = z$, $y + 0 = y$, and $(y + z') = (y + z)'$. These may be compounded by means of truth-functional connectives and quantifiers, as in $\sim(y = z)$, $(y = z) \supset (y' = z')$, and $(x)(y)(x + y = y + x)$. Moreover, there is a descriptive quantifier ℓ that converts formulas into terms, which can then be used to make more formulas, ad infinitum. Let $\phi\{\alpha\}$ be a formula in which α occurs free. The term $(\ell\alpha)\phi\{\alpha\}$ designates the least natural number α satisfying $\phi\{\alpha\}$ if there is such a number, and otherwise it designates zero. For example, $(\ell y)(\exists z)((y = 0'' + z) \;\&\; \sim(z = 0)))$ designates three, but since zero is not the successor of any number, $(\ell y)(y' = 0)$ designates zero.

The descriptive operator ℓ could be defined contextually (though not explicitly) in terms of the rest of Peano arithmetic, but it is more convenient for us to take it as primitive. Since ℓ is a kind of quantifier, it binds variables, and hence Peano arithmetic contains closed terms with variables, e.g., $(\ell y)(y = 0')$, as well as closed terms with no variables, e.g., $0' + 0'''$, and open terms, e.g., $x + y$ and $(\ell y)(y = x'') + z$.

Various arithmetic functions (e.g., exponentiation, factorial) and predicates (e.g., "greater than," "is divisible by," and "is a prime") can be defined recursively in Peano arithmetic.*

We turn now to the axioms and rules of inference of Peano arithmetic.

* The general procedure for expressing primitive recursive functions in this system of Peano arithmetic is outlined in Mendelson, *Introduction to Mathematical Logic*, pp. 131–32.

We start with the axioms and rules of the logic of causal statements, delete the modal operators, and extend universal instantiation to apply to all terms (not just individual variables), with suitable restrictions to preserve the freedom status of variables. Then axioms are added to govern the descriptive quantifier ℓ, and further axioms are added to express the transitivity, symmetry, and reflexivity of equality (see p. 208, above). There is a derived rule of inference permitting the exchange of provably equal terms in all contexts. Finally, we add six axioms and an axiom scheme for arithmetic.

The six arithmetic axioms are

$$\left.\begin{array}{ll}(1) & \sim(0 = x') \\ (2) & (x = y) \equiv (x' = y')\end{array}\right\} \text{Successor function}$$

$$\left.\begin{array}{ll}(3) & (x + 0) = x \\ (4) & (x + y') = (x + y)'\end{array}\right\} \text{Addition}$$

$$\left.\begin{array}{ll}(5) & (x \cdot 0) = 0 \\ (6) & (x \cdot y') = ((x \cdot y) + x)\end{array}\right\} \text{Multiplication.}$$

The axiom scheme is the basis of the rule of mathematical induction (see p. 49). Let $\phi\{\alpha\}$ be a formula in which α occurs free; $\phi\{0\}$ and $\phi\{\alpha'\}$ result from making the indicated substitutions for the free occurrences of α in $\phi\{\alpha\}$. Then every formula of this form is an axiom

$$(7) \qquad [\phi\{0\}\&(\alpha)(\phi\{\alpha\} \supset \phi\{\alpha'\})] \supset (\alpha)\phi\{\alpha\} \qquad .$$

Note that by the rule of axiom generation (p. 349) the closure of each axiom is also an axiom.

Since individual variables are the only variables of Peano arithmetic and these can be quantified, this formal system contains closed formulas, e.g., $0' + 0'' = 0'''$ and $(x)(x + 0'' = x'' + 0)$, as well as open formulas, e.g., $x + 0'' = x'' + 0$. On the standard interpretation of Peano arithmetic, each closed formula expresses a statement about arithmetic that is either true or false. This interpretation can be made more precise by formulating it in terms of an abstract arithmetic structure or model of natural numbers, functions, and relations; it is, of course, the abstract interpretation implicit in our ordinary and mathematical uses of arithmetic. Using this precise interpretation, one can define truth for the closed formulas as we did for the modal models (pp. 359–63). And since all the truths of Peano arithmetic are logical truths, we can drop the qualification "logical" without ambiguity.

Since open formulas (as well as closed ones) can be theorems, we will define truth for them also. An open formula is true if and only if the result of universally quantifying all its free variables is true. A terminological consequence of this definition of "truth" should be noted. If Φ is open, it may happen that neither Φ nor $\sim\Phi$ is true, as is the case with $x = y'$ and $\sim(x = y')$. To avoid confusion, we use the phrase "not true" in such cases, rather than "false." But if Φ is closed, one of the pair $\{\Phi, \sim\Phi\}$ is true and the other false.

We can prove that every theorem of Peano arithmetic is true in the same way we proved that every theorem of the logic of causal statements is logically true (p. 364). An examination of the axioms shows that on this interpretation each axiom is true, while an examination of the rules of inference shows that an immediate consequence of formulas that are true on this interpretation is also true on this interpretation. Consequently, all the theorems of Peano arithmetic are true on the intended interpretation. It follows as a corollary that Peano arithmetic is consistent. In other words, there is no formula Φ, and hence no closed formula Φ, such that both Φ and $\sim\Phi$ are theorems of Peano arithmetic.

The theorems of Peano arithmetic constitute a large body of arithmetic truths. Some examples are: "3 + 5 = 8," "17·23 = 391," "24 is divisible by 4," "7 is the fourth prime," the commutativity and associativity of addition and of multiplication, the distribution principle

$$(x)(y)(z)(((x + y)\cdot z) = ((x\cdot z) + (y\cdot z))) \qquad ,$$

and the rule for exponents

$$(y)(m)(n)((y^m\cdot y^n) = y^{m+n}) \qquad .$$

The question then arises: Is every arithmetic truth a theorem of Peano arithmetic?

This question can be put more precisely. It is plausible to hold that with respect to its expressive power, Peano arithmetic is a complete *formalization* of ordinary intuitive arithmetic: each statement of ordinary arithmetic is expressed by a closed formula of Peano arithmetic. The previous question then becomes: Is every true formula of Peano arithmetic a theorem of this system? Gödel's incompleteness theorem answers this question negatively.

6.4.2 Gödel's incompleteness theorem

Before stating this theorem we must define "completeness" in an appropriate sense.

For Peano arithmetic to be a complete formalization of arithmetic, every true formula should be a theorem. The rules of the system allow both universal generalization and universal instantiation for any variable (pp. 348, 349, 370), so that an open formula is a theorem if and only if the result of universally quantifying all its variables is a theorem. Hence Peano arithmetic would be a complete formalization of arithmetic if every true closed formula were a theorem. But rather than take this as the definition of completeness, we take the following, which is preferable because it makes no reference to the interpretation. A formal language $\mathfrak{L}$ is *complete* if and only if, for every closed formula Φ of $\mathfrak{L}$, either Φ or $\sim\Phi$ is a theorem of $\mathfrak{L}$. Since every theorem of Peano arithmetic is true, Peano arithmetic is complete in this formal sense if and only if every true closed formula is a theorem.

Gödel's incompleteness theorem shows that Peano arithmetic is not complete. Though Gödel proved his theorem for the specific formal language we have called Peano arithmetic, it is important that the theorem applies to any equivalent language and to any more inclusive language. Let us say that an interpreted formal language $\mathfrak{L}$ "contains Peano arithmetic" if all the concepts of Peano arithmetic are expressible in $\mathfrak{L}$ and all the theorems of Peano arithmetic are theorems of $\mathfrak{L}$. For the sake of convenience, we restrict our attention to formal interpreted languages of pure mathematics and logic, so that all truths are logical truths and all falsehoods are logical falsehoods. We also assume that all variables can be universally quantified, so that our formal definition of "complete" will be appropriate. At the end of this section we shall extend Gödel's results to languages in which empirical content can be expressed.

Gödel's incompleteness theorem can now be stated: *Let $\mathfrak{L}$ be an interpreted formal language containing Peano arithmetic whose theorems are all true on the given interpretation; then $\mathfrak{L}$ is incomplete.** We describe the main features of the proof of this theorem in the balance of the present subsection.

Let $\mathfrak{L}_A$ be any interpreted formal language containing Peano arithmetic such that on the given interpretation every theorem of $\mathfrak{L}_A$ is true. The system $\mathfrak{L}_A$ could be Peano arithmetic itself, but it might also be some stronger system whose theorems are all true on the given interpretation. What is essential for our purpose is that $\mathfrak{L}_A$ must contain Peano arithmetic and the given interpretation of $\mathfrak{L}_A$ must include the standard interpretation of Peano arithmetic in terms of natural numbers, arithmetic functions, and arithmetic relations.

Since $\mathfrak{L}_A$ is a formal language, Gödel's coding technique may be applied to it. In our examples, we will assume that $\mathfrak{L}_A$ is Peano arithmetic and has the following coding:

$\sim$	v	(	)	=	′	+	·	ℓ	0	w	x	y	z	...
1	3	5	7	9	11	13	15	17	19	21	23	25	27	... .

Under Gödel's coding, the concepts of formula, axiom, immediate consequence, and proof become numerical concepts. For example, the class of axioms of $\mathfrak{L}_A$ is represented by the class of Gödel numbers of axioms, and

* Gödel's original version was: If $\mathfrak{L}$ is a formal language that contains Peano arithmetic and is consistent, then $\mathfrak{L}$ is incomplete. This version is equivalent to that of the text, since a language of the type under consideration is consistent if and only if it has a model, i.e., an interpretation whereby every theorem is true. This latter equivalence follows from a completeness theorem for higher order quantification theory. See Henkin, "Completeness in the Theory of Types," and Church, *Introduction to Mathematical Logic* 1: 307.

so to say "The formula $(x + 0) = x$ is an axiom" is to say "$\mathbf{g}[(x + 0) = x]$ is an axiom-number," or "$2^5 3^{23} 5^{13} 7^{19} 11^7 13^9 17^{23}$ is an axiom-number."

To say that a sequence $\Theta_1, \Theta_2, \Theta_3$ is a proof in $\mathfrak{L}_A$ of Θ_3 is to say that the Gödel number of the sequence $\Theta_1, \Theta_2, \Theta_3$ is a proof-number and the last exponent in its prime decomposition represents the formula Θ_3. Formal statements about language $\mathfrak{L}_A$ thus become arithmetic statements, and true formal statements about $\mathfrak{L}_A$ become true arithmetic statements. The decision algorithms for formulahood, axiomhood, and proofhood become algorithms for calculating whether or not a given integer belongs to a certain class of natural numbers, while the enumeration algorithms for formulahood and theoremhood become algorithms for enumerating natural numbers. The foregoing shows how Gödel's coding technique converts true statements about the basic propreties of a formal language into true statements about natural numbers and their relations, that is, true statements of arithmetic.

Thus Gödel realized Leibniz's dream of reducing provability to calculation. He then went one very creative step beyond. Taking advantage of the fact that the language $\mathfrak{L}_A$ contains arithmetic, he expressed these arithmetic statements about $\mathfrak{L}_A$ in $\mathfrak{L}_A$ itself. Many (though not all) true statements of arithmetic are theorems of $\mathfrak{L}_A$, and it turns out that the crucial arithmetic statements about the formal properties of $\mathfrak{L}_A$ are theorems of $\mathfrak{L}_A$. In particular, some important facts about the provability of formulas in $\mathfrak{L}_A$ can be both expressed and proved in $\mathfrak{L}_A$! Thus Gödel showed how to represent or embed the formal structure of $\mathfrak{L}_A$ in $\mathfrak{L}_A$ itself.

Let us see in more detail how this can be done. For each specific natural number n there are infinitely many closed terms of Peano arithmetic that designate n. Let $\sigma(n)$ be the closed term of the form $0'''\cdots''$ that designates n, and let $\tau(n)$ be any closed term that designates n. Thus $\sigma(3)$ is $0'''$ and $0' + 0''$ and $(\ell x)(x = 0''')$ are both $\tau(3)$'s.

Since the notion "this sequence of formulas is a proof of that formula" is arithmetic, it can be expressed in $\mathfrak{L}_A$. It is expressed by an open formula $P\{\alpha, \beta\}$, where α and β are free variables ranging over the natural numbers. When terms $\tau(m)$ and $\tau(n)$ are substituted for the variables α and β, the result is a closed formula $P\{\tau(m), \tau(n)\}$ that is true if and only if m is the Gödel number of a proof in $\mathfrak{L}_A$ of the formula whose Gödel number is n. Thus the formula $P\{\alpha, \beta\}$ of $\mathfrak{L}_A$ expresses the concept "α is the Gödel number of a proof in $\mathfrak{L}_A$ of the formula whose Gödel number is β."

Let $P'\{\beta\}$ be the formula $(\exists\alpha)P\{\alpha, \beta\}$. The closed formula $P'\{\tau(n)\}$ is true if and only if $\tau(n)$ is the Gödel number of a theorem of $\mathfrak{L}_A$, and so the open formula $P'\{\beta\}$ expresses the notion "β is the Gödel number of a theorem of $\mathfrak{L}_A$." This shows how the concept of provability or theoremhood is expressed in $\mathfrak{L}_A$.

Certain facts about provability in $\mathfrak{L}_A$ can be proved in $\mathfrak{L}_A$. When we are given two natural numbers m and n, we can calculate whether m is the Gödel number of a proof of the formula whose Gödel number is n. Since $\mathfrak{L}_A$ contains Peano arithmetic, this calculation can be reproduced as a proof in $\mathfrak{L}_A$, with the numbers m and n being given in the form $\sigma(m)$ and $\sigma(n)$. Hence if $P\{\sigma(m), \sigma(n)\}$ is true, it is a theorem of $\mathfrak{L}_A$, and if $\sim P\{\sigma(m), \sigma(n)\}$ is true, it is a theorem of $\mathfrak{L}_A$.

Now suppose Φ is a theorem and m is the Gödel number of a proof of Φ. Then $P\{\sigma(m), \sigma(\mathbf{g}[\Phi])\}$ is a theorem, and by existential generalization $(\exists\alpha)P\{\alpha, \sigma(\mathbf{g}[\Phi])\}$ is also a theorem; hence $P'\{\sigma(\mathbf{g}[\Phi])\}$ is a theorem. This establishes the following metatheorem for $\mathfrak{L}_A$: If Φ is a theorem, then $P'\{\sigma(\mathbf{g}[\Phi])\}$ is a theorem. In other words, if Φ is a theorem of $\mathfrak{L}_A$, an arithmetic statement of this fact is also a theorem of $\mathfrak{L}_A$.

The preceding discussion shows how one can use Gödel's coding technique to translate statements about provability in $\mathfrak{L}_A$ into statements of arithmetic, and how one can then express and prove these statements about $\mathfrak{L}_A$ in $\mathfrak{L}_A$ itself. This double procedure is possible because the interpreted formal language $\mathfrak{L}_A$ is arithmetic in two ways: it is arithmetiz*able*, and it is *about* arithmetic.

We next define an important arithmetic function $\rho(m)$ by means of a reflexive substitution operation and then indicate how $\rho(m)$ can be expressed in $\mathfrak{L}_A$. There are two cases in the definition of $\rho(m)$, according to whether m is or is not the Gödel number of a formula with one free variable. The latter case is the uninteresting case; we will dispose of it first. If m is not the Gödel number of a formula with one free variable, then $\rho(m) = 0$.

In the interesting case, m is the Gödel number of a formula $\phi\{\alpha\}$ with the free numerical variable α, i.e.,

(1) $\mathbf{g}[\phi\{\alpha\}] = m$.

For this case $\rho(m)$ is defined as follows. Substitute the term $\sigma(m)$ for all free occurrences of α in this formula, obtaining $\phi\{\sigma(m)\}$. Then

(2) $\rho(m) = \mathbf{g}[\phi\{\sigma(m)\}]$.

By combining (1) and (2) we get

(3) $\rho(\mathbf{g}[\phi\{\alpha\}]) = \mathbf{g}[\phi\{\sigma(\mathbf{g}[\phi\{\alpha\}])\}]$.

Thus in the interesting case, $\rho(m)$ is the Gödel number of the formula obtained by substituting the term $\sigma(m)$ in the formula whose Gödel number is m. This is shown in the following schema:

Gödel number of formula	m	$\rho(m)$
Formula of $\mathfrak{L}_A$	$\phi\{\alpha\}$	$\phi\{\sigma(m)\}$.

Now the value of $\rho(m)$ for a particular natural number m can be calculated arithmetically, and since $\mathfrak{L}_A$ contains Peano arithmetic, this calculation can be represented in $\mathfrak{L}_A$. Hence there is a term $R\{\alpha\}$ of $\mathfrak{L}_A$ that represents the function ρ as follows.

(4) The formula $R\{\tau(m)\} = \tau(n)$ is true if and only if $\rho(m) = n$.
If $R\{\sigma(m)\} = \sigma(n)$ is true then it is a theorem, and
if $\sim R\{\sigma(m)\} = \sigma(n)$ is true then it is a theorem.

Using the formula $P'\{\alpha\}$ and the term $R\{\beta\}$, Gödel constructed a formula U that on the reflexive interpretation of $\mathfrak{L}_A$ says of itself that it is not provable. This he did as follows. Consider first the formula $\sim P'\{R\{\beta\}\}$; let its Gödel number be u. Consider next the formula $\sim P'\{R\{\sigma(u)\}\}$ and call it "U." By the definition of ρ, the Gödel number of U is $\rho(u)$, as the following application of the preceding schema shows.

Gödel number of formula	u	$\rho(u)$
Formula of $\mathfrak{L}_A$	$\sim P'\{R\{\beta\}\}$	$\sim P'\{R\{\sigma(u)\}\}$ $[=U]$.

Let us interpret U. Applying (4), above, we see that $R\{\sigma(u)\}$ designates the number $\rho(u)$. By the definition of the formula $P'(\alpha)$, above, $P'\{R\{\sigma(u)\}\}$ then says "$\rho(u)$ is the Gödel number of a theorem of $\mathfrak{L}_A$." Hence U says

(U) The formula whose Gödel number is $\rho(u)$ is not a theorem of $\mathfrak{L}_A$.

Since the Gödel number of U is $\rho(u)$, U is self-referring, and it says of itself (via Gödel coding and the reflexive interpretation of $\mathfrak{L}_A$) that it is not a theorem of $\mathfrak{L}_A$. That is, the formula U says, in effect,

(U) Formula U is *not* a theorem of $\mathfrak{L}_A$.

By the interpretation of the tilde ($\sim$), formula $\sim U$ says, in effect,

($\sim U$) Formula U is a theorem of $\mathfrak{L}_A$.

It will turn out that neither U nor $\sim U$ is a theorem, and on this account U is sometimes called an undecidable formula.

We now prove a lemma: *U is a true formula that is not a theorem of $\mathfrak{L}_A$.* (1) The truth of U is easily established by a reductio ad absurdum argument. Assume that U is false, so that $\sim U$ is true. By the content of $\sim U$, formula U is a theorem of $\mathfrak{L}_A$. By hypothesis, every theorem of $\mathfrak{L}_A$ is true, and so U is true. Since the assumption that U is false leads to the conclusion that U is true, U must be true. (2) By the content of U, U is not a theorem of $\mathfrak{L}_A$. This completes the proof of the lemma.

It follows from the lemma that $\sim U$ is false. By hypothesis every theorem of $\mathfrak{L}_A$ is true, so that $\sim U$ is not a theorem of $\mathfrak{L}_A$. Thus we have shown that neither U nor $\sim U$ is a theorem of $\mathfrak{L}_A$. By the definition of "complete," $\mathfrak{L}_A$ is incomplete. This proves Gödel's incompleteness theorem: If $\mathfrak{L}$ is an interpreted formal language containing Peano arithmetic whose theorems are all true on the given interpretation, then $\mathfrak{L}$ is incomplete.

Gödel's theorem is philosophically important because of its implications concerning logical truth. By the lemma, the undecidable formula U is true. Moreover, U expresses an arithmetic truth, namely, that there is no number that represents a proof in $\mathfrak{L}_A$ of the formula whose Gödel number is $\rho(u)$. Since every arithmetic truth is a logical truth, Gödel's incompleteness theorem has this alternate form: *If $\mathfrak{L}$ is an interpreted formal language containing Peano arithmetic, the class of theorems of $\mathfrak{L}$ is different from the class of logical truths expressible in $\mathfrak{L}$.* This shows that the notion of logical truth cannot be completely formalized.

The reader may feel that the foregoing reasoning is incorrect, on the ground that the undecidable formula U is self-referential and that self-reference leads to contradiction. Actually Peano arithmetic is consistent,* and by hypothesis the formal language $\mathfrak{L}_A$ is consistent; so U does *not* lead to contradiction. However, because some self-referential statements do lead to contradiction, it may be helpful to say a few words about the difference between legitimate and illegitimate self-reference.

The sentence "This statement is false" is true if false and false if true and hence both true and false! That is, any attempt to ascertain whether "This statement is false" is true or false ends in a vicious circle. Similarly, any attempt to verify "This statement is true" leads to a vicious circle, even though no contradiction results. But not all self-referring statements are paradoxical. It is obvious that "This sentence contains four words" is false and that "This sentence is grammatical" is true. The statement "This sentence contains five words" refers to a property of its symbols, and it is easy to verify that its symbols are so related.† Now the notions of formula, axiom, immediate consequence, proof, and theorem are all concerned with the formal properties and interrelation of symbols in a formal language, so that the self-reference in U is legitimate.

The difference between legitimate and illegitimate self-reference in $\mathfrak{L}_A$ can best be explained by comparing the syntactical notion of theoremhood with the semantical notion of truth. We have already seen that the former can be expressed in $\mathfrak{L}_A$: the open formula $P'\{\alpha\}$ expresses the notion "α is the Gödel number of a theorem of $\mathfrak{L}_A$." The parallel question for truth is: Can the concept of truth in $\mathfrak{L}_A$ be expressed in $\mathfrak{L}_A$? Our earlier definition of truth for a closed formula of a modal model is an example of a truth defini-

* On pp. 371–72, we mentioned an interpretation on which every theorem of Peano arithmetic is true. A detailed demonstration that every theorem is true on this interpretation establishes, in a way, that Peano arithmetic is consistent, but this proof employs mathematical induction and thus assumes an informal logic that is essentially as strong as Peano arithmetic.

Since the concept of consistency is syntactical, a statement asserting the consistency of $\mathfrak{L}_A$ can be expressed in $\mathfrak{L}_A$. Gödel proved that if Peano arithmetic is consistent, any formula of it that expresses its consistency is unprovable. This shows that if Peano arithmetic is consistent, one cannot prove within it the consistency of any stronger system.

† Likewise, an automaton or biological cell may contain a structural description of itself sufficiently detailed to control self-reproduction. See von Neumann's *Theory of Self-Reproducing Automata*, pp. 122–26.

tion (pp. 358–60). A definition of "Φ is true in $\mathfrak{L}_A$" can be constructed along similar lines. But can this or any equivalent truth definition be expressed in $\mathfrak{L}_A$? In other words, is there an open formula $T\{\alpha\}$ of $\mathfrak{L}_A$ such that a closed formula $T\{\tau(m)\}$ is true if and only if the formula whose Gödel number is m is true on the given interpretation of $\mathfrak{L}_A$?

The answer to this question is negative. That is, the concept of truth for $\mathfrak{L}_A$ cannot be defined in $\mathfrak{L}_A$.* Indeed, if there were such a formula $T\{\alpha\}$, a contradiction could be derived in the following way. Let f be the Gödel number of $\sim T\{R\{\alpha\}\}$, so that $\rho(f)$ is the Gödel number of $\sim T\{R\{\sigma(f)\}\}$:

Gödel number of formula	f	$\rho(f)$
Formula of $\mathfrak{L}_A$	$\sim T\{R\{\alpha\}\}$	$\sim T\{R\{\sigma(f)\}\}$ [$=F$].

Since $R\{\sigma(f)\}$ designates the natural number $\rho(f)$, formula F says, in effect,

(F) The formula with Gödel number $\rho(f)$ is false.

Since $\rho(f)$ is the Gödel number of F, F is self-referring and says of itself (via the reflexive arithmetic interpretation of $\mathfrak{L}_A$) that it is false.

(F) The formula F is false.

If F is true it is false and if it is false it is true, and so it is both true and false, i.e., contradictory.

We can see better now the difference between the legitimate self-reference of the undecidable formula U and the illegitimate self-reference of "This statement is false." The syntactic concept "provable in $\mathfrak{L}_A$" can be expressed in $\mathfrak{L}_A$; hence there are formulas of $\mathfrak{L}_A$ that refer to their own provability, for example, the formula U. In contrast, the semantic concept "true in $\mathfrak{L}_A$" cannot be expressed in $\mathfrak{L}_A$, and so there are no formulas of $\mathfrak{L}_A$ that refer to their own truth-value.

This last result has a bearing on Leibniz's plans for a universal language (pp. 365–67). For if the concept of truth for $\mathfrak{L}_A$ cannot be expressed in $\mathfrak{L}_A$, there are true statements about the truth of $\mathfrak{L}_A$ that cannot be expressed in $\mathfrak{L}_A$. These statements are logically true, so that not all logical truths can be expressed in $\mathfrak{L}_A$. Since $\mathfrak{L}_A$ is any interpreted formal language that contains Peano arithmetic and whose theorems are all true, there is no interpreted formal language of complete expressive power.

A sentence may legitimately refer to the truth-value of another sentence, as in the definition of truth for a model $\mathfrak{M}$-$\mathfrak{L}$ (pp. 358–60). Moreover, these references may be iterated, as in

(3) The next sentence is false

* Tarski, "The Concept of Truth in Formalized Languages" and Gödel, "On Undecidable Propositions of Formal Mathematical Systems," sec. 7.

Gödel has remarked that "it is this theorem which is the true reason for the existence of undecidable propositions in the formal systems containing arithmetic." (Letter to the author, quoted on p. 55 of von Neumann's *Theory of Self-Reproducing Automata*.)

(2) The next sentence is true

(1) $17 \times 23 = 318$,

where sentences (1) and (2) are false and (3) is true. Since these sentences cannot be expressed in a single formal language $\mathfrak{L}_A$, how can they be formalized?

The simplest and best way is to embed them in an infinite hierarchical structure of the form

$$
\begin{array}{ll}
\vdots & \\
\mathfrak{L}^m & \\
\vdots & \\
\mathfrak{L}^2 & \text{(meta-metalanguage)} \\
\mathfrak{L}^1 & \text{(metalanguage)} \\
\mathfrak{L}^0 & \text{(object language } \mathfrak{L}_A) \quad .
\end{array}
$$

Each language $\mathfrak{L}^m$ contains a sublanguage equal in expressive power to the language $\mathfrak{L}^{m-1}$ directly beneath it, so that for each statement of $\mathfrak{L}^{m-1}$ there is an equivalent statement in $\mathfrak{L}^m$. In addition, each language contains means for making statements about the languages below, including predicates for "true" and "provable."

Consider languages $\mathfrak{L}^m$ and $\mathfrak{L}^n$ where $m > n$ ($n = 0, 1, 2, \ldots$), and let "F^m_n" be a symbol (term) of $\mathfrak{L}^m$ designating a formula of $\mathfrak{L}^n$. Then $\mathfrak{L}^m$ contains statements of the form

(P^m) F^m_n is provable in $\mathfrak{L}^n$

(T^m) F^m_n is true in $\mathfrak{L}^n$.

Since the concept of provability of $\mathfrak{L}^n$ can be expressed in $\mathfrak{L}^n$, there is a statement of $\mathfrak{L}^n$ that, under Gödel's arithmetic coding, is equivalent to P^m. But because the concept of truth in a language cannot be defined in that language, there is no statement in $\mathfrak{L}^n$ equivalent to T^m. Thus each language of the hierarchy is richer than the languages below it.*

Gödel's incompleteness theorem can be stated also in terms of computing machines, which we shall discuss next.

* Such a hierarchy goes back to Russell's theory of types. If each language is governed by a simple theory of types, the whole structure is an improved form of the ramified theory of types. See appendix C of Copi's *Symbolic Logic*.

For historical references see the previous note; Russell, "Mathematical Logic as Based on the Theory of Types"; Russell and Whitehead, *Principia Mathematica*, "Introduction," chap. 2; Ramsey, *The Foundation of Mathematics*, pp. 1–81; and Carnap, *The Logical Syntax of Language*, pp. 205–22.

6.4.3 *Machines and algorithms*

The foregoing makes clear that various algorithms lie at the heart of a formal language. Now algorithms are best defined in terms of a quite different kind of formal system, an automaton, which is an idealized model of a digital computing machine. Hence, to paint a complete picture of the essential structure of a formal language, we must relate formal languages to automata. This exercise will also enable us to show exactly how Gödel's incompleteness theorem refutes Leibniz's conjecture (pp. 366–67). Automata play an important role elsewhere in this book, especially in Sections 9.2.3, 9.4.3, and 10.3, so that a brief discussion of them is in order on that account as well.

The two main types of automata are finite automata and Turing machines. These are imagined to operate synchronously and discretely, with time (t) having the integral values 0, 1, 2, 3, ...

A *finite automaton* is a finite network of primitive elements of two sorts: switches and delays.* See Figures 35 and 36. Switches perform logical functions, and delays store ("remember") information. Each wire or node is in one of two states at each moment of time: 0 (zero, false, passive, low voltage, not stimulated, no-pulse) or 1 (one, true, active, high voltage, stimulated, pulse). The output of a switch element is a truth-function of its input; e.g., $D(t) \equiv \{A(t)\&B(t)\&C(t)\}$. The initial output of a delay is zero (0), and the input at one moment (t) becomes the output at the next moment ($t + 1$). Networks of elements are composed by connecting outputs to inputs with the restriction that every cycle must pass through a delay.

By separating the switches and the delays and by using identity switches if necessary, we can arrange any finite automaton in the normal form of Figure 36a. This form shows that a finite automaton is a deterministic system with finite sets of input, internal (delay output), and output states. The complete history of a finite automaton is determined by its input history in the following way. The initial internal state is 0 on every wire; thereafter the internal and input states at t determine the next ($t + 1$) internal state. The output state at each moment is determined truth-functionally by the input and internal states at that moment. An example is given in Figure 36b, where 1 is represented by a pulse and 0 by the absence of a pulse. Automaton $\mathcal{A}$ is a two-stage binary counter that produces an output pulse for every fourth pulse received.

Any alphabet can be expressed in binary form. For example, the Roman alphabet and punctuation marks can be coded into five-bit sequences 00000, 00001, 00010, . . . , 11110, 11111. Viewed in this way, a finite autom-

* Burks and Wright, "Theory of Logical Nets"; Moore, "Gedanken-Experiments on Sequential Machines"; and Burks and Wang, "The Logic of Automata."

A(t)

B(t)

C(t)

$D(t) \qquad D(t) \equiv \{A(t)B(t)C(t)\}$

$E(t) \qquad E(t) \equiv \left[\{A(t)C(t)\} \not\equiv B(t)\right]$

$F(t) \qquad F(t) \equiv \{A(t) \not\equiv C(t)\}$

(a) Switch S

$G(t) \longrightarrow \boxed{} \longrightarrow H(t) \qquad \begin{cases} H(0) \equiv 0 \\ H(t+1) \equiv G(t) \end{cases}$

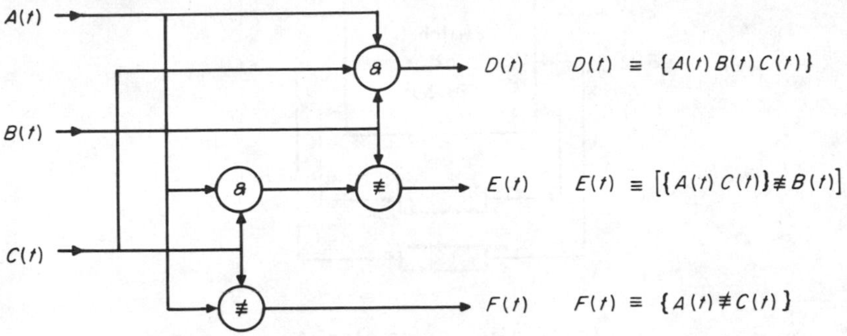

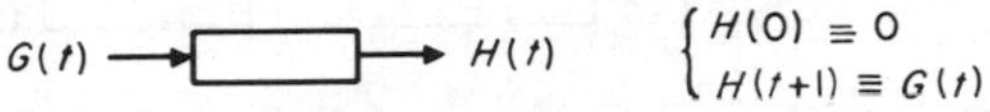

(b) Delay

Fig. 35. Automata primitives

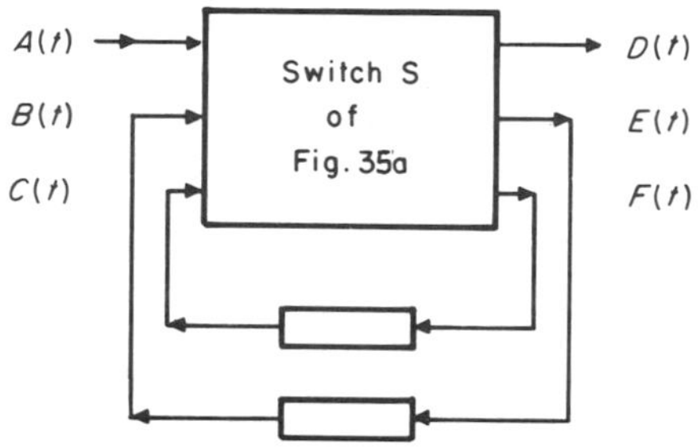

(a) Finite automaton A

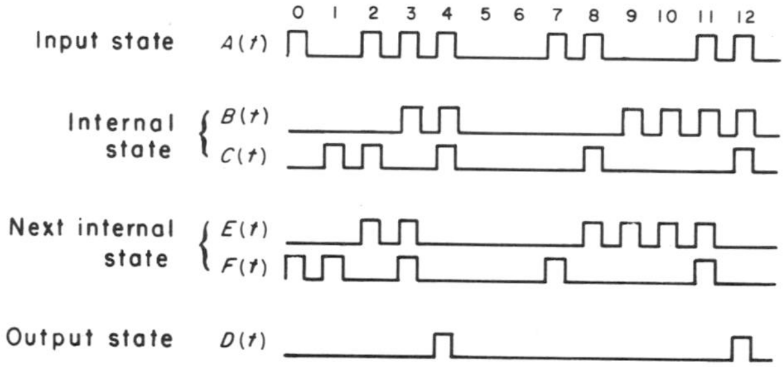

(b) A partial history of finite automaton A

Fig. 36. Finite automaton

aton is a symbol processor that converts a sequence of symbols from one alphabet (the set of input states) into a sequence of symbols from another alphabet (the set of output states).

An actual computing machine is finite, even including all of its magnetic tape, disk, and drum memory; therefore, it can be modeled at a high level of abstraction by a finite automaton.* This point can be expressed in the reverse direction: modern computer technology has produced physical realizations of finite automata composed of billions of switches and delays operating at rates of millions of pulses per second. The simplest organization of these machines involves four interconnected parts: (1) memory for storing information—input data, instructions, intermediate calculations ("scratch work"), and the completed answer; (2) an arithmetic-logical unit for processing information—adding, subtracting, multiplying, comparing, etc.; (3) an input-output unit; (4) a control that interprets and directs the execution of the instructions. The control is capable of ordering different operations conditional on the nature of the data; for example, it may carry out one instruction if a number is positive or zero and a different instruction if that number is negative.

A sequence of instructions is called a "program." The idea of a computing machine that can understand a program is basic to logic as well as to our civilization generally. The concept is over a hundred years old, but its practical realization is quite recent. In the first half of the nineteenth century, Charles Babbage attempted unsuccessfully to construct a general purpose digital computer from mechanical parts, using punched cards for the program. What Babbage wanted to do was not feasible given the mechanical technology of his time; indeed, powerful general-purpose digital computers require an electronic technology. The first electronic general-purpose digital computer was the ENIAC, completed in 1946. The ENIAC had very little capacity to store its own program electronically and to modify it automatically, but electronic computers with this capacity were built soon thereafter and are now very common.†

Despite the finitude of actual computers, for formal purposes an algorithm or program is best defined in terms of an automaton with unbounded storage. When this is done one can see clearly the contrast between the finitude of an algorithm or program and its ability to process indefinitely

* A detailed design for a very simple machine is executed in Burks and Copi, "The Logical Design of an Idealized General Purpose Computer."

† Babbage's ideas are described in *Babbage's Calculating Engines*, pp. 6–50. The ENIAC is described in my article "Electronic Computing Circuits of the ENIAC." The first published design of an electronic computer that could store its own program electronically and modify it automatically is Burks, Goldstine, and von Neumann, *Preliminary Discussion of the Logical Design of an Electronic Computing Instrument.*

For the story of the early development of electronic computers, see Goldstine's *The Computer from Pascal to von Neumann.*

large expressions or problems. For example, the multiplication algorithm we all learn in elementary school can be stated as a finite rule, but in principle it enables us to compute the product of any two decimal numbers, no matter how long. This contrast is expressed in automata theory by embodying the algorithm in a finite automaton and using indefinitely large memories for the input data (the multiplier and multiplicand), the output (the product), and the intermediate calculations (the partial products).

For this purpose we introduce the three tape units of Figure 37: an input tape "reader," an output tape "printer," and a tape "storage unit." Each unit contains a one-way infinite tape divided into squares, a mechanism for moving the tape, and circuitry for communicating symbols between wires and the tape. The tape symbol under the "head" of the reader appears on the output wires; when the "advance" wire is activated, the tape moves forward one square. The printer works analogously to the reader; whenever the advance wire is activated, the symbol is recorded and the tape advanced. The symbols are drawn from a finite alphabet that includes a blank. The storage unit can read from the square under its head and also erase and write on this square. It can move its tape either forward or backward one square per time step. Since all these tape units can be synthesized from switches and delays, no new automaton primitives are needed for them.

The tape of a printer is initially all blank, while the tape of a storage unit or reader has only finitely many (non-blank) symbols written on it initially (at $t = 0$). The effect of having infinitely many symbols on an input tape may be studied by considering an infinite set of tapes, each with finitely many symbols. We make the reader tapes infinitely long so that they may be used inside a system of machines, as in Figures 40 and 41, below.

A *Turing machine* consists of a finite automaton connected to a storage unit, a printer, and perhaps a reader.* See Figure 38. At time $t = 0$ the Turing machine has an initial state in which finitely many non-blank symbols are written on its tapes. Even if it has no tape reader, this machine has infinitely many possible initial states, for there is no bound to the number of non-blank symbols that may be written on its storage tape.

Viewed sub specie aeternitatis, a Turing machine defines a mapping from initial *states* to output *tapes*. The machine is a deterministic system; hence, starting from a given input state it will pass through an infinite succession of states, producing a unique output tape in the process. This tape might be blank, i.e., have no characters printed on it. We call this mapping from initial states to output tapes the *computation* of the Turing machine.

* Turing, "On Computable Numbers, with an Application to the Entscheidungsproblem." Post, "Finite Combinatory Processes—Formulation 1."

Turing and Post did not have separate input and output tapes but placed the input and output information on the storage unit tape.

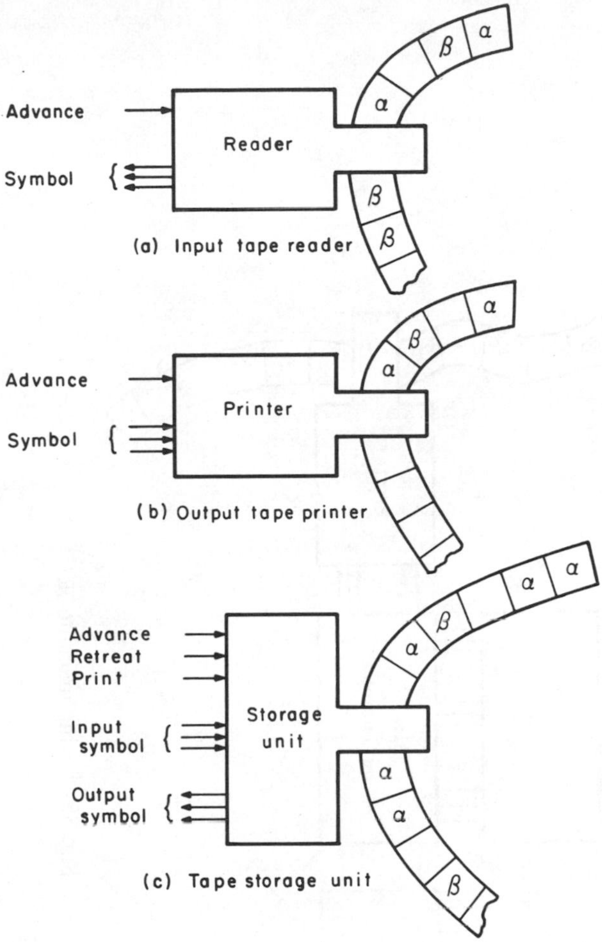

Fig. 37. Tape units

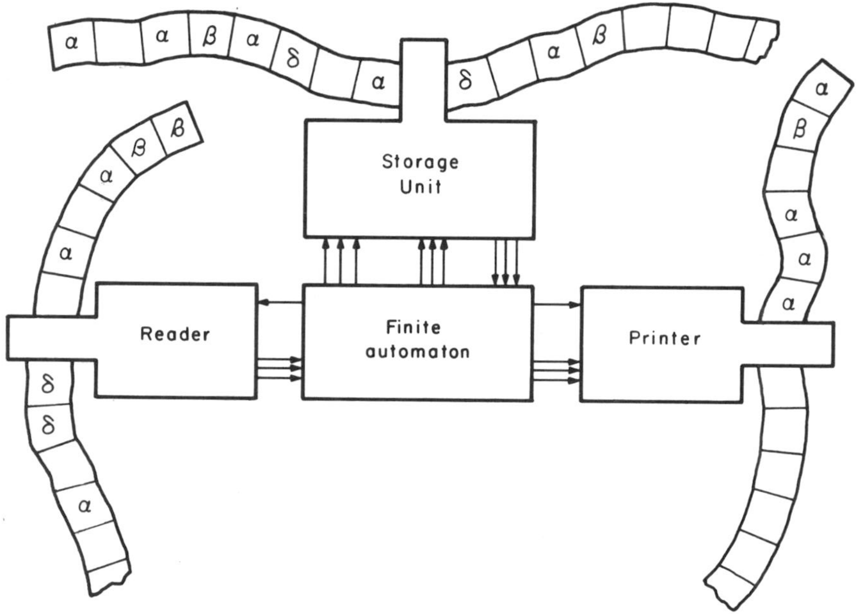

Fig. 38. Turing machine $\mathfrak{M}$

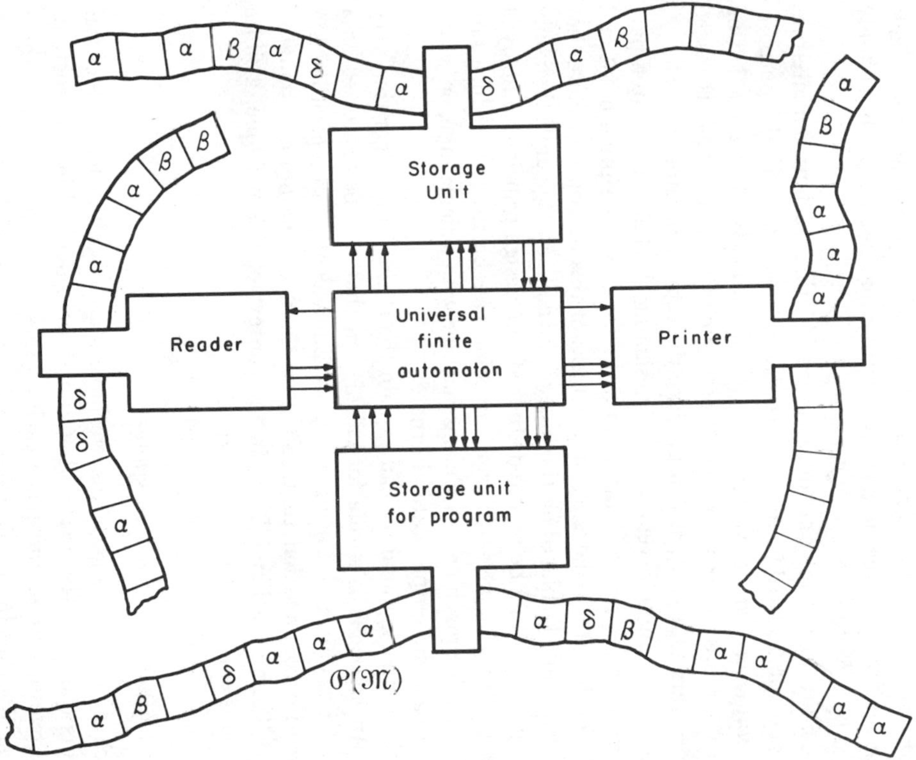

Fig. 39. Universal Turing machine $\mathfrak{U}$

Turing designed a machine that can be programmed to do the computation of any specific Turing machine and thus is appropriately called a "universal Turing machine." See Figure 39. Fix some standard tape alphabet, and consider the class of Turing machines whose tapes all use symbols from this alphabet. There is no loss of generality in this restriction, since expressions written in any alphabet can be translated into expressions written in this alphabet. The finite automaton part of a Turing machine can be described by a finite formula. Let $\mathcal{L}$ be some programming language in which the finite automaton part of a Turing machine $\mathcal{M}$ can be suitably described by a finite program $\mathcal{P}(\mathcal{M})$.

The finite automaton part of a universal Turing machine can interpret any program of $\mathcal{L}$ stored in an auxiliary storage unit added for this purpose. Thus a *universal Turing machine* $\mathcal{U}$ has this property: For each Turing machine $\mathcal{M}$, there is a program $\mathcal{P}(\mathcal{M})$ of $\mathcal{L}$ such that when $\mathcal{P}(\mathcal{M})$ is placed on the program tape of $\mathcal{U}$, $\mathcal{U}$ will produce the same computation as $\mathcal{M}$.

There are many different ways of designing the finite automaton part of a universal machine. One way is to make $\mathcal{P}(\mathcal{M})$ a description of $\mathcal{M}$ and design $\mathcal{U}$ so that it simulates $\mathcal{M}$ on the basis of this description. Note that the program could be placed on the tape of the main storage unit; then only one storage unit would be required. Indeed, the design principles employed in constructing a universal Turing machine can be used to reduce any multitape Turing machine to a Turing machine with a single tape, on which input, storage, and output data alternate.

With this background we can explain the notion of an algorithm very simply. An *algorithm* is a rule for calculation that can be expressed as a program for a universal Turing machine. Equivalently, an algorithm is a procedure for computation that can be realized by the finite automaton part of a Turing machine. Thus, in the context of this machine, a finite automaton is equivalent to a finite rule.

6.4.4 Machines and formal languages

Each of the five algorithms we have stated for the logic of causal statements (pp. 344, 349, 351, and 369) may be converted into a program. Imagine five machines, and place each of these programs in one of these machines. We thereby get *decision machines* for formulahood, axiomhood, and proofhood and *enumeration machines* for formulas and theorems.

Let us look at a machine of each kind in more detail. A decision machine for axiomhood is a computing machine that, when given any formula, will decide in a finite time whether that formula is an axiom or not. That is, it will always correctly answer the question "Is this formula an axiom?" and print the answer on the tape. The output of the theorem enumeration machine is a sequence T_1, T_2, T_3, . . . such that for each theorem T_n of the formal language there is a time at which T_n appears in the sequence. An enumeration machine works forever, never finishing its job. It is still convenient to look at the output of an enumeration machine from the point of view of eternity, though, and to speak of the machine as enumerating a certain infinite class, e.g., the class of theorems.

We are considering machines that process expressions of various kinds: symbols, formulas, and proofs. Each class of expressions α that is processed has the following essential characteristics. There is a machine that will decide of any entity whether or not it belongs to α, and there is a machine that will enumerate the members of α. The following lemma applies to any such class α. Lemma: *Let* α_1, α_2 *be mutually exclusive and jointly exhaustive subsets of* α. *Assume that there is a machine that enumerates the elements of* α. *There are enumeration machines for both* α_1 *and* α_2 *if and only if there is a decision machine that, when given an element of* α, *will decide whether it belongs to* α_1 *or* α_2.

We prove this lemma by the constructions of Figures 40 and 41. In these figures, only the input and output tapes are shown, though the machines also have internal tapes for storing programs and the results of intermediate computations. For the sake of concreteness, we let α be the set of formulas of a formal language $\mathfrak{L}$, α_1 the set of theorems, and α_2 the set of non-theorems. The lemma then becomes: There are a theorem enumeration machine and a non-theorem enumeration machine if and only if there is a decision machine for theoremhood.

To prove the lemma from right to left we combine a formula enumeration machine with the given decision machine for theoremhood as in Figure 40. The output of the formula enumeration machine (from tape head 1) goes into the decision machine for theoremhood (at tape head 2). The decision machine takes each formula F_1, F_2, F_3, . . . in turn and decides whether or not it is a theorem, putting the theorems on output tape 3 and the non-theorems on output tape 4. The result of this construction is a machine with two output tapes, one enumerating the theorems and the other enumerating the non-theorems.

To prove the lemma from left to right, we construct a decision machine for theoremhood from the two given enumeration machines, as in Figure 41. The outputs of these enumeration machines are fed into a formula comparison machine with three input tapes (3, 4, 5) and two output tapes (6, 7) that performs the following simple operations. It accepts formula Φ_n from the question input tape 4 and stores it. It then looks at the theorems on tape 3 and the non-theorems on tape 5 until it finds Φ_n. If it finds Φ_n on tape 3 it writes it on tape 6, and if it finds Φ_n on tape 5 it writes it on tape 7. The formula Φ_n must appear sometime on either tape 3 or tape 5, since by definition every formula is either a theorem or a non-theorem. After deciding whether Φ_n is a theorem or a non-theorem, the formula comparison machine

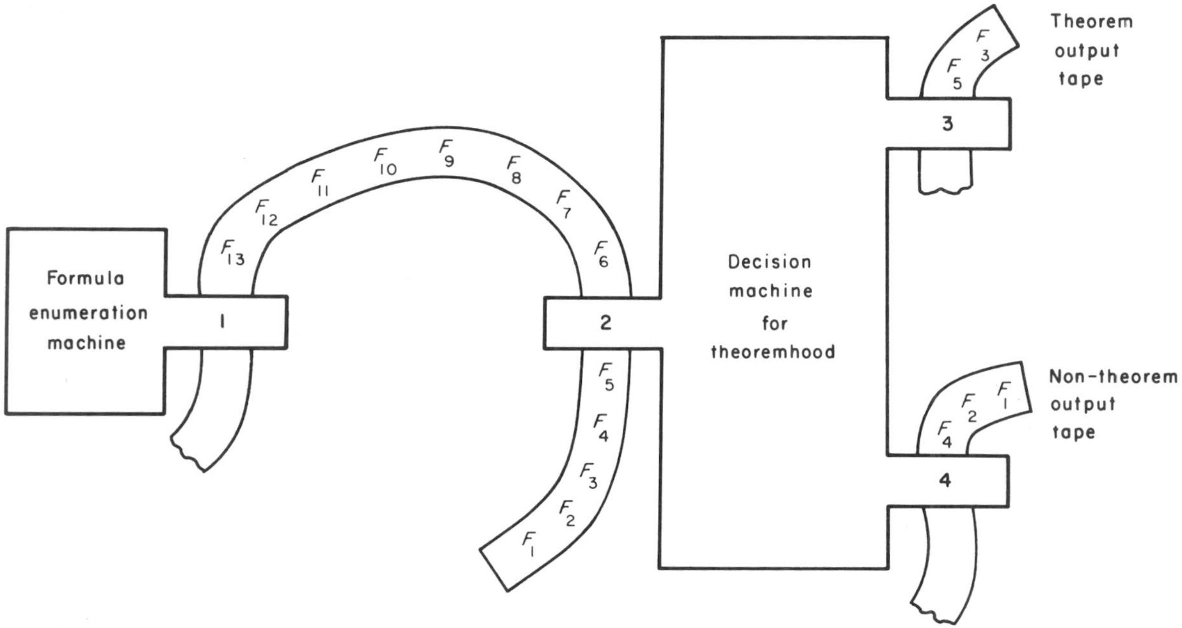

Fig. 40. Construction of theorem and non-theorem enumeration machines from a formula enumeration machine and a decision machine for theoremhood

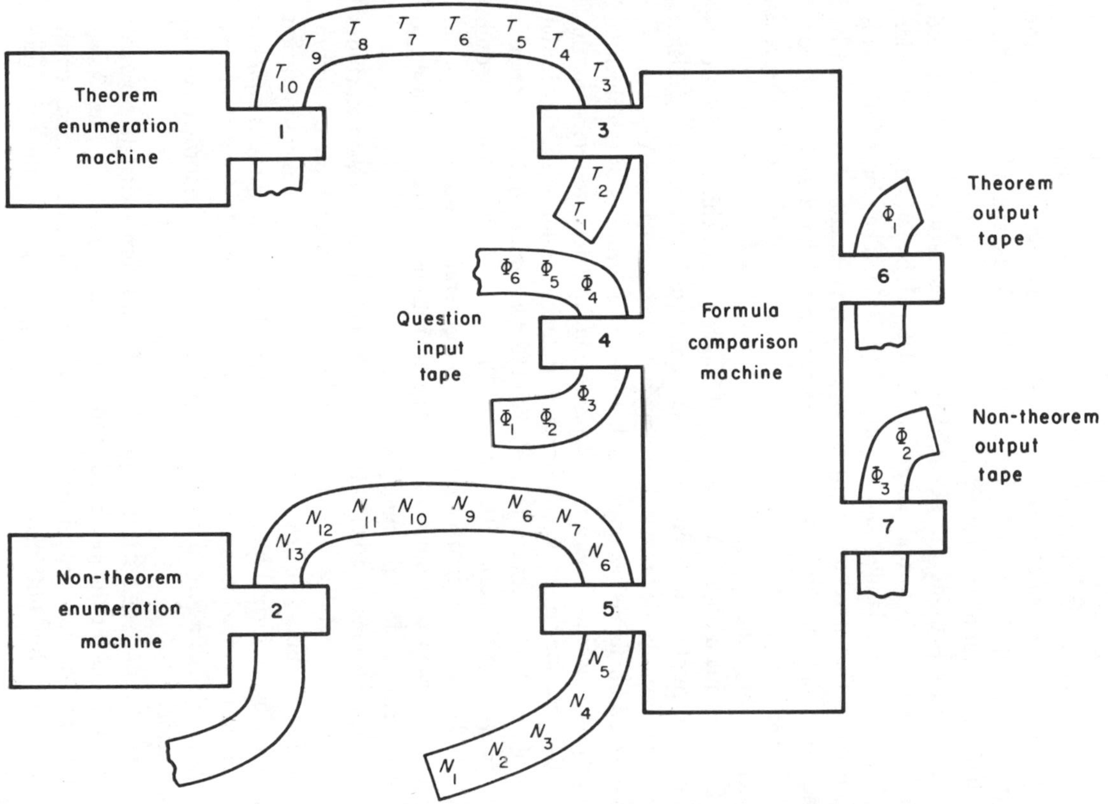

Fig. 41. Construction of a decision machine for theoremhood from theorem and non-theorem enumeration machines

moves the input tapes 3 and 5 back to their beginnings so that it can repeat these operations for the next formula (Φ_{n+1}) on tape 4. Thus the whole mechanism of Figure 41 is a decision machine for theoremhood.

The machines of Figures 40-41 are really systems of machines rather than single Turing machines, as that term was defined. However, the design principles employed in constructing a universal Turing machine can be used to convert the design of a finite system of Turing machines into the design of a computationally equivalent (single) Turing machine. This completes the proof of the lemma.

Let us now examine the essential connections between machines and formal languages. A formal language is defined by specifying decision algorithms for formulahood and proofhood (p. 366). The discussion of this section shows that it is equivalent to say: A formal language is defined by giving the designs for decision machines for formulahood and proofhood. By Gödel's coding, these designs in turn yield the design of a theorem enumeration machine.

Since the main objective of a formal language is to characterize a class of theorems, might one define a formal language in terms of a decision machine for formulahood and a theorem enumeration machine? Yes, because a proof could be defined as any initial sequence of formulas of the theorem enumeration machine. There is a decision machine for proofhood in this sense: this machine merely compares a putative proof with the initial output of the theorem enumeration machine. One might object that it is not as convenient to work with proofs of this sort as with proofs based on axioms and rules of inference. However, no general definition of "formal language" restricts the complexity of the algorithms or machines used to specify a particular formal language.

Our earlier lemma on the relation of enumeration and decision machines shows that a theoremhood decision machine is stronger than a theorem enumeration machine (see figs. 40-41). Since there is a formula enumeration machine for every formal language, a theorem decision machine is equal to two enumeration machines, one for theorems and one for non-theorems. The specification of a formal language yields a design for the former but not for the latter.

This situation suggests the question: Do all formal languages have decision machines for theoremhood, and if not, which ones do? The answer is that there are such machines for weak formal languages, e.g., truth-function theory, but not for stronger ones, e.g., first-order quantification theory.

The truth-table algorithm of page 346 constitutes the basis of a decision machine for theoremhood in truth-function theory. For the theorems are the tautologies, the truth-table algorithm is a decision algorithm for tautologyhood, and this algorithm may be written as a program for a general-purpose digital computer.* In contrast, there is no decision machine for theoremhood in first-order quantification theory† (and hence not for the logic of causal statements), or for theoremhood in Peano arithmetic.

The purpose of a formal language is to characterize and organize a body of truths. The notion of a theorem is a means to that end. Hence it is of great interest to know whether there are enumeration and decision machines for the truths expressible in Peano arithmetic. We will derive a corollary from Gödel's incompleteness theorem stating that neither machine exists. Corollary: *If* $\mathfrak{L}$ *is an interpreted formal language containing Peano arithmetic, then*

(A) *there is no machine that will enumerate the true formulas of* $\mathfrak{L}$, and

(B) *there is no machine that will decide of a formula of* $\mathfrak{L}$ *whether or not it is true.*

The proof of (A) is by reductio ad absurdum. Assume that there is a machine $\mathcal{E}$ whose enumerated output consists of the true formulas of $\mathfrak{L}$. We define a new formal language $\mathfrak{L}'$ that has the same definition of formula as $\mathfrak{L}$ but a different definition of proof. A proof in $\mathfrak{L}'$ is a sequence consisting of the first n ($n = 1, 2, 3, \ldots$) formulas enumerated by $\mathcal{E}$. This definition yields a very simple decision machine for proofhood in $\mathfrak{L}'$, namely, a machine that merely compares a putative proof of length N with the first N formulas enumerated by machine $\mathcal{E}$.

This definition of proof guarantees that every theorem of $\mathfrak{L}'$ is true. Hence $\mathfrak{L}'$ satisfies the conditions of Gödel's incompleteness theorem: it is an interpreted formal language (with the same interpretation as $\mathfrak{L}$) such that every theorem of $\mathfrak{L}'$ is true on the given interpretation. By Gödel's theorem there is some closed formula U' of $\mathfrak{L}'$ such that neither U' nor $\sim U'$ is a theorem of $\mathfrak{L}'$. Since U' is closed, either formula U' or formula $\sim U'$ is true. The true one is enumerated by $\mathcal{E}$ and is therefore a theorem of $\mathfrak{L}'$. This is the contradiction that proves part (A) of the corollary.

Part (B) of the corollary follows from part (A) and the earlier lemma on the relation between enumeration and decision machines (p. 389). If there were a decision machine for truth, there would be a truth enumeration machine. See Figure 42.

Let us now apply the results of this section to Leibniz's conjecture (pp. 366–67). Leibniz envisaged a universal language that had complete expressive power. We saw in discussing illegitimate self-reference that there is no single interpreted language of complete expressive power (p. 378). This

* Alternatively, one can design a special-purpose digital computer to do truth-tables. See, for example, Burks et al., "An Analysis of a Logical Machine Using Parentheses-Free Notation."

† Church, "A Note on the Entscheidungsproblem."

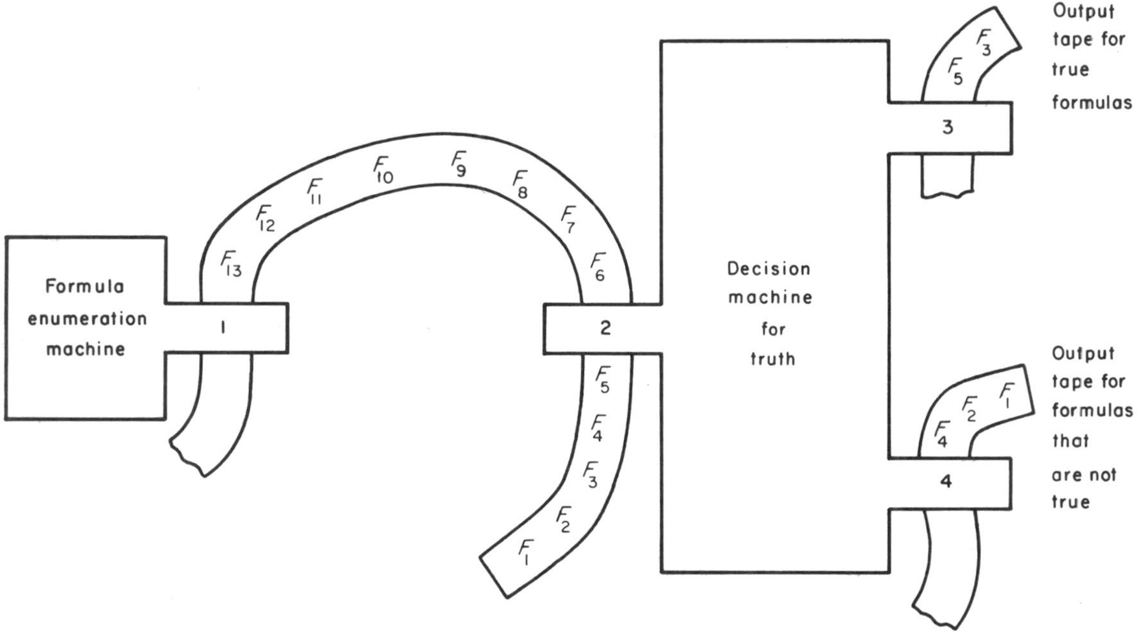

Fig. 42. Construction of a truth enumeration machine from a truth decision machine

fact does not really refute Leibniz's conjecture, however, for there might be an object language sufficiently rich for the practical purposes Leibniz had in mind. That is, there might be an interpreted formal language $\mathfrak{L}_U$ in which all the problems and disputes Leibniz hoped to solve arithmetically could be formulated.

Let us assume that there is an interpreted formal language $\mathfrak{L}_U$ such that its expressive power is sufficient for Leibniz's purposes, it contains Peano arithmetic, and its theorems are all logically true. Leibniz's conjecture then becomes: (1) every theorem of $\mathfrak{L}_U$ is logically true, and (2) there is an algorithm for calculating whether or not a formula of $\mathfrak{L}_U$ is logically true.

It might seem that Gödel's incompleteness theorem and its machine corollary refute this conjecture immediately. But so far we have established these theorems only for interpreted formal languages of pure mathematics and logic, in which every statement is logically true-or-false (p. 373). Leibniz's universal language $\mathfrak{L}_U$ also contains empirically true-or-false statements, and so Gödel's results need to be extended to cover such languages.

This is easily done. For $\mathfrak{L}_U$ has all the properties essential to the proof of the incompleteness theorem: $\mathfrak{L}_U$ contains Peano arithmetic, and every theorem of $\mathfrak{L}_U$ is true. This being the case Gödel's reflexive arithmetical technique can be used to construct a self-referring formula U^* that says of itself that it is not provable in $\mathfrak{L}_U$. The proof procedure of Section 6.4.2 can then be used to prove that U^* is logically true but not a theorem of $\mathfrak{L}_U$. This refutes the first part of Leibniz's conjecture. The second part can be refuted by modifying the proof of the machine corollary of the incompleteness theorem in a similar way to make this corollary cover $\mathfrak{L}_U$.

Our formulation of Leibniz's conjecture does not reflect the practical hopes he had for his universal arithmetic language. He thought that it could be developed in a few years and that it would facilitate the discovery of important mathematical results and help resolve difficult philosophical disputes.

> Nothing is needed, I say, but that philosophic and mathematical procedures, as they call them, be based upon a new method, which I can prescribe and which contains nothing more difficult than other procedures, or more remote from our usual practices, or more foreign to our habits of writing. It will not require much more work than we see already being spent on a good many procedures and on a good many encyclopedias, as they call them. I believe that a number of chosen men can complete the task within five years; within two years they will exhibit the common doctrines of life, that is, metaphysics and morals, in an irrefutable calculus.
>
> Once the characteristic numbers of many ideas have been established, the human race will have a new organon, which will increase the power of the mind much more than the optic glass has aided the

eyes, and will be as much superior to microscopes and telescopes as reason is superior to vision.*

Formal languages might have these practical values even though Leibniz's conjecture is false. Looking backward, however, we can see that Leibniz was grossly optimistic in his practical hopes. Human beings have not produced practical results by using formal languages, except insofar as concepts from these languages are embodied in electronic digital computers. And here the practical values have come and will come in ways very different from those Leibniz envisaged.

This completes our discussion of machines. Short as it is, it suffices to show that the structure of a formal language is fundamentally mechanical in nature and that there can be no mechanical definition of logical truth.

6.5 Some Theorems of the Logic of Causal Statements

6.5.1 Derived rules of inference

In the last section we developed some general properties that the logic of causal statements shares with all formal languages. We return now to expound the specific features of the logic of causal statements by proving some theorems that will be helpful in interpreting it. The reader is reminded that formulas of the logic of causal statements never contain modalities applied to modalities, and hence when the metalinguistic variables Φ, Ψ, Θ, etc., occur in the contexts $\Box\Phi$, $\Box^c \Psi$, etc., they are restricted to nonmodal formulas (p. 344).

Though the existence of a theorem enumeration algorithm is an important structural fact about the logic of causal statements, such an algorithm, even if computerized, would be of no use to us. We shall describe some algorithms that will serve to facilitate the discovery and presentation of proofs of theorems that do concern us.

The first algorithm converts a proof of Ψ from premises $\Phi_1, \Phi_2, \ldots, \Phi_{N-1}, \Phi_N$ into a proof of $\Phi_N \supset \Psi$ from premises $\Phi_1, \Phi_2, \ldots, \Phi_{N-1}$. Let the given proof be the sequence $\Theta_1, \Theta_2, \ldots, \Theta_M$ where Θ_M is Ψ. The proof constructed by the algorithm is related to the given proof in the following schematic way:

$$\Theta_1 \qquad \left\{ \begin{array}{l} \cdot \\ \cdot \\ \cdot \\ \Phi_N \supset \Theta_1 \end{array} \right.$$

* *Philosophische Schriften* 7: 187, translated by Frank O. Copley. For the full text in which this quotation occurs, see Wiener's Leibniz *Selections*, pp. 17–25. Wiener gives a general account of Leibniz's views on method (pp. xi–xxxiii) and translations of many selections (pp. 1–89).

Θ_2 {
.
.
.
$\Phi_N \supset \Theta_2$
}

. .
. .
. .

Θ_M $(=\Psi)$ {
.
.
.
$\Phi_N \supset \Theta_M$ (i.e., $\Phi_N \supset \Psi$) ,
}

where the dots on the right indicate lines to be filled in by the algorithm. The new proof, of course, does not use the premise Φ_N.

The algorithm is formulated as an induction on m $(=1, 2, \ldots, M)$. That is, on the first step the algorithm fills in the lines preceding $\Phi_N \supset \Theta_1$, on the second step it fills in the schema up to $\Phi_N \supset \Theta_2$, and on the m-th step it fills in the schema up to $\Phi_N \supset \Theta_m$. By the definition of "proof" each Θ_m $(m = 1, 2, \ldots, M)$ is a premise, an axiom, or an immediate consequence of preceding Θ's; in the algorithm these three possibilities are regrouped into the following three cases.

Case I. If Θ_m is an axiom or a premise other than Φ_N, replace it by the sequence

(a)	Θ_m	This is an axiom or a premise other than Φ_N
(b)	$\Phi_N \supset \Theta_m$	This is an immediate consequence of (a) by the truth-functional axiom $\Theta_m \supset (\Phi_N \supset \Theta_m)$.

Case II. If Θ_m is Φ_N, replace it by $\Phi_N \supset \Phi_N$, which is a truth-functional axiom.

Case III. If Θ_m is an immediate consequence of earlier formulas, what is done depends on how many of these formulas there are. However, the basic pattern of an immediate inference is the same in every case, so it will suffice to cover the subcase where Θ_m is an immediate consequence of two earlier formulas. Let these two earlier formulas be Θ_i and Θ_j, with $i < j < m$. Since Θ_m is an immediate consequence of Θ_i and Θ_j, $\Theta_i\Theta_j \supset \Theta_m$ is an axiom. Now at step m the algorithm has already completed steps $1, 2, \ldots, m - 1$, and so the part of the new proof already constructed contains $\Phi_N \supset \Theta_i$ and $\Phi_N \supset \Theta_j$. Replace Θ_m of the given proof by the sequence $\Theta_i\Theta_j \supset \Theta_m$, $\Phi_N \supset \Theta_m$. The result is

(a)	$\Phi_N \supset \Theta_i$	This is given
(b)	$\Phi_N \supset \Theta_j$	This is given
(c)	$\Theta_i\Theta_j \supset \Theta_m$	This is an axiom

(d) $\Phi_N \supset \Theta_m$ This is an immediate consequence of (a), (b), and (c) by the truth-functional axiom

$$[(\Phi_N \supset \Theta_i)(\Phi_N \supset \Theta_j)(\Theta_i\Theta_j \supset \Theta_m)] \supset (\Phi_N \supset \Theta_m) .$$

This concludes the algorithm. Table 17 shows the result of applying it to a specific proof. The explanatory comments accompanying the algorithm show that this algorithm does in fact convert a proof of Ψ from premises $\Phi_1, \Phi_2, \ldots, \Phi_{N-1}, \Phi_N$ into a proof of $\Phi_N \supset \Psi$ from premises $\Phi_1, \Phi_2, \ldots, \Phi_{N-1}$. Now that we know of the existence of this algorithm, we can use it to simplify the process of proving theorems. Suppose we have a proof of Ψ from premises $\Phi_1, \Phi_2, \ldots, \Phi_{N-1}, \Phi_N$; that is, a proof of $\Phi_1, \Phi_2, \ldots, \Phi_{N-1}, \Phi_N \vdash \Psi$. We then know that there is a proof of $\Phi_1, \Phi_2, \ldots, \Phi_{N-1} \vdash \Phi_N \supset \Psi$, and in addition we have an algorithm for constructing this proof. There is, therefore, no point in writing out the proof of $\Phi_1, \Phi_2, \ldots, \Phi_{N-1} \vdash \Phi_N \supset \Psi$; we can infer $\Phi_N \supset \Psi$ from $\Phi_1, \Phi_2, \ldots, \Phi_{N-1}$ without further ado.

Thus we have a new rule of inference: Given a proof of $\Phi_1, \Phi_2, \ldots, \Phi_{N-1}, \Phi_N \vdash \Psi$, we may infer $\Phi_N \supset \Psi$ from $\Phi_1, \Phi_2, \ldots, \Phi_{N-1}$. We call this the rule of *conditional proof* and state it in the form

[7a] If $\Phi_1, \Phi_2, \ldots, \Phi_{N-1}, \Phi_N \vdash \Psi$, then $\Phi_1, \Phi_2, \ldots, \Phi_{N-1} \vdash \Phi_N \supset \Psi$.

The rule is stated in this way for convenience, but it should be kept in mind that we have established more than is expressed in [7a]. For [7a] states merely that if there exists a proof of $\Phi_1, \Phi_2, \ldots, \Phi_{N-1}, \Phi_N \vdash \Psi$, then there exists a proof of $\Phi_1, \Phi_2, \ldots, \Phi_{N-1} \vdash \Phi_N \supset \Psi$; whereas we have constructed an algorithm that will convert the former proof into the latter proof. Theorem [7a] is often called the "deduction theorem."

The rule of conditional proof may be used to convert a proof from premises into a categorical proof. For example, given a proof of Ψ from the premises Φ_1 and Φ_2, we can apply the rule of conditional proof twice to obtain a categorical proof of $\Phi_1 \supset (\Phi_2 \supset \Psi)$. This process can be iterated and the result manipulated truth-functionally to give the corollary

If $\Phi_1, \Phi_2, \ldots, \Phi_N \vdash \Psi$, then $\vdash (\Phi_1\Phi_2 \ldots \Phi_N) \supset \Psi$.

We proved earlier that every theorem of the logic of causal statements is logically true (p. 364). It follows that if an argument is valid in the logic of causal statements, the corresponding conditional is logically true (cf. p. 22).

Similarly, when the rule of conditional proof is applied to a proof of $\Psi\bar{\Psi}$ from $\bar{\Phi}$, the result is a categorical proof of $\bar{\Phi} \supset \Psi\bar{\Psi}$. By adding the formula Φ to the end of this proof we obtain a categorical proof of Φ itself, since $(\bar{\Phi} \supset \Psi\bar{\Psi}) \supset \Phi$ is a truth-functional axiom. This justifies the following rule of inference.

[7b] If $\bar{\Phi} \vdash \Psi\bar{\Psi}$, then $\vdash \Phi$.

TABLE 17

Illustration of the Conditional Proof Algorithm

Given proof that $(x)(Ax \supset Bx), \Box^c Ay \vdash By$		Resultant proof that $(x)(Ax \supset Bx) \vdash \Box^c Ay \supset By$	
1. $(x)(Ax \supset Bx)$	Premise	a. $(x)(Ax \supset Bx)$	Premise
		1. $\Box^c Ay \supset (x)(Ax \supset Bx)$	a, primitive rule & truth-functional axiom
2. $\Box^c Ay$	Premise	2. $\Box^c Ay \supset \Box^c Ay$	Truth-functional axiom
3. $Ay \supset By$	1, primitive rule & universal instantiation	b. $(x)(Ax \supset Bx) \supset (Ay \supset By)$	Universal instantiation
		3. $\Box^c Ay \supset (Ay \supset By)$	1, b, primitive rule & truth-functional axiom
4. Ay	2, primitive rule & modal ordering	c. $\Box^c Ay \supset Ay$	Modal ordering
		4. $\Box^c Ay \supset Ay$	2, c, primitive rule & truth-functional axiom
5. By	3, 4, primitive rule & truth-functional axiom	d. $\{(Ay \supset By)Ay\} \supset By$	Truth-functional axiom
		5. $\Box^c Ay \supset By$	3, 4, d, primitive rule & truth-functional axiom

A closely related rule of inference, which also follows from the rule of conditional proof, is

[7c] If $\Phi_1, \Phi_2, \ldots, \Phi_N, \sim\Psi \vdash \Psi$, then $\Phi_1, \Phi_2, \ldots, \Phi_N \vdash \Psi$.

These last two derived rules of inference are called rules of *reductio ad absurdum.*

It is apparent that adding the rules of conditional proof and reductio ad absurdum to our formal language does not enlarge the class of theorems of the language. For this reason these two rules are called *derived rules of inference*. We state and justify two more derived rules, one for generalization and one for exchange.

[8] The *generalization rule* is

[8a] If $\Phi_1, \Phi_2, \ldots, \Phi_N \vdash \Psi$, then $\Box\Phi_1, \Box\Phi_2, \ldots, \Box\Phi_N \vdash \Box\Psi$

[8b] If $\Phi_1, \Phi_2, \ldots, \Phi_N \vdash \Psi$, then $\Box^c \Phi_1, \Box^c \Phi_2, \ldots, \Box^c \Phi_N \vdash \Box^c \Psi$

[8c] If $\Phi_1, \Phi_2, \ldots, \Phi_N \vdash \Psi$, then $(\alpha)\Phi_1, (\alpha)\Phi_2, \ldots, (\alpha)\Phi_N \vdash (\alpha)\Psi$

[8d] If $\Phi \vdash \Psi$, then $\Diamond\Phi \vdash \Diamond\Psi$

[8e] If $\Phi \vdash \Psi$, then $\Diamond^c \Phi \vdash \Diamond^c \Psi$

[8f] If $\Phi \vdash \Psi$, then $(\exists\alpha)\Phi \vdash (\exists\alpha)\Psi$.

Rules [8a], [8b], [8d], and [8e] are subject to the condition that the premises and conclusion of the given argument contain no modal symbols, since otherwise iterated modalities would occur in the derived argument.

Consider rule [8b] first. The use of this as a derived rule is justified by an algorithm converting a proof of Ψ from premises $\Phi_1, \Phi_2, \ldots, \Phi_N$ into a proof of $\Box^c \Psi$ from premises $\Box^c \Phi_1, \Box^c \Phi_2, \ldots, \Box^c \Phi_N$. Let the given proof be the sequence of formulas $\Theta_1, \Theta_2, \ldots, \Theta_M$, where Θ_M is Ψ. The new proof is constructed from the old by applying the following rules to each Θ_m ($m = 1, 2, \ldots, M$). See Table 18 for an example.*

Case I. If Θ_m is a premise, replace it by $\Box^c \Theta_m$, which is a premise of the new proof.

Case II. If Θ_m is an axiom, replace it by the sequence

(a) $\Box\Theta_m$ .This is an axiom by axiom generation

(b) $\Box^c \Theta_m$ This is an immediate consequence of (a) by modal ordering.

* This construction presupposes that the given proof contains no modal operators, for otherwise the derived proof would contain formulas with iterated modalities. However, if there is a proof from nonmodal premises to a nonmodal conclusion that contains modal symbols, then there is also a proof that contains no modal symbols. That such is the case can be shown by using the completeness result for first-order quantification theory (every valid [logically true] formula is a theorem), the result that every theorem of the logic of causal statements is logically true (p. 364), and the deduction theorems (rules of conditional proof) for the two systems (p. 398). I wish to thank Soshichi Uchii for this proof.

TABLE 18

ILLUSTRATION OF THE GENERALIZATION RULE ALGORITHM

Given proof that $P, Q \vdash PQ$			Resultant proof that $\Box^c P, \Box^c Q \vdash \Box^c (PQ)$		
1.	P	Premise	1.	$\Box^c P$	Premise
2.	Q	Premise	2.	$\Box^c Q$	Premise
3.	PQ	1, 2, primitive rule and truth-functional axiom	a.	$\Box(PQ \supset PQ)$	Axiom generation and truth-functional axiom
			b.	$\Box\{(PQ \supset PQ) \supset [P \supset (Q \supset PQ)]\}$	Truth-functional axiom and axiom generation
			c.	$\Box(PQ \supset PQ) \supset \Box[P \supset (Q \supset PQ)]$	b, primitive rule and modal distribution
			d.	$\Box[P \supset (Q \supset PQ)]$	a, c, primitive rule and truth-functional axiom
			e.	$\Box^c [P \supset (Q \supset PQ)]$	d, primitive rule and ordering of modalities
			f.	$\Box^c P \supset \Box^c (Q \supset PQ)$	e, primitive rule and modal distribution
			g.	$\Box^c (Q \supset PQ)$	1, f, primitive rule and truth-functional axiom
			h.	$\Box^c Q \supset \Box^c (PQ)$	g, primitive rule and modal distribution
			j.	$\Box^c (PQ)$	2, h, primitive rule and truth-functional axiom

Case III. If Θ_m is an immediate consequence of earlier formulas, what is done depends on how many of these formulas there are. It will suffice to cover the case where two preceding formulas Θ_i and Θ_j were used and the axiom $\Theta_i\Theta_j \supset \Theta_m$ was appealed to. Replace Θ_m by the sequence

(a)	$\Box(\Theta_i\Theta_j \supset \Theta_m)$	This is an axiom by axiom generation
(b)	$\Box\{(\Theta_i\Theta_j \supset \Theta_m) \supset [\Theta_i \supset (\Theta_j \supset \Theta_m)]\}$	This is an axiom by axiom generation operating on a truth-functional axiom
(c)	$\Box(\Theta_i\Theta_j \supset \Theta_m) \supset \Box[\Theta_i \supset (\Theta_j \supset \Theta_m)]$	This is an immediate consequence of (b) by modal distribution
(d)	$\Box[\Theta_i \supset (\Theta_j \supset \Theta_m)]$	This is an immediate consequence of (a) and (c) by a truth-functional axiom
(e)	$\Box^c [\Theta_i \supset (\Theta_j \supset \Theta_m)]$	This is an immediate consequence of (d) by modal ordering
(f)	$\Box^c \Theta_i \supset \Box^c (\Theta_j \supset \Theta_m)$	This is an immediate consequence of (e) by modal distribution
(g)	$\Box^c (\Theta_j \supset \Theta_m)$	Since Θ_i occurs earlier than Θ_m in the given proof, $\Box^c \Theta_i$ has occurred earlier than (f) in the new proof; (g) is an immediate consequence of $\Box^c \Theta_i$ and (f) by a truth-functional axiom
(h)	$\Box^c \Theta_j \supset \Box^c \Theta_m$	This is an immediate consequence of (g) by modal distribution
(i)	$\Box^c \Theta_m$	Since Θ_j occurs earlier than Θ_m in the given proof, $\Box^c \Theta_j$ has occurred earlier than (h) in the new proof; (i) is an immediate consequence of $\Box^c \Theta_j$ and (h) by a truth-functional axiom.

The algorithm for rule [8b] is now complete. The explanatory comments made concurrently with the algorithm show that when the algorithm is given a proof of Ψ from premises $\Phi_1, \Phi_2, \ldots, \Phi_N$, it produces a proof of $\Box^c \Psi$ from premises $\Box^c \Phi_1, \Box^c \Phi_2, \ldots, \Box^c \Phi_N$. This justifies the use of [8b] as a derived rule of inference.

Now replace every occurrence of $\Box^c$ by $\Box$ in the algorithm for rule [8b] and make the obvious simplifications. The result is an algorithm justifying the use of [8a] as a derived rule. Next, replace every occurrence of $\Box$ in this new algorithm by (α). The result is an algorithm justifying the use of [8c] as a derived rule. In showing that the sequence produced by this last algorithm is a proof, one cites quantifier distribution instead of modal distribution.

Rule [8d] may be derived from rule [8a] by letting $N = 1$, substituting $\sim\Psi$ for Φ, substituting $\sim\Phi$ for Ψ, using the obvious truth-functional fact that $\Theta \vdash X$ if and only if $\sim X \vdash \sim\Theta$, and applying definition [1c]. Rules [8e] and [8f] may be derived similarly from [8b] and [8c], respectively. Note that the rule

$$\text{If } \Phi_1, \Phi_2 \vdash \Psi, \text{ then } \Diamond\Phi_1, \Diamond\Phi_2 \vdash \Diamond\Psi$$

fails, as is obvious from the fact that $P, \bar{P} \vdash P\bar{P}$.

Note finally that the rules

$$\text{If } \vdash\Psi, \text{ then } \vdash\Box\Psi$$

$$\text{If } \vdash\Psi, \text{ then } \vdash\Box^c\Psi$$

$$\text{If } \vdash\Psi, \text{ then } \vdash(\alpha)\Psi$$

are the special cases of [8a], [8b], and [8c], respectively, that occur when there are no premises. The first rule is a formal or syntactic embodiment in the logic of causal statements of the following interpretive fact about that system: If formula Φ is logically true then $\Box\Phi$ is logically true (p. 364). Thus some truths about the system are provable in the system (compare pp. 374–75, 378).

This completes our discussion of the rule of generalization.

Our last derived rule of inference is the *exchange rule.*

[9] Let Φ_2 be the result of replacing one or more occurrences of Θ_1 by Θ_2 in Φ_1. If $\vdash\Theta_1 \equiv \Theta_2$, then $\vdash\Phi_1 \equiv \Phi_2$

Some examples of exchange are:

$$\text{If } \vdash P \equiv \sim\sim P, \text{ then } \vdash\Box(P \vee P) \equiv \Box(\sim\sim P \vee P)$$

$$\text{If } \vdash P \equiv \sim\sim P, \text{ then } \vdash\Box(P \vee P) \equiv \Box(\sim\sim P \vee \sim\sim P)$$

$$\text{If } \vdash(x)Ay \equiv Ay, \text{ then } \vdash\Box^c(y)[\sim(x)Ay \vee By] \equiv \Box^c(y)[\sim Ay \vee By].$$

See Table 19 in connection with the last of these examples.

The use of exchange as a derived rule is justified by an algorithm that constructs a proof of $\Phi_1 \equiv \Phi_2$ from a proof of $\Theta_1 \equiv \Theta_2$. Because this algorithm is geared to the concept of height, we first extend that concept to include quantifiers and modal operators (see pp. 345–46).

[Initial step] Statement variables and formulas of the form $\psi\alpha_1\alpha_2 \ldots \alpha_N$ are of height zero.

[General step] The height of $\sim\Phi$, $(\alpha)\Phi$, $\Box\Phi$, and $\Box^c\,\Phi$ is one greater than the height of Φ. The height of $(\Phi \vee \Psi)$ is one greater than the maximum of the heights of Φ and Ψ.

TABLE 19

ILLUSTRATION OF "HEIGHT" AS DEFINED FOR THE EXCHANGE RULE ALGORITHM

Height	Construction of "$\Box^c\,(y)[\sim(x)Ay \vee By]$" from its subformulas	Construction of "$\Box^c\,(y)[\sim Ay \vee By]$" from its subformulas
4	$\Box^c(y)[\sim(x)Ay \vee By]$	$\Box^c(y)[\sim Ay \vee By]$
3	$(y)[\sim(x)Ay \vee By]$	$(y)[\sim Ay \vee By]$
2	$\sim(x)Ay \vee By$	$\sim Ay \vee By$
1	$\sim(x)Ay$	$\sim Ay$
0	$(x)Ay,\ \ By$	$Ay,\ \ By$

This table shows the structure of two equivalent formulas in terms of corresponding subformulas of equal "height."

Formulas Φ_1 and Φ_2 of metatheorem [9] are the same except for the exchange of Θ_1 and Θ_2. In order to get an exact correspondence of their structures, we redefine the height of all the subformulas contained in them so that corresponding subformulas will have the same height. The height of each subformula is what is given by the previous definition provided that height zero is first assigned to all occurrences of Θ_1 and Θ_2 involved in the exchange. An example is

$$\text{If} \vdash \Theta_1 \equiv \Theta_2, \text{ then} \vdash \Phi_1 \equiv \Phi_2$$

$$\text{If} \vdash \underbrace{(P \vee P)}_{0} \equiv \underbrace{\sim\sim P}_{0}, \text{ then} \vdash \overbrace{\Box\{\overbrace{\underbrace{(P \vee P)}_{0} \vee \underbrace{\sim\underbrace{(\underset{0}{P} \vee \underset{0}{P})}_{1}}_{2}}^{3}\}}^{4} \equiv \overbrace{\Box\{\overbrace{\underbrace{\sim\sim P}_{0} \vee \underbrace{\sim\underbrace{(\underset{0}{P} \vee \underset{0}{P})}_{1}}_{2}}^{3}\}}^{4}$$

Note that occurrences of "$P \vee P$" have height zero or their natural height of one, according as they are or are not involved in the exchange.

There is now a one-to-one correspondence between the subformulas of Φ_1 and Φ_2 such that (1) for each subformula X_1 of Φ_1 the corresponding formula X_2 of Φ_2 is the result of replacing zero or more occurrences of Θ_1 in X_1 by Θ_2, and (2) X_1 and X_2 have the same height by the modified definition just given. This correspondence is illustrated in the preceding example and in Table 19.

The exchange rule algorithm is organized by an induction on height. In the initial step the algorithm takes all the subformulas of Φ_1 and Φ_2 of height zero and constructs proofs of $X_1 \equiv X_2$ for all pairs X_1, X_2 of corresponding formulas. In the general step the algorithm takes all of the subformulas of Φ_1 and Φ_2 of height n $(=1, 2, 3, \ldots)$ and constructs proofs of $X_1 \equiv X_2$ for all pairs X_1, X_2 of corresponding subformulas from the proof of the preceding steps. The proof of equivalence constructed on the last step is a proof of $\Phi_1 \equiv \Phi_2$. The details for the initial and general steps of the algorithm follow.

[Initial step] X_1 and X_2 are both of height zero. There are two cases: $\Theta_1 \equiv \Theta_2$ and $\Psi \equiv \Psi$. The proof of $\Theta_1 \equiv \Theta_2$ is given, and $\Psi \equiv \Psi$ is a truth-functional axiom.

[General step] The algorithm already has proofs of $\Psi_1 \equiv \Psi_2$ and $\Delta_1 \equiv \Delta_2$, and it must construct proofs of equivalence of greater height involving the operations v, $\sim$, (α), $\Box$, and $\Box^c$. It does this by means of five subalgorithms:

$\mathcal{A}_v$ constructs a proof of $(\Psi_1 \vee \Delta_1) \equiv (\Psi_2 \vee \Delta_2)$ from $\Psi_1 \equiv \Psi_2$ and $\Delta_1 \equiv \Delta_2$

$\mathcal{A}_\sim$ constructs a proof of $\sim\Psi_1 \equiv \sim\Psi_2$ from $\Psi_1 \equiv \Psi_2$

$\mathcal{A}_{(\alpha)}$ constructs a proof of $(\alpha)\Psi_1 \equiv (\alpha)\Psi_2$ from $\Psi_1 \equiv \Psi_2$

$\mathcal{A}_\Box$ constructs a proof of $\Box\Psi_1 \equiv \Box\Psi_2$ from $\Psi_1 \equiv \Psi_2$

$\mathcal{A}_{\Box^c}$ constructs a proof of $\Box^c\Psi_1 \equiv \Box^c\Psi_2$ from $\Psi_1 \equiv \Psi_2$

Algorithms $\mathcal{A}_v$ and $\mathcal{A}_\sim$ merely record the formulas to be proved, since these formulas are immediate consequences of the given formulas by truth-functional axioms. Algorithm $\mathcal{A}_{\Box^c}$ first records $\Psi_1 \supset \Psi_2$ and $\Psi_2 \supset \Psi_1$; these are immediate consequences of the given formula by truth-functional axioms. It then applies the generalization rule algorithm to obtain proofs of $\Box^c(\Psi_1 \supset \Psi_2)$ and $\Box^c(\Psi_2 \supset \Psi_1)$. Next, it obtains proofs of $\Box^c\Psi_1 \supset \Box^c\Psi_2$ and $\Box^c\Psi_2 \supset \Box^c\Psi_1$ by means of modal distribution. Finally, it combines these last two proofs to obtain a proof of $\Box^c\Psi_1 \equiv \Box^c\Psi_2$ by means of the primitive rule. Algorithms $\mathcal{A}_{(\alpha)}$ and $\mathcal{A}_\Box$ operate similarly.

We have now finished the algorithm for exchange rule [9]. See Table 20 for an example. Only the main steps of the constructed proof are given

TABLE 20

ILLUSTRATION OF THE EXCHANGE RULE ALGORITHM

Construction of a proof of "$\Box^c (y)[\sim(x)Ay \vee By] \equiv \Box^c (y)[\sim Ay \vee By]$" from a given proof of "$(x)Ay \equiv Ay$"

Height of the formulas flanking "≡"	Main steps of resultant proof	Explanation
0	1. $Ay \equiv (x)Ay$	This is the given proof of "$(x)Ay \equiv Ay$"
	2. $(x)Ay \equiv Ay$	
	3. $By \equiv By$	This is a truth-functional axiom
1	4. $\sim(x)Ay \equiv \sim Ay$	This is the result of applying algorithm $\mathfrak{A}_{\sim}$ to line 2
2	5. $[\sim(x)Ay \vee By] \equiv [\sim Ay \vee By]$	This is the result of applying algorithm $\mathfrak{A}_{\vee}$ to lines 3 and 4
3	6. $(y)[\sim(x)Ay \vee By] \equiv (y)[\sim Ay \vee By]$	This is the result of applying algorithm $\mathfrak{A}_{(\alpha)}$ to line 5
4	7. $\Box^c (y)[\sim(x)Ay \vee By] \equiv \Box^c (y)[\sim Ay \vee By]$	This is the result of applying algorithm $\mathfrak{A}_{\Box^c}$ to line 6

in this table; we will supply the intermediate steps. Line 4 follows from line 2 by the truth-functional axiom "$[(x)Ay \equiv Ay] \supset [\sim(x)Ay \equiv \sim Ay]$" and the primitive rule. Line 5 follows from lines 3 and 4 by the truth-functional axiom "$\{[By \equiv By][\sim(x)Ay \equiv \sim Ay]\} \supset \{[\sim(x)Ay \vee By] \equiv [\sim Ay \vee By]\}$" and the primitive rule. In this case a simpler axiom would do, but we are illustrating the algorithm, which is designed to handle all cases. The derivation of line 6 from line 5 in accordance with algorithm $\mathfrak{A}_{(\alpha)}$ is shown by the following scheme, where Ψ_1 is "$[\sim(x)Ay \vee By]$" and Ψ_2 is "$[\sim Ay \vee By]$."

(a)	$\Psi_1 \equiv \Psi_2$	Given (line 5)
(b)	$\Psi_1 \supset \Psi_2$	From (a) by truth-functional axiom and primitive rule
(c)	$\Psi_2 \supset \Psi_1$	Ditto
(d)	$(y)(\Psi_1 \supset \Psi_2)$	From (b) by generalization
(e)	$(y)(\Psi_2 \supset \Psi_1)$	From (c) by generalization
(f)	$(y)\Psi_1 \supset (y)\Psi_2$	From (d) by quantifier distribution and the primitive rule
(g)	$(y)\Psi_2 \supset (y)\Psi_1$	From (c) as in (f)
(h)	$(y)\Psi_1 \equiv (y)\Psi_2$	From (f) and (g) by truth-functional axiom and primitive rule.

Line 7 is derived from line 6 in an analogous way.

The precise conditions for exchange by the exchange rule should be noted. If the equivalence $\Theta_1 \equiv \Theta_2$ has been proved and Φ_1 $\{\Phi_2\}$ is given, then Φ_2 $\{\Phi_1\}$ follows by the exchange rule, the primitive rule, and a truth-functional axiom. Hence the exchange rule permits the exchange of any two formulas that have been *proved* equivalent. It does not, however, authorize the exchange of two formulas because they are logically equivalent. For example, if $\Box(\Theta_1 \equiv \Theta_2)$ is a premise or is the conclusion of a proof from premises, one cannot exchange Θ_1 and Θ_2 by means of rule [9]. We could add a rule of inference to allow the exchange of logical equivalents (cf. the rule of exchange of the calculus of inductive probability, pp. 47–48), but derived rule [9] is adequate for our purposes.

This concludes our discussion of derived rules.

6.5.2 Some metatheorems

In the preceding subsections we established a number of results for the logic of causal statements. Typical examples are "There is an algorithm for deciding formulahood," "There is an algorithm that will enumerate every theorem," "If $\Phi_1, \Phi_2, \ldots, \Phi_{N-1}, \Phi_N \vdash \Psi$, then $\Phi_1, \Phi_2, \ldots, \Phi_{N-1} \vdash \Phi_N \supset \Psi$," and "There is an algorithm that will convert a proof of $\Psi\overline{\Psi}$ from premise $\overline{\Phi}$ into a categorical proof of Φ." Since these results are stated and proved in the metalanguage, they are appropriately called *metatheorems*. They are to be distinguished from theorems of the formal language itself (p. 350).

In the remainder of this section we establish some further metatheorems. Each of these gives the form of an infinite class of theorems of our formal language. For example, in proving metatheorem [10c], below, we prove the theorems "$(\Box^c P \vee \Box^c Q) \supset \Box^c (P \vee Q)$," "$(\Box^c R \vee \Box^c S) \supset \Box^c (R \vee S)$," "$\{\Box^c P \vee \Box^c (y)By\} \supset \Box^c \{P \vee (y)By\}$," etc.

We begin with some additional principles of distribution.

[10a] $\vdash (\Box^c \Phi \Box^c \Psi) \equiv \Box^c (\Phi\Psi)$

[10b] $\vdash (\Diamond^c \Phi \vee \Diamond^c \Psi) \equiv \Diamond^c (\Phi \vee \Psi)$

[10c] $\vdash (\Box^c \Phi \vee \Box^c \Psi) \supset \Box^c (\Phi \vee \Psi)$

[10d] $\vdash \Diamond^c (\Phi\Psi) \supset \Diamond^c \Phi$

Since the logic of causal statements was designed to make proofs simple and intuitive, it will not be necessary to give proofs of these metatheorems in full detail. Derived rules of inference will be used as well as the primitive rule of inference. Truth-functional axioms will be identified by the abbreviation "**TF**," as in the second line of the proof of [10b], below. Each use of the primitive rule of inference will be annotated by the name of the axiom on which that use depends. For example, in the proof of [10c], line (b) follows from line (a) by modal ordering and the primitive rule. And in the proof of [10d], line (d) results from line (c) by the primitive rule of inference and the truth-functional axiom $\{\Box^c \sim\Phi \supset \Box^c \sim(\Phi\Psi)\} \supset \{\sim\Box^c \sim(\Phi\Psi) \supset \sim\Box^c \sim\Phi\}$.

The proof of metatheorem [10a] is

(a)	$\Phi, \Psi \vdash \Phi\Psi$	**TF**
(b)	$\Box^c \Phi, \Box^c \Psi \vdash \Box^c (\Phi\Psi)$	(a), generalization
(c)	$\vdash \Box^c \Phi \supset [\Box^c \Psi \supset \Box^c (\Phi\Psi)]$	(b), conditional proof
(d)	$\Phi\Psi \vdash \Phi$	**TF**
(e)	$\Box^c (\Phi\Psi) \vdash \Box^c \Phi$	(d), generalization
(f)	$\vdash \Box^c (\Phi\Psi) \supset \Box^c \Phi$	(e), conditional proof
(g)	$\vdash \Box^c (\Phi\Psi) \supset \Box^c \Psi$	As in (d), (e), (f)
(h)	$\vdash (\Box^c \Phi \Box^c \Psi) \equiv \Box^c (\Phi\Psi)$	(c), (f), (g), **TF**.

The proof of metatheorem [10b] uses metatheorem [10a].

(a)	$\vdash (\Box^c \sim\Phi \Box^c \sim\Psi) \equiv \Box^c (\sim\Phi\sim\Psi)$	[10a]
(b)	$\vdash (\sim\Phi\sim\Psi) \equiv \sim(\Phi \vee \Psi)$	**TF**

(c)	$\vdash \Box^c (\sim\Phi \sim\Psi) \equiv \Box^c \sim(\Phi \vee \Psi)$	(b), exchange
(d)	$\vdash (\Box^c \sim\Phi\, \Box^c \sim\Psi) \equiv \Box^c \sim(\Phi \vee \Psi)$	(a), (c), **TF**
(e)	$\vdash (\sim\Box^c \sim\Phi \vee \sim\Box^c \sim\Psi) \equiv \sim\Box^c \sim(\Phi \vee \Psi)$	(d), **TF**
(f)	$\vdash (\Diamond^c \Phi \vee \Diamond^c \Psi) \equiv \Diamond^c (\Phi \vee \Psi)$	(e), [1d].

The proof of metatheorem [10c] is

(a)	$\vdash \Box\{\Phi \supset (\Phi \vee \Psi)\}$	**TF**, axiom generation
(b)	$\vdash \Box^c \{\Phi \supset (\Phi \vee \Psi)\}$	(a), modal ordering
(c)	$\vdash \Box^c \Phi \supset \Box^c (\Phi \vee \Psi)$	(b), modal distribution
(d)	$\vdash \Box^c \Psi \supset \Box^c (\Phi \vee \Psi)$	As in (a), (b), (c)
(e)	$\vdash (\Box^c \Phi \vee \Box^c \Psi) \supset \Box^c (\Phi \vee \Psi)$	(c), (d), **TF**.

And the proof of metatheorem [10d] is

(a)	$\sim\Phi \vdash \sim(\Phi\Psi)$	**TF**
(b)	$\Box^c \sim\Phi \vdash \Box^c \sim(\Phi\Psi)$	(a), generalization
(c)	$\vdash \Box^c \sim\Phi \supset \Box^c \sim(\Phi\Psi)$	(b), conditional proof
(d)	$\vdash \sim\Box^c \sim(\Phi\Psi) \supset \sim\Box^c \sim\Phi$	(c), **TF**
(e)	$\vdash \Diamond^c (\Phi\Psi) \supset \Diamond^c \Phi$	(d), [1d].

Now if we restate the four metatheorems labeled [10] and their proofs, with $\Box$ in place of $\Box^c$ and $\Diamond$ in place of $\Diamond^c$, we obtain four new metatheorems and their proofs, the only difference being that the generalization rule [8a] is appealed to in place of rule [8b]. Similarly, if we restate the four metatheorems labeled [10] and their proofs, with (α) in place of $\Box^c$ and $(\exists\alpha)$ in place of $\Diamond^c$, we obtain four new metatheorems and their proofs. These are special cases of the parallelism of the pair $\Box^c$, $\Diamond^c$ to the pairs $\Box$, $\Diamond$ and (α), $(\exists\alpha)$, respectively. There is a metatheorem covering this parallelism that would allow one to pass directly from [10] to the corresponding metatheorems for the logical modalities and the quantifiers. We need not take time to state and prove it, however, since our interest here is in the causal modalities; only when we wish to make an explicit comparison will we state and prove the corresponding theorems for the logical modalities and quantifiers.

We have already noted that [10a]–[10d] are not theorems of our formal language; rather, they are theorems about formal language theorems, and hence are metatheorems. Correspondingly, the "proofs" just given of [10a]–[10d] are not formal language proofs in the sense of Section 6.2.3. Rather, these proofs of [10a]–[10d] are algorithms or instructions for constructing proofs in the formal language. For example, suppose we want a proof of the formula "$\Diamond^c (PQ) \supset \Diamond^c P$," which is an instance of metatheorem [10d]. Line (a) of the proof of [10d] says that the sequence "$\sim P$, $\sim(PQ)$" is a proof from premise "$\sim P$." By line (b) we apply the algorithm of the generalization rule [8b] to the proof "$\sim P$, $\sim(PQ)$" to obtain a proof of "$\Box^c \sim(PQ)$" from premise "$\Box^c \sim P$." Line (*c*) tells us that this last proof is converted into a categorical proof of "$\Box^c \sim P \supset \Box^c \sim(PQ)$" by the conditional proof algorithm. Appending "$\sim\Box^c \sim(PQ) \supset \sim\Box^c \sim P$" to this categorical proof gives us a categorical proof of "$\sim\Box^c \sim(PQ) \supset \sim\Box^c \sim P$" itself. This last formula is, by definition, the same as "$\Diamond^c (PQ) \supset \Diamond^c P$."

Hereafter, when the proofs of metatheorems are easily constructed we shall not give them in detail. Sometimes we merely indicate the definitions, axioms, theorems, and rules that are needed, as in [11] below. When the proofs of the different metatheorems of a group are similar, we give only some of the proofs, as in [13] below.

To understand the intuitive content of a theorem, it is often helpful to compare it with a closely related formula that is not a theorem. Metatheorems [10a] and [10b] are equivalences, but metatheorem [10c] is only an implication, for its converse

$$\Box^c (\Phi \vee \Psi) \supset (\Box^c \Phi \vee \Box^c \Psi)$$

is not a metatheorem. To see this, consider the instance

$$\Box^c (Pa \vee Qa) \supset (\Box^c Pa \vee \Box^c Qa) \quad .$$

This formula is false in a model in which "$Pa\overline{Qa}$" and "$\overline{Pa}Qa$" describe causally possible universes but "$PaQa$" and "$\overline{Pa}\,\overline{Qa}$" do not. Hence this formula is not logically true and is not a theorem (pp. 362, 364). Metatheorem [10d] is easily extended to

$$\Diamond^c (\Phi\Psi) \supset (\Diamond^c \Phi \, \Diamond^c \Psi) \quad .$$

Its converse is not a metatheorem, for the formula

$$(\Diamond^c Pa \Diamond^c \overline{Pa}) \supset \Diamond^c (Pa\overline{Pa})$$

is false in a model in which "Pa" is true in one causally possible world and "$\overline{Pa}$" is true in a different causally possible world.

We can summarize the principles of distribution [10] as follows. A causal necessity operator can be distributed in both directions across a conjunction, but in only one direction across a disjunction. In contrast, a causal possibility operator can be distributed in both directions across a disjunction, but in only one direction across a conjunction.

The next metatheorems give additional principles of modal ordering.

[11a]	$\vdash \Box\Phi \supset \Phi$	Modal ordering, **TF**
[11b]	$\vdash (\Phi \rightarrow \Psi) \supset (\Phi \underset{c}{\rightarrow} \Psi)$	Modal ordering, [1f], [1g]
[11c]	$\vdash (\Phi \underset{c}{\rightarrow} \Psi) \supset (\Phi \supset \Psi)$	Modal ordering, [1g]

[11d]	$\vdash (\Phi \rightarrow \Psi) \supset (\Phi \supset \Psi)$	[11b], [11c], **TF**
[11e]	$\vdash (\alpha)(\Phi \rightarrow \Psi) \supset (\alpha)(\Phi \underset{c}{\rightarrow} \Psi)$	[11b], generalization, quantifier distribution
[11f]	$\vdash (\alpha)(\Phi \underset{c}{\rightarrow} \Psi) \supset (\alpha)(\Phi \supset \Psi)$	[11c], as in [11e]
[11g]	$\vdash (\alpha)(\Phi \rightarrow \Psi) \supset (\alpha)(\Phi \supset \Psi)$	[11e], [11f], **TF**
[11h]	$\vdash \Phi \supset \Diamond^c \Phi$	Modal ordering, [1d], **TF**
[11i]	$\vdash \Diamond^c \Phi \supset \Diamond \Phi$	Modal ordering, [1d], **TF**
[11j]	$\vdash \Phi \supset \Diamond \Phi$	[11h], [11i], **TF**.

It is easy to construct models to show that the following are not metatheorems: $\Phi \supset \Box^c \Phi$, $\Box^c \Phi \supset \Box \Phi$, $\Phi \supset \Box \Phi$, $\Diamond \Phi \supset \Diamond^c \Phi$, $\Diamond^c \Phi \supset \Phi$, and $\Diamond \Phi \supset \Phi$. These results rank the modalities by strength. In order of decreasing strength they are: logical necessity, causal necessity, and actuality; likewise, logical implication, causal implication, and material implication; and finally, actuality, causal possibility, and logical possibility.

The metatheorem $\Phi \supset (\exists\alpha)\Phi$ is a direct quantificational analog of [11h] and [11j]. The following stronger analog is proved easily from universal instantiation and [1b] by **TF**. It is called *existential generalization.*

[12] Let Ψ be the result of substituting the individual variable β for all free occurrences of α in Φ. If Ψ has exactly as many occurrences of free individual variables as Φ, then $\vdash \Psi \supset (\exists\alpha)\Phi$.

The following properties of causal implication are important enough to deserve names.

[13a]	$\vdash [(\Phi \underset{c}{\rightarrow} \Psi)(\Psi \underset{c}{\rightarrow} \Theta]) \supset (\Phi \underset{c}{\rightarrow} \Theta)$	*Transitivity*
[13b]	$\vdash [(\alpha)(\Phi \underset{c}{\rightarrow} \Psi)(\alpha)(\Psi \underset{c}{\rightarrow} \Theta)] \supset (\alpha)(\Phi \underset{c}{\rightarrow} \Theta)$	
[13c]	$\vdash (\Phi \underset{c}{\rightarrow} \Theta) \supset (\Phi\Psi \underset{c}{\rightarrow} \Theta)$	*Addition of a superfluous condition*
[13d]	$\vdash (\alpha)(\Phi \underset{c}{\rightarrow} \Theta) \supset (\alpha)(\Phi\Psi \underset{c}{\rightarrow} \Theta)$	
[13e]	$\vdash (\Phi\Psi \underset{c}{\rightarrow} \Theta) \equiv (\Phi\bar{\Theta} \underset{c}{\rightarrow} \bar{\Psi})$	*Transposition*
[13f]	$\vdash (\alpha)(\Phi\Psi \underset{c}{\rightarrow} \Theta) \equiv (\alpha)(\Phi\bar{\Theta} \underset{c}{\rightarrow} \bar{\Psi})$	
[13g]	$\vdash (\Phi\Psi \underset{c}{\rightarrow} \Theta) \equiv [\Phi \underset{c}{\rightarrow} (\Psi \supset \Theta)]$	*Exportation.*
[13h]	$\vdash (\alpha)(\Phi\Psi \underset{c}{\rightarrow} \Theta) \equiv (\alpha)[\Phi \underset{c}{\rightarrow} (\Psi \supset \Theta)]$	

It will suffice to give proofs of three of these. The proof of the quantificational form of transitivity is in five steps.

(a)	$\Phi \supset \Psi, \Psi \supset \Theta \vdash \Phi \supset \Theta$	**TF**
(b)	$(\alpha)\Box^c(\Phi \supset \Psi), (\alpha)\Box^c(\Psi \supset \Theta) \vdash (\alpha)\Box^c(\Phi \supset \Theta)$	(a), generalization

(c) $\vdash (\alpha)\Box^c(\Phi \supset \Psi) \supset [(\alpha)\Box^c(\Psi \supset \Theta) \supset (\alpha)\Box^c(\Phi \supset \Theta)]$ (b), conditional proof

(d) $\vdash [(\alpha)\Box^c(\Phi \supset \Psi)(\alpha)\Box^c(\Psi \supset \Theta)] \supset (\alpha)\Box^c(\Phi \supset \Theta)$ (c), **TF**

(e) $\vdash [(\alpha)(\Phi \underset{c}{\rightarrow} \Psi)(\alpha)(\Psi \underset{c}{\rightarrow} \Theta)] \supset (\alpha)(\Phi \underset{c}{\rightarrow} \Theta)$ (d), [1g].

And the proof of both forms of transposition is

(a) $\vdash (\Phi\Psi \supset \Theta) \equiv (\Phi\bar{\Theta} \supset \bar{\Psi})$ **TF**

(b) $\vdash \Box^c(\Phi\Psi \supset \Theta) \equiv \Box^c(\Phi\bar{\Theta} \supset \bar{\Psi})$ (a), exchange

(c) $\vdash (\Phi\Psi \underset{c}{\rightarrow} \Theta) \equiv (\Phi\bar{\Theta} \underset{c}{\rightarrow} \bar{\Psi})$ (b), [1g]

(d) $\vdash (\alpha)(\Phi\Psi \underset{c}{\rightarrow} \Theta) \equiv (\alpha)(\Phi\bar{\Theta} \underset{c}{\rightarrow} \bar{\Psi})$ (c), exchange.

6.5.3 Paradoxes of implication

We shall conclude the formal treatment of the logic of causal statements by proving some metatheorems about the so-called paradoxes of implication and discussing the extent to which these results really are paradoxical.* This exercise will illustrate the use of the logic of causal statements as a model language and will thereby make a natural transition to the next chapter.

A false proposition materially implies, a causal impossibility causally implies, and a logical impossibility logically implies any proposition. Similarly, a true proposition is materially implied by, a causal necessity is causally implied by, and a logical necessity is logically implied by any proposition. Stated symbolically,

[14a] $\vdash \sim\Phi \supset (\Phi \supset \Psi)$ [14b] $\vdash \Psi \supset (\Phi \supset \Psi)$

[14c] $\vdash \sim\Diamond^c\Phi \supset (\Phi \underset{c}{\rightarrow} \Psi)$ [14d] $\vdash \Box^c\Psi \supset (\Phi \underset{c}{\rightarrow} \Psi)$

[14e] $\vdash \sim\Diamond\Phi \supset (\Phi \rightarrow \Psi)$ [14f] $\vdash \Box\Psi \supset (\Phi \rightarrow \Psi)$.

These are called the *paradoxes of material, causal, and logical implication*, respectively, though as we shall see in a moment they are not really paradoxes.

Both [14a] and [14b] are truth-functional axioms. The proof of [14c] is

(a) $\sim\Phi \vdash \Phi \supset \Psi$ **TF**

(b) $\Box^c\sim\Phi \vdash \Box^c(\Phi \supset \Psi)$ (a), generalization

(c) $\vdash \Box^c\sim\Phi \supset \Box^c(\Phi \supset \Psi)$ conditional proof

(d) $\vdash \sim\sim\Box^c\sim\Phi \supset \Box^c(\Phi \supset \Psi)$ (c), **TF**

(e) $\vdash \sim\Diamond^c\Phi \supset (\Phi \underset{c}{\rightarrow} \Psi)$ (d), [1d], [1f].

The proofs of [14d], [14e], and [14f] are similar.

* See Lewis and Langford, *Symbolic Logic*, chap. 8, "Implication and Deducibility."

The "paradoxes" of implication are not really paradoxical, but only appear so to one who has made a bad translation from ordinary language into a formal language. We made this finding for the paradoxes of material implication (p. 43); we will now show that it holds for logical implication; and later we will extend it to include causal implication (p. 428).

The paradoxical character of formulas [14e] and [14f] derives mainly from the association of logical implication with valid deductive arguments. In Chapter 1, we defined a deductive argument to be valid just in case its corresponding conditional is logically true (p. 22). This is equivalent to: a deductive argument is valid if and only if its premises logically imply its conclusion. From this definition it follows directly that an argument with contradictory premises, or with a logically necessary conclusion, is valid. Moreover, the rules of inference normally employed in deduction do permit the derivation of an arbitrary proposition from a contradiction; they also sometimes permit the derivation of a logical truth from no premises at all and hence from an irrelevant premise.

Therefore, it is natural to say that a contradiction logically implies any statement and that a necessary statement is logically implied by any statement. But as we noted in connection with our original definition of deductive validity, the valid deductive arguments people actually construct satisfy not only that definition but other conditions as well; they are deductive proofs of the conclusion from the premises that proceed by intuitively acceptable steps and serve certain purposes.

Usually when one constructs an interpreted deductive argument, his ultimate purpose is to establish the truth of a statement (and, ipso facto, the falsity of its negation) by validly deducing it as a conclusion from certain premises tentatively accepted as true. This purpose is not fulfilled if the premises are contradictory, for they cannot then be true, and both the conclusion and its negation will follow from them. Nor is this purpose fulfilled if the premises are irrelevant to the conclusion and are not needed for its derivation. Thus though "It is raining and it isn't raining" logically implies "Romany came from Sanskrit," no one would claim to *prove* that Romany came from Sanskrit by deriving "Romany came from Sanskrit" from an obviously contradictory premise. In an ordinary valid argument, the conclusion and premises have in common some concept or term that plays an essential role (or at least is thought to play an essential role) in the derivation.

It is appropriate here to view a deductive argument as a miniature axiomatic system, with premises as axioms and conclusions as theorems. Usually when one constructs an interpreted axiomatic system, his purpose is to specify and organize a given class of true statements by so choosing the axioms that this class of statements becomes the class of theorems. Thus the truths of Euclidean geometry may be specified by giving a complete and consistent set of axioms for this subject. If this purpose is to be fulfilled, two conditions, which are directly related to the two paradoxes of logical implication, must also be fulfilled. First, the axioms must be logically consistent; otherwise, all statements follow from them, and they do not distinguish the true from the false. Second, though some of the axioms may be superfluous, there is no point to the axiomatization if none of the axioms are needed for the derivation.

It might seem that a reductio ad absurdum proof constitutes an exception to the foregoing, but it does not. The situation can be explained in terms of the rules

[7b] If $\bar{\Phi} \vdash \Psi\bar{\Psi}$, then $\vdash \Phi$

[7c] If $\Phi_1, \ldots, \Phi_N, \sim\Psi \vdash \Psi$, then $\Phi_1, \ldots, \Phi_N \vdash \Psi$.

These are derived rules of the logic of causal statements, but they also express rules of reductio ad absurdum used in mathematics generally; let us view them in this way. Call the proof from $\bar{\Phi}$ to $\Psi\bar{\Psi}$ (or from $\Phi_1, \Phi_2, \ldots, \Phi_N, \sim\Psi$ to Ψ) an "indirect proof" and the corresponding proof of Φ (or from $\Phi_1, \ldots, \Phi_N$ to Ψ) the corresponding "direct proof." Now, the premises of an indirect proof are indeed contradictory. But an indirect proof is only a stepping stone to a direct proof, which normally does not have contradictory premises. When rule [7c] is used, it is intended that the premises of the direct proof be consistent. Usually, when [7b] is employed, the axioms of some system function as background premises, and it is hoped that this system is consistent.

It should be noted that the indirect proofs actually used in mathematics have an informal feature not captured by the principle that a contradictory statement logically implies any statement. In actual indirect proofs the contradiction generated contains one of the premises or has some content in common with the premises, so that the antecedent and consequent of the conditional corresponding to the indirect proof have some common content. In contrast, according to the principle that a contradiction logically implies any proposition, a logical connection exists between a contradiction and a totally unrelated statement, as in "$(2 + 2 = 5) \rightarrow$ (Today is Monday)."

The preceding shows that the mathematician normally aims at proofs with consistent premises and that he uses proofs with contradictory premises as means to this goal. We include members of the intuitionistic school of mathematics as well as mathematicians generally, although the intuitionist has a different view of the relation of indirect to direct proofs from that just expounded. Derived rules [7b] and [7c] were justified by algorithms that convert indirect proofs into direct proofs. These algorithms employ a law of double negation ($\sim\sim\Phi \supset \Phi$) not accepted by the intuitionist, and so for him an indirect proof does not lead automatically to a direct proof. He does require, however, that a good proof have consistent premises; accordingly, he views indirect proofs as inferior to direct proofs.

The claim that there is a deductive proof from $\Phi_1, \Phi_2, \ldots, \Phi_N$ to Ψ may be expressed by the conditional

If $\Phi_1, \Phi_2, \ldots, \Phi_N$, then Ψ .

Since most proofs actually constructed have premises that are consistent and are needed in the proof, the true conditionals corresponding to these proofs have, for the most part, antecedents that are consistent and are deductively relevant to the consequent. This being so, it is misleading, if not wrong, to use "if . . . , then . . ." when these conditions are not satisfied. Consequently, though

(Today is both Tuesday and Wednesday) $\rightarrow$
(Galli-Curci sang beautifully)
(The moon is coated with Camembert) $\rightarrow$ ($69 \times 71 = 4{,}899$)

are both true,

If today is both Tuesday and Wednesday, then
Galli-Curci sang beautifully
If the moon is coated with Camembert, then
$69 \times 71 = 4{,}899$

are either misleading or false.

Let us summarize the results of this analysis of the paradoxes of logical implication. Consider the definition: a deductive argument is valid if and only if its premises logically imply its conclusion. This definition states the most important condition a deductive argument must satisfy to be valid, but it does not cover some important informal aspects of deductive validity. Normally, when one claims that premises logically imply a conclusion, these informal aspects are present; and it is misleading to make this claim when these aspects are absent, even though the most basic condition for deductive validity (logical implication) is satisfied. One has only to recognize this source of the paradoxes of logical implication to see that they are not actually paradoxical.

The so-called paradoxes of implication are closely related to the following six metatheorems, which are of interest.

[15a] $\vdash [(\Phi \supset \Psi)(\Phi \supset \overline{\Psi})] \equiv {\sim}\Phi$ [15b] $\vdash (\Phi \supset \Psi\overline{\Psi}) \equiv {\sim}\Phi$

[15c] $\vdash [(\Phi \underset{c}{\rightarrow} \Psi)(\Phi \underset{c}{\rightarrow} \overline{\Psi})] \equiv {\sim}\Diamond^c \Phi$ [15d] $\vdash (\Phi \underset{c}{\rightarrow} \Psi\overline{\Psi}) \equiv {\sim}\Diamond^c \Phi$

[15e] $\vdash [(\Phi \rightarrow \Psi)(\Phi \rightarrow \overline{\Psi})] \equiv {\sim}\Diamond\Phi$ [15f] $\vdash (\Phi \rightarrow \Psi\overline{\Psi}) \equiv {\sim}\Diamond\Phi$.

The metatheorems on the left give, for each type of implication, a necessary and sufficient condition under which two hypotheticals "If Φ, then Ψ" and "If Φ, then ${\sim}\Psi$" are both true. In each case the corresponding metatheorem on the right states that this is also a necessary and sufficient condition for "If Φ, then $\Psi\overline{\Psi}$" being true.

Metatheorems [15a] and [15b] are both truth-functional axioms. We prove [15c] and [15d] simultaneously.

(a)	$\vdash (\Phi \supset \Psi\bar{\Psi}) \equiv \sim\Phi$	**TF**
(b)	$\vdash \Box^c (\Phi \supset \Psi\bar{\Psi}) \equiv \Box^c \sim\Phi$	(a), exchange
(c)	$\vdash \Box^c (\Phi \supset \Psi\bar{\Psi}) \equiv \sim\sim\Box^c \sim\Phi$	(b), **TF**
(d)	$\vdash (\Phi \underset{c}{\rightarrow} \Psi\bar{\Psi}) \equiv \sim\Diamond^c \Phi$	(c), [1d], [1g]
(e)	$\vdash (\Phi \supset \Psi\bar{\Psi}) \equiv \{(\Phi \supset \Psi)(\Phi \supset \bar{\Psi})\}$	**TF**
(f)	$\vdash \Box^c (\Phi \supset \Psi\bar{\Psi}) \equiv \Box^c \{(\Phi \supset \Psi)(\Phi \supset \bar{\Psi})\}$	(e), exchange
(g)	$\vdash \{\Box^c (\Phi \supset \Psi)\Box^c (\Phi \supset \bar{\Psi})\}$ $\equiv \Box^c \{(\Phi \supset \Psi)(\Phi \supset \bar{\Psi})\}$	[10a]
(h)	$\vdash \Box^c (\Phi \supset \Psi\bar{\Psi}) \equiv [(\Phi \underset{c}{\rightarrow} \Psi)(\Phi \underset{c}{\rightarrow} \bar{\Psi})]$	(f), (g), **TF**
(i)	$\vdash (\Phi \underset{c}{\rightarrow} \Psi\bar{\Psi}) \equiv [(\Phi \underset{c}{\rightarrow} \Psi)(\Phi \underset{c}{\rightarrow} \bar{\Psi})]$	(h), [1g]
(j)	$\vdash [(\Phi \underset{c}{\rightarrow} \Psi)(\Phi \underset{c}{\rightarrow} \bar{\Psi})] \equiv \sim\Diamond^c \Phi$	(d), (i), **TF**.

Line (j) is metatheorem [15c] and line (d) is metatheorem [15d]. The proofs of [15e] and [15f] are similar.

This concludes for the most part our presentation of the logic of causal statements as a formal language. We shall, however, add several more definitions and metatheorems in the next chapter as their need arises.

6.6 Summary

Our fourth main question was: What is the nature of causal necessity and how are causal necessity and inductive probability related? In order to establish the formal properties of causal necessity, in Chapters 6 and 7 we develop the logic of causal statements and use it as a formal model of ordinary and scientific discourse involving causality.

The present chapter has emphasized the formal structure of the logic of causal statements. We defined this language, gave an abstract interpretation of it, and proved some theorems in it. It was developed as an example of a formal language, so as to bring out its general as well as its specific properties. The next chapter will emphasize the application of the logic of causal statements to ordinary and scientific discourse involving causality.

The need for the causal modalities was established by analyzing a causal subjunctive and showing that none of the usual kinds of implication are adequate for symbolizing it. The logic of causal statements consists of first-order quantification theory extended to include both the logical modalities ($\Box$, $\Diamond$, $\rightarrow$, $\leftrightarrow$) and the causal modalities ($\Box^c$, $\Diamond^c$, $\underset{c}{\rightarrow}$, $\underset{c}{\leftrightarrow}$). These modalities are interpreted in terms of logically possible and causally possible universes. Iterated modalities are not included.

The structure of the logic of causal statements (*sec. 6.2*). The underlying structure of a formal language is defined without reference to its interpretation by means of decision algorithms for formulahood and proofhood. The logic of causal statements was presented as an example of a formal language. The formulas are constructed from the primitive symbols in such a way that there is a simple algorithm for deciding of a sequence of symbols whether it is a formula. Axioms are of the following kinds: truth-functional, quantificational, modal, and those generated from other axioms by the rule of axiom generation. There is an algorithm for axiomhood.

Any axiom of conditional form can be employed by the primitive rule of inference to produce an immediate consequence of a set of formulas. A proof may be either a categorical proof or a proof from premises. The last formula of a categorical proof is a theorem. There is a decision algorithm for proofhood that incorporates the decision algorithm for axiomhood.

An abstract interpretation (*sec. 6.3*). An abstract, idealized interpretation of the logic of causal statements was given by means of simple modal models. This interpretation contrasts with, and is a simple model of, the concrete interpretation of the same language to which the next chapter is devoted.

A modal model $\mathcal{M}$-$\mathcal{L}$ contains a model language $\mathcal{L}$ and a corresponding model $\mathcal{M}$ of the nonlinguistic part of reality. Each language $\mathcal{L}$ contains the logic of causal statements augmented by predicate constants and individual constants. Each individual constant names a basic individual of $\mathcal{M}$ and each n-adic predicate corresponds to an n-adic basic property of $\mathcal{M}$. There may be infinitely many individuals and individual constants.

Logical connections are permitted between atomic statements, so that not every basic conjunction describes a logically possible universe. There is a nested structure of universe descriptions, causally possible universe descriptions, and the true universe description; and there is a corresponding structure of logically possible, causally possible, and actual universes.

The concept of truth was defined for a closed formula relative to a given model $\mathcal{M}$-$\mathcal{L}$. Quantifiers are translated into their truth-functional equivalents; if the model contains infinitely many basic individuals, this produces pseudoformulas rather than formulas. The truth-value of an atomic statement varies from universe to universe. A closed formula is logically necessary if it is true in all logically possible universes, and it is causally necessary if it is true in all causally possible universes.

A formula of the logic of causal statements is logically true if and only if it is true on every interpretation in every modal model. Every theorem of the logic of causal statements is logically true, and hence this language is consistent. The logic of causal statements contains logical truths about the causal and logical modalities. In particular, each theorem of the form $\Box\Phi$ expresses a logical truth about a logical truth (Φ).

The mechanical character of a formal language (sec. 6.4). A discussion of the general properties of formal languages helped to establish the scope and limits of formalization.

Gödel showed how to translate any formal language into a system of arithmetic in which symbols, formulas, and proofs are expressed by positive integers. The decision algorithms for formulahood and proofhood that are definitive of a formal language can then be used to construct enumeration algorithms for formulas and theorems.

Peano arithmetic is an interpreted formal language for arithmetic in which every theorem is true. Since it is a formal language, Gödel's arithmetization procedure can be applied to it. The result is a formal language containing formulas that express statements about itself.

A formal language is complete if for every closed formula Φ, either Φ or $\sim\Phi$ is a theorem. Gödel's incompleteness theorem is: Let $\mathfrak{L}$ be an interpreted formal language containing Peano arithmetic such that every theorem of $\mathfrak{L}$ is true on the given interpretation; then $\mathfrak{L}$ is incomplete.

The proof of this theorem was described in connection with an interpreted formal language $\mathfrak{L}_A$ containing Peano arithmetic and having every theorem true. Since $\mathfrak{L}_A$ is a formal language, the concepts "formula of $\mathfrak{L}_A$" and "proof of $\mathfrak{L}_A$" are arithmetic in character. Since $\mathfrak{L}_A$ contains Peano arithmetic, these concepts can be expressed in $\mathfrak{L}_A$ itself. Thus true statements *about* $\mathfrak{L}_A$ become true statements *of* $\mathfrak{L}_A$, and many of these are theorems of $\mathfrak{L}_A$.

Gödel produced a closed formula U of $\mathfrak{L}_A$ that says on this reflexive interpretation that it is not a theorem of $\mathfrak{L}_A$. Now if $\sim U$ were true, then U would be true. For $\sim U$ says that U is a theorem, and all theorems of $\mathfrak{L}_A$ are true. But since U is closed, exactly one of the pair $\{U, \sim U\}$ is true. Hence U is true and $\sim U$ is false.

Since U is true and says it is not a theorem, U is not a theorem. Since $\sim U$ is false and all theorems are true, $\sim U$ is not a theorem. Hence $\mathfrak{L}_A$ is incomplete, and Gödel's theorem is established.

Not every property of $\mathfrak{L}_A$ can be expressed in $\mathfrak{L}_A$. The concept "Φ is true in $\mathfrak{L}_A$" is an example. If this concept could be defined in $\mathfrak{L}_A$, the procedure used to construct U could be used to construct a formula F that says of itself that it is false. Then the general mode of argument used to prove Gödel's theorem could be used to derive a contradiction.

The foregoing shows that algorithms are the essence of a formal language. Algorithms are best defined in terms of automata. A finite automaton is a finite network of switches and delays. A Turing machine consists of a finite automaton connected to two or three tape units: a storage unit, a printer, and perhaps a reader. A universal Turing machine can perform the computation of any Turing machine when it is given a description or program-equivalent of that machine.

An algorithm is a rule for calculation that can be expressed as a program for a universal Turing machine. Hence the definition of a formal language yields designs for formula enumeration and theorem enumeration machines. Formal languages, however, do not generally have theorem decision machines.

The following corollary gives the essence of Gödel's incompleteness theorem in terms of machines. If $\mathcal{L}$ is an interpreted formal language containing Peano arithmetic, there is no machine that will enumerate the true formulas of $\mathcal{L}$, and there is no machine that will decide of a formula of $\mathcal{L}$ whether or not it is true. Since every arithmetic truth is a logical truth, there can be no purely formal or algorithmic definition of logical truth.

Some theorems of the logic of causal statements (*sec. 6.5*). Some algorithms facilitating the discovery and presentation of proofs of theorems were presented. These algorithms are derived rules of inference: rules of conditional proof and reductio ad absurdum; the rule of generalization; and the rule of exchange, which permits the exchange of proved equivalents.

Some specific metatheorems that will be useful in interpreting the logic of causal statements were proved. These included principles of distribution, modal ordering, transitivity, transposition, and exportation, and also the paradoxes of implication.

The paradoxes of logical implication were resolved. These paradoxes arise from a conflict between our intuitive, informal notion of implication and a certain formal model of it. The definition "a deductive argument is valid if and only if its premises logically imply its conclusion" states the most important condition a deductive argument must satisfy to be valid. But it does not capture some important informal aspects of deductive validity that are normally present in deductive reasoning.

7 The Logic of Causal Statements as a Model of Natural Language

An ordinary *hypothetical proposition*, as propositions containing an antecedent condition and a consequent result are called, relates to what *would* occur in states of things not all coincident with the existing state of things. Suppose I say "If I were to upset the inkstand the tablecloth would be injured." This means that of all the different courses of events that might occur, the disposition of things in the room being what it is, every one is one in which either the inkstand is not upset or the tablecloth is spoiled.

[A law is] general in referring to all possible things, and not merely to those that happen to exist. No collection of facts can constitute a law; for the law goes beyond any accomplished facts and determines how facts that *may be*, but *all* of which never can have happened, shall be characterized.*

7.1 Introduction

In this chapter my logic of causal statements will be used to model certain portions of ordinary and scientific discourse. But first some general comments about formal and natural languages are in order.

Being a formal language, the logic of causal statements contains sharp and rigorous distinctions between certain given "atoms" and the corresponding constructed "compounds": primitive symbols *vs.* formulas, axioms *vs.* theorems, and primitive rules of inference *vs.* derived rules of inference. Natural languages do not contain these distinctions. The distinction between morphemes and sentences is analogous to the distinction between primitive symbols and formulas, but the former lacks the rigorous and simple character of the latter. And while some logical truths are more "self-evident" than others, any division of them into axioms and theorems is quite arbitrary. Also, as a formal language, the logic of causal statements is highly algorithmic and mechanical in structure: there are decision machines for formulahood, axiomhood, and proofhood, and an enumeration machine for theorem-

I have benefited from personal discussions with Charles Stevenson on the subject of this chapter.

* Peirce, *Collected Papers*. The first quotation is 8.380n4 (undated). The second quotation is from 1.420 and was written about 1896.

See also 4.546 and 4.580-4 (both dated 1906) and the quotations on p. 173, above.

hood. Clearly, the structure of the logic of causal statements is very different from the structure of a natural language in these respects.

The technical languages used by mathematicians and scientists fall somewhere between formal and natural languages in these same respects. The proofs and derivations of mathematicians and scientists are not formal, for they depend heavily on intuition and interpretation. Nevertheless, these technical languages are much more rigorous and precise than natural languages.

The preceding comparisons concern the structures of languages, not their expressive powers. The question of what can be expressed in a formal language is much deeper than the question of what its structure is. To see this, compare the structure of a formal language $\mathfrak{L}_A$ for Peano arithmetic and Gödel's proof that this structure can be expressed in $\mathfrak{L}_A$ itself (sec. 6.4.2).

The fact that a natural language has a nonalgorithmic structure does not preclude the possibility that it is ultimately formalizable and mechanizable. For suppose one could construct a finite automaton that used a natural language, not only internally but in dealing with its environment, and thus performed the basic linguistic functions of which humans are capable. An automaton can be specified formally, and a properly working digital computer is a physical realization of this formalism, so that the envisaged automaton would constitute a formal and mechanical realization of a natural language (sec. 6.4.3).* One would then have represented in a formal language many phenomena that are not part of its given structure, such as vagueness (pp. 437-40), the power to apply empirical concepts, and the power to reason deductively and inductively (pp. 610-13). Since this envisaged result concerns the expressive power of a formal language, it would not contradict the fact that natural languages are structurally much less mechanical than formal languages.

Though the logic of causal statements differs greatly from ordinary and scientific languages in the ways discussed above, it is nonetheless a useful model of these in one important regard. As we noted earlier, all reasoning is in terms of rules and is general, there being many cases covered by the same rule (p. 15). Implicit in ordinary discourse is a notion of deductive validity, according to which arguments and rules are classified into the valid and the invalid. This notion is rough and vague, in contrast to the formal notion of deductive validity, which is sharp and precise. Still, the latter may be used to model the former. This commonsense notion of deductive validity may be modeled to some extent by a nonmodal formal language and to an even greater extent by a formal language containing the logical modalities. But as we saw in Section 6.1, a logic of casual modalities is needed for modeling deductive arguments that contain causal statements.

The present chapter is devoted to modeling such arguments in the logic

* See my "Logic, Biology and Automata—Some Historical Reflections," pp. 308–10.

of causal statements. We express causal statements in the symbolism of this formal language and compare the deductive interrelations of the symbolized statements with those of the original statements. As in the case of any model, we are interested in the differences between the model language and the natural language as well as in the similarities.

The following two points should be kept in mind when modeling arguments of ordinary discourse. First, a statement does not always convey its meaning or content by itself; its meaning may also depend on its context. The same is true of an argument, which is a sequence of statements and a claim that one of these follows from the others. Consequently, when symbolizing a statement or argument, one must look at the surrounding discourse as well as at the words to be symbolized. Sometimes a sentence has different meanings in different contexts; for example, the same subjunctive sentence may be counterfactual in one context but not in another (pp. 438–39). Sometimes two different sentences should be symbolized by the same formula. For example, when the context shows that "All gold objects dissolve in aqua regia" expresses a causal law, the symbolization of this indicative should be the same as that of the subjunctive "If a gold object should be placed in aqua regia, it would dissolve" (p. 437). Furthermore, there are cases in which the actual discourse surrounding a statement or argument may not suffice to fix its meaning. In order to ascertain what a speaker means by a sentence, one may need to determine what conclusions he would deduce from it or what he would count as evidence for or against it. It may even be necessary to observe his actions (see the discussion of meaning and action in sec. 4.2). Because of this dependence of meaning on context, our modeling will rely heavily on examples.

Second, in deciding whether a natural language argument is valid it may be helpful to model that argument in a formal language. But it should be emphasized that by symbolizing an argument one does not reduce the question of its validity to a formal question. While the question of the validity of the model is a formal question, the question whether the model preserves the validity status of the original argument is not. Indeed, to answer the latter question one must use the same kind of intuitive considerations he uses to decide whether the original argument is valid. For example, in deciding whether a sentence is symbolized correctly, it is often helpful to decide what conclusions one would or would not draw from that sentence and then to determine whether these conclusions do or do not follow from the proposed symbolization.

As we use the logic of causal statements to model natural discourse we shall be interpreting it. Since this interpretation is in terms of natural language and natural phenomena, it is concrete, in contrast to the interpretation in terms of abstract models given in the last chapter (sec. 6.3). The **logic of causal statements** as concretely interpreted is distinct from the logic of causal statements as a formal language, or as abstractly interpreted, though these three languages are intimately related. The formal language is the core of both interpreted languages. Moreover, the abstract interpretation of Section 6.3 is itself a model of the concrete interpretation that we will give in the current chapter.

Thus each abstract model $\mathfrak{M}$-$\mathfrak{L}$ is a model of reality. $\mathfrak{M}$ models "nature," or the nonlinguistic part of reality, which is extended in space and time. The actual universe of $\mathfrak{M}$ corresponds to our actual universe; the logically possible universes of $\mathfrak{M}$ correspond to the logically possible alternatives of our universe; and the causally possible universes of $\mathfrak{M}$ correspond to the causally possible alternatives to our actual universe, that is, those logically possible universes that obey the laws of nature. Each possible universe is temporal (with past, present, and future) and spatial. The interpreted formal language $\mathfrak{L}$ models natural language insofar as the latter is used to express the causal and logical modalities. Finally, the complex $\mathfrak{M}$-$\mathfrak{L}$ models reality as a whole, so that the interpretation of $\mathfrak{L}$ in terms of $\mathfrak{M}$ models the interpretation of a natural language in terms of reality.

We proceed now to develop the concrete interpretation of the logic of causal statements.

7.2 Laws of Nature

7.2.1 Laws and theories

Sometimes one assumes a law or theory to be true and draws conclusions from it, though he recognizes that the law or theory is only probable and may be revised or replaced later. In the current chapter we model laws of nature and scientific theories from that point of view, then study their deductive consequences. In Chapter 10 we shall examine alternative possible laws and study the probabilistic bearing of data upon them.

Consider first Newton's theory of mechanics: his law of gravitation together with his laws of motion. In this theory a complete state of the universe at time t is given by a list of all the particles of matter together with the position, mass, and momentum of each particle at time t. The scope of the theory is limited to histories of the universe in which no particle hits another. For such histories, the application of Newton's theory of mechanics to a complete state of the universe at time t_1 yields a unique complete state of the universe at any other time t_2. Since his theory expresses a law of nature covering many possible histories of the universe (as well as the actual history), the result of prefixing $\square^c$ to it is a true statement.

The conjunction of Maxwell's equations is a law of nature, holding for a large set of possible boundary and initial conditions. Consequently, the result of prefixing $\square^c$ to Maxwell's equations is a true statement. Another example of a law of nature is

[H] An electron moving in a vacuum perpendicular to a magnetic field (*M*) and subject to no other forces (*N*) is deflected (*D*).

Sentence [H] states a law describing how nature behaves in all cases (actual and hypothetical) when the antecedent condition is satisfied. Hence, the proposition

[H′] It is causally necessary that an electron moving in a vacuum perpendicular to a magnetic field (*M*) and subject to no other forces (*N*) is deflected (*D*)

is true. A principle from Einstein's special theory of relativity exemplifies a different type of law of nature:

> The velocity of light in vacuo is the same in all inertial systems, that is, in all reference systems moving with constant velocity relative to each other.*

This principle, as well as the theory of which it is a part, holds for all causally possible universes; thus the result of prefixing it by $\Box^c$ is also true.

It should be noted that not all laws of nature and scientific theories are to be modeled in the logic of causal statements. Some laws and theories are essentially probabilistic and therefore should be modeled in a probabilistic logic. Classical thermodynamics and quantum mechanics are examples. We call these "empirical probability theories" and model them in the calculus of inductive probability (sec. 8.3). An atomic empirical probability statement is a very special case of an empirical probability theory.

It will be convenient to have a technical name for those theories and **laws** that are to be modeled in the logic of causal statements. We call them **laws of nature.** This term, as well as the closely related concrete notion of a causally possible universe, is too fundamental to be defined explicitly (sec. 1.3); indeed, we argue later that the notion of causal necessity is a priori (sec. 10.2.2). Hence we are specifying the meaning of "law of nature" informally, by examples and general comments.

Most true scientific theories of a nonprobabilistic, nondescriptive sort express laws of nature, provided they are fundamental and are qualified by the proper conditions of application and restrictions of scope. Now a law of nature has three main features: (1) a uniqueness feature, (2) a modal feature, and (3) a uniformity feature.

(1) The uniqueness of a law of nature involves a single-valued mathematical function: there is a mathematical function that, when applied to a property of the system at t_1 (as argument value), gives a unique property of the system at time t_2 (as function value). The properties involved may be either partial states or complete states of the system. The time t_2 is gen-

* Einstein, *The Meaning of Relativity*, pp. 25-27.

erally later than t_1 but need not be. A law of nature may place constraints on a state of the system at any given time, but laws of nature generally connect states of the system at different times.

The uniqueness feature of example [H] is then: when an electron is moving in a vacuum perpendicular to a magnetic field with no other forces present, the electron will be deflected *without exception.* The described state of the system is partial because it does not include the velocity of the electron or the strength of the field.

The uniqueness feature of a law of nature is different from determinism, which is a limiting case of it, and contrasts with the nonuniqueness of an empirical probability theory. Determinism is the limiting case of uniqueness that obtains when the resultant unique property (the function value) is a complete state. For example, Newton's theory of mechanics defines a mathematical function that, when applied to a complete state at t_1 (as argument value), gives a *unique complete state* at any other time t_2 (as function value). Determinism will be discussed later (sec. 9.3.2). An empirical probability theory involves a many-valued mathematical function. In a Markov chain, for instance, the probability of the next state depends on the present state, but the present state does not yield a unique next state.

(2) A law of nature is a general principle, rule, or theory that describes many possible successions of complete states, holds for many possible boundary conditions, or covers many possible circumstances. It is this modal feature of a law of nature that warrants the use of causal necessity ($\Box^c$) in symbolizing it. For convenience the primitive "$\Box^c$" was defined so that a logical necessity is also a causal necessity ($\Box\Phi \supset \Box^c \Phi$). But logical laws are not laws of nature, and so the modal feature of this latter type of law is better expressed by "$\Box^c \Phi \sim \Box\Phi$" than by "$\Box^c \Phi$" alone. See also the definition of nonparadoxical causal implication in the next subsection.

(3) The uniformity feature of laws of nature will be discussed at length in Chapter 9. The essential points are these. In their most fundamental form, laws of nature involve connections between nonindexical properties. Nonindexical properties (e.g., being made of gold, dissolving in aqua regia) are to be contrasted with indexical properties (e.g., occurring today, being a word on this page), which depend on spatial or temporal references (sec. 9.2.2). Causally necessary connections hold basically between nonindexical properties and are uniform over space and time (sec. 9.3.1). In the applications we make of the logic of causal statements in the present chapter, we will interpret the predicate variables as nonindexical predicates and the free individual variables as proper names or terms that are causally neutral, e.g., "this ring," "this event."

We call a law of nature formulated in terms of cause and effect a **causal law.** Sentence [H′] expresses a causal law: in the given conditions, a magnetic field will cause the electron to be deflected, the deflection of the electron being the effect. But Newton's theory of mechanics, Maxwell's equations, and Einstein's principle are not causal in form and hence are not causal laws*

It should be noted that we apply the term "causal necessity" to laws of nature that are not causal laws as well as to those that are. This deviates from ordinary usage (see sec. 7.4), making "causal necessity" a technical term for us. Laws of nature, whether causal or noncausal, concern possibilities as well as actualities and thus have a kind of necessity. It is convenient to have a name for this type of necessity; we have chosen to call it "causal."† This term is appropriate for a number of reasons. The notion of law of nature is a generalization of the notion of causal law; that is, causal laws are often special cases of laws of nature. For example, proposition [H], in which we can distinguish a cause (the magnetic field) and an effect (the deflection), is a special case of Maxwell's equations. Moreover, the status of laws of nature has traditionally been discussed in terms of cause and effect. The first part of our fourth main question is: What is the nature of causal necessity? This is essentially the same as a question discussed by Hume and Kant (see p. 30). Thus, while our use of "causal" in "causal necessity" differs from ordinary usage, it is a natural extension of this usage.

We now proceed to model causal laws in more detail, carrying forward the enumeration of definitions and metatheorems of the preceding chapter. The reader is reminded that formulas of the logic of causal statements never contain modalities applied to modalities. Consequently, when the metalinguistic variables Φ, Ψ, Θ, etc., occur in the contexts $\Box\Phi$, $\Box^c\Psi$, etc., these variables are restricted to non-modal formulas.

7.2.2 Causal laws

The considerations of Section 6.1 show that the formulas "$(x)(MxNx \underset{c}{\rightarrow} Dx)$" and "$\Box^c(x)(MxNx \supset Dx)$" are better models of statement [H′] than nonmodal formulas, formulas using the logical modalities, or probabilistic formulas. There are some essential properties of a causal law that "$(x)(MxNx \underset{c}{\rightarrow} Dx)$" and "$\Box^c(x)(MxNx \supset Dx)$" do not express, however. We will formalize two such properties now.

We noted in the last subsection that the modal feature of a law of

* Sometimes a complete state of a spatio-temporal system is said to be the cause of a later complete state, but this is not the ordinary use of "cause." Rather, it is an extension of the ordinary "local" use of "cause" to a "global" use. For examples, see the quotation from Laplace on p. 574, below, and Bohm, *Causality and Chance in Modern Physics*, p. 3.

† I began to develop the logic of causal statements in 1939 and have used the term "causal" in this sense since that time. Other terms have been used for the causal modalities. Reichenbach called them the physical modalities (*Elements of Symbolic Logic*, p. 392; *Nomological Statements and Admissible Operations*), and Fitch called them the natural modalities (*Symbolic Logic*, p. 69).

nature is better expressed by "$\Box^c \Phi \sim\Box\Phi$" than by "$\Box^c \Phi$" alone. For causal laws, this generalizes to the requirement that the antecedent and consequent of a causal law are logically independent. Logical independence is defined by

[16a] $\Phi \bigcirc \Psi =_{df} \Diamond(\Phi\Psi)\Diamond(\Phi\overline{\Psi})\Diamond(\overline{\Phi}\Psi)\Diamond(\overline{\Phi}\&\overline{\Psi})$.

This is a special case of the definition used in probability theory (p. 50).

The notion of logical independence may also be expressed in terms of logical implication

[16b] $(\Phi \bigcirc \Psi) \equiv \{\sim(\Phi \rightarrow \overline{\Psi})\sim(\Phi \rightarrow \Psi)\sim(\overline{\Phi} \rightarrow \overline{\Psi})\sim(\overline{\Phi} \rightarrow \Psi)\}$.

That is, two statements are logically independent just in case neither the first statement nor its negation logically implies the second statement or its negation. The proof begins

(a) $\vdash \sim(\Phi\Psi) \equiv (\Phi \supset \overline{\Psi})$ **TF**

(b) $\vdash \sim\Box\sim(\Phi\Psi) \equiv \sim\Box(\Phi \supset \overline{\Psi})$ (a), exchange

(c) $\vdash \Diamond(\Phi\Psi) \equiv \sim(\Phi \rightarrow \overline{\Psi})$ (b), [1c], [1f].

Three more equivalences may be proved similarly

(d) $\vdash \Diamond(\Phi\overline{\Psi}) \equiv \sim(\Phi \rightarrow \Psi)$

(e) $\vdash \Diamond(\overline{\Phi}\Psi) \equiv \sim(\overline{\Phi} \rightarrow \overline{\Psi})$

(f) $\vdash \Diamond(\overline{\Phi}\&\overline{\Psi}) \equiv \sim(\overline{\Phi} \rightarrow \Psi)$ As in (a)-(c).

Theorem [16b] now follows from definition [16a] by exchanging the proved equivalents of (c), (d), (e), and (f).

The second respect in which causal implication is inadequate for expressing causal laws concerns the "paradoxes" of implication (sec. 6.5.3). The paradoxes of logical implication are already excluded by the requirement of logical independence (see theorem [18b], below), but the paradoxes of causal implication must also be excluded. For in the normal sense of "cause," a causally impossible situation is not itself the cause of anything, and a causally necessary situation is not caused by anything.

To formalize these two properties of causal laws we define a new kind of implication, called *nonparadoxical causal implication* (**npc**).

[17a] $\Phi\ \mathbf{npc}\ \Psi =_{df} (\Phi \underset{c}{\rightarrow} \Psi)(\Phi \bigcirc \Psi)\Diamond^c \Phi \sim\Box^c \Psi$.

Actually, the full logical independence of Φ and Ψ is not needed in the definiens, as is shown by the following theorem.

[17b] $(\Phi\ \mathbf{npc}\ \Psi) \equiv (\Phi \underset{c}{\rightarrow} \Psi)\Diamond(\Phi\overline{\Psi})\Diamond(\overline{\Phi}\Psi)\Diamond^c \Phi \sim\Box^c \Psi$.

We first prove a lemma.

(a) $\Phi \underset{c}{\rightarrow} \Psi$ Premise

(b) $\Diamond^{c} \Phi$ — Premise

(c) $\sim(\Phi \underset{c}{\rightarrow} \bar{\Psi})$ — (a), (b), [15c], **TF**

(d) $\sim(\Phi \rightarrow \bar{\Psi})$ — (c), [11b], **TF**

(e) $\Diamond(\Phi\Psi)$ — (d), [1], exchange, **TF**

(f) $\Phi \underset{c}{\rightarrow} \Psi, \Diamond^{c} \Phi \vdash \Diamond(\Phi\Psi)$ — (a)-(e).

A special case of this is

(g) $\bar{\Psi} \underset{c}{\rightarrow} \bar{\Phi}, \Diamond^{c} \bar{\Psi} \vdash \Diamond(\bar{\Psi}\bar{\Phi})$.

By means of exchange and **TF** this can be extended to

(h) $\Phi \underset{c}{\rightarrow} \Psi, \sim\Box^{c} \Psi \vdash \Diamond(\bar{\Phi}\bar{\Psi})$.

By combining (f) and (h) and using definition [16a] we obtain

(i) $\Phi \underset{c}{\rightarrow} \Psi, \Diamond(\Phi\bar{\Psi}), \Diamond(\bar{\Phi}\Psi), \Diamond^{c} \Phi, \sim\Box^{c} \Phi \vdash (\Phi \underset{c}{\rightarrow} \Psi)(\Phi \bigcirc \Psi)\Diamond^{c} \Phi \sim\Box^{c} \Psi.$

The converse may be demonstrated by means of **TF** and definition [16a]. Theorem [17b] may now be proved by combining (i) with its converse, using conditional proof and applying definition [17a].

Note that lines (a)-(e) of the preceding paragraph constitute a proof from premises, as indicated in (f). For this reason lines (a)-(e) are not preceded by yield signs "$\vdash$", as are the lines of a categorical proof.

Nonparadoxical causal implication can be used to improve some of our earlier models of causal statements. The causal universal

[H″] $(x)(MxNx$ **npc** $Dx)$

is a better model of the causal law [H′] than is the formula "$(x)(MxNx \underset{c}{\rightarrow} Dx)$." Likewise "$GrAr$ **npc** Dr" is a better model of

[A] If this ring is gold (G) and should be placed in aqua regia (A), it would dissolve (D)

than the formula "$GrAr \underset{c}{\rightarrow} Dr$" given in Section 6.1.

We shall now state some theorems relating nonparadoxical causal implication (**npc**) to the other three kinds of implication: logical ($\rightarrow$), causal ($\underset{c}{\rightarrow}$), and material ($\supset$). The proofs will only be indicated. Whereas a logical conditional implies the corresponding causal conditional (theorems [11b] and [11e]), a logical conditional and the corresponding nonparadoxical causal conditional are incompatible.

[18a] $\vdash (\Phi$ **npc** $\Psi) \supset \sim(\Phi \rightarrow \Psi)$ — [16b], [17], **TF**.

It follows directly that nonparadoxical causal implication is not subject to the paradoxes of logical implication.

[18b] $\vdash (\Phi\ \mathbf{npc}\ \Psi) \supset \Diamond\Phi{\sim}\Box\Psi$ [18a], [14e], [14f], **TF**.

A nonparadoxical causal conditional does imply the corresponding causal and material conditionals.

[18c] $\vdash (\Phi\ \mathbf{npc}\ \Psi) \supset (\Phi \underset{c}{\rightarrow} \Psi)$ [17], **TF**

[18d] $\vdash (\Phi\ \mathbf{npc}\ \Psi) \supset (\Phi \supset \Psi)$ [11c], [18c], **TF**

[18e] $\vdash (\alpha)(\Phi\ \mathbf{npc}\ \Psi) \supset (\alpha)(\Phi \underset{c}{\rightarrow} \Psi)$

[18f] $\vdash (\alpha)(\Phi\ \mathbf{npc}\ \Psi) \supset (\alpha)(\Phi \supset \Psi)$.

These last two quantified forms can be proved from the preceding unquantified forms by generalization, quantifier distribution, and the primitive rule of inference.

It is of interest to ask, of a given kind of implication, whether two conditionals of the form "If Φ, then Ψ" and "If Φ, then ${\sim}\Psi$" can both be true, and whether a conditional with a logically contradictory consequent can be true. Metatheorem [15] shows that both are possible for material, causal, and logical implication. Our next metatheorems show that neither is possible for nonparadoxical causal implication.

[19a] $\vdash {\sim}[(\Phi\ \mathbf{npc}\ \Psi)(\Phi\ \mathbf{npc}\ \overline{\Psi})]$

[19b] $\vdash {\sim}(\Phi\ \mathbf{npc}\ \Psi\overline{\Psi})$.

The first of these may be proved by reductio ad absurdum.

(a) ${\sim}{\sim}[(\Phi\ \mathbf{npc}\ \Psi)(\Phi\ \mathbf{npc}\ \overline{\Psi})] \vdash (\Phi \underset{c}{\rightarrow} \Psi)(\Phi \underset{c}{\rightarrow} \overline{\Psi})$ [18c], **TF**

(b) ${\sim}{\sim}[(\Phi \underset{c}{\rightarrow} \Psi)(\Phi \underset{c}{\rightarrow} \overline{\Psi})] \vdash {\sim}\Diamond^{c}\Phi$ [15c], **TF**

(c) ${\sim}{\sim}[(\Phi\ \mathbf{npc}\ \Psi)(\Phi\ \mathbf{npc}\ \overline{\Psi})] \vdash \Diamond^{c}\Phi$ [17], **TF**.

Combining these three proofs gives

(d) ${\sim}{\sim}[(\Phi\ \mathbf{npc}\ \Psi)(\Phi\ \mathbf{npc}\ \overline{\Psi})] \vdash \Diamond^{c}\Phi{\sim}\Diamond^{c}\Phi$ (a), (b), (c), **TF**

(e) $\vdash {\sim}[(\Phi\ \mathbf{npc}\ \Psi)(\Phi\ \mathbf{npc}\ \overline{\Psi})]$ (d), reductio ad absurdum.

Metatheorem [19b] may be proved by reductio ad absurdum, [17a], [15d], and **TF**.

Metatheorem [13] states that causal implication is transitive, allows a superfluous condition to be added to the antecedent, and is subject to transposition and exportation. Nonparadoxical causal implication has these properties only under restricted conditions. These restrictions pertain to the logical modalities and the paradoxes of metatheorem [14], and they are usually satisfied in deductive inferences involving causal laws.
Weakened transitivity is expressed by

[20a] $\vdash \{\Diamond(\Phi\overline{\Theta})\Diamond(\overline{\Phi}\Theta)\} \supset \{(\Phi\ \mathbf{npc}\ \Psi)(\Psi\ \mathbf{npc}\ \Theta) \supset (\Phi\ \mathbf{npc}\ \Theta)\}$

[20b] $\vdash (\alpha)\{\Diamond(\Phi\bar{\Theta})\Diamond(\bar{\Phi}\Theta)\} \supset$
$\{(\alpha)(\Phi \textbf{ npc } \Psi)(\alpha)(\Psi \textbf{ npc } \Theta) \supset (\alpha)(\Phi \textbf{ npc } \Theta)\}$.

Weakened addition of a superfluous condition is expressed by

[20c] $\vdash \{\Diamond(\Phi\Psi\bar{\Theta})\Diamond(\overline{\Phi\Psi}\Theta)\Diamond^c(\Phi\Psi)\} \supset \{(\Phi \textbf{ npc } \Theta) \supset (\Phi\Psi \textbf{ npc } \Theta)\}$

[20d] $\vdash (\alpha)\{\Diamond(\Phi\Psi\bar{\Theta})\Diamond(\overline{\Phi\Psi}\Theta)\Diamond^c(\Phi\Psi)\} \supset$
$\{(\alpha)(\Phi \textbf{ npc } \Theta) \supset (\alpha)(\Phi\Psi \textbf{ npc } \Theta)\}$.

Weakened transposition is expressed by

[20e] $\vdash \{\Diamond[\sim(\Phi\bar{\Theta})\bar{\Psi}]\Diamond^c(\Phi\bar{\Theta})\} \supset \{(\Phi\Psi \textbf{ npc } \Theta) \supset (\Phi\bar{\Theta} \textbf{ npc } \bar{\Psi})\}$

[20f] $\vdash (\alpha)\{\Diamond[\sim(\Phi\bar{\Theta})\bar{\Psi}]\Diamond^c(\Phi\bar{\Theta})\} \supset$
$\{(\alpha)(\Phi\Psi \textbf{ npc } \Theta) \supset (\alpha)(\Phi\bar{\Theta} \textbf{ npc } \bar{\Psi})\}$.

And weakened exportation is expressed by

[20g] $\vdash \{\Diamond[\bar{\Phi}(\Psi \supset \Theta)]\Diamond^c(\Psi\bar{\Theta})\} \supset \{(\Phi\Psi \textbf{ npc } \Theta) \supset [\Phi \textbf{ npc } (\Psi \supset \Theta)]\}$

[20h] $\vdash (\alpha)\{\Diamond[\bar{\Phi}(\Psi \supset \Theta)]\Diamond^c(\Psi\bar{\Theta})\} \supset$
$\{(\alpha)(\Phi\Psi \textbf{ npc } \Theta) \supset (\alpha)\{\Phi \textbf{ npc } (\Psi \supset \Theta)\}\}$.

Note that "$\overline{\Phi\Psi}$" in [20c] and [20d] abbreviates "$\sim(\Phi\Psi)$."

The proof of weakened transitivity begins with four subordinate proofs.

(a)	$\Phi \textbf{ npc } \Psi, \Psi \textbf{ npc } \Theta \vdash (\Phi \underset{c}{\rightarrow} \Psi)(\Psi \underset{c}{\rightarrow} \Theta)$	[18c], **TF**
(b)	$(\Phi \underset{c}{\rightarrow} \Psi)(\Psi \underset{c}{\rightarrow} \Theta) \vdash \Phi \underset{c}{\rightarrow} \Theta$	[13a], **TF**
(c)	$\Phi \textbf{ npc } \Psi \vdash \Diamond^c\Phi$	[17a], **TF**
(d)	$\Psi \textbf{ npc } \Theta \vdash \sim\Box^c\,\Theta$	[17a], **TF**.

We now combine these four proofs to obtain a proof that

(e) $\Phi \textbf{ npc } \Psi, \Psi \textbf{ npc } \Theta \vdash (\Phi \underset{c}{\rightarrow} \Theta)\Diamond^c\,\Phi{\sim}\Box^c\,\Theta$ (a)-(d), **TF**.

Finally, we modify this proof to obtain a proof that

(f) $\Diamond(\Phi\bar{\Theta})\Diamond(\bar{\Phi}\Theta), \Phi \textbf{ npc } \Psi, \Psi \textbf{ npc } \Theta$
$\vdash \Phi \textbf{ npc } \Theta$ (e), [17b], **TF**.

Metatheorem [20a] now follows by conditional proof and **TF**, while [20b] follows by generalization, conditional proof, and **TF**.

The preceding proof of weakened transitivity illustrates a technique we will use frequently for building proofs from other proofs. The proof began with the four subordinate proofs of (a), (b), (c), and (d), each proof having a different set of premises. These subordinate proofs were then combined to obtain proof (e), which has premises Φ **npc** Ψ and Ψ **npc** Θ. The premise $\Diamond(\Phi\bar{\Theta})\Diamond(\bar{\Phi}\Theta)$ was added to obtain proof (f). Finally, the rule of conditional proof was applied three times to obtain a categorical proof of $\Diamond(\Phi\bar{\Theta})\Diamond(\bar{\Phi}\Theta) \supset$

$\{(\Phi\ \mathbf{npc}\ \Psi) \supset [(\Psi\ \mathbf{npc}\ \Theta) \supset (\Phi\ \mathbf{npc}\ \Theta)]\}$. Theorem [20a] then followed by **TF**.

The proof of the weakened principle for adding a superfluous condition is

(a)	$\Phi\ \mathbf{npc}\ \Theta$	$\vdash (\Phi \underset{c}{\rightarrow} \Theta){\sim}\Box^{c}\,\Theta$	[17a], **TF**
(b)	$\Phi \underset{c}{\rightarrow} \Theta$	$\vdash \Phi\Psi \underset{c}{\rightarrow} \Theta$	[13c], **TF**
(c)	$\Phi\ \mathbf{npc}\ \Theta$	$\vdash (\Phi\Psi \underset{c}{\rightarrow} \Theta){\sim}\Box^{c}\,\Theta$	(a), (b), **TF**
(d)	$\Diamond(\Phi\Psi\overline{\Theta})\Diamond(\overline{\Psi\Phi}\Theta),\ \Diamond^{c}(\Phi\Psi),\ \Phi\ \mathbf{npc}\ \Theta$	$\vdash \Phi\Psi\ \mathbf{npc}\ \Theta$	(c), [17b], **TF**.

Metatheorem [20c] now follows by conditional proof and **TF**, while [20d] follows by generalization, conditional proof, and **TF**.

The proof of weakened transposition is

(a)	$\Phi\Psi\ \mathbf{npc}\ \Theta$	$\vdash (\Phi\Psi \underset{c}{\rightarrow} \Theta)\Diamond^{c}(\Phi\Psi)$	[17a], **TF**
(b)	$\Phi\Psi \underset{c}{\rightarrow} \Theta$	$\vdash \Phi\overline{\Theta} \underset{c}{\rightarrow} \overline{\Psi}$	[13e], **TF**
(c)	$\Diamond^{c}(\Phi\Psi)$	$\vdash {\sim}\Box^{c}\,\overline{\Psi}$	[1d], [10d], exchange, **TF**
(d)	$\Phi\Psi\ \mathbf{npc}\ \Theta$	$\vdash (\Phi\overline{\Theta} \underset{c}{\rightarrow} \overline{\Psi}){\sim}\Box^{c}\,\overline{\Psi}$	(a)-(c), **TF**
(e)	$\Phi\Psi\ \mathbf{npc}\ \Theta$	$\vdash \Diamond(\Phi\overline{\Theta}{\sim}{\sim}\Psi)$	[17b], **TF**, exchange
(f)	$\Diamond[{\sim}(\Phi\overline{\Theta})\overline{\Psi}],\ \Diamond^{c}(\Phi\overline{\Theta}),\ \Phi\Psi\ \mathbf{npc}\ \Theta$	$\vdash \Phi\overline{\Theta}\ \mathbf{npc}\ \overline{\Psi}$	(d), (e), [17b], **TF**.

Metatheorem [20e] now follows by conditional proof and **TF**, while [20f] follows by generalization, conditional proof, and **TF**.

The proof of weakened exportation is

(a)	$\Phi\Psi\ \mathbf{npc}\ \Theta$	$\vdash (\Phi\Psi \underset{c}{\rightarrow} \Theta)\Diamond^{c}(\Phi\Psi)$	[17a], **TF**
(b)	$\Phi\Psi \underset{c}{\rightarrow} \Theta$	$\vdash \Phi \underset{c}{\rightarrow} (\Psi \supset \Theta)$	[13g], **TF**
(c)	$\Diamond^{c}(\Phi\Psi)$	$\vdash \Diamond^{c}\,\Phi$	[10d]
(d)	$\Phi\Psi\ \mathbf{npc}\ \Theta$	$\vdash [\Phi \underset{c}{\rightarrow} (\Psi \supset \Theta)]\Diamond^{c}\,\Phi$	(a)-(c), **TF**
(e)	$\Diamond^{c}(\Psi\overline{\Theta})$	$\vdash {\sim}\Box^{c}\,(\Psi \supset \Theta)$	[1d], exchange, **TF**
(f)	$\Phi\Psi\ \mathbf{npc}\ \Theta$	$\vdash \Diamond[\Phi(\overline{\Psi \supset \Theta})]$	[17b], **TF**, exchange
(g)	$\Diamond[\overline{\Phi}(\Psi \supset \Theta)],\ \Diamond^{c}(\Psi\overline{\Theta}),\ \Phi\Psi\ \mathbf{npc}\ \Theta$	$\vdash \Phi\ \mathbf{npc}\ (\Psi \supset \Theta)$	(d)-(f), [17b], **TF**.

Metatheorem [20g] now follows by conditional proof and **TF**, while [20h] follows by generalization, conditional proof, and **TF**.

Let us now illustrate and discuss some of these metatheorems. Consider exportation first. The formula $\Phi \underset{c}{\rightarrow} (\Psi \supset \Theta)$ may be validly derived from

$\Phi\Psi \underset{c}{\rightarrow} \Theta$ by the exportation principle [13g]. Similarly, Φ **npc** $(\Psi \supset \Theta)$ follows from $\Phi\Psi$ **npc** Θ, together with two added conditions, by weakened exportation [20g]. Note that the final implication of both $\Phi \underset{c}{\rightarrow} (\Psi \supset \Theta)$ and Φ **npc** $(\Psi \supset \Theta)$ is material. This is crucial, for neither of the principles

$$[I_1] \qquad (\Phi\Psi \underset{c}{\rightarrow} \Theta) \supset [\Phi \supset (\Psi \underset{c}{\rightarrow} \Theta)]$$

$$[I_2] \qquad \{\Diamond[\overline{\Phi}(\Psi \supset \Theta)]\Diamond^c(\Psi\overline{\Theta})\} \supset \{(\Phi\Psi \ \mathbf{npc}\ \Theta) \supset [\Phi \supset (\Psi \ \mathbf{npc}\ \Theta)]$$

is a logical truth. To see this, rewrite the first in the form $\Box^c(\Phi\Psi \supset \Theta) \supset [\Phi \supset \Box^c(\Psi \supset \Theta)]$. It might be the case that $\Phi\Psi \supset \Theta$ is true in all causally possible universes, Φ is true in the actual universe, and $\Psi \supset \Theta$ is false in some causally possible universe. This shows that $[I_1]$ is not a logical truth. A slightly more complicated argument shows that $[I_2]$ is not a logical truth.

We illustrate $[I_2]$ with a fallacious argument about the ring that was almost dropped in aqua regia

(a)	$Gr\,Ar$ **npc** Dr	Premise
(b)	$\Diamond[\overline{Gr}(Ar \supset Dr)]$	Premise
(c)	$\Diamond^c(Ar\,\overline{Dr})$	Premise
(d)	$Gr \supset (Ar$ **npc** $Dr)$	INVALID exportation from (a)-(c) by $[I_2]$
(e)	Gr	Premise
(f)	Ar **npc** Dr	(d), (e), **TF.**

Suppose that the ring is in fact gold, so that all four premises are true. The conclusion is nevertheless false, for placing an object in aqua regia is not causally sufficient to make it dissolve; it is required also that the object be composed of a suitable material, e.g., gold or silver. Hence the argument is invalid.

Though the causal conditional "*Ar* **npc** *Dr*" is false, the subjunctive "If the ring should be placed in aqua regia, it would dissolve" is true. It is a true causal subjunctive in which the antecedent does not explicitly contain conditions sufficient to bring about the consequent. We discuss the symbolization of such elliptical causal subjunctives in the next section (sec. 7.3.3).

Thus a nonparadoxical causal conditional $\Phi\Psi$ **npc** Θ is true only when the antecedent $\Phi\Psi$ contains conditions causally sufficient for Θ. If the conditions expressed in the antecedent of a nonparadoxical causal conditional are not causally sufficient to make the consequent true, the causal conditional is false; and even if it is believed now, it will, in all probability, be rejected or revised someday. Similarly, if exceptions are found to a principle that is thought to be a causal law, that principle must be revised or regarded as only an approximation to the truth.

On the other hand, $\Phi\Psi$ **npc** Θ may be true even though Φ **npc** Θ is also true, so that the condition Ψ is superfluous. An example is

[J] $(x)(MxNxWx$ **npc** $Dx)$,

which results from adding the condition "is near a wooden rod (W)" to the causal law that a magnetic field deflects an electron moving perpendicular to it. The argument

$(x)(MxNx$ **npc** $Dx)$

$(x)(MxNxWx \bigcirc Dx)$

$(x)\Diamond^c (MxNxWx)$

$\therefore (x)(MxNxWx$ **npc** $Dx)$

is valid by [20d] and **TF**, and it has true premises. Hence its conclusion is true, even though this conclusion contains the causally superfluous and irrelevant condition "Wx."

Consider now the statement

[J′] *It is a causal law that* an electron moving in a vacuum perpendicular to a magnetic field (M), subject to no other forces (N) and near a wooden rod (W), is deflected (D).

While the unitalicized part of [J′] is true, it does not express a causal law, because the wooden rod is not causally relevant to the behavior of the electron. Consequently, formula [J] is not a good model of the natural language statement [J′]. A similar point can be made about "$(x)\{MxNx$ **npc** $(Dx \vee Wx)\}$," which contains the causally irrelevant disjunct "Wx" in its consequent.

We next define a notion, "nonsuperfluous causal implication (**nsc**)," that excludes these irrelevant factors from antecedent and consequent. $(\Phi_1\Phi_2 \ldots \Phi_N)$ **nsc** $(\Psi_1 \vee \Psi_2 \vee \ldots \vee \Psi_M)$ if and only if (1) $(\Phi_1\Phi_2 \ldots \Phi_N)$ **npc** $(\Psi_1 \vee \Psi_2 \vee \ldots \vee \Psi_M)$, and (2) the result of striking out any disjunct of $\Box^c (\overline{\Phi}_1 \vee \ldots \vee \overline{\Phi}_N \vee \Psi_1 \vee \ldots \vee \Psi_M)$ is false.

This formal notion of nonsuperfluous causal implication is of limited interest, however, because the elimination of irrelevant causal factors cannot be completely formalized. There is nothing in our formal system to prevent one from interpreting the predicate "A" of "$(x)(Ax$ **npc** $Dx)$" so that it includes a large number of superfluous causal conditions. For example, one might interpret "A" to mean "is an electron moving in a vacuum perpendicular to a magnetic field, subject to no other forces, near a wooden rod, and near a desk that is of such and such size and shape and is five feet from an individual with such and such a history." In this case, the result of striking out either disjunct of "$\Box^c (\overline{Ax} \vee Dx)$" is false, and so from a formal point of view "$(x)(Ax$ **npc** $Dx)$" contains no causally irrelevant factors. Note in this connection that "$(Ad\ \mathbf{npc}\ Cd) \equiv (Ad\ \mathbf{nsc}\ Cd)$" is a theorem, following directly from the definitions; nonsuperfluous causal implication is stronger than nonparadoxical causal implication only when the antecedent has more than one conjunct or the consequent has more than one disjunct.

Actually, the elimination of causally irrelevant predicates from a statement is only part of the task of characterizing a more basic property of causal laws: their foundational role in the corpus of scientific results and conclusions. Only the most general and fundamental causal statements are causal laws or laws of nature. And these two properties are relative to the state of development of a science, for the most general and fundamental laws of one era are often derivable from more basic laws of a later era. For example, refinements of Kepler's three laws of planetary motion and of Galileo's law of falling bodies may be deduced from Newton's three laws of motion, Newton's law of universal gravitation, and some empirical facts about the planets.

The foundational role laws play in science is somewhat analogous to the foundational role axioms play in a formal system, but there are essential differences because science is not a formalized discipline. Even if it were possible to formalize all of science at any given stage, it would be impossible to construct a single interpreted formal language that would serve for all science through all time. The truly revolutionary developments in science involve the invention of basically new concepts, and these require a fundamentally new language for their expression. Some examples are: Newton's idea that uniform rectilinear motion is natural and needs no explanation, the combined space-time of Einstein's special theory of relativity, and some of the quantum theoretical concepts associated with Heisenberg's uncertainty principle. Thus the requirement that a scientific law be sufficiently general and basic is very difficult, if not impossible, to formalize, and hence it should be treated informally, outside of our formalism (see sec. 1.6.2).

In the present subsection we have modeled many important features of causal laws by means of nonparadoxical causal implication (**npc**). In subsequent subsections we will use nonparadoxical causal implication to model causal subjunctives, causal dispositions, and deterministic cause-effect relations.

7.3 Subjunctives and Dispositions

7.3.1 Causal modalities and subjunctives

An essential feature of laws of nature, causal laws, and lawlike statements is that, in appropriate contexts, they imply counterfactual conditionals expressed in the subjunctive mood. We shall model this phenomenon in the logic of causal statements.

Because the logic of the causal subjunctive is rather complicated, we develop it by stages. The present section covers the nonelliptical case (sec. 7.3.1), the elliptical use of a subjunctive to express a disposition (sec. 7.3.2), and then elliptical subjunctives generally (sec. 7.3.3). The next section will treat some aspects of the subjunctive connected to the cause-effect relation (sec. 7.4.1) and the relation of a subjunctive to its context (sec. 7.4.2).

Consider the following argument, in which the major premise is intended to express a causal law.

All gold (*G*) objects dissolve (*D*) in aqua regia (*A*)
This ring (*r*) is not a gold object in aqua regia
Therefore, if this ring had been a gold object in aqua regia,
  it would have dissolved.

The minor premise states that "*GrAr*" is false in the actual world. The use of the subjunctive in the conclusion signifies that the conclusion is about causally possible, nonactual universes in which "*GrAr*" is true. The subjunctive clause "This ring had been a gold object in aqua regia" is not a sentence, but by treating it as if it were we can use our already developed logic to symbolize the argument. The result is

$(x)(GxAx \textbf{ npc } Dx)$

$\sim(GrAr)$

$\therefore \sim(GrAr)(GrAr \textbf{ npc } Dr)$.

This formalized argument is valid by universal instantiation and **TF**.

Compare the following invalid argument, in which the major premise expresses an accidental fact about the world.

All the books (*B*) on that desk (*D*) are in Italian (*I*)
This (*t*) is not a book on that desk
Therefore, if this had been a book on that desk,
  it would have been in Italian.

This argument may be symbolized

$(x)(BxDx \supset Ix)$

$\sim(BtDt)$

$\therefore \sim(BtDt)(BtDt \textbf{ npc } It)$.

This formalized argument is invalid, because the material universal "$(x)(BxDx \supset Ix)$" is entirely about the actual world and says nothing about any possible nonactual world. It is easy to show this argument to be invalid by constructing an abstract model: let the actual universe be $Bt\overline{Dt}\overline{It}$ and let there be one other causally possible universe $BtDt\overline{It}$ (see sec. 6.3).

These two arguments, the one valid and the other invalid, bring out the essential difference between a causal universal $(\alpha)(\phi\alpha \textbf{ npc } \psi\alpha)$ and the corresponding material universal $(\alpha)(\phi\alpha \supset \psi\alpha)$.* Under contrary-to-fact conditions the causal universal implies a contrary-to-fact conditional, while the material universal does not. By metatheorem [18f], a causal universal implies the corresponding material universal. Hence the causal universal $(\alpha)(\phi\alpha$ **npc** $\psi\alpha)$ is definitely stronger than the corresponding material universal $(\alpha)(\phi\alpha \supset \psi\alpha)$.

The foregoing discussion shows that the causal modalities are closely connected to the subjunctive mood. This is an important but complicated connection, which we shall be discussing at a number of places in the remainder of this chapter.

In some cases the relations between the subjunctive and the causal modalities are straightforward. The conclusions of the two preceding arguments should be symbolized with nonparadoxical causal implication rather than with material implication because of the subjunctive "would." The causal universal "$(x)(GxAx$ **npc** $Dx)$" may properly be translated into the subjunctive "If a gold object should be placed in aqua regia, it would dissolve." In contrast, the material universal "$(x)(BxDx \supset Ix)$" should not be translated into a subjunctive but into a declarative sentence.

Other cases are more complicated. The correct treatment of an indicative statement such as "All gold objects dissolve in aqua regia" depends very much on the context. In the argument given earlier we intended this sentence to express a causal connection and hence symbolized it "$(x)(GxAx$ **npc** $Dx)$." But one might intend it to assert only that all gold objects that have been, are, or will be put in aqua regia did or will in fact dissolve, saying nothing about what would have happened or would happen in any contrary-to-fact case. If so, it should be symbolized "$(x)(GxAx \supset Dx)$." On each of these interpretations the relation of the indicative "All gold objects dissolve in aqua regia" to the subjunctive "If this gold ring should be placed in aqua regia, it would dissolve" is clear. The causal universal "$(x)(GxAx$ **npc** $Dx)$" definitely implies "$GrAr$ **npc** Dr," whereas the material universal "$(x)(GxAx \supset Dx)$" definitely does not.

Now one can utter "All gold objects dissolve in aqua regia" without being clear as to whether the subjunctive is or is not implied. In this case, neither "valid" nor "invalid" correctly applies to this argument

All gold objects dissolve in aqua regia
Therefore, if this gold ring should be placed in aqua regia,
it would dissolve.

The usage is vague and unclear at this point; neither "$(x)(GxAx$ **npc** $Dx)$"

* Lowercase Greek letters were used in chap. 6 as metalinguistic variables ranging over the individual and predicate variables of our formal language. Hereafter lowercase Greek letters will range over complex predicates as well. Thus "$(x)(GxAx$ **npc** $Dx)$" is of the form $(\alpha)(\phi\alpha$ **npc** $\psi\alpha)$.

nor "$(x)(GxAx \supset Dx)$" is a good model of "All gold objects dissolve in aqua regia."

The idea of a deductive argument being neither valid nor invalid because it is vague deserves some discussion, for vagueness involves borderline cases in an essential way.* Consider the word "bald," and imagine that Adams understands the word and also has full information about the hair on Black's head. If Black has lots of hair, or none at all, Adams will know whether or not to call Black bald. But if the amount of hair on Black's head falls in the ill-defined border area between "bald" and "non-bald," Adams will be unable to decide whether or not Black is bald. This indecision results from the essential vagueness of the term "bald," and not from a lack of empirical information about Black's head or a failure to understand the word "bald."

Another vague term is "some." Logicians always treat "some" in its numerical sense as if it meant precisely "at least one." In ordinary language "some" often connotes "more than one," though exactly how many is unclear. For example, the sentence "Some people voted for the motion" might be uttered in a situation where the following truth-conditions apply: if only one person voted for the motion, the sentence is false; if four or more voted for the motion, the sentence is true; while if only two people voted for the motion, it is uncertain whether the sentence is true or false. Now, if the truth-status of a sentence is uncertain, the validity-status of arguments containing it may also be uncertain. Thus in the situation just described, the argument

> Exactly two people voted for the motion
> Therefore, some people voted for the motion

does not have a definite validity-status.

Now suppose that identity ("=") is added to the logic of causal statements, so that quantitative statements can be expressed. "There are at least two V's" may be symbolized "$(\exists x)(\exists y)[VxVy \sim(x = y)]$," and "There are exactly two V's" may be symbolized

$$(\exists x)(\exists y)\{VxVy \sim(x = y)(z)[Vz \supset (z = x \text{ v } z = y)]\}\quad.$$

How shall "Some people voted for the motion" be symbolized in this extended language? Because every symbolization will be numerically precise, there is no sentence of the formal language that captures or models the vagueness of the ordinary language sentence "Some people voted for the motion."

Subjunctives are often vague with respect to their counterfactual thrust. Take "If her gold ring had been dropped in aqua regia, it would have dissolved" as an example. In certain contexts it implies that the ring was not in fact dropped into aqua regia, and there it is counterfactual. But a detec-

* See my "Empiricism and Vagueness."

tive, in solving a crime, might assert "If her gold ring had been dropped in aqua regia, it would have dissolved" to help him decide whether or not the ring was destroyed; in this case the sentence is not counterfactual. And in other contexts the counterfactual status of "If her gold ring had been dropped in aqua regia, it would have dissolved" is vague.

Precision does not necessarily make a formal language superior to an informal one, however. Vague terms are generally more easily applied than their precise analogues. Terms like "some," "many," "high," and "bald" are so useful just because they are vague.

We saw that in certain circumstances vagueness does not affect the truth-status of a sentence. Thus "Some people voted for the motion" is clearly false if no one voted for it. Similarly, the vagueness of an argument may not affect its validity status. For example, the argument

All gold objects dissolve in aqua regia
This gold ring will be placed in aqua regia
Therefore, this gold ring will dissolve

is valid even if it is unclear whether the major premise implies a subjunctive. Correspondingly, both of the formal arguments

$(x)(GxAx \ \mathbf{npc}\ Dx)$	$(x)(GxAx \supset Dx)$
$GrAr$	$GrAr$
$\therefore Dr$	$\therefore Dr$

are valid in the logic of causal statements.

Let us summarize our conclusions concerning the modal status of the nonsubjunctive "All gold objects dissolve in aqua regia." In certain contexts it is well modeled by the causal universal "$(x)(GxAx \ \mathbf{npc}\ Dx)$," and in others by the material universal "$(x)(GxAx \supset Dx)$"; while in still other contexts the sentence is vague with respect to the difference between a causal and a material universal, and neither model will do. Corresponding possibilities often occur regarding declarative statements, such as the usual formulations of scientific and causal laws.

Scientific discourse is generally vague with respect to its modal status. Nevertheless, scientific practice and inference do reflect modal distinctions. A scientist does sometimes draw subjunctive conclusions from his premises, and he frequently applies his laws to possible situations that he knows may never be realized. As we shall see in Chapter 10, modal distinctions influence his inductive inferences as well as his deductive inferences.

Though scientific practice and inference reflect modal distinctions, the modalities need not appear explicitly in scientific statements. That is, the scientist need not explicitly think of or label his statements as causally necessary or as not causally necessary. I think he is properly vague on this point, since the problem of modality is not a scientific problem, but a philosophical problem about science.

Let us now summarize the results of the present subsection. In appropriate contexts, laws of nature, causal laws, and lawlike statements imply subjunctive conditionals, counterfactual or noncounterfactual. Causal necessity is needed to model the latter, and hence the former. This is so even though the modal status of ordinary and scientific discourse is often vague.

*7.3.2. Causal dispositions**

We next use nonparadoxical causal implication (**npc**) to model causal dispositional statements. Causal dispositions are of interest in their own right and also because of their similarity to probabilistic dispositions (sec. 8.2.2).

Consider again the laboratory assistant's ring (p. 338) and assume that it is in fact made of gold. Since gold is soluble in aqua regia, it is true that

[L] Her ring is soluble in aqua regia.

We call [L] a *causal dispositional*. Other examples of causal dispositionals are "*a* is inflammable," "*b* is malleable," and "*c* is excitable." Dispositions in this wide sense include powers, potentialities, capacities, latencies, and abilities insofar as these are deterministic rather than probabilistic.

Statement [L] is synonymous, or nearly synonymous, with the subjunctive

[L′] Her ring is such that, if it were placed in aqua regia, it would dissolve.

Though the basis of this sentence's being true is that the ring is made of gold, the sentence does not explicitly mention gold, and it would also be true if the ring were made of silver or platinum. This suggests modeling [L] and [L′] by

[L″] Her ring (r) possesses a property X such that $XrAr$ **npc** Dr,

which is symbolized with an existential predicate quantifier

[L‴] $(\exists X)[Xr(XrAr \textbf{ npc } Dr)]$.

Of course, more than one quantifier may be required, as in symbolizing "The ring would dissolve in this liquid."

The formal system of the previous chapter does not allow predicate variables to be quantified. Consequently, formulas representing causal dispositions and arguments involving these formulas do not belong to that system. The same holds for formulas containing statement quantifiers, e.g., [21b] below. For the reasons given on page 344, we shall handle the quantifi-

* See, besides my "Dispositional Statements," Pap's "Disposition Concepts and Extensional Logic" and Sellars' "Counterfactuals, Dispositions, and the Causal Modalities."

cation of predicates and statements informally and by analogy to the quantification of individual variables. In each specific case of an inference involving a predicate or statement quantifier, it will be intuitively clear that the inference is valid. Hereafter, the name "logic of causal statements" will be used both for the formal system and for this informal extension of it, but the yields sign "$\vdash$" will always be restricted to the former.

As an illustration let us derive the causal dispositional "Her ring is soluble in aqua regia" from the premises "Gold dissolves in aqua regia" and "Her ring is gold."

(a)	$(x)(GxAx$ **npc** $Dx)$	Premise
(b)	Gr	Premise
(c)	$GrAr$ **npc** Dr	(a), universal instantiation
(d)	$Gr(GrAr$ **npc** $Dr)$	(b), (c), **TF**
(e)	$(\exists X)[Xr(XrAr$ **npc** $Dr)]$	(d), existential generalization of the predicate "*G*."

The last step is taken by means of the analogue of theorem [12] for an existential predicate quantifier. In theorem [12] the assertion that a particular individual has a property implies that there is at least one individual having that property. Similarly, the assertion that the property *G* satisfies a certain condition implies that there is at least one property satisfying the following condition:

$$Gr(GrAr \textbf{ npc } Dr) \supset (\exists X)[Xr(XrAr \textbf{ npc } Dr)]$$

This formula expresses a logical truth, so that the passage from (d) to (e) by means of it is valid. The corresponding mode of inference for individual symbols is called "existential generalization" (p. 411); accordingly we call this mode of inference ***existential generalization of a predicate.***

A converse principle of inference is used in the argument from "Her ring is soluble in aqua regia" to the material conditional "If her ring is placed in aqua regia, it will dissolve."

(a)	$(\exists X)[Xr(XrAr$ **npc** $Dr)]$	Premise
(b)	$Yr(YrAr$ **npc** $Dr)$	(a), existential instantiation of the predicate "*X*"
(c)	$YrAr \supset Dr$	(b), [18d], **TF**
(d)	Yr	(b), **TF**
(e)	$Ar \supset Dr$	(c), (d), **TF**.

The premise (a) states that there exists a property *X* satisfying a certain condition. The premise does not tell us what this property is; for example, whether or not the ring is made of platinum. But since it is given that the property exists, we can "name" it by an arbitrary predicate symbol ("Y") that has *not* already occurred free in the argument.* The corresponding mode of inference for individual symbols is called "existential instantiation," and we call this mode of inference *existential instantiation of a predicate.*

Let us now see what is expressed by a causal dispositional formula, using "$(\exists X)[Xr(XrAr\ \mathbf{npc}\ Dr)]$" as an example. This formula is true because the laboratory assistant's ring is in fact made of gold (Gr). It would also be true if the ring were made of silver or platinum, for silver and platinum are also soluble in aqua regia. An important feature of the dispositional formula "$(\exists X)[Xr(XrAr\ \mathbf{npc}\ Dr)]$" is that it leaves all of these possibilities open. If one knows that the ring is soluble in aqua regia, he knows that the ring has some property X satisfying the causal condition $XrAr$ **npc** Dr, but he need not know what property this is. Thus it is an essential feature of a causal dispositional that it asserts the existence of a property without identifying that property explicitly. A good model must preserve this feature, and so neither "Gr" nor "$Gr(x)(GxAx\ \mathbf{npc}\ Dx)$" is a good model of "Her ring is soluble in aqua regia."

If the laboratory assistant's ring were placed in aqua regia, it would dissolve; and one could properly say that the ring dissolved *because* it was made of gold. An object might dissolve in aqua regia because it was made of gold, or because it was made of silver, etc. We call the properties by virtue of which an object would dissolve if placed in aqua regia *the properties underlying the disposition* "soluble in aqua regia." Sometimes the properties underlying a disposition are known, and sometimes they are not. Chemists know many properties underlying the disposition "soluble in aqua regia." But psychologists and physiologists do not know the properties of mind or matter (or both) underlying the psychological disposition of excitability.

Later we shall see that changes of dispositions are changes in the properties underlying the dispositions, not changes in the governing causal laws (pp. 572-73).

We have used the form $(\exists\phi)[\phi\alpha(\phi\alpha\psi\alpha\ \mathbf{npc}\ \theta\alpha)]$ to model causal dispositionals. It is not the case, however, that every formula of this form represents a causal disposition, as an example will make clear. Suppose p is a paperweight that is to be placed in aqua regia. We then have

(a)	Ap	Premise
(b)	$(x)(GxAx\ \mathbf{npc}\ Dx)$	Premise

* This restriction is needed because the use of a predicate symbol that has already occurred free in the argument may lead to contradiction. For example, if we also had the premise "The ring (r) is not made of platinum ($\sim P$)" and we used "P" instead of "Y" in line (b), we could infer both "Pr" and "$\sim Pr$."

(c)	$GxAx \equiv AxGx$	**TF**
(d)	$(x)(GxAx$ **npc** $Dx) \equiv (x)(AxGx$ **npc** $Dx)$	(c), exchange
(e)	$(x)(AxGx$ **npc** $Dx)$	(b), (d), **TF**
(f)	$ApGp$ **npc** Dp	(e), universal instantiation
(g)	$Ap(ApGp$ **npc** $Dp)$	(a), (c), **TF**
(h)	$(\exists X)[Xp(XpGp$ **npc** $Dp)]$	(d), existential generalization of the predicate "A."

The conclusion may be translated into the noncounterfactual subjunctive "If this paperweight were gold, it would dissolve." Since both premises are true and the argument is valid, the conclusion is true. But though the conclusion "$(\exists X)[Xp(XpGp$ **npc** $Dp)]$" is of the form $(\exists\phi)[\phi\alpha(\phi\alpha\psi\alpha$ **npc** $\theta\alpha)]$, it and the corresponding subjunctive clearly do not attribute a dispositional property to the paperweight; the reason for this is to be found in the nature of the properties involved in a disposition and in their interrelations, particularly in the nature of the properties underlying a disposition.

There are three properties to consider in connection with the causal dispositional "Her ring is soluble in aqua regia"; namely, being made of gold, being in aqua regia, and dissolving. These properties differ in important ways. The material constitution, e.g., being made of gold, of an object is relatively stable and enduring; it is generally characteristic of a thing over long periods of time, and while a thing may change its constitution, e.g., gold may be transmuted, it is relatively difficult to make it do so. In contrast, the property of being in aqua regia is more transient, generally being possessed by a thing in only a few of its states. The same is true of the process of dissolving, something that happens to the ring over a relatively short span of time. We may summarize this difference by saying that "being made of gold" is an *enduring property* while "being in aqua regia" and "dissolving" are *transient properties*.

The enduring property "being made of gold" underlies the ring's disposition to dissolve in aqua regia. Thus the dispositional statement "This ring is soluble in aqua regia" attributes an enduring property to an object, characterizing this property indirectly by means of transient properties. Accordingly, the expression

[M] $(\exists X)\{Xr(XrAr$ **npc** $Dr)(X$ is an enduring property$)\}$

is a better model of "This ring is soluble in aqua regia" than our earlier formula "$(\exists X)[Xr(XrAr$ **npc** $Dr)]$."

More generally, a causal dispositional statement should be modeled by the form

[M′] $(\exists\phi)\{\phi\alpha(\phi\alpha\psi\alpha$ **npc** $\theta\alpha)(\phi$ is an enduring property$)\}$, where ψ and θ designate transient properties. The individual variable α designates the object to which the disposition is attributed. The dispositional formula attributes an enduring property to the object by means of the quantified predicate variable ϕ. This enduring property is not explicitly mentioned but is characterized by way of its causal connection to the transient properties designated by the predicates ψ and θ.

A property that underlies a disposition is on a more basic level than the transient properties used to characterize it. Often a hierarchy of properties underlie a given disposition, with some of the properties lying on deeper levels than others. Thus the following three properties underlie the ring's disposition to dissolve in aqua regia: "being made of gold," the atomic structure of gold, and the complex of atomic features that are responsible for gold, silver, and platinum all dissolving in aqua regia. Each of these three properties lies on a deeper level than the preceding one. Two points should be noted about such a hierarchy of properties. First, the levels of a hierarchy are closely related to our earlier informal requirement that a scientific law be sufficiently general and fundamental (pp. 434-35); the law that all objects of such-and-such atomic structure dissolve in aqua regia is more basic than the law that gold dissolves in aqua regia. Second, a property underlying a disposition may itself be dispositional; in this event a model of the original disposition may contain causal modalities applied to causal modalities (see sec. 7.5.1).

The foregoing characterization of the difference between an enduring and a transient property is clearly informal and is not expressible in the logic of causal statements, at least in any direct way. We therefore conclude: The causal modalities play an essential role in causal dispositional statements, but these statements also have essential informal aspects.

7.3.3 *Elliptical causal implication*

In our discussion of dispositions we used the pattern $(\exists\phi)[\phi\alpha(\phi\alpha\psi\alpha \mathbf{\ npc\ } \theta\alpha)]$ as a model for causal subjunctives of the form "If it should be the case that $\psi\alpha$, then it would be the case that $\theta\alpha$," where the conditions mentioned in the antecedent are not causally sufficient to make the consequent true. Since most subjunctives take such an elliptical form, the pattern $(\exists\phi)[\phi\alpha(\phi\alpha\psi\alpha \mathbf{\ npc\ } \theta\alpha)]$ has a wide application. For this reason, we symbolize and name the kind of implication expressed by that pattern. *Elliptical causal implication* (**ec**) is defined by

[21a] $\psi\alpha \mathbf{\ ec\ } \theta\alpha =_{\mathrm{df}} (\exists\phi)[\phi\alpha(\phi\alpha\psi\alpha \mathbf{\ npc\ } \theta\alpha)]$

[21b] $\Psi \mathbf{\ ec\ } \Theta =_{\mathrm{df}} (\exists\Phi)[\Phi(\Phi\Psi \mathbf{\ npc\ } \Theta)]$.

In order to simplify symbolizations and proofs, we have given the definition of **ec** in two forms, the first having a predicate quantifier and the second having a statement quantifier. We manipulate statement quantifiers in the same way we manipulate predicate quantifiers, using the rules *existential generalization of a statement* and *existential instantiation of a statement* in place of the corresponding rules for predicate quantifiers (pp. 441-42).

Let us now formally compare elliptical causal implication (**ec**) with causal implication ($\underset{c}{\rightarrow}$) and non-paradoxical causal implication (**npc**). First, all three types of implication are stronger than material implication.

[22] $(\Psi\ \mathbf{ec}\ \Theta) \supset (\Psi \supset \Theta)$.

Compare [11c] and [18d].

The proof of metatheorem [22] is

(a)	$\Psi\ \mathbf{ec}\ \Theta$	Premise
(b)	$(\exists\Phi)[\Phi(\Phi\Psi\ \mathbf{npc}\ \Theta)]$	(a), [21]
(c)	$\Lambda(\Lambda\Psi\ \mathbf{npc}\ \Theta)$	(b), existential instantiation of the statement
(d)	$(\Lambda\Psi\ \mathbf{npc}\ \Theta) \supset (\Lambda\Psi \supset \Theta)$	[18d]
(e)	$\Psi \supset \Theta$	(c), (d), **TF**.

The theorem now follows by conditional proof.

Causal implication is transitive. In contrast, nonparadoxical and elliptical causal implication are transitive only under certain conditions (cf. [13a] with [20a]).

An elliptical causal implication Ψ **ec** Θ differs from a corresponding non-paradoxical causal implication $\Phi\Psi$ **npc** Θ in the status of the clause Φ, which is explicit in the latter conditional but implicit in the former. This difference leads to further interesting differences with respect to exportation and the compatibility of conditionals that have the same antecedent but contradictory consequents. We shall establish the relevant theorems for **ec** and compare them with the corresponding theorems for other types of implication; these comparisons are summarized in Table 21.

Consider exportation first. Going from left to right in metatheorem [13g], we have

$$(\Phi\Psi \underset{c}{\rightarrow} \Theta) \supset [\Phi \underset{c}{\rightarrow} (\Psi \supset \Theta)] \quad .$$

Note that the final implication of this metatheorem is material. This is essential, for the principle

$$(\Phi\Psi \underset{c}{\rightarrow} \Theta) \supset [\Phi \supset (\Psi \underset{c}{\rightarrow} \Theta)]$$

is false. It is false because the final antecedent Ψ may not contain conditions that are causally sufficient for Θ. Similar remarks hold for non-paradoxical causal implication; see metatheorem [20g] and the discussion following its proof. In contrast, elliptical causal implication is exportable in a strong

TABLE 21

COMPARISON OF FIVE KINDS OF IMPLICATION

Kind of implication		Are these expressions theorems when "if . . . then . . ." is replaced by the given implication symbol?		
Name	Symbol	[if ΦΨ, then Θ] ⊃ [Φ ⊃ (if Ψ, then Θ)]	∼[(if Ψ, then Θ) (if Ψ, then $\bar{\Theta}$)]	∼(if Ψ, then Θ$\bar{\Theta}$)
Material	⊃	Yes	No	No
Logical	→	No	No	No
Causal	$\underset{c}{\rightarrow}$	No	No	No
Non-paradoxical causal	**npc**	No	Yes	Yes
Elliptical causal	**ec**	Yes	No	Yes

sense. Moreover, nonparadoxical causal implication may be "exported" to become elliptical causal implication.

[23a] (ΦΨ **ec** Θ) ⊃ {Φ ⊃ (Ψ **ec** Θ)}

[23b] (ΦΨ **npc** Θ) ⊃ {Φ ⊃ (Ψ **ec** Θ)}

The proof of metatheorem [23a] is

(a)	ΦΨ **ec** Θ	Premise
(b)	(∃Γ)[Γ(ΓΦΨ **npc** Θ)]	(a), [21]
(c)	Λ(ΛΦΨ **npc** Θ)	(b), existential instantiation of the statement Γ
(d)	Φ	Premise
(e)	(ΛΦ)(ΛΦΨ **npc** Θ)	(c), (d), **TF**
(f)	(∃Γ)[Γ(ΓΨ **npc** Θ)]	(e), existential generalization of the statement ΛΦ
(g)	Ψ **ec** Θ	(f), [21].

The theorem now follows by conditional proof.

The formula Ψ **ec** Θ may be derived from ΦΨ **npc** Θ and Φ by **TF**, existential generalization of the statement Φ, and definition [21]. Metatheorem [23b] then follows by conditional proof.

Finally, let us compare our three types of causal implication ($\underset{c}{\rightarrow}$, **npc**, **ec**) in regard to the questions: Can the conditionals "If Ψ, then Θ" and "If Ψ, then ∼Θ" both be true? Can a conditional with a logically contradictory consequent be true? For plain causal implication ($\underset{c}{\rightarrow}$), both answers are "yes" (metatheorems [15c] and [15d]). For nonparadoxical causal implication (**npc**), both answers are "no" (metatheorems [19a] and [19b]). And for elliptical causal implication, the answers are "only if a certain condition is satisfied" and "no", respectively.

[24a] $\{(\Psi \textbf{ ec } \Theta)(\Psi \textbf{ ec } \bar{\Theta})\} \supset (\exists\Lambda)\{\Lambda \sim\Diamond^c(\Lambda\Psi)\}$

[24b] $\{(\psi\alpha \textbf{ ec } \theta\alpha)(\psi\alpha \textbf{ ec } \overline{\theta\alpha})\} \supset (\exists\lambda)\{\lambda\alpha \sim\Diamond^c(\lambda\alpha\psi\alpha)\}$

[24c] $\sim(\Psi \textbf{ ec } \Theta\bar{\Theta})$

The proof of [24a] is

(a)	$\Psi \textbf{ ec } \Theta$	Premise
(b)	$\Psi \textbf{ ec } \bar{\Theta}$	Premise
(c)	$(\exists\Lambda_1)[\Lambda_1(\Lambda_1\Psi \textbf{ npc } \Theta)]$	(a), [21]
(d)	$(\exists\Lambda_2)[\Lambda_2(\Lambda_2\Psi \textbf{ npc } \bar{\Theta})]$	(b), [21]
(e)	$\Lambda_1(\Lambda_1\Psi \textbf{ npc } \Theta)$	(c), existential instantiation of the statement Λ_1
(f)	$\Lambda_2(\Lambda_2\Psi \textbf{ npc } \bar{\Theta})$	(d), existential instantiation of the statement Λ_2
(g)	$\Lambda_1\Psi \underset{c}{\rightarrow} \Theta$	(e), [17], **TF**
(h)	$\Lambda_1\Psi\Lambda_2 \underset{c}{\rightarrow} \Theta$	(g), [13c], **TF**
(i)	$\Lambda_1\Lambda_2\Psi \underset{c}{\rightarrow} \Theta$	(h), **TF**, exchange
(j)	$\Lambda_1\Lambda_2\Psi \underset{c}{\rightarrow} \bar{\Theta}$	(f), as in (g)-(i)
(k)	$\sim\Diamond^c[(\Lambda_1\Lambda_2)\Psi]$	(i), (j), [15c], **TF**
(l)	$(\Lambda_1\Lambda_2) \sim\Diamond^c[(\Lambda_1\Lambda_2)\Psi]$	(e), (f), (k), **TF**
(m)	$(\exists\Lambda)\{\Lambda \sim \Diamond^c(\Lambda\Psi)\}$	(l), existential generalization of the statement $\Lambda_1\Lambda_2$.

Metatheorem [24a] now follows by conditional proof. The proof of [24b] is the same, except that the rule of existential instantiation of a predicate is used instead of the rule of existential instantiation of a statement.

The role of the condition $(\exists\Lambda)\{\Lambda\sim\Diamond^c(\Lambda\Phi)\}$ in [24a] is best understood by means of an example. Consider a model with four logically independent statements A, Y_1, Y_2, and B, and these causally possible universe descriptions:

$A\ Y_1\ \bar{Y}_2\ B$

$A\ \bar{Y}_1\ Y_2\ \bar{B}$

$\bar{A}\ Y_1\ Y_2\ \bar{B}$

of which the last is true. In this model all of the following statements are true:

$$Y_1A\ \mathbf{npc}\ B, \qquad Y_1, \qquad Y_1(Y_1A\ \mathbf{npc}\ B), \qquad A\ \mathbf{ec}\ B$$

$$Y_2A\ \mathbf{npc}\ \bar{B}, \qquad Y_2, \qquad Y_2(Y_2A\ \mathbf{npc}\ \bar{B}), \qquad A\ \mathbf{ec}\ \bar{B}$$

$$Y_1Y_2, \qquad \sim\Diamond^c\{(Y_1Y_2)A\}, \qquad (\exists X)\{X \sim\Diamond^c(XA)\}$$

Here we have a case in which A elliptically causes B in one circumstance (Y_1) and elliptically causes $\bar{B}$ in a different circumstance (Y_2). But then it is causally impossible for A to occur jointly with both circumstances (Y_1Y_2). For a similar example, see the discussion of the barbershop paradox, (pp. 460-63).

The proof of metatheorem [24c] is by reductio ad absurdum

(a)	$\sim\sim(\Psi\ \mathbf{ec}\ \Theta\bar{\Theta})$	Premise
(b)	$(\exists\Phi)[\Phi(\Phi\Psi\ \mathbf{npc}\ \Theta\bar{\Theta})]$	(a), [21], **TF**
(c)	$\Phi(\Phi\Psi\ \mathbf{npc}\ \Theta\bar{\Theta})$	(b), existential instantiation of the statement Φ
(d)	$\sim(\Phi\Psi\ \mathbf{npc}\ \Theta\bar{\Theta})$	[19b]
(e)	$(\Phi\Psi\ \mathbf{npc}\ \Theta\bar{\Theta}) \sim (\Phi\Psi\ \mathbf{npc}\ \Theta\bar{\Theta})$	(c), (d), **TF**.

The metatheorem now follows by reductio ad absurdum.

Having established some of the formal properties of elliptical causal implication (**ec**), we now use that connective for modeling subjunctives. In Section 7.3.1, we employed nonparadoxical causal implication (**npc**) to symbolize causal subjunctives in which the antecedent is causally sufficient for the consequent. In the most common use of a causal subjunctive, however, the user does not mean that the antecedent is causally sufficient by itself but only in conjunction with other conditions that, though they are in fact satisfied, are not explicitly mentioned. These uses should be modeled with elliptical causal implication rather than with nonparadoxical causal implication. The forms "If it should be the case that Ψ, then it would be the case that Θ" and "If it had been the case that Ψ, it would have been the case that Θ" should be modeled by $\sim\Psi(\Psi\ \mathbf{ec}\ \Theta)$ if a counterfactual is meant, and by $\Psi\ \mathbf{ec}\ \Theta$ if a noncounterfactual is meant.

We offer some examples. A waiter almost drops a glass tumbler, but does not. Consider the argument

[N_1] All released (R) objects that are heavier than air (H) fall (F)

[N_2] This glass (g), which is heavier than air, was not released

[N_3] Therefore, if this glass had been released, it would have fallen.

It is clear that the major premise is meant to be a causal universal and that the conclusion is meant to be counterfactual, and so the argument is valid.

The validity of this argument is preserved when it is modeled in the logic of causal statements.

(a)	$(x)(RxHx$ **npc** $Fx)$	Premise [N_1]
(b)	$(x)(HxRx$ **npc** $Fx)$	(a), **TF**, exchange
(c)	$HgRg$ **npc** Fg	(b), universal instantiation
(d)	$Hg \sim Rg$	Premise [N_2]
(e)	$Hg(HgRg$ **npc** $Fg)$	(c), (d), **TF**
(f)	$(\exists X)[Xg(XgRg$ **npc** $Fg)]$	(e), existential generalization of the predicate "H"
(g)	Rg **ec** Fg	(f), [21a]
(h)	$\sim Rg(Rg$ **ec** $Fg)$	(d), (g), **TF**.

The last formula symbolizes the counterfactual [N_3].

The informal argument about the glass should be contrasted with the following informal argument.

[N_1*] All the books (B) on that desk (D) are in Italian (I)

[N_2*] This (t) book is not on the desk

[N_3*] Therefore, if this book were on that desk, it would be in Italian.

Suppose it is clear from the context that the major premise is a material universal and the conclusion counterfactual. This informal argument is invalid, as is its formal model:

$$(x)(BxDx \supset Ix)$$

$$Bt \sim Dt$$

$$\therefore \sim Dt(Dt \textbf{ ec } It)$$

A material universal does not support an inference to a contrary-to-fact conditional, because the former concerns only the actual world, whereas the latter concerns possible, nonactual worlds as well.

Thus there are subjunctives that should be modeled with elliptical causal implication (**ec**) as well as subjunctives that should be modeled with nonparadoxical causal implication (**npc**). We call a subjunctive of either kind a *causal subjunctive.* Causal subjunctives may be counterfactual or noncounterfactual. The nature of causal subjunctives may be further elucidated by comparing them with some other kinds of assertive, hypothetical subjunctives. For this purpose it will suffice to consider the elliptical, counterfactual case.*

* For a discussion of subjunctives see also Goodman, "The Problem of Counterfactual Conditionals"; Chisholm, "Law Statements and Counterfactual Inference"; and Stevenson, "IF-FICULTIES." There is a substantial literature on subjunctives in the philosophical journals.

Let us look first at an elliptical, counterfactual causal subjunctive from the point of view of the "user" who asserts it. Take the form "If it had been the case that Ψ, it would have been the case that Θ." The user is considering a causally possible state of affairs $\Phi\Psi$, which he thinks agrees with the actual state of affairs in respect Φ but differs from the actual state of affairs in respect Ψ. The user asserts that the possible state of affairs Θ results from the state of affairs $\Phi\Psi$ by some law of nature. The state Φ is not mentioned explicitly in the subjunctive; we have represented it by means of an existential quantifier $(\exists\Phi)$. The same general remarks hold for elliptical causal subjunctives that are not counterfactual, except that it is left open as to whether the possible state of affairs Ψ is actual or not.

Causal subjunctives are based on what the user believes to be the actual laws of nature. In contrast, when reasoning inductively one considers alternative possible laws of nature (sec. 10.3), and one may for various reasons envisage a change in the laws of nature. Elliptical counterfactual subjunctives used in such cases differ from elliptical, counterfactual causal subjunctives.

An example is "If the theory of relativity were false, and people could be transported faster than the speed of light, man could travel from the earth to Proxima Centauri and back in one year." Symbolize the antecedent of this sentence by Ψ and the consequent by Θ. Let Φ represent the unstated assumptions the user is making about the distance from the earth to Proxima Centauri (approximately four light-years), the power of rocket engines, the laws that are to replace the theory of relativity (Newton's laws), etc. Since the antecedent Ψ is causally impossible, this subjunctive cannot be symbolized adequately with any of our causal implications. For, when Ψ is causally impossible, the truth-status of $\Psi \underset{c}{\rightarrow} \Theta$, of Ψ **npc** Θ, and of Ψ **ec** Θ does not depend upon the content of Θ. But though this type of subjunctive is not a "causal subjunctive" as we defined that term, it has much in common with causal subjunctives. The user is considering a logically possible state of affairs $\Phi\Psi$ that he thinks agrees with the actual state of affairs in respect Φ but differs from the actual state of affairs in respect Ψ. The user asserts that the state of affairs Θ results from the state of affairs $\Phi\Psi$ by certain principles. Moreover, these principles express alternative possible laws of nature, so that the formalism of the logic of causal statements applies to them (cf. pp. 624–26).

There are still other elliptical, counterfactual subjunctives that do not involve the causal modalities at all. For example, "If the premises of this argument were true, then the conclusion would be true" involves the logical modalities. The sentence "If this coin had been tossed many times, it would probably have fallen heads about half the time" is a probabilistic subjunctive; we model such subjunctives in the next chapter. The patterns of many of these subjunctives are similar to the patterns we found in subjunctives involving the causal modalities.

Thus there is a pattern common to many elliptical, counterfactual subjunctives. Consider the form "If Ψ were the case, Θ would be," meant as an elliptical counterfactual. The user is considering a certain state of affairs $\Phi\Psi$ that is factual in respect Φ, counterfactual in respect Ψ. He is asserting that another "state of affairs" Θ follows from $\Phi\Psi$ by certain rules or principles. Subjunctives vary in regard to the logical or epistemological status of $\Phi\Psi$ and the rules and principles used to connect Θ to $\Phi\Psi$. Generally, $\Phi\Psi$ is at least logically possible, but there are important exceptions. For example, suppose one wishes to show, by a reductio ad absurdum proof, that Θ follows from Φ. Using Φ as an unstated premise, he argues: If $\sim\Theta$ were true, Θ would be; therefore Θ is true. If this argument is valid, the state of affairs $\Phi\sim\Theta$ is logically impossible. But even in this case there is a "pretense" that $\Phi\sim\Theta$ is logically possible; for at the start of the argument it has not yet been shown that $\Phi\sim\Theta$ is logically impossible, else there would be no point to the argument (cf. sec. 6.5.3).

All the subjunctives discussed so far are hypothetical and assertive. In contrast, some subjunctives are expressive. Examples are "May we return soon," "Part we in friendship from your land," and "Oh, were he only here!" These also concern possible states of affairs, but here the user is directing wishes and intentions toward possible states of affairs rather than reasoning about them. We conclude that possible states of affairs play a fundamental role in the interpretation of subjunctives.

7.4 Causality

7.4.1 Causes and effects

We shall now use elliptical causal implication (**ec**) to model cause-effect relations. Suppose an electron (e) is deflected by a magnetic field in accordance with the law "$(x)(MxNx$ **npc** $Dx)$" and it is asserted that the magnetic field (M) caused the deflection (D), there being no other forces (N). These conditions may be symbolized "$(MeDe)(Me$ **ec** $De)$," the first conjunct asserting that two events have occurred, the second conjunct asserting that the first caused the second. Elliptical causal implication is appropriate here, because the cause is not sufficient to produce the effect by itself, but only in the presence of an additional condition (that there be no force other than that due to a magnetic field.)

This example comes from physics, which is a well-developed science. As remarked earlier, the notions of causal law, cause, and effect are employed less in such sciences than formerly, having been replaced by notions of theory, system, and state (pp. 30, 427). Consequently, some aspects of causality are best discussed in terms of examples from other sciences and from commonsense knowledge. Quite naturally, though, these examples will be less precise and complete, as our next example illustrates. Attempting to state a causal law on the poisonous effects of potassium cyanide, and aware of the abortive attempt to kill Rasputin with this poison, I asked a pharmacologist friend to specify a minimum fatal dose. He found this hard to do, and he suggested instead a law about strychnine, with the antecedent qualified to exclude abnormal cases.

Strychnine can cause death. More specifically,

[O_1] If a normal adult (N) should take one grain or more of strychnine orally (S) without receiving an antidote (A), he would die (D).

Assume that

[O_2] Grey (g) is a normal adult and will not receive an antidote.

It follows that

[O_3] If Grey takes one grain or more of strychnine orally, it will *cause* his death.

This valid inference is modeled in the logic of causal statements as follows.

(a)	$(x)(NxSx\overline{Ax}\ \mathbf{npc}\ Dx)$	Premise [O_1]
(b)	$Ng\overline{Ag}$	Premise [O_2]
(c)	$[(Ng\overline{Ag})Sg]\ \mathbf{npc}\ Dg$	(a), universal instantiation, exchange, **TF**
(d)	$Ng\overline{Ag} \supset (Sg\ \mathbf{ec}\ Dg)$	(c), [23b], **TF**
(e)	$Sg\ \mathbf{ec}\ Dg$	(b), (d), **TF**.

This last formula models the conclusion [O_3].

Most cause-effect statements are of the form: when the antecedent conditions are satisfied, the effect inevitably follows the cause. But some cause-effect statements claim only that the effect follows the cause probabilistically. Consider "Cigarette smoking causes lung cancer." Applying this generalization to a particular case, one might say

[P] Martin's (m) lung cancer (L) is the effect of cigarette-smoking (S).

Now, not every case of cigarette-smoking results in lung cancer, and so it may be asked what one means by saying that cigarette-smoking caused lung cancer in this particular case. There are several possibilities. One might mean that there is a causal law that, if known, could have been used to predict Martin's lung cancer from his smoking and the other relevant conditions. On this interpretation, [P] may be modeled by

[P′] $(SmLm)(Sm\ \mathbf{ec}\ Lm)$.

Alternatively, one might mean that there is a causal law enabling one to predict that Martin would not have got lung cancer had he not smoked, other relevant conditions remaining the same. On this interpretation, [P] may be modeled by

[P″] $(SmLm)(\overline{Sm}$ **ec** $\overline{Lm})$.

Or one might mean both of these things, so that [P] should be modeled by the conjunction of [P′] and [P″].

But one need not intend [P] to be based on any causal law. Instead, he might intend an empirical probability claim, such as

[P‴] Martin *probably* would not have got lung cancer had he not smoked cigarettes.

On this interpretation the cause (cigarette-smoking) does not inevitably produce the effect (lung cancer), but only with a certain probability. Sentence [P‴] is a probabilistic subjunctive, and it should be modeled in a probabilistic logic rather than the logic of causal statements. We shall do this in the next chapter. In the current chapter we analyze nonprobabilistic causal relations, that is, causal relations based on causal laws. Since this is the most common case, we limit the term **cause-effect statement** to this case.

The causal relation holds primarily between events. In order to simplify the symbolism, we use a single individual symbol to represent a sequence of events, i.e., a process that includes both cause and effect. When $\psi\alpha$ **ec** $\theta\alpha$ (or $\overline{\psi\alpha}$ **ec** $\overline{\theta\alpha}$) is a cause-effect statement, α's exemplifying ψ (or $\bar{\psi}$) is the cause of (has as an effect) α's exemplifying θ (or $\bar{\theta}$). The event or process α may occupy a limited space-time region (as in "The magnetic field caused the deflection of the electron" or "Igniting the gunpowder caused the explosion") or an extended space-time region (as in "The assassination of Archduke Ferdinand caused World War II" or "Smoking caused Martin's cancer").

A comment on our use of the lowercase Greek letters ϕ, ψ, θ, etc., is needed. We have normally used them to refer to symbols (predicates), but in the preceding paragraph they refer to properties. It is convenient to allow both uses so long as the meaning is clear from the context. It will also be convenient to speak of ψ causing θ in instance α ($\psi\alpha$ **ec** $\theta\alpha$), though of course the cause-effect relation holds most directly between events. Similarly, one can speak derivatively of the necessary connection between cause and effect, even though elliptical causal implication (**ec**) connects statements rather than events.

We saw in Section 7.2.2 that nonparadoxical causal implication (**npc**) captures some but not all of the important features of causal laws. Similarly, elliptical causal implication (**ec**) captures some but not all of the important features of deterministic cause-effect relations. We now state some additional conditions that $\psi\alpha$ **ec** $\theta\alpha$ must satisfy for ψ to be the cause of θ in instance α.

It will turn out that these conditions have an important bearing on the proper symbolization of subjunctives.

It is obvious that for ψ to be a cause of θ, ψ must be causally relevant to θ. Consider again the electron (e) that was deflected by a magnetic field (M) when there were no other forces present (N). Let "W" mean there is a wooden rod present. Then "$(x)(MxNxWx$ **npc** $Dx)$," "$(x)(MxNx\overline{Wx}$ **npc** $Dx)$," and "$MeNe$" are all true, and both "We **ec** De" and "$\overline{We}$ **ec** De" can be derived from them. But since the electron would be deflected whether or not a wooden rod was there, neither its being near the wooden rod nor its being far from the wooden rod can cause its deflection. More generally, given Φ **npc** Ψ, Φ, and a suitable causally irrelevant factor Θ, one can obtain $\Phi(\Phi\Theta$ **npc** $\Psi)$ and hence Θ **ec** Ψ, even though Θ is causally irrelevant to Ψ.

This condition of causal relevance applies to the corresponding subjunctives also. The subjunctive "If the electron should move in the vicinity of a wooden rod, it would be deflected" implies that a wooden rod is relevant to the behavior of the electron, and hence this subjunctive is either misleading or false. Since the formula "We **ec** De" is clearly true, it is not a good model of the subjunctive. On the other hand, "$\overline{We}(We$ **ec** $De)$" is a good model of the contrary-to-fact subjunctive "Had there been a wooden rod there, the electron would still have been deflected."

Causal relevance was discussed above (pp. 434-35) in connection with causal laws and the principle of adding a superfluous condition ([20c] and [20d]). As noted there, a better model of causality can be obtained by using the notion of nonsuperfluous causal implication instead of the notion of nonparadoxical causal implication. But as also noted there, only the most general and fundamental statements are causal laws, and these characteristics of being general and fundamental are essentially informal in nature. Similarly, not every event or thing that is causally relevant to the effect qualifies as a cause, but only an event or a thing that plays a key role in producing the effect qualifies. An effect may, of course, have several causes, as in the case of a historical event.

The foregoing considerations show that a subjunctive is subject to certain informal constraints not captured by elliptical causal implication. Another example of such a constraint is discussed below in connection with the rule of completeness for causal subjunctives (p. 459).

Our earlier example of strychnine poisoning illustrates the point that a cause plays a very special role in bringing about its effect. Suppose Grey takes strychnine (Sg) and, being normal (Ng) and receiving no antidote ($\overline{Ag}$), dies (Dg). Then "Sg **ec** Dg," "Ng **ec** Dg," and "$\overline{Ag}$ **ec** Dg" are all true, and the antecedent of each is causally relevant to Grey's death. But of the three factors, strychnine, normalcy, and absence of antidote, only the first was the cause of his death.

It is natural to ask: Of the events or things that are causally relevant to an effect, what differentiates those that are causes from those that are not? The answer to this question is tied up with the temporal aspect of causality.

An essential feature of the relation of cause to effect is this: A cause can occur no later in time than its effect. Since the form $\psi\alpha$ **ec** $\theta\alpha$ does not express temporal order, this aspect of causality is not modeled by elliptical causal implication as such.

Consider, for example, the causal law that all released objects (R) that are heavier than air (H) fall (F), and assume that the glass tumbler (g) was not released, so that it did not fall. The properties $R\bar{F}$ and $\bar{H}$ are logically independent. Moreover, it is causally possible for an object to be released and not fall, for the object might be lighter than air. Consequently, the premises of the following argument are all true.

(a)	$(x)(RxHx \textbf{ npc } Fx)$	Premise
(b)	$\sim Rg \sim Fg$	Premise
(c)	$(x)\{\Diamond[\sim(Rx\overline{Fx})\overline{Hx}]\Diamond^{c}(Rx\overline{Fx})\}$	Premise
(d)	$(x)(Rx\overline{Fx} \textbf{ npc } \overline{Hx})$	(a), (c), [20f], **TF**
(e)	$Rg\overline{Fg} \textbf{ npc } \overline{Hg}$	(d), universal instantiation
(f)	$\overline{Fg}Rg \textbf{ npc } \overline{Hg}$	(e), **TF** exchange
(g)	$\overline{Fg}(\overline{Fg}Rg \textbf{ npc } \overline{Hg})$	(b), (f), **TF**
(h)	$(\exists X)[Xg(XgRg \textbf{ npc } \overline{Hg})]$	(g), existential generalization of predicate "$\bar{F}$"
(i)	$Rg \textbf{ ec } \overline{Hg}$	(h), [21a].

This last formula is true, being derived validly from true premises.

Though the formula "Rg **ec** $\overline{Hg}$" is true, R is not a cause of $\bar{H}$, for releasing an object does not cause it to become lighter than air. Now both "Rg **ec** Fg" and "Rg **ec** $\overline{Hg}$" are of the form $\psi\alpha$ **ec** $\theta\alpha$, and yet while R causes F it does not cause $\bar{H}$. What makes the difference? The answer lies in the relation of each formula to the temporal process of being released and falling.

To begin with (at time t_1), the glass is being held, and is not free to fall. Imagine that the glass is released at a later time (t_2) and begins to fall. Its fall is completed at a still later time (t_3). The causal system thus goes through the following sequence. First, the system was in a stable, unchanging state; this is the background against which the later changes are to be viewed. Second, at time t_2 the system was changed significantly by the release of the glass. Third, this change induced a further change (the falling) in accordance with the law of gravitation. We can think of the releasing of the glass as one event (Rg) and the falling of the glass as another event (Fg).

The first event (Rg) is the cause, and the resultant, succeeding event (Fg) is the effect. The cause (Rg) involves the property that is changed (R), and the effect (Fg) involves the property (F) that appeared because of the change. The property of being heavier than air (H) is invariant through the whole process. In the terminology of page 443, the causal property R and the effect property F are transient properties, while the unchanging background property H is an enduring property.

As this example makes clear, the notions of cause and effect cannot be understood by themselves alone but only in the context of a process. A cause and its effect are events or things that play certain roles in a series of changes taking place in a definite manner and in accordance with causal laws. Very often it is possible in principle for a human being to control a causal process. In such cases a cause is that which one might manipulate in order to produce an effect or to prevent an effect from occurring. Thus the ideas of cause and effect are closely related to the possibility of human control.

We can now give a rough answer to the question: Of the events or things that are causally relevant to an effect, what differentiates those that qualify as causes from those that do not? A cause is, or is intimately related to, a change in a situation leading to the effect. Not any such change qualifies as a cause but only a change that plays an important and positive role in producing the effect. As the dictionary puts it, a cause is "something that brings about an effect or a result."

The form $\psi\alpha$ **ec** $\theta\alpha$ does not express temporal order; so this form does not distinguish cases in which the antecedent occurs earlier than the consequent, e.g., "Rg **ec** Fg," from cases in which it does not, e.g., "Rg **ec** $\overline{Hg}$." The temporal aspect of causality could be expressed by using variables ranging over time. This is not hard to do, but it leads to complex and unwieldy formulas, and we have carried the formal modeling of cause and effect far enough for present purposes. In Section 9.2 (Space-time Systems), we shall introduce a spatio-temporal framework for symbolizing causal statements and discuss the role of temporal succession and spatial contiguity in causality by means of this framework.

Let us now summarize our results concerning cause-effect relations. Many important features of causal laws may be modeled by means of nonparadoxical causal implication (**npc**), and many important features of cause-effect statements may be modeled by means of elliptical causal implication (**ec**). The elliptical character of **ec** is appropriate for symbolizing a cause-effect relation because the cause is not sufficient to produce the effect by itself, but only in the presence of another condition. Specifically, if ψ causes θ in some instance α, then $\psi\alpha$ **ec** $\theta\alpha$ or $\overline{\psi\alpha}$ **ec** $\overline{\theta\alpha}$ is true. On the other hand, there is an important feature of the relation of cause to effect that is not expressed by the form $\psi\alpha$ **ec** $\theta\alpha$: a cause and its effect play certain roles in a process, the cause being a key factor in bringing about its effect.

We draw a philosophical conclusion from our success in using the logic of causal statements to model causal laws, causal dispositionals, causal subjunctives, and cause-effect statements. *At the pragmatic level of ordinary usage and scientific practice, there is a necessary connection between cause and effect.* This is not logical necessity ($\Box$), but causal necessity ($\Box^c$). These two kinds of necessity are formally similar (see chap. 6), but as concretely interpreted they are quite different (see secs. 1.2 and 6.5.3 and the current chapter).

To justify the thesis that cause-effect relations are necessary we have argued from the properties of the model (the logic of causal statements) to the properties of the system modeled (causal discourse). In making this type of argument, one must ask whether the discrepancies between model and modeled invalidate or weaken the argument (sec. 1.6.3). They do not in the present case. An examination of the differences discussed in the present chapter does show that ordinary and scientific causal discourse is more complex structurally than the logic of causal statements. But this examination reveals no basis for thinking that better models of this discourse will not possess the essential modal features of causal necessity ($\Box^c$). Hence the differences between our models of causal discourse and the discourse modeled do not count against the thesis that there is a necessary connection between cause and effect.

We shall argue later that causal necessity has an even deeper and more fundamental status: the concept of causal necessity is a priori and is irreducibly modal (secs. 10.2.2–10.2.3).

7.4.2 *Contravening forces and completeness*

We have noted several times the need, when modeling statements and arguments of natural discourse, to model a sufficiently complete portion of the discourse. Enough of the context of the discourse must be included to avoid ambiguity. On page 20 we invoked the rule of total evidence in accounting for inductive arguments: one should use all the information (evidence, knowledge) available to him in deciding whether a proposition is true or false, probable or improbable, and in deciding what degree of probability to use in acting on a proposition. We saw also that it is often desirable to model sets of interrelated probability statements (e.g., prior probabilities, degrees of prediction, and posterior probabilities) rather than isolated probability statements (p. 92). And we noted in Section 7.1 that the meaning of a sentence is usually not given by that sentence alone, but depends on its context as well. In the present subsection we show the need for another completeness requirement in modeling subjunctives.

Suppose a dictator is about to drink a glass of wine when he is suddenly stopped on the suspicion it is poisoned. A chemist then analyzes the wine and finds it contains several grains of strychnine. The chemist knows that if a normal adult (N) takes one or more grains of strychnine (S) without receiving an antidote (A), he will die. He knows also that the dictator is normal and that no antidote is available. Hence he concludes

[R] If the dictator (d) had taken the strychnine (S), he would have died (D),

which we symbolize

[R′] $\sim Sd(Sd\ \mathbf{ec}\ Dd)$

This formula is true, as the following argument shows.

(a)	$(x)(NxSx\overline{Ax}\ \mathbf{npc}\ Dx)$	Premise
(b)	$Nd\&\overline{Sd}\&\overline{Ad}$	Premise
(c)	$NdSd\overline{Ad}\ \mathbf{npc}\ Dd$	(a), universal instantiation
(d)	$Nd\overline{Ad}Sd\ \mathbf{npc}\ Dd$	(c), **TF**, exchange
(e)	$Nd\overline{Ad}(Nd\overline{Ad}Sd\ \mathbf{npc}\ Dd)$	(b), (d), **TF**
(f)	$(\exists X)[Xd(XdSd\ \mathbf{npc}\ Dd)]$	(e), existential generalization of the predicate $N\bar{A}$
(g)	$Sd\ \mathbf{ec}\ Dd$	(f), [21a]
(h)	$\sim Sd(Sd\ \mathbf{ec}\ Dd)$	(b), (g), **TF**.

But now suppose the dictator is afraid of being poisoned and has arranged for a physician always to be present with a complete stock of antidotes. In these circumstances the sentence "If the dictator had taken the strychnine, he would have died" is false; for had the dictator taken the strychnine, he would have received an antidote and lived. The true state of affairs is described by "Even if he had taken the poison, he would not have died," and perhaps by "If the dictator had taken the strychnine, he would *not* have died." However, the formula "$\sim Sd(Sd\ \mathbf{ec}\ Dd)$" is true in these circumstances, for the dictator is normal (Nd), he did not take strychnine ($\overline{Sd}$), and consequently he was not actually given an antidote ($\overline{Ad}$). Since the sentence "If the dictator had taken the strychnine, he would have died" is false and the formula "$\sim Sd(Sd\ \mathbf{ec}\ Dd)$" is true, the latter is not a good model of the former in these circumstances. It is easy to imagine a third situation in which the dictator's enemy anticipates the dictator's precautions and arranges to prevent the antidote from being used. And, of course, the dictator can anticipate this, too. Thus there may be a succession of forces, contravening forces, contra-contravening forces, etc.

We have noted the importance of context in symbolizing sentences generally and subjunctives in particular. The introduction of contravening forces into the strychnine example constitutes an enlargement of the context.

In the strychnine example as originally envisaged, precautionary measures were not under consideration, and so "$(x)(NxSx\overline{A}x$ **npc** $Dx)$" was a good symbolization. Now a new causal factor has been introduced, influencing the causal factors already present, for whether or not "$NdSd\overline{A}d$" could have been true depends on the absence or presence of precautionary measures. Consequently, the formulation of the law governing the situation must be complicated accordingly. For example, if the precautions taken (P) unconditionally cause an antidote to be used, the law may be expressed as "$(x)(NxSxPx$ **npc** $\overline{Dx})$," while if further conditions are involved, they must be stated. We shall make a detailed analysis of a different example in a moment.

But let us first formulate the general principle we have just applied to the subjunctive "If the dictator had taken strychnine, he would have died." When asserting a causal subjunctive, one is, or should be, dealing with a relatively isolated, self-sufficient system and a relatively definite theory or set of laws governing this system. Correspondingly, when modeling a causal subjunctive, one should include enough of its context to obtain a portion of discourse that is complete and self-sufficient with respect to the relevant forces and laws, and one should model this portion of discourse as a unit. We call this general principle the *rule of completeness for causal subjunctives.*

Since a causal subjunctive is based on a causal law or theory, it is not surprising that the rule of completeness for causal subjunctives is similar to rules used in scientific theorizing and modeling generally. We noted in Section 1.6.2 that a scientific theory or model represents certain aspects or features of reality but not all. A scientific theory or model treats of a system governed by certain laws and not by others, and isolated from outside influences. For example, Galileo's law of falling bodies concerns a system free from electric forces, frictional forces, and hydrodynamic forces. The second law of thermodynamics (the state of maximum entropy is the most probable state of a gas; see pp. 114-17) holds only for a closed system.

The rule of completeness for causal subjunctives is also similar to the rule of total evidence (p. 20).

An application of the rule of completeness may presuppose the notion of causal necessity. Thus, in stating that a system is closed or is subject to certain laws and not to others, one must speak of "all forces" or "all laws," where the ideas of force and law involve causal necessity. Again, in modeling a subjunctive, one may use predicates that are themselves dispositional; in such a case, a better model can be made by using iterated causal modalities (cf. secs. 7.3.2 and 7.5), though the original model may nevertheless be useful. But there is no circularity in presupposing the notion of causal necessity when modeling a portion of discourse by means of the logic of causal statements, since the purpose of this logic is to formalize partially the notion of causal necessity, not to reduce this notion to nonmodal notions. Indeed, we shall argue in Section 10.2.3 that causal necessity cannot be constructed from or defined in terms of nonmodal notions.

The rule of completeness for causal subjunctives may be used to resolve Lewis Carroll's barbershop paradox.* We will present the paradox, model it by means of elliptical causal implication, and then apply the rule of completeness to it.

A barbershop has three barbers, Allen, Brown, and Carr. It is a rule that the shop is always attended; so if Carr and Allen are both out, Brown must be in. Since Allen has been ill recently, there is a second rule that if Allen goes out his friend Brown must accompany him. Carroll then considers the following premises based on the rules,

(a)	If Carr and Allen *were* both out, then Brown *would be* in	Premise, from the first rule
(b)	If Allen *were* out, Brown *would* also be out	Premise, from the second rule
(c)	Carr is out	Premise.

The first two premises are formulated as subjunctives, which seems acceptable since the rules of the barbershop cover various possible situations. Moreover, this set of premises appears to be consistent.

Carroll then reasons as follows.

(d)	If Carr *should be* out, then if Allen *were* out Brown *would be* in	From (a) by exportation
(e)	If Allen *were* out Brown *would be* in	From (c) and (d) by *modus ponens*
(f)	It is not the case that if Allen *were* out Brown *would be* in	From (b), since "If Ψ, then Θ" and "If Ψ, then $\overline{\Theta}$" are incompatible.

Lines (e) and (f) are contradictory, and so Carroll *seems* to deduce a contradiction from consistent premises. Where does the argument go wrong?

Since the first two premises are subjunctives, modal symbols should be used in modeling them. Suppose, for example, that Brown never intended to go out with Allen, but this intention was never manifested because Allen never went out. Then "(Allen is out) $\supset$ (Brown is out)" would always be true, but the premise "If Allen *were* out, Brown *would* also be out" would be false. Insofar as they really accept these two rules and act in accordance with them, the barbers have a disposition to behave in certain ways. It is therefore appropriate to symbolize these rules with elliptical causal implication.

* Carroll, "A Logical Paradox." Burks and Copi, "Lewis Carroll's Barber Shop Paradox." Baker, "Incompatible Hypotheticals and the Barbershop Paradox."

The rules extend over time, but it will suffice to consider the situation at any given time. Let "A" mean "Allen is out at this time," and similarly with "B" and "C." Symbolizing each rule separately, we obtain the following formal model of Carroll's argument (a)–(f).

(a′)	CA **ec** $\bar{B}$	Premise, from the first rule
(b′)	A **ec** B	Premise, from the second rule
(c′)	C	Premise
(d′)	$C \supset (A$ **ec** $\bar{B})$	(a′), [23a]
(e′)	A **ec** $\bar{B}$	(c′), (d′), **TF**
(f′)	$\sim(A$ **ec** $\bar{B})$	(b′), INVALID!

We showed earlier that the last step is invalid in the logic of causal statements, i.e., that "A **ec** B" and "A **ec** $\bar{B}$" are compatible (p. 448).

Thus according to this analysis of the barbershop paradox, if the premises (a)–(c) are true, then

(b) If Allen were out, Brown would be *out*

(e) If Allen were out, Brown would be *in*

are both true. These seemingly incompatible statements reflect two different, but equally acceptable ways of looking at and reasoning about the barbershop situation as it is portrayed by the premises. Note, however, that it would be wrong to combine (b) and (e) in order to infer

If Allen were out, Brown would be both in and out [A **ec** $\bar{B}B$],

for this statement is false by metatheorem [24c].

The circumstances under which both "A **ec** B" and "A **ec** $\bar{B}$" are true can best be understood by means of a simple model in which lines (a′)-(e′) of the preceding argument are true and line (f′) is false. The causally possible universe descriptions of the model are

$C\ A\ R_1\ \bar{R}_2\ \bar{B}$

$\bar{C}\ A\ \bar{R}_1\ R_2\ B$

$C\ \bar{A}\ R_1\ R_2\ B$,

the last of these being true. "R_1" and "R_2" may be thought of as involving the properties that underly the dispositions of the first and second rules, respectively.

All of the following statements are true in this model:

R_1CA **npc** $\bar{B}$, R_1, $R_1(R_1CA$ **npc** $\bar{B})$, CA **ec** $\bar{B}$, C, A **ec** $\bar{B}$

R_2A **npc** B, R_2, $R_2(R_2A$ **npc** $B)$, A **ec** B

R_1CR_2, $\sim\Diamond^c\{(R_1CR_2)A\}$, $(\exists X)\{X\sim\Diamond^c(XA)\}$

Thus A can elliptically cause not-B in one circumstance (R_1C) and elliptically cause B in a different circumstance (R_2). But, in accordance with theorem [24a], it is then causally impossible for A to occur jointly with both circumstances (R_1CR_2). This same point is illustrated by an earlier model on page 448.

Our analysis of the barbershop paradox constitutes a plausible resolution of it. But this resolution is not completely satisfactory, for one can still ask: What really would be the case if Allen were out—would Brown be in or out? One may feel that the subjunctives

(b) If Allen were out, Brown would be *out*

(e) If Allen were out, Brown would be *in*

are incompatible in some way, and since "A **ec** B" and "A **ec** $\bar{B}$" are compatible, they do not fully model these subjunctives. I think this feeling is correct, and the incompatibility can be explained by applying the rule of completeness for causal subjunctives to Carroll's argument.

The rules of the barbershop are causal subjunctives, and in the paradox each is included within the context of the other. By the rule of completeness for causal subjunctives, these rules should be modeled together, rather than separately as is done in model (a′)–(f′). The natural way to model (a) and (b) jointly is by

[S] $(\exists X)[X(XCA \textbf{ npc } \bar{B})(XA \textbf{ npc } B)]$

But this formula is contradictory, for its existential instantiation yields "$\Diamond^c (XCA)$" and also "$\Box^c \sim(XCA)$," which in turn yields "$\sim\Diamond^c (XCA)$." This result confirms our feeling that Carroll's two subjunctive premises are incompatible.

However, the two rules of the barbershop can be modeled in a consistent manner. This is accomplished by the following formula

[T] $(\exists R)[R(R \textbf{ npc } \{(CA \supset \bar{B})(A \supset B)\})]$,

which treats the barbershop situation as a single dispositional system. Here "R" attributes to the barbershop a single property underlying the disposition expressed by the two rules, and thus it plays the role played by "R_1R_2" in the model used above. The subjunctive character of the rules is modeled by nonparadoxical causal implication (**npc**). The truth-functional consequent "$(CA \supset \bar{B})(A \supset B)$" within [T] is logically equivalent to "$B\bar{C} \vee \bar{A}$." In other words "$B\bar{C} \vee \bar{A}$" is the truth-functional component of the combined rules of the barbershop. Since "$B\bar{C} \vee \bar{A}$" implies "$\sim(CA)$," the rules of the barbershop imply that Carr and Allen cannot be out at the same time.

But the situation where Carr and Allen are both out is exactly the situation envisaged in Carroll's first rule

(a) If Carr and Allen were both out, Brown would be in.

Hence in the context of

(b) If Allen were out, Brown would be out,

the situation CA envisaged in (a) becomes causally impossible. Since one normally reasons subjunctively from a causally possible situation, statement (a) becomes misleading or false in context (b). The proper response to the question "Given that Carr is out, what really would be the case if Allen were out?" is to observe that the situation presupposed by the question violates the rules of the barbershop, so that no conclusion should be drawn from it. Thus the barbershop paradox arises from taking two subjunctive chains of reasoning, each acceptable in itself, and combining them without realizing that the combination is unacceptable.

We saw earlier that in using an elliptical causal subjunctive one normally has in mind a situation he takes to be causally possible, and that similar consistency requirements apply to other kinds of subjunctives (p. 451). We see now that for a causal subjunctive to be true and not misleading, its antecedent must be causally possible, not only intrinsically, but also in the wider context in which it is used. This requirement is an informal generalization of the condition that for Φ **npc** Ψ to hold, the antecedent Φ must be causally possible (p. 428). All of these consistency requirements result from a general characteristic of discourse involving hypotheticals: when asserting a conditional statement one is normally considering implicit and explicit antecedent conditions, the totality of which is consistent in an appropriate sense. We used this fact to resolve the paradoxes of implication (pp. 413-15).

Before leaving the barbershop paradox, let us return to the specific role of elliptical causal implication (**ec**) in modeling subjunctives. We compared the subjunctives

(b) If Allen were out, Brown would be *out*

(e) If Allen were out, Brown would be *in*

with the corresponding formulas

(b′) A **ec** B

(e′) A **ec** $\bar{B}$

By the rule of completeness for causal subjunctives, (b) and (e) are incompatible. Since formulas (b′) and (e′) are compatible, they do not fully model the corresponding subjunctives. Thus Carroll's barbershop paradox reveals another aspect of elliptical causal subjunctives not captured by our formal model of elliptical causal implication (**ec**).

Let us summarize what we have learned about elliptical causal subjunctives from modeling them with elliptical causal implication. The form "If Ψ were the case, Θ would be the case" should be modeled by $\sim\Psi(\Psi$ **ec** $\Theta)$ if a counterfactual is meant and by Ψ **ec** Θ if a noncounterfactual is meant. By definition [21b], Ψ **ec** Θ is equivalent to $(\exists\Phi)[\Phi(\Phi\Psi$ **npc** $\Theta)]$. We draw two conclusions from the success of the logic of causal statements in modeling elliptical causal subjunctives. First, an elliptical causal subjunctive asserts that a sentence Φ is true, where Φ satisfies the explicitly given relation $\Phi\Psi$ **npc** Θ but Φ itself is not explicitly given. Second, an elliptical causal subjunctive rests on a nonparadoxical causal implication $\Phi\Psi$ **npc** Θ and hence ultimately on a law of nature.

But Ψ **ec** Θ is not a perfect model for elliptical causal subjunctives of the form "If Ψ were the case, Θ would be the case." In context a subjunctive is governed by certain informal rules such as the rule of completeness for causal subjunctives. These informal conditions are not captured by the formula Ψ **ec** Θ. Consequently, a subjunctive is sometimes false or misleading when the corresponding formula is not.

7.5 Iterated Modalities

7.5.1 Change of dispositions

We have discussed at length the interpretation of the causal ($\Box^c$) and logical ($\Box$) necessity symbols when each is applied to a nonmodal expression. Iterations of these symbols (e.g., $\Box\,\Box$ and $\Box\,\Box^c$) are not allowed in the logic of causal statements, and so far we have not needed them. But iterated modalities do occur in causal and logical discourse, and a complete account must include them. There is no completely satisfactory interpretation of iterated logical modalities, and I do not have a solution to the wider problem of combined causal and logical modalities; but I shall try to indicate the main issues, particularly as they concern causal necessity.

Let us consider first an example of an iterated causal necessity. A thing may change its dispositional properties, doing so in accord with causal laws. For instance, bombarding a substance with high energy particles under the right conditions will transmute it into a substance having different chemical properties. Thus gold may be transmuted into mercury and thereby have its melting point changed from 1,063° C to −39° C. Since a disposition involves a causal modality (sec. 7.3.2.) a law governing a change of dispositions involves a causal modality applied to a causal modality. The sentence

[U] The operations O performed on a gold object (G) will cause it to acquire a melting point of −39° C (P)

is symbolized

$$(x)(OxGx \textbf{ npc } Px)$$

Now "Px" is dispositional, meaning that if x were cooled to −39° C, it would solidify, and if it were heated (H) to −39° C, it would liquefy (L). For simplicity let us take only the latter of these conditionals. Symbolizing it by "Hx **ec** Lx" and substituting for "Px" we obtain

$$(x)[OxGx \ \mathbf{npc} \ (Hx \ \mathbf{ec} \ Lx)] \quad .$$

Applying definition [21a] we get

[U′] $(x)[OxGx \ \mathbf{npc} \ (\exists Y)\{Yx(YxHx \ \mathbf{npc} \ Lx)\}] \quad .$

When this is reduced to primitive terms by definitions [17], [16], and [1], it will contain a causal necessity applied to both a causal necessity and a logical necessity.

Thus, the natural way to symbolize a change of dispositions leads to iterated modalities. There nevertheless might be an adequate symbolization that avoids iterated modalities. Let us see if we can find such a symbolization of [U]. In [U′], the predicate variable "Y" is used to symbolize the property underlying the disposition "having a melting point of −39° C." One can say that performing operation O on a gold object (G) will cause it to acquire Y:

[U″] $(x)(\exists Y)[(OxGx \ \mathbf{npc} \ Yx)(YxHx \ \mathbf{npc} \ Lx)] \quad .$

This last formula has no iterated modalities. But it is a good symbolization of the original sentence [U] only if [U′] and [U″] are logically equivalent, either in themselves or relative to certain acceptable premises about the situation. And we cannot decide whether [U′] and [U″] are logically equivalent until we know whether such a principle as

$$\Box^c \Phi \supset \Box^c \Box^c \Phi$$

is a logical truth. Hence, to decide whether a change of dispositions does or does not involve iterated modalities, we are brought back to our original question: How are iterated modalities to be interpreted?

As a formal basis for discussion, we extend the logic of causal statements by (1) widening the definition of "formula" so that $\Box\Phi$ and $\Box^c \Phi$ are formulas even when Φ contains modal operators (cf. p. 343) and (2) augmenting the rule of axiom generation so that $\Box\Phi$ is an axiom when Φ contains modal operators (cf. p. 349). This extended system will be called "the logic of causal statements with iterated modalities."* In its metalanguage the variables Φ, Ψ, Θ, etc. will range over all formulas, with no restriction in modal contexts to prevent iterated modalities (cf. p. 344). All the results of Section 6.5 (Some Theorems of the Logic of Causal Statements) hold for the logic of causal statements with iterated modalities.

* It is equivalent to the system of my "The Logic of Causal Propositions," sec. 3.

On the concrete interpretation I have in mind, and insofar as I understand iterated modalities, all the theorems of the logic of causal statements with iterated modalities seem logically true.* Let us consider next each of the following forms, to see whether all the formulas of a given form are logically true and might reasonably be added as axioms.

[V_1] $\Box\Phi \equiv \Box\Box\Phi$ $\Diamond\Psi \equiv \Box\Diamond\Psi$

[V_2] $\Box^c\Phi \equiv \Box^c\Box^c\Phi$ $\Diamond^c\Psi \equiv \Box^c\Diamond^c\Psi$

[V_3] $\Box^c\Phi \equiv \Box\Box^c\Phi$ $\Diamond^c\Psi \equiv \Box\Diamond^c\Psi$.

Suppose one reasons about a statement Φ and concludes that it is a logical truth ($\Box\Phi$). Having decided by reasoning alone that $\Box\Phi$, he can then reflect on this process and conclude that $\Box\Box\Phi$. By a similar process he can infer $\Box\Diamond\Psi$ from $\Diamond\Psi$. The converses hold by the principle that $\Box\Theta$ implies Θ. Hence it is at least plausible to accept

[V_1] $\Box\Phi \equiv \Box\Box\Phi$ $\Diamond\Psi \equiv \Box\Diamond\Psi$.

This gives a plausible interpretation for iterated logical modalities. But I do not see how to give a corresponding interpretation for the iterated causal modalities of [V_2].†

Principle [V_3] is false by our concrete interpretation of the necessity symbols. Logical necessity ($\Box$) was originally defined in terms of logical

* Iterated modalities may be interpreted abstractly by means of modal models based on the relation "universe u_1 is possible relative to universe u_2." See the papers by Kripke in the bibliography, Hintikka's papers on modality listed there, and Uchii's "Inductive Logic with Causal Modalities: A Probabilistic Approach."

Uchii has constructed an abstract model of this kind for the logic of causal statements with iterated modalities, and has shown that every theorem of the system is logically true (valid) in this model (cf. p. 364). He has also shown that the system is complete in the sense that every formula valid in the model is a theorem. His results are not yet published.

† In "Eine Interpretation des intuitionistischen Aussagenkälkuls," Gödel pointed out an interesting analogy between logical truth ($\Box$) and provability in certain formal languages. The principle

[V_1*] Φ is provable in $\mathfrak{L}_A$ if and only if Φ is provably provable in $\mathfrak{L}_A$

holds for a language $\mathfrak{L}_A$ containing Peano arithmetic. [V_1*] is the provability analog of $\Box\Phi \equiv \Box\Box\Phi$. The provability analog of $\Diamond\bar{\Psi} \equiv \Box\Diamond\bar{\Psi}$ is

[V_1**] Ψ is not provable in $\mathfrak{L}_A$ if and only if Ψ is provably not provable in $\mathfrak{L}_A$.

[V_1**] implies the existence of a decision machine for theoremhood in $\mathfrak{L}_A$, and hence is false. Compare sec. 6.4.2.

truth: A statement is logically true if it can in principle be shown to be true by reasoning alone (secs. 1.2.1 and 1.2.3). By this criterion it is obvious that

$\Box^c$ (All gold objects dissolve in aqua regia)

is not logically true, for observation and experiment are required for its verification. Hence

$\Box\Box^c$ (All gold objects dissolve in aqua regia)

is false. This shows that some formulas of the form $\Box^c \Phi \equiv \Box\Box^c \Phi$ are false. Similarly, $\Box^c \sim\Psi$ may be empirically false, in which case $\Diamond^c \Psi \equiv \Box\Diamond^c \Psi$ is false. Hence we reject [V_3].

Thus, for the concrete interpretation of the logic of causal statements we intend, all formulas of form [V_1] seem logically true, some formulas of form [V_2] are difficult to interpret, and some formulas of form [V_3] are false. While causal necessity and logical necessity are similar in important respects, they differ on whether their primary statements are empirical or logical.

7.5.2. *Comprehensive modal logics*

Except in the present section, we did not need iterated modalities for analyzing causal statements of ordinary and scientific discourse. Nevertheless, it would be desirable to have a good interpretation of iterated modalities. In order to formulate the problem further, we shall make some points about causal necessity that must be taken into account by any adequate interpretation.

Consider first the relation of causal to logical necessity. A causally necessary statement is one that is true in every causally possible universe, and a causally possible universe is a logically possible universe in which every law of nature governing the actual universe holds. Hence a statement is causally necessary if and only if it is logically implied by the set of causal laws governing the actual universe. In other words,

[W_1] $\Box^c \Phi \equiv$ (The set of causal laws governing the actual universe logically implies Φ).

Since this statement is true because of the way causal necessity was defined, it is logically true. Thus it is the case that

[W_2] $\Box\{\Box^c \Phi \equiv$ (The set of causal laws governing the actual universe logically implies Φ)$\}$.

And since [W_1] is logically true, it is reasonable to convert it into a definition of $\Box^c$ in terms of the notion of a causal law. One way of formalizing this is given by Fitch.* From the logic of causal statements with iterated

* *Symbolic Logic*, p. 69.

modalities, form a new language by the following two steps. Delete $\Box^c$ from all formulas and thus from all axioms; note that [4a] becomes $\Box\Phi \supset \Phi$ (p. 349). Add a statement constant C to the language, modify the definition of "formula" to accommodate C, and adopt

[W$_1$′] $\Box^c \Phi \equiv (C \rightarrow \Phi)$

as a definitional scheme. Here "C" represents itself in the metalanguage, just as "$\Box^c$" does.

It is easy to show that the forms

[4a] $\Box\Phi \supset \Box^c \Phi$

[4d] $\Box^c (\Phi \supset \Psi) \supset \{\Box^c \Phi \supset \Box^c \Psi\}$

[4f] $(\alpha)\Box^c \Phi \equiv \Box^c (\alpha)\Phi$

are metatheorems of the new language. But the important causal principle

[4b] $\Box^c \Phi \supset \Phi$

becomes $\Box(C \supset \Phi) \supset \Phi$, which is not a metatheorem.* Principle [4b] would become a metatheorem if C were added to the axioms, but then $\Box C$ and $\Box^c \Phi \supset \Box\Phi$ would also become metatheorems, and these are clearly unacceptable.

We can partially recover the principle $\Box^c \Phi \supset \Phi$ in the form $C \vdash \Box^c \Phi \supset \Phi$. Even so, the system based on the definition $\Box^c \Phi \equiv (C \rightarrow \Phi)$ is unsatisfactory. For when the principle $\Box\Phi \supset \Box\Box\Phi$ is added to this system, the unacceptable scheme $\Box^c \Phi \supset \Box\Box^c \Phi$ becomes a metatheorem, as the following proof of $\Box\Box^c \Phi$ from the premise $\Box^c \Phi$ shows: $\Box^c \Phi$, $\Box(C \supset \Phi)$, $\Box\Box(C \supset \Phi)$, $\Box\Box^c \Phi$.

The reason why definition [W$_1$′] is unsatisfactory is that it is not a good formalization of [W$_1$]. Imagine that someone has written down a disjunction of the universe descriptions of all causally possible universes; call this disjunction "C." It is then the case that a statement Φ is causally necessary if and only if C logically implies it, as [W$_1$′] states. But since this last statement is not logically true, it is not the case that

[W$_2$′] $\Box\{\Box^c \Phi \equiv (C \rightarrow \Phi)\}$.

To see this, consider a formula Θ that contains no modal operators and is empirically true-or-false. Then $\Box^c \Theta$ is also empirically true-or-false. But whether or not C implies Θ is a logical matter, and so $C \rightarrow \Theta$ is logically true

* This can be shown by extending the definition of truth of p. 359 so that iterated modalities do not alter the truth-value of a formula; that is, $\Box 1$ and $\Diamond 1$ have the value 1, $\Box 0$ and $\Diamond 0$ have the value 0. On this definition of truth, all theorems of the new language are logically true (cf. p. 364), while $\Box(C \supset C) \supset C$ is false when C is assigned "false" (0).

or false. Since the left-hand side of $\Box^c \Theta \equiv (C \rightarrow \Theta)$ is empirical while the right-hand side is logical, $\Box\{\Box^c \Theta \equiv (C \rightarrow \Theta)\}$ is false.

To be satisfactory as a definition of $\Box^c$ in terms of the notion of a causal law, [W_1] needs to be formalized with statement predicates and quantifiers. Abbreviate the statement predicate "is a statement expressing the set of causal laws governing the actual universe" by "**K**." An instance of [W_1] may now be symbolized

$$[W_1''] \quad \Box^c P \equiv (\exists Q)\{\mathbf{K}Q\&(R)(\mathbf{K}R \supset [Q \leftrightarrow R])\&(Q \rightarrow P)\} \qquad ,$$

where "$(\exists Q)$" and "(R)" are statement quantifiers. If we had an adequate formal language for the logical modalities that had statement predicates and quantifiers, we could use scheme [W_1''] as a definition of $\Box^c$ in terms of the primitive statement predicate "**K**."*

The foregoing demonstrates that to understand fully the iterated modalities, we need to view them in the context of a more comprehensive logical system. We next analyze iterated modalities in a different way and draw a similar conclusion.

Consider the definite description "the set of causal laws governing the actual universe." In arriving at formula [W_1''] we treated this definite description as an expression of our formal language, symbolizing it by means of variables for which sentences are substituted. This is accordant with the logic of causal statements, in which modal operators are prefixed to statement variables and statement forms. But the expression "the set of causal laws governing the actual universe" can also be represented in a metalanguage. On this approach, it would be symbolized by means of variables for which terms denoting statements are substituted. This is a special case of a more general approach to the modalities, in which they are analyzed as metalinguistic predicates, such as "is logically necessary," "logically implies," that are attached to terms denoting statements.† Let us see how iterated modalities are interpreted on this approach.

For this purpose we compare an object language that permits iterations of the modal operator "$\Box$" with some hierarchical systems containing the modal predicate "is necessary" ("**N**"). Our discussion will take place in an extrahierarchical language, in which the logical constants "$\Box$" and "**N**" represent themselves.

* Some systems of logical necessity have been developed in which statement and predicate variables may be quantified, but there is much yet to be learned about such systems and their interpretation. See the papers by E. J. Lemmon and Ruth Marcus in *Proceedings of a Colloquium on Modal and Many-Valued Logics*.

† See Frege, "Über Sinn und Bedeutung." In "A Formulation of the Logic of Sense and Denotation," Church attempts to formalize Frege's distinction between Sinn and Bedeutung. See also Carnap, *The Logical Syntax of Language* and *Meaning and Necessity*. The literature on the metalinguistic treatment of modality is reviewed and indexed in the *Journal of Symbolic Logic*.

In the last chapter a hierarchy of languages was used for formalizing statements about truth (p. 379):

.

.

.

$\mathfrak{L}^m$

.

.

.

$\mathfrak{L}^2$ (meta-metalanguage)

$\mathfrak{L}^1$ (metalanguage)

$\mathfrak{L}^0$ (object language $\mathfrak{L}_A$).

The object language $\mathfrak{L}_A$ contains Peano arithmetic, which on its standard interpretation expresses only one kind of truth, logical or necessary truth. For a hierarchy of iterated modalities to be adequate, $\mathfrak{L}_A$ should express at least two other modes of truth, causal necessity and plain truth. However, to show the problems involved here we need only distinguish logical truth from plain truth. Hence we stipulate that each language of the hierarchy above $\mathfrak{L}^0$ contain a predicate "is logically true" (**N**), a predicate "is true" (**T**), plus appropriate axioms and rules for these predicates. The predicate **N** is stronger than the predicate **T**, for every logical truth is true but not conversely; compare the modal principle $\Box\Phi \supset \Phi$.

An assertion is made with one of these predicates by prefixing it to a term naming or designating a statement of a lower language. There are many different ways of forming terms that refer to statements, three of which are illustrated in Table 22. First, we ordinarily name an expression by exhibiting it between quotation marks (column 2). Second, the formulas of an arithmetized language are designated by their Gödel numbers (p. 367); for example, in column 3 "**g**[87x113 = 9831]" represents the Gödel number of "87x113 = 9831" in some suitable coding. Third, descriptive phrases may be employed for referring to formulas (column 4). The particular naming methods available in a hierarchy of languages play an important role, and the system must contain rules governing them.

For our purposes it will suffice to consider, for a given hierarchy, some one primary "name relation" δ. Thus if Φ is a formula of the language of a hierarchy, each higher language contains a term $\delta[\Phi]$ naming Φ. $\mathbf{T}(\delta[\Phi])$ states that Φ is true, while $\mathbf{N}(\delta[\Phi])$ states that Φ is necessarily or logically true. Note that "δ" is an operator in the extrahierarchical language for forming names (in that language) of names that exist in the hierarchy. For example, in column 3 of Table 22, "**g**[87x113 = 9831]" (or "δ[87x113 = 9831]") names that integer of the metalanguage that names (via a Gödel coding) the object language formula "87x113 = 9831." Thus "δ" is a

TABLE 22

ITERATED MODAL OPERATORS COMPARED WITH ITERATED MODAL PREDICATES

ITERATIONS OF THE MODAL OPERATOR □ IN AN OBJECT LANGUAGE	ITERATIONS OF THE MODAL PREDICATE **N** IN A HIERARCHY OF LANGUAGES			
	Method of naming formulas			Hierarchy of languages
	Quotes	Gödel numbers	Descriptions	
α_1 87x113 = 9831	α_2 87x113 = 9831	α_3 87x113 = 9831	α_4 [See p. 3 of the present book]	Object language
β_1 □(87x113 = 9831)	β_2 **N**('87x113 = 9831')	β_3 **N**(**g**[87x113 = 9831])	β_4 Statement [1] on page 3 is necessary	Meta-language
γ_1 □□(87x113 = 9831)	γ_2 **N**('**N**('87x113 = 9831')')	γ_3 **N**(**g**[**N**(**g**[87x113 = 9831])])	γ_4 The statement directly above is necessary	Meta-meta-language
Column 1	Column 2	Column 3	Column 4	

Statement [1] on page 3 is in fact "87 x 113 = 9831."

symbol outside the hierarchy that represents a unary name relation existing in the hierarchy.

Let us now compare modal operators and predicates in a hierarchy. Consider first the case in which necessity is asserted of a nonmodal statement. That is, consider an object language formula Φ with no modal operators and compare $\Box\Phi$ with $\mathbf{N}(\delta[\Phi])$. Assume that the modal operator $\Box$ has been interpreted, so that $\Box\Phi$ has a truth-value. It is natural to interpret the predicate **N** correspondingly, so that $\mathbf{N}(\delta[\Phi])$ has the same truth-value. This gives the principle

[X] If Φ contains no modal operators, then
$\Box\Phi$ is true if and only if $\mathbf{N}(\delta[\Phi])$ is true.

This principle is illustrated in Table 22: compare β_1 with β_2, β_3, and β_4. Note that formula β_1 is in the object language, whereas formulas β_2, β_3, and β_4 are in the metalanguage.

The principle may also be illustrated in connection with the exchangeability of equals in modal logic (cf. pp. 47, 403). Let the object language be the logic of causal statements and interpret it as in Section 6.3 (An Abstract Interpretation). On this interpretation, the predicate **T** means "true in the actual world" and the predicate **N** means "true in all logically possible worlds." Material equivalents cannot always be exchanged in modal logic; thus

[Y⁰] $(P \equiv Q) \supset \Box\{(P \vee \bar{P}) \equiv (Q \vee \bar{P})\}$

is not logically true. But two logically equivalent formulas can be exchanged, and so

[Z⁰] $\Box(P \equiv Q) \supset \Box\{(P \vee \bar{P}) \equiv (Q \vee \bar{P})\}$

is logically true. These two modal operator formulas of $\mathfrak{L}^0$ have their modal predicate equivalents in $\mathfrak{L}^1$.

[Y¹] $\mathbf{T}(\delta[P \equiv Q]) \supset \mathbf{N}(\delta[(P \vee \bar{P}) \equiv (Q \vee \bar{P})])$

[Z¹] $\mathbf{N}(\delta[P \equiv Q]) \supset \mathbf{N}(\delta[(P \vee \bar{P}) \equiv (Q \vee \bar{P})])$.

The second of these two formulas is logically true, while the first is not.

But though $\Box\Phi$ and $\mathrm{N}(\delta[\Phi])$ have the same truth-value when Φ contains no modal operators, they differ in mode of expression or meaning. $\mathbf{N}(\delta[\Phi])$ attributes necessity to Φ indirectly, by using the name $\delta[\Phi]$ to refer to it, whereas $\Box\Phi$ attributes necessity to Φ directly, by prefixing $\Box$ to it. The distinction being made is simply that between *using* a statement of the object language and *referring to* that statement in the metalanguage.

This difference may also be seen in terms of what is involved in understanding the meaning of a modal statement of each kind (cf. pp. 4–5, 172). Consider someone who knows how to use the modal symbols $\Box$ and **N**, who understands the expression "the statement on the board," but who knows no tensor calculus. Suppose there is just one statement on the board, it is about tensors, and he does not understand it. Then he cannot understand the result of prefixing $\Box$ to this statement, but he can understand "The statement on the board is necessary."

Next consider iterated modalities. When the modal predicate **N** is used, iterated modalities take the form $\mathbf{N}(\delta[\mathbf{N}(\delta[\Phi])])$, $\mathbf{N}(\delta[\mathbf{N}(\delta[\mathbf{N}(\delta[\Phi])])])$, etc. See Table 22 for examples. The question arises: Do corresponding modal operators and modal predicate statements have the same truth-values when iterated modalities are involved? For instance, if Φ contains no modal operators, is $\Box\Box\Phi$ true if and only if $\mathbf{N}(\delta[\mathbf{N}(\delta[\Phi])])$ is true? Compare rule [X] above.

The answer to this question depends on the properties of the name relation δ. When formulas are named by their Gödel numbers, a modal operator statement and the corresponding modal predicate statement do have the same truth-value, as in columns 1 and 3 of Table 22. Since one can decide by reasoning alone that β_1 is true, γ_1 is also true (cf. p. 466). Similarly, one can decide by reasoning alone that β_3 is true, for an analysis of the number $\mathbf{g}[\alpha_3]$, i.e., $\mathbf{g}[87\text{x}113 = 9831]$, into its prime factors is an arithmetic calculation. Hence γ_3 is true. More generally, it is plausible to maintain that $\Box\Box\Phi$ and $\mathbf{N}(\mathbf{g}[\mathbf{N}(\mathbf{g}[\Phi])])$ are true or false together, and similarly for further iterations of $\Box$ and **N**.

This correspondence of truth-value breaks down when formulas are named by descriptions of the sort used in column 4 of Table 22. Statement [1] of page 3 of this book *is* logically true, and so β_4 is true. But this is a matter of fact, not a matter of logic. For while a logically true statement is written at this place in our actual world, there are logically possible alternative worlds in which this is not the case; for example, worlds in which an empirically false statement is written at that place. It is thus plausible to hold that the truth of β_4 cannot be decided by reasoning alone and hence that γ_4 is false. Here is a case where the modal operator statement $\Box\Box\Phi$ is true and the corresponding modal predicate statement $\mathbf{N}(\delta[\mathbf{N}(\delta[\Phi])])$ is false. Thus when iterated modalities are involved, the difference in meaning between $\Box$ and $\mathbf{N}\delta$ sometimes produces a difference in truth-value between a modal operator statement and the corresponding modal predicate statement.

This comparison of columns 3 and 4 of Table 22 shows that the behavior of iterated modal predicates in a hierarchy of languages depends critically on the properties of the name relation δ of the hierarchy. A further example will illustrate this point.

We saw earlier that "*provable* in $\mathcal{L}^0$" can be defined in $\mathcal{L}^0$, while "*true* in $\mathcal{L}^0$" can be defined only in $\mathcal{L}^1$ and higher languages, not in $\mathcal{L}^0$ (sec. 6.4.2). It is natural to ask whether the modal predicate "*necessary* (**N**) in $\mathcal{L}^0$" can be defined in $\mathfrak{L}^0$. Montague has shown that the answer is negative if formulas are named by their Gödel numbers and the system contains a minimal set of principles governing necessity (**N**). On the other hand, by naming formulas with quotes Niemi has constructed a consistent object language containing the predicate **N** in which a reasonable amount of modal logic may be expressed.* Hence the answer to the question: "Can the modal predicate **N** be defined in the object language?" depends on the name relation δ that is involved.

This concludes our brief comparison of modal operators and modal predicates. The operator $\Box$ and the predicate **N** behave somewhat similarly, but there are also important differences, which depend in part on the name relation δ of the hierarchy. Actually, very few formal hierarchical systems of modal predicates have been constructed and studied, and not enough is known about the interpretation of iterated modal predicates to clarify the interpretation of iterated modal operators. In my opinion, a good understanding of the iterated modalities will come only after logicians have constructed and studied interpreted hierarchical systems that contain the modal predicate **N** and a name relation δ, as well as the modal operators $\Box$ and $\Box^c$, and that permit iterations, both separately and together, of $\Box$, $\Box^c$, and $\mathbf{N}\delta$.

We have now completed our discussion of the problem of interpreting iterated modalities. We have seen that iterated modalities are closely related to language hierarchies in which expressions refer to other expressions, and to modal logics that contain statement quantifiers and predicates. We saw earlier that predicate and statement quantifiers are needed for symbolizing dispositional statements and other elliptical causal subjunctives (secs. 7.3.2–7.3.3). Hence a complete understanding of the causal modalities requires the development and interpretation of more comprehensive logical systems, based on hierarchies of languages rather than on single languages, containing predicate and statement quantifiers in addition to individual quantifiers, and containing metalinguistic modal predicates as well as modal operators.

7.6 Conclusion

There are two basic aspects to my logic of causal statements: its formal structure and its interpretation.

As a formal language, the logic of causal statements contains sharp and rigorous distinctions between certain given atoms and the corresponding constructed compounds: primitive symbols *vs.* formulas, axioms *vs.* theorems, and primitive rules *vs.* derived rules of inference. These notions

* Montague, "Syntactical Treatments of Modality, with Corollaries on Reflexion Principles and Finite Axiomatizability." Niemi, "On the Existence of a Modal Antinomy."

are all defined without reference to the interpretation of the language. Indeed, there are decision machines for formulahood, axiomhood, and proofhood in the logic of causal statements.

Natural languages do not contain the rigid distinctions characteristic of a formal language and they are therefore much less mechanical in structure than formal languages. Hence the structure of the logic of causal statements is very different from the structure of a natural language. Nevertheless, the precise notion of deductive validity in the logic of causal statements is a useful model of the vague notion of deductive validity of ordinary and scientific discourse.

In the present chapter we have used formulas of the logic of causal statements to model deductive arguments containing causal statements. Differences as well as similarities have been noted. This use of the logic of causal statements to model natural discourse constitutes a concrete (in contrast to an abstract) interpretation of it.

Laws of Nature (*sec. 7.2*). Nonprobabilistic laws of nature and scientific theories are causally necessary, since they hold for sets of possible boundary conditions, most of which are nonactual. Laws of nature have three main features: uniqueness or single-valuedness, of which determinism is a limiting case; modality, or appropriateness of $\Box^c \Phi \sim\Box\Phi$; and invariance over space and time. A causal law is a law of nature formulated in terms of cause and effect.

Causal necessity and causal implication give better models of causal laws than nonmodal, logically modal, or probabilistic symbols. However, still better models are obtained with nonparadoxical implication (**npc**), which requires logical independence of antecedent and consequent and excludes the paradoxes of causal implication.

For $\Phi\Psi$ **npc** Θ to be true, the antecedent must be causally sufficient to produce the consequent. Hence $\Phi\Psi$ **npc** Θ does not export to $\Phi \supset (\Psi$ **npc** $\Theta)$, though it does export to Φ **npc** $(\Psi \supset \Theta)$ when Φ, Ψ, and Θ satisfy certain independence conditions. Transitivity, addition of a superfluous condition, and transposition also hold for **npc** when appropriate independence conditions are satisfied.

Subjunctives and dispositions (*sec. 7.3*). Most subjunctives are elliptical, and elliptical causal implication (**ec**) was introduced to symbolize them. This notion is defined by

$$\Psi \textbf{ ec } \Theta =_{df} (\exists\Phi)[\Phi(\Phi\Psi \textbf{ npc } \Theta)]$$

for the statement variable case, and similarly for the predicate variable case (p. 444). The logic of causal statements was extended informally to cover statement and predicate quantifiers.

In appropriate contexts, laws of nature, causal laws, and lawlike statements imply subjunctive conditionals, counterfactual or noncounterfactual.

These subjunctives are called "causal subjunctives." Good models of them may be constructed by means of **npc** and **ec** but not by the simpler types of implication $\supset$ or $\rightarrow$. An elliptical causal subjunctive "If Ψ were the case, Θ would be the case" should be modeled by $\sim\Psi(\Psi\ \mathbf{ec}\ \Theta)$ if a counterfactual is meant and by $\Psi\ \mathbf{ec}\ \Theta$ if a noncounterfactual is meant. But $\Psi\ \mathbf{ec}\ \Theta$ is not a perfect model for these subjunctives; for the context of the subjunctive may be subject to certain informal constraints or conditions that do not apply to the formula $\Psi\ \mathbf{ec}\ \Theta$, with the result that the subjunctive may be false or misleading when the corresponding formula is not.

An indicative such as "Gold dissolves in aqua regia" should be modeled by **npc** or $\supset$ according to the context; in some contexts it is unclear which symbols should be used. When the modal status of a premise or conclusion is vague, the validity status of the argument may also be vague. Scientific discourse is generally vague with respect to its modal status. But scientific practice and inference do reflect modal distinctions, for scientists draw subjunctive conclusions from their premises and apply their laws to possible situations they know will not be realized.

Causal dispositionals involve elliptical or implicit information that may be symbolized with an existential predicate quantifier. Thus "Her ring (r) is soluble (D) in aqua regia (A)" is symbolized by "$(\exists X)[Xr(XrAr\ \mathbf{npc}\ Dr)]$" or "$Ar\ \mathbf{ec}\ Dr$." If a dispositional statement is true, there is a property underlying the disposition by virtue of which it is true. And the properties underlying a disposition, e.g., being gold, being silver, are more enduring and less transient than the properties mentioned explicitly in the dispositional, e.g., being placed in aqua regia, dissolving.

An elliptical causal implication $\Psi\ \mathbf{ec}\ \Theta$ differs from a corresponding nonparadoxical causal implication $\Phi\Psi\ \mathbf{npc}\ \Theta$ in the status of the clause Φ, which is explicit in the latter conditional but implicit in the former. This difference leads to interesting differences with respect to exportation and the compatibility of conditionals that have the same antecedent but contradictory consequents. The following theorems and non-theorems show the basic similarities and differences, the non-theorems being placed in rectangles:

$$\boxed{(\Phi\Psi\ \mathbf{npc}\ \Theta) \supset \{\Phi \supset (\Psi\ \mathbf{npc}\ \Theta)\}} \qquad (\Phi\Psi\ \mathbf{ec}\ \Theta) \supset \{\Phi \supset (\Psi\ \mathbf{ec}\ \Theta)\}$$

$$\sim(\Psi\ \mathbf{npc}\ \Theta\bar{\Theta}) \qquad \sim(\Psi\ \mathbf{ec}\ \Theta\bar{\Theta})$$

$$\sim\{(\Psi\ \mathbf{npc}\ \Theta)(\Psi\ \mathbf{npc}\ \bar{\Theta})\} \qquad \boxed{\sim\{(\Psi\ \mathbf{ec}\ \Theta)(\Psi\ \mathbf{ec}\ \bar{\Theta})\}}$$

The last formula is not a theorem because Ψ can elliptically cause Θ under one condition (Λ_1) and elliptically cause not-Θ under another condition (Λ_2), though it will then be causally impossible for Ψ to occur jointly with both conditions (theorem [24]).

There is a pattern common to many counterfactual elliptical subjunctives. Consider the form "If Ψ were the case, Θ would be," meant as an elliptical counterfactual. The user is considering a certain state of affairs $\Phi\Psi$ that is factual in respect Φ, counterfactual in respect Ψ. He is asserting that another "state of affairs" Θ follows from $\Phi\Psi$ by certain rules or principles. Causal and noncausal subjunctives vary in regard to the logical or epistemological status of $\Phi\Psi$ and the rules and principles used to connect Θ to $\Phi\Psi$.

Causality (*sec. 7.4*). Many important features of causal laws may be modeled by means of nonparadoxical causal implication (**npc**), and many important features of cause-effect statements may be modeled by means of elliptical causal implication (**ec**). Elliptical causal implication is appropriate for symbolizing cause-effect relations, because the cause is not sufficient to produce the effect by itself but only in the presence of another condition. Specifically, if ψ causes θ in some instance α, then $\psi\alpha$ **ec** $\theta\alpha$, or $\overline{\psi\alpha}$ **ec** $\overline{\theta\alpha}$, or both are true. On the other hand, an important feature of the relation of cause to effect is not expressed by the form $\psi\alpha$ **ec** $\theta\alpha$: a cause and its effect play certain definite roles in a process, the cause being a key factor in bringing about its effect.

When asserting a causal subjunctive, one should be dealing with a relatively isolated, self-sufficient system and a relatively definite theory or set of laws governing this system. Correspondingly, when modeling a causal subjunctive, one should apply the ***rule of completeness for causal subjunctives***: include enough of the context of the subjunctive to obtain a portion of discourse that is complete and self-sufficient with respect to the relevant forces and laws, and model this portion of discourse as a unit. This rule is similar to the rule of total evidence (p. 20).

This rule is illustrated by Lewis Carroll's barbershop paradox. The barbershop rules are dispositional and elliptical, and so a formal model based on **ec** captures many aspects of the situation. But the crucial issue concerns the compatibility of two subjunctives "If A, then $\bar{B}$" and "If A, then B." When the rule of completeness of causal subjunctives is applied to the barbershop paradox, these subjunctives are incompatible. Since the formulas "A **ec** $\bar{B}$" and "A **ec** B" are compatible, they do not capture this feature of the paradox and hence do not fully resolve it.

We drew a philosophical conclusion from our success in using the logic of causal statements to model causal laws, causal dispositionals, causal subjunctives, and cause-effect statements. *At the pragmatic level of ordinary usage and scientific practice, there is a necessary connection between cause and effect.* This necessity is not logical necessity ($\Box$), but causal necessity ($\Box^c$). The concepts of logical and causal necessity are formally similar, but their concrete interpretations are markedly different (p. 457).

Iterated modalities (*sec. 7.5*). We did not need iterated modalities until we symbolized changes of disposition. There is no satisfactory concrete interpretation of iterated modalities.

The principles $\Box\Phi \equiv \Box\Box\Phi$ and $\Diamond\Psi \equiv \Box\Diamond\Psi$ are plausible. The principles $\Box^c \Phi \equiv \Box\Box^c \Phi$ and $\Diamond^c \Psi \equiv \Box\Diamond^c \Psi$ are false, since causal statements are empirically true-or-false.

Iterated modal operators are closely related to statement predicates and quantifiers. They are also related to iterations of modal predicates in a hierarchy of languages. In such a hierarchy, a necessity statement may be formed by prefixing the modal predicate **N** to a term $\delta[\Phi]$ that designates the statement Φ.

The operator $\Box$ and the predicate **N** behave similarly: to each object language statement $\Box\Phi$ there corresponds a metalinguistic statement $\mathbf{N}(\delta(\Phi))$ that has the same truth-value. But this correspondence does not always hold for iterated modalities. For some name relations δ, $\Box\Box\Phi$ and $\mathbf{N}(\delta[\mathbf{N}(\delta[\Phi])])$ may have different truth-values.

A complete understanding of the causal modalities requires the development and interpretation of more comprehensive logical systems, based on hierarchies of languages rather than on single languages, containing predicate and statement quantifiers in addition to individual quantifiers, and containing metalinguistic modal predicates as well as modal operators.

Conclusion. The logic of causal statements is a good model for causal statements and arguments of ordinary discourse, though not a perfect one. It fits actual discourse well enough to show that causal necessity is an essential feature of laws of nature, causal laws, causal dispositionals, causal subjunctives, and cause-effect statements.

This result leads naturally to our fourth main question: What is the nature of causal necessity and how is it related to inductive probability? We shall suggest an answer to this question in Chapters 9 and 10. But first, we shall use the notion of a disposition to answer our third main question.

8 The Dispositional Theory of Empirical Probability

. . . the statement that the *probability*, that if a die be thrown from a dice box it will turn up a number divisible by three, is one-third . . . means that the die has a certain "would-be"; and to say that a die has a "would-be" is to say that it has a property, quite analogous to any *habit* that a man might have. Only the "would-be" of the die is presumably as much simpler and more definite than the man's habit as the die's homogeneous composition and cubical shape is simpler than the nature of the man's nervous system and soul. . . .*

8.1 Introduction

Our third main question was: What is the general nature of a system of atomic empirical probability statements? How are empirical ($\mathbf{P}_e$) and inductive ($\mathbf{P}$) probability related? Why is the traditional calculus of probability applicable to empirical probabilities? (Pp. 29, 144)

The frequency theory of empirical probability holds that atomic empirical probability statements should be analyzed into frequency probability statements and reasoned about by means of the calculus of frequency probability, which is an interpretation of the traditional calculus of probability. This theory partially answers our third question, but it does not explain how empirical probability statements are verified or applied. Frequencies can be observed only in the finite case; whereas frequency probability statements deal with infinite sequences, requiring rules of inductive inference to make the connection. Conversely, empirical probability statements are often applied to single events, and rules of inductive inference are needed to make the connection in this direction also. (Sec. 3.4.1)

In the present chapter we give a better and more complete answer to the third question. We combine ideas taken from our analysis of causal dispositionals (sec. 7.3.2), our pragmatic theory of inductive probability (sec. 5.6), and the frequency theory of empirical probability (sec. 3.4.1) for the purpose of developing a new theory, to be called the "dispositional theory of empirical probability."

This chapter is based on my articles "Dispositional Statements" and "Peirce's Two Theories of Probability."

* Peirce, *Collected Papers* 2.664 (1910). More of this quotation is given on pp. 534–35, below.

Section 8.2.1 contains a dispositional model of the statement

(a) The empirical probability of this coin falling tails is one–half [$\mathbf{P}_e(T) = .5$].

Very roughly, the model states

(b) The coin is such that, were it tossed many times, it would probably (**P**) fall tails approximately half the time.

Two points should be noted about this dispositional model. First, the only sense of "probability" used in the model is that of inductive probability, so that empirical probabilities are accounted for by means of inductive probabilities. Second, an empirical probability statement is explicated in terms of an inductive probability assignment to observable consequences; compare Peirce's pragmatic analysis of empirical statements into their deductive consequences (p. 167).

After constructing this dispositional model, we compare it with our earlier model of the causal dispositional "Her ring is soluble in aqua regia" (sec. 8.2.2). We next show how to construct a dispositional model for any atomic empirical probability statement (sec. 8.2.3).

The notion of an atomic empirical probability statement, which is restricted to independent processes, is then generalized to the notion of an empirical probability theory. Dispositional models are constructed for empirical probability theories, and the dispositional theory of empirical probability is stated in terms of these models. A positivistic version of the dispositional theory is also given. (Sec. 8.3)

The dispositional theory of empirical probability is compared with other theories of empirical probability in Section 8.4, and the whole development is summarized in Section 8.5.

8.2 A Fair Coin

8.2.1 Dispositional model of the fair coin hypothesis

Empirical probability statements occur in many branches of science, and they are often exceedingly complicated. In principle, there is no bound on how complicated they can be, other than man's capacity to deal with them. Fortunately, however, the essential epistemological features of empirical probability are found in simple examples. We shall analyze first our earlier example of the 500-lira piece, dated 1861 and 1961 and commemorating one hundred years of Italian unity (p. 143). Suppose the coin is to be tossed repeatedly by the usual process, and it is asserted that:

The empirical probability of this coin falling tails is one-half,

or, more briefly, $\mathbf{P}_e(T) = .5$. This probability statement is empirical, to be investigated by tossing the coin.

How the coin falls depends on the tossing procedure as well as the coin itself. "This coin is fair" asserts that the coin is such that, if it were randomly or fairly tossed, the resultant sequence of tails and heads would be an independent process of probability one-half. Hence "This is a fair coin, randomly tossed" implies "The sequence of tails and heads is an independent process of probability one-half." The latter assertion does not imply the former, though, because an unfairness in the coin might be compensated for in the tossing procedure. Nevertheless, for convenience of reference we call "$\mathbf{P}_e(T) = 1/2$" the "fair-coin hypothesis."

Let the sequence of possible tosses be $x_1, x_2, x_3, \ldots$, with the outcome of each toss x_i being a tail (T) or a head ($\bar{T}$). The fair-coin hypothesis $\mathbf{P}_e(T) = 1/2$ asserts that the sequence $Tx_1, Tx_2, Tx_3, \ldots$ is an independent process of probability one-half (p. 58).* We explicate this hypothesis by considering the empirical process of verifying or refuting it. If this hypothesis is rejected, some alternative hypothesis will probably be accepted. Consequently, the empirical content of the fair-coin hypothesis is best explicated by considering it along with alternatives to it. The alternatives occur at two different levels. The sequence of tosses may be an independent process of some probability other than one-half; but at a deeper level, the sequence of possible tosses may not be an independent process at all (see sec. 8.3.1).

Any empirical investigation is conducted against a background of information and assumptions. Let us suppose that the process $Tx_1, Tx_2, Tx_3, \ldots$ is an independent process of some unknown probability. This assumption can be formulated in two different ways. In the terminology of Section 2.5.2, it says that the process $Tx_1, Tx_2, Tx_3, \ldots$ is a mixture of independent processes. In the terminology of empirical probabilities, it says that "$\mathbf{P}_e(T) = \alpha$" is true for some unknown α. The number of possible values of α that really matter depends on the precision required. Although there are many interesting problems about continuous probabilities, they are not relevant to our question about the nature of empirical probability. For our purposes it will suffice to divide the probability range into tenths and assume that α is restricted to the eleven values 0, .1, .2, . . . , .9, 1.

Since the probability statements $\mathbf{P}_e(T) = \alpha$ are empirical, they may be confirmed or disconfirmed by observation and experiment. Suppose the coin is thrown 1,000 times and 523 tosses are tails. This result is much more likely on $\mathbf{P}_e(T) = .5$ than on the other alternatives. Correspondingly, the fair-coin hypothesis $\mathbf{P}_e(T) = .5$ is strongly confirmed by this result, and the alternative hypotheses $\mathbf{P}_e(T) = \alpha$ for $\alpha \neq .5$ are strongly disconfirmed.

This verification process may be modeled by means of Bayes' theorem

* Note that we are here talking about the fair-coin hypothesis, not asserting it. This fact is signified by the context, specifically, by the occurrence of the word "hypothesis"; it could also be signified by placing the hypothesis in quotation marks. Our usage in these matters is generally informal, as explained earlier on p. 43.

and Bayes' method of finding an unknown probability (sec. 2.5). It will be recalled that an application of Bayes' theorem involves the following: a set of alternative hypotheses, a prior probability distribution over these hypotheses, an observed result, the degree to which each hypothesis predicts this result, and the probabilities of the hypotheses posterior to this result. In the present example, the alternative hypotheses are the eleven empirical probability statements $\mathbf{P}_e(T) = \alpha$. Nothing was explicitly stated about the prior probabilities of these hypotheses, but the verification of the fair-coin hypothesis $\mathbf{P}_e(T) = 1/2$ on the basis of 1,000 tosses presupposes something about these prior probabilities. For the result of 523 tails in 1,000 tosses was taken as pretty well settling the question: What is the empirical probability of a tail? Now if a person were strongly enough convinced that the coin was biased, he would attribute the observed result to chance and would not accept the fair-coin hypothesis $\mathbf{P}_e(T) = .5$, though further results might cause him to change his mind. Thus the acceptance of $\mathbf{P}_e(T) = .5$ on the basis of 523 tails in 1,000 tosses is incompatible with certain prior probability distributions, even though it is compatible with a wide range of prior probability distributions. More generally, unless there is some restriction on the prior probabilities, no finite amount of evidence can settle the question: What is the empirical probability of a tail? (Pp. 89–91)

For the sake of simplicity, let us assign equal prior probabilities to the eleven hypotheses under consideration. The foregoing inductive reasoning about the coin may then be expressed as follows. The first premise states that the process is a mixture of independent processes, with each empirical probability value having the same prior probability.

[1] $\mathbf{P}_e(T) = 0, .1, \ldots, .9$ or 1; and
$\mathbf{P}(\mathbf{P}_e(T) = \alpha) = 1/11$, for $\alpha = 0, .1, \ldots, .9, 1$.

Symbolize the observed result of tossing the coin by

(*R*) Out of 1,000 tosses, 523 were tails.

The second premise is

[2] It is the case that *R*, and *R* expresses all available information about the results of tossing the coin.*

The traditional calculus of probability gives the following approximate values for the degrees of prediction of *R*.

[3] $\mathbf{P}(R, \mathbf{P}_e(T) = .5) = 8.76 \times 10^{-3}$
$\mathbf{P}(R, \mathbf{P}_e(T) = .6) = 1.34 \times 10^{-7}$
$\mathbf{P}(R, \mathbf{P}_e(T) = \alpha) \leqq 1.07 \times 10^{-15}$ when α is neither .5 nor .6.

* Since the sequence $Tx_1, Tx_2, \ldots$ is a mixture of independent processes, any information beyond the number of heads and the number of tails is inductively irrelevant. But from a theoretical point of view there is no harm in using all the available information. See our earlier discussion of the rule of total evidence (p. 20).

The following approximate posterior probabilities may be inferred by means of Bayes' theorem.

[4] $\mathbf{P}(\mathbf{P}_e(T) = .5, R) = .999985$
$\mathbf{P}(\mathbf{P}_e(T) = .6, R) = .000015$
$\mathbf{P}(\mathbf{P}_e(T) = \alpha, R) \leqq 10^{-13}$ when α is neither .5 nor .6.

Since R expresses all the available information about the results of tossing the coin, the posterior probabilities of [4] are accepted as the correct probabilities to act upon. And the posterior probability of the fair-coin hypothesis is so close to 1 that for most practical purposes we can conclude the true hypothesis is

[5] $\therefore\ \mathbf{P}_e(T) = .5$.

Let us look at some of the epistemological features of the preceding inductive argument. An atomic empirical probability statement is empirically true-or-false (pp. 27–28); hence conclusion [5] is empirically true-or-false. The first part of premise [1] is empirical, for the sequence of tosses might not be a mixture of independent processes; it might, for example, be a Markov chain (see also pp. 490–91, below). Premise [2] is clearly empirically true-or-false. The remaining statements of the argument are atomic inductive probability statements. The prior probabilities are relative to the general information available, and so are the other inductive probabilities.

We now reformulate the inductive argument [1] – [5], eliminating the occurrences of empirical probability and using only conditional inductive probability, while yet keeping the empirical status of the conclusion and the first part of the first premise. The resulting argument [0′] – [6′] is a dispositional model of the original argument [1] – [5].

Premise [1] states that the sequence of tosses $Tx_1, Tx_2, \ldots$ is a mixture of independent processes of probabilities 0, .1, . . . , .9, and 1, and it assigns equal prior probabilities to each of these eleven probability values. Now the notion of a mixture of independent processes was defined relative to a condition G, so that a given process is a mixture of independent processes under some conditions G but not a mixture of independent processes under other conditions G (pp. 58, 75). To say that a sequence $Tx_1, Tx_2, \ldots$ is unconditionally a mixture of independent processes is to say that some condition G is satisfied relative to which the sequence $Tx_1, Tx_2, \ldots$ is a mixture of independent processes. The symbolization of premise [1] therefore calls for the existential statement quantifier "there exists a G." By the definition of a mixture of independent processes, there are hypotheses $H_0, H_{.1}, \ldots, H_{.9}, H_1$ that are mutually exclusive and jointly exhaustive relative to G and such that for each H_α the sequence $Tx_1, Tx_2, \ldots$ is an independent process of probability α relative to $H_\alpha \& G$. The prior probability of each of these hypotheses is also relative to G. Further conditions on statement G are discussed later (pp. 492–93, 500–501, 513).

Premise [1] is thus modeled by the quantified statement

[0′] There exist G and H_α (for $\alpha = 0, .1, \ldots, .9, 1$) such that: it is the case that G; G contains all available information about the process $Tx_1, Tx_2, \ldots$; $Tx_1, Tx_2, \ldots$ is an independent process of probability α relative to $H_\alpha \& G$; the H_α are mutually exclusive and jointly exhaustive relative to G; and $\mathbf{P}(H_\alpha, G) = 1/11$.

To draw conclusions from this premise we drop the existential statement quantifiers on G and H_α by repeated applications of the rule of existential instantiation of a statement (p. 445). The result of this operation is

[1′] It is the case that G; G contains all available information about the process $Tx_1, Tx_2, \ldots$; $Tx_1, Tx_2, \ldots$ is an independent process of probability α relative to $H_\alpha \& G$, for $\alpha = 0, .1, \ldots, .9, 1$; $H_0, H_{.1}, \ldots, H_{.9}, H_1$ are mutually exclusive and jointly exhaustive relative to G; and $\mathbf{P}(H_\alpha, G) = 1/11$, for $\alpha = 0, .1, \ldots, .9, 1$.

Premise [2] appears unchanged, as follows.

[2′] It is the case that R, and R expresses all available information about the results of tossing the coin,

where R states that 523 tosses out of 1,000 were tails. The degrees of prediction of R may be calculated from [1′] by the calculus of inductive probability. They are

[3′] $\mathbf{P}(R, H_{.5}G) = 8.76 \times 10^{-3}$
$\mathbf{P}(R, H_{.6}G) = 1.34 \times 10^{-7}$
$\mathbf{P}(R, H_\alpha G) \leqq 1.07 \times 10^{-15}$ when α is neither .5 nor .6.

The posterior probabilities may now be calculated from [1′] and [3′] by Bayes' theorem.

[4′] $\mathbf{P}(H_{.5}, RG) = .999985$,
$\mathbf{P}(H_{.6}, RG) = .000015$,
$\mathbf{P}(H_\alpha, RG) \leqq 10^{-13}$ when α is neither .5 nor .6,
where RG expresses all available information about the process $Tx_1, Tx_2, \ldots$.

It is essential that the posterior probabilities take into account all the available evidence. For example, if an investigator knows the result of 2,000 tosses of the coin, he should not base his posterior probabilities on just the first 1,000 tosses.

The desired conclusion may now be reached in two steps. By [4′] the posterior probability of the fair-coin hypothesis $H_{.5}$ is nearly 1, and the posterior probabilities of the alternative hypotheses are nearly 0. Hence for most practical purposes one can accept the fair-coin hypothesis. Combining this acceptance with [1′] gives

[5′] ∴ It is the case that $H_{.5}G$; and $Tx_1, Tx_2, \ldots$ is an independent process of probability .5 relative to $H_{.5}G$.

Finally, the statement $H_{.5}G$ is generalized by the rule of existential generalization of a statement (p. 445), giving the desired conclusion.

[6′] ∴ There exists a statement F such that:
it is the case that F; and $Tx_1, Tx_2, \ldots$ is an independent process of probability .5 relative to F.

The conclusion [6′] is a dispositional model of the empirical probability statement $\mathbf{P}_e(T) = .5$, and the whole argument [0′] – [6′] is a dispositional model of the original inductive argument [1] – [5]. This model argument contains two kinds of operations with existential quantifiers. At the beginning of the argument, the existential statement quantifiers on G and the H_α are dropped by the rule of existential instantiation; at the end of the argument the conjunction $H_{.5}G$ is quantified by the rule of existential generalization.

A simpler model may be obtained by treating these statement quantifiers and the manipulation of them externally, i.e., as exterior to the model. The original inductive argument [1] – [5] is then modeled by the argument [1′] – [5′], with each step of the latter modeling the corresponding step of the former. In this dispositional model the symbol "G" represents an arbitrary statement relative to which the sequence of tosses is a mixture of independent processes of probabilities 0, .1, . . . , .9, 1 (with each probability value having the same prior probability); and each symbol "H_α" represents an arbitrary statement relative to which the sequence of tosses is an independent process of probability α. In the model [1′] – [5′], the assumption that the sequence of tosses is a mixture of independent processes is modeled by G and each $\mathbf{P}_e(T) = \alpha$ is modeled by the corresponding H_α. Each $\mathbf{P}_e(T) = \alpha$ and the corresponding H_α imply the same predictions to the same degree (cf. [3] and [3′]) and are supported in the same way by the same observations (cf. [4] and [4′]). Consequently, the empirical tests for each $\mathbf{P}_e(T) = \alpha$ and the corresponding H_α are the same. Hence the hypotheses H_α are good models of the atomic empirical probability statements $\mathbf{P}_e(T) = \alpha$. In particular, hypothesis $H_{.5}$ models the fair-coin hypothesis $\mathbf{P}_e(T) = .5$.

We have now given two dispositional models, [0′] – [6′] and [1′] – [5′], of the original inductive argument [1] – [5], that is, of the process of verifying the empirical probability statement $\mathbf{P}_e(T) = .5$ by tossing the coin. What we have modeled is a specific example of an empirical probability statement and its verification, but we shall see later that any empirical probability statement and its verification by means of Bayes' theorem can be modeled in this way (sec. 8.2.3). Because of the general significance of these dispositional models, two points should be noted about them here: the only concept of probability they employ is the concept of conditional inductive probability, and yet they preserve the empirical status of empirical probability statements. We will conclude this subsection by developing these two points further.

The original inductive argument [1] – [5] uses two concepts of probability: empirical probability ($\mathbf{P}_e$) and inductive probability ($\mathbf{P}$). In contrast, the dispositional models of this argument employ only the latter concept, and that only in its conditional (as opposed to its unconditional) form (sec. 2.6). Consequently, the only inductive rules used in the dispositional models are the formal rules of the calculus of inductive probability, the informal rules governing the application of this calculus, e.g., the rule of total evidence, and the rules of standard inductive logic. Thus our dispositional models make explicit the rules governing the verification of the empirical probability statement $\mathbf{P}_e(T) = .5$. Compare our earlier conclusion that the frequency theory of empirical probability does not say what rules are used in the verification of an empirical probability statement (pp. 149–50).

Our exclusive use of conditional inductive probability in the dispositional models [0′] – [6′] and [1′] – [5′] gives rise to a question. Atomic inductive probability statements are not empirically true-or-false (p. 160). Yet the dispositional models preserve the empirical status of the empirical probability statements they model. How do they do this? They do it by means of the existential statement quantifiers that are explicit in the model [0′] – [6′] and implicit in the model [1′] – [5′]. Let us illustrate this mechanism for the case of $\mathbf{P}_e(T) = .5$.

The empirical probability statement $\mathbf{P}_e(T) = .5$ is modeled by [6′], which asserts that some statement F is true of the coin, where F satisfies the condition

[a] $Tx_1, Tx_2, \ldots$ is an independent process of probability .5 relative to F.

We demonstrate first that this condition is not empirically true-or-false. The notion of an independent process was defined on page 58 in terms of the notion of an independent set of statements, and the latter notion was defined on page 50. When each definiendum is replaced by its definiens, condition [a] becomes an infinite conjunction of two kinds of statements. Those of the first kind are atomic inductive probability statements giving the degree of prediction for each toss, for example, $\mathbf{P}(Tx_7, F) = .5$. Those of the second kind are assertions of independence, such as

$$\mathbf{P}(Tx_2, F) = \mathbf{P}(Tx_2, Tx_1F) .$$

This may be written

$$\text{There is a number } x \text{ such that } \mathbf{P}(Tx_2, F) = x \text{ and } \mathbf{P}(Tx_2, Tx_1F) = x ,$$

which shows that assertions of independence are compounds of atomic inductive probability statements. Now such statements are not empirically true-or-false (p. 160), and so condition [a] is not empirically true-or-false.

But though condition [a] is not itself empirical, whether or not there is a true statement F satisfying this condition is an empirical matter. Thus the quantified statement [6′] is empirically true-or-false, even though its constituent condition [a] is not. This explains how the dispositional models [0′] – [6′] and [1′] – [5′] can use conditional inductive probability as the sole probability concept and yet preserve the empirical status of empirical probability statements.

8.2.2 Causal and probabilistic dispositions

The preceding models of empirical probability statements employ existential statement quantifiers, which have been used in this context to assert the truth of statements not given explicitly but characterized by their inductive probability relations to observable consequences. This is similar to the use of existential predicate and statement quantifiers to model causal dispositions (sec. 7.3.2). While there are important differences between the two cases, the similarities are sufficient to warrant saying that a true atomic empirical probability statement is about a ***probabilistic disposition.***

Let us refer to a dispositional statement as a "dispositional." It is instructive to compare a causal dispositional with a probabilistic dispositional. The causal dispositional

> Her ring (r) is such that, if it were placed in aqua regia (A), it would dissolve (D)

was symbolized

$$(\exists X)[Xr(XrAr \ \mathbf{npc}\ Dr)] \quad ,$$

where "**npc**" signifies nonparadoxical causal implication (p. 428). The probabilistic dispositional

> The empirical probability of this 500-lira piece falling tails (T) is .5 [$\mathbf{P}_e(T) = .5$]

was symbolized

[6′] There exists a statement F such that:
it is the case that F; and Tx_1, Tx_2, . . . is an independent process of probability .5 relative to F.

For the sake of convenience a statement quantifier is used here rather than a predicate quantifier; but a predicate quantifier could have been used, for "$\mathbf{P}_e(T) = .5$" attributes a property to the coin and tossing procedure just as "$(\exists X)[Xr(XrAr \ \mathbf{npc}\ Dr)]$" attributes a property to the ring.

Both causal and probabilistic dispositionals attribute a property to an object without explicitly naming the property. For causal dispositions we called such a property a "property underlying the disposition" (p. 442). In the beginning, we use the same terminology for probabilistic dispositions, although ultimately it will turn out that what underlies a probabilistic disposition is a miniature system involving laws as well as properties. In the case of a causal disposition, a property underlying the disposition is characterized by its causal connections to transient properties such as "dissolving" that are observed in the experimental situation. In the case of a probabilistic disposition, a property underlying the disposition is characterized by its inductive probability connections to possible finite sequences of observable events (falling heads or tails). Note that falling heads (or tails) is a transient property of the coin.

One difference between causal and probabilistic dispositionals concerns the epistemological status of the condition used to characterize the property underlying the disposition. The formula "$(\exists X)[Xr(XrAr$ **npc** $Dr)]$" asserts that the ring has a property X, characterizing this property by means of the causal conditional "$XrAr$ **npc** Dr." This causal conditional is empirically true-or-false. The probabilistic dispositional [6′] asserts that some statement F is true of the coin and tossing procedure, and it characterizes F by its inductive probability connections to the possible outcomes of tossing the coin. Specifically, F must be such that

[a] $Tx_1, Tx_2, \ldots$ is an independent process of probability .5 relative to F.

We saw in the last subsection that this independence condition has the same epistemological status as the atomic inductive probability statements of which it is compounded; the relevant aspect of that status for us here is that the independence condition is not empirically true-or-false. Thus a probability condition used to characterize a property underlying a probabilistic disposition is not empirically true-or-false, whereas a causal condition used to characterize a property underlying a causal disposition is empirically true-or-false.

Despite this difference, there is an important similarity between a condition that characterizes a property underlying a causal disposition and a condition that characterizes a property underlying a probabilistic disposition. Both are fundamentally modal in character. We have used the logic of causal statements to symbolize conditions of the former kind and the calculus of inductive probability to symbolize conditions of the latter kind. There are obvious differences between these two systems, the most important being the central role of numbers in the calculus of inductive probability. But both systems treat of possibilities as well as actualities and hence are modal logics. The logic of causal statements treats logically possible and causally possible universes, as well as the actual universe (sec. 6.1). The calculus of inductive probability treats logically possible as well as actual events. For example, the statement "Tx_1, Tx_2, Tx_3 is an independent process of probability α on condition g" assigns conditional inductive probabilities to all eight possible outcomes of three tosses of a coin (p. 58). If the coin is never tossed, none of these eight possibilities will be actual. Similarly, in Carnap's extension of the calculus of inductive probability, unconditional inductive probabilities are assigned to all logically possible universes belonging to a given model (sec. 3.2.2).

There are two important manifestations of the fact that the logic of causal statements and the calculus of inductive probability are both modal logics. First, the rules for exchanging equivalents of both systems have modal restrictions. The exchange principle of the calculus of inductive probability and of standard inductive logic allows logically equivalent statements to be exchanged in probability contexts, but not statements that are merely truth-functionally equivalent (pp. 47–48). The rule of exchange of the logic of causal statements requires provable equivalence for exchange, and provable equivalence implies logical equivalence (pp. 403, 364). Such restrictions on the exchange of equivalents are to be expected in logical systems dealing with possibilities as well as actualities.

Second, both the logic of causal statements and the calculus of inductive probability may be used to model subjunctive conditionals. We saw in Section 7.3 how to model many subjunctives in the logic of causal statements. In particular, causal dispositionals may be expressed as subjunctives, and they imply subjunctives. Similarly, probabilistic dispositionals imply subjunctives. For example, the fair-coin hypothesis $\mathbf{P}_e(T) = .5$ may be expressed briefly as

> The coin and tossing procedure are such that the sequence Tx_1, Tx_2, . . . is an independent process of probability .5.

By dropping the existential statement quantifier implicit in "such that," using the calculus of inductive probability, and replacing the existential quantifier by existential generalization of a statement, one may infer

> The coin and tossing procedure are such that the probability of from 450 to 550 tails in 1,000 tosses is .999860.*

This implies the subjunctive

> If the coin *were* thrown 1,000 times by this procedure, it *would* very probably fall tails between 450 and 550 times.

Thus both causal and probabilistic dispositionals imply subjunctives.

Another similarity between causal and probabilistic dispositionals emerges from a consideration of the premise with which the investigation of the 500-lira piece began, namely: There is a definite empirical probability of the coin falling tails. We divided the probability range into tenths for convenience, and so this premise became

* *Tables of the Cumulative Binomial Probability Distribution.*

[1] $\mathbf{P}_e(T) = 0, .1, \ldots, .9$, or 1.

This was modeled by [0′], which may be expressed briefly as

[b] The coin is such that the process $Tx_1, Tx_2, \ldots$ is a mixture of independent processes.

Now each of the alternative hypotheses $\mathbf{P}_e(T) = \alpha$ is modeled by

[c] The coin is such that the process $Tx_1, Tx_2, \ldots$ is an independent process of probability α,

and the fair-coin hypothesis is modeled by the specific case of this when $\alpha = .5$. The forms of [b] and [c] are essentially the same. Since [c] is dispositional and empirical, so is [b].

Thus, to assert that the sequence of tosses is a mixture of independent processes is to attribute a disposition to the coin (and tossing procedure). Likewise, to assert that the sequence of tosses is an independent process of probability α, for some fixed α, is to attribute a disposition to the coin and tossing procedure. The former assertion is a disjunction of assertions of the latter kind, for to say that a sequence of tosses is a mixture of independent processes is to say that it is an independent sequence of some unknown probability α. Hence, in determining the unknown probability of the coin falling tails, the investigator began with the premise that the coin had a general probabilistic disposition, i.e., that a sequence of tosses was a mixture of independent processes, and used Bayes' theorem to ascertain that the coin had a more specific probabilistic disposition, i.e., that the coin was in fact fair.

Let us look at the assertion that the sequence of tosses is a mixture of independent processes from an epistemological point of view. Since this assertion is empirical, there are logically conceivable circumstances under which it would be false. We mention two of them, one involving the coin, the other the tossing procedure.

(1) Imagine that the coin has an internal mechanism that shifts its center of gravity according to the way it falls, so that when it falls heads the probability of a tail on the next toss is increased, and when it falls tails the probability of a head on the next toss is increased. One who commits the gambler's fallacy in effect attributes such a mechanism to a normal coin (p. 62). If the coin does have this internal mechanism, and it is not compensated for in the tossing procedure, the sequence of tosses is not a mixture of independent processes.

(2) Suppose the toss is made by one of those rare persons who can control the way the coin lands, though the toss looks normal. He could toss the coin so that the sequence of tosses would not be a mixture of independent processes.

It is natural to ask: What evidence does the investigator have for his premise that the sequence of tosses is a mixture of independent processes? and, How can this premise be confirmed or disconfirmed by tossing the coin? Usually the evidence for this premise consists of information about the behavior of coins already tossed. The inference from such evidence to the conclusion that the sequence is a mixture of independent processes is, of course, inductive. Since the evidence is all from the past and the present, and the conclusion says something about the future behavior of the coin, this inductive inference involves standard inductive logic, as we saw in discussing the frequency theory of probability (sec. 3.4, especially pp. 149–50 and 160).

The hypothesis that the sequence of tosses is a mixture of independent processes can be investigated in the same way that the fair-coin hypothesis can be tested: by tossing the coin and applying Bayes' theorem. A significant correlation between successive events in the sequence is evidence that the process is not a mixture of independent processes. For example, the occurrence of long strings of heads is strong evidence that the sequence of tosses is not a mixture of independent processes.*

Now Bayes' theorem can be applied to the hypothesis that the sequence is a mixture of independent processes only if various alternatives to this hypothesis are formulated and assigned prior probabilities. The disjunction of all these hypotheses would again be dispositional and empirical.

There are thus three probabilistic dispositions attributable to the coin: that expressed by the fair-coin hypothesis, that expressed by the hypothesis that the sequence is an equiprobable mixture of independent processes, and that expressed by a disjunction of this last hypothesis and its alternatives. Each of these dispositions serves as a basis for investigating the preceding one and hence is more basic than the preceding one. Moreover, each of these dispositions has a property underlying it. Hence there is a hierarchy of properties underlying the probabilistic disposition expressed by the fair-coin hypothesis. There is often a hierarchy of properties underlying a causal disposition (p. 444), so that probabilistic and causal dispositions are similar in this respect.

We turn now to another respect in which causal and probabilistic dispositions are similar. It was pointed out (p. 443) that an essential aspect of the meaning of the causal dispositional "Her ring is soluble in aqua regia" is not captured by the formula "$(\exists X)[Xr(XrAr$ **npc** $Dr)]$" but only by a formula with an additional restriction, namely "$(\exists X)[Xr(XrAr$ **npc** $Dr)$ (X is an enduring property)]." Moreover, this restriction "X is an enduring property" cannot be stated precisely or rigorously. A similar restriction is needed for the dispositional model of the fair-coin hypothesis.

* If α is the probability of a head and the sequence of tosses is independent, the probability of a transition, i.e., HT or TH, is $2\alpha(1 - \alpha)$. Hence, for large N, a significant difference between $\sigma_N(HT \text{ v } TH)$ and $2\sigma_N(H)\sigma_N(T)$ is evidence that the sequence of tosses is not a mixture of independent processes.

To see that this is so, look again at the dispositional model of the verification process that led to the acceptance of the fair-coin hypothesis. It was assumed at the beginning of the process that some statement G was true relative to which the process $Tx_1, Tx_2, \ldots$ is a mixture of independent processes of probabilities 0, .1, . . . , .9, and 1. There were thus eleven alternative hypotheses H_α ($\alpha = 0, .1, \ldots, .9, 1$) under investigation, each hypothesis being characterized by the condition

[d] $Tx_1, Tx_2, \ldots$ is an independent process of probability α relative to $H_\alpha G$.

Each such hypothesis H_α is verified in the same way as the corresponding empirical probability statement $\mathbf{P}_e(T) = \alpha$. For example, the result of 523 tails in 1,000 tosses was strong empirical evidence for $H_{.5}$ and against the alternative hypotheses.

We show next that better models of the empirical probability statements $\mathbf{P}_e(T) = \alpha$ can be made by restricting further the class of statements that, when substituted for the variable H_α, result in condition [d] being true. Consider, in particular, condition [d] as it applies to the fair-coin hypothesis $H_{.5}$.

[e] $Tx_1, Tx_2, \ldots$ is an independent process of probability .5 relative to $H_{.5}\,G$.

And consider the effect of substituting either of the following statements for $H_{.5}$ in condition [e].

(*R*) Out of 1,000 tosses, 523 were tails

(*S*) The coin looks symmetrical.

Now the expression obtained by substituting either R or S for $H_{.5}$ in [e] is true, since both R and S favor the probability .5 over the other possible probability values. Yet clearly neither R nor S is a good model of the fair-coin hypothesis $P_e(T) = .5$. This shows that condition [e], and hence condition [d], needs a further restriction.

To see what this restriction should be, we ask: What do the results of tossing the coin tell about the coin and tossing procedure? What changes in the coin and tossing procedure would alter the expected results of tossing the coin? What is the role of laws of nature in this matter?

The way the coin is likely to fall depends on a number of factors: the basic physical constitution of the coin, the actual characteristics of the tossing procedure, and the laws governing the falling of the coin. It is a priori possible that nature should prefer heads to tails, but experience has shown that it does not. Taking laws of nature as fixed, let us see what properties of the coin and tossing procedure affect the probability of the coin falling tails. With the usual tossing procedure, the following property of the coin gives equal probabilities of tails and heads.

(U) The coin is symmetrically shaped and the matter in it is uniformly distributed.*

But the probability of a tail might be one-half even though U were false. For example, the matter in the coin could be distributed nonuniformly but symmetrically. Also, the coin could have a hole on one side compensated for by a hole on the other side, or the coin could have an asymmetry counterbalanced by some feature of the tossing procedure.

The preceding discussion shows three things about the properties underlying the probabilistic disposition of the fair coin. First, many different properties may underlie this disposition. Second, not every property of the coin or tossing procedure is of the proper sort to underlie this disposition; for example, how the coin looks and the outcome of any particular sequence of tosses are excluded. Third, what really underlies this probabilistic disposition is a complex system: a set of physical properties that is complete with respect to properties of a certain kind and a certain level of specificity, together with the causal laws governing these properties. The completeness requirement here is a specific case of the role of total evidence (p. 20).

Thus a probabilistic dispositional is concerned with a miniature system: a relatively isolated, self-sufficient system that produces a probabilistic sequence. For example, a fair coin, the procedure whereby it is tossed, and the causal laws governing these together constitute a miniature system that produces the independent process $Tx_1, Tx_2, \ldots$ of probability 1/2. We call such a miniature system a "system underlying a probabilistic disposition." Different systems may underlie the same probabilistic disposition, but, of course, the systems underlying different probabilistic dispositions must be different. Let $\mathcal{S}$ be a system underlying a probabilistic disposition, and let $\phi x_1, \phi x_2, \ldots$ be the probabilistic process produced by $\mathcal{S}$. We call a description of $\mathcal{S}$ that is complete with respect to properties and laws of a certain kind and of a certain level of specificity a *complete theory of the process* $\phi x_1, \phi x_2, \ldots$.

We can now give an improved dispositional model of the empirical probability statement $\mathbf{P}_e(T) = \alpha$.

[f] There exists a statement H_α such that:
it is the case that H_α; H_α is a complete theory of the process $Tx_1, Tx_2, \ldots$; and $Tx_1, Tx_2, \ldots$ is an independent process of probability α relative to H_α.

A model of the fair-coin hypothesis $\mathbf{P}_e(T) = .5$ may be obtained by substituting .5 for α throughout. An improved dispositional model of the assumption that the sequence is a mixture of independent processes is

* There are, of course, slight deviations from symmetry and uniformity, but these affect the probability very little, if at all.

[g] There exists a statement M such that:
it is the case that M; M is a complete theory of the process $Tx_1, Tx_2, \ldots$; and $Tx_1, Tx_2, \ldots$ is a mixture of independent processes of probability 0, .1, . . . , .9, 1 relative to M.

Compare the probabilistic dispositionals [f] and [g] with the causal dispositional (pp. 443–44).

[h] $(\exists X)[Xr(XrAr\ \mathbf{npc}\ Dr)(X \text{ is an enduring property})]$.

The restriction of the quantified variables in [f] and [g] to a complete theory is similar to the restriction of the quantified variable in [h] to an enduring property. Neither restriction can be expressed precisely or rigorously. The two restrictions differ in that the latter is about a property whereas the former is about a theory, which in turn refers to properties. The properties referred to by a complete theory of the sequence of coin tosses are enduring properties rather than transient properties: the shape of the coin, the distribution of matter in it, etc. But the completeness requirement of the probabilistic case is stronger than the "enduring property" requirement of the causal case; for the former calls for a complete description of the system underlying the disposition, while the latter does not. The difference is not so great as it appears at first sight, however. For we saw that causal subjunctives should deal with relatively isolated, self-sufficient systems governed by a set of causal laws. The rule of completeness for causal subjunctives was introduced to make this desideratum explicit (p. 459).

Two final differences between causal and probabilistic dispositionals need to be mentioned. The first concerns uniqueness. This is a feature of a law of nature (pp. 425–26) and hence of causal dispositionals. Thus the second conjunct of "$(\exists X)[Xr(XrAr\ \mathbf{npc}\ Dr)]$" asserts that wherever X and A are exemplified, D will be exemplified. In contrast, the complete theory $H_{.5}$ does not predict the observed result R but only assigns a higher degree of prediction to it than do the alternative hypotheses. This lack of predictive uniqueness is essential to a probabilistic disposition, and our definition of a "complete theory of the sequence $\phi x_1, \phi x_2, \ldots$" was framed to allow for it.

The contrast here is that between a function with a unique value for each argument and a multivalued function. The causal dispositional $(\exists X)[Xr(XrAr\ \mathbf{npc}\ Dr)]$ "predicts" the unique result Dr under the condition $XrAr$. The probabilistic dispositional $\mathbf{P}_e(T) = .5$ does not predict a unique result when the coin is tossed finitely many times, but rather it allows all possible head-tail sequences, assigning a probability to each. In Peirce's terminology, the causal dispositional $(\exists X)[Xr(XrAr\ \mathbf{npc}\ Dr)]$ has the relatively simple practical consequence $XrAr\ \mathbf{npc}\ Dr$, whereas the probabilistic dispositional $\mathbf{P}_e(T) = .5$ has infinitely many practical consequences (pp. 167, 174, 178–79).

The multivaluedness of probabilistic dispositionals has a bearing on how the completeness condition involved in them is to be formulated. Assume for purposes of discussion that the coin and tossing procedure constitute a deterministic system (cf. sec. 9.4.1). Let $\mathfrak{D}$ be a complete description of the state of this system before the coin is tossed and of the laws governing this system. Then $\mathfrak{D}$ deductively implies exactly how the coin would fall, i.e., $\mathfrak{D}$ determines the sequence $Tx_1, Tx_2, \ldots$. Under these circumstances both of the conditions

$Tx_1, Tx_2, \ldots$ is an independent process of probability 1/2 relative to $\mathfrak{D}$

$Tx_1, Tx_2, \ldots$ is a mixture of independent processes of probabilities 0, .1, . . . , .9, and 1 relative to $\mathfrak{D}$

are clearly false, since $\mathbf{P}(Tx_i, \mathfrak{D})$ is either 0 or 1 for each toss x_i. However, the completeness requirement in the definiens of "complete theory of the process $\phi x_1, \phi x_2, \ldots$" does not demand the absolute completeness that $\mathfrak{D}$ possesses but only completeness relative to a certain type of property and a certain level of specificity. Let us give some examples of this relative completeness. If the distribution of matter in one part of the coin is given by a complete theory $H_{.5}$, then $H_{.5}$ will give the distribution of matter in the rest of the coin. If a complete theory mentions a hole on one side of a coin, then this complete theory will contain similar information about the other side of the coin.

The other difference between causal and probabilistic dispositions concerns our knowledge of the properties and systems underlying the disposition. Scientists know of many properties underlying the causal disposition "soluble in aqua regia." Moreover, these properties enter into many important causal laws, and it is often of practical interest to know, in any particular instance of the disposition, what property does in fact underlie the disposition. In these respects, the disposition "soluble in aqua regia" is typical of causal dispositions generally. In contrast, much less is known about the systems underlying probabilistic dispositions. This lack of knowledge is more important theoretically than practically, however. Let $\mathcal{S}$ be a system underlying a probabilistic disposition, and let $\phi x_1, \phi x_2, \ldots$ be the process $\mathcal{S}$ produces. Consider first the practical implications of our lack of information about $\mathcal{S}$. By the very nature of a probabilistic disposition, $\mathcal{S}$ is characterized by its inductive probability connections to the process $\phi x_1, \phi x_2, \ldots$. Consequently, probabilistic predictions and verifications involving this process can be made without further information about $\mathcal{S}$. Consider next the theoretical implications of our lack of information about $\mathcal{S}$. The system $\mathcal{S}$ is characterized only by its inductive probability connections to the process $\phi x_1, \phi x_2, \ldots$. The rules governing inductive probability are those of the calculus of inductive probability and standard inductive logic.

We saw earlier, in connection with Hume's thesis that there is no noncircular justification of induction, that the application of standard inductive logic to real systems is speculative in character (sec. 3.3.3). Hence our dispositional treatment of empirical probability has a speculative component.

We conclude this section by summarizing the results of our comparison of causal and probabilistic dispositionals. The comparison was based on an example of each. The causal dispositional "Her ring is soluble in aqua regia" was modeled by

[h] $(\exists X)[Xr(XrAr \textbf{ npc } Dr)(X \text{ is an enduring property})]$.

The fair-coin hypothesis "$\mathbf{P}_e(T) = .5$" was modeled by

[i] There exists a statement $H_{.5}$ such that:
it is the case that $H_{.5}$; $H_{.5}$ is a complete theory of the process $Tx_1, Tx_2, \ldots$; and $Tx_1, Tx_2, \ldots$ is an independent process of probability .5 relative to $H_{.5}$.

We have compared these two dispositionals with respect to (I) their content, (II) their modality, and (III) their relation to unique predictability; and we have reached the following conclusions.

(I) A causal dispositional attributes an enduring property to an object without identifying this property explicitly; rather, this enduring property is characterized by way of its causal connections (**npc**) to transient properties explicitly mentioned in the dispositional statement. These causal connections are empirical in nature. The enduring property attributed to the object is called the property underlying the disposition; many different properties may underlie a given causal disposition.

Similarly, an empirical probability statement attributes a miniature system to an object without identifying this system explicitly; rather, this system $\mathcal{S}$ is characterized by way of its inductive probability (**P**) connections to possible finite sequences of an event ϕ explicitly mentioned in the empirical probability statement. These inductive probability connections are nonempirical in nature. The miniature system attributed to the object is called the system underlying the probabilistic disposition; many different systems may underlie a given probabilistic disposition. Any such system $\mathcal{S}$ produces a probabilistic process $\phi x_1, \phi x_2, \ldots$. The empirical probability statement attributes $\mathcal{S}$ to the object by asserting the truth of a hypothesis that gives a complete theory of the process $\phi x_1, \phi x_2, \ldots$.

Three further points should be noted about the content of causal and probabilistic dispositionals. First, both the notion of an enduring property and the notion of a complete theory of a process are informal in nature. The latter notion is stronger than the former, including the former as a special case. Second, there is often a hierarchy of properties underlying a causal disposition, and there is often a hierarchy of systems underlying a probabilistic disposition. Much less is known about the systems underlying probabilistic dispositions than about the properties underlying causal dispositions.

Third, causal and probabilistic dispositionals resemble scientific theories in several important respects. Both dispositionals and theories treat of systems. Both dispositionals and theories are subject to completeness conditions; in this connection, the reader should recall the rule of completeness for causal subjunctives (p. 459) as well as the notion of a "complete theory of a process" used in model [i] above. And both dispositionals and theories have an implicit character. A dispositional does not explicitly identify the property or system underlying the disposition but only implicitly identifies it. Similarly, a scientific theory does not identify its observable phenomena explicitly but only implicitly.

(II) Both causal and probabilistic disposition statements are statements about possibilities and hence are fundamentally modal in character. Causal dispositionals concern causally possible universes and are governed by the logic of causal statements. Probabilistic dispositionals make an assignment of inductive probabilities to various possible finite sequences and are governed by the rules of the calculus of inductive probability and of standard inductive logic. The rules for exchanging equivalents in all these systems have modal restrictions. Both causal and probabilistic dispositionals imply subjunctive conditionals.

(III) Finally, a causal dispositional involves unique predictability, whereas a probabilistic dispositional assigns degrees of prediction to infinitely many possible results.

8.2.3 Dispositional models of atomic empirical probability statements

In the preceding parts of this section we developed and discussed a dispositional model of the fair-coin hypothesis $\mathbf{P}_e(T) = .5$. This hypothesis is a particular case of an atomic empirical probability statement, and we shall now show how to construct a dispositional model for any atomic empirical probability statement. We shall also consider various conclusions that can be drawn by means of Bayes' theorem.*

An atomic empirical probability statement $\mathbf{P}_e(\phi) = \alpha$ relates to a process $\phi x_1, \phi x_2, \ldots,$ asserting that this is an independent process of probability α. The empirical content of $\mathbf{P}_e(\phi) = \alpha$ may be understood in terms of Bayes' theorem. An application of Bayes' theorem involves a set of alternative hypotheses, which consists of $\mathbf{P}_e(\phi) = \alpha$ together with every statement that might be accepted if $\mathbf{P}_e(\phi) = \alpha$ is rejected. There are many

* In dealing with the fair-coin hypothesis, we used letters from the Roman alphabet for predicate variables and statement variables. For the more general case, we shall use Greek letters and script letters for these variables.

possible sets of alternatives, but the simplest and most usual case is where it is assumed that one of the statements $\mathbf{P}_e(\phi) = \alpha_n$ $(n = 1, 2, \ldots, N)$ is true. In other words: it is assumed that the process $\phi x_1, \phi x_2, \ldots$ is a mixture of independent processes of probabilities $\alpha_1, \alpha_2, \ldots,$ and α_N.

Inquiry starts from an assignment of prior probabilities to the hypotheses $\mathbf{P}_e(\phi) = \alpha_n$. A finite portion of the sequence $\phi x_1, \phi x_2, \ldots$ is observed. The degree of prediction of the observed result is calculated for each hypothesis, and then the posterior probabilities of the hypotheses are calculated by Bayes' theorem. The assertion of these posterior probabilities constitutes a conclusion, since, by the rule of total evidence, these posterior probabilities are the probabilities that should now be assigned to the hypotheses. Two further conclusions may be drawn. First, a probabilistic prediction concerning an unobserved part of the sequence $\phi x_1, \phi x_2, \ldots$ may be made. Second, a level of acceptance for a hypothesis may be specified, any hypothesis being accepted when its posterior probability exceeds this level. How high this level of acceptance should be will depend, of course, upon the practical situation.

We wish now to describe the structure of this inductive reasoning, so that we can generalize it later (sec. 8.3.2). Let the statement variable "$\mathcal{R}$" range over truth-functions of a finite number of the events $\phi x_1, \phi x_2, \ldots$. The direct verificational and predictive content of each of the hypotheses $\mathbf{P}_e(\phi) = \alpha_n$ is given by the degree of prediction it assigns to each $\mathcal{R}$. Let this degree of prediction be $f(\mathcal{R}, n)$; that is, define

$$\mathbf{P}(\mathcal{R}, \mathbf{P}_e(\phi) = \alpha_n) =_{\text{df}} f(\mathcal{R}, n) \quad .$$

We refer to "$f(\mathcal{R}, n)$" as the "degrees-of-prediction function."

We next derive a characterizing equation for $f(\mathcal{R}, n)$. Consider some particular result $\mathcal{R}$, and let L be the last event referred to in $\mathcal{R}$. Then $\mathcal{R}$ can be expressed as a disjunctive normal form in which the disjuncts are possible outcomes of the process $\phi x_1, \phi x_2, \ldots, \phi x_L$. Moreover, since by hypothesis this is an independent process (of probability α_n), $\mathcal{R}$ is equivalent to a disjunction of equations of the form $S_L(\phi) = s$, where s is the number of successes (occurrences of ϕ) in L trials (see secs. 2.4, 2.5.2). The probability of $S_L(\phi) = s$ is $C^L_s(\alpha_n)^s(1 - \alpha_n)^{L-s}$, where C^L_s is the number of combinations of L things taken s at a time (p. 53). This shows that the degrees-of-prediction function $f(\mathcal{R}, n)$ is (in this case) completely characterized by the equation

$$f(S_L(\phi) = s, n) = C^L_s(\alpha_n)^s(1 - \alpha_n)^{L-s} \qquad \text{for } n = 1, 2, \ldots, N \, .$$

Let $g(n)$ be the prior probability assigned to the hypothesis $\mathbf{P}_e(\phi) = \alpha_n$. We will call "$g(n)$" the "prior-probabilities function." Each prior-probability is non-zero and they sum to unity, so that

$$g(n) > 0 \text{ for each } n = 1, 2, \ldots, N, \text{ and } \sum_{n=1}^{N} g(n) = 1 .$$

Finally, let $h(n, \mathcal{R})$ be the posterior probability of hypothesis $\mathbf{P}_e(\phi) = \alpha_n$ on result $\mathcal{R}$. We call the function "$h(n, \mathcal{R})$" the "posterior-probabilities function." Bayes' theorem gives the posterior probabilities as a function of the degrees of prediction and the prior probabilities, and thus it defines the function $h(n, \mathcal{R})$ in terms of the functions $f(\mathcal{R}, n)$ and $g(n)$. Since the posterior probabilities sum to one,

$$\sum_{n=1}^{N} h(n, \mathcal{R}) = 1 .$$

We can use the functions $f(\mathcal{R}, n)$, $g(n)$, and $h(n, \mathcal{R})$ to formulate an inductive argument form based on Bayes' method of finding the unknown probability of a mixture of independent processes (p. 76). The hypotheses under consideration are characterized by their degrees of prediction.

[11] $\mathbf{P}(\mathcal{R}, \mathbf{P}_e(\phi) = \alpha_n) = f(\mathcal{R}, n)$, where the function $f(\mathcal{R}, n)$ is defined by
$$f(S_L(\phi) = s, n) = C^L_s(\alpha_n)^s(1 - \alpha_n)^{L-s} \quad \text{for } n = 1, 2, \ldots, N .$$

The inductive argument begins with an "assertion of alternatives."

[12] Exactly one of the hypotheses $\mathbf{P}_e(\phi) = \alpha_n (n = 1, 2, \ldots, N)$ is true.

Non-zero prior probabilities that sum to unity are assigned to these hypotheses:

[13] $\mathbf{P}(\mathbf{P}_e(\phi) = \alpha_n) = g(n)$, where $g(n)$ satisfies the conditions
$$g(n) > 0 \text{ for } n = 1, 2, \ldots, N, \text{ and } \sum_{n=1}^{N} g(n) = 1 .$$

This prior probability assignment, as well as the assertion of alternatives, should be based on all the information available at the beginning of the inductive argument. The observed result is

[15] $\mathcal{R}$,

which should express all available information about the result of tossing the coin. This concludes the premises of the argument.

By the rule of total evidence, the posterior probabilities are the probabilities that should be used after the result $\mathcal{R}$ is known. We therefore assert $\mathcal{R}$ together with the probabilities posterior to $\mathcal{R}$.

[16] $\therefore\ \mathcal{R}$ and $\mathbf{P}(\mathbf{P}_e(\phi) = \alpha_n, \mathcal{R}) = h(n, \mathcal{R})$.

These posterior probabilities may be used in either of two ways. Theorem [19] (p. 66) may be used to calculate the probability of a prediction $\mathcal{P}$ concerning a finite part of the sequence $\phi x_1, \phi x_2, \ldots$. This probabilistic prediction is expressed by

[17] $\therefore \mathcal{R}$, and the probability of a prediction $\mathcal{P}$ is given by

$$\mathbf{P}(\mathcal{P}, \mathcal{R}) = \sum_{n=1}^{N} \mathbf{P}(\mathbf{P}_e(\phi) = \alpha_n, \mathcal{R})\mathbf{P}(\mathcal{P}, \mathbf{P}_e(\phi) = \alpha_n \& \mathcal{R}) \quad .$$

Second, a hypothesis may be accepted when its posterior probability exceeds an acceptance level set by the investigator. Suppose $\mathbf{P}_e(\phi) = \beta$ is such a hypothesis. Then the following categorical conclusion is drawn.

[18] $\therefore \mathbf{P}_e(\phi) = \beta \quad .$

If no hypothesis is sufficiently well confirmed to justify its acceptance, more of the sequence can be observed until some hypothesis is confirmed. Suppose that the sequence $\phi x_1, \phi x_2, \ldots$ is infinite and that successive initial segments of it are examined ad infinitum. The investigation is then an instance of Bayes' method of finding an unknown probability, and the confirmation theorem applies (p. 84). Let β be the true probability value, so that $\mathbf{P}_e(\phi) = \beta$ is the true hypothesis. According to the confirmation theorem, for each assignment of non-zero prior probabilities and for each positive ϵ_s and ϵ_a there is a length of experiment l such that: for every $L > l$, the probability is at least $1 - \epsilon_s$ that the observed result $S_L(\phi) = s$ will be such that $\mathbf{P}(\mathbf{P}_e(\phi) = \beta, S_L(\phi) = s) > 1 - \epsilon_a$. In other words, for any assignment of non-zero prior probabilities to the hypotheses and for each positive ϵ_s and ϵ_a, there is a length of experiment l such that: the probability is at least $1 - \epsilon_s$ that, after performing this experiment, the investigator will know the true probability value β to degree $1 - \epsilon_a$. To put it informally, whatever level of acceptance $1 - \epsilon_a$ is stipulated, the investigator will ultimately adopt the true hypothesis. In short, an investigator who applies Bayes' method of finding an unknown probability to a mixture of independent processes will eventually know the value of the originally unknown probability.

The inductive argument [11]–[18] contains unanalyzed empirical probability statements and unconditional inductive probabilities. The dispositional theory of empirical probability offers a model of this argument that eliminates the occurrences of empirical probability and uses only conditional inductive probability while it yet preserves the validity of the argument and the empirical status of the atomic empirical probability statements of the argument.

According to the dispositional theory, an empirical probability statement $\mathbf{P}_e(\phi) = \alpha_n$ is dispositional in nature. Underlying this probabilistic disposition is a relatively self-sufficient system of properties and laws $\mathcal{S}_n$ that produces an independent process $\phi x_1, \phi x_2, \ldots$ of probability α_n. A description of $\mathcal{S}_n$ that is complete with respect to properties and laws of a certain kind and of a certain level of specificity is called a "complete theory of the process $\phi x_1, \phi x_2, \ldots$" (p. 493). Let $\mathcal{H}_n$ be a complete theory of the process $\phi x_1, \phi x_2, \ldots$ such that relative to $\mathcal{H}_n$ this process is an independent process of probability α_n. A hypothesis $\mathcal{H}_n$ enters into the dispositional model of $\mathbf{P}_e(\phi) = \alpha_n$ indirectly. One who knows that $\mathbf{P}_e(\phi) = \alpha_n$ is true does not know what specific system $\mathcal{S}_n$ among many possible systems produces the independent process $\phi x_1, \phi x_2, \ldots$ of probability α_n. Hence the content of $\mathcal{H}_n$ is not explicitly given in the dispositional model of $\mathbf{P}_e(\phi) = \alpha_n$. Rather, the dispositional model of $\mathbf{P}_e(\phi) = \alpha_n$ asserts that there is a true hypothesis $\mathcal{H}_n$ satisfying the condition

[j] $\mathcal{H}_n$ is a complete theory of the process $\phi x_1, \phi x_2, \ldots$; and $\phi x_1, \phi x_2, \ldots$ is an independent process of probability α_n relative to $\mathcal{H}_n$.

Similarly, the "assertion of alternatives," namely,

[12] Exactly one of the hypotheses $\mathbf{P}_e(\phi) = \alpha_n$ (for $n = 1, 2, \ldots, N$) is true

is dispositional in nature. Underlying this disposition is a relatively self-sufficient system of properties and laws $\mathcal{S}^*$ that produces a mixture of independent processes of probabilities $\alpha_1, \alpha_2, \ldots$, and α_N. Let $\mathcal{G}$ be a complete theory of this process relative to which the process $\phi x_1, \phi x_2, \ldots$ is a mixture of independent processes of probabilities $\alpha_1, \alpha_2, \ldots, \alpha_N$. As in the case of the hypotheses $\mathcal{H}_n$, the content of $\mathcal{G}$ is not explicitly given in the model. Rather, it is asserted that there is some sentence $\mathcal{G}$ satisfying the stated condition.

The dispositional model of argument [11] – [18] is constructed from the argument itself by the following moves. First, relativize everything to $\mathcal{G}$. Second, replace each statement $\mathbf{P}_e(\phi) = \alpha_n$ by the corresponding hypothesis $\mathcal{H}_n$. Third, assert that some $\mathcal{G}$ satisfying the stated conditions is in fact true. Finally, existentially quantify "$\mathcal{G}$" and the "$\mathcal{H}_n$" at the appropriate places. The resultant model [11′] – [18′] is given below, with certain simplifications. Existential quantifiers are omitted, as in the model [1′] – [5′] above (pp. 484–85). Thus the free variables "$\mathcal{G}$," "$\mathcal{H}_1$," . . . , "$\mathcal{H}_N$" represent arbitrary statements satisfying the given conditions. To simplify the presentation we are omitting the completeness requirements needed at various stages of the argument. There are conditions specifying that the statement $\mathcal{G}$ and each hypothesis $\mathcal{H}_n$ be complete theories of the sequence $\phi x_1, \phi x_2, \ldots$. There is a condition that $\mathcal{G}$ be based on all the information available at the beginning of the argument and a condition that $\mathcal{R}$ express all available information about the outcome of tossing the coin.

Thus a dispositional model of the set of empirical probability statements $\mathbf{P}_e(\phi) = \alpha$ (where $\alpha = \alpha_1, \alpha_2, \ldots, \alpha_N$), and of the empirical process of verifying one of these statements, has the following form.

[11′] $\mathbf{P}(\mathcal{R}, \mathcal{H}_n\mathcal{G}) = f(\mathcal{R}, n)$ {Degrees of prediction}

[12′] $\mathcal{H}_1, \mathcal{H}_2, \ldots, \mathcal{H}_N$ are mutually exclusive and jointly exhaustive relative to $\mathcal{G}$

[13′] $\mathbf{P}(\mathcal{H}_n, \mathcal{G}) = g(n)$ {Prior probabilities}.

Consider now the epistemological status of [11′], [12′], and [13′] or, more specifically, the epistemological status of the sentences obtained by substituting sentences for the sentence variables of [11′], [12′], and [13′]. [12′] will be logically true-or-false. [11′] and [13′] will be conjunctions of atomic inductive probability statements and hence by the argument of Section 3.4.2 will not be empirically true-or-false. Therefore, the conjunction of [11′], [12′], and [13′] will not be empirically true-or-false. But clearly the conjunction of [11], [12], and [13] is empirically true-or-false. To model this feature of the original inductive argument, we assert

[14′] $\mathcal{G}$, where $\mathcal{G}$ satisfies [11′], [12′], and [13′].

Whether or not there exists a statement $\mathcal{G}$ satisfying [14′] is an empirical matter.

The dispositional model continues.

[15′] $\mathcal{R}$.

The main conclusion is

[16′] $\therefore$ $\mathcal{R}\mathcal{G}$, where $\mathcal{G}$ satisfies [11′], [12′],
and $\mathbf{P}(\mathcal{H}_n, \mathcal{R}\mathcal{G}) = h(n, \mathcal{R})$ {Posterior probabilities}.

There are two auxiliary conclusions. A further prediction may be made.

[17′] $\therefore$ $\mathcal{R}\mathcal{G}$, and $\mathbf{P}(\mathcal{P}, \mathcal{R}\mathcal{G}) = \sum_{n=1}^{N} \mathbf{P}(\mathcal{H}_n, \mathcal{R}\mathcal{G})\mathbf{P}(\mathcal{P}, \mathcal{H}_n\mathcal{R}\mathcal{G})$.

If the posterior probability $h(\beta, \mathcal{R})$ of hypothesis $\mathcal{H}_\beta$ exceeds the acceptance level set by the investigator, that hypothesis is adopted.

[18′] $\therefore$ $\mathcal{H}_\beta\mathcal{G}$, and $\mathbf{P}(\mathcal{R}, \mathcal{H}_\beta\mathcal{G}) = f(\mathcal{R}, \beta)$.

The dispositional model [11′] – [18′] is a good model of the inductive argument form [11] – [18], and each hypothesis $\mathcal{H}_n$ is a good model of the corresponding empirical probability statement $\mathbf{P}_e(\phi) = \alpha_n$. The validity-status of the argument [11] – [18] is preserved by the model [11′] – [18′]. The empirical status of the conjoint premise [11]&[12]&[13] is preserved by the conjoint premise [11′]&[12′]&[13′]&[14′], and the empirical status of the conclusion [18] is preserved by the conclusion [18′]. Each $\mathcal{H}_n$ and its corresponding $\mathbf{P}_e(\phi) = \alpha_n$ imply the same predictions to the same degree and so they are supported in the same way by the same observations.

The original inductive argument [11] – [18] uses the concepts of empirical probability and unconditional inductive probability as well as the concept of conditional inductive probability, whereas the dispositional model [11′] – [18′] uses only the last of these three concepts. Hence our dispositional models account for empirical probability in terms of conditional inductive probability and account for the verification of an empirical probability statement in terms of the rules governing conditional inductive probability.

Note that in the dispositional model [11′] – [18′], the degrees of prediction, the assertion of alternatives, and the prior probabilities have all been gathered together in the single empirical probability assertion [14′]. It is really this whole system of atomic probability statements that is modified on the basis of the observation $\mathcal{R}$ and from which probabilistic predictions are made.

Let us now summarize the conclusions we have reached thus far concerning the general nature of a set of alternative empirical probability hypotheses. Each hypothesis is dispositional in nature, asserting that the system underlying the disposition is such that each possible outcome has a certain probability (degree of prediction). In the context of an assignment of prior probabilities to the alternatives, these probabilistic predictions may be used to confirm or disconfirm the hypothesis: a finite portion of the actual process produced by the system is observed and Bayes' theorem is applied to the result. Thus empirical probability statements may be modeled by probabilistic dispositional formulas that are verified and manipulated by means of the calculus of inductive probability.

8.3 Dispositional Models of Empirical Probability Theories

8.3.1 Empirical probability theories

Thus far we have modeled only atomic empirical probability statements in the sense originally defined (pp. 26–28). These are of the form $\mathbf{P}_e(\phi) = \alpha$ and concern either independent processes (when a specific value of α is given) or mixtures of independent processes (when different possible values of α are allowed). An independent process is a limiting case of a mixture of independent processes, namely, the case when only one possible value of α is given. Hence our modeling has been limited to mixtures of independent processes.

But there are many probabilistic processes and systems in nature that are not mixtures of independent processes, and science contains many laws and principles applying to such processes and systems. To cover these, we shall now generalize our original concept of an atomic empirical probability statement to what we call an "empirical probability theory." Then in the next subsection we shall show how dispositional models may be constructed for empirical probability theories.

We begin by extending the notion of a process $\phi x_1, \phi x_2, \phi x_3, \ldots$. This was originally defined for the two-state case $(\phi, \overline{\phi})$ and later extended to the multistate case (ϕ is $\phi_1, \phi_2, \ldots$, or ϕ_κ) [pp. 58, 118]. Both of these definitions required that every two distinct atomic statements ϕx_i and ϕx_j $(i \neq j)$ be logically independent. Correspondingly, every basic conjunction of a model $\mathfrak{M}$-$\mathfrak{L}$ was taken to describe a logically possible universe (p. 105). But in developing modal models for the logic of causal statements we allowed atomic statements to be logically dependent, and we took the universe descriptions of a model to be any non-empty subset of basic conjunctions (pp. 354–57). To obtain the same generality for complete probability assignments to processes, we extend the concept of *process* in exactly the same way.

Our concept of an empirical probability theory is based on that of a complete probability assignment, which was introduced in Section 3.2.4 (Inductive logics and Bayes' method). After repeating the definition we discuss several applications of it to natural processes.*

Consider a finite or infinite multistate discrete process $\phi x_1, \phi x_2, \phi x_3, \ldots$ in which each ϕ is one of the states $\phi_1, \phi_2, \ldots, \phi_\kappa$. Let $\mathfrak{R}$ be a truth-function of a finite number of the events $\phi x_1, \phi x_2, \phi x_3, \ldots$, and let $\mathcal{G}$ express the general information relative to which probabilities are assigned to these truth-functions. *A complete probability assignment to the process* $\phi x_1, \phi x_2, \phi x_3, \ldots$ *on condition* $\mathcal{G}$ is defined by a function $\mathbf{P}(\mathfrak{R}, \mathcal{G})$ that assigns a real number to each $\mathfrak{R}$ and satisfies the axioms for unconditional probability of Section 2.6. Note that if $\mathfrak{R}$ is inconsistent relative to $\mathcal{G}$, it automatically receives a probability of zero.

A Markov chain was introduced as an example of a complete probability assignment that is not a mixture of independent processes (pp. 125–26). In a Markov chain, the probability of a given state occurring at x_{i+1} depends on the state of the system at time x_i but not directly on earlier states of the system. A succession of generations in a genetic system is another example of a Markov chain. By Gregor Mendel's laws, the genetic complexion of the offspring, i.e., the $i+1$ generation, depends probabilistically on the genetic complexion of the parent generation, i.e., the ith generation.

The statement form $\mathbf{P}_e(\phi) = \alpha$ by itself is clearly too simple to characterize a Markov chain. For a Markov chain, the following need to be specified: the probability of the first event, the transition probabilities from the ith event to its immediate successor, and the fact that these transition probabilities are independent of information concerning earlier events. For the two-state case (ϕ and $\overline{\phi}$), the general form for a Markov chain is

[k] $\mathbf{P}_e(\phi x_1) = \alpha$ Initial probability

$$\left.\begin{aligned}\mathbf{P}_e(\phi x_{i+1}, \phi x_i) &= \beta\\ \mathbf{P}_e(\phi x_{i+1}, \overline{\phi x_i}) &= \beta'\end{aligned}\right\}\quad \text{Transition probabilities}$$

$$\left.\begin{aligned}\mathbf{P}_e(\phi x_{i+1}, \phi x_i \Psi) &= \mathbf{P}_e(\phi x_{i+1}, \phi x_i)\\ \mathbf{P}_e(\phi x_{i+1}, \overline{\phi x_i}\Psi) &= \mathbf{P}_e(\phi x_{i+1}, \overline{\phi x_i})\end{aligned}\right\}\quad \text{Independence conditions,}$$

* Further examples may be found in probability textbooks. See, for instance, Feller, *An Introduction to Probability Theory and Its Applications*, chaps. 15, 16, and 17, and Kemeny and Snell, *Finite Markov Chains*, chap. 7.

where $i = 1, 2, 3, \ldots$, and where Ψ is any noncontradictory truth-function of $\phi x_1, \phi x_2, \ldots, \phi x_{i-2}, \phi x_{i-1}$.

The notion of an atomic empirical probability statement $\mathbf{P}_e(\phi) = \alpha$ was originally defined for an independent process of probability α (pp. 27, 58). We see now that the essence of empirical probability ($\mathbf{P}_e$) lies in there being an assignment of probabilities to possible outcomes, so that the actual outcome will have evidential bearing on the empirical probability claim; and it does not lie in the fact that this probability assignment is of the particular kind "independent process." Hereafter we shall use the notion of an *atomic empirical probability statement* $\mathbf{P}_e(\phi, \Psi) = \alpha$ in the more general sense illustrated above. An empirical probability theory consists of a set of atomic empirical probability statements. The statement that a process is an independent process of probability α is thus a very simple kind of empirical probability theory.

The behavior of a digital computer that makes random errors may be approximated with a Markov chain.* A machine in the sense of Section 6.4.3 (Machines and algorithms) can operate synchronously, taking on successive states at times $t_1, t_2, \ldots$. A very simple example will suffice to show the relation of digital computers to Markov chains. Consider a device without inputs that has only two states, S and $\bar{S}$. In the error-free case, the initial state of the machine is determined and the next state of the machine is a deterministic (single-valued) function of the present state. For concreteness we specify that the initial state is S and that each state is followed by itself; the sequence of states would then be $Sx_1, Sx_2, Sx_3, \ldots$. But assume now that each component of the computer has a fixed probability of erring at any given moment. In this case neither the initial state nor the transition between states is determined. Rather, the succession of states is a Markov chain with

[k′] $\mathbf{P}_e(St_1) = 1 - \epsilon$ Initial probability

$$\left.\begin{aligned}\mathbf{P}_e(St_{i+1}, St_i) &= 1 - \epsilon\\ \mathbf{P}_e(St_{i+1}, \bar{S}t_i) &= \epsilon\end{aligned}\right\}\quad \text{Transition probabilities,}$$

where ϵ is a real number between 0 and 1 and is, for actual computers, a small number.

We give next an example of a natural process in which the probability of an event ϕx_{i+1} is influenced not only by the preceding event but also by earlier events $\phi x_{i-1}, \phi x_{i-2}$, etc. The events $\phi x_1, \phi x_2, \phi x_3, \ldots$ are successive occurrences (tokens) of type characters (letters, numerals, punctuation

* Von Neumann, "Probabilistic Logics and the Synthesis of Reliable Organisms from Unreliable Components." Burks, "Toward a Theory of Automata Based on More Realistic Primitive Elements."

marks, and spaces) in some written text. The empirical probability of any given character occurring varies from character to character. As any reader of Edgar Allan Poe's "Gold Bug" knows, "e" is the most frequent character of English. Moreover, the probability of a character occurring varies according to what characters have preceded it, so that if one knows the last few characters he can predict the next character more successfully than he could if he did not have this information. In symbols, $\mathbf{P}_e(\phi x_{i+1})$, $\mathbf{P}_e(\phi x_{i+1}, \phi x_i)$, $\mathbf{P}_e(\phi x_{i+1}, \phi x_{i-1}\ \phi x_i)$, etc., are (in general) different.*

Some interesting examples of complete probability assignments occur in the statistics of physical particles (photons, electrons, atoms, molecules, etc.). We discussed the statistics of classical thermodynamics in Section 3.2.3 and saw there that this statistics can be expressed in the framework of a model universe, that it assigns prior probabilities to the microscopic states of a gas in accordance with the rules of random inductive logic (see Table 11), and that random inductive logic treats the basic individuals of the model universe as independent. Since the basic individuals of a model universe can be ordered arbitrarily, random inductive logic, and hence classical thermodynamics, treats a model universe as an independent sequence.

The statistics of classical thermodynamics is sometimes called Maxwell-Boltzmann statistics, named after James Clerk Maxwell and Ludwig Boltzmann. It may be contrasted with two statistics of quantum mechanics: Bose-Einstein statistics and Fermi-Dirac statistics, named for Jagadis Chandra Bose, Albert Einstein, Enrico Fermi, and P. A. M. Dirac. These statistics are sometimes referred to as "distribution laws," because they give probabilistic information about the distribution of particles with respect to particle states. Photons, nuclei, and atoms containing an even number of elementary particles are governed by Bose-Einstein statistics. Electrons, neutrons, and protons are governed by Fermi-Dirac statistics. Maxwell-Boltzmann statistics applies to the molecules of a gas.†

We will present all three statistics as complete probability assignments for model universes and compare them to standard, inverse, and random inductive logics. Consider a model $\mathfrak{M}$-$\mathfrak{L}$ in the sense of Section 3.2. The individuals are to be interpreted as particles *at a given time*. A particle may be either elementary, e.g., photons, electrons; or nonelementary, e.g., atoms, molecules. Each particle is in one of many possible states, called "particle states," "elements of state space," or "elements of the phase space." These particle states correspond to the individual states of $\mathfrak{M}$-$\mathfrak{L}$, except that in

* Shannon, "A Mathematical Theory of Communication," secs. 2 and 3.

† These three statistics and their applications are discussed in sec. 12.9 of Margenau and Murphy, *The Mathematics of Physics and Chemistry*, in chap. 10 of Tolman, *The Principles of Statistical Mechanics*, and on p. 39 of Feller, *An Introduction to Probability Theory and its Applications*.

physics the particle states are taken as primitive, whereas in Section 3.2 individual states are constructed from monadic properties.

Under this interpretation of a model universe in terms of a system of particles, Bose-Einstein, Fermi-Dirac, and Maxwell-Boltzmann statistics can be expressed as inductive logics. Bose-Einstein statistics assigns the same probability to each distribution description and equal probabilities to isomorphic universe descriptions, and it is therefore an interpretation of standard inductive logic. On Fermi-Dirac statistics, no two particles can be in the same state; that is, Fermi-Dirac statistics assigns zero probability to any distribution having two particles in the same state. This is Wolfgang Pauli's exclusion principle: no two electrons can be in the same energy state. Hence Fermi-Dirac statistics presupposes that the number of individuals of a model must be less than or equal to the number of individual states of the model. Except for the exclusion principle, the same probability is assigned to each distribution description and equal probabilities are assigned to isomorphic universe descriptions. The complete probability assignment of Fermi-Dirac statistics is analogous to that of inverse inductive logic, because on both the probability that a given individual will be in a given state is decreased if some other individual is in that state. Fermi-Dirac statistics is not an interpretation of inverse inductive logic, however; for the former assigns zero probability to some universe descriptions, while the latter assigns a positive probability to every universe description. Finally, Maxwell-Boltzmann statistics assigns the same probability to each universe description and is therefore an interpretation of random inductive logic (see sec. 3.2.3).

"Exchangeable" complete probability assignments were defined earlier and were related to mixtures of independent processes (pp. 125–26). A complete probability assignment to a finite or infinite process ϕx_1, ϕx_2, ϕx_3, . . . is exchangeable if and only if it assigns equal probabilities to isomorphic truth-functions of the formulas "ϕx_1," "ϕx_2," . . . . All three statistics of physics are exchangeable complete probability assignments. Bose-Einstein statistics describes mixtures of independent processes, Maxwell-Boltzmann statistics describes independent processes, and Fermi-Dirac statistics describes probabilistic processes that are neither.

We have now illustrated the concept of a complete probability assignment with many examples of natural processes that are not mixtures of independent processes and hence are not covered by our original definition of an empirical probability statement. But before generalizing this latter notion to that of an empirical probability theory, we need to generalize further the notion of a complete probability assignment.

As originally defined, a complete probability assignment rests on a discrete reference frame of events x_1, x_2, x_3, ... Consequently, it does not directly cover probabilistic systems and processes based on a continuous reference frame. A radioactive atom, such as uranium, may change to a different kind of atom by emitting particles or gamma rays, and this new atom may change to another kind of atom by the same process. Since an emission and transition may occur at any time, this probabilistic process takes place in a temporal continuum.

Consider, for example, an atomic process involving N kinds of atoms. Let the succession of states (atoms) be $A_1, A_2, \ldots, A_N$, and let the corresponding transition times be $\tau_1, \tau_2, \ldots, \tau_N$, respectively. Different kinds of atoms tend to live for different lengths of time, so that the probability of transition depends on the kind of atom. But for each kind of atom A_n, the probability of a transition to A_{n+1} remains unchanged so long as the process is in state A_n. In other words, for each A_n there is a constant c_n such that for sufficiently small δ the probability of a transition during the interval τ_n to $\tau_n + \delta$ is $c_n\delta$.

Continuous probability systems may usually be approximated with discrete probability systems. Let us show how this can be done, using the process of radioactive disintegration as an example. Divide time into discrete units of duration δ' and place each transition at the beginning of a temporal unit $t_1, t_2, t_3, \ldots$. The sequence of states of the atomic system is then of the form $At_1, At_2, At_3, \ldots, At_i, \ldots$, where A may be $A_1, A_2, \ldots$, or A_n. This process is a Markov chain in which the probability of transition from A_n to A_{n+1} is $c_n\delta'$.

For this approximation to be satisfactory, the interval δ' must be small compared to the accuracy of time measurement. As instrumental and experimental technology improves, still smaller intervals will be needed. If this improvement were to continue indefinitely, a succession of discrete reference frames in which the intervals become smaller without limit would be needed. Such a succession of discrete reference frames is equivalent to a continuous reference frame.

To cover continuous probability systems like radioactive emission, we extend the notion of a *complete probability assignment* to include continuous reference frames as well as discrete reference frames. A reference frame may be one-dimensional (as in the case of a Markov chain) or multidimensional (as in the case of a thermodynamic system).

We are now in a position to generalize our original concept of an empirical probability statement to that of an empirical probability theory. An **empirical probability theory** is any empirical theory that makes a complete probability assignment to the observable characteristics of a process or system of events. The process or system may have any number of dimensions and may be continuous as well as discrete.* The statement that a process is

* The idea could be generalized even further. One could have an empirical probability theory that did not assign probabilities to *all* possible outcomes or observable characteristics of the system under consideration, provided that it assigned enough probabilities to

an independent process of probability α is a very simple kind of empirical probability theory. Other examples of empirical probability theories are: the claim that a process is a mixture of independent processes together with a prior probability distribution for the unknown probability α, a law of radioactive emission, a description of the probabilistic behavior of a written text, the statement that the behavior of a computer is a Markov chain, the Bose-Einstein statistics of a nucleus, the Fermi-Dirac statistics of an electron, and the second law of thermodynamics.

Since a theory is by definition expressible in a finite number of symbols, not every complete probability assignment can form the basis of an empirical probability theory. Consider, for example, a mixture of independent processes in which the unknown probability α can be any real number between zero and one inclusive (p. 125). There exist, in a purely mathematical sense, prior probability distributions of α that are not finitely expressible and therefore cannot be used in an empirical probability theory.

The concept of an empirical probability theory is basic, and any adequate philosophy of empirical probability must cover all such theories. But since our probability machinery treats only the discrete case and does not cover the continuous case, and since in practice the continuous case can be approximated by the discrete, we restrict our analysis to empirical probability theories of discrete systems.* The significance of this restriction is perhaps debatable; but it is my opinion that all the theories of empirical probability discussed below (secs. 8.3.2 to 8.4.3) can be extended to the continuous case, and when this is done the philosophical conclusions I draw will need only minor alterations.

A discrete system can have any number of dimensions, and each event of the system can have any number of states. While the number of dimensions and states affects the complexity of the theory, it does not affect the fundamentals of the verification process; and so in our formal analysis we consider only one-dimensional, two-state systems. We will give the general form of an empirical probability theory of such a system, and then in the next subsection we will generalize the inductive argument [11] – [18] of the last subsection to cover this case (pp. 499–500).

Verification involves a set of alternative theories about a process. Let $\mathfrak{T}_1, \mathfrak{T}_2, \ldots, \mathfrak{T}_N$ be alternative empirical probability theories of a finite or infinite process $\phi x_1, \phi x_2, \phi x_3, \ldots$ that has two states ϕ and $\overline{\phi}$. Let "$\mathfrak{R}$" be a variable ranging over all truth-functions of a finite number of the events

observable data to make empirical confirmation of itself possible. The statistical analysis of incomplete empirical probability theories is extremely complicated, however, and we will say nothing about them here.

* For a general treatment of continuous probability see Feller, *An Introduction to Probability Theory and its Applications*, vol. 2.

$\phi x_1, \phi x_2, \phi x_3, \ldots$. The specific content of a set of theories varies according to the case, but the general form can be expressed in terms of a degrees-of-prediction function $f(\mathcal{R}, n)$, a prior-probabilities function $g(n)$, and a posterior-probabilities function $h(n, \mathcal{R})$. These functions are like those used in the inductive argument form [11] – [18], except that they are now generalized to cover any empirical probability theory of a one-dimensional, two-state process rather than limited to mixtures of independent processes.

The degrees of prediction of an empirical probability theory $\mathfrak{J}_n$ determine a complete probability assignment for the process $\phi x_1, \phi x_2, \phi x_3, \ldots$. The assignment may be written in terms of a degrees-of-prediction function $f(\mathcal{R}, n)$ as

$$\mathbf{P}(\mathcal{R}, \mathfrak{J}_n) = f(\mathcal{R}, n) \qquad \text{for } n = 1, 2, \ldots, N\,.$$

Here $f(\mathcal{R}, n)$ is any function that is finitely expressible and satisfies the following three conditions.

(1) For each $n = 1, 2, \ldots, N$, $f(\mathcal{R}, n)$ satisfies the axioms for unconditional probability (sec. 2.6).

Second, the theories $\mathfrak{J}_1, \mathfrak{J}_2, \ldots, \mathfrak{J}_N$ are mutually exclusive, i.e., they determine different complete probability assignments:

(2) If $n_1 \neq n_2$, then for some $\mathcal{R}$, $f(\mathcal{R}, n_1) \neq f(\mathcal{R}, n_2)$.

Third, since every empirical fact about the process $\phi x_1, \phi x_2, \phi x_3, \ldots$ must be accounted for by some one or more of the theories, each consistent result $\mathcal{R}$ has a non-zero degree of prediction:

(3) If $\mathcal{R}$ is consistent, there is an $n = 1, 2, \ldots, N$ such that $f(\mathcal{R}, n) > 0$.

Prior probabilities are distributed over these theories by means of a prior-probabilities function $g(n)$:

$$\mathbf{P}(\mathfrak{J}_n) = g(n) \qquad \text{for } n = 1, 2, \ldots, N\,.$$

Here $g(n)$ is any finitely expressible function satisfying the following two conditions. First, the theories under consideration are jointly exhaustive, i.e., no other theory is considered a real alternative, and hence

(4) $$\sum_{n=1}^{N} g(n) = 1 \qquad .$$

A theory with zero prior probability can never be confirmed, and so it need not be considered:

(5) $g(n) > 0 \qquad \text{for } n = 1, 2, \ldots, N$.

Given the degrees-of-prediction function $f(\mathcal{R}, n)$ and the prior-probabilities function $g(n)$, we may define the corresponding posterior-probabilities function by means of Bayes' theorem:

(6) $$h(n, \mathfrak{R}) = \frac{g(n)f(\mathfrak{R}, n)}{\sum_{n=1}^{N} g(n)f(\mathfrak{R}, n)} \quad \text{for } n = 1, 2, \ldots, N.$$

After a particular result $\mathfrak{R}$ is established by observation, the posterior probabilities of the theories take the place of the prior probabilities.

It should be noted that a probabilistic mixture of empirical probability theories is also an empirical probability theory. This follows from the fact that a probabilistic mixture of complete probability assignments is also a complete probability assignment (see theorem [19], p. 66). To obtain the logical form of a mixture of empirical probability theories, we merely combine the degrees of prediction and the prior probabilities into a single statement:

[q] For $n = 1, 2, \ldots, N$:
(a) $\mathbf{P}(\mathfrak{R}, \mathfrak{J}_n) = f(\mathfrak{R}, n)$ {Degrees of prediction}
(b) $\mathbf{P}(\mathfrak{J}_n) = g(n)$ {Prior probabilities},

where the functions $f(\mathfrak{R}, n)$ and $g(n)$ satisfy the conditions given above. Statement [q] is also an empirical probability theory, since it determines a complete probability assignment to the sequence $\phi x_1, \phi x_2, \ldots$:

$$\mathbf{P}(\mathfrak{R}) = \sum_{n=1}^{N} \mathbf{P}(\mathfrak{J}_n)\mathbf{P}(\mathfrak{R}, \mathfrak{J}_n) \quad .$$

Hence [q] is the general form of an empirical probability theory that is a mixture of empirical probability theories.

Since the new notion of an empirical probability theory is broader than the earlier notion of an atomic empirical probability statement, our third main question (pp. 29, 144) needs to be revised by replacing the old notion with the new. The final version of this question is: *What is the general nature of an empirical probability theory? How are empirical and inductive probabilities related? Why is the traditional calculus of probability applicable to empirical probabilities?*

8.3.2 The dispositional theory of empirical probability

We call our answer to this question the **dispositional theory of empirical probability.** Actually, this answer is implicit in the preceding portions of this chapter, but in the present subsection we develop it further and state it explicitly.

Let us first generalize the inductive argument form [11] – [16], which was limited to mixtures of independent processes (p. 499). We rewrite it to cover any set $\mathfrak{J}_1, \mathfrak{J}_2, \ldots, \mathfrak{J}_N$ of empirical probability theories of a one-dimensional, two-state process. Let $\mathcal{R}$ be a truth-function of a finite number of the events $\phi x_1, \phi x_2, \ldots$. For $n = 1, 2, \ldots, N$, let $f(\mathcal{R}, n)$, $g(n)$, and $h(n, \mathcal{R})$ be any probability functions satisfying the conditions given at the end of the preceding subsection.

Inquiry begins with an empirical probability theory that is a probabilistic mixture of the theories $\mathfrak{J}_1, \mathfrak{J}_2, \ldots, \mathfrak{J}_N$. A portion of the sequence $\phi x_1, \phi x_2, \ldots$ is observed, with result $\mathcal{R}$. The prior probabilities $g(n)$ are then replaced by the posterior probabilities $h(n, \mathcal{R})$. Thus the form of the inductive argument is

Premises:

[21] (Empirical probability theory) For $n = 1, 2, \ldots, N$
(a) $\mathbf{P}(\mathcal{R}, \mathfrak{J}_n) = f(\mathcal{R}, n)$ {Degrees of prediction}
(b) $\mathbf{P}(\mathfrak{J}_n) = g(n)$ {Prior probabilities}

[22] (Observed result) $\mathcal{R}$

Conclusion:

[23] (Empirical probability theory) For $n = 1, 2, \ldots, N$
(a) $\mathbf{P}(\mathcal{R}, \mathfrak{J}_n) = f(\mathcal{R}, n)$ {Degrees of prediction}
(b) $\mathbf{P}(\mathfrak{J}_n, \mathcal{R}) = h(n, \mathcal{R})$ {Posterior probabilities}.

The three separate premises [11] – [13] have been replaced by a single premise [21], because the prior probabilities, the degrees of prediction, and the assertion of alternatives should be treated as a unit. It is this unit that is changed as a result of the observation $\mathcal{R}$; that is, theory [21] is replaced by theory [23]. And it is this unit that implies a probabilistic prediction by theorem [19] of page 66. A prediction made on the basis of premise [21] is

$$\mathbf{P}(\mathcal{P}) = \sum_{n=1}^{N} \mathbf{P}(\mathfrak{J}_n)\mathbf{P}(\mathcal{P}, \mathfrak{J}_n) \quad .$$

A prediction made on the basis of the conclusion [23] is

$$\mathbf{P}(\mathcal{P}, \mathcal{R}) = \sum_{n=1}^{N} \mathbf{P}(\mathfrak{J}_n, \mathcal{R})\mathbf{P}(\mathcal{P}, \mathfrak{J}_n \& \mathcal{R}) \quad .$$

The inductive argument [21] – [23] may be iterated: another portion of the sequence $\phi x_1, \phi x_2, \ldots$ is observed and Bayes' theorem is applied to the new result $\mathcal{R}'$. In the resulting sequence of arguments the posterior probabilities of one argument become the prior probabilities of the next argument. The whole verification process is thus a repeated movement from one set of probabilities (degrees of prediction and prior probabilities) to a new set of probabilities (degrees of prediction and new prior probabilities) under the influence of observations made on the process $\phi x_1, \phi x_2, \ldots$.

When the process under consideration is a mixture of independent processes, the confirmation theorem applies (p. 84), guaranteeing that if the investigation is continued long enough the true theory will ultimately be accepted. The confirmation theorem is the result of combining the law of large numbers for independent processes (p. 61) with Bayes' theorem (pp. 66–67, 84). More general forms of the law of large numbers may be combined with Bayes' theorem to obtain generalizations of the confirmation theorem.* Under suitable specification of the conditions, a generalization of the confirmation theorem applies to empirical probability theories, guaranteeing that if the investigation is continued long enough the true theory will ultimately be confirmed.

A dispositional model of the inductive argument [21] – [23] can be made by replacing each "$\mathfrak{I}_n$" by the corresponding variable "$\mathcal{H}_n$" and relativizing all probability statements to $\mathcal{G}$. The result follows.

Premises:

[21′] (Empirical probability theory): $\mathcal{G}$, where $\mathcal{G}$ satisfies

$$\left.\begin{aligned}&\text{(a) } \mathbf{P}(\mathcal{R}, \mathcal{H}_n\mathcal{G}) = f(\mathcal{R}, n)\\ &\text{(b) } \mathbf{P}(\mathcal{H}_n, \mathcal{G}) = g(n)\end{aligned}\right\} \quad \text{for } n = 1, 2, \ldots, N$$

[22′] (Observed result) $\mathcal{R}$

Conclusion:

[23′] (Empirical probability theory): $\mathcal{R}\mathcal{G}$, where $\mathcal{G}$ satisfies

$$\left.\begin{aligned}&\text{(a) } \mathbf{P}(\mathcal{R}, \mathcal{H}_n\mathcal{G}) = f(\mathcal{R}, n)\\ &\text{(b) } \mathbf{P}(\mathcal{H}_n, \mathcal{R}\mathcal{G}) = h(n, \mathcal{R})\end{aligned}\right\} \quad \text{for } n = 1, 2, \ldots, N\,.$$

This dispositional model [21′] – [23′] stands to the inductive argument [21] – [23] as the dispositional model [11′] – [18′] stands to the inductive argument [11] – [18] (sec. 8.2.3). Underlying each of the probabilistic dispositions involved is a relatively self-sufficient system of properties and laws characterized by its inductive probability connections to the process ϕx_1, ϕx_2, ϕx_3, ... In the dispositional model, the statement $\mathcal{G}$ and each hypothesis $\mathcal{H}_n$ is to be a complete theory of the process ϕx_1, ϕx_2, ϕx_3, . . . , describing in each case an underlying system that is complete with respect to properties and laws of a certain kind and a certain level of specificity. The contents of the hypotheses $\mathcal{G}$, $\mathcal{H}_1$, . . . , $\mathcal{H}_N$ are not explicitly given but rather are characterized by various conditions, including the condition that $\mathcal{G}$ be based on all the information available at the beginning of the inquiry.

These completeness conditions are not included explicitly in [21′] – [23′] but are to be understood as present in the argument form. Similarly, existential quantifiers on "$\mathcal{G}$," "$\mathcal{H}_1$," . . . , "$\mathcal{H}_N$" have been omitted, as in some of our earlier dispositional models. Thus the free variables "$\mathcal{G}$,"

* Various forms of the law of large numbers are discussed in Feller, *An Introduction to Probability Theory and its Applications;* Kemeny and Snell, *Finite Markov Chains;* and Doob, *Stochastic Processes.*

"$\mathcal{H}_1$," . . . , "$\mathcal{H}_N$" represent arbitrary statements satisfying the given conditions.

Let us now compare the dispositional model [21′] – [23′] with the original inductive argument [21] – [23]. Each theory $\mathfrak{I}_n$ implies the same predictions to the same degree as its corresponding hypothesis $\mathcal{H}_n$, and is supported in the same way by the same observations. Consequently, the empirical tests for each $\mathfrak{I}_n$ and the corresponding $\mathcal{H}_n$ are the same. Hence the hypotheses $\mathcal{H}_n$ are good models of the empirical probability theories $\mathfrak{I}_n$, and the argument [21′] – [23′], taken as a whole, is a good model of the original inductive argument [21] – [23].

The dispositional pattern [21′] – [23′] reveals the essential epistemological features of empirical probabilities. We illustrate this dispositional pattern by applying it to the Markov chain associated with the two-state machine mentioned earlier. The process under consideration is $St_1, St_2, \ldots,$ and the empirical probability statements to be modeled are [k′] (p. 505), together with the independence conditions characteristic of Markov chains. For the sake of simplicity we consider only three alternative hypotheses

$(H_1)\quad \epsilon = 1/4$
$(H_2)\quad \epsilon = 1/2$
$(H_3)\quad \epsilon = 3/4$.

Since for actual machines the probability of error is usually small, we assign a prior probability of 0.9 to H_1 and a prior probability of 0.05 to each of the other two hypotheses. Suppose events t_1 through t_{20} are observed, with the result

$(R)\qquad SSSS\bar{S}\bar{S}\bar{S}SSS\bar{S}\bar{S}\bar{S}\bar{S}SSSS\bar{S}$.

This result strongly favors the hypothesis that $\epsilon = 1/4$, for on this hypothesis a change from one state to another should occur, on the average, every fourth step. Consequently, the probability of $\overline{St_{21}}$ is very close to 3/4.

The dispositional model of the foregoing inductive reasoning is as follows.

Premises:

[21″] G, where G satisfies

(a) $\mathbf{P}(R, H_1G) = 1.30503 \text{ x } 10^{-5}$
$\mathbf{P}(R, H_2G) = 9.5368 \text{ x } 10^{-7}$ } Degrees of prediction
$\mathbf{P}(R, H_3G) = 2.2 \text{ x } 10^{-10}$

(b) $\mathbf{P}(H_1, G) = .9$
$\mathbf{P}(H_2, G) = \mathbf{P}(H_3, G) = .05$ } Prior probabilities

[22″] R .

Conclusion:

[23″] $\therefore$ RG, where G satisfies

(a) Same degrees of prediction as [21″] (a)

(b) $\left.\begin{array}{l}\mathbf{P}(H_1, RG) = .996 \\ \mathbf{P}(H_2, RG) = .004 \\ \mathbf{P}(H_3, RG) = .000001\end{array}\right\}$ Posterior probabilities.

The probabilistic prediction for the next event t_{21} is

[24″] $\therefore$ RG, where $\mathbf{P}(\overline{St_{21}}, RG) = .749$.

Suppose the criterion for acceptance of a hypothesis is that its posterior probability exceed .99. The investigator can then conclude

[25″] $\therefore$ H_1G, where $St_1, St_2, \ldots$ is a Markov chain with
$\mathbf{P}(St_1, H_1G) = 3/4$
$\mathbf{P}(St_{i+1}, St_iH_1G) = 3/4$
$\mathbf{P}(St_{i+1}, \overline{St_i}H_1G) = 1/4$.

The foregoing shows how to construct dispositional models for a set of empirical probability theories that give complete probability assignments to a process $\phi x_1, \phi x_2, \ldots$. Hypotheses are introduced and characterized by their inductive probability connections to observable properties of the sequence. Portions of the process are observed, Bayes' theorem is applied, and eventually the true hypothesis is adopted. It follows from the very method by which these dispositional models are constructed that an empirical probability theory and its dispositional model are supported in the same way by the same observations and imply the same predictions to the same degree. Hence these dispositional models are good models of empirical probability theories in a very fundamental respect.

They are good models in a further important respect. We saw earlier that the traditional calculus of probability may be applied to empirical probabilities to infer one empirical probability theory from others (pp. 143–44). For example, the argument

[31]	$\mathbf{P}_e(T) = \alpha$	(The empirical probability of a tail is α)
[32]	$\mathbf{P}_e(D) = \beta$	(The empirical probability of a deuce is β)
[33]	$\mathbf{P}_e(D, T) = \mathbf{P}_e(D)$	(Tails and deuces are independent)
[34]	$\therefore$ $\mathbf{P}_e(TD) = \alpha\beta$	(The empirical probability of both a tail and a deuce is $\alpha\beta$)

is valid by the traditional calculus of probability. We shall see now that the dispositional model of this argument is valid by the calculus of inductive probability and hence is a good model in that respect.

Let the hypotheses H_α represent the various possibilities for the coin and let the hypotheses H_β^* represent the various possibilities for the die; the number of alternative hypotheses in each case does not matter. Similarly, the general information G, the prior probabilities, the completeness conditions, and the statement quantifiers may all be omitted as irrelevant to present purposes. For the independence of the coin tosses from the die throws to be made explicit, these events must be placed in the same context, that is, their probabilities must be stated relative to the conjunction $H_\alpha H_\beta^*$. The argument [31] – [34] is then modeled by

[31′] H_α, where $Tx_1, Tx_2, \ldots$ is an independent process of probability α relative to $H_\alpha H_\beta^*$

[32′] H_β^*, where $Dx_1, Dx_2, \ldots$ is an independent process of probability β relative to $H_\alpha H_\beta^*$

[33′] $Tx_1, Dx_1, Tx_2, Dx_2, \ldots$ is an independent process relative to $H_\alpha H_\beta^*$

[34′] $\therefore\ H_\alpha H_\beta^*$, where $Tx_1\&Dx_1, Tx_2\&Dx_2, \ldots$ is an independent process of probability $\alpha\beta$ relative to $H_\alpha H_\beta^*$.

The conclusion follows from the premises by the definition of independent process and the special multiplication principle. The original argument was valid, and the fact that the dispositional model is valid shows that it is a good model in this respect.

More generally, an argument whose premises and conclusion are empirical probability theories is valid by the traditional calculus of probability if and only if its dispositional model is valid by the calculus of inductive probability. Thus in a dispositional model, empirical probabilities are modeled by means of inductive probabilities in such a way that applications of the traditional calculus of probability to empirical probabilities become applications of the calculus of inductive probability to inductive probabilities. That is, the rules for constructing dispositional models of empirical probability arguments are rules of interpretation under which the calculus of inductive probability is applicable to empirical probabilities. So we have answered the question, "Why is the traditional calculus of probability applicable to empirical probabilities?" by showing how that calculus is being interpreted when it is applied to empirical probabilities.

Of course, it is not necessary in practice to trace all the details of the application as we did in the argument [31′] – [34′]. Instead, one can work directly with empirical probabilities. Indeed, the traditional calculus of probability may be interpreted directly in terms of empirical probabilities by rewriting the axioms, theorems, and proofs of Chapter 2 with "$\mathbf{P}_e$" replacing "$\mathbf{P}$." Let us call this interpretation of the traditional calculus the "calculus of empirical probability." Since this calculus is basically an application of the calculus of inductive probability, the former calculus has the same epistemological status as the latter. Hence the theorems of the calculus of empirical probability are true statements that have two aspects, an a priori aspect and a pragmatic aspect (p. 305).

Thus there are three closely related interpretations of the traditional calculus of probability: the inductive (p. 39), the frequency (p. 145), and the empirical. The practicing scientist may use any of these three interpretations in reasoning about empirical probability theories, or if he prefers, he may use the traditional calculus of probability without considering how it should be interpreted. The scientist, qua scientist, wishes to ascertain which empirical probability statements are true and to make correct inferences from some empirical probability statements to others. Either the traditional calculus of probability or any of its three interpretations is satisfactory for these purposes. For example, how the traditional calculus of probability is interpreted makes no essential difference to the physics of quantum mechanics, though it is important for the philosophy of quantum mechanics.

In other words, the three concepts of inductive probability (**P**), empirical probability ($\mathbf{P}_e$), and frequency probability ($\mathbf{P}_f$) are on a par from the point of view of the practicing scientist. But they are not on a par from the point of view of the philosopher of science, as the following considerations show. First, inductive probability is the only kind used in probabilistic dispositional formulas. Second, the calculus of inductive probability and standard inductive logic provide the rules of inductive inference used in verifying a probabilistic dispositional formula; Bayes' theorem is the most important of these rules. Third, the calculus of inductive probability provides the rules for arguing from some probabilistic dispositional formulas to others. Hence the only kind of probability used in probabilistic dispositional formulas is the inductive, and the only rules of probability used in verifying and manipulating probabilistic dispositional formulas are those of inductive probability. This shows that empirical probabilities can be accounted for in terms of inductive probabilities. The converse is not true, as is shown by our refutation of the frequency theory of inductive probability, which identifies frequency, empirical, and inductive probability (sec. 3.4.2). Consequently, the concept of inductive probability is epistemologically more fundamental than the concept of empirical probability.

We saw in Sections 2.4 and 3.4.1 how frequency probability can be accounted for in terms of inductive probability. Again, the converse is not true: inductive probability cannot be accounted for in terms of frequency probability (sec. 3.4.2). Hence the concept of inductive probability is epistemologically more fundamental than either the concept of empirical probability or the concept of frequency probability.

Let us now summarize what we have learned about empirical probabilities. An empirical probability theory makes a complete probability assignment to the possible observable outcomes of a process. It asserts that there is an underlying system that produces the process and is such that each possible observable outcome has a certain probability or degree of prediction.

An empirical probability theory may be confirmed or disconfirmed by means of its predictions. Consider a theory $\mathfrak{T}_1$ of a process $\phi x_1, \phi x_2, \ldots$. The verification of $\mathfrak{T}_1$ takes place in the context of a set $\mathfrak{T}_1, \mathfrak{T}_2, \ldots, \mathfrak{T}_N$ of mutually exclusive and jointly exhaustive theories and an assignment of prior probabilities to these theories. Thus we have a set of empirical probability theories $\mathfrak{T}_1, \mathfrak{T}_2, \ldots, \mathfrak{T}_N$, each theory assigning a degree of prediction to every possible observed result of the process $\phi x_1, \phi x_2, \ldots$. These empirical probability theories can be tested empirically by observing a finite portion of the process $\phi x_1, \phi x_2, \ldots$ and applying Bayes' theorem.

The degrees of prediction of the theories $\mathfrak{T}_1, \mathfrak{T}_2, \ldots \mathfrak{T}_N$ together with the prior probabilities of these theories constitute a broader empirical probability theory. Thus an empirical probability theory $\mathfrak{T}_n$ is investigated by being placed in the context of a broader empirical probability theory, which is a probabilistic mixture of $\mathfrak{T}_n$ and the alternatives to $\mathfrak{T}_n$. This broader empirical probability theory is modified by Bayes' theorem on the basis of the observed characteristics of the process $\phi x_1, \phi x_2, \ldots$.

Empirical probability theories can be inferred from other empirical probability theories by means of the traditional calculus of probability.

According to the dispositional theory of empirical probability, an empirical probability theory $\mathfrak{T}_n$ is dispositional in nature. Underlying this probabilistic disposition is a relatively self-sufficient system of properties and laws $\mathcal{S}_n$, the system $\mathcal{S}_n$ being characterized by its inductive probability connections to the process $\phi x_1, \phi x_2, \ldots$. A dispositional model of $\mathfrak{T}_n$ is constructed by asserting that there exists a true hypothesis $\mathcal{H}_n$ satisfying three requirements. First, $\mathcal{H}_n$ must assign the same degree of prediction to an observed result about $\phi x_1, \phi x_2, \ldots$ as does $\mathfrak{T}_n$. Second, $\mathcal{H}_n$ must be a complete theory of the process $\phi x_1, \phi x_2, \ldots$; that is, $\mathcal{H}_n$ must be a description of the underlying system $\mathcal{S}_n$ that is complete with respect to properties and laws of a certain kind and a certain level of specificity. Third, the prior probability of $\mathcal{H}_n$ must be the same as the prior probability of $\mathfrak{T}_n$. The content of $\mathcal{H}_n$ is not explicitly given; rather, it is characterized by means of these three requirements.

These dispositional models have the property that each empirical probability theory $\mathfrak{T}_n$ is modeled by a hypothesis $\mathcal{H}_n$, so that $\mathfrak{T}_n$ and $\mathcal{H}_n$ are supported in the same way by the same observations and imply the same predictions to the same degree. Moreover, an argument whose premises and conclusion are empirical probability theories is valid by the traditional calculus of probability if and only if its dispositional model is valid by the calculus of inductive probability.

Thus the answer to our third main question (p. 511) is this. *An empirical probability theory is dispositional in nature. It asserts that the system underlying the disposition is such that each possible observable outcome has a certain inductive probability (degree of prediction). In the context of alternative theories and a prior probability assignment, these probabilistic predictions may be used to confirm or disconfirm the theory: a finite portion of the actual process produced by the system is observed and Bayes' theorem is applied to the result.*

Empirical probability theories may be modeled by probabilistic dispositional formulas that are verified and manipulated by means of the calculus of inductive probability. These dispositional models account for the applicability of the traditional calculus of probability to empirical probabilities by revealing that these applications are really applications of the calculus of inductive probability to inductive probabilities. Empirical probabilities can be explained in terms of inductive probabilities, but not conversely. Hence the concept of inductive probability is epistemologically more basic than the concept of empirical probability.

8.3.3 The positivistic theory of empirical probability

We shall now develop a positivistic version of the dispositional theory of empirical probability, to be called the "positivistic theory of empirical probability." Although this theory is not as satisfactory as the dispositional theory itself, it is of interest because it views empirical probabilities in a novel way.

The positivistic theory of empirical probability results from a new approach to the analysis of probability, which differs from the approach we have been following in two important respects. First, our approach has been "global," as contrasted with "local." We have encompassed in one unified account many different applications of the traditional calculus of probability. We have related inductive probability to inductive reasoning, to inductive behavior, to standard inductive logic, and to Hume's problem of induction (chaps. 2–5). In the current chapter, we have related inductive probability to empirical probability and empirical probability to causal dispositions.

Second, we have moved mainly from inductive reasoning to formalism rather than in the reverse direction. We began with inductive reasoning and then developed two mathematical formalisms that can be used to model it: the calculus of inductive probability (chap. 2) and standard inductive logic (chap. 3). There was, of course, constant feedback between application and formalism, and in Chapter 5 the movement was mainly from the pragmatic calculus of choice to its applications rather than in the reverse direction. Nevertheless, our prevailing tendency has been to move from actual inductive reasoning to formal models of it. It is for this reason that the calculus of inductive probability was based on conditional rather than unconditional probability (see sec. 2.6).

In the present subsection, we use opposite procedures on both points. First, we employ a "local" approach, concentrating on a single application of the traditional calculus of probability: the use of Bayes' theorem to confirm an empirical probability theory. Second, we start with the mathematical formalism and then apply it. Thus we begin with Bayes' theorem and show how it may be applied to the process of verifying an empirical probability theory. No attempt will be made to relate this kind of inductive reasoning to other kinds or to general epistemological problems. In other words, we are now considering only one application of the calculus of probability and are not attempting to connect this application to other applications of the same formalism or to broad questions about knowledge.

For our purposes unconditional probability is simpler to work with than conditional probability. The mathematical formalism is thus defined by the unconditional probability system of Section 2.6. In this system, Bayes' theorem becomes

If $h_1, h_2, \ldots, h_N$ are mutually exclusive and jointly exhaustive and $\mathbf{P}(r) > 0$, then

$$\mathbf{P}(h_n, r) = \frac{\mathbf{P}(h_n)\mathbf{P}(r, h_n)}{\sum_{n=1}^{N} \mathbf{P}(h_n)\mathbf{P}(r, h_n)} \qquad \text{for } n = 1, 2, \ldots, N\,.$$

It is important to realize that Bayes' theorem is here a theorem of the uninterpreted system we called the "traditional calculus of probability," rather than a theorem of the interpreted system we call the "calculus of inductive probability" (sec. 2.1). In other words, we are no longer interpreting the symbol "**P**" to mean "inductive probability" as this concept was originally defined in terms of inductive arguments and the notion of evidence (pp. 23–26). At the moment, "**P**" is only partially interpreted: "**P**" represents any concept governed by the rules of the traditional calculus of probability. As we show how Bayes' theorem is used to model the verification process, "**P**" will acquire a fuller interpretation.

The dispositional models of Sections 8.2.1 to 8.3.2 attribute two kinds of content to an empirical probability theory of a process. First, "on the surface" there is the direct verificational and predictional content of the theory. This content consists of the complete probability assignment made by the theory to the sequence. Second, "underneath" there is the content that refers implicitly to a relatively self-sufficient system of properties and laws producing the sequence. Such an underlying system is related to indirect ways of verifying an empirical probability theory; for example, we may conclude that the probability of a coin falling heads is more than one-half because the coin is weighted on the tail side.

Since we are concerned with only one application of the calculus of probability, we may ignore the implicit content of an empirical probability theory and take the direct verificational and predictive content of the theory as its complete meaning. In terms of the inductive argument forms of Section 8.3.2, we use essentially form [21] – [23] rather than [21′] – [23′]. That is, we interpret the probabilities of argument form [21] – [23] so that they stand on their own without being relativized to some general information referred to only implicitly.

We next introduce the appropriate symbolism for applying Bayes' theorem. Consider a finite or infinite process $\phi x_1, \phi x_2, \ldots$ with two states ϕ and $\bar{\phi}$. Let "$\mathfrak{R}$" be a variable ranging over all truth-functions of a finite number of the events $\phi x_1, \phi x_2, \ldots$. Let N be some positive integer and let $n = 1, 2, \ldots, N$. To represent the alternative probabilistic hypotheses concerning the process $\phi x_1, \phi x_2, \ldots$, we use the degrees-of-prediction function $f(\mathfrak{R}, n)$ and the prior-probabilities function $g(n)$ introduced for this purpose in Section 8.3.1. Let $f(\mathfrak{R}, n)$ be a function satisfying the conditions

(1) For each $n = 1, 2, \ldots, N$, $f(\mathfrak{R}, n)$ satisfies the axioms for unconditional probability (sec. 2.6)

(2) If $n' \neq n$, then for some $\mathfrak{R}$, $f(\mathfrak{R}, n') \neq f(\mathfrak{R}, n)$

(3) If $\mathfrak{R}$ is noncontradictory, there is an $n = 1, 2, \ldots, N$ such that $f(\mathfrak{R}, n) > 0$.

Let $g(n)$ be a function satisfying the conditions

(4) $$\sum_{n=1}^{N} g(n) = 1$$

(5) $g(n) > 0 \qquad$ for each $n = 1, 2, \ldots, N$.

Define the posterior-probabilities function $h(n, \mathfrak{R})$ by

(6) $$h(n, \mathfrak{R}) = \frac{g(n)f(\mathfrak{R}, n)}{\sum_{n=1}^{N} g(n)f(\mathfrak{R}, n)} .$$

Since the functions $f(\mathfrak{R}, n)$, $g(n)$, and $h(n, \mathfrak{R})$ are used in formulating theories, they must be finitely expressible.

Now let "$\mathfrak{I}_1$," "$\mathfrak{I}_2$," . . . , "$\mathfrak{I}_N$" be statement symbols representing the alternative empirical probability theories involved in the verification process. The meaning of these symbols is given by their degrees of prediction

(7) $\mathbf{P}(\mathfrak{R}, \mathfrak{I}_n) = f(\mathfrak{R}, n) \qquad .$

Each theory $\mathfrak{I}$ has a prior probability

(8) $\mathbf{P}(\mathfrak{I}_n) = g(n)$

at the beginning of the inquiry. Note that by condition (2) each of the theories $\mathfrak{I}_1, \mathfrak{I}_2, \ldots, \mathfrak{I}_N$ determines a different complete probability assignment and that by condition (4) every complete probability assignment under consideration is determined by one of these theories. These two conditions are verificational analogues of the conditions defining the notions of "mutually exclusive" (p. 40) and "jointly exhaustive" (p. 52). If before any observations $\mathfrak{R}$ are made, there is reason to believe these alternatives are not sufficient, further alternatives should be added. And if none of the alternatives is in fact adequate to the observed characteristics of the process $\phi x_1, \phi x_2, \phi x_3, \ldots$, then the argument form will "fit" badly and should be given up or revised. In other words, if the particular formalism selected is not working well in the given context, it should be modified or abandoned. A discussion of rules for deciding when to modify or abandon the application of a given formalism is beyond the scope of the present approach.

A finite portion of the process $\phi x_1, \phi x_2, \ldots$ is observed; let the result be $\mathfrak{R}$. It follows from conditions (3) and (5) above and theorem [19] (p. 66) that $\mathbf{P}(\mathfrak{R}) > 0$; therefore Bayes' theorem is applicable. Substituting "$\mathfrak{R}$" for "r," "$\mathfrak{I}_1$" for "h_1," "$\mathfrak{I}_2$" for "h_2," etc., we obtain the probabilities posterior to $\mathfrak{R}$.

$$(9) \qquad \mathbf{P}(\mathfrak{I}_n, \mathfrak{R}) = \frac{\mathbf{P}(\mathfrak{I}_n)\mathbf{P}(\mathfrak{R}, \mathfrak{I}_n)}{\sum_{n=1}^{N} \mathbf{P}(\mathfrak{I}_n)\mathbf{P}(\mathfrak{R}, \mathfrak{I}_n)} \quad .$$

By (7) and (8) this becomes

$$(10) \qquad \mathbf{P}(\mathfrak{I}_n, \mathfrak{R}) = \frac{g(n)f(\mathfrak{R}, n)}{\sum_{n=1}^{N} g(n)f(\mathfrak{R}, n)} \quad .$$

By (6) the posterior probabilities are

$$(11) \qquad \mathbf{P}(\mathfrak{I}_n, \mathfrak{R}) = h(n, \mathfrak{R}) \quad .$$

When Bayes' theorem is applied repeatedly to the same process, the posterior probabilities of one inductive argument become the prior probabilities of the next. If the posterior probabilities are expressed as unconditional probabilities

$$(12) \qquad \mathbf{P}(\mathfrak{I}_n) = h(n, \mathfrak{R}) \quad ,$$

the conclusion of one inductive argument becomes the first premise of the next without being modified. Formula (12) does not contradict formula (8), since formula (12) is asserted only after the observation statement $\mathfrak{R}$ is asserted.

We thus arrive at the following inductive argument form for an application of Bayes' theorem.

Premises:

[41] (Empirical probability theory) For $n = 1, 2, \ldots, N$
(a) $\mathbf{P}(\mathfrak{R}, \mathfrak{I}_n) = f(\mathfrak{R}, n)$ {Degrees of prediction}
(b) $\mathbf{P}(\mathfrak{I}_n) = g(n)$ {Prior probabilities}

[42] (Observed result) $\mathfrak{R}$

Conclusion:

[43] (Empirical probability theory) For $n = 1, 2, \ldots, N$
(a) $\mathbf{P}(\mathfrak{R}, \mathfrak{I}_n) = f(\mathfrak{R}, n)$ {Degrees of prediction}
(b) $\mathbf{P}(\mathfrak{I}_n) = h(n, \mathfrak{R})$ {Posterior probabilities}.

The functions $f(\mathfrak{R}, \mathfrak{I}_n)$, $g(n)$ and $h(n, \mathfrak{R})$ should satisfy conditions (1) – (6). Formulas [41] – [43] are identical to the earlier formulas [21] – [23] (p. 512), except that the posterior probabilities are conditional in the earlier case but unconditional now.

Observe that this inductive argument employs empirical probability theories at two levels. The theories $\mathfrak{I}_1, \mathfrak{I}_2, \ldots, \mathfrak{I}_N$ are empirical probability theories, each defined by its degrees of prediction $\mathbf{P}(\mathfrak{R}, \mathfrak{I}_n) = f(\mathfrak{R}, n)$. The premise [41] is a higher level empirical probability theory, being a probabilistic mixture of the theories $\mathfrak{I}_1, \mathfrak{I}_2, \ldots, \mathfrak{I}_N$. It determines a complete probability assignment in accordance with theorem [19] (p. 66):

$$\mathbf{P}(\mathfrak{R}) = \sum_{n=1}^{N} \mathbf{P}(\mathfrak{I}_n)\mathbf{P}(\mathfrak{R}, \mathfrak{I}_n) \quad .$$

The same remarks apply to the conclusion [43]. Thus an empirical probability theory $\mathfrak{I}_n$ is investigated by being placed in the context of a broader empirical probability theory that is a probabilistic mixture of $\mathfrak{I}_n$ and the alternatives to $\mathfrak{I}_n$.

In each application of the argument form, the premises should satisfy some completeness conditions. The empirical probability theory [41] should be based on all the information available at the beginning of the argument. The statement $\mathfrak{R}$ should be a complete report of the observed portion of the process $\phi x_1, \phi x_2, \ldots$. The empirical probability theory [43] will then be based on all the information available at the end of the argument.

The theories [41] and [43] are conjunctions of conditional probability statements (the degrees of prediction) and unconditional probability statements (the prior and posterior probabilities). These conjuncts are not atomic inductive probability statements in the sense of Sections 1.5.2 and 8.3.1, since they do not contain the evidence on which they are based and since atomic inductive probability statements are *not* empirically true-or-false (pp. 129, 318). We need therefore to give an account of the content of empirical probability theories that is faithful to their empirical status. We call this account the **positivistic theory of empirical probability.**

Let us compare the statement variables of theory [41] with the statement variables of the corresponding theory [21′] of the dispositional model of Section 8.3.2. In both cases, the variable "$\mathcal{R}$" ranges over observation statements that have a certain content or meaning definable independently of their probability connections, and upon which these probability connections depend. An example of such an observation statement is "The first three events were successes."

The dispositional theory of empirical probability treats the theory variables "$\mathcal{H}_1$," "$\mathcal{H}_2$," . . . , "$\mathcal{H}_N$" and "$\mathcal{G}$" of [21′] in the same way as it treats the observation variable "$\mathcal{R}$." According to this theory there exist, at least theoretically, descriptions of complete systems underlying various possible dispositions. The variables "$\mathcal{H}_1$," "$\mathcal{H}_2$," . . . , "$\mathcal{H}_N$" and "$\mathcal{G}$" are thought of as ranging over such descriptions. When the rules of standard inductive logic are applied to descriptions $\mathcal{H}_n$, $\mathcal{G}$, and $\mathcal{R}$, these rules yield a degree of prediction $\mathbf{P}(\mathcal{R}, \mathcal{H}_n\mathcal{G})$ and a prior probability $\mathbf{P}(\mathcal{H}_n, \mathcal{G})$. Empirical probability theory [21′] asserts that there are descriptions $\mathcal{H}_1, \mathcal{H}_2, \ldots, \mathcal{H}_N$ and $\mathcal{G}$ having the specified degrees of prediction and the specified prior probabilities and being such that $\mathcal{G}$ is true.

In contrast, the positivistic theory of empirical probability treats the theory variables "$\mathfrak{J}_1$," "$\mathfrak{J}_2$," . . . , "$\mathfrak{J}_N$" differently from the observation variable "$\mathcal{R}$." The variables "$\mathfrak{J}_1$," "$\mathfrak{J}_2$," . . . , "$\mathfrak{J}_N$" do not range over statements that have a meaning definable independently of their probability connections and on which their probability connections depend. Rather, the content of a theory $\mathfrak{J}_n$ consists just of its degrees of prediction, that is, the degree to which it predicts each possible observable result $\mathcal{R}$. These degrees of prediction are interpreted by certain rules. The traditional calculus of probability provides rules for reasoning about them, and the pragmatic theory of inductive probability provides an interpretation for them in terms of action.

It follows from the foregoing that there are four aspects to the meaning of an empirical probability theory: an a priori aspect, an empirical aspect, a pragmatic aspect, and a subjective aspect (cf. pp. 305–6). Let us look at these in turn.

A priori aspect: The probability statements defining an empirical probability theory are governed by the rules of the traditional calculus of probability. This explains why the traditional calculus is applicable to empirical probabilities and thereby answers the last part of our third main question (p. 511). The rules of standard inductive logic are not involved here, because, as we stated at the beginning of this subsection, we are studying only the use of Bayes' theorem to confirm an isolated empirical probability theory.

Empirical aspect: An empirical probability theory is confirmed by empirical observations. The general process of confirmation is this: a theory

$\mathfrak{I}_n$ has a prior probability, an observation $\mathfrak{R}$ is made, and Bayes' theorem is applied to obtain a posterior probability for $\mathfrak{I}_n$. In some cases an empirical probability theory $\mathfrak{I}_1$ is completely confirmed in the following sense: the posterior probability of $\mathfrak{I}_1$ is so close to one that $\mathfrak{I}_1$ is accepted as true and the alternative theories $\mathfrak{I}_2, \mathfrak{I}_3, \ldots, \mathfrak{I}_N$ are rejected as false. Let us call both a prior and a posterior probability of a theory $\mathfrak{I}_n$ its "weight." Thus at each stage of inquiry an empirical probability theory has a certain weight. Empirical observations influence the weight of an empirical theory and may do so to the extent that the theory is accepted as true. This constitutes the empirical aspect of an empirical probability theory.

Pragmatic aspect: The probability statements constituting an empirical probability theory have the pragmatic meaning or action implications described by the pragmatic theory of inductive probability (sec. 5.6). Since standard inductive logic is not involved here, the same practical implications are described by the personalistic theory of inductive probability (sec. 5.7.2). An empirical probability theory makes a complete probability assignment to a process and thereby constitutes a commitment to bet in certain ways on propositions about this process.

Subjective aspect: The prior probability assignment of premise [41] is subjective in an important respect. Suppose that no observations have yet been made on the sequence $\phi x_1, \phi x_2, \ldots$; that is, no direct evidence concerning the probabilistic character of this sequence has yet been gathered. Imagine two investigators who have the same general information about the sequence and who disagree significantly as to what the prior probability assignment $\mathbf{P}(\mathfrak{I}_n) = g(n)$ should be (cf. p. 91). Are there any rules of inductive logic by which one investigator's assignment can be declared correct and the other investigator's assignment declared wrong? The traditional calculus of probability contains no such rules (sec. 3.1). Since it is limited to this calculus, the positivistic theory of empirical probability must treat any fundamental difference between investigators over prior probabilities as a subjective difference (sec. 5.7.2). Hence, according to this theory, the prior probability assignment of the premise of an inductive argument is not subject to inductive rules.

This completes our discussion of the four aspects of the meaning of an empirical probability theory. At the beginning of this subsection the probability symbol "**P**" was only partly interpreted: it represented any concept governed by the rules of the traditional calculus of probability. We have now completed the interpretation given to this symbol by the positivistic theory of empirical probability. We shall show next that on this interpretation the form $\mathbf{P}(c, d) = x$ has a status very different from that which it has had hitherto in this book. The key to this difference is the way the positivistic theory treats the theory variables "$\mathfrak{I}_1$," "$\mathfrak{I}_2$," . . . , "$\mathfrak{I}_N$" (p. 524).

The notion of an atomic inductive probability statement $\mathbf{P}(c, d) = x$

was originally introduced with reference to an inductive argument and was later generalized to be a component of an empirical probability theory (secs. 1.5.2, 8.3.1). In both cases, the form $\mathbf{P}(c, d) = x$ presupposes a universe of discourse consisting of nonprobabilistic statements whose meanings are definable independently of their probability connections. The variables "c" and "d" range over these statements. For any statements c and d and any value x (quantitative or qualitative), the statement $\mathbf{P}(c, d) = x$ has a definite truth-value (it is true or it is false), borderline cases aside. For example, consider the statements

(*T*) This silver dollar will fall tails on the next toss

(*E*) This silver dollar looks symmetrical, and most symmetrical coins fall tails approximately half the time.

In a suitable context, these statements have definite meanings and definite truth-values. Assume that in this context E contains all the relevant evidence available. Then the atomic inductive probability statement $\mathbf{P}(T, E) = 1/2$ has the truth-value "true," and $\mathbf{P}(T, E) = .1$ has the value "false."

According to the dispositional theory, an empirical probability theory involves the quantification of statement variables occurring in atomic inductive probability forms. The empirical probability theory asserts that there is a true statement satisfying various forms $\mathbf{P}(c, d) = x$. If there is such a statement, the theory is true; whereas if there is no such statement the theory is false. Equivalently, an empirical probability theory is true or false according to whether there is or is not a complete system of the sort described in the theory.

Thus an empirical probability theory has one of two truth-values, "true" or "false." Of course, our knowledge of the theory is not two-valued but a matter of degree, for the prior and posterior probabilities of the theory can be any of infinitely many real numbers. Hence, on the dispositional theory, there is a fundamental distinction between truth-status (which is two-valued) and verification status (which is a matter of degree). But on the positivistic theory, this distinction is not fundamental, as we shall now see.

Since the positivistic theory defines the alternative theories $\mathfrak{J}_1, \mathfrak{J}_2, \ldots, \mathfrak{J}_N$ in terms of probability connections alone, it treats the form $\mathbf{P}(c, d) = x$ in a fashion highly different from that of the dispositional theory. On the positivistic theory, an empirical probability theory about a process $\phi x_1, \phi x_2, \ldots$ has the form

[41] For $n = 1, 2, \ldots, N$
(a) $\mathbf{P}(\mathcal{R}, \mathfrak{J}_n) = f(\mathcal{R}, n)$ {Degrees of prediction}
(b) $\mathbf{P}(\mathfrak{J}_n) = g(n)$ {Weights}.

Here the variable "$\mathfrak{R}$" ranges over all truth-functions of a finite number of the events $\phi x_1, \phi x_2, \ldots$. Each such truth-function has a meaning definable independently of and prior to [41]. For example, if the process is a sequence of coin tosses, the statement "$Tx_1\overline{Tx_2}Tx_3$" means that the first three tosses are tail, head, tail, in that order. But the variables "$\mathfrak{I}_1$," "$\mathfrak{I}_2$," . . . , "$\mathfrak{I}_N$" function very differently from "$\mathfrak{R}$," for they have no meaning or content prior to [41]. Rather, the meaning of each theory $\mathfrak{I}_n$ is constituted by its degrees of prediction.

It follows that the notions of truth and falsity applicable to an observation statement $\mathfrak{R}$ are fundamentally different from the notions of truth and falsity applicable to an empirical probability theory $\mathfrak{I}_n$. An observation statement has one of the two truth-values "true" and "false." In contrast, an empirical probability theory $\mathfrak{I}_n$ has a certain weight or probability (prior or posterior), which can be any number between zero and one. If the probability of a theory $\mathfrak{I}_n$ is sufficiently close to one (or zero), the theory may be treated as true (or false), but this is just an approximation, made for practical reasons. More fundamentally, an empirical probability theory has only a certain probability, so that its truth or falsity is really a matter of degree.

This difference between observation statements and theories may be expressed in terms of the distinction between two-valued logics and multivalued logics. A probability is a kind of truth-value; so the traditional calculus of probability is a multivalued logic having infinitely many truth-values. According to the positivistic theory of empirical probability, this calculus is the "logic" of empirical probability theories, the two values "true" and "false" being practical limiting cases. Hence the logic of empirical probability theories is infinitely-valued, while the logic of observation statements is two-valued.

Let us now summarize the answer given by the positivistic theory of empirical probability to our third main question. *An empirical probability theory consists of a complete probability assignment to possible observable outcomes of a process or system of events. The theory is confirmed or disconfirmed by observing the actual outcomes of this sequence or system. At each stage of inquiry the theory has a certain weight (prior probability or posterior probability). An empirical probability theory has an a priori aspect (it is governed by the rules of the traditional calculus of probability), an empirical aspect (it is confirmed or disconfirmed by empirical observations), a pragmatic aspect (belief in it constitutes a commitment to behave in certain ways in conditions of uncertainty), and a subjective aspect (the assignment of prior probabilities to the theory and its alternatives is ultimately subjective and not governed by inductive rules). Except as an approximation, an empirical probability theory is neither true nor false but has only a weight or probability, which is a matter of degree.*

8.3.4 Prior probabilities and empirical probability

It will clarify both the positivistic and the dispositional theories to compare and contrast them. The most important difference concerns the treatment of prior probabilities.

Both theories analyze an empirical probability theory by means of a complete probability assignment to the possible observable outcomes of the process covered by the theory. But the positivistic analysis stops here, whereas the dispositional analysis makes the probability of an observable outcome relative to a statement or theory about the underlying system of properties and laws (pp. 500–503, 513). Our analysis of the fair-coin hypothesis showed how this works (sec. 8.2).

There are two levels of dispositions here: inquiry begins with a general theory G and (if successful) ends with a more specific hypothesis H_α ($\alpha = 0, .1, \ldots, .9, 1$). The coin-tossing process is a mixture of independent processes conditional on G but is an independent process of probability α conditional on $H_\alpha \& G$. The statements G and H_α are defined implicitly by the probability conditions just given. For example, to say the coin is fair and fairly tossed is to say there are true statements $H_{.5}$ and G satisfying, among other conditions, the condition that Tx_1, Tx_2, . . . is an independent process of probability 0.5 relative to $H_\alpha \& G$. Now these conditions consist of conditional probability statements of standard inductive logic: the probability of each predicted outcome is conditional on $H_\alpha \& G$, and the prior probability of each hypothesis H_α is conditional on G.

Thus both the positivistic and the dispositional theory of empirical probability view an empirical probability as a tendency to produce certain observable results with certain frequencies and hence as a kind of disposition. But they differ sharply over the nature of this disposition or tendency. According to the dispositional theory there is a system of properties and laws underlying this disposition, whereas according to the positivistic theory there is not. We have already seen that this difference leads to a difference in the nature of the truth-status of an empirical probability theory: it is two-valued on the dispositional theory and infinitely-valued on the positivistic theory. This difference also leads to further differences with respect to the (a) a priori, (b) empirical, and (c) subjective aspects of an empirical probability theory (pp. 524–25).

(a) On the positivistic theory, the a priori aspect is limited to the rules of the traditional calculus of probability, but the dispositional theory holds that the rules of standard inductive logic are also involved in an empirical probability theory. We shall see in a moment that this difference leads to a further difference concerning the subjective aspect of an empirical probability theory.

(b) Both the positivistic and the dispositional theories of empirical probability are applications of the probabilistic version of the pragmatic principle of meaning, which explicates the empirical content of a statement in terms of its probabilistic consequences and predictions (sec. 4.2.6). But the two theories differ on the kinds of consequences included. The positivistic theory limits these to the directly observable outcomes of the process covered by the theory. The dispositional theory also allows indirect consequences that are connected probabilistically to the implicitly defined theories about the underlying system of properties and laws. In the fair-coin example, information that the coin is weighted on the tail side lowers (in the context of the law of gravity) the prior probability that the coin is fair ($H_{.5}$). Similarly, information that the tossing arrangement is such that one toss has no causal influence on any other toss is evidence that the process is a mixture of independent processes (hypothesis G).

(c) We consider finally the subjective account of prior probabilities given by the positivistic theory. Two kinds of probability statements are involved in an empirical probability theory; one kind consists of the degrees of prediction, while the other consists initially of the prior probabilities and subsequently of the posterior probabilities (pp. 521–23). The positivistic theory interprets the former as conditional and definitive of the empirical probability theory and the latter as unconditional and subjective.

The dispositional theory gives a different account of prior probabilities. It holds that the prior probabilities are conditional and are subject to the norms of standard inductive logic. These norms are common to all men and are thus intersubjective rather than subjective (pp. 103, 136, 305, 326–27). Consequently, the dispositional theory makes prior probabilities intersubjective, in contrast to the positivistic theory that makes them subjective and relative to the individual.

We now show that an intersubjective account of prior probabilities leads to a better theory of empirical probability than a subjective account. The basic inductive argument form of Section 8.3.2 is

Premises:

[21] (Empirical probability theory) For $n = 1, 2, \ldots, N$
(a) $\mathbf{P}(\mathfrak{R}, \mathfrak{I}_n) = f(\mathfrak{R}, n)$ {Degrees of prediction}
(b) $\mathbf{P}(\mathfrak{I}_n) = g(n)$ {Prior probabilities}

[22] (Observed result) $\mathfrak{R}$

Conclusion:

[23] (Empirical probability theory) For $n = 1, 2, \ldots, N$
(a) $\mathbf{P}(\mathfrak{R}, \mathfrak{I}_n) = f(\mathfrak{R}, n)$ {Degrees of prediction}
(b) $\mathbf{P}(\mathfrak{I}_n, \mathfrak{R}) = h(n, \mathfrak{R})$ {Posterior probabilities}.

Suppose several investigators jointly apply this argument form to a process under the following conditions. Each investigator has the same general information and accepts the same observed result $\mathcal{R}$. Moreover, each investigator uses standard inductive logic in determining his prior probability assignment $\mathbf{P}(\mathfrak{T}_n) = g(n)$. The rules of standard inductive logic do not determine unique values for atomic probabilities, but they do set limits on what values are reasonable (pp. 326–27). Assume for purposes of illustration that the prior probability assignments of these investigators are such that, given the result $\mathcal{R}$, all of them agree that the particular theory $\mathfrak{T}_1$ is well confirmed.

Let a representative member of this group of investigators be called "Mr. Standard" (p. 131). Imagine a "Mr. Non-standard" whose reasoning in the present instance has the following characteristics. Mr. Non-standard has the same general information as Mr. Standard and also accepts $\mathcal{R}$ as the total direct evidence available. But Mr. Non-standard does not accept standard inductive logic, and his prior probability assignment $\mathbf{P}(\mathfrak{T}_n) = g'(n)$ is such that, when Bayes' theorem is applied, it turns out that theory $\mathfrak{T}_N$ is well confirmed and theory $\mathfrak{T}_1$ is disconfirmed. Thus Mr. Standard and Mr. Non-standard come to opposite conclusions concerning the confirmation of theory $\mathfrak{T}_1$.

Now an empirical probability theory is in fact confirmable by empirical observation. This means there is a limit to the amount of disagreement that should exist between two rational investigators who have the same evidence, both direct and indirect, concerning an empirical probability theory. Let us express this fact by saying that an empirical probability theory is "intersubjective." In particular, theory $\mathfrak{T}_1$ of our example is intersubjective, so that Mr. Standard and Mr. Non-standard cannot both be right about the status of $\mathfrak{T}_1$.

The rules of induction recognized by the positivistic theory of empirical probability do not include any rules for deciding whether Mr. Standard's or Mr. Non-standard's prior probability assignment is correct. Hence, on this theory, whether $\mathfrak{T}_1$ should be accepted or rejected is a subjective matter. Consequently, the positivistic theory of empirical probability cannot account for the intersubjectivity of empirical probability theories.

It is important to realize that limit theorems do not solve the problem of prior probabilities for the positivistic theory. The confirmation theorem does hold for every non-zero prior probability assignment to a mixture of independent processes, so that in the limit the prior probability assignment makes no difference. But at any given stage of inquiry there is only a finite amount of evidence, and if two investigators disagree too much on the prior probabilities, this evidence will not be sufficient to bring them into agreement on the posterior probabilities. In other words, limit theorems cannot account for the intersubjective character of empirical probabilities as these occur in actual science. Limit theorems can explain only characteristics of the historical scientific process regarded as an infinite institution. The attempt to remove the problem of prior probabilities by means of limit theorems is similar to Peirce's attempt to justify the use of the straight rule of induction by defining truth as "the opinion which is fated to be ultimately agreed to by all who investigate," and is equally fallacious. (See pp. 90–91, 131, 153–55, above.)

In contrast to the positivistic theory, the dispositional theory of empirical probability holds that prior probabilities should conform to the rules of standard inductive logic. These rules are norms held in common by all rational investigators and hence are intersubjective. Under the circumstances described, whether $\mathfrak{J}_1$ should be accepted or rejected is not a subjective matter but an intersubjective matter. According to the dispositional theory, all rational investigators should accept $\mathfrak{J}_1$ and reject $\mathfrak{J}_N$. Thus, by making prior probabilities intersubjective, the dispositional theory accounts for the intersubjectivity of empirical probability theories. For this reason, we have adopted the dispositional theory of empirical probability as the final answer to our third main question.

8.4 Alternative Theories of Empirical Probability

8.4.1 The frequency theory of empirical probability

In the present section we shall compare our dispositional theory of empirical probability with three other theories of empirical probability: the frequency theory, Peirce's dispositional-frequency theory, and de Finetti's personalistic account of empirical probability.

We discussed the frequency theory of empirical probability in Section 3.4.1. It is the oldest and most commonly accepted theory of empirical probability. As we saw, it explains the nature of atomic empirical probability statements by analyzing them into frequency probability statements, that is, statements about the limiting relative frequency of a property in an infinite sequence. Since frequency probability statements can be reasoned about by means of the calculus of frequency probability, this analysis accounts for the applicability of the traditional calculus of probability to empirical probabilities, and it thereby answers part of our third main question (p. 511).

The frequency theory was the first attempt to analyze empirical probability in terms of testable consequences. Relative frequencies can be observed in the finite case, and they constitute evidence for or against an atomic empirical probability statement. In equating $\mathbf{P}_e$ with $\mathbf{P}_f$, the frequency theory seemingly analyzes an atomic $\mathbf{P}_e$-statement into its empirical consequences.

But this analysis fails because of the gap between the finite and the infinite: an observable result concerns a finite sequence, whereas a frequency probability statement concerns an infinite sequence. This gap exists at both the interpretive and the inferential level. Since the concept of frequency probability is defined only for infinite sequences, it is not even defined for the finite or single case. The inferential gap exists in both directions: how do finite observations constitute evidence for unobservable limit properties, and how can a frequency probability statement be applied to a finite case (pp. 149, 157–58)? The frequency theory of empirical probability does not account for inferences in either direction.

Nor does it help to analyze empirical probability into relative frequency in a finite but "long" sequence. The identification cannot be exact but is only approximate, merely blurring the problem at issue: how to make inferences between statements about finite sequences and statements about infinite sequences without using a nonfrequency concept of probability (pp. 150, 154–55).

Consequently, the frequency theory of empirical probability does not give a completely satisfactory answer to the third main question. It does not explain how empirical and inductive probability are related. It does not tell what rules are used in the direct verification of an empirical probability theory. And it does not explain how an empirical probability theory is relevant to a single event.

The dispositional theory of empirical probability, on the other hand, is able to explain these things, and it is therefore more complete and satisfactory than the frequency theory. The dispositional theory models empirical probabilities by inductive probabilities in such a way that the calculus of inductive probability and standard inductive logic are used in the direct verification of an empirical probability theory (sec. 8.3.2). Thus empirical probabilities can be accounted for in terms of inductive probabilities, although the reverse is not the case. By basing empirical probabilities on inductive probabilities, the dispositional theory is able to explain the relevance of an empirical probability to a single event. Inductive probability is defined for finite, including single, cases.

The underlying reason for the superiority of the dispositional theory of empirical probability over the frequency theory is that the former takes into account both actual and possible sequences and both finite and infinite sequences, whereas the latter takes into account only infinite actual sequences. In other words, the dispositional theory accounts for both finite and infinite probabilistic processes, whereas the frequency theory accounts for only infinite actual sequences. This point was made against the frequency theory of inductive probability (pp. 155, 157–58), but it applies to the frequency theory of empirical probability as well. Let us see how this happens.

Consider the statement "$\mathbf{P}_e(T) = 1/2$," which asserts that the empirical probability of a particular coin falling tails is 1/2. The frequency theory analyzes "$\mathbf{P}_e(T) = 1/2$" into "$\mathbf{P}_f(T) = 1/2$," that is, into the assertion that the frequency probability of a tail is 1/2. The concept of frequency probability was defined for infinite sequences (definition [J], p. 144). Specifically, the definiens of "$\mathbf{P}_f(T) = 1/2$" is "The limiting relative frequency of tails in the infinite sequence of tosses of this coin is 1/2." Now in fact this coin will not be tossed infinitely many times; if an attempt were made to do this, the coin would wear out after a finite number of tosses. It is even questionable whether there will be infinitely many tosses of coins in general; but that is irrelevant here, for "$\mathbf{P}_e(T) = 1/2$" is about one particular coin, not all coins. Hence the expression "$\mathbf{P}_f(T) = 1/2$" is not really defined and cannot serve as an analysans for "$\mathbf{P}_e(T) = 1/2$."

The inadequacies of the frequency theory of empirical probability are partly corrected by Peirce's dispositional-frequency theory of probability, which takes into account possible infinite sequences as well as actual infinite sequences. We look at this theory next.

*8.4.2 Peirce's dispositional-frequency theory of probability.**

The philosophic writings of Charles Sanders Peirce fall into two periods, an earlier and a later one, the year 1890 being an approximate dividing line between the two periods. In his early period, Peirce propounded his frequency theory of inductive probability (sec. 3.4.2) and created his pragmatism (sec. 4.2.1); the first of these dates from 1867 and the second from the early 1870s. Both of these doctrines were nominalistic, recognizing only actualities, not possibilities. The frequency theory of inductive probability presupposes that there exists an actual infinite sequence of applications of a given inductive argument form. Pragmatism analyzes statements into practical conditionals, and in his early period Peirce symbolized practical conditionals with material implication ("$\supset$"), thereby limiting them to actualities.

According to the frequency theory, an inductive probability statement is about the actual universe and not about possible universes. Correspondingly, in his early period Peirce held that one could not assign probabilities to possible universes. He argued that if equal probabilities are assigned to them (as in random inductive logic), "reasoning from past to future experience [would be] absolutely worthless." He concluded:

> The relative probability of this or that arrangement of Nature is something which we should have a right to talk about if universes were as plenty as blackberries, if we could put a quantity of them in a bag, shake them well up, draw out a sample, and examine them to see what proportion of them had one arrangement and what proportion another.

* See my "Peirce's Two Theories of Probability" for a full discussion of this topic.

C. I. Lewis and Karl Popper also advocated dispositional theories of probability. Lewis's "real connections" cover probabilistic as well as causal dispositions; see my "A Pragmatic-Humean Theory of Probability and Lewis's Theory," pp. 451 and 457-63, and Lewis's reply at pp. 665-66. Popper's propensity theory is a form of dispositional theory; see his "The Propensity Interpretation of Probability."

But, even in that case, a higher universe would contain us, in regard to whose arrangements the conception of probability could have no applicability.*

In his later period Peirce converted both his frequency theory of probability and his pragmatism into realistic doctrines. He saw that his earlier nominalistic interpretation of practical conditionals was wrong, and he interpreted them realistically, as implying subjunctive conditionals. In our terminology, a practical conditional expresses a causal necessity (chaps. 6 and 7). In Peirce's terminology, a practical conditional describes a "would be" (p. 173). Correspondingly, he said that probabilities are also "would be's." A probabilistic "would be" is a dispositional frequency rather than an actual frequency. Hence I call this later theory *Peirce's dispositional-frequency theory of probability.*

Because this is the oldest dispositional theory of probability, we quote from Peirce at length.

For the sake of simplicity, I will define [probability] in a particular example. If, then, I say that the probability that if a certain die be thrown in the usual way it will turn up a number divisible by 3 (i.e., either 3 or 6) is 1/3, what do I mean? I mean, of course, to state that that die has a certain habit or disposition of behaviour in its present state of wear. It is a *would be* and does not consist in actualities or single events in any multitude finite or infinite. Nevertheless a habit does consist in what *would* happen under certain circumstances if it should remain unchanged throughout an endless series of actual occurrences. I must therefore define that habit of the die in question which we express by saying that there is a probability 1/3 (or odds of 1 to 2) that if it be thrown it will turn up a number divisible by 3 by saying how it *would* behave if, while remaining with its shape, etc., just as they are now, it *were to be* thrown an endless succession of times. Now it is very true that it is quite impossible that it should be thrown an infinite succession of times. But this is no objection to my supposing it, since that impossibility is merely a physical, or if you please, a metaphysical one, and is not due to any logical impossibility to the occurrence in a finite time of an endless succession of events each occupying a finite time. For when Achilles overtook the tortoise he had to go through such an endless series (endless *in the series*, but not endless *in time*) and supposedly actually did so.†

Peirce then goes on to explicate this "would-be." He says that if the die were tossed forever and remained unchanged throughout, the limiting relative frequency of a 3 or a 6 would be 1/3.

Peirce also makes an interesting comparison between the die's probabilistic disposition and a man's habit.

. . . the die has a certain "would-be"; and to say that a die has a "would-be" is to say that it has a property, quite analogous to any

* *Collected Papers* 2.685 (1878).

† *Collected Papers* 8.225 (ca. 1910).

> *habit* that a man might have. Only the "would-be" of the die is presumably as much simpler and more definite than the man's habit as the die's homogeneous composition and cubical shape is simpler than the nature of the man's nervous system and soul; and just as it would be necessary, in order to define a man's habit, to describe how it would lead him to behave and upon what sort of occasion—albeit this statement would by no means imply that the habit *consists* in that action—so to define the die's "would-be," it is necessary to say how it would lead the die to behave on an occasion that would bring out the full consequence of the "would-be"; and this statement will not of itself imply that the "would-be" of the die *consists* in such behaviour.
>
> Now in order that the full effect of the die's "would-be" may find expression, it is necessary that the die should undergo an endless series of throws from the dice box, the result of no throw having the slightest influence upon the result of any other throw, or, as we express it, the throws must be *independent* each of every other.*

Thus the "full consequence" of a probabilistic "would-be" can be manifested only in an infinite sequence.

Peirce's dispositional-frequency theory of probability covers both inductive probability (**P**) and empirical probability ($\mathbf{P}_e$). Let us consider it first as a theory of inductive probability. It does take into account possible sequences as well as actual sequences and hence does not presuppose that an inductive argument form will be used infinitely many times. Thus Peirce's dispositional-frequency theory remedies an important defect of the frequency theory of inductive probability. But it is open to all the other objections made to the frequency theory in Section 3.4.2, and hence it is not a satisfactory theory of inductive probability.

Taken as a theory of empirical probability, Peirce's dispositional-frequency theory holds that atomic empirical probability statements are dispositional. It distinguishes between the manifestation of a probabilistic disposition and the property underlying that disposition. A probabilistic disposition would be manifested by an infinite sequence of events with an appropriate limiting relative frequency. In my opinion, this dispositional approach is basically correct (sec. 8.3). But there are two respects in which Peirce's view of a probabilistic disposition is not sufficiently discerning.

First, Peirce's account of the difference between causal and probabilistic "would-be's" is unsatisfactory. We shall show this when we present Peirce's tychism (pp. 583–85). While there are important similarities between causal dispositions and probabilistic dispositions, there are also significant differences (sec. 8.2.2). Second, Peirce analyzes a probabilistic disposition in terms of the limiting relative frequency of an infinite sequence, rather than in terms of the inductive probabilities of finite sequences. We now develop this difference and trace its consequences.

* *Collected Papers* 2.664-65 (1910).

Consider the atomic statement

(1) The empirical probability of this coin falling tails is one-half.

On both Peirce's theory and ours, this is a statement about the sequence $Tx_1, Tx_2, \ldots$, it being assumed that the coin would remain the same even if it were tossed forever. Peirce's analysans is

(2) The coin and tossing procedure are such that if the coin were tossed forever by this process, the limiting relative frequency of a tail would be one-half.

Our analysans is

(3) The coin and tossing procedure are such that $Tx_1, Tx_2, \ldots$ is an independent process of inductive probability one-half.

Thus Peirce characterizes the property underlying the disposition by a single prediction that an infinite sequence of tosses of the coin would have a certain character, whereas we characterize the property underlying the disposition by degrees of prediction for all finite sequences. We will show that Peirce's characterization is a limiting case of ours.

The complete expansion of our analysans (3) involves conditional probability, but to facilitate comparison with Peirce's analysans, we omit reference to the condition. Then (3) becomes

(3′) The inductive probability that there will be s tails and f heads in $s + f$ tosses is $C_s^{s+f}(1/2)^{s+f}$.

By the law of large numbers,

(4) $$\operatorname*{Limit}_{L\to\infty} \mathbf{P}(.5 - \epsilon \leqq \sigma_L \leqq .5 + \epsilon) = 1$$

for any positive real number ϵ (p. 61). Though a probability of one allows exceptions (p. 147), nevertheless it is plausible to identify a probability of one with certainty. When this is done, (4) becomes

(4′) If the coin were tossed forever, then the limiting relative frequency of tails would be very close to one-half.

Statement (4′) is very similar to (2). Thus we may obtain Peirce's analysans (2) by taking our analysans (3) to the limit.

Unfortunately, the reverse cannot be done, because Peirce's analysans (2) implies nothing about finite sequences. Statement (2) characterizes the probabilistic disposition of the coin in terms of an infinite sequence and does not deductively imply anything about finite sequences. Consider, for example,

(5) If this coin were tossed 10,000 times, it is highly probable that the relative frequency of tails would be close to one-half.

This statement is a logical consequence of the original analysandum (1) and of our analysans (3), but not of Peirce's analysans (2).

This failure to cover finite sequences is a fatal weakness of Peirce's dispositional-frequency theory. Empirical probability theories are verified by observing finite sequences, and most applications of empirical probabilities are to finite sequences, including the single case. Consequently, Peirce's dispositional-frequency theory cannot account for the verification and application of empirical probability theories.

The same is true of the frequency theory of empirical probability (sec. 8.4.1). Both theories fail here because their conceptual apparatus is too weak; the concept of the limiting frequency of an infinite sequence (whether possible or actual) is not sufficient for the analysis of empirical probabilities. In contrast, the dispositional theory of empirical probability has available the concept of the inductive probability of a possible finite sequence, together with the pragmatic implications of this concept (chap. 5). For example, the dispositional theory $\mathfrak{I}_n$ explains the application of an empirical probability theory to a single ϕx_1 in this way: under conditions of total information, the degree of prediction $\mathbf{P}(\phi x_1, \mathfrak{I}_n)$ gives the correct odds for betting on ϕx_1.

Let us summarize our evaluation of Peirce's dispositional-frequency theory as applied to empirical probabilities. His theory is correct in treating empirical probabilities as dispositional. Because it covers possible infinite sequences as well as actual infinite sequences, it is superior to the frequency theory of empirical probability. But it is too narrow when it characterizes a probabilistic disposition in terms of the limiting relative frequency of an infinite sequence. As the dispositional theory of empirical probability holds, frequencies enter into empirical probabilities via degrees of prediction of possible finite sequences. These degrees of prediction may have certain limiting properties, but the content of an empirical probability theory goes beyond these limiting properties. An empirical probability theory says something directly about each possible finite sequence.

The crux of our criticism of frequency theories of empirical probability can be stated briefly as follows. An essential characteristic of an empirical probability statement is its relation to observable frequencies. The frequency theory of empirical probability, the oldest such theory, makes an important contribution in emphasizing this relation. But neither it nor Peirce's frequency-dispositional theory analyzes the relation correctly. The former analyzes it in terms of actual infinite sequences, while the latter analyzes it in terms of possible infinite sequences. But since observations are finite, it is the relation of an empirical probability to the frequency (σ_L) of occurrences of a property in a *possible finite sequence* that is basic to an empirical probability. Since the dispositional theory of empirical probability recognizes and analyzes this relation, it gives a more complete and satisfactory answer to our third main question (p. 511) than does either the frequency theory of empirical probability or Peirce's dispositional-frequency theory of probability.

8.4.3 The personalistic account of empirical probability

Finally, we compare our dispositional theory of empirical probability with the account of empirical probability originated by de Finetti and defended by Savage.* This account is in terms of the personalistic theory of inductive probability (sec. 5.7.2).

The key problem is to reconcile the subjective character of personal probability with the apparently objective character of empirical probability. Consider the proverbial sequence of tosses of a coin. Assume that the sequence of tosses Tx_1, Tx_2, Tx_3, . . . is an independent process or sequence of some unknown probability. In other words, the empirical probability statement $\mathbf{P}_e(T) = \alpha$ is true for some unknown α. Now the empirical probability α appears to be an objective parameter of the coin and tossing procedure, to be determined by empirical investigation. How can this fact be accounted for in terms of a personal concept of probability?

Savage and de Finetti, respectively, formulate the problem as follows.

> A problem often posed by statisticians is to estimate from a sequence of observations the unknown probability p that repeated trials of some sort are successful. On an objectivistic view, this problem is natural and important, for on such a view the probability that a coin falls heads, for example, is a property of the coin that can be determined by experimentation with the coin and in no other way. But on a personalistic view of probability, strictly interpreted, no probability is unknown to the person concerned, or, at any rate, he can determine a probability only by interrogating himself, not by reference to the external world.

> The old definition [of "independent events with constant but unknown probability p"] cannot, in fact, be stripped of its, so to speak, "metaphysical" character: one would be obliged to suppose that beyond the probability distribution corresponding to our judgment, there must be another, unknown, corresponding to something real, and that the different hypotheses about the unknown distribution—according to which the various trials would no longer be dependent, but independent—would constitute *events* whose probability one could consider. From our point of view these statements are completely devoid of sense, and no one has given them a justification which seems satisfactory, even in relation to a different point of view. . . . If . . . one plays heads or tails with a coin of irregular appearance . . . one does not have the right to consider as distinct hypotheses the suppositions that this imperfection has a more or less noticeable influence on the "unknown

* De Finetti, "Foresight: Its Logical Laws, Its Subjective Sources" and "Le vrai et le probable." Savage, *The Foundations of Statistics*, pp. 50-55.

probability," for this "unknown probability" cannot be defined, and the hypotheses that one would like to introduce in this way have no objective meaning.*

The solution that de Finetti offers to this problem rests on his theorem concerning exchangeable sequences, or processes, given earlier (pp. 125–26). A complete probability assignment to a process ϕx_1, ϕx_2, . . . is "exchangeable" if and only if it assigns equal probabilities to isomorphic truth-functions. De Finetti's theorem is: A complete probability assignment to an infinite process ϕx_1, ϕx_2, . . . is exchangeable if and only if that process is a mixture of independent processes.

By virtue of this theorem, the supposedly objectionable expression "independent process of unknown probability" may be replaced by the expression "exchangeable process." Consider, for example, our assertion about the tosses of a coin:

> Tx_1, Tx_2, . . . is an independent process of some unknown probability α.

This can be replaced by the statement

> Tx_1, Tx_2, . . . is an exchangeable process,

in which the phrase "unknown probability" does not occur.

De Finetti and Savage formulate their solution this way.

> The result at which we have arrived gives us the looked-for answer, which is very simple and very satisfactory: the nebulous and unsatisfactory definition of "independent events with fixed but unknown probability" should be replaced by that of "exchangeable events." This answer furnishes a condition which applies directly to the evaluations of the probabilities of individual events and does not run up against any of the difficulties that the subjectivistic considerations propose to eliminate. . . . It leads in all cases to the same practical conclusion: a rich enough experience leads us always to consider as probable future frequencies or distributions close to those which have been observed.

> Examination of situations in which "unknown" probability is appealed to, whether justifiably or not, shows that, from the personalistic standpoint, they always refer to [exchangeable] sequences of events. . . .†

* Savage, *Foundations of Statistics*, pp. 50-51. De Finetti, "Foresight: Its Logical Laws, Its Subjective Sources," pp. 141-42.

† The first quotation is from de Finetti, "Foresight," p. 142.

The second quotation is from Savage, *Foundations of Statistics*, p. 52. In this quotation we have replaced Savage's "symmetric" by "exchangeable." Note that Savage wrongly restricts empirical probabilities to mixtures of independent sequences or processes. We shall see in a moment that de Finetti does not make this error but is nevertheless unable to account for empirical probability theories about processes other than mixtures of independent processes.

Let us now criticize both de Finetti's formulation of the problem of empirical probability and his profferred solution of it. In stating the problem, he confuses the possibility of an empirical probability being unknown with the seemingly objective character of an empirical probability. A probability can be unknown even on the personalistic theory. For on this theory a personal probability is a disposition of the person involved, manifested by his betting behavior in conditions of uncertainty. Now how a person would behave in certain circumstances may be unknown to that person himself, and it cannot always be ascertained by self-interrogation. Thus the problem of how a probability can be unknown is not unique to empirical probabilities. The important problem about empirical probability that the personalistic theory must face is how to explain the apparently objective character of empirical probability in terms of a personal concept of probability. Prima facie, it seems that we should examine the behavior of the coin, i.e., how it falls, rather than the behavior of a person, i.e., how he bets, to determine the empirical probability that the coin will fall tails.

I do not think that de Finetti solves this problem by analyzing "independent process of unknown probability" into "exchangeable process." In the first place, this attempted solution applies only to mixtures of independent processes. As we showed in Section 8.3.1, many empirical probability theories concern other types of processes, such as Markov chains. De Finetti recognizes this problem and suggests generalizing the notion of exchangeability to cover other types of processes.* But he does not make clear what this generalization might be, and so even from his own point of view he cannot account for the empirical character of probabilistic processes that are not mixtures of independent processes.

In the second place, the notion of exchangeability does not solve the real problem even for the case of independent processes of unknown probability. By using "exchangeable process" in place of "independent process of unknown probability," de Finetti avoids the phrase "unknown probability." But this gives only a verbal solution. For without appealing to de Finetti's exchangeability theorem, one can call an independent process of unknown probability a "mixture of independent processes" (a "mip") and thereby avoid the term "unknown probability." Whatever the process is called, the problem of explaining the apparently objective character of empirical probability in terms of a personal concept of probability still remains.

Insofar as there is a solution to this problem, it can be ascertained by looking at the way an empirical probability theory is verified. Since the personalistic theory of probability treats prior probabilities as personal and ultimately subjective, the analysis of confirmation made by the positivistic theory of empirical probability (sec. 8.3.3) is completely consistent with the

* "Foresight," p. 146. De Finetti speaks of "independent events" and Savage of "independent sequences," whereas we speak of "independent processes."

personalistic theory, and I think it would strengthen this theory to replace de Finetti's exchangeability analysis by the positivistic theory of empirical probability. So let us examine the extent to which empirical probabilities turn out to be objective on the positivistic theory.

Inquiry begins with a set of alternative empirical probability theories $\mathfrak{I}_1, \mathfrak{I}_2, \ldots, \mathfrak{I}_N$. Each theory $\mathfrak{I}_n$ is defined by its degrees of prediction $\mathbf{P}(\mathfrak{R}, \mathfrak{I}_n) = f(\mathfrak{R}, n)$, and each theory has a prior probability $\mathbf{P}(\mathfrak{I}_n) = g(n)$. After an observation $\mathfrak{R}$ is made and Bayes' theorem is applied, each theory $\mathfrak{I}$ has a posterior probability:

$$\mathbf{P}(\mathfrak{I}_n, \mathfrak{R}) = \frac{g(n)f(\mathfrak{R}, n)}{\sum_{n=1}^{N} g(n)f(\mathfrak{R}, n)} \quad .$$

This posterior probability $\mathbf{P}(\mathfrak{I}_n, \mathfrak{R})$ depends on two factors: the specific character of the empirical result $\mathfrak{R}$ and the prior probability distribution $g(n)$. The first factor is objective on any view. But the personalistic theory of probability holds the second factor to be personal and ultimately subjective (sec. 5.7.2).

Thus, on the personalistic theory of probability, the apparently objective character of an empirical probability turns out to be partly objective and partly subjective. De Finetti recognizes this consequence of his theory:

> It is thus that when the subjectivistic point of view is adopted, the problem of induction receives an answer which is naturally subjective but in itself perfectly logical. . . . It is true that in many cases—as for example on the hypothesis of exchangeability—these subjective factors never have too pronounced an influence, provided that the experience be rich enough; this circumstance is very important, for it explains how in certain conditions more or less close agreement between the predictions of different individuals is produced, but it also shows that discordant opinions are always legitimate.
>
> . . . observation cannot confirm or refute an opinion, which is and cannot be other than an opinion and thus neither true nor false; observation can only give us information which is capable of *influencing* our opinion.*

We saw earlier that because the positivistic theory of empirical probability makes prior probabilities subjective, it cannot account for the intersubjective character of empirical probabilities (sec. 8.3.4). By the same line of argument, because the personalistic account of empirical probability makes prior probabilities subjective, it cannot explain the intersubjectivity of empirical probabilities either. In contrast, by making prior probabilities intersubjective, the dispositional theory of empirical probability does explain the intersubjectivity of empirical probability.

* "Foresight," pp. 147 and 154, respectively. A footnote reference to Poincaré is omitted from the first quotation.

We therefore conclude that the dispositional theory of empirical probability (sec. 8.3.2) gives a better explanation of empirical probabilities than the positivistic theory of empirical probability (sec. 8.3.3), the frequency theory of empirical probability (secs. 3.4.1 and 8.4.1), Peirce's dispositional-frequency theory of probability (sec. 8.4.2), or the personalistic account of empirical probability.

8.5 Summary

The dispositional theory of empirical probability was developed in several stages in this chapter, with interspersed discussions of the concept of empirical probability and of alternative theories thereof. This summary is organized differently, with all of the material on the dispositional theory brought together last as the culminating solution to our third main question.

The concept of empirical probability ($\mathbf{P}_e$). An empirical probability statement concerns a process, and it is so defined that observable outcomes of that process are evidentially relevant to the statement. If a coin is fairly thrown, the process $Tx_1, Tx_2, Tx_3, \ldots$ (T = falls tails) is a mixture of independent processes. Consider the possible values $\alpha = 0, .1, .2, \ldots, .9, 1$, and any assignment of non-zero prior probabilities to these values. The result "700 tosses out of 1000 were tails" is evidence for $\mathbf{P}_e(T) = 0.7$ and against $\mathbf{P}_e(T) = 0.5$.

Our original concept of empirical probability had a general feature that proved to be essential and a specific feature that required generalization. The general feature was its modal character: a process $\phi x_1, \phi x_2, \phi x_3, \ldots$ is a set of possible finite outcomes, e.g., $\phi x_1 \phi x_2$, $\overline{\phi x}_1 \phi x_2$, $\overline{\phi x}_1 \phi x_2 \overline{\phi x}_3$, each of which has an evidential bearing on the statement $\mathbf{P}_e(\phi) = \alpha$. The specific feature was that an atomic empirical probability statement was taken to be a statement about a mixture of independent processes. But there are many other kinds of probabilistic processes, and so we generalized the notion of an atomic empirical probability statement to the notion of an empirical probability theory, or set of such statements.

A complete probability assignment to a multistate process $\phi x_1, \phi x_2, \phi x_3, \ldots$ is a function $\mathbf{P}(\mathcal{R}, \mathcal{G})$ that assigns a conditional probability to each truth-function $\mathcal{R}$ of a finite number of the events of the process. We used this notion to cover both continuous and discrete systems of any number of dimensions, but our detailed analyses were for one-dimensional, two-state, discrete systems.

An empirical probability theory is any empirical theory that makes a complete probability assignment to the observable characteristics of a process or system of events. The statement that a process is an independent process of probability α is a very simple kind of empirical probability theory. Other examples of empirical probability theories are: the claim that a process is a mixture of independent processes together with a prior probability distribution for the unknown probability α, a law of radioactive emission, a description of the probabilistic behavior of a written text, the statement that the behavior of a computer is a Markov chain, the Bose-Einstein statistics of a nucleus, the Fermi-Dirac statistics of an electron, and the second law of thermodynamics.

Our third main question is: What is the general nature of an empirical probability theory? How are empirical and inductive probabilities related? Why is the traditional calculus of probability applicable to empirical probabilities? (Sec. 8.3.1)

Frequency theories of empirical probability. The frequency theory holds that atomic empirical probability statements should be analyzed into frequency probability statements and reasoned about by means of the calculus of frequency probability, which is an interpretation of the traditional calculus of probability. This theory partially answers the third question, but it fails to explain how empirical probability statements are verified or applied, and hence it does not show how empirical and inductive probability are related. (Sec. 3.4.1)

The frequency theory was the first attempt to analyze empirical probability in terms of testable consequences, or observed relative frequencies. Its inadequacies stem from an overly simple identification of empirical probability with relative frequency. In analyzing $\mathbf{P}_e(\phi)$ into $\mathbf{P}_f(\phi)$, the frequency theory reduces $\mathbf{P}_e(\phi)$ to the limiting relative frequency of ϕ in a single, actual, infinite sequence. We have shown that a satisfactory analysis of empirical probability must cover possible as well as actual sequences and finite as well as infinite sequences. (Sec. 8.4.1)

Peirce's dispositional-frequency theory of probability analyzes an empirical probability into a dispositional frequency rather than an actual frequency. A probability is a "would-be" that is manifested by an infinite sequence of events having a certain limiting relative frequency. Thus this theory takes into account possible infinite sequences as well as actual infinite sequences. But Peirce fails to distinguish causal "would-be's" from probabilistic "would-be's," and his analysis does not cover finite sequences. (Sec. 8.4.2)

Verification of an empirical probability theory. An empirical probability theory is best explicated by analyzing the procedure for verifying or rejecting it. The rationale of this procedure may be expressed in an inductive argument based on Bayes' method of finding an unknown probability. (Sec. 2.5.3)

The premises of the argument contain the following information: the alternative hypotheses, their prior probabilities, and the observed result. The direct verificational and predictional content of a hypothesis is given by the degree of prediction it assigns to each possible observed result. Posterior probabilities are calculated by Bayes' theorem. The main conclusion of the argument asserts that these posterior probabilities are the probabilities that now should be assigned to the hypotheses. Subsidiary conclusions make predictions based on these posterior probabilities or categorically assert a hypothesis whose posterior probability is sufficiently close to unity.

As an example, assume that the sequence of tosses of a particular coin is an independent process of unknown probability α and that the alternative values $\alpha = 0, .1, .2, \ldots, .9, 1$ are equally probable. Out of 1,000 tosses, 523 fall heads. This result has a higher degree of prediction on $\alpha = .5$ than on any of the other values of α. Hence the posterior probability of the fair-coin hypothesis $\mathbf{P}_e(T) = .5$ is very close to 1, and so this hypothesis is well confirmed. (Pp. 480–83, 497–500, and 509–11)

The positivistic theory of empirical probability. The positivistic theory treats this verification process as an isolated unit and models it by means of the traditional calculus of probability. It analyzes an empirical probability theory into a complete probability assignment to possible observable outcomes of a process or system of events.

An empirical probability theory is confirmed or disconfirmed by observing the actual outcomes of this process or system and applying Bayes' theorem. At each stage of inquiry, the theory has a certain weight (prior probability or posterior probability).

Thus an empirical probability theory has an a priori aspect (it is governed by the rules of the traditional calculus of probability), an empirical aspect (it is confirmed or disconfirmed by empirical observations), a pragmatic aspect (belief in it constitutes a commitment to behave in certain ways in conditions of uncertainty), and a subjective aspect (the assignment of prior probabilities to the theory and its alternatives is ultimately subjective and is not governed by inductive rules). Except as an approximation, an empirical probability theory is neither true nor false but has only a weight or probability, which is a matter of degree. (Sec. 8.3.3)

De Finetti's exchangeability analysis of empirical probabilities is not satisfactory. Since his personalistic theory of probability treats prior probabilities as personal and ultimately subjective, it would strengthen that theory to replace his exchangeability analysis by the positivistic theory of empirical probability. (Sec. 8.4.3)

On the positivistic theory, the a priori aspect of an empirical probability theory is limited to the traditional calculus of probability and does not encompass standard inductive logic. Consequently, it must treat any fundamental disagreement between two investigators over the prior probability assignment as subjective; thus it cannot explain the intersubjective character of empirical probabilities. In contrast, the dispositional theory holds that a prior probability assignment should conform to the rules of standard inductive logic. Since these rules are intersubjective, the dispositional theory does explain the intersubjective character of an empirical probability theory. (Sec. 8.3.4)

The Dispositional Theory of Empirical Probability

Dispositional models of inductive arguments. Dispositional models of the verification process were constructed for the coin-tossing case (pp. 484–86), for the general case of finding the unknown probability of a mixture of independent processes (pp. 501–2), and for the verification of an empirical probability theory of any form (pp. 513–15). These models involve existential statement quantifiers on the alternative hypotheses under test and on the general conditions assumed at the beginning of the test.

In these models an empirical probability statement is explicated in terms of a probability assignment to observable consequences. The essential features of the models are illustrated in the simplest case, that of the fair-coin hypothesis.

(a) The empirical probability of this coin falling tails is .5 [$\mathbf{P}_e(T) = .5$].

Very roughly, this empirical probability statement is modeled by

(b) The coin and tossing procedure are such that the process Tx_1, Tx_2, Tx_3, . . . is an independent process of inductive probability .5.

The following form of this statement makes explicit the observable consequences used to verify or refute it.

(c) The coin is such that, should it be tossed L times, the inductive probability ($\mathbf{P}$) of the result $S_L(T) = s$ is $C_s^L(1/2)^L$.

These models are probabilistic versions of Peirce's pragmatic analysis of an empirical statement into its observable consequences. On Peirce's analysis the empirical statement deductively implies its observable consequences, whereas on our dispositional analysis an empirical probability statement inductively implies its observable consequences with appropriate probabilities.

The concept of conditional inductive probability is the only concept of probability employed in these models. The inductive rules are those of standard inductive logic, including the calculus of inductive probability. Since atomic inductive probability statements are not empirically true-or-false (p. 160), it is natural to ask how these dispositional models preserve the empirical status of an empirical probability theory. They do so by means of the existential statement quantifiers: the probability conditions involved in the model are not empirical, but whether or not there are true statements satisfying these conditions is an empirical matter. (Pp. 486–87)

The dispositional nature of an empirical probability theory. These models show that an empirical probability theory of a process ϕx_1, ϕx_2, ϕx_3, . . . is dispositional in nature. Underlying the probabilistic disposition is a relatively self-sufficient system of properties and laws that produces this process. The underlying system is characterized in the theory by its inductive probability connections to possible finite outcomes that are mentioned explicitly. Many different systems could produce the probabilistic process $\phi x_1, \phi x_2, \phi x_3, \ldots$ and hence may underlie the probabilistic disposition.

It is required in a dispositional model that the general statement $\mathcal{G}$ and the alternative hypotheses $\mathcal{H}_1, \mathcal{H}_2, \ldots, \mathcal{H}_N$ be complete theories of the process, each describing an underlying system that is complete with respect to properties and laws of a certain kind and a certain level of specificity. The contents of the hypotheses $\mathcal{G}, \mathcal{H}_1, \mathcal{H}_2, \ldots, \mathcal{H}_N$ are not explicitly given but are characterized by various conditions, including the condition that $\mathcal{G}$ be based on all the information available at the beginning of the inquiry. (Pp. 490–95, 500–502, and 513–14)

There are, besides the directly observable outcomes of a process, indirect consequences connected probabilistically to the implicitly defined theory about the underlying system of properties and laws. In the fair-coin example, information that the coin is weighted on the tail side lowers the prior probability that the coin is fair, and information that the tossing arrangement is such that no toss causally influences any other toss is evidence that the process is a mixture of independent processes. Since the positivistic theory of empirical probability treats the verification process as an isolated unit, it does not take into account these indirect consequences. (Pp. 520, 528–29)

Probabilistic and causal dispositionals. These are similar in several important respects. Both use higher-order existential quantifiers to assert the truth of a statement that is not given explicitly but is rather characterized by its relations to observable consequences. In other words, both attribute a property to an object or system without explicitly naming that property.

A property underlying a causal disposition is characterized by its causal connections to observable events, the characterizing condition being empirically true-or-false. A property underlying a probabilistic disposition is characterized by its inductive probability connections to observable events, but in this case the characterizing conditions are *not* empirically true-or-false. Both types of characterizing conditions are fundamentally modal.

There are other similarities and differences between probabilistic and causal dispositionals. (Sec. 8.2.2)

The dispositional theory of empirical probability. We thus answer our third main question as follows. An empirical probability theory is dispositional in nature. It asserts that the system underlying the disposition is such that each possible observable outcome has a certain probability (degree of prediction). In the context of alternative theories and a prior probability assignment, these probabilistic predictions may be used to confirm or disconfirm the theory: a finite portion of the actual process produced by the system is observed and Bayes' theorem is applied to the result.

Empirical probability theories may be modeled by probabilistic dispositional formulas that are verified and manipulated by means of the calculus of inductive probability. These dispositional models explain the applicability of the traditional calculus of probability to empirical probabilities by revealing that these applications are really applications of the calculus of inductive probability to inductive probabilities.

The dispositional theory holds that a prior probability assignment should conform to the rules of standard inductive logic. Since these rules are intersubjective, the dispositional theory accounts for the intersubjective character of an empirical probabilistic theory.

Empirical probabilities can be explained in terms of inductive probabilities, but not conversely. Hence the concept of inductive probability is epistemologically more basic than the concept of empirical probability. (Sec. 8.3.2)

This completes our answer to the third main question. We turn next to the fourth and final question: What is the nature of causal necessity and how is it related to inductive probability?

9 Cause and Chance in Space-time Systems

With Earth's first Clay they did the Last Man's knead,
And then of the Last Harvest sow'd the Seed:
Yea, the first Morning of Creation wrote
What the Last Dawn of Reckoning shall read.

When the atoms are traveling straight down through empty space by their own weight, at quite indeterminate times and places they swerve ever so little from their course, just so much that you can call it a change of direction. If it were not for this swerve, everything would fall downwards like rain-drops through the abyss of space. No collision would take place and no impact of atom on atom would be created. Thus nature would never have created anything.

. . . the evolution of the world . . . proceeds from one state of things in the infinite past, to a different state of things in the infinite future. The state of things in the infinite past is chaos, tohu bohu, the nothingness of which consists in the total absence of regularity. The state of things in the infinite future is death, the nothingness of which consists in the complete triumph of law and absence of all spontaneity. Between these, we have on *our* side a state of things in which there is some absolute spontaneity counter to all law, and some degree of conformity of law, which is constantly on the increase owing to the growth of *habit*. The tendency to form habits or tendency to generalize, is something which grows by its own action, by the habit of taking habits itself growing. Its first germs arose from pure chance. There were slight tendencies to obey rules that had been followed, and these tendencies were rules which were more and more obeyed by their own action.*

9.1 Introduction

Our last question is: What is the nature of causal necessity, and how are causal necessity and inductive probability related? (P. 30) Our answer to it is "the presupposition theory of induction," which we shall develop in this and the next chapter. So that the reader may know where we are going, we start with a brief outline of the theory.

The presupposition theory holds that inductive reasoning presupposes

* FitzGerald, *Rubaiyat*, stanza 53. Lucretius, *On the Nature of the Universe*, book 2, p. 66; the view expressed in this passage is that of Epicurus. Peirce, *Collected Papers* 8.317.

a very complex a priori and intersubjective conceptual structure. The main concepts are those of causal necessity ($\Box^c$), inductive probability (**P**), and the distinction between nonindexical properties and a space-time matrix in which they may be repeatedly exemplified.

The verification of a causally necessary statement is Bayesian in character. Prior probabilities are assigned to those alternative sets of causally possible universes that satisfy three presuppositions: a causal uniformity principle, a causal existence principle, and a limited variety principle. These alternative sets of causally possible universes are so structured that each causal hypothesis under consideration has a finite prior probability. The hypotheses imply statements about the actual universe with varying degrees of prediction, so that Bayes' theorem may be applied. Causally necessary truths are thus confirmed by repeated instantiation.

In this chapter we lay the groundwork for the presupposition theory, and in so doing formulate the first two presuppositions. In Chapter 10 we shall complete the theory, and in the process develop the limited variety presupposition.

We study first the underlying space-time framework of induction. Induction involves repetition and therefore presupposes both a repeatable factor (nonindexical properties) and a matrix in which repetition can occur (space-time). Cellular automata are discrete, modal, space-time systems that will be useful in formulating the presuppositions of induction. Spatio-temporal contiguity plays an important but subtle role in induction. (Sec. 9.2, Space-time Systems)

The causal uniformity and causal existence principles are postulates of inductive inference. The causal uniformity principle is: If a causal connection between nonindexical properties holds in one region of space-time, it holds throughout space-time. The causal existence principle is: Some space-time region is governed by quasilocal laws, at least for the most part.

We explain these two principles in part by relating them to the traditional doctrine of determinism and its alternatives. Determinism combines the uniformity postulate and a complete form of the existence postulate. Near-determinism combines the uniformity postulate, the existence postulate, and the doctrine that some events are partially uncaused. Peirce's tychism contrasts with both determinism and near-determinism, for it holds that probabilistic laws are more basic than causal laws. (Sec. 9.3, Causality in Nature)

The chapter concludes with two topics only weakly connected to the presupposition theory, but important in a book devoted to the foundations of probability and causality. These are: How does the determinist account for probabilistic processes? What is randomness, and how is it related to determinism? (Sec. 9.4, Determinism and Chance)

As will be evident, the views expressed henceforth are less complete and more speculative than the views of the preceding chapters.

9.2 Space-time Systems

9.2.1 Induction and repetition

We saw earlier that repetition plays an important role in standard inductive logic. The rule of induction by simple enumeration attaches a positive weight to the number of occurrences of a phenomenon: the more often a property has accompanied another, the more likely it is that it will accompany the other (pp. 102, 111, 124). In this respect, induction differs from deduction, as Hume noted:

> Nothing so like eggs: yet no one, on account of this appearing similarity, expects the same taste and relish in all of them. It is only after a long course of uniform experiments in any kind, that we attain a firm reliance and security with regard to a particular event. Now where is that process of reasoning which, from one instance, draws a conclusion, so different from that which it infers from a hundred instances that are no-wise different from that single one? This question I propose as much for the sake of information, as with an intention of raising difficulties. I cannot find, I cannot imagine any such reasoning.*

Since inductive reasoning involves repetition, it presupposes both a repeatable factor and a matrix or framework in which repetition can occur. Properties may have many spatio-temporal instances or exemplifications, so that the matrix is space-time and the repeatable factor is a domain of properties.

Some restriction needs to be placed on the kind of property to which induction by simple enumeration applies, as the following example shows. A person sees swans for the first time on 18 March 1967 and observes many swans on that day. He can truly say, "I have seen many swans on 18 March 1967 and none on any other day." But it is obviously wrong for him to apply induction by simple enumeration to this premise and conclude, "It is probable that I shall see swans only on 18 March 1967."

A repetitive factor is present in this example, for there are many instances or cases in which the subject has seen a swan on that day. But the repeated property involves space-time and is not an ordinary property, so that the rule of induction by simple enumeration does not apply to it. In the next subsection, we shall distinguish those properties (the "nonindexical") to which induction by simple enumeration applies from those (the "indexical") to which it does not.†

There are many different notions of space and time, ranging from our simple commonsense ideas to the highly sophisticated concepts of Einstein's

* *An Enquiry Concerning Human Understanding*, p. 36 (sec. 4, part 2). Hume incorrectly restricts "reasoning" to "deductive reasoning" (see p. 135, above).

† For a theory of induction in which the distinction between indexical and nonindexical properties is not taken as basic, see Nelson Goodman's *Fact, Fiction, & Forecast*.

theories of relativity. The space and time of common sense are sharply separate: If two events are simultaneous for one observer, they are simultaneous for any other, even though he is moving with respect to the first. But according to the special theory of relativity, simultaneity is relative: events occurring simultaneously in one reference frame may occur sequentially in another reference frame. Again, in common sense, curvature is a property of things in space, but not of space itself. According to the general theory of relativity, however, space-time is itself curved by the presence of matter.

Since we are concerned with the foundations of induction, we employ the commonsense notion of space-time as a continuous spatial arrangement combined with an independent temporal order of possible things and events. The observational data used in the first instance to confirm or disconfirm empirically true-or-false statements occur at the commonsense level and hence are located in commonsense space-time. The particular and detailed structure of space-time depicted in physical theory has been learned by means of inductive inference from observations made at the commonsense level.

In this chapter and the next we consider both artificially defined space-time systems, e.g., cellular automata, and natural space-time systems, e.g., an actual gas in a container or nature itself. We use the term *nature* to refer to the single space-time system consisting of all entities (events or substances) with spatio-temporal location and the basic laws governing these entities (cf. the term "reality," p. 108). Nature, then, has the following ontological components: an underlying matrix of space-time points or regions, a set of properties that can be exemplified at any of these points or regions, and a set of laws governing the exemplifications of these properties. These laws may be causal or probabilistic; in either case they involve possible universes (see sec. 9.3).

Cellular automata are discrete spatio-temporal extensions of the models used earlier for inductive logics (sec. 3.2) and for causal laws (sec. 6.3). The space of a cellular automaton is divided into finite cells and its temporal dimension is divided into successive moments. The spatio-temporal structure of a cellular automaton is thus a discrete model of the continuous space-time of nature; we use cellular automata as very simple models of nature. To this end, we extend our earlier terminology for models (the terms "individual," "state," "universe," etc.) to cover both discrete and continuous space-time systems.

The individual events of a *space-time system* are arranged in a *space-time framework* or coordinate system. This generally has three spatial and one temporal dimension, so that each event has coordinates $(x, y, z; t)$. We also consider space-time systems that have one or two spatial dimensions or a time-coordinate that assumes only non-negative values. The space-time framework may be continuous (as in the case of nature) or discrete (as in the case of cellular automata).

The *basic individuals* of a space-time system are the space-time points or regions at which nonindexical properties are exemplified. Note that in our modal models a basic individual generally has different properties in different universes. For example, in Table 10 (p. 111), individual *b* has property *W* in the first universe but property not-*W* in the second. Thus a basic individual possesses a property in the sense of being the position-moment at which it is exemplified, not in the sense of being an event which contains the property as an ontological "part."* Correspondingly, a proper name or individual constant just denotes a basic individual and has no connotations concerning its properties. Our technical usage here contrasts with ordinary usage, in which a proper name has connotations (p. 558) and in which an event, individual, or continuant is a complex containing properties as well as an individuating principle.

We look next at the basic properties of a space-time system. Since a reference frame is itself a relational system, the relational properties of a space-time system may be derived from its monadic properties. For example, the statement "The magnetic field at $(x, y, z; t)$ is stronger than the magnetic field at $(x', y', z'; t')$" follows from appropriate specific statements about the magnetic field strength at each of these points. Hence, it suffices to confine the basic properties of a space-time system to monadic properties. For the reason given above (p. 551), these monadic properties should be nonindexical. The *basic properties* of a space-time system are thus monadic and nonindexical.

The notions of "individual state," "universe," etc., were originally defined linguistically. This linguistic approach often fails for a space-time system, because the complexity of the system exceeds the expressive power of language. The corresponding notions for a space-time system are nevertheless clear, and so we shall employ them. There is a set of *individual states*. *A temporal state* is an assignment of individual states to all basic individuals $(x, y, z; t)$ for fixed t. A *logically possible universe* is a history of temporal states over the range of t. There is an *actual universe*. There will be a set of causally possible universes (logically possible universes in which the laws of nature hold) or a probability assignment to logically possible universes.

This concludes our explanation of the notion of a space-time system. The rest of this section will be devoted to topics relevant to both space-time and induction: the distinction between nonindexical and indexical properties, cellular automata, and the role of spatio-temporal contiguity in induction.

* My ontology of events and continuants is described in sections 6 and 7 of "Ontological Categories and Language."

9.2.2 *Indexical symbols and properties**

We now distinguish those properties (the nonindexical) to which induction by simple enumeration applies from those (the indexical) to which it does not. This distinction is best drawn by considering both its linguistic and its nonlinguistic side. We begin by distinguishing between indexical symbols, e.g., "now," "here," "this book," "that shape," and nonindexical symbols, e.g., "yellow," "time," "man," "pattern."

As we saw when modeling causal statements, the meaning of a symbol depends on its linguistic context (p. 459). For example, the word "yellow" may refer to a color or to a man's lack of courage. Consider only the occurrences of "yellow" signifying the color. Each such occurrence consists of a characteristic pattern in an appropriate linguistic context; this pattern may be a pattern of sound (e.g., the spoken "yellow," the spoken "jaune," "yellow" as heard by a telegrapher in code), a shape (e.g., "yellow," a typewritten occurrence of "yellow," a written occurrence of "yellow"), etc. Each such occurrence of "yellow" is called a "token," and the class of all such occurrences (in all possible languages, media, and codes) is called a "type." Note that the type "yellow" in the sense of the color yellow is different from the type "yellow" in the sense of being a coward.

More generally, the class of all *tokens* of a given symbol in one of its meanings constitutes a *type*. A token of a symbol is thus an event of a certain character in a context of a certain kind, and so has a definite location in space and time. In contrast, a type is a class of tokens, and it has no spatio-temporal location. Using the type-token distinction, we may differentiate between *indexical symbols* and *nonindexical symbols* by giving examples of each kind and making some general remarks about how each kind functions (see sec. 1.3).

The symbol "today" is indexical, because tokens of it uttered on different days refer to different days, and to determine the day referred to by a token of "today" one needs to know the day on which it is uttered.† Consider, in contrast, the symbol "yellow" in a verbal context indicating that the color yellow is being referred to; for example, in the sentence "Alice wore a bright yellow dress to Convocation." This symbol is nonindexical, because each token signifies the same color, no matter what the spatio-temporal location of the token and its context.

"Here" and "now," when used to refer to the present place and time,

* This subsection is based on my "Icon, Index, and Symbol" and "Proper Names." Further details are given in these papers.

† We are considering only the most common use of language, not its fictional, quotational, and similar uses. The meaning of "today" does not change from one performance of a drama to another. Nor does "ago" change its meaning when the sentence "Lincoln began his Gettysburg address with the words 'Four score and seven years ago' " is uttered in different years.

are indexical symbols, for tokens uttered at different places and times denote different places and times. A token of "this chair," together with an act of pointing that singles out one particular chair from among many, is indexical. But "chair" itself is nonindexical, because one does not need to know the spatio-temporal location of a token of "chair" to know the kind of object being specified.

"That color," "that shape," and "that pattern," used to indicate directly a color, a shape, and a pattern, are all indexical symbols, even though the entities indicated are abstract rather than concrete. In both of the sentences

That book was written by John Masters
That book got wet in the monsoon,

the phrase "that book" is indexical; the first token designates an abstract entity, while the second designates a concrete entity. But "color," "shape," "pattern," and "book" are all nonindexical symbols.

Consider symbols that refer to entities, either abstract or concrete; e.g., the symbols "this tree," "this shade of blue," "the smallest prime number," and "the color having a wavelength of 4,000 Angstroms." These symbols are divided into indexical and nonindexical according to whether or not the spatio-temporal location of a token of the type needs to be known in order to find the referent of the symbol. "The smallest prime number" and "the color having a wavelength of 4,000 Angstroms" are therefore nonindexical symbols.

We shall see later that proper names are indexical symbols. The personal pronouns "I," "you," and "he," used in conversation with gestures to refer to the speaker, the listener, and a third person, respectively, are indexical symbols. But in

If anyone tries to swim the Gunga now, he will drown,

the pronoun "he" is nonindexical, functioning similarly to a variable of a formal language (p. 344). Contrast this sentence with

He wants some coffee

used by a waiter to refer to a customer. The referent of "he" does not change as the former sentence is moved from one spatio-temporal context to another, whereas the referent of "he" does generally change as the spatio-temporal location of the latter sentence changes.

"Right" and "left" are indexical when they pertain to the side of a person or thing. Suppose three men are in a straight line, all facing the same direction. When B says "the man on my right" he refers to C. If, now, B turns around and repeats the same phrase, he refers to A. Similar remarks hold for "the box in front of me" and "the box behind me."

An ostensive definition requires acts of pointing, or the equivalent, and thus is closely related to an index (see pp. 13–14). For example, "crimson" may be defined ostensively by pointing out various crimson-colored objects as positive cases and objects of other colors as negative cases. But this does not make "crimson" an indexical symbol, for the classification of symbols into the indexical and the nonindexical is based on how the symbol functions once it is understood, not on how it is defined or how it is learned.

The demonstrative pronouns "this" and "that" and gestures such as pointing are the fundamental indices. But by themselves they cannot pick out definite objects. An act of pointing or a token of "this" leads to many objects and so cannot designate any particular one without the assistance of a descriptive element, supplied either explicitly or by the context. For example, if one is pointing to a book, the reference might be to the book, that copy of the book, the cover of the book, the design of the cover, the color of the book, etc. For this reason, the basic form of an indexical symbol is "this ϕ" where ϕ is a nonindexical symbol. Note in this connection the closeness in meaning of "here" to "this place," of "now" to "this time," of "today" to "this day," etc. Note also that the form "this ϕ" may fail to indicate any object. For example, one might say "That desk is steel," meaning "The desk in the next room is steel," when there was no desk (or were more than one) in the next room.

The foregoing examples provide a sufficient basis for a general analysis of how the indexical form "this ϕ" functions. Consider what one needs to know about a token of "this ϕ" in order to determine whether or not the token denotes an object, and if it does, to locate and identify that object. (1) He needs to know the description ϕ of the object indicated. This may be conveyed by a symbol accompanying a "this" or a "that" (as in "this city," "that shape," "this cup") or by the context, or it may be incorporated in the indexical expression itself. Thus "now" is equivalent to "the present time," "here" means "this place," "I" refers to the person who speaks or writes it, and "you" refers to the person addressed. (2) The spatial, temporal, or spatio-temporal location of the token must be known. For example, to determine the day referred to by a token of "this day" one needs to know the day on which the token was uttered. (3) Finally, one needs to know a set of directions relating the token to its object. These may be conveyed by an act of pointing, a bodily orientation, etc.; examples are "this man," "that man." But the directions can also be conveyed symbolically. Thus it is part of the meaning of "I" that one finds the person referred to by proceeding from the token to the speaker or writer of the token. Similarly, the entity indicated by a token of "now" is the time at which the token is uttered.

The preceding discussion specifies the meanings of "indexical symbol" and "nonindexical symbol." Using these terms, we now specify the meanings of the correlated terms "indexical property" and "nonindexical property." To do this, we first describe a logically possible universe in which each object and event has a mirror-image counterpart, and hence can be picked out by speakers in the universe only by means of an index. Spatially, the universe consists of two halves, one so located as to be a perfect mirror-image of the other, each half having the same internal construction as the other. The history of each half is the same as the history of the other half, except that the events in one half are spatial mirror images of the events in the other half.

Compare a particular object, for example, a cubical red box with a door on it, and its mirror-image counterpart. Most of the intrinsic (monadic) properties of these two objects are the same: both are cubical, hollow, of exactly the same size, of exactly the same shade of red, etc. What is more important, many of their relational properties are also identical; for example, each box is near a brown chair, a yellow triangular plate is behind each box, each box is a mirror-image of an intrinsically identical box, etc.

Nevertheless, the boxes differ in many of their properties. Suppose that by means of indices a speaker in the universe identifies one box as "the first" and the other as "the second." Then the first box is numerically identical with the first box, while the second box is numerically different from the first box. Moreover, the two boxes differ systematically in certain of their relational properties. If someone pointed to a brown chair near one of the boxes, that box would be near that brown chair while the other box would be far from it. Also, to an observer, one box has a left-hand door while the other box has a right-hand door; the symbols "right" and "left" are indexical, as we have already seen. Thus, the relational properties the two boxes share can be referred to by nonindexical symbols, whereas the relational properties they do not share can be specified only by indexical symbols. Correspondingly, either box can be referred to by a suitable indexical phrase of the form "this ϕ"; but neither box can be picked out by a nonindexical phrase of the form "the ϕ," because if the nonindexical symbol ϕ applies to one box, it also applies to the other box.

It is an empirical matter whether or not the actual universe has the structure of our mirror-image model universe; according to available cosmological evidence it probably does not. We can nevertheless define the notions of "indexical property" and "nonindexical property" in terms of the logical possibility that the actual universe is a mirror-image universe. An *indexical property* is a property such that if the actual universe were a mirror-image universe, this property could be specified only by an indexical symbol. A *nonindexical property* is a property that could be specified by a nonindexical symbol even if the actual universe were a mirror-image universe.

It should be noted that we use the word "property" to cover both properties in the ordinary sense, i.e., monadic properties, and relations, i.e., relational "properties."

Greenness, circularity, being made of gold, being taller than, dissolving in aqua regia, being a swan, and riding a horse are all nonindexical properties. Being near the University of Michigan Library, being inside the White House now, occurring today, being a word on this page, and living in the Himalayas are indexical properties. Nonindexical properties can be specified by indexical symbols as well as by nonindexical symbols, as in the sentence "Silver is the color of my watch." But indexical properties can be specified only by means of indexical symbols. Indexical properties are nevertheless genuine properties; they can, for example, be possessed by many objects. To illustrate: there are many people in my house at this moment, each of whom possesses the indexical property "is a person in my house now."

Clearly, proper names play essential roles in many terms denoting indexical properties. They are themselves indexical, as can be demonstrated by means of our mirror-image model universe. Consider a proper name token used by a speaker to name some object. If a listener understands the reference, he must be able to identify that object in certain circumstances. He does so by means of some nonindexical property he associates with the name. In other words, the proper name functions as a definite description or a phrase of the form "the object having property ϕ," in which ϕ is nonindexical. Different people using a name generally associate different properties with it. This does not matter, as long as the name designates the same object for each.

Now for any given nonindexical property associated with a name, there may be two or more objects having that property; such would always be the case if our universe were a mirror-image universe.* This does not make the proper name token ambiguous, however, because the object it denotes has a unique indexical relation to it. Assume, for purposes of illustration, that our universe is a mirror-image universe, and consider my utterance, "I spent the summer of 1965 in the Himalayas." Whatever nonindexical property I use to identify the Himalayas is also possessed by their mirror-image counterpart. But this does not produce any ambiguity in my use of the proper name "Himalayas," for my listeners know I am referring to the Himalayas that are some seven-thousand miles from me, not to their mirror-image counterpart. This analysis shows that the proper name "Himalayas" functions as a definite description that has both an indexical and a nonindexical component. Hence proper names are indexical symbols.

* More explicitly, we are considering nonindexical properties without built-in requirements on the number of their instances. Thus we exclude "being the tallest man," "being one of the five tallest men," etc.

We conclude our specification of the notion of an indexical property by discussing its role in the principle of the identity of indiscernibles.* This principle is sometimes stated as

[1] If two objects have all their properties in common, they are identical.

But this statement is ambiguous until some class of properties, some class of objects, and a kind of identity are specified.

We are interested here in objects and events located in space-time, e.g., Nandi Devi, that explosion, her pain, rather than abstract objects, e.g., the number two, the numeral "two." We are interested in ordinary identity (e.g., Peirce *was* the founder of pragmatism), rather than logical identity (e.g., seven *is necessarily equal to* three plus four). Finally, we are interested in the ordinary properties of things, rather than modal properties (e.g., Mount Everest *is necessarily identical with itself*) or higher-order properties. Higher-order properties require predicate or statement quantifiers for their formulation (see pp. 344, 440–41, 469, 483–85). For example, the ordinary properties that make a teacher good are first-order properties, e.g., capacity to excite interest, clarity of presentation, organization, while the property "x has most of the properties of a good teacher" is second order.

Even with these restrictions, statement [1] is ambiguous. For it expresses many different principles, according as indexical properties and relational properties are or are not included. The following three distinct versions of the identity of indiscernibles are of interest here.

[2] Two objects with the same monadic, nonindexical properties are identical.

[3] Two objects with the same nonindexical properties, monadic and relational, are identical.

[4] Two objects with the same properties, indexical and nonindexical, monadic and relational, are identical.

These are listed in order of decreasing strength.

Statement [2] is an analysis of Leibniz's formulation of the identity of indiscernibles.

> . . . *there cannot be two individual things in nature which differ only numerically*. For surely it must be possible to give a reason why they are different, and this must be sought in some differences within themselves.

> . . . there are never two things in nature which are perfectly alike and

* Kant, *Prolegomena to Any Future Metaphysics*, sec. 13. Langford, "Otherness and Dissimilarity."

This is also called the principle of the dissimilarity of the diverse.

in which it is impossible to find a difference that is internal or founded on an intrinsic denomination.*

It is easy to construct a model to show that principle [2] is *not* logically true in our sense of the term. Imagine two perfect ball bearings of exactly the same size, which are made of the same material, have the same internal arrangement of atoms, etc.

A model that shows that the weaker principle [3] is not logically true is of greater interest. The two ball bearings do not show this, for they may stand in different relations to their surroundings. For example, one may be closer to a rectangular table than the other. To remedy this deficiency it suffices to make the two ball bearings mirror-image counterparts in a mirror-image model universe of the sort described earlier. Any object in one part of the universe has a mirror-image counterpart, and the object and its counterpart have all their nonindexical properties, relational as well as monadic, in common. The identity of indiscernibles, when restricted to nonindexical properties (as in [3]) is false of this universe, and hence it is not logically true, even though it is probably empirically true. Other models that prove the same point are of course possible; the essential feature is systematic repetition, so that there will be more than one object with the same specific nonindexical properties, relational as well as monadic. An old Chinese conception of the universe as temporally cyclic, if construed so that the events of one epoch are repeated identically in all others, is an adequate model.

We have previously used the idealized models $\mathfrak{M}$-$\mathfrak{L}$ to model certain aspects of reality (secs. 3.2, 6.3); it may be helpful to use them also to illustrate our analysis of the identity of indiscernibles. A model with two distinct objects (i and j), one monadic property (P), and one dyadic relation (R) will suffice. Let the logically possible universes be

(a) $\overline{Pi}PjRii\overline{Rjj}Rij\overline{Rji}$ Actual universe

(b) $\overline{Pi}PjRiiRjjRijRji$

(c) $PiPjRii\overline{Rjj}Rij\overline{Rji}$

(d) $PiPjRiiRjjRijRji$

(e) $\overline{Pi}\,\overline{Pj}RiiRjj\overline{Rij}\,\overline{Rji}$.

The two objects are indexically distinguishable in every universe, for j is identical to j but not to i. The situation with respect to the nonindexical properties P and R varies from universe to universe. The two objects differ both intrinsically and relationally in the actual universe, as presumably any

* *Philosophical Papers and Letters*, pp. 268 and 643, respectively; the italics are Leibniz's. See also pp. 303 and 505-6.

See further Leibniz, *New Essays Concerning Human Understanding*, pp. 9, 51-52, 238-39, and 331-32.

two ordinary objects do.* They might have differed only intrinsically, as in (b), or only relationally, as in (c). But they might have had the same properties, monadic and relational, as in the logically possible universes (d) and (e). This confirms that the identity of indiscernibles, when restricted to nonindexical predicates (as in [3]), is not logically true.

On the other hand, the weak version [4] of the identity of indiscernibles *is* logically true. Consider two objects in a space-time system that have the same properties, indexical as well as relational. Let "i" be an indexical symbol, i.e., individual constant or proper name, referring to one of these, and let "j" be an indexical symbol referring to the other. Whether the two objects i and j are distinct ($i \neq j$) or identical ($i = j$) is left open at the beginning of the argument. Let "A" be an indexical predicate and "x" an individual variable. The argument then proceeds as follows.

(a)	$Ax =_{\text{df}} (i = x)$	Definition of the indexical predicate "A"
(b)	$Ai \equiv (i = i)$	Universal instantiation of (a)
(c)	$i = i$	Law of identity
(d)	Ai	(b), (c), **TF**
(e)	Aj	From (d), since j has every property that i has
(f)	$Aj \equiv (i = j)$	Universal instantiation of (a)
(g)	$i = j$	(e), (f), **TF**.

This shows, by conditional proof, that form [4] of the identity of indiscernibles is a logical truth.

This proof can also be put in transpositional form. Suppose i and j are numerically different objects, that is, $i \neq j$. By the law of identity, $j = j$. Consider now the (monadic) property of being identical with j, which may be symbolized by "$x = j$," where "x" is an individual variable. Since $j = j$, j has this property; but since $i \neq j$, i does not have this property. Hence, j has one property that i does not have, and i and j do not have all their properties in common. This shows that when indexical properties are taken into account, two different objects are necessarily dissimilar, and two completely similar objects are necessarily identical.

Thus we conclude our explanation of the distinction between indexical and nonindexical symbols and of the correlated distinction between indexical and nonindexical properties.

* Probably any two ordinary-sized objects of our actual universe differ intrinsically in some respect, perhaps very minute. At an atomic or subatomic level there may well be two or more particles which do not differ intrinsically from each other. Even if there are such they would very probably differ relationally, as our mirror-image universe argument shows (p. 557).

9.2.3 *Cellular automata*

Cellular automata are formal, discrete space-time systems studied in automata theory.* We define two kinds of cellular automata, probabilistic and causal, and within the causal we distinguish two subkinds, deterministic and indeterministic. We shall find these various kinds useful in formulating the presuppositions of induction and in modeling deterministic and near-deterministic systems (secs. 9.3, 10.3).

A *cellular automaton* is a space-time system of the following sort. The spatial reference frame consists of Euclidean three-dimensional space, divided into equal cubical regions or *cells;* we also consider the degenerate two- and one-dimensional cases. Time is divided into discrete moments and can be either one-way infinite ($t = 0, 1, 2, 3, \ldots$) or two-way infinite ($t = \ldots, -2, -1, 0, 1, 2, \ldots$). Properties are exemplified in each cell at each moment, so that a "cell-moment" is a basic individual. There is a finite set of basic properties, which are monadic and nonindexical. A *cell state* (individual state) is described by a conjunction that tells, for each basic property, whether it is present or absent. A *temporal state* is an assignment of a cell state to every cell. A logically possible universe is a sequence of temporal states, one for each moment of time.

Cellular automata are governed by contiguous laws or "transition rules" based on a *neighborhood relation* that is uniform over the cellular space. The neighborhood $N(c)$ of a cell c consists *of itself* and every cell having a boundary in common with it. Figure 43 shows the neighborhood relation of a two-dimensional cellular space. A cell is included in its own neighborhood for brevity of expression. The state of a cell at time $t + 1$ depends only on the state of its neighbors at time t. This dependence limits the rate at which probabilistic or causal influences can propagate through a cellular space.

A *probabilistic cellular automaton* is governed by a "probabilistic transition rule." This rule gives, for each assignment of cell states to the neighborhood $N(c)$, a probability distribution over the possible next state of cell c. If its temporal dimension is one-way infinite ($t = 0, 1, 2, \ldots$), the automaton is also governed by a probabilistic initial state rule. This rule gives a probability distribution over the possible initial states of each cell. Such a probabilistic cellular automaton is a generalized Markov chain (pp. 125–26, 504–5).

Here is a simple example. Time is one-way infinite and space two-dimensional. There are two cell states, "blank" and "marked," to which the initial state rule assigns equal probabilities. The transition rule is: if m is the number of blank cells of $N(c)$ at time t, the probability of a blank in cell c

* See von Neumann's *Theory of Self-Reproducing Automata*, my "Cellular Automata and Natural Systems," and my *Essays on Cellular Automata*. On pp. 52-64 of the latter I discuss the heuristics of using cellular automata to find the laws governing a natural system.

at moment $t + 1$ is $m/5$. Using these rules, one can calculate a probability assignment to the possible histories of any finite area over any finite time span, starting from $t = 0$. Such a probability assignment is like the assignments to possible universes of Section 3.2 (Inductive Logics for Simple Models of Reality).

A *causal cellular automaton* is governed by a "causal transition rule." This rule gives, for each assignment of cell states to the neighborhood $N(c)$, a list of one or more next cell states for c. If its temporal dimension is one-way infinite, the automaton is also governed by an "initial state rule," which specifies a set of allowable (causally possible) initial temporal states. A causally possible universe is a history of temporal states that satisfies both the initial state rule (if there is one) and the transition rule. Note that both probabilistic and causal transition rules are uniform over space (the cells) and time (the moments).

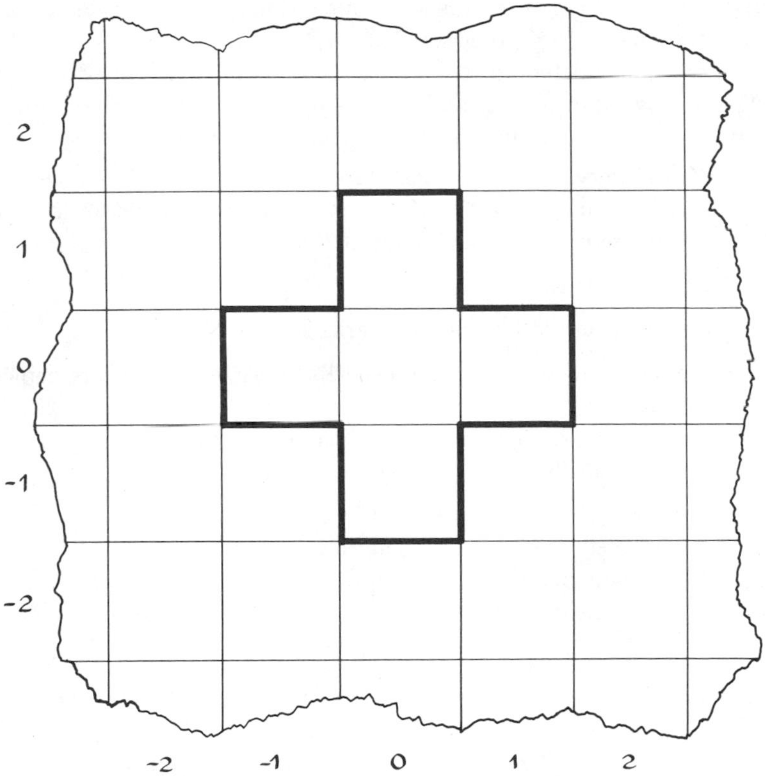

Fig. 43. Two-dimensional cellular space

The neighborhood $N(0, 0)$ of cell $(0, 0)$ is surrounded by a heavy line.

Causal cellular automata are divided into the deterministic and the indeterministic by the criterion: Is the successor of a temporal state always unique? The set of causally possible universes of a *deterministic cellular automaton* satisfies the condition: each temporal state has a unique successor. It follows that each causally possible initial temporal state determines a unique causally possible universe (history of temporal states). In contrast, the set of causally possible universes of an *indeterministic cellular automaton* contains at least one temporal state that has two or more successors.

This global difference between deterministic and indeterministic cellular automata is reflected in a difference between their transition rules. For the deterministic case, each causally possible assignment of states to the neighborhood $N(c)$ determines a unique next state for cell c. This is not so for the indeterministic case. There, at least one assignment of states to the neighborhood $N(c)$ is followed by one cell state for c in one causally possible universe and by a different cell state for c in another causally possible universe. This difference accords with our ordinary notion of determinism and indeterminism (see further sec. 9.3).

A very simple deterministic cellular automaton is illustrated in Figure 44. Space is two-dimensional and time is one-way infinite. There are two cell states, "blank" and "marked." The transition rule is

[5T] A marked cell never changes state
A cell is marked at $t + 1$ if and only if an odd number of its neighbors are in the marked state at t.

The initial state rule is

[5I] Every pattern of blanks and marks is an initial state.

The first seven temporal states of a causally possible universe are depicted in Figure 44.

We define next a simple two-dimensional indeterministic cellular automaton. Its transition rule is

[6T] A marked cell never changes
A blank cell is governed by the rule

Number of marked neighbors at t	State of cell at $t + 1$
0	Blank
1	Blank or marked
2	Marked
3	Marked
4	Blank

Its initial state rule is

[6I] Every pattern of blanks and marks is an initial state.

Different marks are used to indicate the generations.

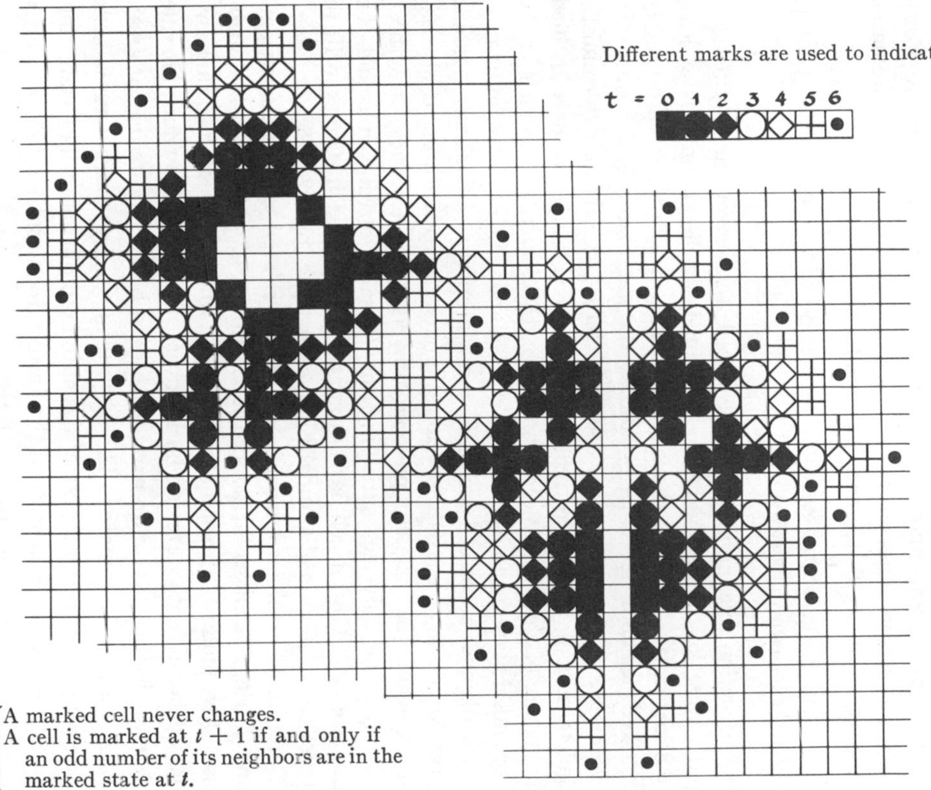

Transition rule [5T]
- A marked cell never changes.
- A cell is marked at $t + 1$ if and only if an odd number of its neighbors are in the marked state at t.

Fig. 44. Partial history of a deterministic cellular automaton

Consider an initial state in which just one cell is marked. By the transition rule, it may be followed by itself or by any state in which one or more of its four neighbors are also marked. Hence this automaton is indeterministic.

Though every indeterministic automaton has an indeterministic transition rule, the converse does not hold. This is demonstrated by the automaton based on transition rule [6T] and the initial state rule

[6I′] In an initial state, every neighborhood of the state must contain at least two marked cells.

By the transition rule, no mark is ever erased; thus every causally possible temporal state has the property that each neighborhood contains at least two marked cells. Therefore, the indeterministic case of a cell with exactly one marked neighbor never arises, and so the automaton is deterministic.

We pause to comment on our use of the term "causal" for deterministic and indeterministic cellular automata. It is a novel usage, but it is justified by the nature of these automata. In essence, they are modal models of the logic of causal statements (sec. 6.3). Each cell-moment is a basic individual and each disjunction of cell states is a cell property. A logically possible universe (or history) consists of an assignment of cell states to all cell-moments, while the causally possible universes (or histories) are those logically possible universes satisfying the causal transition rule and the initial state rule. Causal cellular automata will be used in Chapter 10 to construct causal models of standard inductive logic (pp. 624–25).

Deterministic cellular automata are closely related to the finite automata and Turing machines introduced in Section 6.4.3 (Machines and algorithms). If we modify the original concept of a finite automaton so that any internal (delay output) state can be an initial state, then the transition rule of a deterministic cellular automaton is realized by an infinite regular array of copies of a finite automaton. The outputs of the finite automata in cells $N(c)$ are connected to the inputs of the automaton in cell c. The transition rule gives the next internal state of the finite automaton as a function of its input state and its present internal state.

The relation of Turing machines to deterministic cellular automata is more important; it will be useful when we discuss the question: Can a random sequence occur in a deterministic system? (Sec. 9.4.3) Computationally, Turing machines are equivalent to a species of deterministic cellular automata, which we call "algorithmic cellular automata."

To show this we must make explicit the modal character of a Turing machine. Each machine consists of a finite automaton connected to various tape units, and these tapes may have different initial states or markings (p. 384). Each initial state determines a unique history of temporal states, that is, a causally possible universe. Thus a Turing machine defines a set of causally possible universes. Only finitely many nonblank symbols may be written on the tapes initially, so that the initial state and each subsequent temporal state may be described by a finite formula.

Consider now a deterministic cellular automaton. A subset σ of its cell states is "stable" if and only if the transition rule satisfies this condition: if each cell of $N(c)$ is in a state belonging to σ, then the state of c does not change. A cell state is stable if its unit set is stable. A particular stable cell state may be designated as the "blank state." An "algorithmic temporal state" is one in which only finitely many cells are in nonblank cell states. An *algorithmic cellular automaton* is a deterministic cellular automaton with a one-way infinite temporal dimension ($t = 0, 1, 2, \ldots$), with a blank state, and with all its initial temporal states algorithmic. Because of the local nature of a transition rule, every later temporal state will also be algorithmic.

The deterministic cellular automaton defined by transition rule [5T] (see fig. 44) and the initial state rule

[5I′] Every initial state is algorithmic

is an algorithmic cellular automaton. As in any two-dimensional algorithmic cellular automaton, each temporal state consists of a finite area of cells either blank or marked, surrounded by an infinite blank area. The latter area is like the empty space of traditional physics: nothing happens there until influence comes in from the outside. In Figure 44, the marked state propagates outward indefinitely, but it leaves behind both closed and open areas that are blank forever.

We next extend the notion of "computation" to algorithmic cellular automata. This notion was defined in terms of tapes (p. 384), and so it suffices to show how a tape can be represented in a cellular automaton. Suppose the tape alphabet consists of blank ("0") and one ("1"). Since these states are stable on the tape, we assume that the algorithmic cellular automaton has a pair of stable states ("0" and "1"). A tape is then represented as an infinite row of cells, of which a finite number are in state "one" and the rest are in the blank state.

An algorithmic temporal state can be represented by its multidimensional picture and hence can be described by a finite formula. The next temporal state can be computed from the present temporal state by the transition rule. Thus, for any algorithmic cellular automaton there is a Turing machine that can compute its history from a given initial temporal state. It follows that any computation performed by an algorithmic cellular automaton can also be performed by a Turing machine.

Von Neumann showed that the converse is also the case. He designed a particular algorithmic cellular automaton and showed that it could perform the computation of any Turing machine, and hence of any universal Turing machine. The cellular automaton $\mathcal{A}$ was two-dimensional and had twenty-nine states per cell. Any Turing machine $\mathfrak{M}$ can be embedded in $\mathfrak{A}$ by the following procedure.

Each tape is represented by a one-way infinite row of cells of $\mathfrak{A}$. Let $\mathfrak{I}$ be any initial state of these tapes in which only a finite number of the tape cells are in state one, the remainder being in the blank state. The logical design of the finite automaton part of machine $\mathfrak{M}$ is converted into a finite initial configuration $\mathfrak{F}$ connected to these embedded tapes. The initial states of $\mathfrak{A}$ are restricted to combinations of $\mathfrak{F}$ with some finite tape configuration $\mathfrak{I}$, all other cells of the cellular space being blank.

When cellular automaton $\mathfrak{A}$ is started in such an initial state, it produces the same output tape as machine $\mathfrak{M}$ does when it is started with its tapes in state $\mathfrak{I}$. That is, for each initial state of the Turing machine $\mathfrak{M}$, there is an initial state of the cellular automaton $\mathfrak{A}$ that produces the same output tape. In this manner, the cellular automaton $\mathfrak{A}$, with its initial states so restricted, produces the same computation as Turing machine $\mathfrak{M}$. Therefore, any computation performed by a Turing machine can be performed by an algorithmic cellular automaton.*

Combining this result with the preceding one, we conclude that any computation done by an algorithmic cellular automaton can also be done by a Turing machine, and vice-versa.

9.2.4 Local and global laws

We shall conclude this section by discussing the role of spatio-temporal contiguity in induction.

Hume held that temporal and spatial contiguity are essential to causation.

> . . . whatever objects are consider'd as causes or effects, are *contiguous;* . . . nothing can operate in a time or place which is ever so little remov'd from those of its existence. Tho' distant objects may sometimes seem productive of each other, they are commonly found upon examination to be link'd by a chain of causes, which are contiguous among themselves, and to the distant objects; and when in any particular instance we cannot discover this connexion, we still presume it to exist.†

On Hume's view, a cause may have a remote effect, but there is then an intervening causal chain in which each link consists of a cause producing a spatially contiguous and directly succeeding effect. This accords with common sense.

We call a law of nature or causal law that satisfies Hume's contiguity requirement a *contiguous causal law*. Examples are Maxwell's equations and

* Von Neumann also showed how to construct self-reproducing configurations in $\mathfrak{A}$. See the references given at the beginning of this subsection.

† *A Treatise of Human Nature*, p. 75.

[H] An electron moving in a vacuum perpendicular to a magnetic field (M) and subject to no other forces (N) is deflected (D).

We also count as a contiguous causal law any law that places causal constraints on the simultaneous occurrence of properties at a point.

Contiguous causal laws are modeled in deterministic and indeterministic cellular automata, for the transition rules of these automata are causal rules based on the neighborhood relation $N(c)$. To symbolize these rules in the logic of causal statements, let $\phi\{N(c), t\}$ be any consistent, nontautologous truth-function of atomic statements about the cells $N(c)$ at time t; $\phi\{N(c), t\}$ attributes property ϕ to region $N(c)$ at t. Similarly, $\psi\{c,t'\}$ attributes property ψ to cell c at time $t + 1$. Finally, let the quantifiers "(c)" and "(t)" mean "for any cell c" and "any moment t," respectively. Then the formula

[7] $(c)(t)[\phi\{N(c), t\}$ **npc** $\psi(c, t')]$

expresses a contiguous causal law, describing the passage of causal influence directly from a cell to its neighbors in one time step. The transition rule of a deterministic or indeterministic cellular automaton is equivalent to a consistent set of contiguous causal laws of form [7]. Note that these laws have the uniqueness, modal, and uniformity features characteristic of a law of nature (pp. 425–26).

One could define cellular automata whose transition rules violated spatial contiguity or temporal contiguity or both. The state of a cell at one moment could depend directly on the state of a non-neighboring cell at the previous moment. This is "action-at-a-distance," which violates contiguity in space. The state of a cell at one moment could depend directly on its own state several moments earlier. This is "action-over-a-time-interval," and it violates contiguity in time.

Though most of the laws of nature considered in science are contiguous laws, not all are. Newton's theory of gravity is a classical example of a law that is not. In this theory, the force of gravity acts at a distance directly and instantaneously, without intervening causes. If there is matter at one place, its gravitational field exists simultaneously at a remote place. Thus action-at-a-distance involves causal constraints on the simultaneous occurrence of properties at two distant points. This is a spatial generalization of a causal constraint on the simultaneous occurrence of properties at a single point.

Newton's theory of gravitation seems to refute Hume's claim that spatial contiguity is essential to causation. But one can hold that the law of gravity is an approximation to a more fundamental law that is spatially contiguous. Newton himself felt uncomfortable with action-at-a-distance, and he hypothesized a causal chain from the attracting body through the ether to the attracted body.*

Whether or not gravity acts at a distance without intervening causes is an empirical question, to be settled by physics, not by inductive logic. The same is true of action-over-a-time-interval. However, for reasons of simplicity we ignore the latter possibility and assume that the laws of nature are temporally contiguous. The concept of action-over-a-time-interval has played only a minor role in the history and philosophy of science, and the usual concept of determinism assumes temporal but not spatial contiguity (sec. 9.3.2). In any case, what we say about action-at-a-distance can be extended to action-over-a-time-interval with little modification.

There are other interesting spatial features of laws besides contiguity and noncontiguity. We call a law "local" when it covers a relatively small spatial span and "global" when it covers an infinite spatial span. Contiguous causal laws are local, as are laws allowing limited amounts of action-at-a-distance.

A local law that is uniform over space and time entails a global law. For example, the transition rule of a deterministic cellular automaton defines a global law that gives, for each temporal state, a unique next temporal state.

A global law that is not reducible to a local law is "irreducibly global." An example is

[8] If at time t there are infinitely many cells in state "one," the transition rule of Figure 44 applies; otherwise, no cell changes state.

There is no local law equivalent to [8], because the state of a cell at one moment depends on the state of infinitely many cells at the previous moment.

Newton's inverse square law of gravity is an irreducible global law, for there is no limit in principle to the distance over which gravity operates. Nevertheless, from the point of view of inductive logic and the logic of empirical inquiry, Newton's law has an important local characteristic. Since gravity falls off inversely with the square of the distance, remote objects interact less than nearby objects. Because of this, one can obtain the experimental isolation needed to discover and verify the law of gravity. In contrast, it is not possible to discover and verify empirically an irreducible global law like [8].

To name this feature, we say that Newton's law of gravity is *quasi-local*. Both contiguous and local causal laws are quasi-local. Since observation and experimentation are local activities, successful inquiry presupposes that the laws of nature be quasi-local. A uniformity postulate plays an essential role in inferences from local data to global conclusions. We shall discuss this

* *Mathematical Principles of Natural Philosophy*, pp. 636-37, 671-76.

postulate in a moment, after first stating another practical presupposition of empirical inquiry.

This presupposition concerns the simplicity of causal laws and is most easily explained by means of an automaton model. Suppose an investigator can observe and experiment with a deterministic cellular automaton having a very large number of cell states. The investigator does not know the transition rule of the automaton but is to infer it from his observed data.

Two cases are of interest. At one extreme, the transition rule of the automaton is composed of many contiguous causal laws, each of which is simple in the sense that it connects a quite general property of the neighborhood $N(c)$ to a general property of cell c. Consequently, the method of varying causally relevant qualities (p. 102) can be employed to ascertain the laws of the system. To put the point in different terms: the state of a neighborhood may be described by means of empirical variables that are, for the most part, causally independent of each other or loosely coupled. We say that causal laws of this sort are "inductively simple." In this case the transition rule is composed of many inductively simple contiguous causal laws, each of which can be discovered and verified in relative independence of the others.

At the opposite extreme, we can imagine a transition rule such that very slight differences in the properties of region $N(c)$ can cause large differences in the properties of cell c. The antecedents of the contiguous causal laws of the system refer to complete states of the neighborhood $N(c)$, and these laws cannot in general be reduced to simple laws. Consequently, to learn anything about the transition rule of the automaton, the investigator must observe the complete state of a neighborhood in full detail. If he cannot obtain that much information about the automaton at one time, he can never discover its laws.

The actual relation of the scientist to nature is much more like the first case than the second. A scientist discovers and confirms the laws of nature by making limited observations in a small space-time region. He proceeds by successive approximation, finding a rough law first and then refining it. The progression from Aristotle's qualitative law of falling bodies through Galileo's quantitative law to Newton's theory of gravity is a good example of this.

Thus successful inductive inquiry and verification presuppose that the laws of nature are quasi-local and inductively simple.

9.3 Causality in Nature

9.3.1 Uniformity of nature

According to the presupposition theory, inductive inference rests on three postulates (pp. 632–33). In the present section we shall formulate the first two, the causal uniformity and the causal existence principles, and relate them to the doctrines of determinism, near-determinism, and tychism.

Standard inductive logic contains rules for verifying laws of nature and causal laws. One of the most fundamental of these is the "causal uniformity rule."

[9] Given that a causal connection between nonindexical properties holds in some region of space-time, to conclude that it holds throughout space-time.

When one believes he has established a causal connection between nonindexical properties by certain experiments and observations, he unhesitatingly extrapolates this connection to all space-time. Thus experiments showing that gold dissolves in aqua regia establish that fact for all space-time. The sum total of experiments and observations on which we base our present scientific beliefs is finite, but we take these results to establish laws of nature and causal laws applying to infinitely many actual and possible cases.

The sense of causality involved in rule [9] is the causal necessity of the logic of causal statements, as concretely interpreted in Chapter 7 (The Logic of Causal Statements as a Model of Natural Language). The corresponding rule for a nonmodal language is, of course, invalid. For example, the argument "Someone is a philosopher, therefore everyone is a philosopher" is obviously invalid.

We noted earlier a parallelism between rules of inference and conditional statements. To each deductive argument there is a corresponding conditional that is logically true if and only if the argument is valid (p. 22). Similarly an atomic inductive probability statement corresponds to an inductive argument, the probability statement being true if and only if the argument is valid (p. 25). The same general kind of parallelism exists in the present case. Corresponding to the causal uniformity rule, there is a **causal uniformity principle.**

[9′] If a causal connection between nonindexical properties holds in one region of space-time, it holds throughout space-time.

Since a causal transition rule is invariant over all cells and all moments of a cellular automaton, this principle holds of all causal cellular automata, i.e., of both deterministic and indeterministic cellular automata.

To explain the causal uniformity principle further, we will discuss its relation to changing dispositions and to other kinds of uniformity.

Our analysis of causal dispositions showed that they involve causal laws (sec. 7.3.2). Consider the dispositional statement

[10] This material (m) would melt (M) if it were heated to 1,063° C (H),

which is explicated by

[10′] $(\exists X)[Xm(XmHm \textbf{ npc } Mm)]$.

There is explicit here some property (X) by virtue of which the material would melt if heated to 1,063° C; this property is called "the property underlying the disposition." There is also implicit here a causal law of the form

[11] $(z)(XzHz \textbf{ npc } Mz)$,

for the property (X) underlying the disposition is characterized by an instance ($XmHm$ **npc** Mm) of this law. We refer to [11] as the "causal law underlying the disposition." Suppose, for example, the material is gold. Then the property underlying the disposition is its being gold, and the causal law underlying the disposition is

[11′] $(z)(GzHz \textbf{ npc } Mz)$ [Gold melts at 1,063°].

Now a thing may change its dispositional properties (sec. 7.5.1). For example, gold may be transmuted into mercury, which has a melting point of −39° C. The question then arises: Is this change of disposition a change in the causal law underlying the disposition, and hence a violation of the uniformity of nature principle, or is it only a change in the property underlying the disposition? An examination of the situation shows that the latter is the case. When the given material is transmuted into mercury it loses one disposition and gains another. Underlying the original disposition were a property (being gold) and a law (gold melts at 1,063°). Underlying the new disposition are another property (being mercury) and a different law (mercury melts at −39°). The change of disposition is governed by a third law, the law stating the conditions under which gold is transmuted into mercury. The laws themselves do not change in this process of transmutation, though one law (gold melts at 1,063°) ceases to be applicable and another law (mercury melts at −39°) becomes applicable. What does change when the disposition changes is the property underlying the disposition. Consequently, a change in causal disposition does not violate the causal uniformity principle.

The causal uniformity principle is sometimes called the "principle of the uniformity of nature." This is not a suitable name, because there are other ways in which nature has been thought to be uniform. For example, standard inductive logic is uniform in the sense that it favors statistically uniform universes (pp. 116, 323). And it is uniform in still another sense of "uniform," that of exchangeability. An exchangeable probability assignment to a space-time system treats all space-time regions uniformly: the probability that a complex of properties will occur in a region is invariant from one region to another (p. 125). Finally, determinism is sometimes called a uniformity principle. However, the traditional doctrine of determinism is considerably stronger than our causal uniformity principle, as we shall now see.

9.3.2 Determinism

Though determinism is one of the most widely discussed doctrines of philosophy, we have no satisfactory analytic formulation of it. Actually there are many different kinds of determinism and hence different doctrines of that name. I shall not attempt a complete treatment but shall argue that our ordinary notion of determinism involves causal necessity and causal uniformity as well as uniqueness of succession. Compare our earlier definition of a law of nature (pp. 425–26).

Let us start, as Laplace did, with Newtonian mechanics. A complete temporal state of a mechanical system is given by a list of all the particles of matter together with the position, mass, and momentum of each particle at time t. With the assumption that no particle ever hits another, the system is completely governed by Newton's laws of gravitation together with his laws of motion. When these laws are applied to a temporal state of the system at time t_1 and any other time t_2 is specified, they yield a unique temporal state of the system at time t_2.

Laplace generalized Newton's theory to the doctrine that nature is completely governed by a single all-encompassing causal law.

> We ought then to regard the present state of the universe as the effect of its anterior state and as the cause of the one which is to follow. Given for one instant an intelligence which could comprehend all the forces by which nature is animated and the respective situation of the beings who compose it—an intelligence sufficiently vast to submit these data to analysis—it would embrace in the same formula the movements of the greatest bodies of the universe and those of the lightest atom; for it, nothing would be uncertain and the future, as the past, would be present to its eyes. The human mind offers, in the perfection which it has been able to give to astronomy, a feeble idea of this intelligence. Its discoveries in mechanics and geometry, added to that of universal gravity, have enabled it to comprehend in the same analytical expressions the past and future states of the system of the world. Applying the same method to some other objects of its knowledge, it has succeeded in referring to general laws observed phenomena and in foreseeing those which given circumstances ought to produce. All these efforts in the search for truth tend to lead it back continually to the vast intelligence which we have just mentioned, but from which it will always remain indefinitely removed.*

Note first that Newtonian mechanics and Laplacian determinism are bidirectional: they are both "forward-deterministic" (a present temporal state determines the future) and "backward-deterministic" (a present

* *A Philosophical Essay on Probabilities*, p. 4.

temporal state determines a unique past).* These two kinds of determinism are logically independent, and for most philosophical issues only the former is important. For this reason we limit "determinism" to forward-determinism. The deterministic cellular automaton defined by rules [5T] and [5I] above (p. 564) is not backward-deterministic; one can find two temporal states that are followed by the same next temporal state.

It is obvious that determinism requires uniqueness in the succession of complete states: each temporal state determines a unique future history of the system. Does this uniqueness requirement apply only to the actual universe or to all causally possible universes? I think the latter is the case, for the following reasons.

The traditional formulations of determinism refer to cause and effect or to laws of nature. This is true of Laplace's statement; it is also true of Kant's, "All alterations take place in conformity with the law of connection of cause and effect."† Determinism has often been related to free choice and responsibility, which presuppose the causal modalities (see the next subsection). Finally, the concept of determinism would be too weak if the uniqueness requirement were limited to the actual universe. For it is very likely that no two temporal states of the actual universe are completely identical with respect to their nonindexical properties. Since nonrepetitiveness implies uniqueness, this would suffice to show that nature is deterministic if the definition of determinism were limited to the actual universe. Clearly we mean more than that by "determinism."

Thus the uniqueness requirement of determinism applies to the whole set of causally possible universes, not just to the actual universe. We next define the term "deterministic system" to capture this much of the traditional doctrine of determinism. A *deterministic system* is a causally modal space-time system satisfying the uniqueness condition: If two causally possible universes have a temporal state in common, their subsequent histories are the same.

This definition is expressed in terms of the global law of the system, which treats each temporal state as an "undivided unit." I think the ordinary concept of determinism also includes the following condition on the reducibility of this global law.

* Indeed, most of the forward-deterministic systems studied in physical science are also backward-deterministic. In contrast, all the forward-deterministic cellular automata in which universal Turing machines and self-reproducing automata have been constructed are backward-*in*deterministic. This suggests the question: Can a universal Turing machine or a self-reproducing automaton be embedded in a backward-deterministic cellular automaton?

Recently my student, Tommaso Toffoli, answered this question affirmatively. He showed how to embed any given n-dimensional deterministic cellular automaton in a backwards-deterministic cellular automaton of $n + 1$ dimensions.

† *Critique of Pure Reason*, p. 218 (B232).

[12] The laws of nature are quasi-local and satisfy the causal uniformity principle.

Condition [12] is satisfied by Newtonian mechanics, which is often taken to be a paradigm of determinism. Also, one can be held responsible only for an act over which he has control, and that in turn requires that the laws involved in the act be local and causally uniform (cf. p. 579).

The inclusion of condition [12] in determinism may also be justified by means of an imaginary space-time system whose histories are constructed in a random manner. An infinite creator places infinitely many distinct temporal states in a grab bag and draws them at random, without replacement. He then arranges them into an infinite set of causally possible universes of a space-time system. Finally, he designates one of these universes to be the actual universe.

Since no temporal state occurs twice in the causally possible universes of this system, the uniqueness requirement definitive of a deterministic system is vacuously satisfied. But this imaginary space-time system is too probabilistic to fit under our intuitive notion of determinism, for the laws of the imaginary system are not quasi-local and hence cannot have repeated instances. Even if the real laws of nature were selected at random by a creator, each law has many instances, not necessarily in the actual universe but certainly in the set of causally possible universes. We conclude that determinism involves quasi-local, causally uniform laws.

To capture this aspect of determinism, we define a notion that is stronger than that of a deterministic system. A *tightly deterministic system* is one whose laws are quasi-local and satisfy the causal uniformity principle. Newtonian mechanics is tightly deterministic. And all deterministic cellular automata are tightly deterministic systems.

We can now define "determinism." *Determinism* is the doctrine that nature is a tightly deterministic system. That is, nature is a causally modal space-time system such that if two causally possible universes have a temporal state in common, their subsequent histories are the same. Moreover, the laws of nature are quasi-local and causally uniform.

Notice this is an ontological rather than epistemological concept of determinism. It does not require that there be a "deterministic theory" or progression of such theories adequate to nature. A fortiori, it does not require predictability or computability, even in principle.

Part of our interest in determinism lies in its relation to the causal uniformity principle. Determinism contains this principle but has other requirements as well. The causal uniformity principle is conditional, and it may be incompletely or even vacuously satisfied. For example, all indeterministic cellular automata satisfy it, including the extreme case in which the transition rule allows any cell state to follow any neighborhood state. In contrast, determinism holds that nature is governed by a complete set of quasi-local, causally uniform laws. We shall next discuss near-determinism, which weakens this completeness requirement slightly.

9.3.3 Near-determinism

There are two main alternatives to determinism: near-determinism and tychism. The near-determinist holds that determinism is almost but not completely true; that is, some events are not predetermined. The tychist holds that the basic laws of nature are probabilistic rather than causal. We shall examine these two views in turn.

An event is "not predetermined" or is "partially uncaused" if a prior state of the universe does not causally necessitate it. *Near-determinism* is the doctrine that, though nature is for the most part governed by causally uniform and quasi-local laws, some events are not predetermined. An indeterministic cellular automaton is a near-deterministic system when its transition rule satisfies this approximate condition: the rule gives a unique next state of a cell for "most" states of its neighbors.*

This doctrine is usually called "indeterminism," but I prefer "near-determinism" because it emphasizes the closeness of the doctrine to determinism. Also, "indeterminism" is most often used to name the special case of near-determinism in which the partially uncaused events include acts of free choice.

The near-determinist says very little about the nature of indeterministic phenomena. There are two fundamental ways of conceiving them, and one could hold that there are indeterministic phenomena of both kinds. Lucretius held that indeterministic events occur in a completely arbitrary manner, not being governed by laws of any kind (see the quotations on pp. 549, 578). But one could also hold that indeterministic events are governed by probabilistic rather than causal laws. On this form of near-determinism there are two kinds of basic laws, causal and probabilistic, most events being governed by the former but some events being governed by the latter. Compare Peirce's tychism, according to which *all* basic laws are probabilistic (p. 581).

Near-determinism is closely related to the second postulate of the presupposition theory of induction, so we will introduce this postulate now. The **causal existence principle** is: *Some space-time region is governed by quasi-local laws, at least for the most part.* The notion of "governed by" is modal, applying to what might have happened in the region as well as to what actually happened there.

Consider a specific space-time region $\mathcal{R}$ and laws of hypothetical form: if an antecedent-property occurs, then a consequent-property occurs. The

* More technically, one should consider only those neighborhood states occurring in causally possible universes.

causal existence principle states that the following holds for region $\mathcal{R}$: if the antecedent of a causal law *should* be satisfied, then the consequent of that law *would* also be satisfied. It is not required that the antecedent-property of each causal law be actually exemplified in $\mathcal{R}$, for a causal law may be satisfied vacuously in $\mathcal{R}$.* The space-time region that man occupies has actually displayed a sufficient variety of properties to make possible the knowledge of science we do have.

The causal existence principle requires that some region of space-time exemplify, in a modal sense, a high degree of lawfulness. The causal uniformity principle extends this degree of lawfulness to all space-time. Hence the causal existence and uniformity principles are conjointly equivalent to the disjunction of near-determinism and determinism. We do not take determinism as a presupposition, since it is a stronger principle than is needed for the foundations of induction.

The partially uncaused events that have interested most near-determinists are acts of free choice. Lucretius said:

Again, if all movement is always interconnected, the new arising from the old in a determinate order—if the atoms never swerve so as to originate some new movement that will snap the bonds of fate, the everlasting sequence of cause and effect—what is the source of the free will possessed by living things throughout the earth? What, I repeat, is the source of that willpower snatched from the fates, whereby we follow the path along which we are severally led by pleasure, swerving from our course at no set time or place but at the bidding of our own hearts? There is no doubt that on these occasions the will of the individual originates the movements that trickle through his limbs.†

While the ethical side of the free-will issue lies beyond the scope of this book, an analysis of the relevant causal relations will help to clarify near-determinism.

Our analysis is best carried out on a hypothetical example. Imagine that Maude must choose between firing a gun at someone (**F**) and dropping the gun (**D**), thereby leaving herself unprotected. We stipulate that Maude is normal, has adequate information about her situation, knows what she is doing, is not unduly excited, etc.—indeed, that all the usual practical and legal criteria for her act to be free are satisfied.

To get at the free-will issue one must distinguish the act of choosing

* However, if the causal uniformity principle also holds, every antecedent-property will occur in $\mathcal{R}$ in some causally possible universe. For each antecedent-property is exemplified sometime and somewhere in some causally possible universe. By the causal uniformity principle, there will be another causally possible universe in which this exemplification will occur in $\mathcal{R}$. See sec. 10.3.2 (Verification of causal laws), especially the shifting lemma (p. 629).

† *On the Nature of the Universe*, book 2, p. 67.

from the act chosen. The former will be symbolized with script, the latter with boldface. Let $\mathfrak{F}$ be the decision to fire the gun and $\mathfrak{D}$ the decision to drop it. Suppose that Maude decides to drop the gun ($\mathfrak{D}$) and as a consequence deliberately drops it a short time later (**D**), and that had she decided to fire the gun ($\mathfrak{F}$) she would have done so (**F**).

We have stipulated that, by normal standards, Maude's action was free, and hence she is responsible for the foreseeable consequences of her act.* Her being responsible depends on certain causal links. Those running from the act of choosing to the act chosen are

[13a] $(X\mathfrak{D})\&(X\mathfrak{D}\ \mathbf{npc}\ \mathbf{D})$

[13b] $(X\overline{\mathfrak{F}})\&(X\mathfrak{F}\ \mathbf{npc}\ \mathbf{F})$.

Here "*X*" symbolizes the normal background conditions under which Maude's choice of one act or the other leads to responsible action. For example, she would not be responsible for dropping the gun if she dropped it because she was shot; "*X*" excludes this possibility. The causal links of [13] and similar causal connections from the acts **F** and **D** to their consequences are necessary conditions for Maude's being responsible for her act.

The foregoing analysis shows that the existence of certain causal connections is essential to an act's being free. These connections must be uniform so that the subject can know them in advance, and they must be local so that he can control his actions and their consequences. Hence freedom and responsibility presuppose the existence of local and uniform causal laws.†

The existence of such laws is, of course, compatible with determinism. But many near-determinists hold a thesis about choice and responsibility that is incompatible with determinism. We will call this the "free-will thesis" and formulate it in our terms. Consider an act of choice that leads to a free act. The doctrine of determinism implies this act of choice is predetermined (causally necessitated) by a prior state of the universe. In contrast, the *free-will thesis* holds this act of choice is partially uncaused, and only because it is partially uncaused is one properly held responsible for the free act resulting from it.

The free-will thesis is important enough to warrant restatement and illustration. According to the free-willer, the fact that a person's act satisfies the usual practical and legal criteria for being free, i.e., is a "free act" in our sense, is not sufficient ground for that person's being responsible for his act. Rather, moral responsibility is justified only if the free act results from a partially uncaused act of choice.

* That is, Maude's act satisfies the criteria of responsibility normally applied by society. In a moment we will discuss a further question: If determinism is true, is it proper for society to hold Maude responsible for her free act?

† See my "Laws of Nature and the Reasonableness of Regret."

The notion of a partially uncaused act of choice may be illustrated with Maude's decision $\mathfrak{D}$ to drop the gun. The alternative act of choice was that of deciding to fire the gun ($\mathfrak{F}$). To say that Maude's choice was partially uncaused is to say that whether she would choose to drop the gun or fire it was not predetermined. This indeterministic requirement may be symbolized in the logic of causal statements as follows. Let S_1 be the actual state of nature at some moment slightly prior to the time at which Maude made her decision. The claim that Maude's act of choice was partially uncaused is symbolized

[14a] S_1 does not causally imply $\mathfrak{D}$; that is, $\Diamond^c (S_1 \overline{\mathfrak{D}})$

[14b] S_1 does not causally imply $\mathfrak{F}$; that is, $\Diamond^c (S_1 \overline{\mathfrak{F}})$.

Applied to this example, the free-will thesis is that Maude's act of dropping the gun is not really free unless condition [14] is satisfied and further that unless this condition is satisfied Maude should not be held responsible for her act. Condition [14] clearly violates determinism. Note that this condition involves the temporal antecedents of the act of choice, whereas the causal connections we found to be compatible with determinism all ran in the other direction: from the act of choice to the act chosen and thence to its consequences.

Advocates of the free-will thesis sometimes advance the following type of argument for their position and against determinism. Consider Maude's choice again and pick some moment prior to her birth. Let S_0 be the actual state of nature at that moment. If determinism is true, S_0 causally necessitated the background condition S_1, Maude's decision $\mathfrak{D}$, and hence her act **D**. Since Maude was not alive when S_0 occurred, she had no choice concerning it. Hence her act of choice $\mathfrak{D}$ was predetermined by forces beyond her control and she should not be held responsible for her action. More generally, if determinism is true and every act of choice is determined by a prior state of the universe, no person can properly be held responsible for his actions.

But this argument merely restates the issue of free-will and determinism; it does not contribute to its resolution. For the determinist grants that a person's choices are predetermined by forces beyond his control. He nevertheless holds that the usual practical and legal criteria for free, voluntary, responsible, and unconstrained choice are sufficient to justify the attribution of responsibility.

This concludes our positive presentation of determinism, near-determinism, the causal uniformity postulate, and the causal existence postulate. To explain those doctrines and postulates further, we shall discuss what they exclude. All of them make causal laws basic. We consider next a contrary view, that probabilistic laws are basic and causal laws derivative.

9.3.4 Tychism

Charles Peirce held that there is absolute chance in nature. He called this doctrine "tychism" after the Greek τυχη, meaning "chance."

The word "chance" has many senses. In one sense, the arbitrary events of near-determinism occur by chance (p. 577). Several meanings of "by chance" are applicable to nature even if determinism is true: "by accident," "with inductive probability (**P**)," "with empirical probability ($\mathbf{P}_e$)," "with relative frequency (σ_L and $\mathbf{P}_f$)," and "at random." But the absolute chance of tychism is incompatible with both near-determinism and determinism, for according to these doctrines the basic laws governing all or most phenomena are causal, whereas according to tychism all basic laws are probabilistic.

The probabilistic laws of tychism are the frequency probabilities or dispositional frequencies of Peirce's two theories of probability (secs. 3.4.2, 8.4.2). We found both theories to be inadequate. Indeed, we drew a stronger conclusion: Empirical and frequency probabilities are reducible to inductive probabilities but not vice-versa (see p. 517). On our view then, there is no concept of probabilistic law adequate for the metaphysics of tychism. However, this objection applies to any metaphysics that makes probabilistic laws basic, including a common interpretation of quantum mechanics (cf. pp. 589–91).

Peirce's writings on tychism are murky, fragmentary, undeveloped, and confused; still, one can find interesting issues in them. Also, the general view that chance is more basic than causality is a fundamental alternative to determinism and near-determinism. For these reasons Peirce's ideas on chance deserve discussion.

Tychism is the following doctrine: The basic laws of nature are probabilistic, inexact, and psychical. They are not temporally invariant, but they evolve through time in a way that is roughly analogous to the way natural species evolve. As they develop, these probabilistic laws become increasingly rigid and exact, and nature becomes increasingly regular (uniform). The probabilistic laws become more complex as well, and correspondingly the variety in nature increases. In the limit, a probabilistic law becomes totally rigid and exact; it is then a reversible (both backward- and forward-deterministic), absolute law of physics. Examples are Newtonian mechanics and the law of conservation of energy. This cosmological evolutionary process is governed by a general probabilistic law, the tendency of nature to form habits or generalize. Peirce referred to this variously as the "law of habit," the "law of synechism," and the "law of continuity." It is the most general psychical law and itself evolves.*

* Peirce restricted the word "tychism" to the chance aspect of his evolutionary cosmology and called the evolutionary aspect "synechism." We have adopted one name for the whole because the chance and evolutionary aspects are integrally related.

Peirce describes the difference between psychical probabilistic laws and reversible physical laws as follows.

> The law of habit exhibits a striking contrast to all physical laws in the character of its commands. A physical law is absolute. What it requires is an exact relation. Thus, a physical force introduces into a motion a component motion to be combined with the rest by the parallelogram of forces; but the component motion must actually take place exactly as required by the law of force. On the other hand, no exact conformity is required by the mental law. Nay, exact conformity would be in downright conflict with the law; since it would instantly crystallize thought and prevent all further formation of habit. The law of mind only makes a given feeling *more likely* to arise. It thus resembles the "non-conservative" forces of physics, such as viscosity and the like, which are due to statistical uniformities in the chance encounters of trillions of molecules. . . .
>
> The one intelligible theory of the universe is that of objective idealism, that matter is effete mind, inveterate habits becoming physical laws. [6.23–25]

> I believe the law of habit to be purely psychical. But then I suppose matter is merely mind deadened by the development of habit. While every physical process can be reversed without violation of the law of mechanics, the law of habit forbids such reversal. [8.318]*

Peirce's account of the evolution of physical laws from psychical laws is tantalizingly brief.

> . . . you must deduce the fundamental laws of the physical universe as necessary consequences of something. That is you must explain those laws altogether. . . . the laws of nature are results of an evolutionary process. . . . this evolutionary process [is] still in progress. . . . this evolution must proceed according to some principle; and this principle will itself be of the nature of a law. But it must be such a law that it can evolve or develope itself. . . . it must be a tendency toward generalization,—a generalizing tendency. But any fundamental universal tendency ought to manifest itself in nature. Where shall we look for it? We could not expect to find it in such phenomena as gravitation where the evolution has so nearly approached its ultimate limit, that nothing even simulating irregularity can be found in it. But we must search for this generalizing tendency rather in such departments of nature where we find plasticity and evolution still at work. The most plastic of all things is the human mind, and next after that comes the organic world, the world of protoplasm. Now the generalizing tendency is the great law of mind, the law of association, the law of habit taking. We also find in all active protoplasm a tendency to take habits. Hence . . . the laws of the universe have been formed under a universal tendency of all things toward generalization and habit-taking. [7.510–15]

* These and the following quotations in this subsection are from Peirce's *Collected Papers*, the volume and paragraph being given with each quotation. See also 1.400-416, 6.102-104, and the epigraph of this chapter. Tychism dates from the early 1890s.

His attempt to derive reversible physical laws from probabilistic psychical laws by an evolutionary limiting process is too sketchy and obscure to be satisfactory. But in making it Peirce faced a problem confronting any metaphysical cosmology that holds probabilistic laws basic: How are laws and dispositions involving causal necessity to be accounted for? Peirce's distinction between reversible physical laws and probabilistic psychical laws is a special case of the distinction between causal laws and dispositions, on the one hand, and probabilistic processes and dispositions, on the other (chaps. 7 and 8). While causal and probabilistic dispositions are similar in several respects, the concepts of causal necessity ($\Box^c$) and empirical probability ($\mathbf{P}_e$) are fundamentally different, each with its own complex logic. Whatever the formal similarities between causal necessity and a probability of unity, there is no reason to believe that causal laws have in fact evolved as limiting cases of probabilistic laws.

I find three main arguments for tychism in Peirce's writings, all of the form: tychism explains certain features and processes of nature that determinism cannot explain. These arguments overlook important alternatives to tychism and determinism: near-determinism, the dualistic position that both causal and probabilistic laws are basic, and the view that while the basic laws of nature are probabilistic, they are physical and exact rather than mental and inexact. Thus there is a large gap in Peirce's putative justification of tychism. But even apart from that, I think the determinist can rebut his criticisms.

The first argument is: observational measurements are approximate and contain errors, and these characteristics of observation are due, ultimately, to chance (*Collected Papers* 6.44–48). But the determinist can say that inexactitude and error reflect incomplete information about a deterministic system. See the next subsection (Embedded subsystems and probability).

Peirce's second argument is: tychism explains the statistical uniformities (regularities) of nature, while determinism cannot do so.

Uniformities are precisely the sort of facts that need to be accounted for. That a pitched coin should sometimes turn up heads and sometimes tails calls for no particular explanation; but if it shows heads every time, we wish to know how this result has been brought about. Law is *par excellence* the thing that wants a reason.

Now the only possible way of accounting for the laws of nature and for uniformity in general is to suppose them results of evolution. This supposes them not to be absolute, not to be obeyed precisely. It makes an element of indeterminacy, spontaneity, or absolute chance in nature. [6.12–13]

. . . in the beginning—infinitely remote—there was a chaos of unpersonalized feeling, . . . without connection or regularity . . . . This

> feeling, sporting here and there in pure arbitrariness, would have started the germ of a generalizing tendency. . . .
>
> Thus, the tendency to habit would be started; and from this, with the other principles of evolution, all the regularities of the universe would be evolved. At any time, however, an element of pure chance survives and will remain until the world becomes an absolutely perfect, rational, and symmetrical system, in which mind is at last crystallized in the infinitely distant future. [6.33]

This argument is a petitio principii, for it begs the question of whether the existence of statistical uniformities in nature needs to be explained. Peirce is demanding that causal laws be explained in terms of (reduced to) probabilistic laws. But his opponent, the determinist, thinks that the basic laws of nature are causal and that probabilistic laws should be reduced to them (see secs. 9.4.1, 11.3). A similar objection can be made by the determinist who adopts the presupposition theory of induction (sec. 10.4). The causal uniformity and causal existence postulates limit the statistical randomness of nature and hence entail that there be a certain minimum amount of statistical uniformity in nature (pp. 592–93). But since these postulates are presupposed by inductive inference, any attempt to explain this uniformity is circular.

Also, I do not think that Peirce's tychistic explanation of uniformity is fully successful. His law of habit is a metaphysical generalization of his self-corrective inductive method (p. 153). After analyzing that method, I argued that it requires stronger assumptions than Peirce thought (p. 160). Correspondingly, I think his law of habit must be strengthened before it can explain how regularities evolved from chaos.

Peirce's third main argument for tychism concerns growth, the evolution of natural species, other kinds of evolutionary processes, and the increased variety and complexity that result from evolution. Peirce argues, on the positive side, that tychism can explain these processes and phenomena, and on the negative side, that they are incompatible with determinism. His positive argument is:

> Very well, my obliging opponent, we have now reached an issue. You think all the arbitrary specifications of the universe were introduced in one dose, in the beginning, if there was a beginning, and that the variety and complication of nature has always been just as much as it is now. But I, for my part, think that the diversification, the specification, has been continually taking place. . . .
>
> Question any science which deals with the course of time. Consider the life of an individual animal or plant, or of a mind. Glance at the history of states, of institutions, of language, of ideas. Examine the successions of forms shown by paleontology, the history of the globe as set forth in geology, of what the astronomer is able to make out concerning the changes of stellar systems. Everywhere the main fact is growth and increasing complexity. . . . From these broad and ubiquitous

facts we may fairly infer, by the most unexceptionable logic, that there is probably in nature some agency by which the complexity and diversity of things can be increased; and that consequently the rule of mechanical necessity meets in some way with interference.

By thus admitting pure spontaneity of life as a character of the universe, acting always and everywhere though restrained within narrow bounds by law, producing infinitesimal departures from law continually, and great ones with infinite infrequency, I account for all the variety and diversity of the universe, in the only sense in which the really *sui generis* and new can be said to be accounted for. [6.57–59]

On the negative side, Peirce claims that growth, the evolution of natural species, other kinds of evolutionary processes, and the resultant increase in variety and complexity could not occur in nature if determinism were true. He argues that these phenomena and processes require "real" or "absolute" chance, while determinism only allows "simulated" or "quasi-" chance (*Collected Papers* 6.613). His argument is not carried out and his claim is not entirely clear, but it suggests an interesting issue. We will limit it to the evolution of natural species and express it in terms of our conception of determinism. So limited and explicated, "Peirce's claim" is: The evolution of natural species could not have taken place if nature were a tightly deterministic system. In other words, determinism cannot account for the evolution of natural species.

To evaluate Peirce's claim, we need first to consider the broader questions of whether probabilistic processes and random sequences can exist in a tightly deterministic system. We do this in the next section, returning to Peirce's claim at the end of it (pp. 600).

9.4 Determinism and Chance

9.4.1 Embedded subsystems and probability

We are thus led to consider these questions concerning the relation of causality to chance: How does the determinist account for probabilistic processes? What is randomness, and how is it related to determinism? These are fundamental questions, which should in any case be discussed in a broad study of causality and probability, such as the present book. On the other hand, since the presupposition theory of induction does not assume determinism, these questions are only peripheral to that theory. The reader interested primarily in it may go directly to the next chapter.

Despite their similarities, probabilistic processes and dispositions are fundamentally different from causal laws and dispositions (sec. 8.2.2). The tychist, taking the former to be basic, has the problem of accounting for the latter. Likewise, the determinist, holding that nature is completely governed by laws of nature, needs to explain how probabilistic processes and dispositions can occur within a tightly deterministic system. The near-determinist need not do this, for he can allow his uncaused events to be governed by probabilistic laws.

The traditional determinist thought that probability involved partial information about a deterministic system. Hume said:

> Though there be no such thing as *Chance* in the world; our ignorance of the real cause of any event has the same influence on the understanding, and begets a like species of belief or opinion.*

Laplace said:

> The curve described by a simple molecule of air or vapor is regulated in a manner just as certain as the planetary orbits; the only difference between them is that which comes from our ignorance.
>
> Probability is relative, in part to this ignorance, in part to our knowledge.

This is really only a suggestion, and no determinist has gone beyond such brief remarks in explaining the relation of a probabilistic process to a deterministic system.

We shall develop the determinist's suggestion by means of our dispositional theory of empirical probability and the notion of one system being an "embedded subsystem" of another. This notion will also be useful in discussing how determinism is related to randomness. To specify the meaning of "embedded subsystem," we first illustrate the term and then state its defining characteristics.

Consider a gas in a container at equilibrium conditions. The kinetic theory of gases treats this as two distinct systems, one an embedded subsystem of the other. See our earlier analysis of a gas in terms of microscopic and macroscopic states (pp. 114–16). The gas, as underlying system, is composed of a tremendously large number of rapidly moving, small, hard particles, which bounce elastically against each other and the walls of the container. A temporal state of this system is a microscopic state, which contains the coordinates, velocity, and acceleration of each particle. The underlying system is governed by the laws of moving bodies and of elastic collisions.

The embedded subsystem consists of the gas as defined by its macroscopic states, each with its pressure, volume, temperature, mass, energy, and entropy; and the subsystem is governed by the gas law: pressure times volume equals temperature times a constant. By the kinetic theory of gases the pressure of the subsystem is defined in terms of the forces exerted by the particles on the walls of the container, while the temperature of the gas is defined in terms of the average velocity of the particles. The kinetic theory of gases derives the gas law from the mechanical laws of the underlying

* *An Enquiry Concerning Human Understanding*, p. 56. The next quotation is from Laplace's *A Philosophical Essay on Probabilities*, p. 6.

system and the assumption that the initial states of the particles are randomly distributed.

Consider next a physical system consisting of one or more objects of various sizes, shapes, weights, colors, etc., moving in the earth's gravitational field through a fluid or gas. Galileo's law of falling bodies describes the behavior of a simple system embedded in this more general system. The Galilean system results from the general system through allowing only those initial states in which the buoyancy and friction of the fluid or gas have a negligible effect and through ignoring differences in the size, shape, color, etc., of objects with the same mass. Galileo's law of falling bodies follows from Newton's law of mechanics under these special conditions.

We may now give some finite automata examples of embedded subsystems. Let $\mathcal{A}$ be a finite automaton consisting of three delay elements whose outputs are connected to their inputs via a switch that realizes the transition rule:

Present temporal state	0	1	2	3	4	5	6	7
Next temporal state	1	1	3	3	5	6	7	5

.

We modify our original concept of a finite automaton (p. 380) slightly so that any one of these eight states can be an initial or starting state. A finite automaton is then a modal system, with many possible histories. There are eight causally possible histories of automaton $\mathcal{A}$.

System $\mathcal{A}'$ is derived from $\mathcal{A}$ by identifying states 0 and 2. This can be achieved physically by attaching to $\mathcal{A}$ an output switch that maps states 0 and 2 into the same state and preserves the remaining states. The resultant transition rule of $\mathcal{A}'$ is:

Present state	s	1	3	4	5	6	7
Next state	1,3	1	3	5	6	7	5

,

where $s = \{0,2\}$. System $\mathcal{A}'$ is an embedded subsystem of $\mathcal{A}$. Since state s can be followed by either state 1 or state 3, $\mathcal{A}'$ is indeterministic. But $\mathcal{A}$ is deterministic.

Thus an indeterministic system may be embedded in a deterministic system. The reverse can occur, in either of two ways. First, the states of the system can be grouped together to eliminate the indeterminism. For example, let subsystem $\mathcal{A}''$ result from system $\mathcal{A}'$ by grouping states 1 and 3 in the set s'. The transition rule of $\mathcal{A}''$ is deterministic:

Present state	s	s'	4	5	6	7
Next state	s'	s'	5	6	7	5

.

Second, the states of the system that lead to indeterminism might not occur in the embedded subsystem. For example, let subsystem $\mathcal{A}'''$ consist of those histories of $\mathcal{A}'$ starting with states 4, 5, 6, or 7. The transition rule of $\mathcal{A}'''$ is deterministic:

Present state	4	5	6	7
Next state	5	6	7	5

Thus $\mathcal{A}''$ and $\mathcal{A}'''$ are both deterministic subsystems of the deterministic system $\mathcal{A}$.

Our last example of embedding involves the universal Turing machine $\mathcal{U}$ (p. 388). Suppose that $\mathcal{U}$ is given a description $\mathcal{P}(\mathcal{M})$ of machine $\mathcal{M}$ and a description of the initial state of $\mathcal{M}$. Machine $\mathcal{U}$ simulates $\mathcal{M}$ by calculating its states for $t = 1, 2, 3, \ldots$. Viewed over all time, $\mathcal{U}$ contains the complete history of $\mathcal{M}$ that results from the given initial state. Moreover, $\mathcal{U}$ can calculate the history of $\mathcal{M}$ for any possible initial state of $\mathcal{M}$. Hence $\mathcal{M}$ is an embedded subsystem of $\mathcal{U}$.

In our earlier examples of embedding, a state of the embedded subsystem is a set of states of the underlying system, but in this last example it is more complicated. Machine $\mathcal{U}$ uses several time-steps to simulate one time-step of $\mathcal{M}$, so that finite sequences of states of $\mathcal{U}$ represent single states of $\mathcal{M}$. Thus when the universal machine $\mathcal{U}$ simulates another machine $\mathcal{M}$, a state of the embedded subsystem $\mathcal{M}$ is a set of sequences of states of the underlying system $\mathcal{U}$.

The preceding examples illustrate the essential aspects of embedding, which we now abstract.* The histories or possible universes of an *embedded subsystem* are derived from those of the system in which it is embedded by applying either or both of the following operations. First, a proper subset of the initial states of the system is designated as the set of initial states of the subsystem. Second, sets of system states or sets of sequences of system states are designated as the states of the subsystem. Under these two operations, the law or rule of the system yields a derived law or rule for the subsystem. The derived law may differ from the original law in important respects.

We chose the term "embedded subsystem" for the following reason. A complete description of the system contains a complete description of the subsystem, but not conversely, so that the word "subsystem" is appropriate. The word "embedded" is used to indicate that the subsystem need not be a separable physical part of the system but may be distributed through it in a complicated way. A separable physical part, e.g., the carburetor of an automobile, is an embedded subsystem in our sense of the term, but it is a very special case.

We now use the concept of an embedded subsystem to show in a general way how probabilistic processes and dispositions can occur in a tightly deterministic system. Consider as an example the fair-coin hypothesis

* See also my "Models of Deterministic Systems."

[15] The coin-tossing process Tx_1, Tx_2, Tx_3, . . . is an independent process of probability one-half [$\mathbf{P}_e(T) = .5$].

This is a statement about a probabilistic disposition, asserting that the system underlying the disposition is such that each possible observed outcome has a certain inductive probability (degree of prediction). Let $\mathcal{S}$ be the system underlying the disposition and let $H_{.5}$ be a complete description of $\mathcal{S}$. The core of the dispositional model of [15] consists of inductive probability statements that give, conditional on $H_{.5}$ the degrees of prediction of all possible results of tossing the coin (pp. 480–97, 518–19).

If determinism is true, system $\mathcal{S}$ must be an embedded subsystem of some tightly deterministic system. Call this encompassing system $\mathcal{S}_d$. For purposes of argument, assume there is a statement $\mathfrak{D}$ that gives complete information about the initial state and laws of $\mathcal{S}_d$. Since $\mathcal{S}_d$ is deterministic, $\mathfrak{D}$ deductively implies exactly how the coin will fall (cf. pp. 492–94). In contrast, while $H_{.5}$ gives complete information about system $\mathcal{S}$, it gives only partial information about the encompassing system $\mathcal{S}_d$ and hence only probabilistic information about how the coin will fall. Because the dispositional theory reduces empirical probability to inductive probability, only the latter kind of probability is needed in this analysis.

To summarize: the events of the probabilistic process are deterministic with respect to the full system, but they are probabilistic with respect to the system underlying the disposition, which is an embedded subsystem of the full system. The fundamental kind of probability involved here is inductive probability. This shows in a general way how probabilistic processes and dispositions can occur in a tightly deterministic system.

However, it may not be possible to reconcile quantum mechanics and determinism in this way; the issue is still highly controversial. Because the technical details are beyond the scope of this book, we must confine ourselves to a brief discussion of the problem.

In its fullest formulation, quantum theory describes a probabilistic system. On the basis of a foundational analysis of quantum mechanics, John von Neumann argued that quantum mechanical systems are inherently probabilistic and cannot be embedded in deterministic systems. As he expressed it, there are no "hidden parameters" in quantum mechanics.* If this view is correct, quantum theory is incompatible with determinism. Note that in any case, quantum theory is compatible with near-determinism and hence with our presuppositions of induction.

The proof that there are no hidden parameters in quantum mechanics constitutes the strongest argument there is against determinism, but it is

* *Mathematical Foundations of Quantum Mechanics*, pp. 209-11 and 323-28. Kochen and Specker, "The Problem of Hidden Variables in Quantum Mechanics," prove von Neumann's theorem for a wider and better definition of "hidden variable."

still inconclusive. The determinist can point out that the interpretation of quantum mechanics is incomplete and unsatisfactory. He can also argue that the concept of a basic probabilistic law is itself problematic (see pp. 581, 657).

Albert Einstein held to determinism even in the face of quantum mechanics. With Podolsky and Rosen, he found a paradox in quantum theory. As he interpreted it, the theory has this consequence: If a measurement is made in one part of a quantum system, the probabilities of a remote part of the system are changed from what they would have been if the measurement had not been made. In our terminology, there is action-at-a-distance between the empirical probabilities of one part of the system and those of a remote part of the system (cf. pp. 568–70). Einstein found this result paradoxical, and because of it he concluded that quantum theory does not give a complete description of reality.*

Einstein believed that when a complete theory of quantum phenomena is developed, it will be deterministic. He said:

> I am, in fact, firmly convinced that the essential statistical character of contemporary quantum theory is solely to be ascribed to the fact that this [theory] operates with an incomplete description of physical systems.

He expressed his position picturesquely in a letter to Max Born:

> In our scientific expectations we have grown antipodes. You believe in God playing dice and I in perfect laws in the world of things existing as real objects, which I try to grasp in a wildly speculative way.

Born commented as follows:

> What he is aiming at is a general field-theory which preserves the rigid causality of classical physics and restricts probability to masking our ignorance of the initial conditions or, if you prefer, of the pre-history, of all details of the system considered.†

Einstein's views on quantum mechanics are not widely accepted. Instead, the "Copenhagen interpretation" of quantum mechanics, devised by Niels Bohr, is accepted by most physicists. But though they have used this interpretation for several decades, its foundations are unclear, and it is increasingly under attack. It is open to many objections besides the Einstein-Rosen-Podolsky paradox.‡

* Einstein, Podolsky, and Rosen, "Can Quantum-Mechanical Description of Physical Reality be Considered Complete?"

† The first quotation is from Einstein, "Remarks Concerning the Essays Brought Together in this Cooperative Volume," p. 666.

The last two quotations are from Born, "Einstein's Statistical Theories," p. 176. Born says he received Einstein's letter on November 7, 1944.

‡ Bohr thought he resolved the paradox soon after it was posed; see Bohm, *Quantum Theory*, p. 611. Einstein never accepted Bohr's putative resolution; see pp. 681-82 of his

Actually, David Bohm has suggested a deterministic interpretation of quantum mechanics.* This interpretation is not fully worked out, is itself controversial, and has features such as action-at-a-distance (cf. p. 590) that many physicists would find unacceptable. Thus whether or not the probabilistic system described by quantum theory can be embedded in a deterministic system depends on the kind of deterministic system one is willing to consider. Part of the dispute in the foundations of quantum mechanics is over the nature of an acceptable deterministic system.

It should be emphasized that the difficulties of quantum theory concern its interpretation and not its mathematics, its working principles, or its applications. As a physical theory quantum mechanics is highly successful. But as long as its interpretation is unsatisfactory, the question as to whether a quantum mechanical system can be embedded in a deterministic system will remain unsettled. We therefore conclude that while the nondeterministic character of current quantum theory is a strong argument against determinism, it is not at present decisive.

We mention finally a different embedding relation of quantum mechanics. Neils Bohr's correspondence principle relates this subject to classical mechanics. His principle is: In the limit, where large numbers of quanta are involved, quantum laws lead to classical laws as statistical averages.† The correspondence principle makes the deterministic system of classical mechanics the limit of a sequence of subsystems embedded in the probabilistic system of quantum mechanics. When this view is combined with the view that quantum mechanics can be embedded in a deterministic system, a three-layered system of mechanics results. The deterministic system of classical mechanics is embedded in the probabilistic system of quantum mechanics, which is embedded in the deterministic system described by a complete quantum mechanics!

We have now finished our discussion of the question: How does the

---

"Remarks Concerning the Essays Brought Together in this Cooperative Volume."

For further criticisms of the Copenhagen interpretation, see Feyerabend's "Problems of Microphysics."

The foundations of quantum field theory are also unsatisfactory. See Segal, *Mathematical Problems of Relativistic Physics*, p. 97.

* See his *Causality and Chance in Modern Physics* and the two articles by him listed in the bibliography. Bohm and Bub have given another deterministic interpretation of quantum mechanics. For references and a discussion of some of the issues, see Bub's "What is a Hidden Variable Theory of Quantum Phenomena?"

These deterministic interpretations of quantum mechanics are usually called "hidden variable" theories of quantum mechanics. This terminology is very misleading, for they are not hidden variable theories in the sense of Kochen and Specker and are not excluded by their proof that quantum mechanics cannot be embedded in a deterministic system. See the note on p. 589.

† Bohm, *Quantum Theory*, p. 30.

determinist account for probabilistic processes? We turn next to the question: What is randomness, and how is it related to determinism?

9.4.2 *Entropy and randomness*

Some concepts of probability and chance apply to *single* universes and some involve numerical assignments to *sets* of universes. The notions of relative frequency (σ_L), frequency probability ($\mathbf{P}_f$), entropy, and statistical uniformity are of the first kind, while the concepts of inductive probability ($\mathbf{P}$), random inductive logic, exchangeability, and empirical probability ($\mathbf{P}_e$) are of the second kind.

Randomness concepts are of both kinds. "Entropy" is of the first kind, whereas "independent process" and "random inductive logic" are of the second kind. Randomness that applies to a single sequence or universe is appropriately called *sequence randomness*. In the remainder of this section, we shall study entropy and several related kinds or measures of randomness and examine how they are related to determinism.

Any sequence drawn from a finite alphabet can be coded as a binary sequence or number. Hence, from a foundational point of view, the essential features of sequence randomness are displayed in the binary case, and we will generally work with it. Binary sequences represent the simplest kinds of universes, those with only one monadic property. For example, "10101" represents "$Pa\overline{Pb}Pc\overline{Pd}Pe$" and "11111" represents "$PaPbPcPdPe$."

Consider again the concept of entropy, which is the inverse of statistical uniformity (p. 116). Within a finite model, the entropy $\mathbf{E}(u)$ of a universe u is $c_3 \log \mathbf{I}(u) + c_4$, where $\mathbf{I}(u)$ is the number of universes of the model which are isomorphic to u. For example, among the binary sequences of length twenty, 11111111111111111111 and 00000000000000000000 have minimum entropy, while 00011001001110101011 and 10101010101010101010 have maximum entropy.

There is a connection between tight determinism and entropy that is most easily seen in deterministic cellular automata. Focus on a large cubical region of a three-dimensional cellular automaton and choose a temporal span that has few time-steps compared to the number of cells along the edge of the cube. Since causal influence can travel only one cell per time-step, each causally possible history of this finite space-time system is determined by its initial temporal state, except near the edge of the cube. Consequently, each history has low entropy. The maximum entropy or randomness of each of these histories is limited by the contiguous and deterministic character of the transition rule of the system. This rule limits the extent to which the properties of a cell can change from one moment to the next. Compare a completely indeterministic cellular automaton, which allows every possible transition. Since every logically possible history is also causally possible, there is no restriction on the maximum entropy of a history of this automaton.

Because this comparative result holds for each finite space-time region, it holds on the average for the whole system. Hence, the causally possible universes of a deterministic cellular automaton are limited in average maximum entropy, in contrast to the causally possible universes of a completely indeterministic cellular automaton. Similar but slightly weaker conclusions hold for tightly deterministic systems in general. Hence determinism limits entropy.

These conclusions concern the average randomness or entropy of a tightly deterministic system. It is also of interest to know what types of random sequences can occur as embedded subsystems of tightly deterministic systems. We shall discuss this question in the next subsection, after first generalizing the concept of entropy to obtain other notions of sequence randomness.

Though entropy measures one feature or kind of randomness, it is a very limited measure. This is evident from the following sequences.

[a] 10101010101010101010101010101010101010101010101010

[b] 00011001001110101011111010001101101001010001000111 .

These two sequences have the same entropy, yet the first is clearly more regular and less random than the second. For given length, the entropy of a binary sequence depends only on the relative frequencies of 0's and 1's in it, while the randomness depends on the arrangement of the 0's and 1's as well.

The arrangement of 0's and 1's in a sequence involves the relative frequencies of various possible subsequences: pairs (00, 01, 10, 11), triples (000, 001, . . .), quadruples, etc. To have a way of symbolizing these frequencies, we need to generalize our earlier concepts of the number of successes $S_L(\phi)$, relative frequency $\sigma_L(\phi)$, and frequency probability $\mathbf{P}_f(\phi)$. These concepts were defined for a monadic property (ϕ) applicable to a single event or individual, that is, for a simple statement of the form ϕx_l (pp. 59, 144). We now extend the concepts S_L, σ_L, and $\mathbf{P}_f$ to cover arbitrary truth-functions of finite sequences of such statements.

Consider a finite or infinite binary sequence of the form ϕx_1, ϕx_2, ϕx_3, . . . , ϕx_l, ... Let Φ_l be any truth-function of the statements ϕx_l, ϕx_{l+1}, . . . , ϕx_{l+m-1}, where $l = 1, 2, 3, \ldots$ and m is a fixed positive integer. Each such truth-function produces a derived sequence Φ_1, Φ_2, Φ_3, . . . , Φ_l, ... For example, the truth-function $\phi x_l \& \overline{\phi x}_{l+1}$ produces the sequence $\phi x_1 \& \overline{\phi x}_2$, $\phi x_2 \& \overline{\phi x}_3$, $\phi x_3 \& \overline{\phi x}_4$, . . . , and the truth-function $\phi x_l \equiv \phi x_{l+10}$ gives the sequence $\phi x_1 \equiv \phi x_{11}$, $\phi x_2 \equiv \phi x_{12}$, $\phi x_3 \equiv \phi x_{13}$, ...

The notions of "number of successes," "relative frequency," and "frequency probability" are defined for a truth-function Φ_l in the same way they were defined for a monadic predicate ϕ. The number of successes

$S_L(\Phi_l)$ of Φ_l in L trials is the number of true statements in the sequence $\Phi_1, \Phi_2, \ldots, \Phi_l, \ldots, \Phi_L$. The relative frequency of success $\sigma_L(\Phi_l)$ is $S_L(\Phi_l)/L$. And the frequency probability of Φ_l is defined

$$\mathbf{P}_f(\Phi_l) =_{\text{dt}} \underset{L\to\infty}{\text{Limit}}\ \sigma_L(\Phi_l) \quad .$$

Note that the frequency of any truth-function Φ_l is determined by the frequencies of the basic conjunctions of $\phi x_l, \phi x_{l+1}, \ldots, \phi x_{l+m-1}$, since all other truth-functions of these terms can be expressed as disjunctions of these basic conjunctions (p. 50).

One kind of sequence randomness can now be defined as a natural extension of the concept of frequency probability. Let Φ_l be a basic conjunction of the statements $\phi x_l, \phi x_{l+1}, \ldots, \phi x_{l+m-1}$ in which s statements are true and f are false, so that $s + f = m$. An infinite binary sequence $\phi x_1, \phi x_2, \phi x_3, \ldots$ is *admissible** with associated probability α if and only if $\mathbf{P}_f(\Phi_l) = \alpha^s(1 - \alpha)^f$ for each basic conjunction Φ_l.

In an admissible sequence with associated probability 1/2, every binary sequence of length m has a frequency probability of 2^{-m}. That is,

$$\mathbf{P}_f(0) = \mathbf{P}_f(1) = 1/2$$
$$\mathbf{P}_f(00) = \mathbf{P}_f(01) = \mathbf{P}_f(10) = \mathbf{P}_f(11) = 1/4$$
$$\mathbf{P}_f(000) = \mathbf{P}_f(001) = \mathbf{P}_f(010) = \ldots = 1/8$$
etc.

The sequence defined by the following simple rule is known to be admissible, with associated probability 1/2.

[16] Concatenate the positive integers in natural order, expressed in binary form.†

The positive integers 1, 2, 3, 4, 5, 6, 7, 8, and 9, expressed in binary form, are 1, 10, 11, 100, 101, 110, 111, 1000, and 1001 respectively, so that the sequence begins

[16′] 11011100101110111100010011010101111001101111011111000. . . .

Any printed work, and hence the present work, can be coded in binary form by assigning binary sequences to letters, spaces, circles, lines, etc. Hence *Chance, Cause, Reason* appears in sequence [16′] infinitely often and with the appropriate frequency probability!

The concept of admissibility is a generalization of the concept of

* This is essentially equivalent to Copeland's concept of an "admissible number." See his papers in the bibliography.

An admissible number that has associated probability one-half is the same as a number "normal to the base two." See Borel, "Les Probabilités Dénombrables et Leurs Applications Arithmétiques" and Niven, *Irrational Numbers*, chap. 8.

† Champernowne, "The Construction of Decimals Normal in the Scale of Ten." Champernowne's proof is for the decimal sequence 123456789101112 . . . , but it applies to any digital base.

frequency probability, as is readily seen when the definitions are expressed in terms of the relative frequencies of various finite sequences in an infinite sequence. The condition for admissibility is

[17] Every finite sequence with s 1's and f 0's has a limiting relative frequency of $\alpha^s(1 - \alpha)^f$.

For the sequences of unit length (0,1) this reduces to

[17′] The limiting relative frequency of 1's is α.

But this is just the condition for a binary sequence having a frequency probability of α.

The concept of "admissible sequence" was defined for infinite sequences only, but it can be applied to finite sequences in an approximate manner by requiring that the relative frequencies be nearly correct for sequences that are short compared to the given sequence. We will do this for the case of associated probability 1/2. Let $\mathcal{S}$ be a given finite binary sequence of length L: $\phi x_1, \phi x_2, \phi x_3, \ldots, \phi x_L$. Let s be an arbitrary finite binary sequence of length m, e.g., $\phi x_l, \phi x_{l+1}, \ldots, \phi x_{l+m-1}$, where m is much smaller than L. A finite binary sequence $\mathcal{S}$ is *pseudorandom* if and only if each sequence s that is "short" compared to $\mathcal{S}$ has a relative frequency in $\mathcal{S}$ of "approximately" 2^{-m}. The name "pseudorandom" comes from computer science, where such sequences are used for probabilistic computations (see p. 598). The notion of pseudorandomness is, of course, an approximate one. We could easily convert it into a statistical measure but need not do so for our purpose.

The difference between pseudorandomness and entropy is illustrated by our earlier examples:

[a] 10101010101010101010101010101010101010101010101010

[b] 00011001001110101011111010001101101001010001000111 .

Pseudorandomness depends on the relative frequencies of all subsequences that are short compared to the given sequence. The sequences [a] and [b] are of length 50, and we consider subsequences of length 1, 2, 3, or 4 to be "short" compared to them. Now [a] and [b] differ markedly in the distribution of relative frequencies of subsequences of length 2, 3, and 4. Thus [a] contains only two different pairs, two different triples, and two different quadruples, each occurring with a relative frequency of close to 1/2. In contrast, pairs are roughly equidistributed in [b]: $\sigma_{49}(00) \doteq .225$, $\sigma_{49}(01) \doteq .285$, $\sigma_{49}(10) \doteq .265$, and $\sigma_{49}(11) \doteq .225$. The eight triples occur with relative frequencies ranging from .08 to .16. Fifteen of the sixteen quadruples occur (0000 is absent), and their relative frequencies range from .02 to .11. Hence sequence [a] is not pseudorandom, but sequence [b] is.

Thus the pseudorandomness of a sequence depends on the relative frequencies of all subsequences that are short compared to the sequence, while the entropy of a sequence depends only on the relative frequencies $\sigma(0)$ and $\sigma(1)$ of the unit subsequences 0 and 1. In a sequence of length 50, entropy is maximized when $\sigma_{50}(0) = \sigma_{50}(1) = .5$, so that both [a] and [b] have maximum entropy. This shows that entropy measures only the lowest level of pseudorandomness.

It is of interest to compare the two randomness concepts "admissible sequence" and "independent process." The two concepts differ in level: admissibility is a kind of sequence randomness, whereas independence characterizes inductive probability assignments to sets of sequences. But the frequency probabilities of an admissible sequence are strictly parallel to the inductive probabilities of an independent process. To see this, consider the relative frequencies to be expected in an independent process of probability 1/2 (sec. 2.4). There are 2^m basic conjunctions Φ_l of the m terms $\phi x_l, \phi x_{l+1}, \ldots, \phi x_{l+m-1}$. These all have equal inductive probabilities, so that $\mathbf{P}(\Phi_l) = 2^{-m}$. But in an admissible sequence of probability 1/2, the frequency probability $\mathbf{P}_f(\Phi_l)$ also equals 2^{-m}.

Hence, the concept of an admissible sequence can be derived from the concept of an independent process by simply substituting the frequency probability term "$\mathbf{P}_f(\Phi_l)$" for the inductive probability term "$\mathbf{P}(\Phi_l)$." An admissible sequence of probability α thus typifies an independent process of probability α in that, for each truth-function Φ_l, the frequency probability of Φ_l in the sequence equals the inductive probability of Φ_l in the process. An infinite sequence may be viewed intuitively as a totality composed of subsequences or overlapping parts that are arranged in a certain order. An admissible sequence of probability α typifies an independent process of probability α in that each kind of part has a limiting relative frequency equal to its inductive probability.

We defined the notion of an admissible sequence by requiring the frequency probabilities of the sequence to be equal to the inductive probabilities of an independent process. We can apply this procedure to a wider class of complete probability assignments (p. 119) to obtain a more general kind of sequence randomness. As before, let Φ_l be a basic conjunction of the terms $\phi x_l, \phi x_{l+1}, \ldots, \phi x_{l+m-1}$, where $l = 1, 2, 3, \ldots$ and m is a fixed positive integer. An infinite binary sequence $\phi x_1, \phi x_2, \phi x_3 \ldots, \phi x_l, \ldots$ is *truth-functionally random* if and only if there is a complete probability assignment $\mathbf{P}'$ to the infinite process $\phi x_1, \phi x_2, \phi x_3, \ldots, \phi x_l, \ldots$ such that for every basic conjunction Φ_l, $\mathbf{P}'(\Phi_l)$ is independent of l, and $\mathbf{P}_f(\Phi_l) = \mathbf{P}'(\Phi_l)$. Note that the concept of independence used in the definition of truth-functional randomness concerns the position of the basic conjunction Φ_l in the infinite sequence, not the relation of one event ϕx of the basic conjunction to another, as in our original definition of independence (p. 50).

We call these sequences "truth-functionally random" because in them every truth-function has its appropriate frequency probability. Every admissible sequence is truth-functionally random, but not conversely. A mixture of independent processes satisfies the independence condition on $\mathbf{P}'(\Phi_l)$ in the definition of "truth-functionally random" and hence determines a class of truth-functionally random sequences. Some simple Markov chains, e.g., the one defined on page 126, determine classes of truth-functionally random sequences.

Let us now summarize the results of this brief analysis of randomness. Some concepts of randomness involve inductive probability assignments to sets of universes, e.g., the randomness of an independent process, while others apply to single sequences or universes. Entropy, pseudorandomness, admissibility, and truth-functional randomness are kinds of sequence randomness.

The concept of admissibility is a generalization of the concept of frequency probability, admissibility requiring an appropriate limiting relative frequency for every finite sequence, frequency probability requiring only a limiting relative frequency for the unit sequence "1". Pseudorandomness is a finite version of admissibility. Entropy depends only on the relative frequencies of the unit sequences (0,1), and hence measures only the lowest level of pseudorandomness. Determinism limits entropy.

Though admissibility and truth-functional randomness are kinds of sequence randomness, they are formally similar to certain kinds of inductive probability assignments. The definitions of the former can be obtained from the definitions of the latter by substituting the frequency probability term $\mathbf{P}_f(\Phi_l)$ for the inductive probability term $\mathbf{P}(\Phi_l)$.

9.4.3 Determinism and randomness

Determinism is the doctrine that nature is a tightly deterministic system (p. 576). We saw in the last subsection that determinism limits entropy. We shall now explore the relation of determinism to other kinds of sequence randomness, using deterministic automata as models.

Our definition of "deterministic" was for space-time systems (p. 575). Finite automata and Turing machines have a temporal dimension, but they were not presented as spatial systems. However, it is easy to construe them spatially. When viewed as physical objects—or as networks of ideal switches, delays, and tapes spread out in space—finite automata and Turing machines are discrete, deterministic space-time systems. More important, a Turing machine (a fortiori, a finite automaton without inputs) can be embedded in an algorithmic cellular automaton, which is a tightly deterministic system (p. 568).

Since finite automata and Turing machines are deterministic systems, it is interesting to examine the extent to which these machines can produce random sequences. We saw in the last subsection that the sequence defined by the rule, "Concatenate the positive integers in natural order, expressed in binary form," is an admissible sequence. It is easy to design a Turing machine that will calculate this sequence. Equivalently, one can program a universal Turing machine to compute this sequence. Hence some admissible sequences are computable.

A digital computer usually has tape units of some kind, but the size of these is bounded in any actual computation. For this reason, a digital computer is equivalent to a finite automaton without inputs. Computers are often used to simulate probabilistic systems occurring in nature, such as nuclear diffusion processes. In these applications one knows the probabilistic rules governing the system and wants the answer to certain general questions about the system, such as "Is this reaction self-sustaining?" and "Will this genetic feature survive in that environment?" Though the problem is well-defined, no general formula for the answer is known.

A digital computer solves this kind of problem by the so-called Monte Carlo method. The computer chooses an initial condition at random and calculates a history of the system, making random choices at various points according to the given probabilistic laws. It repeats this process until it has calculated a large sample of histories of the system and then answers the original questions on the basis of these sample histories.

To employ the Monte Carlo method, the computer needs a random source. One could build a natural source of randomness, such as a die-tossing mechanism or a device for measuring a random electronic effect, and equip the computer to sense the sequence produced by this source. In practice it has proved better to compute the random sequences used in Monte Carlo computations.

While there are admissible sequences that can be computed, these sequences are generally not satisfactory for Monte Carlo calculations. Admissibility is defined in terms of limiting relative frequencies of basic conjunctions, and this places no constraint on a finite initial segment of an admissible sequence. Indeed, the result of prefixing any finite sequence to an admissible sequence is also admissible. Though an admissible sequence is random in the long run, the initial segment used in a particular computation may not be random at all.

Instead, pseudorandom sequences are used for Monte Carlo computations. Since these sequences are finite, they can be stored in a computer, but it is usually more efficient to generate their successive terms as they are needed.

The following is a good algorithm for generating pseudorandom sequences.* Take a number χ_1 of M binary digits (or bits), multiply it by ρ in

* This is called the power residue or multiplicative congruential method of generating pseudorandom numbers, and it originated with D. H. Lehmer, "Mathematical Methods

binary form, and let χ_2 be the rightmost M bits of the product. Repeat this operation with χ_2 to obtain χ_3. More generally, χ_n consists of the rightmost M bits of $\rho\chi_{n-1}$. Iterate this operation to obtain the sequence of M-bit numbers

[18] $\chi_1, \chi_2, \chi_3, \ldots, \chi_n, \ldots, \chi_N$.

Now select the leftmost bit of each χ_n to obtain the binary sequence

[19] $\beta_1, \beta_2, \beta_3, \ldots, \beta_n, \ldots, \beta_N$.

For proper choices of M, ρ, χ_1, and N, this last sequence is pseudorandom.

We give as an example a pseudorandom sequence computed by the algorithm

[19′] 10110,01111,00001,00000,00000,00001,11011,11111,00101,11110, 10000,00011,00100,00101,10001 .

This is for the case $M = 28$, $\rho = 2^{14}-3$, and $\chi_1 = 113$, where these parameters are expressed in decimal notation.

While this algorithm produces infinitely long sequences, they are not random in the sense of "admissible" but are only random in finite or "local" regions. Consider a particular choice of the parameters M, ρ, and χ_1. There are only 2^M distinct M-bit numbers, or values for the χ_n's. Within 2^M steps, one of the χ_n's will repeat. Hence the infinite sequence $\chi_1, \chi_2, \chi_3, \ldots$ is periodic, and the derived sequence $\beta_1, \beta_2, \beta_3, \ldots$ is also periodic. Let π be the period of the β-sequence, so that $\beta_l = \beta_{l+\pi}$. The frequency probability $\mathbf{P}_f(\beta_l \equiv \beta_{l+\pi})$ is one, making the infinite β-sequence not admissible. Moreover, any finite β-sequence that is long compared to the period π will not be pseudorandom, for the 2^π different sequences of length π will not have the distribution required for pseudorandomness. Thus for any particular Monte Carlo calculation, the parameters M, ρ, χ_1, and N must be chosen so that they provide sufficient randomness for that calculation.

The foregoing shows that pseudorandom sequences can be generated in a digital computer. Viewed abstractly, this computer is a finite automaton without inputs, and it can be embedded in an algorithmic cellular automaton. We saw earlier that some admissible sequences can be computed on Turing machines (p. 598), and that these machines can also be embedded in algorithmic cellular automata (p. 568). Hence both pseudorandom sequences and admissible sequences occur in single histories of algorithmic cellular automata. These automata are tightly deterministic systems of a very limited kind. A fortiori, pseudorandom and admissible sequences occur in single histories of tightly deterministic systems.

in Large-Scale Computing Units." See Chambers, "Random-Number Generation," and Strome, "Algorithm 294: Uniform Random [G5]."

We apply this result to what we called "Peirce's claim": The evolution of natural species could not have taken place if nature were a tightly deterministic system (p. 585).

I have already expressed the opinion that the theory of evolution will someday be put into quantitative and rigorous form (p. 88).* When this is done, the evolution of natural species can be simulated to any desired degree of accuracy and temporal extent by finite automata. Sample histories of the evolutionary process can be traced in detail by the Monte Carlo method and general questions about evolution answered in this way. Pseudorandom sequences will provide the randomness needed for sampling.

Any actual simulation is finite, whereas evolution might in principle go on forever. But if finite simulations of evolution are possible, then an infinite evolutionary process could in principle be simulated by a universal Turing machine. As a source of randomness this machine could use an admissible sequence whose initial segments are sufficiently pseudorandom. This sequence would provide enough randomness because every truth-function would have a frequency probability equal to its inductive probability in an independent process (pp. 594–95).

The simulation of a natural process by a computer involves a strong analogy between the simulation and the process itself. The computer system for simulation obeys laws similar to those of the natural process and hence has histories resembling the histories of the natural process in the relevant respects. In our earlier terminology, the simulation system constitutes a model of the natural process (p. 31). Therefore, if the evolution of natural species can be simulated in a restricted kind of tightly deterministic system, as seems likely, it is also likely that the evolution of natural species could have taken place in a tightly deterministic system.

While this argument is not conclusive, it seems to show that determinism can account for the evolution of natural species, and thereby it casts considerable doubt on Peirce's claim. Peirce's doctrine of tychism may be true, and the randomness required for evolution may in fact have a nondeterministic source, as Peirce thought. But his argument for tychism, as embodied in his claim that determinism and evolution are incompatible, seems invalid.

We have considered four kinds of sequence randomness: entropy, admissibility, pseudorandomness, and truth-functional randomness. Sequences of each of these kinds can occur in tightly deterministic systems. Before leaving the topic of randomness we need to mention two stronger kinds of sequence of randomness, both of which seem incompatible with tight determinism. These are: von Mises' concept of "collective," as formalized by Church, and the notion of a "patternless sequence," conceived by

* See also my "Logic, Biology and Automata—Some Historical Reflections."

Kolmogorov and Chaitin.* Both of these concepts are defined by means of Turing machines.

A "selection machine" is fed a binary sequence term by term and decides whether to select or reject the *next* term on the basis of all previous terms. An infinite binary sequence is a *collective*, with associated probability α, if and only if there is no selection machine that can select from it an infinite sequence of frequency probability other than α.

The randomness of a collective is analogous to the randomness of an independent process in this respect: past events are not relevant to the prediction of future events. In an independent process of probability α, the unconditional inductive probability of an arbitrary event is α, and information about prior events does not change this probability. Analogously, in a collective, the frequency probability of an arbitrary event is α, and information about prior events does not enable any selection machine to choose an infinite subsequence that has a frequency probability other than α.

The notion of a collective is defined in terms of limits, and so it says nothing about randomness in the finite case. Thus the result of prefixing any finite sequence to a collective is also a collective. Since the notion of a patternless sequence covers both finite and infinite sequences, it is superior to that of a collective.

Patternlessness is defined in terms of Turing machines with two input tapes. A "sequence-producing machine" computes an arbitrary finite binary sequence when given a program for calculating that sequence on one tape and a representation of the length of the sequence on the other tape. For convenience of comparison, let the inputs as well as the outputs be expressed in binary form. Now the program may be thought of as a description of the sequence calculated. As will be clear in a moment, the length of the description relative to the length of the sequence described is central to the concept of patternlessness. It is easy to design a machine that merely copies the contents of the program tape onto the output tape, in which case a sequence is its own description and the lengths of the sequence and of its description are identical.

There is a universal sequence-producing machine that, in a suitable sense, computes sequences almost as efficiently as any other machine. The "complexity" of a sequence is defined to be the length of the shortest program that causes this universal sequence-producing machine to compute the sequence. A finite binary sequence is *patternless* if and only if its complexity is suitably close to its length. In other words, the patternless se-

* Von Mises, "Grundlagen der Wahrscheinlichkeitsrechnung," and *Probability, Statistics, and Truth*, pp. 89-90. Church, "On the Concept of a Random Sequence."

Kolmogorov, "Tri Podhoda k Opredeleniju Ponjatija 'Količestvo Informacii' " and "On Tables of Random Numbers." See also the papers by Chaitin and Martin-Löf listed in the bibliography.

quences are those whose shortest descriptions are almost as long as the sequences themselves. An infinite binary sequence is *patternless* if and only if an infinite number of its finite initial segments are patternless.

Thus patternless sequences are defined in terms of the computer programs generating them rather than in terms of statistical properties. Nevertheless, they are random from a statistical point of view. For example, the relative frequency of any finite sequence of length m in a patternless sequence of length L tends to be close to $L/2^m$. Both finite and infinite patternless sequences satisfy a wide variety of statistical tests. Indeed, an infinite patternless sequence seems to have all the statistical properties one would expect a truly random sequence to have. Patternlessness, then, is a form of statistical randomness. Moreover, since patternlessness is defined in terms of complexity, randomness and complexity are intimately related.

While the notions of patternless sequence and collective are defined in terms of Turing machines that have inputs, a specific collective or a specific infinite patternless sequence cannot be computed by a Turing machine without inputs and hence cannot be defined by a finite rule or program. For a machine that computed a collective could easily be modified into a selection machine that selected just the 1's of the sequence. And if there were a machine that computed an infinite patternless sequence, the finite automaton part could be converted into a program of fixed length that would compute every initial segment of the infinite patternless sequence; this contradicts the definition. Consequently, no collective or patternless sequence can occur in an algorithmic cellular automaton.

It follows that the notions of a collective and of an infinite patternless sequence are stronger than the notion of an admissible sequence. Consider again the admissible sequence defined by the rule "Concatenate the positive integers in natural order, expressed in binary form." This sequence can be computed by a Turing machine without a tape reader and hence is neither a collective nor a patternless sequence. Thus while this sequence is "random" in one perfectly good sense of that term, it is not random in the stronger sense of "collective" and "patternless."

Since collectives and patternless sequences cannot occur in algorithmic cellular automata, they probably cannot occur in any tightly deterministic system. Today Peirce could formulate his evolutionary claim thus: one of these strong kinds of sequence randomness is required as a chance basis for the infinite evolution of natural species, and hence evolution could not take place in a tightly deterministic system. In contrast, I hold that admissibility, a weaker kind of sequence randomness that is compatible with tight determinism, is a sufficient chance basis for the infinite evolution of natural species.

This completes our discussion of the two questions raised at the beginning of this section. The first question was: How does the determinist account for probabilistic processes? He can do this by means of the concepts of "inductive probability" and "embedded subsystem." The events of a probabilistic process are deterministic with respect to the full system, but they are probabilistic with respect to the system underlying the probabilistic process, which is an embedded subsystem of the full system.

The second question was: What is randomness, and how is it related to determinism? We have seen that "random" is a highly ambiguous term. It sometimes characterizes inductive probability assignments to sets of sequences, as in "independent process" and "random inductive logic." The relation of determinism to this kind of randomness is covered by our discussion of embedded subsystems and probability.

"Randomness" also refers to any of several kinds or measures of sequence randomness, of which we have mentioned six: entropy, admissibility, pseudorandomness, truth-functional randomness, collective, and patternless sequence. The concept of admissibility is a generalization of the concept of frequency probability. Pseudorandomness is a finite version of admissibility. Entropy measures only the lowest level of pseudorandomness.

Determinism limits entropy. But pseudorandom and admissible sequences can occur in algorithmic cellular automata and could provide the randomness needed for the evolution of natural species. This counts against Peirce's claim that evolution could not have taken place if determinism were true.

9.5 Summary

The present chapter covers the space-time framework underlying induction, explains two presuppositions of induction (the causal uniformity and the causal existence principles), and discusses the relation of determinism to chance. These materials are the groundwork for the presupposition theory of induction.

Space-time systems (*sec. 9.2*). Induction involves repetition and therefore presupposes both a repeatable factor and a framework in which repetition can occur. We studied these factors by analyzing space-time systems, both natural systems, e.g., nature itself, and discrete artificial systems (cellular automata). Indexical symbols and properties were distinguished from non-indexical symbols and properties, respectively.

The basic individuals of a space-time system are the points or regions at which monadic, non-indexical properties are exemplified or instanced. In nature the basic individuals are space-time points, while in cellular automata they are cells at moments, or small space-time regions. Thus nonindexical properties constitute the repeatable factor of induction, and space-time is the framework in which repetition occurs. Space-time systems are modal, having many alternative histories.

Cellular automata are governed by transition rules (laws) that may be either probabilistic or causal. A causal cellular automaton is deterministic if each temporal state has a unique successor, otherwise indeterministic. A Turing machine (and a fortiori, a finite automaton) can be embedded in an algorithmic cellular automaton, which is a limited kind of deterministic cellular automaton.

Spatio-temporal contingiuty plays an important role in induction. Contiguous causal laws are modeled in deterministic and indeterministic automata, since a causal transition rule is based on the neighborhood relation. Most of the laws of nature considered in science are contiguous, but not all, Newton's theory of gravity being the classical exception. In contrast to a truly global law, Newton's law is quasi-local, because remote objects interact less than nearby objects. Successful inductive inquiry and verification presuppose that the laws of nature are quasi-local and also inductively simple.

Causality in nature (*sec. 9.3*). The causal uniformity principle is: If a causal connection between nonindexical properties holds in one region of space-time, it holds throughout space-time. Since a causal transition rule is invariant over all cells and all moments of a cellular automaton, the causal uniformity principle holds of both deterministic and indeterministic cellular automata.

The causal existence principle is: Some space-time region is governed by quasi-local laws, at least for the most part. An indeterministic cellular automaton whose transition rule gives a unique next state of a cell for most states of its neighborhood satisfies the causal existence principle.

A deterministic system is a causally modal space-time system that satisfies the uniqueness condition: if two causally possible universes have a temporal state in common, their subsequent histories are the same. A tightly deterministic system is a deterministic system whose laws are quasi-local and satisfy the causal uniformity postulate. Newton's mechanics depicts such a system. Determinism is the doctrine that nature is a tightly deterministic system.

Near-determinism is the doctrine that, though nature is for the most part governed by causally uniform and quasi-local laws, some events are not predetermined (are partially uncaused). Such events may occur arbitrarily, or they may be governed by probabilistic laws. The partially uncaused events that have interested most near-determinists are acts of free choice, and these near-determinists have maintained that only uncaused free choices are really free.

Determinism combines the causal uniformity principle and a complete form of the causal existence principle. Near-determinism combines both principles with the claim that some events are partially uncaused. Hence the causal existence and uniformity principles are conjointly equivalent to the disjunction of determinism and near-determinism.

Determinism, near-determinism, and tychism are alternative doctrines concerning the kinds of basic laws governing nature. Determinism holds that all basic laws are causal and that these laws completely govern all phenomena. Near-determinism holds that most natural phenomena are governed by causal laws but some are not, occurring arbitrarily or in accord with probabilistic laws. In contrast to both, Peirce's tychism holds that probabilistic laws are basic and causal laws derivative. Implicit in Peirce's argument for tychism is the claim that the evolution of natural species could not have taken place if nature were a tightly deterministic system.

Determinism and chance (sec. 9.4). The determinist, holding that nature is completely governed by causally uniform and quasi-local laws, needs to explain how probabilistic processes and dispositions can occur within a tightly deterministic system. He does so by means of the concepts of "inductive probability" and "embedded subsystem." The events of a probabilistic process are deterministic with respect to the full system, but they are probabilistic with respect to the system underlying the disposition, which is an embedded subsystem of the full system.

The term "random" is highly ambiguous. It sometimes characterizes inductive probability assignments to sets of sequences, as in "independent process" and "random inductive logic." "Randomness" also refers to any of several kinds or measures of "sequence randomness," or the randomness possessed by a single sequence or universe. We studied these kinds of sequence randomness and their interrelations: entropy, admissibility, pseudorandomness, truth-functional randomness, being a collective, and patternlessness.

The concept of admissibility is a generalization of the concept of frequency probability, for admissibility requires an appropriate limiting relative frequency for every finite sequence, while frequency probability ($\mathbf{P}_f$) requires only a limiting relative frequency for the unit sequence "1". Pseudorandomness is a finite version of admissibility. Entropy measures only the lowest level of pseudorandomness.

Determinism limits entropy. But pseudorandom sequences and admissible sequences can occur in algorithmic cellular automata, which constitute a very restricted kind of tightly deterministic system. Such sequences could provide the randomness needed for the evolution of natural species. This constitutes evidence against Peirce's claim that the evolution of natural species could not have taken place if nature were a tightly deterministic system.

10 The Presupposition Theory of Induction

Reason, holding in one hand its principles, according to which alone concordant appearances can be admitted as equivalent to laws, and in the other hand the experiment which it has devised in conformity with these principles, must approach nature in order to be taught by it. It must not, however, do so in the character of a pupil who listens to everything that the teacher chooses to say, but of an appointed judge who compels the witness to answer questions which he has himself formulated.

All attempts to derive these pure concepts of understanding from experience, and so to ascribe to them a merely empirical origin, are entirely vain and useless. I need not insist upon the fact that, for instance, the concept of a cause involves the character of necessity, which no experience can yield. Experience does indeed show that one appearance customarily follows upon another, but not that this sequence is necessary. . . .

To search in our common knowledge for the concepts which do not rest upon particular experience and yet occur in all knowledge from experience, of which they as it were constitute the mere form of connection, presupposes neither greater reflection nor deeper insight than to detect in a language the rules of the actual use of words generally and thus to collect elements for a grammar (in fact both researches are nearly related), even though we are not able to give a reason why each language has just this and no other formal constitution, and still less why any precise number of such formal determinations in general, neither more nor less, can be found in it.*

10.1 Introduction

We began this inquiry into the nature of scientific evidence with four main questions (sec. 1.6.1). Only the fourth remains: What is the nature of causal necessity ($\Box^c$), and how are causal necessity and inductive probability (**P**) related? My answer is the presupposition theory of induction.

Since causal necessity is an essential feature of laws of nature, causal

This theory was originally formulated in my articles, "The Presupposition Theory of Induction," "On the Presuppositions of Induction," and "Dispositional Statements." It is developed further in this chapter by the application of automata theory, particularly my analysis of the heuristic use of cellular automata to discover the laws governing a natural system (*Essays on Cellular Automata*, pp. 52–64).

* Kant, *Critique of Pure Reason*, p. 20 (B xiii); ibid., p. 139 (A 112); and *Prolegomena to Any Future Metaphysics*, p. 70 (sec. 39); respectively.

laws, and related statements, a complete account of induction must explain how causally necessary statements are verified and what role inductive probability plays in the process. Now, we earlier examined four theories of inductive probability: frequency (sec. 3.4.2), pragmatic (sec. 5.6), a priori (sec. 5.7.1), and personalistic (sec. 5.7.2). With the exception of Keynes' version of the a priori theory (see sec. 10.5.1), none of these theories says anything about the verification of causally necessary statements. My presupposition theory provides a more definitive account.

Briefly, the presupposition theory holds that causal necessity is a priori and modal in nature (sec. 10.2), and that inductive verification rests on three presuppositions (secs. 10.3–10.4). The theory is summarized in Section 10.6. The reader can use that summary as a guide to the contents of the present chapter.

10.2 The Epistemological Status of Causal Necessity

10.2.1 Empirical and a priori concepts

The formal properties of causal necessity are given by the logic of causal statements. We saw in Chapter 7 that this logic is a good model for causal propositions and arguments of ordinary discourse. It fits actual discourse well enough to show that causal necessity is an essential feature of laws of nature, causal laws, causal subjunctives, and cause-effect statements (p. 478).

In the present section we shall investigate the epistemological status of causal necessity, using its formal properties as a guide. Two interrelated questions arise here. *Is the concept of causal necessity empirical or a priori? Is causal necessity ultimately modal, or can it in some sense be reduced to nonmodal concepts?*

Consider the first question. We start with a general but rough characterization of the notions of "empirical concept" and "a priori concept." More specific information about these notions will emerge from our application of them to the specific concept of causal necessity. Note that we are here distinguishing two kinds of concepts or terms, not two kinds of propositions or statements, as we did at the beginning of the book (sec. 1.2.1).

Man has the ability to abstract concepts from experience and to construct compound concepts from them. Concepts obtained in either way are "empirical." For example, the concept of redness is empirical because one can see red objects and also non-red objects and note the difference. The concept of pain is empirical because one can feel pain. In both of these cases one has experienced instances of the concept directly and has abstracted the concept from the experience.*

* The epistemological problem of specifying the meaning of "direct experience" is beyond the scope of this book. It should be noted, however, that a variation in the extension of "direct experience" does not necessarily entail a variation in the extension of

There are no centaurs to be seen (directly experienced), but we can see animals, horses, and men and observe that they have bodies and heads. The concept of "centaur" may then be constructed from empirical concepts according to the definition "a centaur is an animal with the head of a man and the body of a horse." Hence the concept "centaur" is a compound empirical concept.

The operations of abstracting concepts from experience and constructing concepts from other concepts are carried out by means of a certain mental apparatus. One can reflect on his experiences of abstraction and construction and see that certain concepts are involved in them, such as the concept of conjunction, the notion of a relation, and the notion of a mathematical function. Since these concepts are presupposed by the definition of "empirical concept," they cannot themselves be empirical but are "a priori concepts." A priori and empirical concepts do not play the same role in a construction: the former constitute the form and organization, the latter the matter and content, of the constructed concept (see sec. 10.4.1).

We shall argue in the next subsection that the concept of causal necessity ($\Box^c$) cannot be abstracted from experience or constructed from concepts so abstracted, and hence it is not an empirical concept. Rather, it is an a priori concept, since it can be obtained only by reflecting on one's experiences and seeing what is involved in them.

The foregoing remarks are summarized in the following two recursive definitions (p. 343).

A priori concept

[Initial step] A concept that can be obtained only by reflecting on one's experiences and seeing what is involved in them is a priori.

[General step] A concept that can be constructed from a priori concepts alone is a priori.

Empirical concept

[Initial step] If one can directly experience instances of a concept and abstract the concept from these experiences, the concept is empirical.

[General step] A concept that can be constructed from empirical concepts, possibly together with some a priori concepts, is also empirical.

Of course all concepts come from experience in the sense that man must have experiences before he can formulate any concept. Hence the distinction between empirical and a priori concepts hinges on a distinction between two different ways of obtaining a concept from experience. This in turn depends upon the distinction between (1) abstracting a concept from experience, e.g., the concept of redness, and (2) reflecting on one's experiences and seeing

"empirical concept," for what is directly experienced, on one view, may be, on another view, constructed from the directly experienced.

The notions of "direct experience" and "empirical concept" are closely related to ostensive definitions. See my "Empiricism and Vagueness."

that a concept is involved in them, e.g., the concept of causal necessity. Now this last distinction is controversial and difficult, and the same is therefore true of the distinction between empirical and a priori concepts. We do not attempt to resolve this problem fully here but content ourselves with doing two things. First, we connect our empirical–a priori distinction to the historical literature. Second, we give positive characterizations of "empirical concept" and "a priori concept" in terms of ideas from automata theory.

Our notions of "empirical concept" and "a priori concept" come close to those of the British Empiricists (John Locke, George Berkeley, and David Hume), the Continental Rationalists (René Descartes, Baruch Spinoza, and Gottfried Leibniz), and Immanuel Kant. The British Empiricists held that all genuine concepts were empirical. In contrast, the Continental Rationalists and Kant held that several philosophically important concepts were a priori, in particular the concepts of substance and causality. We will argue later that the concepts of causal necessity and inductive probability are indeed a priori (pp. 619, 636).

Automata theory is the study of the fundamental principles common to artificial automata (e.g., digital computers, analog computers, control systems) and natural automata (e.g., the human nervous system, self-reproducing cells, the evolutionary aspects of organisms). This is a new subject, but enough is known to show that there are strong analogies between digital computers and human beings regarded as information-processing systems, and that these analogies are relevant to our present problem. The term "automata theory" is von Neumann's. Wiener coined the term "cybernetics" for a similar subject. Cybernetics emphasizes servomechanisms and continuous mathematics (analysis), whereas automata theory emphasizes digital computers and discrete mathematics (combinatorics and logic). However, von Neumann did attempt to expand automata theory to include the study of continuous mechanisms, and Wiener saw that digital computers were important for cybernetics, so that the difference between them is mainly one of approach and emphasis.*

Earlier we discussed general-purpose digital computers and their relation to programs, algorithms, and formal languages (secs. 6.4.3-6.4.4). A general-purpose digital computer has a basic logical design, or fixed structure, of interconnected switching and storage elements. It can store data and instructions for processing that data. A sequence of instructions is called a "program." Given a program, the computer will execute the instruc-

* I have outlined von Neumann's notion of automata theory in my "Introduction" to his *Theory of Self-Reproducing Automata*. For Wiener's views see his *Cybernetics, or Control and Communication in the Animal and the Machine*.

The following explanation of concepts in terms of automata is taken from my "Ontological Categories and Language." See also my "Logic, Computers, and Men."

tions of the program and thereby perform the task specified by the program.

To make a computer more analogous to a human being, we can augment it with sensing devices, e.g., color television cameras, an instrument for measuring the wave-length of light, thermometers, and with devices for action and control, e.g., artificial hands, servomotors. The sensing devices are designed as integral parts of the devices for action and control; for example, a television camera may have a servomechanism and a feedback circuit, enabling it to track a moving object, and the fingers of an artificial hand can sense pressure and texture.

A computer can be programmed to distinguish colors, recognize simple figures, manipulate objects, play games of the complexity of checkers, perform elementary inductive and deductive reasoning, and also to improve its performance of these tasks by learning from its successes and failures. For example, Arthur Samuel has devised a computer program that not only plays a very good game of checkers, but has improved its own game through experience. Initially the program played an amateur game, but by varying its procedures of play and seeing which procedures were most successful, it learned to play tournament-caliber checkers.* Though there is no decision machine for first-order quantification theory (p. 393), there are programs that, when given a formula of first-order quantification theory, will often decide whether it is a theorem or not.†

A computer programmed in the way just described understands concepts in the following sense: it has the ability to recognize instances of a concept and to verify statements involving that concept. For example, the computer can distinguish red from other colors and circularity from other shapes, and it can verify such propositions as "Yesterday, there was a red object beneath that circular object." The computer also has the power to reason, both deductively and inductively, about such propositions. As we mentioned in connection with the logic of inquiry, computers have potentialities for the mechanization of inquiry (p. 18).

The kind of programmed computer just envisaged begins operation with a fixed structure and a program. By virtue of this fixed structure and program, the computer has, initially, certain abilities to process information and to interact with its environment; let us refer to these abilities as the "innate information-processing capacities" of the machine. During its operation, the computer receives information from the environment, processes this information, interacts with the environment, and improves its performance through learning. Thus in the course of operation it acquires certain abilities it did not have initially; let us call these "acquired informa-

* Samuel, "Some Studies in Machine Learning Using the Game of Checkers."

† See, for example, Wang, "Proving Theorems by Pattern Recognition I," and Prawitz, "Advances and Problems in Mechanical Proof Procedures." By 1968, computers were faster at this than most human beings.

tion-processing capacities." Obviously, a computer must have some innate information-processing capacities before it can perform any task or acquire additional information-processing capacities, though a capacity that is innate for one computer might be an acquired capacity for another computer.

Analogously to a computer, a person at birth has a nervous system with a certain structure, that structure having been determined mainly by the information stored in his genes. It is not known whether or not a program is stored initially in the human nervous system, but that does not matter here, for the information in a program can always be expressed in a structure of computing elements, that is, in the structure of the nervous system itself. Let us refer to this basic initial structure, together with any program stored therein, as *man's innate structure-program complex*. By virtue of the innate structure-program complex of his nervous system, a person at birth has certain abilities to process information and interact with his environment; these abilities constitute the innate information-processing capacities of the person. As he has experiences, his nervous system receives and processes information from his environment, and he gradually acquires new information-processing capacities: the ability to recognize colors and shapes, the ability to use a particular language, the ability to play games, the ability to reason, and so on. The development of these capacities corresponds to a modification of his innate structure-program complex. Thus a person begins life with an innate structure-program complex that is the physiological basis of his innate information capacities, and as he learns from experience he acquires a new structure-program complex that is the physiological basis of all of his capacities, both innate and acquired. This new complex will be called *man's acquired structure-program complex*.*

Let us now look at the notions of "empirical concept" and "a priori concept" in terms of automata theory. The abilities to abstract concepts from experience, to construct concepts from other concepts, and to reflect on one's experiences and see what concepts are involved in them are among man's innate information-processing capacities. If one can directly experience instances of a concept and abstract the concept from these experiences, the concept is empirical; also, a concept that can be constructed from empirical concepts is empirical. A concept that has been acquired empirically is an aspect or feature of a person's acquired structure-program complex but not of his innate structure-program complex.

A concept that is not empirical is a priori. A priori concepts are of two sorts. First, an a priori concept may be a basic aspect or feature of the structure-program complex constituting a person's innate information-processing capacities, in terms of which this complex processes information

* A person's innate and acquired information-processing capacities, taken together, are obviously complex and highly organized. But it is not known how much of this organization and complexity is acquired and how much is innate.

and organizes experience. A person becomes aware of such an a priori concept by having experiences involving the concept and seeing on reflection that the concept is involved in these experiences. Second, a concept that can be constructed from a priori concepts alone is a priori. Note that a compound concept having an empirical constituent is empirical.

Thus, a priori concepts are closely related to the innate structure-program complexes and information-processing capacities of men, while empirical concepts are closely related to the acquired structure-program complexes and information-processing capacities of men.*

This completes our general discussion of the notions of empirical concept and a priori concept. In the next subsection we shall apply these notions to the concept of causal necessity.

10.2.2 Causal necessity is a priori

Since several different symbols involving causal necessity will be used, we list them here. The symbol for causal necessity ($\Box^c$) was taken as a primitive of the logic of causal statements (p. 342). Symbols for causal possibility ($\Diamond^c$), causal implication ($\underset{c}{\rightarrow}$), nonparadoxical causal implication (**npc**), and elliptical causal implication (**ec**) were defined in terms of it and the other primitives of the system (definitions [1d], [1g], [17], and [21], respectively). In this chapter we are interested in philosophic issues concerning the nature of causal necessity, and so it will usually not matter which of these symbols or concepts we are discussing.

The logic of causal statements is an interpreted language. The interpretation of Chapter 7 assigns meanings to the causally modal symbols "$\Box^c$," "$\Diamond^c$," "$\underset{c}{\rightarrow}$," "**npc**," and "**ec**" so that all of these symbols are meaningful. In other words, there are genuine concepts of causal necessity ($\Box^c$), causal possibility ($\Diamond^c$), etc. Consider now the first of these concepts. We are to decide between two alternatives: (1) The concept of causal necessity is empirical, that is, one can directly experience instances of causal necessity and abstract the concept of causal necessity from these instances, or else one can construct the concept of causal necessity from empirical concepts. (2) The concept of causal necessity is not empirical but a priori; we become aware of the concept by having experiences involving causal necessity and seeing on reflection that those experiences involve causal necessity, or by constructing the concept of causal necessity from a priori concepts. In deciding between these alternatives we pursue two different approaches.

* Man is not a fixed species, but has developed from lower forms by evolutionary and adaptive processes. The mechanism by which this occurred is understood only in a very general way. The problem of how the innate information-processing capacities (and corresponding structure-program complex) common to all men have evolved is an important and difficult one.

To begin with, we survey our own experiences to ascertain if the concept of causal necessity is empirically derivable. Later, we shall examine critically Hume's profound analysis of causality.

Let us first survey our own experiences to see if we do directly experience instances of causal necessity from which the concept can be abstracted. Consider once again the gold ring (sec. 6.1). Aqua regia causes gold to dissolve. One can establish by observation that an object is gold, that a liquid is aqua regia, and that gold dissolves when placed in aqua regia and does not dissolve when kept in air. Thus one can observe the cause, the effect, and the regularity with which one event follows the other. But clearly one cannot establish by observation that this causal connection is necessary; that is, the necessity in this example cannot be directly experienced. See the second quotation from Kant at the head of this chapter (p. 607).

The properties related by a causal law often differ in the degree to which they are directly observable. For example, one can see a gold object dissolve, although he may need to make some tests to distinguish real gold from fool's gold. But the cause, the effect, or the background conditions may be less directly observable than in that example. Consider the law that an electron moving in a vacuum perpendicular to a magnetic field and subject to no other forces is deflected (pp. 425, 451). One cannot see a magnetic field, and though the path produced by an electron in a cloud chamber can be seen, the electron itself cannot. Here the causal connection is even more remote from direct experience than in the previous case.

Perhaps the most promising way to find causal necessity in experience is to look at one's own inner experiences. Some writers have maintained that one can directly experience causal necessity by introspecting an act of volition or willing.* For example, I decide to move my arm, and as a consequence I move my arm. Let "$\mathfrak{M}$" mean that I willed to move my arm and "**M**" that in fact I moved my arm. This cause-effect relation should be symbolized with elliptical causal implication as "$\mathfrak{M}$ **ec M**" or "$\overline{\mathfrak{M}}$ **ec** $\overline{\mathbf{M}}$" or both (sec. 7.4.1). We will consider only the first of these two causal statements, since the same analysis applies to both. By definition [21b] the causal statement "$\mathfrak{M}$ **ec M**" is equivalent to "$(\exists X)[X(X\mathfrak{M}$ **npc M**$)]$," where the predicate variable "X" refers to the remaining conditions involved in producing the effect. These are physiological and/or mental conditions that, together with my decision, sufficed to bring about the movement of my arm.

* Stout, *Mind and Matter*, chap. 2. Broad, *The Mind and Its Place in Nature*, pp. 101-3.

Whitehead believed that when a person blinks because of a light flash, he directly experiences the causal nexus between the experience of the flash and the experience of the blink (*Process and Reality*, pp. 263-66).

See also the quotations from Keynes, pp. 641-42, below.

I cannot directly experience these conditions, at least not all of them. Now the causal necessity involved in this example holds from $X\mathcal{M}$ to $\mathbf{M}$, not from $\mathcal{M}$ alone to $\mathbf{M}$. Since I cannot directly experience the antecedent conditions X, I cannot experience the causal necessity from $X\mathcal{M}$ to $\mathbf{M}$. The same argument applies to the causal statement "$\overline{\mathcal{M}}$ **ec** $\overline{\mathbf{M}}$," *mutatis mutandis.*

Consider next the following somewhat similar case. A person resolves to act in a certain way, he does in fact make a practice of acting in that way, and he finally develops a habit of so acting. He then has a disposition or tendency to do something of a certain sort in given circumstances. For example, a patrolman (p) receives orders to arrest every jaywalker he sees on his beat, he resolves to execute that order, he arrests everyone he sees jaywalking, and under normal circumstances he would arrest anyone he saw jaywalking on his beat. He thus has a disposition to act in a certain way, which may be symbolized by the causal dispositional "$(\exists X)[Xpy$ $(XpyJpy$ **npc** $Apy)]$," where "Jpy" abbreviates "patrolman p sees y jaywalk and the circumstances are normal," and "Apy" abbreviates "patrolman p arrests y" (sec. 7.3.2). The second conjunct expresses the causal necessity involved in the disposition. As our preceding discussion of an act of volition showed, this causal necessity could be directly experienced by the patrolman only if he directly experienced the property X on which his disposition is based. But it seems to me that one can never directly experience such a property, because how one acts in a certain type of circumstance depends on aspects of oneself that are beyond direct observation.

Let us now apply the recursive definition of "empirical concept" (sec. 10.2.1) to the concept of causal necessity. With respect to the initial step of the definition, we have examined several types of direct experience and found we could not abstract the concept of causal necessity from those experiences. Personally, I cannot find any experiences from which causal necessity can be abstracted. With respect to the general step of the definition of "empirical concept," I cannot find any empirical concepts from which the concept of causal necessity can be constructed. Hence I conclude that the concept of causal necessity is not empirical but a priori.

This conclusion appears to contradict David Hume's famous claim that there is a kind of causal necessity that is empirical; let us examine his claim. As an empiricist, Hume accepted only empirical concepts:

> . . . *all our simple ideas in their first appearance are deriv'd from simple impressions, which are correspondent to them, and which they exactly represent.*
>
> When we entertain, therefore, any suspicion that a philosophical term is employed without any meaning or idea (as is but too frequent), we need but inquire, *from what impression is that supposed idea derived?**

* *A Treatise of Human Nature*, p. 4, and *An Enquiry Concerning Human Understanding*, p. 22.

He then analyzed the relation between cause and effect into constant conjunction, spatial contiguity, temporal succession, and a customary transition of the mind from an experience of the cause to the idea of its effect. This last factor is the source of our idea of causal necessity.

> It appears, then, that this idea of a necessary connexion among events arises from a number of similar instances which occur of the constant conjunction of these events; nor can that idea ever be suggested by any one of these instances, surveyed in all possible lights and positions. But there is nothing in a number of instances, different from every single instance, which is supposed to be exactly similar; except only, that after a repetition of similar instances, the mind is carried by habit, upon the appearance of one event, to expect its usual attendant, and to believe that it will exist. This connexion, therefore, which we *feel* in the mind, this customary transition of the imagination from one object to its usual attendant, is the sentiment or impression from which we form the idea of power or necessary connexion. Nothing farther is in the case. Contemplate the subject on all sides; you will never find any other origin of that idea.

> There is no internal impression, which has any relation [to necessity], but that propensity, which custom produces, to pass from an object to the idea of its usual attendant. This therefore is the essence of necessity. Upon the whole, necessity is something, that exists in the mind, not in objects. . . .
> . . . the necessity of power, which unites causes and effects, lies in the determination of the mind to pass from the one to the other.*

Thus Hume found a kind of causal necessity in experience: the felt propensity of the mind to pass from the idea of a cause to the idea of its effect.

We agree with Hume that there is such a notion of causal necessity and that it is empirical; let us call this kind of causal necessity *felt causal propensity*. We will show the following to be the case: our notion of causal necessity ($\Box^c$), as developed in Chapter 7, cannot be analyzed into the notion of a felt causal propensity; and hence our conclusion that the concept of causal necessity is a priori does not contradict Hume's finding that the concept of a felt causal propensity is empirical.

Consider a statement describing a correct belief in a causal proposition. Hume included some of the background conditions in the cause, so that for him a cause is sufficient in itself to produce an effect (cf. p. 451). Let C be such a cause and E its effect. The form of a correct belief in a causal connection is then

[1] $\mathcal{A}$ believes *correctly* that $\Box^c (x)(Cx \supset Ex)$.

* The first quotation is from *An Enquiry Concerning Human Understanding*, p. 75, while the second is from *A Treatise of Human Nature*, pp. 165-66. See ibid., pp. 169-74, for Hume's analysis of the cause-effect relation.

I am here combining Hume's definition of cause as a "philosophical relation" with his definition of cause as a "natural relation." See *A Treatise of Human Nature*, pp. 169-70, and *An Enquiry Concerning Human Understanding*, pp. 76-77 and 96.

The notion of a constant conjunction between cause C and effect E may be symbolized by "$(x)(Cx \supset Ex)$," together with the assertion that there are instances of the cause, so that "$(x)(Cx \supset Ex)$" cannot be true vacuously. Applying Hume's analysis of causality to [1], we obtain the following analysans.

[1′] (a) 𝒜 believes *correctly* that $(x)(Cx \supset Ex)$, that there are some cases of C, and that in every case E and C are spatially contiguous and E succeeds C.

(b) 𝒜 has the habit of expecting E when he experiences C, and he has an internal impression of this habit.

This internal impression is the direct experience from which the concept of felt causal propensity is abstracted. Thus the analysis of [1] into [1′] seems to eliminate $\Box^c$ in favor of "felt causal propensity." We will argue that this in fact is not so.

The second conjunct [1′](b) refers to a habit. Since a habit is a mental disposition, [1′](b) states that 𝒜 has a disposition such that if he sees an instance of cause C he expects to see the effect E. Now it is an objective fact about 𝒜 that he has this disposition, and an adequate description of this fact must contain some symbol involving causal necessity (sec. 7.3.2). For example, from [1′](b) one can correctly infer such causal subjunctives as "If 𝒜 had observed the cause C, he would have expected the effect E," which requires causal necessity for its symbolization. Moreover, one cannot directly experience the causal necessity of his own habits, as the argument of the first part of this subsection showed. Thus, the analysans [1′] contains causal necessity in our sense as well as the notion of a felt causal propensity, so that the analysis of [1] into [1′] does not eliminate $\Box^c$. Consequently, the concept of $\Box^c$ cannot be analyzed into the concept of felt causal propensity.

We give a second argument to show that $\Box^c$ cannot be analyzed into the concept of felt causal propensity. For this argument we need to distinguish causal uniformities from contingent uniformities. Let Φ be a true statement with no modal operators; then Φ is said to be *causally true* or *contingently true* according to whether $\Box^c \Phi$ is true or false. Regularities, whether causally necessary or contingent, can be of great complexity, but it will suffice to consider the distinction in a simple case. Consider the causal law "$\Box^c (x)(RxHx \supset Fx)$," which states that all released objects (R) that are heavier than air (H) fall (F). Now let "R^*x" mean that the object x was released within my rented bungalow at Ranikhet during 1966. All the objects released there during that period were in fact heavier than air, so that "$(x)(R^*x \supset Fx)$" is true. But "$\Box^c (x)(R^*x \supset Fx)$" is false, so that "$(x)(R^*x \supset Fx)$" is contingently true rather than causally true.

It is easy to imagine a person who does not know that objects lighter than air, e.g., hydrogen-filled balloons, rise when released, and who hence mistakenly expects every object (whether or not it is heavier than air) to fall when released. Then all of Hume's criteria for the causal relation would be satisfied. In other words, it would be true that

[2′] (a) ℬ believes correctly that $(x)(R^*x \supset Fx)$, that there are some cases of R^*, and that in every case F and R^* are spatially contiguous and F succeeds R^*.

(b) ℬ has the habit of expecting F when he experiences R^*, and he has an internal impression of this habit.

Hence by Hume's analysis of causality it should be true that

[2] ℬ believes *correctly* that $\Box^c (x)(R^*x \supset Fx)$.

But [2] is false, because "$\Box^c (x)(R^*x \supset Fx)$" is false.

Thus, on Hume's analysis of causality, if a material universal $(\alpha)(\phi\alpha \supset \Psi\alpha)$ is believed by someone, there is no difference between its being causally true and its being contingently true. More generally, Hume's analysis of causality fails to distinguish causal truths from contingent truths. Since this distinction is made by means of our concept of $\Box^c$, it follows that this concept cannot be analyzed into the concept of felt causal propensity. And because this is so, our earlier conclusion that the concept of $\Box^c$ is nonempirical is consistent with Hume's result that the concept of felt causal propensity is empirical.

Indeed, even though Hume would reject our conclusion that $\Box^c$ is nonempirical, the result of his survey of experience supports our conclusion. We surveyed experience looking for instances from which the concept of $\Box^c$ could be empirically derived, and we found no such experiences. Hume had no notion of $\Box^c$, but he surveyed his impressions looking for instances from which he could empirically derive one or more notions of causal necessity. Hume found only impressions from which the concept of felt causal propensity could be empirically derived; thus he found no impressions from which the concept of $\Box^c$ could be empirically derived.

The fact that we agree with Hume on what can be empirically derived from experience but differ with him so radically concerning the conclusion to be drawn from this is owing to differences in the principles held at the beginning of the survey of experience. Hume held that all genuine concepts were empirical; and so when he could empirically derive no concept of causal necessity other than that of felt causal propensity, he concluded that this latter concept was the only meaningful concept of causal necessity. In contrast, we held that the concept of $\Box^c$ was meaningful and that there might be nonempirical (a priori) concepts; and so when we could empirically derive no concept of causal necessity other than that of felt causal propensity, we concluded that the concept of $\Box^c$ was nonempirical (a priori).

We reached this conclusion by examining specific attempts to derive the concept of causal necessity from experience. A more general argument is: experiences are limited to the actual world, causal necessity ($\Box^c$) concerns a class of possible worlds, and hence the concept of causal necessity is not derivable from experience.

On the basis of the foregoing discussion we conclude that *the concept of causal necessity* ($\Box^c$) *is not empirical but a priori.*

10.2.3 Causal necessity is irreducibly modal

We have now answered the first of the questions raised at the beginning of this section: Is the concept of causal necessity empirical or a priori? The second question was: Is causal necessity ultimately modal, or can it in some sense be reduced to nonmodal concepts? We shall make two attempts to eliminate causal necessity by reducing it to nonmodal concepts.

Our first attempt employs the distinction between indexical and nonindexical symbols (sec. 9.2.2). As an example, take the contingent truth "$(x)(R^*x \supset Fx)$," which states that all objects released in my bungalow at Ranikhet during 1966 fell. Contrast it with the corresponding unrestricted universal "$(x)(Rx \supset Fx)$," which states falsely that all released objects fall. The contingent universal "$(x)(R^*x \supset Fx)$" is true because the subject term "R^*" has been restricted to a certain region of space and time in which, per accidens, all released objects were in fact heavier than air. This suggests that we might distinguish causal truths from contingent truths by requiring that the *predicates* of a basic causal truth be nonindexical. Such a requirement is reasonable in view of the fact that science studies phenomena that are indefinitely repeatable. Note that this requirement places no limitations on the individual constants or proper names involved in a causal truth. Also, causal truths with indexical predicates could be derived from basic causal truths by substitution.

This first attempt to eliminate causal necessity treats a causal law as a summary of matters of fact (past, present, and future) limited to nonindexical properties. Thus a causal law of the form

[3] $\quad \Box^c (\alpha)(\phi\alpha \supset \psi\alpha)$

is to be analyzed into

[3′] $\quad (\alpha)(\phi\alpha \supset \psi\alpha)$ and both ϕ and ψ are nonindexical properties.

But that analysis fails in the case of a contingent truth whose predicates are nonindexical. To construct such an example, start with the contingent truth "$(x)(R^*x \supset Fx)$." The predicate "x was released in my bungalow at Ranikhet during 1966 (R^*)" is indexical. Now, try to form a nonindexical predicate $R^\dagger$ that applies to exactly the same set of objects as does R^*, i.e., such that in fact $(x)(R^\dagger x \equiv R^*x)$. To construct $R^\dagger$ from R^* we would replace the indexical phrase "my bungalow at Ranikhet" by an extremely detailed and complex nonindexical description of the bungalow, of its relation to other bungalows in Ranikhet, of Ranikhet itself, of its relation to the Himalayas, etc., and we would replace "1966" by an equally detailed and complete nonindexical description of what happened in 1966 and the surrounding years.

This effort to formulate a nonindexical predicate $R^\dagger$ such that $(x)(R^\dagger x \equiv R^*x)$ might fail for either of two reasons. First, the actual universe might be a mirror-image universe in which there is a mirror-image of my bungalow at Ranikhet, though as already noted that is unlikely. Second, $R^\dagger$ might nevertheless be exemplified in a remote part of the universe; but by making $R^\dagger$ sufficiently detailed and complex we can render that possibility highly unlikely also. Hence, very probably it is the case that $(x)(R^\dagger x \equiv R^*x)$. It follows that "$(x)(R^\dagger x \supset Fx)$" is very probably true and it is very probably a contingent truth.

It also follows that the statement

[4] $(x)(R^\dagger x \supset Fx)$ and both $R^\dagger$ and F are nonindexical predicates

is very probably true. By the proposed analysis,

[4′] $\Box^c\, (x)(R^\dagger x \supset Fx)$

is then very probably true. But this result contradicts the previous result that "$(x)(R^\dagger x \supset Fx)$" is very probably a contingent truth. Hence the proposed analysis is incorrect,* and our first attempt to reduce causal necessity to nonmodal concepts fails.

Our second attempt to reduce causal necessity to nonmodal concepts involves the objective basis of causal necessity. We saw in the last subsection that a material universal $(\alpha)(\phi\alpha \supset \psi\alpha)$ that is contingently true may satisfy Hume's criteria for cause and effect and hence that Hume cannot distinguish genuine cases of causality from contingent constant conjunctions. His objective criteria of repetition, spatial contiguity, and temporal succession are not enough to make the distinction, because these features are present in contingent truths as well as in causal truths. Hume gave a subjective account of causal necessity, attempting to reduce it to a felt causal propensity. But his account does not help to distinguish genuine cases of causality from contingent constant conjunctions; rather it presupposes this distinction, for one should treat a connection as necessary only if it is a genuine case of causality.

Now an important task of science is to discover and verify laws of nature and causal laws; consequently the scientist must in practice dis-

* The same is true of the analysis that results from adding the condition "both C and E are nonindexical properties" to Hume's analysans of cause-effect as formulated in [1′] of p. 617.

tinguish causally true statements from contingently true statements (p. 439). The particular conclusions science reaches at any given stage depend on the historical course of inquiry and hence on the logic of inquiry as well as the logic of argument (sec. 1.4.1). But insofar as science arrives at correct theories, it draws the distinction between causally true statements and contingently true statements on the basis of empirical data and by means of inductive inference. This process will be discussed in the next section. There must be some difference in the data of the two cases to warrant saying one is causally true, the other only contingently true. Since empirical data are objective, it follows that there is an objective difference between a statement's being contingently true and its being causally true. Therefore, *causal necessity has an objective basis in nature*, and it is not purely subjective, as Hume thought it was.

Thus some objective difference must obtain between the evidence that a statement is causally true and the evidence that it is contingently true. Suppose this difference were described and used in an analysis of the following sort. A causal law $\Box^c (\alpha)(\phi\alpha \supset \psi\alpha)$ is analyzed into the corresponding material universal $(\alpha)(\phi\alpha \supset \psi\alpha)$ conjoined with the requirement that the evidence for $(\alpha)(\phi\alpha \supset \psi\alpha)$ have the described character. This requirement would be of the form: there exist true sentences of a certain kind that stand in certain inductive probability relations to $(\alpha)(\phi\alpha \supset \psi\alpha)$. Notice that this requirement employs an existential statement quantifier in the same manner as our earlier models of causal dispositions and probabilistic dispositions (p. 487).

Notice, too, that even if this analysis succeeded in eliminating causal necessity, it would not show that causal necessity is nonmodal. For it would reduce causal necessity to inductive probability (**P**). But inductive probability is itself a modal concept (secs. 2.3.1, 8.2.2), so that the effect of the proposed analysis would be to reduce one modal concept to another.

In any case, the analysis cannot eliminate causal necessity. Consider a theory that has not yet been verified. The kind of evidence needed to verify it may include experimental phenomena as well as natural phenomena, and some controlled experiments, not yet performed, may be needed for its verification. Since these experiments have not yet been performed, their description requires practical conditionals of the form "If the experiment θ should be performed in circumstances ψ, the observed result would be χ" (sec. 4.2.1). But a practical conditional involves the subjunctive, hence causal necessity (sec. 4.2.4). Thus the objective characteristic distinguishing a causal truth from a contingent truth requires causal necessity for its description. In other words, the concept of causal necessity is needed to describe the kind of evidence that confirms a causal truth. We conclude that the proposed analysis is circular: it does not really eliminate causal necessity but only seems to do so, the concept of causal necessity reappearing in more subtle form. And our second attempt to reduce causal necessity to nonmodal concepts fails.

There is independent confirmation of our claim that an analysis of causal necessity in terms of evidence and confirmation is circular. Hans Reichenbach made a detailed and lengthy attempt to reduce causal necessity to nonmodal notions. Among other conditions, he required of a causally necessary statement that it be verifiably true. In explaining what "verifiably true" meant, he was forced to speak of "possible observational data." Now a possible observational datum can be described only by means of a subjunctive, such as "If the thermometer had been read, a temperature below freezing would have been observed." Since a subjunctive involves causal necessity (sec. 7.3), Reichenbach's analysis was circular.*

We found a similar circularity in Hume's analysis of causality (sec. 10.2.2). Hume began with an analysandum, the notion of "cause and effect," which really involves causal necessity in the sense of $\Box^c$. He offered an analysans that seems to employ only one notion of causal necessity, his notion of felt causal propensity. But Hume's analysans involves an implicit subjunctive ("If $\mathcal{A}$ had observed the cause C, he would have expected the effect E"), which requires causal necessity in the sense of $\Box^c$ for its symbolization; thus his analysis is also circular.

It is significant that so many attempts to eliminate causal necessity turn out to involve a hidden subjunctive and hence are circular. I think this shows the notion of causal necessity to be both pervasive and deep, so that attempts to eliminate it only make it reappear in more subtle guises. Hence I conclude: Causal necessity is ultimately modal and cannot be reduced to nonmodal concepts.

We have now answered the first part of our fourth question, concerning the nature of causal necessity: *The concept of causal necessity* ($\Box^c$) *is a priori and it is irreducibly modal.*

10.3 Causal Models of Standard Inductive Logic

10.3.1 Possible causal systems

We turn to the second part of our fourth question: How are causal necessity and inductive probability related?

Inductive probability was originally defined in terms of inductive inference (sec. 1.5.2). The rules of inductive inference actually used and aspired to in practice constitute standard inductive logic (sec. 3.1). Scientists

* *Nomological Statements and Admissible Operations*, p. 85.

Reichenbach thought his use of a subjunctive here was not circular, on the ground that the subjunctive did not need to state a definite observed result, but could always be highly general, as in "If the thermometer had been read, *some* temperature would have been observed." However, the empirical content of a causally necessary statement cannot usually be expressed by subjunctives of such generality.

verify laws of nature and causal laws, and thus as a matter of practice they distinguish between causally true and contingently true statements (p. 439). Causally necessary statements are often used to infer nonmodal statements. For example, conclusions about life on Mars depend on our knowledge of the causal conditions of life on earth, and a prediction of a lunar eclipse is inferred from accepted causal laws together with observations of present conditions.

Accordingly, the question of how causal necessity and inductive probability are related becomes: How are causally necessary statements verified in standard inductive logic? We will argue that inductive verification is grounded on three presuppositions: the causal uniformity principle, the causal existence principle, and the limited variety principle.

Some of the traditional rules of inductive logic were intended in part as rules for establishing causal laws and hence indirectly as rules for distinguishing between causal and contingent truths. Bacon's tables of instances, Mill's methods of experimental investigation, and the idea of a controlled experiment are examples. But these rules are rough; they do not take explicit account of inductive probability.

The task of explaining how causally necessary statements are verified is a difficult one, and our answer is incomplete and speculative. We employ some new models, to be called "causal models of standard inductive logic." Since these new models combine features of the models of Chapters 3, 6, and 9, we begin by reviewing those.

Formal models $\mathfrak{M}$-$\mathfrak{L}$ were used in Chapter 3 to study inductive logics. A model $\mathfrak{M}$ contains a set of logically possible universes, one of which is "actual." The corresponding language $\mathfrak{L}$ contains a set of universe descriptions, one of which is "true." Models of standard, inverse, and random inductive logics are obtained by assigning inductive probabilities to logically possible universes. The rule of induction by simple enumeration holds in standard inductive logic but not in inverse or random logic. Let us now call these models *statistical models of induction*, to distinguish them from the new models of induction. Statistical models of induction explain the role of repetition in induction. But they do not include the causal modalities and so cannot explain the verification of causally necessary statements. A model $\mathfrak{M}$ does not contain a class of causally possible universes and the concept of causal necessity is not expressible in language $\mathfrak{L}$.

This deficiency is corrected by the models of Chapter 6, which provide an abstract interpretation of the logic of causal statements. In these models, $\mathfrak{M}$ contains a set of causally possible universes, and the corresponding notion of causal necessity is expressible in $\mathfrak{L}$. Hence causal laws can be expressed in these models. But the concept of probability is not expressible in them. In short, statistical models do not account for causal necessity, and the modal models of the logic of causal statements do not account for inductive probability. In addition, neither type of model has a space-time organization. As we saw in the last chapter, some inductively important features of causal laws, such as uniformity and contiguity, presuppose a space-time framework. We modeled these features by means of causal cellular automata (sec. 9.2.3).

Our new models of inductive logic will explain the verification of causal laws. The foregoing review shows that these models should combine the repetitive feature of a statistical model of standard inductive logic, the modality of a causal model, and the space-time organization of a cellular automaton. We present the models informally, with our subsequent interpretation in mind (see sec. 10.4.1).

TABLE 23

Modal Structure of a Causal Model of Standard Inductive Logic

	Possible Causal Systems All causal cellular automata with m cell states satisfying the uniformity and existence presuppositions				
	$\mathcal{S}_a$ (actual) $(\Box^c)$	$\mathcal{S}_1$ $(\Box_1^c)$	$\mathcal{S}_2$ $(\Box_2^c)$	. . . . . .	$\mathcal{S}_M$ $(\Box_M^c)$
Causally Possible Universes Those histories of temporal states that satisfy the transition rule of the automaton	u_{a1} (actual) u_{a2} u_{a3} . . .	u_{11} u_{12} u_{13} . . .	u_{21} u_{22} u_{23} . . .		u_{M1} u_{M2} u_{M3} . . .

$\mathcal{S}_a$ is the actual causal system and represents nature; u_{a1} is the actual universe of $\mathcal{S}_a$ and represents our actual universe.

A **causal model of standard inductive logic** has two parts, a doubly modal structure and a probability assignment to this structure. The modal structure consists of a finite set of "possible causal systems," each containing a set (generally infinite) of causally possible universes. The second part consists of an assignment of unconditional inductive probabilities to these possible causal systems and to the causally possible universes within them.

The structure of a causal model is shown in Table 23. We will describe the possible causal systems of a model in a general way before defining them. These systems are causal cellular automata representing nature and its inductively possible alternatives. All of them have the space-time framework of common sense, and all of them satisfy the three presuppositions of induction. Since commonsense space has three dimensions and commonsense time is infinite in both past and future, we consider cellular automata that have three spatial dimensions and a two-way infinite temporal dimension. Thus space is divided into cubical cells, and time is divided into discrete moments ($t = \ldots, -2, -1, 0, 1, 2, \ldots$). All the causal cellular automata of a given model have the same number m of cell states (see further pp. 633–34). They differ, then, only with respect to their transition rules. And since a transition rule is equivalent to a finite set of contiguous causal laws (p. 569), they differ only with respect to the causal laws governing them.

We now define the *possible causal systems* of a model to be those cellular automata with m cell states that satisfy the following two presuppositions. The causal uniformity presupposition is: If a causal connection between nonindexical properties holds in one region of space-time, it holds throughout space-time. All causal cellular automata satisfy this principle. The causal existence presupposition is: some space-time region is governed by quasi-local laws, at least for the most part. All deterministic and near-deterministic cellular automata satisfy this principle. Hence the possible causal systems of a model consist of all those deterministic and near-deterministic cellular automata having m cell states (the number of cell states of the model). Our third presupposition, the limited variety principle, will provide the basis for the finitude requirement on the number of cell states (p. 633 below).

Let us relate these causal models to our earlier models $\mathfrak{M}$-$\mathfrak{L}$ by describing them in the same terms (pp. 106–7, 351–67). The earlier models were composed of basic individuals and basic properties, from which individual states, logically possible universes, and causally possible universes were constructed. In a causal model, a cell-moment is a basic individual; and a cell state, i.e., an individual state, is described by a conjunction that tells whether a basic property is present or absent. A logically possible universe is a two-way infinite history of temporal states, where a temporal state is an assignment of cell states to the cells of the automaton (p. 562). Note that every possible causal system of a given model contains the same set of logically possible universes, since every cellular automaton of the model is based on the same finite set of cell states. Finally, the *causally possible universes* of a possible causal system consist of those logically possible universes that satisfy the transition rule of the system.

Nature is the single space-time system consisting of all entities (events or substances) that have spatio-temporal location, together with the basic laws governing these entities (p. 552). On some metaphysical theories, such as Peirce's tychism, these basic laws are probabilistic. We have argued that they are causal (chaps. 7 and 9) and have given an account of probabilistic laws that is compatible with this position (chap. 8). Nature is represented in a causal model of standard inductive logic by one of the possible causal systems, the *actual causal system*. The other possible causal systems are the alternatives to nature that satisfy the three presuppositions of induction and that are accordingly considered in the inductive process. One of the universes of the actual causal system represents our actual universe and is called the *actual universe* of the model.

The modal structure of a causal model is depicted in Table 23 above.

$\mathcal{S}_a$ is the actual causal system. One of its universes, u_{a1}, is the actual universe. The systems $\mathcal{S}_1, \mathcal{S}_2, \ldots, \mathcal{S}_M$ are the inductively possible alternatives to $\mathcal{S}_a$.

Each of the systems $\mathcal{S}_a, \mathcal{S}_1, \mathcal{S}_2, \ldots, \mathcal{S}_M$ is a model of the logic of causal statements and therefore defines a causal necessity operator. We reserve the necessity symbol "$\Box^c$" for the actual causal system $\mathcal{S}_a$ and use the symbols "$\Box^c_1$", "$\Box^c_2$", ..., "$\Box^c_M$" for the alternative systems $\mathcal{S}_1, \mathcal{S}_2, \ldots, \mathcal{S}_M$, respectively. Because "$\Box^c$" is defined in terms of the actual causal system, the following equivalences hold, where Φ is a nonmodal statement.

(*M*) $\Box^c \Phi$ is true if and only if Φ is true in every causally possible universe of the actual causal system $\mathcal{S}_a$.

(*A*) Φ is true if and only if Φ holds in the actual universe u_{a1}.

This completes the description of the first part of a causal model of standard inductive logic, namely, its two-layered structure of possible causal systems and causally possible universes within these systems. Note that a causal model is finitistic in certain respects crucial to induction. The number m of cell states of the cellular automata of the model is fixed. The neighborhood $N(c)$ of a cell c is finitistic; it is capable of only a finite number of different states. A transition rule gives, for each state of the neighborhood $N(c)$, a list of one or more next cell states for c. Since only finitely many states are involved, a transition rule, in principle, can be expressed by a finite table. Consequently, the number of possible transition rules, and of possible causal systems, is finite.

On the other hand, a possible causal system may, and generally does, contain infinitely many causally possible universes. Each near-deterministic system does so, since an exception to its laws can occur in any cell at any moment. A deterministic system also generally contains infinitely many causally possible universes, though there are special cases that do not. An example of an exception is a deterministic cellular automaton that has two cell states, 0 and 1, and the transition rule: a cell in state 0 goes to state 1 and a cell in state 1 remains in state 1, regardless of the states of the other cells in its neighborhood. This system has only one causally possible universe, in which every cell is in state 1 at every moment.

The second part of a causal model of standard inductive logic consists of an *assignment of unconditional inductive probabilities* to its possible causal systems and to the universes within these systems. The guiding rule of this assignment is a principle of indifference: all possible causal systems are treated equally, and within each system all causally possible universes are treated equally. Notice that by this rule each possible causal system is assigned a probability of $(M + 1)^{-1}$, there being $M + 1$ such systems. Since in general infinitely many causally possible universes are in each causal system, equal probabilities cannot be assigned to these directly.

Rather, equal probabilities will be assigned to portions of universes that occur in some finite space-time region. This will be explained in connection with the verification process, to which we now turn.

10.3.2 Verification of causal laws

Since a causal model of standard inductive logic is constructed from causal cellular automata, its basic laws are contiguous causal laws, of the form (p. 569)

$$(L) \qquad (c)(t)[\phi\{N(c), t\} \textbf{ npc } \psi(c, t')]$$

This says that the occurrence of property ϕ in region $N(c)$ at t causes the occurrence of property ψ in cell c at $t + 1$. A statement of form L expresses a *possible causal law*, being true in some possible causal systems and false in others. A possible causal system is defined by a transition rule that gives, for each state of the neighborhood $N(c)$, one or more succeeding states of cell c. One can look at this transition function and ascertain whether or not statement L is true of it. Moreover, each state of the neighborhood $N(c)$ can be expressed as a property ϕ and each state of cell c can be expressed as a property ψ. Consequently, the transition rule of a possible causal system is equivalent to a finite set of possible causal laws. The laws that hold in the actual causal system represent laws of nature and are therefore called *actual causal laws*.

Science uses observation and experiment to learn which possible laws are actual, i.e., which possible causal system is the actual causal system. Now direct observation is limited to the actual universe, whereas a law defines a set of causally possible universes (pp. 174, 426). Our problem, then, is: How do observations about the actual universe confirm statements about causally possible universes?

To analyze this confirmation process within our models, we symbolize a typical instance of a possible causal law. The statement L is a causal universal, asserting that a certain connection holds throughout every universe of the actual causal system. It deductively implies a corresponding "material universal"

$$(U) \qquad (c)(t)[\phi\{N(c), t\} \supset \psi(c, t')]$$

In turn, this material universal deductively implies the instance statement

$$(I) \qquad \phi\{N(c_i), t_i\} \supset \psi(c_i, t'_i) \qquad ,$$

for each cell-moment $\langle c_i, t_i \rangle$ of the space-time framework. Statement I can be confirmed or refuted by direct observation of the neighborhood $N(c_i)$ at moment t_i and the cell c_i at the next moment t'_i.

The case of direct refutation is simple: if instance statement I is false, then possible law L is false, because L deductively implies I. The case of confirmation is more complicated. It is intuitively clear that instance-statement I confirms possible law L to some degree and that a sufficient number of such instances will establish L to an acceptable level. But statements like I concern the actual universe and are nonmodal, while statements like L concern the set of causally possible universes and are modal. How can a nonmodal statement constitute evidencc for a modal statement? This is a fundamental problem of inductive logic, which we call "the problem of instance-confirmation."

To say that instance I confirms L is to say that the probability of L posterior to I exceeds the prior probability of L, i.e., $\mathbf{P}(L, I) > \mathbf{P}(L)$. We seek a probability assignment to the possible universes of a causal model that will lead to this result. A possible causal system generally contains infinitely many causally possible universes, so that we cannot assign probabilities to these universes directly. In such situations, one normally uses a limiting process. I believe there exists a limiting process for assigning probabilities to causally possible universes in such a way as to explain instance-confirmation; but I do not have one. Instead I shall make the assignment for a finite space-time region. Admittedly, this is somewhat ad hoc.

Let $\mathfrak{M}$ be a causal model, as depicted in Table 23, above. Since cellular space-time is infinite, this model contains infinitely many causally possible universes or space-time histories. We may cut down model $\mathfrak{M}$ to a finite version $\mathfrak{M}_f$ in the following way. Consider some finite space-time region $\mathfrak{R}$ large enough to contain all observational data that have been collected by men in the past and will be collected by men in the foreseeable future. Replace each causally possible universe of $\mathfrak{M}$ by that portion of it lying in region $\mathfrak{R}$. These partial histories over $\mathfrak{R}$ constitute the causally possible universes of the finite model $\mathfrak{M}_f$. We shall show how instance-confirmation works for this reduced model and then speculate that it works analogously for the full model $\mathfrak{M}$.

Though region $\mathfrak{R}$ is tremendously large, it is finite; it contains only a finite number of cells, each capable of only a finite number of cell-states. Consequently, the finite model $\mathfrak{M}_f$ contains only finitely many causally possible universes. A non-zero unconditional probability is easily assigned to each of these universes. By our earlier stipulation, each causally possible system of $\mathfrak{M}_f$ has a positive probability value (p. 626). Using a rule of indifference, we now divide the probability value of a possible causal system equally among the causally possible universes belonging to that system. Consequently—and this is the essential point—each causally possible universe of the reduced model has a non-zero unconditional probability.

For the reduced model $\mathfrak{M}_f$ to represent the full model $\mathfrak{M}$ with respect to instance confirmation, it is necessary that the truth-status of each possible law L be preserved by the reduction process. Obviously, if L holds in a causal system $\mathcal{S}$ of $\mathfrak{M}$, it also holds in the corresponding causal system $\mathcal{S}_f$ of $\mathfrak{M}_f$. But might all the counterinstances to a given L in system $\mathcal{S}$ lie outside the region $\mathcal{R}$? Then L would be false in $\mathcal{S}$ but true in $\mathcal{S}_f$. This question is answered by the next two lemmas.

Shifting lemma: Let u be a causally possible universe of some possible causal system $\mathcal{S}$, and let u^* result from shifting u in space-time a finite amount. Then u^* is a causally possible universe of $\mathcal{S}$.

Proof: The transition rule of a cellular automaton is uniform over space-time, and in a causal model time is infinite in both directions. Consequently, the result of shifting any causally possible universe in space-time is also a causally possible universe of the same cellular automaton.

Counterinstance lemma: Consider a possible causal law L of the form $(c)(t)[\phi\{N(c), t\}$ **npc** $\psi(c, t')]$. Let $\mathcal{S}$ be a possible causal system of causal model $\mathfrak{M}$, and let $\mathcal{S}_f$ be the corresponding system of the reduced model $\mathfrak{M}_f$. Let $\langle c_i, t_i\rangle$ be any cell-moment of the finite region $\mathcal{R}$ (over which $\mathfrak{M}_f$ is defined), and let I be the instance-statement $\phi\{N(c_i), t_i\} \supset \psi(c_i, t_i')$. If L is false in $\mathcal{S}$, then (1) there is a causally possible universe of $\mathcal{S}_f$ in which I is false, and hence (2) L is false in $\mathcal{S}_f$.

Proof: Assume that L is false in $\mathcal{S}$ and that $\langle c_i, t_i\rangle$ lies in $\mathcal{R}$. Then there is some causally possible universe u of $\mathcal{S}$ in which a counterinstance to L occurs. By the shifting lemma, this counterinstance can be shifted in space-time to the cell-moment $\langle c_i, t_i\rangle$. Therefore, there is a universe u^* of $\mathcal{S}$ in which I is false. Let u_f^* be u^* cut down to size $\mathcal{R}$; that is, u_f^* is the partial history of u^* that lies in $\mathcal{R}$. Then u_f^* is a causally possible universe of $\mathcal{S}_f$ in which I is false. This proves the first part of the lemma. The second part follows directly.

We have concluded our demonstration that the truth-status of a possible law L is the same in a finite causal model $\mathfrak{M}_f$ as in the original full model $\mathfrak{M}$. We next show that instance-confirmation works in a finite causal model, which is a finite version of the general result we are seeking.

Instance-confirmation may be understood as an application of Bayes' Theorem (sec. 2.5). Corollary [22] is most useful here (p. 70). Applied to possible law L and instance statement I it becomes

[5] $\mathbf{P}(L, I) > \mathbf{P}(L)$ if and only if $\mathbf{P}(I, L) > \mathbf{P}(I, \bar{L})$,
provided that $0 < \mathbf{P}(L) < 1$ and $\mathbf{P}(I, L) > 0$

For our application, this corollary may be simplified as follows. Since L entails I, $\mathbf{P}(I, L) = 1$, and the condition $\mathbf{P}(I, L) > 0$ can be eliminated. By the subtraction principle $1 > \mathbf{P}(I, \bar{L})$ is equivalent to $\mathbf{P}(\bar{I}, \bar{L}) > 0$ (see p. 46). Combining these two results and making a truth-functional inference, we obtain

[6] If $0 < \mathbf{P}(L) < 1$ and $\mathbf{P}(\bar{I}, \bar{L}) > 0$, then $\mathbf{P}(L, I) > \mathbf{P}(L)$

The first condition for instance-confirmation is that L be probabilistically possible and not probabilistically necessary. L is true of some causal systems of a full model $\mathfrak{M}$ and hence of the corresponding systems of the reduced model $\mathfrak{M}_f$. L is false in some causal systems of $\mathfrak{M}$. By the counterinstance lemma, L is false of the corresponding systems of $\mathfrak{M}_f$. Consequently,

[7] $$0 < \mathbf{P}(L) < 1$$

in every finite model.

The second condition of [6] is that $\mathbf{P}(\bar{I}, \bar{L})$ be positive. L is false in some causal system $\mathcal{S}$ of $\mathfrak{M}$, and by the counterinstance lemma there is a causally possible universe of the corresponding system $\mathcal{S}_f$ in which I is false. Each causally possible universe of a finite model has a non-zero unconditional probability. Consequently,

[8] $$\mathbf{P}(\bar{I}) > 0$$

in every finite model. Since $\bar{I}$ logically implies $\bar{L}$, $\bar{I}$ is logically equivalent to $\bar{I}\&\bar{L}$. Exchanging logical equivalents in a probability context (p. 47) we obtain

[9] $$\mathbf{P}(\bar{I}\&\bar{L}) > 0 \quad .$$

Since $\mathbf{P}(\bar{L})$ is positive by [7] and the subtraction principle,

[10] $$\frac{\mathbf{P}(\bar{I}\&\bar{L})}{\mathbf{P}(\bar{L})} > 0 \quad .$$

The reduction principle (p. 93) then yields

[11] $$\mathbf{P}(\bar{I}, \bar{L}) > 0$$

for every finite model.

The result we have been seeking now follows directly from [6], [7], and [11]:

[12] $$\mathbf{P}(L, I) > \mathbf{P}(L) \quad ,$$

for every finite causal model. This explains how instance I confirms possible law L in a finite causal model of standard inductive logic. Repeated instance-confirmation constitutes induction by simple enumeration to a contiguous causal law.

At the beginning of this section we set out to show how causally necessary statements are verified in standard inductive logic. For this purpose we constructed causal models of standard inductive logic. The original problem then became the problem of instance-confirmation: How does a nonmodal instance-statement confirm a modal law?

We have answered this question for causal models restricted to a finite space-time framework. It is my speculation that the general procedure can be extended to infinite space-time.* I conclude with two comments on this speculation, one concerning its importance and one concerning its plausibility.

First, by the pragmatic theory, inductive probability assignments express dispositions to act in certain ways under conditions of uncertainty. These actions express choices or preferences (sec. 5.6). Hence inductive probability is rooted in human interests. Most human interests are finite in scope; that is, a sufficiently large finite space-time region contains all the objects of these interests. To the extent that induction is based on finite interests, our use of a finite space-time region in explaining the verification of causally necessary statements is satisfactory. But this explanation does not directly cover inductive verification insofar as it is relevant to immortality or to a Peircean infinite community of investigators (pp. 131, 154–55).

Second, it is intuitively plausible that there does exist a limiting process for assigning probabilities to the universes of a causally possible system, which process explains how a nonmodal instance confirms a modal law. Our studies of statistical models of induction showed that limiting processes exist for those probability assignments that favor statistically uniform universes over statistically random (high-entropy) universes (secs. 3.2.3–3.2.4). I will show that the probability assignment of a causal model also favors statistically uniform universes, thereby providing some evidence for my speculation.

In a causal model, probabilities are assigned to the causally possible partial histories of a large but finite region $\mathcal{R}$. Finite probabilities are assigned to those partial histories belonging to causally possible universes, and zero probabilities are assigned to the others.† A causally possible universe satisfies the causal existence and uniformity presuppositions, which are conjointly equivalent to the disjunction of determinism and near-determinism (p. 578). The causally possible universes of a deterministic cellular automaton are limited in maximum average entropy (pp. 592–93), while a similar but slightly weaker conclusion holds for near-deterministic cellular automata. Entropy is a kind of statistical randomness. Consequently, the causally possible universes of a causal model of standard inductive logic have a high degree of statistical uniformity. These facts suggest that the explanation of instance-confirmation given above for a finite space-time region can be extended to infinite space-time. They also suggest that a

* Soshichi Uchii has recently shown how to do this. See his forthcoming paper "Induction and Causality in a Cellular Space." Drawing on his earlier results, Uchii assigns probabilities to an infinite causal model to obtain instance-confirmation of causal laws.

† Thus a logically possible partial history that does not belong to any causally possible system is assigned zero probability (cf. pp. 101, 113–14, and 147). Each such partial history is highly random and complex (cf. pp. 592–93, 601–2).

suitable generalization of the confirmation theorem applies to a causal model (sec. 2.5.3).

We have now completed our discussion of causal models of standard inductive logic and how they account for the verification of causally necessary statements. The treatment is sketchy and speculative, but I know of no better account of the verification of causally necessary statements. At any rate, these models are sufficiently well articulated to be used in formulating the presupposition theory of induction.

10.4 The Presupposition Theory of Induction

10.4.1 The a priori aspect of inductive probability

The presupposition theory incorporates the pragmatic theory of inductive probability, which holds that inductive probability has two basic and coequal aspects, the one a priori and the other pragmatic. The a priori aspect concerns the assignment of probability values to statements by formal rules: probability values are and should be assigned according to the rules of standard inductive logic. The pragmatic aspect concerns the application of these probability assignments: an atomic inductive probability statement does and should express a disposition to act in certain ways in conditions of uncertainty, while a system of such statements does and should express a commitment to make one's probability assignments conform to standard inductive logic (sec. 5.6).

The pragmatic theory is correct as far as it goes, but it gives no account of causal necessity, which is an essential feature of laws of nature, causal laws, and cause-effect statements (p. 478). The presupposition theory corrects this deficiency. It includes the concept of causal necessity in its account of the a priori aspect of inductive probability and it explains how causally necessary statements are verified.

According to the presupposition theory, inductive reasoning is based on a complex innate and intersubjective conceptual structure that contributes the a priori aspect of inductive reasoning and is part of man's innate structure-program complex. My account of the inductive part of this complex will employ and integrate various materials developed in the current chapter and the preceding one: the distinction between nonindexical properties and the space-time framework in which they occur (sec. 9.2, especially 9.2.2), the a priori status of causal necessity (sec. 10.2), the causal uniformity and causal existence presuppositions (sec. 9.3, especially 9.3.1 and 9.3.3), and causal models of standard inductive logic (sec. 10.3).

I speculate that in inductive reasoning man's innate structure-program complex functions very roughly in the manner of a causal model of standard inductive logic. Nature is viewed as one possible causal system among a set of possible causal systems, each of which corresponds to a set of possible causal laws. We reason inductively in order to ascertain which of these sets is actual, that is, constitutes the laws of nature. Prior to any evidence, each possible causal law has a finite unconditional probability. We make observations of the actual world, and we modify our probability assignments to possible laws in a Bayesian manner. A possible law is accepted as actual when the evidence for it is sufficient.

All the possible causal systems considered by man's innate structure-program complex are based on the same space-time framework and the same finite set of nonindexical properties. Inductive reasoning involves repetition and thus both a repeatable factor and a matrix in which repetition can occur. Nonindexical properties constitute the repeatable factor, and the space-time framework in which they occur is the matrix.

Our causal models of standard inductive logic model the exemplification of properties in a discrete manner. A cell has a finite volume, a moment has a finite duration, and at each moment a cell exemplifies one of a finite set of states. Moreover, all the cellular automata of a causal model are based on the same finite set of cell states. Now since these finitude requirements played an essential role in our account of how causal laws are verified (pp. 627–30), they constitute a third presupposition of induction.

The **limited variety principle** is: *The laws of nature are based on a finite set of nonindexical, monadic properties, each requiring a minimal space-time region for its exemplification.* The individual states of a minimal region are described by conjunctions that tell whether each basic property is or is not present. This is our final presupposition. It differs from our previous two presuppositions in that it is satisfied by the statistical models of Chapter 3 as well as by the causal models of the present chapter.

The presuppositions of induction characterize the possible causal systems of a causal model of standard inductive logic. Accordingly, they also characterize the possible causal laws considered by man's innate structure-program complex when it infers inductively from observed phenomena to its conclusion that a particular possible causal law is probably the actual causal law governing these phenomena. The limited variety principle states that all the properties involved in causal laws are ultimately derived from a finite set of basic properties. We consider next whether this is a plausible restriction on man's innate conceptual structure for induction.

Man's innate conceptual structure for induction may be understood by analogy with a digital computer or information processing machine (p. 612). The limited variety principle characterizes as finite the input or observational data to be processed. It implies that man works with minimal space-time regions and distinguishes only finitely many observational properties within such a region. I argue next that the limited variety principle does hold for man's innate structure-program complex.*

A very small difference in sensory stimulus may cause a very large difference in motor response, yet there is a limit to the fineness of detail that can make a difference to a human response. It follows that there is a smallest difference in stimuli intensity to which the organism can respond. There is also a time duration so short that the organism cannot respond to physical changes within this interval and likewise a spatial volume so small that the organism cannot detect variations over this region. Consequently, a quantum of space-time exists such that the organism can react to only a finite number of quality differences occurring in it. Since the human body is finite it is divisible into a finite number of spatial quanta, so that it can distinguish only a finite number of different possible input states. In short, man is finite in that he can experience only a finite number of occurrences of a finite number of properties in his lifetime.

In this respect, a finite cellular automaton is a good model of the human being. Man's spatial quantum corresponds to the automaton cell, man's temporal quantum corresponds to the discrete moment of the automaton, and the minimal distinguishable stimulus intensity to which man can respond corresponds to the finite number of states of a cell. Therefore, man's innate structure-program complex distinguishes only finitely many properties in any finite space-time region.

Now actual space-time seems continuous and science normally uses continuous functions to describe nature. Seemingly, then, a minimal space-time region has infinitely many logically possible states, not finitely many. Hence there is a finite-infinite discrepancy between man's innate conceptual structure and his scientific theories. I suggest that the continuity of the latter is an idealized construction from the discreteness of the former. The problem here is closely related to that of reconciling the use of real numbers and similar idealizations in empirical theories with the fact that all scientific measurements and observations are approximate.

I am using causal models of standard inductive logic to suggest in a most general way how man's innate structure-program complex functions in induction. These models are at best simple idealizations of a very complicated structure. I shall now discuss two respects in which the models are overly restrictive and how these restrictions might be relaxed.

A causal model of standard inductive logic is based on contiguous causal laws, which satisfy Hume's requirement that immediate causes be spatially and temporally contiguous to their effects. Though most of the laws science considers satisfy this requirement, not all do. Moreover, whether or not the basic laws of science are contiguous is an empirical question, to be settled by science, not by inductive logic (p. 570).

* See also my "Logic, Computers, and Men."

The contiguity requirement of a causal model can be weakened to accommodate action-at-a-distance. Action-over-a-time-interval could be handled in a similar way. Consider all possible laws based on a finite neighborhood, and let p (=1, 2, 3, . . .) be the number of cells between a given cell and its most remote neighbor. Contiguous causal laws are ones for which $p = 1$, and these are the only possible laws considered in the causal models of Section 10.3.

Better causal models are obtained by considering all laws based on finite neighborhoods. Since there are infinitely many such laws, they cannot be assigned equal prior probabilities. But laws operating over greater distances can be assigned lower probabilities. Thus the laws with $p = 1$ can be assigned a total prior probability of 1/2, those of $p = 2$ a total prior probability of 1/4, and in general those for any fixed p value a total prior probability of 2^{-p}. In these revised models, spatially remote direct causal connections are possible, but they are less likely than contiguous causal connections. Newton's misgivings about action-at-a-distance are thus reflected in these models by the fact that laws involving action-at-a-distance have lower prior probabilities than contiguous laws.

The second respect in which causal models of standard inductive logic are too restrictive is that our causal uniformity principle allows no exceptions. But one can envisage minor variations of the laws of nature under which the Bayesian model of induction would still work. For example, laws of nature could vary slowly over space and time, and these variations might be discovered by inductive inference. The requirement that all causally possible universes satisfy our uniformity principle could be relaxed in the same way as the contiguity restriction. Weaker uniformity principles would also be included in the causal models but would have lower prior probabilities than the causal uniformity principle. On the other hand, there are limits to how much variation can be allowed. If the variation were too great, man would never be able to start the empirical confirmation process. As we argued earlier, successful inductive inquiry presupposes that the laws of nature be quasi-local and inductively simple (p. 571). More generally, induction presupposes a certain degree of simplicity in nature, and so simplicity has a basic evidential value in addition to its economic value (cf. p. 21).

Before closing this discussion of the a priori aspect of inductive probability, we need to consider the epistemological status of the concept of inductive probability. We argued in the first part of this chapter that the concept of causal necessity is a priori (sec. 10.2.2). It is evident now that the notion of inductive probability plays an equally fundamental role in man's innate conceptual structure for induction, indicating that it too is a priori. I think it is. Arguments similar to those adduced for causal necessity show that the concept of inductive probability cannot be abstracted from experience but rather is derived by reflecting on our own use of probability to guide our actions. The concept of inductive probability is clearly modal, involving numerical assignments to possible universes (secs. 2.3.1, 3.2.2, 10.3). Hence we can say of inductive probability, as we said of causal necessity, that it is a priori and irreducibly modal (p. 622).

10.4.2 Epistemological status of the presuppositions

At the outset of this treatise, we distinguished logical from empirical statements in terms of the way each kind of statement is established or refuted. A logically true-or-false statement is one whose truth-value can be established by defining, intuiting, reflecting, calculating, or reasoning alone, without the use of observation or experiment. Logically true statements may be used in the verification or refutation of empirical statements. But an empirically true-or-false statement cannot be confirmed or disconfirmed without the use of observation and/or experiment (p. 6).

After developing the distinction between deductive and inductive reasoning, we saw that our definition of "logically true-or-false" is ambiguous between these two kinds of reasoning. Correspondingly, there are two senses of the term "reason": the broad ordinary sense that encompasses standard inductive logic and a narrower technical sense that is limited to deduction. When we use the term "logically true-or-false" without qualification, it is in the latter sense (sec. 5.6.3).

For convenience, we restate our original definitions of "logical" and "empirical," making explicit the distinction between inductive and deductive reasoning. The truth-value of a **logically true-or-false statement** can be established or refuted, in principle, by *deductive* reasoning alone, without the use of observation or experiment. Included within the scope of deductive reasoning are such activities as defining, intuiting, reflecting, and calculating. An **empirically true-or-false statement** can be confirmed or disconfirmed, in principle, by observation, experiment, *deductive* reasoning, and inductive reasoning; an empirically true-or-false statement cannot be confirmed or disconfirmed without the use of observation and/or experiment, but deductive reasoning and inductive reasoning may not be needed.

Clearly our definitions of "logical" and "empirical" leave room for a third kind of statement. Since the process of verifying empirical statements involves the use of atomic inductive probability statements, the latter cannot be empirical. True atomic inductive probability statements and the theorems of the calculus of inductive probability are logically true in the broad sense; however, because of their pragmatic aspect they are not logically true in the technical sense (pp. 160, 318). Our argument for this conclusion was based on statistical models of induction, but the conclusion still holds when our more realistic causal models of standard inductive logic are included. These models have a richer structure than the statistical models, and using one of them to reason inductively involves a stronger commitment than using a statistical model. Hence true atomic inductive probability statements and the theorems of the calculus of inductive probability are neither logical nor empirical truths but are truths of a third kind.

Our three presuppositions of induction are foundational to standard inductive logic, and hence to atomic inductive probability statements. To reason inductively in the manner of a causal model of standard inductive logic is to presuppose that these three principles are true; thus the validity of an inductive argument is relative to them. This implies that they are also of a third kind. We argue that such indeed is the case. The argument is brief, since it involves the same considerations used to show that inductive probability statements are of a third kind.

The three presuppositions characterize the possible causal systems of a causal model. These systems are the alternative conceptions of nature considered in induction. To show that the presuppositions are not logically true, it suffices to describe conceptions of nature that do not satisfy them.

The limited variety principle states that there are a finite number of basic nonindexical properties, each requiring a minimal space-time region for its exemplification. This principle is satisfied by the possible universes of a statistical model of induction and of a causal model of induction. But it is logically conceivable that there should be infinitely many different properties realizable in a finite space-time region.* Indeed, the ordinary scientific description of physical reality in terms of continuous quantity is of this sort.

The causal existence and uniformity principles involve causal necessity, and thus they describe a modal model of the logic of causal statements (sec. 6.3). There are many models of nature in which these two principles are false. The basic laws governing nature might be probabilistic rather than causal, as in Peirce's tychism. Nature might have no modal structure. For example, in a statistical model of induction nature consists of a single universe, the actual universe. Finally, nature might have the structure of a modal model of standard inductive logic but nevertheless not satisfy the causal uniformity and existence principles.

Let us elaborate the last alternative. The causal existence principle states that some space-time region is governed by quasi-local laws, at least for the most part. Yet it is conceivable that nature is governed by a single global law that is not reducible to quasi-local laws. For example, small variations in the state of one local region might directly produce large variations in the state of a distant local region.

The causal uniformity principle states that if a causal connection

* Carnap has considered statistical models of induction that have infinitely many properties. See Sec. 26 of his "Replies and Systematic Expositions." However, in Carnap's models, the probability of a universal statement (All *A*'s are *B*'s) is always zero.

between nonindexical properties holds in one region of space-time, it holds throughout space-time. However, as Hume said, "we can at least conceive a change in the course of nature."* It is logically possible for causal connections to hold in one region of space-time and not in another. For example, dry gunpowder that is ignited before a certain point in time might explode, but not thereafter. Likewise, Newton's inverse square law of gravity might alternate periodically with an inverse cube law. Note that if causal connections reversed periodically, and one did not know the length of the period, the correct rule of induction would be somewhat like inverse inductive logic. One should reason: the more often this "effect" has followed that "cause," the less likely is it to do so the next time. In all these cases one could correctly infer counterfactual subjunctives from these hypothetical causal laws and theories even though they violate the causal uniformity principle.

Thus the presuppositions of induction are not logically true-or-false. We show next that they are not empirically true-or-false. Some empirical statements are established or refuted by direct observation. But most empirical statements are confirmed or disconfirmed inductively, that is, by means of standard inductive logic. Since the causal uniformity, causal existence, and limited variety principles are presupposed by standard inductive logic, the use of this logic to verify them would be circular. Hume's thesis that there is no noncircular justification of standard inductive logic applies to the presuppositions of induction also (p. 134).

We conclude that the presuppositions of induction are neither logical nor empirical, but are statements of a third kind. True atomic inductive probability statements and theorems of the calculus of inductive probability are also of this third kind. All these statements belong to standard inductive logic and are thus assumed or employed in the confirmation or disconfirmation of nonobservational empirical statements. They are sufficiently important to deserve a name; let us call them **inductive statements.**

To explain further the nature of inductive statements, we relate them to pragmatism. On the one hand, they are exceptions to Peirce's pragmatic principle of meaning. On the other hand, they are essentially pragmatic in character.

Peirce's pragmatic principle of meaning is the principle that the meaning of a nonlogical statement consists in the set of those practical conditionals that are logically implied by the statement. This principle is intended to clarify the meaning of any general statement that is not logically true-or-false in terms of statements of a different kind, practical conditionals. But practical conditionals are causally necessary statements, requiring the use of standard inductive logic for their verification. Since standard inductive

* *Treatise*, p. 89. Cf. p. 135 above.

logic consists of inductive statements, pragmatism does not account for the meaning of these statements.

The pragmatist may counter that inductive statements have no practical consequences and hence by his theory are meaningless. But since his analysis of meaning presupposes them, it cannot be applied to them without begging the very question at issue. Hence Peirce's pragmatic principle of meaning does not cover all nonlogical statements as he claimed. It is at best an analysis of empirically true-or-false statements. The same criticism applies to operationalism and the verifiability principle of meaning (pp. 167 and 172–76).

Yet all inductive statements have a pragmatic aspect and are therefore essentially pragmatic in character. True atomic inductive probability statements and theorems of the calculus of inductive probability are inductive-method commitive, expressing a commitment to use an inductive logic, in particular, standard inductive logic. It is because of this pragmatic aspect that these statements are not logically true (p. 318). The presuppositions of induction are foundational to standard inductive logic, and so they share this pragmatic aspect.

10.5 Historical Antecedents

10.5.1 Keynes' principles of induction

The chief antecedents of my presupposition theory are Hume's views on the justification of induction, Kant's theory of causal necessity, and Keynes' limited variety principle. Because the presupposition theory is speculative and somewhat sketchy, comparing it to its antecedents will help clarify and explain it. We have in effect done this for Hume (sec. 3.3.2), and we do it now for Keynes and Kant.

We saw in our review of a priori theories of probability that Keynes' *A Treatise on Probability* presents a nondeductive version of this theory (sec. 5.7.1). The materials of interest here occur mostly in Chapter 22, entitled "The Justification of These Methods."* Keynes grounds induction on three principles: a principle concerning the plurality of causes, a uniformity of nature principle, and his limited variety principle. Keynes actually states each of these assumptions with a probabilistic qualification. But he does not specify what the alternatives to them are, and he makes no use of this probabilistic qualification in his derivation of standard inductive logic.

His principle concerning the plurality of causes is: For each event, there is a finite probability that it has a single cause. I do not see the need for this principle, even in Keynes' theory; hence I shall say no more about it.

* Pp. 251-64. See also pp. 221, 226, 248-50, 274-77, and 427-28.

His uniformity of nature principle is: "*Mere* position in time and space cannot possibly affect, as a determining cause, any other character" (p. 255). He gives no analysis of causality, but his uniformity principle is consonant with my causal uniformity principle. Keynes calls his third principle "the hypothesis of the limitation of independent variety" and the "Inductive Hypothesis." To distinguish it from our somewhat different limited variety principle, we call it "Keynes' limited variety principle." Because it is Keynes' most important and original contribution to inductive logic, we quote him at length.

Keynes introduces the principle by saying that induction assumes something like

> . . . what mathematicians call the principle of the superposition of small effects, or, as I prefer to call it, in this connection, the *atomic* character of natural law. The system of the material universe must consist, if this kind of assumption is warranted, of bodies which we may term . . . *legal atoms*, such that each of them exercises its own separate, independent, and invariable effect, a change of the total state being compounded of a number of separate changes each of which is solely due to a separate portion of the preceding state. [P. 249]
>
> The ultimate constituents together with the laws of necessary connection make up what I shall term the *independent variety* of the system. [P. 251]

Keynes' limited variety principle asserts that this independent variety is finite.

> . . . the qualities of an object are bound together in a limited number of *groups*, a sub-class of each group being an infallible symptom of the coexistence of certain other members of it also. [P. 252]

> . . . the objects in the field, over which our generalisations extend, do not have an infinite number of independent qualities; . . . in other words, their characteristics, however numerous, cohere together in groups of invariable connection, which are finite in number. [P. 256]

Thus Keynes holds that nature is based on a finite causal atomism.

Keynes argues that his three assumptions yield standard inductive logic. The details are not worked out, but the general idea is this. By his limited variety principle, there are only a finite number of possible laws to consider. Each is assigned a finite prior probability. Keynes is not explicit, but his earlier discussion of indifference suggests that he intended to assign each possible law the same probability. In this discussion he defends a modified form of the traditional Principle of Non-Sufficient Reason, which he calls the "Principle of Indifference." This asserts that

> . . . if there is no *known* reason for predicating of our subject one rather than another of several alternatives, then relatively to such knowledge the assertions of each of these alternatives has an *equal* probability. [P. 42]

After discussing the paradoxes and contradictions to which this principle leads (since there are in general many different ways of arranging data in a symmetrical manner) he qualifies it by saying

> . . . our relevant evidence . . . must be symmetrical with regard to the alternatives, and must be applicable to each in the same manner. [Pp. 55–56]

Keynes' derivation of standard inductive logic from his basic principles is very brief.

> . . . if we find two sets of qualities in coexistence there is a finite probability that they belong to the same group, and a finite probability also that the first set specifies this group uniquely. Starting from this assumption, the object of the methods is to increase the finite probability and make it large. Whether or not anything of this sort is explicitly present to our minds when we reason scientifically, it seems clear to me that we do act exactly as we should act, if this were the assumption from which we set out. [P. 253]

Thus the finite prior possibility of a possible law gives a start, and instantiation raises the probability.*

The influence of Keynes' views on mine should be clear from the above quotations. My limited variety principle was suggested by Keynes', though his encompasses my causal existence principle as well. Likewise, my derivation of standard inductive logic in a causal model stems from his embryonic derivation.

After giving his derivation, Keynes discusses "the justification of these methods." He believes that we have "direct knowledge" (in contrast to "knowledge based on experience") of some causal connections between our own acts.

> We have numerous experiences in our own person of acts which are associated with states of consciousness, and we infer that similar acts in others are likely to be associated with similar states of consciousness. . . . We do seem in this case to have direct knowledge, such as we have in no other case, that our states of consciousness are, sometimes at least, causally connected with some of our acts. [P. 257]

He tentatively suggests an a priori, nondeductive justification for using standard inductive logic.

> . . . we are capable of direct knowledge about empirical entities which goes beyond a mere expression of our understanding or sensation of them. We do believe, and yet have no adequate inductive reason whatever for believing, that mere position in time and space cannot make any difference. This belief arises directly, I think, out of our acquaintance with the objects of experience and our understanding of the concepts of

* See also Nicod, *Foundations of Geometry and Induction*, pp. 222 ff.

'time' and 'space.' . . . In a way analogous to [this], the validity of assuming the Inductive Hypothesis, as applied to a particular class of objects, appears to me to be justified.

Our justification for using inductive methods in an argument about numbers arises out of our perceiving directly, when we understand the meaning of a number, that they are of the required character. (Since numbers are logical entities, it may be thought less unorthodox to make such an assumption in their case.) And when we perceive the nature of our phenomenal experiences, we have a direct assurance that in their case also the assumption is legitimate. We are capable, that is to say, of direct synthetic knowledge about the nature of the objects of our experience. [Pp. 263–64]

I shall formulate in my own terminology what Keynes is saying here and then criticize it. His uniformity of nature and limited variety principles are not logically true in our narrow, technical sense of that term (p. 316), and they are not empirically true. Keynes says that we have "direct synthetic knowledge" of them. Though he does not use the term, it is plausible to say that he regards them as "synthetic a priori truths."* He is explicit that they are intuitive (self-evident) rather than demonstrative. Thus Keynes holds that the uniformity of nature and limited variety principles are intuitively true synthetic a priori statements.

I agree that the principles underlying induction are neither empirical nor logical but belong to a third category. However, I do not believe that Keynes' justification succeeds. When fully formulated, his uniformity of nature and limited variety principles must be stated in terms of causal necessity (secs. 9.3 and 10.3). This concept is a priori, not empirical; we cannot directly experience instances of it (sec. 10.2.2). It is therefore implausible that we can see directly that synthetic a priori principles involving it are true. My analysis of the role of the presuppositions in inductive inference shows that they may be used to transcend immediate experiences, and this also makes it implausible that they are intuitively self-evident. Hence, Keynes' direct justification argument fails, and he has not derived the pragmatic aspect of inductive probability from the a priori aspect.

Let us summarize the relation of the presupposition theory to Keynes' theory. My limited variety principle is closely related to his, and the derivation of standard inductive logic in a causal model stems from his derivation. The presupposition theory and Keynes' theory agree that true atomic inductive probability statements and the theorems of the calculus of inductive probability are neither empirical nor logical. There is nevertheless a crucial difference between the two theories. Keynes attempts an a priori justification for using standard inductive logic. The presupposition theory holds that there is no such justification. For it, the a priori and pragmatic aspects of inductive probability are coequal.

* See my "On the Presuppositions of Induction," p. 606.

10.5.2 Kant's theory of causality

In his *Critique of Pure Reason*, Immanuel Kant developed a grand theory about man's innate structure-program complex. We are directly interested here in only a small part of Kant's theory, but because the theory is highly integrated we must briefly survey the whole.

According to Kant, man's innate structure-program complex provides the a priori forms of all experience. This complex has two levels: a lower level of immediate knowledge (sense and intuition) and a higher level of mediate knowledge (conception and judgment).

> . . . there are two stems of human knowledge, namely, *sensibility* and *understanding*, which perhaps spring from a common, but to us unknown, root. Through the former, objects are given to us; through the latter, they are thought . . . the conditions under which alone the objects of human knowledge are given must precede those under which they are thought. . . .*

Sensibility contains two a priori forms of intuition, space and time. Sensations are arranged in these two forms and thereby acquire a spatio-temporal organization. These spatially and temporally arranged sensations are organized in the understanding by a conceptual structure containing four triads of a priori categories (concepts). The triads of most interest to us are substance-cause-reciprocity and possibility-actuality-necessity.

An important part of Kant's theory is his doctrine of the synthetic a priori. There are synthetic a priori statements associated with both the level of sensibility and the level of understanding. Statements of geometry and arithmetic are synthetic a priori statements of sensibility: geometry studies intuitive space and arithmetic studies intuitive time. Each of the twelve categories of the understanding is governed by a basic synthetic a priori principle; for example, determinism is the synthetic a priori principle of causality.

These two kinds of statements, those of mathematics and those of the categories, have much in common; Kant calls both kinds simply "synthetic a priori." But they differ in respects crucial to the nature of causality and induction, and for a proper grasp of Kant's position on that subject the two kinds of statements must be sharply distinguished. We will call those of geometry and arithmetic "mathematical synthetic a priori," and those associated with the twelve categories "categorial synthetic a priori." Let us now look at each in greater detail.

For Kant, mathematical statements are a priori because they concern our a priori forms of intuition and hence can be certified by reasoning alone. These statements are synthetic because they treat of constructions syn-

* *Critique of Pure Reason*, pp. 61-62 (B29-30).

thesized in intuition. Kant says very little about arithmetic constructions, and he fails to relate them to time in an essential way.* In contrast, his analysis of geometry is careful, plausible, and clear. Geometry treats of Euclidean figures (points, lines, angles, triangles, etc.) synthesized or constructed in intuitive space. To establish a theorem of geometry one inspects or reasons about these intuitive constructions. Hence geometrical statements are both synthetic and a priori.

As we saw earlier, Euclidean geometry does appear to be both synthetic and a priori. But this appearance is best explained by distinguishing interpreted geometric statements, which are empirical, from logical (deductive) interrelations among such statements. Moreover, Kant makes the questionable assumption that physical space has the same structure as intuitive space. Even if his views about intuitive space are correct, geometric statements about physical space are empirically true-or-false (see sec. 1.2.2).

We turn next to the categorial synthetic a priori statements, those associated with the categories of the understanding. Kant offers a proof that these twelve categories apply to all possible experience. This proof is his famous "transcendental deduction" of the categories, which is one of the most recondite arguments in the history of philosophy. But though Kant's transcendental argument is hard to follow, his conclusion is clear enough. It is that every one of the twelve categories is an a priori concept that plays a role in organizing experience; moreover, this is the only way to account for experience. As far as causality is concerned, Kant's transcendental deduction of the categories purports to show, among other things, that this concept is a priori rather than empirical, and it involves necessity. See the second quotation at the head of this chapter (p. 607).

Kant also states a basic categorial synthetic a priori principle for each category and offers a transcendental proof of each such principle. These principles are synthetic because they concern the way in which the understanding synthesizes or constructs experiences from sensations. They are a priori because they are applied to experience by the understanding and hence can be established by transcendental proofs. We are interested in the synthetic a priori principle associated with causality:

* Kant's writings on arithmetic were important historically, for they influenced L. E. J. Brouwer's intuitionism, which also holds that mathematics is about constructions in intuition. See the first few pages of Brouwer's "Intuitionism and Formalism."

I once asked Brouwer if his philosophy of mathematics was influenced historically by Kant. He replied that it was and said that he read Kant as a youth. He found many things difficult to understand, but was stimulated and intrigued. He rejected Kant's doctrine of space, saying that Euclidean geometry applies to rigid physical bodies, and that if we were fish we would not find geometrical concepts useful. But he thought his theory of the relation of time to mathematics was very close to Kant's.

Principle of Succession in time, in accordance with the Law of Causality. All alterations take place in conformity with the law of the connection of cause and effect.*

This is a formulation of determinism; Kant was attempting a transcendental proof of the truth of determinism. He seemed to think this proof constituted a nondeductive demonstrative justification of induction and so was a refutation of Hume's thesis that there is no noncircular justification of induction (sec. 3.3).

With this brief survey of Kant's system as a background, I can now compare and contrast my position with his. As a first step, I compare our

TABLE 24

THREE CLASSIFICATIONS OF STATEMENTS COMPARED

<table>
<tr><th colspan="2">Kant</th><th>Our classification</th><th>Hume</th></tr>
<tr><td colspan="2">SYNTHETIC A POSTERIORI</td><td>EMPIRICAL</td><td>MATTERS OF FACT</td></tr>
<tr><td colspan="2">ANALYTIC A PRIORI</td><td rowspan="2">LOGICAL</td><td rowspan="2">RELATIONS OF IDEAS</td></tr>
<tr><td rowspan="2">SYNTHETIC A PRIORI</td><td>MATHEMATICAL SYNTHETIC A PRIORI</td></tr>
<tr><td>CATEGORIAL SYNTHETIC A PRIORI:
Law of Causality (determinism)

Categorial principles of the other eleven categories (substance, actuality, etc.)</td><td>INDUCTIVE:
Causal uniformity, causal existence, and limited variety principles

Inductive probability statements and theorems</td><td>Hume's uniformity of nature principle</td></tr>
</table>

classifications of statements. In a broad sense these classifications are remarkably similar, and also similar to Hume's. See Table 24. My category of inductive statements includes the three presuppositions, all true atomic inductive probability statements, and the theorems of the calculus of inductive probability. These inductive statements are to be compared and contrasted with Kant's Law of Causality and Hume's uniformity of nature principle. Of course, though the statements in the bottom boxes of Table 24 play comparable roles in our three philosophies, our epistemological theories of them differ.

Kant divided statements into three basic kinds: synthetic a posteriori, analytic a priori, and synthetic a priori. When his synthetic a priori statements are subdivided into the mathematical and categorial, as we have done,

* *Critique of Pure Reason*, p. 218 (B232). Kant also calls this principle the second "analogy."

the classification becomes fourfold. But there is good reason now to group together the analytic a priori and the mathematical synthetic a priori, so that the classification becomes trichotomous again. Kant's analytic a priori statements consisted of definitions and the propositions of traditional logic. Traditional logic studied simple tautologies and simple subject-predicate statements and thus corresponds to a limited part of first-order quantification theory. For Kant, Euclidean geometry and arithmetic constituted the foundations of mathematics. There was a large gap between traditional logic and mathematics in his time, and Kant quite naturally saw these subjects as very different. This gap has since been filled by developments in logic and the foundations of mathematics, so that there is now no sharp dividing line between logic and mathematics (cf. pp. 16–17). It is therefore better to group together Kant's analytic a priori and mathematical synthetic a priori statements, as we have done in our category of logically true-or-false statements.

For Kant, determinism is a synthetic a priori principle of the understanding and hence is what we called a categorial synthetic a priori statement. Determinism entails my causal existence and causal uniformity presuppositions (p. 578); therefore, in Kant's system they would also be categorial synthetic a priori statements. I argued that these presuppositions were neither logical nor empirical, but of a third kind of statement, which I called "inductive" (sec. 10.4.2). Hence my classification of the presuppositions of induction is similar to Kant's. As Table 24 shows, however, there is only a small overlap of the class of categorial synthetic a priori statements with my class of inductive statements.

My reworking of Kant's classification of statements emphasizes the differences between the mathematical and the categorial synthetic a priori more than others have done. Kant himself, though, does treat these two types of statements under two different headings, "transcendental aesthetic" (the theory of sensibility) and "transcendental logic" (the theory of understanding). He uses different kinds of arguments for the two kinds of statements. Finally, on Kant's own account, mathematical proofs, which establish mathematical synthetic a priori statements, are very different from his transcendental proofs, which establish categorial synthetic a priori statements.

Of course, Kant places greater emphasis on the similarities between the mathematical and the categorial synthetic a priori. Both involve synthesis and construction in a general sense. But my classes of logical and inductive statements are also similar in important respects. For me, both deductive and inductive statements are logically true-or-false in the broad sense of "logical" (sec. 5.6.3). Also, the a priori aspect of inductive probability is rich and complicated, involving a great deal of reasoning (sec. 10.4.1). According to my account, the differences between logical (in the narrow sense) and inductive statements appear only in the foundational analysis of deduction and induction.

The preceding historical analysis shows that Kant treated the presuppositions of induction as a third kind of statement, just as I have done. The same is true of Hume and Keynes. Hume's uniformity of nature principle is similar to mine, differing chiefly in the analysis of causal necessity. Hume said explicitly that his principle did not express a relation of ideas, for its negation is conceivable. Moreover, he treated it differently from a matter of fact, saying that we apply it as a matter of "habit" or "custom." Hume's "custom" is similar to the "pragmatic aspect" of a presupposition (pp. 135, 616, 639). Keynes held his uniformity of nature and limited variety principles to be synthetic a priori, thereby also placing them in a third category (p. 642).

Thus in classifying the presuppositions of induction as a third kind of statement I am in essential agreement with Hume, Kant, and Keynes. The differences among us concern primarily the nature of causal necessity and the epistemological status of this third kind of statement.

I agree with Kant as against Hume that the concept of causal necessity is a priori rather than empirical, and my conception of man's innate structure-program complex is similar to Kant's theory of the understanding (sec. 10.2). But my arguments are quite different from Kant's and we place causality in different contexts. He has a complicated theory of how perceptual experience is organized in terms of causality and other categories but says practically nothing about probability. The relation of probability to causality is one of my chief concerns, and for me the concept of inductive probability is also a priori.

On the other hand, I agree with Hume rather than with Kant and Keynes on the justification of induction. Kant's transcendental proof of the law of causality (determinism) is an attempt to give a nondeductive, *demonstrative* justification of induction. Keynes thinks there is a nondeductive *intuitive* justification of induction (p. 642). As against both Kant and Keynes, I advocate Hume's thesis that there is no noncircular justification of induction (sec. 3.3).

10.6 Summary of the Presupposition Theory

Since the **presupposition theory of induction** has been developed over several chapters, a definitive summary of it may be useful. The presupposition theory is my answer to the fourth main question: What is the nature of causal necessity ($\Box^c$) and how are causal necessity and inductive probability (**P**) related? (P. 30) This theory also provides my final answer to the first main question: What is the general nature of a system of inductive probability statements? (Pp. 29, 92)

The presupposition theory incorporates the pragmatic theory of inductive probability and hence the double aspect view of probability. A system of atomic inductive probability statements has two interrelated but coequal aspects, an a priori aspect and a pragmatic aspect. The a priori aspect concerns the assignment of probability values to statements by formal rules. Probability values are and should be assigned according to the rules of standard inductive logic. The presupposition theory conceives these rules in terms of a causal model of standard inductive logic; thus it has a broader view of them than the pragmatic theory, which conceives them in terms of a statistical model of standard inductive logic (cf. secs. 3.2 and 10.3).

The pragmatic aspect of inductive probability concerns the application of these probability assignments. An atomic inductive probability statement does and should express a disposition to act or "bet" in certain ways under conditions of uncertainty; in a generalized sense of "betting," the subject's belief in $\mathbf{P}(c, d) = x$ expresses a commitment to bet on the pair c, d with odds x to $1 - x$. A system of atomic inductive probability statements does and should express a commitment to make one's probability assignments conform to the calculus of probability and standard inductive logic. Since the rule of maximizing utility plays a dominant role in the application of probability theory to action, the pragmatic aspect of inductive probability involves the concept of utility. The calculus of choice explicates the concepts of probability and utility as these concepts are reflected and should be reflected in the choices of a single subject.

The descriptive and the normative claims of the presupposition theory are subject to certain qualifications. Descriptively, the calculus of probability, standard inductive logic, and the calculus of choice are only fair models of actual inductive reasoning and decision-making. Normatively, one should generally follow these three axiomatic systems when reasoning inductively and making decisions. But the difficulties of the traditional theory of utility show that there are important exceptions to this general rule. These difficulties are resolved by limiting informally the scope of some of the axioms of the calculus of choice. (Secs. 5.6, 10.4.1)

The presupposition theory holds that the a priori aspect of inductive probability is contributed by man's innate structure-program complex. Causal necessity and inductive probability are a priori concepts that are part of this innate complex (sec. 10.4.1). In inductive reasoning, nature is viewed as one possible causal system among many, each of which has an unconditional inductive probability.

These possible causal systems are all based on the same space-time framework and the same finite set of nonindexical properties (secs. 9.2.1–9.2.2). The properties constitute the repeatable factor in induction, while the space-time framework is the matrix in which repetition occurs. Each possible causal system contains a set of causally possible universes. Nature is the actual causal system, its set of causally possible universes correspond to causal necessity ($\Box^c$), and one of its universes is the actual universe.

Causally necessary statements are verified by a Bayesian process. Unconditional inductive probabilities (**P**) are assigned to possible causal systems and to the causally possible universes within them. Since a possible causal system corresponds to a set of possible laws, each law of this set has a finite probability prior to any empirical evidence. To confirm or disconfirm a possible law, one makes observations of the actual universe and assesses the law's posterior probability. When a possible causal law has sufficient posterior probability, he accepts it as a law of nature. (Secs. 9.2.4, 10.3–10.4)

The possible causal systems we consider in induction, and a fortiori our concept of nature, satisfy three presuppositions. The causal uniformity principle is: If a causal connection between nonindexical properties holds in one region of space-time, it holds throughout space-time. The causal existence principle is: Some space-time region is governed by quasi-local laws, at least for the most part. These two principles are conjointly equivalent to the disjunction of determinism and near-determinism. The third presupposition is the limited variety principle: The laws of nature are based on a finite set of nonindexical, monadic properties, each requiring a minimal space-time region for its exemplification. These presuppositions entail that there are only a finite number of possible contiguous causal laws. Non-contiguous laws are assigned less prior probability than contiguous laws. (Secs. 9.3, 10.4.1, 10.5.1).

We developed causal models of standard inductive logic to suggest how man's innate structure-program complex functions in induction. These models combine the repetitive feature of a statistical model of standard inductive logic, the modality of a model for the logic of causal statements, and the space-time framework of cellular automata. Cellular automata are discrete space-time systems, space being divided into finite cells and time into discrete moments. Each cell is in one of a finite set of nonindexical cell states at each moment.

A causal cellular automaton is governed by a transition rule describing the direct causal influence of a cell on its contiguous neighbors. For each assignment of cell states to the neighborhood of a cell, the transition rule gives a list of one or more next cell states of that cell. A transition rule is equivalent to a consistent set of contiguous causal laws, and it defines a set of causally possible histories or universes. Thus a causal cellular automaton is a finite discrete space-time system governed by contiguous causal laws. All causal cellular automata satisfy the causal uniformity and limited variety principle by definition. Causal cellular automata that satisfy the causal existence principle are either deterministic or near-deterministic. (Secs. 9.2.3–9.2.4)

A causal model of standard inductive logic consists of a set of possible causal systems and an assignment of unconditional inductive probabilities to these systems. The possible causal systems of a model are those causal cellular automata with some fixed number of cell states that satisfy the causal existence principle. Each system contains a set of causally possible universes. Equal unconditional probabilities are assigned to the possible causal systems of a model and, within each system, to finite space-time portions of its causally possible universes.

A possible causal law holds in some possible causal systems but not in others and hence has a finite unconditional prior probability. The degree of prediction of an instance of a possible law is greater relative to that law than to its negation. By Bayes' theorem, if an instance statement is verified, the posterior probability of the possible law is then greater than its prior probability. Repeated observation of instances establishes a contiguous causal law. This explains how causally necessary statements are confirmed by nonmodal observation statements. (Secs. 10.3–10.4)

At the outset we distinguished two basic kinds of statements involved in scientific inquiry. Logically true-or-false statements are established or refuted by deductive reasoning alone. Empirical statements are confirmed or disconfirmed by the joint use of observation-experiment, deductive reasoning, and inductive reasoning. Our analysis of induction shows that it employs true atomic inductive probability statements, theorems of the calculus of inductive probability, and the presuppositions of induction. These statements are neither logical nor empirical but constitute a third class, that of inductive statements. (Secs. 10.4.2, 10.5.2)

11 Chance, Cause, and Reason

But though [metaphysics] is older than all other sciences, and would survive even if all the rest were swallowed up in an abyss of an all-destroying barbarism, it has not yet had the good fortune to enter upon the secure path of a science.*

11.1 Fundamental Concepts

We have almost completed our inquiry into the nature of scientific evidence. Our treatment has been necessarily long, for the subject is complex and involves many distinct but interrelated issues. The meanings of the most basic terms have been specified in successive stages and our main questions have been revised more than once.

To delineate the central thread of our argument, let us review the key terms, state the main questions in final form, and indicate where our answers are given and the answers of other philosophers discussed. We shall conclude by showing how to combine our answers into a single unified theory of probability, causality, and induction. This last chapter may also serve the reader as a guide to the contents of the book.

The chief concepts fall under the headings "chance," "cause," and "reason."

Chance. Philosophically, the most important kinds of chance are inductive probability ($\mathbf{P}$) and empirical probability ($\mathbf{P}_e$). These concepts are also modal, involving numerical assignments to possible universes or sequences. Other types of chance are nonmodal, pertaining to single universes or sequences. The notions of relative frequency (σ_L), frequency probability ($\mathbf{P}_f$), statistical uniformity, and various forms of sequence randomness (including entropy) are of this type.

Cause. The most fundamental causal notion is the modal concept of causal necessity. Laws of nature, causal laws, causal dispositions, cause-effect relations, determinism, and near-determinism all involve causal necessity ($\Box^c$).

Reason. We have investigated the ultimate nature of the knowledge acquired by the empirical sciences, in which two kinds of reason play essential roles: deduction and induction. Since deduction, the subject matter as well as the tool of mathematics, has already received much scholarly attention, we limit ourselves to a review of deductive reasoning and concentrate primarily on inductive reasoning.

* Kant, *Critique of Pure Reason*, p. 21 (B xiv).

Mathematics differs from the empirical sciences in both methods and results. Statements of mathematics are shown to be true by deductive reasoning, with observation and experiment playing no essential role. In contrast, statements of empirical science cannot be established by deductive reasoning alone; observation or experiment is required, and usually inductive reasoning also. There are thus at least two basically different kinds of statements: a logically true-or-false statement can be established or refuted, in principle, by deductive reasoning alone, whereas an empirically true-or-false statement can be confirmed or disconfirmed only by means of observation and/or experiment. (Secs. 1.2–1.5, 5.6.3, 6.3.3, 10.4.2)

We next review in more detail the fundamental concepts involved in inductive reasoning.

Inductive probability (**P**). Inductive probability is probability in an evidential sense, as it occurs in an inductive argument. An atomic inductive probability statement $\mathbf{P}(c, d) = x$ asserts that condition or premise d supports conclusion c to degree x. The calculus of inductive probability relates atomic inductive probability statements to one another. It is both a descriptive and a normative model of inductive reasoning. The probabilities of actual inductive inference are conditional, but a foundational analysis of induction requires that they be reduced to unconditional form.

Of particular relevance to induction is Bayes' theorem for calculating the probability of a hypothesis after a prediction has been confirmed or disconfirmed. Bayes' theorem, Bayes' method of finding an unknown probability, and the confirmation theorem give a good account of many artificial and natural cases of confirming a hypothesis by testing its observable consequences. (Sec. 1.5.2, chap. 2, secs. 3.2.4, 8.2.1, 8.2.3, 8.3.1, and 10.3.2)

Utility (**U**). An important aspect of inductive probability, involving the concept of utility, is its relation to action in conditions of uncertainty. The utility of a consequence is the value of that consequence to the person making the choice, while the utility of an act is calculated from the probabilities and utilities of the possible consequences of that act. The rule of maximizing utility states that in choosing from among several acts, one should choose an act of maximum utility. (Chap. 4)

My calculus of choice provides a foundation for the rule of maximizing utility and for the calculus of inductive probability. A subject indicates his preferences by marking choice trees in accordance with the axioms of the calculus of choice, which require that his preferences satisfy such conditions as comparability and transitivity. The main theorem states that choices made in conformity with the axioms do in fact maximize utility and satisfy the calculus of inductive probability. Descriptively, the calculus of choice is a fair model of decision-making; normatively, one should generally follow it in making decisions, but there are exceptions. (Chap. 5)

Though the calculi of choice and of inductive probability enable one to infer some atomic inductive probability statements from others, these calculi do not in general determine the truth-status of an atomic inductive probability statement by itself (sec. 3.1). Rules for doing this belong to standard inductive logic, which we shall discuss in a moment, after first reviewing the prior concept of causal necessity.

Causal necessity—formal. The formal properties of causal necessity ($\Box^c$) are given by my logic of causal statements. This logic was presented as an algorithmic structure and then used as a formal model of ordinary and scientific discourse involving causality.

The logic of causal statements consists of first-order quantification theory extended to include both the logical modalities ($\Box, \Diamond, \rightarrow, \leftrightarrow$) and the causal modalities ($\Box^c, \Diamond^c, \underset{c}{\rightarrow}, \underset{c}{\leftrightarrow}$). Its underlying structure was defined without reference to its interpretation, by means of decision algorithms for formulahood, axiomhood, and proofhood. An abstract, idealized interpretation was given by means of simple modal models, which contain logically possible universes, causally possible universes, and an actual universe. (Chap. 6)

Causal necessity—interpreted. The abstract interpretation of Chapter 6 contrasts with the concrete interpretation of Chapter 7, where the logic of causal statements is treated as a model of natural language. Nonprobabilistic laws of nature and scientific theories are causally necessary, since they hold for sets of possible boundary conditions, most of which are nonactual. They have three main features: uniqueness, modality, and invariance over space and time. A causal law is a law of nature formulated in terms of cause and effect. Many important features of these laws may be modeled by means of nonparadoxical causal implication (**npc**).

Causal dispositionals involve elliptical or implicit information that may be symbolized with an existential statement quantifier or, equivalently, with elliptical causal implication (**ec**). Elliptical causal implication is also useful for symbolizing cause-effect relations, since, in most cases, what is ordinarily regarded as the cause is not sufficient by itself to produce the effect. In appropriate contexts, laws of nature, causal laws, and lawlike statements imply subjunctive conditionals, which may be modeled by means of nonparadoxical and elliptical causal implication.

The logic of causal statements is a good model for causal statements and arguments of ordinary discourse; it fits actual discourse well enough to show that causal necessity is an essential feature of laws of nature, causal laws, causal dispositionals, causal subjunctives, and cause-effect statements. Hence an adequate theory of inductive probability must take account of causal necessity. (Chap. 7)

Causal necessity and space-time. Induction involves repetition: nonindexical properties constitute the repeatable factor, and space-time is the framework in which repetition occurs. Space-time systems are modal, having many alternative histories. This modality is causal for the determinist and near-determinist; in contrast, Peirce's tychism holds it to be probabilistic.

Cellular automata are discrete space-time systems with contiguous laws. We used causal cellular automata to model contiguous causal laws, deterministic systems, and near-deterministic systems. (Chap. 9)

Standard inductive logic. An inductive logic is a system of rules for judging the truth-values of atomic inductive probability statements; standard inductive logic is the system of rules of inductive inference actually used and aspired to by the practicing scientist. It has as its core the calculus of inductive probability and includes in addition the method of varying relevant qualities, rules for analogy, and the rule of induction by simple enumeration. This last rule is: the more often one nonindexical property has accompanied another, the higher the likelihood that it will accompany the other.

Statistical models of induction may be defined for some highly simplified models of reality. An inductive logic for a model is constructed by assigning unconditional probabilities to the logically possible universes of the model, thereby determining the truth-value of every atomic inductive probability statement about the model. A statistical model of standard inductive logic is obtained by assigning higher probabilities to statistically uniform universes than to universes with high entropy; this assignment results in the rule of induction by simple enumeration. Other assignments produce statistical models that are deductively consistent alternatives to standard inductive logic. The most important weakness of statistical models of standard inductive logic is their failure to account for causality. (Chap. 3)

To explain how causally necessary statements are verified, we constructed causal models of standard inductive logic. A causal model consists of a set of possible causal systems, each of which is a deterministic or near-deterministic cellular automaton, together with an assignment of unconditional probabilities to these causal systems and to the causally possible universes within them. Induction by simple enumeration to a contiguous causal law results by Bayes' theorem. (Sec. 10.3)

Empirical probability ($\mathbf{P}_e$). An empirical probability statement concerns a probabilistic process or disposition. It is so defined that the observable outcomes of the process are evidentially relevant to the statement. For example, the statement "the empirical probability of this coin falling tails is α" [$\mathbf{P}_e(T) = \alpha$] assigns a degree of prediction to each possible outcome of tossing the coin. If alternative hypotheses are assigned prior probabilities and an outcome observed, the posterior probabilities can be calculated by Bayes' theorem. For example, the result "700 tosses out of 1,000 are tails" will raise the probability of "$\mathbf{P}_e(T) = .7$" and lower that of "$\mathbf{P}_e(T) = .8$". (Secs. 1.5.2, 8.2)

The notion of an empirical probability statement was generalized to that of an empirical probability theory, that is, any empirical theory that makes a complete probability assignment to the observable characteristics of a process. The procedure for verifying or rejecting an empirical probability theory is based on Bayes' theorem. The premises of the argument contain the alternative theories, their prior probabilities, and the observed result; the direct verification and predictive content of each hypothesis is given by the degree of prediction it assigns to each possible result. Probabilities posterior to the observed result are calculated by Bayes' theorem, and a hypothesis whose posterior probability is sufficiently close to unity may be asserted categorically. (Sec. 8.3.1)

11.2 Questions and Answers

We now restate the four main questions of this book and indicate where their answers are given.

(I) *What is the general nature of a system of atomic inductive probability statements?* (Pp. 29, 92) An answer to this question is given by my pragmatic theory of inductive probability, which is based on the calculus of choice developed in Chapter 5. According to the pragmatic theory, a system of atomic inductive probability statements has two interrelated but coequal aspects, an a priori aspect and a pragmatic aspect. The former concerns the assignment of probability values to statements by formal rules, while the latter concerns the application of these probability assignments in conditions of uncertainty. (Sec. 5.6 and pp. 333–35)

The pragmatic theory is satisfactory as far as it goes, but it is incomplete because it fails to account for causal necessity, which is involved in the pragmatic aspect of probability. I later incorporated the pragmatic theory in my presupposition theory of induction, which does explain causal necessity and how it is related to inductive probability.

Other answers to the first question are given by the frequency, a priori, and personalistic theories of inductive probability. The frequency theory of Peirce and Reichenbach identifies inductive probability with frequency probability (sec. 3.4.2); the a priori theory of Keynes and Carnap holds that there is an a priori justification for using standard inductive logic, so that the pragmatic aspect of inductive probability is derivable from the a priori aspect (secs. 5.7.1, 10.5.1). My own pragmatic theory is based on the personalistic theory of Ramsey, de Finetti, and Savage and is similar to it; the main difference is that the pragmatic theory includes the rules of standard inductive logic in the criteria of inductive rationality, whereas the personalistic theory does not (sec. 5.7.2).

(II) *Is a true atomic inductive probability statement logically true, empirically true, or neither? Are the theorems of the calculus of inductive probability logically true*? (Pp. 29, 92, 313) We concluded that true atomic inductive probability statements and the theorems of the calculus of inductive probability belong to a third category, that of inductive statements. Three intermediate results were used to establish this conclusion: the existence of different deductively consistent inductive logics (statistical models of induction) applicable to reality (sec. 3.3.1), my refutation of the frequency theory of inductive probability (sec. 3.4.2), and my pragmatic theory of inductive probability (sec. 5.6.3). Positive information as to the nature of statements of this third kind is given by the pragmatic and the presupposition theories.

(III) *What is the general nature of an empirical probability theory? How are empirical and inductive probabilities related? Why is the traditional calculus of probability applicable to empirical probabilities?* (Pp. 29, 144, 511) My dispositional theory of empirical probability answers this question. As the name implies, it analyzes empirical probability dispositionally. An empirical probability statement asserts that the system underlying the disposition is such that each possible observable outcome has a certain inductive probability (degree of prediction). In a context of alternative hypotheses and an assignment of prior inductive probabilities to them, these probabilistic predictions may be used to confirm or disconfirm the statement. One observes a finite portion of the process produced by the system and applies Bayes' theorem to the result.

Empirical probability theories may be modeled by probabilistic dispositional formulas that are verified and manipulated by means of the calculus of inductive probability. These dispositional models account for the applicability of the traditional calculus of probability to empirical probabilities by revealing that these applications are really applications of the calculus of inductive probability to inductive probabilities.

The dispositional theory holds that a prior probability assignment should conform to the rules of standard inductive logic. Since these rules are intersubjective, the dispositional theory explains the intersubjective character of an empirical probability theory. Inductive probability is the only kind of probability used in the dispositional analysis of an empirical probability theory; hence the dispositional theory reduces empirical probability to inductive probability. But inductive probabilities cannot be explained in terms of empirical probabilities and are therefore more basic than empirical probabilities. (Secs. 8.3.2, 8.3.4, 8.5)

We also formulated the positivistic theory of empirical probability as a possible but less adequate answer to our third question (sec. 8.3.3). Other answers to this question have been given by the frequency theory of empirical probability (secs. 3.4.1, 8.4.1), Peirce's dispositional-frequency theory of probability (sec. 8.4.2) and the personalistic account of empirical probability (sec. 8.4.3).

(IV) *What is the nature of causal necessity and how are causal necessity and inductive probability related?* (P. 30) This question is answered by my presupposition theory of induction, which was developed in Chapters 9 and 10 (with a summary in sec. 10.6).

The presupposition theory incorporates the pragmatic theory and so holds the a priori and pragmatic aspects of probability to be coequal. Further, it holds the concepts of causal necessity and inductive probability to be a priori; thus it grounds the a priori aspect of inductive probability in man's innate structure-program complex.

The presupposition theory employs the logic of causal statements (chaps. 6 and 7) and causal models of standard inductive logic (sec. 10.3). Using these models, the theory explains how causally necessary statements are confirmed by means of nonmodal data.

The possible causal systems we consider in induction satisfy three presuppositions: the causal uniformity principle, the causal existence principle, and the limited variety principle. The first two of these are conjointly equivalent to the disjunction of determinism and near-determinism. (Secs. 9.3, 10.4.1)

Our analysis of inductive reasoning shows that it employs true atomic inductive probability statements, theorems of the calculus of inductive probability, and the presuppositions of induction. These statements are neither logical nor empirical, but constitute a third class, that of inductive statements. (Secs. 5.6.3, 10.4.2, 10.5.2)

11.3 A Unified Theory of Probability, Causality, and Induction

In answering the fourth question, my presupposition theory incorporates the answers to the first and second questions. The third question is answered by my dispositional theory of empirical probability, which reduces empirical probability to inductive probability and is neutral about the nature of the latter concept. The dispositional and presuppositional theories may thus be conjoined to obtain a **unified theory of probability, causality, and induction** that answers all four questions. We now mention some further features of this unified theory and propose its adoption.

Empirical probability reduces to inductive probability, but not vice-versa (p. 517). Hence all basic laws are causal, and there are no basic probabilistic laws. This view is contrary to one form of near-determinism, which holds that some basic laws are causal and some probabilistic, and contrary to Peirce's tychism, which holds that all basic laws are probabilistic (secs. 9.3.3–9.3.4, 9.4.3).

The inductive probabilities implicit in empirical probabilities are subject to the norms of standard inductive logic. These norms are common to all men and are therefore intersubjective (sec. 8.3.4). Since the presupposition theory grounds these norms in man's innate structure-program complex, our unified theory bases the intersubjectivity of empirical probabilities on this complex.

A complete theory of chance must explain frequency concepts of probability and related concepts: number of successes (S_L), relative frequency (σ_L), frequency probability ($\mathbf{P}_f$), and various kinds of sequence randomness. We have explained all of these concepts in the process of explaining inductive probability (secs. 2.4–2.5, 3.2.4, 8.2.3, and 9.4.2). Frequency concepts of probability express properties of single sequences or universes. Frequency probability is the limiting case of relative frequency, applying only to infinite sequences or universes. In contrast, inductive probability involves numerical assignments to sets of universes. There are many interesting theorems relating these two kinds of concepts, such as the law of large numbers and the confirmation theorem. Hence my unified theory relates frequency probability to inductive probability in this way: frequency concepts apply to single universes and are nonmodal, while inductive probability applies to sets of universes and is modal.

We therefore answer the four questions with which this inquiry began by conjoining two theories: the presupposition theory of induction and the dispositional theory of inductive probability. The combination is a unified theory of induction, causality, and three kinds of probability: inductive, empirical, and frequency.

Bibliography

Allais, M. "Le Comportement de l'Homme Rationnel Devant le Risque: Critique des Postulats et Axioms de l'Ecole Americaine." *Econometrica* 21 (1953): 503–46.

Arrow, Kenneth. "Alternative Approaches to the Theory of Choice in Risk-taking Situations." *Econometrica* 19 (1951): 404–37.

Ayer, A. J. *Language, Truth and Logic*, 2d ed. London: Victor Gollancz, 1950.

Babbage, H. P., ed. *Babbage's Calculating Engines—Being a Collection of Papers Relating to Them; Their History, and Construction*. London: Spon, 1889.

Bacon, Francis. *Novum Organum*, trans. by R. Ellis and James Spedding. London: George Routledge & Sons, n.d. Original Latin edition published 1620.

Baker, A. J. "Incompatible Hypotheticals and the Barber Shop Paradox." *Mind* 54 (1955): 384–87.

Ball, W. W. Rouse. *Mathematical Recreations and Essays*, 11th ed. London: Macmillan, 1940.

Barcan, Ruth. *See* Marcus.

Bayes, Thomas. "An Essay Towards Solving a Problem in the Doctrine of Chances. By the late Rev. Mr. Bayes, F. R. S.: communicated by Mr. Price, in a Letter to John Canton, A. M. F. R. S." *Philosophical Transactions Giving Some Account of the Present Undertakings, Studies, and Labours, of the Ingenious in Many Considerable Parts of the World;* vol. 53, for the year 1763: read 23 Dec. 1763, pp. 370–418. London: printed for L. Davis and C. Reymers, printers to the Royal Society [of London for Improving Natural Knowledge], 1764. Reprinted in *Biometrica* 45 (1958): 293–315 with a biographical note by G. A. Barnard. Reprinted, together with another essay by Bayes, in *Facsimiles of Two Papers by Bayes*, ed. by W. Edwards Deming. Washington, D.C.: Graduate School, Department of Agriculture, 1940.

Bernoulli, Daniel. "Specimen Theoriae Novae de Mensura Sortis." *Commentarii Academiae Scientiarum Imperialis Petropolitanae*, for 1730 and 1731, 5 (1738): 175–92. English trans. by Louise Sommer, "Exposition of a New Theory on the Measurement of Risk." *Econometrica 22* (1954): 23–36.

Blackstone, Sir William. *Commentaries on the Laws of England*, 4 vols. New York: Harper, 1854. Originally published 1765–69.

Bohm, David. *Causality and Chance in Modern Physics*. London: Routledge & Kegan Paul, 1957.

———. *Quantum Theory*. New York: Prentice-Hall, 1951.

———. "Quantum theory in terms of 'hidden' variables I." *Physical Review* 85 (1952): 166–79.

———. "A suggested interpretation of quantum theory in terms of 'hidden' variables II." *Physical Review* 85 (1952): 180–93.

Bondi, H. *Cosmology*, 2d ed. Cambridge: Cambridge University Press, 1960.

Bonola, Roberto. *Non-Euclidean Geometry*, trans. by H. S. Carslaw. Chicago: Open Court, 1912.

BOREL, ÉMILE. "Les Probabilités Dénombrables et Leurs Applications Arithmétiques." *Rendiconti del Circolo Matematico di Palermo* 27 (1909) 247–71. Reprinted as Note V in Borel's *Leçons sur la Théorie des Fonctions*, 3d ed. Paris: Gauthier-Villars, 1928.

———. "A propos d'un traité de probabilités." *Revue Philosophique* 98 (1924): 321–36. This was a review of Keynes' *A Treatise on Probability*. English trans. by Howard Smokler, "Apropos of a Treatise on Probability," *Studies in Subjective Probability*, ed. by Henry Kyburg and Howard Smokler. New York: John Wiley, 1964, pp. 45–60.

———. "La théorie du jeu et les équations intégrales à noyau symétrique." *Comptes Rendus Hebdomadaires des Séances de l'Académie des Sciences* 173 (séance due 19 Décembre 1921): 1304–8. English trans. by L. J. Savage, "The Theory of Play and Integral Equations with Skew Symmetric Kernels." *Econometrica* 21 (1953): 97–100. See ibid., pp. 95–96, 101–27, for translations of other papers on game theory by Borel and for commentary by Maurice Fréchet and John von Neumann.

BORN, MAX. "Einstein's Statistical Theories," in *Albert Einstein: Philosopher Scientist*, ed. by P. A. Schilpp. Evanston, Illinois: Library of Living Philosophers, 1949, pp. 161–78.

BRIDGMAN, P. W. *The Logic of Modern Physics*. New York: Macmillan, 1927.

BROAD, C. D. *Induction, Probability, and Causation* (selected papers dating from 1920, with an essay by G. H. von Wright, "Broad on Induction and Probability"). Dordrecht, Netherlands: D. Reidel, 1968.

———. *The Mind and its Place in Nature*. London: Routledge & Kegan Paul, 1925.

BROUWER, L. E. J. *Intuitionisme et Formalisme*. Groningen, 1912, 32 pp. English translation by Arnold Dresden, "Intuitionism and Formalism," *Bulletin of the American Mathematical Society* 20 (1913–14): 81–96. Reprinted in *Philosophy of Mathematics*, ed. by Paul Benacerraf and Hilary Putnam. Englewood Cliffs, New Jersey: Prentice-Hall, 1964, pp. 66–77.

BUB, JEFFREY. "What is a Hidden Variable Theory of Quantum Phenomena?" *International Journal of Theoretical Physics* 2 (1969): 101–23.

BURKS, ARTHUR W. "Cellular Automata and Natural Systems," in *Cybernetics and Bionics* (Proceedings of the 5th Congress of the Deutsche Gesellschaft für Kybernetik, Nurnberg, March 28–30, 1973), ed. by W. D. Keidel, W. Handler, and M. Spreng. Munich: R. Oldenbourg, 1974, pp. 190–204.

———. "Computation, Behavior, and Structure in Fixed and Growing Automata." *Behavioral Science* 6 (1961):5–22. Original version and discussion in *Self-Organizing Systems*, ed. by Marshall Yovits and Scott Cameron. New York: Pergamon Press, 1960, pp. 282–311 and 312–14.

———. "Dispositional Statements." *Philosophy of Science* 22 (1955): 175–93.

———. "Electronic Computing Circuits of the ENIAC." *Proceedings of the Institute of Radio Engineers* 35 (1947): 756–67.

———. "Empiricism and Vagueness." *Journal of Philosophy* 43 (1946): 447–86.

———, ed. *Essays on Cellular Automata*. Urbana, Illinois: University of Illinois Press, 1970.

———. "Icon, Index, and Symbol." *Philosophy and Phenomenological Research* 9 (1949): 673–89.

———. Introduction to Peirce selections, in *Classic American Philosophers*, ed. by Max Fisch. New York: Appleton-Century-Crofts, 1951, pp. 41–53.

———. Introduction to von Neumann's *Theory of Self-Reproducing Automata*. See von Neumann.

———. "Justification in Science," in *Academic Freedom, Logic, and Religion*, ed. by Morton White. Philadelphia: University of Pennsylvania Press, 1953, pp. 109–25.

———. "Laws of Nature and Reasonableness of Regret." *Mind* 55 (1946): 170–72.

———. "Logic, Biology and Automata—Some Historical Reflections." *International Journal of Man-Machine Studies* 7 (1975):297–312.

———. "The Logic of Causal Propositions." *Mind* 60 (1951): 363–82. Abstract, *Journal of Symbolic Logic* 15 (1950): 78.

———. "Logic, Computers, and Men." *Proceedings and Addresses of the American Philosophical Association* 46 (1972–73): 39–57.

———. "Models of Deterministic Systems." *Mathematical Systems Theory* 8 (1974): 295–308.

———. "Ontological Categories and Language." *Visva-Bharati Journal of Philosophy* 3 (1967): 25–46. Visva-Bharati (University), Santiniketan, West Bengal, India.

———. "Peirce's Conception of Logic as a Normative Science." *Philosophical Review* 52 (1943): 187–93.

———. "Peirce's Theory of Abduction." *Philosophy of Science* 13 (1946): 301–6.

———. "Peirce's Two Theories of Probability," in *Studies in the Philosophy of Charles Sanders Peirce, Second Series*, ed. by Edward Moore and Richard Robin. Amherst: University of Massachusetts Press, 1964, pp. 141–50.

———. "A Pragmatic-Humean Theory of Probability and Lewis's Theory," in *The Philosophy of C. I. Lewis*, edited by P. A. Schilpp. La Salle, Illinois: Open Court, 1968, pp. 415–63. This article was completed in 1954. Lewis replies, pp. 665–66 and 668–69.

———. "The Presupposition Theory of Induction." *Philosophy of Science* 20 (1953): 177–97.

———. "On the Presuppositions of Induction." *Review of Metaphysics* 8 (1955): 574–611.

———. "Reichenbach's Theory of Probability and Induction." *Review of Metaphysics* 4 (1951): 371–93.

———. Review of Rudolf Carnap's *Logical Foundations of Probability. Journal of Philosophy* 48 (1951): 524–35.

———. Review of Rudolf Carnap's *The Continuum of Inductive Methods. Journal of Philosophy* 50 (1953): 731–34.

———. "On the Significance of Carnap's System of Inductive Logic for the Philosophy of Induction," in *The Philosophy of Rudolf Carnap*, ed. by P. A. Schilpp. La Salle, Illinois: Open Court, 1963, pp. 739–59. This article was completed in 1954. Carnap replies, pp. 980–83.

———. "A Theory of Proper Names." *Philosophical Studies* 2 (1951): 36–45.

———. "Toward a Theory of Automata Based on More Realistic Primitive Elements," in *Information Processing 1962, Proceedings of IFIP Congress 62*, ed. by C. M. Popplewell. Amsterdam: North-Holland, 1963, pp. 379–85. Reprinted as Essay Three of *Essays on Cellular Automata*, ed. by Arthur W. Burks. Urbana, Illinois: University of Illinois Press, 1970.

———. "Von Neumann's Self-Reproducing Automata." Essay One of *Essays on Cellular Automata*, ed. by Arthur W. Burks. Urbana, Illinois: University of Illinois Press, 1970.

———, and Irving Copi. "Lewis Carroll's Barber Shop Paradox." *Mind* 59 (1950): 219–22.

———. "The Logical Design of an Idealized General-Purpose Computer." *Journal of the Franklin Institute* 261 (March 1956): 299–314, (April 1956): 421–36.

———, H. H. Goldstine, and John von Neumann. *Preliminary Discussion of the Logical Design of an Electronic Computing Instrument*. Princeton: Institute for Advanced Study, 1946, 2d ed., 1947, pp. vi + 42. Reprinted in *John von Neumann—Collected Works* 5, ed. by A. H. Taub. New York: Macmillan, 1963, pp. 34–79.

———, and Hao Wang. "The Logic of Automata." *Journal of the Association for Computing Machinery* 4 (1957): 193–218, 279–97. Reprinted in Hao Wang, *A Survey of Mathematical Logic*. Peking: Science Press, 1962; distributed by North-Holland Publishing Company, Amsterdam, pp. 175–223.

———, D. W. Warren, and J. B. Wright. "An Analysis of a Logical Machine Using Parenthesis-Free Notation." *Mathematical Tables and Other Aids to Computation* 8 (1954): 53–57.

———, and J. B. Wright. "Sequence Generators and Digital Computers." *Recursive Function Theory* (Proceedings of Symposia in Pure Mathematics) 5: 139–99. Providence, Rhode Island: American Mathematical Society, 1962.

———. "Theory of Logical Nets." *Proceedings of the Institute of Radio Engineers* 41 (1953): 1357–65. Reprinted in *Sequential Machines—Selected Papers*, ed. by E. F. Moore. Reading, Mass.: Addison-Wesley, 1964, pp. 193–212.

Butler, Bishop Joseph. *The Analogy of Religion, Natural and Revealed, to the Constitution and Course of Nature*, ed. by G. R. Crooks. New York: Harper, 1868. Originally published 1736.

Carnap, Rudolf. "The Aim of Inductive Logic," in *Logic, Methodology and Philosophy of Science: Proceedings of the 1960 International Congress*, ed. by E. Nagel, P. Suppes, and A. Tarski. Stanford, Cal.: Stanford University Press, 1962, pp. 303–18.

———. *The Continuum of Inductive Methods*. Chicago: University of Chicago Press, 1952.

———. *Logical Foundations of Probability*. Chicago: University of Chicago Press, 1950, 2d ed., 1962.

———. *The Logical Syntax of Language*, trans. by Countess von Zeppelin. New York: Harcourt, Brace, 1937. Original German version published in 1934.

———. *Meaning and Necessity*. Chicago: University of Chicago Press, 1947.

———. "Modalities and Quantification." *Journal of Symbolic Logic* 11 (1946): 33–64.

———. "Replies and Systematic Expositions," in *The Philosophy of Rudolf Carnap*, ed. by P. A. Schilpp. La Salle, Illinois: Open Court, 1963, pp. 859–1013.

———, and Richard Jeffrey (eds.). *Studies in Inductive Logic and Probability* 1. Berkeley: University of California Press, 1971.

Carroll, Lewis. "A Logical Paradox." *Mind* n.s. 3 (1894): 436–38.

Céline, Louis-Ferdinand. *The Life and Work of Semmelweis*, trans. by R. A. Parker. Boston: Little, Brown, 1937.

Chaitin, Gregory. "On the Length of Programs for Computing Finite Binary Sequences." *Journal of the Association for Computing Machinery* 13 (1966): 547–69.

———. "On the Length of Programs for Computing Finite Binary Sequences: Statistical Considerations." *Journal of the Association for Computing Machinery* 16 (1969): 145–59.

Chambers, R. P. "Random-Number Generation." *IEEE* (Institute of Electrical and Electronic Engineers) *Spectrum* 4 (1967): 48–56.

Champernowne, D. G. "The Construction of Decimals Normal in the Scale of Ten." *Journal of the London Mathematical Society* 8 (1933): 254–60.

CHISHOLM, RODERICK. "Law Statements and Counterfactual Inference." *Analysis* 15 (1955): 97–105.

CHURCH, ALONZO. "On the Concept of a Random Sequence." *Bulletin of the American Mathematical Society* 46 (1940): 130–35.

———. "A Formulation of the Logic of Sense and Denotation," in *Structure, Method, and Meaning*, ed. by Paul Henle, H. M. Kallen, and S. K. Langer. New York: Liberal Arts Press, 1951, pp. 3–24.

———. *Introduction to Mathematical Logic* 1. Princeton: Princeton University Press, 1956.

———. "A Note on the Entscheidungsproblem." *Journal of Symbolic Logic* 1 (1936): 40–41. A correction, ibid., pp. 101–2.

COPELAND, ARTHUR H. "Admissible Numbers in the Theory of Probability." *American Journal of Mathematics* 50 (1928): 535–52.

———. "Point Set Theory Applied to the Random Selection of the Digits of Admissible Numbers." *American Journal of Mathematics* 58 (1936): 181–92.

COPI, IRVING. *Symbolic Logic*, 3d ed. New York: Macmillan, 1967.

———. *See* Burks.

COURANT, RICHARD, and H. ROBBINS. *What is Mathematics?* New York: Oxford University Press, 1941.

COXETER, H. S. M. *Non-Euclidean Geometry*. Toronto: University of Toronto Press, 1942.

CRESSWELL, M. J. *See* Hughes.

CROW, JAMES F. and MOTOO KIMURA. *An Introduction to Population Genetics Theory*. New York: Harper & Row, 1970.

DAVIDSON, DONALD, and PATRICK SUPPES, in collab. with Sidney Siegel. *Decision Making, An Experimental Approach*. Stanford, Cal.: Stanford University Press, 1957.

DEDEKIND, RICHARD. *Was Sind und was Sollen die Zahlen?* Braunschweig, 1888. Reprinted in Dedekind's *Gesammelte Werke* 3, Berlin, 1932.

DE FINETTI, BRUNO. "Initial Probabilities: A Prerequisite for any Valid Induction." *Synthese* 20 (1969): 2–16. See also I. J. Good's discussion of this paper, ibid., pp. 17–24.

———. "La Prévision: Ses Lois Logiques, Ses Sources Subjectives." *Annales de l'Institut Henri Poincaré* 7 (1937): 1–68. English trans. by Henry Kyburg, "Foresight: Its Logical Laws, its Subjective Sources," in *Studies in Subjective Probability*, ed. by Henry Kyburg and Howard Smokler. New York: John Wiley, 1964, pp. 93–158.

———. *Probability, Induction, and Statistics*. New York: John Wiley, 1972.

———. "Recent Suggestions for the Reconciliation of Theories of Probability," in *Proceedings of the Second Berkeley Symposium on Mathematical Statistics and Probability*, ed. by J. Neyman. Berkeley: University of California Press, 1951, pp. 217–25.

———. "Sul Significato Soggetivo della Probabilità." *Fundamenta Mathematica* 17 (1931): 298–329.

———. "Le vrai et le probable." *Dialectica* 3 (1949): 78–93.

DIOGENES LÄERTIUS. *Lives of Eminent Philosophers*. With an English translation by R. D. Hicks; 2 vols. London: William Heinemann, 1925. Original Greek manuscript probably written in the third century A.D.

DOOB, J. L. *Stochastic Processes*. New York: John Wiley, 1953.

DUNNINGTON, G. WALDO. *Carl Friedrich Gauss: Titan of Science*. New York Exposition Press, 1955.

EDWARDS, WARD. "Behavioral Decision Theory," in *Annual Review of Psychology* 12, ed. by P. R. Farnsworth, O. McNemar, and Q. McNemar. Palo Alto, Cal.: Annual Reviews, 1961, pp. 473–98.

EINSTEIN, ALBERT, *The Meaning of Relativity; fifth edition, including the Relativistic Theory of the Non-Symmetric Field.* Princeton, New Jersey: Princeton University Press, 1955.

———. "Remarks Concerning the Essays Brought Together in this Co-operative Volume," in *Albert Einstein: Philosopher-Scientist*, ed. by P. A. Schilpp. Evanston, Illinois: Library of Living Philosophers, 1949, pp. 665–88.

———, B. PODOLSKY, and N. ROSEN. "Can Quantum-Mechanical Description of Physical Reality be Considered Complete?" *Physical Review* 47 (May 1935): 777–80.

ELLIS, LESLIE. "On the Foundations of the Theory of Probabilities." *Transactions of the Cambridge Philosophical Society* 8 (1844): 1–6, read 14 Feb. 1842. Reprinted in *The Mathematical and Other Writings*, ed. by William Walton. Cambridge: Deighton, Bell, 1863, pp. 1–11.

ENGEL, FRIEDRICH, and PAUL STÄCKEL. *Die Theorie der Parallellinien von Euklid bis auf Gauss, Eine Urkundensammlung zur Vorgeschichte der Nichteuklidischen Geometrie.* Leipzig: B. G. Teubner, 1895.

EUCLID. *The Thirteen Books of Euclid's Elements*, ed. by Thomas L. Heath; 3 vols. New York: Dover, 1956. Original Greek manuscript written about 300 B.C.

FEIGENBAUM, EDWARD, and JULIAN FELDMAN, eds. *Computers and Thought.* New York: McGraw Hill, 1963.

FELLER, WILLIAM. *An Introduction to Probability Theory and Its Applications;* vol. 1, 2d ed., 1959; vol. 2, 1966. New York: John Wiley & Sons.

FEYERABEND, P. K. "Problems of Microphysics," in *Frontiers of Science and Philosophy*, ed. by Robert Colodny. Pittsburgh: University of Pittsburgh Press, 1962, pp. 189–283.

FISHER, R. A. *The Genetical Theory of Natural Selection*, 2d ed. New York: Dover, 1958; 1st ed. published 1930.

FITCH, FREDERIC. "Intuitionistic Modal Logic with Quantifiers." *Portugaliae Mathematica* 7 (1948): 113–18.

———. *Symbolic Logic.* New York: Ronald Press, 1952.

FITZGERALD, EDWARD. *Rubaiyat of Omar Khayyam.* The four editions with the original prefaces and notes. Leipzig: Bernhard Tauchnitz, 1910. The first edition was published in 1859.

FREGE, GOTTLOB. "Über Sinn und Bedeutung." *Zeitschrift fur Philosophie und philosophische Kritik*, n.s. vol. 100 (1892): 25–50. English trans. by H. Feigl, "On Sense and Nominatum," in *Readings in Philosophical Analysis*, ed. by H. Feigl and W. Sellars. New York: Appleton-Century-Crofts, 1949, pp. 85–102.

FRIEDMAN, MILTON, and L. J. SAVAGE. "The Utility Analysis of Choices Involving Risk." *Journal of Political Economy* 56 (1948): 279–304.

GÖDEL, KURT. "Über formal unentscheidbare Sätze der Principia Mathematica und verwandter Systeme I." *Monatschefte für Mathematik und Physik* 38 (1931): 173–98. English trans. by Elliott Mendelson, "On Formally Undecidable Propositions of the Principia Mathematica and Related Systems. I," in *The Undecidable*, ed. by Martin Davis. Hewlett, New York: Raven Press, 1965, pp. 4–38.

———. "Eine Interpretation des intuitionistischen Aussagenkalküls." *Ergebnisse Eines Mathematischen Kolloquiums* Heft 4 (for 1931–32, pub. 1933): 39–40. English trans. by J. Hintikka and L. Rossi, "An Interpretation of the Intuitionistic Sentential Logic," in *The Philosophy of Mathematics*, ed. by Jaakko Hintikka. London: Oxford University Press, 1969, pp. 128–29.

———. "On Undecidable Propositions of Formal Mathematical Systems." Mimeographed notes on lectures delivered at the Institute of Advanced Study, Princeton, New Jersey. February-May 1934. Reprinted in *The Undecidable*, ed. by Martin Davis. Hewlett, New York: Raven Press, 1965, pp. 39–74.

GOLDSTINE, HERMAN H. *The Computer from Pascal to von Neumann*. Princeton: Princeton University Press, 1972.

———. *See* Burks.

GOOD, I. J. *Probability and the Weighing of Evidence*. London: Charles Griffin, 1950.

GOODMAN, NELSON. *Fact, Fiction, & Forecast*. Cambridge, Mass.: Harvard University Press, 1955.

———. "The Problem of Counterfactual Conditionals." *Journal of Philosophy* 44 (1947): 113-28. Reprinted in Goodman's *Fact, Fiction, & Forecast*.

HALLOCK, GRACE, and C. E. TURNER. *Walter Reed*. New York: Metropolitan Life Insurance Company, 1926.

HEMPEL, CARL G. "A Purely Syntactical Definition of Confirmation." *Journal of Symbolic Logic* 8 (1943): 122–43.

HENKIN, LEON. "Completeness in the Theory of Types." *Journal of Symbolic Logic* 15 (1950): 81–91.

HENLE, PAUL. "Meaning and Verifiability," in *The Philosophy of Rudolf Carnap*, ed. by P. A. Schilpp. La Salle, Ill.: Open Court, 1963, pp. 165–81.

HINTIKKA, JAAKKO. "On a Combined System of Inductive Logic," in *Studia Logico-Mathematica et Philosophica in honorem Rolf Nevanlinna*. Helsinki: *Acta Philosophica Fennica*, fasc. 18, 1965, pp. 21–30.

———. "Induction by Enumeration and Induction by Elimination," in *The Problem of Inductive Logic*, ed. by I. Lakatos. Amsterdam: North-Holland, 1968, pp. 191–216; discussion, pp. 217–31.

———. "Modality and Quantification." *Theoria* 27 (1961): 119–28.

———. "The Modes of Modality," in *Proceedings of a Colloquium on Modal and Many-Valued Logics, Helsinki, 23–26 August 1962*. Helsinki: *Acta Philosophica Fennica*, fasc. 16, 1963, pp. 65–81.

———. "Towards a Theory of Inductive Generalization," in *Proceedings of the 1964 International Congress for Logic, Methodology and Philosophy of Science*, ed. by Y. Bar-Hillel. Amsterdam: North-Holland, 1968, pp. 274–88.

———, and PATRICK SUPPES, eds. *Aspects of Inductive Logic*. Amsterdam: North-Holland, 1966.

HOLLAND, JOHN. *Adaptation in Natural and Artificial Systems—An Introductory Analysis with Applications to Biology, Control, and Artificial Intelligence*. Ann Arbor, Michigan: University of Michigan Press, 1975.

HOSIASSON-LINDENBAUM, JANINA. "On Confirmation." *Journal of Symbolic Logic* 5 (1940): 133–48.

HUGHES, G. E., and M. J. CRESSWELL. *An Introduction to Modal Logic*. London: Methuen, 1968.

HUME, DAVID. *An Enquiry Concerning Human Understanding*, ed. by L. A. Selby-Bigge in volume entitled *Enquiries*, 2d ed. Oxford: Oxford University Press, 1902. Originally published as *Philosophical Essays Concerning Human Understanding* in 1748.

———. *A Treatise of Human Nature*, ed. by L. A. Selby-Bigge. London: Oxford University Press, 1888. Originally published 1739.

JEFFREYS, HAROLD. *Theory of Probability*, 2d ed. Oxford: Oxford University Press, 1948.

JOHNSON, W. E. *Logic*. Cambridge: University Press, part 1, 1921; part 2 (Demonstrative Inference: Deductive and Inductive), 1922; part 3 (The Logical Foundations of Science), 1924.

KANT, IMMANUEL. *Kritik der reinen Vernunft*. Riga: Johann Friedrich Hartknoch, 1781. Second edition published in 1787; the pages of the two editions are referred to by "A" and "B," respectively. English trans. by N. K. Smith, *Critique of Pure Reason*. London: Macmillan, 1933.

———. *Prolegomena to Any Future Metaphysics*, ed. by Lewis Beck. New York: Liberal Arts Press, 1950. Original German ed. published 1783.

KEMENY, J. G. "Fair Bets and Inductive Probabilities." *Journal of Symbolic Logic* 20 (1955): 263–73.

———, and J. L. SNELL. *Finite Markov Chains*. New York: D. Van Nostrand, 1960.

KEYNES, JOHN MAYNARD. *A Treatise on Probability*. London: Macmillan, 1921.

———. *Monetary Reform*. New York: Harcourt, Brace, 1924.

KIMURA, MOTOO, and TOMOKO OHTA. *Theoretical Aspects of Population Genetics*. Princeton, New Jersey: Princeton University Press, 1971.

KIMURA, MOTOO. *See* Crow.

KLEENE, STEPHEN C. *Introduction to Metamathematics*. New York: D. Van Nostrand, 1952.

KOCHEN, SIMON and E. P. SPECKER. "The Problem of Hidden Variables in Quantum Mechanics." *Journal of Mathematics and Mechanics* 17 (1967): 59–87.

KOESTLER, ARTHUR. *The Sleepwalkers*. New York: Macmillan, 1959.

KOLMOGOROV, A. N. *Foundations of the Theory of Probability*. New York: Chelsea, 1950. Original German ed. 1933.

———. "On Tables of Random Numbers." *Sankyā: Indian Journal of Statistics*, Series A, 25 (1963): 369–76.

———. "Tri Podhoda k Opredeleniju Ponjatija 'Količestvo Informacii'." *Problemy Peredači Informacii* 1 (1965): 3–11. ("Three Approaches to the Definition of the Concept 'Quantity of Information'.")

KOOPMAN, B. O. "The Bases of Probability." *Bulletin of the American Mathematical Society* 46 (1940): 763–74.

KRANTZ, DAVID. *See* Luce.

KRIPKE, SAUL A. "A Completeness Theorem in Modal Logic." *Journal of Symbolic Logic* 24 (1959): 1–14.

———. "Semantical Analysis of Modal Logic I: Normal Modal Propositional Calculi." *Zeitschrift für mathematische Logik und Grundlagen der Mathematik* 9 (1963): 67–96.

———. "Semantical Considerations on Modal Logic," in *Proceedings of a Colloquium on Modal and Many-Valued Logics, Helsinki 23–26 August 1962*. Helsinki: *Acta Philosophica Fennica*, fasc. 16, 1963, pp. 83–94.

KYBURG, HENRY, and HOWARD SMOKLER, eds. *Studies in Subjective Probability*. New York: John Wiley, 1964.

LANGFORD, C. H. "The Notion of Analysis in Moore's Philosophy," in *The Philosophy of G. E. Moore*, ed. by P. A. Schilpp. Chicago: Northwestern University, 1942, pp. 321–42.

———. "Otherness and Dissimilarity." *Mind* 39 (1930): 454–61.

———. *See* Lewis.

LAPLACE, MARQUIS PIERRE SIMON DE. *A Philosophical Essay on Probabilities*.

Trans. by F. W. Truscott and F. L. Emory. New York: Dover, 1951. Original French ed. 1814.

LEHMAN, R. SHERMAN. "On Confirmation and Rational Betting." *Journal of Symbolic Logic* 20 (1955): 251–62.

LEHMER, D. H. "Mathematical Methods in Large-Scale Computing Units," in *Proceedings of a Second Symposium on Large-Scale Digital Calculating Machines.* Cambridge, Mass.: Harvard University Press, 1951, pp. 141–46.

LEIBNIZ, BARON GOTTFRIED WILHELM VON. *New Essays Concerning Human Understanding*, trans. by A. G. Langley; 2d ed. Chicago: Open Court, 1916. Written 1704, first published 1765.

———. *Opuscules et Fragments Inédits de Leibniz.* Louis Couturat. Hildesheim: George Olms, 1966. Originally published 1903.

———. *Philosophical Papers and Letters*, trans. and ed. by Leroy Loemker; 2d ed. Dordrecht, Holland: D. Reidel, 1969.

———. *Die Philosophischen Schriften von Gottfried Wilhelm Leibniz* 7, ed. by C. I. Gerhardt. Hildesheim: George Olms, 1961. Originally published 1890.

———. *Selections*, ed. by Philip P. Wiener. New York: Scribners, 1951.

LEMMON, E. J. "A Theory of Attributes Based on Modal Logic," in *Proceedings of a Colloquium on Modal and Many-Valued Logics, Helsinki, 23–26 August 1962.* Helsinki: *Acta Philosophica Fennica*, fasc. 16, 1963, pp. 95–122.

LENZ, JOHN. "Induction as Self-Corrective," in *Studies in the Philosophy of Charles Sanders Peirce. Second Series*, ed. by Edward Moore and Richard Robin. Amherst: University of Massachusetts Press, 1964, pp. 151–62.

LEWIS, C. I. *An Analysis of Knowledge and Valuation.* La Salle, Illinois: Open Court, 1946.

———. *Mind and the World Order.* New York: Dover, 1956. Originally published 1929.

———. "Replies to My Critics," in *The Philosophy of C. I. Lewis*, ed. by P. A. Schilpp. La Salle, Illinois: Open Court, 1968, pp. 653–76.

———, and C. H. LANGFORD. *Symbolic Logic.* New York: Century, 1932.

LOCKE, JOHN. *An Essay Concerning Human Understanding*, ed. by A. C. Fraser; 2 vols. New York: Dover, 1959. Original ed. published 1690.

LUCE, R. DUNCAN, and DAVID KRANTZ. "Conditional Expected Utility." *Econometrica* 39 (March 1971): 253–71.

———, and HOWARD RAIFFA. *Games and Decisions.* New York: John Wiley, 1957.

LUCRETIUS (TITUS LUCRETIUS CARUS). *On the Nature of the Universe*, trans. by R. E. Latham. Harmondsworth, Middlesex: Penguin Books, 1951. Original Latin version circulated about 55 B.C. under the title *De Rerum Natura* (On the Nature of Things).

MARCUS, RUTH BARCAN. "Classes and Attributes in Extended Modal Systems," in *Proceedings of a Colloquium on Modal and Many-Valued Logics, Helsinki, 23–26 August 1962.* Helsinki: *Acta Philosophica Fennica*, fasc. 16, 1963, pp. 123–36.

———. "The Deduction Theorem in a Functional Calculus of First Order Based on Strict Implication." *Journal of Symbolic Logic* 11 (1946): 115–18.

———. "A Functional Calculus of First Order Based on Strict Implication." *Journal of Symbolic Logic* 11 (1946): 1–16.

MARGENAU, HENRY, and G. M. MURPHY. *The Mathematics of Physics and Chemistry.* New York: D. Van Nostrand, 1943.

MARTIN-LÖF, PER. "The Definition of Random Sequences." *Information and Control* 9 (1966): 602–19.

MENDELSON, ELLIOTT. *Introduction to Mathematical Logic*. Princeton, New Jersey: D. Van Nostrand, 1964.

MILL, JOHN STUART. *A System of Logic, Ratiocinative and Inductive*, 8th ed. London: Longmans, Green, 1947. Originally published 1843.

MONTAGUE, RICHARD. "Syntactical Treatments of Modality, with Corollaries on Reflexion Principles and Finite Axiomatizability," in *Proceedings of a Colloquium on Modal and Many-Valued Logics, Helsinki, 23–26 August 1962*. Helsinki: *Acta Philosophica Fennica*, fasc. 16, 1963, pp. 153–67.

MOORE, EDWARD F. "Gedanken-Experiments on Sequential Machines," in *Automata Studies*, ed. by C. E. Shannon and J. McCarthy. Princeton, New Jersey: Princeton University Press, 1956.

MORGENSTERN, OSKAR. *See* von Neumann.

MURPHY, G. M. *See* Margenau.

NEWTON, ISAAC. *Mathematical Principles of Natural Philosophy and The System of the World*, trans. by Andrew Motte and ed. by Florian Cajori. Berkeley: University of California Press, 1946. Original Latin ed. published 1687.

NEYMAN, J. *First Course in Probability and Statistics*. New York: Henry Holt, 1950.

NICOD, JEAN. *Foundations of Geometry and Induction*. This contains two works, "Geometry in the Sensible World" and "The Logical Problem of Induction." Trans. by Philip Wiener. London: Routledge & Kegan Paul, 1930.

NIEMI, GUNNAR. "On the Existence of a Modal Antinomy." *Synthese* 23 (1972): 463–76.

NIVEN, IVAN. *Irrational Numbers*. Published by the Mathematical Association of America and distributed by John Wiley, 1956.

OHTA, TOMOKO. *See* Kimura.

PAGE, LEIGH. *Introduction to Theoretical Physics*. New York: D. Van Nostrand, 1942.

PAP, ARTHUR. "Disposition Concepts and Extensional Logic," in *Concepts, Theories, and the Mind-Body Problem*, ed. by H. Feigl, M. Scriven, and G. Maxwell. Minneapolis: University of Minnesota Press, 1958, pp. 196–224.

PASCAL, BLAISE. *Pensées*, trans. by W. F. Trotter. New York: E. P. Dutton, 1931; 1st ed. appeared in 1670. A good French edition is that of Leon Brunschvicg; 3 vols. Paris, Librairie Hachette et Cie, 1904.

PEANO, GIUSEPPE, et al. *Formulaire de Mathématiques*, 5 vols. Turin, 1895–1908.

PEIRCE, CHARLES S. *Collected Papers of Charles Sanders Peirce*. Vols. 1–6 ed. by Charles Hartshorne and Paul Weiss; vols. 7–8 by Arthur W. Burks. Cambridge, Mass: Harvard University Press. 1: *Principles of Philosophy*, 1931; 2: *Elements of Logic*, 1932; 3: *Exact Logic*, 1933; 4: *The Simplest Mathematics*, 1933; 5: *Pragmatism and Pragmaticism*, 1934; 6: *Scientific Metaphysics*, 1935; 7: *Science and Philosophy*, 1958; 8: *Reviews, Correspondence, and Bibliography*, 1958. References are to volume and paragraph; e.g., 7.361 refers to vol. 7, par. 361.

PLATO. *The Dialogues of Plato*. 3d ed., ed. by B. Jowett. Oxford: Oxford University Press, 1892. Original Greek manuscripts written in the fourth century B.C.

PODOLSKY, B. *See* Einstein.

POLYA, G. *How to Solve It*. New York: Doubleday, 1957.

POPPER, KARL. "The Propensity Interpretation of Probability." *British Journal for the Philosophy of Science* 10 (1959): 25–42.

POST, EMIL L. "Finite Combinatory Processes—Formulation 1." *Journal of Symbolic Logic* 1 (September 1936): 103–5.

PRAWITZ, D. "Advances and Problems in Mechanical Proof Procedures," in

Machine Intelligence 4, ed. by B. Meltzer and D. Michie. New York: American Elsevier, 1969, pp. 59–71.

PRICE, DEREK J. DE S. "Contra-Copernicus: A Critical Re-Estimation of the Mathematical Planetary Theory of Ptolemy, Copernicus, and Kepler," in *Critical Problems in the History of Science*, ed. by Marshall Clagett. Madison: University of Wisconsin Press, 1959, pp. 197–218.

RAIFFA, HOWARD. *See* Luce.

———, and ROBERT SCHLAIFER. *Applied Statistical Decision Theory*. Boston: Graduate School of Business Administration, Harvard University, 1961.

RAMSEY, FRANK. *The Foundations of Mathematics*, ed. by R. B. Braithwaite. New York: Harcourt, Brace, 1931.

———. "Truth and Probability." Pp. 156–98 of *The Foundations of Mathematics*.

REICHENBACH, HANS. *Elements of Symbolic Logic*. New York: Macmillan, 1947.

———. *Nomological Statements and Admissible Operations*. Amsterdam: North-Holland, 1954.

———. *The Theory of Probability*. Berkeley: University of California Press, 1949. Original German ed. 1935.

REID, CONSTANCE. *Hilbert*. New York: Springer-Verlag, 1970.

RICHARDSON, M. *Fundamentals of Mathematics*. New York: Macmillian, 1947.

ROBBINS, H. *See* Courant.

Rosen, N. *See* Einstein.

ROSSER, BARKLEY. "Extensions of Some Theorems of Gödel and Church." *Journal of Symbolic Logic* 1 (1936): 87–91.

RUSSELL, BERTRAND. *Human Knowledge, Its Scope and Limits*. New York: Simon and Schuster, 1948.

———. "Mathematical Logic as Based on the Theory of Types." *American Journal of Mathematics* 30 (1908): 222–62.

———. *Mysticism and Logic and Other Essays*. London: George Allen & Unwin, 1950.

———. *The Problems of Philosophy*. New York: Henry Holt, n. d.

———. *See* Whitehead.

SALMON, WESLEY. *The Foundations of Scientific Inference*. Pittsburgh: University of Pittsburgh Press, 1966.

SAMUEL, A. L. "Some Studies in Machine Learning Using the Game of Checkers." *IBM Journal of Research and Development* 3 (1959): 211–32. "Some Studies in Machine Learning Using the Game of Checkers II—Recent Progress." Ibid. 11 (1967): 601–17.

SAVAGE, L. J. *The Foundations of Statistics*. New York: John Wiley, 1954.

———, et al. *The Foundations of Statistical Inference*. A discussion. New York: John Wiley, 1962.

———. *See* Friedman.

SCHLAIFER, ROBERT. *See* Raiffa.

SCHLICK, MORITZ. "Meaning and Verification." *Philosophical Review* 45 (1936): 339–69.

SEGAL, IRVING E. *Mathematical Problems of Relativistic Physics*. Providence, Rhode Island: American Mathematical Society, 1963.

SELLARS, WILFRID. "Counterfactuals, Dispositions, and the Causal Modalities," in *Concepts, Theories, and the Mind-Body Problem*, ed. by H. Feigl, M. Scriven, and G. Maxwell. Minneapolis: University of Minnesota Press, 1958, pp. 225–308.

SHANNON, C. E. "A Mathematical Theory of Communication." *Bell System Technical Journal* 27 (1948): 379–423, 623–56. Reprinted in C. E. Shannon and

W. Weaver, *The Mathematical Theory of Communication*. Urbana: University of Illinois Press, 1949, pp. 3–91.

SHIMONY, ABNER. "Coherence and the Axioms of Confirmation." *Journal of Symbolic Logic* 20 (1955): 1–28.

SNELL, J. L. *See* Kemeny.

SOMMERVILLE, D. M. Y. *The Elements of Non-Euclidean Geometry*. London: G. Bell and Sons, 1914.

SPECKER, E. P. *See* Kochen.

STABLER, E. R. *An Introduction to Mathematical Thought*. Cambridge, Mass.: Addison-Wesley, 1953.

STÄCKEL, PAUL. *See* Engel.

STEVENSON, CHARLES. "IF-FICULTIES." *Philosophy of Science* 37 (March 1970): 27–49.

STOUT, G. F. *Mind and Matter*. Cambridge: Cambridge University Press, 1931.

STROME, W. MURRAY. "Algorithm 294: Uniform Random [G5]." *Communications of the Association for Computing Machinery* 10 (1967): 40.

SUPPE, FREDERICK, ed. *The Structure of Scientific Theories*. Urbana, Illinois: University of Illinois Press, 1975.

SUPPES, PATRICK. *See* Davidson.

Tables of the Cumulative Binomial Probability Distribution. By the Staff of the Computation Laboratory. Vol. 35 of *The Annals of the Computation Laboratory of Harvard University*. Cambridge, Mass.: Harvard University Press, 1955.

Tables of Probability Functions. Prepared by the Federal Works Agency, Work Projects Administration, for the City of New York, under the sponsorship of the National Bureau of Standards. Arnold Lowan, Technical Director. Vol. 1, 1941; vol. 2, 1942.

TARSKI, ALFRED. "The Concept of Truth in Formalized Languages," in *Logic, Semantics, Metamathematics*, trans. by J. H. Woodger. Oxford: Clarendon Press, 1956, pp. 152–278. Original Polish version 1933, German trans. 1936.

THRALL, R. M., C. H. COOMBS, and R. L. DAVIS, eds. *Decision Processes*. New York: John Wiley, 1954.

TODHUNTER, I. *A History of the Mathematical Theory of Probability From the Time of Pascal to That of Laplace*. New York: Chelsea, 1949. Originally published 1865.

TOLMAN, RICHARD C. *The Principles of Statistical Mechanics*. Oxford: Clarendon Press, 1938.

TURING, A. M. "On Computable Numbers, with an Application to the Entscheidungs-problem." *Proceedings of the London Mathematical Society*, Series 2, 42 (1936–37): 230–65. "A Correction," ibid. 43 (1937): 544–46.

TURNER, C. E. *See* Hallock.

UCHII, SOSHICHI. "The Confirmation of Causal Laws." Ph.D. thesis, University of Michigan, Ann Arbor, Michigan, 1971. University Microfilms, Ann Arbor, Order No. 72-5000.

———. "Induction and Causality in a Cellular Space." To be published in *PSA 1976*, Vol. 2 (Philosophy of Science Association).

———. "Inductive Logic with Causal Modalities: A Deterministic Approach." *Synthese* 26 (1973): 264–303.

———. "Inductive Logic with Causal Modalities: A Probabilistic Approach." *Philosophy of Science* 39 (1972): 162–178.

VENN, JOHN. *The Logic of Chance*. London: Macmillan, 1866, and later eds.

VON KRIES, JOHANNES. *Die Principien der Wahrscheinlichkeitsrechnung. Eine logische Untersuchung*. Freiburg im Breisgau: J. C. B. Mohr, 1886.

VON MISES, RICHARD. *Probability, Statistics, and Truth*, 2d revised English ed., prepared by Hilda Geiringer. New York: Macmillan, 1957. Original German ed. published 1928.

———. "Grundlagen der Wahrscheinlichkeitsrechnung." *Mathematische Zeitschrift* 5 (1919): 52–99.

VON NEUMANN, JOHN. *Mathematische Grundlagen der Quantenmechanik*. Berlin: Springer, 1932. English trans. by R. T. Beyer, *Mathematical Foundations of Quantum Mechanics*. Princeton, New Jersey: Princeton University Press, 1955.

———. "Method in the Physical Sciences," in *The Unity of Knowledge*, ed. by L. Leary. New York: Doubleday, 1955, pp. 157–64. Reprinted in *John von Neumann—Collected Works* 6, ed. by A. H. Taub. New York: Macmillan, 1963, pp. 491–98.

———. "Probabilistic Logics and the Synthesis of Reliable Organisms from Unreliable Components," in *Automata Studies*, ed. by C. E. Shannon and J. McCarthy. Princeton, New Jersey: Princeton University Press, 1956, pp. 43–98. Reprinted in *John von Neumann—Collected Works* 5, ed. by A. H. Taub. New York: Macmillan, 1963, pp. 329–78.

———. "Zur Theorie der Gesellschaftsspiele." *Mathematische Annalen* 100 (1928): 295–320.

———. *Theory of Self-Reproducing Automata*, ed. and completed by Arthur W. Burks. Urbana, Illinois: University of Illinois Press, 1966.

———. *See* Burks.

———, and OSKAR MORGENSTERN. *Theory of Games and Economic Behavior*. Princeton, New Jersey: Princeton University Press, 1944; 2d ed., 1947; 3d ed., 1953.

VON WRIGHT, GEORG H. *An Essay in Modal Logic*. Amsterdam: North-Holland, 1951.

———. *The Logical Problem of Induction*. Helsingfors: Finnish Literary Society, 1941; 2d ed. Oxford: Basil Blackwell, 1957.

WAISMANN, FRIEDRICH. "Logische Analyse des Wahrscheinlichkeitsbegrifts." *Erkenntnis* 1 (1930–31): 228–48.

WANG, HAO. "The Axiomatization of Arithmetic." *Journal of Symbolic Logic* 22 (1957): 145–58.

———. "Proving Theorems by Pattern Recognition I." *Communications of the Association for Computing Machinery* 3 (1960): 220–34.

———. *See* Burks.

WARREN, DON. *See* Burks.

WHITEHEAD, ALFRED NORTH. *Process and Reality*. New York: Macmillan, 1929.

———, and BERTRAND RUSSELL. *Principia Mathematica*. Cambridge: Cambridge University Press. Vol. 1 (1910), vol. 2 (1912), vol. 3 (1913); 2d ed., 1925, 1926, and 1927, respectively.

WHITTAKER, EDMUND. *A History of the Theories of Aether and Electricity*, 2 vols. New York: Harper & Brothers, 1960.

WIENER, NORBERT. *Cybernetics, or Control and Communication in the Animal and the Machine*. New York: John Wiley and Sons, 1948; 2d ed., with supplementary chapters, 1961.

WILDER, RAYMOND L. *Introduction to the Foundations of Mathematics*, 2d ed. New York: John Wiley, 1965.

WILL, FRED. "The Justification of Theories." *Philosophical Review* 64 (1955): 370–88.

WOLFE, HAROLD E. *Introduction to Non-Euclidean Geometry*. New York: Dryden Press, 1945.

WRIGHT, J. B. *See* Burks.

WRIGHT, SEWALL, *The Theory of Gene Frequencies* (vol. 2 of *Evolution and the Genetics of Populations*). Chicago: University of Chicago Press, 1969.

Yellow Fever. A Compilation of Various Publications. Senate Document No. 822, 61st Congress, 3d session. Washington: Government Printing Office, 1911.

YOVITS, M. C., and S. CAMERON, eds. *Self-Organizing Systems*. New York: Pergamon Press, 1960.

Index

The reader is invited to use the index as a key to the interrelationships within groups of concepts that may not have been defined together in the body of the book, as well as for page references. The chief concepts are listed in pairs (see, for example, "cause and effect") or in hierarchical structures (see, for example, "logic"). Further interrelationships among terms are indicated in cross-references.

The index follows the convention of the text, whereby technical terms were printed in boldface when defined, and lesser but still important terms in italics; both the defined terms and the corresponding pages are given in boldface or italics in the index.

Abduction (logic of inquiry), 16
Absolute probability. *See* unconditional probabilities
Absolute value (of a real number), 61
Acceptance parameter ϵ_a, 78
Accuracy parameter ϵ'_a, 79
Acquired. *See* Man, his innate (acquired) structure-program complex
Act, 180, 257
  mixed act, 183
  normal form expression, 258
  partial, 183, 263, *278*
  pseudo-act, 297
  tree, *182*, **257**
    every choice of an act tree maximizes a function $\sum_{n=1}^{N} P(q_n, i)U(a_n, iq_n)$, *290*
  value $V(a)$ of act a, 198
  variance of act a, 195
  See also Chance; Choice; Consequence; Tree; Utility
Action
  at-a-distance, 569
  over-a-time-interval, 569
  and probability, 165, 176–79, 179ff. *See also* Partial belief; Pragmatic aspect of inductive probability; Utility
Actual
  causal law, 627 ff.
  causal system, 625 ff.
  universe, 105, 341, 359, 553, *625* ff.
Addition principle (probability)
  general, 40, *51, 55*
  principle of counting equiprobable cases, 52
  special, 40, *51, 55*
Addition of a superfluous condition, 411
  weakened form, 431
Admissible sequence, 594, 598
Airy, G. B., 86
Algorithm, 388
  casting out nines, 337
  decision algorithm for
    axiomhood, 349
    formulahood, 344
    proofhood, 351
    theoremhood, 347, 392
  derived rule of inference, 396–407
  enumeration algorithm for
    formulas, 369
    theorems, 369
  Leibniz, 337–38, 365–67
  normal form (of a tree), 272–77, *275*
  and randomness, 595, 598–99, 601
  trimming trees, 275
  truth-table, 346
  See also Automaton; Cellular automaton, causal, algorithmic; Decision machine; Enumeration machine; Program; Rule
Allais, M., 194
Analogy, argument by, 101
Analysis, 34, 169
  analysandum and *analysans, 34, 169*
  See also Definition; Language modeling; Meaning
Analytic, 7
A posteriori, 7
A priori
  aspect of inductive probability, 305 ff., 314–19, 322, 326, 632–36, 642
  concept, 607, *609* ff., 612–13, 643–45
    causal necessity ($\square^c$), 613–19
    inductive probability, 635–36
  knowledge, 7. *See also* Innate knowledge; Man, his innate (acquired) structure-program complex
  theory of inductive probability, 321 ff., 655
    deductive version, 321–24
    nondeductive version, 321–22, 639–42

Argument. *See* Deductive argument; Inductive argument; Logic, of argument
Arithmetic. *See* Peano arithmetic
Arithmetization of language (coding)
  causal statements, logic of, 367–68
  Gödel, 367 ff.
  Leibniz, 368–69
  of Peano arithmetic, 373–74
Arrow, Kenneth, 252
Arrowheads, 257, 265
Asymmetrical (relation), *208*
Atomic empirical probability statement $P_e(\phi, \psi)$, **27**, *505*. *See also* Empirical probability theory
Atomic inductive probability statement $\mathbf{P}(c, d) = x$, **26**
  not empirically true-or-false, 160
  not logically true-or-false, 129
  a third kind of statement (inductive), 638, 645
Atomic statement (of a formal language), *104*, *359*
Automaton
  delay, 380
  finite, *380*, 587, 597. *See also* Man, and computers
  and language, 366, 380
  switch, 380
  tape unit, 384
  theory, 610
  Turing machine, *384*, 597, 601–2
    and cellular automaton, 566–68, 575
    computation of, *384*
    and embedded subsystem, 588
    selection machine, 601
    sequence-producing machine, 601
    universal, *388*
  See also Algorithm; Cellular automaton; Computer, electronic; Decision machine; Enumeration machine; Program
Axiomatic system, 7, 12–13, 251. *See also* Decision machine; Definition; Enumeration machine; Formal language; Geometry. *For specific systems, see* Causal statements, logic of; Choice, calculus of; Inductive probability, calculus of; Peano arithmetic; Quantification theory; Truth-functional, logic
Axiom generation, *349*
Ayer, A. J., 167

Babbage, Charles, 383
Bacon, Francis, 24, 102
  tables of instances, 102
Baker, A. J., 460
Ball, W. W. R., 53
Barbershop paradox, 460–64
Barcan, Ruth, 348, 469
Basic. *See* Choice, basis; Conjunction; Individual; Property
Bayes, Thomas, 66
  method of finding an unknown probability, 76–77 ff., 118–28, 155, 159–60
    and Carnap's continuum, 124–27
    and de Finetti's theorem, 125–27
    and empirical probability, 481 ff.
    success in finding true hypothesis, 78 ff
    See also Induction and repetition; Self-corrective inductive method
  theorem, 66, 67 ff., 652
    applications, 85 ff.
    calculation format, 68
    condition for verification, 70
    and instance confirmation, 629–30
    ratio form, 66, 69
  See also Confirmation theorem; Degrees of prediction; Posterior probabilities; Prediction theorem; Prior Probabilities; Standard inductive logic
Belief. *See* Partial belief; Pragmatism, and belief
Berkeley, George, 610
Bernoulli, Daniel, 191
Birdum, 187
Blackstone, William, 62
Bohm, David, 427, 590–91
Bohr, Niels, 32, 590–91
Boltzmann, Ludwig, 117, 506
Bolyai, F., 7
Bondi, H., 187
Bonola, Roberto, 10
Book, *214*, 247, 254–56
  "book" theorem, *214*, 250, 252, 289, 303
    relation to calculus of choice, 213, 216, 251–52, 289–91, 303–4
  See also Coherent (incoherent) set of partial beliefs
Borel, Émile, 252, 594
Born, Max, 590
Bose, J. C., 117, 506
Bound variable. *See* Variable
Brandt, Richard, xvi
Bridge (game), 52–53
Bridgman, Percy, 167
Broad, C. D., 321, 614
Brouwer, L. E. J., 644
Bub, Jeffrey, 591
Butler, Joseph, 165, 188

Calculus. *See* Causal statements, logic of (four entries); Choice, calculus of; Empirical probability, calculus; Frequency, probability, calculus; Inductive probability, calculus of; Peano arithmetic; Quantification theory, first order; Truth-functional, truth-function theory
Cameron, S., 18
Carnap, Rudolph, xv, 104 ff., 110, 140–44, 321–25, 348, 379, 469
a priori theory of inductive probability, 321–25
justification of induction, 322–25
continuum of inductive logics, 121–22, 123, 155 ff.
and Bayes' method, 124–27
and de Finetti's theorem, 125–27
inductive logic, 107–14
See also Inductive logic (assignment of probabilities)
Carroll, Lewis
barbershop paradox, 460–64
definitions, 138
Catholic Church, 19, 189
Causal disposition, 440–51, 479
change of, 464–65, 572–73
compared to probabilistic disposition, 487–97, 535, 583
dispositional, 440, 487
property underlying, 442
enduring vs. *transient, 443*
See also Causal subjunctive; Cause and effect; Disposition; Property, enduring vs. transient; Would-be's
Causal existence principle, 577–78, 625, 641
Causal law, 168–69, **426** ff.
actual, 627 ff.
confirmation of, 627–32, 640–41
contiguous, 568, 630
global vs. local, 568–71
inductively simple, 571
and near-determinism, 577
possible, 450, *627* ff.
properties involved in, 551–54, 619–20, 632–34, 648
quasi-local law, 570
and responsibility, 579
as summary of facts, 619–20. *See also* True, contingently
verification of, 627–32, 640–41
See also Causal model of standard inductive logic; Cellular automaton, causal; Law, global vs. local; True, causally true; Verification; Would-be's
Causal modalities
equivalence ($\underset{c}{\leftrightarrow}$), *341, 345*
implication ($\underset{c}{\rightarrow}$), 174, 339, *341, 345*
elliptical causal implication (**ec**), *444*, 464
nonparadoxical causal implication (**npc**), *428*
nonsuperfluous causal (**nsc**), 434
iterated, 343, 400, 464–69
necessity ($\Box^c$), 174, *341, 342*, 651
is a priori, 613–19
in causal model of standard inductive logic ($\Box^c, \Box^c_1, \Box^c_2, \ldots, \Box^c_M$), 626
cause and effect, 457, 477
compared to logical necessity, 457, 466–67, 477
as a formal concept, 338, 340, 416–17, 653
interpretation, 421 ff., 457, 478, 653
irreducibly modal, 619–22
relation to inductive probability, 622–50
role in science, 439–40, 457, 620–21
space-time and, 551–54, 568–81, 623–24, 653–54
subjective or objective, 620–22
See also Causal disposition; Causal law; Cause and effect; Felt causal propensity
possibility ($\Diamond^c$), *341, 344*
See also Modal logic; Modal operators; Model; Universe and universe description
Causal model of standard inductive logic, 624 ff., 654
assignment of unconditional inductive probabilities, 624, *626* ff.
possible causal law, 627 ff.
actual causal law, 627 ff.
possible causal system, 625 ff.
actual causal system, 625 ff.
actual universe, 625 ff.
causally possible universe, 625 ff.
verification of causal laws, 627–32, 640–41
counterinstance lemma, 629
instance-confirmation, 628 ff.
shifting lemma, 578, *629*
See also Cellular automaton; Inductive logic (assignment of probabilities); Inductive probability; Presupposition theory of induction
Causal statements, logic of (axioms)
axiom generation, 349
modal, 348
distribution, 349
ordering, 349
-quantifier commutation, 349
quantificational, 347
elimination of irrelevant quantifier, 347

quantifier distribution, 347
universal instantiation, 348
truth-functional, 346
Causal statements, logic of (general), **340, 351, 423**
algorithms for. *See* Algorithm
compared to calculus of inductive probability, 488–89
consistent, 364
definitions, 344–45
as a formal language, 338, 342
grammar, 342–45
formula, 343
immediate consequence, 350
interpretation
abstract, 352 ff.
concrete, 352, 365, 424 ff.
with iterated modalities, 465 ff.
logically true statement, 359 ff., *363* ff., 367, 396, 419
premise, 350
proof, 350
categorical, 350
from premises, 350
rule of inference
derived, 400
primitive, 350
theorem, 350
every theorem logically true, 364
Causal statements, logic of (rules)
conditional proof, 398
reductio ad absurdum, 400
exchange, 403
existential generalization
of an individual symbol, *411*
of a predicate, 441
of a statement, 445, 484
existential instantiation
of a predicate, 442
of a statement, 445, 484
generalization, 400
modus ponens, 350
primitive, 350
Causal statements, logic of (theorems)
addition of a superfluous condition, 411
weakened form, 431
distribution, 408
existential generalization, 411
exportation, 411
weakened form, 431
kinds of implication compared, 446 ff.
modal ordering, 410–11
paradoxes of implication, 412
transitivity, 411
weakened form, 430
transposition, 411
weakened form, 431
Causal subjunctive, 338–39, 342, 435 ff., *449* ff., 464
rule of completeness, 459
See also Causal disposition; Cause and effect; Subjunctive conditional
Causal system. See Causal law; Causal model of standard inductive logic; Completeness, rule of, for causal subjunctives; Determinism; Law; Near-determinism; Probabilistic disposition
Causal uniformity principle, 572–73, 625, 635, 640. *See also* Uniformity
Causally true. *See* True
Cause and effect, 30, 451–57
causal relevance, 434–35, 454–56
cause-effect statement, 453 ff.
necessity, 457, 477
See also Causal disposition; Causal law; Causal subjunctive; Hume, David; Method, of varying causally relevant qualities; Theory
Céline, Louis-Ferdinand, 24
Cell. *See* Cellular automaton
Cellular automaton (general), *562* ff.
cell, 562
cell-moment, 562
state 562
history, 563, 566, 624
neighborhood relation $N(c)$, 562
space, 562–63
state
cell, 562
temporal, 562
Cellular automaton, causal, 563–64
and causality, 566, 569, 575–77, 624–25, 632–34
kinds
algorithmic, 567
deterministic, 564
indeterministic, 564
near-deterministic, 577, 625
modality of, 566
and randomness, 592–93, 599, 602
rule
initial state, 563
transition, 563
self-reproducing, 377, 568, 575
and Turing machines, 566–68, 575
See also Causal law, contiguous; Causal model of standard inductive logic
Cellular automaton, probabilistic, 562
rule
initial state, 562
transition, 562
Chaitin, Gregory, 601–2
Chambers, R. P., 599
Champernowne, D. G., 594

Chance, 24, 577, 581 ff., 585 ff., 651
point, 181, 256, 264
See also Determinism; Near-determinism; Probability; Randomness, kinds of; Tychism
Chisholm, Roderick, 449
Choice
basis, 254, *259*
point, 181, 256, 264
trees, *181*, **257**
complete set, 254, **261**
and utility, 180 ff.
See also Act; Chance; Consequence; Paradox, of choice; Prefers; Tree
Choice, calculus of (summarized on pp. 328–33), **254** ff.
axioms
existence, 270, 307
invariance, 268, 307–8
logical equivalence, 264–65, 307
marking, 262, 308–12
normal form, 276, 307–8
ordering of uncertainties, 270, 307
quantitative, nonsymmetrical form [VIII′], *301*, 311
quantitative, symmetrical form [VIII], *288*, 308–12
subset, 266, 307
grammar, 254–62
proof of main theorem [IX], 291–98
relation to
"book" theorem, 213, 216, 251–52, 289–91, 303–4
calculus of inductive probability, 281–83, 288–91
theorems
corollary [X] to main theorem, 304, 309–10
main theorem [IX], *288* ff.
main theorem, alternative version [IX′], 302
main theorem [IX_s] of Savage's system, 302
partial act, 278
permutation, 287
reduction, 276
simple ordering of conditional preferences, 269
simple ordering of conditional uncertainties, 271
simple ordering of preferences, 267
use of, 306–12
See also de Finetti, Bruno; Inductive probability; Savage, L. J.; Utility
Church, Alonzo, 373, 393, 469, 600–1
Coding. *See* Arithmetization of language
Coherent (*incoherent*) *set of partial beliefs, 214*, 247, 249–50, *303*
potential coherence, 303
strictly coherent, 215
See also Book; Partial belief; Rational
Collective, 147, *601*
Combinations
number of combinations C^n_r, *53*
Comparative
preferences, 208 ff., 266–69, 277–81, 309
probabilities, 209 ff., 270–72, 281–86. *See also* Quantitative and qualitative, probabilities; Uncertainties
relation, 208
values, 208 ff., 266–69, 277–81. *See also* Quantitative and qualitative, valuations
Complement
$\bar{\alpha}$ defined as 1-α, 200
Completeness, 13
of calculus of inductive probability, 99–104
complete set of choice trees, 261
for formal language, *372–73*. *See also* Gödel, Kurt, incompleteness theorem
of inductive logic for a model, 108
of a probabilistic process
complete assignment to a process, 119, *504, 508*
complete theory of a process, 493
rule of, for causal subjunctives, 459
See also Total evidence, rule of
Complexity. *See* Patternless sequence; Simplicity
Computation. *See* Turing machine
Computer, electronic, 18, 142, 383, 610–12
and man, 18, 610–13, 633–34
See also Automaton
Concept
a priori, 607, *609* ff., 612–13
causal necessity ($\Box^c$), 613–19
inductive probability (**P**), 635–36
empirical, 609 ff., 612–13
See also Epistemology; Meaning
Conclusion, 22, 350
Conditional
proof, 398
statement. *See* Implication
See also Corresponding conditional; Practical conditional; Prefers
Conditional probability, 39 ff., **92** ff.
axioms, 40–42
See also Unconditional probabilities
Confirmation (and disconfirmation)
of causal laws, 627–32, 640–41
confirmation theorem, 73–74, **84,** 85, 88
See also Bayes, Thomas, theorem; Empirical probability, empirical probability theory; Induction and

repetition; Inductive probability; Verification

Conjunction (&, Ɛ, *pq*), 11, *42*

basic, 50, 359. See also Universe and universe description

Consequence, 166, *180*

name, 254

point, 181, 256, 264

valuation function U(c), 289

stake S(c), 214

See also Act; Choice; Tree; Utility

Consistent. *See* Causal statements, logic of; Logical modalities; Peano arithmetic; Probabilistic modalities

Constant

individual, 358. *See also* Proper name

logical, 342

predicate, 358

statement, 358

Contiguity and law

and cellular automata, 562, 569–71

contiguous causal law, 568 ff., 630, 634–35

and Hume, 568, 634

Contingently true, 617

Coombs, C. H., 252

Copeland, Arthur, 594

Copernicus, Nicolaus, 20

Copi, Irving, 379, 383, 460

Copley, Frank, 337, 396

Corresponding conditional, 22

Counterfactual, 438 ff.

Counterinstance lemma, 629

Courant, Richard, 7, 169

Couturat, Louis, 337

Coxeter, H. S. M., 7

Crow, James, 88

Cybernetics, 610

Davidson, Donald, 306

Davis, R. L., 252

Decision machine (or *algorithm*)

for axiomhood, 349, 388

and formal language, 344, 347, 349, 351, 388, 392, 396

for formulahood, 344, 388

and logical truth, 367, 396, 419

for proofhood, 351, 388

relation to enumeration machine, 389

for theoremhood

in first-order quantification theory (nonexistence of), 392

in truth-function theory, 347, 392

See also Automaton; Enumeration machine; Turing machine

Dedekind, Richard, 369

Deduction theorem, 398

Deductive argument, 22, 413–15. *See also* Corresponding conditional; Premise and conclusion; Proof; Reason and reasoning; Valid and invalid

Deductive logic, 16

relation to inductive logic, 45–48, 216, 262–66, 314–15, 322

deductive justification of induction, 321–25

See also Logically true-or-false statement

Deductively rational, 314 ff.

de Finetti, Bruno, 214, 250 ff., 302, 325, 538–42

and pragmatism, 254

theorem, 126

and Bayes' method, 125–27

and Carnap's continuum of inductive logics, 125–27

and exchangeability, 126

See also Choice, calculus of; Personalistic

Definition

and axiomatic system, 12–13

definiendum and *definiens, 11*

equal by definition ($=_{df}$), 11

explicit, 12

implicit, 13

ostensive, 13–14, 556

recursive, 343

See also Analysis; Interpretation; Language modeling; Meaning

Degree-of-belief function P(q, i), 289. See also Inductive probability; Partial belief

Degrees of prediction, 68

function, 498, 510, 521

Demonstrative, 642, 645, 647. *See also* Deductive argument; Proof

De Morgan's Law, 55

Descartes, René, 610

Descriptive vs. normative

analysis of meaning, 34–35

pragmatic, 170–76, 639

use of calculus of choice, 262, 306–12

use of calculus of inductive probability, 40

Determinism, 573–77, *576*, 644–45

backward vs. forward, 574–75, 581

deterministic system, 576

tightly deterministic system, 576

and embedded subsystems, 588–92

and entropy, 592–93

and quantum mechanics, 589–91

and randomness, 585–86, 589–93, 597–603

and reversibility, 581 ff.

and uniformity, 573–74, 576–77

See also Cellular automaton, causal, deterministic; Free will; Near-determinism; Tychism

Diogenes Läertius, 137

Dirac, P. A. M., 117, 506

Discovery, logic of (**logic of inquiry**), **16**. *See also* Logic
Disjunction (v), *11*, *42*, *342*
disjunctive normal form, 109. *See also* Normal form (of a tree)
Disposition
dispositional model of
empirical probability statement, 483–87, 497–503
empirical probability theory, 512–16
fair-coin hypothesis, 480–87
inductive argument, 484–85, 501–2, 512–16
dispositional (statement), 487
causal, *440*, 487
probabilistic, 487
dispositional theory of empirical probability, 479 ff., **511**, 518–19, 656–58
compared to frequency theories, 532–38
compared to personalistic account, 541–42
compared to positivistic theory, 519–20, 524–31
intersubjective character, 529–31
See also Peirce, Charles S., dispositional-frequency theory of probability; Probabilistic disposition; Property; Unified theory of probability, causality, and induction
See also Causal disposition; Probabilistic disposition
Dissimilarity of the diverse, 559
Distribution
description, *107*
modal, *349*, 408
quantifier, *347*
Doob, J. L., 513
Dunnington, G. W., 10

Edwards, Ward, 306
Effect. *See* Cause and effect
Einstein, Albert, 117, 171–72, 425, 506, 551, 590
Elliptical causal implication (**ec**), *444*, 464
Ellis, Leslie, 148
Embedded subsystem, *588*
and determinism, 588–92
and probability, 588–92
and quantum mechanics, 589–91
and Turing machines, 588
Empirical
concept, *609* ff., 612–13
factor (relative frequency s/L), 122
knowledge. *See* Science
Empirically true-or-false statement, 2-6, 12, 362, **636**. *See also* Inductive logic; Inductive statement
Empirical probability $\mathbf{P}_e(\phi, \psi)$, **27**, 142–50, 160, 654–55
atomic empirical probability statement $\mathbf{P}_e(\phi, \psi) = \alpha$, **27**, *505*
and Bayes' method, 481 ff.
calculus, 516
empirical probability theory, 508
verification, 509–19
and mixture of independent processes, 481 ff.
relation to inductive probability, 485–87, 502–3, 517–19
See also Disposition, dispositional theory of empirical probability; Frequency, theory of empirical probability; Peirce, Charles S., dispositional-frequency theory of probability; Personalistic, account of empirical probability; Positivistic theory of empirical probability; Probabilistic law
Engel, Friedrich, 10
ENIAC, 383
Entropy E(u), *116*
and determinism, 592–93
and randomness, 115–17, 631
See also Isomorphic; Random inductive logic; Randomness, kinds of; Uniformity, statistical
Enumeration machine (or *algorithm*)
and formal language, 344, 347, 349, 351, 388, 392, 396
for formulas, *369*, *388*
and Gödel's incompleteness theorem, 393
relation to decision machine, 389
for theorems, *369*, *388*
See also Automaton; Decision machine; Turing machine
Epicurus, 549
Epistemology, 2, 35
of causal necessity, 608–22
of the presuppositions, 636–39
See also Concept; Knowledge; Statement
Equipartition, *287*
Equiprobable cases, principle of counting, *52*
Equivalence
causal ($\overset{\leftrightarrow}{c}$), *341*, *345*
logical ($\leftrightarrow$), *11*, *340*, *345*, 403
axiom, *264–65*, 307
between trees, 263–64
and probability, 47, 264
material ($\equiv$), *42*, *345*
relation, *208*
Euclid, 7 ff. *See also* Geometry
Event, 552
cell-moment, 562

partially uncaused, 577 ff.
and probability, 41, 57, 118, 144, 262–63
Evidence, 24, 316
and law, 37
rule of total evidence, 20, 457, 459
in science and other disciplines, 36–37
See also Probability
Evolution, 153, 613
computer simulation, 600
and language, 139
Peirce's claim re evolution and determinism, 585, 600, 602
quantitative form, 88, 600
theory of, 88
and tychism, 549, 581 ff.
Exchange
exchangeable probability assignment, *125* ff., 507
and de Finetti's theorem, 126
and mixture of independent processes, 125 ff.
and unknown probabilities, 539–40
logical equivalence axiom of calculus of choice, *264–65*
principle of calculus of probability, *47*, 264
rule of logic of causal statements, *403*
Exclusive and exhaustive
jointly exhaustive on condition, 52
mutually exclusive on condition, 40
See also Partition
Existence axiom, 270, 307
Existential. *See* Causal statements, logic of (rules, theorems); Generalization, existential; Instantiation, existential; Quantifier, existential
Experience, 607–9, 614–19, 642, 643 ff.
Experiment, 6, 71–92, 122, 627
length of, 58, 76, 85
See also Frequency
Exportation, 411
weakened form, 431

Fair-coin hypothesis, 480 ff.
Feigenbaum, Edward, 18
Feldman, Julian, 18
Feller, William, 57, 504, 506, 509, 513
Felt causal propensity, 616
Fermi, Enrico, 117, 506
Feyerabend, P. K., 591
Finite automaton, 380, 587, 597
Fisher, R. A., 88
Fitch, Frederic, 348, 427, 467
FitzGerald, Edward, 549
Fizeau, A. H. L., 86
Formal language
arithmetization (coding), 367 ff.
atomic statement, 104, 359
causal statements, logic of, 338, 342
completeness, 372–73
consistent, 364
and decision machines, 344, 347, 349, 351, 388, 392, 396
defined, *366*
and enumeration machines, 369, 388, 392, 393
grammar, 254 ff., 342 ff., 421
limits of, 421–22, 434–35, 444, 464
mechanical nature of, 367–96, 392
and natural language, 421–22
uninterpreted, 340, 342–43, 365–66
See also Axiomatic system; Causal statements, logic of; Choice, calculus of; Peano arithmetic; Quantification theory, first-order; Truth-functional, truth-function theory
Formula, 104, 343
closed, 358
isomorphic, 107
and model, 31–34, 351–62, 422 ff.
open, 358
pseudoformula, 357
truth-functional, 345
See also Decision machine, for formulahood; Statement; Tree
Foucault, J. B. L., 86
Foundations of inductive arguments, 17. *See also* Causal modalities; Causal model of standard inductive logic; Inductive argument; Inductive probability
Free variable. *See* Variable
Free will (choice), 578–80
free-will thesis, 579
and responsibility, 579
See also Determinism; Near-determinism; Tychism
Frege, Gottlob, 469
Frequency, 57–65
number of successes (S_L)**, 58,** 593–94
probability $\mathbf{P}_f(\phi, \psi)$**, 144,** 146–47, 160, 593–94
applied to finite or single case, 149, 154–55, 157–58
calculus, 145
observation and, 149, 531
relation to inductive probability, 160, 517
relative frequency of success (σ_L)**, 58,** 132, 593–94
theory of empirical probability, *148* ff., 158, 479, 531–33, 536–37
compared to dispositional theory, 532–38

finite version, 150
theory of inductive probability, 150 ff., 160, 655
See also Peirce, Charles S., dispositional-frequency theory of probability; Peirce-Reichenbach justification of induction
Fresnel, Augustin, 86
Friedman, Milton, 203

Galilei, Galileo, 2, 19, 32, 35
Gambling, 189–207, 213–16
anti-gamblers' fallacy theorem, 63
gamblers' fallacy, 62
law of the gambler's ruin, 64
Game, 213–16
marking, 255 ff.
theory, 252–53
Gauss, K. F., 9–10
Generalization
existential
of an individual symbol, *411*
of a predicate, 441
of a statement, 445, 484
rule, 400
Genetics, 88, 612
Geocentric hypothesis, 19 ff., 85
Geometry, 7–10
compared to alternative inductive logics, 128–29
Euclidean, 7–10
Kant, 7, 644
Lobachevskian, 7–10
Riemannian, 7–10
Gödel, Kurt, 367 ff., 378, 466
arithmetization of languages (coding), 367 ff.
Gödel number **g**(Φ), *368*
incompleteness theorem, 373, 377, 393
and enumeration machine for truth, 393
proof, 373–76
indefinability of truth in arithmetic, 378
undecidable formula, 376
Gold, T., 187
Goldstine, H. H., 383
Goodman, Nelson, 449, 551
Grammar. *See* Causal statements, logic of (general); Choice, calculus of; Formal language; Peano arithmetic

Hallock, Grace, 102
Height
for exchange rule, 404
truth-functional, 345–46
Heliocentric hypothesis, 19 ff., 85
Henkin, Leon, 373
Henle, Paul, 175
Heuristic logic (logic of inquiry), 16. *See also* Logic
Hierarchy of languages, 379, 470–74. *See also* Paradox and self-reference
Hilbert, David, 8
Hintikka, Jaakko, 140, 466
History of cellular automaton, 563, 566, 624. *See also* Universe and universe description
Holland, John, 88
Hosiasson-Lindenbaum, Janina, 40
Hume, David, xv, 30, 99, 427, 551, 586, 610, 620, 638, 645
analysis of causality, 616–17
contiguity and causality, 568, 634
custom and causality, 135, 647
felt causal propensity, 616
justification of induction, 134–37
theory of causality, 615–18, 620–22
uniformity of nature principle, 135, 645, 647
Hume's thesis that there is no noncircular justification of induction, 128–42, **134,** 154 ff., 317, 321, 324, 638, 646
historical origin, 134 ff.
speculative character, 137–42
See also Justification of induction
Hypothesis
fair-coin, 480 ff.
simplicity of, 18 ff., 571
See also Bayes, Thomas; Theory
Hypothetical statement. *See* Implication

Icon, 31–32
Identity of indiscernibles, 559–61
If . . . then . . . , 43–45. *See also* Implication
Ignorance and probability, 147–48, 586
Immediate consequence, 23, *350*. *See also* Intuitive; Valid and invalid
Implication
causal ($\underset{c}{\rightarrow}$), 174, 339, *341, 345*
contrary-to-fact conditional, 437
elliptical causal (**ec**), *444*, 464
kinds of implication compared, 446 ff.
logical ($\rightarrow$), 11, *340, 345*
material ($\supset$), *42–44*, 173–74, *345*
nonparadoxical causal (**npc**), *428*
nonsuperfluous causal implication (**nsc**), 434
See also Paradox, of implication
Incoherent. *See* Coherent (incoherent) set of partial beliefs
Incompleteness theorem. *See* Gödel, Kurt, incompleteness theorem; Peano arithmetic

Independence
  logical. *See* Logical modalities
  probabilistic
    independent on condition, 50
    independent process, 58
    See also Mixture of independent processes
Indeterminism. *See* Cellular automaton, causal, indeterministic; Near-determinism
Index, 554–62, 633
  and proper name, 558
  See also Property; Symbol
Indifference
  principle of, 626, 640–41
  relation on acts and on statements (=), *182*, 207–9, 267
    conditional form ($=_i$), 269, 271
Individual (and individual symbol)
  basic, 104, 359, 553, 562
  constant, proper name, 358
  state, 105, 553, 562
  variable, 342–43
Induction, mathematical, 49
Induction and repetition, 551 ff., 633
  confirmation by repeated experimentation, 71 ff., 89. *See also* Bayes, Thomas, method of finding an unknown probability; Confirmation (and disconfirmation), confirmation theorem; Self-corrective inductive method
  induction and property, 104–5, 120–21, 140, 551–54, 625, 632–34
  induction by simple enumeration, rule of, 102, 122, 630
    straight rule of induction, 123–24, *153*
  induction and uniformity, 114–17, 127–28. *See also* Uniformity
  See also Bayes, Thomas, theorem; Carnap, Rudolph, continuum of inductive logics; Causal model of standard inductive logic; Pragmatic theory of inductive probability; Standard inductive logic
Inductive argument
  and probability, 23 ff.
  and rules, 24–25, 101–3, 122–24, 152 ff. *See also* Analogy, argument by; Bacon, Francis, tables of instances; Bayes, Thomas, method of finding an unknown probability; Induction and repetition; Inductive logic (assignment of probabilities); Mill, J. S., methods
  validity, 25, 151–52
  See also Inductive logic; Inductive probability; Reason and reasoning
Inductive hypothesis. *See* Keynes, J. M.
Inductive logic (assignment of probabilities), **103,** *110*
  alternative inductive logics, 103, 109 ff., 128 ff.
    and geometries, 128–29
  Carnap's continuum of inductive logics, 121 ff., 155 ff.
    and mixtures of independent processes, 126
  for a model $\mathfrak{M}$-$\mathfrak{L}$
    completeness of, 108
    infinite case, 119–20
    limitations, 140–41
    called "*statistical model of induction,*" *623,* 654
  See also Induction and repetition; Inductive probability; Inverse inductive logic; Random inductive logic; Standard inductive logic
Inductive logic (subject), **17,** 21. *See also* Deductive logic; Inductive argument; Inductive logic (assignment of probabilities); Inductive probability, calculus of
Inductive-method committive, 314. See also Pragmatic aspect of inductive probability
Inductive probability P(c, d), **26,** 92, 146, 160, 652
  a priori aspect, 305 ff., 314–19, 322, 326, 632–36, 642
  a priori concept, 635–36
  atomic inductive probability statement P(c, d) = x, **26,** 638, 645
  complete probability assignment to a process, 119, *504, 508*
    exchangeable assignment, *125* ff., 507
  degree-of-belief function P(q, i), *289*
  modality, 45–48, 58, 101, 113–14, 155, 636
  pragmatic aspect, 305 ff., 314–19, 322, 326
  relation to
    causal necessity, 622–50
    deduction, 45–48, 216, 262–66, 314–15, 322
    empirical probability, 485–87, 502–3, 518–19
    frequency probability, 160, 517
  See also A priori, theory of inductive probability; Choice, calculus of; Inductive logic; Frequency, theory of inductive probability; Personalistic, theory of inductive probability; Pragmatic theory of inductive probability; Presupposition theory of induction; Probability; Unified theory of probability, causality, and induction

Inductive probability, calculus of, 39 ff., 214
axioms
conditional probability, 40 ff., **92** ff.
unconditional probability, 92–93
compared to logic of causal statements, 488–89
incompleteness of, 99–104. *See also* Completeness, of inductive logic for a model
as a model, 40, 92
relation to
"book" theorem, 213–16
calculus of choice, 281–83, 288–91
theorems
Bayes' theorem, 66, 67 ff. *See also* Bayes, Thomas
counting equiprobable cases, 52
exchange principle, 47–48
general and *special addition principles,* 40, *51,* 55
general and *special multiplication principles,* 40, *49*
prediction theorem, 66
reduction principle, 93, 276
subtraction principle, 46
See also Confirmation (and disconfirmation), confirmation theorem; de Finetti, Bruno, theorem; Large numbers, law of
Inductive statement, 319, **638–39,** 645–47, 650. *See also* Synthetic, a priori
Inductively rational
rational$_i$, *315*
rational$_s$, *315*
See also Coherent (incoherent) set of partial beliefs; Reason and reasoning
Inequivalence, material ($\not\equiv$), *42*
Inference. *See* Deductive argument; Inductive argument; Rule
Infinite
limit, 61
utility, 188–92
vs. finite scope of induction, 127, 131, 139–40, 154–55, 630–31. *See also* Limit, and probability; Prior probabilities, and convergence of opinion
Information
background, 94–95, 138–39
See also Evidence; Ignorance and probability; Man, and computers; Probability, and general information
Initial state rule, 562
Innate knowledge, 1. *See also* A priori, concept; Knowledge; Man, his innate (acquired) structure-program complex
Inquiry, 16 ff., 153 ff., 569–71
logic of empirical, 16, 17 ff., 168
logic of mathematical, 16
paradox, 1
See also Bayes, Thomas, method of finding an unknown probability; Knowledge; Science
Instance-confirmation. *See* Bayes, Thomas, theorem; Causal model of standard inductive logic
Instantiation
existential
of a predicate, 442
of a statement, 445, 484
universal, 348
Insurance, 65, 186, 199–207
Interpretation, 8
abstract, 352 ff.
of calculus of probability, 39
concrete, 352, 365, 424 ff.
See also Definition; Language modeling; Meaning; Model; Pragmatism
Intuitive
intuitively acceptable step, 22–23, 413
justification of induction, 640–42
knowledge, 7, 22–23, 39, 413, 614, 642, 645
See also Immediate consequence; Knowledge; Proof; Valid and invalid
Invalid. *See* Valid and invalid
Invariance axiom, 268, 307–8
Inverse inductive logic, 103, 138
for a model $\mathfrak{M}$-$\mathfrak{L}$, *111*
and Carnap's continuum of inductive logics, 127
and Fermi-Dirac statistics, 117, 506–7
and uniformity, 116, 127
Mr. Inverse, 131, 313–18
Irreflexive (relation), *208*
Irregularity. *See* Entropy
Isomorphic, 125, 127
formulas ($\Phi I \Psi$), *107*
measures $\mathbf{I}(\Phi)$ and $\mathbf{I}'(d)$, *107, 114*
and uniformity, 116–17
See also Distribution, description; Entropy

Jackfield, 210
James, William, 254
Jeffreys, Harold, 140, 321
Justification of induction, 130 ff.
Carnap, 322–25
deductive vs. nondeductive justification, 321
Hume, 134–37
Kant, 645–47
Keynes, 640–42, 647
Peirce-Reichenbach justification of induction, 153 ff.

Russell, 136–37
See also Hume's thesis that there is no noncircular justification of induction

Kant, Immanuel, xv, 7, 30, 427, 559, 575, 651
a priori concept, 643–45
arithmetic, 644
causality, 30, 427, 607
determinism, 644–45
geometry, 7, 644
justification of induction, 645–47
synthetic a priori, 643–46
categorial, 643–46
mathematical, 643–46
transcendental proof of law of causality, 644–47
Kemeny, J. G., 214, 504, 513
Kepler, Johannes, 2, 20
Keynes, J. M., xv, 39, 101, 131, 211, 614
a priori theory of inductive probability, 321–22, 639–42
derivation of standard inductive logic, 640–41
intuitive justification of induction, 640–42, 647
limited variety principle (inductive hypothesis), 640
plurality of causes, 639
relation to presupposition theory of induction, 639–42
uniformity of nature, 640
Kimura, Motoo, 88
Kinetic theory of gases, 31, 115 ff., 506–7, 586
Kleene, S. C., 367
Klein, Felix, 7
Knowledge, 1, 37
a priori, 7
demonstrative, 643–44
innate, 1
intuitive, 7, 22–23, 39, 413, 614, 642, 645
and probability, 85, 159–60
See also A priori, concept; Empirical, concept; Epistemology; Intuitive; Justification of induction; Man, his innate (acquired) structure-program complex; Questions and answers; Science; Statement
Kochen, Simon, 589, 591
Koestler, Arthur, 20
Kolmogorov, A. N., 601–2
Koopman, B. O., 211, 253
Krantz, David, 251
Kripke, Saul, 466

Langford, C. H., xv, 169, 339, 348, 412, 559
Language
arithmetization (coding), 367 ff.
Leibniz, 368–69
and automata, 366, 380
and evolution, 139
formal. *See* Formal language
formal and natural compared, 421–22
hierarchy of languages, 379, 470–74
natural, 4, 139, 421 ff.
universal language (Leibniz), 337–38, 365–67, 393–96
complete expressive power, 366
See also Interpretation; Meaning; Metalanguage and object language
Language modeling, 33 ff., 170–71
descriptive, 34
normative, 34
See also Analysis; Definition; Interpretation; Meaning; Model
Laplace, Pierre, 427, 574, 586
Large numbers, law of, 61
Law
causal. *See* Causal law
global vs. local, 568–71
of nature, 425 ff.
modality, 426
possible, 450
simplicity of, 571, 635
uniformity, 426
uniqueness, 425–26
physical, 581 ff.
probabilistic, 577, 581. *See also* Empirical probability; Tychism
psychical, 581 ff.
reversible, 581 ff.
Law (legal) and probability, 61–62. *See also* Evidence
Lehman, R. S., 214
Lehmer, D. H., 598
Leibniz, Gottfried, 337, 560, 610
and algorithms, 337–38, 365–67
arithmetization of language, 368–69
conjecture, 366–67, 393–95
identity of indiscernibles, 559–61
universal language, 337–38, 365–67, 393–96
complete expressive power, 366
Lemmon, E. J., 469
Lenz, John, 151
Lewis, C. I., 254, 339, 348, 412, 533
Light, theories of, 86
Likes at least as much as
relation on acts and on statements ($\geqq$), *207* ff., 267
conditional form ($\geqq_i$), 269, 271
simple ordering, 208 ff., 266–72
See also Utility

Limit
limit $\lim_{n\to\infty} \sigma_n$, 61
and probability, 61–64, 84–85, 90, 144 ff., 151 ff., 530–37, 593 ff.
See also Infinite
Limited variety principle, 625, **633–34,** 640–41. *See also* Keynes, J. M.
Lobachevski, N. I., 7 ff.
Locke, John, 189, 610
Logic, 15
of argument, 16 *See also* Deductive argument; Deductive logic; Inductive argument; Inductive logic
of inquiry, 16
empirical, 16, 17 ff., 168
mathematical, 16
For specific logical systems see Causal statements, logic of; Choice, calculus of; Inductive probability, calculus of; Peano arithmetic; Quantification theory, first order; Truth-functional, logic
See also Formal language; Logically true-or-false statement; Modal logic; Reasoning; Rule
Logical constant, 342
Logical modalities
consistent
formal language, *364*
logic of causal statements, *364*
equivalence (↔), *11, 340, 345*, 403
axiom, 264–65, 307
between trees, *263–64*
and probability, 47, 264
implication (→), *11, 340, 345*
independence (○), *428*
logically independent on condition, 50
iterated, 343, 400, 466–74
necessity(□), *11, 340, 342*
predicate (**N**), 469 ff.
and proof, 403, 466
possibility (◇), *11, 340, 344*
See also Inductive probability; Modal logic; Modal operators; Model; Universe and universe description
Logically true-or-false statement, 2–6, 11, 22, **316,** 322–23, 466, **636**
and Leibniz's conjecture, 366–67, 393–95
in logic of causal statements, 363 ff., 403, 466
"logically true" in the broad sense, 134–37, 316, 321, 636, 646–47
and machines, 367, 396, 419
modal predicate "is logically true" (**N**), 469–74
Φ is true in 𝔐-𝔏, *359* ff., 371–72
See also Deductive logic; Logical modalities; Rational; Reasoning; Tautology; True
Long run. *See* Frequency, probability
Luce, R. D., 251, 252
Lucretius, 549, 577–78

Machine. *See* Automaton; Decision machine; Enumeration machine
Macroscopic state, 115
Main questions. *See* Questions and answers
Man
and computers, 18, 610–13, 633-34
finitude of, 633–34
his innate (acquired) structure-program complex, 612, 632 ff., 643–47. *See also* Kant, Immanuel
Marcus, Ruth Barcan, 348, 469
Margenau, Henry, 506
Marking
axiom, 262, 308–12
game, 255 ff.
marked set of trees, 262
marked-set equivalent, 278
pay-off path, 255
Markov chain, 125, 504–5
Martin-Löf, Per, 601
Material
equivalence (≡), *42, 345*
implication (⊃), *42–44*, 173–74, *345*
inequivalence (≢), *42*
universal, 436–37, 627. *See also* True, contingently
Mathematical expectation, 184. See also Utility
Mathematical induction, 49, 371
Mathematics, 2 ff., 9, 36
Maximizing utility
every choice of an act tree maximizes the function $\sum_{n=1}^{N} P(q_n, i)U(a_n, iq_n)$, *290*
rule of, 180, 181–216, 251
See also Choice, calculus of; Pay-off path
Maxwell, James, 117, 506
Meaning, 4–5, 166–79, 423
descriptive component, 171–74
normative component, 175–76
Peirce's pragmatic principle of meaning, 167 ff., 177, 480, 638–39
probabilistic version of the pragmatic principle of meaning, 177
sameness of, 168–69
specifying the meaning of a term, 12–15, 138
See also Analysis; Definition; Interpretation; Language modeling; Pragmatism

Mendel, Gregor, 88
Mendelson, Elliott, 369, 370
Mental telepathy, 91
Metalanguage and object language, 42, *344*, 379, 408. *See also* Hierarchy of languages; Paradox, and self-reference
Metaphysics, 175–76, 651
Metatheorem, *408*
Method
of this book, 33
of varying causally relevant qualities, *102*
See also Bacon, Francis, tables of instances; Bayes, Thomas, method of finding an unknown probability; Mill, J. S., methods; Self-corrective inductive method
Michelson, A. A., 6
Microscopic state, 115
Mill, J. S., 25, 102, 188
methods, 102
Mirror-image universe, 557
Mixed act, *183*
Mixture of independent processes, 75, 125–26
and Bayes' method of finding an unknown probability, 76–77 ff., 118–28, 155, 159–60
and Carnap's continuum of inductive logics, 121 ff., 155 ff.
and confirmation theorem, 73–74, 84, 85, 88
and empirical probabilities, 481 ff.
exchangeable, 125 ff.
Modal
axiom, *348*
distribution, *349*, 408
model, 352 ff., *358* ff., 623
ordering, *349*, 410–11
-quantifier commutation, *349*
Modal logic, 10–12, *44*
comprehensive, 467–74
Peirce, 339
See also Causal modalities; Causal statements, logic of; Inductive probability, calculus of; Logical modalities; Probabilistic modalities
Modal operators, 10–12, 340–45
iterated, 343, 400, 467–74
See also Causal modalities; Logical modalities; Probabilistic modalities
Model, *31*, 33 ff., 108
causal model of standard inductive logic, 624 ff., 654
in empirical science, 31–33
and formula, 31–34, 351–62, 422 ff.
and icons, 31–32
modal model 𝔐-𝔏, 352 ff., *358* ff., 623
model 𝔐-𝔏, *106*, 108 ff., 140–41
true in, *359* ff., 371–72
See also Process
simple models of reality, 34, 104–7
statistical model of induction, *623*
See also Inductive logic (assignment of probabilities) for a model; Interpretation; Language modeling; Nature; Reality; Sequence, of events; Theory; Universe and universe description
Modus ponens, *350*
Monadic property, 553
Montague, Richard, 474
Monte Carlo method, 598
Moore, Edward F., 380
Morgenstern, Oskar, 252
Morley, E. W., 6
Multiplication principle
general, 40, *49*, *51*
special, 40, *49*, *51*
Murphy, G. M., 506

Name
relation (δ), 470
See also Consequence; Constant; Proper name
Nature, 424, *552*, 625. *See also* Causal system; Model 𝔐-𝔏; Reality; Space-time system; Uniformity, of nature
Near-determinism, *577* ff.
and arbitrary events, 577
and probabilistic laws, 577
See also Causal law; Cellular automaton, causal, indeterministic, and near-deterministic; Determinism; Free will; Tychism
Necessity
causal ($\Box^c$), *341*, *342*. *See also* Causal modalities, necessity
cause and effect, 457, 477
logical ($\Box$), *11*, *340*, *342*
predicate (**N**), 469 ff.
probabilistic, *272*
Negation ($\sim$, $\bar{p}$), *11*, *42*, *342*
$\bar{\alpha}$ defined as 1-α, 200
Neighborhood relation $N(c)$, *562*
Newton, Isaac, 5, 6, 569–71, 574
mechanics, 2, 21
Neyman, J., 57, 88
Nicod, Jean, 321, 641
Niemi, Gunnar, 474
Niven, Ivan, 594
Nonparadoxical causal implication (**npc**), *428*
causal relevance and, 434–35, 454–56
Nonsufficient reason, principle of, 640
Nonsuperfluous causal implication (**nsc**), 434
Normal form, disjunctive, 109
Normal form (of a tree), 272–77
act expression, *258*

algorithm, 275
axiom, 276, 307–8
choice (act) tree, 258, 272–77
of a tree, 275
See also Act; Consequence; Tree; Trimming trees
Normative. *See* Descriptive vs. normative
Number. *See* Combinations; Frequency; Gödel

Object language. *See* Metalanguage and object language
Observation, 6, 174, 524–26, 614, 627
and frequency probability, 149, 531
See also Experiment
Odds, 69
Ohta, Tomoko, 88
Operationalism, 167
Operator. *See* Causal modalities; Logical modalities; Modal operators; Probability
Ordering. *See* Simple ordering
Ostensive definition, 13–14, 556

Page, Leigh, 116
Pap, Arthur, 440
Papini, G., 254
Paradox
barbershop, 460–64
of choice
sure-thing, 194, 277–78, 307–8
variance, 196
of implication, 412
causal, 412 ff.
logical, 412 ff.
material, 412 ff.
of inquiry, 1
Saint Petersburg, 190–92, 197, 295
of second ace, 52–54
and self-reference, 377–79. *See also* Hierarchy of languages; Metalanguage
Parallax, 19, 86
Partial act, 183, 263, 278
Partial belief, 178–79, 247, 249
set of partial beliefs, 213–14
See also Coherent (incoherent) set of partial beliefs; Degree-of-belief function; Inductive probability
Particle, 114. *See also* Individual
Partition, 52, *287*
Pascal, Blaise, 189
Pascal's wager, 189–90
Patternless sequence, 601–2
Pay-off path, 255. See also Maximizing utility

Peano, Giuseppe, 369
Peano arithmetic, 369 ff.
arithmetization (coding), 373–74
$\sigma(n)$ designates n, 374
$\tau(n)$ designates n, 374
$P\{\alpha, \beta\}$ [α is proof of β], 374
$P'\{\beta\}$ [β is a theorem], 374
$\rho(m)$ [substitute $\sigma(m)$ into formula m], 375
$R\{\alpha\}$ [representation of ρ], 375–76
axioms, 371
consistent, 372, 377
definition in, 370
Gödel number $\mathbf{g}(\Phi)$, *368*
grammar, 370
incompleteness theorem, 373, 377
proof, 373–76
indefinability of truth in arithmetic, 378
$\mathfrak{L}_A$, 373
rules of inference, 371
symbols ($=, 0, ', +, \cdot, \ell$), 370
undecidable formula, 376
Peirce, Charles S., xvi, 16, 31–32, 89, 148, 151, 165 ff., 254, 421, 479, 549
abduction (logic of inquiry), 16
dispositional-frequency theory of probability, 534 ff., 533–38
compared to dispositional theory, 535–37
earlier and later views, 151, 173–74, 533
modal logic, 339
nominalism and realism (would-be's), 172–74, 339, 421, 534–35, 583
pragmatism. *See* Pragmatism
scientific community, 154
synechism, 581
tychism, 577, *581* ff.
claim re evolution and determinism, 585, 600, 602
universes and blackberries, 89, 533–34
See also Frequency, theory of empirical probability; Frequency, theory of inductive probability; Peirce-Reichenbach justification of induction
Peirce-Reichenbach justification of induction, 153 ff.
Permutation theorem, 287
Personalistic
account of empirical probability, 538–42
compared to dispositional theory, 541–42
and positivistic theory of empirical probability, 540–41
subjective character, 538, 541
theory of inductive probability, 253, *325* ff., 655
subjective character, 253–54, 326–27

and unknown probability, 538–42
See also Pragmatic theory of inductive probability
Philosophy of science, 1
Plato, 1
Podolsky, B., 590
Point (of a tree)
chance, choice, and *consequence points, 181, 256,* 264
logically impossible, 257, 264, 272
probabilistically impossible, 272
probabilistically necessary, 272
information at a point, 257
root, 256
Polya, G., 18
Popper, Karl, 533
Positivistic theory of empirical probability, 523 ff., 527, 657
aspects of probability
a priori, 524, 528
empirical, 524–25, 528–29
pragmatic, 525
subjective, 525, 529–31
compared to
dispositional theory, 519–20, 524–31
personalistic account, 540–41
Possibility
causal (◇ᶜ), *341, 344*
logical (◇), *11, 340, 344*
relative, 50
possible causal law, 450, 627 ff.
possible causal system. *See* Causal model of standard inductive logic.
See also Probabilistic modalities; Universe and universe description
Post, E. L., 384
Posterior probabilities, 68
function, 499, 511, 521
See also Bayes, Thomas, theorem
Practical conditional, 167 ff., 178
and subjunctives, 172–74, 320
See also Conditional; Would-be's
Pragmatic aspect of inductive probability, 305 ff., 314–19, 322, 326. *See also* Inductive-method committive
Pragmatic theory of inductive probability, 305, 305–20, 318–20, 479, 655–57
historical background, 249–54
intersubjective character, 94, 108, 116-17, 139–42, 253–54, 326–27, 529–31
See also Causal necessity; Personalistic, theory of inductive probability; Presupposition theory of induction; Unified theory of probability, causality, and induction
Pragmatism
and belief, 166
and operationalism, 167
Peirce's pragmatic principle of meaning, 167 ff., 177, 480
criticism of, 171–78
and metaphysics, 175–76, 638–39
Peirce-Reichenbach justification of induction, 153 ff.
probabilistic version of pragmatic principle of meaning, 177
and verifiability theory of meaning, 167
See also Meaning; Practical conditional; Pragmatic aspect of inductive probability; Pragmatic theory of inductive probability
Prawitz, D., 611
Predicate, 104, 341
constant, 358
variable, 342–43
See also Generalization; Instantiation; Property
Prediction theorem, 66
Prefers
relation on acts and on statements (>), *207* ff., 267
conditional form ($>_i$), 269, 271
transitive, 208 ff., 210 ff., 267, 308
See also Likes at least as much as; Utility
Premise and *conclusion, 22, 350*
Presupposition theory of induction (summarized on pp. 647–50), 549–50, 584, 632–39, **647,** 657
a priori aspect of inductive probability, 305 ff., 314–19, 322, 326, 632–36, 642
causal model of standard inductive logic. *See* Causal model of standard inductive logic
presuppositions of induction, 323–24, 624–25, 632 ff., 645
causal existence principle, 577–78, 625, 641
causal uniformity principle, 572–73, 625, 635, 640
as inductive statements, 637–38,
limited variety principle, 625, **633–34,** 640–41
relation to other theories
Kant's theory of causality, 643–47
Keynes' principle of induction, 639–42
pragmatic theory of inductive probability, 632 ff.
unified theory of probability, causality, and induction, 657 f.
status of causal necessity
a priori, 613–19
irreducibly modal, 619–22
Price, Derek, 20
Primitive
rule of inference, 350, 408
symbol, 342

Prior probabilities, 68
and convergence of opinion, 90–91, 327, 530–31
epistemological status, 91
factor (ω/κ), 122
function, 498, 510, 521
and probabilistic disposition, 482 ff., 498, 510, 521, 528–31, 541
subjective vs. intersubjective, 94, 108, 116–17, 139–42, 253–54, 326–27, 529–31, 538, 541
See also Bayes, Thomas, theorem; Dispositional theory of empirical probability; Positivistic theory of empirical probability
Probabilistic disposition, 487
compared to causal disposition, 487–97, 535, 583
dispositional models of atomic empirical probability statements, 483–87, 497–503
and prior probabilities, 482 ff., 498, 510, 521, 528–31, 541
system underlying a probabilistic disposition, 493, 528
complete theory of a process, 493
Probabilistic law
criticism of the notion, 581
and near-determinism, 577
See also Empirical probability; Tychism
Probabilistic modalities
impossible on condition, 272
impossible (choice, chance, consequence) point, 272
necessary on condition, 272
See also Coherent (incoherent) set of partial beliefs; Inductive probability, modality; Modal logic; Modal operators; Possibility
Probabilistic subjunctive, 453, 489
Probabilistic version of pragmatic principle of meaning, 177
Probability
and action, 165, 176–79, 179 ff. *See also* Partial belief; Pragmatic aspect of inductive probability; Utility
applicable to single universes or to sets of universes, 89, 117–18
conditional vs. **unconditional, 41, 92–94,** 519–20. *See also* Posterior probabilities; Prior probabilities
and embedded subsystems, 588–92
and event, 41, 57, 262–63
and general information, 94–95, 138–39. *See also* Information, background; Total evidence, rule of
and ignorance, 147–48, 586
and inductive argument, 23 ff.
and knowledge, 85, 159–60
quantitative and qualitative, 187–88, 209 ff., 311–12
See also Chance; Conditional probability; Empirical probability; Evidence; Frequency; Inductive probability; Logical modalities; Odds; Randomness, kinds of; Thermodynamic probability; Uncertainties; Unconditional probability; Utility
Probability, traditional calculus of, 39 ff., 517, 520. *See also* Inductive probability, calculus of
Process, 58, 118, 144
probabilistic
complete assignment to, 119, *504, 508*
complete theory of, 493
See also Independent process; Inductive logic (assignment of probabilities); Mixture of independent processes
See also Model $\mathfrak{M}$-$\mathfrak{L}$; Sequence of events; Universe and universe description
Program (computer), 383, 388
Pronoun, demonstrative, 555
Proof, 23, *350,* 413–15
categorical, 350
conditional, 398
definability in arithmetic, 374
from premises, 350
reductio ad absurdum, 400, 414
See also Decision machine, for proofhood; Deductive argument
Proper name, 104
and index, 558
See also Act; Consequence; Constant; Name; Quantifier, descriptive
Property
basic, 104, 359, 553, 562
and causal laws, 551–54, 619–20, 632–34, 648
enduring vs. *transient, 443. See also* Causal disposition
indexical vs. *nonindexical, 557* ff., 633
and identity of indiscernibles, 559–61
and induction, 104–5, 120–21, 140, 551–54, 625, 632–34
monadic, 553
relational, 341, 553
underlying a disposition, 442 ff., 491 ff., 528. *See also* Probabilistic disposition, system underlying
See also Predicate
Proposition. *See* Statement
Pseudo-
act, 297
formula, 357

randomness, 595, 598–99
statement, 295
Ptolemy, 20
Puerperal fever, 23–24
Pyrrho of Elis, 137, 315–18

Qualitative. *See* Quantitative and qualitative
Quantification theory, first-order, 351, 393
Quantifier
descriptive (ℓ), 370
existential
over individuals (∃x), *340*
over predicates (∃P), 344, 440 ff.
over statements (∃φ), 344, 445 ff., 483 ff.
interpretation, 353–54, 357, 359–61
universal (x), 340
See also Causal statements, logic of (axioms, rules, theorems)
Quantitative axiom
nonsymmetrical, 301, 311
symmetrical, 288, 308–12
Quantitative and qualitative
probabilities, 187–88, 209 ff., 311–12. *See also* Comparative; Uncertainties
valuations, 187–88, 209 ff., 311–12. *See also* Utility
Quantum mechanics
and determinism, 589–91
and embedded subsystems, 589–91
Questions and answers, 1–2, 178
main questions (summarized on pp. 655–57)
first, *29*, *92*, 305, 647
second, *29*, *92*, 129, 160, *313*, 318
third, *29*, *144*, 148, 479, *511*, 518–19
fourth, *30*, 174, 320, 337–38, 478, 549, 607, 622, 647
See also Method; Paradox

Raiffa, Howard, 88, 252
Ramsey, Frank, 214, 247, 249 ff., 325, 339, 379
Random inductive logic, 103, 138
compared to second law of thermodynamics, 115–17
for a model 𝔐-𝔏, *112*
and Carnap's continuum of inductive logics, 123
and Maxwell-Boltzmann statistics, 117, 506–7
and uniformity, 116
Mr. Random, 131
See also Entropy
Randomness, kinds of, 592, 603
applicable to single universes
admissible sequence, 594, 598
collective, 147, *601*
entropy **E**(u), 115–17, 592
patternless sequence, 601–2
pseudorandomness, 595, 598–99
sequence randomness, 592
truth-functional randomness, 596
and cellular automaton, causal, 592–93, 599, 602
and determinism, 585–86, 589–93, 597-603
involving numerical assignments to sets of universes, 596–97. *See also* Independence, probabilistic; Mixture of independent processes; Random inductive logic
See also Chance; Determinism, and randomness; Inductive probability; Probability; Uniformity
Rasputin, G. E., 452
Rational
deductively rational, 314 ff.
inductively rational, 315–16
rational$_i$, *315*
rational$_s$, *315*
See also Coherent (incoherent) set of partial beliefs; Logical modalities, consistent; Logically true-or-false statement; Reason and reasoning
Reality, 31, *108*. *See also* Model; Nature
Reason and *reasoning*, *15*, 337 ff., 422, 607, 636, 651
deductive, 2–6, 316 ff.
inductive, 40, 135–37, 315 ff.
See also Deductive argument; Inductive argument; Logic; Logically true-or-false statement; Rational
Recursive definition, 343
of axioms, 345, 349
of a priori and empirical concepts, 609
of formulas, 343
Reductio ad absurdum, 400, 414
Reduction
principle (of calculus of inductive probability), *93*, 276
theorem (of calculus of choice), 276
Reflexive (relation), *208*
Reichenbach, Hans
causal necessity, 427, 622
frequency theory of
empirical probability, 148 ff.
inductive probability, 151 ff.
See also Peirce-Reichenbach justification of induction
Reid, Constance, 8
Relation, 207 ff., 344, 356–57. *See also* Asymmetrical; Cause and effect; Comparative; Equivalence; Indifference; Irreflexive; Likes at least as much as; Name; Prefers; Property;

Reflexive; Simple ordering; Symmetrical; Transitive
Relative
frequency, 122
probability. *See* Conditional probability
width ω/κ, *120*
Repetition and induction. *See* Induction and repetition
Responsibility, 579
Richardson, M., 7
Riemann, G. R., 7 ff.
Robbins, H., 7, 169
Root of a tree, *181*, *256*
Rosen, N., 590
Rosser, Barkley, 367
Rule, *15*, 18
and deduction, 22
and induction, 24–25, 101–3, 122–24, 153. *See also* Analogy, argument by; Bacon, Francis, tables of instances; Bayes, Thomas, method of finding an unknown probability; Induction and repetition; Inductive logic (assignment of probabilities); Mill, J. S., methods
of inference
derived, 396–407, *400*
primitive, *350*
For specific rules see Causal statements, logic of (rules); Completeness, rule of, for causal subjunctives; Exchange; Induction and repetition, Maximizing utility; Total evidence, rule of
See also Algorithm; Initial state rule; Logic; Transition rule
Russell, Bertrand, 23, 136–37, 323, 379

Saint Petersburg paradox, 190–92, 197, 295
Salmon, Wesley, 155
Samuel, A. L., 611
Savage, L. J., 84, 126, 191, 203, 250 ff., 263, 325, 538–42
his axiomatic system, 299–303
See also Choice, calculus of; Personalistic
Schlaifer, Robert, 88
Schlick, Moritz, 167
Science, 1, 2 ff., 36, 439–40
Scientific community, 154
Second law of thermodynamics, 115–17
Segal, Irving E., 591
Self-corrective inductive method, *153* ff., 584. *See also* Bayes, Thomas, method of finding an unknown probability
Self-reference, 377–79
Sellars, Wilfred, 440
Semmelweis, Ignaz, 23–24
Sentential calculus, 347
Sequence
of events, 57 ff., 118 ff., 144 ff.
randomness, *592*
See also Model; Process; Randomness, kinds of
Shannon, C. E., 506
Shifting lemma, 578, *629*
Shimony, Abner, 214
Simple ordering, 267
of preferences, 208, 266–69. *See also* Likes at least as much as; Prefers
relation, *208*
of uncertainties, 209 ff., 270–72. *See also* Uncertainties
Simplicity
of hypotheses and theories, 18 ff., 571
of models, 35
of nature, 635
Single case. *See* Frequency, probability
Snell, J. L., 504, 513
Sommerville, D. M. Y., 7
Sophists, 1
Space, 5, 7–10, 551 ff., 562–63, 643–44
Space-time
framework, *552*
system, *552–53*
See also Automaton; Causal uniformity principle; Time
Specifying the meaning of a term, *12–15*, 138. *See also* Analysis; Definition; Interpretation; Language modeling; Meaning
Specker, E. P., 589, 591
Spinoza, Baruch, 610
Stabler, E R , 7
Stäckel, Paul, 10
Stake $S(c)$, *214*. *See also* Consequence, valuation function
Standard deviation $\sigma(a)$, *195*
Standard inductive logic, 103, 138–39, 155 ff., 622–32, 654
causal model. *See* Causal model of standard inductive logic
for a model $\mathfrak{M}$-$\mathfrak{L}$, *110*
and Bayes' method, 118–28
and Bose-Einstein statistics, 117, 506–7
called "*statistical model of induction*," *623*, 654
and Carnap's continuum of inductive logics, 121 ff.
compared to a causal model of standard inductive logic, 623, 654
and uniformity, 116
Mr. Standard, *131*, 313–18
State
cell, *562*
individual, *105*, *553*, 562

macroscopic, 115
microscopic (complexion), 115
temporal, 553, 562
See also Cellular automaton (general); Universe and universe description
Statement, 3, 8
constant, 358
proposition, 3
pseudostatement, 295
statement calculus, 347
statement form, 8
variable, 342–43
See also Atomic statement; Empirically true-or-false statement; Formula; Inductive statement; Logically true-or-false statement; Variable
Statistical model of induction. See Inductive logic (assignment of probabilities), for a model
Statistics
Bose-Einstein and standard inductive logic, 117, 506–7
Fermi-Dirac and inverse inductive logic, 117, 506–7
Maxwell-Boltzmann and random inductive logic, 117, 506–7
See also Probability; Standard deviation; Uniformity, statistical; Variance
Stevenson, Charles, xvi, 421, 449
Stout, G. F., 614
Straight rule of induction, 153 ff.
Strategy, 252
Strome, W. M., 599
Subjunctive conditional, 435 ff., 449 ff.
counterfactual, 438 ff.
See also Causal subjunctive; Practical conditional; Probabilistic subjunctive
Submodel (subprocess), 119–20
Subset axiom, 266, 307
Substitution instance, 346
Subtraction principle, 46
Sub-tree, 258
Success, 132–34
parameter ϵ_s, 84
See also Bayes, Thomas, method of finding an unknown probability; Frequency
Superfluous condition, addition of a, 411
weakened form, 431
Suppes, Patrick, 140, 306
Sure-thing paradox, 194, 277–78, 307–8
Switch, automaton, 380
Symbol
indexical vs. *nonindexical, 554* ff.
See also Icon; Language; Meaning
Symmetrical
relation, *208*
form of *quantitative axiom, 288,* 308–12
Synechism, 581
Synthetic, 7
a priori, 642–46. *See also* Inductive statement; Kant, Immanuel
System
of bets, 214
deterministic, 576
embedded subsystem, 588
determinism and randomness, 588–92
indeterministic, 564, 577. *See also* Tychism
near-deterministic, 577, 625
probabilistic. *See* Causal model of standard inductive logic; Cellular automaton, probabilistic; Inductive logic (assignment of probabilities); Tychism
underlying a probabilistic disposition, 493, 528
See also Automaton; Axiomatic system; Cellular automaton; Formal language; Space-time system

Tables of instances, 102
Tape unit, 384
Tarski, Alfred, 378
Tautology, 45, 346. See also Logically true-or-false statement
Teleological explanation, 169
Temporal state. *See* State
Theorem, 350. See also Causal statements, logic of (theorems); Choice, calculus of; Decision machine, for theorem-hood; Inductive probability, calculus of; Peano arithmetic
Theory, 31
causal and minimizing theories, 168–69
in empirical science, 424 ff.
compared to dispositionals, 459, 493 ff.
See also Empirical probability, theory; Hypothesis; Law of nature; Model
Thermodynamic probability W(*s*) (configuration number), 115
Thrall, R. M., 252
Time, 380, 551 ff., 562, 643–44. *See also* Space-time; Temporal state
Todhunter, I., 29, 57
Toffoli, Tommaso, 575
Token and *Type*, 259, *554*
Tolman, Richard, 506
Total evidence, rule of, 20, 457, 459. *See also* Completeness, rule of, for causal subjunctives; Probability, and general information
Traditional
theory of utility, 179–212, *185*
calculus of probability, 39 ff., 517, 520.

See also Inductive probability, calculus of
Transition rule, 562
Transitive
preferences, 208 ff., 267, 308
relation, 208
transitivity principle, *411*
weakened form, 430
Transposition, 411
weakened form, 431
Tree, 256
act, ***182*****, 257**
choice, ***181*****, 257**
complete set, 261
extended, 258
marked set, 262
marked-set equivalent, 278
pay-off path, 255
normal form choice (act) tree, 258, 272–77
root, 181, 256
subtree, 258
two *trees (subtrees) are logically equivalent on condition i, 263–64*
See also Act; Chance; Choice; Consequence; Marking; Normal form (of a tree); Point (of a tree); Trimming trees
Trimming trees
trimmed form of a tree, 275
trimming algorithm, 275
True, 153
Φ is true in $\mathcal{M}$-$\mathcal{L}$, *359* ff., 371–72
causally true, 617
contingently true, 617
modal predicate "is logically true" (**N**), 469–74
predicate "is true" (**T**), 371, 470
indefinability of truth in arithmetic. *See* Gödel, Kurt
See also Empirically true-or-false statement; Inductive statement; Logically true-or-false statement
Truth-functional
axioms, 346
formula, 345
height, 345–46
logic, 42–45
randomness, 596
TF (truth-functional axiom and primitive rule), 408
truth-function theory, 347
See also Height; Substitution instance; Tautology
Truth-table, 346
Turing, A. M., 384
Turing machine, 384, 597, 601–2
and cellular automaton, 566–68, 575
computation of, 384
and embedded subsystem, 588
selection machine, 601
sequence-producing machine, 601
universal, 388
See also Algorithm; Decision machine; Enumeration machine; Program
Turner, C. E., 102
Tychism, 549, *581* ff.
Peirce's claim re evolution and determinism, 585, 600, 602
See also Determinism; Near-determinism
Type and *Token,* 259, *554*
Types, theory of. *See* Hierarchy of languages

Uchii, Soshichi, 93, 400, 466, 631
Uncertainties, 179 ff.
ordering of uncertainties axiom, 270, 307
simple ordering, 209 ff., 270–72
See also Comparative, probabilities; Probability; Quantitative and qualitative, probabilities
Unconditional probabilities, 92–93 ff.
assignment to possible universes, 108 ff., 624, *626* ff.
See also Conditional probability
Understanding. *See* Meaning
Unified theory of probability, causality, and induction, 657–58
Uniformity
causal uniformity
and determinism, 573–74, 576–77
principle, 572–73, 625, 635, 640
rule, 572
and induction, 114–17, 127–28
of nature, 135, 571–74, 640
Hume's principle, 135, 645, 647
Keynes, 640
statistical, 116, 583–84
See also Induction and repetition; Randomness, kinds of
Uninterpreted (undefined)
formal language, 340, 342–43, 365–66
term, 8–9, 13, 39
Universal. *See* Instantiation, universal; Language, universal; Material, universal; Quantifier, universal; Turing machine, universal
Universe and universe description
actual universe (true universe description), 105, 341, *359, 553, 625*
causally possible universe (description), 341, *359, 625*
logically possible universe (universe description), 105, 341, *359, 553*
relative to a condition, 50
mirror-image universe, 557
possible state of affairs, 450–51

See also Distribution, description; History of cellular automaton; Model; Process; Peirce, Charles S.; Probability; Randomness, kinds of
Unknown probability
Bayes' **method of finding, 76–77** ff., 118–28, 155, 159–60
of mixture of independent process, 76 ff., 118–28, 155, 159–60
and personalistic theory of inductive probability, 538–42
Utility, 179 ff., 652
and choice, 180 ff.
infinite, 188–92
marginal utility of money, 186, 201
measuring utility by comparison, 298
traditional theory, 179–212, *185*
utile, *185*, 270
utility U(a, g) of act a, **180**
utility U(c) of consequence c, **180**
See also Choice, calculus of; Consequence, valuation function; Mathematical expectation; Maximizing utility; Pragmatic theory of inductive probability; Prefers; Probability; Traditional, theory of utility; Value

Vagueness, 437–40
Vailati, G., 254
Valid and invalid
deductive arguments, *22*
inductive arguments, 25, 151–52
See also Corresponding conditional; Immediate consequence; Inductive argument, validity; Intuitive; Knowledge; Proof
Value
valuations
comparative, 208 ff., 266–69, 277–81
quantitative and qualitative, 187–88, 209 ff., 311–12
transitive, 208–9, 210 ff., 267, 308
value $V(a)$ of act a, 198
See also Utility
Variable, 8, *342*
free and bound occurrences, *347*
individual, *343*
predicate, *343*
and pronoun, 555
statement, *343*
theory vs. observation, 524–26
See also Statement
Variance
of act a, *195*
paradox, *196*
Venn, John, 148
Verification, 92
of causal laws, 627–32, 640–41
and meaning, 167
See also Confirmation; Empirical probability theory
von Kries, Johannes, 321
von Mises, Richard, 147, 148, 600–601
von Neumann, John, 252, 302, 377, 383, 505, 562, 567–68, 589, 610

Wang, Hao, 369, 380, 611
Whitehead, A. N., 379, 614
Whittaker, Edmund, 6, 86
Wiener, Norbert, 337, 396, 610
Wilder, R. L., 13
Will, Fred, 88
Wolfe, H. E., 10
Would-be's, 173, 339, 421, 534-35, 583. *See also* Causal disposition; Causal law; Causal modalities, necessity
Wright, J. B., 380
Wright, Sewall, 88

Yellow fever, 101–2
Young, Thomas, 86
Yovits, M. C., 18